The Norton Reader

The Norton Reader

An Anthology of Expository Prose

REVISED

Arthur M. Eastman, *General Editor*
CARNEGIE-MELLON UNIVERSITY

Caesar Blake
UNIVERSITY OF TORONTO

Hubert M. English, Jr.
UNIVERSITY OF MICHIGAN

Alan B. Howes
UNIVERSITY OF MICHIGAN

Robert T. Lenaghan
UNIVERSITY OF MICHIGAN

Leo F. McNamara
UNIVERSITY OF MICHIGAN

James Rosier
UNIVERSITY OF PENNSYLVANIA

W · W · NORTON & COMPANY · INC · *New York*

Copyright © 1969, 1965 by W. W. Norton & Company, Inc.

Since this page cannot legibly accommodate
all the copyright notices, the pages following
constitute an extension of the copyright page.

Library of Congress Catalog Card No. 68-9281

Book design by John Woodlock

PRINTED IN THE UNITED STATES OF AMERICA

1 2 3 4 5 6 7 8 9 0

ACKNOWLEDGMENTS

Mortimer J. Adler: from *Humanistic Education and Western Civilization*, edited by Arthur A. Cohen. Copyright © 1964 by Holt, Rinehart and Winston, Inc. Reprinted by permission of the publisher.

James Agee: from *Let Us Now Praise Famous Men*. Copyright 1939 by Houghton Mifflin Company. Reprinted by permission of the publisher.

Richard D. Altick: from *The Art of Literary Research*. Copyright © 1963 by W. W. Norton & Company, Inc. Reprinted by permission of the publisher.

Robert Ardrey: from *The Territorial Imperative*. Copyright © 1966 by Robert Ardrey. Reprinted by permission of Atheneum Publishers.

Hannah Arendt: from *Eichmann in Jerusalem*. Copyright © 1963 by Hannah Arendt. Reprinted by permission of The Viking Press, Inc.

W. H. Auden: from *The Dyer's Hand*. Copyright © 1962 by W. H. Auden. Reprinted by permission of Random House, Inc.

Russell Baker: from *All Things Considered*. Copyright © 1962, 1963, 1964, 1965 by The New York Times Company. Published by J. B. Lippincott Company.

James Baldwin: from *Notes of a Native Son*. Copyright © 1955 by James Baldwin. Reprinted by permission of the Beacon Press.

Margaret Banning: from *Letters to Susan*. Copyright 1934 by Margaret Culkin Banning. Reprinted by permission of Brandt & Brandt.

Owen Barfield: from *Essays Presented to Charles Williams*, Oxford University Press, 1947. Edited by C. S. Lewis. Reprinted by permission of the author.

Jacques Barzun and Henry F. Graff: from *The Modern Researcher*. Copyright © 1957 by Jacques Barzun. Reprinted by permission of Harcourt, Brace & World, Inc.

Walter Jackson Bate: from *The Achievement of Samuel Johnson*. Copyright © 1955 by Oxford University Press, Inc. Reprinted by permission of the publisher.

George W. Beadle: from *Phoenix*, Vol. II, No. 1, September 1963. Reprinted by permission of the author and the Michigan Memorial-Phoenix Project.

Carl Becker: from *Modern Democracy*. Copyright 1941 by Yale University Press. Reprinted by permission of the Press.

Max Beerbohm: from *And Even Now*. Copyright 1921 by E. P. Dutton & Company, Inc.; renewal 1949 by Max Beerbohm. Published in Canada by William Heinemann Ltd. Publishers. Reprinted by permission of the publishers.

Henri Bergson: from "Laughter," which is contained in the book, *Comedy*, by Wylie Sypher. Copyright © 1956 by Wylie Sypher. Reprinted by permission of Doubleday & Company, Inc.

Bruno Bettelheim: from *The Informed Heart*. Copyright © 1960 by The Free Press, A Corporation. Reprinted by permission of the publisher.

Wayne C. Booth: "Boring from Within: The Art of the Freshman Essay," from an address to the Illinois Council of College Teachers in 1963. Reprinted by permission of the author.

Wayne C. Booth: from *The Knowledge Most Worth Having*, 1967. Reprinted by permission of the University of Chicago Press.

C. D. Broad: from *A Short History of Science*. Copyright © C. D. Broad, 1963. Reprinted with permission of The Macmillan Company.

J. Bronowski: "The Reach of Imagination," from *The American Scholar*, Spring 1967. Reprinted by permission of The American Academy of Arts and Letters and the author.

Jerome S. Bruner: from *Toward A Theory of Instruction*. Copyright 1966 by the President and Fellows of Harvard College. Reprinted by permission of the Belknap Press of Harvard University Press.

Martin Buber: from *Pointing the Way*. Copyright © 1957 by Martin Buber. Reprinted by permission of Harper & Row, Publishers, Inc.

J. B. Bury: from *Selected Essays of J. B. Bury*, 1930. Reprinted by permission of the Trustees of the Will of the late Mrs. Jane Bury Bagnall.

Truman Capote: from *The Muses Are Heard*. Copyright © 1956 by Truman Capote. Reprinted by permission of Random House, Inc. Originally appeared in *The New Yorker* in different form.

Edward Hallett Carr: from *What Is History?* Copyright © 1961 by Edward Hallett Carr. Reprinted by permission of Alfred A. Knopf, Inc., and The Macmillan Company Ltd. of Canada.

W. J. Cash: from *The Mind of the South*. Copyright 1941 by Alfred A. Knopf, Inc. Reprinted by permission of the publisher.

Francis Christensen: from *Notes Toward a New Rhetoric*. Copyright © 1967 by Francis Christensen. This essay appeared originally in *College English*, October 1963, and is reprinted by permission of the author and Harper & Row, publishers.

Kenneth Clark: from *Encounter*, January 1963. Reprinted by permission of the author and *Encounter*.

Contents

[Entries marked with · are followed by Questions]

xii · Contents

ON EDUCATION

ON MIND

PROSE FORMS: LETTERS   434

ON CIVILIZATION

ON LITERATURE AND THE ARTS

ON ETHICS

ON GOVERNMENT

ON HISTORY

ON SCIENCE

ON RELIGION

Preface to the Revised Edition

The strength of the original *Norton Reader* lay in the excellence and abundance of its materials, in their relevance to the lives of today's students, and in the general usefulness given to the volume by its clear but unobtrusive organization. This new edition attempts to build from the strength of the old in the light of the experience of the editors and of colleagues across the country who have contributed to this venture their criticisms both sharp and generous.

The reader who compares this edition with the first will discover that we have not redefined our standards of excellence. Still we call on such great writers of the past as Ascham, Bacon, Donne, Erasmus, Hopkins, Jefferson, La Rochefoucauld, Lincoln, Machiavelli, Matthew, and Plato. We call also on the vital voices of contemporaries, among whom, appearing for the first time in Personal Report, are Norman Mailer and Truman Capote. Benjamin Whorf and W. K. Wimsatt join the section On Language along with Jacques Barzun and Francis Christensen. John Holt and Jerome Bruner are important newcomers to the discussion On Education. Among other new contributors are Robert Ardrey, Erik Erikson, Northrop Frye, Robert Graves, Eric Hoffer, Martin Luther King Jr., Joseph Wood Krutch, Konrad Lorenz, Marshall McLuhan, Daniel P. Moynihan, and Diana Trilling.

The essays in the *Reader* are gathered into sections titled according to major fields of human experience or concern—Language, Education, Mind, etc. These fields, it seems to us, exert some claim upon selection. Each demands to be represented fairly, with material indicative of basic theory and of significant practice. And here we are confident we have gained on the first edition. The new language section, for example, with its radical theoretical material from the meta-linguist Benjamin Whorf, with its British philosophizing from Barfield and Lewis, with its up-to-date history from Francis, with its discussion of style's relevance to meaning from Wimsatt, and with its application to clear writing and to generative rhetoric by Barzun and Graff on the one hand, by Christensen on the other —the new language section answers to its title more responsibly and effectively than before. To mention but one other section, On Ethics now includes van den Haag and D. H. Lawrence on pornography and crime, morality and the novel; Hare on language and racial discrimination, Erikson on the golden rule in the refractions yielded by psychoanalysis, Shils and Medawar on the sanctity of human life as science sees it; and to its moral portraits it adds Walter Jackson Bate's presentation of the last days of Dr. Johnson.

To improve on the *Reader's* original offerings, we might simply have added, but we have removed as well. Ruskin's essay *Traffic* still seems to the editors excellent, but the evidence is that it is not assigned and, as has been long recognized, that work is good in vain which is not read. Ruskin has gone, and others whom it seems charitable not to name—because they were not assigned, were too long, or appeared to hindsight inferior to present replacements. Perhaps thirty percent of the first edition has thus become a casualty, but the replacements more than fill the ranks. There are sixty-four new essays and eleven new readings in the Prose Forms.

Good writing is always germane: it talks to men where they live. And perhaps the relevance of the material in this *Reader* to to-day's young men and women needs no further warrant than the names of its authors and the topics of their choosing. King on discrimination and Moynihan on contemporary radicalism clearly talk to today's problems. McLuhan is manifestly as timely as timely can be (though whether timeless is another question), as is Leary on LSD or Holt on what goes wrong in our classrooms or Adler on *The Future of Democracy* (an essay tantalizingly subtitled *A Swan Song*). And though other titles and topics may seem a shade further away from the headlines, surely Coffin exploring the forces that crucified Christ and Lorenz searching out the human meanings of the behavior of the water shrew and Theodora Kroeber examining the conduct of a Stone Age savage cataclysmically thrust into the twentieth century are writing about our problems and our world. *The Norton Reader*, we believe, is relevant to its readers.

The usefulness of the *Reader*, as it derives from its ordering by content, its short discussion of journal, letter, character, apothegm, and parable, its questions and its rhetorical appendix, needs perhaps no special discussion. The ordering remains unchanged—unobtrusive, we think, minimal, yet genuinely reflective of the individual's enlarging experience. Teachers who wish to work by topic can use its divisions; those who wish to advance in other ways may do so with equal ease. An Index of Essays Illustrative of Rhetorical Modes and Devices, which groups some hundred of the essays according to their most important structural types, will be of assistance here. The discussions of prose forms have undergone such revision as fits them to this edition but remain in other respects unchanged. The number and proportion of essays accompanied by questions has grown slightly. The terminal Notes on Composition (formerly entitled "A Compendious Rhetoric") directs attention to rhetorical principles as exemplified in the present text.

Teachers are notoriously individualistic, not to say independent, and English teachers traditionally find their own ways to accomplish the common goals of improved reading, writing, thinking, and understanding. The editors have been diffident about their own methods of doing things in the classroom and disinclined to intrude their putative expertise on others. But a good many teachers have wanted a guide, just as hunters and hikers, however experienced, on encountering new territory or new game may want a guide. Their wish has been well met—not in this book but in one that accompanies it. Its title is *An Analytical Guide for Study, Discussion, and Writing,* and it has been prepared by Josephine and Earl Schulze, who combine long experience in freshman English with intense experience using the first edition of *The Norton Reader.*

We acknowledge again the perceptive help, while the First Edition was in the making, of Professors Robert D. Bamberg of the University of Pennsylvania, James H. Broderick of Bryn Mawr College, Frederick Candelaria of the University of Oregon, Don L. Cook of the University of Indiana, John P. Cutts of Wayne State University, David J. DeLaura of the University of Texas, John Doebler of Dickinson University, Scott Elledge of Cornell University, J. R. Gaskin of the University of North Carolina, Donald J. Gray of the University of Indiana, Fabian Gudas of Louisiana State University, Eugene Hardy of the University of Nebraska, W. Donald Head of San Jose State College, Harold D. Kelling of the University of Colorado, Cecil M. McCulley of the College of William and Mary, Joseph P. Roppolo of Tulane University, Fred A. Tarpley of East Texas University, Hulon Willis of Bakersfield College, and Harris W. Wilson of the University of Illinois. Their wise counsel has been augmented in the revision by Professors Donald L. Cross of Upsala College, Scott Elledge, Donald Gray, James W. Groshong of Oregon State University, A. G. Medlicott, Jr., of the University of Connecticut, Byron Patterson of American River College, Charles B. Ruggless of Humboldt State College, Carl E. Stenberg of Rhode Island College, James Wheatley of Trinity College, and Hulon Willis. As before, John Benedict of W. W. Norton & Company, Inc., has helped us immeasurably—with his own nominations, with a critical eye, sensitive, sharp, and wide-ranging, with encouragement, with sanity.

Arthur M. Eastman

An Index of Essays Illustrative of Rhetorical Modes and Devices

THESIS: Saying Something That Matters

STYLE

The Norton Reader

Personal Report

DYLAN THOMAS
Memories of Christmas

One Christmas was so much like another, in those years, around the sea-town corner now, and out of all sound except the distant speaking of the voices I sometimes hear a moment before sleep, that I can never remember whether it snowed for six days and six nights when I was twelve or whether it snowed for twelve days and twelve nights when I was six; or whether the ice broke and the skating grocer vanished like a snowman through a white trap-door on that same Christmas Day that the mince-pies finished Uncle Arnold and we tobogganed down the seaward hill, all the afternoon, on the best tea-tray, and Mrs. Griffiths complained, and we threw a snowball at her niece, and my hands burned so, with the heat and the cold, when I held them in front of the fire, that I cried for twenty minutes and then had some jelly.

All the Christmases roll down the hill towards the Welsh-speaking sea, like a snowball growing whiter and bigger and rounder, like a cold and headlong moon bundling down the sky that was our street; and they stop at the rim of the ice-edged, fish-freezing waves, and I plunge my hands in the snow and bring out whatever I can find; holly or robins or pudding, squabbles and carols and oranges and tin whistles, and the fire in the front room, and bang go the crackers, and holy, holy, holy, ring the bells, and the glass bells shaking on the tree, and Mother Goose, and Struwelpeter[1] —oh! the baby-burning flames and the clacking scissorman!—Billy Bunter[2] and Black Beauty, Little Women and boys who have three helpings, Alice and Mrs. Potter's badgers,[3] penknives, teddy-bears

---

1. The title character of *Struwelpeter (Slovenly Peter), or Merry Tales and Funny Pictures,* a children's book originally in German, by Dr. Heinrich Hoffmann, containing gaily grim admonitory narratives in verse about little Pauline, for example, who played with matches and got burned up; or the little boy who sucked his thumbs until the tall scissorman cut them off.

2. The humorous fat boy in Frank Richards' tales of English school life.

3. Beatrix Potter, creator of *Peter Rabbit* and other animal tales for children, among them *The Tale of Mr. Tod,* a badger.

—named after a Mr. Theodore Bear, their inventor, or father, who died recently in the United States—mouth-organs, tin-soldiers, and blancmange, and Auntie Bessie playing "Pop Goes the Weasel" and "Nuts in May", and "Oranges and Lemons" on the untuned piano in the parlor all through the thimble-hiding musical-chairing blind-man's-buffing party at the end of the never-to-be-forgotten day at the end of the unremembered year.

In goes my hand into that wool-white bell-tongued ball of holidays resting at the margin of the carol-singing sea, and out come Mrs. Prothero and the firemen.

It was on the afternoon of the day of Christmas Eve, and I was in Mrs. Prothero's garden, waiting for cats, with her son Jim. It was snowing. It was always snowing at Christmas; December, in my memory, is white as Lapland, though there were no reindeers. But there were cats. Patient, cold, and callous, our hands wrapped in socks, we waited to snowball the cats. Sleek and long as jaguars and terrible-whiskered, spitting and snarling they would slink and sidle over the white back-garden walls, and the lynx-eyed hunters, Jim and I, fur-capped and moccasined trappers from Hudson's Bay off Eversley Road, would hurl our deadly snowballs at the green of their eyes. The wise cats never appeared. We were so still, Eskimo-footed arctic marksmen in the muffling silence of the eternal snows—eternal, ever since Wednesday—that we never heard Mrs. Prothero's first cry from her igloo at the bottom of the garden. Or, if we heard it at all, it was, to us, like the far-off challenge of our enemy and prey, the neighbor's Polar Cat. But soon the voice grew louder. "Fire!" cried Mrs. Prothero, and she beat the dinner-gong. And we ran down the garden, with the snowballs in our arms, towards the house, and smoke, indeed, was pouring out of the dining-room, and the gong was bombilating, and Mrs. Prothero was announcing ruin like a town-crier in Pompeii. This was better than all the cats in Wales standing on the wall in a row. We bounded into the house, laden with snowballs, and stopped at the open door of the smoke-filled room. Something was burning all right; perhaps it was Mr. Prothero, who always slept there after midday dinner with a newspaper over his face; but he was standing in the middle of the room, saying "A fine Christmas!" and smacking at the smoke with a slipper.

"Call the fire-brigade," cried Mrs. Prothero as she beat the gong.

"They won't be there," said Mr. Prothero, "it's Christmas."

There was no fire to be seen, only clouds of smoke and Mr. Prothero standing in the middle of them, waving his slipper as though he were conducting.

"Do something," he said.

And we threw all our snowballs into the smoke—I think we

missed Mr. Prothero—and ran out of the house to the telephone-box.

"Let's call the police as well," Jim said.

"And the ambulance."

"And Ernie Jenkins, he likes fires."

But we only called the fire-brigade, and soon the fire-engine came and three tall men in helmets brought a hose into the house and Mr. Prothero got out just in time before they turned it on. Nobody could have had a noisier Christmas Eve. And when the firemen turned off the hose and were standing in the wet and smoky room, Jim's aunt, Miss Prothero, came downstairs and peered in at them. Jim and I waited, very quietly, to hear what she would say to them. She said the right thing, always. She looked at the three tall firemen in their shining helmets, standing among the smoke and cinders and dissolving snowballs, and she said: "Would you like something to read?"

Now out of that bright white snowball of Christmas gone comes the stocking, the stocking of stockings, that hung at the foot of the bed with the arm of a golliwog dangling over the top and small bells ringing in the toes. There was a company, gallant and scarlet but never nice to taste though I always tried when very young, of belted and busbied and musketed lead soldiers so soon to lose their heads and legs in the wars on the kitchen table after the tea-things, the mince-pies, and the cakes that I helped to make by stoning the raisins and eating them, had been cleared away; and a bag of moist and many-colored jelly-babies and a folded flag and a false nose and a tram-conductor's cap and a machine that punched tickets and rang a bell; never a catapult; once, by a mistake that no one could explain, a little hatchet; and a rubber-buffalo, or it may have been a horse, with a yellow head and haphazard legs; and a celluloid duck that made, when you pressed it, a most unducklike noise, a mewing moo that an ambitious cat might make who wishes to be a cow; and a painting-book in which I could make the grass, the trees, the sea, and the animals any color I pleased: and still the dazzling sky-blue sheep are grazing in the red field under a flight of rainbow-beaked and pea-green birds.

Christmas morning was always over before you could say Jack Frost. And look! suddenly the pudding was burning! Bang the gong and call the fire-brigade and the book-loving firemen! Some-one found the silver three-penny-bit with a currant on it; and the someone was always Uncle Arnold. The motto in my cracker read:

> Let's all have fun this Christmas Day,
> Let's play and sing and shout hooray!

and the grown-ups turned their eyes towards the ceiling, and Auntie Bessie, who had already been frightened, twice, by a clockwork mouse, whimpered at the sideboard and had some elderberry wine. And someone put a glass bowl full of nuts on the littered table, and my uncle said, as he said once every year: "I've got a shoe-nut here. Fetch me a shoehorn to open it, boy."

And dinner was ended.

And I remember that on the afternoon of Christmas Day, when the others sat around the fire and told each other that this was nothing, no, nothing, to the great snowbound and turkey-proud yule-log-crackling holly-berry-bedizined and kissing-under-the-mistletoe Christmas when *they* were children, I would go out, school-capped and gloved and mufflered, with my bright new boots squeaking, into the white world on to the seaward hill, to call on Jim and Dan and Jack and to walk with them through the silent snowscape of our town.

We went padding through the streets, leaving huge deep footprints in the snow, on the hidden pavements.

"I bet people'll think there's been hippoes."

"What would you do if you saw a hippo coming down Terrace Road?"

"I'd go like this, bang! I'd throw him over the railings and roll him down the hill and then I'd tickle him under the ear and he'd wag his tail . . ."

"What would you do if you saw *two* hippoes . . . ?"

Iron-flanked and bellowing he-hippoes clanked and blundered and battered through the scudding snow towards us as we passed by Mr. Daniel's house.

"Let's post Mr. Daniel a snowball through his letter box."

"Let's write things in the snow."

"Let's write 'Mr. Daniel looks like a spaniel' all over his lawn."

"Look," Jack said, "I'm eating snow-pie."

"What's it taste like?"

"Like snow-pie," Jack said.

Or we walked on the white shore.

"Can the fishes see it's snowing?"

"They think it's the sky falling down."

The silent one-clouded heavens drifted on to the sea.

"All the old dogs have gone."

Dogs of a hundred mingled makes yapped in the summer at the sea-rim and yelped at the trespassing mountains of the waves.

"I bet St. Bernards would like it now."

And we were snowblind travelers lost on the north hills, and the great dewlapped dogs, with brandy-flasks round their necks, ambled and shambled up to us, baying "Excelsior."

We returned home through the desolate poor sea-facing streets where only a few children fumbled with bare red fingers in the thick wheel-rutted snow and catcalled after us, their voices fading away, as we trudged uphill, into the cries of the dock-birds and the hooters of ships out in the white and whirling bay.

Bring out the tall tales now that we told by the fire as we roasted chestnuts and the gaslight bubbled low. Ghosts with their heads under their arms trailed their chains and said "whooo" like owls in the long nights when I dared not look over my shoulder; wild beasts lurked in the cubby-hole under the stairs where the gasmeter ticked. "Once upon a time," Jim said, "there were three boys, just like us, who got lost in the dark in the snow, near Bethesda Chapel, and this is what happened to them . . ." It was the most dreadful happening I had ever heard.

And I remember that we went singing carols once, a night or two before Christmas Eve, when there wasn't the shaving of a moon to light the secret, white-flying streets. At the end of a long road was a drive that led to a large house, and we stumbled up the darkness of the drive that night, each one of us afraid, each one holding a stone in his hand in case, and all of us too brave to say a word. The wind made through the drive-trees noises as of old and unpleasant and maybe web-footed men wheezing in caves. We reached the black bulk of the house.

"What shall we give them?" Dan whispered.

" 'Hark the Herald'? 'Christmas comes but Once a Year' ?"

"No," Jack said: "We'll sing 'Good King Wenceslas.' I'll count three."

One, two, three, and we began to sing, our voices high and seemingly distant in the snow-felted darkness round the house that was occupied by nobody we knew. We stood close together, near the dark door.

> Good King Wenceslas looked out
> On the Feast of Stephen.

And then a small, dry voice, like the voice of someone who has not spoken for a long time, suddenly joined our singing: a small, dry voice from the other side of the door: a small, dry voice through the keyhole. And when we stopped running we were outside *our* house; the front room was lovely and bright; the gramophone was playing; we saw the red and white balloons hanging from the gas-bracket; uncles and aunts sat by the fire; I thought I smelt our supper being fried in the kitchen. Everything was good again, and Christmas shone through all the familiar town.

"Perhaps it was a ghost," Jim said.

"Perhaps it was trolls," Dan said, who was always reading.

"Let's go in and see if there's any jelly left," Jack said. And we did that.

WALLACE STEGNER
The Town Dump

The town dump of Whitemud, Saskatchewan, could only have
been a few years old when I knew it, for the village was born in
1913 and I left there in 1919. But I remember the dump better
than I remember most things in that town, better than I remember most of the people. I spent more time with it, for one thing;
it has more poetry and excitement in it than people did.

It lay in the southeast corner of town, in a section that was
always full of adventure for me. Just there the Whitemud River
left the hills, bent a little south, and started its long traverse
across the prairie and international boundary to join the Milk. For
all I knew, it might have been on its way to join the Alph: simply,
before my eyes, it disappeared into strangeness and wonder.

Also, where it passed below the dumpground, it ran through
willowed bottoms that were a favorite campsite for passing teamsters, gypsies, sometimes Indians. The very straw scattered around
those camps, the ashes of those strangers' campfires, the manure
of their teams and saddle horses, were hot with adventurous
possibilities.

It was as an extension, a living suburb, as it were, of the
dumpground that we most valued those camps. We scoured them
for artifacts of their migrant tenants as if they had been
archaeological sites full of the secrets of ancient civilizations. I
remember toting around for weeks the broken cheek strap of a
bridle. Somehow or other its buckle looked as if it had been
fashioned in a far place, a place where they were accustomed to
flatten the tongues of buckles for reasons that could only be
exciting, and where they made a habit of plating the metal with
some valuable alloy, probably silver. In places where the silver was
worn away the buckle underneath shone dull yellow: probably
gold.

It seemed that excitement liked that end of town better than
our end. Once old Mrs. Gustafson, deeply religious and a little
raddled in the head, went over there with a buckboard full of
trash, and as she was driving home along the river she looked and
saw a spent catfish, washed in from Cypress Lake or some other
part of the watershed, floating on the yellow water. He was two
feet long, his whiskers hung down, his fins and tail were limp. He
was a kind of fish that no one had seen in the Whitemud in the
three or four years of the town's life, and a kind that none of us
children had ever seen anywhere. Mrs. Gustafson had never seen
one like him either; she perceived at once that he was the devil,

and she whipped up the team and reported him at Hoffman's elevator.

We could hear her screeching as we legged it for the river to see for ourselves. Sure enough, there he was. He looked very tired, and he made no great effort to get away as we pushed out a half-sunken rowboat from below the flume, submerged it under him, and brought him ashore. When he died three days later we experimentally fed him to two half-wild cats, but they seemed to suffer no ill effects.

At that same end of town the irrigation flume crossed the river. It always seemed to me giddily high when I hung my chin over its plank edge and looked down, but it probably walked no more than twenty feet above the water on its spidery legs. Ordinarily in summer it carried about six or eight inches of smooth water, and under the glassy hurrying of the little boxed stream the planks were coated with deep sun-warmed moss as slick as frogs' eggs. A boy could sit in the flume with the water walling up against his back, and grab a cross brace above him, and pull, shooting himself sledlike ahead until he could reach the next brace for another pull and another slide, and so on across the river in four scoots.

After ten minutes in the flume he would come out wearing a dozen or more limber black leeches, and could sit in the green shade where darning needles flashed blue, and dragonflies hummed and darted and stopped, and skaters dimpled slack and eddy with their delicate transitory footprints, and there stretch the leeches out one by one while their sucking ends clung and clung, until at last, stretched far out, they let go with a tiny wet *puk* and snapped together like rubber bands. The smell of the river and the flume and the clay cutbanks and the bars of that part of the river was the smell of wolf willow.

But nothing in that end of town was as good as the dumpground that scattered along a little runoff coulee dipping down toward the river from the south bench. Through a historical process that went back, probably, to the roots of community sanitation and distaste for eyesores, but that in law dated from the Unincorporated Towns Ordinance of the territorial government, passed in 1888, the dump was one of the very first community enterprises, almost our town's first institution.

More than that, it contained relics of every individual who had ever lived there, and of every phase of the town's history.

The bedsprings on which the town's first child was begotten might be there; the skeleton of a boy's pet colt; two or three volumes of Shakespeare bought in haste and error from a peddler, later loaned in carelessness, soaked with water and chemicals in a house fire, and finally thrown out to flap their stained eloquence in the prairie wind.

Broken dishes, rusty tinware, spoons that had been used to mix paint; once a box of percussion caps, sign and symbol of the carelessness that most of those people felt about all matters of personal or public safety. We put them on the railroad tracks and were anonymously denounced in the *Enterprise*. There were also old iron, old brass, for which we hunted assiduously, by night conning junkmen's catalogues and the pages of the *Enterprise* to find how much wartime value there might be in the geared insides of clocks or in a pound of tea lead carefully wrapped in a ball whose weight astonished and delighted us. Sometimes the unimaginable outside world reached in and laid a finger on us. I recall that, aged no more than seven, I wrote a St. Louis junk house asking if they preferred their tea lead and tinfoil wrapped in balls, or whether they would rather have it pressed flat in sheets, and I got back a typewritten letter in a window envelope instructing me that they would be happy to have it in any way that was convenient for me. They added that they valued my business and were mine very truly. Dazed, I carried that windowed grandeur around in my pocket until I wore it out, and for months I saved the letter as a souvenir of the wondering time when something strange and distinguished had singled me out.

We hunted old bottles in the dump, bottles caked with dirt and filth, half buried, full of cobwebs, and we washed them out at the horse trough by the elevator, putting in a handful of shot along with the water to knock the dirt loose; and when we had shaken them until our arms were tired, we hauled them off in somebody's coaster wagon and turned them in at Bill Anderson's pool hall, where the smell of lemon pop was so sweet on the dark pool-hall air that I am sometimes awakened by it in the night, even yet.

Smashed wheels of wagons and buggies, tangles of rusty barbed wire, the collapsed perambulator that the French wife of one of the town's doctors had once pushed proudly up the planked sidewalks and along the ditchbank paths. A welter of foul-smelling feathers and coyote-scattered carrion which was all that remained of somebody's dream of a chicken ranch. The chickens had all got some mysterious pip at the same time, and died as one, and the dream lay out there with the rest of the town's history to rustle to the empty sky on the border of the hills.

There was melted glass in curious forms, and the half-melted office safe left from the burning of Bill Day's Hotel. On very lucky days we might find a piece of the lead casing that had enclosed the wires of the town's first telephone system. The casing was just the right size for rings, and so soft that it could be whittled with a jackknife. It was a material that might have made

artists of us. If we had been Indians of fifty years before, that
bright soft metal would have enlisted our maximum patience and
craft and come out as ring and metal and amulet inscribed with
the symbols of our observed world. Perhaps there were too many
ready-made alternatives in the local drug, hardware, and general
stores; perhaps our feeble artistic response was a measure of the
insufficiency of the challenge we felt. In any case I do not remember that we did any more with the metal than to shape it into
crude seal rings with our initials or pierced hearts carved in them;
and these, though they served a purpose in juvenile courtship,
stopped something short of art.

The dump held very little wood, for in that country anything
burnable got burned. But it had plenty of old iron, furniture,
papers, mattresses that were the delight of field mice, and jugs
and demijohns that were sometimes their bane, for they crawled
into the necks and drowned in the rain water or redeye that was
inside.

If the history of our town was not exactly written, it was at
least hinted, in the dump. I think I had a pretty sound notion
even at eight or nine of how significant was that first institution
of our forming Canadian civilization. For rummaging through its
foul purlieus I had several times been surprised and shocked to
find relics of my own life tossed out there to rot or blow away.

The volumes of Shakespeare belonged to a set that my father
had bought before I was born. It had been carried through successive moves from town to town in the Dakotas, and from Dakota
to Seattle, and from Seattle to Bellingham, and Bellingham to
Redmond, and from Redmond back to Iowa, and from there to
Saskatchewan. Then, stained in a stranger's house fire, these volumes had suffered from a house-cleaning impulse and been thrown
away for me to stumble upon in the dump. One of the Cratchet
girls had borrowed them, a hatchet-faced, thin, eager, transplanted
Cockney girl with a frenzy, almost a hysteria, for reading. And
yet somehow, through her hands, they found the dump, to become
a symbol of how much was lost, how much thrown aside, how
much carelessly or of necessity given up, in the making of a new
country. We had so few books that I was familiar with them all,
had handled them, looked at their pictures, perhaps even read
them. They were the lares and penates, part of the skimpy im-
pedimenta of household gods we had brought with us into
Latium.[1] Finding those three thrown away was a little like finding
my own name on a gravestone.

And yet not the blow that something else was, something that

1. In Roman families the lares and
penates were the ancestral, household
gods; they came to embody the continuity of the family. Cf. Virgil, *Aeneid*
I. 1-7.

impressed me even more with the dump's close reflection of the town's intimate life. The colt whose picked skeleton lay out there was mine. He had been incurably crippled when dogs chased our mare, Daisy, the morning after she foaled. I had labored for months to make him well; had fed him by hand, curried him, exercised him, adjusted the iron braces that I had talked my father into having made. And I had not known that he would have to be destroyed. One weekend I turned him over to the foreman of one of the ranches, presumably so that he could be cared for. A few days later I found his skinned body, with the braces still on his crippled front legs, lying on the dump.

Not even that, I think, cured me of going there, though our parents all forbade us on pain of cholera or worse to do so. The place fascinated us, as it should have. For this was the kitchen midden of all the civilization we knew; it gave us the most tantalizing glimpses into our lives as well as into those of the neighbors. It gave us an aesthetic distance from which to know ourselves.

The dump was our poetry and our history. We took it home with us by the wagonload, bringing back into town the things the town had used and thrown away. Some little part of what we gathered, mainly bottles, we managed to bring back to usefulness, but most of our gleanings we left lying around barn or attic or cellar until in some renewed fury of spring cleanup our families carted them off to the dump again, to be rescued and briefly treasured by some other boy with schemes for making them useful. Occasionally something we really valued with a passion was snatched from us in horror and returned at once. That happened to the mounted head of a white mountain goat, somebody's trophy from old times and the far Rocky Mountains, that I brought home one day in transports of delight. My mother took one look and discovered that his beard was full of moths.

I remember that goat; I regret him yet. Poetry is seldom useful, but always memorable. I think I learned more from the town dump than I learned from school: more about people, more about how life is lived, not elsewhere but here, not in other times but now. If I were a sociologist anxious to study in detail the life of any community, I would go very early to its refuse piles. For a community may be as well judged by what it throws away —what it has to throw away and what it chooses to—as by any other evidence. For whole civilizations we have sometimes no more of the poetry and little more of the history than this.

QUESTIONS

1. Stegner begins his reminiscence of the town dump by saying that it had "poetry and excitement" in it. In what ways does he seek to convey those qualities to the reader?

2. Is Stegner's description of the dump and its surroundings vivid? Where does his writing directly appeal to the senses, and which senses are called into play?

3. In his second paragraph Stegner speaks of the Alph, the "sacred river" of Coleridge's poem "Kubla Khan." Why? How does allusion to that poem help him convey the strangeness and wonder he then felt?

4. In paragraphs 5-8 Stegner departs, as he had departed to a lesser degree in the two preceding paragraphs, from his description of the dump. Explain how that departure is justified and whether the writing there is appropriate to the essay as a whole.

5. Why does Stegner say (p. 9) that finding the three volumes of Shakespeare in the dump was "a little like finding my own name on a gravestone"? What is the purpose and effect of his allusion to Virgil's Aeneid in the sentence just before that?

6. Through what particular details does Stegner portray the dump as a record of his childhood? How is it shown to be also a record of the brief history of the town? In what respects does it reflect and suggest more widely yet, European and American history and culture and, ultimately, the ancient past, the foundations of civilization? Explain how and to what effect Stegner's focus on the dump enables these considerations to widen in scope but remain associated.

BIL GILBERT

Pop Angler

I have always considered myself a fisherman. This morning, for example, I have been out chumming black-nosed dace into a seine and have already caught 162 of them, more than a day's supply for our household raccoons, shrews, and fish crow. It is true that these are not very large fish—trophy dace run about 4¾ inches—but they are ever so game. A big bull dace will muscle his way right between the interstices of mesh if you don't get the net out of the water smartly.

Catches like this, which I have been making for many years, have led me to believe that I am a fisherman, yet I admit that for a long time I seem to have been drifting farther and farther out of the angling mainstream. I have fished and I have caught fish, but I have been sneered at by other fishermen because I do not fish for the right things at the right time in the right way. In fact, if you go to many of my fishing friends they will tell you flatly, patronizingly, "Bil does not fish." Until recently I never contradicted them, realizing that according to their high artistic standards—a black curmudgeon hackle is used only between 7:30 and 9 A.M. on eastward-flowing streams—I did not fish. Recently, however, I have ceased to be shy and sensitive about my fishing. Good, approved-of High Fishing, as I understand it, means catching fish in sporty ways. This being the case, I now see myself as having gone so far out that I am in. After all these defensive years I am now holding my head up proudly as an avant-garde angler, an innovator of style and technique. As Dick Tracy is now to serious art, I am to fishing—the first of the Pop Anglers. No longer do I feel it necessary to hide my fishing experiences. Rather, it seems to me that, for the betterment of the whole sport, I must make my position known.

I started fishing 35 years ago in a shallow, reedy Michigan lake, on the shore of which I more or less grew up. In those days and in that place the conventional way to fish was to anchor a rowboat, throw out a line tied to a long cane pole, sit back, and wait for a fish, whose presence would be indicated by the agitation of a red cork bobber. The object of a morning spent in this fashion was to catch a dozen or so bluegills, maybe a bass or pickerel, to eat for supper.

Even in those days I was made restless by the academic restrictions of the Fishing Establishment. So restless was I that most older, more serious fishermen would not take me in their rowboats. This did not fill my childhood with the bitter wine of frustration but rather with relief. I did not really enjoy sitting on a hard seat staring at a piece of cork as intently as a mystic at a point of flame.

However, our family had a mania for competition, and thus it was that among other curious contests we always held a Fourth of July fishing tournament. The rules were simple: two people fished together as a team, their score being computed on the basis of total inches caught, but the play was fierce. (It marks a child to find his great-grandfather trying to stretch another inch out of a bluegill with two pairs of pliers.) Because feeling ran so high, I had no chance of being chosen as a fishing partner, and I never was. But regardless of what the family record book shows, my partner and I won the 1938 fishing contest, and in so doing I for the first time suffered the unreasoning barbs of angling's purists.

My partner was a large, shaggy Airedale named Mike. Like myself, Mike was a pariah among polite anglers. Hour after hour, summer after summer, he would gallop through the shallow offshore waters trying to catch carp, bullheads, frogs, and turtles. If a line, a bobber, or even a boat got in his way, he simple ran over the obstacle. He was a happy, dedicated fisherman, though he never caught much working alone, and neither did I. But together we were effective. Our favorite spot was not the lake at all but a small, narrow, bush-draped outlet creek. Though beneath contempt as far as serious fishermen were concerned, this little stream teemed with aquatic game. Mike and I went there mostly for turtles and mud puppies, species which we both found more interesting than mere fish. Our method was for Mike to tromp through the stream, barking wildly to flush out the creatures, which I would then grab.

On July 4th, 1938, Mike and I, both unselected—to put it kindly—for the fishing contest, took ourselves off to this creek. I had a large butterfly net and Mike his unquenchable enthusiasm for pursuing water varmints. We went to a place where the creek was partially blocked by the roots of a large pin oak. I put the butterfly net across this narrow chute, and Mike began moving downstream toward me, floundering, thrashing, diving in the muck. In an hour or so we had netted, among other things, four goodish largemouth bass, two carp, and a bowfin, a large prehistoric-looking type which, so help me, is called in southern Michigan a dogfish.

Though our total inches were twice those of the nearest competitor—the carp alone almost was enough to win—our record was disallowed. "It doesn't count. They didn't catch them," stormed the traditionalists. So here was the beef that has plagued me through the years. To say that Mike and I had not caught anything, or that what we had caught were not fish, was plainly at odds with evidence. We looked like we had fish, and we smelled like we had fish. But fishermen are like thought police—two and two are five. We had not caught fish because we had not caught fish as other fishermen had tried to catch them. The rules committee agreed that the seven carcasses we submitted were nonfish and stuck to their decision even after they had eaten our four bass.

As time passed and I got out of the southern Michigan provinces, I met more worldly fishermen—those with old, frail-looking poles, delicate, expensive reels, hats stuck full of okapi-skin lures. Such people, I found, regarded fishing with a bobber and cane pole as scornfully as my family did fishing with an Airedale. Yet even these sophisticates were not sufficiently advanced to understand and admire my style.

One such high fisherman was a newspaper editor. He and I were fairly close acquaintances, but he stopped speaking to me in August 1952 after hearing an account of one of my most successful fishing trips. This chap, whom we shall call Dryden Flye, had been away to a fancy school where, among other things, he had learned about trout and when to whisper reverently, "The hatch is on." (One is not born with a taste for High Fishing. It is an acquired habit like wearing velvet collars, drinking martinis on the rocks, and reading T. S. Eliot.)

Meeting Dry one day in the early summer, I told him that my wife and I were planning a canoe trip down the Pere Marquette River, a clear, swift stream in western Michigan. The Pere Marquette has a fast enough current and enough mild rapids to make a float trip on it one of the most pleasant, effortless experiences imaginable. Also it has the reputation of being one of the premier trout rivers of the upper Midwest. Dry Flye was all praise for our trip until told that the principal purpose, other than simply to float along the river, was to look for goshawk nests—that we were not taking rods, not even cane poles. The thought of spending a week on the Pere Marquette without so much as a length of monofilament filled Dryden Flye with a disgust that he expressed quite openly. Thus it was with considerable pleasure that I reported back to him after the trip that we had caught a lot of trout after all. As I told Dryden, I have nothing against fish in their proper place, which is in a frying pan with plenty of butter, so long as I can get them there without going through the slow, square business of impaling them on the end of a hook. On the Pere Marquette we were able to get fish easily and eat them three days running. Since fishermen, like Arab poets, are always talking about fate, I suppose there is no harm in admitting that it was luck, not planning, that enabled us to do so well. Our good fortune consisted of starting downstream at about the same time as did two officers of the Michigan Conservation Department. They were poling a scow holding tanks containing hatchery-reared trout, which they periodically dumped over the side of their boat by the bucketful. Neither we nor the game wardens were much interested in speed, and therefore our two craft drifted downstream close together, giving us a fine opportunity to observe and profit from the stocking operation. One phenomenon we immediately noted was that a hatchery trout, unexpectedly dumped into a cold, swift-flowing stream, acts very much like a canoeist will under the same circumstances. The trout is immediately chilled, befuddled, and frightened. In such a state of shock he has no interest in eating okapi-skin-covered hooks or any other exotic lure that anglers may present to him. However, these shivering, displaced fish were imminently vulnerable to our more sophisticated techniques. It was the work of a moment to unpack our cooking bag, swing in abeam of one of these dazed fish, and scoop him up in a 12-cup coffeepot. For three days we had only to wait until just before mealtime, then lean over the thwart and draw a couple of quarts of fresh trout.

It seemed to us that this was exciting, modern fishing, but it did not strike Dryden Flye that way when he heard our story. I expected him to be a little envious of our good luck, but the very last words Dry ever spoke to me were, "There should be laws against people like you."

Fishing for trout from a canoe with a coffeepot marked, I believe, the turning point in my career as a truly creative angler. After Dryden Flye's stuffy reaction, I decided to turn my back on the whole arid, arbitrary Fishing Establishment. But I had to wait several years until another opportunity arose to advance the cause of free-form fishing. The chance came one afternoon on the Shenandoah River while I was on another canoe trip with a fellow we can identify as Red Popper. Actually, it was not much of a canoe trip, since Red was a fanatical bass fisherman. A weakness for bass has ruined more of my old canoe friends than obesity and wives put together. Taking a fisherman on a canoe trip is like trying to hurry a child through a carnival. A fisherman in a canoe is always lagging behind, absentmindedly getting stuck on rocks, drifting obliviously into rapids, and having to be rescued.

On the Shenandoah, Red and I were each using a canvas foldboat and paddling solo, for a canoeist will not paddle tandem with a known fisherman any more than he will share a canoe with a pyromaniac, a drunk, or a photographer. By late afternoon we had, in painful stages, reached a section of the river that canoeists call the Staircase and fishermen call Great Bass Water. The Staircase is a three-mile stretch just above the confluence of the Shenandoah and the Potomac, where narrow ledges of rock cross the river-bed at intervals of 50 feet or so. This formation creates a sort of natural slalom run, a series of rapids and rocks that must be watched carefully to be both appreciated and avoided. Unfortunately, the ledges also back the water up into a maze of small pools and flumes, each of which, according to the mythology of local bassmen, harbors enormous fish.

Once into the Staircase, no amount of wheedling, threatening, pleading, or even backwatering could keep Red in sight. Nevertheless, as I threaded through the rapids, I kept looking backward, trying to be sure I would see him when he capsized. While looking over my shoulder, I heard a startling grinding sound from the front of my kayak. My first thought was that I had got what dogooders usually get—a hole in my canoe from trying to be my fisherman's keeper. However, investigation proved that what I had really got was a 21-inch bass that had leaped out of the shallow water into the foldboat, where he was now lunging about noisily. To restrain the beast from punching a hole in the canvas with his wicked-looking dorsal fin, I strung him on the bow painter. Then, pulling up on a flat rock, I draped my catch over the side of the boat and struck a studied, casual pose as Red finally came into sight.

I knew how the conversation would go and was not disappointed:

"My God! Put him back in the water!"

"Put him back, hell. I'm going to put him in the frying pan. There's more to him than a hot dog, which is what we'd have to eat if we were depending on you."

"You can't eat that fish!"

"Just watch me, old buddy."

"But you didn't catch him. Bass like that are for sportsmen."

Red was overwrought, perhaps subconsciously feeling that he was a victim of technological displacement. Therefore I let his last needle pass, but he was, of course, dead wrong in his implication. Catching bass with a canoe rather than from it is a real sport, requiring split-second timing, a cool head, and a steady hand. Since that afternoon in the Staircase I have taken three more legal-size bass in canoes, and for those who may wish to take up this challenging pastime the following technical information is provided. First, you must have the proper equipment. After some experimentation, I recommend the same rig in which I took my first bass—a canvas kayak. A foldboat is low enough to fit nicely under a leaping fish, and the decking holds him once he is in. The gunwales on a Canadian-style canoe are too high for good bass-catching. Aluminum and fiber-glass canoes have too much spring. Because of this I lost what I believe would have been a canoe-bass record on the Susquehanna River. As a monstrous fish leaped, I pushed the bow of a 15-foot aluminum model under him. He came down straight and true but rebounded from the metal floor like a Russian gymnast and disappeared back in the river. It was a heartbreaking experience, but of course it is the big ones that get away that keep us canoe fishermen coming back for more.

The best time to fish with a canoe is early evening. The setting sun seems to blind bass, giving the paddler a better shot at them. The proper paddling maneuver for, so to speak, raising a fish is a splashy sweep stroke delivered with a beaver-tail paddle. Properly executed, bass cannot resist this action.

Canoe fishing is a real thrill sport, but I do not want to misrepresent it as a means of catching fish in large numbers. However, I am told by fishy friends that low yield should not discourage me. Leading fishing metaphysicians now hold that the fewer fish a man catches the better a fisherman he is. This seemingly paradoxical view has been explained to me at some length by another friend, M.T. Creel, a fanatical trout fisherman. M.T. is a purist and a power in something called Trout Unlimited. The principal plank of the TU platform is to encourage real fishermen to fish a lot but when they catch a fish, even a legal-size one, to throw it back. The boys in Trout Unlimited reason that if everyone does this there will be—well, there will be trout unlimited.

Naturally, someone with M.T.'s outlook and a fishing hipster like myself are different breeds. However, we still see M.T. every spring, because through our front yard, a sloping bit of land in the central Pennsylvania highlands, there flows a stream in which brook and rainbow trout, if not unlimited, are plentiful. This stream and the trout therein were plugged hard by the real estate agent who sold us the place six years back. Fortunately for the salesman, we are broadminded, willing to tolerate a bunch of fish in our stream.

As it has turned out, these trout, except for drawing fishermen, bother us very little. Sometimes we go months on end never remembering they are there. Not so, of course, with people like M.T. He shows up every May with $500 worth of mysterious equipment, carefully designed to enable him not to catch trout elegantly. I was delighted to have M.T. on hand as a witness, weakminded as he is, when one day last spring I pushed my canoe-fishing system to its ultimate.

Our stream also serves as a swimming hole. Below the house there is a movable dam, which when raised to its full height backs the water up into a pool 80 feet long and six feet deep. Trout are free to use the pool, but we do not cater to them, and when the dam is raised it plays havoc with their social life. Trout below the dam are unable to visit trout above it, but it takes them a long time to learn this. Downstream trout come to the six-foot barricade and will tenaciously try to leap it. They will keep trying until they lie panting and wheezing in the spillway. I had often observed this behavior but thought little more about it than to note that it proves what nonfishermen have always known—while trout are tasty, they are short on brains. One day, however, while M.T. was splashing about the creek artistically not catching fish, it occurred to me that these stupid trout offered a chance to do something quite gaudy in the way of avant-garde angling.

A large, silly rainbow was at the moment resting at the foot of the dam, after having spent 15 minutes vainly trying to jump the barrier. Looking from the trout to M.T. to a canoe rack that stands on the house side of the stream, I experienced a genuine eureka moment. Going to the boat rack, I selected a well-balanced, 12-foot kayak paddle, a double blade, both ends of which were slightly scoop-shaped. Reaching down gently with this fine instrument, I slipped the tip of one concave blade under the trout, which lay fanning itself like a Victorian matron who has just been frightened by a mouse. As deftly as a bear gulling a salmon, I flipped the fish high in the air over the dam onto the lawn. This was it, canoe fishing without a canoe. You cannot do more. Smiling with restrained modesty I turned to accept M.T.'s congratulations. Unfortunately, he was totally speechless and remained so while I carried the trout in to the frying pan.

Among the many efforts that have been made to discredit my New Fishing theories and to smear me personally, bad-mouthing agents of the Fishing Establishment have claimed that I have no finesse. The slander is that though I sometimes overpower fish with a dog, coffeepot, canoe, or kayak paddle, I never outsmart them. This charge rankles, for even the hint that one cannot think better than a fish constitutes character assassination. Therefore it gave me great pleasure, just a few weeks ago, to finally lay this lie by its heels.

In the late summer the creek goes down, and our swimming hole becomes the only sizable pool of water in the neighborhood. This attracts trout and, inevitably, fishermen. However, under the conditions that now prevail I do not mind the fishermen and am even ready to eat with them. (If I had an unmarried sister, they could marry her, for all of me.) The problem is that by August there are so many trout in our swimming pool—we had seven rainbows and four brooks this year—that they interfere with my serious fishing for black-nosed dace. As I said earlier in this essay, we need a steady supply of these minnows, about a hundred a day, for four raccoons, one fish crow who will not fish for himself, and a smattering of shrews. Ordinarily, catching dace is not a difficult task. You simple throw out a net, chum well with bread—Mother Slonaker's Super Creamy Vitamin Enriched Loaf is the best, I have found—and then haul in on the net lines. However, in midsummer, with all the trout milling around the pool, the minnows never get a chance at the bread. If they try for a chum ball, they get knocked on their tails by greedy rainbows. It is for this reason, the hope that they can clean out the verminous trout, that fishermen are welcome at this time of year. Unfortunately, they can't cut the mustard. They are too far gone on the it's-not-whether-you-catch-or-don't-catch-but-how-you-play-the-line jazz to be effective fish exterminators.

Matters finally came to a head when the fisherman on duty was a colonel, USMC (ret.). He had fished according to the code in troubled waters from Saigon to Santo Domingo. At our pool he tried his okapi lures, purple grackle hackles, things that looked like rabbits' feet, and objects crafted by witch doctors. In desperation he tried canned corn, cheese niblets, and pickled salmon eggs. But though he was forced to stand back a good distance from the pool to keep from getting splashed by the trout that were cavorting through my dace nets, the colonel could not catch a fish. The obvious difficulty—beyond the fact that the colonel's tackle, like all that of most modern fishing purists, was designed not to catch fish—was that the trout had grown accustomed to bread. Even a fish is not so stupid as to want to take a piece of dead okapi when, if he hangs around for awhile, he is sure of getting a few nibbles of Mother Slonaker's finest. When it was suggested that the colonel try a little Vitamin Enriched, he refused rather stiffly. "There are some things a fisherman will not do," he said, standing tall and proud.

Being a freethinking fisherman who will try anything, I borrowed the colonel's flimsy rod, only to find out that, while bread bait may not be immoral, it was in this case impractical. Mother Slonaker's loaf was so creamy good that it simply melted off the hook, and the trout would gobble it up as it drifted toward the bottom of the pool. At this point a conventional fisherman would have given up, but not an iconoclast with a fish crow to feed. Looking around for a bread substitute, I could hardly fail to see the piles of cigarette butts with which the colonel, while nervously dueling the trout, had littered the bank of the pool. Fortunately, he smoked Brand X, a filtered fag, suitably safe and masculine for a marine. Breaking off a firm, fibrous, buoyant filter, I put it on the hook and threw it in the water. A rainbow immediately rose, trout-lipped the butt, swallowed it, and was pulled out on the grass.

"Throw that #$)&+ fish back in the %$&+$&% water," bellowed the colonel, reverting in his shock to his Parris Island manners. He looked as if he might explode.

"Put it back? I'm trying to get them out of here," I said.

"You," the colonel said coldly, as if dealing with some dirty Comsymp, "took that trout on a cigarette."

It was, I believe, my finest fishing hour. I felt I was complete, and I now saw myself for what I truly am, a prophet scorned, who nonetheless will lead the Fishing Establishment kicking and screaming into the bright promise of the post-Walton world.

ALLAN SEAGER
The Joys of Sport at Oxford

During my first week at Oxford I decided not to go out for any sports in the fall, or Michaelmas, term. My college offered Rugby, soccer, field hockey and something referred to as "the boats." I had never done any of these. They were all outdoor sports, and outdoors was where it was raining. For a fee I could also have joined a team of chaps who trotted informally through the dripping countryside in mild competition with a group from another college. Or I could have subscribed to a beagling club and worn a green coat, stout laced boots and a hemispheric little green velvet cap and legged it over the fields behind the dogs in search of hares and perhaps gotten a furry paw glued to a wooden shield as a trophy to hang in my room. The rain discouraged me, however. I got soggy enough walking to lectures. The fall term seemed a good time to lie up in front of a fire and get a good start on my reading.

I did this. I read heavily, but after three weeks I noticed a nervousness coming over me. And after the fourth week I knew what it was. I had been getting up every half hour to look out of the window. Now, there was nothing to look at out of my window but the college coal pile and beyond it a 15-foot wall topped with broken glass to keep students from climbing in after midnight. I was looking for a girl. I had got used to having dates at home but, after a day or two of scrutiny, I could tell that I was not likely to see one poised like a mountain goat on top of the coal.

I had won a Rhodes scholarship because I was the only man at the state examination who had worn a stiff collar—an Arrow, I believe. I did not wear it to Oxford. Instead I bought shirts with what we used to call bootlegger (tab) collars, a tweed jacket and gray flannel "bags." Not knowing that Americans move differently from the English—looser, somehow—and that you can identify one as far as you can see him, I believed my attire made me indistinguishable from an Old Etonian, and I had peeped at the English girls in the lecture halls, thinking that I had at least an even start with the Englishmen. I was appalled at what I saw.

There are four women's colleges at Oxford. Most of their undergraduates were going to be schoolmistresses and looked it. They wore rugged tweeds full of sticks of heather and twigs of gorse that stank in the wet weather, and they had big, frightening muscles in their legs from bike riding. A beautiful American girl would, I thought, be glad to make the acquaintance of a compatriot because of her loneliness.

I spotted an American girl in one of my lectures and she was beautiful. By asking around among other Americans I learned her name, which I have forgotten, and her address. I called. A maid let me in and went to fetch her. When she came in I said, "I wonder if you would care to drink some sherry with me this afternoon and bring a friend." I didn't want her friend, but the university had ruled that young women could visit young men's rooms only in pairs.

"I don't think so," she said coldly.

"Tea, perhaps?"

"No."

"Ah, milk?"

She walked out.

I didn't know then, as I came to later, that American girls in Oxford don't want to meet Americans; they want to meet Englishmen.

After this rebuff I might have lingered before my fire until spring in a dangerous inertia, dangerous because the elements of English diet are extremely reluctant to move without help after you have ingested them. But I was asked to go on the river. I was flattered to be asked, and I went.

The river is the Thames, but it is mysteriously called the Isis where it flows through Oxford, and the way to it is past the walled garden where Lewis Carroll, himself an admirer of girls—but girls rather younger than those who interested me—wrote *Alice in Wonderland* while he was a don at Christ Church. Then you go down a long alley under tremendous elms and you come to the college barges. They are houseboats, really, and they never go any-place. They are moored tight to the bank and are used as dressing rooms. They are painted white, highly ornamented with colored moldings, and they made a pretty sight lined up along the riverbank.

The only rowing I had done was to pull a flat-bottomed rowboat over the weed beds of small lakes after bass. I was not the only novice, however, and we all had to put up with two or three days of "we call this an oar" kind of instruction before they let us sit down and try to put our backs into it. The president of the Boat Club, Tom Smith, was the coach. There was no professional coaching in any sport—there still isn't—except that the varsity cricketers and swimmers had professionals come to look at them occasionally during the season. Tom Smith told me I might make a No. 6, and he gave me politely to know that Six was supposed to move a lot of water. At 12 stone 9 (180 and one-half pounds) I was the biggest man in the boat and, as I found out later, in the college. The English had been children during World War I. They had grown up on rationed food, and I think this is why they were not very big.

At my college we were lucky. We began the season in a proper shell no thicker than a cigar box. I saw an unfortunate youth step right through it into the river because he had not set his foot exactly on the keel when he climbed in. We also had movable seats on little wheels and swivel rowlocks (pronounced "rollocks"). I kept hearing a saying: "English rowing is 10 years behind the times; Cambridge rowing is 20 years behind the times. Oxford rowing is 40 years behind the times."

The varsity boat and those of some of the colleges began training exactly as their forefathers had done when Victoria was a young queen. In the first weeks of the season the varsity eight swung grandly down the river in a craft that resembled the war canoe of some obscure tribe. It was heavy enough for the open sea. It had board seats and the rowlocks were merely two straight pegs you laid the oars between. A month's workouts in this scow certainly pre-served tradition, but it also gave a man a set of boils as big as walnuts. A varsity oarsman spent more time on his feet than a cop, and when he sat down he bellowed. With such a fine start, the boils lasted all season even after the varsity shifted to the shell they would use against Cambridge. At my college, Oriel, we avoided all this pain. Daringly unorthodox, we rowed the Jesus style.

This was not blasphemy and we did not kneel in prayer before taking to the water. The Jesus style was developed at Jesus College, Cambridge by a man named Steve Fairbairn. Succinctly put, it was "blade form." This meant that if your oar blade was right, nothing else mattered. Opposed to this was the practice of the varsity, all the other colleges and, I believe, American crews, called body form, which meant that if your body was correctly poised, the blade had to be right.

A body-form crew was coached right down to its fingernails. You were supposed to keep a straight back, to stare perpetually at the fifth or sixth cervical vertebra of the man in front of you and never move your head. A body form crew is impressive to watch. The muscular decorum makes its members look virtuous and clean-limbed. Perhaps this is its own reward, for a blade-form crew, rowing with backs bending comfortably and gandering around at the blades, may look raffish and sloppy but probably is going as fast as the body-form boys.

We trained all the fall into December. It was mostly just rowing. The Thames is a canal with locks all the way to London and, if we were taking a long paddle, say, eight or 10 miles, we had to pass Iffley lock when we went one way and Osney lock when we went the other. I can remember sitting in Osney lock one dark afternoon, waiting for it to fill, with ice forming on the oars and flakes of snow as big as goose feathers wetting the back of my skimpy little Jaegar shirt, and it was no consolation to remember that the Miller's Wife in *The Canterbury Tales* had probably lived within a furlong.

On short days when we stayed within Iffley lock we were coached by Tom Smith riding a bicycle beside us on the towpath. I doubt if we rowed as much as Washington or Yale. There was no other training. Beer was believed strengthening; gin would keep coxswains small. No one spoke of cigarettes at all. As green as I was, I didn't know whether I was in shape or not, but it didn't make much difference, because term ended about the middle of December and I took off for six weeks in Paris.

The Bump Races come in two sets, late in January and early in May. They are rowed for six days, Thursday through Saturday and Monday through Wednesday. The colloquial name for the January races is Toggers; the formal one, Torpids; but no one could tell me why. The May races are called Eights, and they are quite social. If you have a girl, you bring her, give her luncheons of hock and lobster mayonnaise and she sits on the top of your barge to watch you sweat. Toggers are grimmer because January is grimmer.

Bump races are examples of much made of little. The Thames is a small river at Oxford; in fact, I think Ralph Boston could jump over it at a place called the Gut if he took a good run. There were about 25 rowing colleges at Oxford, and each college put two boats in the river, the larger colleges, like Balliol, three, sometimes four, so there were perhaps 60 in all. I doubt if you could row 60 eight-oared shells abreast at Poughkeepsie, and you certainly can't on the Isis, so they start one behind another and chase the one in front.

Small stakes are driven into the bank 60 feet apart. To each stake a rope 60 feet long is fixed. The cox holds the other end and lets the boat drift until it is taut. Each boat has a starter. Five minutes before time all the starters gather at a little brass cannon in a hayfield to synchronize their stopwatches with a chronometer. Then they come back and stand on the bank beside their boats saying, "Two minutes gone. Three minutes gone," to the yawning oarsmen in the river below. In the last minute they count off the quarters, and finally, "10, 9, 8, 7, 6, 5, 4, come forward, are you ready?" and "Bang!" goes the little brass cannon. The college bargeman gives you a hell of a shove with a boathook and away you go, the cox howling the beat at about 50 strokes a minute. It is very common to black out completely during the first 30 seconds. As soon as you are under way, the stroke drops to about 40, but not much less, because the course from Iffley lock to the top of the barges is only about a mile and a half.

Most of the members of your college are scrambling along the towpath beside you, yelling and shooting off guns. You can't tell whether the boat behind you is gaining, because you are watching Stroke's oar or your own, but if the cox's voice rises to a scream and he starts counting to raise the beat you know you are overtaking the boat ahead. When your bow overlaps his stern, the cox turns the rudder sharply. Bow touches stern. This is the bump.

When you make a bump, the next day your boat starts in the place of the bumped boat. You go up or down each day according to your prowess. The final aim, which may take several years to achieve, is to become Head of the River, the first boat in line.

I came back from Paris not in the best of shape. A wisdom tooth had started acting up. It ached and swelled monotonously. I made my apologies to Tom Smith, and he found another Six. For a week I tried to ignore it, hoping the swelling would go away. It didn't and I asked the dean to recommend a dentist. I found this man in what I took to be a large bedroom with the bed moved out. The walls were covered with flowered wallpaper, and a chromo of Watts's *Hope*[1] hung on the wall. He sat me down in a chair with four legs. He took a look and, as God is my judge, he prescribed an infusion of camomile and poppyhead—not opium, poppyhead—with which to bathe the afflicted parts. I was not sleeping much and I was smoking about 50 Players a day, but I bathed away conscientiously. It didn't do any good. The swelling went gruesomely on. When I looked as if I were trying to conceal a scarlet pippin in my cheek I went back to the dentist and said, "Lance this, will you?" He bumbled and said at last, "I can't. I'm not a dental surgeon." So he took me to a real surgeon, who had his learning son in the office, and

1. An allegorical painting of a female figure seated on the globe, peeping from beneath a blindfold. She bends over a lyre on which only one string remains; the sky is dark except for one star.

there before a blazing coal fire the three together gave me gas and lanced it. Afterward I didn't feel good, but at least I didn't feel like a bomb about to go off.

That night I was sitting in front of my fire, reading and bathing my wound with a little neat whisky when Tom Smith knocked at my door. He said that his No. 6 had just come down with a bad case of flu. Toggers started the next day. Would I care to fill in? It was so casual and the honor of the U.S.A. depended so heavily on it that I said I would be delighted—which was a lie.

On the first day of Toggers I was personally lucky. I had to row only the first six strokes. When the little brass cannon went off, we laid into the first strokes hard. The cox had just shouted, "Six!" when No. 7 in front of me caught a crab. If you are quick you can sometimes lie flat and let the oar pass over your head. Seven was not quick. He was probably blacked out, and the butt of the oar caught him in the belly and jackknifed him out of the boat. Falling, he broke his oar smack off at the rowlock. The boat staggered. There were cries of "Man overboard!" and Dawson-Grove, the cox, was yelling oaths like a banshee. I don't believe it is possible to overturn an eight-oared boat, but we nearly made it. In the confusion, Exeter came tearing into us from behind and sheared off all the oars on the bow side. It was a mess. No. 7 avoided having Exeter's keel bash his head in by cannily staying under water until after the collision; then he swam soggily ashore. Our race was over for that day and I was barely winded.

The next day, with new oars, we caught St. John's on the Green Bank and made a bump. In fact, we made five bumps in all during Toggers. If a boat makes five bumps in Toggers or four in Eights the college is required by custom to stand its members a Bump supper. It is a big jollification in honor of the Boat Club. The manciple (head chef) outdoes himself and provides a really good meal, with fresh soup (I think) and champagne at will. Alumni gather and there are sherry parties. Since many Oriel undergraduates study theology, many of its graduates are parsons, but Church of England clergy are not stuffy. They go to sherry parties, and they don't stand around with a glass in their hands for the look of things, either.

At our Bump supper the hall was in an uproar because of the sherry parties beforehand. Cheers were started but forgotten. Boating songs were begun, broken off and begun again. A stately portrait of Matthew Arnold, once an Oriel don, hung on the wall. A swaying youth, his boiled shirt coming out in welts from spilled champagne, pegged an orange from the centerpiece clean through Matthew's jaw just at the muttonchop. A bonfire sprang up in the front quad, fed by side tables, chairs and Van Gogh reproductions. The son of a Scottish laird broke into the provost's lodgings, stole all the shoes belonging to that good old man (now knighted for his translations of Aristotle) and hurled them all into the flames.

High above the quad in a third-floor bedroom a man named Antony Henley crouched, waiting for the supper to finish. Tony had collected half the chamber pots in the college. (They used them then, and it is no more than even money they use them now.) In a room directly opposite, another man had collected the other half. A rope hung in a curve from one window to the other. At last the dons appeared under the porch of the hall, chatting only less than boisterously from the champagne. They were in full fig—dinner jackets, long M.A. gowns and mortarboards. They walked down the steps in the wavering light of the bonfire. At that moment a shower of broken crockery fell on their heads. Tony and his friend were sticking the rope ends through the pot handles and letting them slide down the rope two at a time. When they met they broke and fell on the dean, the provost, the bursar, the Goldsmith's reader, a bishop or two and other dignitaries. Big joke. The party went on all night, consuming untold bottles of Pommery and Piper-Heidsieck and much of the movable furniture of the college. At one point, I was told, seven drunken archdeacons danced around the bonfire, a spectacle very likely unmatched since the martyrdom of Ridley and Latimer, who were burned years earlier in Broad Street and from the top of whose Gothic monument the Oxford Alpine Club hangs a chamber pot each year.

The next morning the groans of hangover were decently stifled by the mists in the quad. The scouts were out with rakes and shovels, cleaning away the empties, the shards of crockery and the ashes of the bonfire strewn with the nails and eyelets of the provost's shoes. Antony Henley was haled before the dean, presented with a bill for upward of 150 chamber pots and laughingly fined £10. Toggers were over. I have never rowed since nor drunk so much champagne.

I was not, so to speak, an oarsman by trade, I was a swimmer. The rowing I had done, while exhausting and in some ways amusing, merely passed the time until the swimming season opened in the third, or Hilary, term. The trouble was I couldn't find anyplace to "go out" for swimming. There was no varsity pool, I discovered. But I heard somewhere that the swimmers used the Merton Street Baths.

The Baths were in a grubby brick building, built long before with what seemed an ecclesiastical intent, for they had long Gothic windows in front. The pool itself, gently steaming in the cold of the building, was a gloomy tank, trapezoidal in shape, and I learned later that it was 25 yards long on one side and exactly 22 and one-half yards long on the other—which made for some tricky finishes in a race. The bathing master said there hadn't been any gentlemen from the varsity near the place in months. He suggested that I see Mr. Pace in Merton College, the club president.

After I had knocked, Pace opened his door six inches, no more. "Yes?" he said.

"Mr. Pace?"

"Yes," he said.

"My name is Seager."

"Yes?" he said.

"I wanted to ask you about the swimming."

"Oh. Ah," he said. Then he opened the door. "Do come in." I went in.

"Seager? Oh, yes. Someone mentioned your name. From the States, aren't you? Mitchigan? A good club, I believe."

"We were national champions last year."

"Really? Just what did you want to know?"

"When do you start training?"

"Oh, I'll let you know. I'll send you a note round the week before we begin. Will that do?"

It was the Oxford manner again. He was effortlessly making my enthusiasm seem not only comic but childishly comic. However, it is just as well to be candid. I was after their records, and I didn't know then that he was Oxford's best sprinter. "I'd like to start now," I said, "I'm not in very good shape."

"I daresay you could use the Baths. Cost you a bob a time until we start meeting."

He waved his hand nonchalantly.

"Cheers," he said, and I left.

It was only later that I learned I had committed a faux pas. I was always finding out things later. You did not "go out" for the varsity. College sports, O.K.—you could turn up whenever you liked. But the varsity was strictly invitational, so much so that in my day the Varsity Boat Club had never used an American oar. There was a faint general resentment of Americans and Colonials taking over Oxford sports. However, I paid my shilling and trundled a slow half mile every day up and down the bath. It was like swimming in church.

In a couple of weeks Pace sent his note round and the season opened. I was astounded. It was not so much that they swam badly —I had more or less expected that from their record times—it was that they worked so little. In fact, they didn't *work* at all. They swam until they felt tired and quit for the day, refreshed. Where was the old pepper, the old fight? Slowly I began to comprehend the English attitude toward sports, which, unless Dr. Bannister changed it drastically with his great meticulous mile, is this: sports are for fun. If you are good at one or two of them, it is somewhat in the nature of a divine gift. Since the gift is perpetual, it is there every day and you can pull out a performance very near your best any time. With a little practice to loosen the muscles and clear the pipes, you are ready for the severest tests.

I was drinking beer one night in Balliol College with several men, one of them an Olympic runner, a 1,500-meter man. It is rare that a subject so trivial as sports would come up in Balliol, the intellectual center of England, but it came up and eventually came down to the question of how fast could this Olympic man run 1,500 meters at the moment? We all piled into a couple of taxis and drove out to the Oxford Sports Ground, where there was a cinder track. The runner, full of confidence and beer, supplied a stopwatch and a flashlight, and there in his street clothes, in the rain, in the dead of night, this man took off and ran 1,500 meters in just over four minutes. This proved to me that the English were right, but it did not prove to me that I was wrong. I knew I could not swim 100 yards in less than a minute, untrained.

But I stayed untrained. It seemed to be overly zealous to go on chugging up and down after all the other members of the club had showered, dressed and come to stand at the edge of the bath to watch me as if I were a marine curiosity, like a dugong. I tried it a couple of times and quit. I swam as little as they did, no more. Then there was the problem of entertainment after the matches—they didn't call them meets. There was little university swimming in England, so our competition was usually a town club whose members might be aquatic plumbers and carpenters—not gentlemen, you see. With a splendid condescension, we set out a table loaded with whisky, beer and wine after each match, and we had to drink to make our guests feel at home so that caste differences would be concealed and we could pretend to be all jolly good sportsmen together. After a match, say, in London with the Paddington police, the coppers would set out a table of whisky, beer and wine, and we had to drink to show our appreciation of their hospitality. This drinking was not a detestable chore, but it meant that, with two matches a week, we were getting mildly stoned twice a week just in the way of business. This was not how I had been taught to train, and it came over me suddenly how far morality had invaded sports in the U.S.

I won all my races except one, but the times were shamefully slow and I was chased right down to the wire in all of them. In May, John Pace had the whole club to tea in his rooms. There was an hour of conversation interspersed with tomato and cucumber sandwiches. Then Pace stood up by the chimney piece. "Now, chaps," he began facetiously (I never heard anyone use "chaps" except facetiously). "You know we swim the Tabs two weeks from now." "Tabs" meant Cambridge, from the latin *Cantabrigia*. "Please smoke only after meals and cut down your beer to a pint a day. And do try to swim every day between now and then."

People clapped and cried, "Hear! Hear!" as if Pace had been in the House of Commons. I gathered we were in hard training from then on. I had not gone under 61 seconds for 100 yards yet, and I had heard that Cambridge had a fancy Dan named Hill who had done 58. I was scared.

Someone said, "This rationing of beer, John. What if we're sconced?"

"Behave yourselves and you won't be," Pace said.

In Oxford dining halls a sconce is a penalty exacted in the spring of the year for some breach of taste or decorum. It is a welcome penalty, eagerly exacted. If you showed up late for dinner or wearing something odd like a turtleneck sweater or if you said something that could be remotely construed as offensive, you were sconced. Once I said something slightly off color.

"We'll have a sconce on you for that," the man next to me said. He wrote my offense in Latin on the back of a menu, *"Seager dixit obscenissime"*[2] and had a waiter take it up to high table to be approved by the dean. It was a formality. The dean always approved sconces. "What will you take it in?" I was asked. In theory you had to drink a silver quart pot of some liquid, bottoms up. In practice you had no choice; custom said old beer. Once I saw a man take it in fresh cow's milk and he never lived it down. It is the sort of thing planters discuss in Kenya and Borneo 20 years later.

The strength of English beer is indicated by the number of Xs on the barrel. Ale is the weakest, one X. Bitter beer is two Xs. Old beer is five Xs, about as strong as sherry. It is never iced, but in college it comes from the cellars and it might as well be. It looks almost coal-black and it is as thick as stout. It is hard but not impossible to drink it all down at one go. If you do, the man who sconced you has to pay for it. If you fail, it is passed around the table like a loving cup. But the minute you set the pot down empty, you're drunk.

The Cambridge match was held at the Bath Club, then on Dover Street, London. It was a posh club. (I like the origin of posh. When people used to tour the Orient from England the most expensive cabins on the P&O boats, those that made the most of the prevailing winds and the least of the sun, were on the port side going and the starboard side returning, so the luggage for those cabins was marked P.O.S.H., that is "port out, starboard home.") We took an afternoon train down to London already dressed in white ties, black trousers and our blazers, and with an affectation of gaiety we sauntered up Piccadilly in the early evening and into the Bath Club. I knew I had to fear this Cambridge speedster, Hill, who had done 58 seconds, because I had done only 61 that season. (I had done 61 when I was a long, wheyfaced boy of 15 in high school in Tennessee.) My fear was degrading. That's why I was mad: it was a real

---

2. "Seager spoke most obscenely."

fear. And I felt that my teammates had begun to wonder when I was going to demonstrate that I didn't fit one of the stock British images of the American, lots of noise and no performance.

I figured I could take Hill in the 50 if I scrambled, but in the 100 I knew I would have to swim and I figured I could swim about 75 yards before I blew up. Since the English started slow and finished fast, I figured I would start fast, get a big lead, frighten him and finish on whatever I had left.

The Bath Club looked like a court levee, the ladies in those English evening gowns, the men in white ties and tail coats, and the Old Blues[3] wore their blazers. Diamonds glittered. I detected dowagers with lorgnons, a colorful throng, posh. The club pool was 25 yards long on both sides, but it was dark at one end. Since you can bump your head into a goose egg or even oblivion if you slam into a turn you can't see, I wet a towel and hung it over the far end in my lane to make a white spot. As I walked back I heard resentful murmurs from the spectators. "He's an Ameddican," as if what I had done were cunning and illicit.

The 50-yard race went as I had expected. I scrambled. I won in a record time of 25 seconds. I went back to the dressing room to worry about the 100. Hill was a little fleshy fellow whose fat might hide more stamina than I had.

I swam the first two lengths of the 100 in 25 seconds, and after the third length I looked back at Hill. He was 30 feet behind, but I was not encouraged because I could tell I was going to blow up. I blew and finished the last 25 yards with a frantic overhand, dazzled by fatigue, my head out all the way so I could breathe. But I won by a yard, and they said it was a new record, 57 seconds. My teammates shouted and pounded me on the back as if I had done well. My shabby little victories gave Oxford the match.

The adulation of the English for sports figures is greater than that in this country, possibly because a sound sports record keeps a chap from being too "clever"—which is repugnant (Churchill was too clever by half, right up until the blitz). Let a man die who has not specially distinguished himself as an admiral, a cabinet member or a press lord, and if he has been a Blue, Oxon or Cantab, the obituary will very likely be headed OLD BLUE'S DEMISE. That is what is important. A few months after my victories I was having tea with some people at a public tearoom in Oxford.

A man came up to the table, a student, and said to me, "Is this Mr. Seager, the famous swimmer?"

I looked him straight in the eye for maybe three seconds. He seemed to be perfectly serious. "I'm Seager," I answered finally.

"May I shake your hand?" he said.

I shook hands and he went away pleased, apparently. Nobody at

---

3. Former varsity athletes from Oxford and Cambridge.

my table seemed to think that any of this was strange, and I let my self-esteem expand a little.

I didn't get punctured for two years. I was back in Ann Arbor then and happened to run into Matt Mann, my former coach.

"Say, I hear you got a couple of English records," he said. Matt was born in Yorkshire, and he had held English records himself.

"Yes," I said. I couldn't look at him.

"What were your times?"

"Twenty-five. Fifty-seven," I mumbled. I had been a bad boy.

"Fifty-seven! Were you dragging something?" he said jovially.

Surprising myself, I said defiantly, "Matt, it was fun."

And it had been, all of it, the massive courtesy of the swimming policemen, the singing in the pub afterward, the soiree at the Bath Club—not real glory, which means work, but a hell of a lot of fun.

QUESTIONS

1. At some points Seager describes the Oxford manner and pictures himself as an outsider. Give some examples. Are there instances where Seager presents himself in the Oxford manner?
2. What characteristics of the English view of sports does Seager stress? How are these characteristics reflected in other areas of Oxford life?
3. Seager's narrative permits him to use a wide range of language, including British and American diction, and of usage, reaching from the relatively formal to slang. What kinds of effects does Seager achieve with this variety of language?
4. When Seager draped a wet towel at the end of his lane, was that gamesmanship (see Potter, pp. 824–832)? Did he display Rhodesmanship in the state examination?
5. What is Seager's attitude toward the experiences he recounts? How is that attitude expressed in his tone? Does it vary?
6. Consider a nation or smaller social group with which you are familiar. What does its attitude toward sports reveal about the nation or group? Write an essay showing the evidence for your view.

A. J. LIEBLING
Poet and Pedagogue

When Floyd Patterson regained the world heavyweight championship by knocking out Ingemar Johansson in June, 1960, he so excited a teenager named Cassius Marcellus Clay, in Louisville, Kentucky, that Clay, who was a good amateur light heavyweight, made up a ballad in honor of the victory. (The tradition of pugilistic poetry is old; according to Pierce Egan, the Polybius of the London Prize Ring, Bob Gregson, the Lancashire Giant, used "to recount the deeds of his Brethren of the Fist in heroic verse, like the Bards of Old." A sample Gregson couplet was "The British lads that's here/Quite strangers are to fear." He was not a very good fighter, either.) At the time, Clay was too busy training for the Olympic boxing tournament in Rome that summer to set his ode down on paper, but he memorized it, as Homer and Gregson must have done with their things, and then polished it up in his head. "It took me about three days to think it up," Clay told me a week or so ago, while he was training in the Department of Parks gymnasium, on West Twenty-eighth Street, for his New York debut as a professional, against a heavy-weight from Detroit named Sonny Banks. In between his composition of the poem and his appearance on Twenty-eighth Street, Clay had been to Rome and cleaned up his Olympic opposition with aplomb, which is his strongest characteristic. The other finalist had been a Pole with a name that it takes two rounds to pronounce, but Cassius had not tried. A book that I own called *Olympic Games: 1960*, translated from the German, says "Clay fixes the Pole's punch-hand with an almost hypnotic stare and by nimble dodging renders his attacks quite harmless." He thus risked being disqualified for holding and hitting, but he got away with it. He had then turned professional under social and financial auspices sufficient to launch a bank, and had won ten tryout bouts on the road. Now he told me that Banks, whom he had never seen, would be no problem.

I had watched Clay's performance in Rome and had considered it attractive but not probative. Amateur boxing compares with professional boxing as college theatricals compare with stealing scenes from Margaret Rutherford. Clay had a skittering style, like a pebble scaled over water. He was good to watch, but he seemed to make only glancing contact. It is true that the Pole finished the three-round bout helpless and out on his feet, but I thought he had just run out of puff chasing Clay, who had then cut him to pieces. ("Pietrzykowski is done for," the Olympic book says. "He gazes helplessly into his corner of the ring; his legs grow heavier and he cannot escape his rival.") A boxer who uses his legs as much as Clay used his in Rome risks deceleration in a longer bout. I had been more impressed by Patterson when he was an Olympian, in 1952; he had knocked out his man in a round.

At the gym that day, Cassius was on a mat doing situps when Mr. Angelo Dundee, his trainer, brought up the subject of the ballad. "He is smart," Dundee said. "He made up a poem." Clay had his hands locked behind his neck, elbows straight out, as he bobbed up and down. He is a golden-brown young man, big-chested and long-legged, whose limbs have the smooth, rounded look that Joe Louis's used to have, and that frequently denotes fast muscles. He is twenty years old and six feet two inches tall, and he weighs a hundred and ninety-five pounds.

"I'll say it for you," the poet announced, without waiting to be wheedled or breaking cadence. He began on a rise: "You may talk about Sweden [down and up again], You may talk about Rome [down and up again], But Rockville Centre is Floyd Patterson's home [down]."

He is probably the only poet in America who can recite this way. I would like to see T. S. Eliot try.

Clay went on, continuing his ventriflexions: "A lot of people said that Floyd couldn't fight, But you should have seen him on that comeback night."

There were some lines that I fumbled; the tempo of situps and poetry grew concurrently faster as the bardic fury took hold. But I caught the climax as the poet's voice rose: "He cut up his eyes and mussed up his face, And that last left hook knocked his head out of place!"

Cassius smiled and said no more for several situps, as if waiting for Johansson to be carried to his corner. He resumed when the Swede's seconds had had time to slosh water in his pants and bring him around. The fight was done; the press took over: "A reporter asked: 'Ingo, will a rematch be put on?' Johansson said: 'Don't know. It might be postponed.' "

The poet did a few more silent strophes, and then said:

"If he would have stayed in Sweden, He wouldn't have took that beatin'."

Here, overcome by admiration, he lay back and laughed. After a minute or two, he said, "That rhymes. I like it."

There are trainers I know who, if they had a fighter who was a poet, would give up on him, no matter how good he looked, but Mr. Dundee is of the permissive school. Dundee has been a leading Italian name in the prize-fighting business in this country ever since about 1910, when a manager named Scotty Monteith had a boy named Giuseppe Carrora whom he rechristened Johnny Dundee. Johnny became the hottest lightweight around; in 1923, in the twilight of his career, he boiled down and won the featherweight championship of the world. Clay's trainer is a brother of Chris Dundee, a promoter in Miami Beach, but they are not related to Johnny, who is still around, or to Joe and Vince Dundee, brothers out of Baltimore, who were welterweight and middleweight champions, respectively, in the late twenties and early thirties, and who are not related to Johnny, either.

"He is very talented," Dundee said while Clay was dressing. It was bitter cold outside, but he did not make Clay take a cold shower before putting his clothes on. "He likes his shower better at the hotel," he told me. It smacked of progressive education. Elaborating on Clay's talent, Dundee said, "He will jab you five or six times going away. Busy hands. And he has a left uppercut." He added that Clay, as a business enterprise, was owned and operated by a syndicate of ten leading citizens of Louisville, mostly distillers. They had given the boy a bonus of ten thousand dollars for signing up, and paid him a monthly allowance and his training expenses whether he fought or not—a research fellowship. In return, they took half his earnings when he had any. These had been inconsiderable until his most recent fight, when he made eight thousand dollars. His manager of record (since somebody has to sign contracts) was a member of this junta—Mr. William Faversham, a son of the old matinee idol. Dundee, a tutor in attendance, was a salaried employee. "The idea was he shouldn't be rushed," Dundee said. "Before they hired me, we had a conference about his future like he was a serious subject."

It sounded like flying in the face of the old rule that hungry fighters make the best fighters. I know an old-style manager named Al Weill, who at the beginning of the week used to give each of his fighters a five-dollar meal ticket that was good for five dollars and fifty cents in trade at a coffeepot on Columbus Avenue. A guy had to win a fight to get a second ticket before the following Monday. "It's good for them," Weill used to say. "Keeps their mind on their work."

That day in the gym, Clay's boxing had consisted of three rounds with an amateur light heavyweight, who had been unable to keep away from the busy hands. When the sparring partner covered his head with his arms, the poet didn't bother to punch to the body. "I'm a head-hunter," he said to a watcher who called his attention to this omission. "Keep punching at a man's head, and it mixes his mind." After that, he had skipped rope without a rope. His flippancy would have horrified Colonel John R. Stingo, an ancient connoisseur, who says, "Body-punching is capital investment," or the late Sam Langford, who, when asked why he punched so much for the body, said, "The head got eyes."

Now Cassius reappeared, a glass of fashion in a snuff-colored suit and one of those lace-front shirts, which I had never before known anybody with nerve enough to wear, although I had seen them in shirt-shop windows on Broadway. His tie was like two shoestring ends laid across each other, and his smile was white and optimistic. He did not appear to know how badly he was being brought up.

Just when the sweet science appears to lie like a painted ship upon a painted ocean, a new Hero, as Pierce Egan would term him, comes along like a Moran tug to pull it out of the doldrums. It was because Clay had some of the Heroic aura about him that I went uptown the next day to see Banks, the *morceau*[1] chosen for the

1. Short musical piece.

prodigy to perform in his big-time debut. The exhibition piece is usually a fighter who was once almost illustrious and is now beyond ambition, but Banks was only twenty-one. He had knocked out nine men in twelve professional fights, had won another fight on a decision, and had lost two, being knocked out once. But he had come back against the man who stopped him and had knocked him out in two rounds. That showed determination as well as punching power. I had already met Banks, briefly, at a press conference that the Madison Square Garden Corporation gave for the two incipient Heroes, and he seemed the antithesis of the Kentucky bard—a grave, quiet young Deep Southerner. He was as introverted as Clay was extro. Banks, a lighter shade than Clay, had migrated to the automobile factories from Tupelo, Mississippi, and boxed as a professional from the start, to earn money. He said at the press conference that he felt he had "done excellently" in the ring, and that the man who had knocked him out, and whom he had subsequently knocked out, was "an excellent boxer." He had a long, rather pointed head, a long chin, and the kind of inverted-triangle torso that pro-proletarian artists like to put on their steelworkers. His shoulders were so wide that his neat ready-made suit floated around his waist, and he had long, thick arms.

Banks was scheduled to train at two o'clock in the afternoon at Harry Wiley's Gymnasium, at 137th Street and Broadway. I felt back at home in the fight world as soon as I climbed up from the subway and saw the place—a line of plate-glass windows above a Latin-American bar, grill, and barbecue. The windows were flecked with legends giving the hours when the gym was open (it wasn't), the names of fighters training there (they weren't and half of them had been retired for years), and plugs for physical fitness and boxing instruction. The door of the gym—"Harry Wiley's Clean Gym," the sign on it said—was locked, so I went into the Latin-American place and had a beer while I waited. I had had only half the bottle when a taxi drew up at the curb outside the window and five colored men—one little and four big—got out, carrying bags of gear. They had the key for the gym. I finished my beer and followed them.

By the time I got up the stairs, the three fellows who were going to spar were already in the locker room changing their clothes, and the only ones in sight were a big, solid man in a red jersey, who was laying out the gloves and bandages on a rubbing table, and a wispy little chap in an olive-green sweater, who was smoking a long rattail cigar. His thin black hair was carefully marcelled along the top of his narrow skull, a long gold watch chain danged from his fob pocket, and he exuded an air of elegance, precision, and authority, like a withered but still peppery mahout in charge of a string of not quite bright elephants. Both men appeared occupied with their thoughts, so I made a tour of the room before intruding, reading a series of didactic signs that the proprietor had put up among the photographs of prize fighters and pin-up girls. "Road Work Builds Your Legs," one sign said, and another, "Train Every Day—Great Fighters Are Made That Way." A third admonished, "The Gentleman Boxer Has the Most Friends." "Ladies Are Fine—At the Right Time," another said. When I had absorbed them all, I got around to the big man.

"Clay looks mighty fast," I said to him by way of an opening.

He said, "He may not be if a big fellow go after him. That amateur stuff don't mean too much." He himself was Johnny Summerlin, he told me, and he had fought a lot of good heavyweights in his day. "Our boy don't move so fast, but he got fast hands," he said. "He don't discourage easy, either. If we win this one, we'll be all set." I could see that they would be, because Clay has been getting a lot of publicity, and a boxer's fame, like a knight's armor, becomes the property of the fellow who licks him.

Banks now came out in ring togs, and, after greeting me, held out his hands to Summerlin to be bandaged. He looked even more formidable without his street clothes. The two other fighters, who wore their names on their dressing robes, were Cody Jones, a heavyweight as big as Banks, and Sammy Poe, nearly as big. Poe, although a Negro, had a shamrock on the back of his robe—a sign that he was a wag. They were both Banks stablemates from Detroit, Summerlin said, and they had come along to spar with him. Jones had had ten fights and had won eight, six of them by knockouts. This was rougher opposition than any amateur light heavyweight. Banks, when he sparred with Jones, did not scuffle around but practiced purposefully a pattern of coming in low, feinting with head and body to draw a lead, and then hammering in hooks to body and head, following the combination with a right cross. His footwork was neat and geometrical but not flashy —he slid his soles along the mat, always set to hit hard. Jones, using his right hand often, provided rough competition but no substitute for Clay's blinding speed. Poe, the clown, followed Jones. He grunted and howled "Whoo-huh-huh!" every time he threw a punch, and Banks howled back; it sounded like feeding time at a zoo. This was a lively workout.

After the sparring, the little man, discarding his cigar, got into the ring alone with Banks. He wore huge sixteen- or eighteen-ounce sparring gloves, which he held, palm open, toward the giant, leading him in what looked like a fan dance. The little man, covering his meager chest with one glove, would hold up the other, and Banks would hit it. The punch coming into the glove sounded like a fast ball striking a catcher's mitt. By his motions the trainer indicated a scenario, and Banks, from his crouch, dropped Clay ten or fifteen times this way, theoretically. Then the slender man called a halt and sent Banks to punch the bag. "Remember," he said, "you got to keep on top of him—keep the pressure on."

As the little man climbed out of the ring, I walked around to him and introduced myself. He said that his name was Theodore McWhorter, and that Banks was his baby, his creation—he had taught him everything. For twenty years, McWhorter said, he had run a gymnasium for boxers in Detroit—the Big D. (I supposed it must be pretty much like Wiley's, where we were talking.) He had trained hundreds of neighborhood boys to fight, and had had some good fighters in his time, like Johnny Summerlin, but never a champion. Something always went wrong.

There are fellows like this in almost every big town. Cus D'Amato, who brought Patterson through the amateurs and still has him, used to be one of them, with a one-room gym on Fourteenth Street, but he is among the few who ever hit the mother lode. I could see that McWhorter was a good teacher—such men often are. They are never former champions or notable boxers. The old star is impatient with beginners. He secretly hopes that they won't be as good as he was, and this is a self-defeating quirk in an instructor. The man with the little gym wants to prove himself vicariously. Every promising pupil, consequently, is himself, and he gets knocked out with every one of them, even if he lives to be eighty. McWhorter, typically, said he had been an amateur bantamweight in the thirties but had never turned pro, because times were so hard then that you could pick up more money boxing amateur. Instead of medals, you would get certificates redeemable for cash—two, three, five dollars, sometimes even ten. Once you were a pro, you might not get two fights a year. Whatever his real reason, he had not gone on.

"My boy never got nothing easy," he said. "He don't expect it. Nobody give him nothing. And a boy like that, when he got a chance to be something, he's dangerous."

"You think he's really got a chance?" I asked.

"If we didn't think so, we wouldn't have took the match," Mr. McWhorter said. "You can trap a man," he added mysteriously. "Flashy boxing is like running. You got a long lead, you can run freely. The other kid's way behind, you can sit down and play, get up fresh, and run away from him again. But you got a man running after you with a knife or a gun, pressing it in your back, you feel the pressure. You can't run so free. I'm fighting Clay my way." The substitution of the first for the third person in conversation is managerial usage. I knew that McWhorter would resubstitute

Banks for himself in the actual fight.

We walked over to the heavy bag, where Banks was working. There was one other downtown spectator in the gym, and he came over and joined us. He was one of those anonymous experts, looking like all his kind, whom I have been seeing around gyms and fight camps for thirty years. "You can tell a Detroit fighter every time," he said. "They're well trained. They got the fundamentals. They can hit. Like from Philadelphia the fighters got feneese."

Mr. McWhorter acknowledged the compliment. "We have some fine trainers in Detroit," he said.

Banks, no longer gentle, crouched and swayed before the bag, crashing his left hand into it until the thing jigged and clanked its chains.

"Hit him in the belly like that and you got him," the expert said. "He can't take it there."

Banks stopped punching the bag and said, "Thank you, thank you," just as if the expert had said something novel.

"He's a good boy," McWhorter said as the man walked away. "A polite boy."

When I left to go downtown, I felt like the possessor of a possibly valuable secret. I toyed with the notion of warning the butterfly Cassius, my fellow-litterateur, of his peril, but decided that I must remain neutral and silent. In a dream the night before the fight, I heard Mr. McWhorter saying ominously, "You can trap a man." He had grown as big as Summerlin, and his cigar had turned into an elephant goad.

The temperature outside the Garden was around fifteen degrees on the night of the fight, and the crowd that had assembled to see Clay's debut was so thin that it could more properly be denominated a quorum. Only fans who like sociability ordinarily turn up for a fight that they can watch for nothing on television, and that night the cold had kept even the most gregarious at home. (The boxers, however, were sure of four thousand dollars apiece from television.) Only the sportswriters, the gamblers, and the fight mob were there—nonpayers all—and the Garden management, solicitous about how the ringside would look to the television audience, had to coax relative strangers into the working press section. This shortgage of spectators was too bad, because there was at least one red-hot preliminary, which merited a better audience. It was a six-rounder between a lad infelicitously named Ducky Dietz—a hooker and body puncher—and a light heavy from western Pennsylvania named Tommy Gerarde, who preferred a longer range but punched more sharply. Dietz, who shouldn't have, got the decision, and the row that followed warmed our little social group and set the right mood for the main event.

The poet came into the ring first, escorted by Dundee; Nick Florio, the brother of Patterson's trainer, Dan Florio; and a fellow named Gil Clancy, a physical-education supervisor for the Department of Parks, who himself manages a good welterweight named Emile Griffith. (Griffith, unlike Clay, is a worrier. "He is always afraid of being devalued," Clancy says.) As a corner, it was the equivalent of being represented by Sullivan & Cromwell.[2] Clay, who I imagine regretted parting with his lace shirt, had replaced it with a white robe that had a close-fitting red collar and red cuffs. He wore white buckskin bootees that came high on his calves, and taking hold of the ropes in his corner, he stretched and bounced like a ballet dancer at the bar. In doing so, he turned his back to the other, or hungry, corner before Banks and his faction arrived.

Banks looked determined but slightly uncertain. Maybe he was trying to remember all the things McWhorter had told him to do. He was accompanied by McWhorter, Summerlin, and Harry Wiley, a plump, courtly colored man, who runs the clean gym. McWhorter's parchment brow was wrinkled with concentration, and his mouth was set. He looked like a producer who thinks he may have a hit and doesn't want to jinx it. Summerlin was stolid; he may have been remembering the nights when he had not quite made it. Wiley was comforting and solicitous. The weights were announced: Clay, 194½; Banks, 191¼. It was a difference too slight to count between heavyweights. Banks, wide-shouldered, narrow-waisted, looked as if he would be the better man at slinging a sledge or lifting weights; Clay, more cylindrically formed—arms, legs, and torso—moved more smoothly.

When the bell rang, Banks dropped into the crouch I had seen him rehearse, and began the stalk after Clay that was to put the pressure on him. I felt a species of complicity. The poet, still wrapped in certitude, jabbed, moved, teased, looking the *Konzertstück*[3] over before he banged the ivories. By nimble dodging, as in Rome, he rendered the hungry fighter's attack quite harmless, but this time without keeping his hypnotic stare fixed steadily enough on the punch-hand. They circled around for a minute or so, and then Clay was hit, but not hard, by the left hand. He moved to his own left, across Bank's field of vision, and Banks, turning with him, hit him again, but this time full, with the rising left hook he had worked on so faithfully. The poet went down, and the three men crouching below Banks's corner must have felt, as they listened to the count, like a Reno tourist who hears the silver-dollar jackpot come rolling down. It had been a solid shot—no fluke—and where one shot succeeds, there is no reason to think that another won't. The poet rose at the count of

2. A prominent New York law firm. 3. A freer form of the concerto.

two, but the referee, Ruby Goldstein, as the rules in New York require, stepped between the boxers until the count reached eight, when he let them resume. Now that Banks knew he could hit Clay, he was full of confidence, and the gamblers, who had made Clay a 5-1 favorite, must have had a bad moment. None of them had seen Clay fight, and no doubt they wished they hadn't been so credulous. Clay, I knew, had not been knocked down since his amateur days, but he was cool. He neither rushed after Banks, like an angry kid, nor backed away from him. Standing straight up, he boxed and moved—cuff, slap, jab, and stick, the busy hands stinging like bees. As for Banks, success made him forget his whole plan. Instead of keeping the pressure on—he forgot his right hand and began winging left hooks without trying to set Clay up for them. At the end of the round, the poet was in good shape again, and Banks, the more winded of the two, was spitting a handsome quantity of blood from the jabs that Clay had landed going away. Nothing tires a man more than swinging uselessly. Nevertheless, the knockdown had given Banks the round. The hungry fighter who had listened to his pedagogue was in front, and if he listened again, he might very well stay there.

It didn't happen. In the second round, talent asserted itself. Honest effort and sterling character backed by solid instruction will carry a man a good way, but unlearned natural ability has a lot to be said for it. Young Cassius, who will never have to be lean, jabbed the good boy until he had spread his already wide nose over his face. Banks, I could see, was already having difficulty breathing, and the intellectual pace was just too fast. He kept throwing that left hook whenever he could get set, but he was like a man trying to fight off wasps with a shovel. One disadvantage of having had a respected teacher is that whenever the pupil gets in a jam he tries to remember what the professor told him, and there just isn't time. Like the Pole's in the Olympics, Bank's legs grew heavier, and he could not escape his rival. He did not, however, gaze helplessly into his corner of the ring; he kept on trying. Now Cassius, having mixed the mind, began to dig in. He would come in with a flurry of busy hands, jabbing and slapping his man off balance, and then, in close, drive a short, hard right to the head or a looping left to the slim waist. Two-thirds of the way through the round, he staggered Banks, who dropped forward to his glove tips, though his knees did not touch canvas. A moment later, Clay knocked him down fairly with a right hand, but McWhorter's pupil was not done.

The third round was even less competitive; it was now evident that Banks could not win, but he was still trying. He landed the last, and just about the hardest, punch of the round—a good left hook to the side of the poet's face. Clay looked surprised.

Between the third and fourth rounds, the Boxing Commission physician, Dr. Schiff, trotted up the steps and looked into Banks' eyes. The Detroit lad came out gamely for the round, but the one-minute rest had not refreshed him. After the first flurry of punches, he staggered, helpless, and Goldstein stopped the match. An old fighter, brilliant but cursed with a weak jaw, Goldstein could sympathize.

When it was over, I felt that my first social duty was to the stricken. Clay, I estimated, was the kind of Hero likely to be around for a long while, and if he felt depressed by the knock-down, he had the contents of ten distilleries to draw upon for stimulation. I therefore headed for the loser's dressing room to condole with Mr. McWhorter, who had experienced another almost. When I arrived, Banks, sitting up on the edge of a rubbing table, was shaking his head, angry at himself, like a kid outfielder who has let the deciding run drop through his fingers. Summerlin was telling him what he had done wrong: "You can't hit any-body throwing just one punch all the time. You had him, but you lost him. You forgot to keep crowding." Then the unquench-able pedagogue said, "You're a better fighter than he is, but you lost your head. If you can only get him again. . . ." But poor Banks looked only half convinced. What he felt, I imagine, was that he had had Clay, and that it might be a long time before he caught him again. If he had followed through, he would have been in line for dazzling matches—the kind that bring you five figures even if you lose. I asked him what punch had started him on the downgrade, but he just shook his head. Wiley, the gym proprietor, said there hadn't been any one turning point. "Things just went sour gradually all at once," he declared. "You got to respect a boxer. He'll pick you and peck you, peck you and pick you, until you don't know where you are."

NORMAN MAILER

A Television Show with Nelson Algren

A couple of months ago Nelson Algren brought out a book called *Who Lost an American?* (Macmillan—$5.95). It's a work which gets better as it goes along, but the worst to be said about the first chapter is that somebody might read it. It has a parody of James Baldwin and myself which hits at everything but the ring rope, and keeps missing altogether. I don't know about Baldwin, but it ought to be relatively easy to do a job on me. Only Algren was throwing too hard. The first chapter read like the prose of a girl who has broken into hysteria trying to beat up her big big boyfriend. Indeed it was so bad it sounded like a parody of what one's best friend on *Time* might write.

I went through these pages the night before I was scheduled to go on a television show with Algren. This act of reading startled me. What had I done to Nelson? We hardly knew each other. The only crime I could remember was that once some years ago in *Advertisements for Myself* I had shaded lukewarm praise for Algren's books with a few tart remarks, the worst of which maybe in Nelson's eyes was to call him "The Grand Odd-Ball" of American letters. Of course "odd-ball" was not an altogether unsympathetic word, and "grand" was fine, but then Algren's eye might see it in other focus. Still? The parody was frantic, I decided, too frantic to keep one awake. I went to bed pleased (about something else, naturally) and aroused myself at six-thirty with four hours of sleep, to make my way to the television studio. Our show was *Calendar*, Harry Reasoner's C.B.S. morning production; they tape early. To my surprise, I was not suffering. I had had a good night and a good four hours of sleep, and I was alert. Which put me in a most excellent mood. I hadn't felt this good with four hours of sleep in quite a while.

Algren, when I saw him, was not looking his best. He too obviously had had four hours of sleep, but he looked like he'd awakened with somebody else's liver in his windpipe. Nelson has an interesting face when you get a chance to study it, but at first sight he slides into your vision like an ex-con who's put twenty years in the can. Pallor for one thing, and a skinny flick in his eyes which promises nothing but angles.

"You're looking well, Norman," was his formal greeting.

"Fat and pretty." I was feeling genial and I was acting even more genial than I felt. I think he was feeling a classic embarrassment. There's nothing exactly so dim as meeting somebody you've written about savagely if you no longer feel savage.

Perhaps the television promoters of this show had the idea we would offer a literary war for their camera—their introduction was calculated to nip the tail feathers of two fighting cocks, which is what novelists usually are not—but in any case Reasoner's questions cast Algren and me willy-nilly together. We expended most of our first ten minutes in defense of authors who write about the "seamy side of life." Since we were banded together against the common enemy—most of America out there in televisionland—we could hardly throw any roundhouses at each other. Occasionally I'd stick a jab at Algren, but he was on his bicycle. Nelson seemed to be looking for no fight. If it were going to be a personality contest, obviously I was going to win going away. One of the things I sometimes distrust about myself is that I'm fairly good on television. Nelson isn't. He's a gentle voice, and needs time and a coterie around him to be very funny. Then he can be so funny. This morning he was just doing his hangover best, a club fighter out of training who would like to go the distance, pick up his paycheck and not get hurt.

But he dropped a bomb on me. The show was a half-hour offering, with two stops for commercials. Just before the second half Algren was asked who he considered the best American writer around, and he said William Styron was far and away the best because Styron'd written two major novels which nobody else in the generation had done. Yes, said Algren, queried by Harry Reasoner, Styron was better than say a writer like Scott Fitzgerald. Came the commercial. Silence.

My feud with Styron was not exactly a young widow's secret. During the break for the product, I realized Algren had done it. I had the choice of keeping my mouth shut, or shoving into a back-and-forth. (I don't think he's that good—I say he is.) I took the first option. Nobody up at that hour would be able to remember Styron's name anyway. Best to drop the matter cold. Only I was mad. Algren had gotten into me. That tired hungover club fighter had studied me enough to know where my guard was cute, and he dropped a big one in. I was as mad as a lazybitch boxer (a cassius-clay so to speak) who has been winning every round by a fraction and gets decked in the ninth with a manager's punch. That is to say, a punch which was conceived in training camp before the fight. I was mad enough to ignore my own decision and talk about Styron, but the questions went to another direction and we rode out the rest of the show with nothing further for a happening.

I told myself to hold my temper, but succeeded merely by half. "Listen," I said, coming on Algren the moment the cameras were done, "you're twice the writer Styron is, and you aren't even that good."

"Well, I was impressed with him," Algren said.

"Come on." We were talking with the quick intricacy of cellmates. "You know that second novel is as full of shit as a Yuletide turkey."

"But the first is good," said Algren. "I just read *Lie Down in Darkness* last summer. It's a most remarkable book."

"It is," I said, "but the second . . ."

"Well . . ." said Algren. I had the feeling he didn't necessarily disagree with me. Nelson put on his twenty-years-in-the pen look again. "Tell you," he said, "you know what I admire about Styron. He gets a picture taken of Mr. and Mrs. William Styron on the S.S. United States that the S.S. United States puts in its ads in all the magazines. I got to admire that," said Nelson out of the side of his mouth. "I always got to slink over."

"Nelson, you'd give a testimonial to the Miami Hilton if they put your picture in a magazine."

Algren looked hurt. He shook his head quietly as if to say, "You're going too far," but he ended with a carny grin. "I think I'll call Styron up the day this show goes on, tell him to look at it, and then pay him a visit for a month."

"After he sees the show, Styron'll put you up for a year."

Well, there we were. I couldn't help it. I liked Algren.

We started to talk about middleweight prizefighters. We talked of Henry Hank for a while, and of Reuben Carter who Nelson was certain could take Dick Tiger. I told him Tiger was the best fighter pound for pound in the world. "He was," said Algren, "but Fullmer took a lot out of him."

"Well, we'll see."

"Yes."

We stepped out of the studio together. Algren was going to get an hour of sleep before taking off to Aqueduct for the day. I had an impression he was wondering whether to ask me along. On the street, we hesitated. Then I stuck out my arm and we shook hands. Two middleweight artists had fought a draw in Baltimore.

SAMUEL L. CLEMENS
Overland Stagecoaching[1]

As the sun went down and the evening chill came on, we made preparation for bed. We stirred up the hard leather letter-sacks, and the knotty canvas bags of printed matter (knotty and uneven because of projecting ends and corners of magazines, boxes and books). We stirred them up and redisposed them in such a way as to make our bed as level as possible. And we *did* improve it, too, though after all our work it had an upheaved and billowy look about it, like a little piece of a stormy sea. Next we hunted up our boots from odd nooks among the mail-bags where they had settled, and put them on. Then we got down our coats, vests, pantaloons and heavy woolen shirts, from the arm-loops where they had been swinging all day, and clothed ourselves in them—for, there being no ladies either at the stations or in the coach, and the weather being hot, we had looked to our comfort by stripping to our underclothing, at nine o'clock in the morning. All things being now ready, we stowed the uneasy Dictionary where it would lie as quiet as possible, and placed the water-

<hr>

1. From Chapter IV of *Roughing It.* Twain's synoptic headings run as follows: "Making Our Bed—Assaults by the Unabridged—At a Station—Our Driver a Great and Shining Dignitary—Strange Place for a Front Yard—Accommodations—Double Portraits—An Heir-loom—Our Worthy Landlord—'Fixings and Things'—An Exile—Slumgullion—A Well Furnished Table—The Landlord Astonished—Table Etiquette—Wild Mexican Mules—Stage-Coaching and Railroading."

canteens and pistols where we could find them in the dark. Then we smoked a final pipe, and swapped a final yarn; after which, we put the pipes, tobacco and bag of coin in snug holes and caves among the mail-bags, and then fastened down the coach curtains all around, and made the place as "dark as the inside of a cow," as the conductor phrased it in his picturesque way. It was certainly as dark as any place could be—nothing was even dimly visible in it. And finally, we rolled ourselves up like silk-worms, each person in his own blanket, and sank peacefully to sleep.

Whenever the stage stopped to change horses, we would wake up, and try to recollect where we were—and succeed—and in a minute or two the stage would be off again, and we likewise. We began to get into country, now, threaded here and there with little streams. These had high, steep banks on each side, and every time we flew down one bank and scrambled up the other, our party inside got mixed somewhat. First we would all be down in a pile at the forward end of the stage, nearly in a sitting posture, and in a second we would shoot to the other end, and stand on our heads. And we would sprawl and kick, too, and ward off ends and corners of mail-bags that came lumbering over us and about us; and as the dust rose from the tumult, we would all sneeze in chorus, and the majority of us would grumble, and probably say some hasty thing, like: "Take your elbow out of my ribs! Can't you quit crowding?"

Every time we avalanched from one end of the stage to the other, the Unabridged Dictionary would come too; and every time it came it damaged somebody. One trip it "barked" the Secretary's elbow; the next trip it hurt me in the stomach, and the third it tilted Bemis's nose up till he could look down his nostrils—he said. The pistols and coin soon settled to the bottom, but the pipes, pipe-stems, tobacco and canteens clattered and floundered after the Dictionary every time it made an assault on us, and aided and abetted the book by spilling tobacco in our eyes, and water down our backs.

Still, all things considered, it was a very comfortable night. It wore gradually away, and when at last a cold gray light was visible through the puckers and chinks in the curtains, we yawned and stretched with satisfaction, shed our cocoons, and felt that we had slept as much as was necessary. By and by, as the sun rose up and warmed the world, we pulled off our clothes and got ready for breakfast. We were just pleasantly in time, for five minutes afterward the driver sent the weird music of his bugle winding over the grassy solitudes, and presently we detected a low hut or two in the distance. Then the rattling of the coach, the clatter of our six horses' hoofs, and the driver's crisp commands, awoke to a louder and stronger emphasis, and we went sweeping down on the station at our smartest speed. It was fascinating—that old overland stagecoaching.

We jumped out in undress uniform. The driver tossed his gathered reins out on the ground, gaped and stretched complacently, drew off his heavy buckskin gloves with great deliberation and insufferable dignity—taking not the slightest notice of a dozen solicitious inquiries after his health, and humbly facetious and flattering accostings, and obsequious tenders of service, from five or six hairy and half-civilized station-keepers and hostlers who were nimbly unhitching our steeds and bringing the fresh team out of the stables—for in the eyes of the stage-driver of that day, station-keepers and hostlers were a sort of good enough low creatures, useful in their place, and helping to make up a world, but not the kind of beings which a person of distinction could afford to concern himself with; while, on the contrary, in the eyes of the station-keeper and the hostler, the stage-driver was a hero—a great and shining dignitary, the world's favorite son, the envy of the people, the observed of the nations. When they spoke to him they received his insolent silence meekly, and as being the natural and proper conduct of so great a man; when he opened his lips they all hung on his words with admiration (he never honored a particular individual with a remark, but addressed it with a broad generality to the horses, the stables, the surrounding country *and* the human underlings); when he discharged a facetious insulting personality at a hostler, that hostler was happy for the day; when he uttered his one jest —old as the hills, coarse, profane, witless, and inflicted on the same audience, in the same language, every time his coach drove up there—the varlets roared, and slapped their thighs, and swore it was the best thing they'd ever heard in all their lives. And how they would fly around when he wanted a basin of water, a gourd of the same, or a light for his pipe—but they would instantly insult a passenger if he so far forgot himself as to crave a favor at their hands. They could do that sort of insolence as well as the driver they copied it from—for, let it be borne in mind, the overland driver had but little less contempt for his passengers than he had for his hostlers.

The hostlers and station-keepers treated the really powerful *conductor* of the coach merely with the best of what was their idea of civility, but the *driver* was the only being they bowed down to and worshipped. How admiringly they would gaze up at him in his high seat as he gloved himself with lingering deliberation, while some happy hostler held the bunch of reins aloft, and waited patiently for him to take it! And how they would bombard him with glorifying ejaculations as he cracked his long whip and went careering away.

The station buildings were long, low huts, made of sun-dried, mud-colored bricks, laid up without mortar (*adobes*, the Spaniards call these bricks, and Americans shorten it to *'dobies*). The roofs, which had no slant to them worth speaking of, were thatched and then sodded or covered with a thick layer of earth, and from this sprung a pretty rank growth of weeds and grass. It was the first time we had ever seen a man's front yard on top of his house. The buildings consisted of barns, stable-room for twelve or fifteen horses, and a hut for an eating-room for passengers. This latter had bunks in it for the station-keeper and a hostler or two. You could rest your elbow on its eaves, and you had to bend in order to get in at the door. In place of a window there was a square hole about large enough for a man to crawl through, but this had no glass in it. There was no flooring, but the ground was packed hard. There was no stove, but the fireplace served all needful purposes. There were no shelves, no cupboards, no closets. In a corner stood an open sack of flour, and nestling against its base were a couple of black and venerable tin coffee-pots, a tin tea-pot, a little bag of salt, and a side of bacon.

By the door of the station-keeper's den, outside, was a tin wash-basin, on the ground. Near it was a pail of water and a piece of yellow bar soap, and from the eaves hung a hoary blue woolen shirt, significantly—but this latter was the station-keeper's private towel, and only two persons in all the party might venture to use it—the stage-driver and the conductor. The latter would not, from a sense of decency; the former would not because he did not choose to encourage the advances of a station-keeper. We had towels—in the valise; they might as well have been in Sodom and Gomorrah. We (and the conductor) used our handkerchiefs, and the driver his pantaloons and sleeves. By the door, inside, was fastened a small old-fashioned looking-glass frame, with two little fragments of the original mirror lodged down in one corner of it. This arrangement afforded a pleasant double-barreled portrait of you when you looked into it, with one half of your head set up a couple of inches above the other half. From the glass frame hung the half of a comb by a string—but if I had to describe that patriarch or die, I believe I would order some sample coffins. It had come down from Esau and Samson, and had been accumulating hair ever since—along with certain impurities. In one corner of the room stood three or four rifles and muskets, together with horns and pouches of ammunition. The station-men wore pantaloons of coarse, country-woven stuff, and into the seat and the inside of the legs were sewed ample additions of buckskin, to do duty in place of leggings, when the man rode horseback—so the pants were half dull blue and half yellow, and unspeakably pictur-esque. The pants were stuffed into the tops of high boots, the heels whereof were armed with great Spanish spurs, whose little iron clogs and chains jingled with every step. The man wore a huge beard and mustachios, an old slouch hat, a blue woolen shirt, no suspenders, no vest, no coat—in a leathern sheath in his belt, a great long "navy" revolver (slung on right side, ham-mer to the front), and projecting from his boot a horn-handled bowie-knife. The furniture of the hut was neither gorgeous nor much in the way. The rocking-chairs and sofas were not present, and never had been, but they were represented by two three-legged stools, a pine-board bench four feet long, and two empty candle-boxes. The table was a greasy board on stilts, and the table-cloth and napkins had not come—and they were not look-ing for them, either. A battered tin platter, a knife and fork, and a tin pint cup, were at each man's place, and the driver had a queensware[2] saucer that had seen better days. Of course this duke sat at the head of the table. There was one isolated piece of table furniture that bore about it a touching air of grandeur in misfortune. This was the caster.[3] It was German silver, and crippled and rusty, but it was so preposterously out of place there that it was suggestive of a tattered exiled king among bar-barians, and the majesty of its native position compelled respect even in its degradation. There was only one cruet left, and that was a stopperless, fly-specked, broken-necked thing, with two inches of vinegar in it, and a dozen preserved flies with their heels up and looking sorry they had invested there.

The station-keeper up-ended a disk of last week's bread, of the shape and size of an old-time cheese, and carved some slabs from it which were as good as Nicholson pavement, and tenderer.

He sliced off a piece of bacon for each man, but only the ex-perienced old hands made out to eat it, for it was condemned army bacon which the United States would not feed to its soldiers in the forts, and the stage company had bought it cheap for the sustenance of their passengers and employes. We may have found this condemned army bacon further out on the plains than the section I am locating it in, but we *found* it—there is no gainsaying that.

Then he poured for us a beverage which he called "*Slumgul-lion*," and it is hard to think he was not inspired when he named it. It really pretended to be tea, but there was too much dish-rag, and sand, and old bacon-rind in it to deceive the intelligent traveler. He had no sugar and no milk—not even a spoon to stir the in-gredients with.

2. Cream-colored, glazed English earthenware.
3. Lazy Susan.

We could not eat the bread or the meat, nor drink the "slum-gullion." And when I looked at that melancholy vinegar cruet, I thought of the anecdote (a very, very old one, even at that day) of the traveler who sat down to a table which had nothing on it but a mackerel and a pot of mustard. He asked the landlord if this was all. The landlord said:

"*All!* Why, thunder and lightning, I should think there was mackerel enough there for six."

"But I don't like mackerel."

"Oh—then help yourself to the mustard."

In other days I had considered it a good, a very good, anecdote, but there was a dismal plausibility about it, here, that took all the humor out of it.

Our breakfast was before us, but our teeth were idle.

I tasted and smelt, and said I would take coffee, I believed. The station-boss stopped dead still, and glared at me speechless. At last, when he came to, he turned away and said, as one who communes with himself upon a matter too vast to grasp:

"*Coffee!* Well, if that don't go clean ahead of me, I'm d———d!"

We could not eat, and there was no conversation among the hostlers and herdsmen—we all sat at the same board. At least there was no conversation further than a single hurried request, now and then, from one employe to another. It was always in the same form, and always gruffly friendly. Its western freshness and novelty startled me, at first, and interested me, but it presently grew monotonous, and lost its charm. It was:

"Pass the bread, you son of a skunk!" No, I forget—skunk was not the word; it seems to me it was still stronger than that; I know it was, in fact, but it is gone from my memory, apparently. However, it is no matter—probably it was too strong for print, anyway. It is the landmark in my memory which tells me where I first encountered the vigorous new vernacular of the occidental plains and mountains.

We gave up the breakfast, and paid our dollar apiece and went back to our mail-bag bed in the coach, and found comfort in our pipes. Right here we suffered the first diminution of our princely state. We left our six fine horses and took six mules in their place. But they were wild Mexican fellows, and a man had to stand at the head of each of them and hold him fast while the driver gloved and got himself ready. And when at last he grasped the reins and gave the word, the men sprung suddenly away from the mules' heads and the coach shot from the station as if it had issued from a cannon. How the frantic animals did scamper! It was a fierce and furious gallop—and the gait never altered for a moment till we reeled off ten or twelve miles and swept up to the next collection of little station-huts and stables.

So we flew along all day. At 2 P.M. the belt of timber that fringes the North Platte and marks its windings through the vast level floor of the Plains came in sight. At 4 P.M. we crossed a branch of the river, and at 5 P.M. we crossed the Platte itself, and landed at Fort Kearney, *fifty-six hours out from St. Joe*—THREE HUNDRED MILES!

QUESTIONS

1. Why does Twain make so much of the driver's gloves?
2. Today a bus driver is not a hero for most people. Why is Twain's driver a hero? Why aren't the passengers heroes?
3. Can you think of comparable examples of hero worship? What qualities are worshipped? What does the hero worship reveal about some fact or aspect of language? Explain.
4. Twain mentions many rather unpleasant details—the dirty comb, the "greasy board," the inedible food, etc. What modifies the unpleasantness of the impression?
5. What are the humorous devices Twain uses in such sentences as:
   a. "And we would sprawl and kick, too, and ward off ends and corners of mail-bags that came lumbering over us and about us; and as the dust rose from the tumult, we would all sneeze in chorus, and the majority of us would grumble, and probably say some hasty thing, like: 'Take your elbow out of my ribs! Can't you quit crowding?' "
   b. "One trip it [the unabridged dictionary] 'barked' the Secretary's elbow; the next trip it hurt me in the stomach, and the third it tilted Bemis's nose up till he could look down his nostrils—he said."
   c. "From the glass frame hung the half of a comb by a string— but if I had to describe that patriarch or die, I believe I would order some sample coffins."
   d. "The furniture of the hut was neither gorgeous nor much in the way. . . . The table was a greasy board on stilts, and the table-cloth and napkins had not come—and they were not looking for them, either."
   e. "There was only one cruet left, and that was a stopperless, fly-specked, broken-necked thing, with two inches of vinegar in it, and a dozen preserved flies with their heels up and looking sorry they had invested there."
   f. "The station-keeper up-ended a disk of last week's bread, of the shape and size of an old-time cheese, and carved some slabs from it which were as good as Nicholson pavement, and tenderer."
6. Twain once wrote: "The humorous story is told gravely: the teller does his best to conceal the fact that he even dimly suspects that there is anything funny about it. . . ." How accurately does this describe "Overland Stagecoaching"?

TRUMAN CAPOTE

Meeting a Norwegian in Brest Litovsk[1]

Since Brest Litovsk is one of Russia's most strategic railroad centers, its station is among the country's largest. Looking for somewhere to buy a drink, we explored lofty corridors and a series of waiting rooms, the principal one furnished with handsome oak benches occupied by many passengers with very few suitcases. Children and paper bundles filled their laps. The stone floors, soggy with black slush, made slippery walking, and there was an odor in the air, a saturation so heavy it seemed less a smell than a pressure. Travelers to Venice often remark on the vivid scents of that city. The public places of Russia, terminals and department stores, restaurants and theaters, also have a reek instantly recognizable. And Miss Ryan, taking her first sniff of it, said, "Boy, I wouldn't want a bottle of this. Old socks and a million yawns."

In the search for a bar, we began opening doors at random. Miss Ryan sailed through one and out again. It was a men's room. Then, spotting a pair of deaddrunks as they emerged from behind a small red door, she decided, "That's the place we're looking for." The red door led into an extraordinary restaurant. The size of a gymnasium, it looked as if it had been done over for a school prom by a decorating committee with Victorian tastes. Plush crimson draperies were looped along the walls. Other-era chandeliers distributed a tropic glare that beat down on a jungle of borscht-stained tablecloths and withering rubber plants. The maître d'hôtel seemed appropriate to this atmosphere of grandeur gone to seed. He was at least eighty years old, a white-bearded patriarch with ferocious eyes that peered at us, through a sailor's-dive haze of cigarette smoke, as though questioning our right to be there.

Miss Ryan smiled at him and said, "Vodka, *pjolista*." The old man stared at her with more hostility then comprehension. She tried varying pronunciations, "Woedka . . . Wadka . . . Woodka," and even performed a bottoms-up pantomime. "The poor thing's deaf," she said, and shouted, "V*odka*. For God's sake."

Although his expression remained unenlightened, the old man beckoned us forward and, following the Russian custom of seating strangers together, put us at a table with two men. They both were drinking beer, and the old man pointed at it, as if asking, was this what we wanted? Miss Ryan, resigning herself, nodded.

Our companions at the table were two very different specimens. One, a beefy boy with a shaved head and wearing some sort of

1. From *The Muses Are Heard*, 1956.

faded uniform, was well on his way to being drunk, a condition shared by a surprising lot of the restaurant's clientele, most of whom were male, many of them either boisterous or slumped across their tables mumbling to themselves. The second man was an enigma. In appearance he might have been a Wall Street partner of Herman Sartorius, the kind of person better imagined dining at the Pavillon than sipping beer in Brest Litovsk. His suit was pressed, and one could see that he hadn't sewn it himself. There were gold cuff links in his shirt, and he was the only man in the room sporting a tie.

After a moment the shaven-headed soldier spoke to Miss Ryan. "I'm afraid I don't speak Russian," she told him. "We're Americans. Amerikansky." Her declaration had a somewhat sobering effect. His reddened eyes slowly came into semifocus. He turned to the well-dressed man and made a long statement, at the end of which the man answered him with several chiseled, cold-sounding sentences. There followed between them a sharp repartee, then the soldier took his beer and stalked to another table, where he sat glowering. "Well," said Miss Ryan, glowering back, "not *all* the men are attractive, that's for sure." However, she considered our apparent defender, the well-dressed man: "Very attractive. Sort of Otto Kruger. Funny, I've always liked older men. Stop staring. He'll know we're talking about him. Listen," she said, after calling attention to his shirt, his cuff links, his clean fingernails, "do you suppose there's such a thing as a Russian millionaire?"

The beer arrived. A quart bottle and two glasses. The maître d'hôtel poured an inch of beer into my glass, then waited expectantly. Miss Ryan saw the point before I did. "He wants you to *taste* it, like wine." Lifting the glass, I wondered if beer-tasting was a Soviet commonplace, or if it was a ceremony, some confused champagne-memory of Czarist elegance that the old man had revived to impress us. I sipped, nodded, and the old man proudly filled our glasses with a warm and foamless brew. But Miss Ryan said suddenly, "Don't touch it. It's dreadful!" I told her I didn't think it was that bad. "I mean, we're in dreadful trouble," she said. "I mean, my God, we can't pay for this. I completely forgot. We haven't any rubles."

"Please, won't you be my guests?" inquired a soft voice in beautifully accented English. It was the well-dressed man who had spoken, and though his face was perfectly straight, his eyes, a bright Nordic blue, wrinkled with an amusement that took full measure of our discomfort. "I am not a Russian millionaire. They do exist—I know quite a few—but it would give me pleasure to pay for your drink. No, please, there is no cause to apologize," he said, in response to Miss Ryan's stammered efforts, and openly smiling, "it's been the keenest enjoyment. Very unusual. Very unusual to run across Americans in this part of the world. Are you Communists?"

After disabusing him of that notion, Miss Ryan told him where we were going, and why. "You are fortunate that you go to Leningrad first. A lovely city," he said, "very quiet, really European, the one place in Russia I could imagine living, not that I do, but still . . . Yes, I like Leningrad. It's not the least like Moscow. I'm on my way to Warsaw, but I've just been two weeks in Moscow. That's equal to two months anywhere else." He told us that he was Norwegian, and that his business, lumber, had required him to visit the Soviet Union several weeks of every year, except for a gap during the war, since 1931. "I speak the language quite well, and among my friends I don't mind passing as a Russian authority. But to be honest, I can't say I understand much more about it now than I did in 1931. Whenever I go to your country—I've been there, oh, I guess a half dozen times—it always strikes me that Americans are the only people who remind me of Russians. You don't object to my saying that? Americans are so generous. Energetic. And underneath all that brag they have such a wishing to be loved, they want to be petted, like dogs and children, and told that they are just as good and even better than the rest of us. Well, Europeans are inclined to agree with them. But they simply won't believe it. They go right on feeling inferior and far away. Alone. Like Russians. Precisely."

Miss Ryan wanted to know the substance of his dialogue with the soldier who had left the table. "Oh, silly rot," he said. "Alcoholic bravado. For some foozled reason he thought you had insulted him. I told him he was being *nye kulturni*. Remember that: *nye kulturni*. You'll find it extremely useful, because when these chaps are rude and you feel obliged to tick them off, it means not a whit to call them a bastard, a son of a dog, but to tell him he's *uncultured*, that really strikes home."

Miss Ryan was growing anxious about the time. We shook hands with the gentleman and thanked him for the beer. "You've been very *kulturni*," she said. "And by the way, I think you're *more* attractive than Otto Kruger."

"I shall certainly tell my wife," he said grinning. "*Dazvedanya.* Good luck."

BRUNO BETTELHEIM
A Victim[1]

Many students of discrimination are aware that the victim often reacts in ways as undesirable as the action of the aggressor. Less attention is paid to this because it is easier to excuse a defendant than an offender, and because they assume that once the aggression stops the victim's reactions will stop too. But I doubt if this is of real service to the persecuted. His main interest is that the persecution cease. But that is less apt to happen if he lacks a real understanding of the phenomenon of persecution, in which victim and persecutor are inseparably interlocked.

Let me illustrate with the following example: in the winter of 1938 a Polish Jew murdered the German attaché in Paris, vom Rath. The Gestapo used the event to step up anti-Semitic actions, and in the camp new hardships were inflicted on Jewish prisoners. One of these was an order barring them from the medical clinic unless the need for treatment had originated in work accident.

Nearly all prisoners suffered from frostbite which often led to gangrene and then amputation. Whether or not a Jewish prisoner was admitted to the clinic to prevent such a fate depended on the whim of an SS private. On reaching the clinic entrance, the prisoner explained the nature of his ailment to the SS man, who then decided if he should get treatment or not.

I too suffered from frostbite. At first I was discouraged from trying to get medical care by the fate of Jewish prisoners whose attempts had ended up in no treatment, only abuse. Finally things got worse and I was afraid that waiting longer would mean amputation. So I decided to make the effort.

When I got to the clinic, there were many prisoners lined up as usual, a score of them Jews suffering from severe frostbite. The main topic of discussion was one's chances of being admitted to the clinic. Most Jews had planned their procedure in detail. Some thought it best to stress their service in the German army during World War I: wounds received or decorations won. Others planned to stress the severity of their frostbite. A few decided it was best to tell some "tall story," such as that an SS officer had ordered them to report at the clinic.

Most of them seemed convinced that the SS man on duty would not see through their schemes. Eventually they asked me about my plans. Having no definite ones, I said I would go by the way

1. From "Behavior in Extreme Situations: Defenses," Chapter 5 of *The Informed Heart*, 1960.

the SS man dealt with other Jewish prisoners who had frostbite like me, and proceed accordingly. I doubted how wise it was to follow a preconceived plan, because it was hard to anticipate the reactions of a person you didn't know.

The prisoners reacted as they had at other times when I had voiced similar ideas on how to deal with the SS. They insisted that one SS man was like another, all equally vicious and stupid. As usual, any frustration was immediately discharged against the person who caused it, or was nearest at hand. So in abusive terms they accused me of not wanting to share my plan with them, or of intending to use one of theirs; it angered them that I was ready to meet the enemy unprepared.

No Jewish prisoner ahead of me in the line was admitted to the clinic. The more a prisoner pleaded, the more annoyed and violent the SS became. Expressions of pain amused him; stories of previous services rendered to Germany outraged him. He proudly remarked that *he* could not be taken in by Jews, that fortunately the time had passed when Jews could reach their goal by lamentations.

When my turn came he asked me in a screeching voice if I knew that work accidents were the only reason for admitting Jews to the clinic, and if I came because of such an accident. I replied that I knew the rules, but that I couldn't work unless my hands were freed of the dead flesh. Since prisoners were not allowed to have knives, I asked to have the dead flesh cut away. I tried to be matter-of-fact, avoiding pleading, deference, or arrogance. He replied: "If that's all you want, I'll tear the flesh off myself." And he started to pull at the festering skin. Because it did not come off as easily as he may have expected, or for some other reason, he waved me into the clinic.

Inside, he gave me a malevolent look and pushed me into the treatment room. There he told the prisoner orderly to attend to the wound. While this was being done, the guard watched me closely for signs of pain but I was able to suppress them. As soon as the cutting was over, I started to leave. He showed surprise and asked why I didn't wait for further treatment. I said I had gotten the service I asked for, at which he told the orderly to make an exception and treat my hand. After I had left the room, he called me back and gave me a card entitling me to further treatment, and admittance to the clinic without inspection at the entrance.

* * *

Because my behavior did not correspond to what he expected of Jewish prisoners on the basis of his projection, he could not use his prepared defenses against being touched by the prisoner's plight. Since I did not act as the dangerous Jew was expected to, I did not activate the anxieties that went with his stereotype. Still he did not altogether trust me, so he continued to watch while I received treatment.

Throughout these dealings, the SS felt uneasy with me, though he did not unload on me the annoyance his uneasiness aroused. Perhaps he watched me closely because he expected that sooner or later I would slip up and behave the way his projected image of the Jew was expected to act. This would have meant that his delusional creation had become real.

HERBERT GOLD

A Dog in Brooklyn, a Girl in Detroit: A Life Among the Humanities

What better career for a boy who seeks to unravel the meaning of our brief span on earth than that of philosopher? We all wonder darkly, in the forbidden hours of the night, punishing our parents and building a better world, with undefined terms. Soon, however, most of us learn to sleep soundly; or we take to pills or love-making; or we call ourselves insomniacs, not philosophers. A few attempt to define the terms.

There is no code number for the career of philosophy in school, the Army, or out beyond in real life. The man with a peculiar combination of melancholic, nostalgic, and reforming instincts stands at three possibilities early in his youth. He can choose to be a hero, an artist, or a philosopher. In olden times, war, say, or the need to clean out the old west, might make up his mind for him. The old west had been pretty well cleaned up by the time I reached a man's estate, and Gary Cooper could finish the job. Heroism was an untimely option. With much bureaucratic confusion I tried a bit of heroic war, got stuck in the machine, and returned to the hectic, Quonset campus of the G.I. Bill, burning to Know, Understand, and Convert. After a season of ferocious burrowing in books, I was ready to be a Teacher, which seemed a stern neighbor thing to Artist and Philosopher. I took on degrees, a Fulbright fellowship, a wife, a child, a head crammed with foolish questions and dogmatic answers despite the English school of linguistic analysis. I learned to smile, pardner, when I asked questions of philosophers trained at Oxford or Cambridge, but I asked them nonetheless. I signed petitions against McCarthy, wrote a novel, went on a treasure hunt, returned to my roots in the Middle West and stood rooted there, discussed the menace of the mass media, and had another child.

By stages not important here, I found myself teaching the Humanities at Wayne University in Detroit. I am now going to report a succession of classroom events which, retrospectively, seems to have determined my abandonment of formal dealing with this subject. The evidence does not, however, render any conclusion about education in the "Humanities" logically impregnable. It stands for a state of mind and is no substitute for formal argument. However, states of mind are important in this area of experience and meta-experience. However and however: it happens that most of the misty exaltation of the blessed vocation of the teacher issues from the offices of deans, editors, and college presidents. The encounter with classroom reality has caused many teachers, like Abelard meeting the relatives of Eloïse, to lose their bearings. Nevertheless this is a memoir, not a campaign, about a specific life in and out of the Humanities. Though I am not a great loss to the History of Everything in Culture, my own eagerness to teach is a loss to me.

News item of a few years ago. A young girl and her date are walking along a street in Brooklyn, New York. The girl notices that they are being followed by an enormous Great Dane. The dog is behaving peculiarly, showing its teeth and making restless movements. A moment later, sure enough, the dog, apparently maddened, leaps slavering upon the girl, who is borne to earth beneath its weight. With only an instant's hesitation, the boy jumps on the dog. Its fangs sunk in one, then in the other, the dog causes the three of them to roll like beasts across the sidewalk.

A crowd gathers at a safe distance to watch. No one interferes. They display the becalmed curiosity of teevee viewers.

A few moments later a truckdriver, attracted by the crowd, pulls his vehicle over to the curb. This brave man is the only human being stirred personally enough to leave the role of passive spectator. Instantaneously analyzing the situation, he leaps into the struggle—*attacking and beating the boy.* He has naturally assumed that the dog must be protecting an innocent young lady from the unseemly actions of a juvenile delinquent.

I recounted this anecdote in the classroom in order to introduce a course which attempted a summary experience of Humanities 610 for a monumental nine credits. There were a number of points to be made about the passivity of the crowd ("don't get involved," "not my business") and the stereotypical reaction of the truck driver who had been raised to think of man's best friend as not another human being but a dog. In both cases, addicted to entertainment and clichés, the crowd and the trucker could not recognize what was actually happening before their eyes; they responded irrelevantly to the suffering of strangers; they were not a part of the main. This led us to a discussion of the notion of "community." In a closely-knit society, the people on the street would have known the couple involved and felt a responsibility towards them. In a large city, everyone is a stranger. (Great art can give a sense of the brotherhood of men. Religion used to do this, too.) "Any questions?" I asked, expecting the authority of religion to be defended.

An eager hand shot up. Another. Another. Meditative bodies sprawled in their chairs. "Are all New Yorkers like that?" "Well, what can you do if there's a mad dog and you're not expecting it?" "Where does it say in what great book how you got to act in Brooklyn?"

I took note of humor in order to project humorousness. I found myself composing my face in the look of thought which teevee panelists use in order to project thinking. I discovered a serious point to elaborate—several. I mentioned consciousness and relevance and the undefined moral suggestion implied by the labor which produces any work of art or mind. A girl named Clotilda Adams asked me: "Why don't people try to get along better in this world?"

Somewhat digressively, we then discussed the nature of heroism, comparing the behavior of the boy and the truck driver. Both took extraordinary risks; why? We broke for cigarettes in the autumn air outside. Then, for fifty minutes more, we raised these interesting questions, referring forward to Plato, Aristotle, St. Thomas, Dostoevsky, Tolstoy, William James, and De Gaulle; and then boy, dog, girl, truck driver and crowd were left with me and the crowned ghosts of history in the deserted room while my students went on to Phys Ed, Music Appreciation, Sosh, and their other concerns. Having been the chief speaker, both dramatist and analyst, I was exalted by the lofty ideas floated up into the air around me. I was a little let down to return to our real life in which dog-eat-dog is man's closest pal. Fact. Neither glory nor pleasure nor power, and certainly not wisdom, provided the goal of my students. Not even wealth was the aim of most of them. They sought to make out, to do all right, more prideful than amorous in love, more security-hungry than covetous in status. I saw my duty as a teacher: Through the Humanities, to awaken them to the dream of mastery over the facts of our lives. I saw my duty plain: Through the Humanities, to lead them toward the exaltation of knowledge and the calm of control. I had a whole year in which to fulfill this obligation. It was a two-semester course.

Before she left the room, Clotilda Adams said, "You didn't answer my question." Fact.

Outside the university enclave of glass and grass, brick and trees, Detroit was agonizing in its last big year with the big cars. Automation, dispersion of factories, and imported automobiles were eroding a precarious confidence. Fear was spreading; soon the landlords would offer to decorate apartments and suffer the pain. Detroit remembered the war years with nostalgia. Brave days, endless hours, a three-shift clock, insufficient housing, men sleeping in the all-night, triple-feature movies on Woodward and Grand River. Though the area around the Greyhound and Trailways stations was still clotted with the hopeful out of the hill country of the mid-South and the driven from the deep South—they strolled diagonally across the boulevards, entire families holding hands—some people suspected what was already on its way down the road: twenty per cent unemployment in Detroit.

The semester continued. We churned through the great books. One could classify my students in three general groups, intelligent, mediocre, and stupid, allowing for the confusions of three general factors—background, capacity, and interest. This was how we classified the Humanities, too: ancient, medieval, and modern. It made a lot of sense, and it made me itch, scratch, and tickle. Series of three form nice distinctions. According to Jung and other authorities, they have certain mythic significances. The course was for nine credits. All the arts were touched upon. We obeyed Protagoras; man, just man, was our study. When I cited him—"the proper study of man is Man"—Clotilda Adams stirred uneasily in her seat. "By which Protagoras no doubt meant woman, too," I assured her. She rested.

Now imagine the winter coming and enduring, with explosions of storm and exfoliations of gray slush, an engorged industrial sky overhead and sinus trouble all around. The air was full of acid and a purplish, spleeny winter mist. Most of Detroit, in Indian times before the first French trappers arrived, had been a swamp and below sea level. The swamp was still present, but invisible; city stretched out in all directions, crawling along the highways. Though Detroit was choked by a dense undergrowth of streets and buildings, irrigated only by super-highways, its work was done with frantic speed. The Rouge plant roared, deafened. The assembly lines clanked to the limit allowed by the UAW. The old Hudson factory lay empty, denuded, waiting to become a parking lot. Then the new models were being introduced! Buick! Pontiac! Dodge! Ford and Chevrolet! Ford impudently purchased a huge billboard faced towards the General Motors Building on Grand Boulevard. General Motors retaliated by offering free ginger ale to all comers, and a whole bottle of Vernor's to take home if you would only consent to test-drive the new Oldsmobile, the car with the . . . I've forgotten what it had that year. All over town the automobile companies were holding revival meetings; hieratic salesmen preached to the converted and the hangers-back alike; lines at the loan companies stretched through the revolving doors and out on to the winter pavements. But many in those lines were trying to get additional financing on their last year's cars. The new models were an indifferent success despite all the uproar of display and Detroit's patriotic attention to it. Searchlights sliced up the heavens while the city lay under flu.

Teachers at Wayne University soon learn not to tease the American Automobile. *Lèse*[1] Chrysler was a moral offense, an attack on the livelihood and the sanctity of the American garage. Detroit was a town in which men looked at hub caps as men elsewhere have sometimes looked at ankles. The small foreign car found itself treated with a violent Halloween kidding-on-the-square, scratched, battered, and smeared (another Jungian series of three!). A passionate and sullen town, Detroit had no doubts about its proper business. All it doubted was everything else.

I often failed at inspiring my students to do the assigned reading. Many of them had part-time jobs in the automobile industry or its annexes. Even a Philosopher found it difficult to top the argument, "I couldn't read the book this week, I have to *work*," with its implied reproach for a scholar's leisure. But alas, many of these stricken proletarians drove freshly-minted automobiles. They worked in order to keep up the payments, racing like laboratory mice around the cage of depreciation. Certain faculty deep thinkers, addicted to broad understanding of the problems of others, argued that these students were so poor they *had* to buy new cars in order to restore their confidence. The finance companies seemed to hear their most creative expressions, not me. Deep in that long Detroit winter, I had the task of going from the pre-Socratic mystics all the way to Sartre, for nine credits. Like an audio-visual monkey, I leapt from movie projector to records to slides, with concurrent deep labor in book and tablet. We read *The Brothers Karamazov*, but knowing the movie did not give credit. We studied *The Waste Land*, and reading the footnotes did not suffice. We listened to Wanda Landowska play the harpsichord on records. We sat in the dark before a slide of Seurat's "La Grande Jatte"[2] while I explained the importance of the measles of *pointillisme* to students who only wanted to see life clear and true. see it comfortably. Clotilda Adams said that this kind of painting hurt her eyes. She said that there was too much reading for one course— "piling it on. This isn't the only course we take." She said that she liked music, though. Moses only had to bring the Law down the mountain to the children of Israel; I had to bring it pleasingly.

We made exegeses. I flatly turned down the request of a dean that I take attendance. As a statesmanlike compromise, I tested regularly for content and understanding.

Then, on a certain morning, I handed back some quiz papers at the beginning of class. Out on the street, a main thoroughfare through town, it was snowing; this was one of those magical days of late winter snowfall—pale, cold, clean, and the entire city momentarily muffled by the silence of snow. The room hissed with steam heat; a

1. Injured. Cf. *lèse majesté:* injured majesty, *i.e.,* treason.
2. River park in Paris, subject of Seurat's painting.

smell of galoshes and mackinaws arose from the class. "Let us not discuss the test—let us rise above grades. Let us try to consider nihilism as a byproduct of the Romantic revival—" I had just begun my lecture when an odd clashing, lumping noise occurred on Cass Avenue. "Eliot's later work, including *The Four Quartets*, which we will not discuss here. . . ."

But I was interrupted by a deep sigh from the class. A product of nihilism and the romantic revival? No. It was that strange tragic sigh of horror and satisfaction. Out in the street, beyond the window against which I stood, a skidding truck had sideswiped a taxi. The truckdriver had parked and gone into a drugstore. The cab was smashed like a cruller. From the door, the driver had emerged, stumbling drunkenly on the icy road, holding his head. There was blood on his head. There was blood on his hands. He clutched his temples. The lines of two-way traffic, moving very slowly in the snow and ice, carefully avoided hitting him. There were streaks of perforated and patterned snow, frothed up by tires. He was like an island around which the sea of traffic undulated in slow waves; but he was an island that moved in the sea and held hands to head. He slid and stumbled back and forth, around and about his cab in the middle of the wide street. He was in confusion, in shock. Even at this distance I could see blood on the new-fallen snow. Drivers turned their heads upon him like angry Halloween masks, but did not get involved. Snow spit at his feet.

No one in the class moved. The large window through which we gazed was like a screen, with the volume turned down by habit, by snow, by a faulty tube. As the teacher, my authority took precedence. I ran out to lead the cab driver into the building. An elderly couple sat huddled in the car, staring at the smashed door, afraid to come out the other. They said they were unhurt.

I laid the man down on the floor. He was bleeding from the head and his face was a peculiar purplish color, with a stubble of beard like that of a dead man. There was a neat prick in his forehead where the union button in his cap had been driven into the skin. I sent a student to call for an ambulance. The cab driver's color was like that of the bruised industrial sky. "You be okay till the ambulance——?"

Foolish question. No alternative. No answer.

We waited. The class was restless. When they weren't listening to me, or talking to themselves, or smudging blue books in an exam, they did not know what to do in this room devoted to the specialized absorption of ideas. Silence. Scraping of feet, crisping of paper. We watched the slow-motion traffic on the street outside.

The cab driver moved once in a rush, turning over face down against the floor, with such force that I thought he might break his nose. Then slowly, painfully, as if in a dream, he turned back and lay staring at the ceiling. His woollen lumberjack soaked up the blood trickling from one ear; the blood traveled up separated cilia of wool which drew it in with a will of their own. There was a swaying, osmotic movement like love-making in the eager little wisps of wool. An astounded ring of Humanities 610 students watched, some still holding their returned quiz papers. One girl in particular, Clotilda Adams, watched him and me with her eyes brilliant, wet and bulging, and her fist crumpling the paper. I tried by imagining it to force the ambulance through the chilled and snow-fallen city. I saw it weaving around the injured who strutted with shock over ice and drift, its single red Cyclops' eye turning, the orderlies hunched over on benches, chewing gum and cursing the driver. The ambulance did not arrive. Clotilda Adams' eye had a thick, impenetrable sheen over it. She watched from the cab driver to me as if we were in some way linked. When would the authorities get there? When the medics? There must have been many accidents in town, and heart attacks, and fires with cases of smoke inhalation.

Before the ambulance arrived, the police were there. They came strolling into the classroom with their legs apart, as if they remembered ancestors who rode the plains. Their mouths were heavy in thought. They had noses like salamis, red and mottled with fat. They were angry at the weather, at the school, at the crowd, at me, and especially at the prostrate man at our feet. He gave them a means to the creative expression of pique. (Everyone needs an outlet.)

Now Clotilda Adams took a step backward, and I recall thinking this odd. She had been treading hard near the pool of blood about the cab-driver, but when the cops strolled up, she drifted toward the outer edge of the group of students, with a sly look of caution in her downcast, sideways-cast eyes. Her hand still crisped at the returned exam paper. This sly, lid-fallen look did not do her justice. She was a hard little girl of the sort often thought to be passionate—skinny but well-breasted, a high hard rump with a narrow curve, a nervous mouth.

The two policemen stood over the body of the cab-driver. They stared at him in the classic pose—one cop with a hand resting lightly on the butt of his gun and the other on his butt, the younger cop with lips so pouted that his breath made a snuffling sound in his nose. They both had head colds. Their Ford was pulled up on the snow-covered lawn outside, with raw muddled marks of tread in the soft dirt. When the snow melted, there would be wounded streaks in the grass. The cab driver closed his eyes under the finicking, distasteful examination. At last one spoke: "See your driver's license."

The cab driver made a clumsy gesture towards his pocket. The cop bent and went into the pocket. He flipped open the wallet, glanced briefly at the photographs and cash, glanced at me, and then began lip-reading the license.

The cab-driver was in a state of shock. There was a mixture of thin and thick blood on his clothes and messing the floor. "This man is badly hurt," I said. "Can't we get him to the hospital first?"

"This is only your *driver* license," the cop said slowly, having carefully read through Color of Hair: *Brn*, Color of Eyes: *Brn*, and checked each item with a stare at the man on the floor. "Let me see your chauffeur license."

"He's badly hurt," I said. "Get an ambulance."

"Teach'," said the older cop, "you know your business? We know ours."

"It's on the way," said the other. "Didn't you call it yourself?"

"No, one of the students. . . ." I said.

He grinned with his great victory. "So—don't you trust your pupils neither?"

Shame. I felt shame at this ridicule of my authority in the classroom. A professor is not a judge, a priest, or a sea captain; he does not have the right to perform marriages on the high seas of audio-visual aids and close reasoning. But he is more than an intercom between student and fact; he can be a stranger to love for his students, but not to a passion for his subject; he is a student himself; his pride is lively. The role partakes of a certain heft and control. There is power to make decisions, power to abstain, power to bewilder, promote, hold back, adjust, and give mercy; power, an investment of pride, a risk of shame.

Clotilda Adams, still clutching her exam, stared at me with loathing. She watched me bested by the police. She barely glanced, and only contemptuously, at the man bleeding from the head on the floor. She moved slightly forward again in order to participate fully in an action which apparently had some important meaning for her. She had lost her fear of the police when she saw how we all stood with them. The limits were established.

The police were going through the cab-driver's pockets. They took out a folding pocket-knife and cast significant looks at it and at each other. It had a marbled plastic hilt, like a resort souvenir. It was attached to a key ring.

"Hey!" one said to the half-conscious man. "What's this knife for?"

"Where'd you get them keys?" the other demanded, prodding the cabbie with his toe.

"A skeleton key. These cab companies," one of the cops decided to explain to Clotilda Adams, who was standing nearby, "they get the dregs. Hillbillies, you know?"

I said nothing, found nothing to say. I now think of Lord Acton's famous law, which is accepted as true the way it was uttered. The opposite is also true—the commoner's way: Having no power corrupts; having absolutely no power corrupts absolutely.

The bleeding seemed to have stopped. The cab driver sat up, looking no better, with his bluish, greenish, drained head hanging between his knees. His legs were crumpled stiffly. He propped himself on his hands. The police shot questions at him. He mumbled, mumbled, explained, explained.

"How long you been in Detroit? How come you come out of the mountains?"

"Why you pick up this fare?"

"What makes you think Cass is a one-way street?"

Mumbling and mumbling, explaining and explaining, the cab-driver tried to satisfy them. He also said: "Hurt. Maybe you get me to the hospital, huh? Hurt real bad."

"Maybe," said one of the cops, "maybe we take you to the station house first. That boy you hit says reckless driving. I think personally you'd flunk the drunk test—what you think, Teach'?"

I sent one of the students to call for an ambulance again. In the infinitesimal pause between my suggestion and his action, an attentive reluctant expectant caesura, I put a dime in his hand for the call. One of the cops gave me that long look described by silent movie critics as the slow burn. "They drive careful," he finally said. "It's snowing. They got all that expensive equipment."

The snow had started again outside the window. The skid-marks on the lawn were covered. Though the sky was low and gray, the white sifting down gave a peaceful village glow to this industrial Detroit. Little gusts barely rattled the windows. With the class, the cops, and the driver, we were living deep within a snowy paper-weight. I felt myself moving very slowly, swimming within thick glass, like the loosened plastic figure in a paper-weight. The snow came down in large torn flakes, all over the buildings of Wayne University, grass, trees, and the pale radiance of a network of slow-motion super-highways beyond. Across the street a modern building —glass and aluminum strips—lay unfinished in this weather. Six months ago there had been a student boardinghouse on that spot, filled with the artists and the beat, the guitar-wielders and the modern dancers, with a tradition going all the way back to the Korean war. Now there were wheelbarrows full of frozen cement; there were intentions to build a Japanese garden, with Japanese proportions and imported goldfish.

My student returned from the telephone. He had reached a hospital.

The cab driver was fading away. Rootlets of shock hooded his eyes: the lid was closing shut. A cop asked him another question—what the button on his cap stood for—it was a union button—and then the man just went reclining on his elbow, he slipped slowly down, he lay in the little swamp of crusted blood on the floor. You know what happens when milk is boiled? The crust broke like the crust of boiled milk when a spoon goes into coffee. The cop stood with a delicate, disgusted grimace on his face. What a business to be in, he seemed to be thinking. In approximately ten years, at age forty-two, he could retire and sit comfortable in an undershirt, with a non-returnable can of beer, before the color TV. He could relax. He could *start* to relax. But in the meanwhile—nag, nag, nag. Drunk cabbies, goddam hillbillies. The reckless driver on the floor seemed to sleep. His lips moved. He was alive.

Then a puffing intern rushed into the room. I had not heard the ambulance. The policeman gave room and the intern kneeled. He undid his bag. The orderlies glanced at the floor and went back out for their stretcher.

I stood on one side of the body, the kneeling intern with his necklace of stethoscope, and the two meditative cops. On the other side was the group of students, and at their head, like a leader filled with wrath, risen in time of crisis, stood Clotilda Adams, still clutching her exam paper. There were tears in her eyes. She was in a fury. She had been thinking all this time, and now her thinking had issue: *rage*. Over the body she handed me a paper, crying out, "I don't think I deserved a D on that quiz. I answered all the questions. I can't get my credit for Philo of Ed without I get a B off you."

I must have looked at her with pure stupidity on my face. There is a Haitian proverb: Stupidity won't kill you, but it'll make you sweat a lot. She took the opportunity to make me sweat, took my silence for guilt, took my open-mouthed gaze for weakness. She said: "If I was a white girl, you'd grade me easier."

Guilty, a hundred years, a thousand years of it; pity for the disaster of ignorance and fear, pity for ambition rising out of ignorance; adoration of desire; trancelike response to passion—passion which justifies itself because passionate. . . . I looked at her with mixed feelings. I could not simply put her down. In order to *put down* your own mind must be made up, put down. She had beauty and dignity, stretched tall and wrathful, with teeth for biting and eyes for striking dead.

"But I know my rights," she said, "*mister*. My mother told me about your kind—lent my father money on his car and then hounded him out of town. He's been gone since fifty-three. But you can't keep us down forever, no sir, you can't always keep us down—"

She was talking and I was yelling. She was talking and yelling about injustice and I, under clamps, under ice, was yelling in a whisper about the sick man. She was blaming me for all her troubles, all the troubles she had seen, and I was blaming her for not seeing what lay before her, and we were making an appointment to meet in my office and discuss this thing more calmly, Miss Adams. Okay. All right. Later.

The police, the doctor, the orderlies, and the injured cab-driver were gone. The police car out front was gone and the snow was covering its traces. The janitor came in and swept up the bloodstains with green disinfectant powder. The frightened couple in the cab were released. They all disappeared silently into the great city, into the routine of disaster and recovery of a great city. I dismissed the class until tomorrow.

The next day I tried to explain to Miss Adams what I meant about her failing to respond adequately to the facts of our life together. Her mouth quivered. Yesterday rage; today a threat of tears. What did I mean she wasn't *adequate*? What did I know about adequate anyhow? Nothing. Just a word. Agreed, Miss Adams. I was trying to say that there were two questions at issue between us—her exam grade and her choice of occasion to dispute it. I would like to discuss each matter separately. I tried to explain why putting the two events together had disturbed me. I tried to explain the notions of empirical evidence and metaphor. Finally I urged her to have her exam looked at by the head of the department, but she refused because she knew in advance that he would support me. "White is Right," she said.

"Do you want to drop out of the class?"

"No. I'll stay," she said with a sudden patient, weary acceptance of her fate. "I'll do what I can."

"I'll do what I can too," I said.

She smiled hopefully at me. She was tuckered out by the continual alert for combat everywhere. She was willing to forgive and go easy. When she left my office, this smile, shy, pretty, and conventional, tried to tell me that she could be generous—a friend.

We had come to Thomas Hobbes and John Locke in our tour through time and the river of humanities. I pointed out that the English philosophers were noted for clarity and eloquence of style. I answered this question: The French? Isn't French noted for clarity? Yes, they too, but they were more abstract. On the whole. In general.

The class took notes on the truths we unfolded together. Spring came and the snow melted. There was that brief Detroit flowering of the new season—jasmine and hollyhocks—which, something like it, must have captivated the Frenchman Antoine de la Mothe Cadillac when he paused on the straits of Detroit in 1701. University gardeners planted grass seed where the patrol car had parked on the lawn. The new models, all except the Cadillac, were going at mean discounts.

"The 'Humanities,' " wrote Clotilda Adams in her final essay, "are a necessary additive to any teacher's development worth her 'salt' in the perilous times of today. The West and the 'Free World' must stand up to the war of ideas against the 'Iron' Curtain." This was in answer to a question about Beethoven, Goethe, and German romanticism. She did not pass the course, but she was nevertheless admitted on probation to the student teacher program because of the teacher shortage and the great need to educate our children in these perilous times. Of today.

Humanities 610 provided ballast for the ship of culture as it pitched and reeled in the heavy seas of real life; I lashed myself to the mast, but after hearing the siren song of ground course outlines, I cut myself free and leaned over the rail with the inside of my lip showing.

It would be oversimplifying to say that I left off teaching Humanities merely because of an experience. Such an argument is fit to be published under the title "I was a Teen-Age Humanities Professor." I also left for fitter jobs, more money, a different life. Still, what I remember of the formal study of Truth and Beauty, for advanced credit in education, is a great confusion of generalities, committees, conferences, audio-visual importunities, and poor contact. "Contact!" cried the desperate deans and chairmen, like radio operators in ancient war movies. And much, much discussion of how to get through to the students. How to get through? Miss Adams and Mr. Gold, cab-driver and Thomas Hobbes, policemen and the faceless student who paused an instant for a dime for the telephone—we all have to discover how relevant we are to each other. Or do we *have* to? No, we can merely perish, shot down like mad dogs or diminished into time with no more than a glimpse of the light.

Words fade; our experience does not touch; we make do with bab-. ble and time-serving. We need to learn the meaning of words, the meaning of the reality those words refer to; we must clasp reality close. We cannot flirt forever, brown-nosing or brow-beating. We must act and build out of our own spirits. How? How? We continually need new politics, new cities, new marriages and families, new ways of work and leisure. We also need the fine old ways. For me, the primitive appeal to pleasure and pain of writing stories is a possible action, is the way in and out again, as teaching was not. As a teacher, I caught my students too late and only at the top of their heads, at the raw point of pride and ambition, and I had not enough love and pressure as a teacher to open the way through their intentions to the common humanity which remains locked within. As a writer, I could hope to hit them in their bodies and needs, where lusts and ideals are murkily nurtured together, calling to the prime fears and joys directly, rising with them from the truths of innocence into the truths of experience.

The peculiar combination of ignorance and jadedness built into most institutions is a desperate parody of personal innocence, personal experience. Nevertheless, education, which means a drawing out—even formal education, a formal drawing out—is a variety of experience, and experience is the only evidence we have. After evidence comes our thinking upon it. Do the scientists, secreting their honey in distant hives, hear the barking of the black dog which follows them? Will the politicians accept the lead of life, or will they insist on a grade of B in Power and Dominion over a doomed race? We need to give proper answers to the proper questions.

Particular life is still the best map to truth. When we search our hearts and strip our pretenses, we all know this. Particular life—we know only what we *know*. Therefore the policemen stay with me: I have learned to despise most authority. The cab-driver remains in his sick bleeding: pity for the fallen and helpless. And I think of Clotilda Adams in her power and weakness; like the cops, she has an authority of stupidity; like the victim of an accident, she is fallen and helpless. But some place, since we persist in our cold joke against the ideal of democracy, the cops still have the right to push people around, Clotilda is leading children in the Pledge of Allegiance. We must find a way to teach better and to learn.

MAX BEERBOHM

A Relic

Yesterday I found in a cupboard an old, small, battered portmanteau which, by the initials on it, I recognized as my own property. The lock appeared to have been forced. I dimly remembered having forced it myself, with a poker, in my hot youth, after some journey in which I had lost the key; and this act of violence was probably the reason why the trunk had so long ago ceased to travel. I unstrapped it, not without dust; it exhaled the faint scent of its long closure; it contained a tweed suit of Late Victorian pattern, some bills, some letters, a collar stud, and—something which, after I had wondered for a moment or two what on earth it was, caused me suddenly to murmur, "Down below, the sea rustled to and fro over the shingle."

Strange that these words had, year after long year, been existing in some obscure cell at the back of my brain—forgotten but all the while existing like the trunk in that cupboard. What released them, what threw open the cell door, was nothing but the fragment of a fan; just the butt-end of an inexpensive fan. The sticks are of white bone, clipped together with a semicircular ring that is not silver. They are neatly oval at the base, but variously jagged at the other end. The longest of them measures perhaps two inches. Ring and all, they have no market value; for a farthing is the least coin in our currency. And yet, though I had so long forgotten them, for me they are not worthless. They touch a chord. . . . Lest this confession raise false hope in the reader, I add that I did not know their owner.

I did once see her, and in Normandy, and by moonlight, and her

name was Angélique. She was graceful, she was even beautiful. I was
but nineteen years old. Yet even so I cannot say that she impressed
me favorably. I was seated at a table of a café on the terrace of a
casino. I sat facing the sea, with my back to the casino. I sat listening
to the quiet sea, which I had crossed that morning. The hour was
late, there were few people about. I heard the swing-door behind
me flap open, and was aware of a sharp snapping and crackling sound
as a lady in white passed quickly by me. I stared at her erect thin
back and her agitated elbows. A short fat man passed in pursuit of
her—an elderly man in a black alpaca jacket that billowed. I saw that
she had left a trail of little white things on the asphalt. I watched
the efforts of the agonized short fat man to overtake her as she swept
wraithlike away to the distant end of the terrace. What was the matter? What had made her so spectacularly angry with him? The three
or four waiters of the café were exchanging cynical smiles and shrugs,
as waiters will. I tried to feel cynical, but was thrilled with excitement, with wonder and curiosity. The woman out yonder had
doubled on her tracks. She had not slackened her furious speed, but
the man waddlingly contrived to keep pace with her now. With every
moment they became more distinct, and the prospect that they would
presently pass by me, back into the casino, gave me that physical
tension which one feels on a wayside platform at the imminent passing of an express. In the rushingly enlarged vision I had of them, the
wrath on the woman's face was even more saliently the main thing
than I had supposed it would be. That very hard Parisian face must
have been as white as the powder that coated it. "*Écoute, Angélique,*" gasped the perspiring bourgeois, "—*écoute, je te supplie—.*"[1]
The swing-door received them and was left swinging to and fro. I
wanted to follow, but had not paid for my bock. I beckoned my
waiter. On his way to me he stooped down and picked up something
which, with a smile and a shrug, he laid on my table: "*Il semble
que Mademoiselle ne s'en servira plus.*"[2] This is the thing I now
write of, and at sight of it I understood why there had been that
snapping and crackling, and what the white fragments on the
ground were.

I hurried through the rooms, hoping to see a continuation of that
drama—a scene of appeasement, perhaps, or of fury still implacable.
But the two oddly-assorted players were not performing there.
My waiter had told me he had not seen either of them before. I suppose they had arrived that day. But I was not destined to see either
of them again. They went away, I suppose, next morning; jointly
or singly; singly, I imagine.

They made, however, a prolonged stay in my young memory, and

1. "Listen, Angelique . . . listen, I beg you—."
2. "It seems that Mademoiselle will not be using this any more."

would have done so even had I not had that tangible memento of them. Who were they, those two of whom that one strange glimpse had befallen me? What, I wondered, was the previous history of each? What, in particular, had all that tragic pother been about? Mlle. Angélique I guessed to be thirty years old, her friend perhaps fifty-five. Each of their faces was as clear to me as in the moment of actual vision—the man's fat shiny bewildered face; the taut white face of the woman, the hard red line of her mouth, the eyes that were not flashing, but positively dull, with rage. I presumed that the fan had been a present from him, and a recent present—bought perhaps that very day, after their arrival in the town. But what, *what* had he done that she should break it between her hands, scattering the splinters as who should sow dragon's teeth? I could not believe he had done anything much amiss. I imagined her grievance a trivial one. But this did not make the case less engrossing. Again and again I would take the fan-stump from my pocket, examining it on the palm of my hand, or between finger and thumb, hoping to read the mystery it had been mixed up in, so that I might reveal that mystery to the world. To the world, yes; nothing less than that. I was determined to make a story of what I had seen—a conte in the manner of great Guy de Maupassant. Now and again, in the course of the past year or so, it had occurred to me that I might be a writer. But I had not felt the impulse to sit down and write something. I did feel that impulse now. It would indeed have been an irresistible impulse if I had known just what to write.

I felt I might know at any moment, and had but to give my mind to it. Maupassant was an impeccable artist, but I think the secret of the hold he had on the young men of my day was not so much that we discerned his cunning as that we delighted in the simplicity which his cunning achieved. I had read a great number of his short stories, but none that had made me feel as though I, if I were a writer, mightn't have written it myself. Maupassant had an European reputation. It was pleasing, it was soothing and gratifying, to feel that one could at any time win an equal fame if one chose to set pen to paper. And now, suddenly, the spring had been touched in me, the time was come. I was grateful for the fluke by which I had witnessed on the terrace that evocative scene. I looked forward to reading the MS. of *The Fan*—tomorrow, at latest. I was not wildly ambitious. I was not inordinately vain. I knew I couldn't ever, with the best will in the world, write like Mr. George Meredith. Those wondrous works of his, seething with wit, with poetry and philosophy and what not, never had beguiled me with the sense that I might do something similar. I had full consciousness of not being a philosopher, of not being a poet, and of not being a wit. Well, Maupassant was none of these things. He was just an observer like me. Of course he was a good deal older than I, and had observed a good deal more.

But it seemed to me that he was not my superior in knowledge of life. I knew all about life through *him*.

Dimly, the initial paragraph of my tale floated in my mind. I—not exactly I myself, but rather that impersonal *je* familiar to me through Maupassant—was to be sitting at that table, with a bock before me, just as I *had* sat. Four or five short sentences would give the whole scene. One of these I had quite definitely composed. You have already heard it. "Down below, the sea rustled to and fro over the shingle."

These words, which pleased me much, were to do double duty. They were to recur. They were to be, by a fine stroke, the very last words of my tale, their tranquillity striking a sharp ironic contrast with the stress of what had just been narrated. I had, you see, advanced further in the form of my tale than in the substance. But even the form was as yet vague. What, exactly, was to happen after Mlle. Angélique and M. Joumand (as I provisionally called him) had rushed back past me into the casino? It was clear that I must hear the whole inner history from the lips of one or the other of them. Which? Should M. Joumand stagger out on to the terrace, sit down heavily at the table next to mine, bury his head in his hands, and presently, in broken words, blurt out to me all that might be of interest? . . .

" 'And I tell you I gave up everything for her—everything.' He stared at me with his old hopeless eyes. 'She is more than the fiend I have described to you. Yet I swear to you, monsieur, that if I had anything left to give, it should be hers.'

"Down below, the sea rustled to and fro over the shingle."

Or should the lady herself be my informant? For a while, I rather leaned to this alternative. It was more exciting, it seemed to make the writer more signally a man of the world. On the other hand, it was less simple to manage. Wronged persons might be ever so communicative, but I surmised that persons in the wrong were reticent. Mlle. Angélique, therefore, would have to be modified by me in appearance and behavior, toned down, touched up; and poor M. Joumand must look like a man of whom one could believe anything. . . .

"She ceased speaking. She gazed down at the fragments of her fan, and then, as though finding in them an image of her own life, whispered, 'To think what I once was, monsieur—what, but for him, I might be, even now!' She buried her face in her hands, then stared out into the night. Suddenly she uttered a short, harsh laugh.

"Down below, the sea rustled to and fro over the shingle."

I decided that I must choose the first of these two ways. It was the less chivalrous as well as the less lurid way, but clearly it was the more artistic as well as the easier. The *chose vue*, the *tranche de la vie*[3]— this was the thing to aim at. Honesty was the best policy. I must be nothing if not merciless. Maupassant was nothing if not merciless. He

3. The "thing seen," the "slice of life."

would not have spared Mlle. Angélique. Besides, why should I libel M. Joumand? Poor—no, not *poor* M. Joumand! I warned myself against pitying him. One touch of "sentimentality," and I should be lost. M. Joumand was ridiculous. I must keep him so. But—what was his position in life? Was he a lawyer perhaps—or the proprietor of a shop in the Rue de Rivoli? I toyed with the possibility that he kept a fan shop—that the business had once been a prosperous one, but had gone down, down, because of his infatuation for this woman to whom he was always giving fans—which she *always* smashed. . . .

" 'Ah monsieur, cruel and ungrateful to me though she is, I swear to you that if I had anything left to give, it should be hers; but,' he stared at me with his old hopeless eyes, 'the fan she broke tonight was the last—the last, monsieur—of my stock.' Down below,"—but I pulled myself together, and asked pardon of my Muse.

It may be that I had offended her by my fooling. Or it may be that she had a sisterly desire to shield Mlle. Angélique from my mordant art. Or it may be that she was bent on saving M. de Maupassant from a dangerous rivalry. Anyway, she withheld from me the inspiration I had so confidently solicited. I *could not* think what had led up to that scene on the terrace. I tried hard and soberly. I turned the *chose vue* over and over in my mind, day by day, and the fan-stump over and over in my hand. But the *chose à figurer*[4]—what, oh what, was that? Nightly I revisited the café, and sat there with an open mind—a mind wide-open to catch the idea that should drop into it like a ripe golden plum. The plum did not ripen. The mind remained wide-open for a week or more, but nothing except that phrase about the sea rustled to and fro in it.

A full quarter of a century has gone by. M. Joumand's death, so far too fat was he all those years ago, may be presumed. A temper so violent as Mlle. Angélique's must surely have brought its owner to the grave, long since. But here, all unchanged, the stump of her fan is; and once more I turn it over and over in my hand, not learning its secret—no, nor even trying to, now. The chord this relic strikes in me is not one of curiosity as to that old quarrel, but (if you will forgive me) one of tenderness for my first effort to write, and for my first hopes of excellence.

4. The "thing to imagine."

QUESTIONS

1. Each time Beerbohm speaks of the man, he changes or adds something. First he is "a short fat man," then he is "the agonized short fat man"; later he is "the perspiring bourgeois." Is this simply variety for variety's sake? Is it elegant variation—a demonstration of literary cleverness? If not, what is it?
2. Beerbohm chose to have the man rather than the woman tell him the story, he says, because "it was . . . more artistic as well

as . . . easier." What precisely did he mean by "artistic"? What has honesty to do with it? Mercilessness? The "chose vue," the "tranche de la vie"?

3. Beerbohm seems to feel that his last version of the tale was more absurd, more offensive to his Muse than the earlier versions. Why?

4. The sentence which Beerbohm originally intended to use as a refrain in his tale of Mlle. Angélique and M. Joumand he uses as a refrain in this essay. Is the effect the same, different, or what? Explain.

5. Beerbohm might have ended his essay on a note of amusement at his youthful folly, at the absurd naiveté of hoping to achieve excellence cheaply and without effort. Would such an ending have been more in keeping with the essay's tone and values than the one he chose? More surprising? More satisfactory? Why or why not?

6. Young men, says Beerbohm, delighted in the simplicity which Maupassant's cunning achieved. Explain the paradox. In what senses might it be applied to Beerbohm's own writing?

GARET GARRETT

Remembrance of the *Times*[1]

May 7, 1915. When I came to the council room (2:30) only Mr. Ochs[2] and Mortimer are there. I have a feeling that they have been keeping silence between them. Mr. O. sits a little forward in his chair. His two hands are flat down on the table in front of him. They are short and thick. He looks at me as I come in, with wide eyes, the left one wider than the right one, and I notice again the symptoms of incipient paralysis. The left side of his face is falling. It is most noticeable when he is feeling emotion deeply. He does not speak, but continues to look at me as I take my seat facing him from the opposite side of the table. Then he says faintly, "The *Lusitania* has been sunk!" He pushes toward me the bulletin, two or three typewritten lines, telling that the great Cunarder was torpedoed by a German submarine off the Irish coast and sank in fifteen minutes. When I looked up he said: "I don't believe it."

Then the others begin to come in, B. and V. and G. and, at last, C. R. M., who sits next to me. More bulletins are received. She sank in thirty minutes and all were saved. She sank instantly, and nobody was saved. She did not sink at all, but has been beached. Each bulletin starts a new circle of conjecture, like a stone heaved into a pond of thought, and we talk a great deal to no purpose at

---

1. From the private papers of Garet Garrett, collected by R. C. Cornuelle for an article in *The American Scholar*.

2. Adolph Ochs (1858–1935), publisher of *The New York Times*.

all. At length it is 3:30 and Mr. O. by force of habit says, "Well, Mr. Mortimer?" which is to ask him what he thought to write about. M. says that nothing he had been thinking of seems now suitable or interesting. Mr. O., still moved helplessly by habit, said: "Well, Mr. Dithmar?" and it was the same with Dithmar as with Mortimer, and the same with the rest of us as with them, except C. R. M., who sat in a heap in his chair, meditative. He would write the lead, of course. That decided itself, and nothing else was decided at all. Mr. O. brought his hands down with a smack on the table, and we all went out—to make tomorrow's *Times*. And it would make itself, as we all knew. Obvious things would suggest themselves. The Washington man would send everything he had; the London man everything he could get; the Associated Press would send in masses of stuff; and somehow it would all fall into divisions: a news layout would in a way evolve, and tomorrow there would be a great paper.

After dinner C. R. M. came in, got the latest news, and went off to write the lead editorial, which also would suggest itself. The nation should be calm. It should trust the President. It should be ready to support him in any steps he might resolve to take to protect the lives of American citizens, the rights of neutrals at sea, and the cause of civilization against barbarism. This crime against humanity only proved what everybody already knew about Germany. At 12:30, with the editorial page still open, and not a line of M.'s copy, I went to his room. Mr. O. was with him. They were reading the editorial. I got it from them a sheet at a time, and on the way to the composing room put extra paragraph marks into it, so that it could be cut into short pieces for distribution among a number of compositors.

July 1, 1915. The sinking of the mule ship *Armenian* by a German submarine, killing a lot of Negro muleteers, is introduced for discussion in a most unexpected way. Mr. O., grinning as he does when he offers something he isn't sure of, and wants to be able to retreat on the pretext of not having meant it too seriously, turns to Mortimer and says: "It occurred to me—about those mules on the *Armenian*—that you might like to write something. Don't it seem cruel to sink a lot of mules that way? Eleven hundred of them! They are loaded on a boat at Newport News and start across the ocean and suddenly they are all drowned by the Germans." He simply couldn't express it in any way not to make it ludicrous, and began to blush furiously. He has really a great tenderness for life. He visualized eleven hundred dumb beasts, existing only to serve man, wantonly destroyed by man. He could see eleven hundred frightened big-eyed mules drowning in one herd, and he was sorry. It moved him almost to tears. Therefore, he grinned absurdly. Mortimer couldn't see it a bit at first. I said the British had used a herd of mules as a screen at the Dardanelles. Ochs said: "Gus, be sure to put that in, too." His feelings were not anti-German. He was sorry for mules, by whomsoever destroyed. Mortimer said at last that he would try, and he did very well with it, too. That ended our discussion of the sinking of the *Armenian*. The diplomatic problems were forgotten.

Sept. 28, 1915. To suggest that the *Times* is first of all a commercial success is to Ochs the unpardonable insult. He does not rage. He will not allow himself to rage. He has never been known outwardly to lose his temper. But to hear this obvious truth about his paper sends him home and to bed sick. His ambition (and it is not strange, seeing how all men long for that which in themselves is unattainable), his ambition is to produce a highbrow newspaper for the intellectuals. Today in council we were talking about the *Tribune*. He said he would not be afraid to take the *Tribune*, make it very "high class," charge five cents a copy for it, and risk his reputation on success. We asked him how he should go about doing it. He would make it important in art, politics, literature, music, etc. (using these terms vaguely), and to do this he would require the services of ten $10,000 men. That was very startling to some of those present. Ochs higgles terrifically over pay. Van Anda, the executive editor, and Mr. Miller, editor-in-chief and part owner, were probably the only two at table who receive as much as $10,000 a year. I come next. We pressed him for further details. Well, beyond doing what he had said, he would use the Associated Press news and nothing else. That would make a great paper. Van Anda said that was exactly what the *Evening Post* did. Mr. O. said the *Evening Post* was a very fine paper. It didn't do enough, he added, probably meaning that it lacked the ten $10,000 men. It has not one such, in fact.

Oct. 1, 1915. Every man is a kind of stranger to his own success. He but dimly understands it. Yesterday as we gathered in the council room we found Mr. O. sitting alone with the latest circulation figures before him, in the form of a four-column advertisement which would appear not only in the *Times* but also in all the other morning papers that would take it. (All but the *World* accepted it.) It was the quarterly statement, made up of the reports required by the P. O. Department. Along with the figures was some boastful text, especially emphasizing the belief that the *Times* is made for "intelligent" people and read by more "intelligent" people than any other American newspaper—a statement as easy to make as hard to prove. The circulation figures, of course, were the largest in the history of the paper—exceeding $318,000 average for the preceding three months. Mr. O.'s attitude contained both reverence and diffidence. His air was that of a man who might be admiring a bust of himself, objectively as a piece of sculpture, subjectively in a very different way. I think he has a feeling that he never knew before how great a man he is.

He cannot see—perhaps nobody ever did in his position—the disadvantages of success. The *Times* is beginning to be a haughty paper, haughty with its customers, as the *Herald* used to be, and that comes of being able to refuse advertising. One night last week we actually left out 12 columns, as there was not enough room in 24 pages for news and 122 columns of advertising together. Mr. O. had said: "Don't spoil the paper for a few columns of advertising." But a part of the success of the *Times* is owing to the art of being gentle with its customers. That is now forgotten. Mr. Wiley could not help showing his private elation at an incident of ungentleness which he reported. The bankers advertising the International Mercantile Marine reorganization had been given a poor position on first insertion, and had specified, for second insertion, a position top of page next to financial, "or omit." Mr. Wiley had said that the *Times* could not accept business in that way at all. People could not call for their own positions. The I. M. M. bankers could take what there was or stay out. We heard the sequel later. The advertisement was withdrawn, but late in the evening it was tendered again on Mr. Wiley's terms, and it got, as might have been expected, no better position than on the day before.

Oct. 15, 1915. Monday, I think it was, Mr. O. spread his hands out on the table and, looking at all of us at once, said, "Mr. T. has sent in his resignation," almost as if Mr. T. were dead. Poor T. He happens only to be weak in a way the rest of us are intolerant of. He went over into New Jersey to do a special story on woman suffrage and was not heard of again for many days. This has happened, oh, so often! And yet, how could we spare him? It was T. who, last Summer, did offhand in the office one night an essay on William J. Bryan, to meet the occasion of his resigning from the State Department, which besides being an excellent and stylish piece of writing, caught and fixed by a kind of inspiration all that spirit of Bryan's Western background—the frame-built town around a square where he was born, the aspirations amid which he grew, etc. T. was not at council meeting the next day, but his piece was commented upon enthusiastically. Mr. O. said it was remarkable that a man could do it out of his head; and it was so. And one of us said one thing and another of us another until it came Mortimer's turn. He got up on his crutches, swinging himself and sighing pessimistically, as he does. "Well," he said, "it makes me regret not drinking rum." The rest of us could only howl, forgetting the make-believe among us that nobody drinks rum, least of all T.

Mr. O. wondered if T.'s resignation would have to be accepted. Mr. Miller quoted somebody as having once said that the kindest thing to do with a man like T. was to take him down to a river dock and push him off; anything short of that was of no earthly use.

I said, just as merchandise, T. was worth all he cost, allowing for damage, breakage, and an occasional incident of total loss of transit. So it was left.

Today I met T. I said he had done a foolish thing. He thought I meant getting drunk. I meant resigning. He asked me how the resignation was received. I said I thought nothing would be done about it. All he needed to do was to sit tight, and the worst that could happen to him would be to take a moral lecturing from two or three superiors, probably Van Anda and, of course, Mr. O. I said he ought not to have resigned. "Oh," he said, "You meant that I was a fool to do that. Well, Payne told me Van Anda was going to fire me, and I resigned to beat him to it. Of course I don't want to leave the *Times*. I've been here eighteen years and I shouldn't know how to work anywhere else."

I told him Payne was a damned old gossip who didn't know what he was talking about.

Poor T. One eyebrow gouged; face all puffed; air of resolve, of beginning all over again from the beginning, of willingness to take his medicine. My last glimpse of him was as he stood waiting for Van Anda to see him, in the corridor, knowing that Van Anda did see him and was pretending that he didn't. So a man pays.

Oct. 19, 1915. Yesterday, on arriving at Council, I found Mr. Ochs discussing the sudden death of Arthur Greaves, city editor, eighteen years with the *Times*. My acquaintance with him was not intimate. He was a man who waved long thin fingers in the air and talked out of a loose, sensitive mouth. Mr. O. had been to the house. He is always the first one to go. He told us about it in a hushed kind of voice, his hands flat down on the table and his eyes wide open and rolling about at us. He had talked with the widow:

"I said perhaps there was someone on the *Times* she could feel more at ease with than with me, someone she could talk to more freely and with whom she would rather discuss arrangements, and she thought a while and said, yes, she thought she would rather talk with Joseph. So I've sent Joseph. She wants to keep the body until Thursday and then send it to Hartford, where some others are buried and where there is a family lot."

And so he went on telling us little things and asking here and there a question, as who had seen him last, and what he said, etc., and for a time everybody was silent. I was thinking of the Jewish character, generalizing about it. I wondered again at its simple, reverent, mystic attitude toward the three great enigmas—birth, marriage, and death. I have noticed it often. I was trying to associate it with the wonderful family ego of Jewish existence, when Mr. O. spoke again, or rather, came out loud with his thoughts, as if he had been speaking all the time, saying—

"He has a house and some life insurance. Not much. I think we ought to print his picture in the *Times*."

Today at Council he was pleased with the picture and with the obituary notice, a column long, written by Joseph. The arrangements had been all made.

"I'd like the editorial staff to be at the church," he said. "I'll have carriages, and we'll either meet here and go to the church or meet at the church, as you like, only we'll all ride behind the body to the Grand Central Station. We'll come down Eighth Avenue and through 43rd street, past the *Times*. All work will be discontinued in the building for half an hour, from ten to ten-thirty, and all the employees of the *Times* will stand outside as the funeral procession passes—as a mark of respect."

So, he was going to make a spectacle of it. I wondered whether he was thinking of Greaves or of the *Times*.

Wiley said it might not be feasible to bring a procession through 43rd street, owing to the torn-up condition of the crossing at 43rd and Seventh Avenue, where subway work is going on. Mr. O. waived the objection aside lightly. That could be arranged for. No such trifle should mar the éclat with which it might seem proper to him to bury the city editor of the New York *Times*, "thought by some people," as he wrote, "to be the greatest newspaper in the world."

Oct. 20, 1915. A Protestant Episcopal low church is probably the barrenest, emptiest thing in the world. The Greaves funeral service was held in that kind of place. I was a few minutes late, or at least the service had already begun, so I was spared the task of sitting close up with the high editorial staff, Mr. O. at the top of it. Passing to a seat which the usher deemed appropriate for one of my appearance, away back and on the other side, I bowed to several persons who acknowledged the salutation very stiffly, not to say, in several cases, imperceptibly. It appears that I am not funeral-broken. I don't know the manners, or I should have known better than to recognize people and expect to be recognized by them. I noticed it directly afterward. Others came in late, and were stared at by intimate acquaintances as if they were total strangers—not the slightest sign of recognition. You are to recognize only one thing here, and that is death, and the living are non-existent. Funerals have a singular fascination for old people. I presently noticed that. I discovered too the reason for the special strain upon one's nerves at a funeral service. It is that one doesn't dare to look bored. So they have that other look, which I have no name for, but which is the funeral look of those who are neither old nor young enough to find it morbidly fascinating and yet must not look bored.

Two men in gowns took turns at reading from a limp, gold-edged book. They were very bad readers. They did not know where exactly to scumble their voices and put in the emotion, so they made sure and put it in everywhere, because they thought Arthur Greaves must have been an important person and deserving of it, seeing that so many distinguished people came to the service. Reading from text was only bad. What followed was banal to the point of being horrible. One of the priests read from a manuscript concealed in the gold-edged book.

"We are gathered here from far and wide—" "It is indeed an imposing spectacle—" "—to cast upon his coffin the forgetmenots of love." "But yesterday [slight pause to look closer, light being bad] Arthur Greaves was with us. Now we have a feeling that he is gone." "I will not, cannot say, I will not say that he is dead. He has just gone away, with a cheery smile and a wave of his hand." "What does the history of his life teach us?" "And now we come to the closing word? Shall it be sad? Oh, no."

I recall these by the squirms they gave me. The "Oh, no," made me want to shriek. The inflection was upside down, as three-year-olds get it in their recitations.

It is shocking how little I know about funerals—so little, indeed, that I think them barbarous. If I should go to bury a friend I'm sure I would wish to lend a hand, to help carry the coffin, to help lower it into the grave, to feel my nerves and muscles straining at least a little bit in the last service for one to whom I had attached my heart. But pallbearers have nothing to do but to come in long coats and high hats and keep the eye of the undertaker. He tells them when to rise and precede the coffin to the door, and how to arrange themselves there in two rows, through which the undertaker's young men, very expert, carry the coffin on their shoulders without touching it with their hands.

I was taken into a carriage with Mr. O. and Mr. Miller, Thompson, and Kingsbury. Somebody asked what anybody thought of it. I said the possibility of having to lie helpless under all that banality was enough to take all the zest out of the thought of dying. And at length we were all agreed that a Roman Catholic service, with its rather fine ritual, would have been much better: Mrs. Greaves is a Roman Catholic.

Then Ochs began to tell us of having seen the Chicago *Tribune*'s war pictures, in a moving-picture theater. The cheerfulness and gaiety of the people in all the war scenes had impressed him greatly, almost as much, in fact, as the statement—written on the frame in which each set of pictures was shown—that the Chicago *Tribune* was the greatest newspaper in the world. Suddenly he shook my arm; "See," he said. "We're coming to it. Isn't it nice?" We had turned into 43rd street, and there, in front of the Times

Annex, were all the employees of "what some men think the greatest paper in the world," bareheaded, waiting for us to pass. "Isn't that nice?" he said again. There were a lot of them. "That's a real tribute," he said. He hated to part with the sight of it. He turned around in his seat to get it again through the little window in the back of the cab. "Look again," he said to Mr. Miller. "Isn't it nice?" Mr. Miller agitated his large frame, as an earnest of fair intentions, but did not get far enough around to see. "Yes," he said. "I saw it all."

"Arthur Greaves would like that better than anything else in the world," said Mr. Ochs, in the middle of the next block.

So the burial of the city editor of the New York *Times* was a public event of some displacement.

Feb. 19, 1916. Littlefield tells me this story, for truth. At a dinner Mr. Ochs was introduced to a person who exclaimed: "What a strong resemblance you bear to the first Napoleon!"

Mr. O. replied: "Oh, I am very much taller than Napoleon."

Feb. 21, 1916. Mr. O. likes to be sentimental, and funerals give him a pretext. Besides, funerals have a kind of fascination for him, I believe. Today, in a still spot of editorial conversation, he looked all around, with his hands pressed hard down on the table, and said: "That was a very sad funeral." It was Crippen's funeral. Between Crippen and O. there could never have been anything in common, except their bipedness, until Crippen died, wherupon he became the sentimental property of the New York *Times*. Mr. O.'s notion of the decent way, the only decent way, to leave the service of the *Times* is at the end of twenty-eight years continuous service to die and have a *Times* funeral. There is not another appropriate exit. If you have waited twenty-eight years you get at least a column obituary. Crippen got only a little more than a quarter of a column. But, anyhow, he was a strange person, who did not lend himself exactly to a New York *Times* obituary. He was a very tiny man with very long legs and walked with a great hammering stride. His face was always very red and his teeth were small and wide apart. He was full of deep and terrible cravings. One he tried to pacify by consuming two quarts of whiskey a day. He was never in the least drunk. Another craving was of the soul, and led him into the dark and devious ways of Eastern occultism, if not of sorcery. He wrote a strange book, *Fire and Clay*, which was really a very fine thing. He was an Englishman, had been long with the London *Times*, and was the kind of man whose private affairs you touch gently, with the fingertips. . . .

I was thinking how difficult it would be for Mr. O. to understand Crippen at all, when suddenly he turned to Ralph Graves, saying:

"We must keep track of that undertaker."

"Yes," said Graves, and I wonder why.

Mr. O. continued, "He was very reasonable. Only two hundred dollars for the whole thing. It was a very good-looking casket. It looked as good as some we've paid four hundred for."

April 21st, 1916. Mr. O. is back, looking very much better, but still with a trace of pallor under the tan he acquired on the Pacific coast. He told us a story. A man named Strauss or Meyers, who had recently made a great deal of money in speculation, who had been reputed to have won a quarter of a million in one Bethlehem Steel stock deal, who had been very successful, who was very shrewd (Mr. O. always stresses these facts about a person), this man had said to Mrs. O.: "Don't let anybody persuade you to go down that Grand Canyon trail. It's terrible. Don't mind what anybody tells you to the contrary. Just make up your mind to believe me and don't go." She had asked him to explain, and he had said: "I went. They persuaded me to go. You have to trust yourself to a mule. The trail is only a few feet wide. If the mule lost its head or decided to commit suicide you would be plunged into that awful abyss and instantly killed. The mule I rode was hungry. Evidently they don't feed them very well. It would go to one side for a bite of something, and then to the other for something else that went with it, one thing calling for another, stretching its neck out over that abyss; and I said to myself, 'What a fool I am. I have made all the money I want. I am only thirty-five. I have nothing more to worry about. And here I am trusting my life to this mule. I don't know what he will do next. Of the two I am the greater ass.' "

But in spite of this warning the Ochs party went, and it was safe enough. Thousands of women go every year. The mules are very trustworthy. We asked Mr. O. if he was not afraid. He said his only uneasiness was that he was continually expecting it to be worse. But after all it wasn't worth it.

Suddenly he turned to Graves with a piece of information he had picked up, about a man who had taken charge of the eastern business of a Chicago packing company at a salary of $250,000 a year. He thought it was a good news item. Graves promised to get something on it. Mr. O. is always impressed by large figures of wealth or income. I especially thought of it today. Also I particularly commented upon the fact that though he talks volubly and easily and tells a story well, with a sense of human weakness that enriches it, his grammar is faulty and his words are badly chosen. This is expecially true when he is expressing thoughts. Often he breaks off suddenly, and lets the rest of it be implied. He thinks out loud.

He asked me suddenly what I thought of the last note to Germany, the so-called ultimatum, dated April 19. I said I thought it was a further invitation to conversations, a statement that threw the council board into a first-rate commotion. I was asked to make it good. I said that nine months ago we had written to Germany that a repetition of the acts then complained of, namely, the wanton sinking of merchant steamers without regard for the lives of passengers and crew, would be regarded as "deliberately unfriendly," and now, in what we believed to be an ultimatum, we were citing many repetitions, that is, many deliberately unfriendly acts, committed in the meantime, and saying that "if" the German Government proposed to continue in this way, and unless the German Government abandoned its "present methods" of illegal submarine warfare, we should be unable to see any other course than the one that led to a severance of diplomatic relations. In the first *Lusitania* note, May, 1915, we took the position that submarine warfare against merchant vessels was inherently inhumane and should be abandoned for that reason. In this so-called ultimatum, April 1916, we repeat that opinion, but do not specifically demand that submarine warfare be abandoned. We specify "present methods," which remain to be defined, and we leave in an "if," which can be denied. The argument goes around the table. One says the inference is clear; another that the implication is final, etc., whereat, after a time, I remark that the fact of our debating it proves it to be debatable: an ultimatum that is debatable is not an ultimatum at all.

Mr. O. thinks there will not be a break with Germany. Yet we are all agreed that she will not abandon her submarine warfare.

I am aware, however, that the presence of Mr. O. gives our thoughts and expressions an elasticity that they did not have in his absence. None of us values his mental processes highly, and yet, he has a way of seeing always the other side that stimulates discussion, statement, and restatement, and leaves a better product altogether than is approached in his absence. Mr. Miller, when he presides, sees only one side of a thing, and smothers any effort to discuss the other. His mind is closed. It was a better mind than Mr. O.'s, and still is, within the limits of its movement. But Mr. O., for his lack of reasoned conviction, is all the more seeing. He can see right and wrong on both sides. He has a tolerance for human nature in the opponent.

May 4, 1916. I begin to get my finger on the riddle of Mr. Ochs. Intellectually he is the inferior of any man at the council table. He cannot think his way through a problem. He works around it, leaping from this aspect to that one, making now an utterly absurd suggestion or deduction and then immediately a very shrewd one. When he is beaten or trapped or finds himself in an awkward place, he says, "No, my thought is—," and then he is off at a new angle entirely. It is nevertheless dangerous to meet him lightly, because he is very often right in some unexpected way. And it is a remarkable fact that although his presence at council tends to lower the intellectual average, his absence leaves the whole thing inert and without spontaneity. He has in him a kind of emotional tolerance of humanity, bordering upon sheer sentimentality, which continually expresses itself in the other point of view, whatever that happens to be. Without fixed convictions on anything, he can let his feelings run. One day this week in his absence the Irish revolt was discussed for the first time. Mr. Miller characterized it, agreeably to his fast political principles; and those of us who suggested aught to the contrary, or felt in the least charitable, were treated with his silence. But on the next day Mr. Ochs, moved by the drama of events in Dublin, especially I believe by the character of the Irish Joan of Arc,[3] made one of his flying leaps and landed flat on the other side. "At least," he said, "they were willing to lay down their lives for what they believed in, right or wrong. That is one of the finest qualities." He expressed it badly, but he did force the other point of view, and Mr. Miller was obliged to relax a bit. Mr. Ochs thought Mr. Mortimer might write "a paragraph about it" in his Topics, which, of course, was no place for the treatment of such a subject. Frequently Mr. O. refers a thing that way to Mortimer, knowing either that Mortimer will write it as he wants it written, or that Mr. Miller, rather than allow Mortimer to slop over into political subjects, will do it himself on a basis of compromise. And that is what happened in this case.

The secret—the secret of the man himself and of his success with the *Times* as well—is that Mr. O. has crowd-consciousness. He, with a newspaper, is like the orator. Both of them address a crowd, with an understanding of its emotions, or rather, with a likeness of emotions, and as the orator and the crowd react on each other, so Mr. O. and the *Times* readers react on each other.

Mr. Ochs is a crowd.

June 5, 1916. It is agreed at last that I shall leave the *Times* not later than July 1, and earlier if there is no strain of work. I managed it to save everybody's feelings. In my note of resignation to Mr. O. I expressed a feeling of personal affection for both him and Mr. Miller, deep regret at breaking away from a number of very pleasant associations, and said that my work with the *Times* could not be worth as much either to me or to the *Times* as the work I was going to do would be worth both to me and to the newspaper to which I intended to transfer it. Before sending for me Mr. Ochs had Mr. Miller and Van Anda up, to tell them. Then he asked me to come up, and on seeing me he said: "I am very much surprised." I said again that I was very sorry to feel that I had to do it,

---

3. **Probably Constance (Gore-Booth) Markiewicz, sentenced to death for her part in the Easter Rising; a sen-** tence later commuted to a term of imprisonment.

and that the thing that hurt me most was to break my personal contact with him, since I had come to feel not only an attachment for him but a very deep regard. That disarmed him. He asked me if it was irrevocable. I said in one sense it was; I had given it all the thought it deserved. But I had not definitely promised myself away; in courtesy to him I had withheld that. He evidently expected me to say something about counter-inducements, but I did not. Instead I complimented him on the *Times* obliquely, by saying that none better than he should understand the passion of one to help in the making of a thing. I was going to the *Tribune*, a paper in the making. The *Times* was made. Thanks to his genius, it was so well and solidly made that there was almost nothing an individual could do to it. I was impatient to do things; and it was hard to get anything done on the *Times*—anything new. He said: "But you will not be as comfortable on the *Tribune* as here." I said: "I don't expect to be. The trouble is that I am too comfortable here. The comfort is killing." He looked at that with some surprise. Suddenly I said: "Why don't you buy the *Post*, and round out your career with an achievement in the way of a highbrow paper?" He responded enthusiastically. "I'm glad to hear you say that," he answered. "I've often thought of it. I could make a big success of the *Post*. Just the announcement that I had bought it would add a million dollars to its value. I know exactly what I should do with it. I'd use only the A.P. news, and bother no more about that end of it; but I'd spend a great deal of money on features of correspondence, articles on art and music and literature and politics. But tell me one thing—how would that help the *Times*?"

"It wouldn't help the Times," I said, "but what of that?"

"It would divide my energies," he replied, "and in that way it would hurt the *Times*." Then as if remembering what I had said about the *Times* being made he added: "I've hardly begun here yet." That is his dream—that he has yet a great deal more to do to the *Times*. The fact is that he is afraid to do anything more.

"You do not realize it," I said, "but you yourself are limited in your own expression by the traditions of this great institution that your industry and genius have created." That he definitely declined to believe. He talked of the great future of the *Times*, and of how futile the *Tribune's* competition would turn out to be.

FRANKLIN RUSSELL

The Running Eiders[1]

An island is a place of refuge for men and animals; its isolation slows the insistent thrust of time. For a moment, as I stand on the highest part of the island, sea water all around me, I believe I am immortal. Nothing can reach me here. I touch rough bark, feel the scrunch of stones underfoot, look into silent pools, and hear the sound of the sea and of my own heart.

Then I laugh because it is all a delusion.

The fact is, an island may have to be deserted. Life can be affirmed only by the denial of its security; this is as true for animals as it is for men. Hay Island, ten miles from Grand Manan,[2] is a monument to this. Men have long gone from it, and their remains suggest how illusory was the security of their island. No one has lived on Hay Island for many years. Two abandoned houses, walls sagging and windows empty, are littered with the debris of another century; they are the decaying nests of extinct creatures.

There are no ghosts on Hay, no flicker of spirits in the presence of the artifacts. A grocery bill from the 1800's evokes nothing. Nail holes in the walls, a black fingerprint on a board, the name Anne carved on a joist, none of these things suggest human occupancy. Perhaps this is because Hay Island is retrogressing, going back to an earlier millennium under the stimulus of a really enduring form of life: ducks.

In the prime of man's occupancy of the island, beginning in the eighteenth century, he decimated the eider ducks. He pillaged their nests for the eggs, which are delicious, and for the valuable eider down. Now, the men have gone, protective laws are in force, and the eider ducks of Hay Island are making their comeback.

This was the southernmost island on my summer trip, the easiest to reach, and it had special significance for me. For years, I had heard stories of how the eiders were taking over the island. Two years before, I had made a quick trip into the area, but the Grand Mananers, residents of a large island nearby, had said, "You're too early. The ducks aren't leaving yet." The next year, I had tried again, to be told, "You're too late. The ducks have gone."

I knew my entire summer could be plagued by such uncertainties, might even turn into a disaster. Therefore, after landing on Grand Manan and waiting for several days while a heavy sea subsided, I was very anxious. It was one thing to sit comfortably in a

---

1. Chapter 2 of *The Secret Islands*, 1965.
2. An island off the southwest coast of New Brunswick at the entrance to the Bay of Fundy.

New York City apartment and compute duck habits, quite another thing to be a prisoner behind surf roaring along an island shoreline.

Anxiety increased when my boat eventually eased me cautiously through mist to reach Hay Island one late afternoon. The tide was down and the boatman was fearful of hidden shoals. "Very dangerous at low tide," he muttered. "I shouldn't have brought you." He anchored, unshipped the dinghy and began rowing me through shallowing water. Abruptly the mist lifted and I had a Neptunian view of Hay Island. We were well below it, so great is the fall of the Fundy tide, and it looked as though the island had suffered a calamity; the sea had been drained from it.

"Good luck," said the boatman. "I'll be back in two tides."

My boots squelched among thick, lank weeds. The sun appeared, ten of its diameters from the horizon and its passage veiled by hurdles of clouds. I felt the urgency of its fall and quickened my pace up an embankment of stones that surrounds the island and protects it from the sea.

"You're too late. The ducks have gone."

I rounded the curve of the shore, trees, shrubs, and ponds on my left, sunset on my right. The shore was luminous from the sunlight now filtered through orange, red, and pink clouds. It was a spectacle but not what I sought. I walked and faced down the long western shore of the island. With the tide out, it was a grand sweep of shingle pouring into the withdrawn sea. As far as I could see, eider ducks walked toward the water. They hobbled and tripped on stones; those nearest to me skittered and fell in their haste. Each duck led a small, compact group of ducklings. I had arrived in time to see the eider ducks deserting the island with their new families. The eiders make their run to the sea, usually at dusk, as soon as the ducklings are strong enough to walk well. In the nest, concealed under a mother's breast or a covering of feathers, the ducklings are reasonably safe. In the water, capable of diving from predators, they have a fair chance of survival. But walking on land before they can fly, they are terribly vulnerable. This gives their passage from the nest to the sea a peculiar and touching urgency.

Forty ducks were in sight at once, all leading ducklings. I paused, watched, then walked forward into the world of the running eiders.

The ducks were Lilliputians on the shingled barrier to the sea. Behind them lay scrub, long grass, and spruce where they had brooded their eggs. Ahead of them lay the sun; easy to imagine it was their beacon. Ducks floated inshore, a communal body which certainly drew the running ducks on; I could see family groups, already in the water, swimming rapidly toward the main group.

As I walked, I was subject to multilayered sensation. My eyes moved back and forth but I knew I was always missing something. I walked high on the shore to avoid cutting off the seagoing families. If I scared ducks from their families, they left the ducklings in the refuge of the shore grasses.

But my feet crashing on the stones generated a general alarm and ducks which had not yet hatched their families began to flee. The first duck was a blur in my eye and a rush of wind in my face, so close did she fly past me. She had fled at the last moment, only when she was sure that I would stumble over her nest. Her flight set the tempo. Ducks came out of the grass and shrub like missiles. Each time harsh clatter of wings beat through dead sticks, a crash of heavy body flung through the undergrowth, then the sleek, speedy body of the duck appeared, eyes bright as she appraised the intruder, the sunset, and her path of escape.

I walked a hundred paces, fascinated, almost willing to be cut down by the ducks, now coming out of the undergrowth by the score. Many of them collided in mid-air; twice, they flew directly at me, blind to me specifically, but unnerving at high speed. Each duck saw me a moment before collision. Wings splayed desperately, tails fanned, and I was enveloped in a gale of ruptured air.

The sun glowed and threw out profuse color. I became ultrasensitive. Demonstrably, I was the only man experiencing this place and time; such a peak of awareness, exhilarant and tingling, might not come to me again. At the same time, it was frightening to be so close to the reality of wild lives, like taking a front-row seat at a boxing match and realizing, for the first time, the ferocious power of the blows.

The sea-run was at its peak. The shore swarmed with duck families. In the sea, back-lit by a dying sun, the offshore ducks had withdrawn slightly in deference to my presence. A score of duck families hurried across the intervening water. For the ducklings, the relief of being in the water was enormous. They dived, flapped stubby wings, shook themselves, skittered around their mothers in tight, excited circles. Then, the family groups set out, big ships followed by lines of small tenders, toward the waiting presence of the main duck flock.

For a moment, I was happy to watch; but such was the insistence of the sea-run to express itself that I could not remain an observer. A concerned quack behind me warned that a duck was close. I turned and saw a duck and ducklings at the edge of the undergrowth. She was in a quandary, the decision to head for the sea already made, the nest deserted, the undergrowth navigated only to find an enemy barring her path. For a moment, we watched each other in a common comprehension of the situation. Then, she made her choice, launched herself suddenly, and flew past me. The dilemma was transferred to the eight ducklings who met my gaze, as baffled as their mother had been a moment before. Their urge to reach the sea was irresistible. To turn back was impossible.

Their hesitation was neither fear nor doubt, merely consideration of their chances of getting *past* me.

They made their run in a group, stomping across the rocks like a phalanx of tiny Martians, as if the impetus of their miniature charge could sweep me out of the way. I stepped back and they were underfoot. I tried to stop one with my boot but he hurdled it in a sprawl of paddles and stub wings. I ran around them and tried to stop them again, drive them back into the shelter of the grass. Impossible. The run for the sea was manic. Their anxiety was so great they knocked each other down, jostled, and blundered. Yet despite interposing stones and debris, they stuck together all the way.

I watched them move down the shingle and hit the water. Almost immediately, a duck flew over their heads, calling. As one creature, the ducklings dived. One second, eight tiny forms bobbed; the next instant, eight circles of displaced water expanded. The ducklings reappeared fifty feet offshore; the duck landed and led her family quickly away.

Until this moment, I thought I had been seeing the full scope of events; but with slow-rising horror, I saw what was really happening along this shore. I had observed gulls everywhere, but on offshore islands they are omnipresent and almost unnoticed.

A duck appeared out of the undergrowth, about a hundred yards away. She led a straggle of fifteen ducklings, probably a coalition of two families. One duckling, smaller than the rest, trailed by six inches, and that was enough. A gull plucked him aloft, his fall and rise so swift it looked like one clean movement. The big bird passed over my head and choked the duckling down audibly as he flew. The remaining ducklings spurted into a more compact mass. The sea-run did not waver. The hovering, gliding gulls, so apparently casual, so outwardly benign, were everywhere, awaiting a chance for a duckling. The running eiders were neither comic nor touching; they were involved in a mathematical experiment in survival.

The equation was simple. Any duckling, on land or on water, who lagged more than five or six inches from his fellows, was killed immediately. The gulls twisted down, beaks agape and paddle feet lowered, struck stone or water, and rebounded buoyantly with their quarry. The ducks were unconcerned at the loss of the ducklings and did not even flinch as the gulls came down. Their presence was, apparently, anticipated, an historic fact of the sea-run. Even when gulls struck so close to the family group that their outflung wings swept the air above the ducks' heads, they provoked no threatening move, no quack of fear or rage. The ducks kept leading their broods, erect-necked and watchful, toward the haven of the water.

The sun disappeared with a final flourish; the run for the sea was thinning. Fewer than a score of ducks were visible. I walked down to the water's edge and looked back toward the heart of the island. The fringe of grass, the undergrowth and spruces, were washed with soft light. At that moment, one last duck appeared among the grasses and headed toward me as though I did not exist. Midway down the gravel, she saw me, turned diagonally, and revealed her family. It was enormous, more than twenty nestlings; probably she had picked up two other families of ducklings who had been temporarily deserted by their mothers. She watched me closely, made no attempt to fly, then hit the water with her big family and fled offshore. The tiny birds showed their elbowed paddle legs as they swam rapidly to keep up with her.

I took one last look up the shore, and as if I had summoned him, a lone duckling appeared. He stood motionless, facing two hundred feet of cruelly stoned beach, himself only hours out of the egg, the light of the sunken sun blinding his new eyes, alone. But he had no doubts. To the sea! He began his run.

At the same instant, a passing gull turned to investigate, apparently puzzled that any duckling could be *alone* on this beach. As he hovered, I hurled a stone and the gull veered away. Another gull took his position. I hurled more stones and the duckling stumbled downhill to the clatter of falling stones and the inquiring kaa's of the watchful gulls.

Even as I threw the stones, I knew that alone, the duckling was doomed. I must catch him and try to find a way to see him safely into the custody of his family. He zigzagged, fell, rolled, ran into my waiting hand. A gull hovered overhead, lit cold as steel in the moldering light. I remembered how wood ducklings could jump and fall a hundred feet to the ground without injury. Most young sea birds can fall from steep cliffs, smash onto rocks, and swim away unharmed. I decided to take a risk.

By this time, the conglomerate duck family was fully a hundred and fifty feet offshore. I hurled the duckling with all my strength at the sunset. He turned over and over silently, a splay of wing stubs and tiny paddle feet, and hit the water. Immediately, a gull was there. But the duckling whisked under the water; the gull hovered, watching. The duckling appeared but went down again before the gull could move toward him.

Finally, a long underwater swim brought the youngster up at the flank of the big family. He shot among them and disappeared.

The desertion of the island was a hint, a clue. I looked forward into the summer and wondered what else I might know. How much would these islands tell me about my own life?

The ducks withdrew and were lost in dusk; I sat till it was dark and contemplated life's urge to have its way and to survive.

QUESTIONS

1. Has Russell made the running of the eiders dramatic? Point out specific details that set the scene.
2. Explain the appropriateness of Russell's speaking of the ducks as "Lilliputians" (p. 85) and, later, as "a phalanx of tiny Martians" (p. 87). What implications does the essay as a whole give to these figures of speech?
3. Early in his essay Russell writes "It was one thing to sit comfortably in a New York City apartment and compute duck habits, quite another thing to be a prisoner behind surf roaring along an island shoreline." (p. 84). What attitudes are implicit in the contrast of these two postures? How does the essay realize, give substance to, the contrast?
4. Russell writes (p. 86) ". . . . could not remain an observer." How does the essay bear this out? Does Russell's ceasing to remain an observer negate or reduce the scientific value of his account of the running eiders?
5. Many students have been taught not to use "I" in an essay. Why? Russell uses "I" very frequently. Does he use it too much? Is he incorrect in using it? Explain.
6. What are some of the implications of the essay's closing sentence? Has the writer prepared for it, given it valid effect?

E. B. WHITE

Once More to the Lake (August 1941)

One summer, along about 1904, my father rented a camp on a lake in Maine and took us all there for the month of August. We all got ringworm from some kittens and had to rub Pond's Extract on our arms and legs night and morning, and my father rolled over in a canoe with all his clothes on; but outside of that the vacation was a success and from then on none of us ever thought there was any place in the world like that lake in Maine. We returned summer after summer—always on August 1st for one month. I have since become a salt-water man, but sometimes in summer there are days when the restlessness of the tides and the fearful cold of the sea water and the incessant wind which blows across the afternoon and into the evening make me wish for the placidity of a lake in the woods. A few weeks ago this feeling got so strong I bought myself a couple of bass hooks and a spinner and returned to the lake where we used to go, for a week's fishing and to revisit old haunts.

I took along my son, who had never had any fresh water up his nose and who had seen lily pads only from train windows. On the journey over to the lake I began to wonder what it would be like. I wondered how time would have marred this unique, this holy spot—the coves and streams, the hills that the sun set behind, the camps and the paths behind the camps. I was sure the tarred road would have found it out and I wondered in what other ways it would be desolated. It is strange how much you can remember about places like that once you allow your mind to return into the grooves which lead back. You remember one thing, and that suddenly reminds you of another thing. I guess I remembered clearest of all the early mornings, when the lake was cool and motionless, remembered how the bedroom smelled of the lumber it was made of and of the wet woods whose scent entered through the screen. The partitions in the camp were thin and did not extend clear to the top of the rooms, and as I was always the first up I would dress softly so as not to wake the others, and sneak out into the sweet outdoors and start out in the canoe, keeping close along the shore in the long shadows of the pines. I remembered being very careful never to rub my paddle against the gunwale for fear of disturbing the stillness of the cathedral.

The lake had never been what you would call a wild lake. There were cottages sprinkled around the shores, and it was in farming country although the shores of the lake were quite heavily wooded. Some of the cottages were owned by nearby farmers, and you would live at the shore and eat your meals at the farmhouse. That's what our family did. But although it wasn't wild, it was a fairly large and undisturbed lake and there were places in it which, to a child at least, seemed infinitely remote and primeval.

I was right about the tar: it led to within half a mile of the shore. But when I got back there, with my boy, and we settled into a camp near a farmhouse and into the kind of summertime I had known, I could tell that it was going to be pretty much the same as it had been before—I knew it, lying in bed the first morning, smelling the bedroom, and hearing the boy sneak quietly out and go off along the shore in a boat. I began to sustain the illusion that he was I, and therefore, by simple transposition, that I was my father. This sensation persisted, kept cropping up all the time we were there. It was not an entirely new feeling, but in this setting it grew much stronger. I seemed to be living a dual existence. I would be in the middle of some simple act, I would be picking up a bait box or laying down a table fork, or I would be saying something, and suddenly it would be not I but my father who was saying the words or making the gesture. It gave me a creepy sensation.

We went fishing the first morning. I felt the same damp moss covering the worms in the bait can, and saw the dragonfly alight on the tip of my rod as it hovered a few inches from the surface of the water. It was the arrival of this fly that convinced me beyond any doubt that everything was as it always had been, that the years were a mirage and there had been no years. The small waves were the same, chucking the rowboat under the chin as we fished at anchor, and the boat was the same boat, the same color green and the ribs broken in the same places, and under the floor-boards the same fresh-water leavings and débris—the dead helgramite,[1] the wisps of moss, the rusty discarded fishhook, the dried blood from yesterday's catch. We stared silently at the tips of our rods, at the dragonflies that came and went. I lowered the tip of mine into the water, tentatively, pensively dislodging the fly, which darted two feet away, poised, darted two feet back, and came to rest again a little farther up the rod. There had been no years between the ducking of this dragonfly and the other one—the one that was part of memory. I looked at the boy, who was silently watching his fly, and it was my hands that held his rod, my eyes watching. I felt dizzy and didn't know which rod I was at the end of.

We caught two bass, hauling them in briskly as though they were mackerel, pulling them over the side of the boat in a businesslike manner without any landing net, and stunning them with a blow on the back of the head. When we got back for a swim before lunch, the lake was exactly where we had left it, the same number of inches from the dock, and there was only the merest suggestion of a breeze. This seemed an utterly enchanted sea, this lake you could leave to its own devices for a few hours and come back to, and find that it had not stirred, this constant and trustworthy body of water. In the shallows, the dark, water-soaked sticks and twigs, smooth and old, were undulating in clusters on the bottom against the clean ribbed sand, and the track of the mussel was plain. A school of minnows swam by, each minnow with its small individual shadow, doubling the attendance, so clear and sharp in the sunlight. Some of the other campers were in swimming, along the shore, one of them with a cake of soap, and the water felt thin and clear and unsubstantial. Over the years there had been this person with the cake of soap, this cultist, and here he was. There had been no years.

Up to the farmhouse to dinner through the teeming, dusty field, the road under our sneakers was only a two-track road. The middle track was missing, the one with the marks of the hooves and the splotches of dried, flaky manure. There had always been three tracks to choose from in choosing which track to walk in; now the choice was narrowed down to two. For a moment I missed terribly the middle alternative. But the way led past the tennis court, and something about the way it lay there in the sun reassured me; the tape had loosened along the backline, the alleys were green with plantains and other weeds, and the net (installed in June and removed in September) sagged in the dry noon, and the whole place steamed with midday heat and hunger and emptiness. There was a choice of

1. The nymph of the May-fly, used as bait.

pie for dessert, and one was blueberry and one was apple, and the waitresses were the same country girls, there having been no passage of time, only the illusion of it as in a dropped curtain—the waitresses were still fifteen; their hair had been washed, that was the only difference—they had been to the movies and seen the pretty girls with the clean hair.

Summertime, oh summertime, pattern of life indelible, the fade-proof lake, the woods unshatterable, the pasture with the sweetfern and the juniper forever and ever, summer without end; this was the background, and the life along the shore was the design, the cottagers with their innocent and tranquil design, their tiny docks with the flagpole and the American flag floating against the white clouds in the blue sky, the little paths over the roots of the trees leading from camp to camp and the paths leading back to the outhouses and the can of lime for sprinkling, and at the souvenir counters at the store the miniature birch-bark canoes and the post cards that showed things looking a little better than they looked. This was the American family at play, escaping the city heat, wondering whether the newcomers in the camp at the head of the cove were "common" or "nice," wondering whether it was true that the people who drove up for Sunday dinner at the farmhouse were turned away because there wasn't enough chicken.

It seemed to me, as I kept remembering all this, that those times and those summers had been infinitely precious and worth saving. There had been jollity and peace and goodness. The arriving (at the beginning of August) had been so big a business in itself, at the railway station the farm wagon drawn up, the first smell of the pine-laden air, the first glimpse of the smiling farmer, and the great importance of the trunks and your father's enormous authority in such matters, and the feel of the wagon under you for the long ten-mile haul, and at the top of the last long hill catching the first view of the lake after eleven months of not seeing this cherished body of water. The shouts and cries of the other campers when they saw you, and the trunks to be unpacked, to give up their rich burden. (Arriving was less exciting nowadays, when you sneaked up in your car and parked it under a tree near the camp and took out the bags and in five minutes it was all over, no fuss, no loud wonderful fuss about trunks.)

Peace and goodness and jollity. The only thing that was wrong now, really, was the sound of the place, an unfamiliar nervous sound of the outboard motors. This was the note that jarred, the one thing that would sometimes break the illusion and set the years moving. In those other summertimes all motors were inboard; and when they were at a little distance, the noise they made was a sedative, an ingredient of summer sleep. They were one-cylinder and two-cylinder engines, and some were make-and-break and some were jump-spark,[2] but they all made a sleepy sound across the lake. The one-lungers throbbed and fluttered, and the twin-cylinder ones purred and purred, and that was a quiet sound too. But now the campers all had outboards. In the daytime, in the hot mornings, these motors made a petulant, irritable sound; at night, in the still evening when the afterglow lit the water, they whined about one's ears like mosquitoes. My boy loved our rented outboard, and his great desire was to achieve singlehanded mastery over it, and authority, and he soon learned the trick of choking it a little (but not too much), and the adjustment of the needle valve. Watching him I would remember the things you could do with the old one-cylinder engine with the heavy flywheel, how you could have it eating out of your hand if you got really close to it spiritually. Motor boats in those days didn't have clutches, and you would make a landing by shutting off the motor at the proper time and coasting in with a dead rudder. But there was a way of reversing them, if you learned the trick, by cutting the switch and putting it on again exactly on the final dying revolution of the flywheel, so that it would kick back against compression and begin reversing. Approaching a dock in a strong following breeze, it was difficult to slow up sufficiently by the ordinary coasting method, and if a boy felt he had complete mastery over his motor, he was tempted to keep it running beyond its time and then reverse it a few feet from the dock. It took a cool nerve, because if you threw the switch a twentieth of a second too soon you would catch the flywheel when it still had speed enough to go up past center, and the boat would leap ahead, charging bull-fashion at the dock.

We had a good week at the camp. The bass were biting well and the sun shone endlessly, day after day. We would be tired at night and lie down in the accumulated heat of the little bedrooms after the long hot day and the breeze would stir almost imperceptibly outside and the smell of the swamp drift in through the rusty screens. Sleep would come easily and in the morning the red squirrel would be on the roof, tapping out his gay routine. I kept remembering everything, lying in bed in the mornings—the small steamboat that had a long rounded stern like the lip of a Ubangi, and how quietly she ran on the moonlight sails, when the older boys played their mandolins and the girls sang and we ate doughnuts dipped in sugar, and how sweet the music was on the water in the shining night, and what it had felt like to think about girls then. After breakfast we would go up to the store and the things were in the same place—the minnows in a bottle, the plugs and spinners disarranged and pawed over by the youngsters from the boys' camp, the fig newtons and the Beeman's gum. Outside, the road was tarred and cars stood in front of the store. Inside, all was just as it had always been, except there was

2. Methods of ignition timing.

more Coca-Cola and not so much Moxie and root beer and birch beer and sarsaparilla. We would walk out with a bottle of pop apiece and sometimes the pop would backfire up our noses and hurt. We explored the streams, quietly, where the turtles slid off the sunny logs and dug their way into the soft bottom; and we lay on the town wharf and fed worms to the tame bass. Everywhere we went I had trouble making out which was I, the one walking at my side, the one walking in my pants.

One afternoon while we were there at that lake a thunderstorm came up. It was like the revival of an old melodrama that I had seen long ago with childish awe. The second-act climax of the drama of the electrical disturbance over a lake in America had not changed in any important respect. This was the big scene, still the big scene. The whole thing was so familiar, the first feeling of oppression and heat and a general air around camp of not wanting to go very far away. In midafternoon (it was all the same) a curious darkening of the sky, and a lull in everything that had made life tick; and then the way the boats suddenly swung the other way at their moorings with the coming of a breeze out of the new quarter, and the premonitory rumble. Then the kettle drum, then the snare, then the bass drum and cymbals, then crackling light against the dark, and the gods grinning and licking their chops in the hills. Afterward the calm, the rain steadily rustling in the calm lake, the return of light and hope and spirits, and the campers running out in joy and relief to go swimming in the rain, their bright cries perpetuating the deathless joke about how they were getting simply drenched, and the children screaming with delight at the new sensation of bathing in the rain, and the joke about getting drenched linking the generations in a strong indestructible chain. And the comedian who waded in carrying an umbrella.

When the others went swimming my son said he was going in too. He pulled his dripping trunks from the line where they had hung all through the shower, and wrung them out. Languidly, and with no thought of going in, I watched him, his hard little body, skinny and bare, saw him wince slightly as he pulled up around his vitals the small, soggy, icy garment. As he buckled the swollen belt suddenly my groin felt the chill of death.

QUESTIONS

1. White had not been back to the lake for many years. What bearing has this fact on the experience which the essay describes?
2. What has guided White in his selection of the details he gives about the trip? Why, for example, does he talk about the road, the dragonfly, the bather with the cake of soap?
3. How do the differences between boats of the past and boats of today relate to or support the point of the essay?

4. What is the meaning of White's last sentence? What relation has it to the sentence just preceding? How has White prepared us for this ending?
5. How would the narrative differ if it were told by the boy? What details of the scene might the boy emphasize? Why? Show what point the boy's selection of details might make.

Prose Forms: Journals

[Occasionally a man catches himself having said something aloud, obviously with no concern to be heard, even by himself. And all of us have overheard, perhaps while walking, a solitary person muttering or laughing softly or exclaiming abruptly. For oneself or another, something floats up from the world within, forces itself to be expressed, takes no real account of the time or the place, and certainly intends no conscious communication.

With more self-consciousness, and yet without a specific audience, a man sometimes speaks out at something that has momentarily filled his attention from the world without. A sharp play at the ball game, the twist of a political speech, an old photograph—something from the outer world impresses the mind, stimulates it, focuses certain of its memories and values, interests and needs. Thus stimulated, the man may wish to share his experience with another, to inform or amuse him, to rouse him to action or persuade him to a certain belief. Often, though, the man experiencing may want most to talk to himself, to give a public shape in words to his thoughts and feelings but for the sake of a kind of private dialogue with himself. Communication to another may be an ultimate desire, but the immediate motive is to articulate the experience for himself.

To articulate, to shape the experience in language for his own sake, one may keep a journal. Literally a day-book, the journal enables one to write down something about the experiences of a day which for a great variety of reasons may have been especially memorable or impressive. The journal entry may be merely a few words to call to mind a thing done, a person seen, a menu enjoyed at a dinner party. It may be concerned at length with a political crisis in the community, or a personal crisis in the home. It may even be as noble as it was with some pious men in the past who used the journal to keep a record of their consciences, a periodic reckoning of their moral and spiritual accounts. In its most public aspect, the idea of a journal calls to mind the newspaper or the record of proceedings like the Congressional Record. In its most closely private form, the journal becomes the diary.

For the person keeping a journal, whatever he experiences and wants to hold he can write down. But to get it down on paper begins another adventure. For he has to focus on what he has experienced,

and to be able to say what, in fact, the experience is. What of it is
new? What of it is remarkable because of associations in the memory
it stirs up? Is this like anything I—or others—have experienced before? Is it a good or a bad thing to have happened? And why, specifically? The questions multiply themselves quickly, and as the journalist seeks to answer the appropriate ones, he begins to know what it is
he contemplates. As he tries next to find the words that best represent
his discovery, the experience becomes even more clear in its shape
and meaning. We can imagine Emerson going to the ballet, being
absorbed in the spectacle, thinking casually of this or that association
the dancer and the movements suggest. When he writes about the
experience in his journal, a good many questions, judgments, and
speculations get tied up with the spectacle, and it is this complex of
event and his total relation to it that becomes the experience he records. The simple facts of time, place, people, and actions drop down
into a man's consciousness and set in motion ideas and feelings which
give those facts their real meaning to that man.

Once this consciousness of events is formulated in words, the jour-
nal-keeper has it, not only in the sense of understanding what he has
seen or felt or thought, but also in the sense of having it there before
him to contemplate long after the event itself. When we read a carefully kept journal covering a long period and varied experiences, we
have the pleasure of a small world re-created for us in the consciousness of one who experienced it. Even more, we feel the continuity,
the wholeness, of the person himself. Something of the same feeling
is there for the person who kept the journal: a whole world of events
preserved in the form of their experienced reality, and with it the
persistent self in the midst of that world. That world and that self are
always accessible on the page, and ultimately, therefore, usably real.

Beyond the value of the journal as record, there is the instructive
value of the habit of mind and hand journal keeping can assure. One
begins to attend more carefully to what happens to him and around
him. To have discovered, like Katherine Mansfield, that so apparently
simple a thing as a pigeon sitting proudly on a tree can bring to mind
the profoundest questions about the relation of God to His creatures,
is to be thereafter a little more sensitive to all kinds of "simple" experience. Fact begins to be related to fact more readily, apparently
dissimilar experiences may not be entirely different, the more and the
less important begin to be discriminated. Even in so unlikely a situation for calm contemplation as war is, it is possible, like Pearce, to
achieve that moment of detachment which focuses the immediate
scene or event for what it is by seeing how it matters in relation to
ideas or meanings beyond the battle or the beleaguered city or the
soldiers' worm game. One begins to see what he is looking at, if he
becomes accustomed to the characteristic method and form of the
journal entry. All the while, one is learning the resources of lan-

guage as a means of representing what he sees, and gaining skill and certainty in doing justice to experience and to his own consciousness when he writes.

The journal represents a discipline. It brings together an individual and a complex environment in a relation that teaches the individual something of himself, something of his world, and something of the meaning of their relation. There is scarcely a moment in a person's life when he is not poised for the lesson. When it comes with the promise of special force, there is the almost irresistible temptation to catch the impulse, give it form, make it permanent, assert its meaning. And so one commits himself to language. To have given up one's experience to words is to have begun marking out the limits and potential of its meaning. In the journal that meaning is developed and clarified to oneself primarily. When the whole intention of the development and the clarification is the consideration of another reader, the method of the journal redirects itself to become that of the essay.]

RALPH WALDO EMERSON: *from* Journal

I like to have a man's knowledge comprehend more than one class of topics, one row of shelves. I like a man who likes to see a fine barn as well as a good tragedy.   [1828]

The Religion that is afraid of science dishonors God and commits suicide.   [1831]

The things taught in colleges and schools are not an education, but the means of education.   [1831]

Don't tell me to get ready to die. I know not what shall be. The only preparation I can make is by fulfilling my present duties. This is the everlasting life.   [1832]

My aunt [Mary Moody Emerson] had an eye that went through and through you like a needle. "She was endowed," she said, "with the fatal gift of penetration." She disgusted everybody because she knew them too well.   [1832]

I am sure of this, that by going much alone a man will get more of a noble courage in thought and word than from all the wisdom that is in books.   [1833]

I fretted the other night at the hotel at the stranger who broke into my chamber after midnight, claiming to share it. But after his lamp had smoked the chamber full and I had turned round to the wall in despair, the man blew out his lamp, knelt down at his bedside, and made in low whisper a long earnest prayer. Then was the relation entirely changed between us. I fretted no more, but respected and liked him.   [1835]

I believe I shall some time cease to be an individual, that the eternal tendency of the soul is to become Universal, to animate the last extremities of organization.   [1837]

It is very hard to be simple enough to be good.   [1837]

A man must have aunts and cousins, must buy carrots and turnips, must have barn and woodshed, must go to market and to the blacksmith's shop, must saunter and sleep and be inferior and silly.   [1838]

How sad a spectacle, so frequent nowadays, to see a young man after ten years of college education come out, ready for his voyage of life—and to see that the entire ship is made of rotten timber, of rotten, honeycombed, traditional timber without so much as an inch of new plank in the hull.   [1839]

A sleeping child gives me the impression of a traveler in a very far country. [1840]

In reading these letters of M.M.E. I acknowledge (with surprise that I could ever forget it) the debt of myself and my brothers to that old religion which, in those years, still dwelt like a Sabbath peace in the country population of New England, which taught privation, self-denial, and sorrow. A man was born, not for prosperity, but to suffer for the benefit of others, like the noble rock-maple tree which all around the villages bleeds for the service of man. Not praise, not men's acceptance of our doing, but the Spirit's holy errand through us, absorbed the thought. How dignified is this! how all that is called talents and worth in Paris and in Washington dwindles before it! [1841]

All writing is by the grace of God. People do not deserve to have good writing, they are so pleased with bad. In these sentences that you show me, I can find no beauty, for I see death in every clause and every word. There is a fossil or a mummy character which pervades this book. The best sepulchers, the vastest catacombs, Thebes and Cairo, Pyramids, are sepulchers to me. I like gardens and nurseries. Give me initiative, spermatic, prophesying, man-making words. [1841]

When summer opens, I see how fast it matures, and fear it will be short; but after the heats of July and August, I am reconciled, like one who has had his swing, to the cool of autumn. So will it be with the coming of death. [1846]

In England every man you meet is some man's son; in America, he may be some man's father. [1848]

Every poem must be made up of lines that are poems. [1848]

Love is necessary to the righting the estate of woman in this world. Otherwise nature itself seems to be in conspiracy against her dignity and welfare; for the cultivated, high-thoughted, beauty-loving, saintly woman finds herself unconsciously desired for her sex, and even enhancing the appetite of her savage pursuers by these fine ornaments she has piously laid on herself. She finds with indignation that she is herself a snare, and was made such. I do not wonder at her occasional protest, violent protest against nature, in fleeing to nunneries, and taking black veils. Love rights all this deep wrong. [1848]

Natural Aristocracy. It is a vulgar error to suppose that a gentleman must be ready to fight. The utmost that can be demanded of the gentleman is that he be incapable of a lie. There is a man who has good sense, is well informed, well-read, obliging, cultivated, capable, and has an absolute devotion to truth. He always means what he says, and says what he means, however courteously. You may spit upon him—nothing could induce him to spit upon you—no praises, and no possessions, no compulsion of public opinion. You may kick him—he will think it the kick of a brute—but he is not a brute, and will not kick you in return. But neither your knife and pistol, nor your gifts and courting will ever make the smallest impression on his vote or word; for he is the truth's man, and will speak and act the truth until he dies.   [1849]

Love is temporary and ends with marriage. Marriage is the perfection which love aimed at, ignorant of what it sought. Marriage is a good known only to the parties—a relation of perfect understanding, aid, contentment, possession of themselves and of the world—which dwarfs love to green fruit.   [1850]

I found when I had finished my new lecture that it was a very good house, only the architect had unfortunately omitted the stairs.   [1851]

This filthy enactment [The Fugitive Slave Law] was made in the nineteenth century, by people who could read and write. I will not obey it, by God.   [1851]

Henry [Thoreau] is military. He seemed stubborn and implacable; always manly and wise, but rarely sweet. One would say that, as Webster could never speak without an antagonist, so Henry does not feel himself except in opposition. He wants a fallacy to expose, a blunder to pillory, requires a little sense of victory, a roll of the drums, to call his powers into full exercise.   [1853]

Shall we judge the country by the majority or by the minority? Certainly, by the minority. The mass are animal, in state of pupilage, and nearer the chimpanzee.   [1854]

All the thoughts of a turtle are turtle.   [1854]

Resources or feats. I like people who can do things. When Edward and I struggled in vain to drag our big calf into the barn, the Irish girl put her finger into the calf's mouth, and led her in directly.   [1862]

George Francis Train said in a public speech in New York, "Slavery is a divine institution." "So is hell," exclaimed an old man in the crowd.   [1862]

You complain that the Negroes are a base class. Who makes and keeps the Jew or the Negro base, who but you, who exclude them from the rights which others enjoy?   [1867]

KATHERINE MANSFIELD: *from* Journal[1]

March 21. Traveled with two brown women. One had a basket of chickweed on her arm, the other a basket of daffodils. They both carried babies bound, somehow, to them with a torn shawl. Neat spare women with combed and braided hair. They slung talk at each other across the bus. Then one woman took a piece of bread from her sagging pocket and gave it to the baby, the other opened her bodice and put the child to her breast. They sat and rocked their knees and darted their quick eyes over the bus load. Busy and indifferent they looked. [1914]

April 5. No bird sits a tree more proudly than a pigeon. It looks as though placed there by the Lord. The sky was silky blue and white, and the sun shone through the little leaves. But the children, pinched and crooked, made me feel a bit out of love with God. [1914]

I'm so hungry, simply empty, and seeing in my mind's eye just now a sirloin of beef, well browned with plenty of gravy and horse-radish sauce and baked potatoes, I nearly sobbed. There's nothing here to eat except omelettes and oranges and onions. It's a cold, sunny, windy day—the kind of day when you want a tremendous feed for lunch and an armchair in front of the fire to boaconstrict in afterwards. I feel sentimental about England now— English food, *decent* English *waste!* How much better than these thrifty French, whose flower gardens are nothing but potential salad bowls. There's not a leaf in France that you can't *faire une infusion avec,* not a blade that isn't *bon pour la cuisine.*[2] By God, I'd like to buy a pound of the best butter, put it on the window sill and watch it melt to spite 'em. They are a stingy, uncomfortable crew for all their lively scrapings. . . . For instance, their houses—what appalling furniture—and never one comfortable chair. If you want to talk the only possible thing to do is to go to bed. It's a case of either standing on your feet or lying in comfort under a puffed-up eiderdown. I quite understand the reason for what is called French moral laxity. You're simply forced into bed—no matter with whom. There's no other place for you. Supposing a *young* man comes to see about the electric light and will go on talking and pointing to the ceiling—or a friend drops in to tea and asks you if you believe in Absolute Evil. How can you give your mind to these things when you're sitting on four knobs

1. The triple dots in these entries are Mansfield's; they do not indicate deletions.
2. "make tea with" . . . "good for eating."

and a square inch of cane? How much better to lie snug and *give yourself up to it.* [1916]

If only one could tell true love from false love as one can tell mushrooms from toadstools. With mushrooms it is so simple— you salt them well, put them aside and have patience. But with love, you have no sooner lighted on anything that bears even the remotest resemblance to it than you are perfectly certain it is not only a genuine specimen, but perhaps *the* only genuine mushroom ungathered. It takes a dreadful number of toadstools to make you realize that life is not one long mushroom. [1917]

The man in the room next to mine has the same complaint as I. When I wake in the night I hear him turning. And then he coughs. And I cough. And after a silence I cough. And he coughs again. This goes on for a long time. Until I feel we are like two roosters calling to each other at false dawn. From far-away hidden farms. [1918]

She is little and grey, with a black velvet band round her hair, false teeth, and skinny little hands coming out of frills like the frills on cutlets.

As I passed her room one morning I saw her "worked" brush-and-comb bag and her Common Prayerbook.

Also, when she goes to the "Ladies," for some obscure reason she wears a little shawl. . . .

At the dining table, smiling brightly: "This is the first time I have ever traveled alone, or stayed by myself in a Strange Hotel. But my husband does not mind. As it is so Very Quiet. Of course, if it were a Gay Place—" And she draws in her chin, and the bead chain rises and falls on her vanished bosom. [1918]

May 31. Work. Shall I be able to express one day my love of work—my desire to be a better writer—my longing to take greater pains. And the passion I feel. It takes the place of religion—it *is* my religion—of people—I create my people: of "life"—it *is* Life. The temptation is to kneel before it, to adore, to prostrate myself, to stay too long in a state of ecstasy before the idea of it. I must be more busy about my master's business. [1919]

December 15. When I had gone to bed I realized what it was that had caused me to "give way." It was the effort of being up, with a heart that won't work. Not my lungs at all. My despair simply disappeared—yes, simply. The weather was lovely. Every morning the sun came in and drew more squares of golden light on the wall, I looked round my bed on to a sky like silk. The day opened slowly, slowly like a flower, and it held the sun long, long before it slowly, slowly folded. Then my homesickness went. I not only didn't want to be in England, I began to love Italy, and the thought of it—the sun—even when it was too hot—always the sun —and a kind of *wholeness* which was good to bask in.

All these two years I have been obsessed by the fear of death. This grew and grew and grew gigantic, and this it was that made me cling so, I think. Ten days ago it went, I care no more. It leaves me perfectly cold. . . . Life either stays or goes.

I must put down here a dream. The first night I was in bed here, *i.e.* after my first day in bed, I went to sleep. And suddenly I felt my whole body *breaking up*. It broke up with a violent shock—an earthquake—and it broke like glass. A long terrible shiver, you understand—the spinal cord and the bones and every bit and particle quaking. It sounded in my ears a low, confused din, and there was a sense of floating greenish brilliance, like broken glass. When I woke I thought that there had been a violent earthquake. But all was still. It slowly dawned upon me—the conviction that in that dream I died. I shall go on living now—it may be for months, or for weeks or days or hours. Time is not. In that dream I died. The *spirit* that is the enemy of death and quakes so and is so tenacious was shaken out of me. I am (December 15, 1919) a dead woman, and *I don't care.* It might comfort others to know that one gives up caring; but they'd not believe any more than I did until it happened. And, oh, how strong was its hold upon me! How I *adored* life and *dreaded* death!

I'd like to write my books and spend some happy time with J. (not very much faith withal) and see L. in a sunny place and pick violets—all kinds of flowers. I'd like to do heaps of things, really. But I don't mind if I do not do them. . . . Honesty (why?) is the only thing one seems to prize beyond life, love, death, everything. It alone remaineth. O you who come after me, will you believe it? At the end *truth* is the only thing *worth having*: it's more thrilling than love, more joyful and more passionate. It simply *cannot* fail. All else fails. I, at any rate, give the remainder of my life to it and it alone. [1919]

What I feel is: She is never for one fraction of a second unconscious. If I sigh, I know that her head lifts. I know that those grave large eyes solemnly fix on me: Why did she sigh? If I turn she suggests a cushion or another rug. If I turn again, then it is my back. Might she try to rub it for me? There is no escape. All night: a faint rustle, the smallest cough, and her soft voice asks: "Did you speak? Can I do anything?" If I do absolutely nothing then she discovers my fatigue under my eyes. There is something profound and terrible in this eternal desire to establish contact. [1920]

August. A sudden idea of the relationship between "lovers."
We are neither male nor female. We are a compound of
both. I choose the male who will develop and expand the male in
me; he chooses me to expand the female in him. Being made
"whole." Yes, but that's a process. By love serve ye one another. . . . And why I choose *one* man for this rather than many
is for safety. We bind ourselves within a ring and that ring is as it
were a wall against the outside world. It is our refuge, our shelter.
Here the tricks of life will not be played. Here is *safety* for us to
grow.

Why, I talk like a child!. . [1921]

Tidied all my papers. Tore up and ruthlessly destroyed much.
This is always a great satisfaction. Whenever I prepare for a journey
I prepare as though for death. Should I never return, all is in
order. This is what life has taught me. [1922]

My first conversation with O. took place on August 30, 1922.
On that occasion I began by telling him how dissatisfied I was
with the idea that Life must be a lesser thing than we were
capable of imagining it to be. I had the feeling that the same
thing happened to nearly everybody whom I knew and whom I did
not know. No sooner was their youth, with the little force and impetus characteristic of youth, done, than they stopped growing. At
the very moment that one felt that now was the time to gather
oneself together, to use one's whole strength, to take control, to be
an adult, in fact, they seemed content to swap the darling wish of
their hearts for innumerable little wishes. Or the image that suggested itself to me was that of a river flowing away in countless little trickles over a dark swamp.

They deceived themselves, of course. They called this trickling
away—greater tolerance—wider interests—a sense of proportion—
so that work did not rule out the possibility of "life." Or they
called it an escape from all this mind-probing and self-consciousness—a simpler and therefore a better way of life. But sooner or
later, in literature at any rate, there sounded an undertone of deep
regret. There was an uneasiness, a sense of frustration. One
heard, one thought one heard, the cry that began to echo in one's
own being: "I have missed it. I have given up. This is not what
I want. If this is all, then Life is not worth living."

But I *know* it is not all. How does one know that? Let me take
the case of K.M. She has led, ever since she can remember, a very
typically false life. Yet, through it all, there have been moments,
instants, gleams, when she has felt the possibility of something
quite other. [1922]

HENRY DAVID THOREAU: *from* Journal

As the least drop of wine tinges the whole goblet, so the least particle of truth colors our whole life. It is never isolated, or simply added as treasure to our stock. When any real progress is made, we unlearn and learn anew what we thought we knew before. [1837]

Not by constraint or severity shall you have access to true wisdom, but by abandonment, and childlike mirthfulness. If you would know aught, be gay before it. [1840]

It is the man determines what is said, not the words. If a mean person uses a wise maxim, I bethink me how it can be interpreted so as to commend itself to his meanness; but if a wise man makes a commonplace remark, I consider what wider construction it will admit. [1840]

Nothing goes by luck in composition. It allows of no tricks. The best you can write will be the best you are. Every sentence is the result of a long probation. The author's character is read from title-page to end. Of this he never corrects the proofs. We read it as the essential character of a handwriting without regard to the flourishes. And so of the rest of our actions; it runs as straight as a ruled line through them all, no matter how many curvets about it. Our whole life is taxed for the least thing well done: it is its net result. How we eat, drink, sleep, and use our desultory hours, now in these indifferent days, with no eye to observe and no occasion [to] excite us, determines our authority and capacity for the time to come. [1841]

What does education often do? It makes a straight-cut ditch of a free, meandering brook. [1850]

All perception of truth is the detection of an analogy; we reason from our hands to our head. [1851]

To set down such choice experiences that my own writings may inspire me and at last I may make wholes of parts. Certainly it is a distinct profession to rescue from oblivion and to fix the sentiments and thoughts which visit all men more or less generally, that the contemplation of the unfinished picture may suggest its harmonious completion. Associate reverently and as much as you can with your loftiest thoughts. Each thought that is welcomed and recorded is a nest egg, by the side of which more will be laid. Thoughts accidentally thrown together become a frame in which more may be developed and exhibited. Perhaps this is the main value of a habit of writing, of keeping a journal—that so we remember our best hours and stimulate ourselves. My thoughts are my company. They have a certain individuality and separate existence, aye, personality. Having by chance recorded a few disconnected thoughts and then brought them into juxtaposition, they suggest a whole new field in which it was possible to labor and to think. Thought begat thought. [1852]

It is pardonable when we spurn the proprieties, even the sanctities, making them stepping-stones to something higher. [1858]

There is always some accident in the best things, whether thoughts or expressions or deeds. The memorable thought, the happy expression, the admirable deed are only partly ours. The thought came to us because we were in a fit mood; also we were unconscious and did not know that we had said or done a good thing. We must walk consciously only part way toward our goal, and then leap in the dark to our success. What we do best or most perfectly is what we have most thoroughly learned by the longest practice, and at length it falls from us without our notice, as a leaf from a tree. It is the *last* time we shall do it—our unconscious leavings. [1859]

The expression "a *liberal* education" originally meant one worthy of freemen. Such is education simply in a true and broad sense. But education ordinarily so called—the learning of trades and professions which is designed to enable men to earn their living, or to fit them for a particular station in life—is *servile*. [1859]

DONALD PEARCE: *from* Journal of a War

December 5, [1944]. The things that enter men's minds. Chaplin, Benchley, the Marx Brothers, and the rest only imitate what is right there in life. I visited a convalescent depot near here, and found that one of the favorite sports was racing angleworms. Heavy bets were placed on the worms and large amounts of money were won and lost daily. It was arranged on the model of horse racing, with tracks, jockeys, stalls, and a complete set of regulations governing everything. The racetrack consisted of eight parallel shallow grooves cut into the ground, about six feet long and one foot apart; these grooves kept the worms racing down the course in the right direction. Small stalls, about the size of a soap dish, were cut into the ground at the starting line for the accommodation of each worm. A straw was struck in front of each for a gate. The soldiers were the jockeys. Each jockey provided himself with a lighted cigarette. When the bets were all laid and the worms all installed, the timekeeper counted out the seconds and shouted "Go!" Up came the straws with the right hand and lighted cigarette ends were applied to the worms' posteriors with the left. They squirmed forward at different speeds, working their way along the little trenches. At the end of exactly thirty seconds, the timekeeper called "Go!" again, and cigarettes were again touched to the worms. And again they would spurt forward. This continued until the winner crossed the finish line.

The shouting and rooting during a race could be heard far across on the other side of the parade ground. One Sunday morning, the Colonel came over to see what kind of game they were playing that was so noisy, and stood there watching a whole race, very fascinated, apparently without anyone noticing him. When someone finally did, the men all came to attention and he started in to lecture them about the cruel sport they were practicing; but the worms were still racing, and everyone kept watching them out of the corners of their eyes, the Colonel included, till in the midst of his remarks, one excited man burst out, "My God! My worm's won!" and the whole group huddled around the finish line to see.

One day a jockey got the great idea of spitting on his worm and stroking its body in his hands till it was nice and smooth, in the hope that maybe he would slide over the ground better the next time. This proved a revolutionary idea, for his worm won the next race by a couple of lengths. So all contestants in the next race spit liberally on their worms, smoothed them down, and said loving and hopeful things to them; but when the race was run, the worms all bogged down, their bodies so packed with mud and bits of grass they could barely move, and the race was a miserable failure. In a flash, the whole group set off after the man who had introduced this modification into the game and chased him around the camp with the intention of beating him up. Down the graveled roads they ran. The Regimental Sergeant-Major stuck his head out of the mess as they ran by and demanded in stentorian tones to know "What the hell's going on out there?" and received the baffling reply, "He made us spit on our worms!"—and they rushed on.

It was found, after a good many of these worm races, that the large dew-worms, because they had more brute strength and energy, were—not always, but as a rule—better than the smaller angle-worms, especially since the smaller worms tended to squirm when touched with a cigarette rather than plunge forward. But it was also found that dew-worms with pronounced annular rings were bad, because the ring often acted as an anchor or drag. Also, a good worm had a distinctly horny feeling in the hand. It was very important which way you placed your worm in the stall—head first, or tail first. If the head was singed rather than the tail, the worm, if he did not go into paroxysms of pain and wrap himself into a tight ball, had to hunch around and face the right way before beginning the race. Several favorites lost races by being placed wrong-end-to in the stall. A worm was good for possibly three races. After that he was more likely to squirm than worm when "spurred."

* * *

December 28. We have been patroling the Rhine and guarding the bridge across it at Nijmegen continuously for so long now that they have begun to acquire a positive hold over our minds and imaginations. Our thoughts seem polarized by them, and turn to them like compasses to a magnet. This bridge is the only one over the Rhine left intact for a hundred miles, and we must keep it that way for our own no doubt imminent invasion of Germany. At the same time, if Jerry decides to counter-attack in force through here, and there has been a good deal of fresh evidence that he's getting ready to do just that, the bridge would become just as important to him. A really ambiguous prize. But he keeps sending explosives downstream at it. Damn strange. We shoot into the river at everything that moves, sometimes exploding mines tied to boards, or logs, or branches. Our engineers have run a huge net across the river about fifty yards upstream from the bridge to catch whatever floats downstream; but things get through or under the net somehow and that's what we shoot at. New rumor: German frogmen have been attempting to swim under the net; also, they have small one-man submarines in the river. Probably fairy lore.

But I was going to say—the bridge and river no longer appear ordinary to us, but seem to have acquired personalities, or to have been endowed with them. Sometimes the river seems less the watched one than the watcher, reflecting back our searchlight beams, and breaking the half-moon into a thousand yellow eyes as we steal along the edge on night patrols. The bridge's single span is unmistakably a high, arched eyebrow over an invisible eye peering across the Rhine. Everything we do here revolves around the bridge and river. As we go back for a rest or, as recently, for Christmas dinner, miles from the line, we cross the iced-flats that follow along the curving windswept dykes, and the great iron eyebrow is right behind us, lifting higher and higher above the mist, in a kind of inscrutable surmise, and as we return to those god-awful flats again, the eyebrow and invisible eye are at it again, staring back at us, watching the Rhine. Perhaps someone should put on a campaign to establish the ordinariness of this bridge and river, put up signs. But it would do no good, I tell myself, because this was Caesar's Rhine, Siegfried's Rhine, Wagner's Rhine, and you can't silence all that mystery. I hate it here.

Whipping the company jeep at top speed along a mile-long windswept section of one of the dykes that stretches between our company and the next is one of the low diversions we have worked out. It's completely exposed and utterly bare; so for two minutes you are an A-number one moving target. An insane game, but we play it. Once I heard the loud, flat snap of a bullet going past my head on one of these mad runs. We are, as they say, very definitely under observation.

* * *

March 3 [1945]. The city[1] was quite heavily defended. First, a steep, raw, anti-tank ditch completely girdling the city had to be negotiated, with continuous covering fire from both flanks. Then we ran into a connected system of crawl- and weapons-trenches forming a secondary ring about the interior. Our covering artillery fire was practically saturational; so he resisted only lightly till we were more than halfway in. There followed some sporadic street fighting and house clearing, nothing very spectacular, and the city fell to us shortly after daybreak; i.e., they simply pulled out and disappeared at about 4:00 A.M.

I had a couple of close ones during this show. On the way in, my platoon was evidently silhouetted against the night sky, and was fired on four times at a range of maybe 300 yards by an eighty-eight. (This is a notorious and vicious gun. The velocity of the shell is so high that you hear it pass or explode near you almost at the same instant that you hear the sound of its being fired. You really can't duck it. Also, it's an open-sights affair—you are aimed at particularly; not, as with mortars, aimed at only by approximation.) Anyway, they went past me about an arm's length above or in front of me, I don't know which. We hit the ditches. After pointing a few more, the gun was forced off by our return tank fire.

During the house-clearing phase, at one spot, I walked instead of ran from one house to another and got my helmet spun around on my head with a close shot. There was an extremely loud, flat "snap," like two hands clapped together hard beside my ear; that was all. Plus a crease in my helmet, which gave me immense prestige with the men all morning.

We had two tanks along with us, and their support made the assignment 100 per cent easier. At one point a handful of German snipers, who were perched in the attic of a three-story house at a bend in the main street, held up the battalion for over an hour. They were finally silenced by one of the tanks. In the half-dark, we circled around behind their house during the tank fire and cut off their escape route. Presently they came out through the back garden, dangling in front of them white cloths on long poles. It was vastly disconcerting. Instead of a squad of Nazi supermen in shiny boots, and packing Lugers, we were confronted by five of the most unkempt, stunted, scrubby specimens I have ever had the pleasure of capturing. Two of them couldn't have been more than

1. Udem, in The Netherlands.

fourteen on their next birthday. Possibly they were on some kind of dope; at least they acted that way, a little dazed, grinning, and rather immune to voice control. One of them had nearly shot me a few hours earlier in the dark before dawn. At the time, I remember, I had thought it wasn't any more than I had expected; but later on, seeing them, I felt that it would have been an unfortunate end to my life. I am obviously getting choosy. What I mean is that I would simply like to be well killed, if killed I am to be. I came to the conclusion that they were from the bottom of Germany's recruiting barrel.

The men in the platoon seemed to think so too, for I caught them in the middle of a queer performance. They had lined the five of them up against a schoolhouse wall and were pretending, quite ceremoniously, that they were going to shoot them. The prisoners certainly believed they were about to be shot; three of them had their hands on their heads and their faces turned to the wall, as for execution; the other two were pleading desperately with three or four of our men. I was astonished to find my best corporal in the thick of this business. I stopped it, of course. Not that they would have carried out the execution; I feel sure of that.

We passed through the town and seized a road-and-rail junction about 800 yards past the outskirts and dug in under moderate shelling. A child would know that that junction would become a hot target—which it very shortly did. We sat it out. He sent several salvos of rockets in on us. These you always hear coming, if it's any comfort. The first salvo was the best, but there was time for my sergeant and me to flatten out in a shallow ditch alongside the track. One rocket hit about four or five feet from us, practically shattering my hearing; it chewed up a couple of railway ties, took two or three chunks out of the rails, and turned me over from my stomach to my back. The blast stung my whole left side. Nothing more really close happened there all night.

Next day, I went back to have a look at Udem. In daylight it seemed in worse condition than I remembered it from the night before. Enemy shelling accounted for much of the destruction; but looters, busy rooting around before daybreak, accounted for some too. The houses that had not been shelled were practically turned inside out by our troops. I came across one soldier telling an admiring group about his morning exploits: "First I took a hammer and smashed over 100 plates, and the cups along with them. Then I took an ax to the china cabinets and buffets. Next I smashed all the furniture and pulled the stuffing out of the big chairs. Then I took the hammer again and smashed all the elements on two electric stoves and broke the enamel off the stove fronts and sides. Then I put a grenade in the big piano, and after that I poured a jar of molasses into it. I broke all the French doors and all the doors with mirrors in them and threw the lamps out into the street. I was so mad."

I turned him over to the Provost Corps in the afternoon.

Udem had a large church made of red stone with high twin towers. German artillery scouts had stationed themselves in these towers in order to direct fire onto our positions five miles away. So the church had to be "neutralized," as they say. We engaged it with 17-pounders for about an hour, I believe successfully. Anyway, I went in to see what we had done. It was full of gaping holes; the stone pillars had even been shot off far within the building. The only unharmed thing I saw was the font. The walls had had blue and gold paintings of religious scenes extending all around the interior; these were mostly peeled or ripped off. One painting was of the Descent from the Cross. It had come loose from its frame and seemed heading for a nosedive; the pale belly of Christ had a group of machine-gun bullets through it. The Germans had made a brief stand at the church and had obviously used it as a temporary strongpoint. As I left, engineers were already laying dynamite charges at critical points along the foundations, with the intention of using the stones as rubble for roads, almost the only reasonable use left for it.

On the way back, I met a number of civilians carrying bundles. Most of them were covered with mud from head to foot. They were staggering along rather than walking, and started every time a gun went off far away or close up. One tall thin man was leading two small children, one by each hand. The children were around his back. The man limped; I saw that he was weeping. My limited German enabled me to discover that he was wounded in a couple of places, that his wife had been killed by shrapnel in the morning, and that he didn't know what to do with his tiny children who were wet, cold, and hungry. I took them down into our cellar where the stretcher bearer dressed his wounds and evacuated him. I offered the two children food—chocolate, bread and jam, biscuits. They only tightened their lips and refused. So I tried a sort of game with the names of the articles of furniture in the cellar, deliberately making silly mistakes, and after a while they laughed at my stupidity. I kept this up, and before long they gobbled whatever I put in front of them. I would like to have done more; but instead I turned them over to the Civil Affairs people, not without complicated feelings of concern and regret. I will never know what happened to them.

Kept rummaging around in the town. Went to the place where I was nearly shot, stood on the exact spot, in fact, and determined the window at the end of the street where the shots had come from. An impulse sent me inside the house itself, where I climbed to the upper room. The machine gun was there on its heavy mounting, still pointing out the window and down the street. I sat behind it and took aim on the doorway I had disappeared into at the moment I was fired on, and waited for someone to pass the spot just to see how I must have looked through his sights. No one came and I got tired of the melodrama and went back to our forward positions.

* * *

March 4. When will it all end? The idiocy and the tension, the dying of young men, the destruction of homes, of cities, starvation, exhaustion, disease, children parentless and lost, cages full of shivering, staring prisoners, long lines of hopeless civilians plodding through mud, the endless pounding of the battle line. I can scarcely remember what it is like to be where explosions are not going off around me, some hostile, some friendly, all horrible; an exploding shell is a terrible sound. What keeps this war going, now that its end is so clear? What do the Germans think of us, and we of them? I do not think we think of them at all, or much. Do they think of us? I can think of their weapons, their shells, their machine guns, but not of the men behind them. I do not feel as if I were fighting against men, but against machines. I need to go up in an airplane and actually see German transport hauling guns and ammunition, see their actual armies; for everything that happens merely comes from a vague beyond, and I cannot visualize the people who are fighting against me. The prisoners that come over hills with their hands up, or who come out of houses with white cloths waving—they have no relation, almost, to anything for me. I can't connect them with the guns they have just laid down, it seems like forcing something to do so. It is becoming hard for me not to feel sometimes that both sides are the common victims of a common terror, that everybody's guns are against everybody ultimately.

These are times when I feel that every bit of fighting is defensive. Self defense. If a machine-gun nest is attacked and wiped out by us, by my own platoon, I do not feel very aggressive, as if I had attacked somebody. It is always that I have defended myself against something that was attacking me. And how often I have thought that there might be a Rilke out there in a German pill box. If I could only see them, as in battles long ago, at close range, before engaging them. In our wars, the warring sides are getting farther and farther apart and war is getting more and more meaningless for the field warriors, and more meaningful for the domestic warriors in factories and homes. Will there come a time when hundreds of miles separate the warring fronts? When long-range weapons and the ghastly impersonality of air attacks are the means of war? It is already a very impersonal thing. When a soldier is killed or wounded his buddies, shaking their heads, merely say, "Poor old Joe. He just got it. Just as he was going up that hill, he got it." As if to imply that he was merely in the wrong place at the wrong time, and that life and death are only matters of luck and do not depend on the calculations of human beings at the other end of an S.P. gun. When we were in our static positions around Wyler Meer and Nijmegen, the enemy became real to me for the first time. I watched him for weeks, saw him dig, run, hide, fire, walk. And when I went on patrols into his territory, there was meaning in that, too, for I knew where he was, I knew his habits. So that while we were probing the cuticle of the enemy, so to speak, he was real; but now when we are ripping into his body, he has disappeared and has turned into something read about in the papers. But the guns remain, manned by soldiers who are so meaningless to us that when they shoot a fellow, all we can say is, "He got it."

Once I could say you cannot be disgusted with the war, because it is too big for disgust, that disgust is too shallow an emotion for something involving millions of people. But I am disgusted now, and I know what I am saying. Once I used to get quite a thrill out of seeing a city destroyed and left an ash heap from end to end. It gave me a vicarious sense of power. I felt the romantic and histrionic emotion produced by seeing "retribution" done; and an aesthetic emotion produced by beholding ruins; and the childish emotion that comes from destroying man-made things. But it is not that way any more. All I experience is revulsion every time a fresh city is taken on. I am no longer capable of thinking that the systematic destruction of a city is a wonderful or even a difficult thing, though some seem to think it even a heroic thing. Well, how is it done? Dozens upon dozens of gun crews stationed some two or three miles away from the city simply place shell after shell into hundreds of guns and fire away for a few hours—the simplest and most elementary physical and mental work—and then presently the firing stops, the city has been demolished, has become an ash heap, and great praise is bestowed on the army for the capture of a new city.

I am not suggesting that cities shouldn't be captured in this way; actually it saves lives. But it fills me with disgust because it is all so abysmally foolish, so lunatic. It has not the dramatic elements of mere barbarism about it; it is straight scientific debauchery. A destroyed city is a terrible sight. How can anyone record it?—the million smashed things, the absolutely innumerable tiny tragedies, the crushed life-works, the jagged homes, army tanks parked in living rooms—who could tell of these things I don't know; they are too numerous to mention, too awful in their meanings. Perhaps everyone should be required to spend a couple of hours examining a single smashed home, looking at the fragmentation of every little thing, especially the tiniest things from kitchen to attic, if he could find an attic; be required, in fact, to list the ruined contents of just one home; something would be served, a little sobriety perhaps honored.

It is disgusting (that it should be necessary, is what galls me to the bones) that a towering cathedral, built by ages of care and effort, a sweet labor of centuries, should be shot down by laughing artillerymen, mere boys, because somebody with a machine gun is hiding in a belfry tower. When I see such a building, damaged perhaps beyond repair after one of these "operations," I know only disgust. The matter of sides in this war temporarily becomes irrelevant, especially if someone at my elbow says, like a conquering hero: "Well, we sure did a job on the old church, eh?"

A job has been done on Europe, on the world, and the resulting trauma will be generations long in its effects. It is not just the shock of widespread destruction, of whole cities destroyed, nor the shock which the defeated and the homeless must have suffered, that I am thinking of: it is even more the conqueror's trauma, the habit of violence, the explosion of values, the distortion of relations, the ascending significance of the purely material, the sense of power, and the pride of strength. These things will afflict the victors as profoundly and for quite as long a time as the other things will afflict the victims; and of the two I am not sure that a crass superiority complex is the more desirable. Perhaps I underestimate our ability to return to normal again.

On Language

WILLIAM MARCH

WILLIAM MARCH

The Unspeakable Words

There were words in the Brett language considered so corrupting in their effect on others that if anyone wrote them or was heard to speak them aloud, he was fined and thrown into prison. The King of the Bretts was of the opinion that the words were of no importance one way or the other, and besides, everybody in the country knew them anyway; but his advisers disagreed, and at last, to determine who was right, a committee was appointed to examine the people separately.

At length everyone in the kingdom had been examined, and found to know the words quite well, without the slightest damage to themselves. There was then left only one little girl, a five-year-old who lived in the mountains with her deaf and dumb parents. The committee hoped that this little girl, at least, had never heard the corrupting words, and on the morning they visited her, they said solemnly: "Do you know the meaning of *poost, gist, duss, feng?*"

The little girl admitted that she did not, and then, smiling happily, she said, "Oh, you must mean *feek, kusk, dalu,* and *liben!*"

Those who don't know the words must make them up for themselves.

RALPH WALDO EMERSON

The Language of the Street

The language of the street is always strong. What can describe the folly and emptiness of scolding like the word *jawing?* I feel too the force of the double negative, though clean contrary to our grammar rules. And I confess to some pleasure from the stinging

116

rhetoric of a rattling oath in the mouths of truckmen and teamsters. How laconic and brisk it is by the side of a page of the *North American Review*. Cut these words and they would bleed; they are vascular and alive; they walk and run. Moreover they who speak them have this elegancy, that they do not trip in their speech. It is a shower of bullets, whilst Cambridge men and Yale men correct themselves and begin again at every half sentence.

OWEN BARFIELD
Poetic Diction and Legal Fiction

The house of poetry contains many mansions. These mansions are so diverse in their qualities and in their effect on the indweller and some of them are so distant from others that the inhabitants of one mansion have been heard to deny that another is part of the same building at all. For instance, Edgar Allen Poe said that there is no such thing as a long poem, and the difference between a long narrative poem and a short lyric is admittedly rather baffling, seeming almost to be one of kind. What I have to say here touches mainly lyric poetry, and will interest those who love to dwell with recurring delight on special felicities of expression more than those to whom poetry means taking their *Iliad* or their *Faerie Queene* a thousand lines at a time and enjoying the story. It is highly specialized. Think for a moment of poems as of pieces of fabric, large tapestries, or minute embroideries as the case may be. What I have to say does not concern the whole form of even one of the embroideries, but only the texture itself, the nature of the process at any given point, as the fabric comes into being, the movements which the shuttle or the needle must have made. It is still more specialized than this; for in examining the texture of poetry one of the most important elements (a mansion to itself) is rhythm, sound, music; and all this is of necessity excluded. I am fully aware that this involves the corollary that the kind of poetry I am talking about may also be written in prose; but that is a difficulty which is chronic to the subject. I wish, however, to treat of that element in poetry which is best called "meaning" pure and simple. Not the meaning of poetry, nor the meaning of any poem as a whole, but just meaning. If this sounds like an essay in microscopy, or if it be objected that what I am talking about is not poetic diction, but etymology or philosophy or even genetic psychology, I can only reply that whatever it ought to be called, it is, to some people, extraordinarily interesting, and that if, in all good faith, I have given it a wrong address, it is still to me the roomiest, the most commodious, and the most exciting of all the mansions which

I rightly or wrongly include in the plan and elevation of the great house.

The language of poetry has always been in a high degree *figurative*; it is always illustrating or expressing what it wishes to put before us by comparing that with something else. Sometimes the comparison is open and avowed, as when Shelley compares the skylark to a poet, to a high-born maiden, and to a rose embowered in its own green leaves; when Keats tells us that a summer's day is:

> like the passage of an angel's tear
> That falls through the clear ether silently.

or when Burns writes simply: "My love is like a red red rose." And then we call it a "simile." Sometimes it is concealed in the form of a bare statement, as when Shelley says of the west wind, not that it is *like* but that it *is* "the breath of Autumn's being," calls upon it to "make him its lyre" and says of himself that *his* leaves are falling. This is known as "metaphor." Sometimes the element of comparison drops still farther out of sight. Instead of saying that A is like B or that A is B, the poet simply talks about B, without making any overt reference to A at all. You know, however, that he intends A all the time, or, better say that you know he intends *an* A; for you may not have a very clear idea of what A is and even if you have got an idea, somebody else may have a different one. This is generally called "symbolism."

I do not say that these particular methods of expression are an absolute *sine qua non* of poetic diction. They are not. Poetry may also take the form of simple and literal statement. But figurative expression is found everywhere; its roots descend very deep, as we shall see, into the nature, not only of poetry, but of language itself. If you took away from the stream of European poetry every passage of a metaphorical nature, you would reduce it to a very thin trickle indeed, pure though the remainder beverage might be to the taste. Perhaps our English poetry would suffer the heaviest damage of all. Aristotle, when treating of diction in his *Poetics*, provides the right expression by calling the element of metaphor πολὺ μέγιστον—far the most important.

It may be noticed that I am now using the word "metaphor" in a slightly different and wider sense than when I placed it in the midst between simile on the one hand and symbol on the other. I am now using it, and shall use it frequently throughout this article, to cover the whole gamut of figurative language including simile and symbol. I do not think this need confuse us. Strict metaphor occurs about the middle of the gamut and expresses the essential nature of such language more perfectly perhaps than either of the extremes. In something the same way Goethe found that the leaf of a plant expressed its essential nature as plant, while the blossom and the root could be considered as metamorphoses of the leaf. Here I want to try and consider a little more closely what the essential nature of figurative language is and how that nature is most clearly apparent in the figure called metaphor.

But first of all let us return to the "gamut" and take some examples. This time let us move along it in the reverse direction, beginning from symbolism.

> Does the road wind uphill all the way?
>   Yes, to the very end.
> Will the day's journey take the whole long day?
>   From morn to night, my friend.
>
> But is there for the night a resting-place?
>   A roof for when the slow, dark hours begin.
> May not the darkness hide it from my face?
>   You cannot miss that inn.
>
> Shall I meet other wayfarers at night?
>   Those who have gone before.
> Then must I knock or call when just in sight?
>   They will not keep you waiting at that door.
>
> Shall I find comfort, travel-sore and weak?
>   Of labor you shall find the sum.
> Will there be beds for me and all who seek?
>   Yea, beds for all who come.

As I have already suggested, the ordinary way of characterizing this kind of language would be to say that the poet says one thing and means another. Is this true? Is it fair to say that Christina Rossetti says B but she really means A? I do not think this is a question which can be answered with a simple "yes" or "no." In fact the difficult and elusive relation between A and B is the heart of my matter. For the time being let me hazard, as a rather hedging sort of answer, that the truer it is to say "yes," the worse is the poem, the truer it is to say "no," the better is the poem. We feel that B, which is actually said, ought to be necessary, even inevitable in some way. It ought to be in some sense the best, if not the only way, of expressing A satisfactorily. The mind should dwell on it as well as on A and thus the two should be somehow inevitably fused together into one simple meaning. But if A is too obvious and could be equally or almost as well expressed by other and more direct means, then the mind jumps straight to A, remains focused on it, and loses interest in B, which shrinks to a kind of dry and hollow husk. I think this is a fault of Christina Rossetti's poem. We know just what A is. A = "The good life is an effort" plus "All men are mortal." Consequently it detaches itself from B, like a soul leaving a body, and the road and the inn and the beds are not a real road and inn and beds, they look faintly heraldic—or as if portrayed in lacquer. They are not even poetically real. We never ᵧᵉt a fair chance to accord to their existence that willing suspension of disbelief which we are told constitutes "poetic faith." Let us try another:

> "Is there anybody there?" said the Traveler,
>   Knocking on the moonlit door;
> And his horse in the silence champed the grasses
>   Of the forest's ferny floor:
> And a bird flew up out of the turret,
>   Above the Traveler's head:
> And he smote upon the door again a second time:
>   "Is there anybody there?" he said.
> But no one descended to the Traveler;
>   No head from the leaf-fringed sill
> Leaned over and looked into his grey eyes,
>   Where he stood perplexed and still.
> But only a host of phantom listeners
>   That dwelt in the lone house then
> Stood listening in the quiet of the moonlight
>   To that voice from the world of men:
> Stood thronging the faint moonbeams on the dark stair,
>   That goes down to the empty hall,
> Hearkening in an air stirred and shaken
>   By the lonely Traveler's call.
> And he felt in his heart their strangeness,
>   Their stillness answering his cry,
> While his horse moved, cropping the dark turf,
>   'Neath the starred and leafy sky;
> For he suddenly smote on the door, even
>   Louder, and lifted his head:—
> "Tell them I came, and no one answered,
>   That I kept my word," he said.
> Never the least stir made the listeners,
>   Though every word he spake
> Fell echoing through the shadowiness of the still house
>   From the one man left awake:
> Ay, they heard his foot upon the stirrup
>   And the sound of iron on stone,
> And how the silence surged softly backward,
>   When the plunging hoofs were gone.[1]

This poem seems to me to possess as symbolism most of the virtues which I miss in Christina Rossetti's. First it obviously *is* a symbol. There *is* an A and a good solid one, though we do not know what it is, because we cannot put it into a separate container of words. But that is just the point. A has not got (perhaps I should say, it has not *yet* got) a separate existence in our apprehension; so it makes itself felt by modifying and enriching the meaning of B—it hides itself in B, hides itself in language which still *could* on the face of it be heard and interpreted as though no A came into the question at all.

I must here remark that merely making A obscure is not in itself

1. Walter de la Mare, "The Listeners."

a recipe for writing good symbolical poetry. William Blake at his worst, and, I fancy, many modern poets who write or intend to write symbolically, go astray here. They are so anxious to avoid the error of intending too obvious an A, so anxious to avoid a mere old-fashioned simile, that we end by being mystified or disgusted by the impossibility of getting any sort of feeling at all of what they are talking about, or why. Why are they talking about B at all, we ask ourselves. If they are doing it simply for the sake of B, it is pure drivel. On the other hand, if they intend an A, what evidence is there of it? We do not mind A being intangible, because it is still only half born from the poet's unconscious, but you cannot make poetry by cunningly removing all the clues which, if left, would discover the staleness of your meaning. In other words, if you set out to say one thing and mean another, you must really mean another, and that other must be worth meaning.

It will be observed that when we started from the simile and moved towards the symbol, the criterion or yardstick by which we measured our progress was the element of *comparison*—paramount in the simile and very nearly vanished out of sight in the symbol. When, on the other hand, we move backwards, starting from the symbol, we find ourselves with another yardstick, viz. the fact of saying one thing and meaning another. The poet says B but he means A. He hides A in B. B is the normal everyday meaning which the words so to speak "ought" to have on the face of them, and A is what the poet *really* has to say to us, and which he can only say through or alongside of, or by modifying, these normal everyday meanings. A is his own new, original, or poetic meaning. If I were writing this article in Greek or German, my public would no doubt be severly restricted, but there would be this advantage to me—that I could run the six words "say-one-thing-and-mean-another" together and use the resulting conglomerate as a noun throughout the rest of it. I cannot do this, but I will make bold to borrow another German word instead. The word *Tarnung* was, I believe, extensively used under the heel of the Nazi tyranny in Germany for the precautionary practice of hiding one meaning in another, the allusion being to the *Tarnhelm* of the Nibelungs.[2] I shall give it an English form and call it "Tarning." When I say "Tarning," therefore, the reader is asked to substitute mentally the concept of saying one thing and meaning another, in the sense in which I have just been trying to expound it. We have already seen that the more A lives as a modification or enrichment of B, the better is the tarning.

Now let us proceed to the next step in our backward progress from symbol to simile. We come to the metaphor. And here we find both the best and the most numerous examples of tarning.

---

2. The *Tarnhelm* was a helmet which made its wearer invisible.

Almost any poem, almost any passage of really vivid prose which you pick up is sure to contain them in abundance. I will choose an example (the source of which he does not disclose) given by Dr. Hugh Blair, the eighteenth-century writer on style.

> Those persons who gain the hearts of most people, who are chosen as the companions of their softer hours, and their reliefs from anxiety and care, are seldom persons of shining qualities or strong virtues: it is rather the soft green of the soul on which we rest our eyes, that are fatigued with beholding more glaring objects.

Consider how the ordinary literal meaning of the word "green" blends with the ineffable psychic quality which it is the writer's object to convey! How much weaker it would be, had he written: "It is rather persons whose souls we find restful, as the eye finds green fields restful, etc." Put it that way and nearly all the tarning, and with it half the poetry, is lost. The passage reminds me of this from Andrew Marvell's *Garden*:

> The Mind, that Ocean where each kind
> Does straight its own resemblance find;
> Yet it creates, transcending these,
> Far other Worlds, and other Seas;
> Annihilating all that's made
> To a green Thought in a green Shade.

What a lot of tarning can be done with the word "green"!

We see that any striking and original use of even a single word tends to be metaphorical and shows us the process of tarning at work. On the whole, I think it is true to say that the fewer the words containing the metaphor, the more the expression is in the strict sense a "trope" rather than a metaphor—the more tarning we shall feel. For the long and elaborate metaphor is already almost a simile—a simile with the word "like" missed out. We must, however, remember that the tarning may not have actually occurred in the particular place where we find it. People copy one another and the metaphor may be a cliché, or, if not a cliché part of our common heritage of speech. Thus when Tennyson writes:

> When the happy Yes
> Falters from her lips,
> Pass and blush the news
> Over glowing ships

we feel that the peculiarly effective use of the word "blush" throughout this lyric is a tarning of his own. It actually goes on in us as we read. When, on the other hand, Arnold writes in the *Scholar Gypsy*:

> O Life unlike to ours!
> Who fluctuate idly without term or scope

or:

> Vague half-believers of our casual creeds,
> Who never deeply felt, nor clearly willed,
> Whose insight never has borne fruit in deeds

though none of this writing can be described as cliché, yet we feel
that the metaphorical element in "fluctuate" and in "borne fruit"
is the product of a tarning that happened before Arnold was born.
So, too, in the passage I first quoted the *"shining* qualities" and the
"softer hours" are metaphors of the kind we are all using every day,
almost without thinking of them as metaphors. We all speak of
clear heads, of brilliant wit, of *seeing* somebody's meaning, of so
and so being the *pick of the bunch*, and so on; and most of us
must use at least, say, a hundred of these dead or half-dead metaphors every day of our lives. In fact, in dealing with metaphor, we
soon find outselves talking, not of poetry, but of language itself.
Everywhere in language we seem to find that the process of tarning,
or something very like it, either is or has been at work.

We seem to owe all these tropes and metaphors embedded in
language to the fact that somebody at some time had the wit to say
one thing and mean another, and that somebody else had the wit
to tumble to the new meaning, to detect the bouquet of a new
wine emanating from the old bottle. We owe them all to tarning, a
process which we find prolifically at work wherever there is
poetry—from the symbol, where it shouts at us and is all too easily
mishandled, to the simile, where we already hear the first faint stir-
rings of its presence, inasmuch as the B image even here is modified, enriched, or colored by the A image with which it is this time
overtly compared.

> Then fly our greetings, fly our speech and smiles!
> —As some grave Tyrian trader, from the sea,
>   Descried at sunrise an emerging prow
> Lifting the cool-hair'd creepers stealthily,
>   The fringes of a southward-facing brow
>   Among the Aegean isles;
> And saw the merry Grecian coaster come,
>   Freighted with amber grapes, and Chian wine,
>   Green bursting figs, and tunnies steep'd in brine;
> And knew the intruders on his ancient home,
>
> The young light-hearted masters of the waves.

The grave Tyrian trader and the merry Grecian coaster are not
the same figures that we should meet in a history book. They have
their own life, they take in the imagination a special color from the
things with which they are compared—that is, the *Scholar Gypsy*
on the one hand and our too modern selves on the other. They
are pregnant with the whole of the poem that has gone before.

I said at the beginning that I might be accused of indulging in a kind of aesthetic microscopy. The drawback of the microscope is this, that even if the grain of sand which we see through it does indeed contain a world, mere magnification is not enough to enable us to see that world. Unfortunately the processes which are said to give to the infinitesimal a cosmic character are not merely minute; they are also very rapid. This is certainly true of the process of tarning as it takes place in the mind of the poet and his reader. It is both rapid and delicate and, as the reader may have felt already, it is difficult to take it out and examine it without rushing in where angels fear to tread. But there is another modern invention which may be brought to the aid of the microscope in order to meet this drawback; and that is the slow-motion film. Can we find in any sphere of human life something analogous to a slow-motion picture of the tarning process? I think we can. I have said that tarning can be detected not only in accredited poetry or literature but also in the history of language as a whole. Is there any other human institution in which tarning also happens, and in which it happens on a broader scale and at a more leisurely pace? I think there is. I think we shall find such an illustration as we want in the law, notably in the development of law by means of fictions.

We are accustomed to find something crabbed and something comic in legal fictions. When we read in an old pleading an averment that the plaintiff resides in the Island of Minorca, "to wit in the parish of St. Mary le Bow in the Ward of Cheap"—or, in a Note in the *Annual Practice* for 1945, that every man-of-war is deemed to be situated permanently in the parish of Stepney—it sounds funny. But it must be admitted that it is not any funnier *per se* than Shelley's telling us that his leaves are falling or Campion informing us as to his mistress that "there is a garden in her face." It is funny when we take it literally, not particularly funny when we understand what is meant and why it is expressed in that particular way.

There is one kind of metaphor which occurs both in law and in poetry and which is on the whole commoner and less odd-sounding in modern law than it is in modern poetry. This is personification of abstractions:

> Let not Ambition mock their useful toil,
>   Their homely joys, and destiny obscure;
> Nor Grandeur hear with a disdainful smile
>   The short and simple annals of the poor.[3]

We find this particular usage almost vanished from English poetry by the beginning of the twentieth century. The personification of abstractions and attributes which we find in the more

---

3. From Thomas Gray's "Elegy Written in a Country Church-Yard."

high-flown sort of eighteenth-century poetry or in the occasional
allegorical papers which Johnson inserted in the *Rambler* sound stiff
and unnatural to us, and a modern poet would hardly bring himself
to try and introduce the device at all. On the other hand, the personification of limited companies by which they are enabled to sue
and be sued at law, to commit trespasses, and generally to be
spoken of as carrying on all sorts of activities which can only *really*
be carried on by sentient beings, is as common as dirt and no one
ever dreams of laughing at it. But these examples will hardly do for
our slow-motion picture. On the contrary, in them the gap between
the B meaning and the A meaning is as wide and the *prima facie*
absurdity of the B or surface-meaning is hardly less than in, let us
say, Ossian's description of the Hero: "In peace, thou art the Gale
of Spring, in war, the Mountain Storm."

The important thing is to see how and why the legal fiction
comes into being and what is its positive function in the life of
human beings. If you have suffered a wrong at the hands of
another human being, the practical question for you, the point at
which law really touches your life as a member of society, is, can
you do anything about it? Can you bring the transgressor to book
and obtain restitution? In other words, can you bring an action
against him, obtain judgment, and get that judgment executed?
Now the answer to that question must always depend to some
extent, and in the earlier stages of a society governed by law it
depends to a very large extent indeed on the answer to another
question. It is not enough simply to show that the transgressor has,
in common parlance, broken the law. What you or your advisers
have to make up your mind about is something rather different and
often much more complicated. You have to ask yourselves, Is there
a form of procedure under which I can move against him? If so, is
it sufficiently cheap and expeditious for me to be able to adopt it
with some hope of success? Where, as in the case of English
Common Law down to the middle of the nineteenth century, these
forms of procedure, or forms of action as they are more often
called, are severely restricted in number, these questions are very
serious ones indeed.

Now suppose you had a good claim to the ownership of a piece
of land, perhaps with a pleasant house on it, which was in the possession of somebody else who also, but wrongfully, claimed to be
the owner. Your proper normal form of action, say, five hundred
years ago, was by Writ of Right, a form of action which was very
much of the first type and hedged about accordingly with all sorts
of ceremonies, difficulties, and delays.

At trahere atque moras tantis licet addere rebus![4]

4. "But it is lawful to draw out and add delays with such things!"

One of the drawbacks of this type of action was that it was subject to things called *Essoins*. Essoins seem to have corresponded roughly to what we should call "adjournments"; they no doubt grew up procedurally with a view to preventing an unscrupulous plaintiff from taking unfair advantage of the defendant's ill health, absence, or other accidental disability. But they must have been corn in Egypt[5] for a usurping defendant. I am tempted to let Glanville,[6] in his own sedate language and at his own pace, give the reader some idea of their nature and complexity:

If the Tenant, being summoned, appear not on the first day, but Essoin himself, such Essoin shall, if reasonable, be received; and he may, in this manner, essoin himself three times successively; and since the causes on account of which a person may justly essoin himself are various, let us consider the different kinds of Essoins.

Of Essoins, some arise on account of ill health, others from other sources.

(I will here interpose that, among the Essoins arising from other sources were the *de ultra mare* and the *de esse in peregrinatione*[7] and that, if a person cast the Essoin *de esse in peregrinatione*, "it must be distinguished whether he went to Jerusalem or to another place. If to the former place, then a year and a day at least is generally allowed him." And with that I will let Glanville proceed again in his own order:)

Of those Essoins which arise from ill health, one kind is that *ex infirmitate veniendi*, another *ex infirmitate de reseantisa*.[8]

If the Tenant, being summoned, should on the first day cast the Essoin *de infirmitate veniendi*, it is in the election of his Adversary, being present, either to require from the Essoiner a lawful proof of the truth of the Essoin in question on that very day, or that he should find pledges or bind himself solemnly that at the day appointed he will have his Warrantor of the Essoin...and he may thus Essoin himself three times successively. If on the third day, he neither appear nor essoin himself, then let it be ordered that he be forthcoming in person on another day; or that he send a fit Attorney in his place, to gain or lose for him.... It may be asked, what will be the consequence if the Tenant appear at the fourth day, after having cast three Essoins, and warrant all the Essoins? In that case, he shall prove the truth of each Essoin by his own oath and that of another; and, on the same day, he shall answer to the suit....

If anyone desire to cast the Essoin *de infirmitate de reseantisa*, he may thrice do it. Yet should the Essoiner, on the third day preceding that appointed, at a proper place and before a proper person, present his Essoin. If, on the third Summons the Tenant appear not, the Court should direct that it may be seen whether his indisposition amount to a languor, or not. For this purpose let the following Writ issue, direct to the Sheriff of the County...:

---

5. See Genesis, xlii. 1–2.

6. Beame's *Translation of Glanville*, London, 1812 [Barfield's note].

7. Essoins arising from being "beyond the sea or on a pilgrimage."

8. Essoins arising from "being too sick to appear" or from "a long-standing infirmity or confinement."

"The King to the Sheriff, Health. I command you that, without delay
you sent 4 lawful men of your County to see if the infirmity of which
B. hath essoined himself in my Court, against R., be a languor or not.
And, if they perceive that it is a languor, then, that they should put to
him a day of one year and one day, from that day of the view, to
appear before me or my justices. . . ."

Nor was it forgotten that Essoiners themselves may be subject to
infirmities and languors:

The principal Essoiner is also at liberty, if so disposed, to essoin himself by another Essoiner. In this case the second Essoiner must state to
the Court that the Tenant, having a just cause of Essoin, had been
detained, so that he could not appear at the day appointed, neither to
lose nor gain, and that therefore he had appointed a certain other person
to essoin him; and that the Essoiner himself had met with such an
impediment, which had prevented his appearance on that day: and this
he is prepared to prove according to the practice of the Court. . . .

Having at last succeeded in getting your opponent out of bed
and fixing the day for the trial, you still could not be certain that
he would not appear in Court followed (subject, no doubt, to
Essoins) by a professional boxer or swordsman, whom you would
have to tackle in lieu of calling evidence. And so on. And all this
may be about a claim so clear that you could get it disposed of in
five minutes if you could only bring it to the stage of being tried at
all!

It would have been a very different matter, so perhaps your
Counsel would advise you, if only the issue were about *personal*
property instead of real property. We could go to a different Court
with a different form of action. No essoins. No wager of law. No
trial by battle. No trial by ordeal. Everything up to date and
efficient. What *is* personal property, you might ask. Well, your
horse for one thing and your hawk and your clothes and your money—oh! yes, and oddly enough if you were a leaseholder instead of
a freeholder and had only a term of years in this precious piece of
land, *that* would be personal property too. But can't I get *my* case
heard by these people? Don't they understand anything about fee
simple?[9] Oh! yes, they understand it all right; in fact they often
have to decide the point. For instance, if a leaseholder in possession
is ousted by a trespasser—by Jove! I've just thought of something!
And then if your Counsel had a touch of creative genius, he might
perhaps evolve the following device. It was evolved at all events, by
Tudor times or thereabouts and continued in use down to the
middle of the nineteenth century.

Remember the situation: You are the rightful owner of a piece

9. An estate in land without limitation to any class of heirs or restrictions on transfer of ownership.

of land of which X, who is in possession, wrongfully claims to be the owner. The device was this: you proceeded to inform the Court by your pleadings that you, as owner of the land, had recently leased it to a person whose name was John Doe, and John Doe had been ousted from his possession violently, *vi et armis*,[1] by X, the Defendant. *You* were not bringing the action, you pretended; John Doe was. But as X might aver in his defense that the blameless Doe had no title, Doe has joined you, his landlord, in the proceedings to prove that you did have a good title at the time when you leased the land to him. By this means you got your case before the Court that had jurisdiction to deal with the action known as Ejectment, and were able to take advantage of the simpler and more effective procedure. Sometimes the fiction was a little more elaborate. Instead of alleging that X had ejected John Doe, you said that another gentleman called Richard Roe, or possibly William Stiles, had done so. Richard Roe having subsequently allowed X to take possession now claimed no interest in the proceedings, but he had given X notice that they were pending, so as to give X a chance to defend his title. In this case the first thing X heard of it all was a letter, signed "your loving friend, Richard Roe," telling him what had happened. Needless to say, John Doe and Richard Roe had no existence.

Many thousands of actions of this pattern and using these names must have been brought between the fifteenth and the nineteenth centuries and before long the whole procedure was no doubt so much a matter of course that it was little more than a kind of mathematical formula. There must, however, have been some earlier occasions on which it was a good deal more, and it is upon any one of these—perhaps the first of all—that I want the reader to bend his mind. Picture to yourself the Court, with Counsel on his feet opening the case. The story of John Doe and Richard Roe is being unfolded. At one point the Judge suddenly looks up and looks very hard at Counsel, who either winks very slightly or returns a stolid uncomprehending stare according to his temperament and the intimacy of his acquaintance with the Judge out of hours. But Counsel knows all the same what has happened. The Bench has tumbled to it. The Judge has guessed that there is no John Doe, no Richard Roe, no lease, no entry, no ouster. At the same moment, however, the Judge has seen the point of the whole fiction, the great advantage in the speedy administration of justice (for the real issue—the validity of X's title and yours—will be heard fairly and in full) and in the extended jurisdiction of his own Court. He decides to accord to the pleadings that willing suspension of disbelief which hundreds of years later made Mr. Bumble

1. "By force of arms."

say that the law was a "hass."[2] The case proceeds. Place this picture before your mind's eye and there I think you will have a slow-motion picture of "tarning."

Has new law been made? It is much the same as asking whether new language has been made when a metaphor disappears into a "meaning." At all events, we begin to understand more fully what Maitland meant, when he wrote of English law that "substantive law has at first the look of being gradually secreted in the interstices of procedure." This is particularly true of an unwritten system like the English Common Law, where the law itself lay hidden in the unconscious, until it was expressed in a judgment, and where rights themselves depended on the existence of remedies. Consider that very important fiction, which is very much alive and flourishing all round us today—the fiction on which the law of trusteeship is based. Anyone who is a trustee will know how absurdly remote from reality is the B interpretation of his position, according to which he is the "owner" of the trust property. Yet this fiction, which permeates the whole of our jurisprudence, which most certainly is law, and not merely procedure, was introduced in the first place by devices strictly procedural, devices and circumstances which had their origin in that same contrast between the genealogical and the personal conceptions of Society which gave us John Doe and Richard Roe.

Moreover, this fictitious ownership, which we call trusteeship, has been strong enough to have other fictions erected on it. By the Common Law the personal property of a married woman became her husband's as soon as she married. But by a particularly ingenious piece of tarning the equity judges expressed in the form of law, and in doing so no doubt partly created, a more modern view of the rights of married women. They followed the Common Law doctrine that the husband owned everything but, as to property which someone had given to the wife with the intention that she should have it for her own separate use, the Courts of Equity began in the eighteenth century to say that the husband did indeed own this, but he owned it as *trustee* for his wife; and they would prevent him from dealing with it in any other way.

In the same way a metaphor may be strong enough to support a metaphor, as when Shelley bids the west wind "Make me thy lyre even as the forest is." If Shelley is not a lyre, neither is the forest; yet he illustrates the one fiction with the other. Nor is there anything grotesque or strained in this magnificent line. It is only when we begin to ponder and analyze it that we see how daring it is.

---

2. In Charles Dickens' *Oliver Twist* (Chap. 51), Mr. Bumble, after being told that the law "supposes that your wife acts under direction," replies: "If the law supposes that, * * * the law is a ass * * * the law's a bachelor * * * "

The long analogy which I have been drawing may be expressed more briefly in the formula:—metaphor: language: meaning:: legal fiction: law: social life. It has no particular significance if poetry is to be regarded *only* as either a pleasurable way of diverting our leisure hours or a convenient vehicle for the propagation of doctrine. For it must be conceded that there is all the difference in the world between the propagation of a doctrine and the creation of a meaning. The doctrine is already formulated and, if we choose to express it by tarning, that is simply a matter of technique or political strategy. The creation of meaning is a very different matter. I hope I may have succeeded in showing in the earlier part of this article that metaphor is something more than a piece of the technique of one of the fine arts. It is πολὺ μέγιστον[3] not merely in the diction of poetry but in the nature and growth of language itself. So far we have only considered in this connection those ubiquitous figures of speech which are, or used to be, called "tropes," as when we speak of our lives *fluctuating*, of our insight *bearing fruit* in deeds, of *seeing the point*, and so on. But if we proceed to study language with a more definitely historical bias, and look into the etymologies and derivations of words, then the vast majority even of those meanings which we normally regard as "literal" are seen to have originated either in metaphors or in something like them. Such words as *spirit, sad, humor, perceive, attend, express, understand*, and so on immediately spring to the mind as examples. Indeed the difficulty here would rather be to find words that are *not* examples. There is no doubt that they were once metaphorical. The question which a good many people have asked themselves, a little uneasily, is, Are they *still* metaphors? And, if not, when—and still more *how*—precisely, did they cease to be so?

What is essential to the nature and growth of language is clearly essential to the nature and growth of our thought, or rather of our consciousness as a whole. In what way then is metaphor or tarning essential to that nature and that growth? Here we begin to tread on metaphysical ground and here I think the analogy of legal fictions can really help us by placing our feet on one or two firmer tufts in the quaking bog. It can help us to realize in firmer outlines certain concepts which, like all those relating to the nature of thought itself, are tenuous, elusive, and difficult of expression.

Students of history will have observed that rebellions and agitations arising out of dissatisfaction with the law tend, at any rate in the earlier stages of society, to demand, not so much a reform of the law as its *publication*. People complain that they do not know what the law is. They want to know what it is, because otherwise they cannot be sure that it will be the same tomorrow as it is today. In fact it is the very essence of a law that it should apply to

---

3. "By far the most important" (see p. 118 above).

every case. It follows that the forms of action must be limited in number, and they must not change from day to day. If there is a different law for every case that arises, then what is being administered is simply not law at all but the arbitrary (though not necessarily unjust) decisions of those who govern us. But that is exactly what the word law *means*—something which is *not* such a series of arbitrary decisions or events, something which will be *the same* for the next case as it was for the last. This is where the difficulty arises; for it is the nature of life itself (certainly of human life) never to repeat itself exactly. Phenomena exactly repeated are not life, they are mechanism. Life varies, law is of its nature unvarying. Yet at the same time it is the function of law to serve, to express, and indeed partly to *make* the social life of the community. That is the paradox, the diurnal solution of which constitutes the process called society. One solution is legislation, the other is fiction. Legislation is drastic, *a priori*, and necessary. Fiction is flexible, empirical, and also necessary. "Without the Fiction of Adoption," says Maine in his *Ancient Law*, "it is difficult to understand how Society would ever have escaped from its swaddling clothes."

In the paradoxical relation of law to social life I think we have a useful picture of the paradoxical relation of language to consciousness. Formal logic is not much studied nowadays, but that does not alter the fact that logic is essential to the very existence of language and the forms of proposition and syllogism underlie all expression. Now logic presupposes first and foremost that the same word means the same thing in one sentence as it does in another. Humpty Dumpty may speak of making his words "mean" what he chooses, and if somebody made a noise never heard before or since he might possibly manage to convey some sort of vague sympathetic impression of the state of his feelings. Yet repetition is inherent in the very meaning of the word "meaning." To say a word "means" something implies that it means that same something more than once.

Here then is the paradox again. The logical use of language presupposes the meanings of the words it employs and presupposes them constant. I think it will be found to be a corollary of this, that the logical use of language can never add any meaning to it. The conclusion of a syllogism is implicit already in the premises, that is, in the *meanings* of the *words* employed; and all the syllogism can do is to make that meaning clearer to us and remove any misconception or confusion. But life is not constant. Every man, certainly every original man, has something new to say, something new to mean. Yet if he wants to express that meaning (and it may be that it is only when he tries to express it, that he knows what he means) he must use language—a vehicle which presupposes that he must either mean what was meant before or talk nonsense!

If therefore he would say anything really new, if that which was hitherto unconscious is to become conscious, he must resort to tarning. He must talk what is nonsense on the face of it, but in such a way that the recipient may have the new meaning suggested to him. This is the true importance of metaphor. I imagine this is why Aristotle, in calling metaphor "the most important," gives us a reason that "it alone does not mean borrowing from someone else." In terms of mixed law and logic we might perhaps say that the metaphorical proposition contains a judgment, but a judgment pronounced with a wink at the Court. Bacon put it more clearly in the *Advancement of Learning* when he said:

> Those whose conceits are seated in popular opinions need only but to prove or dispute; but those whose conceits are beyond popular opinions have a double labor; the one to make themselves conceived, and the other to prove and demonstrate. So that it is of necessity with them to have recourse to similitudes and translations to express themselves.

If we consider Bacon's position in the history of thought, it will not surprise us that the problem should have presented itself to him so clearly. Himself a lawyer, was he not attempting to do for science the very thing which Maitland tells us those old legal fictions were contrived for, that, is "to get modern results out of medieval premises"?

At all events there is a sentence in the *Novum Organum* which provides one of the most striking illustrations of tarning that it would be possible to imagine. It is a double illustration: first, there was an attempt at deliberate and fully conscious meaning-making, which failed: Bacon tried to inject new meaning into a word by *saying* precisely what he wanted it to mean. But we have seen that what is said precisely cannot convey new meaning. But, since his meaning *was* really new, there had at some point in the process to be a piece of actual tarning. There was—and it succeeded. He did in fact inject new meaning into another word—not by saying, but by just meaning it!

> Licet enim in natura nihil vere existat praeter corpora individua eden-tia actus puros individuos ex lege; in doctrinis tamen, illa ipsa lex, ejus-que inquisitio et inventio atque explicatio, pro fundamento est tam ad sciendum quam ad operandum. Eam autem legem ejusque paragraphos *formarum* nomine intelligimus; praesertim cum hoc vocabulum inval-uerit, et familiariter occurrat.[4]

The "forms" of which Bacon here speaks were none other than the Platonic ideas, in which Bacon, of course, did not believe.

---

4. Although it is true that in nature nothing exists beyond separate bodies producing separate motions according to law; still for the *study* of nature that very law and its investigation, discovery, and exposition are the essential thing, for the purpose both of science and of practice. Now it is that law and its clauses which we understand by the term "forms"—principally because this word is a familiar one and has become generally accepted. *Novum Organum*, ii. 2 [Barfield's note].

What he did believe in was that system of abstract causes or uniformity which we have long since been accustomed to express by the phrase "the laws of nature," but for which there was then no name, because the meaning was a new one. He therefore tried deliberately by way of a *simile* to put this new meaning into the old word *"forma"*; but he failed, inasmuch as the new meaning never came into general use. Yet at the same time, more unconsciously, and by way of *metaphor*, he was putting the new meaning into the word *"lex"* itself—that curious meaning which it now bears in the expression "the laws of nature." This is one of those pregnant metaphors which pass into the language, so that much of our subsequent thinking is based on them. To realize that after all they *are* metaphors, and to ask what that entails, opens up avenues of inquiry which are beyond the province of this article. Certainly, they may be misleading, as well as illuminating. Long after Bacon's time, two great men—a lawyer who was concerned with the nature of law and a poet who was concerned with the nature of Nature—felt bound to draw attention to this very metaphor.

"When an atheist," wrote Austin,[5] "speaks of laws governing the irrational world, the metaphorical application is suggested by an analogy still more slender and remote.... He means that the uniformity of succession and co-existence resembles the uniformity of conduct produced by an imperative rule. If, to draw the analogy closer, he ascribes these laws to an author, he personifies a verbal abstraction and makes it play the legislator. He attributes the uniformity of succession and co-existence to laws set by nature: meaning by nature, the world itself; or perhaps that very uniformity which he imputes to nature's commands."

The introduction of the atheist into this passage does not, I think, weaken its force as an illustration, for whatever the strength of Bacon's religious faith, it is quite plain that the "laws" of which he speaks in the *Novum Organum* have very little to do with the "commands" of any being other than nature itself.

"Long indeed," says Coleridge in The Friend, "will man strive to satisfy the inward querist with the phrase, laws of nature. But though the individual may rest content with the seeming metaphor, the race cannot. If a law of nature be a mere generalization, it is included ... as an act of the mind. But if it be other and more, and yet manifestable only in and to an intelligent spirit, it must in act and substance be itself spiritual; for things utterly heterogeneous can have no intercommunion."

Perhaps we may supplement the last sentence by saying that an *apparent* intercommunion between things utterly heterogeneous is the true mark of metaphor and may be significant of spiritual substance. If this is so, and if the aptness of a metaphor to mislead varies inversely with the extent to which it continues to be felt and

5. *Jurisprudence* (1869), i. 213 [Barfield's note].

understood *as* a metaphor and is not taken in a confused way semi-literally, then the contemplation by the mind of legal fictions may really be a rather useful exercise. For these are devices of expression, of which the practical expediency can easily be understood, and whose metaphorical nature is not so easily forgotten as they pass into general use.

There is not much that is more important for human beings than their relations with each other, and it is these which laws are designed to express. The making and application of law are thus fundamental human activities, but what is more important for my purpose is that they bear the same relation to naked thinking as traveling does to map reading or practice to theory. It is not by accident that such key words as *judgment* and *cause* have two distinct meanings; the practical task of fixing personal responsibility must surely have been the soil from which, as the centuries passed, the abstract notion of cause and effect was laboriously raised. Accordingly it would be strange indeed if the study of jurisprudence were not well adapted to throw light on the mind and its workings.

That study was formerly regarded as an essential element in a liberal education. It was a distinguished Italian jurist, Giovanni Battista Vico, who at the turn of the seventeenth and eighteenth centuries became interested in the figurative element in language and evolved therefrom a theory of the evolution of human consciousness from an instinctive "poetic" wisdom (*sapienza poetica*) to the modern mode of analytical thought.

It is perhaps a pity that this respectful attitude to legal studies has long since been abandoned; a pity both on general grounds and because the vast change in man's idea of himself wrought by the new notions of evolution and development, and by the comparatively recent birth of historical imagination, have opened up rich new fields of speculation both in language and in law. A better and more widely diffused knowledge of the latter could hardly fail to be beneficial in far-reaching ways at a time when the whole theory of human society is in the melting pot. For instance, a deeper, more sympathetic understanding of the long, slow movement of the human mind from the feudal, or genealogical, way of regarding human relationships towards what I have called the "personal" way would do no harm.

But I have been mainly concerned here with the subject of fictions. Properly understood, are they not a telling illustration of the fact that knowledge—the fullest possible awareness—of the nature of law is the true way of escape from its shackles? ἐγὼ γὰρ διὰ νόμου νόμῳ ἀπέθανον, "I, by the law, died unto the law," wrote St. Paul; and the *nature* of law, as law, is the same, whether it be moral, or logical, or municipal. If it be important for men to get a deep feeling for this process of liberation in general, it is equally important, for special reasons, that they should better comprehend the particular problem of the part played by metaphor in the operation and development of language. Here too the way to achieve liberation from the "confusion" of thought on which metaphor is based is not by attack or rebellion. The intrinsic nature of language makes all such attitudes puerile. It is not those who, like the optimistic Mr. Stuart Chase,[6] set out to cut away and expose all metaphorical usage who escape the curse of Babel. No. The best way to talk clearly and precisely and to talk sense is to understand as fully as possible the relation between predication and suggestion, between "saying" and "meaning." For then you will at least know what you are *trying* to do. It is not the freemen of a city who are likeliest to lose their way, and themselves, in its labyrinth of old and mazy streets; it is the simple-minded foreign nihilist making, with his honest-to-god intentions and suitcase, straight for the center, like a sensible man.

6. *The Tyranny of Words*, London, 1938 [Barfield's note].

QUESTIONS

1. Why does Barfield have to invent a new term? How does "tarning" differ from metaphor? from symbol? Discuss whether Barfield's "quaking bog" (p. 130) is an example of tarning. Analyze E. B. White's definition of democracy (p. 1000) to determine whether or not it has examples of tarning.

2. To what extent does one "say one thing and mean another" in ordinary conversation? in an expository essay? in a short story? in an argument? in a poem? Do the purpose and occasion of each of these affect the possibility or desirability of tarning?

3. Test Barfield's assertions about the prevalence of metaphor in legal writing by an analysis of Frankfurter, "Haley vs. Ohio" (pp. 1041–1045) or Smith, "Salmon vs. Bagley Laundry Company" (pp. 1045–1049).

4. On p. 134 Barfield makes a distinction between the "genealogical way" and the "personal way" of looking at human beings. Which way does Lincoln view man in "Liberty" (pp. 999–1000)? Does Machiavelli view man the same way in "The Prince" (pp. 954–960)? What implications does each view have for systems of government?

C. S. LEWIS
Bluspels and Flalansferes

Philologists often tell us that our language is full of dead metaphors. In this sentence, the word "dead" and the word "metaphors" may turn out to be ambiguous; but the fact, or group of facts, referred to, is one about which there is no great disagreement. We all know in a rough and ready way, and all admit, these things which are being called "dead metaphors," and for the moment I do not propose to debate the propriety of the name. But while their existence is not disputed, their nature, and their relation to thought, gives rise to a great deal of controversy. For the benefit of any who happen to have avoided this controversy hitherto, I had better make plain what it is, by a concrete example. Bréal in his *Semantics* often spoke in metaphorical, that is consciously, rhetorically, metaphorical language itself. Messrs. Ogden and Richards in *The Meaning of Meaning* took Bréal to task on the ground that "it is impossible thus to handle a scientific subject in metaphorical terms." Barfield in his *Poetic Diction* retorted that Ogden and Richards were, as a matter of fact, just as metaphorical as Bréal. They had forgotten, he complained, that all language has a figurative origin and that the "scientific" terms on which they piqued themselves—words like *organism, stimulus, reference*—were not miraculously exempt. On the contrary, he maintained, "these authors who professed to eschew figurative expressions were really confining themselves to one very old kind of figure; they were rigid under the spell of those verbal ghosts of the physical sciences which today make up practically the whole meaning-system of so many European minds."[1] Whether Ogden and Richards will see fit, or have seen fit, to reply to this, I do not know; but the lines on which any reply would run are already traditional. In fact the whole debate may be represented by a very simple dialogue.

A. You are being metaphorical.

B. You are just as metaphorical as I am, but you don't know it.

A. No, I'm not. Of course I know all about *attending* once having meant *stretching*, and the rest of it. But that is not what it means now. It may have been a metaphor to Adam—but I am not using it metaphorically. What I *mean* is a pure concept with no metaphor about it at all. The fact that it was a metaphor is no more relevant than the fact that my pen is made of wood. You are simply confusing derivation with meaning.

1. A. O. Barfield, *Poetic Diction*, 1928, pp. 139, 140. New ed. (London: Faber & Faber, Ltd., 1952) [Lewis' note].

There is clearly a great deal to be said for both sides. On the one hand it seems odd to suppose that what we *mean* is conditioned by a dead metaphor of which we may be quite ignorant. On the other hand, we see from day to day, that when a man uses a current and admitted metaphor without knowing it, he usually gets led into nonsense; and when, we are tempted to ask, does a metaphor become so old that we can ignore it with impunity? It seems harsh to rule that a man must know the whole semantic history of every word he uses—a history usually undiscoverable—or else talk without thinking. And yet, on the other hand, an obstinate suspicion creeps in that we cannot entirely jump off our own shadows, and that we deceive ourselves if we suppose that a new and purely conceptual notion of *attention* has replaced and superseded the old metaphor of stretching. Here, then, is the problem which I want to consider. How far, if at all, is thinking limited by these dead metaphors? Is Anatole France in any sense right when he reduces "The soul possesses God" to "the breath sits on the bright sky"? Or is the other party right when it urges "Derivations are one thing. Meanings are another"? Or is the truth somewhere between them?

The first and easiest case to study is that in which we ourselves invent a new metaphor. This may happen in one of two ways. It may be that when we are trying to express clearly to ourselves or to others a conception which we have never perfectly understood, a new metaphor simply starts forth, under the pressure of composition or argument. When this happens, the result is often as surprising and illuminating to us as to our audience; and I am inclined to think that this is what happens with the great, new metaphors of the poets. And when it does happen, it is plain that our new understanding is bound up with the new metaphor. In fact, the situation is for our purpose indistinguishable from that which arises when we hear a new metaphor from others; and for that reason, it need not be separately discussed. One of the ways, then, in which we invent a new metaphor, is by *finding* it, as unexpectedly as we might find it in the pages of a book; and whatever is true of the new metaphors that we find in books will also be true of those which we reach by a kind of lucky chance, or inspiration. But, of course, there is another way in which we invent new metaphors. When we are trying to explain, to someone younger or less instructed than ourselves, a matter which is already perfectly clear in our own minds, we may deliberately, and even painfully, pitch about for the metaphor that is likely to help him. Now when this happens, it is quite plain that our thought, our power of meaning, is not much helped or hindered by the metaphor that we use. On the contrary, we are often acutely aware of the discrepancy between our meaning and our image. We know that our metaphor is in some respects misleading; and probably, if we have acquired the tutorial shuffle, we warn our audience that it is "not to be pressed." It is apparently possible, in this case at least, to use metaphor and yet to keep our thinking independent of it. But we must observe that it is possible, only because we have other methods of expressing the same idea. We have already our own way of expressing the thing: we could say it, or we suppose that we could say it, literally instead. This clear conception we owe to other sources—to our previous studies. We can adopt the new metaphor as a temporary tool, which we dominate and by which we are not dominated ourselves, only because we have other tools in our box.

Let us now take the opposite situation—that in which it is we ourselves who are being instructed. I am no mathematician; and someone is trying to explain to me the theory that space is finite. Stated thus, the new doctrine is, to me, meaningless. But suppose he proceeds as follows.

"You," he may say, "can intuit only three dimensions; you therefore cannot conceive how space should be limited. But I think I can show you how that which must appear infinite in three dimensions, might nevertheless be finite in four. Look at it this way. Imagine a race of people who knew only two dimensions—like the Flatlanders. And suppose they were living on a globe. They would have no conception, of course, that the globe was curved—for it is curved round in that third dimension of which they have no inkling. They will therefore imagine that they are living on a plane; but they will soon find out that it is a plane which nowhere comes to an end; there are no edges to it. Nor would they be able even to imagine an edge. For an edge would mean that, after a certain point, there would be nothing to walk on; nothing below their feet. But that *below* and *above* dimension is just what their minds have not got; they have only backwards and forwards, and left and right. They would thus be forced to assert that their globe, which they could not see as a globe, was infinite. You can see perfectly well that it is finite. And now, can you not conceive that as these Flatlanders are to you, so you might be to a creature that intuited four dimensions? Can you not conceive how that which seems necessarily infinite to your three-dimensional consciousness might nonetheless be really finite?" The result of such a metaphor on my mind would be—in fact, has been—that something which before was sheerly meaningless acquires at least a faint hint of meaning. And if the particular example does not appeal to everyone, yet everyone has had experiences of the same sort. For all of us there are things which we cannot fully understand at all, but of which we can get a faint inkling by means of metaphor. And in such cases the relation between the thought and the metaphor is precisely the opposite of the relation which arises when it is we ourselves who understand and then invent the metaphors to help others. We are here entirely at the mercy of the metaphor. If our instructor has chosen it badly, we shall be thinking nonsense. If we have not got the imagery clearly before us, we shall be thinking nonsense. If we have it before us without knowing that it is metaphor—if we forget that our Flatlanders on their globe are a copy of the thing and mistake them for the thing itself—then again we shall be thinking nonsense. What truth we can attain in such a situation depends rigidly on three conditions. First, that the imagery should be originally well chosen; secondly, that we should apprehend the exact imagery; and thirdly that we should know that the metaphor is a metaphor. (That metaphors, misread as statements of fact, are the source of monstrous errors, need hardly be pointed out.)

I have now attempted to show two different kinds of metaphorical situation as they are at their birth. They are the two extremes, and furnish the limits within which our inquiry must work. On the one hand, there is the metaphor which we invent to teach by; on the other, the metaphor from which we learn. They might be called the Master's metaphor, and the Pupil's metaphor. The first is freely chosen; it is one among many possible modes of expression; it does not at all hinder, and only very slightly helps, the thought of its maker. The second is not chosen at all; it is the unique expression of a meaning that we cannot have on any other terms; it dominates completely the thought of the recipient; his truth cannot rise above the truth of the original metaphor. And between the Master's metaphor and the Pupil's there comes, of course, an endless number of types, dotted about in every kind of intermediate position. Indeed, these Pupil-Teachers' metaphors are the ordinary stuff of our conversation. To divide them into a series of classes and sub-classes and to attempt to discuss these separately would be very laborious, and, I trust, unnecessary. If we can find a true doctrine about the two extremes, we shall not be at a loss to give an account of what falls between them. To find the truth about any given metaphorical situation will merely be to plot its position. Insofar as it inclines to the "magistral" extreme, so far our thought will be independent of it; insofar as it has a "pupillary" element, so far it will be the unique expression, and therefore the iron limit of our thinking. To fill in this framework would be, as Aristotle used to say, "anybody's business."

Our problem, it will be remembered, was the problem of "dead" or "forgotten" metaphors. We have now gained some light on the relation between thought and metaphor as it is at the outset, when the metaphor is first made; and we have seen that this relation varies greatly according to what I have called the "metaphorical situation." There is, in fact, one relation in the case of the Master's metaphor, and an almost opposite relation in that of the Pupil's metaphor. The next step must clearly be to see what becomes of

these two relations as the metaphors in question progress to the
state of death or fossilization.

The question of the Master's Metaphor need not detain us long.
I may attempt to explain the Kantian philosophy to a pupil by the
following metaphor. "Kant answered the question 'How do I know
that whatever comes round the corner will be blue?' by the supposition 'I am wearing blue spectacles.'" In time I may come to use
"the blue spectacles" as a kind of shorthand for the whole Kantian
machinery of the categories and forms of perception. And let us
suppose, for the sake of analogy with the real history of language,
that I continue to use this expression long after I have forgotten
the metaphor which originally gave rise to it. And perhaps by this
time the form of the word will have changed. Instead of the "blue
spectacles" I may now talk of the *bloospel* or even the *bluspel*. If I
live long enough to reach my dotage I may even enter on a philo-
logical period in which I attempt to find the derivation of this mysterious word. I may suppose that the second element is derived
from the word *spell* and look back with interest on the supposed
period when Kant appeared to me to be magical; or else, arguing
that the whole word is clearly formed on the analogy of *gospel*,
may indulge in unhistorical reminiscenses of the days when the *Critique* seemed to me irrefragably true. But how far, if at all, will my
thinking about Kant be affected by all this linguistic process? In
practice, no doubt, there will be some subtle influence; the mere
continued use of the word *bluspel* may have led me to attribute to
it a unity and substantiality which I should have hesitated to attribute to "the whole Kantian machinery of the categories and forms
of perception." But that is a result rather of the noun-making than
of the death of the metaphor. It is an interesting fact, but hardly
relevant to our present inquiry. For the rest, the mere forgetting of
the metaphor does not seem to alter my thinking about Kant, just
as the original metaphor did not limit my thinking about Kant;
provided always—and this is of the last importance—that it was, to
begin with, a genuine Master's metaphor. I had my conception of
Kant's philosophy before I ever thought of the blue spectacles. If I
have continued philosophical studies I have it still. The "blue spectacles" phrase was from the first a temporary dress assumed by my
thought for a special purpose, and ready to be laid aside at my
pleasure; it did not penetrate the thinking itself, and its subsequent
history is irrelevant. To any one who attempts to refute my later
views on Kant by telling me that I don't know the real meaning of
bluspel, I may confidently retort "Derivations aren't meanings." To
be sure, if there was any *pupillary* element in its original use, if I
received, as well as gave, new understanding when I used it, then
the whole situation will be different. And it is fair to admit that in
practice very few metaphors can be purely magistral; only that

which to some degree enlightens ourselves is likely to enlighten others. It is hardly possible that when I first used the metaphor of the blue spectacles I did not gain some new awareness of the Kantian philosophy; and, so far, it was not purely magistral. But I am deliberately idealizing for the sake of clarity. Purely magistral metaphor may never occur. What is important for us is to grasp that *just insofar* as any metaphor began by being magistral, so far I can continue to use it long after I have forgotten its metaphorical nature, and my thinking will be neither helped nor hindered by the fact that it was originally a metaphor, nor yet by my forgetfulness of that fact. It is a mere accident. Here, derivations are irrelevant to meanings.

Let us now turn to the opposite situation, that of the Pupil's Metaphor. And let us continue to use our old example of the unmathematical man who has had the finitude of space suggested to him (we can hardly say "explained") by the metaphor of the Flatlanders on their sphere. The question here is rather more complicated. In the case of the Master's metaphor, by hypothesis, the master knew, and would continue to know, what he meant, independently of the metaphor. In the present instance, however, the fossilization of the metaphor may take place in two different ways. The pupil may himself become a mathematician, or he may remain as ignorant of mathematics as he was before; and in either case, he may continue to use the metaphor of the Flatlanders while forgetting its real content and its metaphorical nature.

I will take the second possibility first. From the imagery of the Flatlanders' sphere I have got my first inkling of the new meaning. My thought is entirely conditioned by this imagery. I do not apprehend the thing at all, except by seeing "it could be something like this." Let us suppose that in my anxiety to docket this new experience. I label the inkling or vague notion, "the Flatlanders' sphere." When I next hear the fourth dimension spoken of, I shall say, "Ah yes—the Flatlanders' sphere and all that." In a few years (to continue our artificial parallel) I may be talking glibly of the *Flalansfere* and may even have forgotten the whole of the imagery which this word once represented. And I am still, according to the hypothesis, profoundly ignorant of mathematics. My situation will then surely be most ridiculous. The meaning of *Flalansfere* I never knew except through the imagery. I could get beyond the imagery, to that whereof the imagery was a copy, only by learning mathematics; but this I have neglected to do. Yet I have lost the imagery. Nothing remains, then, but the conclusion that the word *Flalansfere* is now really meaningless. My thinking, which could never get beyond the imagery, at once its boundary and its support, has now lost that support. I mean strictly nothing when I speak of the *Flalansfere*. I am only talking, not thinking, when I use the word. But this fact will be long concealed from me, because *Flalansfere*, being a noun, can be endlessly fitted into various contexts, so as to conform to syntactical usage and to give an appearance of meaning. It will even conform to the logical rules; and I can make many judgments about the *Flalansfere*; such as *it is what it is*, and has *attributes* (for otherwise of course it wouldn't be a thing, and if it wasn't a thing, how could I be talking about it?), and is a *substance* (for it can be the subject of a sentence). And what *affective* overtones the word may have taken on by that time, it is dangerous to predict. It had an air of mystery from the first: before the end I shall probably be building temples to it, and exhorting my countrymen to fight and die for the *Flalansfere*. But the *Flalansfere*, when once we have forgotten the metaphor, is only a noise.

But how if I proceed, after once having grasped the metaphor of the Flatlanders, to become a mathematician? In this case, too, I may well continue to use the metaphor, and may corrupt it in form till it becomes a single noun, the *Flalansfere*. But I shall have advanced, by other means, from the original symbolism; and I shall be able to study the thing symbolized without reference to the metaphor that first introduced me to it. It will then be no harm though I should forget that *Flalansfere* had ever been metaphorical. As the metaphor, even if it survived, would no longer limit my thoughts, so its fossilization cannot confuse them.

The results which emerge may now be summarized as follows. Our thought is independent of the metaphors we employ, insofar as these metaphors are optional: that is, insofar as we are able to have the same idea without them. For that is the real characteristic both of the magistral metaphors and of those which become optional, as the Flatlanders would become, if the pupil learned mathematics. On the other hand, where the metaphor is our only method of reaching a given idea at all, there our thinking is limited by the metaphor so long as we retain the metaphor; and when the metaphor becomes fossilized, our "thinking" is not thinking at all, but mere sound or mere incipient movements in the larynx. We are now in a position to reply to the statement that "Derivations are not meanings," and to the claim that "we know what we mean by words without knowing the fossilized metaphors they contain." We can see that such a statement, as it stands, is neither wholly true nor wholly false. The truth will vary from word to word, and from speaker to speaker. No rule of thumb is possible, we must take every case on its merits. A word can bear a meaning in the mouth of a speaker who has forgotten its hidden metaphor, and a meaning independent of that metaphor, but only on certain conditions. Either the metaphor must have been optional from the beginning, and have remained optional through all the generations of its use, so that the conception has always used and still uses the imagery as a mere tool; or else, at some period subsequent to its creation, we must have gone on to acquire, independently of the metaphor, such new knowledge of the object indicated by it as enables us now, at last, to dispense with it. To put the same thing in another way, meaning is independent of derivation, only if the metaphor was originally "magistral"; or if, in the case of an originally pupillary metaphor, some quite new kind of apprehension has arisen to replace the metaphorical apprehension which has been lost. The two conditions may be best illustrated by a concrete example. Let us take the word for *soul* as it exists in the Romance language. How far is a man entitled to say that what he means by the word *âme* or *anima* is quite independent of the image of *breathing*, and that he means just the same (and just as much) whether he happens to know that "derivation" or not? We can only answer that it depends on a variety of things. I will enumerate all the formal possibilities for the sake of clearness: one of them, of course, is too grotesque to appear for any other purpose.

1. The metaphor may originally have been magistral. Primitive men, we are to suppose, were clearly aware, on the one hand, of an entity called *soul*; and, on the other, of a process or object called *breath*. And they used the second figuratively to suggest the first—presumably when revealing their wisdom to primitive women and primitive children. And we may suppose, further, that this magistral relation to the metaphor has never been lost: that all generations, from the probably arboreal to the man saying "Blast your soul" in a pub this evening, have kept clearly before them these two separate entities, and used the one metaphorically to denote the other, while at the same time being well able to conceive the soul unmetaphorically, and using the metaphor merely as a color or trope which adorned but did not influence their thought. Now if all this were true, it would unquestionably follow that when a man says *anima* his meaning is not affected by the old image of breath; and also, it does not matter in the least whether he knows that the word once suggested that image or not. But of course all this is not true.

2. The metaphor may originally have been pupillary. So far from being a voluntary ornament or pedagogic device, the ideas of *breath* or *something like breath* may have been the only possible inkling that our parents could gain of the soul. But if this was so, how does the modern user of the word stand? Clearly, if he has ceased to be aware of the metaphorical element in *anima*, without replacing the metaphorical apprehension by some new knowledge of the soul, borrowed from other sources, then he will mean nothing by it; we must not, on that account, suppose that he will cease to use it, or even to use it (as we say) intelligibly—i.e. to use it in sentences constructed according to the laws of grammar, and to

insert these sentences into those conversational and literary contexts where usage demands their insertion. If, on the other hand, he has some independent knowledge of the entity which our ancestors indicated by their metaphor of breath, then indeed he may mean something.

I take it that it is this last situation in which we commonly suppose ourselves to be. It doesn't matter, we would claim, what the majestic root GNA really stood for: we have learned a great deal about *knowing* since those days, and it is these more recent acquisitions that we use in our thinking. The first name for a thing may easily be determined by some inconsiderable accident. As we learn more, we mean more; the radical meaning of the old syllables does not bind us; what we have learned since has set us free. Assuredly, the accident which led the Romans to call all Hellenes *Graeci* did not continue to limit their power of apprehending Greece. And as long as we are dealing with sensible objects this view is hardly to be disputed. The difficulty begins with objects of thought. It may be stated as follows.

Our claim to independence of the metaphor is, as we have seen, a claim to know the object otherwise than through that metaphor. If we can throw the Flatlanders overboard and still think the fourth dimension, then, and not otherwise, we can forget what *Flalansfere* once meant and still think coherently. That was what happened, you will remember, to the man who went on and learned mathematics. He came to apprehend that of which the Flatlanders' sphere was only the image, and consequently was free to think beyond the metaphor and to forget the metaphor altogether. In our previous account of him, however, we carefully omitted to draw attention to one very remarkable fact: namely, that when he deserted metaphor for mathematics, he did not really pass from symbol to symbolized, but only from one set of symbols to another. The equations and what-nots are as unreal, as metaphorical, if you like, as the Flatlanders' sphere. The mathematical problem I need not pursue further; we see at once that it casts a disquieting light on our linguistic problem. We have hitherto been speaking as if we had two methods of thought open to us: the metaphorical, and the literal. We talked as if the creator of a magistral metaphor had it always in his power to think the same concept *literally* if he chose. We talked as if the present-day user of the word *anima* could prove his right to neglect that word's buried metaphor by turning round and giving us an account of the soul which was not metaphorical at all. That he has power to dispense with the particular metaphor of *breath*, is of course agreed. But we have not yet inquired what he can substitute for it. If we turn to those who are most anxious to tell us about the soul—I mean the psychologists—we shall find that the word *anima* had simply been replaced by complexes, repressions, censors, engrams, and the like. In other words the *breath* has been exchanged for *tyings-up, shovings-back, Roman magistrates,* and *scratchings.* If we inquire what has replaced the metaphorical *bright sky* of primitive theology, we shall only get a *perfect substance,* that is, a *completely made lying-under,* or—which is very much better, but equally metaphorical—a universal Father, or perhaps (in English) a *loaf-carver,* in Latin a *householder,* in Romance *a person older than.* The point need not be labored. It is abundantly clear that the freedom from a given metaphor which we admittedly enjoy in some cases is often only a freedom to choose between that metaphor and others.

Certain reassurances may, indeed, be held out. In the first place, our distinction between the different kinds of metaphorical situation can stand; though it is hardly so important as we had hoped. To have a choice of metaphors (as we have in some cases) is to know more than we know when we are the slaves of a unique metaphor. And, in the second place, all description or identification, all direction of our own thought or another's, is not so metaphorical as definition. If, when challenged on the word *anima,* we proceed to define, we shall only reshuffle the buried metaphors; but if we simply say (or think) "what I am," or "what is going on in here," we shall have at least something before us which we do not know by metaphor. We shall at least be no worse off than the arboreal psychologists. At the same time, this method will not really carry us far. "What's going on here" is really the content of *hæc anima:* for *anima* we want *"The sort of thing* that is going on here," and once we are committed to *sorts* and *kinds* we are adrift among metaphors.

We have already said that when a man claims to think independently of the buried metaphor in one of his words, his claim may sometimes be allowed. But it was allowed only insofar as he could really supply the place of that buried metaphor with new and independent apprehension of his own. We now see that this new apprehension will usually turn out to be itself metaphorical; or else, what is very much worse, instead of new apprehension we shall have simply words—each word enshrining one more ignored metaphor. For if he does not know the history of *anima,* how should he know the history of the equally metaphorical words in which he defines it, if challenged? And if he does not know their history and therefore their metaphors, and if he cannot define *them* without yet further metaphors, what can his discourse be but an endless ringing of the changes on such *bluspels* and *Flalansferes* as seem to mean, indeed, but do not mean? In reality, the man has played us a very elementary trick. He claimed that he could think without metaphor, and in ignorance of the metaphors fossilized in his words. He made good the claim by pointing to the knowledge of his object which he possessed independently of the metaphor; and the proof of this knowledge was the definition or description which he could produce. We did not at first observe that where we were promised a freedom from metaphor we were given only a power of changing the metaphors in rapid succession. The things he speaks of he has never apprehended *literally*. Yet only such genuinely literal apprehension could enable him to forget the metaphors which he was actually using and yet to have a meaning. Either literalness, or else metaphor understood: one or other of these we must have; the third alternative is nonsense. But literalness we cannot have. The man who does not consciously use metaphors talks without meaning. We might even formulate a rule: the meaning in any given composition is in inverse ratio to the author's belief in his own literalness.

If a man has seen ships and the sea, he may abandon the metaphor of a *sea-stallion* and call a boat a boat. But suppose a man who has never seen the sea, or ships, yet who knows of them just as much as he can glean, say from the following list of *Kenningar*[2]—sea-stallions, winged logs, wave riders, ocean trains. If he keeps all these together in his mind, and knows them for the metaphors they are, he will be able to think of ships, very imperfectly indeed, and under strict limits, but not wholly in vain. But if instead of this he pins his faith on the particular kenning, *ocean trains*, because that kenning, with its comfortable air of machinery, seems to him somehow more safely prosaic, less flighty and dangerous than its fellows, and if, contracting that to the form *oshtrans*, he proceeds to forget that it was a metaphor, then, while he talks grammatically, he has ceased to think of anything. It will not avail him to stamp his feet and swear that he is literal; to say "An *oshtran* is an *oshtran*, and there's an end. I mean what I mean. What I mean is what I say."

The remedy lies, indeed, in the opposite direction. When we pass beyond pointing to individual sensible objects, when we begin to think of causes, relations, of mental states or acts, we become incurably metaphorical. We apprehend none of these things except through metaphor: we know of the ships only what the *Kenningar* will tell us. Our only choice is to use the metaphors and thus to think something, though less than we could wish; or else to be driven by unrecognized metaphors and to think nothing at all. I myself would prefer to embrace the former choice, as far as my ignorance and laziness allow me.

To speak more plainly, he who would increase the meaning and decrease the meaningless verbiage in his own speech and writing, must do two things. He must become conscious of the fossilized

2. The Norse plural for "kenning," a metaphorical compound word (e.g., "whale road" for "sea") used especially in Old English and Old Norse poetry.

metaphors in his words; and he must freely use new metaphors, which he creates for himself. The first depends upon knowledge, and therefore on leisure; the second on a certain degree of imaginative ability. The second is perhaps the more important of the two: we are never less the slaves of metaphor than when we are making metaphor, or hearing it new made. When we are thinking hard of the Flatlanders, and at the same time fully aware that they *are* a metaphor, we are in a situation almost infinitely superior to that of the man who talks of the *Flalansfere* and thinks that he is being literal and straightforward.

If our argument has been sound, it leads us to certain rather remarkable conclusions. In the first place it would seem that we must be content with a very modest quantity of thinking as the core of all our talking. I do not wish to exaggerate our poverty. Not all our words are equally metaphorical, not all our metaphors are equally forgotten. And even where the old metaphor is lost there is often a hope that we may still restore meaning by pointing to some sensible object, some sensation, or some concrete memory. But no man can or will confine his cognitive efforts to this narrow field. At the very humblest we must speak of things in the plural; we must point not only to isolated sensations, but to groups and classes of sensations; and the universal latent in every group and every plural inflection cannot be thought without metaphor. Thus far beyond the security of literal meaning all of us, we may be sure, are going to be driven by our daily needs; indeed, not to go thus far would be to abandon reason itself. In practice we all really intend to go much farther. Why should we not? We have in our hands the key of metaphor, and it would be pusillanimous to abandon its significant use, because we have come to realize that its meaningless use is necessarily prevalent. We must indeed learn to use it more cautiously; and one of the chief benefits to be derived from our inquiry is the new standard of criticism which we must henceforward apply both to our own apparent thought and to that of others. We shall find, too, that real meaning, judged by this standard, does not come always where we have learned to expect. *Flalansferes* and *bluspels* will clearly be most prevalent in certain types of writers. The percentage of mere syntax masquerading as meaning may vary from something like 100 per cent in political writers, journalists, psychologists, and economists, to something like forty per cent in the writers of children's stories. Some scientists will fare better than others: the historian, the geographer, and sometimes the biologist will speak significantly more often than their colleagues; the mathematician, who seldom forgets that his symbols are symbolic, may often rise for short stretches to ninety per cent of meaning and ten of verbiage. The philosophers will differ as widely from one another as any of the other groups differ among themselves: for a good metaphysical library contains at once some of the most verbal, and some of the most significant literature in the world. Those who have prided themselves on being literal, and who have endeavored to speak plainly, with no mystical tomfoolery, about the highest abstractions, will be found to be among the least significant of writers: I doubt if we shall find more than a beggarly five per cent of meaning in the pages of some celebrated "tough minded" thinkers, and how the account of Kant or Spinoza stands, none know but heaven. But open your Plato, and you will find yourself among the great creators of metaphor, and therefore among the masters of meaning. If we turn to Theology—or rather to the literature of religion—the result will be more surprising still; for unless our whole argument is wrong, we shall have to admit that a man who says *heaven* and thinks of the visible sky is pretty sure to mean more than a man who tells us that heaven is a state of mind. It may indeed be otherwise; the second man may be a mystic who is remembering and pointing to an actual and concrete experience of his own. But it is long, long odds. Bunyan and Dante stand where they did; the scale of Bishop Butler, and of better men than he, flies up and kicks the beam.[3]

It will have escaped no one that in such a scale of writers the poets will take the highest place; and among the poets those who have at once the tenderest care for old words and the surest instinct for the creation of new metaphors. But it must not be supposed that I am in any sense putting forward the imagination as the organ of truth. We are not talking of truth, but of meaning: meaning which is the antecedent condition both of truth and falsehood, whose antithesis is not error but nonsense. I am a rationalist. For me, reason is the natural organ of truth; but imagination is the organ of meaning. Imagination, producing new metaphors of revivifying old, is not the cause of truth, but its condition. It is, I confess, undeniable that such a view indirectly implies a kind of truth or rightness in the imagination itself. I said at the outset that the truth we won by metaphor could not be greater than the truth of the metaphor itself; and we have seen since that all our truth, or all but a few fragments, is won by metaphor. And thence, I confess, it does follow that if our thinking is ever true, then the metaphors by which we think must have been good metaphors. It does follow that if those original equations, between good and light, or evil and dark, between breath and soul and all the others, were from the beginning arbitrary and fanciful—if there is not, in fact, a kind of psycho-physical parallelism (or more) in the universe—then all our

3. Joseph Butler (1692–1752), Bish
-op of Durham, was noted for abstract religious speculation. Lewis believes Bunyan's and Dante's physical
descriptions of heaven would tip the
scales in their favor.

thinking is nonsensical. But we cannot, without contradiction, believe it to be nonsensical. And so, admittedly, the view I have taken has metaphysical implications. But so has every view.

QUESTIONS

1. What are the main points of Lewis' argument? How persuasively has he presented his case? Is the main line of his argument weakened by his admission (p. 143) that words which were originally metaphors may have come to reflect "new knowledge of the object"? Do his conclusions, especially those in the last two paragraphs of the essay, follow from what has preceded?
2. Lewis summarizes some of his conclusions about the relationship of metaphor to meaning on pages 143 ff. Test these conclusions by tracing the derivation of the following words in a dictionary. Are there any of these words in which some of the different senses or meanings represent one kind of development, some of them another?

nothing	biology	symbol	imagination
communism	freedom	evolution	personality
prose	religion	ritual	grammar
fossil	science	virtue	metaphor
definition	democracy	literal	literature
meaning	evil		

3. Analyze the following brief poem. Is its metaphor a Master's or Pupil's? Would Barfield consider this a good example of "tarning"? Is tarning more like the magistral or the pupillary metaphor?

> We dance round in a ring and suppose,
> But the Secret sits in the middle and knows.
> —Robert Frost, "The Secret Sits"

BENJAMIN LEE WHORF
Science and Linguistics

Every normal person in the world, past infancy in years, can and does talk. By virtue of that fact, every person—civilized or uncivilized—carries through life certain naive but deeply rooted ideas about talking and its relation to thinking. Because of their firm connection with speech habits that have become unconscious and automatic, these notions tend to be rather intolerant of opposition. They are by no means entirely personal and haphazard; their basis is definitely systematic, so that we are justified in calling them a system of natural logic—a term that seems to me preferable to the term common sense, often used for the same thing.

According to natural logic, the fact that every person has talked fluently since infancy makes every man his own authority on the process by which he formulates and communicates. He has merely to consult a common substratum of logic or reason which he and everyone else are supposed to possess. Natural logic says that talking is merely an incidental process concerned strictly with communication, not with formulation of ideas. Talking, or the use of language, is supposed only to "express" what is essentially already formulated nonlinguistically. Formulation is an independent process, called thought or thinking, and is supposed to be largely indifferent to the nature of particular languages. Languages have grammars, which are assumed to be merely norms of conventional and social correctness, but the use of language is supposed to be guided not so much by them as by correct, rational, or intelligent *thinking*.

Thought, in this view, does not depend on grammar but on laws of logic or reason which are supposed to be the same for all observers of the universe—to represent a rationale in the universe that can be "found" independently by all intelligent observers, whether they speak Chinese or Choctaw. In our own culture, the formulations of mathematics and of formal logic have acquired the reputation of dealing with this order of things, i.e., with the realm and laws of pure thought. Natural logic holds that different languages are essentially parallel methods for expressing this one-and-the-same rationale of thought and, hence, differ really in but minor ways which may seem important only because they are seen at close range. It holds that mathematics, symbolic logic, philosophy, and so on, are systems contrasted with language which deal directly with this realm of thought, not that they are themselves specialized extensions of language. The attitude of natural logic is well shown in an old quip about a German grammarian who devoted his whole life to the study of the dative case. From the point of view of natural logic, the dative case and grammar in general are an extremely minor issue. A different attitude is said to have been held by the ancient Arabians: Two princes, so the story goes, quarreled over the honor of putting on the shoes of the most learned grammarian of the realm; whereupon their father, the caliph, is said to have remarked that it was the glory of his kingdom that great grammarians were honored even above kings.

The familiar saying that the exception proves the rule contains a good deal of wisdom, though from the standpoint of formal logic it became an absurdity as soon as "prove" no longer meant "put on trial." The old saw began to be profound psychology from the time it ceased to have standing in logic. What it might well suggest to us today is that if a rule has absolutely no exceptions, it is not recognized as a rule or as anything else; it is then part of the background of experience of which we tend to remain unconscious. Never having experienced anything in contrast to it, we cannot isolate it and formulate it as a rule until we so enlarge our experience and expand our base of reference that we encounter an interruption of its regularity. The situation is somewhat analogous to that of not missing the water till the well runs dry, or not realizing that we need air till we are choking.

For instance, if a race of people had the physiological defect of being able to see only the color blue, they would hardly be able to formulate the rule that they saw only blue. The term blue would convey no meaning to them, their language would lack color terms, and their words denoting their various sensations of blue would answer to, and translate, our words light, dark, white, black, and so on, not our word blue. In order to formulate the rule or norm of seeing only blue, they would need exceptional moments in which they saw other colors. The phenomenon of gravitation forms a rule without exceptions; needless to say, the untutored person is utterly unaware of any law of gravitation, for it would never enter his head to conceive of a universe in which bodies behaved otherwise than they do at the earth's surface. Like the color blue with our hypothetical race, the law of gravitation is a part of the untutored individual's background, not something he isolates from that background. The law could not be formulated until bodies that always fell were seen in terms of a wider astronomical world in which bodies moved in orbits or went this way and that.

Similarly, whenever we turn our heads, the image of the scene passes across our retinas exactly as it would if the scene turned around us. But this effect is background, and we do not recognize it; we do not see a room turn around us but are conscious only of having turned our heads in a stationary room. If we observe critically while turning the head or eyes quickly, we shall see, no motion it is true, yet a blurring of the scene between two clear views. Normally we are quite unconscious of this continual blurring but seem to be looking about in an unblurred world. Whenever we walk past a tree or house, its image on the retina changes just as if the tree or house were turning on an axis; yet we do not see trees or houses turn as we travel about at ordinary speeds. Sometimes ill-fitting glasses will reveal queer movements in the scene as we look about, but normally we do not see the relative motion of the environment when we move; our psychic makeup is somehow adjusted to disregard whole realms of phenomena that are so all-pervasive as to be irrelevant to our lives and needs.

Natural logic contains two fallacies: First, it does not see that the phenomena of a language are to its own speakers largely of a background character and so are outside the critical consciousness and control of the speaker who is expounding natural logic. Hence, when anyone, as a natural logician, is talking about reason, logic, and the laws of correct thinking, he is apt to be simply marching in step with purely grammatical facts that have somewhat of a background character in his own language or family of languages but are by no means universal in all languages and in no sense a common substratum of reason. Second, natural logic confuses agreement about subject matter, attained through use of language, with knowledge of the linguistic process by which agreement is attained, i.e., with the province of the despised (and to its notion superfluous) grammarian. Two fluent speakers, of English let us say, quickly reach a point of assent about the subject matter of their speech; they agree about what their language refers to. One of them, A, can give directions that will be carried out by the other, B, to A's complete satisfaction. Because they thus understand each other so perfectly, A and B, as natural logicians, suppose they must of course know how it is all done. They think, e.g., that it is simply a matter of choosing words to express thoughts. If you ask A to explain how he got B's agreement so readily, he will simply repeat to you, with more or less elaboration, what he said to B. He has no notion of the process involved. The amazingly complex system of linguistic patterns and classifications which A and B must have in common before they can adjust to each other at all, is all background to A and B.

These background phenomena are the province of the grammarian—or of the linguist, to give him his more modern name as a scientist. The word linguist in common, and especially newspaper, parlance means something entirely different, namely, a person who can quickly attain agreement about subject matter with different people speaking a number of different languages. Such a person is better termed a polyglot or a multilingual. Scientific linguists have long understood that ability to speak a language fluently does not necessarily confer a linguistic knowledge of it, i.e., understanding of its background phenomena and its systematic processes and structure, any more than ability to play a good game of billiards confers or requires any knowledge of the laws of mechanics that operate upon the billiard table.

The situation here is not unlike that in any other field of science. All real scientists have their eyes primarily on background phenomena that cut very little ice, as such, in our daily lives; and yet their studies have a way of bringing out a close relation between these unsuspected realms of fact and such decidedly foreground activities as transporting goods, preparing food, treating the sick, or growing potatoes, which in time may become very much modified simply because of pure scientific investigation in no way concerned with these brute matters themselves. Linguistics is in quite a similar case; the background phenomena with which it deals are involved in all our foreground activities of talking and of reaching agreement, in all reasoning and arguing of cases, in all law, arbitration, conciliation, contracts, treaties, public opinion, weighing of scientific theories, formulation of scientific results. Whenever agreement or assent is arrived at in human affairs, and whether or not mathematics or other specialized symbolisms are made part of the procedure, *this agreement is reached by linguistic processes, or else it is not reached.*

As we have seen, an overt knowledge of the linguistic processes by which agreement is attained is not necessary to reaching some sort of agreement, but it is certainly no bar thereto; the more complicated and difficult the matter, the more such knowledge is a distinct aid, till the point may be reached—I suspect the modern world has about arrived at it—when the knowledge becomes not only an aid but a necessity. The situation may be likened to that of navigation. Every boat that sails is in the lap of planetary forces; yet a boy can pilot his small craft around a harbor without benefit of geography, astronomy, mathematics, or international politics. To the captain of an ocean liner, however, some knowledge of all these subjects is essential.

When linguists became able to examine critically and scientifically a large number of languages of widely different patterns, their base of reference was expanded; they experienced an interruption of phenomena hitherto held universal, and a whole new order of significances came into their ken. It was found that the background linguistic system (in other words, the grammar) of each language is not merely a reproducing instrument for voicing ideas but rather is itself the shaper of ideas, the program and guide for the individual's mental activity, for his analysis of impressions, for his synthesis of his mental stock in trade. Formulation of ideas is not an independent process, strictly rational in the old sense, but is part of a particular grammar and differs, from slightly to greatly, as between different grammars. We dissect nature along lines laid down by our native languages. The categories and types that we isolate from the world of phenomena we do not find there because they stare every observer in the face; on the contrary, the world is presented in a kaleidoscopic flux of impressions which has to be organized by our minds—and this means largely by the linguistic systems in our minds. We cut nature up, organize it into concepts, and ascribe significances as we do, largely because we are parties to an agreement to organize it in this way—an agreement that holds throughout our speech community and is codified in the patterns of our language. The agreement is, of course, an implicit and unstated one, *but its terms are absolutely obligatory*; we cannot talk at all except by subscribing to the organization and classification of data which the agreement decrees.

This fact is very significant for modern science, for it means that no individual is free to describe nature with absolute impartiality but is constrained to certain modes of interpretation even while he thinks himself most free. The person most nearly free in such respects would be a linguist familiar with very many widely different linguistic systems. As yet no linguist even is in any such position. We are thus introduced to a new principle of relativity, which holds that all observers are not led by the same physical evidence to the same picture of the universe, unless their linguistic backgrounds are similar, or can in some way be calibrated.

This rather startling conclusion is not so apparent if we compare only our modern European languages, with perhaps Latin and Greek thrown in for good measure. Among these tongues there is a unanimity of major pattern which at first seems to bear out natural logic. But this unanimity exists only because these tongues are all Indo-European dialects cut in the same basic plan, being historically transmitted from what was long ago one speech community; because the modern dialects have long shared in building up a common culture; and because much of this culture, on the more intellectual side, is derived from the linguistic backgrounds of Latin and Greek. Thus this group of languages satsifies the special case of the clause beginning "unless" in the statement of the linguistic relativity principle at the end of the preceding paragraph. From this condition follows the unanimity of description of the world in the community of modern scientists. But it must be emphasized that "all modern Indo-European-speaking observers" is not the same thing as "all observers." That modern Chinese or Turkish scientists describe the world in the same terms as Western scientists means, of course, only that they have taken over bodily the entire Western system of rationalizations, not that they have corroborated that system from their native posts of observation.

When Semitic, Chinese, Tibetan, or African languages are contrasted with our own, the divergence in analysis of the world becomes more apparent; and when we bring in the native languages of the Americas, where speech communities for many millenniums have gone their ways independently of each other and of the Old World, the fact that languages dissect nature in many different ways becomes patent. The relativity of all conceptual systems, ours included, and their dependence upon language stand revealed. That American Indians speaking only their native tongues are never called upon to act as scientific observers is in no wise to the point. To exclude the evidence which their languages offer as to what the human mind can do is like expecting botanists to study nothing but food plants and hothouse roses and then tell us what the plant world is like!

Let us consider a few examples. In English we divide most of our words into two classes, which have different grammatical and logical properties. Class 1 we call nouns, e.g., "house," "man"; Class 2, verbs, e.g., "hit," "run." Many words of one class can act secondarily as of the other class, e.g., "a hit," "a run," or "to man" the boat, but on the primary level the division between the classes is absolute. Our language thus gives us a bipolar division of nature. But nature herself is not thus polarized. If it be said that strike, turn, run, are verbs because they denote temporary or short-lasting events, i.e., actions, why then is fist a noun? It also is a temporary event. Why are lightning, spark, wave, eddy, pulsation, flame, storm, phase, cycle, spasm, noise, emotion, nouns? They are temporary events. If man and house are nouns because they are long-lasting and stable events, i.e., things, what then are keep, adhere, extend, project, continue, persist, grow, dwell, and so on, doing among the verbs? If it be objected that possess, adhere, are verbs because they are stable relationships rather than stable percepts, why then should equilibrium, pressure, current, peace, group, nation, society, tribe, sister, or any kinship term, be among the nouns? It will be found that an "event" to *us* means "what our language classes as a verb" or something analogized therefrom. And it will be found that it is not possible to define event, thing, object, relationship, and so on, from nature, but that to define them always involves a circuitous return to the grammatical categories of the definer's language.

In the Hopi language, lightning, wave, flame, meteor, puff of smoke, pulsation, are verbs—events of necessarily brief duration cannot be anything but verbs. Cloud and storm are at about the lower limit of duration for nouns. Hopi, you see, actually has a classification of events (or linguistic isolates) by duration type, something strange to our modes of thought. On the other hand, in Nootka, a language of Vancouver Island, all words seem to us to be verbs, but really there are no Classes 1 and 2; we have, as it were, a monistic view of nature that gives us only one class of word for all kinds of events. "A house occurs" or "it houses" is the way of saying "house," exactly like "a flame occurs" or "it burns." These terms seem to us like verbs because they are inflected for durational and temporal nuances, so that the suffixes of the word for house event make it mean long-lasting house, temporary house, future house, house that used to be, what started out to be a house, and so on.

Hopi has a noun that covers every thing or being that flies, with the exception of birds, which class is denoted by another noun. The former noun may be said to denote the class (FC–B)—flying class minus bird. The Hopi actually call insect, airplane, and aviator all by the same word, and feel no difficulty about it. The situa-

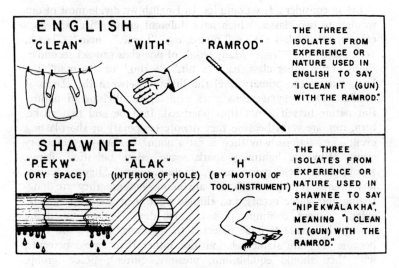

FIGURE 1. Languages dissect nature differently. The different isolates of meaning (thoughts) used by English and Shawnee in reporting the same experience, that of cleaning a gun by running the ramrod through it. The pronouns "I" and "it" are not shown by symbols, as they have the same meaning in each case. In Shawnee "ni-" equals "I"; "-a" equals "it."

tion, of course, decides any possible confusion among very disparate members of a broad linguistic class, such as this class (FC—B). This class seems to us too large and inclusive, but so would our class "snow" to an Eskimo. We have the same word for falling snow, snow on the ground, snow packed hard like ice, slushy snow, wind-driven flying snow—whatever the situation may be. To an Eskimo, this all-inclusive word would be almost unthinkable; he would say that falling snow, slushy snow, and so on, are sensuously and operationally different, different things to contend with; he uses different words for them and for other kinds of snow. The Aztecs go even farther than we in the opposite direction, with cold, ice, and snow all represented by the same basic word with different terminations; ice is the noun form; cold, the adjectival form; and for snow, "ice mist."

What surprises most is to find that various grand generalizations of the Western world, such as time, velocity, and matter, are not essential to the construction of a consistent picture of the universe. The psychic experiences that we class under these headings are, of course, not destroyed; rather, categories derived from other kinds of experiences take over the rulership of the cosmology and seem to function just as well. Hopi may be called a timeless language. It

FIGURE 2. Languages classify items of experience differently. The class corresponding to one word and one thought in language A may be regarded by language B as two or more classes corresponding to two or more words and thoughts.

recognizes psychological time, which is much like Bergson's "duration," but this "time" is quite unlike the mathematical time, T, used by our physicists. Among the peculiar properties of Hopi time are that it varies with each observer, does not permit of simultaneity, and has zero dimensions, i.e., it cannot be given a number greater than one. The Hopi do not say, I "stayed five days," but "I left on the fifth day." A word referring to this kind of time, like the word day, can have no plural. The puzzle picture (Fig. 3, page 158) will give mental exercise to anyone who would like to figure out how the Hopi verb gets along without tenses. Actually, the only practical use of our tenses, in one-verb sentences, is to distinguish among five typical situations, which are symbolized in the picture. The timeless Hopi verb does not distinguish between the present, past, and future of the event itself but must always indicate what type of validity the speaker intends the statement to have: (a) report of an event (situations 1, 2, 3 in the picture); (b) expectation of an event (situation 4); (c) generalization or law

OBJECTIVE FIELD	SPEAKER (SENDER)	HEARER (RECEIVER)	HANDLING OF TOPIC, RUNNING OF THIRD PERSON
SITUATION 1 a.			ENGLISH... "HE IS RUNNING" HOPI... "WARI" (RUNNING. STATEMENT OF FACT)
SITUATION 1 b. OBJECTIVE FIELD BLANK DEVOID OF RUNNING			ENGLISH... "HE RAN" HOPI... "WARI" (RUNNING, STATEMENT OF FACT)
SITUATION 2			ENGLISH... "HE IS RUNNING" HOPI... "WARI" (RUNNING, STATEMENT OF FACT)
SITUATION 3 OBJECTIVE FIELD BLANK			ENGLISH... "HE RAN" HOPI... "ERA WARI" (RUNNING, STATEMENT OF FACT FROM MEMORY)
SITUATION 4 OBJECTIVE FIELD BLANK			ENGLISH... "HE WILL RUN" HOPI... "WARIKNI" (RUNNING, STATEMENT OF EXPECTATION)
SITUATION 5 OBJECTIVE FIELD BLANK			ENGLISH... "HE RUNS" (E.G. ON THE TRACK TEAM) HOPI... "WARIKNGWE" (RUNNING, STATEMENT OF LAW)

FIGURE 3. Contrast between a "temporal" language (English) and a "timeless" language (Hopi). What are to English differences of time are to Hopi differences in the kind of validity.

about events (situation 5.) Situation 1, where the speaker and listener are in contact with the same objective field, is divided by our language into the two conditions, 1a and 1b, which it calls present and past, respectively. This division is unneccessary for a language which assures one that the statement is a report.

Hopi grammar, by means of its forms called aspects and modes, also makes it easy to distinguish between momentary, continued, and repeated occurrences, and to indicate the actual sequence of reported events. Thus the universe can be described without recourse to a concept of dimensional time. How would a physics constructed along these lines work, with no T (time) in its equations? Perfectly, as far as I can see, though of course it would require different ideology and perhaps different mathematics. Of course V (velocity) would have to go too. The Hopi language has no word really equivalent to our "speed" or "rapid." What translates these terms is usually a word meaning intense or very, accompanying any verb of motion. Here is a clue to the nature of our new physics. We may have to introduce a new term I, intensity. Every thing and event will have an I, whether we regard the thing or event as moving or as just enduring or being. Perhaps the I of an electric charge will turn out to be its voltage, or potential. We shall use clocks to measure some intensities, or, rather, some *relative* intensities, for the absolute intensity of anything will be meaningless. Our old friend acceleration will still be there but doubtless under a new name. We shall perhaps call it V, meaning not velocity but variation. Perhaps all growths and accumulations will be regarded as V's. We should not have the concept of rate in the temporal sense, since, like velocity, rate introduces a mathematical and linguistic time. Of course we know that all measurements are ratios, but the measurements of intensities made by comparison with the standard intensity of a clock or a planet we do not treat as ratios, any more than we so treat a distance made by comparison with a yardstick.

A scientist from another culture that used time and velocity would have great difficulty in getting us to understand these concepts. We should talk about the intensity of a chemical reaction; he would speak of its velocity or its rate, which words we should at first think were simply words for intensity in his language. Likewise, he at first would think that intensity was simply our own word for velocity. At first we should agree, later we should begin to disagree, and it might dawn upon both sides that different systems of rationalization were being used. He would find it very hard to make us understand what he really meant by velocity of a chemical reaction. We should have no words that would fit. He would try to explain it by likening it to a running horse, to the difference between a good horse and a lazy horse. We should try to show him, with a superior laugh, that his analogy also was a matter of different intensities, aside from which there was little similarity between a horse and a chemical reaction in a beaker. We should point out that a running horse is moving relative to the ground, whereas the material in the beaker is at rest.

One significant contribution to science from the linguistic point of view may be the greater development of our sense of perspective. We shall no longer be able to see a few recent dialects of the Indo-European family, and the rationalizing techniques elaborated from their patterns, as the apex of the evolution of the human mind; nor their present wide spread as due to any survival from fitness or to anything but a few events of history—events that could be called fortunate only from the parochial point of view of the favored parties. They, and our own thought processes with them, can no longer be envisioned as spanning the gamut of reason and knowledge but only as one constellation in a galactic expanse. A fair realization of the incredible degree of diversity of linguistic system that ranges over the globe leaves one with an inescapable feeling that the human spirit is inconceivably old; that the few thousand years of history covered by our written records are no more than the thickness of a pencil mark on the scale that measures our past experience on this planet; that the events of these recent millenniums spell nothing in any evolutionary wise, that the race has taken no sudden spurt, achieved no commanding synthesis during recent millenniums, but has only played a little with a few of the linguistic formulations and views of nature bequeathed from an inexpressibly longer past. Yet neither this feeling nor the sense of precarious dependence of all we know upon linguistic tools which themselves are largely unknown need be discouraging to science but should, rather, foster that humility which accompanies the true scientific spirit, and thus forbid that arrogance of the mind which hinders real scientific curiosity and detachment.

QUESTIONS

1. Whorf points out that different languages "cut up" reality differently. Consider the following lists of words and in each case imagine another language which does not contain all of the words (just as English does not have all the words for "snow" that Eskimo does), but rather covers more than one English word with a single word. Then describe the principle by which each of your hypothetical languages cuts up that particular part of reality.

confession	fast	package	move
thought	gradually	envelope	stop
speech	slow	milk	stand
dream	accelerate	sky	run
song	continuum	rib	fall
idea	coat	heart	remain

2. Assume the following are sentences and literal translations from a hypothetical language. Using Whorf's approach as a model, derive as many grammatical rules and tell as much as you can about this language, explaining how it differs from English.

Frigii.	Reidi.	Happio da.
It is cold.	It is red.	I am happy.
Sadio datta.	Laughion da.	Laughionta datta.
I was sad.	I am laughing.	They were laughing.
Sadioha da.	Happiohe datta.	Warmioha.
He is sad.	She was happy.	He will be warm.
Warmii.	Warmiohe da.	Frigii tun.
It is warm.	She is warm.	It will be cold.

W. NELSON FRANCIS
The Inner History of English[1]

Indo-European to Old English

The changes which constitute the inner history of a language usually affect, in varying degrees, all three major aspects of the language: vocabulary, grammar, and pronunciation. Evidence for all three kinds of change prior to the earliest surviving documents is entirely indirect: it is derived by reconstructing the original forms from which divergent known forms are most likely to have evolved. Since changes in grammar and pronunciation usually affect not individual items but groups of similar items, it is possible to make general statements that cover these systematic changes. Changes in vocabulary are more likely to be individual, though even here some generalizations can be made, especially about change of meanings.

After the dates when documents became available, the evidence for changes in grammar and vocabulary is direct. But the only direct evidence for pronunciation would· be audible recordings of speech, which did not exist before the present century. So the reconstruction of older pronunciation must be based upon the skillful interpretation of written evidence. As we know from the situation in the English of our own time, spelling is not always a very accurate guide to pronunciation. But combined with the evidence of comparative reconstruction and some direct comments on and descriptions of pronunciation by earlier writers, the written records can lead to at least a plausible reconstruction of older pronunciations.

Since the speakers of the Indo-European parent language had no writing system, all the evidence about its nature is indirect. The branch of linguistics which deals with the reconstruction of this language on the basis of comparative study of its descendants is known as Indo-European philology, and it is highly detailed and technical. For our purposes it is enough to observe certain broad features of hypothetically reconstructed Proto-Indo-European, and to note how some of them became modified in the course of the development of Germanic and later of Old English.

In pronunciation, Proto-Indo-European seems to have had a system of strong accents, whose position in the word shifted when various affixes appeared, and in so doing affected the sound of vowels. This same phenomenon, known by both the German name

1. From Chapter 3 of *The English Language*, 1965. Francis has previously made a distinction between "inner" history (changes in the language itself) and "outer" history (cultural developments that play some part in linguistic change).

"ablaut" and the English name "gradation," also characterizes modern English, in contrast to a language like French or Spanish, where the vowels have the same value whether accented or not. Thus in English the syllabic of the accented first syllable of *native* is a full dipthong, /ey/, but that of the unaccented first syllable of *nativity* is a much shorter and weaker central vowel, /e/. Similar vowel contrasts in Proto-Indo-European account for the still-existing variation in some irregular verbs, such as *ride, rode, ridden*. Sets of words with similar root meanings, like *sit, sat, set, seat, settle*, also show survival of Indo-European ablaut variation in modern English.

Another characteristic of the Proto-Indo-European sound-system was the existence of three sets of "stops," the kind of consonants made by a temporary complete interruption of the air-flow. In modern English the /k/ sounds at the beginning of *cat* and *quarter* and following the /s/ in *skit*, though phonetically quite a bit different, are to all significant purposes the same. But in Proto-Indo-European they were separate sounds, which had different subsequent development in different languages. Thus English *wheel* and Greek *kyklos* (from which English subsequently borrowed *cycle*), though now very different, go back to a common Proto-Indo-European original which began with a lip-rounded kind of /k^w/ sound. Germanic preserved the lip-rounding, as /w/, while Greek preserved only the /k/.

The most sweeping changes in the sound system, as one branch of Indo-European developed into Germanic and subsequently into Old English, were in the consonants. Systematic correspondences, such as the contrast of English *father* and *foot* with Latin *pater* and *pedem*, illustrate the effect of these changes, which were worked out and formulated by nineteenth-century linguists under the misleading titles of Grimm's and Verner's "Laws." They are not laws in the usual sense at all, but simply general statements describing systematic changes in pronunciation.

In its grammar, Proto-Indo-European was very much a "synthetic" language, that is, one which depended heavily on morphological markers, especially inflections, to indicate grammatical relationships and meanings. Thus its nouns seem to have had as many as eight cases to express meanings conveyed in modern English by prepositions, word order, and other devices characteristic of analytic languages. In the course of the development of Germanic and Old English, several of these cases (such as the "locative" and the "ablative," both of which survived in Latin) disappeared, probably because sound changes caused their inflections to become identical with those of other cases. By Old English times only four cases— "nominative," "accusative," "genitive," and "dative"—are common to all nouns, with traces of a fifth, the instrumental, surviving.

Modern English has preserved a combined dative-accusative only in pronouns, and the genitive survives as the possessive marker, -'s.

Another feature of Proto-Indo-European nouns was grammatical gender: the assignment of nouns to different classes based originally on some aspect of meaning. In spite of the terms "masculine" and "feminine" applied to two of these genders, the original distinction does not seem to have been based on sex. One theory holds that it was based on a contrast between individual (masculine) and type (feminine.) In any case, grammatical gender carried with it the requirement of agreement between noun and adjective: adjectives had distinctive forms to be used with the different genders. Anyone who has studied Latin has become familiar with agreement in gender. Both gender and associated agreement were preserved in Germanic and Old English, and have persisted in German to the present day, though modern English has discarded them.

The verb system of Proto-Indo-European seems to have included both aspect and tense, with distinctive endings also for person. There were probably five tenses: present, imperfect, perfect, aorist, and future. In Germanic and subsequent Old English the tenses were reduced to two, the present and the past, or preterit. Proto-Indo-European had four moods: indicative (for statements), imperative (for commands), subjunctive (for unreal statements), and optative (for wishes). In Germanic the last two of these fell together (as they also did in Latin); the resulting subjunctive appears in Old English and survives in a few vestiges in modern English. But the elaborate development of modal auxiliaries, which now express many of the shades of meaning formerly expressed by moods, occurred in Germanic and later in English.

Another morphological complexity of Proto-Indo-European was an inflected passive, which almost totally disappeared in Germanic and shows only vestiges in Old English. Old English developed instead the phrasal passive (*be* with the past participle) which we use in modern English. Proto-Indo-European also had a set of dual number forms, both in nouns and verbs, which survived in Greek and Gothic but disappeared in West Germanic except for a few pronoun forms. In sum, the principal grammatical development as the Germanic branch of the Indo-European family diverged from the others was a tendency to reduce the number of grammatical categories marked by distinctive inflections, and thus to carry out to a considerable degree the change from a synthetic to an analytic language which has been the continuing trend of English grammar.

Although the English vocabulary can be taken up separately, one point ought to be considered here: the distinction between "native" and "borrowed" words. Native words are those which can be shown to have come down in the direct line of descent from the oldest known form of the language, which in the case of English is

Proto-Indo-European. Borrowed words are those which have been adopted into the language from an outside source. A borrowed word, once it has been adapted to the uses of the borrowing language, usually becomes so thoroughly naturalized that only scholars know about its foreign origin. The notion sometimes put forward that somehow "native Anglo-Saxon" words are better than those borrowed from other languages has no basis in fact. Certainly *table* and *chair*, for all they were borrowed from French, are just as good words as the native *board* and *stool*.

To the historian of language, however, the distinction is important because he bases his inferences about earlier states of the language upon a knowledge of the sources of its words. Thus a pair of words like *chalk* and *calcium* is interesting because, while both are borrowed from Latin *calcem*, the appearance of the initial *ch*-sound in *chalk* shows that it was borrowed before the so-called palatalization of initial /k/ in early Old English. This instance also illustrates the fact that, when a borrowed word has became naturalized, it is subject to the same sound changes which affect the pronunciation of native words.

In general a word is considered to be a native Indo-European word if it exists in two or more of the main Indo-European families, without evidence that it was borrowed from one into the other or others. Thus English *father*, which is paralleled not only by German V*ater*, but also by Latin *pater*, Sanskrit *pita*, and others, is clearly a native word.

One use to which the study of the native Indo-European vocabulary has been put is to supply evidence for speculation about the culture of the original speakers of Proto-Indo-European and the location of their homeland. Thus the fact that there are native words for *cow* and *wheel* but not for *plow* has been taken as evidence that they were herdsmen, possibly nomadic, rather than tillers of the soil. The existence of common words for *winter*, *snow*, *beech* (tree), and *salmon* has been considered to prove that their home was in north-central Europe. But such evidence is risky and cannot be carried too far, since even though common words may exist in several languages, their meanings may be so different as to make it impossible to be sure of the meaning of the Indo-European original.

In general the vocabulary of Germanic and hence of early Old English was principally made up of native Indo-European words. Already the Germanic fondness for compounding as a source of new words was strongly in evidence. Early contact of the Germanic tribes with Roman traders had given rise to some borrowing of Latin words, such as *wine* and *kettle*, both of which go back to pre-Anglo-Saxon Germanic. But the great influx of foreign borrowings which was later to characterize the English vocabulary had not yet begun.

Old English to Middle English

The passage of Old English given with its translation on pages 166–167 is a sample of the language as it was at the end of the ninth century. It is the beginning of the Preface to Pope Gregory's book called *Pastoral Care* in an English translation made for or perhaps actually by the great King Alfred, about the year 890. After the devastating wars with the Danes had been halted by Alfred's agreements with Guthrum, the king set out to restore learning and culture in his kingdom. Part of his program was to prepare a translation of this manual for parish priests and to send a copy to each of the bishops in England. Our passage is quoted from the copy destined for Wærferth, Bishop of Worcester, which is now in the Bodleian Library at Oxford.

At first sight the passage seems so strange as not to bear any relation to English at all. But upon closer examination, expecially after a few adjustments to the spelling are made, familiar words begin to appear. The character ð is used as we use *th* in modern English, and æ spells the sound of *a* in cat. Knowing this we can recognize ðæt as *that*. Other words that look much like their modern descendants are *wordum* (*word*, with dative plural ending), *freondlice* (*friendly*, with -*e* ending to mark it as adverb), *folces* (*folk*, with genitive singular ending), *wisdom*, and many others. Some have passed through sound changes which have been reflected in altered spellings; thus the combination æg became in Middle English a diphthong æy, which is illustrated in *mæge* (modern *may*) and *æðer* (modern *either*). Actually more than half the words in this passage are still in use, though altered in shape, pronunciation, and sometimes in meaning.

As an illustration of some of the grammatical features which Old English inherited from Indo-European but which have since passed out of the language, consider the clause *hu ða kyningas ðe ðone ónwald hæfdon ðæs folces on ðdm dagum Gode & his ærendwrecum hersumedon*, which we may represent word for word as "how the kings that the rule had the folk's on those days God and his ministers ['errand-workers'] obeyed." The word order is clearly not that of modern English, and in the modern English rendering is ambiguous. But the Old English is not ambiguous, because the grammatical function of virtually every word is marked by inflectional endings. Even the function word that serves the purposes of both definite article and demonstrative takes on different forms—ða, ðone, ðæs, ðam—in agreement with the noun it modifies. ða kyningas could be either nominative (hence subject) or accusative

Ælfred kyning hateð gretan Wærferð biscep his wordum
luflice & freondlice; & ðe cyðan hate ðæt me com swiðe oft
ón gemynd, hwelce wiotan iu wæron giond Angelcynn, ægðer
ge godcundra hada ge worul[d]cundra; & hu gesæliglica tida
5 ða wæron giond Angelcynn; & hu ða kyningas ðe ðone ónwald
hæfdon ðæs folces [on ðam dagum] Gode & his ærendwrecum
hersumedon; & hie ægðer ge hiora sibbe ge hiora siodo ge hiora
ónweald innanbordes gehioldon, & eac út hiora eðel gerymdon;
& hu him ða speow ægðer ge mid wige ge mid wisdome; & eac
10 ða godcundan hadas hu giorne hie wæron ægðer ge ymb lare
ge ymb liornunga, ge ymb ealle ða ðiowotdomas ðe hie Gode
[don] scoldon; & hu man utanbordes wisdom & lare hieder ón
lond sohte, & hu we hie nu sceoldon ute begietan gif we hie
habban sceoldon. Swæ clæne hio wæs oðfeallenu ón Angel-
15 cynne ðæt swiðe feawa wæron behionan Humbre ðe hiora
ðeninga cuðen understondan ón Englisc, oððe furðum án
ærendgewrit óf Lædene ón Englisc areccean; & ic wene ðæt[te]
noht monige begiondan Humbre næren. Swæ feawa hiora
wæron ðæt ic furðum anne ánlepne ne mæg geðencean besuðan
20 Temese ða ða ic to rice feng. Gode ælmihtegum sie ðonc
ðæt[te] we nu ænigne ón stal habbað lareowa. & forðon ic
ðe bebiode ðæt ðu dó swæ ic geliefe ðæt ðu wille, ðæt ðu
ðe ðissa woruldðinga to ðæm geæmetige swæ ðu oftost mæge,
ðæt ðu ðone wisdom ðe ðe God sealde ðær ðær ðu hiene
25 befæstan mæge, befæste.
—*from* Alfred's *Preface* to Gregory's *Pastoral Care*[2]

(hence direct object), but since the verb *hæfdon* is plural and *ðone
ónwald* is accusative singular, we know that the passage means "the
kings that had the rule." The noun phrase *ðæs folces* is separated
from *ónwald*, to which it is closely related, by the verb, but since it
is doubly marked as a genitive, we know that this phrase is to be
read "rule of the people." Following the preposition *on* we have
the dative *ðam dagum* for "those days"; if it were subject or direct
object, it would be *ða dagas*. *Gode & his ærendwrecum* are the nearest nouns preceding the verb *hersumedon* ("obeyed," plural),
which would mark them as its subject in modern English, but
because they are marked as datives by the ending -*e* (singular) and
-*um* (plural) respectively, we know that they are objects (*hersu-
mian* is one of a group of verbs whose direct objects are in the
dative rather than the usual accusative). When all these markers
are taken into account, there is only one thing the passage could
mean: "how the kings who had the rule over the people in those
days obeyed God and his ministers."

Preservation of Germanic grammatical gender is illustrated in
this passage by pronoun reference. Thus in line 14 the pronoun *hio*
is feminine and thus refers all the way back to the feminine noun
liornunga in line 11. In line 24, the pronoun *hiene* is masculine

2. MS Hatton 20, Bodleian Library, ed. H. Sweet, EETS, O.S. 45, 1871 [Francis'
note].

King Alfred bids greet bishop Wærferth with his words lovingly and friendlily; and I let thee know that it very often came to [my] mind what wise men formerly were throughout England, either of the sacred orders or the secular; and how happy times then were throughout England; and how the kings that then had rule of the folk in those days obeyed God and his ministers; and they maintained their peace, their morality, and their control within the country and also enlarged their domain outside; and how they then prospered both with war and with wisdom; and also the sacred orders how eager they were both with teaching and with learning and concerning all the services that they ought to do for God; and how people from outside [the country] sought wisdom and teaching here in this land, and how we now would have to get them from outside if we were to have them. So complete was its falling off in England that there were very few this side of Humber who could understand their liturgies in English, or translate a letter from Latin into English; and I believe that there were not many beyond Humber. So few of them there were that I cannot think of a single one south of Thames when I came to the throne. To God Almighty be thanks that we now have any teachers in the place. And therefore I bid thee that thou do as I believe thou will, separate thyself from these worldly matters as often as thou canst, that thou apply the wisdom that God gave thee wherever thou mayest.

---

singular accusative and refers back to the masculine noun *wisdom* earlier in the sentence. In modern English, which has switched from grammatical to semantic gender, we would use *it* to refer to both *learning* and *wisdom*, unless we were personifying these abstractions as feminine goddesses.

Even in this short passage there is much more to be observed. But enough has been said to illustrate the major grammatical difference between Old and Modern English—the dependence on inflectional markers rather than word order to indicate grammatical relationships. The contrast in pronunciation could only be brought out clearly by reading the passage aloud, though the spelling is often a signal that the sound was quite different. All three of these aspects—grammar, pronunciation, and spelling—underwent gradual change during the two centuries following Alfred, and more rapid and sweeping change during the two centuries following the Norman Conquest. Let us next look at a passage of Middle English from about the year 1200 to see what some of those changes were.

The brief passage printed with its translation on pages 168–169 is from the opening chapter of *Ancrene Riwle*, or *Rule for Anchoresses*, which was written sometime between 1175 and 1200, probably in the southwest of England. Our selection is taken from the

Nu aski ȝe hwat riwle ȝe ancren schullen holden. ȝe schullen allesweis mid alle mihte & mid alle strencðe wel witen þe inre, & te vttre vor hire sake. þe inre is euere iliche, þe vttre is misliche. vor eurich schal holden þe vttre, efter þet ðe licome
[5] mei best mid hire serui ðe inre. nu þeonne, is hit so þet alle ancren muwen wel holden one riwle? *quantum ad puritatem cordis circa quam uersatur tota religio.* þet is, alle muwen & owen holden one riwle, onont purte of heorte, þet is cleane, schir inwit, wið vte wite of sunne þet ne beo þuruh schrift
[10] ibet. ðis makeð ðe leafdi riwle, ðe riwleð & rihteð & smeðeð ðe heorte, & tet inwit of sunne. vor nout ne makeð hire woc, bute sunne one. Rihten hire & smeðen hire is of euch religiun, & of efrich ordre þe god & alðe strengðe. þeos riwle is imaked nout of monnes fundleas, auh is of godes hestes. for þi heo is
[15] euer on, & schal beon wið vte monglunge & wið vte chaungunge, & all owen hire in on euer to holden.

—*from* the *Ancrene Riwle*[3]

---

manuscript known as Cotton Nero A.xiv (after its seventeenth-century owner and his shelf-mark), now in the British Museum. The manuscript was copied as much as fifty years after the book was written, and therefore may include some scribal changes. But it is a good sample of English of the early part of the thirteenth century. It shows some features of the dialect of its region, inherited from the West Saxon of Alfred but not continuing in standard English, which derives from the dialect of London.

A few points about the spelling will reduce the unfamiliar look of the text considerably. In addition to the ð, which we encountered in our selection from Alfred, there are two unfamiliar letters. The first of these, ȝ (called "yogh"), is here used where modern English uses an initial *y*, as in the pronoun ȝe (the old nominative form of *you*). Later this letter was also used after vowels to spell the velar spirant (like German *ch*), which even later came to be spelled *gh*. But in this manuscript the Old English spelling of this sound with *h* still persists, as in *mihte* (*might*) and *þuruh* (*through*). The runic letter "thorn," þ, which was also used in Old English (though not, as it happens, in our selection from Alfred), is here used interchageably with ð where we use the digraph *th* . The usage of *v* and *u* differs from modern practice: instead of *v* being restricted to the consonant and *u* to the vowel, both are used for both consonant and vowel, the *v* being used at the beginnings of words and the *u* elsewhere. Thus in *vttre*, *v* is the vowel, but in *vor* it is the consonant; and in *eurich*, *u* is the consonant but in *schullen* it is the vowel. This practice prevailed into the seventeenth century. We might also note that the aspirated *w*-sound is spelled *hw* as in Old English, rather than *wh* as in modern English.

3. MS Cotton Nero A. XIV, f. I verso, ed. M. Day, EETS, O.S.,225, 1952. [Francis' note].

Now you ask what rule you anchoresses shall hold. You shall always with all [your] might and with all [your] strength well keep the inner [rule] and the outer for her [i.e., its] sake. The inner rule is ever alike; the outer is different, for every [one] shall hold the outer according as the body best may well hold one rule? "with regard to purity of heart, about which all religion is concerned"—that is, all may and ought to hold one rule concerning purity of heart, that is clean, pure conscience, without reproach of sin that be not bettered through shrift. This the lady's rule brings about, which rules and corrects and smooths the heart and the conscience of sin. For naught makes it crooked but sin only. To correct it and smooth it is of each religion and of every order the good and strength of all. This rule is made not by man's invention, but is of God's commandment. Therefore it is ever one and shall be without mingling and without changing and all ought as one ever to hold it.

In vocabulary, this passage is interesting because it shows the beginning of the influx of French words which was to become a veritable flood as the thirteenth and fourteenth centuries progressed. There are six words of French origin in our brief passage: *riwle, serui, purte, religiun, ordre, and chaungunge* (modern *rule, serve, purity, religion, order, and changing*). According to the Oxford Dictionary, four of these—*riwle, purte, ordre, and chaungunge*—make their first appearance in written English in this text. The others first appeared not long before. The word *ancre* itself (of which *ancrene* is a genitive plural) first appeared as a borrowing from Latin in Old English, but it had very little use before this very widely circulated book made it popular.

Except for these seven words, the vocabulary of this passage is all native. It is of interest to note some of the words which were later to be replaced by borrowings from French and hence to become obsolete or archaic:

witen	: obey	schrift	: confession
schire	: pure	fundleas	: invention
inwit	: conscience	hestes	: commandments
wite	: fault		

Other native words have been supplanted by words themselves native, as *licome* by *body* and *woc* by *crooked*. Even though the Norman occupation was more than a century old, the remaking of the English vocabulary which was one of its consequences had barely begun when the author of the *Ancrene Riwle* wrote.

In grammar, however, we can see many changes in the direction of modern English, particularly in word order. A word-for-word "translation" does not produce the ambiguities which resulted from a similar treatment of the Alfred passage, though in a few places the order is not that of today's English. Thus in the first sentence the inversion of verb and subject after the initial adverb (*Nu aski ʒe . . .*) is no longer current, and the moving of the past participle of a passive verb to the end of the clause in *þat ne beo þuruh schrift ibet*, though possible in today's English, is less common. On the other hand, verb phrases with modal auxiliaries, as in *schullen holden, muwen wel holden*, are in the modern order, rather than the inverted order of Alfred's *habban sceoldon* ("should have"). And since the characteristic case inflections of Old English have virtually disappeared, such grammatical functions as direct object are indicated by position, as in *alle ancren muwen holden one riwle*. But some relationships which must today be indicated wholly by order could still be indicated by inflections: the singular-plural distinction is still preserved in the auxiliaries *mei-muwen* and *schal-schullen*, where modern English has lost the distinctive plural forms.

One feature of Old English grammar that is still evident in the text is grammatical gender, as it is revealed by pronoun reference. The word *riwle* derives from Old French *reule*, which in turn comes from the Latin feminine noun *regula*. The author of the *Ancrene Riwle* regularly uses the feminine pronoun (nominative *heo*, genitive, dative and accusative *hire*) to refer to *riwle*. But by this time the definite article has ceased to be inflected for gender and case, and has become the unchanging *þe* (or in one case *te*) as in modern English.

Once again little can be said about pronunciation without an oral rendering. But some features of the spelling indicate changes that had occurred in pronunciation during the three centuries since Alfred. The making of new diphthongs is illustrated by *mei*, which we saw as *mæge* in the Alfred passage. Spellings like *heorte* and *beo*, though seeming to preserve Old English diphthongs, are probably here intended to represent a rounded front vowel (as in German *horen* or French *boeuf*), which was a normal West Midland feature. The change of Old English *a* to an *o* sound (probably like the *au* of modern English *taut*) is shown in *holden* (Anglian Old English *haldan*) and *on, one* (Old English *an*). The change of initial *f* to *v* in *vor* (*for*) and the u-spelling in *sunne* (*sin*), representing a rounded front vowel as in German *dünn*, are characteristic of the southwest Midland dialect of this manuscript.

In sum, then, we may conclude that this sample of early Middle English, though it still looks very much like a foreign language at first glance, is perceptibly less so than the English of Alfred, especially in its grammar. The next two centuries, during which English reestablished itself as a language of literature and culture worthy of the art of a Chaucer, were to see sweeping changes in vocabulary, and in the century following Chaucer the pronunciation was rather radically altered while the spelling remained relatively fixed. It is in this late Middle English and early modern English period that the language becomes recognizably the language we know in the literature since Shakespeare.

Middle English to Modern English

The following passage is from William Caxton's preface to his second edition of Chaucer's *Canterbury Tales*, printed in 1484. It is obvious at once that the language has changed greatly, especially in vocabulary, during the three centuries since the *Ancrene Riwle* was written. Although the spelling is different from modern practice in minor ways and there are a few grammatical differences, this is recognizably modern English. The modern reader needs no translation.

Grete thanks laude and honour / ought to be gyuen vnto the clerkes / poetes / and historiographs that haue wreton many noble bokes of wysedom of the lyues / passions / & myracles of holy sayntes of hystoryes / of noble and famous Actes / and faittes / And of the cronycles sith the begynnyng of the creacion of the world / vnto thys present tyme / by whyche we ben dayly enformed / and haue knowleche of many thynges / of whom we shold not haue knowen / yf they had not left to vs theyr monumentis wreton / Emong whom and inespecial to fore alle other we ought to gyue a synguler laude vnto that noble & grete philosopher Gefferey chaucer the whiche for his ornate wrytyng in our tongue may wel haue the name of a laureate poete / For to fore that he by hys labour enbelysshyd / ornated / and made faire our englisshe / in thys Royame was had rude speche & Incongrue / as yet it appiereth by olde bookes / whyche at thys day ought not to haue place ne be compared among ne to hys beauteuous volumes / and aournate writynges / of whom he made many bokes and treatyces of many a noble historye as wel in metre as in ryme and prose / and them so craftyly made / that he comprehended hys maters in short / quyck and hye sentences / eschewyng prolyxyte / castyng away the chaf of superfluyte / and shewyng the pyked grayn of sentence / vtteryd by crafty and sugred eloquence / of whom emonge all other of hys bokes / I purpose temprynte by the grace of god the book of the tales of cauntyrburye / in whiche I fynde many a noble hystorye / of euery astate and degre / Fyrst rehercyng the condicions / and tharraye of eche of them as properly as possyble is to be sayd / And after theyr tales whyche ben of noblesse / wysedom / gentylesse / Myrthe / and also of veray holynesse and vertue / wherin he fynysshyth thys sayd booke / whyche book I haue dylygently ouersen and duly examyned to thende that it be made acordyng vnto his owen makyng /

> —from Caxton's Preface to Chaucer's
> Canterbury Tales, 2nd Ed., 1484[4]

Although, as Caxton remarks in another preface, the language has changed considerably from that of Chaucer, Caxton's spelling

---

4. Sig. a ij recto. Ed. W. J. B. Crotch, EETS, O.S. 176, 1928, p. 90 [Francis' note].

is essentially the same as that of Chaucer's day. It is true that the alphabet has been revised by dropping ð, þ, and ȝ in favor of the rather more clumsy modern use of *th* and *gh*. But Caxton uses the same vowel characters as Chaucer, although his pronunciation, especially of long vowels, was probably quite different. For example, Chaucer pronounced *name* as *na:m* or *na:me*, while Caxton, although using the same spelling, probably pronounced the word to rhyme with modern *ham*. Further change since Caxton's time has produced the modern pronunciation /neym/ with the same diphthong as in *may*. This freezing of English spelling according to the conventions of the early fifteenth century in spite of subsequent changes of pronunciation is one of the principal causes of the difficulties and inconsistencies of modern English spelling.

But Caxton's spelling is still not as rigorously standarized as that of today. He is free to spell *book* alternatively with or without a final *-e*, and the plural appears once as *bokes* and once as *bookes*. The latter points raises the question as to whether the plural ending still had syllabic value for Caxton, or whether it had been reduced to /s/ or /z/ except after sibilants, as in present-day English. Spellings like *clerkes, actes, thynges*, and *monumentis* seem to indicate a distinct syllable, but *passions, maters*, and *condicions* argue for a nonsyllabic ending. It is probable that his usage was about the same as ours, and that the *-es* and *-is* spellings are conventional survivals from a time when the ending was pronounced as a separate syllable.

Caxton's grammar shows further development in the direction of modern English, though in some places his word order is not ours. Where he has *monumentis wreton*, we would have written *monuments*. It is still possible for him to invert verb and subject in a statement beginning with an adverbial modifier, as in *in thys Royame was had rude speche*. In modern English if we wish to put the subject after the verb, we supply an expletive or temporary subject, *it* or *there*, in the normal subject position: "in this realm there was rude and incongruous speech." Note that we only use the passive of *have* in some special idioms, like the traditional country newspaper expression, "a good time was had by all." In other respects Caxton's verb phrases have characteristically modern structure, as in *ought to be gyuen, shold not have knowen*. But he still uses the *-th* form of the third person singular, which was to be largely supplanted during the next century by the *-s* form, derived from Northern dialect.

One or two grammatical points are worthy of notice. As in Chaucer's English, Caxton commonly uses *that* with subordinating conjunctions: compare the conjunction *to fore that* ("before") with the preposition *to fore*. He uses *the whyche* as a relative pronoun referring to a personal noun and *whom* referring to an impersonal one (*writynges*). Forms like *thende*, *tharraye*, and *temprynte* indicate elision of the unstressed vowels of *the* and *to*, which is no longer characteristic of standard English. He uses the *th*- forms of the third plural pronoun, which were borrowed from Old Norse into the Northern dialect, in all three cases (*they, theyr, them*), in contrast to the practice of Chaucer, who uses the native English forms in *h*- in the possessive and objective cases. In general Caxton's grammar, though unmistakably of an older day, presents no problems to the modern reader.

But it is in vocabulary that Caxton's English shows the greatest change from that of the *Ancrene Riwle*. The great enrichment of the English vocabulary by borrowings from French, which took place during the period from 1250 to 1400, is very apparent in this passage. If we exclude function words, more than half the words are of French origin. Of sixty-one French words in the passage, only eleven were in the language when the *Ancrene Riwle* was written. Nine more appeared in the thirteenth century, thirty-eight during the fourteenth, and three in the fifteenth. Thus, exclusive of the function words, almost all of which are native, more than a third of the vocabulary of this passage came into the language during the two centuries before Caxton wrote. It is no wonder that he considered pre-Chaucerian English "rude and Incongrue."

The importance of this addition to the vocabulary is emphasized by the fact that almost all of the French borrowings in this passage are still in use, though sometimes with altered meanings. A few, such as *historiograph*, *royame*, *incongrue*, and *gentylesse*, have yielded to the closely related forms *historiographer*, *realm*, *incongruous*, and *gentility*. But the rest are still with us. Nor are they all literary or high-flown words like *superfluity* and *embellish*. Many have become essential items in the workaday vocabulary, where they have replaced or supplemented Old English words of similar meaning. Such are *poet*, *saint*, *famous*, *act*, *present*, *labor*, *rude*, *appear*, *place*, *very*, *virtue*, *finish*, *duly*, and *examine*. Our vocabulary would indeed be impoverished without words of this sort. Often the retention of the Old English word alongside the French import has given us pairs of near-synonyms with delicate differences of meaning, as in

deed	: act	work	: labor
stead	: place	seem	: appear
end	: finish		

Caxton, who, to judge by his prefaces, thought and worried quite a bit about the state of English in his day, was aware of this great change in its vocabulary. In the preface to one of his translations from French, he describes his effort to strike a mean between the "rude" old words of the older English and the "curious" new vocabulary borrowed from French. It is interesting to note that he describes the French words as "the comyn termes, that be dayli vsed."

One more three-hundred-year leap forward brings us to the language of the later eighteenth century. The passage below is from Boswell's *Life of Johnson*, first published in 1791. Even though Boswell was a Scotsman, he had mastered standard English, and this passage may be considered a fair sample of the more formal literary English of the period.

It is apparent at once that the spelling is completely standardized and is almost exactly that of our own day. The only exception in this passage is the *-ck* ending of *characteristick*. Punctuation has changed somewhat since Boswell's time, mostly in the direction of fewer and less strong marks. We would not use the colons in lines eight and sixteen, but most likely a comma in the first case and no mark at all in the second. A good many of Boswell's commas would be omitted in modern practice. Apart from these points, however, the conventions of the writing system are modern and standardized.

> That superiority over his fellows, which he maintained with so much dignity in his march through life, was not assumed from vanity and ostentation, but was the natural and constant effect of those extraordinary powers of mind, of which he could not but be conscious by comparison; the intellectual difference, which in other cases of comparison of characters is often a matter of undecided contest, being as clear in his case as the superiority of stature in some men above others. Johnson did not strut or stand on tip-toe: He only did not stoop. From his earliest years, his superiority was perceived and acknowledged.... His schoolfellow, Mr. Hector, has obligingly furnished me with many particulars of his boyish days: and assured me that he never knew him corrected at school, but for talking and diverting other boys from their business. He seemed to learn by intuition; for though indolence and procrastination were inherent in his constitution, whenever he made an exertion he did more than any one else. In short, he is a memorable instance of what has been often observed, that the boy is the man in miniature: and that the distinguishing characteristics of each individual are the same, through the whole course of life. His favourites used to receive very liberal assistance from him; and such was the submission and deference with which he was treated, such the desire to obtain his regard, that three of the boys, of whom Mr. Hector was sometimes one, used to come in the morning as his humble attendants, and carry him to school.
>
> —from Boswell's Life of Johnson[5]

Boswell's grammar, also, is little different from ours. The use of the empty auxiliary *do* in the modern way, which was worked out in the eighteenth century, is illustrated in the negative verb phrases *did not strut* and *did not stoop*. Not illustrated in this passage but occurring elsewhere in the work is the verb phrase marked for aspect (e.g., "When he and I were traveling"), which, though going back in its origins to Old English, became much more fre-

5. Ed. G. B. Hill and L. F. Powell, 1934, p. 47 [Francis' note].

quent in the seventeenth and eighteenth centuries. The catenative verbs, characteristic of modern English, are illustrated by *seemed to learn* and *used to come*.

Some of Boswell's turns of phrase, though perfectly in accord with modern English grammar, have an old-fashioned ring. Thus "he never knew him corrected at school but for talking" would nowadays be something like "he never knew him to be corrected at school except for talking," and we might render "three of the boys, of whom Mr. Hector was sometimes one" as "three of the boys, sometimes including Mr. Hector." But these differences are more stylistic than grammatical. Perhaps the principal difference in grammar between Boswell's English and ours is the relative scarcity of the noun-adjunct construction. There is no example of it in this passage, and (excluding a few compounds) there are only three— *gunpowder plot, Christmas exercise,* and *college vacation*—in a ten-page passage of which this is a part. Again the noun-adjunct construction was perfectly grammatical in Boswell's day, so we must attribute its increased frequency in present-day English to a stylistic rather than a grammatical change.

Boswell's vocabulary reflects the increase in the number of words of Latin and sometimes Greek origin which was a result of the Renaissance revival of the classical languages. This passage contains twelve words which entered the language after Caxton's preface, our last sample. These words, with the dates of their earliest citation in the Oxford Dictionary, are *superiority* (1526), *obligingly* (1654), *intuition* (1497), *indolence* (1603), *procrastination* (before 1548), *inherent* (1578), *exertion* (1677), *miniature* (1586), *distinguish* (1561), *characteristic* (1664), *favorite* (1583), and *deference* (1647). In addition, five words—*character, particular, constitution, individual,* and *attendant*—though they were in the language in 1484, are here used in meanings or functions which they acquired later. It is interesting to note that in this passage Boswell does not use a single word which had been in the language less than a hundred years. This is evidence of the fact that the influx of classical borrowings was a phenomenon of the period roughly from 1550 to 1675. On the whole the eighteenth century was a period of stabilization of the vocabulary—a good time for the development of lexicography, which was crowned by the publication of Johnson's great dictionary in 1755.

As we look back over the nine hundred years separating Boswell's biography from Alfred's preface, we can see that, while the English language maintained its identity unbroken throughout this long period, it underwent changes which, though gradual, were so great as to be revolutionary. In grammar, it changed from a largely synthetic language, depending principally on inflectional markers to indicate syntactic relations, to an analytic one, depending principally on word order and function words. Its pronunciation went through two periods of radical change, which would make a speaker of old English, if one should miraculously appear, totally unable to understand the language of Boswell's or our own day. During the first half of this period, the spelling system was adjusted from time to time to reflect the changes in pronunciation. But it became virtually fixed at a point representing the pronunciation of approximately the year 1400, so that modern spelling cannot be learned by ear. Finally, its vocabulary underwent two periods of extensive borrowing, from French in the thirteenth and fourteenth centuries and from Latin in the sixteenth and seventeenth. And even as Boswell wrote, the third period of extensive vocabulary change, resulting from the vast scientific, intellectual, and technological revolutions of the nineteenth and twentieth centuries, was beginning.

GEORGE ORWELL
The Principles of Newspeak[1]

Newspeak was the official language of Oceania and had been devised to meet the ideological needs of Ingsoc, or English Socialism. In the year 1984 there was not as yet anyone who used Newspeak as his sole means of communication, either in speech or writing. The leading articles in the *Times* were written in it, but this was a tour de force which could only be carried out by a specialist. It was expected that Newspeak would have finally superseded Oldspeak (or Standard English, as we should call it) by about the year 2050. Meanwhile it gained ground steadily, all Party members tending to use Newspeak words and grammatical constructions more and more in their everyday speech. The version in use in 1984, and embodied in the Ninth and Tenth Edition of the Newspeak dictionary, was a provisional one, and contained many superfluous words and archaic formations which were due to be suppressed later. It is with the final, perfected version, as embodied in the Eleventh Edition of the dictionary, that we are concerned here.

The purpose of Newspeak was not only to provide a medium of expression for the world-view and mental habits proper to the devotees of Ingsoc, but to make all other modes of thought impossible. It was intended that when Newspeak had been adopted once and for all and Oldspeak forgotten, a heretical thought—that is, a thought diverging from the principles of Ingsoc—should be literally unthinkable, at least so far as thought is dependent on words. Its vocabulary was so constructed as to give exact and often

1. Appendix to *1984*, Orwell's novel about the efforts of his hero, Winston Smith, to preserve his own identity in a totalitarian society of the future ruled by the dictator Big Brother.

very subtle expression to every meaning that a Party member could properly wish to express, while excluding all other meanings and also the possibility of arriving at them by indirect methods. This was done partly by the invention of new words, but chiefly by eliminating undesirable words and by stripping such words as remained of unorthodox meanings, and so far as possible of all secondary meanings whatever. To give a single example. The word *free* still existed in Newspeak, but it could only be used in such statements as "This dog is free from lice" or "This field is free from weeds." It could not be used in its old sense of "politically free" or "intellectually free," since political and intellectual freedom no longer existed even as concepts, and were therefore of necessity nameless. Quite apart from the suppression of definitely heretical words, reduction of vocabulary was regarded as an end in itself, and no word that could be dispensed with was allowed to survive. Newspeak was designed not to extend but to *diminish* the range of thought, and this purpose was indirectly assisted by cutting the choice of words down to a minimum.

Newspeak was founded on the English language as we now know it, though many Newspeak sentences, even when not containing newly created words, would be barely intelligible to an English-speaker of our own day. Newspeak words were divided into three distinct classes, known as the A vocabulary, the B vocabulary (also called compound words), and the C vocabulary. It will be simpler to discuss each class separately, but the grammatical peculiarities of the language can be dealt with in the section devoted to the A vocabulary, since the same rules held good for all three categories.

The A vocabulary. The A vocabulary consisted of words needed for the business of everyday life—for such things as eating, drinking, working, putting on one's clothes, going up and down stairs, riding in vehicles, gardening, cooking, and the like. It was composed almost entirely of words that we already possess—words like *hit*, *run*, *dog*, *tree*, *sugar*, *house*, *field*—but in comparison with the present-day English vocabulary, their number was extremely small, while their meanings were far more rigidly defined. All ambiguities and shades of meaning had been purged out of them. So far as it could be achieved, a Newspeak word of this class was simply a staccato sound expressing *one* clearly understood concept. It would have been quite impossible to use the A vocabulary for literary purposes or for political or philosophical discussion. It was intended only to express simple, purposive thoughts, usually involving concrete objects or physical actions.

The grammar of Newspeak had two outstanding peculiarities. The first of these was an almost complete interchangeability between different parts of speech. Any word in the language (in

principle this applied even to very abstract words such as *if* or *when*)
could be used either as verb, noun, adjective, or adverb. Between
the verb and the noun form, when they were of the same root, there
was never any variation, this rule of itself involving the destruction
of many archaic forms. The word *thought,* for example, did not
exist in Newspeak. Its place was taken by *think,* which did duty for
both noun and verb. No etymological principle was involved here;
in some cases it was the original noun that was chosen for retention,
in other cases the verb. Even where a noun and verb of kindred
meaning were not etymologically connected, one or other of them
was frequently suppressed. There was, for example, no such word
as *cut,* its meaning being sufficiently covered by the noun-verb
knife. Adjectives were formed by adding the suffix *-ful* to the noun-
verb, and adverbs by adding *-wise.* Thus, for example, *speedful*
meant "rapid" and *speedwise* meant "quickly." Certain of our
present-day adjectives, such as *good, strong, big, black, soft,* were
retained, but their total number was very small. There was little
need for them, since almost any adjectival meaning could be arrived
at by adding *-ful* to a noun-verb. None of the now-existing adverbs
was retained, except for a very few already ending in *-wise;* the
-wise termination was invariable. The word *well,* for example, was
replaced by *goodwise.*

In addition, any word—this again applied in principle to every
word in the language—could be negatived by adding the affix *un-,*
or could be strengthened by the affix *plus-,* or, for still greater
emphasis *doubleplus-.* Thus, for example, *uncold* meant "warm,"
while *pluscold* and *doublepluscold* meant, respectively, "very cold"
and "superlatively cold." It was also possible, as in present-day
English, to modify the meaning of almost any word by prepositional affixes such as *ante-, post-, up-, down-,* etc. By such methods
it was found possible to bring about an enormous diminution
of vocabulary. Given, for instance, the word *good,* there was no
need for such a word as *bad,* since the required meaning was
equally well—indeed, better—expressed by *ungood.* All that
was necessary, in any case where two words formed a natural pair
of opposites, was to decide which of them to suppress. *Dark,* for
example, could be replaced by *unlight,* or *light* by *undark,* according to preference.

The second distinguishing mark of Newspeak grammar was its
regularity. Subject to a few exceptions which are mentioned below,
all inflections followed the same rules. Thus, in all verbs the preterit
and the past participle were the same and ended in *-ed.* The preterit
of *steal* was *stealed,* the preterit of *think* was *thinked,* and so on
throughout the language, all such forms as *swam, gave, brought,
spoke, taken,* etc., being abolished. All plurals were made by adding
-s or *-es* as the case might be. The plurals of *man, ox, life* were

mans, oxes, lifes. Comparison of adjectives was invariabiy made by adding *-er, est* (*good, gooder, goodest*), irregular forms and the *more, most* formation being suppressed.

The only classes of words that were still allowed to inflect irregularly were the pronouns, the relatives, the demonstrative adjectives, and the auxiliary verbs. All of these followed their ancient usage, except that *whom* had been scrapped as unnecessary, and the *shall, should* tenses had been dropped, all their uses being covered by *will* and *would.* There were also certain irregularities in word formation arising out of the need for rapid and easy speech. A word which was difficult to utter, or was liable to be incorrectly heard, was held to be ipso facto a bad word; occasionally therefore, for the sake of euphony, extra letters were inserted into a word or an archaic formation was retained. But this need made itself felt chiefly in connection with the B vocabulary. *Why* so great an importance was attached to ease of pronunciation will be made clear later in this essay.

The B vocabulary. The B vocabulary consisted of words which had been deliberately constructed for political purposes: words, that is to say, which not only had in every case a political implication, but were intended to impose a desirable mental attitude upon the person using them. Without a full understanding of the principles of Ingsoc it was difficult to use these words correctly. In some cases they could be translated into Oldspeak, or even into words taken from the A vocabulary, but this usually demanded a long paraphrase and always involved the loss of certain overtones. The B words were a sort of verbal shorthand, often packing whole ranges of ideas into a few syllables, and at the same time more accurate and forcible than ordinary language.

The B words were in all cases compound words.[2] They consisted of two or more words, or portions of words, welded together in an easily pronounceable form. The resulting amalgam was always a noun-verb, and inflected according to the ordinary rules. To take a single example: the word *goodthink,* meaning, very roughly, "orthodoxy," or, if one chose to regard it as a verb, "to think in an orthodox manner." This inflected as follows: noun-verb, *goodthink;* past tense and past participle, *goodthinked;* present participle, *goodthinking;* adjective, *goodthinkful;* adverb, *goodthinkwise;* verbal noun, *goodthinker.*

The B words were not constructed on any etymological plan. The words of which they were made up could be any parts of speech, and could be placed in any order and mutilated in any way which

2. Compound words, such as *speak-write,* were of course to be found in the A vocabulary, but these were merely con-venient abbreviations and had no special ideological color [Orwell's note].

made them easy to pronounce while indicating their derivation. In the word *crimethink* (thought-crime), for instance, the *think* came second, whereas in *thinkpol* (Thought Police) it came first, and in the latter word *police* had lost its second syllable. Because of the greater difficulty in securing euphony, irregular formations were commoner in the B vocabulary than in the A vocabulary. For example, the adjectival forms of *Minitrue, Minipax,* and *Miniluv* were, respectively, *Minitruthful, Minipeaceful,* and *Minilovely,* simply because *-trueful, -paxful,* and *-loveful* were slightly awkward to pronounce. In principle, however, all B words could inflect, and all inflected in exactly the same way.

Some of the B words had highly subtilized meanings, barely intelligible to anyone who had not mastered the language as a whole. Consider, for example, such a typical sentence from a *Times* leading article as *Oldthinkers unbellyfeel Ingsoc.* The shortest rendering that one could make of this in Oldspeak would be: "Those whose ideas were formed before the Revolution cannot have a full emotional understanding of the principles of English Socialism." But this is not an adequate translation. To begin with, in order to grasp the full meaning of the Newspeak sentence quoted above, one would have to have a clear idea of what is meant by Ingsoc. And, in addition, only a person thoroughly grounded in Ingsoc could appreciate the full force of the word *bellyfeel,* which implied a blind, enthusiastic acceptance difficult to imagine today; or of the word *oldthink;* which was inextricably mixed up with the idea of wickedness and decadence. But the special function of certain Newspeak words of which *oldthink* was one, was not so much to *express* meanings as to destroy them. These words, necessarily few in number, had had their meanings extended until they contained within themselves whole batteries of words which, as they were sufficiently covered by a single comprehensive term, could now be scrapped and forgotten. The greatest difficulty facing the compilers of the Newspeak dictionary was not to invent new words, but, having invented them, to make sure what they meant; to make sure, that is to say, what ranges of words they canceled by their existence.

As we have already seen in the case of the word *free,* words which had once borne a heretical meaning were sometimes retained for the sake of convenience, but only with the undesirable meanings purged out of them. Countless other words such as *honor, justice, morality, internationalism, democracy, science,* and *religion* had simply ceased to exist. A few blanket words covered them, and, in covering them, abolished them. All words grouping themselves round the concepts of liberty and equality, for instance, were contained in the single word *crimethink,* while all words grouping themselves round the concepts of objectivity and rationalism were contained in the single word *oldthink.* Greater precision would have been dangerous. What was required in a Party member was an outlook similar to that of the ancient Hebrew who knew, without knowing much else, that all nations other than his own worshipped "false gods." He did not need to know that these gods were called Baal, Osiris, Moloch, Ashtaroth, and the like; probably the less he knew about them the better for his orthodoxy. He knew Jehovah and the commandments of Jehovah; he knew, therefore, that all gods with other names or other attributes were false gods. In somewhat the same way, the Party member knew what constituted right conduct, and in exceedingly vague, generalized terms he knew what kinds of departure from it were possible. His sexual life, for example, was entirely regulated by the two Newspeak words *sexcrime* (sexual immorality) and *goodsex* (chastity). *Sexcrime* covered all sexual misdeeds whatever. It covered fornication, adultery, homosexuality, and other perversions, and, in addition, normal intercourse practiced for its own sake. There was no need to enumerate them separately, since they were all equally culpable, and in principle, all punishable by death. In the C vocabulary, which consisted of scientific and technical words, it might be necessary to give specialized names to certain sexual aberrations, but the ordinary citizen had no need of them. He knew what was meant by *goodsex*—that is to say, normal intercourse between man and wife, for the sole purpose of begetting children, and without physical pleasure on the part of the woman; all else was *sexcrime*. In Newspeak it was seldom possible to follow a heretical thought further than the perception that it *was* heretical; beyond that point the necessary words were non-existent.

No word in the B vocabulary was ideologically neutral. A great many were euphemisms. Such words, for example, as *joycamp* (forced-labor camp) or *Minipax* (Ministry of Peace, i.e., Ministry of War) meant almost the exact opposite of what they appeared to mean. Some words, on the other hand, displayed a frank and contemptuous understanding of the real nature of Oceanic society. An example was *prolefeed*, meaning the rubbishy entertainment and spurious news which the Party handed out to the masses. Other words, again, were ambivalent, having the connotation "good" when applied to the Party and "bad" when applied to its enemies. But in addition there were great numbers of words which at first sight appeared to be mere abbreviations and which derived their ideological color not from their meaning but from their structure.

So far as it could be contrived, everything that had or might have political significance of any kind was fitted into the B vocabulary. The name of every organization, or body of people, or doctrine, or country, or institution, or public building, was invariably cut down into the familiar shape; that is, a single easily pronounced word with the smallest number of syllables that would preserve the original derivation. In the Ministry of Truth, for example, the Records Department, in which Winston Smith worked, was called *Recdep*, the Fiction Department was called *Ficdep*, the Teleprograms Department was called *Teledep*, and so on. This was not done solely with the object of saving time. Even in the early decades of the twentieth century, telescoped words and phrases had been one of the characteristic features of political language; and it had been noticed that the tendency to use abbreviations of this kind was most marked in totalitarian countries and totalitarian organizations. Examples were such words as *Nazi, Gestapo, Comintern, Inprecorr, Agitprop.* In the beginning the practice had been adopted as it were instinctively, but in Newspeak it was used with a conscious purpose. It was perceived that in thus abbreviating a name one narrowed and subtly altered its meaning, by cutting out most of the associations that would otherwise cling to it. The words *Communist International*, for instance, call up a composite picture of universal human brotherhood, red flags, barricades, Karl Marx, and the Paris Commune. The word *Comintern*, on the other hand, suggests merely a tightly knit organization and a well-defined body of doctrine. It refers to something almost as easily recognized, and as limited in purpose, as a chair or a table. *Comintern* is a word that can be uttered almost without taking thought, whereas *Communist International* is a phrase over which one is obliged to linger at least momentarily. In the same way, the associations called up by a word like *Minitrue* are fewer and more controllable than those called up by *Ministry of Truth*. This accounted not only for the habit of abbreviating whenever possible, but also for the almost exaggerated care that was taken to make every word easily pronounceable.

In Newspeak, euphony outweighed every consideration other than exactitude of meaning. Regularity of grammar was always sacrificed to it when it seemed necessary. And rightly so, since what was required, above all for political purposes, were short clipped words of unmistakable meaning which could be uttered rapidly and which roused the minimum of echoes in the speaker's mind. The words of the B vocabulary even gained in force from the fact that nearly all of them were very much alike. Almost invariably these words—*goodthink, Minipax, prolefeed, sexcrime, joycamp, Ingsoc, bellyfeel, thinkpol,* and countless others—were words of two or three syllables, with the stress distributed equally between the first syllable and the last. The use of them encouraged a gabbling style of speech, at once staccato and monotonous. And this was exactly what was aimed at. The intention was to make speech, and especially speech on any subject not ideologically neutral, as nearly as possible independent of consciousness. For the purposes of everyday life it was no doubt necessary, or sometimes necessary, to reflect before speaking, but a Party member called upon to make a political or ethical judgment should be able to spray forth the correct opinions as automatically as a machine gun spraying forth bullets. His training fitted him to do this, the language gave him an almost foolproof instrument, and the texture of the words, with their harsh sound and a certain willful ugliness which was in accord with the spirit of Ingsoc, assisted the process still further.

So did the fact of having very few words to choose from. Relative to our own, the Newspeak vocabulary was tiny, and new ways of reducing it were constantly being devised. Newspeak, indeed, differed from almost all other languages in that its vocabulary grew smaller instead of larger every year. Each reduction was a gain, since the smaller the area of choice, the smaller the temptation to take thought. Ultimately it was hoped to make articulate speech issue from the larynx without involving the higher brain centers at all. This aim was frankly admitted in the Newspeak word *duckspeak*, meaning "to quack like a duck." Like various other words in the B vocabulary, *duckspeak* was ambivalent in meaning. Provided that the opinions which were quacked out were orthodox ones, it implied nothing but praise, and when the *Times* referred to one of the orators of the Party as a *doubleplusgood duckspeaker* it was paying a warm and valued compliment.

The C vocabulary. The C vocabulary was supplementary to the others and consisted entirely of scientific and technical terms. These resembled the scientific terms in use today, and were constructed from the same roots, but the usual care was taken to define them rigidly and strip them of undesirable meanings. They followed the same grammatical rules as the words in the other two vocabularies. Very few of the C words had any currency either in everyday speech or in political speech. Any scientific worker or technician could find all the words he needed in the list devoted to his own specialty, but he seldom had more than a smattering of the words occurring in the other lists. Only a very few words were common to all lists, and there was no vocabulary expressing the function of Science as a habit of mind, or a method of thought, irrespective of its particular branches. There was, indeed, no word for "Science," any meaning that it could possibly bear being already sufficiently covered by the word *Ingsoc*.

From the foregoing account it will be seen that in Newspeak the expression of unorthodox opinions, above a very low level, was well-nigh impossible. It was of course possible to utter heresies of a very crude kind, a species of blasphemy. It would have been possible, for example, to say *Big Brother is ungood*. But this statement, which to an orthodox ear merely conveyed a self-evident absurdity, could not have been sustained by reasoned argument, because the necessary words were not available. Ideas inimical to Ingsoc could only be entertained in a vague wordless form, and could only be named in very broad terms which lumped together and condemned whole groups of heresies without defining them in doing so. One could, in fact, only use Newspeak for unorthodox purposes by illegitimately translating some of the words back into Oldspeak. For example, *All mans are equal* was a possible Newspeak sentence, but only in the same sense in which *All men are redhaired* is a possible Oldspeak sentence. It did not contain a grammatical error, but it expressed a palpable untruth, i.e., that all men are of equal size, weight, or strength. The concept of political equality no longer existed, and this secondary meaning had accordingly been purged out of the word *equal*. In 1984, when Oldspeak was still the normal means of communication, the danger theoretically existed that in using Newspeak words one might remember their original meanings. In practice it was not difficult for any person well grounded in *doublethink* to avoid doing this, but within a couple of generations even the possibility of such a lapse would have vanished. A person growing up with Newspeak as his sole language would no more know that *equal* had once had the secondary meaning of "politically equal," or that *free* had once meant "intellectually free," than, for instance, a person who had never heard of chess would be aware of the secondary meanings attaching to *queen* and *rook*. There would be many crimes and errors which it would be beyond his power to commit, simply because they were nameless and therefore unimaginable. And it was to be foreseen that with the passage of time the distinguishing characteristics of Newspeak would become more and more pronounced—its words growing fewer and fewer, their meanings more and more rigid, and the chance of putting them to improper uses always diminishing.

When Oldspeak had been once and for all superseded, the last link with the past would have been severed. History had already been rewritten, but fragments of the literature of the past survived here and there, imperfectly censored, and so long as one retained one's knowledge of Oldspeak it was possible to read them. In the future such fragments, even if they chanced to survive, would be unintelligible and untranslatable. It was impossible to translate any passage of Oldspeak into Newspeak unless it either referred to some technical process or some very simple everyday action, or was already orthodox (*goodthinkful* would be the Newspeak expression) in tendency. In practice this meant that no book written before approximately 1960 could be translated as a whole. Prerevolutionary literature could only be subjected to ideological translation—that is, alteration in sense as well as language. Take for example the well-known passage from the Declaration of Independence:

> We hold these truths to be self-evident, that all men are created equal, that they are endowed by their Creator with certain inalienable rights, that among these are life, liberty and the pursuit of happiness. That to

secure these rights, Governments are instituted among men, deriving their powers from the consent of the governed. That whenever any form of Government becomes destructive of those ends, it is the right of the People to alter or abolish it, and to institute new Government...

It would have been quite impossible to render this into Newspeak while keeping to the sense of the original. The nearest one could come to doing so would be to swallow the whole passage up in the single word *crimethink*. A full translation could only be an ideological translation, whereby Jefferson's words would be changed into a panegyric on absolute government.

A good deal of the literature of the past was, indeed, already being transformed in this way. Considerations of prestige made it desirable to preserve the memory of certain historical figures, while at the same time bringing their achievements into line with the philosophy of Ingsoc. Various writers, such as Shakespeare, Milton, Swift, Byron, Dickens and some others were therefore in process of translation; when the task had been completed, their original writings, with all else that survived of the literature of the past, would be destroyed. These translations were a slow and difficult business, and it was not expected that they would be finished before the first or second decade of the twenty-first century. There were also large quantities of merely utilitarian literature—indispensable technical manuals and the like—that had to be treated in the same way. It was chiefly in order to allow time for the preliminary work of translation that the final adoption of Newspeak had been fixed for so late a date as 2050.

QUESTIONS

1. What is the purpose of Newspeak? What assumptions about the nature and uses of language make it possible to try to accomplish that purpose?

2. Why are three vocabularies necessary in Newspeak? How do they differ and what do they have in common? Are there comparable divisions into "vocabularies" in present-day English?

3. In the A vocabulary what, if anything, is lost by such substitutions as "ungood" for "bad," "unlight" for "dark," etc.? Why are the forms for verb inflections and for comparison of adjectives all made consistent?

4. In the B vocabulary why are all the words compound words? Why are words telescoped as much as possible? How do the purposes represented by these two facts about the B vocabulary differ from the purposes of language as we know it?

5. Why is there no word for science in the C vocabulary, although it is described as consisting "entirely of scientific and technical terms"?

6. Find a brief passage (from the Album of Styles, pp. 214–229, or the section On Ethics) and translate it into Newspeak.

ALFRED NORTH WHITEHEAD
On Style[1]

Finally, there should grow the most austere of all mental qualities; I mean the sense for style. It is an aesthetic sense, based on admiration for the direct attainment of a foreseen end, simply and without waste. Style in art, style in literature, style in science, style in logic, style in practical execution have fundamentally the same aesthetic qualities, namely, attainment and restraint. The love of a subject in itself and for itself, where it is not the sleepy pleasure of pacing a mental quarter-deck, is the love of style as manifested in that study.

Here we are brought back to the position from which we started, the utility of education. Style, in its finest sense, is the last acquirement of the educated mind; it is also the most useful. It pervades the whole being. The administrator with a sense for style hates waste; the engineer with a sense for style economizes his material; the artisan with a sense for style prefers good work. Style is the ultimate morality of mind.

But above style, and above knowledge, there is something, a vague shape like fate above the Greek gods. That something is Power. Style is the fashioning of power, the restraining of power. But, after all, the power of attainment of the desired end is fundamental. The first thing is to get there. Do not bother about your style, but solve your problem, justify the ways of God to man, administer your province, or do whatever else is set before you.

Where, then, does style help? In this, with style the end is attained without side issues, without raising undesirable inflammations. With style you attain your end and nothing but your end. With style the effect of your activity is calculable, and foresight is the last gift of gods to men. With style your power is increased, for your mind is not distracted with irrelevancies, and you are more likely to attain your object. Now style is the exclusive privilege of the expert. Whoever heard of the style of an amateur painter, of the style of an amateur poet? Style is always the product of specialist study, the peculiar contribution of specialism to culture.

1. From Chapter 1 of *The Aims of Education*, 1929.

J. ROBERT OPPENHEIMER
On Style[1]

The problem of doing justice to the implicit, the imponderable, and the unknown is of course not unique to politics. It is always with us in science, it is with us in the most trivial of personal affairs, and it is one of the great problems of writing and of all forms of art. The means by which it is solved is sometimes called style. It is style which complements affirmation with limitation and with humility; it is style which makes it possible to act effectively, but not absolutely; it is style which, in the domain of foreign policy, enables us to find a harmony between the pursuit of ends essential to us and the regard for the views, the sensibilities, the aspirations of those to whom the problem may appear in another light; it is style which is the deference that action pays to uncertainty; it is above all style through which power defers to reason.

1. From a speech (1948) entitled "The Open Mind," later included in a book of the same name.

WALKER GIBSON
A Note on Style and the Limits of Language[1]

Questions about style can most usefully be approached if we think of a style as the expression of a personality. I do not mean at all that our words necessarily reveal what we are "really like." I do mean that every writer and talker, more or less consciously, chooses a role which he thinks appropriate to express for a given time and situation. The personality I am expressing in this written sentence is not the same as the one I orally express to my three-year-old who at this moment is bent on climbing onto my typewriter. For each of these two situations, I choose a different "voice," a different mask, in order to accomplish what I want accomplished. There is no point in asking here which of these voices is closer to the Real Me. What may be worth asking is this: what kinds of voices, in written prose, may be said to respond most sensitively and efficiently to the sort of contemporary world that this book has been describing?

First, let's be logical about it. Given the kind of dilemma with respect to knowledge and language that this book defines, what sort of style might we *expect* in our own time? What sort of speaking

1. Conclusion of *The Limits of Language*, 1962.

voice adopted by the writer, what mask, would be appropriate in a world where, as we have seen, the very nature of nature may be inexpressible? If we live in a pluralistic and fluxlike universe, what manner of word-man should we become in order to talk about it? Well, we might at least expect a man who knows his limits, who admits the inevitably subjective character of his wisdom. We might expect a man who knows that he has no right in a final sense to consider himself any wiser than the next fellow, including the one he is talking to. The appropriate tone, therefore, might be informal, a little tense and self-conscious perhaps, but genial as between equals. With our modern relativistic ideas about the impossibility of determining any "standard dialect" for expressing Truth in all its forms, we might expect the cautious writer to employ many dialects, to shift from formal to colloquial diction, to avoid the slightest hint of authoritarianism. The rhythm of his words will be an irregular, conversational rhythm—not the symmetrical periods of formal Victorian prose. Short sentences alternating erratically with longer sentences. Occasional sentence fragments. In sum we might expect a style rather like *this!*[2]

This style, indeed, is easily recognizable and can be discovered all around us in modern prose. Thirty years ago in a book called *Modern Prose Style*, Bonamy Dobrée described it much as we have done here. "Most of us have ceased to believe, except provisionally, in truths," he wrote, "and we feel that what is important is not so much truth as the way our minds move toward truth." The consequence is a kind of self-searching need for frankness and humility on the part of the writer. "The modern prose-writer, in returning to the rhythms of everyday speech, is trying to be more honest with himself than if he used, as is too wreckingly easy, the forms and terms already published as the expression of other people's minds." Finally, in a touching sentence, "In our present confusion our only hope is to be scrupulously honest with ourselves." That was written in 1933: since then the confusion has multiplied spectacularly, while our hopes of ever being "scrupulously honest" about anything look pretty dim. Still, the relation Dobrée made, between an intellectual difficulty and a style, is essentially the relation we are making here.

The trouble with it—and a reminder of the awful complexity of our subject—is that sometimes this proposition simply doesn't work. Some contemporary writers, sensitively aware of the limits of language, indeed conceding them explicitly, nevertheless write in a *style*

2. A few of the writer's obvious attempts to echo a conversational tone in that paragraph can be quickly summarized. Contractions (let's). Colloquialisms (well . . ., the next fellow). Some very short sentences. Capitalization in an effort to place an ironical turn on a Big Fat Abstraction (Truth)—an effort that is of course much easier to accomplish with the actual voice. Italics (*except*, like *this!*), again in mimicry of the way one speaks in conversation. And so on. The purpose of such devices, to compensate for the loss of oral intonation, is strictly speaking impossible to achieve. If only you were here I could *say* all this to you [Gibson's note].

that sounds like the wisdom of Moses, or like Winston Churchill. Far from echoing the rhythms of ordinary speech, they pontificate or chant in authoritarian rhythms the assertion that one cannot be authoritarian. We have a fine example of this paradox in the paragraph by Oppenheimer that I have so much admired (page 187). Oppenheimer uses a vocabulary, sentence structure, tone, and rhythm all highly structured and formalized; there is no unbending there. The theme of his discourse—that style is "the deference that action pays to uncertainty"—seems at odds with the *personality* we hear uttering this theme. That personality, because of the way the words are chosen and arranged, appears curiously self-confident, even dictatorial, with echoes perhaps of Johnsonian prose, or Macaulay's elegant sentences. Thus the first sentence is built around a handsome triplet of alliterative abstractions ("the implicit, the imponderable, and the unknown"); the second sentence is built out of another triplet of nicely balanced clauses. The extraordinary final sentence approaches incantation in its parallel repetitions of structure. The "voice" we hear, remote indeed from ordinary conversation, seems to *know* even as it asserts its own humility. Different readers will explain all this in different ways: some will argue that the traditional manner lends sincerity and persuasiveness to the message, while others will be set off by what they consider a real discrepancy between matter and manner. We recall that the passage was taken from an address delivered at a formal occasion. I have heard Mr. Oppenheimer's platform manner described as "arrogant"; our stylistic observations might well account in part for such an impression. In any case it is clear that no easy formula—Dobrée's or anyone else's—is going to account for all the vagaries of modern prose.

Other writers in this collection will illustrate Dobrée's thesis with less embarrassment—that is, will show clear evidence of a "conversational" voice. Thus Muller:

> Emerson remarked that it is a good thing, now and then, to take a look at the landscape from between one's legs. Although this stunt might seem pointless when things are already topsy-turvy, it can be the more helpful then. One may say that what this chaotic world needs first of all is *dis*-sociation; by breaking up factitious alliances and oppositions, one may get at the deep uniformities. Or...

The simplicity of the diction in that first sentence, and the absurdity of the described action, support a familiar relation of equality between the speaking voice and the reader. There is no talking down; we all know who Emerson is. (Not "That great American Transcendentalist, Ralph Waldo Emerson. . . .") "Now and then," "stunt," "topsy-turvy" contribute the colloquial touch. The slightly awkward "then" at the end of the second sentence suggests that in this particular communication formal grace would be inappropriate. But with the third sentence the writer boldly shifts his tone as his diction becomes more polysyllabic and his sentence structure more complex. "Enough of geniality," he seems to say, "you must now follow me into a serious tangle." With this abruptness, Muller is perhaps "breaking up factitious alliances" *in his style*, so that his own prose both expresses and dramatizes the point he is making.

The trick, if that is what it is, of mingling formal and colloquial vocabulary can convey a kind of ironical thrust by the writer at his own pretensions. Thus he can have it both ways—make his great assertion and kid himself for his own gall. It is a device much employed in circles that are verbally sophisticated, including academic circles. Consider an extreme example, from a professor of law at Chicago, here discussing a flexible approach to problems of judicial interpretation:

> But it leads to *good* rules of law and in the main toward flexible ones, so that most cases of a given type can come to be handled not only well but easily, and so that the odd case can normally come in also for a smidgeon of relief. The whole setup leads above all—a recognition of imperfection in language and in officer—to *on-going and unceasing judicial review of prior judicial decision* on the side of rule, tool, and technique. That, plus freedom and duty to do justice *with* the rules but *within* both them and their whole temper, that is the freedom, the leeway for own-contribution, the scope for the person, which the system offers.[3]

Here style and message work with a degree of co-operation: a call for unceasing flexibility in the operations of judicial review is expressed in an idiom that is itself almost wildly flexible. The speaker in this passage betrays the strains of an impassioned conversationalist, with his heavy reliance on italics and his interrupted sentence structures. We are buttonholed. This is a technical discussion, and most of the vocabulary has to be fairly heavy, but we have "smidgeon" and "whole setup" to cut across the formality. We have even a jazzy bit of alliteration and rhyme—"rule, tool, and technique." The "recognition of imperfection in language," therefore, which is explicitly granted by the text, is implicitly conveyed as well by the unorthodox scramblings of language. Nobody has to like this style (many are simply irritated), but at least one can see what is going on, and why.

Or consider another extreme example, from a professor of English at Wisconsin, here discussing problems of usage:

> Bad, fair, good, better, best. Only the best is Correct. No busy man can be Correct. But his wife can. That's what women are for. That's why we have women to teach English and type our letters and go to church for us and discover for us that the English say "Aren't I?" while we sinfully hunt golf-balls in the rough on Sunday and, when our partner finds two of them, ask "Which is me?" (Webster: *colloq.*—Professor K of Harvard: I speak colloq myself, and sometimes I write it.) . . . Only a few of us today are aware of the other scales of English usage. It is our business to

3. From Karl N. Llewellyn, *The Common Law Tradition: Deciding Appeals*, Little, Brown, 1960 [Gibson's note].

consciously know about their social utility.[4]

These sentences from a treatise on language admirably demonstrate that self-consciously unbuttoned informality which the subject nowadays seems to demand. To some, again, it will appear offensively "cute," idiosyncratic. Short sentences, some without predicates, surround one almost endless rambling sentence. The ironical capital in Correct (cf. Truth *supra*). Indifference to the rule that pronouns should have specific antecedents ("That's what women are for. That's why . . ."). Muddled number in using personal pronouns (we hunt golf balls, our partner [sing.] finds, [we] ask 'Which is me?'). Deliberately split infinitive in the last sentence quoted, at a point in the utterance when a conventionally formal tone has begun to enter. We may anticipate, I am sure, a time when writers will endeavor to carefully split their infinitives, at whatever cost in awkwardness, just as writers of a former generation endeavored so elaborately to avoid the "error." All this should prove to at least be amusing.

To many readers, the style displayed by a Professor Llewellyn or a Professor Joos will seem undisciplined, vulgar, and chaotic. A sign of academic deterioration. A result of wild "permissiveness" in education and in society generally. But such readers will be missing the point. There is nothing indiscriminately permissive in this style, but the writers do accept and reject different kinds of language from those accepted and rejected by traditional stylists. They express different personalities. Without insisting on the merits of these particular passages, which are certainly debatable, it ought nevertheless to be clear that you do not write in this way simply by saying anything that occurs to you. The process of selection can be, indeed, *more* discriminating because the available supply of language and experience is larger. As this is being written, in the autumn of 1961, a mild flurry about such extensions of language is going on in the press, relating to the publication of a new edition of Webster's *New International Dictionary*. The New York *Times* has editorialized as follows:

A passel of double-domes at the G. & C. Merriam Company joint in Springfield, Mass., have been confabbing and yakking for twenty-seven years—which is not intended to infer that they have not been doing plenty work—and now they have finalized Webster's Third New International Dictionary, Unabridged, a new edition of that swell and esteemed word book.

Those who regard the foregoing paragraph as acceptable English prose will find that the new Webster's is just the dictionary for them. The words in that paragraph all are listed in the new work with no suggestion that they are anything·but standard.

Webster's has, it is apparent, surrendered to the permissive school that has been busily extending its beachhead on English instruction in the schools. This development is disastrous....

4. From Martin Joos, *The Five Clocks*. Copyright 1961 by Martin Joos [Gibson's note].

The *Times* goes on to acknowledge "the lexical explosion that has showered us with so many words in recent years," and to congratulate the Dictionary for including 100,000 new words or new definitions. "These are improvements, but they cannot outweigh the fundamental fault." Webster's has always been a "peerless authority on American English," and therefore its editors have "to some degree a public responsibility." "A new start is needed."

There is, I think, something wrong about all this. If you are acknowledging a "lexical explosion," a language changing with accelerating rapidity, then it seems rather difficult to insist at the same time on a "peerless authority." The editors of the Dictionary may have fulfilled their public responsibility by taking the only wise course—by including as many new words and definitions as they could without making "authoritative" judgments about "standard," "colloquial," and "slang." This is not to say that the modern writer ignores such distinctions; on the contrary he is sensitively aware of them as never before. But he knows, and the dictionary editors know, that no such label is good for long in a culture as volatile as this one. Yesterday's slang is today's standard, and the writer who remains resonant to these shifts has at his disposal a huge and varicolored vocabulary for his art.

The reason we call that opening paragraph in the *Times* editorial "unacceptable English" is not that it contains slang. The reason is that it contains too many kinds of slang at once, without any awareness of their differences. You do not say "passel of double-domes" unless you have some good reason for juxtaposing terms from utterly distinct language worlds. "Passel" is presumably of western-frontier origin and now has a kind of weary whimsy about it, while "double-domes" is recent, cheaply anti-intellectual, with a history something like "egghead" but without the popular acceptance of "egghead." It is conceivable that these words could be included in one sentence, but it would take more skill that the *Times* man has employed. Of course the appearance of clumsiness was just what served his purpose.

Meanwhile the writer who looks backward to "authority," who takes a static view of Standard Language, is likely to sound like the "straight" paragraphs of that editorial. The voice there is closer to a chiding or dictatorial professor than were the voices of the actual professors quoted. And when such a writer uses "modern" terms, he uses them in ways that are long overused before he gets to them—ways like "extending its beachhead on English instruction" or "lexical explosion that has showered us with so many words." It is this sort of thing that is the true vulgarity in our time.

Nevertheless our society remains generous with half-conscious concessions to the imperfections of its language. It may be, for example, that the language of the beatniks, especially their oral conventions, could be looked at in the light of such concessions. Consider just one curious symptom of jive-talk (now dated)—the suffix-plus-prefix *like.* "We came to this big town like and all the streets were like crazy, man." This attempt at rendering beat dialect is doubtless inaccurate but it should serve to make the point. That point is that the beats have (deliberately?) modified or qualified their nouns and adjectives by suggesting that they are not quite accurate, not quite the way things are. "This big town like"—it is a one-ended metaphor. Like what? We have a tenor but no vehicle, or is it a vehicle without a tenor? I have been told that many beats are determinedly antiverbal, preferring to listen to jazz while lying on beaches in Zenlike silence. It fits. The skepticism about the validity of words that "like" implies is a peculiarly twentieth-century skepticism, it seems to me, though there may be analogies with other ages such as the seventeenth century, when scientific developments encouraged similar self-scrutinies and self-doubts. In any event the beats, in their crude and sloppy way of course, have surrounded much of their language with a metaphorical blur by using (among other things) the simple device of "like." They suggest, with this blur, their convicton of the impossibility of anybody else's doing any better with words. Only squares believe you can speak "precisely."

The complexities of experience do occasionally get faced one way or another—if not with the beats' pose of inarticulateness, then with some other pose that will serve to avoid the charge of *really knowing.* Modern novelists adopt a "point of view" which is often no point of view at all, but several points of view from which to indicate various inadequate interpretations of various fictitious characters. It is a technique that will show how two novels as apparently unlike as *The Waves*[5] * * * and Faulkner's *As I Lay Dying* belong after all to the same age. There is no narrator, no one of whom the reader might conceivably say, "There! That's the author talking." The technique is not new; there is *The Ring and the Book,* to mention one example. But the difference is that when you read *The Ring and the Book,* you feel how firmly and finally Browning is on Pompilia's "side," in spite of his wonderful multiplicity throughout that great poem. Whereas in many modern novels you scarcely know who is on anybody's side—you must simply flow in the flux. Sometimes it is so lifelike you can hardly stand it.

And of course that road—the road of chaos chaotically expressing chaos—is a dead end of imitative form where we end with a grunt, or maybe a whimper. The very point is that language will never say our experience "as is," and recognizing this truth, we have immense freedom of possibility to make, create, form what we can out of words or out of anything else. The most elaborate of villanelles is not much further removed from Real Life than the latest Allen Gins-

5. A novel by Virginia Woolf, 1931.

berg[6] poem, or a slice of Mr. Bloom's day.[7] So write a villanelle if that
will meet your need. But whatever it is, there remains this simple
blasphemy to be avoided, and that is the blasphemy of ignoring the
limits, of assuming that one's words do indeed tell the reader what is
going on. There is an important sense in which nobody knows what
he is talking about.

I hope I do not except myself and everything uttered here.

6. Author of unconventional poems
such as *Howl*, 1956.
7. A day in the life of Leopold Bloom,
conveyed mainly through interior monologue, provides the framework of James
Joyce's novel *Ulysses*, 1922.

QUESTIONS

1. Explain the importance of Gibson's distinction between a
   "speaking voice" and a "real" personality.
2. Examine several of the selections in *Personal Report* (pp. 1–95)
   or the *Album of Styles* (pp. 214–229) and characterize the
   speaking voice of each. Compare one or two of these with the
   "voices" of the letters (pp. 434–452) or the journals (pp. 96–115).
3. Gibson refers to Oppenheimer's definition of style (p. 189). How
   closely does the definition of style that Gibson implies correspond with Oppenheimer's? Where do the two differ?
4. Write two brief descriptions of the same scene (or person or
   object or event), using a different "voice" for each. What advantages can one "voice" have over another for handling a given
   subject?

W. SOMERSET MAUGHAM
Lucidity, Simplicity, Euphony[1]

I have never had much patience with the writers who claim from
the reader an effort to understand their meaning. You have only to
go to the great philosophers to see that it is possible to express with
lucidity the most subtle reflections. You may find it difficult to
understand the thought of Hume, and if you have no philosophical
training its implications will doubtless escape you; but no one with
any education at all can fail to understand exactly what the meaning
of each sentence is. Few people have written English with more
grace than Berkeley. There are two sorts of obscurity that you find
in writers. One is due to negligence and the other to willfulness.
People often write obscurely because they have never taken the trouble to learn to write clearly. This sort of obscurity you find too often

1. Chapters 11, 12, and 13 of *The Summing Up*, 1938.

in modern philosophers, in men of science, and even in literary critics. Here it is indeed strange. You would have thought that men who passed their lives in the study of the great masters of literature would be sufficiently sensitive to the beauty of language to write if not beautifully at least with perspicuity. Yet you will find in their works sentence after sentence that you must read twice to discover the sense. Often you can only guess at it, for the writers have evidently not said what they intended.

Another cause of obscurity is that the writer is himself not quite sure of his meaning. He has a vague impression of what he wants to say, but has not, either from lack of mental power or from laziness, exactly formulated it in his mind and it is natural enough that he should not find a precise expression for a confused idea. This is due largely to the fact that many writers think, not before, but as they write. The pen originates the thought. The disadvantage of this, and indeed it is a danger against which the author must be always on his guard, is that there is a sort of magic in the written word. The idea acquires substance by taking on a visible nature, and then stands in the way of its own clarification. But this sort of obscurity merges very easily into the willful. Some writers who do not think clearly are inclined to suppose that their thoughts have a significance greater than at first sight appears. It is flattering to believe that they are too profound to be expressed so clearly that all who run may read, and very naturally it does not occur to such writers that the fault is with their own minds which have not the faculty of precise reflection. Here again the magic of the written word obtains. It is very easy to persuade oneself that a phrase that one does not quite understand may mean a great deal more than one realizes. From this there is only a little way to go to fall into the habit of setting down one's impressions in all their original vagueness. Fools can always be found to discover a hidden sense in them. There is another form of willful obscurity that masquerades as aristocratic exclusiveness. The author wraps his meaning in mystery so that the vulgar shall not participate in it. His soul is a secret garden into which the elect may penetrate only after overcoming a number of perilous obstacles. But this kind of obscurity is not only pretentious; it is short-sighted. For time plays it an odd trick. If the sense is meagre time reduces it to a meaningless verbiage that no one thinks of reading. This is the fate that has befallen the lucubrations of those French writers who were seduced by the example of Guillaume Apollinaire. But occasionally it throws a sharp cold light on what had seemed profound and thus discloses the fact that these contortions of language disguised very commonplace notions. There are few of Mallarmé's poems now that are not clear; one cannot fail to notice that his thought singularly lacked originality. Some of his phrases were beautiful; the materials of his verse were the poetic platitudes of his day.

Simplicity is not such an obvious merit as lucidity. I have aimed at it because I have no gift for richness. Within limits I admire richness in others, though I find it difficult to digest in quantity. I can read one page of Ruskin with delight, but twenty only with weariness. The rolling period, the stately epithet, the noun rich in poetic associations, the subordinate clauses that give the sentence weight and magnificence, the grandeur like that of wave following wave in the open sea; there is no doubt that in all this there is something inspiring. Words thus strung together fall on the ear like music. The appeal is sensuous rather than intellectual, and the beauty of the sound leads you easily to conclude that you need not bother about the meaning. But words are tyrannical things, they exist for their meanings, and if you will not pay attention to these, you cannot pay attention at all. Your mind wanders. This kind of writing demands a subject that will suit it. It is surely out of place to write in the grand style of inconsiderable things. No one wrote in this manner with greater success than Sir Thomas Browne, but even he did not always escape this pitfall. In the last chapter of *Hydriotaphia* the matter, which is the destiny of man, wonderfully fits the baroque splendor of the language, and here the Norwich doctor produced a piece of prose that has never been surpassed in our literature; but when he describes the finding of his urns in the same splendid manner the effect (at least to my taste) is less happy. When a modern writer is grandiloquent to tell you whether or no a little trollop shall hop into bed with a commonplace young man you are right to be disgusted.

But if richness needs gifts with which everyone is not endowed, simplicity by no means comes by nature. To achieve it needs rigid discipline. So far as I know ours is the only language in which it has been found necessary to give a name to the piece of prose which is described as the purple patch; it would not have been necessary to do so unless it were characteristic. English prose is elaborate rather than simple. It was not always so. Nothing could be more racy, straightforward and alive than the prose of Shakespeare; but it must be remembered that this was dialogue written to be spoken. We do not know how he would have written if like Corneille he had composed prefaces to his plays. It may be that they would have been as euphuistic as the letters of Queen Elizabeth. But earlier prose, the prose of Sir Thomas More, for instance, is neither ponderous, flowery nor oratorical. It smacks of the English soil. To my mind King James's Bible has been a very harmful influence on English prose. I am not so stupid as to deny its great beauty. It is majestical. But the Bible is an oriental book. Its alien imagery has nothing to do with us. Those hyperboles, those luscious metaphors, are foreign to our genius. I cannot but think that not the least of the misfortunes that the Secession from Rome brought upon the spiritual life of our country is that this work for so long a period became the daily, and with many the only, reading of our people. Those rhythms, that powerful vocabulary, that grandiloquence, became part and parcel of the national sensibility. The plain, honest English speech was overwhelmed with ornament. Blunt Englishmen twisted their tongues to speak like Hebrew prophets. There was evidently something in the English temper to which this was congenial, perhaps a native lack of precision in thought, perhaps a naïve delight in fine words for their own sake, an innate eccentricity and love of embroidery, I do not know; but the fact remains that ever since, English prose has had to struggle against the tendency to luxuriance. When from time to time the spirit of the language has reasserted itself, as it did with Dryden and the writers of Queen Anne, it was only to be submerged once more by the pomposities of Gibbon and Dr. Johnson. When English prose recovered simplicity with Hazlitt, the Shelley of the letters and Charles Lamb at his best, it lost it again with De Quincey, Carlyle, Meredith and Walter Pater. It is obvious that the grand style is more striking than the plain. Indeed many people think that a style that does not attract notice is not style. They will admire Walter Pater's, but will read an essay by Matthew Arnold without giving a moment's attention to the elegance, distinction and sobriety with which he set down what he had to say.

The dictum that the style is the man is well known. It is one of those aphorisms that say too much to mean a great deal. Where is the man in Goethe, in his birdlike lyrics or in his clumsy prose? And Hazlitt? But I suppose that if a man has a confused mind he will write in a confused way, if his temper is capricious his prose will be fantastical, and if he has a quick, darting intelligence that is reminded by the matter in hand of a hundred things, he will, unless he has great self-control, load his pages with metaphor and simile. There is a great difference between the magniloquence of the Jacobean writters, who were intoxicated with the new wealth that had lately been brought into the language, and the turgidity of Gibbon and Dr. Johnson, who were the victims of bad theories. I can read every word that Dr. Johnson wrote with delight, for he had good sense, charm and wit. No one could have written better if he had not willfully set himself to write in the grand style. He knew good English when he saw it. No critic has praised Dryden's prose more aptly. He said of him that he appeared to have no art other than that of expressing with clearness what he thought with vigor. And one of his Lives he finished with the words: "Whoever wishes to attain an English style, familiar but not coarse, and elegant but not ostentatious, must give his days and nights to the volumes of Addison." But when he himself sat down to write it was with a very different aim. He mistook the orotund for the dignified. He had not the good breeding to see that simplicity and naturalness are the truest marks of distinction.

For to write good prose is an affair of good manners. It is, unlike verse, a civil art. Poetry is baroque. Baroque is tragic, massive and mystical. It is elemental. It demands depth and insight. I cannot but feel that the prose writers of the baroque period, the authors of King James's Bible, Sir Thomas Browne, Glanville, were poets who had lost their way. Prose is a rococo art. It needs taste rather than power, decorum rather than inspiration and vigor rather than grandeur. Form for the poet is the bit and the bridle without which (unless you are an acrobat) you cannot ride your horse; but for the writer of prose it is the chassis without which your car does not exist. It is not an accident that the best prose was written when rococo with its elegance and moderation, at its birth attained its greatest excellence. For rococo was evolved when baroque had become declamatory and the world, tired of the stupendous, asked for restraint. It was the natural expression of persons who valued a civilized life. Humor, tolerance and horse sense made the great tragic issues that had pre-occupied the first half of the seventeenth century seem excessive. The world was a more comfortable place to live in and perhaps for the first time in centuries the cultivated classes could sit back and enjoy their leisure. It has been said that good prose should resemble the conversation of a well-bred man. Conversation is only possible when men's minds are free from pressing anxieties. Their lives must be reasonably secure and they must have no grave concern about their souls. They must attach importance to the refinements of civilization. They must value courtesy, they must pay attention to their persons (and have we not also been told that good prose should be like the clothes of a well-dressed man, appropriate but unobtrusive?), they must fear to bore, they must be neither flippant nor solemn, but always apt; and they must look upon "enthusiasm" with a critical glance. This is a soil very suitable for prose. It is not to be wondered at that it gave a fitting opportunity for the appearance of the best writer of prose that our modern world has seen, Voltaire. The writers of English, perhaps owing to the poetic nature of the language, have seldom reached the excellence that seems to have come so naturally to him. It is in so far as they have approached the ease, sobriety and precision of the great French masters that they are admirable.

Whether you ascribe importance to euphony, the last of the three characteristics that I mentioned, must depend on the sensitiveness of your ear. A great many readers, and many admirable writers, are devoid of this quality. Poets as we know have always made a great use of alliteration. They are persuaded that the repetition of a sound gives an effect of beauty. I do not think it does so in prose. It seems to me that in prose alliteration should be used only for a special reason; when used by accident it falls on the ear very disagreeably. But its accidental use is so common that one can only suppose that the sound of it is not universally offensive. Many writers without distress will put two rhyming words together, join a monstrous long adjective to a monstrous long noun, or between the end of one word and the beginning of another have a conjunction of consonants that almost breaks your jaw. These are trivial and obvious instances. I mention them only to prove that if careful writers can do such things it is only because they have no ear. Words have weight, sound and appearance; it is only by considering these that you can write a sentence that is good to look at and good to listen to.

I have read many books on English prose, but have found it hard to profit by them; for the most part they are vague, unduly theoretical, and often scolding. But you cannot say this of Fowler's *Dictionary of Modern English Usage.* It is a valuable work. I do not think anyone writes so well that he cannot learn much from it. It is lively reading. Fowler liked simplicity, straightforwardness and common sense. He had no patience with pretentiousness. He had a sound feeling that idiom was the backbone of a language and he was all for the racy phrase. He was no slavish admirer of logic and was willing enough to give usage right of way through the exact demesnes of grammar. English grammar is very difficult and few writers have avoided making mistakes in it. So heedful a writer as Henry James, for instance, on occasion wrote so ungrammatically that a schoolmaster, finding such errors in a schoolboy's essay, would be justly indignant. It is necessary to know grammar, and it is better to write grammatically than not, but it is well to remember that grammar is common speech formulated. Usage is the only test. I would prefer a phrase that was easy and unaffected to a phrase that was grammatical. One of the differences between French and English is that in French you can be grammatical with complete naturalness, but in English not invariably. It is a difficulty in writing English that the sound of the living voice dominates the look of the printed word. I have given the matter of style a great deal of thought and have taken great pains. I have written few pages that I feel I could not improve and far too many that I have left with dissatisfaction because, try as I would, I could do no better. I cannot say of myself what Johnson said of Pope: "He never passed a fault unamended by indifference, nor quitted it by despair." I do not write as I want to; I write as I can.

But Fowler had no ear. He did not see that simplicity may sometimes make concessions to euphony. I do not think a far-fetched, an archaic or even an affected word is out of place when it sounds better than the blunt, obvious one or when it gives a sentence a better balance. But, I hasten to add, though I think you may without misgiving make this concession to pleasant sound, I think you should make none to what may obscure your meaning. Anything is better than not to write clearly. There is nothing to be said against lucidity, and against simplicity only the possibility of dryness. This is a risk that is well worth taking when you reflect how much better it is to be bald than to wear a curly wig. But there is in euphony a danger that must be considered. It is very likely to be monotonous. When George Moore began to write, his style was poor; it gave you the impression that he wrote on wrapping paper with a blunt pencil. But he developed gradually a very musical English. He learnt to write sentences that fall away on the ear with a misty languor and it delighted him so much that he could never have enough of it. He did not escape monotony. It is like the sound of water lapping a shingly beach, so soothing that you presently cease to be sensible of it. It is so mellifluous that you hanker for some harshness, for an abrupt dissonance, that will interrupt the silky concord. I do not know how one can guard against this. I suppose the best chance is to have a more lively faculty of boredom than one's readers so that one is wearied before they are. One must always be on the watch for mannerisms and when certain cadences come too easily to the pen ask oneself whether they have not become mechanical. It is very hard to discover the exact point where the idiom one has formed to express oneself has lost its tang. As Dr. Johnson said: "He that has once studiously formed a style, rarely writes afterwards with complete ease." Admirably as I think Matthew Arnold's style was suited to his particular purposes, I must admit that his mannerisms are often irritating. His style was an instrument that he had forged once for all; it was not like the human hand capable of performing a variety of actions.

If you could write lucidly, simply, euphoniously and yet with liveliness you would write perfectly: you would write like Voltaire. And yet we know how fatal the pursuit of liveliness may be: it may result in the tiresome acrobatics of Meredith. Macaulay and Carlyle were in their different ways arresting; but at the heavy cost of naturalness. Their flashy effects distract the mind. They destroy their persuasiveness; you would not believe a man was very intent on ploughing a furrow if he carried a hoop with him and jumped through it at every other step. A good style should show no sign of effort. What is written should seem a happy accident. I think no one in France now writes more admirably than Colette, and such is the ease of her expression that you cannot bring yourself to believe that she takes any trouble over it. I am told that there are pianists who have a natural technique so that they can play in a manner that most executants can achieve only as the result of unremitting toil, and I am willing to believe that there are writers who are equally fortunate. Among them I was much inclined to place Colette. I asked her. I was exceedingly surprised to hear that she wrote everything over and over again. She told me that she would often spend a whole morning working upon a single page. But it does not matter how one gets the effect of ease. For my part, if I get it at all, it is only by strenuous effort. Nature seldom provides me with the word, the turn of phrase, that is appropriate without being far-fetched or common-place.

QUESTIONS

Maugham draws attention to the two conflicting yet complementary approaches to style that have been traditional in literary criticism. One approach maintains that style is primarily a combination of qualities and devices that can be learned and produced; the other, that "style is the man," the reflection in language of a personality with all its attitudes and idiosyncracies. Using passages from *An Album of Styles* (pp. 214–229), explore the two approaches. In any given passage what appears as impersonal technique or device, what as reflecting the special temperament or character of the author?

W. K. WIMSATT
Style as Meaning[1]

"Betwixt the formation of words and that of thought there is this difference," said Cicero, "that that of the words is destroyed if you change them, that of the thoughts remains, whatever words you think proper to use."[2] This is a clear statement of the view of style and meaning which today may be conveniently called "the ornamental." The ancient rhetoricians all seem to have something like this in mind.[3] They may stress the need of meaning, or may in their metaphysics insist on the interdependence of matter and form, but when they reach the surface of meaning, the plane of most detailed organization, they are not able to speak so as to connect this with meaning. It is as if, when all is said for meaning, there remains an irreducible something that is superficial, a kind of scum—which they call style. One may consult as representative the whole treatment of rhetorical figures in Quintilian's *Institute*.

There is the opposite theory of style, one that has been growing on us since the seventeenth century. "So many things, almost in an

1. Introduction to *The Prose Style of Samuel Johnson*, 1941.
2. *De Oratore*, III, lii, in *Cicero on Oratory and Orators*, ed. J. S. Watson (New York, 1890), p. 252 [Wimsatt's note].
3. Cf. Benedetto Croce, *Aesthetic as Science of Expression and General Linguistic*, trans. Douglas Ainslee (London, 1929), pp. 422-9 [Wimsatt's note].

equal number of words," says Sprat.[4] And Pascal, "La vraie éloquence se moque de l'éloquence."[5] And somewhat later Swift, "Proper words in proper places, make the true definition of a style";[6] and Buffon, "Style is simply the order and movement one gives to one's thoughts."[7] By the nineteenth century the doctrine is proclaimed on every hand—very explicitly, for example, by Cardinal Newman:

Thought and speech are inseparable from each other. Matter and expression are parts of one: style is a thinking out into language.... When we can separate light and illumination, life and motion, the convex and the concave of a curve...then will it be conceivable that the...intellect should renounce its own double.[8]

In one of the best books on style to appear in our own day, Mr. Middleton Murry has said:

Style is not an isolable quality of writing; it is writing itself.[9]

It is hardly necessary to adduce proof that the doctrine of identity of style and meaning is today firmly established. This doctrine is, I take it, one from which a modern theorist hardly can escape, or hardly wishes to.

The chief difficulty with the modern doctrine of style lies in its application to rhetorical study. The difficulty appears in two ways: partly in the implicit abandonment of the doctrine when rhetorical study is attempted, but more largely in a wide, silent rejection of the whole system of rhetoric. "We have done with the theory of style," proclaims an eminent critic in Crocean vein, "with meta-

4. Thomas Sprat, *History of the Royal Society* (London, 1702), p. 113. Cf. Richard F. Jones, "Science and English Prose Style in the Third Quarter of the Seventeenth Century," *PMLA*, XLV (1930), 977-1009 [Wimsatt's note].

5. *Pensées*, VII, 34, ed. Ernest Havet (Paris, 1866), Vol. I, p. 106; cf. VII, 28, *op. cit.*, Vol. I, p. 105 [Wimsatt's note].

6. *A Letter to a Young Clergyman, Lately Entered into Holy Orders*, 1721, *Prose Works*, ed. Temple Scott (London, 1898), III, 200-01 [Wimsatt's note].

7. *An Address Delivered Before the French Academy* [generally known as the *Discours sur le Style*], 1753, in Lane Cooper, *Theories of Style* (New York, 1907), p. 171. This, rather than the too-often-quoted "The style is the man," is Buffon's real definition of style —a point well taken by W. C. Brownell, *The Genius of Style* (New York, 1924), p. 46 [Wimsatt's note].

8. "Literature, a Lecture in the School of Philosophy and Letters." 1858, in *The Idea of a University* (London, 1907), pp. 276-7. In Lane Cooper's *Theories of Style* one may conveniently find similar expressions by Coleridge, Wackernagel, De Quincey,

Schopenhauer, Lewes, Pater, and Brunetière (esp. pp. 10, 207, 222-3, 252, 320, 391, 399, 401, 422). See also *Pensées de J. Joubert*, ed. Paul Raynal (Paris, 1888), II, 275-8, Titre XXII, paragraphs IX–XXV; August Boeckh, *Encyklopädie und Methodologie der Philologischen Wissenschaften* (Leipzig, 1886), p. 128.

For the opposite way of thinking, see William Minto, *Manual of English Prose Literature* (Edinburgh and London, 1881) (first published in 1872), Introduction, pp. 14–15; George Saintsbury, "Modern English Prose," 1876, in *Miscellaneous Essays* (London, 1892), pp. 83, 84, 99 [Wimsatt's note].

9. J. Middleton Murry, *The Problem of Style* (Oxford, 1922), p. 77; cf. pp. 16, 71. Cf. Walter Raleigh, *Style* (London, 1897), esp. p. 62; Herbert Read, *English Prose Style* (London, 1932), *passim*. Mr. Logan Pearsall Smith would probably admit that the rich and poetic prose for which he pleads is as much a matter of expression as the plainest (*S.P.E. Tract No. XLVI, Fine Writing* [Oxford, 1936], esp. pp. 203, 220). For a cross-section of opinion from modern professional writers, see Burges Johnson, *Good Writing* (Syracuse University, 1932) [Wimsatt's note].

phor, simile, and all the paraphernalia of Graeco-Roman rhetoric."[1] Now it must be contended that we have not done with "metaphor"—that we still have an important use for the term. But for scarcely any other term of rhetoric have we better than a shrug. We no longer are willing to take seriously a set of terms which once —for centuries—were taken seriously, and which must, no matter how unhappy their use, have stood for something. In throwing away the terms it is even possible we have thrown away all definite concept of the things they once stood for. The realities of antithesis and climax, for example, are perhaps less and less a part of our consciousness. But literary history without these old realities and their terms is impossible; without an evaluation of them it is superficial. The fact is that Cicero used "figures" of this and that sort—moreover, he wrote criticism about them. Hooker and Donne and Johnson used such figures too. And the old terms when used to describe these old writings do mean something. We cannot avoid admitting that we recognize certain things as denoted by the terms, that we know the nominal definitions. Furthermore, we are not ready to call Cicero and the rest simply bad writers. We may insist, and properly, that the accounts they give of their devices, their theories of rhetoric, are insufficient—even baneful as guides to composition; as for the living use they made of what they called "devices," their actual saying of things, in this we see that their intuition was better than their theory.

ii

Any discourse about a definition of "style" is fruitless if it concerns itself too simply with protesting: style *is this* or *is that*. Definitions are impervious to the "lie direct," mere "intrenchant air" for the sword of evidence. The only reason a term should mean something is the history of its application, the fact that it has meant something. We may say that dubious terms have a kind of repertoire of related meanings. But the meaning of a term in a given instance is what any man decides to make it, and if I dislike what he makes it, I may not tell him he is mistaken.

Nevertheless I may dislike it, and justly. This is the problem in facing definitions—that they do often bother us as bad definitions and make us wish vehemently to reject them. The basis for our uneasiness is ultimately one of relevance, relevance of a definition to the principles of the whole science of which the term is accepted as a part. If there is not a fixed real meaning for a term, there is at least an ideal one, a something to which the term should refer if it is to be used in its science without producing nonsense. It is the purpose of definition to determine *what* is referred to, and the business of him who formulates a definition to determine what should

1. J. E. Spingarn, *Creative Criticism* (New York, 1917), p. 30 [Wimsatt's note].

be referred to, as most relevant to the presiding science. The first step toward forming a definition, a theory, of "style" must be taken in the science of literary esthetics, more specifically in a consideration of the nature of words as esthetic medium.

It is the nature of words to mean. To consider words only as sounds, like drum taps, or to consider written letters as patterned objects, as in alphabet soup, is the same as to consider a Stradivarius as material for kindling wood. There is, to be sure, a certain truth in the contention that it is useless to speak of the limits of each art. If a painter of abstractions succeeded in conveying a concept which he described as rhythmic, it would be pointless to contend that such a concept should properly be expressed in music. Insofar as the painting did succeed as an expression, there would simply be *that* expression. On the other hand, even Croce will admit that different artistic intuitions need different media for their "externalization."[2] Even when the various media are considered as forming a continuum, a spectrum, one point in the spectrum is not another point. Red is not green. Stone is not B flat. Stone can be used for a statue; B flat cannot. Words can be used to "mean" in a way that nothing else can. In various senses the other arts may be called expressive or communicative. But it is not in any such senses that words are expressive. When Maritain says that "music imitates with sound and rhythms . . . the movements of the soul,"[3] and when Dewey says that architecture " 'expresses' . . . enduring values of collective human life,"[4] they are speaking of the kind of representation we should speak of if we said that the images of autumn, nightfall, and a dying fire in Shakespeare's sonnet stand for his sense of mortality, or if we said that the whole poem is a symbol of his sense of mortality. While the music and the architecture *are* the symbols of what they represent, the words of a writing must *express* a meaning which *is* a symbol. "A poem should not mean But be," writes Mr. Archibald MacLeish. But a poem cannot *be* in the simple sense that a statue or a piece of Venetian glass *is*. For each thing insofar as it *is*, must *be*, have *being*, according to its nature. The nature of words is to mean, and a poem *is* through its meaning.

There are such things as the Caroline shape poems, the winged or altar shapes of Herbert or Quarles; there are the typographical oddities of E. E. Cummings. There are illuminated manuscripts or illustrated books, Gothic books of Gospels, arabesque texts of the Koran on mosque walls. And people may even have wondered what

2. Benedetto Croce, *op. cit.*, pp. 114–16. Cf. C. K. Ogden *et al.*, *The Foundations of Aesthetics* (London, 1925), p. 28; David Daiches, *The Place of Meaning in Poetry* (Edinburgh, 1935), esp. pp. 30, 61–3 [Wimsatt's note].

3. Jacques Maritain, *Art and Scholasticism*, trans. J. F. Scanlan (London,

1930), p. 58 [Wimsatt's note].

4. John Dewey, *Art as Experience* (New York, 1934), p. 221. Cf. Gilbert Murray, "An Essay on the Theory of Poetry," *Yale Review*, x (1921), 484; Theodore M. Greene, *The Arts and the Art of Criticism* (Princeton, 1940), esp. p. 108 [Wimsatt's note].

they ought to think of Cummings. But nobody thinks that the Gospel suffers when not read in the Book of Kells. It is clear that in the case of illuminations and illustrations of a text there is not a single art expression, but two running side by side. Words, music, costume, and stage may make one expression in an opera; the poetry of Vachel Lindsay read aloud and the accompanying dance may have made one expression; it may be possible to conceive a text so referred to and interrelated with a series of pictures that the two make one expression.[5] Yet it remains true that what we call literature, whether prose or poetry, has not been a graphic medium. It has not been possible or worthwhile to employ words in this way.

But language is spoken before it is written; even after it is written it is implicitly spoken; and language as sound has potentialities far beyond those of language as written or visual.[6] Sound is in some sense the medium of literature, no matter how words are considered as expressive. What is more questionable is how near this medium ever can come to being that of music. Sound in its conventional semantic value is certainly not a musical medium. Further it is not musical in its whole complex of suggestive or directly imitative values, onomatopoeia, and all the more mysteriously felt shades of sound propriety.[7]

A more difficult problem of sound in literature is that of meter and such associates as rhyme and alliteration. But it is usual to insist that these elements of verse are in some way expressive. They express the emotion of poetic experience; or, by inducing in us a pattern of expectancy and playing against that the surprise of variation, they make us realize more intensely both sense and emotion. Or, the verse of a whole poem may be considered as a form, an aspect or way of being known, which gives unity and particularity to the whole—makes it the special poetic symbol that it is.[8] It may be possible to say that this second kind of expressiveness is on the same level as that of music and architecture mentioned above, a

---

5. Mr. Archibald MacLeish's *Land of the Free* (New York, 1938) is "a book of photographs illustrated by a poem. . . . The original purpose had been to write some sort of text to which these photographs might serve as commentary. But so great was the power and the stubborn inward livingness of these vivid American documents that the result was a reversal of that plan" (p. 89) [Wimsatt's note].

6. Cf. Otto Jespersen, *Language, Its Nature, Development and Origin* (London, 1922), *passim;* D. W. Prall, *Aesthetic Judgment* (New York, 1929), pp. 289–90.

7. Many of these values, as a matter of fact, are not, as has been commonly thought, due to any direct expressiveness of sounds but rather to linguistic analogies as ancient as the roots of language (Leonard Bloomfield, *Language* [New York, 1933] pp. 244–5: I. A. Richards, *The Philosophy of Rhetoric* [New York, 1936], pp. 63-5). For a treatment of word sounds as suggestive of or appropriate to meaning, see Otto Jespersen, *Language* (London, 1922), pp. 396–406 [Wimsatt's note].

Cf. I. A. Richards, *Principles of Literary Criticism* (New York, 1934), "Rhythm and Metre," pp. 137–42. It may be too that meter has a hypnotic function. See Edward D. Snyder, *Hypnotic Poetry* (Philadelphia, 1930), pp. 19, 39 ff. [Wimsatt's note].

8. Cf. Lascelles Abercrombie, *Principles of English Prosody* (London, 1923), pp. 15–18, 31; *The Theory of Poetry* (New York, 1926), pp. 70, 95, 138, 140–6 [Wimsatt's note].

direct symbol of experience. But in this case it will be necessary to remember that the expression of the verse coalesces with and is in effect the same as that of the words in their semantic function.

Here we might let the question of language as sound medium rest were it not for the persistent appearance of the mysterious critical term "prose rhythm." From what has been said of verse it is plain that a prose rhythm is conceivable—that is, some alternation of sounds akin to meter, though more variable. If such a succession of sounds could be detected with certainty in any body of prose, and if one had no sense that this was unconnected with the meaning or detracted from it, then it would have to be admitted that in the given case a prose rhythm as an expressive medium did exist. The general question, then, is not whether there can be a prose rhythm but whether there is. And a particular question, such as that concerning English literature, is but the general question narrowed—whether there is. Certain things may be asserted: 1) The rhetoricians of antiquity found in Greek and Latin oratory a rhythm which they analyzed almost as definitely as verse meter, particularly in the sequence of syllables ending clauses, the cursus.[9] 2) The cursus was also a part of Medieval Latin prose.[1] 3) There are some who hold that variations of the cursus occur in English prose.[2] 4) There is, however, no agreement, but the widest divergence of opinion, among those who have made extended studies of the nature of rhythm in English prose. Their number is not small (and each is at odds in some respect with almost all the others): those who would scan, or make meter; those who are interested in some vaguer kind of periodicity, time measurement; those who rely on the cursus; and those who find rhythm in the movement of phrases.[3]

9. See, for example, John W. Sandys, *A Companion to Latin Studies* (Cambridge, 1921), p. 655. François Novotny, *État Actuel des Études sur le Rhythme de la Prose Latine* (Livów, 1929), sees "un bel avenir dans notre science," but confesses: "Ces essais et leur résultats dépendent bien souvent du sentiment esthétique subjectif de l'observateur" (p. 33) [Wimsatt's note].

1. See, for example, Karl Strecker, *Introduction à l'Étude du Latin Médiéval*, trad. par Paul van der Woestijne (Gand, 1933), pp. 51–3; Edouard Norden, *Die Antike Kunstpros*a (Leipzig, 1898), II, 950–1 [Wimsatt's note].

2. See, for example, Oliver Elton, "English Prose Numbers," *Essays and Studies by Members of the English Association*, IV (Oxford, 1913), 29–54; Morris W. Croll, "The Cadence of English Oratorical Prose," *Studies in Philology*, XVI (1919), 1–55 [Wimsatt's note].

3. Cf. John Hubert Scott, *Rhythmic Prose*, "University of Iowa Humanistic Studies," Vol. III, No. 1 (Iowa City, 1925), p. 11. Norton R. Tempest, a more recent writer, is a scanner and at the same time belongs to the cursus school (*The Rhythm of English Prose* [Cambridge University Press, 1930], p. 134). André Classe is a timer with a kymograph, who proposes "only . . . to investigate the question of rhythm from the phonetic point of view" (*The Rhythm of English Prose* [Oxford, 1939], pp. 1, 4, 135). Such investigation doubtless does discover physical facts, but just as phoneticians distinguish between the gross acoustic quality of words and that part of the acoustic quality which has semantic value, so literary students may distinguish between the gross discoverable physical facts about "rhythm" and that part of the facts which relates to expression. Professor Sapir has distinguished between the phonetic and the esthetic analysis of rhythm ("The Musical Foundations of Verse," *Journal of English and Germanic Philology*, XX [1921], 223–4 [Wimsatt's note].

It would be within the province only of a very special investigation to dare say what English prose rhythm is. And I have admitted
above that the question is not whether there can be a prose
rhythm. Yet there are some things that can be said about the possibilities of prose rhythm. If it is a quality of sound, it is either
expressive of something or not. If not (if, say, it is like the number
of times the letter "t" occurs on a given page), it is not a medium
of art and therefore claims no interest; it is not in fact prose
rhythm at all. Secondly, if it is expressive, it expresses either the
same meaning as the words do otherwise, or it does not. If it
expresses the same meaning, it may, like meter, express perhaps
from the same level as words do otherwise, perhaps from a level
more like that of music. These possibilities are admissible.[4] But
thirdly, if it expresses other than the same meaning, then it must
express some meaning which is proper to nonverbal sounds—some
kind of musical meaning. This is perhaps conceivable, that words
should do two separate things, convey their language meaning, and
at the same time be a nonlinguistic tune—perhaps even harmonious
with the language meaning. This, however, seems improbable in
view of the limited musical value of spoken word sounds. It is like
the pictorial value of print in typographical poems, very slight.[5]
Music is not written words, but in tones and time.

The notion of a separate music is further crippled if we consider
that it is impossible for any system of sound in prose to be unconnected with its meaning—that is, neither contribute to it nor
detract from it. Suppose a man to be writing a double composition,
both prose and music; then in the use of any given piece of language he must, consciously or unconsciously, choose for the meaning or for the music. (It is impossible that two such disconnected
effects should often coincide.) Or, to change the sense of "must,"
he must choose for the meaning and sacrifice the music, for the
meaning of words is their nature, while the music of words is negligible. "In the vast majority of those words which can be said to
have an independent musical value," says Mr. Middleton Murry,
"the musical suggestion is at odds with the meaning. When the
musical suggestion is allowed to predominate, decadence of style
has begun."[6]

4. Under this head, rather than under
what follows, should be considered meter in prose, in Dickens, for example.
Here there is a linguistic expressiveness, just as in poetry, but not a coales-
cence, as in poetry, with the rest of
the meaning of the words. Cf. *post* pp.
209–11, what I call "bad style." For
some flagrant examples of meter in
prose, see H. W. and F. G. Fowler, *The
King's English* (Oxford, 1906), p. 295
[Wimsatt's note].

5. Cf. D. W. Prall, *Aesthetic Judgment* (New York, 1929), pp. 289, 295;

Aesthetic Analysis (New York, 1936),
pp. 105–6 [Wimsatt's note].

6. J. Middleton Murry, *The Problem
of Style* (Oxford, 1922), p. 86. And it
seems to me that this is also true of
criticism: when the musical suggestion
predominates, decadence has begun. The
authors of books on prose rhythm are
aware of their danger but they cannot
save themselves. See, for example, William M. Patterson, *The Rhythm of
Prose* (New York, 1916), p. 84; John
Hubert Scott, *op. cit.*, pp. 24, 36–7,
127, 133 [Wimsatt's note].

Let me close this part of the discussion by indicating my own notion of what ought to be called prose rhythm—if something must be called that. The notion has been well expressed by H. W. Fowler: "A sentence or a passage is rhythmical if, when said aloud, it falls naturally into groups of words each well fitted by its length & intonation for its place in the whole & its relation to its neighbors. Rhythm is not a matter of counting syllables & measuring the distance between accents."[7] Prose rhythm is a matter of emphasis; it is putting the important words where they sound important. It is a matter of coherence; it is putting the right idea in the right place.[8]

"Rhythm" as applied to prose is a metaphor. "Rhythm," when used literally, means "measure" or "regularity," and since the movement of good prose is precisely not regular but varied with the sense, the union of the terms "prose" and "rhythm" has been none the happiest.

iii

A first step toward a theory of style might be the reflection that one may say different things about the same topic—or different things which are very much alike.[9] A rose and a poppy are different, but both are flowers. Sidney writes, "Come sleep! O sleep, the certain knot of peace, etc." Shakespeare writes, "O sleep, O gentle sleep, Nature's soft nurse, etc.," and again, "Sleep that knits up the ravell'd sleave of care, etc." It is not that these writers have had the same meaning and have "dressed" it, or expressed it, differently. Rather they have had the same subject, the benefits of sleep, or beneficent sleep, but have had different thoughts, different meanings, which have found expression in different language. They have expressed different, if similar, meanings. Even Betterton, when he recasts one of Shakespeare's passages on sleep, has not merely re-expressed the same meaning; he has actually changed the meaning. Different words make different meanings.

It is true that meanings is not identical with words.[1] Meaning is

---

7. *A Dictionary of Modern English Usage* (Oxford, 1927), "Rhythm," p. 504 [Wimsatt's note].

8. Mr. Ezra Pound says: "The attainment of a style consists in so knowing words that one will communicate the various parts of what one says with the various degrees and weights of importance which one wishes" (*Guide to Kulchur*, quoted in *Times Literary Supplement*, xxxvii [1938], p. 489) [Wimsatt's note].

For a detailed study of inversion of subject and predicate and position of adverbs in English according to sense, see August Western, *On Sentence-Rhythm and Word-Order in Modern English* (Christiania, 1908), esp. p. 9. P. Fijn van Draat, "The Place of the Adverb, A Study in Rhythm," *Neophil-*

ologus, vi (1921), 56–88, esp. 62, 87, admits Western's general principle but would connect certain variations not with sense but with "rhythmic formulas."

9. Cf. A. C. Bradley, *Poetry for Poetry's Sake* (Oxford, 1901), pp. 12–13 [Wimsatt's note].

1. Cf. Alfred North Whitehead, *Modes of Thought* (New York, 1938), pp. 48–9; Alan H. Gardiner, *The Theory of Speech and Language* (Oxford, 1932), p. 70; Edward Sapir, *Language* (New York, 1921), pp. 14, 238; I. A. Richards, *The Philosophy of Rhetoric* (New York, 1936), p. 13; Louis H. Gray, *Foundations of Language* (New York, 1939), pp. 88, 93–4 [Wimsatt's note].

the psychic entity, the something in the mind—for which material is not adequate. In the language of the scholastics: *Voces referuntur ad res significandas mediante conceptione intellectus.*[2] Nevertheless, words do determine meanings relentlessly. To come at it another way, meanings vary persistently with variations of words.[3] It may be well to recall one of Newman's figures, "the convex and the concave of a curve." The convex is not the concave, but if we conceive the curve as a line, then every change in the concave produces a corresponding change in the convex. There is that much truth in the contention of Croce: "Language is a perpetual creation. What has been linguistically expressed is not repeated. . . . Language is not an arsenal of arms already made, and it is not a vocabulary, a collection of abstractions, or a cemetery of corpses more or less well embalmed."[4]

We may be tempted to believe that we have at length distilled words or style away from meaning when we think of bad style. It might be plausible and would probably be useful to formulate some rule like this: Style occurs in isolation only when it is bad, when it fails to coincide with meaning.[5] This might be almost the truth where writing is so bad that it is meaningless—for example, in errors of expression made by one unfamiliar with a language, matters of syntax and elementary vocabulary. But poor expression in the wider sense cannot be reduced to this. The nature of words is against it—their constant tendency to mean. It is not as if we could forget or fail to put meaning in words. They persist in meaning, no matter what we intend or are conscious of. We may fail to say what we intend, but we can scarcely fail to say something.

Bad style is not a deviation of words from meaning, but a deviation of meaning from meaning. Of what meaning from what meaning? Of the actually conveyed meaning (what a reader receives) from the meaning an author intended or ought to have intended.

2. St. Thomas Aquinas, *Summa Theologica*, I, q. 13, a. 1, quoted by Désiré Cardinal Mercier, *A Manual of Modern Scholastic Philosophy* (London, 1919), II, 154. Cf. Alan H. Gardiner, *op. cit.*, pp. 44 ff., 70 ff., 102–3 [Wimsatt's note].

3. The term "meaning" as I am using it may be taken to include all that Ogden and Richards have divided into different kinds of language meaning—the really referential, symbolic, intellectual meaning, and the group of emotive meanings (C. K. Ogden and I. A. Richards, *The Meaning of Meaning* [New York, 1936], pp. 11–12, 126, 186–7, 224–30). Obviously if such is the meaning to which we refer, if we are thinking of works of literature, not treatises of mathematics or philosophy, it is much easier to see how meaning depends on the very words in which

it is cast. I choose not to emphasize this, however, because, as will be seen shortly, some of the effects of style in which I am interested are very slightly if at all dependent on emotive meaning [Wimsatt's note].

4. *Op. cit.*, pp. 150–1; cf. p. 68, on translation. Cf. Leone Vivante, *Intelligence in Expression* (London, 1925), pp. 2–3 [Wimsatt's note].

5. Frederick Schlegel has said: "Although, in strict application and rigid expression, thought and speech always are, and always must be regarded as two things metaphysically distinct,—yet there only can we find these two elements in disunion, where one or both have been employed imperfectly or amiss" (*Lectures on the History of Literature* [New York, 1841], pp. 7–8) [Wimsatt's note].

This is true even of those cases where we might be most tempted to say that the fault of style is mere "awkwardness," since the meaning is conveyed completely. In such cases, the awkwardness consists in some absence of meaning (usually but implicit) or in some contrary or irrelevant meaning, which we disregard, inferring the writer's real meaning, at least so far as it would be explicit. We must do this so continually for most writing—seek out the meaning, put the most relevant construction on every word and phrase, disregard what tries to say the wrong thing—that we fail to sense any lack of meaning and dub the cause of our annoyance metaphorically and conveniently "awkwardness."

The question what the author ought to have said is the true difficulty in judging style. *Ut jam nunc dicat*, says Horace, *jam nunc debentia dici*.[6] It is the only difficulty, for it is the only question, and it is one we implicitly answer every time we judge style. We do it by our sense, more or less definite, of what the author intends to say as a whole, of his central and presiding purpose. The only consideration that can determine an author in a given detail is the adequacy of the detail to his whole purpose.[7] It does not follow that when we are sure this or that phrase or passage is bad style we shall always refer our judgment precisely to our impression of the whole.[8] The steps in subordination are too complicated. Furthermore, a fault in one whole can have something in common with a fault in another whole; whence arises the classification of faults of style and a tendency to refer individual faults only to the class definition.[9] The whole is usually forgotten.

From the foregoing one may begin to infer that a detailed study of style can be fruitful—even in the hands of those who least connect style with meaning. If faults can be classed, so to some extent can merits. That which has for centuries been called style differs from the rest of writing only in that it is one plane or level of the organization of meaning; it would not be happy to call it the outer cover or the last layer; rather it is the furthest elaboration of the one concept that is the center. As such it can be considered. The terms of rhetoric, spurned by Croce and other moderns, did have a

---

6. "To say what ought to be said, and at the proper time." The quotation is from *The Art of Poetry*.

7. H. B. Lathrop, in arguing that emphasis is an aspect of coherence, and coherence an aspect of unity, has shown admirably how the school-book terms may be squared with this philosophy of style ("Unity, Coherence, and Emphasis," *University of Wisconsin Studies in Language and Literature*, No. 2, *Studies by Members of the Department of English* [Madison, 1918], pp. 77–98 [Wimsatt's note].

8. For small faults of inconsistency and irrelevancy in a composition largely good, one would have to examine only a short section of the surrounding text. At the other extreme might be a composition by a schoolboy, where one could guess the central meaning only from the title or from what the schoolboy said when asked, or where there might not be any at all [Wimsatt's note].

9. An operation essential to the economy of thinking, but one which can lead to error when the reason for considering the class as faulty is forgotten, and faults of one type of whole are referred to another—for example, when what would be a fault in a poem of heroic couplets is adduced against the verse of *Christabel* [Wimsatt's note].

value for the ancients, even though they failed to connect all of rhetoric with meaning. To give the terms of rhetoric a value in modern criticism it would be necessary only to determine the expressiveness of the things in language to which the terms refer. This has been done for metaphor, which used to be an ornament, but has now been made "the unique expression of a writer's individual vision" or "the result of the search for a precise epithet."[1] Mr. Empson has spoken ingeniously of that highly "artificial" figure the zeugma.[2] Mr. Bateson has praised a hypallage.[3]

The greatest obstacle to recognizing the expressive value of rhetorical devices is the fact that they recur. One notices that Cicero uses a *litotes* or a *praeteritio*[4] several times in a few pages, or so many hundreds of balances are counted in the *Ramblers* of Johnson. This suggests play with words, disregard of meaning. One is likely to reflect: if these devices express something, then the author must be expressing, or saying, much the same thing over and over—which is useless; therefore the author is really not trying to say anything; he is using words viciously, for an inexpressive purpose.

Such an attitude would not have been possible if the theoretical rhetoricians had not thrust forward the repertory of devices so as to throw them out of focus and conceal their nature as part of language. No one thinks, for example, that sentences because they recur are artificial, that they say the same thing over or say nothing. This is the key to what our attitude toward devices ought to be. Sentences are expressive; so also are declensions, and conjugations; they are expressive forms.[5] They express, not ideas like "grass" or "green," but relations. The so-called "devices," really no more devices than a sentence is a device, express more special forms of meaning, not so common to thinking that they cannot be avoided, like the sentence, but common enough to reappear frequently in certain types of thinking and hence to characterize the thinking, or the style. They express a kind of meaning[6] which may

1. J. Middleton Murry, *The Problem of Style* (Oxford, 1922), pp. 13, 83 [Wimsatt's note].

2. William Empson, *Seven Types of Ambiguity* (New York, 1931), pp. 89–90 [Wimsatt's note].

3. F. W. Bateson, *English Poetry and the English Language* (Oxford, 1934), p. 22 [Wimsatt's note]. Hypallage is the transferring of an epithet from the more to the less natural part of a group of nouns (as when Spenser speaks of "Sansfoy's dead dowry" rather than "the dead Sansfoy's dowry").

4. Litotes is a kind of understatement, often one in which something is asserted by negation of the contrary ("not a few," "not unkind"); praeteritio is a kind of omission in which a brief mention emphasizes what is omitted ("I confine to this page the volume of his treacheries").

5. Cf. Alan H. Gardiner, *The Theory of Speech and Language* (Oxford, 1932), pp. 130–4, 158–61 [Wimsatt's note].

6. The better modern treatments of rhetoric have recognized this. See, for example, Alexander Bain, *English Composition and Rhetoric* (New York, 1886), esp. pp. 20–64, though it is hard to think the doctrine of expressiveness is an abiding principle when he says that one of the functions of metaphor is to "give an agreeable surprise" (pp. 30–1). For a treatment of figures as common elements of speech, see James B. Greenough and George L. Kittredge, *Words and Their Ways in English Speech* (New York, 1901), pp. 14–17 [Wimsatt's note].

be discussed as legitimately as the more obvious kinds such as what a man writes about—the vanity of human wishes or the River Duddon.

It might be better if the term "device" were never used, for its use leads almost immediately to the carelessness of thinking of words as separable practicably from meaning. That is, we think of a given meaning as if it may be weakly expressed in one way but more forcefully in another. The latter is the device—the language applied, like a jack or clamp, or any dead thing, to the meaning, which itself remains static and unchanged, whether or not the device succeeds in expressing it. There is some convenience in this way of thinking, but more philosophy in steadily realizing that each change of words changes the meaning actually expressed. It is better to think of the "weak" expression and the "strong" expression as two quite different expressions, or, elliptically, two different meanings, of which one is farther from, one nearer to, what the author ought to say, or what he intends to say. The whole matter of emphasis, which is the real truth behind Herbert Spencer's wooden theory of economy in words, seems to be best considered in this light. (To keep the mind from being fatigued while receiving ideas—this is Spencer's function for style.[7] One may object that the most important thing about the mind is not that it can be fatigued—but that it can entertain splendid, though often difficult and fatiguing, conceptions.) If a word is to be placed here or there in a sentence in order to be effective, to have due weight, this ought to be thought of not as a juggling of words round a meaning to give the meaning emphatic expression, but as a choice of a more emphatic rather than a less emphatic meaning, or, strictly, the choice of the meaning needed, for meaning exists through emphasis; a change of emphasis is a change of meaning. We must preserve a notion of words, even in their most purely suggestive functions, as something transparently intellectual, not intervening between us and the meaning but luminous and full of their meaning and as if conscious of it.

The expressiveness of the rhetorical device is not always so easily analyzed as that of the sentence or declension—frequently it is a form of implicit expressiveness, one which is certainly present but not simply in virtue of meanings of words or of syntax or of morphology. For example, one of the most frequent forms of implicit expressiveness, or meaning, is that of equality or likeness—with its opposite, inequality or unlikeness. Any succession of words, phrases, or sentences must in any given degree be either like or unlike, and

---

7. "The Philosophy of Style," in Lane Cooper's *Theories of Style* (New York, 1907), pp. 273–4. What if a passage were read twice or pondered at length? Would it not lose most of its force—through being relieved of the duty of preventing our misconceptions? Spencer's essay appeared first in the *Westminster Review* of 1852 [Wimsatt's note].

appropriately or inappropriately so in accordance with whether the successive explicit meanings are like or unlike. The "jingles" collected by H. W. and F. G. Fowler[8] are admirable illustrations of the fault which consists in a likeness of word sounds and hence of implicit meaning where there is no corresponding explicit meaning to be sustained. "To read his tales is a baptism of optimism," they quote from the *Times*. Here there is a nasty jingle of "ptism," "ptimism"—nasty just because the two combinations so nearly alike strive to make these words parallel, whereas they are not; one qualifies the other. The case is even plainer if we take an example of the common "ly" jingle, "He lived practically exclusively on milk," and set beside it something like this: "We are swallowed up, irreparably, irrevocably, irrecoverably, irremediably."[9] In the second we are not conscious of the repeated "ly" as a jingle, any more than of the repeated "irre." The reason is that behind each of these parallel sounds (implicit parallel meanings) there is a parallel explicit meaning. So far as we advert to the sounds as sounds at all it is with a sense of their concordance with the structure of meaning. Such is perhaps the most frequently underlying reason why expressions are approved of or objected to as "euphonious" or "cacophonous," "harmonious" or "inharmonious."

And matters of sound are not the only ones to which the principle of equality and inequality applies. Even so basically wrong a thing as parataxis, the monotony of a schoolboy's writing, consists just in that he is using the same form of meaning in successive clauses and hence fails to relate his meanings, that is, fails to express the really different meanings which lurk dimly in his mind as his real intention or are at least what he should intend. Hypotaxis, the rare-sounding opposite of parataxis, but no other than all modulated writing, consists in the use of different forms of meaning to sustain the sequence of the complex whole meaning * * *.

8. *The King's English* (Oxford, 1906), p. 291. Cf. H. W. Fowler, *A Dictionary of Modern English Usage* (Oxford, 1927), "Jingles," pp. 308–9 [Wimsatt's note].

9. The first is from E. F. Benson, quoted in *The King's English*, p. 292; the second, from John Donne, Sermon LXVI, in *Donne's Sermons*, ed. Logan Pearsall Smith (Oxford, 1919), p. 10 [Wimsatt's note].

AN ALBUM OF STYLES

I

The wind is sometime plain up and down, which is commonly most certain, and requireth least knowledge, wherein a mean shooter, with mean gear, if he can shoot home, may make best shift. A side wind trieth an archer and good gear very much. Sometime it bloweth aloft, sometime hard by the ground; sometime it bloweth by blasts, and sometime it continueth all in one; sometime full side wind, sometime quarter with him, and more; and likewise against him, as a man with casting up light grass, or else if he take good heed, shall sensibly learn by the experience. To see the wind with a man his eyes it is unpossible, the nature of it is so fine and subtile; yet this experience of the wind had I once myself, and that was in the great snow that fell four years ago. I rode in the high way betwixt Topcliff-upon-Swale and Boroughbridge, the way being somewhat trodden before, by wayfaring men; the fields on both sides were plain, and lay almost yard-deep with snow; the night afore had been a little frost, so that the snow was hard and crusted above; that morning the sun shone bright and clear, the wind was whistling aloft, and sharp, according to the time of the year; the snow in the high way lay loose and trodden with horses' feet; so as the wind blew, it took the loose snow with it, and made it so slide upon the snow in the field, which was hard and crusted by reason of the frost over night, that thereby I might see very well the whole nature of the wind as it blew that day. And I had a great delight and pleasure to mark it, which maketh me now far better to remember it. Sometime the wind would be not past two yards broad, and so it would carry the snow as far as I could see. Another time the snow would blow over half the field at once. Sometime the snow would tumble softly; by and by it would fly wonderful fast. And this I perceived also, that the wind goeth by streams, and not whole together. For I should see one stream within a score on me; then the space of two score, no snow would stir; but, after so much quantity of ground, another stream of snow, at the same very time, should be carried likewise, but not equally, for the one would stand still, when the other flew apace and so continue sometime swiftlier, sometime slowlier, sometime broader, sometime narrower, as far as I could see. Nor it flew not straight, but sometime it crooked this way, sometime that way, and sometime it ran round about in a compass. And sometime the snow would be lift clean from the ground up to the air, and by and by it would be all clapt to the ground, as though there had been no wind at all, straightway it would rise and fly again. And that which was the most marvel of all, at one time two drifts of snow flew, the one out of the west into the east, the other out of the north into the east. And I saw two winds, by reason of the snow, the one cross over the other, as it had been two high ways. And, again, I should hear the wind blow in the air, when nothing was stirred at the ground. And when all was still where I rode, not very far from me the snow should be lifted wonderfully. This experience made me more marvel at the nature of the wind, than it made me cunning in the knowledge of the wind; but yet thereby I learned perfectly that it is no marvel at all though men in wind lose their length in shooting, seeing so many ways the wind is so variable in blowing.

—Roger Ascham, from *Toxophilus:*
A Treatise on the Art of Shooting with the Bow

II

I am not ignorant that by "law eternal" the learned for the most part do understand the order, not which God hath eternally purposed himself in all his works to observe, but rather that which with himself he hath set down as expedient to be kept by all his creatures, according to the several conditions wherewith he hath endued them. They who thus are accustomed to speak apply the name of Law unto that only rule of working which superior authority imposeth; whereas we somewhat more enlarging the sense thereof term any kind of rule or canon, whereby actions are framed, a law. Now that law which, as it is laid up in the bosom of God, they call *Eternal,* receiveth according unto the different kinds of things which are subject unto it different and sundry kinds of names. That part of it which ordereth natural agents we call usually Nature's law; that which Angels do clearly behold and without any swerving observe is a law Celestial and heavenly; the law of *Reason,* that which bindeth creatures reasonable in this world, and with which by reason they may most plainly perceive themselves bound; that which bindeth them, and is not known but by special revelation from God, Divine law; Human law, that which out of the law either of reason or of God men probably gathering to be expedient, they make it a law. All things therefore, which are as they ought to be, are conformed unto *this second law eternal;* and even those things which to this eternal law are not conformable are notwithstanding in some sort ordered by *the first eternal law.* For what good or evil is there under the sun, what action correspondent or repugnant unto the law which God hath imposed upon his creatures, but in or upon it God doth work according to the law which himself hath eternally purposed to keep; that is to say, the *first law eternal!* So that a twofold law eternal being thus made, it is not hard to conceive how they both take place in all things.

Wherefore to come to the law of nature: albeit thereby we sometimes mean that manner of working which God hath set for each created thing to keep; yet forasmuch as those things are termed most properly natural agents, which keep the law of their kind unwittingly, as the heavens and elements of the world, which can do no otherwise than they do; and forasmuch as we give unto intellectual natures the name of Voluntary agents, that so we may distinguish them from the other; expedient it will be, that we sever the law of nature observed by the one from that which the other is tied unto. Touching the former, their strict keeping of one tenure, statute, and law, is spoken of by all, but hath in it more than men have as yet attained to know, or perhaps ever shall attain, seeing the travail of wading herein is given of God to the sons of men,[1] that perceiving how much the least thing in the world hath in it more than the wisest are able to reach unto, they may by this means learn humility. Moses, in describing the work of creation, attributeth speech unto God: "God said, Let there be light: let there be a firmament: let the waters under the heaven be gathered together into one place: let the earth bring forth: let there be lights in the firmament of heaven." Was this only the intent of Moses, to signify the infinite greatness of God's power by the easiness of his accomplishing such effects, without travail, pain, or labor? Surely it seemeth that Moses had herein besides this a further purpose, namely, first to teach that God did not work as a necessary but a voluntary agent, intending beforehand and decreeing with himself that which did outwardly proceed from him: secondly, to show that God did then institute a law natural to be observed by creatures, and therefore according to the manner of laws, the institution thereof is described, as being established by solemn injunction. His commanding those things to be which are, and to be in such sort as they are, to keep that tenure and course which they do, importeth the establishment of nature's law. This world's first creation, and the preservation since of things created, what is it but only so far forth a manifestation by execution, what the eternal law of God is concerning things natural? And as it cometh to pass in a kingdom rightly ordered, that after a law is once published, it presently takes effect far and wide, all states framing themselves thereunto; even so let us think it fareth in the natural course of the world: since the time that God did first proclaim the edicts of his law upon it, heaven and earth have hearkened unto his voice, and their labor hath been to do his will: He "made a law for the rain;"[2] He gave his "decree unto the sea, that the waters should not pass his commandment."[3] Now if nature should intermit her course, and

---

1. Eccles. III. 9, 10. "I have seen the travail which God hath given to the sons of men to be exercised in it. He hath made every thing beautiful in his time: also he hath set the world in their heart, so that no man can find out the work that God maketh from the beginning to the end" [Hooker's note].

2. Job xxviii. 26 [Hooker's note].

3. Jer. v. 22 [Hooker's note].

leave altogether though it were but for a while the observation of
her own laws; if those principal and mother elements of the world,
whereof all things in this lower world are made, should lose the
qualities which now they have; if the frame of that heavenly arch
erected over our heads should loosen and dissolve itself; if celestial
spheres should forget their wonted motions, and by irregular volubility turn themselves any way as it might happen; if the prince of
the lights of heaven, which now as a giant doth run his unwearied
course,[4] should as it were through a languishing faintness begin to
stand and to rest himself; if the moon should wander from her
beaten way, the times and seasons of the year blend themselves by
disordered and confused mixture, the winds breathe out their last
gasp, the clouds yield not rain, the earth be defeated of heavenly
influence, the fruits of the earth pine away as children at the
withered breasts of their mother no longer able to yield them relief:
what would become of man himself, whom these things now do all
serve? See we not plainly that obedience of creatures unto the law
of nature is the stay of the whole world?

—Richard Hooker, from *Of the Laws of Ecclesiastical Piety*

4. Psalm xix. 5 [Hooker's note].

III

Men fear death as children fear to go in the dark; and as that
natural fear in children is increased with tales, so is the other. Certainly, the contemplation of death as the wages of sin, and passage
to another world, is holy and religious; but the fear of it, as a
tribute due unto nature, is weak. Yet in religious meditations there
is sometimes mixture of vanity and of superstition. You shall read in
some of the friars' books of mortification that a man should think
with himself what the pain is if he have but his finger's end pressed
or tortured; and thereby imagine what the pains of death are, when
the whole body is corrupted and dissolved; when many times death
passeth with less pain than the torture of a limb; for the most vital
parts are not the quickest of sense. And by him that spake only as a
philosopher, and natural man, it was well said, *Pompa mortis màgis
terret, quam mors ipsa.*[1] Groans and convulsions, and a discolored
face, and friends weeping, and blacks and obsequies, and the like,
show death terrible. It is worthy the observing that there is no passion in the mind of man so weak, but it mates and masters the
fear of death; and therefore death is no such terrible enemy when a
man hath so many attendants about him that can win the combat
of him. Revenge triumphs over death; love slights it; honor aspireth
to it; grief flieth to it; fear preoccupateth it; nay, we read, after Otho
the emperor had slain himself, pity, which is the tenderest of affec-

1. "The retinue of death terrifies more than death itself."

tions, provoked many to die out of mere compassion to their sovereign, and as the truest sort of followers. Nay, Seneca adds, niceness and satiety: *Cogita quamdiu eadem feceris; mori velle, non tantum fortis, aut miser, sed etiam fastidiosus potest.*[2] A man would die, though he were neither valiant nor miserable, only upon a weariness to do the same thing so oft over and over. It is no less worthy to observe, how little alteration in good spirits the approaches of death make: for they appear to be the same men till the last instant. Augustus Caesar died in a compliment, *Livia, conjugii nostri memor, vive et vale.*[3] Tiberius in dissimulation, as Tacitus saith of him, *Jam Tiberium vires et corpus, non dissimulatio, deserebant,*[4] Vespasion in a jest, sitting upon the stool, *Ut puto Deus fio.*[5] Galba with a sentence, *Feri, si ex re sit populi Romani,*[6] holding forth his neck; Septimus Severus in dispatch, *Adeste, se quid mihi restat agendum,*[7] and the like. Certainly the Stoics bestowed too much cost upon death, and by their great preparations made it appear more fearful. Better, saith he, *qui finem vitae extremum inter munera ponit naturae.*[8] It is as natural to die as to be born; and to a little infant, perhaps, the one is as painful as the other. He that dies in an earnest pursuit, is like one that is wounded in hot blood; who for the time scarce feels the hurt; and therefore a mind fixed and bent upon somewhat that is good, doth avert the dolors of death. But, above all, believe it, the sweetest canticle is *Nunc dimittis,*[9] when a man hath obtained worthy ends and expectations. Death hath this also, that it openeth the gate to good fame, and extinguisheth envy; *Extinctus amabitur idem.*[10]

—Francis Bacon, "Of Death"

2. "Consider how long you have been doing the same things: a man may be willing to die not only because he is brave, or wretched, but because he is sick of living."

3. "Farewell, Livia; live on remembering our marriage."

4. "Strength and spirit were deserting Tiberius then, but not his duplicity."

5. A pun is involved: "As I (cleanse myself; think), I am becoming a god."

6. "Strike, if it be for the good of the Roman people."

7. "Approach, if there is anything left for me to do."

8. "Who considers the end of life among the gifts of nature."

9. "Now dismiss [Thy servant, O Lord]": the words spoken by the Prophet Simeon (Luke ii, 29-32).

10. "The same man [who was envied in life] will be loved in death."

IV

We are all conceived in close prison; in our Mothers wombs, we are close prisoners all; when we are born, we are born but to the liberty of the house;[1] prisoners still, though within larger walls; and then all our life is but a going out to the place of execution, to death. Now was there ever any man seen to sleep in the cart, between

1. Donne distinguishes between a prisoner confined to a cell and one given somewhat more liberty.

Newgate, and Tyburn?[2] Between the prison and the place of execution, does any man sleep? And we sleep all the way; from the womb to the grave we are never thoroughly awake; but pass on with such dreams, and imaginations as these, I may live as well, as another, and why should I die, rather than another? But awake, and tell me, says this text *Quis homo?*[3] Who is that other that thou talkest of? *What man is he that liveth, and shall not see death?*

—John Donne, from a sermon delivered at Easter communion, March 28, 1619, when the king was dangerously ill at Newmarket.

2. London prisoners were taken in carts from Newgate prison to nearby Tyburn for execution.
3. "Who [is] the man?"

V

And therefore, restless inquietude for the diuturnity of our memories unto present considerations seems a vanity almost out of date, and superannuated piece of folly. We cannot hope to live so long in our names, as some have done in their persons. One face of Janus holds no proportion unto the other. 'Tis too late to be ambitious. The great mutations of the world are acted, or time may be too short for our designs. To extend our memories by monuments, whose death we daily pray for, and whose duration we cannot hope, without injury to our expectations in the advent of the last day, were a contradiction to our beliefs. We whose generations are ordained in this setting part of time, are providentially taken off from such imaginations; and, being necessitated to eye the remaining particle of futurity, are naturally constituted unto thoughts of the next world, and cannot excusably decline the consideration of that duration, which maketh pyramids pillars of snow, and all that's past a moment.

—Thomas Browne, from *Hydriotaphia*, or *Urn Burial*

VI

Whether others have this wonderful faculty of abstracting their ideas, they best can tell. For myself, I find indeed I have a faculty of imagining, or representing to myself, the ideas of those particular things I have perceived, and of variously compounding and dividing them. I can imagine a man with two heads, or the upper parts of a man joined to the body of a horse. I can consider the hand, the eye, the nose, each by itself abstracted or separated from the rest of the body. But then whatever hand or eye I imagine, it must have some particular shape and color. Likewise the idea of a man that I frame to myself, must be either of a white, or a black, or a tawny, a straight, or a crooked, a tall, or a low, or a middle-sized man. I cannot by any effort of thought conceive the abstract idea above described. And it is equally impossible for me to form the abstract idea of motion distinct from the body moving, and which is neither swift nor slow, curvilinear nor rectilinear; and the like may be said of all other abstract general ideas whatsoever. To be plain, I own myself able to abstract in one sense, as when I consider some particular parts or qualities separated from others, with which though they are united in some object, yet it is possible they may really exist without them. But I deny that I can abstract one from another, or conceive separately, those qualities which it is impossible should exist so separated; or that I can frame a general notion by abstracting from particulars in the manner aforesaid—which two last are the proper acceptations of *abstraction*. And there is ground to think most men will acknowledge themselves to be in my case. The generality of men which are simple and illiterate never pretend to abstract notions. It is said they are difficult, and not to be attained without pains and study. We may therefore reasonably conclude that, if such there be, they are confined only to the learned.

—George Berkeley, from *The Principles of Human Knowledge*

VII

Of the wall [of China] it is very easy to assign the motives. It secured a wealthy and timorous nation from the incursions of Barbarians, whose unskillfulness in arts made it easier for them to supply their wants by rapine than by industry, and who from time to time poured in upon the habitations of peaceful commerce, as vultures descend upon domestic fowl. Their celerity and fierceness made the wall necessary, and their ignorance made it efficacious.

But for the pyramids no reason has ever been given adequate to the cost and labor of the work. The narrowness of the chambers proves that it could afford no retreat from enemies, and treasures might have been reposited at far less expense with equal security. It seems to have been erected only in compliance with that hunger of imagination which preys incessantly upon life, and must be always appeased by some employment. Those who have already all that they can enjoy, must enlarge their desires. He that has built for use, till use is supplied must begin to build for vanity, and extend his plan to the utmost power of human performance, that he may not be soon reduced to form another wish.

I consider this mighty structure as a monument of the insufficiency of human enjoyments. A king, whose power is unlimited, and whose treasures surmount all real and imaginary wants, is compelled to solace, by the erection of a pyramid, the satiety of dominion and tastelessness of pleasures, and to amuse the tediousness of declining life, by seeing thousands laboring without end, and one stone, for no purpose, laid upon another. Whoever thou art, that, not content with a moderate condition, imaginest happiness in royal magnificence, and dreamest that command or riches can feed the appetite of novelty with perpetual gratifications, survey the pyramids, and confess thy folly!

—Samuel Johnson, from *Rasselas*

VIII

Moral philosophy, or the science of human nature, may be treated after two different manners; each of which has its peculiar merit, and may contribute to the entertainment, instruction, and reformation of mankind. The one considers man chiefly as born for action; and as influenced in his measures by taste and sentiment; pursuing one object, and avoiding another, according to the value which these objects seem to possess, and according to the light in which they present themselves. As virtue, of all objects, is allowed to be the most valuable, this species of philosophers paint her in the most amiable colors; borrowing all helps from poetry and eloquence, and treating their subject in an easy and obvious manner, and such as is best fitted to please the imagination, and engage the affections. They select the most striking observations and instances from common life; place opposite characters in a proper contrast; and alluring us into the paths of virtue by the views of glory and most illustrious examples. They make us *feel* the difference between vice and virtue; they excite and regulate our sentiments; and so they can but bend our hearts to the love of probity and true honor, they think, that they have fully attained the end of all their labors.

The other species of philosophers consider man in the light of a reasonable rather than an active being, and endeavor to form his understanding more than cultivate his manners. They regard human nature as a subject of speculation; and with a narrow scrutiny examine it, in order to find those principles, which regulate our understanding, excite our sentiments, and make us to approve or blame any particular object, action, or behavior. They think it a reproach to all literature, that philosophy should not yet have fixed, beyond controversy, the foundation of morals, reasoning, and criticism; and should forever talk of truth and falsehood, vice and virtue, beauty and deformity, without being able to determine the source of these distinctions. While they attempt this arduous task, they are deterred by no difficulties; but proceeding from particular instances to general principles they still push on their inquiries of principles more general, and rest not satisfied till they arrive at those original principles, by which, in every science, all human curiosity must be bounded. Though their speculations seem abstract, and even unintelligible to common readers, they aim at the approbation of the learned and the wise; and think themselves sufficiently compensated for the labor of their whole lives, if they can discover some hidden truths, which may contribute to the instruction of posterity.

—David Hume, from *An Enquiry Concerning Human Understanding*

IX

Every day for at least ten years together did my father resolve to have it mended—'tis not mended yet: no family but ours would have borne with it an hour—and what is most astonishing, there was not a subject in the world upon which my father was so eloquent, as upon that of door-hinges. And yet at the same time, he was certainly one of the greatest bubbles to them, I think, that history can produce: his rhetoric and conduct were at perpetual handy-cuffs. Never did the parlor-door open—but his philosophy or his principles fell a victim to it; three drops of oyl with a feather, and a smart stroke of a hammer, had saved his honor for ever. Inconsistent soul that man is—languishing under wounds, which he has the power to heal —his whole life a contradiction to his knowledge—his reason, that precious gift of God to him—(instead of pouring in oyl) serving but to sharpen his sensibilities, to multiply his pains and render him more melancholy and uneasy under them—poor unhappy creature, that he should do so! Are not the necessary causes of misery in this life enow, but he must add voluntary ones to his stock of sorrow, struggle against evils which cannot be avoided, and submit to others, which a tenth part of the trouble they create him, would remove from his heart forever?

By all that is good and virtuous! if there are three drops of oyl to be got, and a hammer to be found within ten miles of Shandy-Hall, the parlor-door hinge shall be mended this reign.

—Laurence Sterne, from *Tristram Shandy*

X

The division of Europe into a number of independent states, connected, however, with each other, by the general resemblance of religion, language, and manners, is productive of the most beneficial consequences to the liberty of mankind. A modern tyrant, who should find no resistance either in his own breast, or in his people, would soon experience a gentle restraint from the example of his equals, the dread of present censure, the advice of his allies, and the apprehension of his enemies. The object of his displeasure, escaping from the narrow limits of his dominions, would easily obtain, in a happier climate, a secure refuge, a new fortune adequate to his merit, the freedom of complaint, and perhaps the means of revenge. But the empire of the Romans filled the world, and when that empire fell into the hands of a single person, the world became a safe and dreary prison for his enemies. The slave of Imperial despotism, whether he was condemned to drag his gilded chain in Rome and the senate, or to wear out a life of exile on the barren rock of Seriphus, or the frozen banks of the Danube, expected his fate in silent despair. To resist was fatal, and it was impossible to fly. On every side he was encompassed with a vast extent of sea and land, which he could never hope to traverse without being discovered, seized, and restored to his irritated master. Beyond the frontiers, his anxious view could discover nothing, except the ocean, inhospitable deserts, hostile tribes of barbarians, of fierce manners and unknown language, or dependent kings, who would gladly purchase the emperor's protection by the sacrifice of an obnoxious fugitive. "Wherever you are," said Cicero to the exiled Marcellus, "remember that you are equally within the power of the conqueror."

—Edward Gibbon, from *The Decline and Fall of the Roman Empire*

XI

The human species, according to the best theory I can form of it, is composed of two distinct races, *the men who borrow,* and *the men who lend.* To these two original diversities may be reduced all those impertinent classifications of Gothic and Celtic tribes, white men, black men, red men. All the dwellers upon earth, "Parthians, and Medes, and Elamites," flock hither, and do naturally fall in with one or other of these primary distinctions. The infinite superiority of the former, which I choose to designate as the *great race,* is discernible in their figure, port, and a certain instinctive sovereignty. The latter are born degraded. "He shall serve his brethren." There is something in the air of one of this cast, lean and suspicious; contrasting with the open, trusting, generous manners of the other.

Observe who have been the greatest borrowers of all ages—Alcibiades—Falstaff—Sir Richard Steele—our late incomparable Brinsley—what a family likeness in all four!

What a careless, even deportment hath your borrower! what rosy gills! what a beautiful reliance on Providence doth he manifest—taking no more thought than lilies! What contempt for money—accounting it (yours and mine especially) no better than dross. What a liberal confounding of those pedantic distinctions of *meum* and *tuum!* or rather, what a noble simplification of language (beyond Tooke), resolving these supposed opposites into one clear, intelligible pronoun adjective! What near approaches doth he make to the primitive *community*—to the extent of one half of the principle at least!

—Charles Lamb, from "The Two Races of Men"

XII

There is hardly anything that shows the shortsightedness or capriciousness of the imagination more than traveling does. With change of place we change our ideas; nay, our opinions and feelings. We can by an effort indeed transport ourselves to old and long-forgotten scenes, and then the picture of the mind revives again; but we forget those that we have just left. It seems that we can think but of one place at a time. The canvas of the fancy is but of a certain extent, and if we paint one set of objects upon it, they immediately efface every other. We cannot enlarge our conceptions, we only shift our point of view. The landscape bares its bosom to the enraptured eye, we take our fill of it, and seem as if we could form no other image of beauty or grandeur. We pass one, and think no more of it: the horizon that shuts it from our sight also blots it from our memory like a dream. In traveling through a wild barren country I can form no idea of a woody and cultivated one. It appears to me that all the world must be barren, like what I see of it. In the country we forget the town, and in town we despise the country. "Beyond Hyde Park," says Sir Fopling Flutter, "all is a desert." All that part of the map that we do not see before us is a blank. The world in our conceit of it is not much bigger than a nutshell. It is not one prospect expanded into another, county joined to county, kingdom to kingdom, lands to seas, making an image voluminous and vast; the mind can form no larger idea of space than the eye can take in at a single glance. The rest is a name written in a map, a calculation of arithmetic. For instance, what is the true signification of that immense mass of territory and population known by the name of China to us? An inch of pasteboard on a wooden globe, of no more account than a China orange! Things near us are seen of the size of life; things at a distance are diminished to the size of the understanding. We measure the universe by ourselves, and even comprehend the texture of our own being only piecemeal. In this way, however, we remember an infinity of things and places. The mind is like a mechanical instrument that plays a great variety of tunes, but it must play them in succession. One idea recalls another, but it at the same time excludes all others. In trying to renew old recollections, we cannot as it were unfold the whole web of our existence; we must pick out the single threads. So in coming to a place where we have formerly lived, and with which we have intimate associations, everyone must have found that the feeling grows more vivid the nearer we approach the spot, from the mere anticipation of the actual impression: we remember circumstances, feelings, persons, faces, names, that we had not thought of for years; but for the time all the rest of the world is forgotten!

—William Hazlitt, from "On Going a Journey"

XIII

In that great social organ which, collectively, we call literature, there may be distinguished two separate offices that may blend and often do so, but capable, severally, of a severe insulation, and naturally fitted for reciprocal repulsion. There is, first, the literature of *knowledge*, and secondly, the literature of *power*. The function of the first is to *teach*; the function of the second is to *move*; the first is a rudder, the second an oar or a sail. The first speaks to the mere discursive understanding; the second speaks ultimately, it may happen, to the higher understanding or reason, but always through affections of pleasure and sympathy. Remotely, it may travel towards an object seated in what Lord Bacon calls *dry* light; but, proximately, it does and must operate—else it ceases to be a literature of *power* —and on through that *humid* light which clothes itself in the mists and glittering *iris* of human passions, desires, and genial emotions. Men have so little reflected on the higher functions of literature as to find it a paradox if one should describe it as a mean or subordinate purpose of books to give information. But this is a paradox only in the sense which makes it honorable to be paradoxical. Whenever we talk in ordinary language of seeking information or gaining knowl- edge, we understand the words as connected with something of ab- solute novelty. But it is the grandeur of all truth which *can* occupy a very high place in human interests that it is never absolutely novel to the meanest of minds: it exists eternally by way of germ or latent principle in the lowest as in the highest, needing to be developed, but never to be planted. To be capable of transplantation is the immediate criterion of a truth that ranges on a lower scale. Besides which, there is a rarer thing than truth—namely, *power*, or deep sympathy with truth. What is the effect, for instance, upon society, of children? By the pity, by the tenderness, and by the peculiar modes of admiration, which connect themselves with the helpless- ness, with the innocence, and with the simplicity of children, not only are the primal affections strengthened and continually renewed, but the qualities which are dearest in the sight of heaven—the frailty, for instance, which appeals to forbearance, the innocence which sym- bolizes the heavenly, and the simplicity which is most alien from the worldly—are kept up in perpetual remembrance, and their ideals are continually refreshed. A purpose of the same nature is answered by the high literature, viz., the literature of power. What do you learn from *Paradise Lost?* Nothing at all. What do you learn from a cookery book? Something new, something that you did not know before, in every paragraph. But would you therefore put the wretched cookery book on a higher level of estimation than the divine poem? What you owe to Milton is not any knowledge, of which a million separate items are still but a million of advancing steps on the same earthly level; what you owe is *power*—that is, exercise and expansion to your own latent capacity of sympathy with the infinite, where every pulse and each separate influx is a step upwards, a step ascending as upon a Jacob's ladder from earth to mysterious altitudes above the earth. All the steps of knowledge, from first to last, carry you further on the same plane, but could never raise you one foot above your ancient level of earth: whereas the very *first* step in power is a flight—is an ascending movement into another element where earth is forgotten.

—Thomas De Quincey, from "Literature of Knowledge and
Literature of Power"

XIV

Visible and tangible products of the Past, again, I reckon-up to the extent of three: Cities, with their Cabinets and Arsenals; then tilled Fields, to either or to both of which divisions Roads with their Bridges may belong; and thirdly—Books. In which third truly, the last invented, lies a worth far surpassing that of the two others. Wondrous indeed is the virtue of a true Book. Not like a dead city of stones, yearly crumbling, yearly needing repair; more like a tilled field, but then a spiritual field: like a spiritual tree, let me rather say, it stands from year to year, and from age to age (we have Books that already number some hundred-and-fifty human ages); and yearly comes its new produce of leaves (Commentaries, Deductions, Philosophical, Political Systems; or were it only Sermons, Pamphlets, Journalistic Essays), every one of which is talismanic and thaumaturgic, for it can persuade men. O thou who art able to write a Book, which once in the two centuries or oftener there is a man gifted to do, envy not him whom they name City-builder, and inexpressibly pity him whom they name Conqueror or City-burner! Thou too art a Conqueror and Victor: but of the true sort, namely over the Devil: thou too hast built what will outlast all marble and metal, and be a wonder-ringing City of the Mind, a Temple and Seminary and Prophetic Mount, whereto all kindreds of the Earth will pilgrim. Fool! why journeyest thou wearisomely, in thy antiquarian fervor, to gaze on the stone pyramids of Geeza, or the clay ones of Sacchara? These stand there, as I can tell thee, idle and inert, looking over the Desert, foolishly enough, for the last three thousand years: but canst thou not open thy Hebrew BIBLE, then, or even Luther's Version thereof?

—Thomas Carlyle, from *Sartor Resartus*

XV

To write history respectably—that is, to abbreviate dispatches, and make extracts from speeches, to intersperse in due proportion epithets of praise and abhorrence, to draw up antithetical characters of great men, setting forth how many contradictory virtues and vices they united, and abounding in *withs* and *withouts*—all this is very easy. But to be a really great historian is perhaps the rarest of intellectual distinctions. Many scientific works are, in their kind, absolutely perfect. There are poems which we would be inclined to designate as faultless, or as disfigured only by blemishes which pass unnoticed in the general blaze of excellence. There are speeches, some speeches of Demosthenes particularly, in which it would be impossible to alter a word without altering it for the worse. But we are acquainted with no history which approaches to our notion of what a history ought to be—with no history which does not widely depart, either on the right hand or on the left, from the exact line.

The cause may easily be assigned. This province of literature is a debatable land. It lies on the confines of two distinct territories. It is under the jurisdiction of two hostile powers; and, like other districts similarly situated, it is ill-defined, ill-cultivated, and ill-regulated. Instead of being equally shared between its two rulers, the Reason and the Imagination, it falls alternately under the sole and absolute dominion of each. It is sometimes fiction. It is sometimes theory.

History, it has been said, is philosophy teaching by examples. Unhappily, what the philosophy gains in soundness and depth the examples generally lose in vividness. A perfect historian must possess an imagination sufficiently powerful to make his narrative affecting and picturesque. Yet he must control it so absolutely as to content himself with the materials which he finds, and to refrain from supplying deficiences by additions of his own. He must be a profound and ingenious reasoner. Yet he must possess sufficient self-command to abstain from casting his facts in the mold of his hypothesis. Those who can justly estimate these almost insuperable difficulties will not think it strange that every writer should have failed, either in the narrative or in the speculative department of history.

—Thomas Babington Macaulay, from "History"

XVI

Knowledge is one thing, virtue is another; good sense is not conscience, refinement is not humility, nor is largeness and justness of view faith. Philosophy, however enlightened, however profound, gives no command over the passions, no influential motives, no vivifying principles. Liberal Education makes not the Christian, not the Catholic, but the gentleman. It is well to be a gentleman, it is well to have a cultivated intellect, a delicate taste, a candid, equitable, dispassionate mind, a noble and courteous bearing in the conduct of life—these are the connatural qualities of a large knowledge; they are the objects of a University; I am advocating, I shall illustrate and insist upon them; but still, I repeat, they are no guarantee for sanctity or even for conscientiousness, they may attach to the man of the world, to the profligate, to the heartless, pleasant, alas, and attractive as he shows when decked out in them. Taken by themselves, they do but seem to be what they are not; they look like virtue at a distance, but they are detected by close observers, and on the long run; and hence it is that they are popularly accused of pretense and hypocrisy, not, I repeat, from their own fault, but because their professors and their admirers persist in taking them for what they are not, and are officious in arrogating for them a praise to which they have no claim. Quarry the granite rock with razors, or moor the vessel with a thread of silk; then may you hope with such keen and delicate instruments as human knowledge and human reason to contend against those giants, the passion and the pride of man.

—John Henry Newman, from *The Idea of a University*

XVII

But there is of culture another view, in which not solely the scientific passion, the sheer desire to see things as they are, natural and proper in an intelligent being, appears as the ground of it. There is a view in which all the love of our neighbor, the impulses towards action, help, and beneficence, the desire for removing human error, clearing human confusion, and diminishing human misery, the noble aspiration to leave the world better and happier than we found it—motives eminently such as are called social—come in as part of the grounds of culture, and the main and pre-eminent part. Culture is then properly described not as having its origin in curiosity, but as having its origin in the love of perfection; it is *a study of perfection*. It moves by the force, not merely or primarily of the scientific passion for pure knowledge, but also of the moral and social passion for doing good. As, in the first view of it, we took for its worthy motto Montesquieu's words: "To render an intelligent being yet more intelligent!" so, in the second view of it, there is no better motto which it can have than these words of Bishop Wilson: "To make reason and the will of God prevail!"

Only, whereas the passion for doing good is apt to be overhasty in determining what reason and the will of God say, because its turn is for acting rather than thinking, and it wants to be beginning to act; and whereas it is apt to take its own conceptions, which proceed from its own state of development and share in all the imperfections and immaturities of this, for a basis of action; what distinguishes culture is, that it is possessed by the scientific passion as well as by the passion of doing good; that it demands worthy notions of reason and the will of God, and does not readily suffer its own crude conceptions to substitute themselves for them. And knowing that no action or institution can be salutary and stable which is not based on reason and the will of God, it is not so bent on acting and instituting, even with the great aim of diminishing human error and misery ever before its thoughts, but that it can remember that acting and instituting are of little use, unless we know how and what we ought to act and to institute.

—Matthew Arnold, from "Sweetness and Light"

XVIII

The presence that rose thus so strangely beside the waters, is expressive of what in the ways of a thousand years men had come to desire. Hers is the head upon which all "the ends of the world are come," and the eyelids are a little weary. It is a beauty wrought out from within upon the flesh, the deposit, little cell by cell, of strange thoughts and fantastic reveries and exquisite passions. Set it for a moment beside one of those white Greek goddesses or beautiful women of antiquity, and how would they be troubled by this beauty, into which the soul with all its maladies has passed! All the thoughts and experience of the world have etched and molded there, in that which they have of power to refine and make expressive the outward form, the animalism of Greece, the lust of Rome, the mysticism of the middle ages with its spiritual ambition and imaginative loves, the return of the Pagan world, the sins of the Borgias. She is older than the rocks among which she sits; like the vampire, she has been dead many times, and learned the secrets of the grave; and has been a diver in deep seas, and keeps their fallen day about her; and trafficked for strange webs with Eastern merchants: and, as Leda, was the mother of Helen of Troy, and, as Saint Anne, the mother of Mary; and all this has been to her but as the sound of lyres and flutes, and lives only in the delicacy with which it has molded the changing lineaments, and tinged the eyelids and the hands. The fancy of a perpetual life, sweeping together ten thousand experiences, is an old one; and modern philosophy has conceived the idea of humanity as wrought upon by, and summing up in itself, all modes of thought and life. Certainly Lady Lisa might stand as the embodiment of the old fancy, the symbol of the modern idea.

—Walter Pater, from *The Renaissance*

JACQUES BARZUN and HENRY F. GRAFF

Clear Sentences: Right Emphasis and Right Rhythm[1]

Live Sentences for Living Thoughts

As everybody knows, meaning does not come from single words but from words put together in groups—phrases, clauses, sentences. A mysterious bond links these groups of words with our ideas, and this relation leads in turn to the miracle by which ideas pass from one mind to another. The reason for weighing words with care is to make sure that these units of speech shall correspond truly to one's inner vision; the reason for building sentences with care is to make

---

1. Chapter 13 of *The Modern Researcher*, 1957.

sure that all the portions of our thought hang together correctly for truth, and conveniently for understanding.

Everyone's mind, however eager it may be for information, opposes a certain resistance to the reception of somebody else's ideas. Before one can take in another's intent, the shape, connection, and tendency of one's own ideas have to yield to those same features in the other person's. Accordingly, the writer must somehow induce in that other the willingness to receive the foreign matter. He does so with the aid of a great many devices which, when regularly used, are called the qualities of his speech or writing.

These qualities go by such names as: Clarity, Order, Logic, Ease, Unity, Coherence, Rhythm, Force, Simplicity, Naturalness, Grace, Wit, and Movement. But these are not distinct things; they overlap and can reinforce or obscure one another, being but aspects of the single power called Style. Neither style nor any of its qualities can be aimed at separately. Nor are the pleasing characteristics of a writer's style laid on some pre-existing surface the way sheathing and plaster are laid on the rough boards of a half-finished house. Rather, they are the by-product of an intense effort to make words work. By "working" we mean here reaching the mind of another and affecting it in such a way as to reproduce there *our* state of mind.

You cannot aim directly at style, at clarity, precision, and all the rest: you can only remove the many possible obstacles to understanding, while preserving as much as you can of your spontaneous utterance. All attempts at reproducing a recognized style, whether Biblical, Lincolnesque, or "stark" for modernity, defeat themselves. You cannot be someone other than yourself. The qualities we have listed, and others you can name, should therefore be regarded as so many tests that you apply in the course of revision by self-questioning. You do not, while writing, say to yourself: "Now I am going to be clear, logical, coherent." You write a sentence and ask, as you go over it "Can anyone else follow? Perhaps not. Then what is the matter? I see: this does not match that. And here—is this in any way absurd?" Clarity comes when others can follow; coherence when thoughts hang together; logic when their sequence is valid. You achieve these results by changing, cutting, transposing. You may ask: "Is there no way to write so as to avoid all this patching after-the-fact?" There is—and learning how is the subject of this chapter. But note at the outset that any helpful hints will only reduce the amount of rewriting to be done, never remove its necessity.

It is an interesting proof of what has just been said that no satisfactory definition of a sentence has ever been given: there is no specification to which you can build. Yet every educated person recognizes a sentence when he sees one. The mystery of its connection with a train of thought is the point of departure for our effort to make the sentence and the total thought coincide. To say this is to say that notions of correctness or proffers of approved models for sentences will be useless, and even paralyzing, unless they are taken with imagination. Whatever image you may have in mind when you see or hear the word "sentence," that image should not be of something rigid, static, and absolute; a sentence is above all functional, dynamic, and relative. A sentence, perfectly good when taken by itself, may be all wrong when it follows or precedes another. For the thought has to keep moving and its track must be smooth. If you need a structural image of The Sentence, think of it as an organism possessing a skeleton, muscles, and flesh.

Like a skeleton, a sentence is a piece of construction. Traditional grammar in fact speaks of related words as forming "a construction," and calls it awkward or harmonious, allowable or contrary to usage. But do not let the idea of a construction suggest a table or a house; to be sure, a sentence has to stand on its feet, but we liken it to a skeleton because a sentence, like the thought it carries, has to move. Motion is perhaps the fundamental quality of good writing. Motion is what makes writing correspond to thought, which is also a movement from one idea or vision to the next. A reader who knows nothing about the principles of writing may be incapable of analyzing what is wrong as he makes heavy weather through a book. But he feels very keenly whether his mind advances or sticks, goes straight or in circles, marches steadily forward or jerks two steps ahead and three back.

In order to move, the parts of the sentence skeleton must be properly jointed, articulated; the muscles and connective tissue must be strong and inserted at the right places; the burden of ideas must not be too great for the structure. And to cover all this machinery and make it pleasing, the surface must be reasonably varied and polished. Translating this into writers' terms, we say: clauses and phrases must fall into the right pattern of syntax, and the words must be chosen so that the tone and rhythm of the whole are appropriate. A telegraphic message may be exact and well knit, but it lacks grace and sounds unnatural. It moves but does not flow. One cannot imagine reading three hundred pages in telegraphic style. The words omitted in that style and which are restored in ordinary prose are no decoration or added charm; they are simply the rounded contour of the thought, reduced in the telegram to the bare bones.

The return of this image of the skeleton tells us that we have come full circle in our attempt to define at one and the same time what a sentence is and what is does. You may as a result be a little wiser about the virtues to aim at in writing. But you probably think, with reason, that what you need even more than a definition is direct advice, and for this we must look at examples. Yet, we repeat: if you want the examples to be serviceable beyond their immediate instruction, you should study them with the force of our definition behind them.

Five-Legged Sheep and Other Monsters

Let us begin with the schoolbook example: "The wind blew across the desert where the corpse lay and whistled." The sentence moves indeed, and the *information* it contains is not hard to find; but before we quite grasp it we laugh. And this alters the *meaning*, which was not intended to be jocular in the last three words. How to fix it? Our first impulse is to insert a comma after "lay." But reading the result gives an odd impression, as if "and whistled" was a dangling afterthought. Try it aloud and you will hear that a comma pause after "lay" makes "and whistled" sound not simply silly but a trifle puzzling. The only way the sentence sounds rhythmically satisfying is without the pause.

Clearly the diagnosis is that the meaning and the construction are at odds; bad rhythm gives the flaw away, the trouble being that the limb "and whistled" is attached to the wrong part of the body. Since the joke comes from the close link between the corpse and the whistling, we derive from this our first rule of sentence making: *bring as close together as possible the parts that occur together in the world or go together in your mind.*

Now try to apply the rule to our sentence: "The wind blew across the desert and whistled where the corpse lay." No longer comic, but wrong again, because the new close-linking suggests that the whistling took place only near the corpse. In framing a sentence the need to link and connect implies the need to unlink and detach. Try again: "The wind blew and whistled across the desert where the corpse lay." At last we have the limbs correctly distributed—no front leg is hitched on to the hindquarters. Our sentence passes the test as far as avoiding absurdity and false suggestion goes.

But say it aloud once more and you will notice that it still sounds odd. It leaves the voice up in the air, and with the voice, the meaning. This is because the emphases are off beat. In an ordinary declarative sentence, the two spots of emphasis are the beginning and the end. Hence the two most important elements in the thought must occupy those spots. In our example the main elements obviously are: the whistling wind and the corpse. Whether the corpse lay or stood or leaned is a detail. The last idea sounding in our mind's ear must be "the corpse." Can this be managed? Let us see. "The wind blew and whistled across the desert where lay the corpse." A trifle better, but far from perfect. Why? Because modern English shies away from inversions. Idiomatic turns make a language what it is; to defy idiom is to lose force. In short, to sound natural we must stick to "where the corpse lay."

By this time we are sick and tired of wrestling with these twelve words and we conclude that they cannot be juggled into a proper shape. We are ready to scrap the sentences and go at the idea by a different route when a fresh form occurs to us. "The corpse lay in the desert, across which the wind blew and whistled." This is the best yet. The form is right and if the whole subject were only a little less dramatic we could let it stand. But there is a stiffness about "across which" that suits a description of scenery rather than of lonely death. This impression simply means that we have been made aware of Tone while trying to secure Right Emphasis, Right Linking, and Right Rhythm. These features of the sentence, we repeat, are not separable. On the contrary, a sentence is to be regarded as a compromise among their various demands.

If the Tone of "across which" is unsuitable, what *can* we do with the wretched corpse on our hands? Having twisted and turned it about, all that occurs is to abandon our second construction and try a third: "The corpse lay in the desert, and over it the wind blew and whistled."[2] This is still disappointing: a compound sentence is too weak for this gruesome vision; it separates what eye and ear bring together to the mind. We have dismembered and reconstructed without success. What next?

The true solution lies in the so-called periodic sentence, whose form heightens suspense and generally favors rhythm: "Across the desert where the corpse lay, the wind blew and whistled." A peculiarity of the periodic sentence is that its suspensive opening phrase does not monopolize the emphasis we associate with beginnings. The second portion is still emphatic because the forepart rushes down toward it, so to speak, in an effort to complete its own meaning by finding a subject and a verb.

From our experience with a single bad sentence, we can now confirm our first rule of thumb and add to it others for similar use in framing and straightening sentences:

1. Right linking is the prime requisite. Begin by seeing to it that things related are not divided, and that things remote are not falsely joined.

2. Right emphasis comes next. It is what gives momentum to the thought, what makes the sentence move. It starts from a point of superior interest, travels through a valley of detail, and reaches a second point of high interest, which ends the journey by completing or advancing our understanding of the first.

3. When the emphases are right, the rhythm is likely to be right also, for our speaking habits naturally follow our habits of

2. The inveterate verifier is curious about the fact and he asks: *Does the* wind whistle when it blows across an unobstructed waste? [Barzun and Graff's note].

wording and of thought.[3]

4. At any point in the structure, the phrasing must be in keeping with the tenor of the whole. This is a matter partly of diction and partly of construction. The two together produce Tone.

To these four propositions there is an important negative corollary: Although a comma that is missing from a sound sentence should be put in, no putting in of commas will cure a defective sentence. When you are tempted to waste time in this effort, just remember "and whistled."

With these truths in mind, we can refine a little on the art of construction, though with no hope of exhausting the subject of improved sentence building. We go back to the difficult art of linking. The desire to bring kindred things together often tempts the unwary to use phrases which can be read in two or more ways. Ambiguity sets the reader on the wrong track; he must back up and make a fresh start, or perhaps remain in doubt about the right fusion of ideas. When this happens too often, he is understandably aggrieved. Suppose he reads:

If there is lost motion in the rods and boxes in a boiler of steam generating capacity and a valve distributing power properly when the lever is hooked down, it develops into a pound that is annoying and detrimental to the machinery.

The reader's trouble begins at "steam generating capacity." Should this be "steam-generating," a hyphenated adjective modifying "capacity"? Or should it be "a boiler of steam, generating [power at] capacity"? Below, a similar hesitation arises at "valve distributing power." Doubt is settled by our knowledge that valves distribute power and not the other way round ("valve-distributing power" is nonsense). But we have had to stop and figure this out. The second phrase exactly parallels the first—"steam-generating capacity"—and our retentive ear entices us to give their parallel forms a parallel meaning. Next we are stopped for a further instant at whatever "it" is that "develops into a pound." After talk of steam power, the word "pound" is ambiguous. We see at once that it is not a pound of pressure that is meant by a pounding. Still, we have been jerked to a halt a third time. Finally, another, somewhat different, parallel between the two adjectives in the last sentence tells us that this pounding is "annoying . . . to the machinery."

On the whole, this sentence intended for the instruction of engineers can tell us more about writing than about locomotives. And here is what it tells us: Parallelism is so important a device in writ-

---

3. This does not mean that in speaking we usually place our words right for emphasis but that we sound them right, and hence the rhythm is natural. One says: "They *are* good—in *my* opinion." To convey the same meaning in print, one must write: "They are, in my opinion, good." Still judging the written word, explain the rather different meanings of: "In my opinion, they are good" and "They, in my opinion, are good" [Barzun and Graff's note].

ing that its use must be kept pure. Do not give parallel forms to disparate ideas, and always carry out the parallels you start out with. Do not ever suppose that variation is more elegant. Note the accumulation of horrors in:

> When it came right down to it, he was no more able to spell out a conceptual pattern than, in the last analysis, he felt he could muster up the imagination to face such explosive problems of ethics as his sadly unhappy life had left him no room to size up with detachment.

At the words "he was no more able to," the writer has made a contract with the reader. Those words forecast a "than," to be followed by a second action parallel to the first. The contract here is broken. The "than" duly comes, but its proper adjunct is forgotten while the writer pursues his wandering thought down winding channels. Jargon and rank images ("spell out a pattern," "explosive problems," "room to size up") are mixed with clichés ("in the last analysis"), tautologies ("sadly unhappy"), and the redundancies which spoil the parallel—"he [felt he] could," and the words following "imagination." The cure is to give up the "no more than" construction and make two sentences, one about conceptual patterns—whatever they may be—and one about the ethical problems of a sadly unhappy life without room.

An observation made in passing when we examined the sentence from the engineer's manual furnishes a second rule of good construction: the antecedents of pronouns must always be unmistakable. In the welter of rods, boxes, and valves no one can tell what "it" is that "develops into a pound." It cannot be the engine, which is not even mentioned. The motion, no doubt, develops into a pound, but the only motion mentioned is four lines above and it is lost motion—it doesn't exist. In any event, no less than six nouns in the singular precede "it," and two would be enough to create confusion. By rights, the last in order should be the true antecedent, but that happens to be "lever," which makes nonsense. The "it" is an orphaned relative with no references to show when questioned.

Modern Prose: Its Virtues and Vices

After so much wallowing in uncertainty we are eager for a good sentence. Here is one embodying a double parallel and making of it a dramatic image: "Too blind to avert danger, too cowardly to withstand it, the most ancient government of Europe made not an instant's resistance: the peasants of Underwald died upon their mountains, the holders of Venice clung to their lives."[4]

4. Marguerite, Lady Blessington, in her *Conversations of Lord Byron*, Philadelphia, 1836, p. 96, reports that he exclaimed about this passage from Hallam's *Middle Ages*: "This is the way to write history if it is wished to impress it on the memory" [Barzun and Graff's note].

The modern reader who appreciates this sentence may say that in spite of its clarity, richness, and rhythmical excellence, it is alien to his mode of thought and hence beyond his power to imitate. We no longer enjoy these complex and balanced forms; they seem to us artificial. We prefer to write as we speak—or so we like to believe. If the engineer's sentence above, and the biographer's right after, are fair samples of serious prose in our century, we are forced to admit that the elements of complexity are still with us, though unorganized. We are not so simple and straightforward as we pretend, and the truth is that we could not follow the advice to "write as we speak" even if we wanted to.

What prevents the written word from reproducing speech is that in speaking the voice, stress, facial expression, and gesture contribute a quantity of meaning which fills out the insufficiency of colloquial speech. Read the transcript of court testimony and you will see how difficult it is to understand. You have to guess how every remark was spoken, inflected, made clear by something other than words. In good writing the writer has to supply these elements which give point and direction to utterance. Hence the use of those transitional and qualifying words which are almost entirely absent from conversation.

And it is this necessity, of course, which leads to the other extreme. The writer may think as he would speak; but half-conscious of a lack, he fills out his spontaneous sentence with many words—to stop the gaps, to bottle up his meaning which always threatens to fizz away. Up to a point the effort succeeds. But superfluous words destroy explicitness. The fault of beginners is that their sentences say the same thing twice over. Here is a brief example from a business newsletter: "All aspects of our life today bear the marked imprint of science."[5] An imprint *is* a mark, so "marked imprint" is no more than "imprint" by itself. But—and this is the important point—the needless word is not simply canceled and dropped by the reader. It arrests his mind long enough to make him decide whether some special imprint is meant or no. Since it is no, the effort has been wasted. Multiply this kind of fault throughout a paragraph and the reader bogs down.

From this we infer the generality that, all else being equal, *the ease with which thought can be gathered from words is in inverse ratio to their combined length.*

We did not say "to their number," for the length of the words themselves may be part of the impediment; and we did say "all else being equal," which means that occasions are frequent in which long words and long sentences are preferable. But a simple thought buried in a sentence stuffed with long words, inevitably produces

---

[5] First National Bank of Boston,   p. 1 [Barzun and Graff's note].
England Letter, Aug. 31, 1956,

the effect commonly called "a mouthful." Like the mouth, the mind cannot ingest it. The moral is: any sentence of yours which grows on and on in a string of words in "-ity" or "-tion," hooked together with "of's" and "to's," must be whittled down to size with a hatchet.

Consider this, which purports to *make clearer* one of Shakespeare's plays:

> The creation of character, indeed, is not to be regarded as the unique, or even principal, end of Shakespeare's dramatic creations, in which plot and motive, themselves handled with great flexibility and insight, tend increasingly to find their proper context in a more ample artistic unity which embraces and illuminates them; but in the delineation of personality beyond the limits of convention his language first attained some sense of its full possibilities

No mind, including the author's, can take in at one scoop the message of this clumsy compound. Therefore he had no excuse for printing it, even if when he writes his mind does work on the rocket principle, shooting out fresh phrases at intervals as he proceeds where we cannot follow. He should make a first stop after "creations"; and a second after "unity." Rereading this, the author would see that the portion beginning with "but" is so flabbily contrasted with what went before that he should ask himself what, in fact, he did have in mind.

Nor is sprawling his only sin against sense. He gives us an anthology of faults: (1) Awkward repetition: "creation" in line 1, "creations" in line 2. (2) Tautology: "themselves" in line 3, and the whole phrase beginning "find their proper context . . ." down to "embraces" ("context," "unity," and "embraces" say the same thing three times). (3) Illogic: how are we to interpret the comparison in "greater" and "more ample"? Than what? "Increasingly" suggests "as time went on," but we must guess this. (4) Pronouns adrift: "their" in line 4 and "them" in line 5 have two possible antecedents—"dramatic creations," on the one hand, and "plot and motive," on the other. (5) The vagueness of perpetual abstraction: what does it *mean* "to handle plot and motive with greater flexibility and insight"? "to find a proper context"? "to be embraced and illuminated by a more ample artistic unity"? "to delineate personality beyond the limits of convention"? And how in the name of heaven does a writer's *language* "attain some sense of its full possibilities"?

We see in this example what it means to be ponderous without being scholarly. The worst faults of "serious writing" are here conveniently grouped, the "noun plague" dominating them all. Not one plausible agent performs a recognizable act denoted by a strong verb. All is passive and diffuse and jargon-ridden.

As an antidote, let us turn to another writer on Shakespeare:

Structurally, Tate has made few serious alterations. The most important is Bolingbroke's winning of the rabble. This is amusingly done and probably acted well enough. More serious is the "elevation" of Richard's character, a feat on which Tate plumes himself in the Preface. As a matter of fact, it spoils the play.[6]

Despite its choppiness, which might become tedious, and a lack of charm, which would preclude subtle thoughts, this passage at least answers the reader's prayer for simple and straightforward prose. What makes it such is the presence of what was absent in the former passage: plausible agents, recognizable acts, strong verbs. Of these last, there are still too few. A more searching writer would, for instance, have preferred: "Tate has altered but few structural parts . . ." Then the logic could be stricter: if "the most important" alteration is the one about Bolingbroke, how can the one about Richard be "more serious"? And to a good ear— pronouns and parallels again!—the sentence "This is amusingly done and probably acted well enough" sounds disjointed. The shift in voice calls for a second subject: "and *it* probably acted . . ."; for the passive "is done" will not go in harness with the active verb "acted."

Carpentry or Cabinetmaking?

All we have been saying is an extension of our original proposition that "good writing is an intense effort to make words work." The complaints and suggestions about the passages we have examined boil down to the demand that each word—noun, verb, adverb, or any other kind—should contribute something to the sense; and this with economy. If one word can do the work of two, use one. If you absolutely need a phrase, make it short. If the thought is complex and the sentence has to contain several clauses, see to it that each clause expends its energy where none will be wasted, that is, close to the idea it enlarges or qualifies.

A good rule to follow in order to achieve coherence with the least trouble is to stick to your subject, voice, or construction. Do not start with one idea or form and change it in mid-career. The writer above switched from a passive verb to an active and lost momentum. Another will write: "The topic one selects should be clear and precise and when one comes to look for the materials on it, it will be found that the subject itself serves as a guide to their selection." This is no doubt a faithful transcript of the way the thought came out, but its form is ill adapted to its going in. In a second draft the writer should cling to his grammatical subject and see where it leads him: "The topic selected should be clear and pre-

6. Hazelton Spencer, *Shakespeare Im-*, Cambridge, Mass., 1927, p. 262 n and Graff's note].

Spencer is discussing Nahum Tate's eighteenth-century revision of Shakespeare's play.

cise—*so that* IT will guide the researcher—*when* HE comes to look for *his* materials." Twenty-three words in place of thirty-five, and a *continuous motion* instead of three hitches—from "the topic" to "when one comes" to an indefinite "it" and back to "the subject" again.

Only remain faithful to your subject and construction, making everything follow the one and fit into the other, and you will be surprised at the ease, speed, and clarity that you attain. All the thick connective tissue—or clanking chains, rather ("as regards," "as far as . . . is concerned," "in relation to," and the like)—will automatically fall away; associated ideas will be next to next; and your thought will be accessible to the reader who, by definition, is always on the run.

For models of this kind of writing, study the advertising cards in any public vehicle. The ideas conveyed may be stupid, commonplace, or untrue; the words themselves may be flossy or jargon-like, but the construction is usually impeccable. One reason is that advertisers know they have only thirty seconds to make an impression. Another and a clinching reason is that they employ first-rate writing talents. When these are exerted in publicizing welfare agencies or, occasionally, political appeals, they produce classic utterances. What could be better than: "Sixteen million New Yorkers need a fighting Senator with experience, ideas, and a heart."

Note how the attention is arrested, without fuss, by the opening phrase which addresses every voter in the state, and how adroitly the emphases are managed: having started with our interesting selves we wind up with an appeal to the feelings. But "ideas" are not wholly forgotten, though "experience," as the chief political virtue, comes first in the series. Notice also the function of the single adjective "fighting." It is a strong word, but here it is more than that. Without it, the sentence might be a bare statement of need, suggesting no candidate to fill it. But with the epithet, it is clear that the declaration aims at someone, and behold! his picture is underneath it.

You may say that the ease, lucidity, and force of this bid for votes comes from the inherent simplicity of the idea. Not so. It is always easy to write a muddy sentence, and it would be surprising if the one we have been admiring had been struck off impromptu. The normal tendency is to join chunks of wordage each to each as they come and tap them here and there with a hammer till they more or less resemble a structure.

Here are examples of two phases of composition—if indeed the first fragment can claim the name. The writer is a high-school teacher of English whose examination paper was first quoted in an article showing how illiterate are some of those who "educate" our young:

Hemingway works is the beginning of all modern American Literature. He doesn't write too much conversation in his books. Just enough to make the idea go across and his descriptions are brief with many adverbs.[7]

Now comes a hammered-down affair which is brisker and more literate but not much more satisfactory:

Thousands of years ago men first learned the secret of conducting water through crude pipes. ["Crude" is out of place here, since the secret sought was how to conduct water through pipes—which turned out to be crude.] Long before the birth of Christ, the Chinese transported water through bamboo. [Christ is brought in for vividness, but the effect fails by making one wonder what His birth contributed to plumbing.] . . . and there is much evidence of the fine water supply system of the Romans. [By this point, the writer has given up, lost his grip on vividness, fact, and rhythm.][8]

The unpalatable truth is that since a really well-made sentence is not born, like the live body we compared it to, it can only be the result of much planing and fitting, of close measuring for balance, and of hidden jointing for solidity and smoothness—it is cabinet-maker's work, plus the living force which gives movement and stirs the inert frame into an animated whole.

The joiner's task calls at first for an adroit handling of words which, by referring backward or forward, knit thoughts together. Doing this consciously, in second draft, implies knowing when to omit such cross references. Where the reader's mind will take the jump alone, it is a waste to prod him. An example will show what is meant:

What course of procedure does this suggest? In spite of all the study on the broad topic of productivity, the sum total of knowledge useful to management is small. Government and economic research agencies should be encouraged to expand studies of productivity.[9]

This passage is clear and rapid because in the first sentence "this" refers adequately to the preceding paragraph and because in the second sentence the subject (productivity) is named again in a passing manner which allows our attention to dwell on the aspect of it that matters, namely, the *study* of productivity. The writer then omits a further reference after "the sum total of knowledge"—we know very well it is not knowledge at large, but knowledge about productivity. At the last gasp, however, the writer's art broke down: he repeated "studies of productivity" at an emphatic place, almost as if this were a new topic he was introducing. He might have said instead: "Government, etc., should be encouraged to enlarge this sum by extending [not 'expanding'] their researches."

7. James D. Koerner, "Can Our Teachers Read and Write?" *Harper's Magazine*, CCIX (November 1954), 80 [Barzun and Graff's note].

8. Steel Plate Fabricators' Association, *History of Steel Pipe*, Chicago, 1955, p. 3 [Barzun and Graff's note].

9. First National Bank of Boston, *New England Letter*, July 31, 1956, p. 3 [Barzun and Graff's note].

The paragraph that follows the one just quoted gives up the struggle. The writer falls back repeatedly on clumsy reference by means of the phrase "such information . . ."—would be useful, etc. This makes the passage read like a lawyer's brief. Indeed it cannot be read, but must be worked out, studied.

Now there is one place in any article or book where this sort of failure is fatal to the circulation of the work. That place is the beginning. To catch your reader, the hook must be baited with palatable stuff. A good writer will therefore toil over his opening sentence.

Let his model be the one which opens Jane Austen's *Pride and Prejudice*: "It is a truth universally acknowledged that a single man in possession of a good fortune must be in want of a wife." This far from truthful proposition is an ideal opening, because it foretells in the smallest compass what we are about to be concerned with—marriage and money; and how we are to be concerned with them—in the spirit of irony.

Conclusions, too, are important, being the last word ringing in the departing reader's ear. They may be as difficult as beginnings if you have said a great deal and want to recall it in one, final, pregnant sentence. Here is a good example dealing with England's defeat of the Great Armada: "This triumph of sea power insured the survival of the Reformation in England and to a lesser extent in Germany, and helped maintain Holland's independence from Spain."

The Sound of the Sense

These two examples of opening and closing are models only to the extent that they combine a number of the qualities we spoke of earlier as desirable in all writing—clarity, balance, movement, force, and ease. Jane Austen's, it need hardly be pointed out, has grace and wit besides.

But the models further resemble each other in that they disclose a characteristic tone: we hear a voice and it is pleasing. Tone cannot be defined except negatively, when it is bad. Anyone can tell when a writer is talking down to him—that is the condescending tone. But there is also the pompous, the chattering, the precious, the chummy, the toplofty, the cynical and sneering, the vulgar out of the corner of the mouth—the varieties of bad tones are infinite, for they correspond to the mixtures of human emotions.

The curious thing is that a good writer will occasionally fall into a tone which he himself would reprove, yet will never notice the lapse. Either he is seduced by "language," as in preciosity or pedantry; or else he is betrayed by his feelings about the subject, as in cynicism or arrogance. These are reasons, not excuses. The reader is quick to notice what rings false and to resent it as a personal insult. Hence it behooves a writer to watch his tone. To do this he may have to put himself on guard against his most congenial adult attitudes. Until spoiled by sophistication, children who write are free of these. In consequence, a writer such as the nine-year-old author of *The Young Visiters*[1] has perfect tone. Pick up the book anywhere and no matter how difficult the subject, the tone suits:

> The Abbey was indeed thronged next day when Ethel and Bernard cantered up in a very fine carrage drawn by two prancing steeds who foamed a good deal. In the porch stood several clean altar boys who conducted the lucky pair up the aile while the organ pealed a merry blast. The mighty edifice was packed and seated in the front row was the Earl of Clincham looking very brisk as he was going to give Ethel away at the correct moment. Beside him sat Mr. Salteena all in black and looking bitterly sad and he ground his teeth as Ethel came marching up.[2]

What admirable control of rhythm and tone! The difficulty of doing this has led to the maxim: "If you are especially fond of a passage, strike it out." But this advice evidently goes too far, since "fondness" can express a sound judgment about a sentence well worked over. No. The only clue to bad tone is reading oneself after an interval and responding to the text like an unprepared reader. Phrases will then begin to sound hollow, and they will be judged falsehoods or padding or irrelevance.

To sum up, the search for complete adequacy is, first and last, the only general rule for good writing. Try to find out what you mean—what you would go to the stake for—and put it down without frills or depreciatory gestures. Exhaust the means of literary expression, and you will produce sentences that parse and move and carry the ring of your voice. Keep your eye constantly on your subject—that portion occupying your field of vision at the moment—and you will achieve, in addition to ease and lucidity, force. Contrary to common belief, this trinity of virtues does not mean that sentences must bark, or be cast in the same mold, or remain drearily declarative. Nor does keeping the subject ever in view mean that the writer's own personality vanishes. It mingles, rather, with every phrase he sets down, yet without interposing a thick mist of ego between the reader and the page.

Examine, by way of conclusion and summary of our suggestions, the following paragraph, taken from an English scholar's introduction to a volume of letters. Notice how much information is amassed and conveyed without being thrust at the reader; and respond also to the quiet efficiency of a style in which no word is wasted and through which the native impulses of an urbane mind are revealed:

> Saint Evremond admits that the company of his friends and their conversation were more important to him than his writings, which occupied

1. By Daisy Ashford, New York, 1919 [Barzun and Graff's note].

2. *Op. cit.*, p. 99 [Barzun and Graff's note].

his time only when there was nothing better to do. Like his contemporaries at the courts of Louis XIV and Charles II, he regarded literature as one of the necessary accomplishments of a person of quality, not as a means of earning money or reputation. And though posterity remembers him as a man of letters, he himself claimed to be remembered as a soldier first and afterwards as a courtier. For the fate of his compositions after they had left his pen he cared as little as tradition says he cared about his personal appearance in his old age. He wrote, as it has been said of another, for his own and his friends' delight, and for the delight also, though he could not have foreseen it, of the pirate printers. They, of course, turned his carelessness to good account, and flourished on the proceeds of innumerable and horribly garbled impressions of his essays, exposed for sale on the bookstalls of London, Paris, and Amsterdam. Hitherto he has given no delight to the bibliographer, and I confess that I have profited little from an examination of a very large number of those unauthorized publications. At the same time my acquaintance with them, and with the one authentic edition of his collected works, has not altered my belief that a selection of his writings, even in translation, is worth reading, and therefore worth reprinting.[3]

3. John Hayward, ed., *The Letters of Saint Evremond*, London, 1930, p. xiii   [Barzun and Graff's note].

FRANCIS CHRISTENSEN
A Generative Rhetoric of the Sentence[1]

* * *

If the new grammar is to be brought to bear on composition, it must be brought to bear on the rhetoric of the sentence. We have a workable and teachable, if not a definitive, modern grammar; but we do not have, despite several titles, a modern rhetoric.

In composition courses we do not really teach our captive charges to write better—we merely *expect* them to. And we do not teach them how to write better because we do not know how to teach them to write better. And so we merely go through the motions. Our courses with their tear-out work books and four-pound anthologies are elaborate evasions of the real problem. They permit us to put in our time and do almost anything else we'd rather be doing instead of buckling down to the hard work of making a difference in the student's understanding and manipulation of language.

With hundreds of handbooks and rhetorics to draw from, I have never been able to work out a program for teaching the sentence as I find it in the work of contemporary writers. The chapters on the sentence all adduce the traditional rhetorical classification of sentences as loose, balanced, and periodic. But the term *loose* seems to be taken as a pejorative (it sounds immoral); our students, no Bacons or Johnsons, have little occasion for balanced sentences;

1. The present reprinting omits, with the author's permission, a fe   intro-   ductory paragraphs and a "Postscript."

and some of our worst perversions of style come from the attempt to teach them to write periodic sentences. The traditional grammatical classification of sentences is equally barren. Its use in teaching composition rests on a semantic confusion, equating complexity of structure with complexity of thought and vice versa. But very simple thoughts may call for very complex grammatical constructions. Any moron can say "I don't know who done it." And some of us might be puzzled to work out the grammar of "All I want is all there is," although any chit can think it and say it and act on it.

The chapters on the sentence all appear to assume that we think naturally in primer sentences, progress naturally to compound sentences, and must be taught to combine the primer sentences into complex sentences—and that complex sentences are the mark of maturity. We need a rhetoric of the sentence that will do more than combine the ideas of primer sentences. We need one that will *generate* ideas.

For the foundation of such a generative or productive rhetoric I take the statement from John Erskine, the originator of the Great Books courses, himself a novelist. In an essay "The Craft of Writing" (*Twentieth Century English*, Philosophical Library, 1946) he discusses a principle of the writer's craft which, though known he says to all practitioners, he has never seen discussed in print. The principle is this: "When you write, you make a point, not by subtracting as though you sharpened a pencil, but by adding." We have all been told that the formula for good writing is the concrete noun and the active verb. Yet Erskine says, "What you say is found not in the noun but in what you add to qualify the noun . . . The noun, the verb, and the main clause serve merely as the base on which meaning will rise . . . The modifier is the essential part of any sentence." The foundation, then, for a generative or productive rhetoric of the sentence is that composition is essentially a process of *addition*.

But speech is linear, moving in time, and writing moves in linear space, which is analogous to time. When you add a modifier, whether to the noun, the verb, or the main clause, you must add it either before the head or after it. If you add it before the head, the direction of modification can be indicated by an arrow pointing forward; if you add it after, by an arrow pointing backward. Thus we have the second principle of a generative rhetoric—the principle of *direction of modification* or *direction of movement*.

Within the clause there is not much scope for operating with this principle. The positions of the various sorts of close, or restrictive, modifiers are generally fixed and the modifiers are often obligatory—"The man who came to dinner remained till midnight." Often the only choice is whether to add modifiers. What I have seen of attempts to bring structural grammar to bear on composition usually boils down to the injunction to "load the patterns." Thus "pattern practice" sets students to accreting sentences like this: "The small boy on the red bicycle who lives with his happy parents on our shady street often coasts down the steep street until he comes to the city park." This will never do. It has no rhythm and hence no life; it is tone-deaf. It is the seed that will burgeon into gobbledygook. One of the hardest things in writing is to keep the noun clusters and verb clusters short.

It is with modifiers added to the clause—that is, with sentence modifiers—that the principle comes into full play. The typical sentence of modern English, the kind we can best spend our efforts trying to teach, is what we may call the *cumulative sentence*. The main clause, which may or may not have a sentence modifier before it, advances the discussion; but the additions move backward, as in this clause, to modify the statement of the main clause or more often to explicate or exemplify it, so that the sentence has a flowing and ebbing movement, advancing to a new position and then pausing to consolidate it, leaping and lingering as the popular ballad does. The first part of the preceding compound sentence has one addition, placed within it; the second part has 4 words in the main clause and 49 in the five additions placed after it.

The cumulative sentence is the opposite of the periodic sentence. It does not represent the idea as conceived, pondered over, reshaped, packaged, and delivered cold. It is dynamic rather than static, representing the mind thinking. The main clause ("the additions move backward" above) exhausts the mere fact of the idea; logically, there is nothing more to say. The additions stay with the same idea, probing its bearings and implications, exemplifying it or seeking an analogy or metaphor for it, or reducing it to details. Thus the mere form of the sentence generates ideas. It serves the needs of both the writer and the reader, the writer by compelling him to examine his thought, the reader by letting him into the writer's thought.

Addition and direction of movement are structural principles. They involve the grammatical character of the sentence. Before going on to other principles, I must say a word about the best grammar as the foundation for rhetoric. I cannot conceive any useful transactions between teacher and students unless they have in common a language for talking about sentences. The best grammar for the present purpose is the grammar that best displays the layers of structure of the English sentence. The best I have found in a textbook is the combination of immediate constituent and transformation grammar in Paul Roberts's *English Sentences*. Traditional grammar, whether over-simple as in the school tradition or over-complex as in the scholarly tradition, does not reveal the language as it operates; it leaves everything, to borrow a phrase from Wordsworth, "in disconnection dead and spiritless." *English Sentences* is oversimplified and it has gaps, but it displays admirably the struc- tures that rhetoric must work with—primarily sentence modifiers, including nonrestrictive relative and subordinate clauses, but, far more important, the array of noun, verb, and adjective clusters. It is paradoxical that Professor Roberts, who has done so much to make the teaching of composition possible, should himself be one of those who think that it cannot be taught. Unlike Ulysses, he does not see any work for Telemachus to work.

Layers of structure, as I have said, is a grammatical concept. To bring in the dimension of meaning, we need a third principle—that of *levels of generality* or *levels of abstraction.* The main or base clause is likely to be stated in general or abstract or plural terms. With the main clause stated, the forward movement of the sentence stops, the writer shifts down to a lower level of generality or abstraction or to singular terms, and goes back over the same ground at this lower level.[2] There is no theoretical limit to the number of structural layers or levels, each[3] at a lower level of generality, any or all of them compounded, that a speaker or writer may use. For a speaker, listen to Lowell Thomas; for a writer, study William Faulkner. To a single independent clause he may append a page of additions, but usually all clear, all grammatical, once we have learned how to read him. Or, if you prefer, study Hemingway, the master of the simple sentence: "George was coming down in the telemark position, kneeling, one leg forward and bent, the other trailing, his sticks hanging like some insect's thin legs, kicking up puffs of snow, and finally the whole kneeling, trailing figure coming around in a beautiful right curve, crouching, the legs shot forward and back, the body leaning out against the swing, the sticks accenting the curve like points of light, all in a wild cloud of snow." Only from the standpoint of school grammar is this a simple sentence.

This brings me to the fourth, and last, principle, that of texture. *Texture* provides a descriptive or evaluative term. If a writer adds to few of his nouns or verbs or main clauses and adds little, the tex- ture may be said to be thin. The style will be plain or bare. The writing of most of our students is thin—even threadbare. But if he adds frequently or much or both, then the texture may be said to be dense or rich. One of the marks of an effective style, especially in narrative, is variety in the texture, the texture varying with the

2. Cf. Leo Rockas, "Abstract and Concrete Sentences," *CCC*, May 1963. Rockas describes sentences as abstract or concrete, the abstract implying the concrete and vice versa. Readers and writers, he says, must have the knack of apprehending the concrete in the ab- stract and the abstract in the concrete. This is true and valuable. I am saying that within a single sentence the writer may present more than one level of generality, translating the abstract into the more concrete in added levels [Christensen's note].

3. This statement is not quite ten- able. Each helps to make the idea of the base clause more concrete or specific, but each is not more concrete or specific than the one immediately above it * * * [Christensen's note].

change in pace, the variation in texture producing the change in pace. It is not true, as I have seen it asserted, that fast action calls for short sentences; the action is fast in the sentence by Hemingway above. In our classes, we have to work for greater density and variety in texture and greater concreteness and particularity in what is added.

I have been operating at a fairly high level of generality. Now I must downshift and go over the same points with examples. The most graphic way to exhibit the layers of structure is to indent the word groups of a sentence and to number the levels. The first three sentences illustrate the various positions of the added sentence modifiers—initial, medial, and final. The symbols mark the grammatical character of the additions: SC, subordinate clause; RC, relative clause; NC, noun cluster; VC, verb cluster; AC, adjective cluster; A + A, adjective series; Abs, absolute (i.e., a VC with a subject of its own); PP, prepositional phrase. The elements set off as on a lower level are marked as sentence modifiers by junctures or punctuation. The examples have been chosen to illustrate the range of constructions used in the lower levels; after the first few they are arranged by the number of levels. The examples could have been drawn from poetry as well as from prose. Those not attributed are by students.

1
1 He dipped his hands in the bichloride solution and shook them,
  2 a quick shake, (NC)
    3 fingers down, (Abs)
      4 like the fingers of a pianist above the keys. (PP)—Sinclair Lewis

2
  2 Calico-coated, (AC)
  2 small-bodied, (AC)
    3 with delicate legs and pink faces in which their mismatched eyes rolled wild and subdued, (PP)
1 they huddled,
  2 gaudy motionless and alert, (A + A)
  2 wild as deer, (AC)
  2 deadly as rattlesnakes, (AC)
  2 quiet as doves. (AC)—William Faulkner

3
1 The bird's eye, / , remained fixed upon him;
  2 / bright and silly as a sequin (AC)
1 its little bones, / , seemed swooning in his hand.
  2 / wrapped . . . in a warm padding of feathers (VC)—Stella Benson

4
1 The jockeys sat bowed and relaxed,
  2 moving a little at the waist with the movement of their horses. (VC)
          —Katherine Anne Porter

5
1 The flame sidled up the match,
  2 driving a film of moisture and a thin strip of darker grey before it. (VC)

6
1 She came among them behind the man,
  2 gaunt in the gray shapeless garment and the sunbonnet, (AC)
  2 wearing stained canvas gymnasium shoes. (VC)—Faulkner

7
1 The Texan turned to the nearest gatepost and climbed to the top of it,
  2 his alternate thighs thick and bulging in the tight trousers, (Abs)
  2 the butt of the pistol catching and losing the sun in pearly gleams.
    (Abs)—Faulkner

8
1 He could sail for hours,
  2 searching the blanched grasses below him with his telescopic eyes,
    (VC)
  2 gaining height against the wind, (VC)
  2 descending in mile-long, gently declining swoops when he curved and
    rode back, (VC)
  2 never beating a wing. (VC)—Walter Van Tilburg Clark

9
1 They regarded me silently,
  2 Brother Jack with a smile that went no deeper than his lips, (Abs)
    3 his head cocked to one side, (Abs)
    3 studying me with his penetrating eyes; (VC)
  2 the other blank-faced, (Abs)
    3 looking out of eyes that were meant to reveal nothing and to stir
      profound uncertainty. (VC)—Ralph Ellison

10
1 He stood at the top of the stairs and watched me,
  2 I waiting for him to call me up, (Abs)
  2 he hesitating to come down, (Abs)
    3 his lips nervous with the suggestion of a smile, (Abs)
    3 mine asking whether the smile meant come, or go away. (Abs)

11
1 Joad's lips stretched tight over his long teeth for a moment, and
1 he licked his lips,
  2 like a dog, (PP)
    3 two licks, (NC)
      4 one in each direction from the middle. (NC)—Steinbeck

12
1 We all live in two realities:
  2 one of seeming fixity, (NC)
    3 with institutions, dogmas, rules of punctuation, and routines, (PP)
      4 the calendared and clockwise world of all but futile round on
        round; (NC) and
  2 one of whirling and flying electrons, dreams, and possibilities, (NC)
    3 behind the clock. (PP)—Sidney Cox

13
1 It was as though someone, somewhere, had touched a lever and shifted
  gears, and
1 the hospital was set for night running,
  2 smooth and silent, (A + A)
  2 its normal clatter and hum muffled, (Abs)
  2 the only sounds heard in the whitewalled room distant and unreal:
    (Abs)

  3 a low hum of voices from the nurses' desk, (NC)
    4 quickly stifled, (VC)
  3 the soft squish of rubber-soled shoes on the tiled corridor, (NC)
  3 starched white cloth rustling against itself, (NC) and, outside,
  3 the lonesome whine of wind in the country night (NC) and
  3 the Kansas dust beating against the windows. (NC)

14

1 The beach sounds are jazzy,
  2 percussion fixing the mode—(Abs)
    3 the surf cracking and booming in the distance, (Abs)
    3 a little nearer dropped bar-bells clanking, (Abs)
    3 steel gym rings, / , ringing, (Abs)
        /4 flung together, (VC)
    3 palm fronds rustling above me, (Abs)
      4 like steel brushes washing over a snare drum, (PP)
    3 troupes of sandals splatting and shuffling on the sandy cement, (Abs)
      4 their beat varying, (Abs)
        5 syncopation emerging and disappearing with changing paces. (Abs)

15

1 A small Negro girl develops from the sheet of glare-frosted walk,
  2 walking barefooted, (VC)
    3 her bare legs striking and coiling from the hot cement, (Abs)
      4 her feet curling in, (Abs)
        5 only the outer edges touching. (Abs)

16

1 The swells moved rhythmically toward us,
  2 irregularly faceted, (VC)
  2 sparkling, (VC)
  2 growing taller and more powerful until the shining crest bursts, (VC)
    3 a transparent sheet of pale green water spilling over the top, (Abs)
      4 breaking into blue-white foam as it cascades down the front of the wave, (VC)
      4 piling up in a frothy mound that the diminishing wave pushes up against the pilings, (VC)
        5 with a swishsmash, (PP)
      4 the foam drifting back, (Abs)
        5 like a lace fan opened over the shimmering water as the spent wave returns whispering to the sea. (PP)

The best starting point for a composition unit based on these four principles is with two-level narrative sentences, first with one second-level addition (sentences 4, 5), then with two or more parallel ones (6, 7, 8). Anyone sitting in his room with his eyes closed could write the main clause of most of the examples; the discipline comes with the additions, provided they are based at first on immediate observation, requiring the student to phrase an exact observation in exact language. This can hardly fail to be exciting to a class: it is life, with the variety and complexity of life; the workbook exercise is death. The situation is ideal also for teaching diction —abstract-concrete, general-specific, literal-metaphorical, denotative-connotative. When the sentences begin to come out right, it is time to examine the additions for their grammatical character. From then on the grammar comes to the aid of the writing and the writing reinforces the grammar. One can soon go on to multi-level narrative sentences (1, 9–11, 15, 16) and then to brief narratives of three to six or seven sentences on actions with a beginning, a middle, and an end that can be observed over and over again—beating eggs, making a cut with a power saw, or following a record changer's cycle or a wave's flow and ebb. (Bring the record changer to class.) Description, by contrast, is static, picturing appearance rather than behavior. The constructions to master are the noun and adjective clusters and the absolute (13, 14). Then the descriptive noun cluster must be taught to ride piggy-back on the narrative sentence, so that description and narration are interleaved: "In the morning we went out into a new world, a glistening crystal and white world, each skeleton tree, each leafless bush, even the heavy, drooping power lines sheathed in icy crystal." The next step is to develop the sense for variety in texture and change in pace that all good narrative demands.

* * *

I want to anticipate two possible objections. One is that the sentences are long. By freshman English standards they are long, but I could have produced far longer ones from works freshmen are expected to read. Of the sentences by students, most were written as finger exercises in the first few weeks of the course. I try in narrative sentences to push to level after level, not just two or three, but four, five, or six, even more, as far as the students' powers of observation will take them. I want them to become sentence acrobats, to dazzle by their syntactic dexterity. I'd rather have to deal with hyperemia than anemia. I want to add my voice to that of James Coleman (*College Composition and Communication*, December 1962) deploring our concentration on the plain style.

The other objection is that my examples are mainly descriptive and narrative—and today in freshman English we teach only exposition. I deplore this limitation as much as I deplore our limitation to the plain style. Both are a sign that we have sold our proper heritage for a pot of message. In permitting them, the English department undercuts its own discipline. Even if our goal is only utilitarian prose, we can teach diction and sentence structure far more effectively through a few controlled exercises in description and narration than we can by starting right off with exposition (Theme One, 500 words, precipitates *all* the problems of writing). There is no problem of invention; the student has something to communicate—his immediate sense impressions, which can stand a bit of exercising. The material is not already verbalized—he has to match language to sense impressions. His acuteness in observation and in choice of words can be judged by fairly objective standards—is the sound of a bottle of milk being set down on a concrete step suggested better by *clink* or *clank* or *clunk*? In the examples, study the diction for its accuracy, rising at times to the truly imaginative. Study the use of metaphor, of comparison. This verbal virtuosity and syntactical ingenuity can be made to carry over into expository writing.

But this is still utilitarian. What I am proposing carries over of itself into the study of literature. It makes the student a better reader of literature. It helps him thread the syntactical mazes of much mature writing, and it gives him insight into that elusive thing we call style. Last year a student told of rereading a book by her favorite author, Willa Cather, and of realizing for the first time *why* she liked reading her: she could understand and appreciate the style. For some students, moreover, such writing makes life more interesting as well as giving them a way to share their interest with others. When they learn how to put concrete details into a sentence, they begin to look at life with more alertness. If it is liberal education we are concerned with, it is just possible that these things are more important than anything we can achieve when we set our sights on the plain style in expository prose.

I want to conclude with a historical note. My thesis in this paragraph is that modern prose like modern poetry has more in common with the seventeenth than with the eighteenth century and that we fail largely because we are operating from an eighteenth century base. The shift from the complex to the cumulative sentence is more profound than it seems. It goes deep in grammar, requiring a shift from the subordinate clause (the staple of our trade) to the cluster and the absolute (so little understood as to go almost unnoticed in our textbooks). And I have only lately come to see that this shift has historical implications. The cumulative sentence is the modern form of the loose sentence that characterized the anti-Ciceronian movement in the seventeenth century. This movement, according to Morris W. Croll,[4] began with Montaigne and Bacon and continued with such men as Donne, Browne, Taylor, Pascal. To Montaigne, its art was the art of being natural; to Pascal, its eloquence was the eloquence that mocks formal eloquence; to Bacon, it presented knowledge so that it could be examined, not so that it must be accepted.

But the Senecan amble was banished from England when "the direct sensuous apprehension of thought" (T. S. Eliot's words) gave way to Cartesian reason or intellect. The consequences of this

4. "The Baroque Style in Prose," *Studies in English Philology: A Miscellany in Honor of Frederick Klaeber* (1929), reprinted in *Style, Rhetoric, and Rhythm: Essays by Morris W. Croll* (1966) and A. M. Witherspoon and F. J. Warnke, *Seventeenth-Century Prose and Poetry*, 2nd ed. (1963). I have borrowed from Croll in my description of the cumulative sentence [Christensen's note].

shift in sensibility are well summarized by Croll:

To this mode of thought we are to trace almost all the features of modern literary education and criticism, or at least of what we should have called modern a generation ago: the study of the precise meaning of words; the reference to dictionaries as literary authorities; the study of the sentence as a logical unit alone; the careful circumscription of its limits and the gradual reduction of its length; . . .[5] the attempt to reduce grammar to an exact science; the idea that forms of speech are always either correct or incorrect; the complete subjection of the laws of motion and expression in style to the laws of logic and standardization—in short, the triumph, during two centuries, of grammatical over rhetorical ideas.

Here is a seven-point scale any teacher of composition can use to take stock. He can find whether he is based in the eighteenth century or in the twentieth and whether he is consistent—completely either an ancient or a modern—or is just a crazy mixed-up kid.

5. The omitted item concerns punctuation and is not relevant here. In using this scale, note the phrase "what we should have called modern a generation ago" and remember that Croll was writing in 1929 [Christensen's note].

QUESTIONS

1. Compare Christensen's approach to the sentence with Barzun and Graff's (p. 230). What definition of the sentence lies behind each essay? Why does Christensen call his approach "generative"? Do the two essays aim ultimately to promote the same stylistic virtues? Where do they agree, where do they disagree about what makes an effective sentence? How do the different audiences for each essay affect the manner of presentation in each?

2. Christensen talks about four principles: "addition," "direction of modification," "levels of generality," and "texture." Which of these are handled from another point of view by Barzun and Graff, and which are not discussed?

3. Is Christensen's device equally sound for all kinds of writing? For example, is it more appropriate to description and narration than to exposition and argument? Choose some examples of each kind of writing and analyze them.

4. Analyze the quotation about St. Evremond at the end of Barzun and Graff's essay according to Christensen's principles. This selection might be considered a kind of "character." Compare it with one or two of the characters on pages 790–807, still using Christensen's principles for analyzing sentences.

5. At the end of his essay Christensen quotes Croll's seven-point scale for testing whether one's notion of language "is based on the eighteenth century or the twentieth." Test Barzun and Graff's attitude toward language (as far as it can be inferred from their essay) against this scale.

6. How does Christensen distinguish between the "complex" sentence and the "cumulative" sentence? Analyze the passage from Boswell quoted by Francis (p. 174) or a passage or two from the "Album of Styles" (pp. 214–229) in the light of his distinc-

tion. Try rewriting one of the passages in which there are mainly complex sentences in a style which employs mainly cumulative sentences. What is gained and what is lost by the change?

WAYNE C. BOOTH
Boring from Within: The Art of the Freshman Essay[1]

Last week I had for about the hundredth time an experience that always disturbs me. Riding on a train, I found myself talking with my seat-mate, who asked me what I did for a living. "I teach English." Do you have any trouble predicting his response? His face fell, and he groaned, "Oh, dear, I'll have to watch my language." In my experience there are only two other possible reactions. The first is even less inspiriting: "I hated English in school; it was my worst subject." The second, so rare as to make an honest English teacher almost burst into tears of gratitude when it occurs, is an animated conversation about literature, or ideas, or the American language— the kind of conversation that shows a continuing respect for "English" as something more than being sure about *who* and *whom, lie* and *lay.*

Unless the people you meet are a good deal more tactful or better liars than the ones I meet, you've had the two less favorable experiences many times. And it takes no master analyst to figure out why so many of our fellow citizens think of us as unfriendly policemen: it is because too many of us have seen ourselves as unfriendly policemen. I know of a high school English class in Indiana in which the students are explicitly told that their paper grades will not be affected by anything they say; required to write a paper a week, they are graded simply on the number of spelling and grammatical errors. What is more, they are given a standard form for their papers: each paper is to have three paragraphs, a beginning, a middle, and an end —or is it an introduction, a body, and a conclusion? The theory seems to be that if the student is not troubled about having to say anything, or about discovering a good way of saying it, he can then concentrate on the truly important matter of avoiding mistakes.

What's wrong with such assignments? What's wrong with getting the problem of correctness focused sharply enough so that we can really work on it? After all, we do have the job of teaching correct English, don't we? We can't possibly teach our hordes of students to be colorful writers, but by golly, we can beat the bad grammar out of them. Leaving aside the obvious fact that we *can't* beat the bad grammar out of them, not by direct assault, let's think a bit about what

1. Adapted by Mr. Booth from a speech delivered in May 1963 to the Illinois Council of College Teachers of English.

that kind of assignment does to the poor teacher who gives it. Those papers must be read, by someone, and unless the teacher has more trained assistance than you and I have, *she's* the victim. She can't help being bored silly by her own paper-reading, and we all know what an evening of being bored by a class's papers does to our attitude toward that class the next day. The old formula of John Dewey was that any teaching that bores the student is likely to fail. The formula was subject to abuse, quite obviously, since interest in itself is only one of many tests of adequate teaching. A safer formula, though perhaps also subject to abuse, might be: Any teaching that bores the teacher is sure to fail. And I am haunted by the picture of that poor woman in Indiana, week after week reading batches of papers written by students who have been told that nothing they say can possibly affect her opinion of those papers. Could any hell imagined by Dante or Jean-Paul Sartre match this self-inflicted futility?

I call it self-inflicted, as if it were a simple matter to avoid receiving papers that bore us. But unfortunately it is not. It may be a simple matter to avoid the *total* meaninglessness that the students must give that Indiana teacher, but we all know that it is no easy matter to produce interesting papers; our pet cures for boredom never work as well as they ought to. Every beginning teacher learns quickly and painfully that nothing works with all students, and that on bad days even the most promising ideas work with nobody.

As I try to sort out the various possible cures for those batches of boredom—in ink, double-spaced, on one side of the sheet, only, please —I find them falling into three groups: efforts to give the students a sharper sense of writing to an audience, efforts to give them some substance to express, and efforts to improve their habits of observation and of approach to their task—what might be called improving their mental personalities.

This classification, both obvious and unoriginal, is a useful one not only because it covers—at least I hope it does—all of our efforts to improve what our students can do but also because it reminds us that no one of the three is likely to work unless it is related to each of the others. In fact each of the three types of cure—"develop an awareness of audience," "give them something to say," and "enliven their writing personalities"—threatens us with characteristic dangers and distortions; all three together are indispensable to any lasting cure.

Perhaps the most obvious omission in that Indiana teacher's as-signments is all sense of an audience to be persuaded, of a serious rhetorical purpose to be achieved. One tempting cure for this omis-sion is to teach them to put a controversial edge on what they say. So we ask them to write a three-page paper arguing that China should be allowed into the UN or that women are superior to men or that American colleges are failing in their historic task. Then we are sur-prised when the papers turn out to be as boring as ever. The papers

on Red China are full of abstract pomposities that the students themselves obviously do not understand or care about, since they have
gleaned them in a desperate dash through the most readily available
courses listed in the *Readers' Guide*. Except for the rare student who
has some political background and awareness, and who thus might
have written on the subject anyway, they manage to convey little
more than their resentment at the assignment and their boredom in
carrying it out. One of the worst batches of papers I ever read came
out of a good idea we had at Earlham College for getting the whole
student body involved in controversial discussion about world affairs.
We required them to read Barbara Ward's *Five Ideas that Changed
the World*; we even had Lady Barbara come to the campus and talk
to everyone about her concern for the backward nations. The papers,
to our surprise, were a discouraging business. We found ourselves in
desperation collecting the boners that are always a sure sign, when
present in great numbers, that students are thoroughly disengaged.
"I think altruism is all right, so long as we practice it in our own
interest." "I would be willing to die for anything fatal." "It sure is
a doggie dog world."

It is obvious what had gone wrong: though we had ostensibly given
the student a writing purpose, it had not become *his* purpose, and
he was really no better off, perhaps worse, than if we had him writing
about, say, piccolos or pizza. We might be tempted in revulsion from
such overly ambitious failures to search for controversy in the students'
own mundane lives. This may be a good move, but we should not be
surprised when the papers on "Let's clean up the campus" or "Why
must we have traffic fatalities?" turn out to be just as empty as the
papers on the UN or the Congo. They may have more exclamation
points and underlined adjectives, but they will not interest any teacher
who would like to read papers for his own pleasure or edification.
"People often fail to realize that nearly 40,000 people are killed on our
highways each year. Must this carnage continue?" Well, I suppose it
must, until people who write about it learn to see it with their own
eyes, and hearts, instead of through a haze of cliché. The truth is that
to make students assume a controversial pose before they have any
genuine substance to be controversial about is to encourage dishonesty and slovenliness, and to ensure our own boredom. It may very
well lead them into the kind of commercial concern for the audience
which makes almost every *Reader's Digest* article intelligible to everyone over the chronological age of ten and boring to everyone over
the mental age of fifteen. *Newsweek* magazine recently had a readability survey conducted on itself. It was found to be readable by the
average twelfth grader, unlike *Time*, which is readable by the average eleventh grader. The editors were advised, and I understand are
taking the advice, that by improving their "readability" by one year
they could improve their circulation by several hundred thousand.

Whether they will thereby lop off a few thousand adult readers in the process was not reported.

The only protection from this destructive type of concern for the audience is the control of substance, of having something solid to say. Our students bore us, even when they take a seemingly lively controversial tone, because they have nothing to say, to us or to anybody else. If and when they discover something to say, they will no longer bore us, and our comments will no longer bore them. Having something to say, they will be interested in learning how to say it better. Having something to say, they can be taught how to give a properly controversial edge to what will by its nature be controversial—nothing, after all, is worth saying that everybody agrees on already.

When we think of providing substance, we are perhaps tempted first to find some way of filling students' minds with a goodly store of general ideas, available on demand. This temptation is not necessarily a bad one. After all, if we think of the adult writers who interest us, most of them have such a store; they have read and thought about man's major problems, and they have opinions and arguments ready to hand about how men ought to live, how society ought to be run, how literature ought to be written. Edmund Wilson, for example, one of the most consistently interesting men alive, seems to have an inexhaustible flow of reasoned opinions on any subject that comes before him. Obviously our students are not going to interest us until they too have some ideas.

But it is not easy to impart ideas. It is not even easy to impart opinions, though a popular teacher can usually manage to get students to parrot his views. But ideas—that is, opinions backed with genuine reasoning—are extremely difficult to develop. If they were not, we wouldn't have a problem in the first place; we could simply send our students off with an assignment to prove their conviction that God does or does not exist or that the American high school system is the best on God's earth, and the interesting arguments would flow.

There is, in fact, no short cut to the development of reasoned ideas. Years and years of daily contact with the world of ideas are required before the child can be expected to begin formulating his own ideas and his own reasons. And for the most part the capacity to handle abstract ideas comes fairly late. I recently saw a paper of a bright high school sophomore, from a good private school, relating the economic growth of China and India to their political development and relative supply of natural resources. It was a terrible paper; the student's hatred of the subject, his sense of frustration in trying to invent generalizations about processes that were still too big for him, showed in every line. The child's parent told me that when the paper was returned by the geography teacher, he had pencilled on the top of one page, "Why do you mix so many bad ideas with your good ones?"

The son was almost in tears, his father told me, with anger and help-lessness. "He talks as if I'd put bad ideas in on purpose. I don't know a bad idea from a good one on this subject."

Yet with all this said, I am still convinced that general ideas are not only a resource but also a duty that cannot be dodged just because it is a dangerous one. There is nothing we touch, as English teachers, that is immune to being tainted by our touch; all the difference lies in how we go about it.

Ideas are a resource because adolescents are surprisingly responsive to any real encouragement to think for themselves, *if* methods of forced feeding are avoided. The seventeen-year-old who has been given nothing but commonplaces and clichés all his life and who final-ly discovers a teacher with ideas of his own may have his life changed, and, as I shall say in my final point, when his life is changed his writing is changed. Perhaps some of you can remember, as I can, a first experience with a teacher who could think for himself. I can remember going home from a conversation with my high school chemistry teacher and audibly vowing to myself: "Someday I'm going to be able to think for myself like that." There was nothing especially unconventional about Luther Gidding's ideas—at least I can remem-ber few of them now. But what I cannot forget is the way he had with an idea, the genuine curiosity with which he approached it, the pause while he gave his little thoughtful cough, and then the bulldog tenacity with which he would argue it through. And I am convinced that though he never required me to write a line, he did more to improve my writing during the high school years than all of my English teachers put together. The diary I kept to record my sessions with him, never read by anyone, was the best possible writing prac-tice.

If ideas, in this sense of speculation backed up with an attempt to think about things rigorously and constructively, are a great and often neglected resource, they are also our civic responsibility—a far more serious responsibility than our duty to teach spelling and grammar. It is a commonplace to say that democracy depends for its survival on an informed citizenry, but we all know that mere information is not what we are talking about when we say such things. What we mean is that democracy depends on a citizenry that can reason for themselves, on men who know whether a case has been proved, or at least made probable. Democracy depends, if you will forgive some truisms for a moment, on free choices, and choices cannot be in any sense free if they are made blind: free choice is, in fact, choice that is based on knowledge—not just opinions, but knowledge in the sense of reasoned opinion. And if that half of our population who do not go beyond high school do not learn from us how to put two and two together and how to test the efforts of others to do so, and if the colleges continue to fail with most of the other half, we are doomed to become even more sheeplike, as a nation, than we are already.

Papers about ideas written by sheep are boring; papers written by thinking boys and girls are interesting. The problem is always to find ideas at a level that will allow the student to *reason*, that is, to provide support for his ideas, rather than merely assert them in half-baked form. And this means something that is all too often forgotten by the most ambitious teachers—namely, that whatever ideas the student writes about must somehow be connected with his own experience. Teaching machines will never be able to teach the kind of writing we all want, precisely because no machine can ever know which general ideas relate, for a given student, to some meaningful experience. In the same class we'll have one student for whom philosophical and religious ideas are meaningful, another who can talk with confidence about entropy and the second law of thermodynamics, a third who can write about social justice, and a fourth who can discuss the phony world of Holden Caulfield. Each of them can do a good job on his own subject, because he has as part of his equipment a growing awareness of how conclusions in that subject are related to the steps of argument that support conclusions. Ideally, each of these students ought to have the personal attention of a tutor for an hour or so each week, someone who can help him sharpen those connections, and not force him to write on topics not yet appropriate to his interests or experience. But when these four are in a class of thirty or forty others, taught by a teacher who has three or four other similar sections, we all know what happens: the teacher is forced by his circumstances to provide some sort of mold into which all of the students can be poured. Although he is still better able to adapt to individual differences than a machine, he is unfortunately subject to boredom and fatigue, as a machine would not be. Instead of being the philosopher, scientist, political analyst, and literary critic that these four students require him to be, teaching them and learning from them at the same time, the teacher is almost inevitably tempted to force them all to write about the ideas he himself knows best. The result is that at least three of the four must write out of ignorance.

Now clearly the best way out of this impasse would be for legislatures and school boards and college presidents to recognize the teaching of English for what it is: the most demanding of all teaching jobs, justifying the smallest sections and the lightest course loads. No composition teacher can possibly concentrate on finding special interests, making imaginative assignments, and testing the effectiveness and cogency of papers if he has more than seventy-five students at a time; the really desirable limit would be about forty-five—three sections of fifteen students each. Nobody would ever expect a piano teacher, who has no themes to read, to handle the great masses of pupils that we handle. Everyone recognizes that for all other technical skills individual attention is required. Yet for this, the most delicate of all skills, the one requiring the most subtle interrelationships of training, character, and experience, we fling students and teachers into hopelessly impersonal patterns.

But if I'm not careful I'll find myself saying that our pupils bore us because the superintendents and college presidents hire us to be bored. Administrative neglect and misallocation of educational funds are basic to our problem, and we should let the citizenry know of the scandal on every occasion. But meanwhile, back at the ranch, we are faced with the situation as it now is: we must find some way to train a people to write responsibly even though the people, as represented, don't want this service sufficiently to pay for it.

The tone of political exhortation into which I have now fallen leads me to one natural large source of ideas as we try to encourage writing that is not just lively and controversial but informed and genuinely persuasive. For many students there is obviously more potential interest in social problems and forces, political controversy, and the processes of everyday living around them than in more general ideas. The four students I described a moment ago, students who can say something about philosophy, science, general political theory, or literary criticism, are rare. But most students, including these four, can in theory at least be interested in meaningful argument about social problems in which they are personally involved.

As a profession we have tried, over the past several decades, a variety of approaches attempting to capitalize on such interests. Papers on corruption in TV, arguments about race relations, analyses of distortions in advertising, descriptions of mass communication—these have been combined in various quantities with traditional subjects like grammar, rhetoric, and literature. The "communications" movement, which looked so powerful only a few years ago and which now seems almost dead, had at its heart a perfectly respectable notion, a notion not much different from the one I'm working with today: get them to write about something they know about, and make sure that they see their writing as an act of communication, not as a meaningless exercise. And what better material than other acts of communication.

The dangers of such an approach are by now sufficiently understood. As subject matter for the English course, current "communications media" can at best provide only a supplement to literature and analysis of ideas. But they can be a valuable supplement. Analysis in class of the appeals buried in a *New Yorker* or *Life* advertisement followed by a writing assignment requiring similar analyses can be a far more interesting introduction to the intricacies of style than assignments out of a language text on levels of usage or emotion-charged adjectives. Analysis of a *Time* magazine account, purporting to be objective news but in actual fact a highly emotional editorial, can be not only a valuable experience in itself, but it can lead to papers in which the students do say something to us. Stylistic analysis of the treatment of the same news events by two newspapers or weeklies of different editorial policy can lead to an intellectual awakening of great importance, and thus to papers that will not, cannot, bore the teacher. But this will happen only if the students' critical powers are genuinely developed. It will not do simply to teach the instructor's own prejudices.

There was a time in decades not long past when many of the most lively English teachers thought of their job as primarily to serve as handmaids to liberalism. I had one teacher in college who confessed to me that his overriding purpose was to get students to read and believe *The Nation* rather than the editorials of their daily paper. I suppose that his approach was not entirely valueless. It seems preferable to the effort to be noncontroversial that marks too many English teachers in the '60's, and at least it stirred some of us out of our dogmatic slumbers. But unfortunately it did nothing whatever about teaching us to think critically. Though we graduated from his course at least aware—as many college graduates do not seem to be today— that you can't believe anything you read in the daily press until you have analyzed it and related it to your past experience and to other accounts, it failed to teach us that you can't believe what you read in *The Nation* either. It left the job undone of training our ability to think, because it concentrated too heavily on our opinions. The result was, as I remember, that my own papers in that course were generally regurgitated liberalism. I was excited by them, and that was something. But I can't believe that the instructor found reading them anything other than a chore. There was nothing in them that came from my own experience, my own notions of what would constitute evidence for my conclusions. There I was, in Utah in the depths of the depression, writing about the Okies when I could have been writing about the impoverished farmers all around me. I wrote about race relations in the south without ever having talked with a Negro in my life and without recognizing that the bootblack I occasionally saw in Salt Lake City in the Hotel Utah was in any way related to the problem of race relations.

The third element that accounts for our boring papers is the lack of character and personality in the writer. My life, my observations, my insights were not included in those papers on the Okies and race relations and the New Deal. Every opinion was derivative, every observation second-hand. I had no real opinions of my own, and my eyes were not open wide enough for me to make first-hand observations on the world around me. What I wrote was therefore characterless, without true personality, though often full of personal pronouns. My opinions had been changed, my *self* had not. The style was the boy, the opinionated, immature, uninformed boy; whether my teacher knew it or not—and apparently he did not—his real job was to make a man of me if he wanted me to write like a man.

Putting the difficulty in this way naturally leads me to what perhaps many of you have been impatient about from the beginning. Are not the narrative arts, both as encountered in great literature and as practiced by the students themselves, the best road to the infusion of individuality that no good writing can lack? Would not a real look at the life of that bootblack, and an attempt to deal with him in narrative, have led to a more interesting paper than all of my generalized attacks on the prejudiced southerners?

I think it would, but once again I am almost more conscious of the dangers of the cure than of the advantages. As soon as we make our general rule something like, "Have the students write a personal narrative on what they know about, what they can see and feel at first hand," we have opened the floodgates for those dreadful assignments that we all find ourselves using, even though we know better: "My Summer Vacation," "Catching My First Fish," and "Our Trip to the Seattle World's Fair." Here are personal experiences that call for personal observation and narration. What's wrong with them?

Quite simply, they invite triviality, superficiality, puerility. Our students have been writing essays on such non-subjects all their lives, and until they have developed some sort of critical vision, some way of looking at the world they passed through on their vacations or fishing trips, they are going to feed us the same old bromides that have always won their passing grades. "My Summer Vacation" is an invitation to a grocery list of items, because it implies no audience, no point to be made, no point of view, no character in the speaker. A bright student will make something of such an invitation, by dramatizing the comic family quarrel that developed two days out, or by comparing his view of the American motel system with Nabokov's in *Lolita*, or by remembering the types of people seen in the campgrounds. If he had his own eyes and ears open he might have seen, in a men's room in Grand Canyon last summer, a camper with a very thick French accent trying to convert a Brooklyn Jew into believing the story of the Mormon gold plates. Or he could have heard, at Mesa Verde, a young park ranger, left behind toward the end of the season by all of the experienced rangers, struggling ungrammatically through a set speech on the geology of the area and finally breaking down in embarrassment over his lack of education. Such an episode, really *seen*, could be used narratively to say something to other high school students about what education really is.

But mere narration can be in itself just as dull as the most abstract theorizing about the nature of the universe or the most derivative opinion-mongering about politics. Even relatively skilful narration, used too obviously as a gimmick to catch interest, with no real relation to the subject, can be as dull as the most abstract pomposities. We all know the student papers that begin like *Reader's Digest* articles, with stereotyped narration that makes one doubt the event itself: "On a dark night last January, two teen agers were seen etc., etc." One can open any issue of *Time* and find this so-called narrative interest plastered throughout. From the March 29 issue I find, among many others, the following bits of fantasy: #1: "A Bolivian father sadly surveyed his nation's seven universities, then made up his mind. 'I don't want my son mixed up in politics.' . . . So saying, he sent his son off to West Germany to college." So writing, the author sends me into hysterical laughter: the quote is phony, made up for the occasion to disguise the generality of the news item. #2: "Around 12:30 P.M. every Monday and Friday, an aging Cubana Airlines turbo-prop Britannia whistles to a halt at Mexico City's International Airport. Squads of police stand by. All passengers . . . without diplomatic or Mexican passports are photographed and questioned. . . . They always dodge questions. 'Why are you here? Where are you going?' ask the Mexicans. 'None of your business,' answer the secretive travelers." "Why should I go on reading?" ask I. #3: "At 6:30 one morning early this month, a phone shrilled in the small office off the bedroom of Egypt's President. . . Nasser. [All early morning phones "shrill" for *Time*.] Already awake, he lifted the receiver to hear exciting news: a military coup had just been launched against the anti-Nasser government of Syria. The phone rang again. It was the Minister of Culture. . . . How should Radio Cairo handle the Syrian crisis? 'Support the rebels,' snapped Nasser." Oh lucky reporter, I sigh, to have such an efficient wiretapping service. #4: "In South Korea last week, a farmer named Song Kyu Il traveled all the way from the southern provinces to parade before Seoul's Duk Soo Palace with a placard scrawled in his own blood. . . . Farmer Song was thrown in jail, along with some 200 other demonstrators." That's the last we hear of Song, who is invented as an individual for this opening and then dropped. #5: "Defense Secretary Robert McNamara last spring stood beside President Kennedy on the tenth-deck bridge of the nuclear-powered carrier *Enterprise*. For as far as the eye could see, other U. S. ships deployed over the Atlantic seascape." Well, maybe. But for as far as the eye can see, the narrative clichés are piled, rank on rank. At 12:00 midnight last Thursday a gaunt, harried English professor could be seen hunched over his typewriter, a pile of *Time* magazines beside him on the floor. "What," he murmured to himself, sadly, "Whatever can we do about this trashy imitation of narration?"

Fortunately there is something we can do, and it is directly within our province. We can subject our students to models of genuine narration, with the sharp observation and penetrating critical judgment that underlies all good story telling, whether reportorial or fictional.

It is a truth universally acknowledged, that a single man in possession of a good fortune must be in want of a wife.

However little known the feelings or views of such a man may be on his first entering a neighborhood, this truth is so well fixed in the minds of the surrounding families, that he is considered as the rightful property of someone or other of their daughters.

"My dear Mr. Bennet," said his lady to him one day, "have you heard that Netherfield Park is let at last?"

And already we have a strong personal tone established, a tone of mocking irony which leaves Jane Austen's Mrs. Bennet revealed before us as the grasping, silly gossip she is. Or try this one:

I am an American, Chicago-born—Chicago, that somber city—and go at things as I have taught myself, free-style, and will make the record in my own way: first to knock, first admitted; sometimes an innocent knock, sometimes a not so innocent. But a man's character is his fate, says Heraclitus, and in the end there isn't any way to disguise the nature of the knocks by acoustical work on the door or gloving the knuckles.

Everybody knows there is no fineness or accuracy of suppression; if you hold down one thing you hold down the adjoining.

My own parents were not much to me, though I cared for my mother. She was simple-minded, and what I learned from her was not what she taught....

Do you catch the accent of Saul Bellow here, beneath the accent of his Augie March? You do, of course, but the students, many of them, do not. How do you know, they will ask, that Jane Austen is being ironic? How do you know, they ask again, that Augie is being characterized by his author through what he says? In teaching them how we know, in exposing them to the great narrative voices, ancient and modern, and in teaching them to hear these voices accurately, we are, of course, trying to change their lives, to make them new, to raise their perceptions to a new level altogether. Nobody can really catch these accents who has not grown up sufficiently to see through cheap substitutes. Or, to put it another way, a steady exposure to such voices is the very thing that will produce the maturity that alone can make our students ashamed of beclouded, commercial, borrowed spectacles for viewing the world.

It is true that exposure to good fiction will not in itself transform our students into good writers. Even the best-read student still needs endless hours and years of practice, with rigorous criticism. Fiction will not do the job of discipline in reasoned argument and of practice in developing habits of addressing a living audience. But in the great fiction they will learn what it means to look at something with full attention, what it means to see beneath the surface of society's platitudes. If we then give them practice in writing about things close to the home base of their own honest observations, constantly stretching their powers of generalization and argument but never allowing them to drift into pompous inanities or empty controversiality, we may have that rare but wonderful pleasure of witnessing the miracle: a man and a style where before there was only a bag of wind or a bundle of received opinions. Even when, as with most of our students, no miracles occur, we can hope for papers that we can enjoy reading. And as a final bonus, we might hope that when our students encounter someone on a train who says that he teaches English, their automatic response may be something other than looks of pity or cries of mock alarm.

QUESTIONS

1. Booth is writing for an audience of English teachers. In what ways might the essay differ if he were writing for an audience of students?
2. On page 259 Booth says he has "now fallen" into a "tone of political exhortation." (Tone may be defined as the reflection in language of the attitude a writer takes toward his subject or his audience or both.) What other "tones" are there in the essay? Why does Booth find it necessary to vary the tone?
3. What steps are necessary before an "opinion" can become a "reasoned opinion"? Select some subject on which you have a strong opinion and decide whether it is a reasoned opinion.
4. Booth characterizes the writing in the Reader's Digest and Time (pp. 261–263). What does he feel the two magazines have in common? Analyze an article from either one of these magazines to see how accurate Booth's characterization is.

On Education

WAYNE C. BOOTH

Is There Any Knowledge That a Man *Must* Have?

Everyone lives on the assumption that a great deal of knowledge is not worth bothering about; though we all know that what looks trivial in one man's hands may turn out to be earth-shaking in another's, we simply cannot know very much, compared with what might be known, and we must therefore choose. What is shocking is not the act of choice which we all commit openly but the claim that some choices are wrong. Especially shocking is the claim implied by my title: There is some knowledge that a man *must* have.

There clearly is no such thing, if by knowledge we mean mere acquaintance with this or that thing, fact, concept, literary work, or scientific law. When C. P. Snow and F. R. Leavis exchanged blows on whether knowledge of Shakespeare is more important than knowledge of the second law of thermodynamics, they were both, it seemed to me, much too ready to assume as indispensable what a great many wise and good men have quite obviously got along without. And it is not only nonprofessionals who can survive in happy ignorance of this or that bit of lore. I suspect that many successful scientists (in biology, say) have lost whatever hold they might once have had on the second law; I know that a great many literary scholars survive and even flourish without knowing certain "indispensable" classics. We all get along without vast loads of learning that other men take as necessary marks of an educated man. If we once begin to "reason the need" we will find, like Lear, that "our basest beggars/Are in the poorest thing superfluous." Indeed, we can survive, in a manner of speaking, even in the modern world, with little more than the bare literacy necessary to tell the "off" buttons from the "on."

Herbert Spencer would remind us at this point that we are interpreting *need* as if it were entirely a question of private survival. Though he talks about what a man must know to stay alive, he is

265

more interested, in his defense of science, in what a *society* must know to survive: "Is there any knowledge that *man* must have?"—not a man, but *man*. This question is put to us much more acutely in our time than it was in Spencer's, and it is by no means as easy to argue now as it was then that the knowledge needed for man's survival is scientific knowledge. The threats of atomic annihilation, of engulfing population growth, of depleted air, water, and food must obviously be met, if man is to survive, and in meeting them man will, it is true, need more and more scientific knowledge; but it is not at all clear that more and more scientific knowledge will by itself suffice. Even so, a modern Herbert Spencer might well argue that a conference like this one, with its emphasis on the individual and his cognitive needs, is simply repeating the mistakes of the classical tradition. The knowledge most worth having would be, from his point of view, that of how to pull mankind through the next century or so without absolute self-destruction. The precise proportions of different kinds of knowledge—physical, biological, political, ethical, psychological, historical, or whatever—would be different from those prescribed in Spencer's essay, but the nature of the search would be precisely the same.

We can admit the relevance of this emphasis on social utility and at the same time argue that our business here is with other matters entirely. If the only knowledge a man *must* have is how to cross the street without getting knocked down—or, in other words, how to navigate the centuries without blowing himself up—then we may as well close the conference and go home. We may as well also roll up the college and mail it to a research institute, because almost any place that is not cluttered up with notions of liberal education will be able to discover and transmit practical bits of survival-lore better than we can. Our problem of survival is a rather different one, thrust at us as soon as we change our title slightly once again to "Is there any knowledge (other than the knowledge for survival) that a man must have?" That slight shift opens a new perspective on the problem, because the question of what it is to be a man, of what it is to be fully human, is the question at the heart of liberal education.

To be human, to be human, to be fully human. What does it mean? What is required? Immediately, we start feeling nervous again. Is the speaker suggesting that some of us are not fully human *yet?* Here come those hierarchies again. Surely in our pluralistic society we can admit an unlimited number of legitimate ways to be a man, without prescribing some outmoded aristocratic code!

Who—or what—is the creature we would educate? Our answer will determine our answers to educational questions, and it is therefore, I think, worth far more vigorous effort than it usually receives. I find it convenient, and only slightly unfair, to classify the educational talk I encounter these days under four notions of man, three of them metaphorical, only one literal. Though nobody's position, I suppose, fits my types neatly, some educators talk as if they were programming machines, some talk as if they were conditioning rats, some talk as if they were training ants to take a position in the anthill, and some—precious few—talk as if they thought of themselves as men dealing with men.

One traditional division of the human soul, you will remember, was into three parts: the vegetable, the animal, and the rational. Nobody, so far as I know, has devised an educational program treating students as vegetables, though one runs into the analogy used negatively in academic sermons from time to time. Similarly, no one ever really says that men are ants, though there is a marvelous passage in Kwame Nkrumah's autobiography in which he meditates longingly on the order and pure functionality of an anthill. Educators do talk of men as machines or as animals, but of course they always point out that men are much more complicated than any other known animals or machines. My point here is not so much to attack any one of these metaphors—dangerous as I think they are—but to describe briefly what answers to our question each of them might suggest.

Ever since Descartes, La Mettrie,[1] and others explicitly called a man a machine, the metaphor has been a dominant one in educational thinking. Some have thought of man as a very complex machine, needing very elaborate programming; others have thought of him as a very simple machine, requiring little more than a systematic pattern of stimuli to produce foretellable responses. I heard a psychologist recently repeat the old behaviorist claim (first made by John B. Watson, I believe) that if you would give him complete control over any normal child's life from birth, he could turn that child into a great musician or a great mathematician or a great poet—you name it and he could produce it. On being pressed, the professor admitted that this claim was only "in theory," because we don't yet have the necessary knowledge. When I pushed further by asking why he was so confident in advance of experimental proof, it became clear that his faith in the fundamental metaphor of man as a programmable machine was unshakable.

When the notion of man as machine was first advanced, the machine was a very simple collection of pulleys and billiard balls and levers. Such original simplicities have been badly battered by our growing awareness both of how complex real machines can be

1. René Descartes (1596-1650), French philosopher and mathematician; Julian Offray de La Mettrie (1709- 1751), French physician and philosopher.

and of how much more complex man is than any known machine. Modern notions of stimulus-response patterns are immeasurably more complicated than anything Descartes imagined, because we are now aware of the fantastic variety of stimuli that the man-machine is subject to and of the even more fantastic complexity of the responding circuits.

But whether the machine is simple or complex, the educational task for those who think of man under this metaphor is to program the mechanism so that it will produce the results that we have fore-ordained. We do not simply fill the little pitchers, like Mr. Grad-grind in Dickens' *Hard Times;*[2] we are much too sophisticated to want only undigested "pour-back," as he might have called his product. But we still program the information channels so that the proper if-loops and do-loops will be followed and the right feedback produced. The "programming" can be done by human teachers, of course, and not only by machines; but it is not surprising that those whose thinking is dominated by this metaphor tend to discover that machines are better teachers than men. The more ambitious programmers do not hesitate to claim that they can teach both thought and creativity in this way. But I have yet to see a program that can deal effectively with any subject that cannot be reduced to simple yes and no answers, that is, to answers that are known in advance by the programmer and can thus be fixed for all time.

We can assume that subtler machines will be invented that can engage in simulated dialogue with the pupil, and perhaps even recognize when a particularly bright pupil has discovered something new that refutes the program. But even the subtlest teaching machine imaginable will still be subject, one must assume, to a final limitation: it can teach only what a machine can "learn." For those who believe that man is literally nothing but a very compli-cated machine, this is not in fact a limitation; machines will ulti-mately be able to duplicate all mental processes, thus "learning" everything learnable, and they will be able in consequence to teach everything.

I doubt this claim for many reasons, and I am glad to find the testimony of Norbert Wiener, the first and best known cyberneti-cist, to the effect that there will always remain a radical gap between computers and the human mind. But "ultimately" is a long way off, and I am not so much concerned with whether ulti-mately man's mind will closely resemble some ultimately inventable machine as I am with the effects, here and now, of thinking about men under the analogy with machines of today. Let me simply close this section with an illustration of how the mechanistic model can permeate our thought in destructive ways. Ask yourselves what

2. Thomas Gradgrind thought of his students as "little pitchers . . . who were to be filled so full of facts."

picture of creature-to-be-educated emerges from this professor of teacher education:

> To implement the TEAM Project new curriculum proposal ... our first concerns are with instructional systems, materials to feed the system, and personnel to operate the system. We have defined an instructional system as the optimal blending of the demands of content, communication, and learning. While numerous models have been developed, our simplified model of an instructional system would look like Figure 2. . . . We look at the process of communication—communicating content to produce learning—as something involving the senses: ... [aural, oral, tactile, visual]. And I think in teacher education we had better think of the communications aspect of the instructional system as a package that includes the teacher, textbook, new media, classroom, and environment. To integrate these elements to more effectively transmit content into permanent learning, new and better instructional materials are needed and a new focus on the teacher of teachers is required. The teacher of teachers must: (1) examine critically the content of traditional courses in relation to desired behavioral outcomes; (2) become more sophisticated in the techniques of communicating course content; and (3) learn to work in concert with media specialists to develop the materials and procedures requisite to the efficient instructional system. And if the media specialist were to be charged with the efficient operation of the system, his upgrading would demand a broad-based "media generalist" orientation.[3]

I submit that the author of this passage was thinking of human beings as stimulus-response systems on the simplest possible model, and that he was thinking of the purpose of education as the transfer of information from one machine to another. Though he would certainly deny it if we asked him, he has come to think about the human mind so habitually in the mechanistic mode that he doesn't even know he's doing it.[4]

But it is time to move from the machine metaphor to animal metaphors. They are closely related, of course, because everybody who believes that man is a machine also believes that animals are machines, only simpler ones. But many people who would resist the word "machine" do tend to analogize man to one or another characteristic of animals. Since man is obviously an animal in one sense, he can be studied as an animal, and he can be taught as an animal is taught. Most of the fundamental research in learning theory underlying the use of teaching machines has been done, in fact, on animals like rats and pigeons. You can teach pigeons to play Ping-Pong rather quickly by rewarding every gesture they make that moves them toward success in the game and refusing to reward those gestures that you want to efface. Though everybody admits

3. Desmond P. Wedberg, *Teacher Education Looks to the Future,* Twelfth Biennial School for Executives (Washington, D. C.: American Association of Colleges for Teacher Education, 1964) [Booth's note].

4. I am not of course suggesting

that *any* use of teaching machines implies a mechanistic reduction of persons to machines; programmers rightly point out that machines *can* free teachers from the mechanical and save time for the personal [Booth's note].

that human beings are more complicated than rats and pigeons, just as everyone admits that human beings are more complicated than computers, the basic picture of the animal as a collection of drives or instincts, "conditioned" to learn according to rewards or punishments, has underlain much modern educational theory.

The notion of the human being as a collection of drives different from animal drives only in being more complex carries with it implications for education planners. If you and I are motivated only by sex or hunger or more complex drives like desire for power or for ego-satisfaction, then of course all education depends on the provision of satisfactions along our route to knowledge. If our teachers can just program carrots along the path at the proper distance, we donkey-headed students will plod along the path from carrot to carrot and end up as educated men.

I cannot take time here to deal with this view adequately, but it seems to me that it is highly questionable even about animals themselves. What kind of thing, really, is a rat or a monkey? The question of whether animals have souls has been debated actively for at least nine centuries; now psychologists find themselves dealing with the same question under another guise: What *are* these little creatures that we kill so blithely for the sake of knowledge? What *are* these strangely resistant little bundles of energy that will prefer—as experiments with rats have shown—a complicated interesting maze without food to a dull one *with* food?

There are, in fact, many experiments by now showing that at the very least we must postulate, for animals, a strong independent drive for mastery of the environment or satisfaction of curiosity about it. All the more advanced animals will learn to push levers that produce interesting results—clicks or bells or flashing lights or sliding panels—when no other reward is offered.[5] It seems clear that even to be a fulfilled animal, as it were, something more than "animal satisfaction" is needed!

I am reminded here of the experiments on mother-love in monkeys reported by Harry F. Harlow in the *Scientific American* some years ago. Harlow called his article "Love in Infant Monkeys," and the subtitle of his article read, "Affection in infants was long thought to be generated by the satisfactions of feeding. Studies of young rhesus monkeys now indicate that love derives mainly from close bodily contact." The experiment consisted of giving infant monkeys a choice between a plain wire figure that offered the infant milk and a terry-cloth covered figure without milk. There was a pathetic picture of an infant clinging to the terry-cloth figure, and a caption that read "The infants spent most of their time clinging to the soft cloth 'mother' even when nursing bottles were

5. See Robert W. White, "Motivation Reconsidered: The Concept of Competence," *Psychological Review*, 66 (1959), 297–333 [Booth's note].

attached to the wire mother." The article concluded—rather prematurely, I thought—that "contact comfort" had been shown to be a "prime requisite in the formation of an infant's love for its mother," that the act of nursing had been shown to be unimportant if not totally irrelevant in forming such love (though it was evident to any reader, even at the time, that no genuine "*act* of nursing" had figured in the experiment at all), and that "our investigations have established a secure experimental approach to this realm of dramatic and subtle emotional relationships." The only real problem, Harlow said, was the availability of enough infant monkeys for experiment.

Now I would not want to underrate the importance of Harlow's demonstration to the scientific community that monkeys do not live by bread alone. But I think that most scientists and humanists reading the article would have been struck by two things. The first is the automatic assumption that the way to study a subject like love is to break it down into its component parts; nobody looking at that little monkey clinging to the terry-cloth could possibly have said, "This is love," unless he had been blinded by a hidden conviction that love in animals is—must be—a mere cumulative result of a collection of drive satisfactions. This assumption is given quite plainly in Harlow's concluding sentence: "Finally with such techniques established, there appears to be no reason why we cannot at some future time investigate the fundamental neurophysiological and biochemical variables underlying affection and love." For Harlow monkeys (and people) seem to be mere collections of neurophysiological and biochemical variables, and love will be best explained when we can explain the genesis of each of its parts. The second striking point is that for Harlow animals do not matter, except as they are useful for experiment. If he had felt that they mattered, he might have noticed the look on his infant's face—a look that predicted for me, and for other readers of the *Scientific American* I've talked with, that these monkeys were doomed.

And indeed they were. A year or so later another article appeared, reporting Harlow's astonished discovery that all of the little monkeys on which he had earlier experimented had turned out to be incurably psychotic. Not a single monkey could mate, not a single monkey could play, not a single monkey could in fact become anything more than the twisted half-creatures that Harlow's deprivations had made of them. Harlow's new discovery was that monkeys needed close association with their peers during infancy and that such association was even more important to their development than genuine mothering. There was no sign that Harlow had learned any fundamental lessons from his earlier gross mistakes; he had landed nicely on his feet, still convinced that the way to study love is to break it down into its component parts and that the way to study animals is to maim them or reduce them to something less than themselves. As Robert White says, summarizing his reasons for rejecting similar methods in studying human infancy, it is too often assumed that the scientific way is to analyze behavior until one can find a small enough unit to allow for detailed research, but in the process "very vital common properties" are lost from view.

I cite Harlow's two reports not, of course, to attack animal experimentation—though I must confess that I am horrified by much that goes on in its name—nor to claim that animals are more like human beings than they are. Rather, I want simply to suggest that the danger of thinking of men as animals is heightened if the animals we think of are reduced to machines on a simple model.

The effects of reducing education to conditioning can be seen throughout America today. Usually they appear in subtle forms, disguised with the language of personalism; you will look a long time before you find anyone (except a very few Skinnerians) saying that he thinks of education as exactly like conditioning pigeons. But there are plenty of honest, blunt folk around to let the cat out of the bag—like the author of an article this year in *College Composition and Communications*: "The Use of a Multiple Response Device in the Teaching of Remedial English." The author claimed to have evidence that if you give each student four buttons to be pushed on multiple-choice questions, with all the buttons wired into a lighted grid at the front of the room, the resulting "instantaneous feedback"—every child learning immediately whether he agrees with the rest of the class—speeds up the learning of grammatical rules considerably over the usual workbook procedures. I daresay it does—but meanwhile what has happened to education? Or take the author of an article on "Procedures and Techniques of Teaching," who wrote as follows: "If we expect students to learn skills, they have to practice, but practice doesn't make perfect. Practice works if the learner *learns the results* of his practice, i.e., if he receives feedback. Feedback is most effective when it is contiguous to the response being learned. One of the chief advantages of teaching machines is that the learner finds out quickly whether his response is right or wrong . . . [Pressey] has published the results of an extensive program of research with tests that students score for themselves by punching alternatives until they hit the correct one. . . . [Thus] teaching machines or workbooks have many theoretical advantages over lecturing or other conventional methods of instruction." But according to what theory, one must ask, *do* systematic feedback mechanisms, perfected to whatever degree, have "theoretical advantages" over human contact? Whatever else can be said for such a theory, it will be based on the simplest of comparisons with animal learning. Unfortunately, the author goes on, experimental evidence is on the whole rather discouraging: "Experiments at the Systems Development Corporation . . . suggest that teaching incorporating . . . human characteristics is more effective than the typical fixed-sequence machines. (In this experiment instead of using teaching machines to simulate human teachers, the experimenters used humans to simulate teaching machines!)"

So far I have dealt with analogies for man that apply only to individuals. My third analogy turns to the picture of men in groups, and it is given to me partly by discussions of education, like those of Admiral Rickover, that see it simply as filling society's needs. I know of only one prominent educator who has publicly praised the anthill as a model for the kind of society a university should serve—a society of specialists each trained to do his part. But the notion pervades many of the defenses of the emerging multiversities.

If knowledge is needed to enable men to function as units in society, and if the health of society is taken as the purpose of their existence, then there is nothing wrong in training the ants to fill their niches; it would be wrong not to. "Education is our first line of defense—make it strong," so reads the title of the first chapter of Admiral Rickover's book, *Education and Freedom* (New York: Dutton, 1959). "We must upgrade our schools" in order to "guarantee the future prosperity and freedom of the Republic." You can tell whether the ant-analogy is dominating a man's thinking by a simple test of how he orders his ends and means. In Admiral Rickover's statement, the schools must be upgraded in order to guarantee future prosperity, that is, we improve education for the sake of some presumed social good.

I seldom find anyone putting it the other way round: we must guarantee prosperity so that we can improve the schools, and the reason we want to improve the schools is that we want to insure the development of certain kinds of persons, both as teachers and as students. You cannot even say what I just said so long as you are really thinking of ants and anthills. Ants are not ends in themselves, ultimately more valuable than the hills they live in (I *think* they are not; maybe to themselves, or in the eyes of God, even ants are ultimate, self-justifying ends). At least from our point of view, ants are expendable, or to put it another way, their society is more beautiful, more interesting, more admirable than they are. And I would want to argue that too many people think of human beings in the same way when they think of educating them. The Communists make this quite explicit: the ends of Communist society justify whatever distortion or destruction of individual purposes is necessary to achieve them; men are educated for the state, not for their own well-being. They are basically political animals, not in the Aristotelian sense that they require society if they are to achieve their full natures and thus their own special, human kind of happiness, but in the sense that they exist, like ants, for the sake of the body politic.

If the social order is the final justification of what we do in education, then a certain attitude toward teaching and research will result: all of us little workmen, down inside the anthill, will go on happily contributing our tiny bit to the total scheme without worrying much about larger questions of the why and wherefore. I know a graduate student who says that she sometimes sees her graduate professors as an army of tiny industrious miners at the bottom of a vast mine, chipping away at the edges and shipping their bits of knowledge up to the surface, blindly hoping that someone up there will know what to do with it all. An order is received for such-and-such new organic compounds; society needs them. Another order is received for an atomic bomb; it is needed, and it is therefore produced. Often no orders come down, but the chipping goes on anyway, and the shipments are made, because everyone knows that the health of the mine depends on a certain tonnage of specialized knowledge each working day.

We have learned lately that "they" are going to establish a great new atom-smasher, perhaps near Chicago. The atom-smasher will employ two thousand scientists and technicians. I look out at you here, knowing that some of you are physics majors, and I wonder whether any of you will ultimately be employed in that new installation, and if you are, whether it will be as an ant or as a human being. Which it will be must depend not on your ultimate employers but on yourself and on what happens to your education between now and then: if you have been given nothing but training to be that ultimate unit in that ultimate system, only a miracle can save you from formic dissolution of your human lineaments.

But it is long past time for me to turn from these negative, truncated portraits of what man really is not and attempt to say what he is. And here we encounter a difficulty that I find very curious. You will note that each of these metaphors has reduced man to something less than man, or at least to a partial aspect of man. It is easy to say that man is not a machine, though he is in some limited respects organized like a machine and even to some degree "programmable." It is also easy to say that man is not simply a complicated rat or monkey, though he is in some ways like rats and monkeys. Nor is man an ant, though he lives and must function in a complicated social milieu. All these metaphors break down not because they are flatly false but because they *are* metaphors, and any metaphorical definition is inevitably misleading. The ones I have been dealing with are especially misleading, because in every case they have reduced something more complex to something much less complex. But even if we were to analogize man to something more complex, say, the universe, we would be dissatisfied. What we want is some notion of what man really *is*, so that we will know what or whom we are trying to educate.

And here it is that we discover something very important about man, something that even the least religious person must find himself mystified by: man is the one "thing" we know that is completely resistant to our efforts at metaphor or analogy or image-making. What seems to be the most important literal characteristic of man is his resistance to definitions in terms of anything else. If you call me a machine, even a very complicated machine, I know that you deny what I care most about, my selfhood, my sense of being a person, my consciousness, my conviction of freedom and dignity, my awareness of love, my laughter. Machines have none of these things, and even if we were generous to their prospects, and imagined machines immeasurably superior to the most complicated ones now in existence, we would still feel an infinite gap between them and what we know to be a basic truth about ourselves: machines are expendable, ultimately expendable, and men are mysteriously ends in themselves.

I hear people deny this, but when they do they always argue for their position by claiming marvelous feats of super-machine calculation that machines can now do or will someday be able to do. But that is not the point; of course machines can outcalculate us. The question to ask is entirely a different one: Will they ever outlove us, outlive us, outvalue us? Do we build machines because machines are good things in themselves? Do we nurture them for their own good, as we nurture our children? An obvious way to test our sense of worth in men and machines is to ask ourselves whether we would ever campaign to liberate the poor drowntrodden machines who have been enslaved. Shall we form a National Association for the Advancement of Machinery? Will anyone ever feel a smidgeon of moral indignation because this or that piece of machinery is not given equal rights before the law? Or put it another way: Does anyone value Gemini more than the twins? There may be men now alive who would rather "destruct," as we say, the pilot than the experimental rocket, but most of us still believe that the human being in the space ship is more important than the space ship.

When college students protest the so-called depersonalization of education, what they mean, finally, is not simply that they want to meet their professors socially or that they want small classes or that they do not want to be dealt with by IBM machines. All these things are but symptoms of a deeper sense of a violation of their literal reality as persons, ends in themselves rather than mere expendable things. Similarly, the current deep-spirited revolt against racial and economic injustice seems to me best explained as a sudden assertion that people, of whatever color or class, are not reducible to social conveniences. When you organize your labor force or your educational system as if men were mere social conveniences, "human resources," as we say, contributors to the gross national product, you violate something that we all know, in a form of knowledge much deeper than our knowledge of the times tables or the second law of thermodynamics: those field hands, those children crowded into the deadening classroom, those men laboring without dignity in the city anthills are *men*, creatures whose worth is mysteriously more than any description of it we might make in justifying what we do to them.

Ants, rats, and machines can all learn a great deal. Taken together, they "know" a very great part of what our schools and colleges are now designed to teach. But is there any kind of knowledge that a creature must have to qualify as a man? Is there any part of the educational task that is demanded of us by virtue of our claim to educate this curious entity, this *person* that cannot be reduced to mechanism or animality alone?

You will not be surprised, by now, to have me sound, in my answer, terribly traditional, not to say square: the education that a *man* must have is what has traditionally been called liberal education. The knowledge it yields is the knowledge or capacity or power of how to act freely as a man. That's why we call liberal education liberal: it is intended to liberate from whatever it is that makes animals act like animals and machines act like machines.

I'll return in a moment to what it means to act freely as a man. But we are already in a position to say something about what knowledge a man must have—he must first of all be able to learn for himself. If he cannot learn for himself, he is enslaved by his teachers' ideas, or by the ideas of his more persuasive contemporaries, or by machines programmed by other men. He may have what we call a good formal education, yet still be totally bound by whatever opinions happen to have come his way in attractive grab. One wonders how many of our graduates have learned how to take hold of a subject and "work it up," so that they can make themselves experts on what other men have concluded. In some ways this is not a very demanding goal, and it is certainly not very exciting. It says nothing about that popular concept, creativity, or about imagination or originality. All it says is that anyone who is dependent on his teachers *is* dependent, not free, and that anyone who knows how to learn for himself is less like animals and machines than anyone who does not know how to learn for himself.

We see already that a college is not being merely capricious or arbitrary when it insists that some kinds of learning are more important than some others. The world is overflowing with interesting subjects and valuable skills, but surely any college worth the name will put first things first: it will try to insure, as one inescapable goal, that every graduate can dig out from the printed page what he needs to know. And it will not let the desire to tamp in additional tidbits of knowledge, however delicious, interfere with training minds for whom a formal teacher is no longer required.

To put our first goal in this way raises some real problems that we cannot solve. Obviously no college can produce self-learners in very many subjects. Are we not lucky if a graduate can learn for himself even in one field, now that knowledge in all areas has advanced as far as it has? Surely we cannot expect our graduates to reach a stage of independence in mathematics and physics, in political science and psychology, in philosophy and English, *and* in all the other nice subjects that one would like to master.

Rather than answer this objection right away, let me make things even more difficult by saying that it is not enough to learn how to learn. The man who cannot *think* for himself, going beyond what other men have learned or thought, is still enslaved to other men's ideas. Obviously the goal of learning to think is even more difficult than the goal of learning to learn. But difficult as it is we must add it to our list. It is simply not enough to be able to get up a subject on one's own, like a good encyclopedia employee, even though any college would take pride if all its graduates could do so. To be fully human means in part to think one's own thoughts, to reach a point at which, whether one's ideas are different from or similar to other men's, they are truly one's own.

The art of asking oneself critical questions that lead either to new answers or to genuine revitalizing of old answers, the art of making thought live anew in each new generation, may not be entirely amenable to instruction. But it is a necessary art nonetheless, for any man who wants to be free. It is an art that all philosophers have tried to pursue, and many of them have given direct guidance in how to pursue it. Needless to say, it is an art the pursuit of which is never fully completed. No one thinks for himself very much of the time or in very many subjects. Yet the habitual effort to ask the right critical questions and to apply rigorous tests to our hunches is a clearer mark than any other of an educated man.

But again we stumble upon the question, "Learn to think about *what?*" The modern world presents us with innumerable subjects to think about. Does it matter whether anyone achieves this rare and difficult point in more than one subject? And if not, won't the best education simply be the one that brings a man into mastery of a narrow specialty as soon as possible, so that he can learn to think for himself as soon as possible? Even at best most of us are enslaved to opinions provided for us by experts in *most* fields. So far, it might be argued, I still have not shown that there is any kind of knowledge that a man must have, only that there are certain skills that he must be able to exercise in at least one field.

To provide a proper grounding for my answer to that objection would require far more time than I have left, and I'm not at all sure that I could do so even with all the time in the world. The question of whether it is possible to maintain a human stance toward any more than a tiny fraction of modern knowledge is not clearly answerable at this stage in our history. It will be answered, if at all, only when men have learned how to store and retrieve all "machinable" knowledge, freeing themselves for distinctively human tasks. But in the meantime, I find myself unable to surrender, as it were, three distinct kinds of knowledge that seem to me indispensable to being human.

To be a man, a man must first know something about his own nature and his place in Nature, with a capital N—something about the truth of things, as men used to say in the old-fashioned days before the word "truth" was banned from academia. Machines are not curious, so far as I can judge; animals are, but presumably they never go, in their philosophies, even at the furthest, beyond a kind of solipsistic existentialism. But in science, in philosophy (ancient and modern), in theology, in psychology and anthropology, and in literature (of some kinds), we are presented with accounts of our universe and of our place in it that as men we can respond to in only one manly way: by thinking about them, by speculating and testing our speculations.

We know before we start that our thought is doomed to incompleteness and error and downright chanciness. Even the most rigorously scientific view will be changed, we know, within a decade, or perhaps even by tomorrow. But to refuse the effort to understand is to resign from the human race; the unexamined life can no doubt be worth living in other respects—after all, it is no mean thing to be a vegetable, an oak tree, an elephant, or a lion. But a man, a man will want to see, in this speculative domain, beyond his next dinner.

By putting it in this way, I think we can avoid the claim that to be a man I must have studied any one field—philosophy, science, theology. But to be a man, I *must speculate*, and I must learn how to test my speculations so that they are not simply capricious, unchecked by other men's speculations. A college education, surely, should throw every student into a regular torrent of speculation, and it should school him to recognize the different standards of validation proper to different kinds of claims to truth. You cannot distinguish a man who in this respect is educated from other men by whether or not he believes in God, or in UFO's. But you can tell an educated man by the way he takes hold of the question of whether God exists, or whether UFO's are from Mars. Do you know your own reasons for your beliefs, or do you absorb your beliefs from whatever happens to be in your environment, like plankton taking in nourishment?

Second, the man who has not learned how to make the great human achievements in the arts his own, who does not know what it means to *earn* a great novel or symphony or painting for himself, is enslaved either to caprice or to other men's testimony or to a life of ugliness. You will notice that as I turn thus to "beauty"— another old-fashioned term—I do not say that a man must know how to prove what is beautiful or how to discourse on aesthetics. Such speculative activities are pleasant and worthwhile in themselves, but they belong in my first domain. Here we are asking that a man be educated to the experience of beauty; speculation about it can then follow. My point is simply that a man is less than a man if he cannot respond to the art made by his fellow man.

Again I have tried to put the standard in a way that allows for the impossibility of any one man's achieving independent responses in very many arts. Some would argue that education should insure some minimal human competence in all of the arts, or at least in music, painting, and literature. I suppose I would be satisfied if all of our graduates had been "hooked" by at least one art, hooked so deeply that they could never get free. As in the domain of speculation, we could say that the more types of distinctively human activity a man can master, the better, but we are today talking about floors, not ceilings, and I shall simply rest content with saying that to be a man, a man must know artistic beauty, in some form, and know it in the way that beauty can be known. (The distinction between natural and man-made beauty might give me trouble if you pushed me on it here, but let me just say, dogmatically, that I would not be satisfied simply to know natural beauty—women and sunsets, say—as a substitute for art).

Finally, the man who has not learned anything about how to understand his own intentions and to make them effective in the world, who has not, through experience and books, learned something about what is possible and what impossible, what desirable and what undesirable, will be enslaved by the political and social intentions of other men, benign or malign. The domain of practical wisdom is at least as complex and troublesome as the other two, and at the same time it is even more self-evidently indispensable. How should a man live? How should a society be run? What direction should a university take in 1966? For that matter what should be the proportion, in a good university, of inquiry into truth, beauty, and "goodness"? What kind of knowledge of self or of society is pertinent to living the life proper to a man? In short, the very question of this conference falls within this final domain: What knowledge, if any, is most worthy of pursuit? You cannot distinguish the men from the boys according to any one set of conclusions, but you *can* recognize a man, in this domain, simply by discovering whether he can think for himself about practical questions, with some degree of freedom from blind psychological or political or economic compulsions. Ernest Hemingway tells somewhere of a man who had "moved one dollar's width to the [political] right for every dollar that he'd ever earned." Perhaps no man ever achieves the opposite extreme, complete freedom in his choices from irrelevant compulsions. But all of us who believe in education believe that it is possible for any man, through study and conscientious thought, to school his choices—that is, to free them through coming to understand the forces working on them.

Even from this brief discussion of the three domains, I think we are put in a position to see how it can be said that there is some knowledge that a man must have. The line I have been pursuing will not lead to a list of great books, or even to a list of indispensable departments in a university. Nor will it lead, in any clear-cut fashion, to a pattern of requirements in each of the divisions. Truth, beauty, and goodness (or "right choice") are relevant to study in every division within the university; the humanities, for example, have no corner on beauty or imagination or art, and the sciences have no corner on speculative truth. What is more, a man can be ignorant even of Shakespeare, Aristotle, Beethoven, and Einstein, and be a man for a' that—*if* he has learned how to think his own thoughts, experience beauty for himself, and choose his own actions.

It is not the business of a college to determine or limit what a man will know; if it tries to, he will properly resent its impositions, perhaps immediately, perhaps ten years later when the imposed information is outmoded. But I think that it *is* the business of a college to help teach a man how to use his mind for himself, in at least the three directions I have suggested. * * * To think for oneself is, as we all know, hard enough. To design a program and assemble faculty to assist rather than hinder students in their efforts to think for themselves is even harder. But in an age that is oppressed by huge accumulations of unassimilated knowledge, the task of discovering what it means to educate a man is perhaps more important than ever before.

RALPH WALDO EMERSON
The American Scholar[1]

Mr. President and Gentlemen:

I greet you on the recommencement of our literary year. Our anniversary is one of hope, and, perhaps, not enough of labor. We do not meet for games of strength or skill, for the recitation of histories, tragedies, and odes, like the ancient Greeks; for parliaments of love and poesy, like the Troubadours; nor for the advancement of science, like our contemporaries in the British and European capitals. Thus far, our holiday has been simply a friendly sign of the survival of the love of letters amongst a people too busy to give to letters any more. As such it is precious as the sign of an indestructible instinct. Perhaps, the time is already come when it ought to be, and will be, something else; when the sluggard intellect of this continent will look from under its iron lids and fill the postponed expectation of the world with something better than the exertions of mechanical skill. Our day of dependence, our long apprenticeship to the learning of other lands, draws to a close. The millions that around us are rushing into life, cannot always be fed on the sere remains of foreign harvests. Events, actions arise, that must be sung, that will sing themselves. Who can doubt that poetry will revive and lead in a new age, as the star in the constellation Harp, which now flames in our zenith, astronomers announce, shall one day be the pole-star for a thousand years?

In this hope I accept the topic which not only usage but the nature of our association seem to prescribe to this day—the American Scholar. Year by year we come up hither to read one more chapter of his biography. Let us inquire what light new days and events have thrown on his character and his hopes.

It is one of those fables which out of an unknown antiquity convey an unlooked-for wisdom, that the gods, in the beginning, divided Man into men, that he might be more helpful to himself; just as the hand was divided into fingers, the better to answer its end.

The old fable covers a doctrine ever new and sublime; that there is One Man—present to all particular men only partially, or through one faculty; and that you must take the whole society to find the whole man. Man is not a farmer, or a professor, or an engineer, but he is all. Man is priest, and scholar, and statesman, and producer, and soldier. In the *divided* or social state these functions are parceled out to individuals, each of whom aims to do his stint of the joint work, whilst each other performs his. The fable implies that the individual, to possess himself, must sometimes return from his

1. The Phi Beta Kappa address at Harvard College, August 31, 1837.

own labor to embrace all the other laborers. But, unfortunately, this original unit, this fountain of power, has been so distributed to multitudes, has been so minutely subdivided and peddled out, that it is spilled into drops, and cannot be gathered. The state of society is one in which the members have suffered amputation from the trunk, and strut about so many walking monsters—a good finger, a neck, a stomach, an elbow, but never a man.

Man is thus metamorphosed into a thing, into many things. The planter, who is Man sent out into the field to gather food, is seldom cheered by any idea of the true dignity of his ministry. He sees his bushel and his cart, and nothing beyond, and sinks into the farmer, instead of Man on the farm. The tradesman scarcely ever gives an ideal worth to his work, but is ridden by the routine of his craft, and the soul is subject to dollars. The priest becomes a form; the attorney a statute-book; the mechanic a machine; the sailor a rope of the ship.

In this distribution of functions the scholar is the delegated intellect. In the right state he is *Man Thinking*. In the degenerate state, when the victim of society, he tends to become a mere thinker, or still worse, the parrot of other men's thinking.

In this view of him, as Man Thinking, the theory of his office is contained. Him Nature solicits with all her placid, all her monitory pictures; him the past instructs; him the future invites. Is not indeed every man a student, and do not all things exist for the student's behoof? And, finally, is not the true scholar the only true master? But the old oracle said, "All things have two handles: beware of the wrong one." In life, too often, the scholar errs with mankind and forfeits his privilege. Let us see him in his school, and consider him in reference to the main influences he receives.

The first in time and the first in importance of the influences upon the mind is that of nature. Every day, the sun; and, after sunset, Night and her stars. Ever the winds blow; ever the grass grows. Every day, men and women, conversing—beholding and beholden. The scholar is he of all men whom this spectacle most engages. He must settle its value in his mind. What is nature to him? There is never a beginning, there is never an end, to the inexplicable continuity of this web of God, but always circular power returning into itself. Therein it resembles his own spirit, whose beginning, whose ending, he never can find—so entire, so boundless. Far too as her splendors shine, system on system shooting like rays, upward, downward, without center, without circumference—in the mass and in the particle, Nature hastens to render account of herself to the mind. Classification begins. To the young mind every thing is individual, stands by itself. By and by, it finds how to join two things and see in them one nature; then three, then three thousand; and so, tyrannized over by its own unifying instinct, it goes on tying things together, diminishing anomalies, discovering roots, running under ground whereby contrary and remote things cohere and flower out from one stem. It presently learns that since the dawn of history there has been a constant accumulation and classifying of facts. But what is classification but the perceiving that these objects are not chaotic, and are not foreign, but have a law which is also a law of the human mind? The astronomer discovers that geometry, a pure abstraction of the human mind, is the measure of planetary motion. The chem-ist finds proportions and intelligible method throughout matter; and science is nothing but the finding of analogy, identity, in the most remote parts. The ambitious soul sits down before each refractory fact; one after another reduces all strange constitutions, all new powers, to their class and their law, and goes on forever to animate the last fiber of organization, the outskirts of nature, by insight.

Thus to him, to this schoolboy under the bending dome of day, is suggested that he and it proceed from one root; one is leaf and one is flower; relation, sympathy, stirring in every vein. And what is that root? Is not that the soul of his soul? A thought too bold; a dream too wild. Yet when this spiritual light shall have revealed the law of more earthly natures—when he has learned to worship the soul, and to see that the natural philosophy that now is, is only the first gropings of its gigantic hand, he shall look forward to an ever expanding knowledge as to a becoming creator. He shall see that nature is the opposite of the soul, answering to it part for part. One is seal and one is print. Its beauty is the beauty of his own mind. Its laws are the laws of his own mind. Nature then becomes to him the measure of his attainments. So much of nature as he is ignorant of, so much of his own mind does he not yet possess. And, in fine, the ancient precept, "Know thyself," and the modern precept, "Study nature," become at last one maxim.

II. The next great influence into the spirit of the scholar is the mind of the Past—in whatever form, whether of literature, of art, of institutions, that mind is inscribed. Books are the best type of the influence of the past, and perhaps we shall get at the truth—learn the amount of this influence more conveniently—by considering their value alone.

The theory of books is noble. The scholar of the first age received into him the world around; brooded thereon; gave it the new arrangement of his mind, and uttered it again. It came into him life; it went out from him truth. It came to him short-lived actions; it went out from him immortal thoughts. It came to him business; it went from him poetry. It was dead fact; now, it is quick thought. It can stand, and it can go. It now endures, it now flies, it now inspires. Precisely in proportion to the depth of mind from which it issued, so high does it soar, so long does it sing.

Or, I might say, it depends on how far the process had gone, of transmuting life into truth. In proportion to the completeness of the distillation, so will the purity and imperishableness of the product be. But none is quite perfect. As no air-pump can by any means make a perfect vacuum, so neither can any artist entirely exclude the conventional, the local, the perishable from his book, or write a book of pure thought, that shall be as efficient, in all respects, to a remote posterity, as to contemporaries, or rather to the second age. Each age, it is found, must write its own books; or rather, each generation for the next succeeding. The books of an older period will not fit this.

Yet hence arises a grave mischief. The sacredness which attaches to the act of creation, the act of thought, is transferred to the record. The poet chanting was felt to be a divine man: henceforth the chant is divine also. The writer was a just and wise spirit: henceforward it is settled the book is perfect; as love of the hero corrupts into worship of his statue. Instantly the book becomes noxious: the guide is a tyrant. The sluggish and perverted mind of the multitude, slow to open to the incursions of Reason, having once so opened, having once received this book, stands upon it, and makes an outcry if it is disparaged. Colleges are built on it. Books are written on it by thinkers, not by Man Thinking; by men of talent, that is, who start wrong, who set out from accepted dogmas, not from their own sight of principles. Meek young men grow up in libraries, believing it their duty to accept the views which Cicero, which Locke, which Bacon, have given; forgetful that Cicero, Locke, and Bacon were only young men in libraries when they wrote these books.

Hence, instead of Man Thinking, we have the bookworm. Hence the book-learned class, who value books, as such; not as related to nature and the human constitution, but as making a sort of Third Estate with the world and the soul. Hence the restorers of readings, the emendators, the bibliomaniacs of all degrees.

Books are the best of things, well used; abused, among the worst. What is the right use? What is the one end which all means go to effect? They are for nothing but to inspire. I had better never see a book than to be warped by its attraction clean out of my own orbit, and made a satellite instead of a system. The one thing in the world, of value, is the active soul. This every man is entitled to; this every man contains within him, although in almost all men obstructed and as yet unborn. The soul active sees absolute truth and utters truth, or creates. In this action it is genius; not the privilege of here and there a favorite, but the sound estate of every man. In its essence it is progressive. The book, the college, the school of art, the institution of any kind, stop with some past utterance of genius. This is good, say they, let us hold by this. They pin me down. They look backward and not forward. But genius looks forward: the eyes of man are set in his forehead, not in his hind-head: man hopes: genius creates. Whatever talents may be, if the man create not, the pure efflux of the Deity is not his; cinders and smoke there may be, but not yet flame. There are creative manners, there are creative actions, and creative words; manners, actions, words, that is, indicative of no custom or authority, but springing spontaneous from the mind's own sense of good and fair.

On the other part, instead of being its own seer, let it receive from another mind its truth, though it were in torrents of light, without periods of solitude, inquest, and self-recovery, and a fatal disservice is done. Genius is always sufficiently the enemy of genius by over-influence. The literature of every nation bears me witness. The English dramatic poets have Shakspearized now for two hundred years.

Undoubtedly there is a right way of reading, so it be sternly subordinated. Man Thinking must not be subdued by his instruments. Books are for the scholar's idle times. When he can read God directly, the hour is too precious to be wasted in other men's transcripts of their readings. But when the intervals of darkness come, as come they must—when the sun is hid and the stars withdraw their shining—we repair to the lamps which were kindled by their ray, to guide our steps to the East again, where the dawn is. We hear, that we may speak. The Arabian proverb says, "A fig tree, looking on a fig tree, becometh fruitful."

It is remarkable, the character of the pleasure we derive from the best books. They impress us with the conviction that one nature wrote and the same reads. We read the verses of one of the great English poets, of Chaucer, of Marvell, of Dryden, with the most modern joy—with a pleasure, I mean, which is in great part caused by the abstraction of all *time* from their verses. There is some awe mixed with the joy of our surprise, when this poet, who lived in some past world, two or three hundred years ago, says that which lies close to my own soul, that which I also had well-nigh thought and said. But for the evidence thence afforded to the philosophical doctrine of the identity of all minds, we should suppose some pre-established harmony, some foresight of souls that were to be, and some preparation of stores for their future wants, like the fact observed in insects, who lay up food before death for the young grub they shall never see.

I would not be hurried by any love of system, by any exaggeration of instincts, to underrate the Book. We all know, that as the human body can be nourished on any food, though it were boiled grass and the broth of shoes, so the human mind can be fed by any knowledge. And great and heroic men have existed who had almost no other information than by the printed page. I only would say that it needs a strong head to bear that diet. One must be an inventor to read well. As the proverb says, "He that would bring home the wealth of the Indies, must carry out the wealth of the Indies." There is then creative reading as well as creative writing. When the mind is braced by labor and invention, the page of whatever book we read becomes luminous with manifold allusion. Every sentence is doubly significant, and the sense of our author is as broad as the world. We then see, what is always true, that as the seer's hour of vision is short and rare among heavy days and months, so is its record, perchance, the least part of his volume. The discerning will read, in his Plato or Shakespeare, only that least part, only the authentic utterances of the oracle; all the rest he rejects, were it never so many times Plato's and Shakespeare's.

Of course there is a portion of reading quite indispensable to a wise man. History and exact science he must learn by laborious reading. Colleges, in like manner, have their indispensable office—to teach elements. But they can only highly serve us when they aim not to drill, but to create; when they gather from far every ray of various genius to their hospitable halls, and by the concentrated fires, set the hearts of their youth on flame. Thought and knowledge are natures in which apparatus and pretension avail nothing. Gowns and pecuniary foundations, though of towns of gold, can never countervail the least sentence or syllable of wit. Forget this, and our American colleges will recede in their public importance, whilst they grow richer every year.

III. There goes in the world a notion that the scholar should be a recluse, a valetudinarian—as unfit for any handiwork or public labor as a penknife for an axe. The so-called "practical men" sneer at speculative men, as if, because they speculate or see, they could do nothing. I have heard it said that the clergy—who are always, more universally than any other class, the scholars of their day—are addressed as women; that the rough, spontaneous conversation of men they do not hear, but only a mincing and diluted speech. They are often virtually disfranchised; and indeed there are advocates for their celibacy. As far as this is true of the studious classes, it is not just and wise. Action is with the scholar subordinate, but it is essential. Without it he is not yet man. Without it thought can never ripen into truth. While the world hangs before the eye as a cloud of beauty, we cannot even see its beauty. Inaction is cowardice, but there can be no scholar without the heroic mind. The preamble of thought, the transition through which it passes from the unconscious to the conscious, is action. Only so much do I know, as I have lived. Instantly we know whose words are loaded with life, and whose not.

The world—this shadow of the soul, or *other me*—lies wide around. Its attractions are the keys which unlock my thoughts and make me acquainted with myself. I run eagerly into this resounding tumult. I grasp the hands of those next me, and take my place in the ring to suffer and to work, taught by an instinct that so shall the dumb abyss be vocal with speech. I pierce its order; I dissipate its fear; I dispose of it within the circuit of my expanding life. So much only of life as I know by experience, so much of the wilderness have I vanquished and planted, or so far have I extended my being, my dominion. I do not see how any man can afford, for the sake of his nerves and his nap, to spare any action in which he can partake. It is pearls and rubies to his discourse. Drudgery, calamity, exasperation, want, are instructors in eloquence and wisdom. The true scholar grudges every opportunity of action past by, as a loss of power. It is the raw material out of which the intellect moulds her splendid products. A strange process too, this by which experience is converted into thought, as a mulberry leaf is converted into satin. The manufacture goes forward at all hours.

The actions and events of our childhood and youth are now matters of calmest observation. They lie like fair pictures in the air. Not so with our recent actions, with the business which we now have in hand. On this we are quite unable to speculate. Our affections as yet circulate through it. We no more feel or know it than we feel the feet, or the hand, or the brain of our body. The new deed is yet a part of life, remains for a time immersed in our unconscious life. In some contemplative hour it detaches itself from the life like a ripe fruit, to become a thought of the mind. Instantly it is raised, transfigured; the corruptible has put on incorruption. Henceforth it is an object of beauty, however base its origin and neighborhood. Observe too the impossibility of antedating this act. In its grub state, it cannot fly, it cannot shine, it is a dull grub. But suddenly, without observation, the selfsame thing unfurls beautiful wings, and is an angel of wisdom. So is there no fact, no event, in our private history, which shall not, sooner or later, lose its adhesive, inert form, and astonish us by soaring from our body into the empyrean. Cradle and infancy, school and playground, the fear of boys, and dogs, and ferules, the love of little maids and berries, and many another fact that once filled the whole sky, are gone already; friend and relative, profession and party, town and country, nation and world, must also soar and sing.

Of course, he who has put forth his total strength in fit actions has the richest return of wisdom. I will not shut myself out of this globe of action, and transplant an oak into a flowerpot, there to hunger and pine; nor trust the revenue of some single faculty, and exhaust one vein of thought, much like those Savoyards, who, getting their livelihood by carving shepherds, shepherdesses, and smoking Dutchmen, for all Europe, went out one day to the mountain to find stock, and discovered that they had whittled up the last of their pine trees. Authors we have, in numbers, who have written out their vein, and who, moved by a commendable prudence, sail for Greece or Palestine, follow the trapper into the prairie, or ramble round Algiers, to replenish their merchantable stock.

If it were only for a vocabulary, the scholar would be covetous of action. Life is our dictionary. Years are well spent in country labors; in town; in the insight into trades and manufactures; in frank intercourse with many men and women; in science; in art; to the one end of mastering in all their facts a language by which to illustrate and embody our perceptions. I learn immediately from any speaker how much he has already lived, through the poverty or the splendor of his speech. Life lies behind us as the quarry from whence we get ties and copestones for the masonry of to-day. This is the way to learn grammar. Colleges and books only copy the language which the field and the work-yard made.

But the final value of action, like that of books, and better than books, is that it is a resource. That great principle of Undulation in nature, that shows itself in the inspiring and expiring of the breath; in desire and satiety; in the ebb and flow of the sea; in day and night; in heat and cold; and, as yet more deeply ingrained in every atom and every fluid, is known to us under the name of Polarity— these "fits of easy transmission and reflection," as Newton called them, are the law of nature because they are the law of spirit.

The mind now thinks, now acts, and each fit reproduces the other. When the artist has exhausted his materials, when the fancy no longer paints, when thoughts are no longer apprehended and books are a weariness, he has always the resource to live. Character is higher than intellect. Thinking is the function. Living is the functionary. The stream retreats to its source. A great soul will be strong to live, as well as strong to think. Does he lack organ or medium to impart his truths? He can still fall back on this elemental force of living them. This is a total act. Thinking is a partial act. Let the grandeur of justice shine in his affairs. Let the beauty of affection cheer his lowly roof. Those "far from fame," who dwell and act with him, will feel the force of his constitution in the doings and passages of the day better than it can be measured by any public and designed display. Time shall teach him that the scholar loses no hour which the man lives. Herein he unfolds the sacred germ of his instinct, screened from influence. What is lost in seemliness is gained in strength. Not out of those on whom systems of education have exhausted their culture, comes the helpful giant to destroy the old or to build the new, but out of unhandselled savage nature; out of terrible Druids and Berserkers come at last Alfred and Shakespeare.

I hear therefore with joy whatever is beginning to be said of the dignity and necessity of labor to every citizen. There is virtue yet in the hoe and the spade, for learned as well as for unlearned hands. And labor is everywhere welcome; always we are invited to work; only be this limitation observed, that a man shall not for the sake of wider activity sacrifice any opinion to the popular judgments and modes of action.

I have now spoken of the education of the scholar by nature, by books, and by action. It remains to say somewhat of his duties. They are such as become Man Thinking. They may all be comprised in self-trust. The office of the scholar is to cheer, to raise, and to guide men by showing them facts amidst appearances. He plies the slow, unhonored, and unpaid task of observation. Flamsteed and Herschel, in their glazed observatories, may catalogue the stars with the praise of all men, and the results being splendid and useful, honor is sure. But he, in his private observatory, cataloguing obscure and nebulous stars of the human mind, which as yet no man has thought of as such—watching days and months sometimes for a few facts; correcting still his old records—must relinquish display and immediate fame. In the long period of his preparation he must betray often an ignorance and shiftlessness in popular arts, incurring the disdain of the able who shoulder him aside. Long he must stammer in his speech; often forgo the living for the dead. Worse yet, he must accept—how often!—poverty and solitude. For the ease and pleasure of treading the old road, accepting the fashions, the education, the religion of society, he takes the cross of making his own, and, of course, the self-accusation, the faint heart, the frequent uncertainty and loss of time, which are the nettles and tangling vines in the way of the self-relying and self-directed; and the state of virtual hostility in which he seems to stand to society, and especially to educated society. For all this loss and scorn, what offset? He is to find consolation in exercising the highest functions of human nature. He is one who raises himself from private considerations and breathes and lives on public and illustrious thoughts. He is the world's eye. He is the world's heart. He is to resist the vulgar prosperity that retrogrades ever to barbarism, by preserving and communicating heroic sentiments, noble biographies, melodious verse, and the conclusions of history. Whatsoever oracles the human heart, in all emergencies, in all solemn hours, has uttered as its commentary on the world of actions, these he shall receive and impart. And whatsoever new verdict Reason from her inviolable seat pronounces on the passing men and events of to-day, this he shall hear and promulgate.

These being his functions, it becomes him to feel all confidence in himself, and to defer never to the popular cry. He and he only knows the world. The world of any moment is the merest appearance. Some great decorum, some fetish of a government, some ephemeral trade, or war, or man, is cried up by half mankind and cried down by the other half, as if all depended on this particular up or down. The odds are that the whole question is not worth the poorest thought which the scholar has lost in listening to the controversy. Let him not quit his belief that a popgun is a popgun, though the ancient and honorable of the earth affirm it to be the crack of doom. In silence, in steadiness, in severe abstraction, let him hold by himself; add observation to observation, patient of neglect, patient of reproach, and bide his own time—happy enough if he can satisfy himself alone that this day he has seen something truly. Success treads on every right step. For the instinct is sure, that prompts him to tell his brother what he thinks. He then learns that in going down into the secrets of his own mind he has descended into the secrets of all minds. He learns that he who has mastered any law in his private thoughts, is master to that extent of all men whose language he speaks, and of all into whose language his own can be translated. The poet, in utter solitude remembering his spontaneous thoughts and recording them, is found to have recorded that which men in crowded cities find true for them also. The orator distrusts at first the fitness of his frank confessions, his want of knowledge of the persons he addresses, until he finds that he is the complement of his hearers—that they drink his words because he fulfils for them their own nature; the deeper he dives into his privatest, secretest presentiment, to his wonder he finds this is the most acceptable, most public, and universally true. The people delight in it; the better part of every man feels, This is my music; this is myself.

In self-trust all the virtues are comprehended. Free should the scholar be—free and brave. Free even to the definition of freedom, "without any hindrance that does not arise out of his own constitution." Brave; for fear is a thing which a scholar by his very function puts behind him. Fear always springs from ignorance. It is a shame to him if his tranquillity, amid dangerous times, arise from the presumption that like children and women his is a protected class; or if he seek a temporary peace by the diversion of his thoughts from politics or vexed questions, hiding his head like an ostrich in the flowering bushes, peeping into microscopes, and turning rhymes, as a boy whistles to keep his courage up. So is the danger a danger still; so is the fear worse. Manlike let him turn and face it. Let him look into its eye and search its nature, inspect its origin—see the whelping of this lion—which lies no great way back; he will then find in himself a perfect comprehension of its nature and extent; he will have made his hands meet on the other side, and can henceforth defy it and pass on superior. The world is his who can see through its pretension. What deafness, what stone-blind custom, what overgrown error you behold is there only by sufferance—by your sufferance. See it to be a lie, and you have already dealt it its mortal blow.

Yes, we are the cowed—we the trustless. It is a mischievous notion that we are come late into nature; that the world was finished a long time ago. As the world was plastic and fluid in the hands of God, so it is ever to so much of his attributes as we bring to it. To igorance and sin, it is flint. They adapt themselves to it as they may; but in proportion as a man has any thing in him divine, the firmament flows before him and takes his signet and form. Not he is great who can alter matter, but he who can alter my state of mind. They are the kings of the world who give the color of their present thought to all nature and all art, and persuade men by the cheerful serenity of their carrying the matter, that this thing which they do is the apple which the ages have desired to pluck, now at last ripe, and inviting nations to the harvest. The great man makes the great thing. Wherever Macdonald sits, there is the head of the table.[2] Linnaeus makes botany the most alluring of studies, and wins it from the farmer and the herb-woman; Davy, chemistry; and Cuvier, fossils. The day is always his who works in it with serenity and great aims. The unstable estimates of men crowd to him whose mind is filled with a truth, as the heaped waves of the Atlantic follow the moon.

For this self-trust, the reason is deeper than can be fathomed—darker than can be enlightened. I might not carry with me the feeling of my audience in stating my own belief. But I have already shown the ground of my hope, in adverting to the doctrine that man is one. I believe man has been wronged; he has wronged himself. He has almost lost the light that can lead him back to his prerogatives. Men are become of no account. Men in history, men in the world of to-day, are bugs, are spawn, and are called "the mass" and "the herd." In a century, in a millennium, one or two men; that is to say, one or two approximations to the right state of every man. All the rest behold in the hero or the poet their own green and crude being—ripened; yes, and are content to be less, so *that* may attain to its full stature. What a testimony, full of grandeur, full of pity, is borne to the demands of his own nature, by the poor clansman, the poor partisan, who rejoices in the glory of his chief. The poor and the low find some amends to their immense moral capacity, for their acquiescence in a political and social inferiority. They are content to be brushed like flies from the path of a great person, so that justice shall be done by him to that common nature which it is the dearest desire of all to see enlarged and glorified. They sun themselves in the great man's light, and feel it to be their own element. They cast the dignity of man from their downtrod selves upon the shoulders of a hero, and will perish to add one drop of blood to make that great heart beat, those giant sinews combat and conquer. He lives for us, and we live in him.

Men, such as they are, very naturally seek money or power; and power because it is as good as money—the "spoils," so called, "of office." And why not? for they aspire to the highest, and this, in their sleep-walking, they dream is highest. Wake them and they shall quit the false good and leap to the true, and leave governments to clerks and desks. This revolution is to be wrought by the gradual domestication of the idea of Culture. The main enterprise of the

2. This sentence is proverbial. MacDonald is unidentified.

world for splendor, for extent, is the upbuilding of a man. Here are the materials strewn along the ground. The private life of one man shall be a more illustrious monarchy, more formidable to its enemy, more sweet and serene in its influence to its friend, than any kingdom in history. For a man, rightly viewed, comprehendeth the particular natures of all men. Each philosopher, each bard, each actor has only done for me, as by a delegate, what one day I can do for myself. The books which once we valued more than the apple of the eye, we have quite exhausted. What is that but saying that we have come up with the point of view which the universal mind took through the eyes of one scribe; we have been that man, and have passed on. First, one, then another, we drain all cisterns, and waxing greater by all these supplies, we crave a better and more abundant food. The man has never lived that can feed us ever. The human mind cannot be enshrined in a person who shall set a barrier on any one side to this unbounded, unboundable empire. It is one central fire, which, flaming now out of the lips of Etna, lightens the capes of Sicily, and now out of the throat of Vesuvius, illuminates the towers and vine-yards of Naples. It is one light which beams out of a thousand stars. It is one soul which animates all men.

But I have dwelt perhaps tediously upon this abstraction of the Scholar. I ought not to delay longer to add what I have to say of nearer reference to the time and to this country.

Historically, there is thought to be a difference in the ideas which predominate over successive epochs, and there are data for marking the genius of the Classic, of the Romantic, and now of the Reflective or Philosophical age. With the views I have intimated of the oneness or the identity of the mind through all individuals, I do not much dwell on these differences. In fact, I believe each individual passes through all three. The boy is a Greek; the youth, romantic; the adult, reflective. I deny not, however, that a revolution in the leading idea may be distinctly enough traced.

Our age is bewailed as the age of Introversion. Must that needs be evil? We, it seems, are critical; we are embarrassed with second thoughts; we cannot enjoy any thing for hankering to know whereof the pleasures consists; we are lined with eyes; we see with our feet; the time is infected with Hamlet's unhappiness—

Sicklied o'er with the pale cast of thought.

It is so bad then? Sight is the last thing to be pitied. Would we be blind? Do we fear lest we should outsee nature and God, and drink truth dry? I look upon the discontent of the literary class as a mere announcement of the fact that they find themselves not in the state of mind of their fathers, and regret the coming state as untried; as a boy dreads the water before he has learned that he can swim. If there is any period one would desire to be born in, is it not the age of Revolution; when the old and the new stand side by side and admit of being compared; when the energies of all men are searched by fear and by hope; when the historic glories of the old can be compensated by the rich possibilities of the new era? This time, like all times, is a very good one, if we but know what to do with it.

I read with some joy of the auspicious signs of the coming days, as they glimmer already through poetry and art, through philosophy and science, through church and state.

One of these signs is the fact that the same movement which effected the elevation of what was called the lowest class in the state, assumed in literature a very marked and as benign an aspect. Instead of the sublime and beautiful, the near, the low, the common, was explored and poetized. That which had been negligently trodden under foot by those who were harnessing and provisioning themselves for long journeys into far countries, is suddenly found to be richer than all foreign parts. The literature of the poor, the feeling of the child, the philosophy of the street, the meaning of the household life, are the topics of the time. It is a great stride. It is a sign—is it not?—of new vigor when the extremities are made active, when currents of warm life run into the hands and the feet. I ask not for the great, the remote, the romantic; what is doing in Italy or Arabia; what is Greek art, or Provençal minstrelsy; I embrace the common, I explore and sit at the feet of the familiar, the low. Give me insight into to-day, and you may have the antique and future worlds. What would we really know the meaning of? The meal in the firkin; the milk in the pan; the ballad in the street; the news of the boat; the glance of the eye; the form and the gait of the body—show me the ultimate reason of these matters; show me the sublime presence of the highest spiritual cause lurking, as always it does lurk, in these suburbs and extremities of nature; let me see every trifle bristling with the polarity that ranges it instantly on an eternal law; and the shop, the plough, and the ledger referred to the like cause by which light undulates and poets sing—and the world lies no longer a dull miscellany and lumber-room, but has form and order; there is no trifle, there is no puzzle, but one design unites and animates the farthest pinnacle and the lowest trench.

This idea has inspired the genius of Goldsmith, Burns, Cowper, and, in a newer time, of Goethe, Wordsworth, and Carlyle. This idea they have differently followed and with various success. In contrast with their writing, the style of Pope, of Johnson, of Gibbon, looks cold and pedantic. This writing is blood-warm. Man is surprised to find that things near are not less beautiful and wondrous than things remote. The near explains the far. The drop is a small ocean. A man is related to all nature. This perception of the worth of the vulgar is fruitful in discoveries. Goethe, in this very thing the most modern of the moderns, has shown us, as none ever did, the genius of the ancients.

There is one man of genius who has done much for this philosophy of life, whose literary value has never yet been rightly estimated; I mean Emanuel Swedenborg. The most imaginative of men, yet writing with the precision of a mathematician, he endeavored to engraft a purely philosophical Ethics on the popular Christianity of his time. Such an attempt of course must have difficulty which no genius could surmount. But he saw and showed the connection between nature and the affections of the soul. He pierced the emblematic or spiritual character of the visible, audible, tangible world. Especially did his shade-loving muse hover over and interpret the lower parts of nature; he showed the mysterious bond that allies moral evil to the foul material forms, and has given in epical parables a theory of insanity, of beasts, of unclean and fearful things.

Another sign of our times, also marked by an analogous political movement, is the new importance given to the single person. Everything that tends to insulate the individual—to surround him with barriers of natural respect, so that each man shall feel the world is his, and man shall treat with man as a sovereign state with a sovereign state—tends to true union as well as greatness. "I learned," said the melancholy Pestalozzi, "that no man in God's wide earth is either willing or able to help any other man." Help must come from the bosom alone. The scholar is that man who must take up into himself all the ability of the time, all the contributions of the past, all the hopes of the future. He must be an university of knowledges. If there be one lesson more than another which should pierce his ear, it is, The world is nothing, the man is all; in yourself is the law of all nature, and you know not yet how a globule of sap ascends; in yourself slumbers the whole of Reason; it is for you to know all; it is for you to dare all. Mr. President and Gentlemen, this confidence in the unsearched might of man belongs, by all motives, by all prophecy, by all preparation, to the American Scholar. We have listened too long to the courtly muses of Europe. The spirit of the American freeman is already suspected to be timid, imitative, tame. Public and private avarice make the air we breathe thick and fat. The scholar is decent, indolent, complaisant. See already the tragic consequence. The mind of this country, taught to aim at low objects, eats upon itself. There is no work for any but the decorous and the complaisant. Young men of the fairest promise, who begin life upon our shores, inflated by the mountain winds, shined upon by all the stars of God, find the earth below not in unison with these, but are hindered from action by the disgust which the principles on which business is managed inspire, and turn drudges, or die of disgust, some of them suicides. What is the remedy? They did not yet see, and thousands of young men as hopeful now crowding to the barriers for the career do not yet see, that if the single man plant himself indomitably on his instincts, and there abide, the huge world will come round to him. Patience, patience; with the shades of all the good and great for company; and for solace the perspective of your own infinite life; and for work the study and the communication of principles, the making those instincts prevalent, the conversion of the world. Is it not the chief disgrace in the world, not to be an unit—not to be reckoned one character—not to yield that peculiar fruit which each man was created to bear, but to be reckoned in the gross, in the hundred, or the thousand, of the party, the section, to which we belong; and our opinion predicted geographically, as the north, or the south? Not so, brothers and friends—please God, ours shall not be so. We will walk on our own feet; we will work with our own hands; we will speak our own minds. The study of letters shall be no longer a name for pity, for doubt, and for sensual indulgence. The dread of man and the love of man shall be a wall of defence and a wreath of joy around all. A nation of men will for the first time exist, because each believes himself inspired by the Divine Soul which also inspires all men.

QUESTIONS

1. Outline this oration, showing how its four major parts relate to the main topic. Are the parts accorded equal or different treatment, in length and detail? in development? Why? What are the main points within each part?

2. What distinction does Emerson make between "Man thinking" and "a mere thinker"? What foundation does he provide for the distinction? What view of the nature of society does the distinction imply?

3. Why does Emerson emphasize the influence of action upon the scholar? Is there any incompatibility between an active and an intellectual life?

4. At the outset Emerson states the "doctrine of One Man" and that idea recurs several times in the work. Define the doctrine and explain its significance at each reappearance.

5. What relation exists between the "doctrine of One Man" and the idea of self-trust? In what other contexts is that doctrine, if not stated directly, an implicit governing principle?

6. Locate some of Emerson's citations of proverbs and maxims. What effects does he produce by using them? To what degree and in what ways does Emerson's style embody, apart from direct citation, the qualities of proverb and maxim?

7. Has Emerson's thought been incorporated into or reflected by American educational practice? To what degree? In what ways? Draw upon your own experience of American schools as well as upon what you know of educational theory.

LEARNED HAND
Sources of Tolerance[1]

I am going to ask you to go with me, not into questions which have direct relation to the law or to government, but to those which concern the mental habits of our people, since these, indirectly at any rate, in the end determine its institutions. This is not an easy, maybe it is an impossible undertaking, but at any rate, nobody can very effectually challenge what you say about such vague things, and you are exempt from the need of citation—blessed exoneration to a judge. It may be worth discussion, if only for discussion's sake. At least it can serve to bring out differences of opinion.

By way of prelude may I then ask you for a moment to go back in our country for nearly a century and a half? We were substantially a nation of farmers; towns were few; cities, as we should now rate them, did not exist. Life was, as we like to believe, simple. Maybe it was not so in fact, for simplicity depends rather on one's inner state of mind; but at any rate it was less pressed and hurried; people did not think so much about how complicated they were, and less dissipated their attention.

The political notions of the time were divided into two contrasting groups which it has been the custom to associate with the great names of Jefferson and Hamilton. It is easy to associate Jefferson's ideas with those of Rousseau, from whom on the outside they seem to have been drawn. This, as I understand it, is wrong, but he had drunk deeply at the springs of Physiocracy, and in any event he believed in the basic virtue of mankind, once set free from artificial restraints. He found his ideal in a community of independent families, each entrenched in its farm, self-subsistent, independent, needing no regulation, and tolerant of little interference, especially by government. Those who invoke his name today must be shocked at his scorn of the mob of mechanics and artisans, whose turbulence and separation from some particular plot of earth unfitted them in his eyes for sharing in the Good Life. A nation in which information, or what passes as such, can be instantaneously sent from one end to the other, in which the craving for conformity demands uniformity in belief, which for that reason wears the same clothes, reads the same print and follows the same fashions, amusements and conventions, would have seemed to him scurvy and sordid. He would have found little in the America of today to justify that Utopia of which he had dreamed.

1. An address delivered before the Juristic Society of the University of Pennsylvania in June 1930.

The extraordinary richness of his own nature, his omnivorant interest in all the activities of man, no doubt colored his picture of a life on the land; yet it also enabled him to transmute into a rosy ideal the dumb aspirations of his people, and so they looked to him for their leadership for a quarter of a century after his accession to power, and if we count Jackson as his dubious disciple, for that much longer. Clearly there was something in his outlook which responded to the needs of those among whom he lived.

Hamilton was a horse of another color, always an exotic, succeeding in his statecraft only because of the disorders which immediately followed the Revolution; whose genius needed the cloak of Washington beneath which his real work was hid for near a century. He was no Utopian; he did not believe in the perfectibility of human nature. Government was a combination of those interests in the community which collectively would be irresistible; a combination resting upon self-interest. When he secured the passage of the Constitution, it was by means of such a combination; the landed class, the manufacturers and the public creditors. In the doubtful contest for ratification, as Beard has shown, it was these votes which eventually won, and it was under the aegis of Washington that he managed to carry on for those critical eight years. With the constant movement of the frontier westward, the underlying, but less articulate, aspirations of a rural people finally asserted themselves, after Adams had run off Hamilton's momentum.

The animosity between the two men was well founded and inevitable. They represented, and we are right still to take them as our most shining examples of, two theories of human society; that which demands external control, and that which insists upon the opportunity for personal expression. Jefferson's victory seemed to him to be the sanction of all that the Revolution had implied; the liberation of a free people from the domination of greed and corruption, opening vistas of human felicity not theretofore known on earth. For its fuller expression he was willing, forced by a sad necessity, to sacrifice his constitutional scruples and forever compromise his party by the acquisition of Louisiana. To Hamilton, Jefferson's accession was the beginning of the end, the last step in a plunge towards anarchy. The squalid political quarrel for the domination of the rump of Federalism which ended in his death, had for him a deeper significance than the leadership in a party then apparently writhing to dissolution. The Eighteenth Brumaire[2] was five years past, and though the Coronation at Notre Dame was still some months away, recent events already foreshadowed it. In the final breakdown of that Jacobinism which he and his associates thought certain and early, the

2. Brumaire was the second month in the French revolutionary calendar. The Eighteenth Brumaire of the year VIII (Nov. 9, 1799) was the day on which Napoleon assumed supreme power of France as first Consul. His coronation at Notre Dame as emperor occurred on December 2, 1804.

need would arise for some transatlantic Bonaparte to gather the shreds of society, and build a state upon surer foundations than that weak instrument in which at heart he had never really believed. To prevent Federalism, the sacred chalice, from passing into the obscene hands of a turncoat and a traitor was worth the chance that cost him his life.[3]

Each man would have said that he was the champion of liberty, and each would have been right. To one the essential condition of any tolerable life was the free expression of the individual, the power to lead his life on his own terms, to enjoy the fruits of his industry, to garner the harvest of his hands and brain, without subtraction by a horde of office-holders, locusts who laid waste the land and spread the venal doctrine of their right to eat what others had sown, the blight, the virus, of a society of honest men, enjoying the earth which God, at least in this blessed country, had patently spread out for their satisfaction. The other saw in all this no more than the maunderings of a toxic dream. What was the assurance of man's capacity to deal with his own fate? Was it not clear that virtue and intelligence among the sons of Adam was as rare as physical prowess, indeed much rarer? Liberty could not rest upon anarchy; it was conditioned upon an ordered society, in which power should rest where power should be, with the wise and the good, who could be at least presumptively ascertained as those who in the battle of life had already given some signs of capacity. It was an empty phantom to assume some automatic regulation by which without plan and direction public affairs manage themselves. The concerns of a great people are not all individual; they have collective interests without which their life can scarcely rise above that of savages, each shifting for himself, without comfort, security, or the leisure which alone makes existence endurable. Jacobins might bawl of liberty, but really they meant no more than the tyranny of their own domination over the mob.

Placed as we now are, with an experience of over a century behind us, we can say that the future was apparently to justify Hamilton as against his great rival. Our knowledge of the ways of Nature, our command of her energies, and the materials which she has set so freely at our hands, has made it no longer possible to think of a society of families, isolated and non-communicating, each weaving its own fate independently of the rest. We have fabricated a nexus of relations which makes even rural life impossible as Jefferson understood it. The motor, the airplane, the telephone and telegraph, the radio, the railroad, the Linotype, the modern newspaper, the "movie" —and most horrible, the "talkie"—have finally destroyed it. Liberty is irretrievably gone in any sense that it was worth having to him. A farmer must have complicated machinery; he depends upon mar-

3. In the presidential campaign of 1800 Hamilton supported Jefferson against Aaron Burr and subsequently lost his life in a duel with Burr arising from this political opposition.

kets thousands of miles away; he will win by a crop shortage in India, and lose by a fall in industrial shares. He must "listen in" on Amos an' Andy, have camping places in the National Parks and tour in the Ford in winter. So be it; I welcome his larger life, but it has its price; he is tied to all men, as all men are tied to him, in a web whose threads no eye can follow and no fingers unravel.

Nor would there still be many, though doubtless some there are, who would deny that government must be the compromise of conflicting interests, as Hamilton supposed. While there lingers in political platforms and other declamatory compositions the notion that each man, if only he could be disabused of false doctrine, would act and vote with an enlightened eye to the public weal, few really believe it. We know well that an objective calculus of human values is impossible, and if it were available, would be so thin and speculative that men would not accept it. For any times that can count in human endeavor, we must be content with compromises in which the more powerful combination will prevail. The most we can hope is that if the maladjustment becomes too obvious, or the means too offensive to our conventions, the balance can be re-established without dissolution, a cost greater than almost any interests can justify. The method of Hamilton has had its way; so far as we can see must always have its way; in government, as in marriage, in the end the more insistent will prevails.

Liberty is so much latitude as the powerful choose to accord to the weak. So much perhaps must be admitted for abstract statement; anything short of it appears to lead to inconsistencies. At least no other formula has been devised which will answer. If a community decides that some conduct is prejudicial to itself, and so decides by numbers sufficient to impose its will upon dissenters, I know of no principle which can stay its hand. Perhaps indeed it is no more than a truism to say so; for, when we set ourselves this or that limitation, religion for example, we find that we wince in application. Who can say that the polygamy of the Mormons was not a genuine article of that faith? When we forbade it in the name of our morals, was it not an obvious subterfuge still to insist that we recognized religious freedom? Should we tolerate suttee? If we forbid birth-control in the interest of morals, is it inconceivable that we should tax celibacy? We call that conduct moral about whose effect upon our common interest we have unusually strong convictions. We do not hesitate to impose this upon those who do not share our views; and tolerance ends where faith begins. Plato may have been right about the proper relations of the sexes; we should not allow his experiment to be tried.[4] I do not see how we can set any limits to legitimate coercion beyond those which our forbearance concedes.

4. See *The Republic*, Book V, where Socrates advocates the propagation of the human species by selective breeding.

And yet, so phrased, we should all agree, I think, that the whole substance of liberty has disappeared. It is intolerable to feel that we are each in the power of the conglomerate conscience of a mass of Babbitts, whose intelligence we do not respect, and whose standards we may detest. Life on their terms would be impossible to endure; of their compunctions we have no guarantee. Who shall deliver us from the body of this death? Certainly there was a meaning in Jefferson's hatred of the interposition of collective pressure, though he extended it to so much of what we now accept as government. We may believe that his emphasis was wrong; that it required a great war eventually to clear away the centrifugal tendencies that underlay it; but shall we not feel with him that it is monstrous to lay open the lives of each to whatever current notions of propriety may ordain? That feeling was the energy that lay back of the first ten amendments to the Constitution, which were really a part of the document itself. Impossible though they be of literal interpretation, like a statute, as counsels of moderation rather than as parts of our constituent law, they represent a mood, an attitude towards life, deep rooted in any enduring society.

Jefferson thought that they could be made to prevail by weakening the central power, but he was too astute an observer to rely upon political device alone. It was in the social, not in the political, constitution of his society that real security lay. For it was impossible to sweep a community of small eighteenth century farmers with mob hysteria. His dislike of cities was in part at any rate because they were subject to just such accesses. He did not, and he could not, see that time was to make rural life as susceptible to moral epidemics as the city mobs which he feared and mistrusted. He set his faith upon isolation and isolation in the end has failed him. The shores are no longer studded with rows of solid columns to break the waves of propaganda; they are not studded with anything whatever, and the waves sweep over them without obstacle and run far up into the land. The question I wish to put before you, which all this introduction is to prepare, is this—which I trust you will forgive me for putting in colloquial form—how far is liberty consistent with the methods of the modern "high-power" salesman? If it is not, what is to be done about it? Being Americans, we are not likely to agree that nothing can.

It has always interested me to read of the observations of those patient anthropologists who associate intimately with our cousin, the chimpanzee. I know a woman who endured the embrace of her son's pet for two hours, lest if disturbed in its caresses it might furiously strangle her. Devotion could scarcely ask more. We may learn much of ourselves from what are now, I believe, called the "conduct patterns" of the anthropoids, but it will not interest me so much as if the study could be of the herds. What I want to know is, why we have become so incurably imitative. I can improvise reasons, but you know how worthless that kind of anthropology is, so I shall spare you. But you will agree about the fact I fancy; you will agree that ideas are as infectious as bacteria and appear to run their course like epidemics. First, there is little immunity, nearly all individuals are susceptible, so that the disease spreads like a prairie fire. Next, a period where the curve of infection, as the pathologists say, remains level; this may last a long time. Last a decline of the curve which, so far as is known, nothing can check. The virus has lost its potency, or some immunity has established itself in a wholly mysterious way.

Ideas, fashions, dogmas, literary, political, scientific, and religious, have a very similar course; they get a currency, spread like wildfire, have their day and thereafter nothing can revive them. Were the old questions ever answered? Has anyone ever proved or disproved the right of secession? Most issues are not decided; their importance passes and they follow after. But in their day they rack the world they infest; men mill about them like a frantic herd: not understanding what their doctrines imply, or whither they lead. To them attach the noblest, and the meanest, motives, indifferent to all but that there is a cause to die, or to profit by. Such habits are not conducive to the life of reason; that kind of devotion is not the method by which man has raised himself from a savage. Rather by quite another way, by doubt, by trial, by tentative conclusion.

In recent times we have deliberately systematized the production of epidemics in ideas, much as a pathologist experiments with a colony of white mice, who are scarcely less protected. The science of propaganda by no means had its origin in the Great War, but that gave it a greater impetus than ever before. To the advertiser we should look for our best technique. I am told that if I see McCracken's tooth-paste often enough in street cars, on billboards and in shop windows, it makes no difference how determined I may be not to become one of McCracken's customers, I shall buy McCracken's tooth-paste sooner or later, whether I will or no; it is as inevitable as that I shut my eyes when you strike at my face. In much the same way political ideas are spread, and moral too, or for that matter, religious. You know the established way of raising money for the School of Applied and Theoretical Taxidermy. One employs a master mind in group suggestion, with lieutenants and field workers. The possible "prospects" are bombarded with a carefully planned series of what for some unknown reason is called "literature" —leaflets, pictures, pathetic appeals, masterful appeals, appeals to patriotism. Shall American animals suffer the indignity of inadequate stuffing, having themselves given their lives to the cause? Will not you as a loyal American do your bit too; they having made the last supreme sacrifice? Taxidermy is a patriotic duty; are you for taxidermy? If not, you are against it, a taxidermical outlaw at best, at worst a taxidermical Laodicean.[5] Brother, show your colors, join some group, at all costs join, be not a non-joiner, a detestable, lily-livered, half-hearted, supercilious, un-American, whom we would exile if we could and would not pass if he sought entrance.

I submit that a community used to be played on in this way, especially one so large and so homogeneous as we have become, is not a favorable soil for liberty. That plant cannot thrive in such a forcing bed; it is slow growing and needs a more equitable climate. It is the product, not of institutions, but of a temper, of an attitude towards life; of that mood that looks before and after and pines for what is not. It is idle to look to laws, or courts, or principalities, or powers, to secure it. You may write into your constitutions not ten, but fifty, amendments, and it shall not help a farthing, for casuistry will undermine it as casuistry should, if it have no stay but law. It is secure only in that *constans et perpetua voluntas suum cuique tribuendi*[6]; in that sense of fair play, of give and take, of the uncertainty of human hypothesis, of how changeable and passing are our surest convictions, which has so hard a chance to survive in any times, perhaps especially in our own.

There are some who, looking on the American scene, see remedy in trying to introduce and maintain local differences. Especially in matters of government, let us be astute to preserve local autonomy, not to concentrate all power in our capital. There are reasons enough for this in any case, but as a relief from the prevalent mood it seems to me a delusion. That served very well in Jefferson's time; it will not do today. We cannot set our faces against a world enraptured with the affluence which comes from mass production; and what has served so magically in material things, is it not proved to be good for our ideas, our amusements, our morals, our religion? The heretic is odious in proportion as large industry is successful. Rapidity of communication alone makes segregation a broken reed; for men will talk with one another, visit one another, join with one another, listen collectively, look collectively, play collectively, and in the end, for aught I know, eat and sleep collectively, though they have nothing to say, nothing to do, no eyes or ears with which to enjoy or to value what they see and hear. You cannot set up again a Jeffersonian world in separate monads, each looking up to heaven. For good or evil, man, who must have lived for long in groups, likes too much the warm feeling of his mental and moral elbows in touch with his neighbors'.

Well, then, shall we surrender; shall we agree to submit to the dictation of the prevalent fashion in morals and ideas, as we do in dress? Must we capture surreptitiously such independence as we can, "bootleg" it, as it were, and let the heathen rage, the cattle mill, the

5. The early Christians of Laodicea were notoriously lukewarm or indifferent.
6. "the constant and personal desire to accord to each his own."

air resound with imperious nostrums which will brook no dissi-
dence? Maybe it will come to that; sometimes I wonder whether to
be a foe of war, for example—which might be thought a blameless
disposition—is not a stigma of degeneracy. Again I have pondered
on what it is to be a Bolshevik, and once I learned. There was a
time when Congress thought it could reach the salaries of my brothers
and myself by an income tax, until the Supreme Court manfully
came to our rescue. A judge of much experience was talking with
me one day about it; I was wrong enough in my law, as it afterwards
turned out, and disloyal enough in temper to my class, to say that
I thought the tax valid. "Do you know anything about it?" he asked
with some asperity. "No," said I, "not a thing." "Have you ever
read Taney's letter?" "No," said I again, for I was innocent of any
learning. "Why, they can't do that," said he; "they can't do that,
that's Bolshevism." And so it turned out, to my personal gratification,
since when, freed from that Red Peril, I have enjoyed an immunity
which the rest of you, alas, cannot share. Far be it from me to suggest
that there are graver thrusts at the structure of society than to tax
a Federal judge. Properly instructed, I have recanted my heresy, and
yet there hangs about "Bolshevism" a residual vagueness, a lack of
clear outline, as of a mountain against the setting sun; which only
goes to show, I suppose, that a fundamentally corrupt nature can
never be wholly reformed.

As I say, we may have to lie low like Bre'r Rabbit, and get our
freedom as best we can, but that is the last resort. Perhaps if we
cannot build breakwaters, we may be able to deepen the bottom.
The Republic of Switzerland is cut into deep valleys; it has been a
traditional home of freedom. Greece is made in the same way; to
Greece we owe it that our civilization is not Asian. Our own country
has not that protection; and in any event, of what value would it be
in these later days, when Fords climb Pikes Peak and Babe Ruth is
the local divinity at once in San Diego and Bangor? But what nature
has not done for us, perhaps time can. I conceive that there is nothing
which gives a man more pause before taking as absolute what his
feelings welcome, and his mind deems plausible, than even the
flicker of a recollection that something of the sort has been tried
before, felt before, disputed before, and for some reason or other has
now quite gone into Limbo. Historians may be dogmatists, I know,
though not so often now as when history was dogma. At least you
will perhaps agree that even a smattering of history and especially
of letters will go far to dull the edges of uncompromising conviction.
No doubt one may quote history to support any cause, as the devil
quotes scripture; but modern history is not a very satisfactory side-
arm in political polemics; it grows less and less so. Besides, it is not
so much history one learns as the fact that one is aware that man
has had a history at all. The liberation is not in the information but

in the background acquired, the sense of mutability, and of the transcience of what seems so poignant and so pressing today. One may take sides violently over the execution of Charles the First, but he has been dead a long while; the issue is not bitter unless we connect it with what is going on today. Many can of course do this, but that in itself requires considerable knowledge of intervening events, and those who can achieve a sustained theory are almost entitled to their partisanship, in reward of their ingenuity. After all, we can hope only for palliatives.

With history I class what in general we call the Liberal Arts, Fiction, Drama, Poetry, Biography, especially those of other countries; as far as that be possible, in other tongues. In short, I argue that the political life of a country like ours would get depth and steadiness, would tend to escape its greatest danger, which is the disposition to take the immediate for the eternal, to press the advantage of present numbers to the full, to ignore dissenters and regard them as heretics, by some adumbration of what men have thought and felt in other times and at other places. This seems to me a surer resort than liberal weeklies, societies for the promotion of cultural relations, sermons upon tolerance, American Civil Liberty Unions. I know very well how remote from the possibilities of most men anything of the kind must be, but good temper, as well as bad, is contagious. And today in America vast concourses of youth are flocking to our colleges, eager for something, just what they do not know. It makes much difference what they get. They will be prone to demand something they can immediately use; the tendency is strong to give it them; science, economics, business administration, law in its narrower sense. I submit that the shepherds should not first feed the flocks with these. I argue for the outlines of what used to go as a liberal education—not necessarily in the sense that young folks should waste precious years in efforts, unsuccessful for some reason I cannot understand, to master ancient tongues; but I speak for an introduction into the thoughts and deeds of men who have lived before them, in other countries than their own, with other strifes and other needs. This I maintain, not in the interest of that general cultural background, which is so often a cloak for the superior person, the prig, the snob and the pedant. But I submit to you that in some such way alone can we meet and master the high-power salesman of political patent medicines. I come to you, not as an advocate of education for education's sake, but as one, who like you, I suppose, is troubled by the spirit of faction, by the catch-words with the explosive energy of faith behind them, by the unwillingness to live and let live with which we are plagued. It is well enough to put one's faith in education, but the kind makes a vast difference. The principles of a common pump are in my opinion not so important politically as Keat's *Ode on a Grecian Urn*, to crib a phrase from

Augustine Birrell.

May I take an illustration nearer to the field with which you are especially concerned? I venture to believe that it is as important to a judge called upon to pass on a question of constitutional law, to have at least a bowing acquaintance with Acton and Maitland, with Thucydides, Gibbon and Carlyle, with Homer, Dante, Shakespeare and Milton, with Machiavelli, Montaigne and Rabelais, with Plato, Bacon, Hume and Kant, as with the books which have been specifically written on the subject. For in such matters everything turns upon the spirit in which he approaches the questions before him. The words he must construe are empty vessels into which he can pour nearly anything he will. Men do not gather figs of thistles, nor supply institutions from judges whose outlook is limited by parish or class. They must be aware that there are before them more than verbal problems; more than final solutions cast in generalizations of universal applicability. They must be aware of the changing social tensions in every society which make it an organism; which demand new schemata of adaptation; which will disrupt it, if rigidly confined.

This is only an illustration of the much wider question of our political life at large. I submit that the aim is not so fanciful as it may seem; though at the moment I agree the outlook is not promising. Young people are not much disposed to give their time to what seems like loose browsing in the past. Though there are signs of a turn, of the significance of the insignificant, I shall try no forecast. All I want to emphasize is the political aspect of the matter, of the opportunity to preserve that spirit of liberty without which life is insupportable, and nations have never in the past been able to endure.

Jefferson is dead; time has disproved his forecasts; the society which he strove to preserve is gone to chaos and black night, as much as the empire of Genghis Khan; what has succeeded he would disown as any get of his. Yet back of the form there is still the substance, the possibility of the individual expression of life on the terms of him who has to live it. The victory is not all Hamilton's, nor can it be unless we are all to be checked as anonymous members regulated by some bureaucratic machine, impersonal, inflexible, a Chronos to devour us, its children. We shall not succeed by any attempt to put the old wine in new bottles; liberty is an essence so volatile that it will escape any vial however corked. It rests in the hearts of men, in the belief that knowledge is hard to get, that man must break through again and again the thin crust on which he walks, that the certainties of today may become the superstitions of tomorrow; that we have no warrant of assurance save by everlasting readiness to test and test again. William James was its great American apostle in modern times; we shall do well to remember him.

Surely we, the children of a time when the assumptions of even the science of our fathers have been outworn; surely we ought not to speak in apocalyptic verities, nor scourge from the temple those who do not see with our eyes. All the devices of our ingenuity, all our command over the materials of this earth, all the organization and differentiation of our industry and our social life, all our moral fetishes and exaltations, all our societies to ameliorate mankind, our hospitals, our colleges, our institutes—all these shall not save us. We shall still need some knowledge of ourselves, and where shall we better look than to the fate of those who went before? Would we hold liberty, we must have charity—charity to others, charity to ourselves, crawling up from the moist ovens of a steaming world, still carrying the passional equipment of our ferocious ancestors, emerging from black superstition amid carnage and atrocity to our perilous present. What shall it profit us, who come so by our possessions, if we have not charity?

QUESTIONS

1. What are the "sources of tolerance" named in the title? At what point in his address does Hand speak directly to that topic? Why does he not do so at the start?
2. What conditions, according to Hand, diminish liberty and tolerance? What proposed remedies does he consider and find insufficient?
3. To what purpose does Hand contrast Jefferson and Hamilton? What essentially is the contrast? Of what are they representative figures?
4. Consider whether, and in what ways, Hand's speech resembles a conversation, or dialogue. Is that mode of speech a suitable way of rendering the ideas he recommends? Explain.
5. Both Hand and Emerson ("The American Scholar," pp. 281–295) discuss the influence of the past and knowledge of history in forming the mind of a thinking man. Compare their views of the value and uses of that knowledge.

GEOFFREY CROWTHER

English and American Education[1]

For the past three years I have been engaged, with my colleagues of the Central Advisory Council on Education in England, in a comprehensive study of the English educational system. I had some of my own education in the United States, and I have been a frequent visitor to America ever since. This double experience has bred in me a growing sense of astonishment that two countries

1. First presented as an address to the Conference of High School Principals and Supervisors in Baltimore, Maryland.

which share the same language, so many of the same cultural traditions and ways of life, whose political, religious, and social aspirations are so largely identical, should have educational systems so utterly different as to provide almost no basis for a comparison between them.

That is a strong statement, and my present purpose is to try to justify it. Let me first say, however, that I have no intention whatever of trying to show that one national system is, on balance, better than the other; only that they are much more different than is usually realized.

The American and the English educational systems are different in purpose, structure, and method. Let us start with purpose. The two systems grew up in response to very different pressures and needs. In America, you have always been very conscious of the need to build up a new society. You have wanted to construct something bigger, richer, better than you have. This is said to arise from something in the American national character, but that seems to me to turn the logic upside down; it is the American national character that has arisen from the circumstances in which the American people have found themselves. From the start it was necessary to create a supply of ministers of religion, of lawyers, and of skilled artisans—I place them in the order of importance in which they were regarded at the time. Later on there came the obvious necessity of incorporating the great waves of immigrants into your society. Still later came the great task, in which you are still engaged, of knitting your varied economic, social, and racial groups into the harmonious and balanced society in which the principles of democratic government can work properly.

Consciously or unconsciously, American education has at all times been designed to serve these social purposes. It has been regarded as an instrument by which society can build its own future. From its nature, it has inescapably been concerned with the rank and file of the people. Its chief concern for many generations has been to do something to the masses—and I think the word is *to*, not *for*—in the interests of the American dream.

All this, of course, is platitude in America. What may not be quite so familiar is the contrast in the historical situation in England. We have never been very conscious of the necessity to build a new society. At all relevant times we have had a fully developed society already in being. And at all relevant times we have also, I am sorry to say, been on the whole pretty satisfied with the society we have. For most of the last two hundred years, American education has been designed to do a job of construction; English education has been designed primarily for maintenance, with improvement coming second. In the very latest period, perhaps, those attitudes have started to change. As with so many aspects of education, there seem to be the first signs of a tendency to change sides. Your education is becoming socially more conservative just when ours is becoming more consciously radical.

But that is a speculation for the future, on which I will not enlarge. I am talking of the influences of the past, which have shaped the structures of today. American education has always had to concern itself with the common man in his multitudes. The concern of English education has until very recently been with the maintenance of society, in the words of the old prayer which you will often hear in school and college chapels, "that there may never be wanting a succession of persons duly qualified to serve God in church and state." This is a conception which does not necessarily embrace the education of the great mass. There is a fine, rich, broad educational tradition in England. But it is not a tradition of education, above the minimum level, for the multitude. Post-primary education has always been thought of as a privilege in England; it was not until 1944 that the principle of secondary education for all was established, and it is hardly yet fully effective.

Let me pursue this contrast a little further. Let me give you two of the consequences, of which I would guess that one will shock you, while the other may perhaps surprise you more favorably.

I will start with the shocker. The consequence of our different attitude is that the sheer size, the volume or quantity, of English education is very much smaller than American. The age at which the legal compulsion to attend school expires is still only fifteen. Moreover, that is an effective leaving age, and more than four children out of five in fact leave school before they are sixteen. Of the sixteen-year-old age group—those between their sixteenth and seventeenth birthdays—only 22 per cent are still in full-time education. In the seventeen-year-olds, the figure falls to 13 per cent of the boys and 11 per cent of the girls. Among eighteen-year-olds, it is 8 per cent of the boys and 5.5 per cent of the girls.

What strikes Americans, I find, as even odder than these figures is the fact that we are not, as a nation, greatly disturbed by them, although many of us think they ought to be larger. But we cannot assume that public opinion is on our side. I am very doubtful whether there would be any support in public opinion for a policy of keeping the majority of children in school after sixteen, and I am certain that you would find hardly anyone in England who believes, as you do, in keeping all children at school until eighteen. Our college students represent about 3 per cent of each age group, and there is an expansion program in hand that will raise it to about 5 per cent. Anybody who suggested that we needed any more than that would meet with the strongest resistance, and not least from the universities themselves.

This attitude does not arise from any lack of love for our children. It is not because we think we can't afford it. The proportion of our national income that we spend on general welfare services—social security, health, and the like—is about the highest in the world. It is not from lack of generosity or lack of means that we confine education after the middle teens to a minority. It is because we sincerely believe that it is the right thing to do, in the interests of the children themselves. After all, there can be no absolute rules about education. Nobody believes that any child should be allowed to leave school at twelve. I do not suppose a time will ever come when, even in America, it will become legal or compulsory for everyone to stay in full-time education until twenty-five. Where you fix the age between those limits is surely a matter of judgment. And why should it be the same age for all children? Our belief in England is that, balancing what can be got out of school against what can be got out of life, the average boy or girl has probably had the optimum dose after eleven years of schooling—and do not forget that we begin, by legal compulsion, at the age of five. Eleven years, after all, is one year out of every six or seven of the average lifetime.

Now let me give you the other side of the medal. Because education after fifteen or sixteen is confined to a minority, that minority gets every assistance that the state can provide. It is nowadays, to an overwhelming extent, a minority chosen for intelligence and attainment. There are, of course, still the independent schools, where very substantial fees have to be paid. But the pressure of numbers upon them is such that a stupid boy or girl will have great difficulty getting in. And in the state schools, selection is by merit only. But once selected, a boy finds himself with his foot not so much on a ladder as an escalator. He will have the best resources of the best schools concentrated on him. If he can secure a place in a university, and that also is a matter of selection by merit, the state will pay his tuition fees and his living expenses, not only during the session but during the vacation as well. There is no such thing as working your way through college in England. We do not need a National Merit Scholarship scheme because we have one already. Nor is this a recent thing. It has been expanded in recent years, but it has always existed.

Let me move on to structure. The outstanding difference here lies in the fact that we have a very much smaller degree of local control than you do. There are about 50,000 schools boards in the United States, each of them, I suppose, more or less free to run the schools as it thinks best. That gives a total population in the average school board area of about 3500 persons. In England there are about 130 local education authorities, which gives an average population per area of about 300,000. Moreover, there are two other differences, apart from this sharp difference in size. Your school boards consist,

I believe, in most states, of persons specially elected for the purpose, with no other duties. In England the schools are run by the county council, or the borough council, which is the general-purpose government of the area.

Second, your school boards raise their own money by direct taxes, or at least the greater part of it. In England about 70 per cent of the expenditure of the local education authorities is met out of grants from the central government in London. There are advantages and disadvantages in this. It means that we do not have the enormous range in standards between rich areas and poor areas that you do. It means a much greater degree of standardization of conditions of employment among the teachers, and therefore of interchangeability between school and school and between area and area. But it also inevitably means a greater degree of uniformity imposed from the center. We think our system is decentralized, because it allows much more local freedom and variety than exist in the school systems of most Continental European countries. But there is no doubt that it is much more highly centralized than the American system.

The other great difference under the heading of structure is the principle of selection upon which our system is based. All children, except the minority in fee-paying schools, go to undifferentiated schools from the age of five to the age of eleven. At eleven or thereabouts, a proportion of them, varying from area to area but averaging between 20 and 25 per cent, is selected for what we call grammar schools, which include children to the age of eighteen, though not all the pupils stay that long. The remainder go to what are called secondary modern schools, which include children to age fifteen and increasingly to sixteen, but no older.

You will see from this description that the crucial time for an English child is at the age of eleven or a little more. The selection test then applied—the famous or infamous eleven-plus examination—is supposed to be a classification purely by ability and aptitude, without any suspicion of being derogatory to those who are not selected. But, of course, everybody wants to be selected, and with the growing pressure of numbers as a result of the post-war bulge of population, the selection has been getting steadily more competitive. As the result of agitation, the Labor Party has adopted the policy of abolishing the eleven-plus examination by sending all children at that age to the same schools, the so-called comprehensive secondary schools. The Labor Party has moved toward this system in several of the areas where it controls the local council, and even in Conservative areas there is a distinct movement to experiment with systems that do not involve sending children to different schools at the age of eleven.

I have several times seen this movement quoted in America as evidence that English education is turning away from selection. I think this is a grave misunderstanding. The public objection to selection at eleven is social and political, not educational. It is an objection on the part of parents to having their children sent to different schools, not to their having different educations. And the remedies that are being applied are wholly in terms of institutions, not in terms of the education they provide. I know, for example, one large new comprehensive school built by a Labor council. Every child entering that school is tested and placed in one of fifteen "streams," differentiated by the children's intelligence and aptitude. This selection is done by the teachers; the parents have nothing to do with it; and the children are not even supposed to know which stream is which in intelligence grading. A child placed in one of the top streams will have an almost wholly different education from a child placed even in one of the middle streams. If this is not selection, I do not know the meaning of the term. But this is what we mean by a comprehensive school. Many people in England will tell you that the comprehensive school has been copied from the American comprehensive high school, some meaning it as a compliment, some as the reverse. I have often told them that they could hardly be more mistaken.

Nonselection—if that is the opposite of selection—as it is practiced in America is totally unknown in England. By nonselection I mean the principle of treating all children alike, allowing them to sort themselves out by their choice of courses, by what they find easy and difficult, or by their varying ambitions—with counseling assistance, no doubt, but without any compulsory segregations. I am sure that your system seems as odd to us as ours does to you. There is no retreat from selection in England; the only change is that a growing number of people—but still a minority—think that the selection should be within a common school, not between schools.

The differences between the two countries in educational method make an enormous subject, and I must restrict myself to four points out of many that it would be possible to make.

The first of these differences in method lies in the position of the teacher, in the relative positions of the teacher and the textbook. One of the things about American education that most strikes the English visitor is the importance you attach to textbooks. We have no parallel to that. To begin with, I do not think there are more than two or three, at most, of the local education authorities in England that tell their schools what textbooks to use. That is left to the teacher, occasionally the principal, or the head of the department in a large school. And in the higher grades, more often than not, there is not a textbook at all. A teacher will often recommend a book as covering the subject pretty well and as being useful for reference but will not make any attempt to go through it chapter by chapter.

This system places a much greater responsibility on the individual teacher, and I have often been asked in America whether we do not have a lot of trouble with it. So far as the political and social responsibility of the teacher is concerned, I cannot recall having heard of a single case arising through a teacher's being accused of using a book which seems offensive or objectionable to somebody in authority. That is partly, perhaps mainly, because our system of large authorities and rather remote and indirect public control puts the individual teacher largely out of the reach of vigilance committees, whether of parents or of the local chamber of commerce. There is also a strong tradition against anything that smacks of political interference with the schools.

Educational responsibility, however, is another matter. Quite clearly, a system like ours, which places so much responsibility on the individual teacher, cannot work well unless the average standard of intelligence, knowledge, and teaching competence is high. Up to the present, we have been able to maintain that standard. It is partly, of course, a matter of numbers. In the whole of England last year there were only some 260,000 schoolteachers. We were a little short, but 300,000 would have given us all we need. And this is in a country about one quarter the size of the United States. I do not know how many schoolteachers there are in the United States, but I am very sure it is many more than four times 300,000. I do not see how you could possibly have coped with the enormous increase in the American school population in the past forty years without being willing to take thousands of young men and women who needed close support from a textbook before they could teach. Indeed, under the pressure of rising numbers in the schools, I fear we shall find before long that we shall have to give the teacher more assistance, and that implies more external control on his teaching. This particular contrast is not, however, entirely a matter of numbers. It is partly also the result of a different tradition of teacher training, which, in England, has always laid a much greater emphasis on the content of what is to be taught than in America and much less on questions of pedagogic method.

The second difference in method is the absence in England of the course system which is so universal in your schools and colleges. Indeed, the word "course" has a wholly different meaning in the two countries. If you asked an English school child what courses he was taking, he wouldn't know what you meant. If you asked him what subjects he was taking, he would answer English, Latin, mathematics, history, and so forth. But that would not mean, as it would in America, that those were the subjects he had chosen to take. They would be the subjects that his form, or class, was taking, and therefore that he was taking with the rest of the class. Until the boy is about fifteen or sixteen, it is unlikely that he or his parents have had any say in the choice of form in which he is placed. And at no age does he have any say in deciding the curriculum of that form. At the higher ages, there is a choice between three of four different curriculums, but each curriculum has to be taken, within narrow limits, as it stands.

Here, indeed, is a contrast with the American system. Perhaps it is not quite so sharp a contrast in practice as it is in principle, as I observe that, more and more, those American boys and girls who have ambition to gain admittance to a good college find their choice of courses in high school made for them by the college entrance requirements. But there is one important consequence for teaching that is worth bringing out. In an English school, in any year but one (and that one is what we call the fifth form year, about the age of fourteen or fifteen), you can assume that the pupils who are taking a subject in one year will be taking the same subject next year. The study of a subject can therefore be planned as a continuous process over a period of years. That is what we mean when we use the word "course." We mean a whole balanced curriculum of six or seven or eight subjects, planned to continue over three or four or five years. Once a boy or girl enters on such a course, he or she will normally pursue it to the end. And all the boys and girls in a course will take substantially the same subjects, with perhaps slight options, as between a second classical or a second modern language. You will therefore understand how bewildered we are when we contemplate one of your neat, packaged, self-contained, nine-month courses, such as high school physics. It is no good asking an English schoolboy when he enters college how many years of French he has had at school. Two boys might both truthfully answer nine years. But they might mean totally different things, and neither one would mean what you thought he meant.

How, then, do we measure what a student has accomplished, if we cannot count up the number of courses he has satisfactorily taken? The answer is that we rely, to an extent wholly unknown to you, on general examinations. Every year—sometimes every term— the pupil has to take a written examination in all the subjects of the curriculum, and his further progress depends, sometimes entirely, on his performance in that examination. Most of these examinations are set and assessed within the school itself, by his own teachers. But at three crucial points in his career the examination is set and assessed by an external body. The first of these is the eleven-plus examination, which determines to which sort of secondary school the child should go. The second comes at fifteen or sixteen and is called the Ordinary Level of the General Certificate of Education, set and assessed by one of nine examining boards closely associated with the universities. This examination can be taken in any number of subjects from one upwards, but the most usual practice is to take it in from five to nine subjects. Third, there is the Adanced Level of the General Certificate of Education, which is taken at eighteen or thereabouts and which plays a large part in university entrance.

I have been describing the practice of the grammar schools; that is, the schools for the brightest 20 to 25 percent of the children. Examinations, especially written examinations, play a much smaller part in the life of the less intelligent children. Even in this case, however, they play a much larger part than they do in America; and there is a rising demand for public examinations, at lower standards of intelligence than those of the General Certificate of Education, for these less gifted children. I cannot honestly say that the children themselves clamor for examinations, but employers do, and therefore so do the parents. All the questions that Americans ask and answer in terms of the number and variety of courses a student has taken we ask and answer in terms of the examinations he has passed.

I have left to the last what is the sharpest difference of all between our two systems. This is our system of specialization, in which England is, I think, unique in the world. A student will take the examination for the Ordinary Level of the General Certificate of Education at the age of fifteen or sixteen in a wide range of subjects drawn both from the humanities and from the natural sciences. But once he has passed that examination, he will specialize. That is to say, he will devote two thirds, or perhaps even more, of his time in school to a narrow range of subjects. In one boy's case it may be physics, chemistry, and mathematics; in another's it may be chemistry and biology, or it may be history or modern languages and literature, or classical languages and philosophy. But, whatever the choice, the greater part of the pupil's attention, in the classroom and in his private study time, is given to his specialty, and he will take the advanced level examination at eighteen in his special subjects only. When he gets to the university, the specialization is even more intense. The range of subjects does not usually get any narrower, but the student gives 100 per cent of his time to it.

I have found that to Americans, and indeed to educationalists from every country in the world except England, this seems a very strange system indeed. Perhaps you will have difficulty in believing that I really mean what I say. So let me cite my own case, though it is now more than thirty years old. I was a modern languages specialist. For my last three years at school, from the age of fifteen to eighteen, I studied mostly French and German language and literature, perhaps three or four hours a week of history, and one hour of Scripture on Sundays. For another two years at Cambridge, even the history and the Scripture were cut out, and I studied French and German exclusively. Five years of my life were given to those languages. My experience was perhaps a little extreme; I think the admixture of general and contrasting subjects would nowadays, in a good school, be a little bigger. But the difference would not be great. The English boy or girl is a specialist from the age of fifteen or sixteen.

The advisory council of which I am chairman was specifically requested by the Minister of Education to review this system of specialization. We examined it most carefully and discussed it at great length, both with witnesses and among ourselves. In the end we came to the conclusion that we wanted to see it continued. We found that it was being pushed too far, and we have made a number of suggestions for removing what we think are abuses. But we have reported in favor of this system of specialization. And that is a unanimous conclusion reached by a council made up of educators of all kinds. Perhaps you will find that fact as extraordinary as the system itself, and I must try to give you some of our reasons for thinking that, in this matter, we in England are in step and the whole of the rest of the world is out of step.

Let me begin by telling you of one argument that we reject. This is the argument that every intelligent citizen, or every educated man, ought to know something about each subject in a range so wide that it compels a balanced curriculum; that no one can afford to be ignorant of history, government, science, languages, and so forth. To this, we would give our answer in two parts. First, it is true that there are certain elementary skills and knowledges that everyone must have—reading, writing, arithmetic, and several more. But these essential elements can be, and should be, provided by the age of sixteen. If you go on with them after that age, you will be wasting your time, because the knowledge you instill will be forgotten unless it can be attached to the main intellectual interest of a boy's or girl's life, which begins to emerge at about that age.

The second part of the answer is that it is only when you have got these essential elementary skills and knowledges out of the way that you can confront the real task of education. The acquisition of factual knowledge is by itself a poor test of any education and a lamentably poor test of the education of boys and girls of seventeen and eighteen. It has been said that the process of education is not to be compared to that of filling up an empty pot, but rather to that of lighting a fire. The proper test of an education is whether it teaches the pupil to think and whether it awakens his interest in applying his brain to the various problems and opportunities that life presents. If these have once been done, then factual knowledge can easily be assimilated. If these have not been done, then no amount of nodding acquaintance with widely varying fields of human knowledge will equip a boy or girl with an educated mind. We in England argue the case for specialization not primarily on the score of the information it provides but because it awakens interest, teaches clear thinking, and induces self-discipline in study.

We believe that, if you can find which of the recognized intellectual disciplines most arouses a boy's interest—and we confine his choice to five or six recognized disciplines, chosen for their intellectual content, not for their vocational value—if you can let him spend his time on what interests him, but insist that he must work hard at it, go deep into it, follow it up in the library or the laboratory, get around behind the stage scenery that defines the formal academic subject, you will really be teaching him how to use the mind that God has given him. This sort of intensive study takes a great deal of time, and that is why it can only be applied, for any one student, to a restricted range of subjects. No doubt you will say that the boy must be very narrow as a result. That may be. Are you sure that being narrow is worse than being shallow?

I find that English education has a high reputation among Americans. I am often asked, for example, whether it is not true that the eighteen-year-old boy in England is a year or two ahead of his American contemporary. I always answer that question, or assertion, by asking some others. What boy? If an English boy is still at school at eighteen, he is necessarily in the upper quartile in intelligence. Are you comparing him with the average American high school graduate, who is of average intelligence? And ahead in what? In the subjects to which he has been giving nearly all his time and attention for two years? It would be strange if he were not a long way ahead in those. Or over the whole range of a broad curriculum? He has been taught different things, by different methods, with a different purpose in view, in a different sort of school. There is no fair basis for a comparative judgment.

QUESTIONS

1. What three principal contrasts does Crowther draw between English and American education? Does Crowther develop each of the principal contrasts in the same manner? In the same detail? In what ways does he effect transitions from point to point within each of the principal sections? From section to section?

2. What are Crowther's sources of information? What kinds of authority does he employ to support his statements? Does he give equal weight to each kind of authority? How does he convey a sense of the kind and degree of authority in support of his statements?

3. Crowther's description of the system of American education must necessarily be general. Does it appear to be accurate? Does your own experience of American schools yield observations departing from Crowther's in particular ways? To what extent do these par-

ticular differences, if any, offer a general picture at variance with Crowther's?

4. Crowther asserts that in America education "has been regarded as an instrument by which society can build its own future" (p. 307). Find evidence to support or refute this thesis in the preceding essays of this section. Determine in what ways and to what extent the assertion fits American views of education today.

ÉTIENNE GILSON

Education and Higher Learning[1]

The aim and purpose of this address will be to describe the proper relationship that obtains, or should obtain, between education and higher learning. By the word "education" I intend to signify the system of schools now existing in most American and European countries, from primary schools up to universities, together with the programs and the general spirit that inspire their teaching methods. Naturally, since there is a great deal of variety within this system, my remarks will be of a general nature. They will deal with tendencies rather than with concrete facts. If and where exceptions are to be found, it should be understood beforehand that my remarks simply do not apply. If there is any truth in what I am about to say, it can be a global truth only. As to "higher learning," it will always signify that part of any complete school system that deals with liberal learning and, in consequence, with creative learning. We may have to use one or two concrete examples; yet, thus considered in its entire abstraction and generality, our problem will not be discussed in terms of any local, national, or continental situation. Even the political notions it may have to touch upon will not be borrowed from practical politics, but from political philosophy. I trust, however, that the main consequences of these reflections will not appear irrelevant to practical life. For education is a field of human activity in which it is most necessary that speculation go before action.

Let us first consider teaching as it is commonly understood in European as well as in American public schools, or even high schools, below the university level. Its object is an immediately practical one. A civilized country is made up of citizens who can read and write, perform elementary arithmetical operations, say something about the place of their own country in both space and time; last, not the least, it is made up of citizens who know enough in order to discharge one of the many functions necessary to the welfare of the community. Incidentally, this is what justifies the right of intervention by the State in matters of education, and this right extends much farther

1. An address delivered at the University of Toronto as part of the centennial celebration of St. Michael's College in 1952.

than some of us would feel willing to concede. In his encyclical letter *Repraesentanti in terra*, December 31, 1929, Pope Pius XI expressly says: "The State can demand, and therefore see to it, that all citizens be endowed with the necessary knowledge of their civic and national duties, nay, with a certain amount of intellectual, moral, and physical culture which, given the conditions prevailing in our own times, is necessarily required for the common good." Education, then, has become a public service to the full extent to which it has become a public necessity. At the same time, and to the same extent, education is tending to become more and more practical in nature, because, for the State, the common good of the body politic is a practical end. Such is the reason why our schools are progressively tending either to become vocational schools or, at least, to prepare children in view of such schools, wherein they will ultimately qualify for some specialized job.

The same remark applies even to colleges and universities. From a mere glance at their programs, it appears that their proper function is to turn out, year in, year out, the right number of trained engineers, physicians, lawyers, farmers, and businessmen necessary to the welfare of a civilized country. Professors and teachers of all types are no exceptions to the rule. Our students express themselves correctly when they say that they are looking for a teaching *job*. To teach is not to speculate, an avocation for which nobody ever was paid. To teach is to act. What do we require from future teachers at all levels? Simply that they know what they will have to teach. In many cases we content ourselves with making sure that they will be able to learn it a week ahead of their pupils. Indeed, there would be no sense in protesting against the generalized tendency that now prevails to assign useful ends to our modern system of education.

Here, however, a distinction should be made between the two notions of "practicality" and of "usefulness." Were these identical, there would be for us no problem to discuss. We could then quote with unqualified approval the forceful remarks of A. N. Whitehead on the subject.[2] "Pedants," Whitehead says, "sneer at an education which is useful. But if education is not useful, what is it? Is it a talent, to be hidden away in a napkin? Of course education should be useful, whatever your aim in life. It was useful to St. Augustine and it was useful to Napoleon. It is useful, because understanding is useful." To this, which is undoubtedly true, we nevertheless beg to add that understanding is not always useful in the same way. What Napoleon learned at the artillery school of Brienne was the art of handling guns; a useful art in its own way, to be sure, but a very practically useful one. As to what St. Augustine had learned from St. Ambrose and from Plotinus, it was infinitely more useful still, since it was the

2. A. N. Whitehead, *The Aims of Education* (Mentor Books, 1949), p. 14 [Gilson's note].

way to achieve salvation, than which nothing can be more useful to man; yet, at the same time, he had also learned that salvation was beatitude; that is, the love of truth for its own sake, than which nothing less practical and more speculative can possibly be conceived. Understanding is alway useful indeed, but when he himself wrote about the "divine beauty" of Lagrange's equations, Whitehead would have been much better understood by St. Augustine than by Napoleon. *Gaudium de veritate*, the joy born in us from the mere sight of truth: is it useful? Of course it is. But because it is an end in itself, not a means to any other end, it is not at all practical.

Seen from this precise point of view, the practical trend now prevailing in modern education raises a difficult problem. Does it provide boys and girls, students in all fields, with the proper feeling for the supreme importance of that type of knowledge which, precisely because it is not practical, might well be the most useful of all? In protesting against those who believe in the possibility of useless knowledge, Whitehead probably had in mind the distinction drawn by Cardinal Newman, whose works he knew so well, between a "liberal" education and a "useful" education. But a more careful examination of his text clearly shows that where he was writing "useful," what the Cardinal had in mind was "practical." In his Fifth Discourse, *On the Scope and Nature of University Education,* Newman has lovingly described what he used to call "liberal knowledge" as a knowledge "sufficient for itself, apart from every external and ulterior object."[3] To which he added that to educate for such knowledge is the true scope of a university. Even after granting to Whitehead that this knowledge is eminently useful, the fact remains that its own type of usefulness has nothing to do with practicality. How is it, then, that instead of keeping faith with Newman's ideal, the general trend of our modern school system is to stress the kind of knowledge that is not sufficient for itself, but always aims at some external and ulterior object?

Let us honestly face the difficulty. "Liberal knowledge" is not a new formula. Originally it pointed out the knowledge of the so-called "liberal arts"; that is to say, according to Cicero's own commentary, the knowledge of those arts which it is befitting for a free man to know: *artes libero dignae.* As to the other arts—namely, the mechanical ones—they were good for hand workers or, to say it more bluntly, for slaves. Of course legal slaves have long ceased to exist, yet, unless

3. Newman was well aware of this derivation as well as of its ideological implications. Speaking of the word "liberal," Newman says: "Now, first, in its grammatical sense it is opposed to *servile;* and by 'servile work' is understood, as our catechisms inform us, bodily labor, mechanical employment, and the like, in which the mind has little or no part." (*The Idea of a University,* London: Longman's, Green and Co., 1912, p. 106.) Liberal knowledge, Newman has just observed, is "the especial property of a University and a gentleman" (p. 106). When such expressions are used in their literal meaning, "we contrast a liberal education with a commercial education or a professional" (p. 107) [Gilson's note].

I am mistaken, more than a shade of this ancient meaning is still hovering over the language of Cardinal Newman[4] especially where he identifies "liberal knowledge" with "a gentleman's knowledge."[5] Not being myself an Englishman, I cannot pretend to know what it is to be a "gentleman." Yet I will make bold to say that, in Cardinal Newman's own mind, to study in view of becoming a skilled carpenter, a bricklayer, or even a trained mechanic would not have answered his definition of a gentleman's knowledge. When, to his own dismay, a true gentleman finds himself afflicted with a natural gift for such mechanical avocations, to resort to the British category of "hobby" is for him the only way to indulge his taste without losing his social dignity. Whatever else he may have been, the student described by Newman as a gentleman could certainly afford a university training free from immediate professional preoccupations. A truly Oxonian ideal indeed, at least as Oxford used to be in the good old times, but one which, in most parts of the world today, looks more like a dream than a reality. This gentlemanly type of education presupposes a measure of those worldly possessions which only wealthy men can afford to despise. Without in the least denying that modern universities are still successfully engaged in the task of turning out gentlemen, one may at least observe that the meaning of the word no longer is exactly what it used to be. In our own day, just as all women are ladies, all men are gentlemen.

The reason for this change is a political one. A democratic type of society has progressively replaced the aristocratic social order of Newman's England. This is not a question of political regimes, but rather a change in social structures, coming in the wake of political revolutions. There is no other choice than between aristocracy, which stands for inequality, and democracy, which stands for equality. Whether it calls itself a kingdom, an empire, a republic or even a democratic republic, a society remains an aristocracy to the full extent that it maintains a privileged class, be it only that of those who "have" as against those who "have not." In modern democracies, this measure is steadily becoming an always smaller and smaller one, and this fact is not without deeply affecting the nature and the spirit of their systems of education, especially with respect to their attitude toward liberal knowledge and higher learning.

From the time of its very origins, which, for Western civilization, is that of ancient Greece, free and liberal speculation has always been made possible by the existence of a leisured class whose members, if they felt so inclined, could dedicate themselves to speculative research and to contemplation. For this reason, Aristotle says, the first men to philosophize were priests. The remark clearly applies to the middle ages, when nobody could become a scholar unless

---

4. Newman, *The Idea of a University*, pp. 107-108 [Gilson's note].

5. Newman, *The Idea of a University*, p. 111 [Gilson's note].

he was a cleric.[6] When both in Greece and in modern societies laymen became interested in learning, the existence of lay philosophers, scientists, and scholars of any sort was made possible either because they themselves belonged to the aristocracy of their time, which was the case for Francis Bacon and for Descartes, or else because some enlightened members of that aristocracy provided them with the intellectual leisure necessary for disinterested speculation. The Florence of the Medici, Elizabethan England, the France of Louis XIV, where writers, artists, and scientists of all countries stood a fair chance of being supported by the King or by the nobility, are so many outstanding examples of what aristocratic societies can do for liberal knowledge. This type of culture was truly liberal, because it was not expected to bring about any practical results either for those who paid for it or for those who were being paid to produce it. Princes would then find it natural to favor the development of the arts and the sciences simply because they knew that beauty and truth were good things to be enjoyed for their own sake. Artists and scientists had no idea of making a fortune out of their work. So long as their protectors gave them enough to live, they considered themselves highly privileged, as indeed they were, since they were free to live a wholly unpractical life, the only one in which they were interested.

The kind of education that befits such a type of aristocratic culture is easy to define: it is the education of the elite, by an elite, and for an elite. In such circumstances, education is the received method whereby an aristocracy recruits its future members or, at least, the competent body of citizens who, sharing in the benefits of the prevailing social system, are interested in insuring its survival. No wonder, then, that at the very times when it gave birth to a Dante, a Shakespeare, or a Descartes, Europe had practically no system of public schools; so much so, that by far the larger number of its inhabitants were illiterate. Aristocracy is a great producer of higher learning and of liberal knowledge, only it keeps it to itself; it is a spring rather than a stream.

Not so in democratic societies, whose systems of education naturally follow the rule of their political life. What they want is an education of the whole people, given by men who themselves belong among the people and, consequently, intended for the greater benefit of the people in its entirety. This time we find ourselves confronted with a powerful system of intellectual irrigation whose streams are visible everywhere; the only questions are: Where is the spring? Where are

6. One of the most revolutionary effects of Christianity was to call *all* men, slaves or not, ignorant or learned, to the most liberal type of knowledge, which is that of truth embraced for its own sake. Faith made it accessible to all. This is the deep-seated reason why the Catholic Church has always favored liberal studies. In as much as they are truly liberal, studies aim to lead human minds to truth enjoyed for its own sake; that is, to contemplation. And what is eternal life, if not the eternal enjoyment of absolute Truth? [Gilson's note].

the sources? Can there still be sources in a society whose natural tendency is to universalize education and, consequently, to equalize it?

This is a genuine issue, which we must have the courage to face, not in any spirit of criticism, and still less of hostility, toward democracy, but with the sincere desire to understand its educational problems and thus throw some light on its difficulties. There are several interrelated reasons why, whereas aristocracies were more interested in creating intellectual culture than in spreading it, democracies seem to be more eager to distribute higher learning than to create it. Among these reasons there is a particularly obvious one. If our school system exists, not in view of a chosen minority, but in view of all, its average level should answer the average level of the population as a whole. Hence the unavoidable consequence that the best gifted among the pupils will be discriminated against. Nor should we imagine that creative minds will multiply in direct proportion to the growth of the school population. The reverse is much more likely to happen. In aristocratic societies, genius has often found access to higher culture, even under adverse circumstances; in democratic societies, it will have no higher culture to which to gain access. Since equality in ignorance is easier than equality in learning, each and every teacher will have to equalize his class at the bottom level rather than at the top one, and the whole school system will spontaneously obey the same law. It is anti-democratic to teach all children what only some of them are able to learn. Nay, it is anti-democratic to teach what all children can learn by means of methods which only a minority of pupils are able to follow. Since, as has been said, democracy stands for equality, democratic societies have a duty to teach only what is accessible to all and to see to it that it be made accessible to all. The overwhelming weight of their school population is therefore bound to lower the center of gravity in their school systems. The first peril for democracies, therefore, is to consider it their duty, in order to educate all citizens, to teach each of them less and less and in a less and less intelligent way.

It is not easy to say such things without sounding satirical, which I have no intention of being. I myself am an old teacher, and I would not let it be thought either that I am pining for a return of our countries to some aristocratic type of society, or that, when I remember what schools used to be around 1890, I see things deteriorating from bad to worse. Much progress has been achieved; the only point I am stressing is: Has there been progress all along the line? We are teaching more and more, but are we teaching better and better? And, if not, is it not because, confronted as they are with the legitimate task of providing learning for all their citizens, modern democracies have to cope with entirely new problems for which they are not prepared? The task of turning learning into a commodity and education into a public service is something both necessary and unheard of, for which there is no historical precedent. We should not feel too surprised to see the democratic State handling education like coal, hydroelectric power, or public means of transportation. The State must control everything in order to insure the equal distribution of all necessary goods among all citizens, including even education. We do not want this progress to stop, we simply do not want it to defeat its own purpose; and this is what the democratic State is going to do if it does not handle learning according to its own nature, which, because it is born of the mind, is wholly unlike any other kind of commodity.

We have reached such a pass that pedagogical authorities are beginning to think that learning is there in view of the schools, not the schools in view of learning.[7] This very year some schoolteachers made once more the time-honored discovery that the spelling of their mother tongue stood in need of being simplified. I need not quote the name of the country, because there is not a single language in the world whose spelling could not be made simpler than it is. The only trouble is that, in order to be perfectly simple, spelling has to be purely phonetic, in which case nobody can understand what he reads. This, however, is not my point. What I am interested in is the main rule set up by the committee on the simplification of spelling in that country. According to the school inspector who wrote the report, the committee decided either to accept, or else to reject, all suggested changes "according as they could, or could not, facilitate the teaching of the language." This curious pedagogical imperialism implies that the proper function of spelling is to be taught. Such teachers do not consider themselves the servants of learning, but its owners; so they have a full right to change it in order to facilitate their work. And indeed, why not? If all citizens have an equal right to know spelling, spelling should be made foolproof and equally available to all citizens. I am sorry to say, without any trace of irony, that this is the principle which we now apply to practically all disciplines, from spelling to metaphysics. We do not impart learning such as it is, but such as it ought to be in order to be teachable to the millions. From time to time, some simple-minded professor attempts to make his pupils understand, not himself, but that which he teaches. The rumor soon

7. A striking symptom of this disease, and one that deserves special study, is the present tendency of pedagogy to become an independent discipline. There are pedagogues whose ambition it is to teach how to teach. As often as not, such teachers undertake to teach disciplines which they themselves do not know, or know imperfectly, to those who know them. Their attitude implies that the divorce of teaching from learning is now complete. Moreover, this also turns teaching itself into a "servile work." What is more, the divorce of teaching from learning threatens our whole educational system with failure; for the only effective pedagogical methods are those that proceed from learning itself, through the person of the teacher, to the person of the pupil [Gilson's note].

begins to spread that the poor man cannot make himself understood. So he is a bad teacher, and we turn *him* out of his class, not the pupils.

Besides the general lowering of its level, another consequence follows from this democratic treatment of education at the hands of the State; namely, its predominately practical character. Nothing is more logical; and this time, since all citizens are part and parcel of the democratic State, all we have to do is to consult ourselves in order to know its will. Time and again, we have heard fathers say with solemn gravity: "I want my son to have an education." In point of fact, we all have said it ourselves, but what we really have meant is: "I want my son to get a job." A perfectly legitimate desire indeed. At the end of their studies, good students should get jobs that will turn them into citizens equally useful to themselves, to their future families, and to their country. Since such is the wish of the vast majority of its citizens, the democratic State will naturally tend to give them what they want; that is, a sound, practical education with no frills. This is what all teaching States are now doing, and they do it pretty well. Once more, I am not criticizing; I am merely trying to observe facts, and the outstanding fact, in this case, is that what we agreed to call "liberal knowledge," precisely because it has no practical usefulness, is bound to be eliminated together with the frills. The steady decline of classical studies, in Europe as well as in America, is a clear instance of what I have in mind. Even their strongest supporters cannot pretend that classical humanities are practically useful in everyday life; those among us who try to defend them on this ground are simply betraying their cause. Even if classical humanities may be put to practical use, this cannot be the reason why they should be taught. Such an aristocratic type of education simply cannot be universalized. As a consequence, no room can be made for it in the programs of schools which must cater to all citizens. So we teach them too little, or too late, which is little better than not to teach them at all. Why complain? Liberal knowledge, Newman says, is to itself its own end; in our industrial age, contemplation is a luxury which very few States can afford to subsidize. The cold truth is that the practical uselessness which recommended liberal education to Cardinal Newman's mind today justifies its exclusion from the curriculum of our democratic schools. Even societies cannot have their cake and eat it.

Yet there should be somebody to make the cake, and it is to be feared that, unless they re-examine their own educational problem, democracies will soon find themselves with nothing to eat. First of all, democratic education rests upon the principle of equality applied to the human understanding. But this application is a fallacy of the well-known type, which consists in applying to two different orders what is true of only one of them. The notion of democracy is a social one; it expresses the common will of a people to deal with its own members as if all men were born free and equal. On the contrary, human understanding is a fact of nature, and whether we like it or not, facts of nature are not equal. Nature is not democratic. Physical and intellectual inequalities can be corrected, or compensated; the democratic State can see to it that even the less gifted among its citizens be given a fair chance to learn and to know something; it can narrow the gap that separates creative genius from merely normal intellects, and even from abnormally backward ones; above all, democracy can prevent natural inequalities from begetting social privileges sometimes worse than the natural ones; yet, when all is said and done, nature can be corrected, not suppressed. Understanding is not equal in men. Intellectual life is just what it is, not what society would like it to be. Unless democracies accept its laws just as they are, they may well turn out an always larger number of teachers, they will have less and less to teach.

We are simply forgetting that intellectual superiority and fitness for speculative knowledge are one and the same thing. In this sense, liberal knowledge is the only source of all practically useful knowledge, without any exception. Classical humanities are not the only relevant example. As a token of the general nature of the problem, I beg to quote the growing misconception of what science itself actually is. On June 16, 1952, the continental edition of the British *Daily Mail* announced to its readers that the United States had their first atom submarine "nearly ready." To this the same newspaper added the following personal comment of the President of the United States: "The day that the propellers of this new submarine first bite into the water will be the most momentous day in the field of atomic science, since the first flash of light down in the desert seven years ago." A typically democratic statement indeed, in which "science" merely means "engineering." The first flash of light in the field of atomic science did not shine in any desert seven years ago, but in the minds of Einstein and of other scientists who were speculating about the structure of matter and not looking for atom bombs or for atom submarines. True science is liberal knowledge; scientists seek after it for its own sake; engineers put it to practical use; they do not want to know in order to know, but in order to make. Yet it is a positive and well-established fact that the more speculative and liberal it is, the more fruitful scientific knowledge proves to be in its practical applications. Pasteur saved millions of human lives although he himself was not a physician. Nearer home, I do not think that Dr. Banting, who was a physician, ever intended to find a specific for diabetes; yet when he first isolated insulin, the specific was found. Science found it; medicine applied it.

If this be true, our democratic system of education now finds itself at a crossroad. It has done wonders in the past and we do not want it to undo them. There must be an education for the millions; the learning included in this type of mass education should be both practical and simple, that is to say, adapted to the general needs and to the average intellectual aptitudes of its pupils; yet, at the same time, even a thoroughly democratic system of education should not allow its ceaselessly growing body to lead its head. Unless they themselves provide, not a new aristocratic social class, but their own intellectual elite, which is something different, the social and technical progress of which our modern democratic States are so justly proud will soon come to an end. In peace and war, the powerful industrial equipment of the greatest among modern nations can be rendered obsolete at any time by the abstract speculation of some unknown scientist using a few sheets of paper and a pencil in the solitude of his own study. Nor should we forget that the times of the greatest national perils are also those when foreign scientists are no longer an available commodity.[8] This is not for democracies a matter of choice. None of them can hope indefinitely to consume the products of natural aristocracy without adding its own contribution to the common good. What we now need, within our present system of universal education, is another system, this time of selection, whose proper object will be not to thwart the best gifted intellects which it is our task to educate. Unless it follows such a policy, no nation can hope to prosper for a very long time. True democracy in education certainly consists in insuring the intellectual survival of even the unfit; it cannot possibly consist in preventing the natural superiority of the fittest from bearing their fruits to the greater benefit of all.

This obvious truth should not be so hard to understand. There is nothing less democratic, in the usual sense of the word, than sports and games. Championship is the triumph of carefully cultivated natural inequalities. There is no point in pretending that, in a democracy, every citizen should be able to beat Olympic records. We simply could not do it, however hard we might try, but we do not resent the fact. We do not ask our directors of athletics to prevent some students from running as fast as they can because if they did they would run faster than the others. We do not consider it democratic to set athletic standards as low as possible. On the

8. Even this very practical point is not always understood. In the Toronto *Globe and Mail*, Sept. 12, 1952, Sir Eric Rideal, a distinguished British scientist then visiting Ottawa, issued the timely warning: "You cannot trade on the originality of another country forever." If there is an obvious truth, this is one. Yet the next issue of the same paper (Sept. 13) summed up the consensus of a group of leading Canadian industrialists in this terse sentence: "Sir Eric is all wet." Their main objection was that, to carry out his suggestion "would definitely not be good for the Canadian pocketbook," the more so as "the importation of ideas is easy and there is no tax on them." This statement deserves to endure as an outstanding specimen in the history of mental parasitology. At any rate, the complete failure of Sir Eric to convey an exceedingly simple idea is enough to show that the task of importing them is not as easy as it might seem [Gilson's note].

contrary, we fully realize the fact that the exceptional performances of a few world champions act as a fruitful challenge whose effects are actually felt in all stadiums and on all athletic fields. What is democratic, here as everywhere else, is to keep both competition and selection as widely open as possible, and then to set up the highest conceivable standard as a standing invitation to all. In short, the only sound policy for any democracy is to raise the average level of its people[9] by cultivating the excellency of the best among its citizens.

What we understand so well concerning the education of the body, could we not understand concerning the education of the mind? Unless we do, we shall go on drifting along the same way which has already led us to make pedagogy the judge of learning. It can be concisely described in Shakespeare's terse words: "My foot my tutor." High school programs adapted to the kind of pupils they receive; university programs adapted to the kind of pupils that high schools are permitted by law to provide; and no provision made for the free development of liberal knowledge under all its forms, whose creative activity is the life and blood of any system of education! Things have gone so far that I might cite several countries in which, despairing as it were of saving higher learning, their governments have erected, outside universities, new institutions specialized in research work, where scholars seek but do not teach, while university professors teach but do not seek. I beg to say that, in so far as public education is concerned, wholly to surrender to this new tendency would be nothing less than the beginning of the end. The remedy we need should not consist in killing the patient. Since it is the course of nature that education derives its substance from the creative activity of a few speculative minds, let us rather help nature to follow its course. Where there is no higher learning, the presence of creative minds becomes less probable, intellectual light ceases to shine, routine and pedantry set in, and living truths shrivel into desiccated formulas. Then we begin complaining about the general decay of studies, as if students could still take an interest in matters which, even for those who teach them, have already lost their

9. Many professors and college presidents bitterly complain about the fact that students exhibit a much more marked taste for athletics than for academic studies. I beg to suggest that the students are right on this point. To the extent that they are not "professional," sports and athletics are enjoyed for their own sake and are to themselves their own end. From this point of view, which has not escaped the perspicacity of Cardinal Newman (*op. cit.*, pp. 107-108), "manly games, or games of skill, or military prowess, though bodily, are, it seems, accounted liberal." And rightly so. But if this is true, then athletics is now the only part of our school programs which is, officially and unrestrictedly, animated by a liberal spirit. Instead of asking for less athletics, we should rather bring back to the classroom the liberal spirit which once inspired it and still inspires athletics. Our only choice, therefore, is either to eliminate from our programs everything whose practical usefulness is not perceptible to students themselves, or else to say to them frankly that practical usefulness should not be the end of their education. Where the liberal spirit still prevails, students derive as much pleasure from the classroom as from the athletic field [Gilson's note].

meaning. The situation needs attention, but it is not desperate. All we have to do in order to mend it is refuse to allow our educational body to grow too big for its soul, and to remember that its soul is liberal knowledge, itself the source of higher learning.

QUESTIONS

1. What is Gilson's thesis concerning the correct relationship between education and higher learning?
2. What distinction does Gilson draw between "practical" and "useful"? How does that distinction help to advance his argument?
3. Part of Gilson's purpose is to detach the idea of liberal knowledge from certain political and social values historically associated with that idea. What are those values? Why does Gilson wish to detach the idea of liberal knowledge from them?
4. What consequences does Gilson see following from "the democratic treatment of education at the hands of the State"? Which of these consequences does he acknowledge as inevitable in a democracy? Which does he contend are unnecessary, and why?
5. What assumption about democratic equality in education, with respect to intelligence, does Gilson find fallacious? Do you agree? Does his analogy between education and athletics illuminate his argument? In what ways?
6. What point is Gilson making in footnote 8? How does this citation of impractical "practicality" help advance his thesis?
7. Gilson says that "Even their strongest supporters cannot pretend that classical humanities are practically useful in everyday life" (p. 324). Yet many would disagree. Develop the case that the classical humanities are practically useful in everyday life. Is the argument valid?
8. The analogy Gilson draws between education and athletics and his assertions in footnote 9 affirm a relation between liberal knowledge and the spirit of play. Explore this relation. Read Perry's "Examsmanship and the Liberal Arts" (pp. 328–338). Do Gilson and Perry agree?

WILLIAM G. PERRY, JR.

Examsmanship and the Liberal Arts: A Study in Educational Epistemology

"But sir, I don't think I really deserve it, it was mostly bull, really." This disclaimer from a student whose examination we have awarded a straight "A" is wondrously depressing. Alfred North Whitehead invented its only possible rejoinder: "Yes sir, what you wrote is nonsense, utter nonsense. But ah! Sir! It's the right *kind* of nonsense!"

Bull, in this university,[1] is customarily a source of laughter, or a problem in ethics. I shall step a little out of fashion to use the subject as a take-off point for a study in comparative epistemology. The phenomenon of bull, in all the honor and opprobrium with which it is regarded by students and faculty, says something, I think, about our theories of knowledge. So too, the grades which we assign on examinations communicate to students what these theories may be.

We do not have to be out-and-out logical-positivists to suppose that we have something to learn about "what we think knowledge is" by having a good look at "what we do when we go about measuring it." We know the straight "A" examination when we see it, of course, and we have reason to hope that the student will understand why his work receives our recognition. He doesn't always. And those who receive lesser honor? Perhaps an understanding of certain anomalies in our customs of grading good bull will explain the students' confusion.

I must beg patience, then, both of the reader's humor and of his morals. Not that I ask him to suspend his sense of humor but that I shall ask him to go beyond it. In a great university the picture of a bright student attempting to outwit his professor while his professor takes pride in not being outwitted is certainly ridiculous. I shall report just such a scene, for its implications bear upon my point. Its comedy need not present a serious obstacle to thought.

As for the ethics of bull, I must ask for a suspension of judgment. I wish that students could suspend theirs. Unlike humor, moral commitment is hard to think beyond. Too early a moral judgment is precisely what stands between many able students and a liberal education. The stunning realization that the Harvard Faculty will often accept, as evidence of knowledge, the cerebrations of a student who has little data at his disposal, confronts every student with an ethical dilemma. For some it forms an academic focus for what used to be thought of as "adolescent disillusion." It is irrelevant that rumor inflates the phenomenon to mythical proportions. The students know that beneath the myth there remains a solid and haunting reality. The moral "bind" consequent on this awareness appears most poignantly in serious students who are reluctant to concede the competitive advantage to the bullster and who yet feel a deep personal shame when, having succumbed to "temptation," they themselves receive a high grade for work they consider "dishonest."

I have spent many hours with students caught in this unwelcome bitterness. These hours lend an urgency to my theme. I have found that students have been able to come to terms with the ethical problem, to the extent that it is real, only after a refined study of the

1. Harvard.

true nature of bull and its relation to "knowledge." I shall submit grounds for my suspicion that we can be found guilty of sharing the students' confusion of moral and epistemological issues.

I

I present as my "premise," then, an amoral *fabliau*. Its hero-villain is the Abominable Mr. Metzger '47. Since I celebrate his virtuosity, I regret giving him a pseudonym, but the peculiar style of his bravado requires me to honor also his modesty. Bull in pure form is rare; there is usually some contamination by data. The community has reason to be grateful to Mr. Metzger for having created an instance of laboratory purity, free from any adulteration by matter. The more credit is due him, I think, because his act was free from premeditation, deliberation, or hope of personal gain.

Mr. Metzger stood one rainy November day in the lobby of Memorial Hall. A junior, concentrating in mathematics, he was fond of diverting himself by taking part in the drama, a penchant which may have had some influence on the events of the next hour. He was waiting to take part in a rehearsal in Sanders Theatre, but, as sometimes happens, no other players appeared. Perhaps the rehearsal had been canceled without his knowledge? He decided to wait another five minutes.

Students, meanwhile, were filing into the Great Hall opposite, and taking seats at the testing tables. Spying a friend crossing the lobby toward the Great Hall's door, Metzger greeted him and extended appropriate condolences. He inquired, too, what course his friend was being tested in. "Oh, Soc. Sci. something-or-other." "What's it all about?" asked Metzger, and this, as Homer remarked of Patroclus, was the beginning of evil for him.

"It's about Modern Perspectives on Man and Society and All That," said his friend. "Pretty interesting, really."

"Always wanted to take a course like that," said Metzger. "Any good reading?"

"Yeah, great. There's this book"—his friend did not have time to finish.

"Take your seats please" said a stern voice beside them. The idle conversation had somehow taken the two friends to one of the tables in the Great Hall. Both students automatically obeyed; the proctor put blue-books before them; another proctor presented them with copies of the printed hour-test.

Mr. Metzger remembered afterwards a brief misgiving that was suddenly overwhelmed by a surge of curiosity and puckish glee. He wrote "George Smith" on the blue book, opened it, and addressed the first question.

I must pause to exonerate the Management. The Faculty has a rule that no student may attend an examination in a course in which he is not enrolled. To the wisdom of this rule the outcome of this deplorable story stands witness. The Registrar, charged with the enforcement of the rule, has developed an organization with procedures which are certainly the finest to be devised. In November, however, class rosters are still shaky, and on this particular day another student, named Smith, was absent. As for the culprit, we can reduce his guilt no further than to suppose that he was ignorant of the rule, or, in the face of the momentous challenge before him, forgetful.

We need not be distracted by Metzger's performance on the "objective" or "spot" questions on the test. His D on these sections can be explained by those versed in the theory of probability. Our interest focuses on the quality of his essay. It appears that when Metzger's friend picked up his own blue book a few days later, he found himself in company with a large proportion of his section in having received on the essay a C +. When he quietly picked up "George Smith's" blue book to return it to Metzger, he observed that the grade for the essay was A−. In the margin was a note in the section man's hand. It read "Excellent work. Could you have pinned these observations down a bit more closely? Compare . . . in . . . pp. . . ."

Such news could hardly be kept quiet. There was a leak, and the whole scandal broke on the front page of Tuesday's *Crimson*. With the press Metzger was modest, as becomes a hero. He said that there had been nothing to it at all, really. The essay question had offered a choice of two books, Margaret Mead's *And Keep Your Powder Dry* or Geoffrey Gorer's *The American People*. Metzger reported that having read neither of them, he had chosen the second "because the title gave me some notion as to what the book might be about." On the test, two critical comments were offered on each book, one favorable, one unfavorable. The students were asked to "discuss." Metzger conceded that he had played safe in throwing his lot with the more laudatory of the two comments, "but I did not forget to be balanced."

I do not have Mr. Metzger's essay before me except in vivid memory. As I recall, he took his first cue from the name Geoffrey, and committed his strategy to the premise that Gorer was born into an "Anglo-Saxon" culture, probably English, but certainly "English speaking." Having heard that Margaret Mead was a social anthropologist, he inferred that Gorer was the same. He then entered upon his essay, centering his inquiry upon what he supposed might be the problems inherent in an anthropologist's observation of a culture which was his own, or nearly his own. Drawing in part from memories of table-talk on cultural relativity[2] and in part from creative logic, he rang changes on the relation of observer to observed, and

2. "An important part of Harvard's education takes place during meals in the Houses." An Official Publication [Perry's note].

assessed the kind and degree of objectivity which might accrue to an observer through training as an anthropologist. He concluded that the book in question did in fact contribute a considerable range of " 'objective', and even 'fresh'," insights into the nature of our culture. "At the same time," he warned, "these observations must be understood within the context of their generation by a person only partly freed from his embeddedness in the culture he is observing, and limited in his capacity to transcend those particular tendencies and biases which he has himself developed as a personality in his interraction with this culture since his birth. In this sense the book portrays as much the character of Geoffrey Gorer as it analyzes that of the American people." It is my regrettable duty to report that at this moment of triumph Mr. Metzger was carried away by the temptations of parody and added, "We are thus much the richer."

In any case, this was the essay for which Metzger received his honor grade and his public acclaim. He was now, of course, in serious trouble with the authorities.

I shall leave him for the moment to the mercy of the Administrative Board of Harvard College and turn the reader's attention to the section man who ascribed the grade. He was in much worse trouble. All the consternation in his immediate area of the Faculty and all the glee in other areas fell upon his unprotected head. I shall now undertake his defense.

I do so not simply because I was acquainted with him and feel a respect for his intelligence; I believe in the justice of his grade! Well, perhaps "justice" is the wrong word in a situation so manifestly absurd. This is more a case in "equity." That is, the grade is equitable if we accept other aspects of the situation which are equally absurd. My proposition is this: if we accept as valid those C grades which were accorded students who, like Metzger's friend, demonstrated a thorough familiarity with the details of the book without relating their critique to the methodological problems of social anthropology, then "George Smith" deserved not only the same, but better.

The reader may protest that the C's given to students who showed evidence only of diligence were indeed not valid and that both these students and "George Smith" should have received E's. To give the diligent E is of course not in accord with custom. I shall take up this matter later. For now, were I to allow the protest, I could only restate my thesis: that "George Smith's" E would, in a college of liberal arts, be properly a "better" E.

At this point I need a short-hand. It is a curious fact that there is no academic slang for the presentation of evidence of diligence alone. "Parroting" won't do; it is possible to "parrot" bull. I must beg the reader's pardon, and, for reasons almost too obvious to bear, suggest "cow."

Stated as nouns, the concepts look simple enough:

> cow (pure): data, however relevant, without relevancies.
> bull (pure): relevancies, however relevant, without data.

The reader can see all too clearly where this simplicity would lead. I can assure him that I would not have imposed on him this way were I aiming to say that knowledge in this university is definable as some neuter compromise between cow and bull, some infertile hermaphrodite. This is precisely what many diligent students seem to believe: that what they must learn to do is to "find the right mean" between "amounts" of detail and "amounts" of generalities. Of course this is not the point at all. The problem is not quantitative, nor does its solution lie on a continuum between the particular and the general. Cow and bull are not poles of a single dimension. A clear notion of what they really are is essential to my inquiry, and for heuristic purposes I wish to observe them further in the celibate state.

When the pure concepts are translated into verbs, their complexities become apparent in the assumptions and purposes of the students as they write:

To cow (*v. intrans.*) or the act of cowing:
To list data (or perform operations) without awareness of, or comment upon, the contexts, frames of reference, or points of observation which determine the origin, nature, and meaning of the data (or procedures). To write on the assumption that "a fact is a fact." To present evidence of hard work as a substitute for understanding, without any intent to deceive.

To bull (*v. intrans.*) or the act of bulling:
To discourse upon the contexts, frames of reference and points of observation which would determine the origin, nature, and meaning of data if one had any. To present evidence of an understanding of form in the hope that the reader may be deceived into supposing a familiarity with content.

At the level of conscious intent, it is evident that cowing is more moral, or less immoral, than bulling. To speculate about unconscious intent would be either an injustice or a needless elaboration of my theme. It is enough that the impression left by cow is one of earnestness, diligence, and painful naiveté. The grader may feel disappointment or even irritation, but these feelings are usually balanced by pity, compassion, and a reluctance to hit a man when he's both down and moral. He may feel some challenge to his teaching, but none whatever to his one-ups-manship. He writes in the margin: "See me."

We are now in a position to understand the anomaly of custom: As instructors, we always assign bull an E, *when we detect it*; whereas we usually give cow a C, *even though it is always obvious*.

After all, we did not ask to be confronted with a choice between morals and understanding (or did we?). We evince a charming humanity, I think, in our decision to grade in favor of morals and pathos. "I simply *can't* give this student an E after he has *worked* so hard." At the same time we tacitly express our respect for the bullster's strength. We recognize a colleague. If he knows so well how to dish it out, we can be sure that he can also take it.

Of course it is just possible that we carry with us, perhaps from our own school-days, an assumption that if a student is willing to work hard and collect "good hard facts" he can always be taught to understand their relevance, whereas a student who has caught onto the forms of relevance without working at all is a lost scholar.

But this is not in accord with our experience.

It is not in accord either, as far as I can see, with the stated values of a liberal education. If a liberal education should teach students "how to think," not only in their own fields but in fields outside their own—that is, to understand "how the other fellow orders knowledge," then bulling, even in its purest form, expresses an important part of what a pluralist university holds dear, surely a more important part than the collecting of "facts that are facts" which schoolboys learn to do. Here then, good bull appears not as ignorance at all but as an aspect of knowledge. It is both relevant and "true." In a university setting good bull is therefore of more value than "facts," which, without a frame of reference, are not even "true" at all.

Perhaps this value accounts for the final anomaly: as instructors, we are inclined to reward bull highly, *where we do not detect its intent*, to the consternation of the bullster's acquaintances. And often we do not examine the matter too closely. After a long evening of reading blue books full of cow, the sudden meeting with a student who at least understands the problems of one's field provides a lift like a draught of refreshing wine, and a strong disposition toward trust.

This was, then, the sense of confidence that came to our unfortunate section man as he read "George Smith's" sympathetic considerations.

II

In my own years of watching over students' shoulders as they work, I have come to believe that this feeling of trust has a firmer basis than the confidence generated by evidence of diligence alone. I believe that the theory of a liberal education holds. Students who have dared to understand man's real relation to his knowledge have shown themselves to be in a strong position to learn content rapidly and meaningfully, and to retain it. I have learned to be less concerned about the education of a student who has come to understand the nature of man's knowledge, even though he has not yet committed himself to hard work, than I am about the education of the student who, after one or two terms at Harvard is working desperately hard and still believes that collected "facts" constitute knowledge. The latter, when I try to explain to him, too often understands me to be saying that he "doesn't *put in enough generalities.*" Surely he has "put in *enough* facts."

I have come to see such quantitative statements as expressions of an entire, coherent epistemology. In grammar school the student is taught that Columbus discovered America in 1492. The *more* such items he gets "right" on a given test the more he is credited with "knowing." From years of this sort of thing it is not unnatural to develop the conviction that knowledge consists of the accretion of hard facts by hard work.

The student learns that the more facts and procedures he can get "right" in a given course, the better will be his grade. The more courses he takes, the more subjects he has "had," the more credits he accumulates, the more diplomas he will get, until, after graduate school, he will emerge with his doctorate, a member of the community of scholars.

The foundation of this entire life is the proposition that a fact is a fact. The necessary correlate of this proposition is that a fact is either right or wrong. This implies that the standard against which the rightness or wrongness of a fact may be judged exists *someplace* —perhaps graven upon a tablet in a Platonic world outside and above *this* cave of tears. In grammar school it is evident that the tablets which enshrine the spelling of a word or the answer to an arithmetic problem are visible to my teacher who need only compare my offerings to it. In high school I observe that my English teachers disagree. This can only mean that the tablets in such matters as the goodness of a poem are distant and obscured by clouds. They surely exist. The pleasing of befuddled English teachers degenerates into assessing their prejudices, a game in which I have no protection against my competitors more glib of tongue. I respect only my science teachers, authorities who *really know.* Later I learn from them that "this is only what we think *now.*" But eventually, surely. . . . Into this epistemology of education, apparently shared by teachers in such terms as "credits," "semester hours" and "years of French" the student may invest his ideals, his drive, his competitiveness, his safety, his self-esteem, and even his love.

College raises other questions: by whose calendar is it proper to say that Columbus discovered America in 1492? How, when and by whom was the year 1 established in this calendar? What of other calendars? In view of the evidence for Leif Ericson's previous visit (and the American Indians), what historical ethnocentrism is suggested by the use of the word "discover" in this sentence? As for

Leif Ericson, in accord with what assumptions do you order the evidence?

These questions and their answers are not "more" knowledge. They are devastation. I do not need to elaborate upon the epistemology, or rather epistemologies, they imply. A fact has become at last "an observation or an operation performed in a frame of reference." A liberal education is founded in an awareness of frame of reference even in the most immediate and empirical examination of data. Its acquirement involves relinquishing hope of absolutes and of the protection they afford against doubt and the glib-tongued competitor. It demands an ever widening sophistication about systems of thought and observation. It leads, not away from, but *through* the arts of gamesmanship to a new trust.

This trust is in the value and integrity of systems, their varied character, and the way their apparently incompatible metaphors enlighten, from complementary facets, the particulars of human experience. As one student said to me: "I used to be cynical about intellectual games. Now I want to know them thoroughly. You see I came to realize that it was only when I knew the rules of the game cold that I could tell whether what I was saying was tripe."

We too often think of the bullster as cynical. He can be, and not always in a light-hearted way. We have failed to observe that there can lie behind cow the potential of a deeper and more dangerous despair. The moralism of sheer work and obedience can be an ethic that, unwilling to face a despair of its ends, glorifies its means. The implicit refusal to consider the relativity of both ends and means leaves the operator in an unconsidered proprietary absolutism. History bears witness that in the pinches this moral superiority has no recourse to negotiation, only to force.

A liberal education proposes that man's hope lies elsewhere: in the negotiability that can arise from an understanding of the integrity of systems and of their origins in man's address to his universe. The prerequisite is the courage to accept such a definition of knowledge. From then on, of course, there is nothing incompatible between such an epistemology and hard work. Rather the contrary.

I can now at last let bull and cow get together. The reader knows best how a productive wedding is arranged in his own field. This is the nuptial he celebrates with a straight A on examinations. The masculine context must embrace the feminine particular, though itself "born of woman." Such a union is knowledge itself, and it alone can generate new contexts and new data which can unite in their turn to form new knowledge.

In this happy setting we can congratulate in particular the Natural Sciences, long thought to be barren ground to the bullster. I have indeed drawn my examples of bull from the Social Sciences, and by analogy from the Humanities. Essay-writing in these fields has long been thought to nurture the art of bull to its prime. I feel, however, that the Natural Sciences have no reason to feel slighted. It is perhaps no accident that Metzger was a mathematician. As part of my researches for this paper, furthermore, a student of considerable talent has recently honored me with an impressive analysis of the art of amassing "partial credits" on examinations in advanced physics. Though beyond me in some respects, his presentation confirmed my impression that instructors of Physics frequently honor on examinations operations structurally similar to those requisite in a good essay.

The very qualities that make the Natural Sciences fields of delight for the eager gamesman have been essential to their marvelous fertility.

III

As priests of these mysteries, how can we make our rites more precisely expressive? The student who merely cows robs himself, without knowing it, of his education and his soul. The student who only bulls robs himself, as he knows full well, of the joys of inductive discovery—that is, of engagement. The introduction of frames of reference in the new curricula of Mathematics and Physics in the schools is a hopeful experiment. We do not know yet how much of these potent revelations the very young can stand, but I suspect they may rejoice in them more than we have supposed. I can't believe they have never wondered about Leif Ericson and that word "discovered," or even about 1492. They have simply been too wise to inquire.

Increasingly in recent years better students in the better high schools and preparatory schools are being allowed to inquire. In fact they appear to be receiving both encouragement and training in their inquiry. I have the evidence before me.

Each year for the past five years all freshmen entering Harvard and Radcliffe have been asked in freshman week to "grade" two essays answering an examination question in History. They are then asked to give their reasons for their grades. One essay, filled with dates, is 99% cow. The other, with hardly a date in it, is a good essay, easily mistaken for bull. The "official" grades of these essays are, for the first (alas!) C+ "because he has worked so hard," and for the second (soundly, I think) B+. Each year a larger majority of freshmen evaluate these essays as would the majority of the faculty, and for the faculty's reasons, and each year a smaller minority give the higher honor to the essay offering data alone. Most interesting, a larger number of students each year, while not overrating the second essay, award the first the straight E appropriate to it in a college of liberal arts.

For us who must grade such students in a university, these developments imply a new urgency, did we not feel it already. Through our grades we describe for the students, in the showdown, what we believe about the nature of knowledge. The subtleties of bull are not peripheral to our academic concerns. That they penetrate to the center of our care is evident in our feelings when a student whose good work we have awarded a high grade reveals to us that he does not feel he deserves it. Whether he disqualifies himself because "there's too much bull in it," or worse because "I really don't think I've worked that hard," he presents a serious educational problem. Many students feel this sleaziness; only a few reveal it to us.

We can hardly allow a mistaken sense of fraudulence to undermine our students' achievements. We must lead students beyond their concept of bull so that they may honor relevancies that are really relevant. We can willingly acknowledge that, in lieu of the date 1492, a consideration of calendars and of the word "discovered," may well be offered with intent to deceive. We must insist that this does not make such considerations intrinsically immoral, and that, contrariwise, the date 1492 may be no substitute for them. Most of all, we must convey the impression that we grade understanding qua understanding. To be convincing, I suppose we must concede to ourselves in advance that a bright student's understanding is understanding even if he achieved it by osmosis rather than by hard work in our course.

These are delicate matters. As for cow, its complexities are not what need concern us. Unlike good bull, it does not represent partial knowledge at all. It belongs to a different theory of knowledge entirely. In our theories of knowledge it represents total ignorance, or worse yet, a knowledge downright inimical to understanding. I even go so far as to propose that we award no more C's for cow. To do so is rarely, I feel, the act of mercy it seems. Mercy lies in clarity.

The reader may be afflicted by a lingering curiosity about the fate of Mr. Metzger. I hasten to reassure him. The Administrative Board of Harvard College, whatever its satanic reputations, is a benign body. Its members, to be sure, were on the spot. They delighted in Metzger's exploit, but they were responsible to the Faculty's rule. The hero stood in danger of probation. The debate was painful. Suddenly one member, of a refined legalistic sensibility, observed that the rule applied specifically to "examinations" and that the occasion had been simply an hour-test. Mr. Metzger was merely "admonished."

JOHN HOLT
How Teachers Make Children Hate Reading

When I was teaching English at the Colorado Rocky Mountain School, I used to ask my students the kinds of questions that English teachers usually ask about reading assignments—questions designed to bring out the points that *I* had decided *they* should know. They, on their part, would try to get me to give them hints and clues as to what I wanted. It was a game of wits. I never gave my students an opportunity to say what they really thought about a book.

I gave vocabulary drills and quizzes too. I told my students that every time they came upon a word in their book they did not understand, they were to look it up in the dictionary. I even devised special kinds of vocabulary tests, allowing them to use their books to see how the words were used. But looking back, I realize that these tests, along with many of my methods, were foolish.

My sister was the first person who made me question my conventional ideas about teaching English. She had a son in the seventh grade in a fairly good public school. His teacher had asked the class to read Cooper's *The Deerslayer*. The choice was bad enough in itself; whether looking at man or nature, Cooper was superficial, inaccurate and sentimental, and his writing is ponderous and ornate. But to make matters worse, this teacher had decided to give the book the microscope and x-ray treatment. He made the students look up and memorize not only the definitions but the derivations of every big word that came along—and there were plenty. Every chapter was followed by close questioning and testing to make sure the students "understood" everything.

Being then, as I said, conventional, I began to defend the teacher, who was a good friend of mine, against my sister's criticisms. The argument soon grew hot. What was wrong with making sure that children understood everything they read? My sister answered that until this class her boy had always loved reading, and had read a lot on his own; now he had stopped. (He was not really to start again for many years.)

Still I persisted. If children didn't look up the words they didn't know, how would they ever learn them? My sister said, "Don't be silly! When you were little you had a huge vocabulary, and were always reading very grown-up books. When did you ever look up a word in a dictionary?"

She had me. I don't know that we had a dictionary at home; if we did, I didn't use it. I don't use one today. In my life I doubt that I have looked up as many as fifty words, perhaps not even half that.

Since then I have talked about this with a number of teachers. More than once I have said, "according to tests, educated and literate people like you have a vocabulary of about twenty-five thousand words. How many of these did you learn by looking them up in a dictionary?" They usually are startled. Few claim to have looked up even as many as a thousand. How did they learn the rest?

They learned them just as they learned to talk—by meeting words over and over again, in different contexts, until they saw how they fitted.

Unfortunately, we English teachers are easily hung up on this matter of understanding. Why should children understand everything they read? Why should anyone? Does anyone? I don't, and I never did. I was always reading books that teachers would have said were "too hard" for me, books full of words I didn't know. That's how I got to be a good reader. When about ten, I read all the D'Artagnan stories and loved them. It didn't trouble me in the least that I didn't know why France was at war with England or who was quarreling with whom in the French court or why the Musketeers should always be at odds with Cardinal Richelieu's men. I didn't even know who the Cardinal was, except that he was a dangerous and powerful man that my friends had to watch out for. This was all I needed to know.

Having said this, I will now say that I think a big, unabridged dictionary is a fine thing to have in any home or classroom. No book is more fun to browse around in—*if* you're not made to. Children, depending on their age, will find many pleasant and interesting things to do with a big dictionary. They can look up funny-sounding words, which they like, or words that nobody else in the class has ever heard of, which they like, or long words, which they like, or forbidden words, which they like best of all. At a certain age, and particularly with a little encouragement from parents or teachers, they may become very interested in where words came from and when they came into the language and how their meanings have changed over the years. But exploring for the fun of it is very different from looking up words out of your reading because you're going to get into trouble with your teacher if you don't.

While teaching fifth grade two years or so after the argument with my sister, I began to think again about reading. The children in my class were supposed to fill out a card—just the title and author and a one-sentence summary—for every book they read. I was not running a competition to see which child could read the most books, a competition that almost always leads to cheating. I just wanted to know what the children were reading. After a while it became clear that many of these very bright kids, from highly literate and even literary backgrounds, read very few books and deeply disliked reading. Why should this be?

At this time I was coming to realize, as I described in my book *How Children Fail*, that for most children school was a place of danger, and their main business in school was staying out of danger as much as possible. I now began to see also that books were among the most dangerous things in school.

From the very beginning of school we make books and reading a constant source of possible failure and public humiliation. When children are little we make them read aloud, before the teacher and other children, so that we can be sure they "know" all the words they are reading. This means that when they don't know a word, they are going to make a mistake, right in front of everyone. Instantly they are made to realize that they have done something wrong. Perhaps some of the other children will begin to wave their hands and say, "Ooooh! O-o-o-oh!" Perhaps they will just giggle, or nudge each other, or make a face. Perhaps the teacher will say, "Are you sure?" or ask someone else what he thinks. Or perhaps, if the teacher is kindly, she will just smile a sweet, sad smile—often one of the most painful punishments a child can suffer in school. In any case, the child who has made the mistake knows he has made it, and feels foolish, stupid, and ashamed, just as any of us would in his shoes.

Before long many children associate books and reading with mistakes, real or feared, and penalties and humiliation. This may not seem sensible, but it is natural. Mark Twain once said that a cat that sat on a hot stove lid would never sit on one again—but it would never sit on a cold one either. As true of children as of cats. If they, so to speak, sit on a hot book a few times, if books cause them humiliation and pain, they are likely to decide that the safest thing to do is to leave all books alone.

After having taught fifth-grade classes for four years I felt quite sure of this theory. In my next class were many children who had had great trouble with schoolwork, particularly reading. I decided to try at all costs to rid them of their fear and dislike of books, and to get them to read oftener and more adventurously.

One day soon after school had started, I said to them, "Now I'm going to say something about reading that you have probably never heard a teacher say before. I would like you to read a lot of books this year, but I want you to read them only for pleasure. I am not going to ask you questions to find out whether you understand the books or not. If you understand enough of a book to enjoy it and want to go on reading it, that's enough for me. Also I'm not going to ask you what words mean.

"Finally," I said, "I don't want you to feel that just because you start a book, you have to finish it. Give an author thirty or forty pages or so to get his story going. Then if you don't like the char-acters and don't care what happens to them, close the book, put it away, and get another. I don't care whether the books are easy or hard, short or long, as long as you enjoy them. Furthermore I'm put-ting all this in a letter to your parents, so they won't feel they have to quiz and heckle you about books at home."

The children sat stunned and silent. Was this a teacher talking? One girl, who had just come to us from a school where she had had a very hard time, and who proved to be one of the most interest-ing, lively, and intelligent children I have ever known, looked at me steadily for a long time after I had finished. Then, still looking at me, she said slowly and solemnly, "Mr. Holt, do you really mean that?" I said just as solemnly, "I mean every word of it."

Apparently she decided to believe me. The first book she read was Dr. Seuss's *How the Grinch Stole Christmas*, not a hard book even for most third graders. For a while she read a number of books on this level. Perhaps she was clearing up some confusion about reading that her teachers, in their hurry to get her up to "grade level," had never given her enough time to clear up. After she had been in the class six weeks or so and we had become good friends, I very tentatively suggested that, since she was a skillful rider and loved horses, she might like to read *National Velvet*. I made my sell as soft as possible, saying only that it was about a girl who loved and rode horses, and that if she didn't like it, she could put it back. She tried it, and though she must have found it quite a bit harder than what she had been reading, finished it and liked it very much.

During the spring she really astonished me, however. One day, in one of our many free periods, she was reading at her desk. From a glimpse of the illustrations I thought I knew what the book was. I said to myself, "It can't be," and went to take a closer look. Sure enough, she was reading *Moby Dick*, in the edition with woodcuts by Rockwell Kent. When I came close to her desk she looked up. I said, "Are you really reading that?" She said she was. I said, "Do you like it?" She said, "Oh, yes, it's neat!" I said, "Don't you find parts of it rather heavy going?" She answered "Oh, sure, but I just skip over those parts and go on to the next good part."

This is exactly what reading should be and in school so seldom is—an exciting, joyous adventure. Find something, dive into it, take the good parts, skip the bad parts, get what you can out of it, go on to something else. How different is our mean-spirited, picky insistence that every child get every last little scrap of "under-standing" that can be dug out of a book.

For teachers who really enjoy doing it, and will do it with gusto, reading aloud is a very good idea. I have found that not just fifth graders but even ninth and eleventh graders enjoy it. Jack London's

"To Build a Fire" is a good read-aloud story. So are ghost stories, and "August Heat," by W. F. Harvey, and "The Monkey's Paw," by Saki (H. H. Munro), are among the best. Shirley Jackson's "The Lottery" is sure-fire, and will raise all kinds of questions for discussion and argument. Because of a TV program they had seen and that excited them, I once started reading my fifth graders William Golding's *Lord of the Flies*, thinking to read only a few chapters, but they made me read it to the end.

In my early fifth-grade classes the children usually were of high IQ, came from literate backgrounds and were generally felt to be succeeding in school. Yet it was astonishingly hard for most of those children to express themselves in speech or in writing. I have known a number of five-year-olds who were considerably more articulate than most of the fifth graders I have known in school. Asked to speak, my fifth graders were covered with embarrassment; many refused altogether. Asked to write, they would sit for minutes on end, staring at the paper. It was hard for most of them to get down a half page of writing, even on what seemed to be interesting topics or topics they chose themselves.

In desperation I hit on a device that I named the Composition Derby. I divided the class into teams, and told them that when I said, "Go," they were to start writing something. It could be about anything they wanted, but it had to be about something—they couldn't just write "dog dog dog dog" on the paper. It could be true stories, descriptions of people or places or events, wishes, made-up stories, dreams—anything they liked. Spelling didn't count, so they didn't have to worry about it. When I said, "Stop," they were to stop and count up the words they had written. The team that wrote the most words would win the derby.

It was a success in many ways and for many reasons. The first surprise was that the two children who consistently wrote the most words were two of the least successful students in the class. They were bright, but they had always had a very hard time in school. Both were very bad spellers, and worrying about this had slowed down their writing without improving their spelling. When they were free of this worry and could let themselves go, they found hidden and unsuspected talents.

One of the two, a very driven and anxious little boy, used to write long adventures, or misadventures, in which I was the central character—"The Day Mr. Holt Went to Jail," "The Day Mr. Holt Fell Into the Hole," "The Day Mr. Holt Got Run Over," and so on. These were very funny, and the class enjoyed hearing me read them aloud. One day I asked the class to write a derby on a topic I would give them. They groaned; they liked picking their own. "Wait till you hear it," I said. "It's 'The Day the School Burned Down.' "

With a shout of approval and joy they went to work, and wrote furiously for 20 minutes or more, laughing and chuckling as they wrote. The papers were all much alike; in them the children danced around the burning building, throwing in books and driving me and the other teachers back in when we tried to escape.

In our first derby the class wrote an average of about ten words a minute; after a few months their average was over 20. Some of the slower writers tripled their output. Even the slowest, one of whom was the best student in the class, were writing 15 words a minute. More important, almost all the children enjoyed the derbies and wrote interesting things.

Some time later I learned that Professor I. S. Hayakawa, teaching freshman English, had invented a better technique. Every day in class he asked his students to write without stopping for about half an hour. They could write on whatever topic or topics they chose, but the important thing was not to stop. If they ran dry, they were to copy their last sentence over and over again until new ideas came. Usually they came before the sentence had been copied once. I use this idea in my own classes, and call this kind of paper a Non-Stop. Sometimes I ask students to write a Non-Stop on an assigned topic, more often on anything they choose. Once in a while I ask them to count up how many words they have written, though I rarely ask them to tell me; it is for their own information. Sometimes these papers are to be handed in; often they are what I call private papers, for the students' eyes alone.

The private paper has proved very useful. In the first place, in any English class—certainly any large English class—if the amount the students write is limited by what the teacher can find time to correct, or even to read, the students will not write nearly enough. The only remedy is to have them write a great deal that the teacher does not read. In the second place, students writing for themselves will write about many things that they would never write on a paper to be handed in, once they have learned (sometimes it takes a while) that the teacher means what he says about the papers' being private. This is important, not just because it enables them to get things off their chest, but also because they are most likely to write well, and to pay attention to how they write, when they are writing about something important to them.

Some English teachers, when they first hear about private papers, object that students do not benefit from writing papers unless the papers are corrected. I disagree for several reasons. First, most students, particularly poor students, do not read the corrections on their papers; it is boring, even painful. Second, even when they do read these corrections, they do not get much help from them, do not build the teacher's suggestions into their writing. This is true even when they really believe the teacher knows what he is talking about.

Third, and most important, we learn to write by writing, not by reading other people's ideas about writing. What most students need above all else is practice in writing, and particularly in writing about things that matter to them, so that they will begin to feel the satisfaction that comes from getting important thoughts down in words and will care about stating these thoughts forcefully and clearly.

Teachers of English—or, as some schools say (ugh!), Language Arts—spend a lot of time and effort on spelling. Most of it is wasted; it does little good, and often more harm than good. We should ask ourselves, "How do good spellers spell? What do they do when they are not sure which spelling of a word is right?" I have asked this of a number of good spellers. Their answer never varies. They do not rush for a dictionary or rack their brains trying to remember some rules. They write down the word both ways, or several ways, look at them and pick the one that looks best. Usually they are right.

Good spellers know what words look like and even, in their writing muscles, feel like. They have a good set of word images in their minds, and are willing to trust these images. The things we do to "teach" spelling to children do little to develop these skills or talents, and much to destroy them or prevent them from developing.

The first and worst thing we do is to make children anxious about spelling. We treat a misspelled word like a crime and penalize the misspeller severely; many teachers talk of making children develop a "spelling conscience," and fail otherwise excellent papers because of a few spelling mistakes. This is self-defeating. When we are anxious, we don't perceive clearly or remember what we once perceived. Everyone knows how hard it is to recall even simple things when under emotional pressure; the harder we rack our brains, the less easy it is to find what we are looking for. If we are anxious enough, we will not trust the messages that memory sends us. Many children spell badly because although their first hunches about how to spell a word may be correct, they are afraid to trust them. I have often seen on children's papers a word correctly spelled, then crossed out and misspelled.

There are some tricks that might help children get sharper word images. Some teachers may be using them. One is the trick of air writing; that is, of "writing" a word in the air with a finger and "seeing" the image so formed. I did this quite a bit with fifth graders, using either the air or the top of a desk, on which their fingers left no mark. Many of them were tremendously excited by this. I can still hear them saying, "There's nothing there, but I can see it!" It seemed like black magic. I remember that when I was little I loved to write in the air. It was effortless, voluptuous, satisfying, and it was fun to see the word appear in the air. I used to write "Money Money Money," not so much because I didn't have any as because I liked the way it felt, particularly that *y* at the end, with its swooping tail.

Another thing to help sharpen children's image-making machinery is taking very quick looks at words—or other things. The conventional machine for doing this is the tachistoscope. But these are expensive, so expensive that most children can have few chances to use them, if any at all. With some three-by-five and four-by-eight file cards you can get the same effect. On the little cards you put the words or the pictures that the child is going to look at. You hold the larger card over the card to be read, uncover it for a split second with a quick wrist motion, then cover it up again. Thus you have a tachistoscope that costs one cent and that any child can work by himself.

Once when substituting in a first-grade class, I thought that the children, who were just beginning to read and write, might enjoy some of the kind of free, nonstop writing that my fifth graders had. One day about 40 minutes before lunch, I asked them all to take pencil and paper and start writing about anything they wanted to. They seemed to like the idea, but right away one child said anxiously, "Suppose we can't spell a word."

"Don't worry about it," I said. "Just spell it the best way you can."

A heavy silence settled on the room. All I could see were still pencils and anxious faces. This was clearly not the right approach. So I said, "All right, I'll tell you what we'll do. Any time you want to know how to spell a word, tell me and I'll write it on the board."

They breathed a sigh of relief and went to work. Soon requests for words were coming fast; as soon as I wrote one, someone asked me another. By lunchtime, when most of the children were still busily writing, the board was full. What was interesting was that most of the words they had asked for were much longer and more complicated than anything in their reading books or workbooks. Freed from worry about spelling, they were willing to use the most difficult and interesting words that they knew.

The words were still on the board when we began school next day. Before I began to erase them, I said to the children, "Listen, everyone. I have to erase these words, but before I do, just out of curiosity, I'd like to see if you remember some of them."

The result was surprising. I had expected that the child who had asked for and used a word might remember it, but I did not think many others would. But many of the children still knew many of the words. How had they learned them? I suppose each time I wrote a word on the board a number of children had looked up, relaxed yet curious, just to see what the word looked like, and these images and the sound of my voice saying the word had stuck in their minds until the next day. This, it seems to me, is how children may best learn to write and spell.

What can a parent do if a school, or a teacher, is spoiling the language for a child by teaching it in some tired way? First, try to get them to change, or at least let them know that you are eager for change. Talk to other parents; push some of these ideas in the PTA; talk to the English department at the school; talk to the child's own teacher. Many teachers and schools want to know what the parents want.

If the school or teacher cannot be persuaded, then what? Perhaps all you can do is try not to let your child become too bored or discouraged or worried by what is happening in school. Help him meet the school's demands, foolish though they may seem, and try to provide more interesting alternatives at home—plenty of books and conversation, and a serious and respectful audience when a child wants to talk. Nothing that ever happened to me in English classes at school was as helpful to me as the long conversations I used to have every summer with my uncle, who made me feel that the difference in our ages was not important and that he was really interested in what I had to say.

At the end of her freshman year in college a girl I know wrote home to her mother, "Hooray! Hooray! Just think—I never have to take English any more!" But this girl had always been an excellent English student, had always loved books, writing, ideas. It seems unnecessary and foolish and wrong that English teachers should so often take what should be the most flexible, exciting, and creative of all school courses and make it into something that most children can hardly wait to see the last of. Let's hope that we can and soon will begin to do much better.

QUESTIONS

1. What are the major indictments Holt makes and what alternatives does he propose?
2. Booth discusses various metaphors (including man as machine and man as animal) that underline different theories of education ("Is There Any Knowledge That a Man Must Have?," pp. 265–280). Might Holt accept any of these metaphors? If Holt constructed a different metaphor of his own, what might it be?
3. Is the kind of teaching that Holt describes likely to lead to students' having the knowledge that Booth believes essential? Explain. How far would it go toward producing Emerson's ideal of "man thinking" ("The American Scholar," pp. 281–295)?

4. McLuhan says that we "are entering the new age of education that is programmed for discovery rather than instruction ("Preface to the Third Printing of Understanding Media," pp. 580–584). Holt says reading should be "an exciting, joyous adventure," rather than being associated with "mistakes, real or feared, and penalties and humiliation." How are the two writers' attitudes similar, how different? Would Holt approve of the metaphor implied in "programmed"? Explain.
5. Here are two accounts of a young boy's going to school, the second a summary or précis of the first. Determine what has been removed from the original in the summary. Then write a short comparison of original and summary from Holt's educational point of view, as it can be inferred from his essay.

His days were rich in formal experience. Wearing overalls and an old sweater (the accepted uniform of the private seminary), he sallied forth at morn accompanied by a nurse or a parent and walked (or was pulled) two blocks to a corner where the school bus made a flag stop. This flashy vehicle was as punctual as death: seeing us waiting at the cold curb, it would sweep to a halt, open its mouth, suck the boy in, and spring away with an angry growl. It was a good deal like a train picking up a bag of mail. At school the scholar was worked on for six or seven hours by half a dozen teachers and a nurse, and was revived on orange juice in midmorning. In a cinder court he played games supervised by an athletic instructor, and in a cafeteria he ate lunch worked out by a dietitian.

—E. B. White, "Education"

His days followed a set routine. He wore overalls and an old sweater, as everyone else did in his school. In the morning, a parent or nurse walked the two blocks with him to the corner where he met the school bus. The bus was always on time. During the six or seven hours of the school day, he had six teachers. The school also employed a nurse and a dietitian. Games were supervised. The children ate in the cafeteria. Orange juice was served during the morning session.

—End-of-Year Examinations in English for college bound students grades 9-12, Commission on English.

JEROME S. BRUNER
The Will to Learn[1]

The single most characteristic thing about human beings is that they learn. Learning is so deeply ingrained in man that it is almost involuntary, and thoughtful students of human behavior have even

1. Chapter 6 of *Toward a Theory of Instruction*, 1966.

speculated that our specialization as a species is a specialization for learning. For, by comparison with organisms lower in the animal kingdom, we are ill equipped with prepared reflex mechanisms. As William James put it decades ago, even our instinctive behavior occurs only once, thereafter being modified by experience. With a half century's perspective on the discoveries of Pavlov, we know that man not only is conditioned by his environment, but may be so conditioned even against his will.

Why then invoke the idea of a "will to learn"? The answer derives from the idea of education, a human invention that takes a learner beyond "mere" learning. Other species begin their learning afresh each generation, but man is born into a culture that has as one of its principal functions the conservation and transmission of past learning. Given man's physical characteristics, indeed, it would be not only wasteful but probably fatal for him to reinvent even the limited range of technique and knowledge required for such a species to survive in the temperate zone. This means that man cannot depend upon a casual process of learning; he must be "educated." The young human must regulate his learning and his attention by reference to external requirements. He must eschew what is vividly right under his nose for what is dimly in a future that is often incomprehensible to him. And he must do so in a strange setting where words and diagrams and other abstractions suddenly become very important. School demands an orderliness and neatness beyond what the child has known before; it requires restraint and immobility never asked of him before; and often it puts him in a spot where he does not *know* whether he knows and can get no indication from anybody for minutes at a time as to whether he is on the right track. Perhaps most important of all, school is away from home with all that fact implies in anxiety, or challenge, or relief.

In consequence of all this the problem of "the will to learn" becomes important, indeed exaggerated. Let us not delude ourselves: it is a problem that cannot be avoided, though it can be made manageable, I think. We shall explore what kinds of factors lead to satisfaction in "educated" learning, to pleasure in the practice of learning as it exists in the necessarily artificial atmosphere of the school. Almost all children possess what have come to be called "intrinsic" motives for learning. An intrinsic motive is one that does not depend upon reward that lies outside the activity it impels. Reward inheres in the successful termination of that activity or even in the activity itself.

Curiosity is almost a prototype of the intrinsic motive. Our attention is attracted to something that is unclear, unfinished, or uncertain. We sustain our attention until the matter in hand becomes clear, finished, or certain. The achievement of clarity or merely the search for it is what satisfies. We would think it preposterous if somebody thought to reward us with praise or profit for having satisfied our curiosity. However pleasant such external reward might be, and however much we might come to depend upon it, the external reward is something added. What activates and satisfies curiosity is something inherent in the cycle of activity by which we express curiosity. Surely such activity is biologically relevant, for curiosity is essential to the survival not only of the individual but of the species. There is considerable research that indicates the extent to which even nonhuman primates will put forth effort for a chance to encounter something novel on which to exercise curiosity. But it is clear that unbridled curiosity is little more than unlimited distractibility. To be interested in everything that comes along is to be interested in nothing for long. Studies of the behavior of three-year-olds, for example, indicate the degree to which they are dominated from the outside by the parade of vivid impressions that pass their way. They turn to this bright color, that sharp sound, that new shiny surface. Many ends are beyond their reach, for they cannot sustain a steady course when the winds shift. If anything, they are "too curious." They live by what psychologists have long called the laws of primary attention: attention dominated by vividness and change in the environment. There has been much speculation about the function of this early and exhausting tempo of curiosity. One neuropsychologist, Donald Hebb, has suggested that the child is drinking in the world, better to construct his neural "models" of the environment. And it is plain that a stunted organism is produced by depriving an infant of the rich diet of impressions on which his curiosity normally feeds with such extravagance. Animals raised in homogenized environments show crippling deficits in their later ability to learn and to transfer what they have learned. Children "kept in the attic" by misguided or psychotic parents show the same striking backwardness. Indeed, even the children who have suffered the dull, aseptic environment of backward foundling homes often show a decline in intelligence that can be compensated only by vigorous measures of enrichment. So surely, then, an important early function is served by the child's omnivorous capacity for new impressions. He is sorting the world, storing those things that have some recurrent regularity and require "knowing," discriminating them from the parade of random impressions.[2]

But if attention is to be sustained, directed to some task and held there in spite of temptations that come along, then obviously constraints must be established. The voluntary deployment of curiosity, so slowly and painfully mastered, seems to be supported

2. For a further account of the functions of early curiosity, see J. S. Bruner, "The Cognitive Consequences of Early Sensory Deprivation," *Psychosomatic Medicine*, 21.2:89–95 (1959) [Bruner's note].

in part by the young child's new-found capacity to "instruct himself," literally to talk to himself through a sustained sequence. And in part the steadying force seems to be the momentum of concrete overt acts that have a way of sustaining the attention required for their completion by shutting off irrelevant impressions. In time, and with the development of habitual activities, and of language, there emerges more self-directed attention, sometimes called derived primary attention. The child is held steady not so much by vividness as by the habitual round of activity that now demands his attention. Little enough is known about how to help a child become master of his own attention, to sustain it over a long, connected sequence. But while young children are notoriously wandering in their attention, they can be kept in a state of rapt and prolonged attentiveness by being told compelling stories. There may be something to be learned from this observation. What makes the internal sequence of a story even more compelling than the distractions that lie outside it? Are there comparable properties inherent in other activities? Can these be used to train a child to sustain his curiosity beyond the moment's vividness?

Observe a child or group of children building a pile of blocks as high as they can get them. Their attention will be sustained to the flashing point until they reach the climax when the pile comes crashing down. They will return to build still higher. The drama of the task is only its minor virtue. More important is the energizing lure of uncertainty made personal by one's own effort to control it. It is almost the antithesis of the passive attraction of shininess and the vivid. To channel curiosity into more powerful intellectual pursuits requires precisely that there be this transition from the passive, receptive, episodic form of curiosity to the sustained and active form. There are games not only with objects, but with ideas and questions—like Twenty Questions—that provide such a disciplining of the channeling of curiosity. Insofar as one may count on this important human motive—and it seems among the most reliable of the motives—then it seems obvious that our artificial education can in fact be made less artificial from a motivational standpoint by relating it initially to the more surfacy forms of curiosity and attention, and then cultivating curiosity to more subtle and active expression. I think it is fair to say that most of the success in contemporary curriculum building has been achieved by this route. When success comes, it takes the form of recognition that beyond the few things we know there lies a domain of inference: that putting together the two and two that we have yields astonishing results. But this raises the issue of competence, to which we must turn next.

For curiosity is only one of the intrinsic motives for learning.

The drive to achieve competence is another. Professor Robert White puts the issue well:

> According to Webster, competence means fitness or ability, and the suggested synonyms include capability, capacity, efficiency, proficiency, and skill. It is therefore a suitable word to describe such things as grasping and exploring, crawling and walking, attention and perception, all of which promote an effective—a competent—interaction with the environment. It is true, of course, that maturation plays a part in all these developments, but this part is heavily overshadowed by learning in all the more complex accomplishments like speech or skilled manipulation. I shall argue that it is necessary to make competence a motivational concept; there is *competence motivation* as well as competence in its more familiar sense of achieved capacity. The behavior that leads to the building up of effective grasping, handling, and letting go of objects, to take one example, is not random behavior that is produced by an overflow of energy. It is directed, selective, and persistent, and it continues not because it serves primary drives, which indeed it cannot serve until it is almost perfect, but because it satisfies an intrinsic need to deal with the environment.[3]

Observations of young children and of the young of other species suggest that a good deal of their play must be understood as practice in coping with the environment. Primatologists describe, for example, how young female baboons cradle infant baboons in their arms long before they produce their own offspring. In fact, baboon play can be seen almost entirely as the practice of interpersonal skills. Unlike human children, baboons never play with objects, and this, the anthropologists believe, is connected with their inability to use tools when they grow up. And there is evidence that early language mastery, too, depends on such early preparation. One linguist recently has shown how a two-year-old goes on exploring the limits of language use even after the lights are out, parents removed, communication stopped, and sleep imminent.[4]

The child's metalinguistic play is hard to interpret as anything other than pleasure in practicing and developing a new skill. Although competence may not "naturally" be directed toward school learning, it is certainly possible that the great access of energy that children experience when they "get into a subject they like" is made of the same stuff.

We get interested in what we get good at. In general, it is difficult to sustain interest in an activity unless one achieves some degree of competence. Athletics is the activity par excellence where the young need no prodding to gain pleasure from an increase in skill, save where prematurely adult standards are imposed on little leagues formed too soon to ape the big ones. A custom introduced some years ago at the Gordonstoun School in Scotland has become legendary. In addition to conventionally competitive track and field

3. R. W. White, "Motivation Reconsidered: The Concept of Competence," *Psychological Review*, 66:297–333 (1959) [Bruner's note].

4. Ruth H. Weir, *Language in the Crib* (The Hague: Mouton, 1962) [Bruner's note].

events within the school, there was established a novel competition in which boys pitted themselves against their own best prior record in the events. Several American schools have picked up the idea and, while there has been no "proper evaluation," it is said that the system creates great excitement and enormous effort on the part of the boys.

To achieve the sense of accomplishment requires a task that has some beginning and some terminus. Perhaps an experiment can serve again as a parable. There is a well-known phenomenon known to psychologists by the forbidding name of the Zeigarnik Effect. In brief, tasks that are interrupted are much more likely to be returned to and completed, and much more likely to be remembered, than comparable tasks that one has completed without interruption. But that puts the matter superficially, for it leaves out of account one factor that is crucial. The effect holds only if the tasks that the subject has been set are ones that have a structure—a beginning, a plan, and a terminus. If the tasks are "silly" in the sense of being meaningless, arbitrary, and without visible means for checking progress, the drive to completion is not stimulated by interruption.

It seems likely that the desire to achieve competence follows the same rule. Unless there is some meaningful unity in what we are doing and some way of telling how we are doing, we are not very likely to strive to excel ourselves. Yet surely this too is only a small part of the story, for everybody does not want to be competent in the same activities, and some competencies might even be a source of embarrassment to their possessors. Boys do not thrill to the challenge of sewing a fine seam (again, in our culture), nor girls to becoming competent street fighters. There are competencies that are appropriate and activating for different ages, the two sexes, different social classes. But there are some things about competence motives that transcend these particulars. One is that an activity (given that it is "approved"), must have some meaningful structure to it if it requires skill that is a little bit beyond that now possessed by the person—that it be learned by the exercise of effort. It is probably the combination of the two that is critical.

Experienced teachers who work with the newer curricula in science and mathematics report that they are surprised at the eagerness of students to push ahead to next steps in the course. Several of the teachers have suggested that the eagerness comes from increased confidence in one's ability to understand the material. Some of the students were having their first experience of understanding a topic in some depth, of going somewhere in a subject. It is this that is at the heart of competence motives, and surely our schools have not begun to tap this enormous reservoir of zest.

While we do not know the limits within which competence

drives can be shaped and channeled by external reward, it seems quite likely that they are strongly open to external influence. But channelization aside, how can education keep alive and nourish a drive to competence—whether expressed in farming, football, or mathematics? What sustains a sense of pleasure and achievement in mastering things for their own sake—what Thorstein Veblen referred to as an instinct for workmanship? Do competence motives strengthen mainly on their exercise, in whatever context they may be exercised, or do they depend also upon being linked to drives for status, wealth, security, or fame?

There are, to begin with, striking differences among cultures and between strata within any particular society with respect to the encouragement given to competence drives. David McClelland, for example, in writing about the "achieving society," comments upon the fact that in certain times and places one finds a flowering of achievement motivation strongly supported by the society and its institutions and myths alike.[5] Emphasis upon individual responsibility and initiative, upon independence in decision and action, upon perfectibility of the self—all of these things serve to perpetuate more basic competency motives past childhood.

But cultures vary in their evaluation of *intellectual mast*ery as a vehicle for the expression of competence. Freed Bales, for example, in comparing Irish and Jewish immigrant groups in Boston, remarks that the Jewish, much more than the Irish, treat school success and intellectuality as virtues in their own right as well as ways of upward mobility.[6] The reasons can be found in history. Herzog and Zborowski, in their book on eastern European Jewish communities, suggest that the barrier erected against Jews' entering other professions may have helped foster the cultivation of intellectual excellence as a prized expression of competence.[7]

A culture does not "manage" these matters consciously by the applications of rewards and reproofs alone. The son of the rabbi in the eastern European *stetl*[8] was not punished if he wished to become a merchant rather than a Talmudic scholar, and, indeed, if he chose to become the latter he typically went through long, extrinsically unrewarding, and arduous training to do so. More subtle forces are at work, all of them fairly familiar but too often overlooked in discussing education. One of them is "approval." The professional man is more "respected" than the manual worker. But that scarcely exhausts the matter. Respected by whom? Con-

5. David C. McClelland, *The Achieving Society* (Princeton, N.J.: Van Nostrand, 1961) [Bruner's note].

6. R. Freed Bales, "The 'Fixation Factor' in Alcohol Addiction: A Hypothesis Derived from a Comparative Study of Irish and Jewish Social Norms," unpublished doctoral disserta-

tion, Harvard University, 1944 [Bruner's note].

7. Mark Zborowski and Elizabeth Herzog, *Life Is with People: The Jewish Little-Town of Eastern Europe* (New York: International Universities Press, 1952) [Bruner's note].

8. Ghetto or religious community.

temporary sociologists speak of the approval of one's "reference group"—those to whom one looks for guides to action, for the definition of the possible, for ultimate approbation. But what leads *this* individual to look to *that* particular reference group?

What appears to be operative is a process we cavalierly call identification. The fact of identification is more easily described than explained. It refers to the strong human tendency to model one's "self" and one's aspirations upon some other person. When we feel we have succeeded in "being like" an identification figure, we derive pleasure from the achievement and, conversely, we suffer when we have "let him down." Insofar as the identification figure is also "a certain kind of person"—belongs to some group or category—we extend our loyalties from an individual to a reference group. In effect, then, identification relates one not only to individuals, but to one's society as well.

While this account is oversimplified, it serves to underline one important feature of identification as a process—its self-sustaining nature. For what it accomplishes is to pass over to the learner the control of punishment and reward. Insofar as we now carry our standards with us, we achieve a certain independence from the immediate rewards and punishments meted out by others.

It has been remarked by psychologists that identification figures are most often those who control the scarce psychological resources that we most desire—love, approval, sustenance. Let me skip this issue for a moment and return to it later.

The term identification is usually reserved for those strong attachments where there is a considerable amount of emotional investment. But there are "milder" forms of identification that are also important during the years of childhood and after. Perhaps we should call those who serve in these milder relationships "competence models." They are the "on the job" heroes, the reliable ones with whom we can interact in some way. Indeed, they control a rare resource, some desired competence, but what is important is that the resource is attainable by interaction. The "on the job" model is nowhere better illustrated than in the manner in which the child learns language from a parent. The tryout-correction-revision process continues until the child comes to learn the rules whereby sentences are generated and transformed appropriately. Finally he develops a set of productive habits that enable him to be his own sentence maker and his own corrector. He "learns the rules of the language." The parent is the model who, by interaction, teaches the skill of language.

In the process of teaching a skill the parent or teacher passes on much more. The teacher imparts attitudes toward a subject and, indeed, attitudes toward learning itself. What results may be quite inadvertent. Often, in our schools, for example, this first lesson is that learning has to do with remembering things when asked, with maintaining a certain undefined tidiness in what one does, with following a train of thought that comes from outside rather than from within and with honoring right answers. Observant anthropologists have suggested that the basic values of the early grades are a stylized version of the feminine role in the society, cautious rather than daring, governed by a ladylike politeness.

One recent study by Pauline Sears underlines the point.[9] It suggests that girls in the early grades, who learn to control their fidgeting earlier and better than boys, are rewarded for excelling in their "feminine" values. The reward can be almost too successful, so that in later years it is difficult to move girls beyond the orderly virtues they learned in their first school encounters. The boys, more fidgety in the first grade, get no such reward and as a consequence may be freer in their approach to learning in later grades. Far more would have to be known about the other conditions present in the lives of these children to draw a firm conclusion from the findings, but it is nonetheless suggestive. There are surely many ways to expand the range of competence models available to children. One is the use of a challenging master teacher, particularly in the early grades. And there is film or closed-circuit television, opening up enormously the range of teachers to whom the student can be exposed. Filmed teaching has, to be sure, marked limits, for the student cannot interact with an image. But a kind of pseudo interaction can be attained by including in the television lesson a group of students who are being taught right on the screen, with whom the student can take common cause. Team teaching provides still another approach to the exemplification of a range of competences, particularly if one of the teachers is charged specially with the role of gadfly. None of the above is yet a tried practice, but pedagogy, like economics and engineering, often must try techniques to find not only whether they work, but how they may be made to work.

I would like to suggest that what the teacher must be, to be an effective competence model, is a day-to-day working model with whom to interact. It is not so much that the teacher provides a model to *imitate*. Rather, it is that the teacher can become a part of the student's internal dialogue—somebody whose respect he wants, someone whose standards he wishes to make his own. It is like becoming a speaker of a language one shares with somebody. The language of that interaction becomes a part of oneself, and the standards of style and clarity that one adopts for that interaction become a part of one's own standards.

Finally, a word about one last intrinsic motive that bears closely upon the will to learn. Perhaps it should be called reciprocity. For

9. Pauline Sears, "Attitudinal and Affective Factors Affecting Children's Approaches to Problem Solving," in J. S. Bruner, ed., *Learning about Learning* (Washington, D.C.: U.S. Office of Education, in press) [Bruner's note].

it involves a deep human need to respond to others and to operate jointly with them toward an objective. One of the important insights of modern zoology is the importance of this intraspecies reciprocity for the survival of individual members of the species. The psychologist Roger Barker[10] has commented that the best way he has found to predict the behavior of the children whom he has been studying in great detail in the midst of their everyday activities is to know their situations. A child in a baseball game behaves baseball; in the drugstore the same child behaves drugstore. Situations have a demand value that appears to have very little to do with the motives that are operative. Surely it is not simply a "motive to conform"; this is too great an abstraction. The man who is regulating his pressure on the back of a car, along with three or four others, trying to "rock it out," is not so much conforming as "fitting his efforts into an enterprise." It is about as primitive an aspect of human behavior as we know.

Like the other activities we have been discussing, its exercise seems to be its sole reward. Probably it is the basis of human society, this response through reciprocity to other members of one's species. Where joint action is needed, where reciprocity is required for the group to attain an objective, then there seem to be processes that carry the individual along into learning, sweep him into a competence that is required in the setting of the group. We know precious little about this primitive motive to reciprocate, but what we do know is that it can furnish a driving force to learn as well. Human beings (and other species as well) fall into a pattern that is required by the goals and activities of the social group in which they find themselves. "Imitation" is not the word for it, since it is usually not plain in most cases what is to be imitated. A much more interesting way of looking at what is involved is provided by the phenomenon of a young child learning to use the pronouns "I" and "you" correctly. The parent says to the child, "You go to bed now." The child says, "No, you no go to bed." We are amused. "Not me but *you*," we say. In time, and after a surprisingly brief period of confusion, the child learns that "you" refers to himself when another uses it, and to another person when he uses it—and the reverse with "I." It is a prime example of reciprocal learning. It is by much the same process that children learn the beautifully complicated games they play (adult and child games alike), that they learn their role in the family and in school, and finally that they come to take their role in the greater society.

The corpus of learning, using the word now as synonymous with knowledge, is reciprocal. A culture in its very nature is a set of values, skills, and ways of life that no one member of the society

10. Roger Barker, "On the Nature of the Environment," *Journal of Social* *Issues,* 19.4:17–38 (1963) [Bruner's note].

masters. Knowledge in this sense is like a rope, each strand of which extends no more than a few inches along its length, all being intertwined to give a solidity to the whole. The conduct of our educational system has been curiously blind to this interdependent nature of knowledge. We have "teachers" and "pupils," "experts" and "laymen." But the community of learning is somehow overlooked.

What can most certainly be encouraged—and what is now being developed in the better high schools—is something approximating the give and take of a seminar in which discussion is the vehicle of instruction. This is reciprocity. But it requires recognition of one critically important matter: you cannot have both reciprocity and the demand that everybody learn the same thing or be "completely" well rounded in the same way all the time. If reciprocally operative groups are to give support to learning by stimulating each person to join his efforts to a group, then we shall need tolerance for the specialized roles that develop—the critic, the innovator, the second helper, the cautionary. For it is from the cultivation of these interlocking roles that the participants get the sense of operating reciprocally in a group. Never mind that this pupil for this term in this seminar has a rather specialized task to perform. It will change. Meanwhile, if he can see how he contributes to the effectiveness of the group's operations on history or geometry or whatnot, he is likely to be the more activated. And surely one of the roles that will emerge is that of auxiliary teacher—let it, encourage it. It can only help in relieving the tedium of a classroom with one expert up here and the rest down there.

At the risk of being repetitious, let me restate the argument. It is this. The will to learn is an intrinsic motive, one that finds both its source and its reward in its own exercise. The will to learn becomes a "problem" only under specialized circumstances like those of a school, where a curriculum is set, students confined, and a path fixed. The problem exists not so much in learning itself, but in the fact that what the school imposes often fails to enlist the natural energies that sustain spontaneous learning—curiosity, a desire for competence, aspiration to emulate a model, and a deep-sensed commitment to the web of social reciprocity. Our concern has been with how these energies may be cultivated in support of school learning. If we know little firmly, at least we are not without reasonable hypotheses about how to proceed. The practice of education does, at least, produce interesting hypotheses. After all, the Great Age of Discovery was made possible by men whose hypotheses were formed before they had developed a decent technique for measuring longitude.

You will have noted by now a considerable de-emphasis of "extrinsic" rewards and punishments as factors in school learning.

There has been in these pages a rather intentional neglect of the so-called Law of Effect, which holds that a reaction is more likely to be repeated if it has previously been followed by a "satisfying state of affairs." I am not unmindful of the notion of reinforcement. It is doubtful, only, that "satisfying states of affairs" are *reliably to* be found outside learning itself—in kind or harsh words from the teacher, in grades and gold stars, in the absurdly abstract assurance to the high school student that his lifetime earnings will be better by 80 percent if he graduates. External reinforcement may indeed get a particular act going and may even lead to its repetition, but it does not nourish, reliably, the long course of learning by which man slowly builds in his own way a serviceable model of what the world is and what it can be.

QUESTIONS

1. Bruner discusses four "natural energies that sustain spontaneous learning." What are they? Why does he find it necessary to repeat them in a summary toward the end of his essay? Why has he given more stress to some of these "energies" than to others?
2. Why, at the end of his essay, does Bruner talk about the "Law of Effect"? Does his last paragraph seem necessary? How does it strengthen or weaken his main position?
3. Bruner introduces what he calls "a parable" on page 353. Compare this with one of the parables on pages 1374–1400. Does Bruner's idea of "parable" differ from the one on pages 1374–1375? Explain.
4. Compare the implications in Bruner's and Holt's essays about the role of the teacher. Explain where they agree and disagree.

On Mind

HENRY DAVID THOREAU

Observation

There is no such thing as pure *objective* observation. Your observation, to be interesting, *i.e.* to be significant, must be *subjective*. The sum of what the writer of whatever class has to report is simply some human experience, whether he be poet or philosopher or man of science. The man of most science is the man most alive, whose life is the greatest event. Senses that take cognizance of outward things merely are of no avail. It matters not where or how far you travel—the farther commonly the worse—but how much alive you are. If it is possible to conceive of an event outside to humanity, it is not of the slightest significance, though it were the explosion of a planet. Every important worker will report what life there is in him. It makes no odds into what seeming deserts the poet is born. Though all his neighbors pronounce it a Sahara, it will be a paradise to him; for the desert which we see is the result of the barrenness of our experience. No mere willful activity whatever, whether in writing verses or collecting statistics, will produce true poetry or science. If you are really a sick man, it is indeed to be regretted, for you cannot accomplish so much as if you were well. All that a man has to say or do that can possibly concern mankind, is in some shape or other to tell the story of his love—to sing, and, if he is fortunate and keeps alive, he will be forever in love. This alone is to be alive to the extremities. It is a pity that this divine creature should ever suffer from cold feet; a still greater pity that the coldness so often reaches to his heart. I look over the report of the doings of a scientific association and am surprised that there is so little life to be reported; I am put off with a parcel of dry technical terms. Anything living is easily and naturally expressed in popular language. I cannot help suspecting that the life of these learned professors has been almost as inhuman and wooden as a rain-gauge or self-registering magnetic machine. They communicate no fact which rises to the temperature of blood-heat. It doesn't all amount to one rhyme.

GEORGE SANTAYANA

Imagination

Men are ruled by imagination: imagination makes them into men, capable of madness and of immense labors. We work dreaming. Consider what dreams must have dominated the builders of the Pyramids—dreams geometrical, dreams funereal, dreams of resurrection, dreams of outdoing the pyramid of some other Pharoah! What dreams occupy that fat man in the street, toddling by under his shabby hat and bedraggled rain-coat? Perhaps he is in love; perhaps he is a Catholic, and imagines that early this morning he has partaken of the body and blood of Christ; perhaps he is a revolutionist, with the millennium in his heart and a bomb in his pocket. The spirit bloweth where it listeth; the wind of inspiration carries our dreams before it and constantly refashions them like clouds. Nothing could be madder, more irresponsible, more dangerous than this guidance of men by dreams. What saves us is the fact that our imaginations, groundless and chimerical as they may seem, are secretly suggested and controlled by shrewd old instincts of our animal nature, and by continual contact with things. The shock of sense, breaking in upon us with a fresh irresistible image, checks wayward imagination and sends it rebounding in a new direction, perhaps more relevant to what is happening in the world outside.

When I speak of being governed by imagination, of course I am indulging in a figure of speech, in an ellipsis; in reality we are governed by that perpetual latent process within us by which imagination itself is created. Actual imaginings—the cloud-like thoughts drifting by—are not masters over themselves nor over anything else. They are like the sound of chimes in the night; they know nothing of whence they came, how they will fall out, or how long they will ring. There is a mechanism in the church tower; there was a theme in the composer's head; there is a beadle who has been winding the thing up. The sound wafted to us, muffled by distance and a thousand obstacles, is but the last lost emanation of this magical bell-ringing. Yet in our dream it is all in all; it is what first entertains and absorbs the mind. Imagination, when it chimes within us, apparently of itself, is no less elaborately grounded; it is a last symptom, a rolling echo, by which we detect and name the obscure operation that occasions it; and not this echo in its aesthetic impotence, but the whole operation whose last witness it is, receives in science the name of imagination, and may be truly said to rule the human world.

This extension of names is inevitable although unfortunate, because language and perception are poetical before they become scientific, if they ever do; as Aristotle observes that the word anger is used indifferently for two different things: dialectically, or as I call it, imaginatively, for the desire for revenge, but physically for a boiling of the humors. And utterly different as these two things are in quality, no great inconvenience results from giving them the same name, because historically they are parts of the same event. Nature has many dimensions at once, and whenever we see anything happen, much else is happening there which we cannot see. Whilst dreams entertain us, the balance of our character is shifting beneath: we are growing while we sleep. The young think in one way, the drunken in another, and the dead not at all; and I imagine—for I have imagination myself—that they do not die because they stop thinking, but they stop thinking because they die. How much veering and luffing before they make that port! The brain of man, William James used to say, has a hair-trigger organization. His life is terribly experimental. He is perilously dependent on the oscillations of a living needle, imagination, that never points to the true north.

There are books in which the footnotes, or the comments scrawled by some reader's hand in the margin, are more interesting than the text. The world is one of these books. The reciprocal interference of magnetic fields (which I understand is the latest conception of matter) may compose a marvelous moving pattern; but the chief interest to us of matter lies in its fertility in producing minds and presenting recognizable phenomena to the senses; and the chief interest of any scientific notion of its intrinsic nature lies in the fact that, if not literally true, it may liberate us from more misleading conceptions. Did we have nothing but electrical physics to think of, the nightmare would soon become intolerable. But a hint of that kind, like a hasty glance into the crater of a volcano, sends a wholesome shudder through our nerves; we realize how thin is the crust we build on, how mythical and remote from the minute and gigantic scale of nature are the bright images we seem to move among, all cut out and fitted to our human stature. Yet these bright images are our natural companions, and if we do not worship them idolatrously nor petrify them into substances, forgetting the nimble use of them in mental discourse, which is where they belong, they need not be more misleading to us, even for scientific purposes, than are words or any other symbols.

It is fortunate that the material world, whatever may be its intrinsic structure or substance, falls to our apprehension into such charming units. There is the blue vault of heaven, there are the twinkling constellations, there are the mountains, trees, and rivers, and above all those fascinating unstable unities which we call animals and persons; magnetic fields I am quite ready to believe them, for such in a vast vague way I feel them to be, but individual bodies they will remain to my sensuous imagination, and dramatic personages to my moral sense. They, too, are animate: they, too, compose a running commentary on things and on one another, adding their salacious footnotes to the dull black letter of the world. Many of them are hardly aware of their own wit; knowing they are but commentators, they are intent on fidelity and unconscious of invention. Yet against their will they gloss everything, willy-nilly we are all scholiasts together. Heaven forbid that I should depreciate this prodigious tome of nature, or question in one jot or tittle the absolute authority of its Author; but it is like an encyclopedia in an infinite number of volumes, or a directory with the addresses of everybody that ever lived. We may dip into it on occasion in search of some pertinent fact, but it is not a book to read; its wealth is infinite, but so is its monotony; it is not composed in our style nor in our language, we could not have written one line of it. Yet the briefest text invites reflection, and we may spin a little homily out of it in the vernacular for our own edification.

In the *Mahabharata*, a learned friend tells me, a young champion armed for the combat and about to rush forward between the two armies drawn up in battle array, stops for a moment to receive a word of counsel from his spiritual adviser—and that word occupies the next eighteen books of the epic; after which the battle is allowed to proceed. The Indian poets had spiritual minds, they measured things by their importance to the spirit, not to the eye. They despised verisimilitude and aesthetic proportion; they despised existence, the beauties of which they felt exquisitely nevertheless, and to which their imagination made such stupendous additions. I honor their courage in bidding the sun stand still, not that they might thoroughly vanquish an earthly enemy, but that they might wholly clarify their own soul. For this better purpose the sun need not stand still materially. For the spirit, time is an elastic thing. Fancy is quick and brings the widest vistas to a focus in a single instant. After the longest interval of oblivion and death, it can light up the same image in all the greenness of youth; and if cut short, as it were at Pompeii, in the in the midst of a word, it can, ages after, without feeling the break, add the last syllable. Imagination changes the scale of everything, and makes a thousand patterns of the woof of nature, without disturbing a single thread. Or rather—since it is nature itself that imagines—it turns to music what was only strain; as if the universal vibration, suddenly ashamed of having been so long silent and useless, had burst into tears and laughter at its own folly, and in so doing had become wise.

QUESTIONS

1. What effect does Santayana achieve by beginning with what he later identifies as a figure of speech, an ellipsis?
2. The language of this essay is highly figurative throughout. Find examples of the various kinds of figures of speech used. How are they appropriate to the subject? How far are they necessary to it?
3. How does analogy contribute to Santayana's definition of imagination? Why does he use the analogy between the process of imagination and the production of music, first introduced in the second paragraph, to conclude the essay? Where does it recur, directly or by implication, in the essay?
4. It is not unusual to compare the world to a book, but Santayana's comparison involves some rather special features and implications. What are these?
5. Santayana asks the reader to "consider what dreams must have dominated the builders of the Pyramids." Can dreams be said to dominate the builders of rockets and missiles? Or of research laboratories? Or do these differ fundamentally from the Pyramids? How, or why? Does Santayana's discussion illuminate, in this connection, such terms as space race and medical breakthrough?

JACOB BRONOWSKI
The Reach of Imagination

For three thousand years, poets have been enchanted and moved and perplexed by the power of their own imagination. In a short and summary essay I can hope at most to lift one small corner of that mystery; and yet it is a critical corner. I shall ask, What goes on in the mind when we imagine? You will hear from me that one answer to this question is fairly specific: which is to say, that we can describe the working of the imagination. And when we describe it as I shall do, it becomes plain that imagination is a specifically *human* gift. To imagine is the characteristic act, not of the poet's mind, or the painter's, or the scientist's, but of the mind of man.

My stress here on the word *human* implies that there is a clear difference in this between the actions of men and those of other animals. Let me then start with a classical experiment with animals and children which Walter Hunter thought out in Chicago about 1910. That was the time when scientists were agog with the success of Ivan Pavlov in forming and changing the reflex actions of dogs, which Pavlov had first announced in 1903. Pavlov had been given a Nobel prize the next year, in 1904; although in fairness I should say that the award did not cite his work on the conditioned reflex, but on the digestive gland.

Hunter duly trained some dogs and other animals on Pavlov's lines. They were taught that when a light came on over one of three tunnels out of their cage, that tunnel would be open; they could escape down it, and were rewarded with food if they did. But once he had fixed that conditioned reflex, Hunter added to it a deeper idea: he gave the mechanical experiment a new dimension, literally—the dimension of time. Now he no longer let the dog go to the lighted tunnel at once; instead, he put out the light, and then kept the dog waiting a little while before he let him go. In this way Hunter timed how long an animal can remember where he has last seen the signal light to his escape route.

The results were and are staggering. A dog or a rat forgets which one of three tunnels has been lit up within a matter of seconds—in Hunter's experiment, ten seconds at most. If you want such an animal to do much better than this, you must make the task much simpler: you must face him with only two tunnels to choose from. Even so, the best that Hunter could do was to have a dog remember for five minutes which one of two tunnels had been lit up.

I am not quoting these times as if they were exact and universal: they surely are not. Hunter's experiment, more than fifty years old now, had many faults of detail. For example, there were too few animals, they were oddly picked, and they did not all behave consistently. It may be unfair to test a dog for what he *saw*, when he commonly follows his nose rather than his eyes. It may be unfair to test any animal in the unnatural setting of a laboratory cage. And there are higher animals, such as chimpanzees and other primates, which certainly have longer memories than the animals that Hunter tried.

Yet when all these provisos have been made (and met, by more modern experiments) the facts are still startling and characteristic. An animal cannot recall a signal from the past for even a short fraction of the time that a man can—for even a short fraction of the time that a child can. Hunter made comparable tests with six-year-old children, and found, of course, that they were incomparably better than the best of his animals. There is a striking and basic difference between a man's ability to imagine something that he saw or experienced, and an animal's failure.

Animals make up for this by other and extraordinary gifts. The salmon and the carrier pigeon can find their way home as we cannot: they have, as it were, a practical memory that man cannot match. But their actions always depend on some form of habit: on instinct or on learning, which reproduce by rote a train of known responses. They do not depend, as human memory does, on calling to mind the recollection of absent things.

Where is it that the animal falls short? We get a clue to the answer, I think, when Hunter tells us how the animals in his experiment tried to fix their recollection. They most often pointed themselves at the light before it went out, as some gun dogs point rigidly at the game they scent—and get the name *pointer* from the posture. The animal makes ready to act by building the signal into its action. There is a primitive imagery in its stance, it seems to me; it is as if the animal were trying to fix the light on its mind by fixing it in its body. And indeed, how else can a dog mark and (as it were) name one of three tunnels, when he has no such words as *left* and *right*, and no such numbers as *one, two, three?* The directed gesture of attention and readiness is perhaps the only symbolic device that the dog commands to hold on to the past, and thereby to guide himself into the future.

I used the verb *to imagine* a moment ago, and now I have some ground for giving it a meaning. *To imagine* means to make images and to move them about inside one's head in new arrangements. When you and I recall the past, we imagine it in this direct and homely sense. The tool that puts the human mind ahead of the animal is imagery. For us, memory does not demand the preoccupation that it demands in animals, and it lasts immensely longer, because we fix it in images or other substitute symbols. With the same symbolic vocabulary we spell out the future—not one but many futures, which we weigh one against another.

I am using the word *image* in a wide meaning, which does not restrict it to the mind's eye as a visual organ. An image in my usage is what Charles Peirce called a *sign*, without regard for its sensory quality. Peirce distinguished between different forms of signs, but there is no reason to make his distinction here, for the imagination works equally with them all, and that is why I call them all images.

Indeed, the most important images for human beings are simply words, which are abstract symbols. Animals do not have words, in our sense: there is no specific center for language in the brain of any animal, as there is in the human being. In this respect at least we know that the human imagination depends on a configuration in the brain that has only evolved in the last one or two million years. In the same period, evolution has greatly enlarged the front lobes in the human brain, which govern the sense of the past and the future; and it is a fair guess that they are probably the seat of our other images. (Part of the evidence for this guess is that damage to the front lobes in primates reduces them to the state of Hunter's animals.) If the guess turns out to be right, we shall know why man has come to look like a highbrow or an egghead: because otherwise there would not be room in his head for his imagination.

The images play out for us events which are not present to our senses, and thereby guard the past and create the future—a future that does not yet exist, and may never come to exist in that form.

By contrast, the lack of symbolic ideas, or their rudimentary poverty, cuts off an animal from the past and the future alike, and imprisons him in the present. Of all the distinctions between man and animal, the characteristic gift which makes us human is the power to work with symbolic images: the gift of imagination.

This is really a remarkable finding. When Philip Sidney in 1580 defended poets (and all unconventional thinkers) from the Puritan charge that they were liars, he said that a maker must imagine things that are not. Halfway between Sidney and us, William Blake said, "What is now proved was once only imagined." About the same time, in 1796, Samuel Taylor Coleridge for the first time distinguished between the passive fancy and the active imagination, "the living Power and prime Agent of all human Perception." Now we see that they were right, and precisely right: the human gift is the gift of imagination—and that is not just a literary phrase.

Nor is it just a literary gift; it is, I repeat, characteristically human. Almost everything that we do that is worth doing is done in the first place in the mind's eye. The richness of human life is that we have many lives; we live the events that do not happen (and some that cannot) as vividly as those that do; and if thereby we die a thousand deaths, that is the price we pay for living a thousand lives. (A cat, of course, has only nine.) Literature is alive to us because we live its images, but so is any play of the mind—so is chess: the lines of play that we foresee and try in our heads and dismiss are as much a part of the game as the moves that we make. John Keats said that the unheard melodies are sweeter, and all chess players sadly recall that the combinations that they planned and which never came to be played were the best.

I make this point to remind you, insistently, that imagination is the manipulation of images in one's head; and that the rational manipulation belongs to that, as well as the literary and artistic manipulation. When a child begins to play games with things that stand for other things, with chairs or chessmen, he enters the gateway to reason and imagination together. For the human reason discovers new relations between things not by deduction, but by that unpredictable blend of speculation and insight that scientists call induction, which—like other forms of imagination—cannot be formalized. We see it at work when Walter Hunter inquires into a child's memory, as much as when Blake and Coleridge do. Only a restless and original mind would have asked Hunter's questions and could have conceived his experiments, in a science that was dominated by Pavlov's reflex arcs and was heading toward the behaviorism of John Watson.

Let me find a spectacular example for you from history. What is the most famous experiment that you had described to you as a child? I will hazard that it is the experiment that Galileo is said to have made in Sidney's age, in Pisa about 1590, by dropping two unequal balls from the Leaning Tower. There, we say, is a man in the modern mold, a man after our own hearts: he insisted on questioning the authority of Aristotle and St. Thomas Aquinas, and seeing with his own eyes whether (as they said) the heavy ball would reach the ground before the light one. Seeing is believing.

Yet seeing is also imagining. Galileo did challenge the authority of Aristotle, and he did look at his mechanics. But the eye that Galileo used was the mind's eye. He did not drop balls from the Leaning Tower of Pisa—and if he had, he would have got a very doubtful answer. Instead, Galileo made an imaginary experiment in his head, which I will describe as he did years later in the book he wrote after the Holy Office silenced him: the *Discorsi . . . intorno a due nuove scienze*, which was smuggled out to be printed in the Netherlands in 1638.

Suppose, said Galileo, that you drop two unequal balls from the tower at the same time. And suppose that Aristotle is right— suppose that the heavy ball falls faster, so that it steadily gains on the light ball, and hits the ground first. Very well. Now imagine the same experiment done again, with only one difference: this time the two unequal balls are joined by a string between them. The heavy ball will again move ahead, but now the light ball holds it back and acts as a drag or brake. So the light ball will be speeded up and the heavy ball will be slowed down; they must reach the ground together because they are tied together, but they cannot reach the ground as quickly as the heavy ball alone. Yet the string between them has turned the two balls into a single mass which is heavier than either ball—and surely (according to Aristotle) this mass should therefore move faster than either ball? Galileo's imaginary experiment has uncovered a contradiction; he says trenchantly, "You see how, from your assumption that a heavier body falls more rapidly than a lighter one, I infer that a (still) heavier body falls more slowly." There is only one way out of the contradiction: the heavy ball and the light ball must fall at the same rate, so that they go on falling at the same rate when they are tied together.

This argument is not conclusive, for nature might be more subtle (when the two balls are joined) than Galileo has allowed. And yet it is something more important: it is suggestive, it is stimulating, it opens a new view—in a word, it is imaginative. It cannot be settled without an actual experiment, because nothing that we imagine can become knowledge until we have translated it into, and backed it by, real experience. The test of imagination is experience. But then, that is as true of literature and the arts as it is of science. In science, the imaginary experiment is tested by confronting it with physical experience; and in literature, the imaginative conception is tested by confronting it with human experience. The superficial speculation in science is dismissed because it is found to falsify nature; and the shallow work of art is discarded because it is found to be untrue to our own nature. So when Ella Wheeler Wilcox died in 1919, more people were reading her verses than Shakespeare's; yet in a few years her work was dead. It had been buried by its poverty of emotion and its trivialness of thought: which is to say that it had been proved to be as false to the nature of man as, say, Jean Baptiste Lamarck and Trofim Lysenko[1] were false to the nature of inheritance. The strength of the imagination, its enriching power and excitement, lies in its interplay with reality— physical and emotional.

I doubt if there is much to choose here between science and the arts: the imagination is not much more free, and not much less free, in one than in the other. All great scientists have used their imagination freely, and let it ride them to outrageous conclusions without crying "Halt!" Albert Einstein fiddled with imaginary experiments from boyhood, and was wonderfully ignorant of the facts that they were supposed to bear on. When he wrote the first of his beautiful papers on the random movement of atoms, he did not know that the Brownian motion which it predicted could be seen in any laboratory. He was sixteen when he invented the paradox that he resolved ten years later, in 1905, in the theory of relativity, and it bulked much larger in his mind than the experiment of Albert Michelson and Edward Morley[2] which had upset every other physicist since 1881. All his life Einstein loved to make up teasing puzzles like Galileo's, about falling lifts and the detection of gravity; and they carry the nub of the problems of general relativity on which he was working.

Indeed, it could not be otherwise. The power that man has over nature and himself, and that a dog lacks, lies in his command of imaginary experience. He alone has the symbols which fix the past and play with the future, possible and impossible. In the Renaissance, the symbolism of memory was thought to be mystical, and devices that were invented as mnemonics (by Giordano Bruno, for example, and by Robert Fludd) were interpreted as magic signs. The symbol is the tool which gives man his power, and it is the same tool whether the symbols are images or words, mathematical signs or mesons. And the symbols have a reach and a roundness that goes beyond their literal and practical meaning. They are the rich concepts under which the mind gathers many particulars into one name, and many instances into one general induction. When a

1. Lamarck was a French biologist (1744–1829) who held that characteristics acquired by experience were biologically transmittable. Lysenko is a Russian biologist (1898–   ) who has held that hereditary properties of organisims could be changed by manipulating the environment.

2. This was an experiment designed to measure the drag exerted on the passage of light by a hypothetical stationary medium. Its negative results eliminated the concept of a motionless, measurable ether and cleared the way for the development of the theory of relativity.

man says *left* and *right*, he is outdistancing the dog not only in looking for a light; he is setting in train all the shifts of meaning, the overtones and the ambiguities, between *gauche* and *adroit* and *dexterous*, between *sinister* and the sense of right. When a man counts *one*, *two*, *three*, he is not only doing mathematics; he is on the path to the mysticism of numbers in Pythagoras and Vitruvius and Kepler, to the Trinity and the signs of the Zodiac.

I have described imagination as the ability to make images and to move them about inside one's head in new arrangements. This is the faculty that is specifically human, and it is the common root from which science and literature both spring and grow and flourish together. For they do flourish (and languish) together; the great ages of science are the great ages of all the arts, because in them powerful minds have taken fire from one another, breathless and higgledy-piggledy, without asking too nicely whether they ought to tie their imagination to falling balls or a haunted island. Galileo and Shakespeare, who were born in the same year, grew into greatness in the same age; when Galileo was looking through his telescope at the moon, Shakespeare was writing *The Tempest* and all Europe was in ferment, from Johannes Kepler to Peter Paul Rubens, and from the first table of logarithms by John Napier to the Authorized Version of the Bible.

Let me end with a last and spirited example of the common inspiration of literature and science, because it is as much alive today as it was three hundred years ago. What I have in mind is man's ageless fantasy, to fly to the moon. I do not display this to you as a high scientific enterprise; on the contrary, I think we have more important discoveries to make here on earth than wait for us, beckoning, at the horned surface of the moon. Yet I cannot belittle the fascination which that ice-blue journey has had for the imagination of men, long before it drew us to our television screens to watch the tumbling astronauts. Plutarch and Lucian, Ariosto and Ben Jonson wrote about it, before the days of Jules Verne and H. G. Wells and science fiction. The seventeenth century was heady with new dreams and fables about voyages to the moon. Kepler wrote one full of deep scientific ideas, which (alas) simply got his mother accused of witchcraft. In England, Francis Godwin wrote a wild and splendid work, *The Man in the Moone*, and the astronomer John Wilkins wrote a wild and learned one, *The Discovery of a New World*. They did not draw a line between science and fancy; for example, they all tried to guess just where in the journey the earth's gravity would stop. Only Kepler understood that gravity has no boundary, and put a law to it—which happened to be the wrong law.

All this was a few years before Isaac Newton was born, and it was all in his head that day in 1666 when he sat in his mother's garden, a young man of twenty-three, and thought about the reach of gravity. This was how he came to conceive his brilliant image, that the moon is like a ball which has been thrown so hard that it falls exactly as fast as the horizon, all the way round the earth. The image will do for any satellite, and Newton modestly calculated how long therefore an astronaut would take to fall round the earth once. He made it ninety minutes, and we have all seen now that he was right; but Newton had no way to check that. Instead he went on to calculate how long in that case the distant moon would take to round the earth, if indeed it behaves like a thrown ball that falls in the earth's gravity, and if gravity obeyed a law of inverse squares. He found that the answer would be twenty-eight days.

In that telling figure, the imagination that day chimed with nature, and made a harmony. We shall hear an echo of that harmony on the day when we land on the moon, because it will be not a technical but an imaginative triumph, that reaches back to the beginning of modern science and literature both. All great acts of imagination are like this, in the arts and in science, and convince us because they fill out reality with a deeper sense of rightness. We start with the simplest vocabulary of images, with *left* and *right* and *one, two, three,* and before we know how it happened the words and the numbers have conspired to make a match with nature: we catch in them the pattern of mind and matter as one.

QUESTIONS

1. How does the Hunter experiment provide Bronowski with the ground for defining the imagination?
2. Bronowski discusses the work of Galileo and Newton in the middle and at the end of his essay; what use does he make of their work? Does it justify placing them in the central and final positions?
3. On page 366 Bronowski attributes the imagination to a "configuration" in the brain. Configuration seems vague here; what else shows uncertainty about exactly what happens in the brain? Does this uncertainty compromise the argument of this essay?
4. What function is given to the mind by the title metaphor of reaching (later extended to symbols on page 369)? What words does Bronowski use to indicate the objects reached for? What is the significance of his selecting these words?

BENEDETTO CROCE
Intuition and Expression[1]

Knowledge has two forms: it is either *intuitive* knowledge or *logical* knowledge; knowledge obtained through the *imagination* or knowledge obtained through the *intellect*; knowledge of the *individual* or knowledge of the *universal*, of *individual things* or of the *relations* between them: it is, in fact, productive either of *images* or of *concepts*.

In ordinary life, constant appeal is made to intuitive knowledge. It is said that we cannot give definitions of certain truths; that they are not demonstrable by syllogisms; that they must be learned intuitively. The politician finds fault with the abstract reasoner, who possesses no lively intuition of actual conditions; the educational theorist insists upon the necessity of developing the intuitive faculty in the pupil before everything else; the critic in judging a work of art makes it a point of honor to set aside theory and abstractions, and to judge it by direct intuition; the practical man professes to live rather by intuition than by reason.

But this ample acknowledgment granted to intuitive knowledge in ordinary life, does not correspond to an equal and adequate acknowledgment in the field of theory and of philosophy. There exists a very ancient science of intellectual knowledge, admitted by all without discussion, namely, Logic; but a science of intuitive knowledge is timidly and with difficulty asserted by but a few. Logical knowledge has appropriated the lion's share; and if she does not slay and devour her companion outright, yet yields to her but grudgingly the humble place of maidservant or doorkeeper. What can intuitive knowledge be without the light of intellectual knowledge? It is a servant without a master; and though a master find a servant useful, the master is a necessity to the servant, since he enables him to gain his livelihood. Intuition is blind; intellect lends her eyes.

Now, the first point to be firmly fixed in the mind is that intuitive knowledge has no need of a master, nor to lean upon anyone; she does not need to borrow the eyes of others, for she has excellent eyes of her own. Doubtless it is possible to find concepts mingled with intuitions. But in many other intuitions there is no trace of such a mixture, which proves that it is not necessary. The impression of a moonlight scene by a painter; the outline of a country drawn by a cartographer; a musical motive, tender or energetic; the words of a sighing lyric, or those with which we ask, command,

1. Chapter 1 of *Aesthetic as Science of Expression.*

and lament in ordinary life, may well all be intuitive facts without a shadow of intellectual relation. But, think what one may of these instances, and admitting further the contention that the greater part of the intuitions of civilized man are impregnated with concepts, there yet remains to be observed something more important and more conclusive. Those concepts which are found mingled and fused with the intuitions are no longer concepts, insofar as they are really mingled and fused, for they have lost all independence and autonomy. They have been concepts, but have now become simple elements of intuition. The philosophical maxims placed in the mouth of a personage of tragedy or of comedy, perform there the function, not of concepts, but of characteristics of such personage; in the same way as the red in a painted face does not there represent the red color of the physicists, but is a characteristic element of the portrait. The whole is that which determines the quality of the parts. A work of art may be full of philosophical concepts; it may contain them in greater abundance and they may there be even more profound than in a philosophical dissertation, which in its turn may be rich to overflowing with descriptions and intuitions. But notwithstanding all these concepts the total effect of the work of art is an intuition; and notwithstanding all those intuitions, the total effect of the philosophical dissertation is a concept. The *Promessi Sposi* contains copious ethical observations and distinctions, but does not for that reason lose as a whole its character of simple story or intuition. In like manner the anecdotes and satirical effusions to be found in the works of a philosopher like Schopenhauer do not deprive those works of their character of intellectual treatises. The difference between a scientific work and a work of art, that is, between an intellectual fact and an intuitive fact, lies in the difference of the total effect aimed at by their respective authors. This it is that determines and rules over the several parts of each, not these parts separated and considered abstractly in themselves.

But to admit the independence of intuition as regards concept does not suffice to give a true and precise idea of intuition. Another error arises among those who recognize this, or who at any rate do not explicitly make intuition dependent upon the intellect, to obscure and confuse the real nature of intuition. By intuition is frequently understood *perception*, or the knowledge of actual reality, the apprehension of something as *real*.

Certainly perception is intuition: the perceptions of the room in which I am writing, of the ink bottle and paper that are before me, of the pen I am using, of the objects that I touch and make use of as instruments of my person, which, if it write, therefore exists—these are all intuitions. But the image that is now passing through my brain of a me writing in another room, in another town, with different paper, pen, and ink, is also an intuition. This means that the distinction between reality and non-reality is extraneous, secondary, to the true nature of intuition. If we imagine a human mind having intuitions for the first time, it would seem that it could have intuitions of actual reality only, that is to say, that it could have perceptions of nothing but the real. But since knowledge of reality is based upon the distinction between real images and unreal images, and since this distinction does not at the first moment exist, these intuitions would in truth not be intuitions either of the real or of the unreal, not perceptions, but pure intuitions. Where all is real, nothing is real. The child, with its difficulty of distinguishing true from false, history from fable, which are all one to childhood, can furnish us with a sort of very vague and only remotely approximate idea of this ingenuous state. Intuition is the undifferentiated unity of the perception of the real and of the simple image of the possible. In our intuitions we do not oppose ourselves as empirical beings to external reality, but we simply objectify our impressions, whatever they be.

Those, therefore, who look upon intuition as sensation formed and arranged simply according to the categories of space and time would seem to approximate more nearly to the truth. Space and time (they say) are the forms of intuition; to have an intuition is to place it in space and in temporal sequence. Intuitive activity would then consist in this double and concurrent function of spatiality and temporality. But for these two categories must be repeated what was said of intellectual distinctions, when found mingled with intuitions. We have intuitions without space and without time: the color of a sky, the color of a feeling, a cry of pain and an effort of will, objectified in consciousness: these are intuitions which we possess, and with their making space and time have nothing to do. In some intuitions, spatiality may be found without temporality, in others, *vice versa*; and even where both are found, they are perceived by later reflection: they can be fused with the intuition in like manner with all its other elements: that is, they are in it *materialiter* and not *formaliter*, as ingredients and not as arrangement. Who, without an act of reflection which for a moment breaks in upon his contemplation, can think of space while looking at a drawing or a view? Who is conscious of temporal sequence while listening to a story or a piece of music without breaking into it with a similar act of reflection? What intuition reveals in a work of art is not space and time, but *character, individual physiognomy*. The view here maintained is confirmed in several quarters of modern philosophy. Space and time, far from being simple and primitive functions, are nowadays conceived as intellectual constructions of great complexity. And further, even in some of those who do not altogether deny to space and time the quality of formative principles, categories, and functions, one observes an effort to unite them and to regard them in a different manner from that in which these categories are generally conceived. Some limit intuition to the sole category of spatiality, maintaining that even time can only be intuited in terms of space. Others abandon the three dimensions of space as not philosophically necessary, and conceive the function of spatiality as void of all particular spatial determination. But what could such a spatial function be, a simple arrangment that should arrange even time? It represents, surely, all that criticism and refutation have left standing—the bare demand for the affirmation of some intuitive activity in general. And is not this activity truly determined, when one single function is attributed to it, not spatializing nor temporalizing, but characterizing? Or rather, when it is conceived as itself a category or function which gives us knowledge of things in their concreteness and individuality?

Having thus freed intuitive knowledge from any suggestion of intellectualism and from every later and external addition, we must now explain it and determine its limits from another side and defend it from a different kind of invasion and confusion. On the hither side of the lower limit is sensation, formless matter, which the spirit can never apprehend in itself as simple matter. This it can only possess with form and in form, but postulates the notion of it as a mere limit. Matter, in its abstraction, is mechanism, passivity; it is what the spirit of man suffers, but does not produce. Without it no human knowledge or activity is possible; but mere matter produces animality, whatever is brutal and impulsive in man, not the spiritual dominion, which is humanity. How often we strive to understand clearly what is passing within us! We do catch a glimpse of something, but this does not appear to the mind as objectified and formed. It is in such moments as these that we best perceive the profound difference between matter and form. These are not two acts of ours, opposed to one another; but the one is outside us and assaults and sweeps us off our feet, while the other inside us tends to absorb and identify itself with that which is outside. Matter, clothed and conquered by form, produces concrete form. It is the matter, the content, which differentiates one of our intuitions from another: the form is constant: it is spiritual activity, while matter is changeable. Without matter spiritual activity would not forsake its abstractness to become concrete and real activity, this or that spiritual content, this or that definite intuition.

It is a curious fact, characteristic of our times, that this very form, this very activity of the spirit, which is essentially ourselves, is so often ignored or denied. Some confound the spiritual activity of man with the metaphorical and mythological activity of what is called nature, which is mechanism and has no resemblance to human activity, save when we imagine, with Æsop, that "*arbores loquuntur non tantum ferae.*"[2] Some affirm that they have never observed in themselves this "miraculous" activity, as though there were no difference, or only one of quantity, between sweating and thinking, feeling cold and the energy of the will. Others, certainly with greater reason, would unify activity and mechanism in a more general concept, though they are specifically distinct. Let us, however, refrain for the moment from examining if such a final unification be possible, and in what sense, but admitting that the attempt may be made, it is clear that to unify two concepts in a third implies to begin with the admission of a difference between the two first. Here it is this difference that concerns us and we set it in relief.

Intuition has sometimes been confused with simple sensation. But since this confusion ends by being offensive to common sense, it has more frequently been attenuated or concealed with a phraseology apparently designed at once to confuse and to distinguish them. Thus, it has been asserted that intuition is sensation, but not so much simple sensation as *association* of sensations. Here a double meaning is concealed in the word "association." Association is understood, as either memory, mnemonic association, conscious recollection, and in that case the claim to unite in memory elements which are not intuited, distinguished, possessed in some way by the spirit and produced by consciousness, seems inconceivable: or it is understood as association of unconscious elements, in which case we remain in the world of sensation and of nature. But if with certain associationists we speak of an association which is neither memory nor flux of sensations, but a *productive* association (formative, constructive, distinguishing), then our contention is admitted and only its name is denied to it. For productive association is no longer association in the sense of the sensationalists, but *synthesis*, that is to say, spiritual activity. Synthesis may be called association; but with the concept of productivity is already posited the distinction between passivity and activity, between sensation and intuition.

Other psychologists are disposed to distinguish from sensation something which is sensation no longer, but is not yet intellectual concept: the *representation* or *image*. What is the difference between their representation or image and our intuitive knowledge? Everything and nothing: for "representation" is a very equivocal word. If by representation be understood something cut off and standing out from the psychic basis of the sensations, then representation is intuition. If, on the other hand, it be conceived as complex sensation, we are back once more in crude sensation, which does not vary in quality according to its richness or poverty,

2. "The trees speak, not only the beasts." Phaedrus.

or according to whether the organism in which it appears is rudimentary or highly developed and full of traces of past sensations. Nor is the ambiguity remedied by defining representation as a psychic product of secondary degree in relation to sensation, defined as occupying the first place. What does secondary degree mean here? Does it mean a qualitative, formal difference? If so, representation is an elaboration of sensation and therefore intuition. Or does it mean greater complexity and complication, a quantitative, material difference? In that case intuition is once more confused with simple sensation.

And yet there is a sure method of distinguishing true intuition, true representation, from that which is inferior to it: the spiritual fact from the mechanical, passive, natural fact. Every true intuition or representation is also *expression*. That which does not objectify itself in expression is not intuition or representation, but sensation and mere natural fact. The spirit only intuits in making, forming, expressing. He who separates intuition from expression never succeeds in reuniting them.

Intuitive activity *possesses intuitions to the extent that it expresses them.* Should this proposition sound paradoxical, that is partly because, as a general rule, a too restricted meaning is given to the word "expression." It is generally restricted to what are called verbal expressions alone. But there exist also nonverbal expressions, such as those of line, color, and sound, and to all of these must be extended our affirmation, which embraces therefore every sort of manifestation of the man, as orator, musician, painter, or anything else. But be it pictorial, or verbal, or musical, or in whatever other form it appear, to no intuition can expression in one of its forms be wanting; it is, in fact, an inseparable part of intuition. How can we really possess an intuition of a geometrical figure, unless we possess so accurate an image of it as to be able to trace it immediately upon paper or on the blackboard? How can we really have an intuition of the contour of a region, for example of the island of Sicily, if we are not able to draw it as it is in all its meanderings? Everyone can experience the internal illumination which follows upon his success in formulating to himself his impressions and feelings, but only so far as he is able to formulate them. Feelings or impressions, then, pass by means of words from the obscure region of the soul into the clarity of the contemplative spirit. It is impossible to distinguish intuition from expression in this cognitive process. The one appears with the other at the same instant, because they are not two, but one.

The principal reason which makes our view appear paradoxical as we maintain it, is the illusion or prejudice that we possess a more complete intuition of reality than we really do. One often hears people say that they have many great thoughts in their minds, but that they are not able to express them. But if they really had them, they would have coined them into just so many beautiful sounding words, and thus have expressed them. If these thoughts seem to vanish or to become few and meager in the act of expressing them, the reason is that they did not exist or really were few and meager. People think that all of us ordinary men imagine and intuit countries, figures, and scenes like painters, and bodies like sculptors; save that painters and sculptors know how to paint and carve such images, while we bear them unexpressed in our souls. They believe that anyone could have imagined a Madonna of Raphael; but that Raphael was Raphael owing to his technical ability in putting the Madonna upon canvas. Nothing can be more false than this view. The world which as a rule we intuit is a small thing. It consists of little expressions, which gradually become greater and wider with the increasing spiritual concentration of certain moments. They are the words we say to ourselves, our silent judgments: "Here is a man, here is a horse, this is heavy, this is sharp, this pleases me," etc. It is a medley of light and color, with no greater pictorial value than would be expressed by a haphazard splash of colors, from among which one could barely make out a few special, distinctive traits. This and nothing else is what we possess in our ordinary life; this is the basis of our ordinary action. It is the index of a book. The labels tied to things (it has been said) take the place of the things themselves. This index and these labels (themselves expressions) suffice for small needs and small actions. From time to time we pass from the index to the book, from the label to the thing, or from the slight to the greater intuitions, and from these to the greatest and most lofty. This passage is sometimes far from easy. It has been observed by those who have best studied the psychology of artists that when, after having given a rapid glance at anyone, they attempt to obtain a real intuition of him, in order, for example, to paint his portrait, then this ordinary vision, that seemed so precise, so lively, reveals itself as little better than nothing. What remains is found to be at the most some superficial trait, which would not even suffice for a caricature. The person to be painted stands before the artist like a world to discover. Michaelangelo said, "One paints, not with the hands, but with the brain." Leonardo shocked the prior of the Convent of the Graces by standing for days together gazing at the "Last Supper," without touching it with the brush. He remarked of this attitude: "The minds of men of lofty genius are most active in invention when they are doing the least external work." The painter is a painter because he sees what others only feel or catch a glimpse of, but do not see. We think we see a smile, but in reality we have only a vague impression of it, we do not perceive all the characteristic traits of which it is the sum, as the painter discovers them after he has worked upon them and is thus able to fix them on the canvas. We do not intuitively possess more even of our intimate friend, who is with us every day and at all hours, than at most certain traits of physiognomy which enable us to distinguish him from others. The illusion is less easy as regards musical expression; because it would seem strange to everyone to say that the composer had added or attached notes to a motive which was already in the mind of him who is not the composer; as if Beethoven's Ninth Symphony were not his own intuition and his intuition the Ninth Symphony. Now, just as one who is deluded as to the amount of his material wealth is confuted by arithmetic, which states its exact amount, so he who nourishes delusions as to the wealth of his own thoughts and images is brought back to reality, when he is obliged to cross the *Pons Asinorum*[3] of expression. Let us say to the former, count; to the latter, speak; or, here is a pencil, draw, express yourself.

Each of us, as a matter of fact, has in him a little of the poet, of the sculptor, of the musician, of the painter, of the prose writer: but how little, as compared with those who bear those names, just because they possess the most universal dispositions and energies of human nature in so lofty a degree! How little too does a painter possess of the intuitions of a poet! And how little does one painter possess those of another painter! Nevertheless, that little is all our actual patrimony of intuitions or representations. Beyond these are only impressions, sensations, feelings, impulses, emotions, or whatever else one may term what still falls short of the spirit and is not assimilated by man; something postulated for the convenience of exposition, while actually nonexistent, since to exist also is a fact of the spirit.

We may thus add this to the various verbal descriptions of intuition, noted at the beginning: intuitive knowledge is expressive knowledge. Independent and autonomous in respect to intellectual function; indifferent to later empirical discriminations, to reality and to unreality, to formations and apperceptions of space and time, which are also later: intuition or representation is distinguished as *form* from what is felt and suffered, from the flux or wave of sensation, or from psychic matter; and this form, this taking possession, is expression. To intuit is to express, and nothing else (nothing more, but nothing less) than to *express*.

3. The geometrical proposition that if a triangle has two of its sides equal, the angles opposite these sides will also be equal: so named ("the bridge of asses") from the difficulty experienced by beginners in mastering it.

JOHN SELDEN
The Measure of Things

We measure from ourselves; and as things are for our use and purpose, so we approve them. Bring a pear to the table that is rotten, we cry it down, 'tis naught; but bring a medlar that is rotten, and 'tis a fine thing; and yet I'll warrant you the pear thinks as well of itself as the medlar[1] does.

We measure the excellency of other men by some excellency we conceive to be in ourselves. Nash, a poet, poor enough (as poets use to be), seeing an alderman with his gold chain, upon his great horse, by way of scorn said to one of his companions, "Do you see yon fellow, how goodly, how big he looks? Why, that fellow cannot make a blank verse."

Nay, we measure the goodness of God from ourselves; we measure his goodness, his justice, his wisdom, by something we call just, good, or wise in ourselves; and in so doing, we judge proportionally to the country-fellow in the play, who said, if he were King, he would live like a lord, and have peas and bacon every day, and a whip that cried Slash.

---

1. The medlar, a fruit like the crab apple, becomes edible only after it begins to decay.

QUESTIONS

1. What pattern of parallels do you discern among the three parts of Selden's statement? How does this principle of structure enforce the thesis he is setting forth?
2. Can the three paragraphs be rearranged without damage? Explain. What principle or principles appear to govern the present arrangement? Does it imply anything about value? About the kind of universe in which Selden conceives man to live?
3. Consider the three desires of the country fellow who would be king. Has Selden arranged these desires in any particular order? If so, what relation does that order bear to the order of the whole statement?

FRANCIS BACON
The Idols of the Mind[1]

There are four classes of idols which beset men's minds. To these for distinction's sake I have assigned names—calling the first class *Idols of the Tribe*; the second, *Idols of the Cave*; the third, *Idols of the Market-place*; the fourth, *Idols of the Theater*.

* * *

The Idols of the Tribe have their foundation in human nature itself, and in the tribe or race of men. For it is a false assertion that the sense of man is the measure of things. On the contrary, all perceptions, as well of the sense as of the mind, are according to the measure of the individual and not according to the measure of the universe. And the human understanding is like a false mirror, which, receiving rays irregularly, distorts and discolors the nature of things by mingling its own nature with it.

The Idols of the Cave are the idols of the individual man. For everyone (besides the errors common to human nature in general) has a cave or den of his own, which refracts and discolors the light of nature; owing either to his own proper and peculiar nature or to his education and conversation with others; or to the reading of books, and the authority of those whom he esteems and admires; or to the differences of impressions, accordingly as they take place in a mind preoccupied and predisposed or in a mind indifferent and settled; or the like * * *

There are also idols formed by the intercourse and association of men with each other, which I call Idols of the Market-place, on account of the commerce and consort of men there. For it is by discourse that men associate; and words are imposed according to the apprehension of the vulgar. And therefore the ill and unfit choice of words wonderfully obstructs the understanding. Nor do the definitions or explanations wherewith in some things learned men are wont to guard and defend themselves, by any means set the matter right. But words plainly force and overrule the understanding, and throw all into confusion, and lead men away into numberless empty controversies and idle fancies.

Lastly, there are idols which have immigrated into men's minds from the various dogmas of philosophies, and also from wrong laws of demonstration. These I call Idols of the Theater; because in my

1. This selection comes from Bacon's *Novum Organum (New Instrument)*, the work that in a series of apothegms describes the method by which man is to achieve universal knowledge. The source of knowledge, says Bacon, is experience; the method, induction, the reasoning from particulars to generalities. But our inductions are confused by the false images or *idols* which beset our minds.

judgment all the received systems[2] are but so many stage-plays, representing worlds of their own creation after an unreal and scenic fashion. Nor is it only of the systems now in vogue, or only of the ancient sects and philosophies, that I speak: for many more plays of the same kind may yet be composed and in like artificial manner set forth; seeing that errors the most widely different have nevertheless causes for the most part alike. Neither again do I mean this only of entire systems, but also of many principles and axioms in science, which by tradition, credulity, and negligence have come to be received.

But of these several kinds of idols I must speak more largely and exactly, that the understanding may be duly cautioned.

The human understanding is of its own nature prone to suppose the existence of more order and regularity in the world than it finds. And though there be many things in nature which are singular and unmatched, yet it devises for them parallels and conjugates and relatives which do not exist. Hence the fiction that all celestial bodies move in perfect circles * * *

The human understanding when it has once adopted an opinion (either as being the received opinion or as being agreeable to itself) draws all things else to support and agree with it. And though there be a greater number and weight of instances to be found on the other side, yet these it either neglects and despises, or else by some distinction sets aside and rejects; in order that by this great and pernicious predetermination the authority of its former conclusions may remain inviolate. And therefore it was a good answer that was made by one who when they showed him hanging in a temple a picture of those who had paid their vows as having escaped shipwreck, and would have him say whether he did not now acknowledge the power of the gods —"Aye," asked he again, "but where are they painted that were drowned after their vows?" And such is the way of all superstition, whether in astrology, dreams, omens, divine judgments, or the like; wherein men, having a delight in such vanities, mark the events where they are fulfilled, but where they fail, though this happen much oftener, neglect and pass them by. But with far more subtlety does this mischief insinuate itself into philosophy and the sciences; in which the first conclusion colors and brings into conformity with itself all that come after, though far sounder and better. Besides, independently of that delight and vanity which I have described, it is the peculiar and perpetual error of the human intellect to be more moved and excited by affirmatives than by negatives; whereas it ought properly to hold itself indifferently disposed towards both alike. Indeed in the establishment of any true axiom, the negative instance is the more forcible of the two.

The human understanding is moved by those things most which

2. Philosophical systems.

strike and enter the mind simultaneously and suddenly, and so fill the imagination; and then it feigns and supposes all other things to be somehow, though it cannot see how, similar to those few things by which it is surrounded. But for that going to and fro to remote and heterogeneous instances, by which axioms are tried as in the fire, the intellect is altogether slow and unfit, unless it be forced thereto by severe laws and overruling authority.

The human understanding is unquiet; it cannot stop or rest, and still presses onward, but in vain. Therefore it is that we cannot conceive of any end or limit to the world; but always as of necessity it occurs to us that there is something beyond. Neither again can it be conceived how eternity has flowed down to the present day: for that distinction which is commonly received of infinity in time past and in time to come can by no means hold; for it would thence follow that one infinity is greater than another, and the infinity is wasting away and tending to become finite. The like subtlety arises touching the infinite divisibility of lines, from the same inability of thought to stop. But this inability interferes more mischievously in the discovery of causes: for although the most general principles in nature ought to be held merely positive, as they are discovered, and cannot with truth be referred to a cause; nevertheless the human understanding being unable to rest still seeks something prior in the order of nature. And then it is that in struggling towards that which is further off it falls back upon that which is more nigh at hand—namely, on final causes[3]; which have relation clearly to the nature of man rather than to the nature of the universe, and from this source have strangely defined philosophy. But he is no less an unskilled and shallow philosopher who seeks causes of that which is most general, than he who in things subordinate and subaltern omits to do so.

The human understanding is no dry light, but receives an infusion from the will and affections[4]; whence proceed sciences which may be called "sciences as one would." For what a man had rather were true he more readily believes. Therefore he rejects difficult things from impatience of research; sober things, because they narrow hope; the deeper things of nature, from superstition; the light of experience, from arrogance and pride, lest his mind should seem to be occupied with things mean and transitory; things not commonly believed, out of deference to the opinion of the vulgar. Numberless in short are the ways, and sometimes imperceptible, in which the affections color and infect the understanding.

But by far the greatest hindrance and aberration of the human understanding proceeds from the dullness, incompetency, and deceptions of the senses; in that things which strike the sense outweigh things which do not immediately strike it, though they be more important. Hence it is that speculation commonly ceases

3. Roughly, the purposes of God.   4. Partialities, prejudices.

where sight ceases, insomuch that of things invisible there is little or no observation. * * * So again the essential nature of our common air, and of all bodies less dense than air (which are very many), is almost unknown. For the sense by itself is a thing infirm and erring; neither can instruments for enlarging or sharpening the senses do much: but all the truer kind of interpretation of nature is effected by instances and experiments fit and apposite; wherein the sense decides touching the experiment only, and the experiment touching the point in nature and the thing itself.

The human understanding is of its own nature prone to abstractions and gives a substance and reality to things which are fleeting. But to resolve nature into abstractions is less to our purpose than to dissect her into parts; as did the school of Democritus, which went further into nature than the rest. Matter rather than forms[5] should be the object of our attention, its configurations and changes of configuration, and simple action, and law of action or motion; for forms are figments of the human mind, unless you will call those laws of action forms.

Such then are the idols which I call *Idols of the Tribe*; and which take their rise either from the homogeneity of the substance of the human spirit, or from its preoccupation, or from its narrowness, or from its restless motion, or from an infusion of the affections, or from the incompetency of the senses, or from the mode of impression.

The *Idols of the Cave* take their rise in the peculiar constitution, mental or bodily, of each individual; and also in education, habit, and accident. Of this kind there is a great number and variety; but I will instance those the pointing out of which contains the most important caution, and which have most effect in disturbing the clearness of the understanding.

Men become attached to certain particular sciences and speculations, either because they fancy themselves the authors and inventors thereof, or because they have bestowed the greatest pains upon them and become most habituated to them. But men of this kind, if they betake themselves to philosophy and contemplations of a general character, distort and color them in obedience to their former fancies; a thing especially to be noticed in Aristotle, who made his natural philosophy a mere bondservant to his logic, thereby rendering it contentious and well nigh useless. * * *

There is one principal and as it were radical distinction between different minds, in respect of philosophy and the sciences; which is this: that some minds are stronger and apter to mark the differences of things, others to mark their resemblances. The steady and acute mind can fix its contemplations and dwell and fasten on the subtlest

5. The *form* of a thing is its idea or essential nature, as distinguished from its *matter*.

distinctions; the lofty and discursive mind recognizes and puts together the finest and most general resemblances. Both kinds however easily err in excess, by catching the one at gradations the other at shadows.

There are found some minds given to an extreme admiration of antiquity, others to an extreme love and appetite for novelty; but few so duly tempered that they can hold the mean, neither carping at what has been well laid down by the ancients, nor despising what is well introduced by the moderns. This however turns to the great injury of the sciences and philosophy; since these affectations of antiquity and novelty are the humors of partisans rather than judgments; and truth is to be sought for not in the felicity of any age, which is an unstable thing, but in the light of nature and experience, which is eternal. These factions therefore must be abjured, and care must be taken that the intellect be not hurried by them into assent.

Contemplations of nature and of bodies in their simple form break up and distract the understanding, while contemplations of nature and bodies in their composition and configuration overpower and dissolve the understanding: a distinction well seen in the school of Leucippus and Democritus as compared with the other philosophies. For that school is so busied with the particles that it hardly attends to the structure; while the others are so lost in admiration of the structure that they do not penetrate to the simplicity of nature. These kinds of contemplation should therefore be alternated and taken by turns; that so the understanding may be rendered at once penetrating and comprehensive, and the inconveniences above mentioned, with the idols which proceed from them, may be avoided.

Let such then be our provision and contemplative prudence for keeping off and dislodging the Idols of the Cave, which grow for the most part either out of the predominance of a favorite subject, or out of an excessive tendency to compare or to distinguish, or out of partiality for particular ages, or out of the largeness or minuteness of the objects contemplated. And generally let every student of nature take this as a rule—that whatever his mind seizes and dwells upon with peculiar satisfaction is to be held in suspicion, and that so much the more care is to be taken in dealing with such questions to keep the understanding even and clear.

But the *Idols of the Market-place* are the most troublesome of all: idols which have crept into the understanding through the alliances of words and names. For men believe that their reason governs words; but it is also true that words react on the understanding; and this it is that has rendered philosophy and the sciences sophistical and inactive. Now words, being commonly framed and applied according to the capacity of the vulgar, follow those lines of division which are most obvious to the vulgar understanding. And whenever an understanding of greater acuteness or a more diligent observation would alter those lines to suit the true divisions of nature, words stand in the way and resist the change. Whence it comes to pass that the high and formal discussions of learned men end oftentimes in disputes about words and names; with which (according to the use and wisdom of the mathematicians) it would be more prudent to begin, and so by means of definitions reduce them to order. Yet even definitions cannot cure this evil in dealing with natural and material things; since the definitions themselves consist of words, and those words beget others: so that it is necessary to recur to individual instances, and those in due series and order; as I shall say presently when I come to the method and scheme for the formation of notions and axioms.

The idols imposed by words on the understanding are of two kinds. They are either names of things which do not exist (for as there are things left unnamed through lack of observation, so likewise are there names which result from fantastic suppositions and to which nothing in reality corresponds), or they are names of things which exist, but yet confused and ill-defined, and hastily and irregularly derived from realities.

* * *

Idols of the Theater, or *of Systems*, are many, and there can be and perhaps will be yet many more. For were it not that now for many ages men's minds have been busied with religion and theology; and were it not that civil governments, especially monarchies, have been averse to such novelties, even in matters speculative; so that men labor therein to the peril and harming of their fortunes —not only unrewarded, but exposed also to contempt and envy: doubtless there would have arisen many other philosophical sects like to those which in great variety flourished once among the Greeks. For as on the phenomena of the heavens many hypotheses may be constructed, so likewise (and more also) many various dogmas may be set up and established on the phenomena of philosophy. And in the plays of this philosophical theater you may observe the same thing which is found in the theater of the poets, that stories invented for the stage are more compact and elegant, and more as one would wish them to be, than true stories out of history.

In general however there is taken for the material of philosophy either a great deal out of a few things, or a very little out of many things; so that on both sides philosophy is based on too narrow a foundation of experiment and natural history, and decides on the authority of too few cases. For the rational school of philosophers snatches from experience a variety of common instances, neither duly ascertained nor diligently examined and weighed, and leaves all the rest to meditation and agitation of wit.

There is also another class of philosophers, who having bestowed much diligent and careful labor on a few experiments, have thence made bold to educe and construct systems; wresting all other facts in a strange fashion to conformity therewith.

And there is yet a third class, consisting of those who out of faith and veneration mix their philosophy with theology and traditions; among whom the vanity of some has gone so far aside as to seek the origin of science among spirits and genii. So that this parent stock of errors—this false philosophy—is of three kinds; the *sophistical*, the *empirical*, and the *superstitious*.

BENJAMIN FRANKLIN
The Convenience of Being "Reasonable"[1]

I believe I have omitted mentioning that, in my first voyage from Boston, being becalmed off Block Island, our people set about catching cod, and hauled up a great many. Hitherto I had stuck to my resolution of not eating animal food, and on this occasion I considered, with my master Tryon, the taking every fish as a kind of unprovoked murder, since none of them had, or ever could do us any injury that might justify the slaughter. All this seemed very reasonable. But I had formerly been a great lover of fish, and, when this came hot out of the frying-pan, it smelled admirably well. I balanced some time between principle and inclination, till I recollected that, when the fish were opened, I saw smaller fish taken out of their stomachs; then thought I, "if you eat one another, I don't see why we mayn't eat you." So I dined upon cod very heartily, and continued to eat with other people, returning only now and then occasionally to a vegetable diet. So convenient a thing it is to be a *reasonable creature*, since it enables one to find or make a reason for everything one has a mind to do.

1. From the *Autobiography*.

WILLIAM MARCH
The Dog and Her Rival

A dog who had been greatly loved by her master found her life less pleasant after he married. She came one night to talk things over with the mare and said, "I wish them both happiness. Perhaps it would be better if I went away, because it must grieve my master to see the way his wife humiliates me all day long."

The mare thought that would be a sensible thing to do, but the dog sighed, shook her head, and continued. "No, that would never work out, because if I disappeared without a word, the uncertainty of my fate would break my master's heart; and, besides, that wife of his would make him believe I was fickle and had abandoned him, and he'd never know how much I had suffered or how great my love was. On second thought, it might be even simpler if I took poison and died on his doorstep. That I think would be the noblest thing to do, the final proof of my love."

The mare said that such renunciation seemed a generous gesture indeed, and the dog lifted her head and stared at the moon. "I'd do it, too," she said; "I'd kill myself on my master's doorstep if only I could hear his pleas for forgiveness when he finds my body, or see him beating his worthless wife for having driven me to such an end."

Love can be the most dreadful disguise that hate assumes.

BERTRAND RUSSELL
On the Nature of Truth and Falsehood

The question "What is Truth?" is one which may be understood in several different ways, and before beginning our search for an answer, it will be well to be quite clear as to the sense in which we are asking the question. We may mean to ask what things are true: Is science true? Is revealed religion true? and so on. But before we can answer such questions as these, we ought to be able to say what these questions *mean*: what is it, exactly, that we are asking when we say, "Is science true?" It is this preliminary question that I wish to discuss. The question whether this or that is true is to be settled, if at all, by considerations concerning this or that, not by general considerations as to what "truth" means; but those who ask the question presumably have in their minds already some idea as to what "truth" means, otherwise the question and its answer could have no definite meaning to them.

When, however, we have agreed that the question we are concerned with is "What does 'truth' mean?" we have by no means come to an end of possible ambiguities. There is the question "How is the word 'truth' properly used?" This is a question for the dictionary, not for philosophy. Moreover, the word has some perfectly proper uses which are obviously irrelevant to our inquiry: a "true" man, a "true" poet, are "true" in a different sense from that with which we are concerned. Again, there is the question "What do people usually have in mind when they use the word 'truth'?" This question comes nearer to the question we have to ask, but is still different from it. The question what idea people have when they use a word is a question of psychology; moreover, there is very little in common between the ideas which two different people in fact attach to the same word, though there would often be more agreement as to the ideas which they would consider it proper to attach to the word.

The question we have to discuss may be explained by pointing out that, in the case of such a word as "truth," we all feel that some fundamental concept, of great philosophical importance, is involved, though it is difficult to be clear as to what this concept is. What we wish to do is to detach this concept from the mass of irrelevancies in which, when we use it, it is normally embedded, and to bring clearly before the mind the abstract opposition upon which our distinction of true and false depends. The process to be gone through is essentially one of analysis: we have various complex and more or less confused beliefs about the true and the false, and we have to reduce these to forms which are simple and clear, without causing any avoidable conflict between our initial complex and confused beliefs and our final simple and clear assertions. These final assertions are to be tested partly by their intrinsic evidence, partly by their power of accounting for the "data"; and the "data," in such a problem, are the complex and confused beliefs with which we start. These beliefs must necessarily suffer a change in becoming clear, but the change should not be greater than is warranted by their initial confusion.

Although the question what things are true rather than false does not form part of our inquiry, yet it will be useful to consider for a moment the nature of the things to which we attribute either truth or falsehood. Broadly speaking, the things that are true or false, in the sense with which we are concerned, are statements, and beliefs or judgments.[1] When, for example, we see the sun shining, the sun itself is not "true," but the judgment "the sun is shining" is true. The truth or falsehood of statements can be defined in terms of the truth or falsehood of beliefs. A statement is true when a person who believes it believes truly, and false when a person who believes it believes falsely. Thus in considering the nature of truth we may confine ourselves to the truth of beliefs, since the truth of statements is a notion derived from that of beliefs. The question we have to discuss is therefore: What is the difference between a true belief and a false belief? By this I mean, What is the difference which actually *constitutes* the truth or falsehood of a belief? I am not asking for what is called a *criterion* of truth, i.e. for some quality, other than truth, which belongs to whatever is true and to nothing else. This distinction between the

---

1. I shall use the words "belief" and "judgment" as synonyms [Russell's note].

nature of truth and a *criterion* of truth is important, and has not always been sufficiently emphasized by philosophers. A criterion is a sort of trademark, i.e. some comparatively obvious characteristic which is a guarantee of genuineness. "None genuine without the label": thus the label is what assures us that such and such a firm made the article. But when we say that such and such a firm made the article we do not *mean* that the article has the right label; thus there is a difference between meaning and criterion. Indeed, it is just this difference which makes a criterion useful. Now I do not believe that truth has, universally, any such trademark: I do not believe that there is any one label by which we can always know that a judgment is true rather than false. But this is not the question which I wish to discuss: I wish to discuss what truth and falsehood actually are, not what extraneous marks they have by which we can recognize them.

The first point upon which it is important to be clear is the relation of truth and falsehood to the mind. If we were right in saying that the things that are true or false are always judgments, then it is plain that there can be no truth or falsehood unless there are minds to judge. Nevertheless it is plain, also, that the truth or falsehood of a given judgment depends in no way upon the person judging, but solely upon the facts about which he judges. If I judge that Charles I died in his bed, I judge falsely, not because of anying to do with me, but because in fact he did not die in his bed. Similarly, if I judge that he died on the scaffold, I judge truly, because of an event which in fact occurred 260 years ago. Thus the truth or falsehood of a judgment always has an objective ground, and it is natural to ask whether there are not objective truths and falsehoods which are the objects, respectively, of true and false judgments. As regards truths, this view is highly plausible. But as regards falsehoods, it is the very reverse of plausible; yet, as we shall see, it is hard to maintain it with regard to truths without being forced to maintain it also as regards falsehoods.

In all cognitive acts, such as believing, doubting, disbelieving, apprehending, perceiving, imagining, the mind has objects other than itself to which it stands in some one of these various relations. In such a case as perception this is sufficiently obvious: the thing perceived is necessarily something different from the act of perceiving it, and the perceiving is a relation between the person perceiving and the thing perceived. The same thing holds, though less obviously, with regard to imagination. If I imagine, say, a certain color, the color is an object before my mind just as truly as if I perceived the color, though the relation to my mind is different from what it would be if I perceived the color, and does not lead me to suppose that the color exists in the place where I imagine it. Judgments, also, consist of relations of the mind to objects. But here a distinction has to be made between two different theories as to the relation which constitutes judgment. If I judge (say) that Charles I died on the scaffold, is that a relation between me and a single "fact," namely, Charles I's death on the scaffold, or "that Charles I died on the scaffold," or is it a relation between me and Charles I and dying and the scaffold? We shall find that the possibility of false judgments compels us to adopt the latter view. But let us first examine the view that a judgment has a single object.

If every judgment, whether true or false, consists in a certain relation, called "judging" or "believing," to a single object, which is what we judge or believe, then the distinction of true and false as applied to judgments is derivative from the distinction of true and false as applied to the objects of judgments. Assuming that there are such objects, let us, following Meinong, give them the name "Objectives." Then every judgment has an objective, and true judgments have true objectives, while false judgments have false objectives. Thus the question of the meaning of truth and falsehood will have to be considered first with regard to objectives, and we shall have to find some way of dividing objectives into those that are true and those that are false. In this, however, there is great difficulty. So long as we only consider true judgments, the view that they have objectives is plausible: the actual event which we describe as "Charles I's death on the scaffold" may be regarded as the objective of the judgment "Charles I died on the scaffold." But what is the objective of the judgment "Charles I died in his bed"? There was no event such as "Charles I's death in his bed." To say that there ever was such a thing as "Charles I's death in his bed" is merely another way of saying that Charles I died in his bed. Thus, if there is an objective, it must be something other than "Charles I's death in his bed." We may take it to be "that Charles I died in his bed." We shall then have to say the same of true judgments: the objective of "Charles I died on the scaffold" will be "that Charles I died on the scaffold."

To this view there are, however, two objections. The first is that it is difficult to believe that there are such objects as "that Charles I died in his bed," or even "that Charles I died on the scaffold." It seems evident that the phrase "that so and so" has no complete meaning by itself, which would enable it to denote a definite object as, e.g. the word "Socrates" does. We feel that the phrase "that so and so" is essentially incomplete, and only acquires full significance when words are added so as to express a judgment, e.g. "I believe that so and so," "I deny that so and so," "I hope that so and so." Thus, if we can avoid regarding "that so and so" as an independent entity, we shall escape a paradox. This argument is not decisive, but it must be allowed a certain weight. The second objection is more fatal, and more germane to the consideration of truth and falsehood. If we allow that all judgments have objectives, we shall have to allow that there are objectives which are false. Thus there will be in the world entities, not dependent upon the existence of judgments, which can be described as objective falsehoods. This is in itself almost incredible: we feel that there could be no falsehood if there were no minds to make mistakes. But it has the further drawback that it leaves the difference between truth and falsehood quite inexplicable. We feel that when we judge truly some entity "corresponding" in some way to our judgment is to be found outside our judgment, while when we judge falsely there is no such "corresponding" entity. It is true we cannot take as this entity simply the grammatical subject of our judgment: if we judge, e.g. "Homer did not exist," it is obvious that Homer is not the entity which is to be found if our judgment is true, but not if it is false. Nevertheless it is difficult to abandon the view that, in some way, the truth or falsehood of a judgment depends upon the presence or absence of a "corresponding" entity of some sort. And if we do abandon this view, and adhere to the opinion that there are both true and false objectives, we shall be compelled to regard it as an ultimate and not further explicable fact that objectives are of two sorts, the true and the false. This view, though not logically impossible, is unsatisfactory, and we shall do better, if we can, to find some view which leaves the difference between truth and falsehood less of a mystery.

It might be thought that we could say simply that true judgments have objectives while false ones do not. With a new definition of objectives this view might become tenable, but it is not tenable so long as we hold to the view that judgment actually is a relation of the mind to an objective. For this view compels us, since there certainly are false judgments, and a relation cannot be a relation to nothing, to admit that false judgments as well as true ones have objectives. We must therefore abandon the view that judgments consist in a relation to a single object. We cannot maintain this view with regard to true judgments while rejecting it with regard to false ones, for that would make an intrinsic difference between true and false judgments, and enable us (what is obviously impossible) to discover the truth or falsehood of a judgment merely by examining the intrinsic nature of the judgment. Thus we must turn to the theory that *no* judgment consists in a relation to a single object.

The difficulty of the view we have been hitherto considering was that it compelled us either to admit objective falsehoods, or to admit that when we judge falsely there is nothing that we are judging. The way out of the difficulty consists in maintaining that, whether we judge truly or whether we judge falsely, there is no one thing that we are judging. When we judge that Charles I died on the scaffold, we have before us, not one object, but several objects, namely Charles I and dying and the scaffold. Similarly, when we judge that Charles I died in his bed, we have before us the objects Charles I, dying, and his bed. These objects are not fictions: they are just as good as the objects of the true judgment. We therefore escape the necessity of admitting objective falsehoods, or of admitting that in judging falsely we have nothing before the mind. Thus in this view judgment is a relation of the mind to several other terms: when these other terms have *inter se* a "corresponding" relation, the judgment is true; when not, it is false. This view, which I believe to be the correct one, must now be further expanded and explained.

In saying that judgment is a relation of the mind to several things, e.g. to Charles I and the scaffold and dying, I do not mean that the mind has a certain relation to Charles I and also has this relation to the scaffold and also has it to dying. I do not, however, wish to deny that, when we are judging, we have *a* relation to each of the constituents of our judgment separately, for it would seem that we must be in some way conscious of these constituents, so that during any judgment we must have, to each constituent of the judgment, that relation which we may call "being conscious of it." This is a very important fact, but it does not give the essence of judgment. Nothing that concerns Charles I and dying and the scaffold separately and severally will give the judgment "Charles I died on the scaffold." In order to obtain this judgment, we must have one single unity of the mind and Charles I and dying and the scaffold, i.e., we must have, not several instances of a relation between two terms, but one instance of a relation between more than two terms. Such relations, though familiar to mathematicians, have been unduly ignored by philosophers. Since they appear to me to give the key to many puzzles about truth, I shall make a short digression to show that they are common and ought to be familiar.

One of the commonest ways in which relations between more than two terms occur is in propositions about what happened at some particular time. Take such a proposition as "A loved B in May and hated him in June," and let us suppose this to be true. Then we cannot say that, apart from dates, A has to B either the relation of loving or that of hating. This necessity for a date does not arise with *all* ordinary relationships; for example, if A is the brother of B, no date is required: the relationship holds always or never, or (more strictly) holds or does not hold without regard to time. But love and hate are "time's fool": they are not relations which hold without regard to date. "A loved B in May" is a relation, not between A and B simply, but between A and B and

May.[2] This relation between A and B and May cannot be analyzed into relations between A and B, A and May, B and May: it is a single unity. It is partly the failure to perceive that the date is one of the terms in such relations which has caused such difficulty in the philosophy of time and change.

As another illustration, take the relation of jealousy. Time comes in here exactly as it did with love and hate, but we will for the moment ignore time, because the point to be noticed about jealousy is that it involves three people. The simplest possible proposition asserting jealousy is such as "A is jealous of B's love for C," or "A is jealous of B on account of C." It might be thought that "B's love for C" was one term, and A the other term. But this interpretation will not apply to cases of mistaken jealousy: if A is Othello, there is no such thing as "B's love for C." Thus this interpretation is impossible, and we are compelled to regard jealousy as a relation of three persons, i.e. as having for its unit a relation which is what we may call "triangular." If we further take into account the necessity for a date, the relation becomes "quadrangular," i.e. the simplest possible proposition involving the relation will be one which concerns four terms, namely, three people and a date.

We will give the name "*multiple* relations" to such as require more than two terms. Thus a relation is "multiple" if the simplest propositions in which it occurs are propositions involving more than two terms (not counting the relation). From what has been said it is obvious that multiple relations are common, and that many matters cannot be understood without their help. Relations which have only two terms we shall call "dual relations."

The theory of judgment which I am advocating is that judgment is not a dual relation of the mind to a single objective, but a multiple relation of the mind to the various other terms with which the judgment is concerned. Thus if I judge that A loves B, that is not a relation of me to "A's love for B," but a relation between me and A and love and B. If it were a relation of me to "A's love for B," it would be impossible unless there were such a thing as "A's love for B," i.e. unless A loved B, i.e. unless the judgment were true; but in fact false judgments are possible. When the judgment is taken as a relation between me and A and love and B, the mere fact that the judgment occurs does not involve any relation between its objects A and love and B; thus the possibility of false judgments is fully allowed for. When the judgment is true, A loves B; thus *in this case* there *is* a relation between the objects of the judgment. We may therefore state the difference between truth and falsehood as follows: Every judgment is a relation of a mind to several objects,

2. I do not want to assume any theory as to the nature of time: "May" can be interpreted as the reader likes. The statement in the text may then have to be made a little more complicated, but the necessity for a relation of more than two terms will remain [Russell's note].

one of which is a relation; the judgment is *true* when the relation which is one of the objects relates the other objects, otherwise it is false. Thus in the above illustration, love, which is a relation, is one of the objects of the judgment, and the judgment is true if love relates A and B. The above statement requires certain additions which will be made later; for the present, it is to be taken as a first approximation.

One of the merits of the above theory is that it explains the difference between judgment and perception, and the reason why perception is not liable to error as judgment is. When we were considering the theory that judgment is a dual relation of the mind to a single objective, we found that so far as true judgments were concerned this theory worked admirably, but that it would not account for false judgments. Now this difficulty will not apply against a corresponding theory of perception. It is true that there are cases where perception *appears* to be at fault, such as dreams and hallucinations. But I believe that in all these cases the perception itself is correct, and what is wrong is a judgment based upon the perception. It would take us too far from our subject to develop this theme, which requires a discussion of the relation between sense-data (i.e. the things we immediately perceive) and what we may call physical reality, i.e. what is there independently of us and our perceptions. Assuming the result of this discussion, I shall take it as agreed that perception, as opposed to judgment, is never in error, i.e. that, whenever we perceive anything, what we perceive exists, at least so long as we are perceiving it.

If the infallibility of perception is admitted, we may apply to perception the theory of the single objective which we found inapplicable to judgment. Take, for example, such a case as spatial relations. Suppose I see simultaneously on my table a knife and a book, the knife being to the left of the book. Perception presents me with a complex object, consisting of the knife and the book in certain relative positions (as well as other objects, which we may ignore). If I attend to this complex object and analyze it, I can arrive at the judgment "the knife is to the left of the book." Here the knife and the book and their spatial relation are severally before my mind; but in the perception I had the single whole "knife-to-left-of-book." Thus in perception I perceive a single complex object, while in a judgment based upon the perception I have the parts of the complex object separately though simultaneously before me. In order to perceive a complex object, such as "knife-to-left-of-book," there must be such an object, since otherwise my perception would have no object, i.e. there would not be any perceiving, since the relation of perception requires the two terms, the perceiver and the thing perceived. But if there is such an object as "knife-to-left-of-book," then the knife must be to the left of the book; hence the judgment "the knife is to the left of the book" must be true. Thus any judgment of perception, i.e. any judgment derived immediately from perception by mere analysis, must be true. (This does not enable us, in any given case, to be quite certain that such and such a judgment is true, since we may inadvertently have failed merely to analyze what was given in perception.) We see that in the case of the judgment of perception there is, corresponding to the judgment, a certain complex object which is perceived, as one complex, in the perception upon which the judgment is based. It is because there is such a complex object that the judgment is true. This complex object, in the cases where it is perceived, is the objective of the perception. Where it is not perceived, it is still the necessary and sufficient condition of the truth of the judgment. There was such a complex event as "Charles I's death on the scaffold"; hence the judgment "Charles I died on the scaffold" is true. There never was such a complex event as "Charles I's death in his bed"; hence "Charles I died in his bed" is false. If A loves B, there is such a complex object as "A's love for B," and vice versa; thus the existence of this complex object gives the condition for the truth of the judgment "A loves B." And the same holds in all other cases.

We may now attempt an exact account of the "correspondence" which constitutes truth. Let us take the judgment "A loves B." This consists of a relation of the person judging to A and love and B, i.e. to the two terms A and B and the relation "love." But the judgment is not the same as the judgment "B loves A"; thus the relation must not be abstractly before the mind, but must be before it as proceeding from A to B rather than from B to A. The "corresponding" complex object which is required to make our judgment true consists of A related to B by the relation which was before us in our judgment. We may distinguish two "senses" of a relation according as it goes from A to B or from B to A. Then the relation as it enters into the judgment must have a "sense," and in the corresponding complex it must have the same "sense." Thus the judgment that two terms have a certain relation R is a relation of the mind to the two terms and the relation R with the appropriate sense: the "corresponding" complex consists of the two terms related by the relation R with the same sense. The judgment is true when there is such a complex, and false when there is not. The same account, *mutatis mutandis,* will apply to any other judgment. This gives the definition of truth and falsehood.

We see that, according to the above account, truth and falsehood are primarily properties of judgments, and therefore there would be no truth or falsehood if there were no minds. Nevertheless, the truth or falsehood of a given judgment does not depend upon the person making it or the time when it is made, since the "corresponding" complex, upon which its truth or falsehood depends, does not contain the person judging as a constituent (except, of course, when the judgment happens to be about oneself). Thus the mixture of dependence upon mind and independence of mind, which we noticed as a characteristic of truth, is fully preserved by our theory.

The questions what things are true and what false, whether we know anything, and if so, how we come to know it, are subsequent to the question "What is truth?" and except briefly in the case of the judgment of perception, I have avoided such questions in the above discussion, not because they are of less interest, but in order to avoid confusing the issue. It is one of the reasons for the slow progress of philosophy that its fundamental questions are not, to most people, the most interesting, and therefore there is a tendency to hurry on before the foundations are secure. In order to check this tendency, it is necessary to isolate the fundamental questions, and consider them without too much regard to the later developments; and this is what, in respect of one such question, I have tried to do in the foregoing pages.

ROBERTA WOHLSTETTER

Surprise[1]

If our intelligence system and all our other channels of information failed to produce an accurate image of Japanese intentions and capabilities, it was not for want of the relevant materials. Never before have we had so complete an intelligence picture of the enemy. And perhaps never again will we have such a magnificent collection of sources at our disposal.

Retrospect

To review these sources briefly, an American cryptanalyst, Col. William F. Friedman, had broken the top-priority Japanese diplomatic code, which enabled us to listen to a large proportion of the privileged communications between Tokyo and the major Japanese embassies throughout the world. Not only did we know in advance how the Japanese ambassadors in Washington were advised, and how much they were instructed to say, but we also were listening to top-secret messages on the Tokyo-Berlin and Tokyo-Rome circuits, which gave us information vital for conduct of the war in the Atlantic and Europe. In the Far East this source provided minute details on movements connected with the Japanese program of expansion into Southeast Asia.

1. This selection is the seventh and final chapter in the author's *Pearl Harbor: Warning and Decision*.

Besides the strictly diplomatic codes, our cryptanalysts also had some success in reading codes used by Japanese agents in major American and foreign ports. Those who were on the distribution list for MAGIC[2] had access to much of what these agents were reporting to Tokyo and what Tokyo was demanding of them in the Panama Canal Zone, in cities along the east and west coasts of the Americas from northern Canada as far south as Brazil, and in ports throughout the Far East, including the Philippines and the Hawaiian Islands. They could determine what installations, what troop and ship movements, and what alert and defense measures were of interest to Tokyo at these points on the globe, as well as approximately how much correct information her agents were sending her.

Our naval leaders also had at their disposal the results of radio traffic analysis. While before the war our naval radio experts could not read the content of any Japanese naval or military coded messages, they were able to deduce from a study of intercepted ship call signs the composition and location of the Japanese Fleet units. After a change in call signs, they might lose sight of some units, and units that went into port in home waters were also lost because the ships in port used frequencies that our radios were unable to intercept. Most of the time, however, our traffic analysts had the various Japanese Fleet units accurately pinpointed on our naval maps.

Extremely competent on-the-spot economic and political analysis was furnished by Ambassador Grew and his staff in Tokyo. Ambassador Grew was himself a most sensitive and accurate observer, as evidenced by his dispatches to the State Department. His observations were supported and supplemented with military detail by frequent reports from American naval attachés and observers in key Far Eastern ports. Navy Intelligence had men with radio equipment located along the coast of China, for example, who reported the convoy movements toward Indochina. There were also naval observers stationed in various high-tension areas in Thailand and Indochina who could fill in the local outlines of Japanese political intrigue and military planning. In Tokyo and other Japanese cities, it is true, Japanese censorship grew more and more rigid during 1941, until Ambassador Grew felt it necessary to disclaim any responsibility for noting or reporting overt military evidence of an imminent outbreak of war. This careful Japanese censorship naturally cut down visual confirmation of the decoded information but very probably never achieved the opaqueness of Russia's Iron Curtain.

During this period the data and interpretations of British intelligence were also available to American officers in Washington and the Far East, though the British and Americans tended to distrust each other's privileged information.

2. The name given to information obtained from decoded Japanese diplomatic dispatches.

In addition to secret sources, there were some excellent public ones. Foreign correspondents for *The New York Times,* the *Herald Tribune,* and the Washington *Post* were stationed in Tokyo and Shanghai and in Canberra, Australia. Their reporting as well as their predictions on the Japanese political scene were on a very high level. Frequently their access to news was more rapid and their judgment of its significance as reliable as that of our Intelligence officers. This was certainly the case for 1940 and most of 1941. For the last weeks before the Pearl Harbor strike, however, the public newspaper accounts were not very useful. It was necessary to have secret information in order to know what was happening. Both Tokyo and Washington exercised very tight control over leaks during this crucial period, and the newsmen accordingly had to limit their accounts to speculation and notices of diplomatic meetings with no exact indication of the content of the diplomatic exchanges.

The Japanese press was another important public source. During 1941 it proclaimed with increasing shrillness the Japanese government's determination to pursue its program of expansion into Southeast Asia and the desire of the military to clear the Far East of British and American colonial exploitation. This particular source was rife with explicit signals of aggressive intent.

Finally, an essential part of the intelligence picture for 1941 was both public and privileged information on American policy and activities in the Far East. During the year the pattern of action and interaction between the Japanese and American governments grew more and more complex. At the last, it became especially important for anyone charged with the responsibility of ordering an alert to know what moves the American government was going to make with respect to Japan, as well as to try to guess what Japan's next move would be, since Japan's next move would respond in part to ours. Unfortunately our military leaders, and especially our Intelligence officers, were sometimes as surprised as the Japanese at the moves of the White House and the State Department. They usually had more orderly anticipations about Japanese policy and conduct than they had about America's. On the other hand, it was also true that State Department and White House officials were handicapped in judging Japanese intentions and estimates of risk by an inadequate picture of our own military vulnerability.

All of the public and private sources of information mentioned were available to America's political and military leaders in 1941. It is only fair to remark, however, that no single person or agency ever had at any given moment all the signals existing in this vast information network. The signals lay scattered in a number of different agencies; some were decoded, some were not; some traveled through rapid channels of communication, some were blocked by technical or procedural delays; some never reached a center of decision. But it is legitimate to review again the general sort of picture that emerged during the first week of December from the signals readily at hand. Anyone close to President Roosevelt was likely to have before him the following significant fragments.

There was first of all a picture of gathering troop and ship movements down the China coast and into Indochina. The large dimensions of this movement to the south were established publicly and visually as well as by analysis of ship call signs. Two changes in Japanese naval call signs—one on November 1 and another on December 1—had also been evaluated by Naval Intelligence as extremely unusual and as signs of major preparations for some sort of Japanese offensive. The two changes had interfered with the speed of American radio traffic analysis. Thousands of interceptions after December 1 were necessary before the new call signs could be read. Partly for this reason American radio analysts disagreed about the locations of the Japanese carriers. One group held that all the carriers were near Japan because they had not been able to identify a carrier call sign since the middle of November. Another group believed that they had located one carrier division in the Marshalls. The probability seemed to be that the carriers, wherever they were, had gone into radio silence; and past experience led the analysts to believe that they were therefore in waters near the Japanese homeland, where they could communicate with each other on wavelengths that we could not intercept. However, our inability to locate the carriers exactly, combined with the two changes in call signs, was itself a danger signal.

Our best secret source, MAGIC, was confirming the aggressive intention of the new military cabinet in Tokyo, which had replaced the last moderate cabinet on October 17. In particular, MAGIC provided details of some of the preparations for the move into Southeast Asia. Running counter to this were increased troop shipments to the Manchurian border in October. (The intelligence picture is never clear-cut.) But withdrawals had begun toward the end of that month. MAGIC also carried explicit instructions to the Japanese ambassadors in Washington to pursue diplomatic negotiations with the United States with increasing energy, but at the same time it announced a deadline for the favorable conclusion of the negotiations, first for November 25, later postponed until November 29. In case of diplomatic failure by that date, the Japanese ambassadors were told, Japanese patience would be exhausted, Japan was determined to pursue her Greater East Asia policy, and on November 29 "things" would automatically begin to happen.

On November 26 Secretary Hull rejected Japan's latest bid for American approval of her policies in China and Indochina. MAGIC had repeatedly characterized this Japanese overture as the "last," and it now revealed the ambassadors' reaction of consternation and despair over the American refusal and also their country's characterization of the American Ten Point Note as an "ultimatum."

On the basis of this collection of signals, Army and Navy Intelligence experts in Washington tentatively placed D-day *for the Japanese Southeastern campaign* during the week end of November 30, and when this failed to materialize, during the week end of December 7. They also compiled an accurate list of probable British and Dutch targets and included the Philippines and Guam as possible American targets.

Also available in this mass of information, but long forgotten, was a rumor reported by Ambassador Grew in January, 1941. It came from what was regarded as a not-very-reliable source, the Peruvian embassy, and stated that the Japanese were preparing a surprise air attack on Pearl Harbor. Curiously the date of the report is coincident roughly with what we now know to have been the date of inception of Yamamoto's plan; but the rumor was labeled by everyone, including Ambassador Grew, as quite fantastic and the plan as absurdly impossible. American judgment was consistent with Japanese judgment at this time, since Yamamoto's plan was in direct contradition to Japanese naval tactical doctrine.

Perspective

On the basis of this rapid recapitulation of the highlights in the signal picture, it is apparent that our decisionmakers had at hand an impressive amount of information on the enemy. They did not have the complete list of targets, since none of the last-minute estimates included Pearl Harbor. They did not know the exact hour and date for opening the attack. They did not have an accurate knowledge of Japanese capabilities or of Japanese ability to accept very high risks. The crucial question then, we repeat, is, If we could enumerate accurately the British and Dutch targets and give credence to a Japanese attack against them either on November 30 or December 7, why were we not expecting a specific danger to *ourselves?* And by the word "expecting," we mean expecting in the sense of taking specific alert actions to meet the contingencies of attack by land, sea, or air.

There are several answers to this question that have become apparent in the course of this study. First of all, it is much easier *after* the event to sort the relevant from the irrelevant signals. After the event, of course, a signal is always crystal clear; we can now see what disaster it was signaling, since the disaster has occurred. But before the event it is obscure and pregnant with conflicting meanings. It comes to the observer embedded in an atmosphere of "noise," *i.e.,* in the company of all sorts of information that is useless and irrelevant for predicting the particular disaster. For example, in Washington, Pearl Harbor signals were competing with a vast number of signals from the European theater. These European signals announced danger from the European theater. These European signals announced danger more frequently and more specifically than any coming from the Far East. The Far Eastern signals were also arriving at a center of decision where they had to compete with the prevailing belief that an unprotected offensive force acts as a deterrent rather than a target. In Honolulu they were competing *not* with signals from the European theater, but rather with a large number of signals announcing Japanese intentions and preparations to attack Soviet Russia rather than to move southward; here they were also competing with expectations of local sabotage prepared by previous alert situations.

In short, we failed to anticipate Pearl Harbor not for want of the relevant materials, but because of a plethora of irrelevant ones. Much of the appearance of wanton neglect that emerged in various investigations of the disaster resulted from the unconscious suppression of vast congeries of signs pointing in every direction except Pearl Harbor. It was difficult later to recall these signs since they had led nowhere. Signals that are characterized today as absolutely unequivocal warnings of surprise air attack on Pearl Harbor become, on analysis in the context of December, 1941, not merely ambiguous but occasionally inconsistent with such an attack. To recall one of the most controversial and publicized examples, the winds code,[3] both General Short and Admiral Kimmel testified that if they had had this information, they would have been prepared on the morning of December 7 for an air attack from without. The messages establishing the winds code are often described in the Pearl Harbor literature as Tokyo's declaration of war against America. If they indeed amounted to such a declaration, obviously the failure to inform Honolulu of this vital news would have been criminal negligence. On examination, however, the messages proved to be instructions for code communication after normal commercial channels had been cut. In one message the recipient was instructed on receipt of an execute to destroy all remaining codes in his possession. In another version the recipient was warned that the execute would be sent out "when relations are becoming dangerous" between Japan and three other countries. There was a different code term for each country: England, America, and the Soviet Union.

There is no evidence that an authentic execute of either message was ever intercepted by the United States before December 7. The message ordering code destruction was in any case superseded by a much more explicit code-destruction order from Tokyo that was intercepted on December 2 and translated on December 3. After December 2, the receipt of a winds-code execute for code destruction would therefore have added nothing new to our information, and

3. A Japanese code which, by means of specious weather information inserted in the daily Japanese-language short-wave news broadcast, signaled danger-ously deteriorated diplomatic relations between Japan and the United States, the USSR, or Great Britain.

code destruction in itself cannot be taken as an unambiguous sub-
titute for a formal declaration of war. During the first week of
December the United States ordered all American consulates in the
Far East to destroy all American codes, yet no one has attempted to
prove that this order was equivalent to an American declaration of
war against Japan. As for the other winds-code message, provided an
execute had been received warning that relations were dangerous
between Japan and the United States, there would still have been no
way on the basis of this signal alone to determine whether Tokyo was
signaling Japanese intent to attack the United States or Japanese fear
of an American surprise attack (in reprisal for Japanese aggressive
moves against American allies in the Far East). It was only after the
event that "dangerous relations" could be interpreted as "surprise
air attack on Pearl Harbor."

There is a difference, then, between having a signal available somewhere in the heap of irrelevancies, and perceiving it as a warning;
and there is also a difference between perceiving it as a warning, and
acting or getting action on it. These distinctions, simple as they are,
illuminate the obscurity shrouding this moment in history.

Many instances of these distinctions have been examined in the
course of this study. We shall recall a few of the most dramatic now.
To illustrate the difference between having and perceiving a signal,
let us return to Colonel Fielder.[4] * * * Though he was an untrained
and inexperienced Intelligence officer, he headed Army Intelligence
at Pearl Harbor at the time of the attack. He had been on the job
for only four months, and he regarded as quite satisfactory his sources
of information and his contacts with the Navy locally and with Army
Intelligence in Washington. Evidently he was unaware that Army
Intelligence in Washington was not allowed to send him any "action"
or policy information, and he was therefore not especially concerned
about trying to read beyond the obvious meaning of any given communication that came under his eyes. Colonel Bratton, head of Army
Far Eastern Intelligence in Washington, however, had a somewhat
more realistic view of the extent of Colonel Fielder's knowledge.
At the end of November, Colonel Bratton had learned about the
winds-code setup and was also apprised that the naval traffic analysis
unit under Commander Rochefort in Honolulu was monitoring 24
hours a day for an execute. He was understandably worried about the
lack of communication between this unit and Colonel Fielder's office, and by December 5 he finally felt that the matter was urgent
enough to warrant sending a message directly to Colonel Fielder
about the winds code. Now any information on the winds code, since
it belonged to the highest classification of secret information, and
since it was therefore automatically evaluated as "action" information, could not be sent through normal G-2 channels. Colonel Brat-

4. An officer discussed earlier in the book.

ton had to figure out another way to get the information to Colonel Fielder. He sent this message: "Contact Commander Rochefort immediately thru Commandant Fourteenth Naval District regarding broadcasts from Tokyo reference weather." Signal Corps records establish that Colonel Fielder received this message. How did he react to it? He filed it. According to his testimony in 1945, it made no impression on him and he did not attempt to see Rochefort. He could not sense any urgency behind the lines because he was not expecting immediate trouble, and his expectations determined what he read. A warning signal was available to him, but he did not perceive it.

Colonel Fielder's lack of experience may make this example seem to be an exception. So let us recall the performance of Captain Wilkinson, the naval officer who headed the Office of Naval Intelligence in Washington in the fall of 1941 and who is unanimously acclaimed for a distinguished and brilliant career. His treatment of a now-famous Pearl Harbor signal does not sound much different in the telling. After the event, the signal in question was labeled "the bomb-plot message." It originated in Tokyo on September 24 and was sent to an agent in Honolulu. It requested the agent to divide Pearl Harbor into five areas and to make his future reports on ships in harbor with reference to those areas. Tokyo was especially interested in the locations of battleships, destroyers, and carriers, and also in any information on the anchoring of more than one ship at a single dock.

This message was decoded and translated on October 9 and shortly thereafter distributed to Army, Navy, and State Department recipients of MAGIC. Commander Kramer, a naval expert on MAGIC, had marked the message with an asterisk, signifying that he thought it to be of particular interest. But what was its interest? Both he and Wilkinson agreed that it illustrated the "nicety" of Japanese intelligence, the incredible zeal and efficiency with which they collected detail. The division into areas was interpreted as a device for shortening the reports. Admiral Stark was similarly impressed with Japanese efficiency, and no one felt it necessary to forward the message to Admiral Kimmel. No one read into it a specific danger to ships anchored in Pearl Harbor. At the time, this was a reasonable estimate, since somewhat similar requests for information were going to Japanese agents in Panama, Vancouver, Portland, San Diego, San Francisco, and other places. It should be observed, however, that the estimate was reasonable only on the basis of a very rough check on the quantity of espionage message passing between Tokyo and these American ports. No one in Far Eastern Intelligence had subjected the messages to any more refined analysis. An observer assigned to such a job would have been able to record an increase in the frequency and specificity of Tokyo's requests concerning Manila and Pearl Harbor in the last weeks before the outbreak of war, and he would have noted that Tokyo was not displaying the same interest in other American ports. These observations, while not significant in isolation, might have been useful in the general signal picture.

There is no need, however, to confine our examples to Intelligence personnel. Indeed, the crucial areas where the signals failed to communicate a warning were in the operational branches of the armed services. Let us take Admiral Kimmel and his reaction to the information that the Japanese were destroying most of their codes in major Far Eastern consulates and also in London and Washington. Since the Pearl Harbor attack, this information has frequently been characterized by military experts who were not stationed in Honolulu as an "unmistakable tip-off." As Admiral Ingersoll explained at the congressional hearings, with the lucidity characteristic of statements after the event:

> If you rupture diplomatic negotiations you do not necessarily have to burn your codes. The diplomats go home and they can pack up their codes with their dolls and take them home. Also, when you rupture diplomatic negotiations, you do not rupture consular relations. The consuls stay on.
> Now, in this particular set of dispatches that did not mean a rupture of diplomatic negotiations, it meant war, and that information was sent out to the fleets as soon as we got it. . . .[5]

The phrase "it meant war" was, of course, pretty vague; war in Manila, Hong Kong, Singapore, and Batavia is not war 5000 miles away in Pearl Harbor. Before the event, for Admiral Kimmel, code burning in major Japanese consulates in the Far East may have "meant war," but it did not signal danger of an air attack on Pearl Harbor. In the first place, the information that he received was not the original MAGIC. He learned from Washington that Japanese consulates were burning "almost all" of their codes, not all of them, and Honolulu was not included on the list. He knew from a local source that the Japanese consulate in Honolulu was burning secret papers (not necessarily codes), and this back-yard burning had happened three or four times during the year. In July, 1941, Kimmel had been informed that the Japanese consulates in lands neighboring Indochina had destroyed codes, and he interpreted the code burning in December as a similar attempt to protect codes in case the Americans or their British and Dutch allies tried to seize the consulates in reprisal for the southern advance. This also was a reasonable interpretation at the time, though not an especially keen one.

Indeed, at the time there was a good deal of evidence available to support all the wrong interpretations of last-minute signals, and the interpretations appeared wrong only *after* the event. There was, for example, a good deal of evidence to support the hypothesis that Japan would attack the Soviet Union from the east while the Russian Army was heavily engaged in the west. Admiral Turner, head of

5. *Hearings*, Part 9, p. 4226.

Navy War Plans in Washington, was an enthusiastic adherent of this view and argued the high probability of a Japanese attack on Russia up until the last week in November, when he had to concede that most of Japan's men and supplies were moving South. Richard Sorge, the expert Soviet spy who had direct access to the Japanese Cabinet, had correctly predicted the southern move as early as July, 1941, but even he was deeply alarmed during September and early October by the large number of troop movements to the Manchurian border. He feared that his July advice to the Soviet Union had been in error, and his alarm ultimately led to his capture on October 14. For at this time he increased his radio messages to Moscow to the point where it was possible for the Japanese police to pinpoint the source of the broadcasts.

It is important to emphasize here that most of the men that we have cited in our examples, such as Captain Wilkinson and Admirals Turner and Kimmel—these men and their colleagues who were involved in the Pearl Harbor disaster—were as efficient and loyal a group of men as one could find. Some of them were exceptionally able and dedicated. The fact of surprise at Pearl Harbor has never been persuasively explained by accusing the participants, individually or in groups, of conspiracy or negligence or stupidity. What these examples illustrate is rather the very human tendency to pay attention to the signals that support current expectations about enemy behavior. If no one is listening for signals of an attack against a highly improbable target, then it is very difficult for the signals to be heard.

For every signal that came into the information net in 1941 there were usually several plausible alternative explanations, and it is not surprising that our observers and analysts were inclined to select the explanations that fitted the popular hypotheses. They sometimes set down new contradictory evidence side by side with existing hypotheses, and they also sometimes held two contradictory beliefs at the same time. We have seen this happen in G-2[6] estimates for the fall of 1941. Apparently human beings have a stubborn attachment to old beliefs and an equally stubborn resistance to new material that will upset them.

Besides the tendency to select whatever was in accord with one's expectations, there were many other blocks to perception that prevented our analysts from making the correct interpretation. We have just mentioned the masses of conflicting evidence that supported alternative and equally reasonable hypotheses. This is the phenomenon of noise in which a signal is embedded. Even at its normal level, noise presents problems in distraction; but in addition to the natural clatter of useless information and competing signals, in 1941 a number of factors combined to raise the usual noise level. First of all,

6. Intelligence.

it had been raised, especially in Honolulu, by the background of previous alert situations and false alarms. Earlier alerts, as we have seen, had centered attention on local sabotage and on signals supporting the hypothesis of a probable Japanese attack on Russia. Second, in both Honolulu and Washington, individual reactions to danger had been numbed, or at least dulled, by the continuous international tension.

A third factor that served to increase the natural noise level was the positive effort made by the enemy to keep the relevant signals quiet. The Japanese security system was an important and successful block to perception. It was able to keep the strictest cloak of secrecy around the Pearl Harbor attack and to limit knowledge only to those closely associated with the details of military and naval planning. In the Japanese Cabinet only the Navy Minister (who was also Prime Minister) knew of the plan before the task force left its final port of departure.

In addition to keeping certain signals quiet, the enemy tried to create noise, and sent false signals into our information system by carrying on elaborate "spoofs." False radio traffic made us believe that certain ships were maneuvering near the mainland of Japan. The Japanese also sent to individual commanders false war plans for Chinese targets, which were changed only at the last moment to bring them into line with the Southeastern movement.

A fifth barrier to accurate perception was the fact that the relevant signals were subject to change, often very sudden change. This was true even of the so-called static intelligence, which included data on capabilities and the composition of military forces. In the case of our 1941 estimates of the infeasibility of torpedo attacks in the shallow waters of Pear Harbor, or the underestimation of the range and performance of the Japanese Zero, the changes happened too quickly to appear in an intelligence estimate.

Sixth, our own security system sometimes prevented the communication of signals. It confronted our officers with the problem of trying to keep information from the enemy without keeping it from each other, and, as in the case of MAGIC, they were not always successful. As we have seen, only a very few key individuals saw these secret messages, and they saw them only briefly. They had no opportunity or time to make a critical review of the material, and each one assumed that others who had seen it would arrive at identical interpretations. Exactly who those "others" were was not quite clear to any recipient. Admiral Stark, for example, thought Admiral Kimmel was reading all of MAGIC. Those who were not on the list of recipients, but who had learned somehow of the existence of the decodes, were sure that they contained military as well as diplomatic information and believed that the contents were much fuller and more precise than they actually were. The effect of carefully limiting the reading and dis-

cussion of MAGIC, which was certainly necessary to safeguard the secret of our knowledge of the code, was thus to reduce this group of
signals to the point where they were scarcely heard.

To these barriers of noise and security we must add the fact that
the necessarily precarious character of intelligence information and
predictions was reflected in the wording of instructions to take action.
The warning messages were somewhat vague and ambiguous. Enemy
moves are often subject to reversal on short notice, and this was true
for the Japanese. They had plans for canceling their attacks on American possessions in the Pacific up to 24 hours before the time set for
attack. A full alert in the Hawaiian Islands, for example, was one
condition that might have caused the Pearl Harbor task force to
return to Japan on December 5 or 6. The fact that intelligence predictions must be based on moves that are almost always reversible
makes understandable the reluctance of the intelligence analyst to
make bold assertions. Even if he is willing to risk his reputation on
a firm prediction of attack at a definite time and place, no commander will in turn lightly risk the penalties and costs of a full alert.
In December, 1941, a full alert required shooting down any unidentified aircraft sighted over the Hawaiian Islands. Yet this might have
been interpreted by Japan as the first overt act. At least that was
one consideration that influenced General Short to order his lowest
degree of alert. While the cautious phrasing in the messages to
the theater is certainly understandable, it nevertheless constituted
another block on the road to perception. The sentences in the final
theater warnings—"A surprise aggressive move in any direction is a
possibility" and "Japanese future action unpredictable but hostile
action possible at any moment"—could scarcely have been expected
to inform the theater commanders of any change in their strategic
situation.

Last but not least we must also mention the blocks to perception
and communication inherent in any large bureaucratic organization,
and those that stemmed from intraservice and interservice rivalries.
The most glaring example of rivalry in the Pearl Harbor case was
that between Naval War Plans and Naval Intelligence. A general
prejudice against intellectuals and specialists, not confined to the
military but unfortunately widely held in America, also made it difficult for intelligence experts to be heard. McCollum, Bratton, Sadt-
ler, and a few others who felt that the signal picture was ominous
enough to warrant more urgent warnings had no power to influence
decision. The Far Eastern code analysts, for example, were believed
to be too immersed in the "Oriental point of view." Low budgets
for American Intelligence departments reflected the low prestige of
this activity, whereas in England, Germany, and Japan, 1941 budgets
reached a height that was regarded by the American Congress as
quite beyond reason.

In view of all these limitations to perception and communication, is the fact of surprise at Pearl Harbor, then, really so surprising? Even with these limitations explicitly recognized, there remains the step between perception and action. Let us assume that the first hurdle has been crossed: An available signal has been perceived as an indication of imminent danger. Then how do we resolve the next questions: What specific danger is the signal trying to communicate, and what specific action or preparation should follow?

On November 27, General MacArthur had received a war warning very similar to the one received by General Short in Honolulu. MacArthur's response had been promptly translated into orders designed to protect his bombers from possible air attack from Formosan land bases. But the orders were carried out very slowly. By December 8, Philippine time, only half of the bombers ordered to the south had left the Manila area, and reconnaissance over Formosa had not been undertaken. There was no sense of urgency in preparing for a Japanese air attack, partly because our intelligence estimates had calculated that the Japanese aircraft did not have sufficient range to bomb Manila from Formosa.

The information that Pearl Harbor had been attacked arrived at Manila early in the morning of December 8, giving the Philippine forces some 9 or 10 hours to prepare for an attack. But did an air attack on Pearl Harbor necessarily mean that the Japanese would strike from the air at the Philippines? Did they have enough equipment to mount both air attacks successfully? Would they come from Formosa or from carriers? Intelligence had indicated that they would have to come from carriers, yet the carriers were evidently off Hawaii. MacArthur's headquarters also pointed out that there had been no formal declaration of war against Japan by the United States. Therefore approval could not be granted for a counterattack on Formosan bases. Furthermore there were technical disagreements among airmen as to whether a counterattack should be mounted without advance photographic reconnaissance. While Brereton was arranging permission to undertake photographic reconnaissance, there was further disagreement about what to do with the aircraft in the meantime. Should they be sent aloft or should they be dispersed to avoid destruction in case the Japanese reached the airfields? When the Japanese bombers arrived shortly after noon, they found all the American aircraft wingtip to wingtip on the ground. Even the signal of an actual attack on Pearl Harbor was not an unambiguous signal of an attack on the Philippines, and it did not make clear what response was best.

Prospect

The history of Pearl Harbor has an interest exceeding by far any tale of an isolated catastrophe that might have been the result of negligence or stupidity or treachery, however lurid. For we have found the roots of this surprise in circumstances that affected honest, dedicated, and intelligent men. The possibility of such surprise at any time lies in the conditions of human perception and stems from uncertainties so basic that they are not likely to be eliminated, though they might be reduced.

It is only to be expected that the relevant signals, so clearly audible after an event, will be partially obscured before the event by surrounding noise. Even past diligence constructs its own background of noise, in the form of false alarms, which make less likely an alarm when the real thing arrives: the old story of "cry wolf" has a permanent relevance. A totalitarian aggressor can draw a tight curtain of secrecy about his actions and thus muffle the signals of attack. The Western democracies must interpret such signals responsibly and cautiously, for the process of commitment to war, except *in extremis*, is hedged about by the requirements of consultation. The precautions of secrecy, which are necessary even in a democracy to keep open privileged sources of information, may hamper the use of that information or may slow its transmission to those who have the power of decision. Moreover, human attention is directed by beliefs as to what is likely to occur, and one cannot always listen for the right sounds. An all-out thermonuclear attack on a Western power would be an unprecedented event, and some little time (which might be vital) would surely have to pass before that power's allies could understand the nature of the event and take appropriate action.

There is a good deal of evidence, some of it quantitative, that in conditions of great uncertainty people tend to predict that events that they want to happen actually will happen. Wishfulness in conditions of uncertainty is natural and is hard to banish simply by exhortation—or by wishing. Further, the uncertainty of strategic warning is intrinsic, since an enemy decision to attack might be reversed or the direction of the attack changed; and a defensive action can be taken only at some cost. (For example, at Pearl Harbor, flying a 360-degree reconnaissance would have meant sacrificing training, would have interrupted the high-priority shipment program to the Philippines, and would have exhausted crews and worn out equipment within a few weeks.) In general, an extraordinary state of alert that brings about a peak in readiness must be followed by a trough at a later date. In some cases the cost of the defensive actions is hard to estimate and their relevance is uncertain. Therefore the choice of action in response to strategic warning must also be uncertain. Finally, the balance of technical and military factors that might make an attack infeasible at one time can change swiftly and without notice to make it feasible at another. In our day such balances are changing with unprecedented speed.

Pearl Harbor is not an isolated catastrophe. It can be matched by many examples of effective surprise attack. The German attack on

Russia in the summer of 1941 was preceded by a flood of signals, the massing of troops, and even direct warnings to Russia by the governments of the United States and the United Kingdom, both of whom had been correctly informed about the imminence of the onslaught. Yet it achieved total surprise.[7] Soviet arguments current today that Stalin and Marshal Zhukov, his Chief of the General Staff, knew and failed to act have obvious parallels with the accusations about President Roosevelt's conspiracy of silence. These Soviet reinterpretations of history aim not only to downgrade Stalin, but also to establish that Soviet leaders were not *really* surprised in 1941, and the Soviet Union can therefore count on adequate warning in any future conflict.[8] But the difficulties of discerning a surprise attack on oneself apply equally to totalitarian and democratic states.

The stunning tactical success of the Japanese attack on the British at Singapore was made possible by the deeply held British faith in the impregnability of that fortress. As Captain Grenfell put it, newspapers and statesmen like their fortresses to be impregnable. "Every fortress," he wrote, "that has come into the news in my lifetime—Port Arthur, Tsing Tao, the great French defensive system of the Maginot Line—has been popularly described as impregnable before it has been attacked. . . . One way or another it became a virtually accepted fact in Britain and the Dominions that Singapore was an impregnable bastion of Imperial security."[9] Yet the defenses of Singapore were rendered useless by military surprise in the form of an attack from an unexpected, northerly direction.

More recently, the Korean War provided some striking examples of surprise. The original North Korean attack was preceded by almost weekly maneuvers probing the border. These regular week-end penetrations built up so high a level of noise that on June 25, 1950, the actual initiation of hostilities was not distinguished from the preceding tests and false alarms. The intervention of the Chinese, at a later stage of the Korean War, was preceded by mass movements of Chinese troops and explicit warnings by the Chinese government to our own, by way of India, that this was precisely what they would do if we crossed the 38th parallel. Nonetheless, in important respects, we were surprised by the Chinese Communist forces in November, 1950.[10]

7. I am grateful to William W. Kaufmann of the MIT Center for International Studies for permission to read his unpublished paper, "Operation Barbarossa," which deals with the background of the German surprise attack [Wohlstetter's note].

8. For a recent Russian view of the Pearl Harbor attack and its lessons on the "launching of aggression by imperialist states," see Maj. Gen. N. Pavlenko, "Documents on Pearl Harbor," *Voenno-Istoricheskii Zhurnal (Military-Historical Journal)*, No. 1, January, 1961, pp.

85-105. I am indebted for this reference to John Thomas of the Institute of Defense Analysis and to Arnold Horelick, Soviet analyst of The RAND Corporation [Wohlstetter's note].

9. Grenfell, *Main Fleet to Singapore*, p. 64 [Wohlstetter's note].

10. For a succinct and lucid account, see "Strategic Surprise in the Korean War," an unpublished paper by Harvey DeWeerd of The RAND Corporation and the National Security Studies Program, University of California at Los Angeles [Wohlstetter's note].

How do matters stand with reference to a future thermonuclear aggression by a totalitarian power? Would such an attack be harder or easier to conceal than the Japanese aggression against Pearl Harbor? There have been many attempts in recent years to cheer us with the thought that the H-bomb has so outmoded general war that this question may appear unimportant. However, such attempts to comfort ourselves really beg the question. The question is, Will it be possible in the future for a totalitarian power so to conceal an impending attack on the forces that we have disposed for retaliation as to have a high probability of virtually eliminating them before they receive warning or have time to respond to it? In this connection it is important to observe that there is no cause for complacency. In spite of the vast increase in expenditures for collecting and analyzing intelligence data and in spite of advances in the art of machine decoding and machine translation, the balance of advantage seems clearly to have shifted since Pearl Harbor in favor of a surprise attacker. The benefits to be expected from achieving surprise have increased enormously and the penalties for losing the initiative in an all-out war have grown correspondingly. In fact, since only by an all-out surprise attack could an attacker hope to prevent retaliation, anything less would be suicidal, assuming that some form of attack is contemplated by one major power against another.

In such a surprise attack a major power today would have advantages exceeding those enjoyed by the Japanese in 1941. It is a familiar fact that with the ever-increasing readiness of bomber and missile forces, strategic warning becomes harder and harder to obtain; and with the decrease in the flight time for delivery of massive weapons of destruction, tactical warning times have contracted from weeks to minutes. It is no longer necessary for the aggressor to undertake huge movements of troops and ships in the weeks immediately preceding an all-out war, such as we described in our account of the Japanese war plan. Manned bombers capable of delivering a blow many times more devastating then anything dreamed of by the Japanese might be on their way from bases deep inside their homeland without yielding any substantial intelligence warning; they might conceivably follow routes that, by avoiding detection or at least identification among the friendly and unknown traffic appearing on radars, would be unlikely to give even any considerable tactical warning. Submarines might be kept on station several hundred miles off our coast during years of peace and might launch ballistic missiles on the receipt of a prearranged signal. Finally, intercontinental ballistic missiles might be kept for years at a high degree of readiness, and, if there were enough of them, they might be launched after simply being "counted down," with no further visible preparation. Total flight time for such rockets between continents might be less than fifteen minutes and radar warning less than that. Most important, such blows, unlike those leveled by the Japanese at Pearl Harbor, might determine the outcome not merely of a battle, but of the war itself. In short, the subject of surprise attack continues to be of vital concern. This fact has been suggested by the great debate among the powers on arms control and on the possibilities of using limitation and inspection arrangements to guard against surprise attack. The very little we have said suggests that such arrangements present formidable difficulties.

This study has not been intended as a "how-to-do-it" manual on intelligence, but perhaps one major practical lesson emerges from it. We cannot *count* on strategic warning. We *might* get it, and we might be able to take useful preparatory actions that would be impossible without it. We certainly ought to plan to exploit such a possibility should it occur. However, since we cannot rely on strategic warning, our defenses, if we are to have confidence in them, must be designed to function without it. If we accept the fact that the signal picture for impending attacks is almost sure to be ambiguous, we shall prearrange actions that are right and feasible in response to ambiguous signals, including signs of an attack that might be false. We must be capable of reacting repeatedly to false alarms without committing ourselves or the enemy to wage thermonuclear war.

It is only human to want some unique and univocal signal, to want a guarantee from intelligence, an unambiguous substitute for a formal declaration of war. This is surely the unconscious motivation of all the rewriting of Pearl Harbor history, which sees in such wavering and uncertain sources of information as the winds code and all of the various and much-argued MAGIC texts a clear statement of Japanese intent. But we have seen how drastically such an interpretation oversimplifies the task of the analyst and decisionmaker. If the study of Pearl Harbor has anything to offer for the future, it is this: We have to accept the fact of uncertainty and learn to live with it. No magic, in code or otherwise, will provide certainty. Our plans must work without it.

STANLEY MILGRAM
A Behavioral Study of Obedience[1]

This article describes a procedure for the study of destructive obedience in the laboratory. It consists of ordering a naive S to administer increasingly more severe punishment to a victim in the context of a learning experiment. Punishment is administered by means of a shock generator with 30 graded switches ranging from Slight Shock

1. This research was supported by a grant (NSF G-17916) from the National Science Foundation. Exploratory studies conducted in 1960 were supported by a grant from the Higgins Fund at Yale University. The research assistance of Alan C. Elms and Jon Wayland is gratefully acknowledged [Milgram's note].

to Danger: Severe Shock. The victim is a confederate of the E. The primary dependent variable is the maximum shock the S is willing to administer before he refuses to continue further. 26 Ss obeyed the experimental commands fully, and administered the highest shock on the generator. 14 Ss broke off the experiment at some point after the victim protested and refused to provide further answers. The procedure created extreme levels of nervous tension in some Ss. Profuse sweating, trembling, and stuttering were typical expressions of this emotional disturbance. One unexpected sign of tension— yet to be explained—was the regular occurrence of nervous laughter, which in some Ss developed into uncontrollable seizures. The variety of interesting behavioral dynamics observed in the experiment, the reality of the situation for the S, and the possibility of parametric variation within the framework of the procedure, point to the fruitfulness of further study.[2]

Obedience is as basic an element in the structure of social life as one can point to. Some system of authority is a requirement of all communal living, and it is only the man dwelling in isolation who is not forced to respond, through defiance or submission, to the commands of others. Obedience, as a determinant of behavior is of particular relevance to our time. It has been reliably established that from 1933–1945 millions of innocent persons were systematically slaughtered on command. Gas chambers were built, death camps were guarded, daily quotas of corpses were produced with the same efficiency as the manufacture of appliances. These inhumane policies may have originated in the mind of a single person, but they could only be carried out on a massive scale if a very large number of persons obeyed orders.

Obedience is the psychological mechanism that links individual action to political purpose. It is the dispositional cement that binds men to systems of authority. Facts of recent history and observation in daily life suggest that for many persons obedience may be a deeply ingrained behavior tendency, indeed, a prepotent impulse overriding training in ethics, sympathy, and moral conduct. C. P. Snow (1961) points to its importance when he writes:

When you think of the long and gloomy history of man, you will find more hideous crimes have been committed in the name of obedience than have ever been committed in the name of rebellion. If you doubt that, read William Shirer's *Rise and Fall of the Third Reich.* The German Officer Corps were brought up in the most rigorous code of obedience ... in the name of obedience they were party to, and assisted in, the most wicked large-scale actions in the history of the world [p. 24].

While the particular form of obedience dealt with in the present

2. This headnote, written by the au-   originally published. S means subject;
thor, appeared with the article as it was   E the experimenter.

study has its antecedents in these episodes, it must not be thought all obedience entails acts of aggression against others. Obedience serves numerous productive functions. Indeed, the very life of society is predicated on its existence. Obedience may be ennobling and educative and refer to acts of charity and kindness, as well as to destruction.

GENERAL PROCEDURE

A procedure was devised which seems useful as a tool for studying obedience (Milgram, 1961). It consists of ordering a naive subject to administer electric shock to a victim. A simulated shock generator is used, with 30 clearly marked voltage levels that range from 15 to 450 volts. The instrument bears verbal designations that range from Slight Shock to Danger: Severe Shock. The responses of the victim, who is a trained confederate of the experimenter, are standardized. The orders to administer shocks are given to the naive subject in the context of a "learning experiment" ostensibly set up to study the effects of punishment on memory. As the experiment proceeds the naive subject is commanded to administer increasingly more intense shocks to the victim, even to the point of reaching the level marked Danger: Severe Shock. Internal resistances become stronger, and at a certain point the subject refuses to go on with the experiment. Behavior prior to this rupture is considered "obedience," in that the subject complies with the commands of the experimenter. The point of rupture is the act of disobedience. A quantitative value is assigned to the subject's performance based on the maximum intensity shock he is willing to administer before he refuses to participate further. Thus for any particular subject and for any particular experimental condition the degree of obedience may be specified with a numerical value. The crux of the study is to systematically vary the factors believed to alter the degree of obedience to the experimental commands.

The technique allows important variables to be manipulated at several points in the experiment. One may vary aspects of the source of command, content and form of command, instrumentalities for its execution, target object, general social setting, etc. The problem, therefore, is not one of designing increasingly more numerous experimental conditions, but of selecting those that best illuminate the *process* of obedience from the socio-psychological standpoint.

RELATED STUDIES

The inquiry bears an important relation to philosophic analyses of obedience and authority (Arendt, 1958; Friedrich, 1958; Weber, 1947), an early experimental study of obedience by Frank (1944), studies in "authoritarianism" (Adorno, Frenkel-Brunswik, Levinson, & Sanford, 1950; Rokeach, 1961), and a recent series of analytic and empirical studies in social power (Cartwright, 1959). It owes much to the long concern with *suggestion* in social psychology, both in its normal forms (*e.g.*, Binet, 1900) and in its clinical manifestations (Charcot, 1881). But it derives, in the first instance, from direct observation of a social fact; the individual who is commanded by a legitimate authority ordinarily obeys. Obedience comes easily and often. It is a ubiquitous and indispensable feature of social life.

Method

SUBJECTS

The subjects were 40 males between the ages of 20 and 50, drawn from New Haven and the surrounding communities. Subjects were obtained by a newspaper advertisement and direct mail solicitation. Those who responded to the appeal believed they were to participate in a study of memory and learning at Yale University. A wide range of occupations is represented in the sample. Typical subjects were postal clerks, high school teachers, salesmen, engineers, and laborers. Subjects ranged in educational level from one who had not finished elementary school, to those who had doctorate and other professional degrees. They were paid $4.50 for their participation in the experiment. However, subjects were told that payment was simply for coming to the laboratory, and that the money was theirs no matter what happened after they arrived. Table 1 shows the proportion of age and occupational types assigned to the experimental condition.

TABLE 1

DISTRIBUTION OF AGE AND OCCUPATIONAL TYPES IN THE EXPERIMENT

Occupations	20-29 *years* n	30-39 *years* n	40-50 *years* n	*Percentage of total (Occupations)*
Workers, skilled and unskilled	4	5	6	37.5
Sales, business, and white-collar	3	6	7	40.0
Professional	1	5	3	22.5
Percentage of total (age)	20	40	40	

Note. Total $N = 40$.

PERSONNEL AND LOCALE

The experiment was conducted on the grounds of Yale University in the elegant interaction laboratory. (This detail is relevant to the perceived legitimacy of the experiment. In further variations, the experiment was dissociated from the university, with consequences for performances.) The role of experimenter was played by a 31-year-old high school teacher of biology. His manner was impassive, and his appearance somewhat stern throughout the experiment. He was dressed in a gray technician's coat. The victim was played by a 47-year-old accountant, trained for the role; he was of Irish-American stock, whom most observers found mild-mannered and likable.

PROCEDURE

One naive subject and one victim (an accomplice) performed in each experiment. A pretext had to be devised that would justify the administration of electric shock by the naive subject. This was effectively accomplished by the cover story. After a general introduction on the presumed relation between punishment and learning, subjects were told:

But actually, we know *very little* about the effect of punishment on learning, because almost no truly scientific studies have been made of it in human beings.

For instance, we don't know how *much* punishment is best for learning —and we don't know how much difference it makes as to who is giving the punishment, whether an adult learns best from a younger or an older person than himself—or many things of that sort.

So in this study we are bringing together a number of adults of different occupations and ages. And we're asking some of them to be teachers and some of them to be learners.

We want to find out just what effect different people have on each other as teachers and learners, and also what effect *punishment* will have on learning in this situation.

Therefore, I'm going to ask one of you to be the teacher here tonight and the other one to be the learner.

Does either of you have a preference?

Subjects then drew slips of paper from a hat to determine who would be the teacher and who would be the learner in the experiment. The drawing was rigged so that the naive subject was always the teacher and the accomplice always the learner. (Both slips contained the word "Teacher.") Immediately after the drawing, the teacher and learner were taken to an adjacent room and the learner was strapped into an "electric chair" apparatus.

The experimenter explained that the straps were to prevent excessive movement while the learner was being shocked. The effect was to make it impossible for him to escape from the situation. An electrode was attached to the learner's wrist, and electrode paste was applied "to avoid blisters, and burns." Subjects were told that the electrode was attached to the shock generator in the adjoining room.

In order to improve credibility the experimenter declared, in response to a question by the learner: "Although the shocks can be extremely painful, they cause no permanent tissue damage."

Learning task. The lesson administered by the subject was a paired-associate learning task. The subject read a series of word pairs to the learner, and then read the first word of the pair along with four terms. The learner was to indicate which of the four terms had originally been paired with the first word. He communicated his answer by pressing one of four switches in front of him, which in turn lit up one of four numbered quadrants in an answer-box located atop the shock generator.

Shock generator. The instrument panel consists of 30 lever switches set in a horizontal line. Each switch is clearly labeled with a voltage designation that ranges from 15 to 450 volts. There is a 15-volt increment from one switch to the next going from left to right. In addition, the following verbal designations are clearly indicated for groups of four switches going from left to right: Slight Shock, Moderate Shock, Strong Shock, Very Strong Shock, Intense Shock, Extreme Intensity Shock, Danger: Severe Shock. (Two switches after this last designation are simply marked XXX.)

Upon depressing a switch: a pilot light corresponding to each switch is illuminated in bright red; an electric buzzing is heard; an electric blue light, labeled "voltage energizer," flashes; the dial on the voltage meter swings to the right; various relay clicks are sounded.

The upper left-hand corner of the generator is labeled Shock Generator, Type ZLB, Dyson Instrument Company, Waltham, Mass. Output 15 Volts-450 Volts.

Details of the instrument were carefully handled to insure an appearance of authenticity. The panel was engraved by precision industrial engravers, and all components were of high quality. No subject in the experiment suspected that the instrument was merely a simulated shock generator.[3]

Sample shock. Each naive subject is given a sample shock on the shock generator, prior to beginning his run as teacher. This shock is always 45 volts, and is applied by pressing the third switch of the generator. The shock is applied to the wrist of the naive subject, and has its source in a 45-volt battery wired into the generator. This further convinces the subject of the authenticity of the generator.

Shock instructions. The subject is told to administer a shock to the learner each time he gives a wrong response. Moreover—and this is the key command—the subject is instructed to "move one level higher on the shock generator each time the learner flashes a wrong answer." He is also instructed to announce the voltage level before administering a shock. This serves to continually remind subjects of the increasing intensity of shocks administered to the learner.

Preliminary and regular run. Pretests revealed that the procedure of reading words and administering shocks requires some practice before it can be handled smoothly. Therefore, immediately preceding the regular run, the teacher is given a preliminary series of 10 words to read to the learner. There are 3 neutral words in the practice

3. A related technique, making use of a shock generator, was reported by Buss (1961) for the study of aggression in the laboratory. Despite the considerable similarity of technical detail in the experimental procedures, both investigators proceeded in ignorance of the other's work. Milgram provided plans and photographs of his shock generator, experimental procedure, and first results in a report to the National Science Foundation in January, 1961. This report received only limited circulation. Buss reported his procedure 6 months later, but to a wider audience. Subsequently, technical information and reports were exchanged. The present article was first received in the Editor's office on December 27, 1961; it was resubmitted with deletions on July 27, 1962 [Milgram's note].

series (*i.e.*, words that the learner answers correctly), so that shocks are administered for 7 of the words, with the maximum shock at 105 volts (moderate shock). Almost all subjects master the procedure by the time the preliminary run is over.

Subjects are then presented with a second list, and are told that the procedure is the same as for the first list; the experimenter adds, however:

When you get to the bottom of the list, repeat it over again, and continue giving shocks, until the learner has learned all the pairs correctly.

The experimenter instructs the subject to,

start from 15 volts and increase the shock level one step each time the learner gives a wrong answer.

Feedback from the victim. In all conditions the learner gives a predetermined set of responses to the word pair test, based on a schedule of approximately three wrong answers to one correct answer. In the present experimental condition no vocal response or other sign of protest is heard from the learner until Shock Level 300 is reached. When the 300-volt shock is administered, the learner pounds on the wall of the room in which he is bound to the electric chair. The pounding can be heard by the subject. From this point on, the learner's answers no longer appear on the four-way panel.

At this juncture, subjects ordinarily turn to the experimenter for guidance. The experimenter instructs the subject to treat the absence of a response as a wrong answer, and to shock the subject according to the usual schedule. He advises the subjects to allow 5–10 seconds before considering no response as a wrong answer, and to increase the shock level one step each time the learner fails to respond correctly. The learner's pounding is repeated after the 315-volt shock is administered; afterwards he is not heard from, nor do his answers reappear on the four-way signal box.

Experimenter feedback. At various points in the experiment the subject may turn to the experimenter for advice on whether he should continue to administer shocks. Or he may indicate that he does not wish to go on. It was important to standardize the experimenter's responses to these inquiries and reactions.

If the subject indicated his unwillingness to go on, the experimenter responded with a sequence of "prods," using as many as necessary to bring the subject into line.

Prod 1: Please continue, *or* Please go on.
Prod 2: The experiment requires that you continue.
Prod 3: It is absolutely essential that you continue.
Prod 4: You have no other choice, you *must* go on.

The prods were always made in sequence: Only if Prod 1 had been unsuccessful, could Prod 2 be used. If the subject refused to obey the experimenter after Prod 4, the experiment was terminated. The experimenter's tone of voice was at all times firm, but not impolite. The sequence was begun anew on each occasion that the subject balked or showed reluctance to follow orders.

Special prods. If the subject asked if the learner was liable to suffer permanent physical injury, the experimenter said:

Although the shocks may be painful, there is no permanent tissue damage, so please go on. [Followed by Prods 2, 3, and 4 if necessary.]

If the subject said that the learner did not want to go on, the experimenter replied:

Whether the learner likes it or not, you must go on until he has learned all the word pairs correctly. So please go on. [Followed by Prods 2, 3, and 4 if necessary.]

DEPENDENT MEASURES

The primary dependent measure for any subject is the maximum shock he administers before he refuses to go any further. In principle this may vary from 0 (for a subject who refuses to administer even the first shock) to 30 (for a subject who administers the highest shock on the generator). A subject who breaks off the experiment at any point prior to administering the thirtieth shock level is termed a *defiant subject*. One who complies with experimental commands fully, and proceeds to administer all shock levels commanded, is termed an *obedient* subject.

Further records. With few exceptions, experimental sessions were recorded on magnetic tape. Occasional photographs were taken through one-way mirrors. Notes were kept on any unusual behavior occurring during the course of the experiments. On occasion, additional observers were directed to write objective descriptions of the subjects' behavior. The latency and duration of shocks were measured by accurate timing devices.

Interview and dehoax. Following the experiment, subjects were interviewed; open-ended questions, projective measures, and attitude scales were employed. After the interview, procedures were undertaken to assure that the subject would leave the laboratory in a state of well being. A friendly reconciliation was arranged between the subject and the victim, and an effort was made to reduce any tensions that arose as a result of the experiment.

Results
PRELIMINARY NOTIONS

Before giving an account of the experimental results, it is instructive to consider how persons predict others will perform when commanded to administer powerful shocks to another person. Fourteen Yale seniors, all psychology majors, were provided with a detailed description of the experimental situation. They were asked to reflect carefully on it, and to predict the behavior of 100 hypothetical subjects. More specifically, they were instructed to plot the distribution of obedience of "100 Americans of diverse occupations, and ranging in age from 20 to 50 years," who were placed in the experimental situation.

There was considerable agreement among the respondents on the expected behavior of hypothetical subjects. All respondents predicted that only an insignificant minority would go through to the end of the shock series. (The estimates ranged from 0 to 3%; *i.e.*, the most "pessimistic" member of the class predicted that of 100 persons, 3 would continue through to the most potent shock available on the shock generator—450 volts.) The class mean was 1.2%. The question was also posed informally to colleagues of the author, and the most general feeling was that few if any subjects would go beyond the designation Very Strong Shock.

RESULT OF EXPERIMENT I

Subjects accept situation. With few exceptions subjects were convinced of the reality of the experimental situation, that they were administering shocks to another person, and the most potent shocks were extremely painful. In the post-experimental interview subjects were asked: "How painful to the learner were the last few shocks that you administered to him?" Subjects were instructed to indicate their answers on a printed 14-point scale ranging from "Not at all painful" to "Extremely painful." The modal[4] response was 14 (Extremely painful), with the mean at 13.42.

Signs of extreme tension. Many subjects showed signs of nervousness in the experimental situation, and especially upon administering the more powerful shocks. In a large number of cases the degree of tension reached extremes that are rarely seen in sociopsychological laboratory studies. Subjects were observed to sweat, tremble, stutter, bite their lips, groan, and dig their fingernails into their flesh. These were characteristic rather than exceptional responses to the experiment.

One sign of tension was the regular occurrence of nervous laughing fits. Fourteen of the 40 subjects showed definite signs of nervous laughter and smiling. The laughter seemed entirely out of place, even bizarre. Full-blown, uncontrollable seizures were observed for 3 subjects. On one occasion we observed a seizure so violently convulsive that it was necessary to call a halt to the experiment. The subject, a 46-year-old encyclopedia salesman, was seriously embarrassed by his untoward and uncontrollable behavior. In the post-experimental interviews subjects took pains to point out that they were not sadistic types, and that the laughter did not mean they enjoyed shocking the victim.

Distribution of scores. It had been conjectured that persons

4. Most frequent.

would not, in general, agree to administer shocks beyond the level designated as Very Strong Shock. The distribution of maximum shocks for this experiment is shown in Table 2. The obtained distribution of scores deviates radically from the prediction.

Upon command of the experimenter, each of the 40 subjects went beyond the expected breakoff point. No subject stopped prior to administering Shock Level 20. (At this level—300 volts—the victim kicks on the wall and no longer provides answers to the teacher's multiple-choice questions.)

Of the 40 subjects, 5 refused to obey the experimental commands beyond the 300-volt level. Four more subjects administered one further shock, and then refused to go on. Two broke off at the 330-volt level, and 1 each at 345, 360, and 375 volts. Thus a total of 14 subjects defied the experimenter. It is instructive to reprint their remarks at the point of defiance, as transcribed from the tape recordings:

[0124] I think he's trying to communicate, he's knocking....Well it's not fair to shock the guy...these are terrific volts. I don't think this is very humane....Oh, I can't go on with this; no, this isn't right. It's a hell of an experiment. The guy is suffering in there. No, I don't want to go on. This is crazy. [Subject refused to administer more shocks.]

[0123] He's banging in there. I'm gonna chicken out. I'd like to continue, but I can't do that to a man....I'm sorry I can't do that to a man. I'll hurt his heart. You take your check....No really, I couldn't do it.

These subjects were frequently in a highly agitated and even angered state. Sometimes, verbal protest was at a minimum, and the subject simply got up from his chair in front of the shock generator, and indicated that he wished to leave the laboratory.

Of the 40 subjects, 26 obeyed the orders of the experimenter to the end, proceeding to punish the victim until they reached the most potent shock available on the shock generator. At that point, the experimenter called a halt to the session. (The maximum shock is labeled 450 volts, and is two steps beyond the designation: Danger: Severe Shock.) Although obedient subjects continued to administer shocks, they often did so under extreme stress. Some expressed reluctance to administer shocks beyond the 300-volt level, and displayed fears similar to those who defied the experimenter; yet they obeyed.

After the maximum shocks had been delivered, and the experimenter called a halt to the proceedings, many obedient subjects heaved sighs of relief, mopped their brows, rubbed their fingers over their eyes, or nervously fumbled cigarettes. Some shook their heads, apparently in regret. Some subjects had remained calm throughout the experiment, and displayed only minimal signs of tension from beginning to end.

TABLE 2
DISTRIBUTION OF BREAKOFF POINTS

Verbal designation and voltage indication	Number of subjects for whom this was maximum shock
Slight Shock	
15	0
30	0
45	0
60	0
Moderate Shock	
75	0
90	0
105	0
120	0
Strong Shock	
135	0
150	0
165	0
180	0
Very Strong Shock	
195	0
210	0
225	0
240	0
Intense Shock	
255	0
270	0
285	0
300	5
Extreme Intensity Shock	
315	4
330	2
345	1
360	1
Danger: Severe Shock	
375	1
390	0
405	0
420	0
XXX	
435	0
450	26

Discussion

The experiment yielded two findings that were surprising. The first finding concerns the sheer strength of obedient tendencies manifested in this situation. Subjects have learned from childhood that it is a fundamental breach of moral conduct to hurt another person against his will. Yet, 26 subjects abandon this tenet in following the instructions of an authority who has no special powers to enforce his commands. To disobey would bring no material loss to the subject; no punishment would ensue. It is clear from the remarks and outward behavior of many participants that in punishing the victim they are often acting against their own values. Subjects often expressed deep disapproval of shocking a man in the face of his objections, and others denounced it as stupid and senseless. Yet the majority complied with the experimental commands. This outcome was surprising from two perspectives: first, from the standpoint of predictions made in the questionnaire described earlier. (Here, however, it is possible that the remoteness of the respondents from the actual situation, and the difficulty of conveying to them the concrete details of the experiment, could account for the serious underestimation of obedience.)

But the results were also unexpected to persons who observed the experiment in progress, through one-way mirrors. Observers often uttered expressions of disbelief upon seeing a subject administer more powerful shocks to the victim. These persons had a full acquaintance with the details of the situation, and yet systematically underestimated the amount of obedience that subjects would display.

The second unanticipated effect was the extraordinary tension generated by the procedures. One might suppose that a subject would simply break off or continue as his conscience dictated. Yet, this is very far from what happened. There were striking reactions of tension and emotional strain. One observer related:

I observed a mature and initially poised businessman enter the laboratory smiling and confident. Within 20 minutes he was reduced to a twitching, stuttering wreck, who was rapidly approaching a point of nervous collapse. He constantly pulled on his earlobe, and twisted his hands. At one point he pushed his fist into his forehead and muttered: "Oh God, let's stop it." And yet he continued to respond to every word of the experimenter, and obeyed to the end.

Any understanding of the phenomenon of obedience must rest on an analysis of the particular conditions in which it occurs. The following features of the experiment go some distance in explaining the high amount of obedience observed in the situation.

1. The experiment is sponsored by and takes place on the grounds of an institution of unimpeachable reputation, Yale University. It may be reasonably presumed that the personnel are competent and reputable. The importance of this background authority is now being studied by conducting a series of experiments outside of New Haven, and without any visible ties to the university.

2. The experiment is, on the face of it, designed to attain a worthy purpose—advancement of knowledge about learning and

memory. Obedience occurs not as an end in itself, but as an instrumental element in a situation that the subject construes as significant, and meaningful. He may not be able to see its full significance, but he may properly assume that the experimenter does.

3. The subject perceives that the victim has voluntarily submitted to the authority system of the experimenter. He is not (at first) an unwilling captive impressed for involuntary service. He has taken the trouble to come to the laboratory presumably to aid the experimental research. That he later becomes an involuntary subject does not alter the fact that, initially, he consented to participate without qualification. Thus he has in some degree incurred an obligation toward the experimenter.

4. The subject, too, has entered the experiment voluntarily, and perceives himself under obligation to aid the experimenter. He has made a commitment, and to disrupt the experiment is a repudiation of this initial promise of aid.

5. Certain features of the procedure strengthen the subject's sense of obligation to the experimenter. For one, he has been paid for coming to the laboratory. In part this is canceled out by the experimenter's statement that:

Of course, as in all experiments, the money is yours simply for coming to the laboratory. From this point on, no matter what happens, the money is yours.[5]

6. From the subject's standpoint, the fact that he is the teacher and the other man the learner is purely a chance consequence (it is determined by drawing lots) and he, the subject, ran the same risk as the other man in being assigned the role of learner. Since the assignment of positions in the experiment was achieved by fair means, the learner is deprived of any basis of complaint on this count. (A similar situation obtains in Army units, in which—in the absence of volunteers—a particularly dangerous mission may be assigned by drawing lots, and the unlucky soldier is expected to bear his misfortune with sportsmanship.)

7. There is, at best, ambiguity with regard to the prerogatives of a psychologist and the corresponding rights of his subject. There is a vagueness of expectation concerning what a psychologist may require of his subject, and when he is overstepping acceptable limits. Moreover, the experiment occurs in a closed setting, and thus provides no opportunity for the subject to remove these ambiguities by discussion with others. There are few standards that seem directly applicable to the situation, which is a novel one for most subjects.

8. The subjects are assured that the shocks administered to the subject are "painful but not dangerous." Thus they assume that the

5. Forty-three subjects, undergraduates at Yale University, were run in the experiment without payment. The results are very similar to those obtained with paid subjects [Milgram's note].

426 · Stanley Milgram

discomfort caused the victim is momentary, while the scientific gains resulting from the experiment are enduring.

9. Through Shock Level 20 the victim continues to provide answers on the signal box. The subject may construe this as a sign that the victim is still willing to "play the game." It is only after Shock Level 20 that the victim repudiates the rules completely, refusing to answer further.

These features help to explain the high amount of obedience obtained in this experiment. Many of the arguments raised need not remain matters of speculation, but can be reduced to testable propositions to be confirmed or disproved by further experiments.[6]

The following features of the experiment concern the nature of the conflict which the subject faces.

10. The subject is placed in a position in which he must respond to the competing demands of two persons: the experimenter and the victim. The conflict must be resolved by meeting the demands of one or the other; satisfaction of the victim and the experimenter are mutually exclusive. Moreover, the resolution must take the form of a highly visible action, that of continuing to shock the victim or breaking off the experiment. Thus the subject is forced into a public conflict that does not permit any completely satisfactory solution.

11. While the demands of the experimenter carry the weight of scientific authority, the demands of the victim spring from his personal experience of pain and suffering. The two claims need not be regarded as equally pressing and legitimate. The experimenter seeks an abstract scientific datum; the victim cries out for relief from physical suffering caused by the subject's actions.

12. The experiment gives the subject little time for reflection. The conflict comes on rapidly. It is only minutes after the subject has been seated before the shock generator that the victim begins his protests. Moreover, the subject perceives that he has gone through but two-thirds of the shock levels at the time the subject's first protests are heard. Thus he understands that the conflict will have a persistent aspect to it, and may well become more intense as increasingly more powerful shocks are required. The rapidity with which the conflict descends on the subject, and his realization that it is predictably recurrent may well be sources of tension to him.

13. At a more general level, the conflict stems from the opposition of two deeply ingrained behavior dispositions: first, the disposition not to harm other people, and second, the tendency to obey those whom we perceive to be legitimate authorities.

---

6. A series of recently completed experiments employing the obedience paradigm is reported in Milgram (1964) [Milgram's note].

References

Adorno, T., Else Frenkel-Brunswik, D. J. Levinson, and R. N. Sanford, *The Authoritarian Personality*. New York: Harper & Row, 1950.

Arendt, H., "What Was Authority?" In C. J. Friedrich (ed.), *Authority*. Cambridge, Mass.: Harvard University Press, 1958. Pp. 81-112.

Binet, S., *La suggestibilité*. Paris: Schleicher, 1900.

Buss, A. H., *The Psychology of Aggression*. New York: Wiley, 1961.

Cartwright, S. (ed.), *Studies in Social Power*. Ann Arbor: University of Michigan Institute for Social Research, 1959.

Chacot, J. M., *Oeuvres complètes*. Paris: Bureaux du Progrès Médical, 1881.

Frank, J. D., "Experimental Studies of Personal Pressure and Resistance." *Journal of General Psychology*, 30 (1944), 23-64.

Friedrich, C. J. (ed.), *Authority*. Cambridge, Mass.: Harvard University Press, 1958.

Milgram, S., *Dynamics of Obedience*. Washington, D.C.: National Science Foundation, January 25, 1961. (Mimeographed.)

Milgram, S., "Some Conditions of Obedience and Disobedience to Authority." *Human Relations* (1964).

Rokeach, M., "Authority, Authoritarianism, and Conformity." In I. A. Berg and B. M. Bass (eds.), *Conformity and Deviation*. New York: Harper & Row, 1961. Pp. 230-257.

Snow, C. P., "Either-or." *The Progressive*, 24 (Feburary 1961).

Weber, M., *The Theory of Social and Economic Organization*. Oxford, Eng.: Oxford University Press, 1947.

QUESTIONS

1. The opening paragraph states that "from 1933–1945 millions of innocent persons were systematically slaughtered on command." Does this study help to explain how that could have happened? What is the purpose of the study? What do you learn from it?

2. Does this experiment involve an actual shock to anybody?

3. What explanation is offered for the subjects' continuing the experiment even when they believed that they were inflicting intense physical pain upon the "learner"? What explains the experimenters' continuing the experiment even when they knew that they were inflicting evident psychological pain upon the subjects? How many subjects refused to complete the experiment? How many times did the experimenters find it necessary to stop?

4. Milgram points out (p. 425) that "There is, at best, ambiguity with regard to the prerogatives of a psychologist and the corresponding rights of his subject. There is a vagueness of expectation concerning what a psychologist may require of his subject, and when he is overstepping acceptable limits." Does this study appear to bear out that observation?

5. "The orders to administer shocks are given to the naive subject in the context of a 'learning experiment' ostensibly set up to study the effects of punishment on memory" (p. 415). This sentence is in the passive voice; recast it in the active. How frequent is the passive voice in this piece of writing? Does the passive voice indicate scientific precision? Or objectivity? Or what?

6. What is a prod? A dehoax? (See pp. 419–420.) How do these terms help define the role of the experimental scientist?

WILLIAM JAMES
The Ethical and Pedagogical Importance of the Principle of Habit[1]

"Habit a second nature! Habit is ten times nature," the Duke of Wellington is said to have exclaimed; and the degree to which this is true no one probably can appreciate as well as one who is a veteran soldier himself. The daily drill and the years of discipline end by fashioning a man completely over again, as to most of the possibilities of his conduct.

"There is a story," says Prof. Huxley, "which is credible enough, though it may not be true, of a practical joker who, seeing a discharged veteran carrying home his dinner, suddenly called out, 'Attention!' whereupon the man instantly brought his hands down, and lost his mutton and potatoes in the gutter. The drill had been thorough, and its effects had become embodied in the man's nervous structure."

Riderless cavalry-horses, at many a battle, have been seen to come together and go through their customary evolutions at the sound of the bugle-call. Most domestic beasts seem machines almost pure and simple, undoubtingly, unhesitatingly doing from minute to minute the duties they have been taught, and giving no sign that the possibility of an alternative ever suggests itself to their mind. Men grown old in prison have asked to be readmitted after being once set free. In a railroad accident a menagerie-tiger, whose cage had broken open, is said to have emerged, but presently crept back again, as if too much bewildered by his new responsibilities, so that he was without difficulty secured.

Habit is thus the enormous fly-wheel of society, its most precious conservative agent. It alone is what keeps us all within the bounds of ordinance, and saves the children of fortune from the envious uprisings of the poor. It alone prevents the hardest and most repulsive walks of life from being deserted by those brought up to tread therein. It keeps the fisherman and the deck-hand at sea through the winter; it holds the miner in his darkness, and nails the countryman to his log-cabin and his lonely farm through all the months of snow; it protects us from invasion by the natives of the desert and the frozen zone. It dooms us all to fight out the battle of life upon the lines of our nurture or our early choice, and to make the best of a pursuit that disagrees, because there is no other for which we are fitted, and it is too late to begin again. It keeps different social strata from mixing. Already at the age of

1. From "Habit," Chapter 10 of *The Principles of Psychology*.

twenty-five you see the professional mannerism settling down on the young commercial traveler, on the young doctor, on the young minister, on the young counselor-at-law. You see the little lines of cleavage running through the character, the tricks of thought, the prejudices, the ways of the "shop," in a word, from which the man can by-and-by no more escape than his coat-sleeve can suddenly fall into a new set of folds. On the whole, it is best he should not escape. It is well for the world that in most of us, by the age of thirty, the character has set like plaster, and will never soften again.

If the period between twenty and thirty is the critical one in the formation of intellectual and professional habits, the period below twenty is more important still for the fixings of *personal* habits, properly so called, such as a vocalization and pronunciation, gesture, motion, and address. Hardly ever is a language learned after twenty spoken without a foreign accent; hardly ever can a youth transferred to the society of his betters unlearn the nasality and other vices of speech bred in him by the associations of his growing years. Hardly ever, indeed, no matter how much money there be in his pocket, can he even learn to *dress* like a gentleman-born. The merchants offer their wares as eagerly to him as to the veriest "swell," but he simply *cannot* buy the right things. An invisible law, as strong as gravitation, keeps him within his orbit, arrayed this year as he was the last; and how his better-clad acquaintances contrive to get the things they wear will be for him a mystery till his dying day.

The great thing, then, in all education, is to *make our nervous system our ally instead of our enemy.* It is to fund and capitalize our acquisitions, and live at ease upon the interest of the fund. *For this we must make automatic and habitual, as early as possible, as many useful actions as we can,* and guard against the growing into ways that are likely to be disadvantageous to us, as we should guard against the plague. The more of the details of our daily life we can hand over to the effortless custody of automatism, the more our higher powers of mind will be set free for their own proper work. There is no more miserable human being than one in whom nothing is habitual but indecision, and for whom the lighting of every cigar, the drinking of every cup, the time of rising and going to bed every day, and the beginning of every bit of work, are subjects of express volitional deliberation. Full half the time of such a man goes to the deciding, or regretting, of matters which ought to be so ingrained in him as practically not to exist for his consciousness at all. If there be such daily duties not yet ingrained in any one of my readers, let him begin this very hour to set the matter right.

In Professor Bain's chapter on "The Moral Habits" there are some admirable practical remarks laid down. Two great maxims emerge from his treatment. The first is that in the acquisition of a new habit, or the leaving off of an old one, we must take care to *launch ourselves with as strong and decided an initiative as possible.* Accumulate all the possible circumstances which shall re-enforce the right motives; put yourself assiduously in conditions that encourage the new way; make engagements incompatible with the old; take a public pledge, if the case allows; in short, envelop your resolution with every aid you know. This will give your new beginning such a momentum that the temptation to break down will not occur as soon as it otherwise might; and every day during which a breakdown is postponed adds to the chances of its not occurring at all.

The second maxim is: *Never suffer an exception to occur till the new habit is securely rooted in your life.* Each lapse is like the letting fall of a ball of string which one is carefully winding up; a single slip undoes more than a great many turns will wind again. *Continuity* of training is the great means of making the nervous system act infallibly right. As Professor Bain says:

"The peculiarity of the moral habits, contradistinguishing them from the intellectual acquisitions, is the presence of two hostile powers, one to be gradually raised into the ascendant over the other. It is necessary, above all things, in such a situation, never to lose a battle. Every gain on the wrong side undoes the effect of many conquests on the right. The essential precaution, therefore, is so to regulate the two opposing powers that the one may have a series of uninterrupted successes, until repetition has fortified it to such a degree as to enable it to cope with the opposition, under any circumstances. This is the theoretically best career of mental progress."

The need of securing success at the *outset* is imperative. Failure at first is apt to damp the energy of all future attempts, whereas past experiences of success nerve one to future vigor. Goethe says to a man who consulted him about an enterprise but mistrusted his own powers: "Ach! you need only blow on your hands!" And the remark illustrates the effect on Goethe's spirits of his own habitually successful career.

The question of "tapering off," in abandoning such habits as drink and opium-indulgence comes in here, and is a question about which experts differ within certain limits, and in regard to what may be best for an individual case. In the main, however, all expert opinion would agree that abrupt acquisition of the new habit is the best way, *if there be a real possibility of carrying it out.* We must be careful not to give the will so stiff a task as to insure its defeat at the very outset; but, *provided one can stand it*, a sharp period of suffering, and then a free time, is the best thing to aim at, whether in giving up a habit like that of opium, or in simply changing one's hours of rising or of work. It is surprising how soon a desire will die of inanition if it be *never* fed.

One must first learn, unmoved, looking neither to the right nor left, to walk firmly on the strait and narrow path, before one can begin "to make one's self over again." He who every day makes a fresh resolve is like one who, arriving at the edge of the ditch he is to leap, forever stops and returns for a fresh run. Without *unbroken* advance there is no such thing as *accumulation* of the ethical forces possible, and to make this possible, and to exercise us and habituate us in it, is the sovereign blessing of regular work.[2]

A third maxim may be added to the preceding pair: *Seize the very first possible opportunity to act on every resolution you make, and on every emotional prompting you may experience in the direction of the habits you aspire to gain.* It is not in the moment of their forming, but in the moment of their producing *motor effects*, that resolves and aspirations communicate the new "set" to the brain. As the author last quoted remarks:

The actual presence of the practical opportunity alone furnishes the fulcrum upon which the lever can rest, by means of which the moral will may multiply its strength, and raise itself aloft. He who has no solid ground to press against will never get beyond the stage of empty gesture-making.

No matter how full a reservoir of *maxims* one may possess, and no matter how good one's *sentiments* may be, if one have not taken advantage of every concrete opportunity to *act,* one's character may remain entirely unaffected for the better. With mere good intentions, hell is proverbially paved. And this is an obvious consequence of the principles we have laid down. A "character," as J. S. Mill says, "is a completely fashioned will"; and a will, in the sense in which he means it, is an aggregate of tendencies to act in a firm and prompt and definite way upon all the principal emergencies of life. A tendency to act only becomes effectively ingrained in us in proportion to the uninterrupted frequency with which the actions actually occur, and the brain "grows" to their use. When a resolve or a fine glow of feeling is allowed to evaporate without bearing practical fruit it is worse than a chance lost; it works so as positively to hinder future resolutions and emotions from taking the normal path of discharge. There is no more contemptible type of human character than that of the nerveless sentimentalist and dreamer, who spends his life in a weltering sea of sensibility and emotion, but who never does a manly concrete deed. Rousseau, inflaming all the mothers of France, by his eloquence, to follow Nature and nurse their babies themselves, while he sends his own children to the foundling hospital, is the classical example of what I mean. But every one of us in his measure, whenever, after glow-

2. J. Bahnsen: "Beitäge zu Charakterologie" (1867), vol. I, p. 209 [James' note].

ing for an abstractly formulated Good, he practically ignores some actual case, among the squalid "other particulars" of which that same Good lurks disguised, treads straight on Rousseau's path. All Goods are disguised by the vulgarity of their concomitants, in this work-a-day world; but woe to him who can only recognize them when he thinks them in their pure and abstract form! The habit of excessive novel-reading and theater-going will produce true monsters in this line. The weeping of the Russian lady over the fictitious personages in the play, while her coachman is freezing to death on his seat outside, is the sort of thing that everywhere happens on a less glaring scale. Even the habit of excessive indulgence in music, for those who are neither performers themselves nor musically gifted enough to take it in a purely intellectual way, has probably a relaxing effect upon the character. One becomes filled with emotions which habitually pass without prompting to any deed, and so the inertly sentimental condition is kept up. The remedy would be, never to suffer one's self to have an emotion at a concert, without expressing it afterward in *some* active way. Let the expression be the least thing in the world—speaking genially to one's grandmother, or giving up one's seat in a horse-car, if nothing more heroic offers—but let it not fail to take place.

These latter cases make us aware that it is not simply *particular lines* of discharge, but also *general forms* of discharge, that seem to be grooved out by habit in the brain. Just as, if we let our emotions evaporate, they get into a way of evaporating; so there is reason to suppose that if we often flinch from making an effort, before we know it the effort-making capacity will be gone; and that, if we suffer the wandering of our attention, presently it will wander all the time. Attention and effort are, as we shall see later, but two names for the same psychic fact. To what brain-processes they correspond we do not know. The strongest reason for believing that they do depend on brain-processes at all, and are not pure acts of the spirit, is just this fact, that they seem in some degree subject to the law of habit, which is a material law. As a final practical maxim, relative to these habits of the will, we may, then, offer something like this: *Keep the faculty of effort alive in you by a little gratuitous exercise every day.* That is, be systematically ascetic or heroic in little unnecessary points, do every day or two something for no other reason than that you would rather not do it, so that when the hour of dire need draws nigh, it may find you not unnerved and untrained to stand the test. Asceticism of this sort is like the insurance which a man pays on his house and goods. The tax does him no good at the time, and possibly may never bring him a return. But if the fire *does* come, his having paid it will be his salvation from ruin. So with the man who has daily inured himself to habits of concentrated attention, energetic volition, and self-denial in unnecessary things. He will stand like a tower when everything rocks around him, and when his softer fellow-mortals are winnowed like chaff in the blast.

The physiological study of mental conditions is thus the most powerful ally of hortatory ethics. The hell to be endured hereafter, of which theology tells, is no worse than the hell we make for ourselves in this world by habitually fashioning our characters in the wrong way. Could the young but realize how soon they will become mere walking bundles of habits, they would give more heed to their conduct while in the plastic state. We are spinning our own fates, good or evil, and never to be undone. Every smallest stroke of virtue or of vice leaves its never so little scar. The drunken Rip Van Winkle, in Jefferson's play, excuses himself for every fresh dereliction by saying, "I won't count this time!" Well! he may not count it, and a kind Heaven may not count it; but it is being counted none the less. Down among his nerve cells and fibres the molecules are counting it, registering and storing it up to be used against him when the next temptation comes. Nothing we ever do is, in strict scientific literalness, wiped out. Of course this has its good side as well as its bad one. As we become permanent drunkards by so many separate drinks, so we become saints in the moral, and authorities and experts in the practical and scientific spheres, by so many separate acts and hours of work. Let no youth have any anxiety about the upshot of his education, whatever the line of it may be. If he keep faithfully busy each hour of the working day, he may safely leave the final result to itself. He can with perfect certainty count on waking up some fine morning, to find himself one of the competent ones of his generation, in whatever pursuit he may have singled out. Silently, between all the details of his business, the *power of judging* in all that class of matter will have built itself up within him as a possession that will never pass away. Young people should know this truth in advance. The ignorance of it has probably engendered more discouragement and faint-heartedness in youths embarking on arduous careers than all other causes put together.

QUESTIONS

1. What, according to James, is the utility of habit for society? For the individual person?
2. Will conformity result from cultivating habits according to the maxims here presented?
3. James and Milgram ("A Behavioral Study of Obedience," pp. 413 – 427) are both psychologists. Do they appear to be working in similar ways? If dissimilar, how do you explain the difference? Is one more scientific than the other? How do the two pieces of writing compare as to subject, method of presentation, assumptions, purpose, style?
4. Compare this essay by James with his letter to his daughter (pp. 819–820). What similarities and what differences are there in content, treatment, tone? Explain these.

Prose Forms: Letters

[In 1870 a certain Perez Cowan received this short letter:

DEAR PETER,

It is indeed sweet news. I am proud of your happiness. To Peter, and Peter's, let me give both hands. Delight has no competitor, so it is always most.

"Maggie" is a warm name. I shall like to take it.

Home is the definition of God.

EMILY

Cowan had recently married Maggie, and with customary good feeling and form for such an occasion, Emily Dickinson wrote to congratulate her friend. The familiar associations of sentiment are there: Love-Marriage-Joy-Home-Blessedness. But these sentiments are felt and expressed in so uncommon a way that the reader's start of pleasure makes him attend specially to the letter. To move from one sentiment to another ordinarily requires connected development, but here one almost feels the silences between the remark about "delight" and the compliment on the bride's name, between "home" and "definition" and "God." Cowan doubtless knew Emily Dickinson's peculiar quality of mind and personality. And he must have been unsurprised at her characteristically terse, oblique expression. The letter might have been for him as if Emily spoke these things; its whole idiom and tone seem just that personal.

The letter is probably the most directly personal gesture in written language. What the letter is about may be an extra allowance, the death of a close relative, or a purchase from a business firm. But the letter is equally about the writer of it, because he inevitably, though not always self-consciously, addresses another person to whom it matters who is speaking and how. The voice of the writer, his individuality, is important because it becomes his style, his characteristic use of the language to express that complicated thing we call his perception of experience, and to express it in a way that anticipates the expectations of his reader. When Lord Chesterfield writes to his son a letter on the art of pleasing, we hear a father's voice clearly enough, but we also hear a man whose whole way of seeing life is everywhere implied in a language that insists on the formal but reconciles it with the individual's sentiment.

434

An occasion and an exchange between two people about it: the situation is not far removed in its essentials from the abundant and accustomed experience of us all. If the occasion is something a person wants to hold for himself only, he may commit his thoughts and impressions to his journal. As soon, though, as he desires to share the occasion with another, he begins to take account of the person to whom he addresses himself. He has an audience importantly different from and importantly like himself: different in that combination of personality, temperament, taste, and judgment that makes each of them a unique person; alike in a common ground of knowledge, experience, and interests which each may reasonably assume the other to be aware of. The novelist Henry James kept very full notebooks in which his persistent concern was to clarify for himself ideas and experiences of many kinds, always in terms of his own mind's needs. But James' ideas about stoicism in the face of death in his splendid letter to Grace Norton are not set down as for a journal; he takes account of Miss Norton's situation, anticipates her frame of mind, subtly gauges her feelings about the death of a loved one. His ideas assume a shape in language that takes equal measure of him as sender and Miss Norton as receiver of the letter.

Everybody, of course, writes letters which convey things of an essentially private nature: chatty, abbreviated, "secret." But it is hard for a thoughtful adult to write even so privately without verging continually on reflection, analysis, judgment of the shared intimacies. Behind James's letter to Grace Norton there is obviously a close personal relationship that permits him to take some things for granted, to assume mutual knowledges and understanding, but also to move from these to remarks that are more impersonally true and important about death and sorrow and life. In Mrs. Banning's letter to Susan the mother and daughter are involved in a specific world of manners and morals which gives much more than a private point to the mother's first remark: "No, you can't drive to Detroit for Thanksgiving with the two boys and Ann."

When the impetus to communicate through a letter becomes less personal or private, and more "public" in its interests and its manner, the essential impetus to the essay has begun. The personal essay, especially when the author speaks unequivocally as "I," is very much like a letter in the relation of Self and Occasion. The important differences is the Other, the audience, for in the essay the audience has broadened and the common ground of fact and experience is less specific. In the essay therefore, assumptions have to be more carefully considered for their appropriateness, implications have usually to be grounded in specific facts and arguments, terms and ideas must be defined, developed, clarified, the relationships of ideas have to be spelled out rather than taken for granted. At the conclusion of Baldwin's "Stranger in the Village," we are deeply involved in his assessment of the moral meaning the black-white race dilemma poses to Americans and the world, but at the beginning of the essay, we were quickly immersed in a fascinating account of the author's experience as a lone Negro in a Swiss village. Almost imperceptibly, the limits of that very personal experience expand to a sharply critical view of a complex historical and cultural problem. Baldwin maintains the unapologetic "I" in his essay with sufficient tact not to call undue attention to himself as a private person, but rather to show the continuity of his own experience and a public problem. The first part of the essay could easily have been a letter to a friend; the latter part is sufficiently public to command that general audience to which an essay is addressed. So conscious is he of his audience that the essay defines and explains, illustrates and argues, develops and extends what, in a letter, might well have been merely asserted.

But the basic considerations remain the same: something to write about; a writer; someone to read him. All that the writer is as a person affects his mode of seeing, his consciousness of what he sees. The effect he would have on a reader disciplines that consciousness. The relationship of these three—an occasion, a self, and others—underlies the letter. It is also, with suitable adjustments in the content of the terms, the relationship which underlies the essay.]

MARGARET CULKIN BANNING: Letter to Susan

November 15, 1934

DEAR SUSAN

No, you can't drive to Detroit for Thanksgiving with the two boys and Ann. I thought that I'd better put that simple, declarative sentence at the beginning of this letter so that you wouldn't be kept in suspense even if you are put in a bad temper. I'm sorry to have to be so definite and final. I would like to leave the decision to your own judgment, but this is one of the few times when I can't do that. For the judgment of so many people, young and old, is a little askew about just such propositions as four young people motoring together for most of two days and a night without any stops except for breath and coffee.

I do agree with much of what you wrote me. It would be delightful to be there for that Thanksgiving dance and it wouldn't be expensive to carry out your plan. I quite understand that you can manage the complicated schedules all around by leaving Wednesday afternoon, driving all that night and most of Thursday, and I don't doubt that you would have a grand time until Saturday noon and all be back in college by Sunday night. Also I know that Mark is probably the best driver of all your friends and that he behaves well. His father was like that too. He was also—though this bit of history may not interest you—rather dashing in his ways, like Mark. I don't know the other boy, David, or is it Daniel? (your handwriting certainly doesn't get any better) but I'll take your word for all the sterling qualities you say he has. Nobody need argue with me about Ann, after the way she measured up to family troubles and kept gay all last summer. Even you are all that I sometimes say you are, but it doesn't affect the situation.

In fact, I think it aggravates it. Such young people as you four have no right to do things that confuse you with people who are quite different in habits and ideas of control. You write, quote, please don't say that I can't go because of the looks of the thing because that's such rubbish and not like you, unquote. You're wrong on both counts. It is not rubbish and it is like me. I get a little angry about this highhanded scrapping of the looks of things. What else have we to go by? How else can the average person form an opinion of a girl's sense of values or even of her chastity except by the looks of her conduct? If looks are so unimportant, why do you yourself spend so much time on your physical looks before you go out with strangers? In your own crowd you will go around all day wearing shorts and a sweat shirt and that eternal and dreadful red checked scarf that should be burned. But if you are going to be with people you don't know or who don't know who you are, it is different.

Then you are careful to make yourself look as if you were decently bred, as if you could read and write, and as if you had good taste in clothes and cosmetics. You wouldn't be caught wearing cheap perfume, would you? Then why do you want to wear cheap perfume on your conduct?

Looks do matter and I do not mean just hair and skin and teeth and clothes. Looks are also your social contact with the world. Suppose you take this drive. How would it look to strangers? Two young men (of marriageable age) take two young women (also of marriageable age) on a forty-hour drive. Everyone knows that many girls go on forty-hour drives with men with extremely bad results, such as overexcited emotions, reckless conduct, and road accidents. How is anyone to make a special case of you? Why should anyone? It looks as if you deliberately assumed the pathetic privileges of girls who want to be with men at any cost to their reputations.

You wrote also that you think that it is nobody's business except your own what you do, but you are wrong. This is the kind of world—and there doesn't seem to be any other—in which conduct is social as well as individual. The main point of your education, from kindergarten up, has been to make you understand that, and I don't want you to break down at this small test. Your conduct is not entirely your own business, though it begins there. Afterwards it affects other people's conduct. Other girls, seeing you go off on an unchaperoned motor jaunt, think it's all right to do the same thing. Parents doubt and wonder. Men, and even boys, grow skeptical and more careless. You confuse things by such conduct.

I must also point out, even in the face of your cool young rage, that you ask a great deal more than gasoline and company of Mark and David—who may be Daniel. An unchaperoned girl, for whom a young man is responsible to parents whom he knows and respects, is a great burden to a young man. You are—so you said yourself—decent. Mark would have you on his hands in situations when people would not know whether you are decent or not. Suppose you all had an accident. Suppose, for example, that you couldn't make this trip without a long stop, speed being so eminently respectable but stops always so questionable. If you trail into some hotel after midnight, though a tourist camp should be all any of you can afford this year, it wouldn't be so easy for either of those boys. Did it ever occur to you that there's something almost crooked in the way decent girls nowadays use the shelter of their established respectability to make things awkward for men?

There's another thing in my mind which is only partly relevant. You make no mention of it, assuming the coolest of friendly relations between the four of you. But suppose that David-Daniel (I'm beginning to love that name) found himself more excited than you anticipate by the proximity—and what proximity!—of you two good-looking girls. That happens. I seem to remember having mentioned it before. It might happen to one of those two boys. And how about you and Ann? Are you quite frank with me or yourselves? Isn't part of the lure of this trip the fact that you yourself do like Mark very much? Your plan really is to drive a car full of high explosives for forty hours, from dark to dawn, and enjoy your own daring no matter who blows up.

You wrote me that it would be such fun that you hope I'll see it your way. That's always a very disarming argument, but I think it's on my side this time. You see, if there were any necessity for this trip I would feel differently about it. If you were compelled for some real reason to travel that way, if there were a war or a *siege* to make it necessary, or if it were the only way you could see Mark for years, I would say that you could do it. But fun—that so-transient fun—of just missing being hit by a bus or finding the best hamburgers in the world at a roadside inn, or being cut in on twenty times at that Thanksgiving dance—isn't a good enough reason.

It is no fun for me either, to disappoint you like this. It isn't easy to be the person who sometimes has to try to preserve your happiness at the expense of your fun. After Thanksgiving—I know you probably can't do it until then—will you please believe that's true?

With love to you, Ann, Mark and David-Daniel,

Mother

LORD CHESTERFIELD: Letter to His Son

London, October 16, O.S. 1747

Dear Boy

The art of pleasing is a very necessary one to possess, but a very difficult one to acquire. It can hardly be reduced to rules; and your own good sense and observation will teach you more of it than I can. "Do as you would be done by," is the surest method that I know of pleasing. Observe carefully what pleases you in others, and probably the same things in you will please others. If you are pleased with the complaisance and attention of others to your humors, your tastes, or your weaknesses, depend upon it, the same complaisance and attention on your part to theirs will equally please them. Take the tone of the company that you are in, and do not pretend to give it; be serious, gay, or even trifling, as you find the present humor of the company; this is an attention due from every individual to the majority. Do not tell stories in company; there is nothing more tedious and disagreeable; if by chance you know a very short story, and exceedingly applicable to the present subject of conversation, tell it in as few words as possible; and even then, throw out that you do not love to tell stories, but that the shortness of it tempted you.

Of all things banish the egotism out of your conversation, and never think of entertaining people with your own personal concerns or private affairs; though they are interesting to you, they are tedious and impertinent to everybody else; besides that, one cannot keep one's own private affairs too secret. Whatever you think your own excellencies may be, do not affectedly display them in company; nor labor, as many people do, to give that turn to the conversation, which may supply you with an opportunity of exhibiting them. If they are real, they will infallibly be discovered, without your pointing them out yourself, and with much more advantage. Never maintain an argument with heat and clamor, though you think or know yourself to be in the right; but give your opinion modestly and coolly, which is the only way to convince; and, if that does not do, try to change the conversation, by saying, with good-humor, "We shall hardly convince one another; nor is it necessary that we should, so let us talk of something else."

Remember that there is a local propriety to be observed in all companies; and that what is extremely proper in one company may be, and often is, highly improper in another.

The jokes, the *bon-mots*, the little adventures, which may do very well in one company, will seem flat and tedious, when related in another. The particular characters, the habits, the cant of one company may give merit to a word, or a gesture, which would have none at all if divested of those accidental circumstances. Here people very commonly err; and fond of something that has entertained them in one company, and in certain circumstances, repeat it with emphasis in another, where it is either insipid, or, it may be, offensive, by being ill-timed or misplaced. Nay, they often do it with this silly preamble: "I will tell you an excellent thing," or, "I will tell you the best thing in the world." This raises expectations, which, when absolutely disappointed, make the relator of this excellent thing look, very deservedly, like a fool.

If you would particularly gain the affection and friendship of particular people, whether men or women, endeavor to find out their predominant excellency, if they have one, and their prevailing weakness, which everybody has; and do justice to the one, and something more than justice to the other. Men have various objects in which they may excel, or at least would be thought to excel; and, though they love to hear justice done to them, where they know that they excel, yet they are most and best flattered upon those points where they wish to excel, and yet are doubtful whether they do or not. As for example: Cardinal Richelieu, who was undoubtedly the ablest statesman of his time, or perhaps of any other, had the idle vanity of being thought the best poet too; he envied the great Corneille his reputation, and ordered a criticism to be written upon the *Cid*. Those, therefore, who flattered skillfully, said little to him of his abilities in state affairs, or at least but *en passant*, and as it might naturally occur. But the incense which they gave him, the smoke of which they knew would turn his head in their favor, was as a *bel esprit* and a poet. Why? Because he was sure of one excellency, and distrustful as to the other.

You will easily discover every man's prevailing vanity by observing his favorite topic of conversation; for every man talks most of what he has most a mind to be thought to excel in. Touch him but there, and you touch him to the quick. The late Sir Robert Walpole (who was certainly an able man) was little open to flattery upon that head, for he was in no doubt himself about it; but his prevailing weakness was, to be thought to have a polite and happy turn to gallantry— of which he had undoubtedly less than any man living. It was his favorite and frequent subject of conversation, which proved to those who had any penetration that it was his prevailing weakness, and they applied to it with success.

Women have, in general, but one object, which is their beauty; upon which scarce any flattery is too gross for them to follow. Nature has hardly formed a woman ugly enough to be insensible to flattery upon her person; if her face is so shocking that she must, in some degree, be conscious of it, her figure and air, she trusts, make ample amends for it. If her figure is deformed, her face, she thinks, counterbalances it. If they are both bad, she comforts herself that she has graces, a certain manner, a *je ne sais quoi* still more engaging than beauty. This truth is evident from the studied and elaborate dress of the ugliest woman in the world. An undoubted, uncontested, conscious beauty is, of all women, the least sensible of flattery upon that head; she knows it is her due, and is therefore obliged to nobody for giving it her. She must be flattered upon her understanding; which, though she may possibly not doubt of herself, yet she suspects that men may distrust.

Do not mistake me, and think that I mean to recommend to you abject and criminal flattery: no; flatter nobody's vices or crimes: on the contrary, abhor and discourage them. But there is no living in the world without a complaisant indulgence for people's weaknesses, and innocent, though ridiculous vanities. If a man has a mind to be thought wiser, and a woman handsomer, than they really are, their error is a comfortable one to themselves, and an innocent one with regard to other people; and I would rather make them my friends by indulging them in it, than my enemies by endeavoring (and that to no purpose) to undeceive them.

There are little attentions, likewise, which are infinitely engaging, and which sensibly affect that degree of pride and self-love, which is inseparable from human nature, as they are unquestionable proofs of the regard and consideration which we have for the persons to whom we pay them. As, for example, to observe the little habits, the likings, the antipathies, and the tastes of those whom we would gain; and then take care to provide them with the one, and to secure them from the other; giving them, genteelly, to understand, that you had observed they liked such a dish, or such a room, for which reason you had prepared it: or, on the contrary, that having observed they had an aversion to such a dish, a dislike to such a person, etc., you had taken care to avoid presenting them. Such attention to such trifles flatters self-love much more then greater things, as it makes people think themselves almost the only objects of your thoughts and care.

These are some of the arcana necessary for your initiation in the great society of the world. I wish I had known them better at your age; I have paid the price of three and fifty years for them, and shall not grudge it if you reap the advantage. Adieu.

EMILY DICKINSON: Letters to
Thomas Wentworth Higginson[1]

April 26, 1862

MR. HIGGINSON

Your kindness claimed earlier gratitude, but I was ill, and write to-day from my pillow.

Thank you for the surgery; it was not so painful as I supposed. I bring you others, as you ask, though they might not differ. While my thought is undressed, I can make the distinction; but when I put them in the gown, they look alike and numb.

You asked how old I was? I made no verse, but one or two, until this winter, sir.

I had a terror since September, I could tell to none; and so I sing, as the boy does of the burying ground, because I am afraid.

You inquire my books. For poets, I have Keats, and Mr. and Mrs. Browning. For prose, Mr. Ruskin, Sir Thomas Browne, and the *Revelations*. I went to school, but in your manner of the phrase had no education. When a little girl, I had a friend who taught me Immortality; but venturing too near, himself, he never returned. Soon after my tutor died, and for several years my lexicon was my only companion. Then I found one more, but he was not contented I be his scholar, so he left the land.

You ask of my companions. Hills, sir, and the sundown, and a dog large as myself, that my father bought me. They are better than

1. Thomas Wentworth Higginson—minister, literary figure, and man of public affairs—wrote in 1862 for the *Atlantic Monthly* an essay of encouragement addressed to young American writers. Some time later he received a letter from Emily Dickinson containing four poems for which she asked his judgment and advice ("Are you too deeply occupied to say if my verse is alive?"). Higginson replied, making some restrained suggestions about her writing, and inviting her to write him again. The first letter printed here resumed the exchange.

beings because they know, but do not tell; and the noise in the pool at noon excels my piano.

I have a brother and sister; my mother does not care for thought, and father, too busy with his briefs to notice what we do. He buys me many books, but begs me not to read them, because he fears they joggle the mind. They are religious, except me, and address an eclipse, every morning, whom they call their "Father."

But I fear my story fatigues you. I would like to learn. Could you tell me how to grow, or is it unconveyed, like melody or witchcraft?

You speak of Mr. Whitman. I never read his book, but was told that it was disgraceful.

I read Miss Prescott's *Circumstance*, but it followed me in the dark, so I avoided her.

Two editors of journals came to my father's house this winter, and asked me for my mind, and when I asked them "why" they said I was penurious, and they would use it for the world.

I could not weigh myself, myself. My size felt small to me. I read your chapters in *The Atlantic*, and experienced honor for you. I was sure you would not reject a confiding question.

Is this, sir, what you asked me to tell you?

> Your friend,
> E. DICKINSON

Amherst, 1868

DEAR FRIEND

A letter always feels to me like Immortality because it is the mind alone without corporeal friend. Indebted in our talk to attitude and accent, there seems a spectral power in thought that walks alone. I would like to thank you for your great kindness, but never try to lift the words which I cannot hold.

Should you come to Amherst, I might then succeed, though gratitude is the timid wealth of those who have nothing. I am sure that you speak the truth, because the noble do, but your letters always surprise me.

My life has been too simple and stern to embarrass any. "Seen of angels," scarcely my responsibility.

It is difficult not to be fictitious in so fair a place, but tests' severe repairs are permitted all.

When a little girl I remember hearing that remarkable passage and preferring the "power," not knowing at the time that "kingdom" and "glory" were included.

You noticed my dwelling alone. To an emigrant, country is idle except it be his own. You speak kindly of seeing me; could it please your convenience to come so far as Amherst, I should be very glad, but I do not cross my father's ground to any house or town.

Of our greatest acts we are ignorant. You were not aware that you saved my life. To thank you in person has been since then one of my few requests. . . . You will excuse each that I say, because no one taught me.

EMILY DICKINSON: Letters to Mrs. Henry Hills

March, 1879

DEAR FRIEND

The only balmless wound is the departed human life we had learned to need.

For that, even Immortality is a slow solace. All other peace has many roots and will spring again.

With cheer from one who knows.

[SALUTATION OMITTED]

Vocal is but one form of remembrance, dear friend—the cherishing that is speechless is equally warm.

EMILY DICKINSON: Letter to Her Cousins

November, 1882

DEAR COUSINS

I hoped to write you before, but mother's dying almost stunned my spirit.

I have answered a few inquiries of love, but written little intuitively. She was scarcely the aunt you knew. The great mission of pain had been ratified—cultivated to tenderness by persistent sorrow, so that a larger mother died than had she died before. There was no earthly parting. She slipped from our fingers like a flake gathered by the wind, and is now part of the drift called "the infinite."

We don't know where she is, though so many tell us.

I believe we shall in some manner be cherished by our Maker—that the One who gave us this remarkable earth has the power still farther to surprise that which He has caused. Beyond that all is silence. . . .

Mother was very beautiful when she had died. Seraphs are solemn artists. The illumination that comes but once paused upon her features, and it seemed like hiding a picture to lay her in the grave; but the grass that received my father will suffice his guest, the one he asked at the altar to visit him all his life.

I cannot tell how Eternity seems. It sweeps around me like a sea. . . . Thank you for remembering me. Remembrance—mighty word.

"Thou gavest it to me from the foundation of the world."

Lovingly,

EMILY

THOMAS HENRY HUXLEY: Letter to Charles Kingsley

14 Waverly Place, Sept. 23, 1860

MY DEAR KINGSLEY

I cannot sufficiently thank you, both on my wife's account and my own, for your long and frank letter, and for all the hearty sympathy which it exhibits—and Mrs. Kingsley will, I hope, believe that we are no less sensible of her kind thought of us. To myself your letter was especially valuable, as it touched upon what I thought even more than upon what I said in my letter to you.

My convictions, positive and negative, on all the matters of which you speak, are of long and slow growth and are firmly rooted. But the great blow which fell upon me seemed to stir them to their foundation, and had I lived a couple of centuries earlier I could have fancied a devil scoffing at me and them—and asking me what profit it was to have stripped myself of the hopes and consolations of the mass of mankind? To which my only reply was and is—Oh devil! truth is better than much profit. I have searched over the grounds of my belief, and if wife and child and name and fame were all to be lost to me one after the other as the penalty, still I will not lie.

And now I feel that it is due to you to speak as frankly as you have done to me. An old and worthy friend of mine tried some three or four years ago to bring us together—because, as he said, you were the only man who would do me any good. Your letter leads me to think he was right, though not perhaps in the sense he attached to his own words.

To begin with the great doctrine you discuss. I neither deny nor affirm the immortality of man. I see no reason for believing in it, but, on the other hand, I have no means of disproving it.

Pray understand that I have no *a priori* objections to the doctrine. No man who has to deal daily and hourly with nature can trouble himself about *a priori* difficulties. Give me such evidence as would justify me in believing anything else, and I will believe that. Why should I not? It is not half so wonderful as the conservation of force, or the indestructibility of matter. Whoso clearly appreciates all that is implied in the falling of a stone can have no difficulty about any doctrine simply on account of its marvelousness.

But the longer I live, the more obvious it is to me that the most sacred act of a man's life is to say and to feel, "I believe such and such to be true." All the greatest rewards and all the heaviest penalties of existence cling about that act.

The universe is one and the same throughout; and if the condition of my success in unraveling some little difficulty of anatomy or physiology is that I shall rigorously refuse to put faith in that which does not rest on sufficient evidence, I cannot believe that the great mysteries of existence will be laid open to me on other terms.

It is no use to talk to me of analogies and probabilities. I know what I mean when I say I believe in the law of the inverse squares, and I will not rest my life and my hopes upon weaker convictions. I dare not if I would.

Measured by this standard, what becomes of the doctrine of immortality?

You rest in your strong conviction of your personal existence, and in the instinct of the persistence of that existence which is so strong in you as in most men.

To me this is as nothing. That my personality is the surest thing I know—may be true. But the attempt to conceive what it is leads me into mere verbal subtleties. I have champed up all that chaff about the ego and the non-ego, about noumena and phenomena, and all the rest of it, too often not to know that in attempting even to think of these questions, the human intellect flounders at once out of its depth.

It must be twenty years since, a boy, I read Hamilton's essay on the unconditioned, and from that time to this, ontological speculation has been a folly to me. When Mansel took up Hamilton's argument on the side of orthodoxy (!) I said he reminded me of nothing so much as the man who is sawing off the sign on which he is sitting, in Hogarth's picture. But this by the way.

I cannot conceive of my personality as a thing apart from the phenomena of my life. When I try to form such a conception I discover that, as Coleridge would have said, I only hypostatize a word, and it alters nothing if, with Fichte, I suppose the universe to be nothing but a manifestation of my personality. I am neither more nor less eternal than I was before.

Nor does the infinite difference between myself and the animals alter the case. I do not know whether the animals persist after they disappear or not. I do not even know whether the infinite difference between us and them may not be compensated by *their* persistence and *my* cessation after apparent death, just as the humble bulb of an annual lives, while the glorious flowers it has put forth die away.

Surely it must be plain that an ingenious man could speculate without end on both sides, and find analogies for all his dreams. Nor does it help me to tell me that the aspirations of mankind—that my own highest aspirations even—lead me toward the doctrine of immortality. I doubt the fact, to begin with, but if it be so even, what is this but in grand words asking me to believe a thing because I like it.

Science has taught to me the opposite lesson. She warns me to be careful how I adopt a view which jumps with my preconceptions, and to require stronger evidence for such belief than for one to which I was previously hostile.

My business is to teach my aspirations to conform themselves to fact, not to try and make facts harmonize with my aspirations.

Science seems to me to teach in the highest and strongest manner the great truth which is embodied in the Christian conception of entire surrender to the will of God. Sit down before fact as a little child, be prepared to give up every preconceived notion, follow humbly wherever and to whatever abysses nature leads, or you shall learn nothing. I have only begun to learn content and peace of mind since I have resolved at all risks to do this.

There are, however, other arguments commonly brought forward in favor of the immortality of man, which are to my mind not only delusive but mischievous. The one is the notion that the moral government of the world is imperfect without a system of future rewards and punishments. The other is: that such a system is indispensable to practical morality. I believe that both these dogmas are very mischievous lies.

With respect to the first, I am no optimist, but I have the firmest belief that the Divine Government (if we may use such a phrase to express the sum of the "customs of matter") is wholly just. The more I know intimately of the lives of other men (to say nothing of my own), the more obvious it is to me that the wicked does *not* flourish nor is the righteous punished. But for this to be clear we must bear in mind what almost all forget, that the rewards of life are contingent upon obedience to the *whole* law—physical as well as moral—and that moral obedience will not atone for physical sin, or *vice versa*.

The ledger of the Almighty is strictly kept, and every one of us has the balance of his operations paid over to him at the end of every minute of his existence.

Life cannot exist without a certain conformity to the surrounding universe—that conformity involves a certain amount of happiness in excess of pain. In short, as we live we are paid for living.

And it is to be recollected in view of the apparent discrepancy between men's acts and their rewards that Nature is juster than we. She takes into account what a man brings with him into the world, which human justice cannot do. If I, born a bloodthirsty and savage brute, inheriting these qualities from others, kill you, my fellow-men will very justly hang me, but I shall not be visited with the horrible remorse which would be my real punishment if, my nature being higher, I had done the same thing.

The absolute justice of the system of things is as clear to me as any scientific fact. The gravitation of sin to sorrow is as certain as that of the earth to the sun, and more so—for experimental proof of the fact is within reach of us all—nay, is before us all in our own lives, if we had but the eyes to see it.

Not only, then, do I disbelieve in the need for compensation, but I believe that the seeking for rewards and punishments out of this life leads men to a ruinous ignorance of the fact that their inevitable rewards and punishments are here.

If the expectation of hell hereafter can keep me from evil-doing, surely *a fortiori* the certainty of hell now will do so? If a man could be firmly impressed with the belief that stealing damaged him as much as swallowing arsenic would do (and it does), would not the dissuasive force of that belief be greater than that of any based on mere future expectations?

And this leads me to my other point.

As I stood behind the coffin of my little son the other day, with my mind bent on anything but disputation, the officiating minister read, as a part of his duty, the words, "If the dead rise not again, let us eat and drink, for tomorrow we die." I cannot tell you how inexpressibly they shocked me. Paul had neither wife nor child, or he must have known that his alternative involved a blasphemy against all that was best and noblest in human nature. I could have laughed with scorn. What! because I am face to face with irreparable loss, because I have given back to the source from whence it came, the cause of a great happiness, still retaining through all my life the blessings which have sprung and will spring from that cause, I am to renounce my manhood, and, howling, grovel in bestiality? Why, the very apes know better, and if you shoot their young, the poor brutes grieve their grief out and do not immediately seek distraction in a gorge.

Kicked into the world a boy without guide or training, or with worse than none, I confess to my shame that few men have drunk deeper of all kinds of sin than I. Happily, my course was arrested in time—before I had earned absolute destruction—and for long years I have been slowly and painfully climbing, with many a fall, towards better things. And when I look back, what do I find to have been the agents of my redemption? The hope of immortality or of future reward? I can honestly say that for these fourteen years such a consideration has not entered my head. No, I can tell you exactly what has been at work. *Sartor Resartus* led me to know that a deep sense of religion was compatible with the entire absence of theology. Secondly, science and her methods gave me a resting place independent of authority and tradition. Thirdly, love opened up to me a view of the sanctity of human nature, and impressed me with a deep sense of responsibility.

If at this moment I am not a worn-out, debauched, useless carcass of a man, if it has been or will be my fate to advance the cause of science, if I feel that I have a shadow of a claim on the love of those about me, if in the supreme moment when I looked down into my boy's grave my sorrow was full of submission and without bitterness, it is because these agencies have worked upon me, and not because I have ever cared whether my poor personality shall remain distinct for ever from the All from whence it came and whither it goes.

And thus, my dear Kingsley, you will understand what my position is. I may be quite wrong, and in that case I know I shall have to pay the penalty for being wrong. But I can only say with Luther, "*Gott helfe mir, Ich kann nichts anders.*"[1]

I know right well that 99 out of 100 of my fellows would call me atheist, infidel, and all the other usual hard names. As our laws stand, if the lowest thief steals my coat, my evidence (my opinions being known) would not be received against him.

But I cannot help it. One thing people shall not call me with justice, and that is—a liar. As you say of yourself, I too feel that I lack courage; but if ever the occasion arises when I am bound to speak, I will not shame my boy.

I have spoken more openly and distinctly to you than I ever have to any human being except my wife.

If you can show me that I err in premises or conclusion, I am ready to give up these as I would any other theories. But at any rate you will do me the justice to believe that I have not reached my conclusions without the care befitting the momentous nature of the problems involved.

And I write this the more readily to you, because it is clear to me that if that great and powerful instrument for good or evil, the Church of England, is to be saved from being shivered into fragments by the advancing tide of science—an event I should be very sorry to witness, but which will infallibly occur if men like Samuel of Oxford are to have the guidance of her destinies—it must be by the efforts of men who, like yourself, see your way to the combination of the practice of the Church with the spirit of science. Understand that all the younger men of science whom I know intimately are *essentially* of my way of thinking. (I know not a scoffer or an irreligious or an immoral man among them, but they all regard orthodoxy as you do Brahmanism.) Understand that this new school of the prophets is the only one that can work miracles, the only one that can constantly appeal to nature for evidence that it is right, and will constantly appeal to nature for evidence that it is right, and you will comprehend that it is of no use to try to barricade us with shovel hats and aprons, or to talk about our doctrines being "shocking."

I don't profess to understand the logic of yourself, Maurice, and the rest of your school, but I have always said I would swear by your truthfulness and sincerity, and that good must come of your efforts.

1. "God help me, I can do no other."

The more plain this was to me, however, the more obvious the necessity to let you see where the men of science are driving, and it has often been in my mind to write to you before.

If I have spoken too plainly anywhere, or too abruptly, pardon me, and do the like to me.

My wife thanks you very much for your volume of sermons. Ever yours very faithfully,

T. H. HUXLEY

ABRAHAM LINCOLN: Letter to James M. Cutts, Jr.[1]

Executive Mansion
Washington, Oct. 26, 1863

CAPT. JAMES M. CUTTS.

Although what I am now to say is to be, in form, a reprimand, it is not intended to add a pang to what you have already suffered

1. This reprimand may have been delivered to Captain Cutts in a personal interview. Never published by Nicolay and Hay for obvious reasons, a portion was, however, incorporated in their footnote to Lincoln's letter to William G. Anderson, October 31, 1840, as an unidentified bit of advice "given many years afterward to a young officer condemned to be court-martialed for quarreling" (NH, I, 152).

The court-martial trial on June 30, 1863, of Captain James Madison Cutts, Jr., brother of Stephen A. Douglas' second wife, on the charge of "conduct unbecoming an officer and a gentleman," involved three subordinate specifications: (1) that Cutts had used unbecoming language in addressing Captain Charles G. Hutton, aide-de-camp to General Burnside, when Hutton attempted to take over Cutts' desk; (2) that Cutts had sent a written communication to Major William Cutting derogatory to the accomplishments of Captain Hutton as an officer; and (3) that the said "*James M. Cutts* . . . did, on or about the 10th day of April, 1863, while occupying room No. 79, Burnet House, Cincinnati, Ohio, on the afternoon of said day, attempt to look through the key-hole of room No. 80 of said house, occupied by a gentleman and his wife, and did, in the evening of said day, at about half past eleven o'clock, after said lady had retired to her room, and while her husband was in the corridor below, said lady being at the time partly undressed, previous to retiring, take a valise or portmanteau from his room and . . . placing himself thereon, did look through the Venetian blind or transom light in or over the door into said room and at said lady while undressing. . . ." (AGO *General Orders No. 330*, October 8, 1863). To the first

and second specifications Cutts pleaded not guilty; to the third, he acknowledged the facts" with deep regret," and pleaded guilty. The court found him guilty on all three specifications and sentenced him to be dismissed from the service.

In connection with this episode, John Hay's *Diary* on July 18 records Lincoln's humorous remark that Cutts "should be elevated to the peerage for it with the title of Count Peeper." Lincoln's pun and allusion were probably suggested by the name of the Swedish minister, Edward Count Piper.

Tried before the same court-martial, Captain Hutton was found guilty of having sent Captain Cutts a challenge to a duel, but was sentenced merely to a presidential reprimand. Major Cutting was found not guilty of the charge of having carried the challenge from Hutton to Cutts.

Lincoln approved the proceedings in the cases of Cutting and Cutts, but in view of Cutts' previous good character . . . and gallant conduct in battle" remitted the sentence after reprimand. (*General Orders No. 330*). The proceedings in the case of Captain Hutton, Lincoln disapproved, because "The penalty fixed by the 25th Article of War for the offence of which the accused is found guilty, viz., sending a challenge to another officer, is cashiering, and admits of no alternative. . . . The President directs that Captain Hutton be dismissed the service of the United States from the 28th day of September, 1863." (*Ibid.*). Hutton was reappointed, however, as of October 30, 1863, and served throughout the war. [This note comes from *The Collected Works of Abraham Lincoln*, Roy P. Basler, ed., Marion Dolores Pratt and Lloyd A. Dunlap, asst. eds., Vol. VI.]

upon the subject to which it relates. You have too much of life yet before you, and have shown too much of promise as an officer, for your future to be lightly surrendered. You were convicted of two offences. One of them, not of great enormity, and yet greatly to be avoided, I feel sure you are in no danger of repeating. The other you are not so well assured against. The advice of a father to his son "Beware of entrance to a quarrel, but being in, bear it that the opposed may beware of thee,"[2] is good, and yet not the best. Quarrel not at all. No man resolved to make the most of himself, can spare time for personal contention. Still less can he afford to take all the consequences, including the vitiating of his temper, and the loss of self-control. Yield larger things to which you can show no more than equal right; and yield lesser ones, though clearly your own. Better give your path to a dog, than be bitten by him in contesting for the right. Even killing the dog would not cure the bite.

In the mood indicated deal henceforth with your fellow men, and especially with your brother officers; and even the unpleasant events you are passing from will not have been profitless to you.

2. Polonius to Laertes, *Hamlet* I, iii, 65-67.

HENRY JAMES: Letter to Grace Norton

131 Mount Vernon St., Boston
July 28 [1883]

MY DEAR GRACE

Before the sufferings of others I am always utterly powerless, and your letter reveals such depths of suffering that I hardly know what to say to you. This indeed is not my last word—but it must be my first. You are not isolated, verily, in such states of feeling as this—that is, in the sense that you appear to make all the misery of all mankind your own; only I have a terrible sense that you give all and receive nothing—that there is no reciprocity in your sympathy—that you have all the affliction of it and none of the returns. However—I am determined not to speak to you except with the voice of stoicism. I don't know *why* we live—the gift of life comes to us from I don't know what source or for what purpose; but I believe we can go on living for the reason that (always of course up to a certain point) life is the most valuable thing we know anything about, and it is therefore presumptively a great mistake to surrender it while there is any yet left in the cup. In other words consciousness is an illimitable power, and though at times it may seem to be all consciousness of misery, yet in the way it propagates itself from wave to wave, so that we never cease to feel, and though at moments we appear to, try to, pray to, there is something that holds one in one's place, makes it a standpoint in the universe which it is probably good not to forsake. You are right in your consciousness that we are all echoes and reverberations of the *same*, and you are noble when your interest and pity as to everything that surrounds you, appears to have a sustaining and harmonizing power. Only don't, I beseech you, *generalize* too much in these sympathies and tendernesses—remember that every life is a special problem which is not yours but another's, and content yourself with the terrible algebra of your own. Don't melt too much into the universe, but be as solid and dense and fixed as you can. We all live together, and those of us who love and know, live so most. We help each other—even unconsciously, each in our own effort, we lighten the effort of others, we contribute to the sum of success, make it possible for others to live. Sorrow comes in great waves—no one can know that better than you—but it rolls over us, and though it may almost smother us it leaves us on the spot, and we know that if it is strong we are stronger, inasmuch as it passes and we remain. It wears us, uses us, but we wear it and use it in return; and it is blind, whereas we after a manner see. My dear Grace, you are passing through a darkness in which I myself in my ignorance see nothing but that you have been made wretchedly ill by it; but it is only a darkness, it is not an end, or *the* end. Don't think, don't feel, any more than you can help, don't conclude or decide—don't do anything but *wait*. Everything will pass, and serenity and *accepted* mysteries and disillusionments, and the tenderness of a few good people, and new opportunities and ever so much of life, in a word, will remain. You will do all sorts of things yet, and I will help you. The only thing is not to *melt* in the meanwhile. I insist upon the necessity of a sort of mechanical condensation—so that however fast the horse may run away there will, when he pulls up, be a somewhat agitated but perfectly identical G. N. left in the saddle. Try not to be ill—that is all; for in that there is a failure. You are marked out for success, and you must not fail. You have my tenderest affection and all my confidence. Ever your faithful friend—

HENRY JAMES

On Civilization

JOHN STUART MILL

Civilization: Signs of the Times

The word "civilization," like many other terms of the philosophy of human nature, is a word of double meaning. It sometimes stands for *human improvement* in general, and sometimes for *certain kinds* of improvement in particular.

We are accustomed to call a country more civilized if we think it more improved; more eminent in the best characteristics of man and society; farther advanced in the road to perfection; happier, nobler, wiser. This is one sense of the word "civilization." But, in another sense, it stands for that kind of improvement only which distinguishes a wealthy and powerful nation from savages or barbarians. It is in this sense that we may speak of the vices or the miseries of civilization; and that the question has been seriously propounded, whether civilization is, on the whole, a good or an evil. Assuredly, we entertain no doubt on this point: we hold that civilization is a good; that it is the cause of much good, and not incompatible with any; but we think there is other good, much even of the highest good, which civilization in this sense does not provide for, and some which it has a tendency (though that tendency may be counteracted) to impede.

The inquiry into which these considerations would lead is calculated to throw light upon many of the characteristic features of our

and manufacturing classes, the gradual emancipation of the agricultural, the tumults and *bouleversements*[2] which accompanied these changes in their course, and the extraordinary alterations in institutions, opinions, habits, and the whole of social life, which they brought in their train. We need only ask the reader to form a conception of all that is implied in the words "growth of a middle class," and then to reflect on the immense increase of the numbers and property of that class throughout Great Britain, France, Germany, and other countries, in every successive generation, and the novelty of a laboring class receiving such wages as are now commonly earned by nearly the whole of the manufacturing, that is, of the most numerous, portion of the operative classes of this country—and ask himself, whether, from causes so unheard of, unheard-of effects ought not to be expected to flow. It must at least be evident, that if, as civilization advances, property and intelligence become thus widely diffused among the millions, it must also be an effect of civilization, that the portion of either of these which can belong to an individual must have a tendency to become less and less influential, and all results must more and more be decided by the movements of masses, provided that the power of combination among the masses keeps pace with the progress of their resources. And that it does so, who can doubt? There is not a more accurate test of the progress of civilization than the progress of the power of co-operation.

Consider the savage: he has bodily strength, he has courage, enterprise, and is often not without intelligence. What makes all savage communities poor and feeble? The same cause which prevented the lions and tigers from long ago extirpating the race of men—incapacity of co-operation. It is only civilized beings who can combine. All combination is compromise: it is the sacrifice of some portion of individual will for a common purpose. The savage cannot bear to sacrifice, for any purpose, the satisfaction of his individual will. His social cannot even temporarily prevail over his selfish feelings, nor his impulses bend to his calculations. Look again at the slave: he is used, indeed, to make his will give way, but to the commands of a master, not to a superior purpose of his own. He is wanting in intelligence to form such a purpose: above all, he cannot frame to himself the conception of a fixed rule; nor, if he could, has he the capacity to adhere to it. He is habituated to control, but not to self-control: when a driver is not standing over him with a whip, he is found more incapable of withstanding any temptation, or restraining any inclination, than the savage himself.

We have taken extreme cases, that the fact we seek to illustrate might stand out more conspicuously. But the remark itself applies universally. As any people approach to the condition of savages or of slaves, so are they incapable of acting in concert. Consider even war,

2. Commotions.

the most serious business of a barbarous people: see what a figure rude nations, or semi-civilized and enslaved nations, have made against civilized ones, from Marathon downwards! Why? Because discipline is more powerful than numbers, and discipline—that is, perfect co-operation—is an attribute of civilization. To come to our own times, the whole history of the Peninsular War bears witness to the incapacity of an imperfectly civilized people for co-operation. Amidst all the enthusiasm of the Spanish nation struggling against Napoléon, no one leader, military or political, could act in concert with another; no one would sacrifice one iota of his consequence, his authority, or his opinion, to the most obvious demands of the common cause: neither generals nor soldiers could observe the simplest rules of the military art. If there be an interest which one might expect to act forcibly upon the minds even of savages, it is the desire of simultaneously crushing a formidable neighbor whom none of them are strong enough to resist single-handed; yet none but civilized nations have ever been capable of forming an alliance. The native states of India have been conquered by the English, one by one; Turkey made peace with Russia in the very moment of her invasion by France; the nations of the world never could form a confederacy against the Romans, but were swallowed up in succession, some of them being always ready to aid in the subjugation of the rest. Enterprises requiring the voluntary co-operation of many persons independent of one another, in the hands of all but highly civilized nations, have always failed.

It is not difficult to see why this incapacity of organized combination characterizes savages, and disappears with the growth of civilization. Co-operation, like other difficult things, can be learnt only by practice; and, to be capable of it in great things, a people must be gradually trained to it in small. Now, the whole course of advancing civilization is a series of such training. The laborer in a rude state of society works singly; or, if several are brought to work together by the will of a master, they work side by side, but not in concert: one man digs his piece of ground; another digs a similar piece of ground close by him. In the situation of an ignorant laborer, tilling even his own field with his own hands, and associating with no one except his wife and his children, what is there that can teach him to co-operate? The division of employments; the accomplishment, by the combined labor of several, of tasks which could not be achieved by any number of persons singly—is the great school of co-operation. What a lesson, for instance, is navigation, as soon as it passes out of its first simple stage!—the safety of all constantly depending upon the vigilant performance, by each, of the part peculiarly allotted to him in the common task. Military operations, when not wholly undisciplined, are a similar school; so are all the operations of commerce and manufactures which require the employment of many hands upon the same thing at the same time. By these operations, mankind learn the value of combination; they see how much and with what ease it accomplishes, which never could be accomplished without it; they learn a practical lesson of submitting themselves to guidance, and subduing themselves to act as interdependent parts of a complex whole. A people thus progressively trained to combination by the business of their lives become capable of carrying the same habits into new things. For it holds universally, that the only mode of learning to do any thing is actually doing something of the same kind under easier circumstances. Habits of discipline, once acquired, qualify human beings to accomplish all other things for which discipline is needed. No longer either spurning control, or incapable of seeing its advantages, whenever any object presents itself which can be attained by co-operation, and which they see or believe to be beneficial, they are ripe for attaining it.

The characters, then, of a state of high civilization being the diffusion of property and intelligence, and the power of co-operation, the next thing to observe is the unexampled development which all these elements have assumed of late years.

The rapidity with which property has accumulated and is accumulating in the principal countries of Europe, but especially in this island, is obvious to every one. The capital of the industrious classes overflows into foreign countries, and into all kinds of wild speculations. The amount of capital annually exported from Great Britain alone, surpasses, probably, the whole wealth of the most flourishing commercial republics of antiquity. But this capital, collectively so vast, is mainly composed of small portions; very generally so small, that the owners cannot, without other means of livelihood, subsist on the profits of them. While such is the growth of property in the hands of the mass, the circumstances of the higher classes have undergone nothing like a corresponding improvement. Many large fortunes have, it is true, been accumulated; but many others have been wholly or partially dissipated: for the inheritors of immense fortunes, as a class, always live at least up to their incomes when at the highest; and the unavoidable vicissitudes of those incomes are always sinking them deeper and deeper into debt. A large proportion of the English landlords, as they themselves are constantly telling us, are so overwhelmed with mortgages, that they have ceased to be the real owners of the bulk of their estates. In other countries, the large properties have very generally been broken down; in France, by revolution, and the revolutionary law of inheritance; in Prussia, by successive edicts of that substantially democratic though formally absolute government.

With respect to knowledge and intelligence, it is the truism of the age, that the masses, both of the middle and even of the working classes, are treading upon the heels of their superiors.

If we now consider the progress made by those same masses in the capacity and habit of co-operation, we find it equally surprising. At what period were the operations of productive industry carried on upon any thing like their present scale? Were so many hands ever before employed at the same time, upon the same work, as now in all the principal departments of manufactures and commerce? To how enormous an extent is business now carried on by joint-stock companies!—in other words, by many small capitals thrown together to form one great one. The country is covered with associations. There are societies for political, societies for religious, societies for philanthropic purposes. But the greatest novelty of all is the spirit of combination which has grown up among the working classes. The present age has seen the commencement of benefit societies; and they now, as well as the more questionable Trades Unions, overspread the whole country. A more powerful, though not so ostensible, instrument of combination than any of these, has but lately become universally accessible—the newspaper. The newspaper carries home the voice of the many to every individual among them: by the newspaper, each learns that others are feeling as he feels; and that, if he is ready, he will find them also prepared to act upon what they feel. The newspaper is the telegraph which carries the signal throughout the country, and the flag round which it rallies. Hundreds of newspapers speaking in the same voice at once, and the rapidity of communication afforded by improved means of locomotion, were what enabled the whole country to combine in that simultaneous energetic demonstration of determined will which carried the Reform Act. Both these facilities are on the increase, every one may see how rapidly; and they will enable the people on all decisive occasions to form a collective will, and render that collective will irresistible.

To meet this wonderful development of physical and mental power on the part of the masses, can it be said that there has been any corresponding quantity of intellectual power or moral energy unfolded among those individuals or classes who have enjoyed superior advantages? No one, we think, will affirm it. There is a great increase of humanity, a decline of bigotry, as well as of arrogance and the conceit of caste, among our conspicuous classes; but there is, to say the least, no increase of shining ability, and a very marked decrease of vigor and energy. With all the advantages of this age, its facilities for mental cultivation, the incitements and the rewards which it holds out to exalted talents, there can scarcely be pointed out in the European annals any stirring times which have brought so little that is distinguished, either morally or intellectually, to the surface.

That this, too, is no more than was to be expected from the tendencies of civilization, when no attempt is made to correct them, we shall have occasion to show presently. But, even if civilization did nothing to lower the eminences, it would produce an exactly similar effect by raising the plains. When the masses become powerful, an individual, or a small band of individuals, can accomplish nothing considerable except by influencing the masses; and to do this becomes daily more difficult, from the constantly increasing number of those who are vying with one another to attract the public attention. Our position, therefore, is established, that, by the natural growth of civilization, power passes from individuals to masses, and the weight and importance of an individual, as compared with the mass, sink into greater and greater insignificance.

The change which is thus in progress, and to a great extent consummated, is the greatest ever recorded in social affairs; the most complete, the most fruitful in consequences, and the most irrevocable. Whoever can meditate on it, and not see that so great a revolution vitiates all existing rules of government and policy, and renders all practice and all predictions grounded only on prior experience worthless, is wanting in the very first and most elementary principle of statesmanship in these times.

"*Il faut,*" as M. de Tocqueville has said, "*une science politique nouvelle à un monde tout nouveau.*"[3] The whole face of society is reversed; all the natural elements of power have definitely changed places; and there are people who talk of standing up for ancient institutions, and the duty of sticking to the British Constitution settled in 1688! What is still more extraordinary, these are the people who accuse others of disregarding variety of circumstances, and imposing their abstract theories upon all states of society without discrimination.

We put it to those who call themselves conservatives, whether, when the chief power in society is passing into the hands of the masses, they really think it possible to prevent the masses from making that power predominant as well in the government as elsewhere. The triumph of democracy, or, in other words, of the government of public opinion, does not depend upon the opinion of any individual, or set of individuals, that it ought to triumph, but upon the natural laws of the progress of wealth, upon the diffusion of reading, and the increase of the facilities of human intercourse. If Lord Kenyon or the Duke of Newcastle could stop these, they might accomplish something. There is no danger of the prevalence of democracy in Syria or Timbuctoo. But he must be a poor politician who does not know, that whatever is the growing power in society will force its way into the government by fair means or foul. The distribution of constitutional power cannot long continue very different from that of real power, without a convulsion; nor, if the institutions which impede the progress of democracy could be by any miracle preserved, could even they do more than render that progress a little slower. Were the constitution of Great Britain to remain henceforth unaltered, we are

3. "An entirely new world requires a new science of government."

not the less under the dominion, becoming every day more irresistible, of public opinion.

With regard to the advance of democracy, there are two different positions which it is possible for a rational person to take up, according as he thinks the masses prepared or unprepared to exercise the control which they are acquiring over their destiny, in a manner which would be an improvement upon what now exists. If he thinks them prepared, he will aid the democratic movement; or, if he deem it to be proceeding fast enough without him, he will at all events refrain from resisting it. If, on the contrary, he thinks the masses unprepared for complete control over their government—seeing at the same time, that, prepared or not, they cannot long be prevented from acquiring it—he will exert his utmost efforts in contributing to prepare them: using all means, on the one hand, for making the masses themselves wiser and better; on the other, for so rousing the slumbering energy of the opulent and lettered classes, so storing the youth of those classes with the profoundest and most valuable knowledge, so calling forth whatever of individual greatness exists or can be raised up in the country, as to create a power which might partially rival the mere power of the masses, and might exercise the most salutary influence over them for their own good. When engaged earnestly in works like these, one can understand how a rational person might think, that, in order to give more time for the performance of them, it were well if the current of democracy, which can in no sort be stayed, could be prevailed upon, for a time, to flow less impetuously. With conservatives of this sort, all democrats of corresponding enlargement of aims could fraternize as frankly and cordially as with most of their own friends; and we speak from an extensive knowledge of the wisest and most high-minded of that body, when we take upon ourselves to answer for them, that they would never push forward their own political projects in a spirit or with a violence which could tend to frustrate any rational endeavors towards the object nearest their hearts—the instruction of the understandings, and the elevation of the characters, of all classes of their countrymen.

But who is there, among the political party calling themselves conservatives, that professes to have any such object in view? Do they seek to employ the interval of respite, which they might hope to gain by withstanding democracy, in qualifying the people to wield the democracy more wisely when it comes? Would they not far rather resist any such endeavor, on the principle that knowledge is power, and that its further diffusion would make the dreaded evil come sooner? Do the leading conservatives in either house of Parliament feel that the character of the higher classes needs renovating, to qualify them for a more arduous task and a keener strife than has yet fallen to their lot? Is not the character of a Tory lord or country gentleman, or a Church-of-England parson, perfectly satisfactory to them? Is not the existing constitution of the two universities—those bodies whose especial duty it was to counteract the debilitating influence of the circumstances of the age upon individual character, and to send forth into society a succession of minds, not the creatures of their age, but capable of being its improvers and regenerators—the universities, by whom this, their especial duty, has been basely neglected, until, as is usual with all neglected duties, the very consciousness of it as a duty has faded from their remembrance —is not, we say, the existing constitution, and the whole existing system of these universities, down to the smallest of their abuses—the exclusion of Dissenters—a thing for which every Tory, though he may not, as he pretends, die in the last ditch, will at least vote in the last division? The Church, professedly the other great instrument of national culture, long since perverted (we speak of rules, not exceptions) into a grand instrument for discouraging all culture inconsistent with blind obedience to established maxims and constituted authorities—what Tory has a scheme in view for any changes in this body, but such as may pacify assailants, and make the institution wear a less disgusting appearance to the eye? What political Tory will not resist to the very last moment any alteration in that Church, which would prevent its livings from being the provision for a family, its dignities the reward of political or of private services? The Tories, those at least connected with Parliament or office, do not aim at having good institutions, or even at preserving the present ones; their object is to profit by them while they exist.

We scruple not to express our belief, that a truer spirit of conservation, as to every thing good in the principles and professed objects of our old institutions, lives in many who are determined enemies of those institutions in their present state, than in most of those who call themselves conservatives. But there are many well-meaning people who always confound attachment to an end with pertinacious adherence to any set of means by which it either is, or is pretended to be, already pursued; and have yet to learn, that bodies of men who live in honor and importance upon the pretence of fulfilling ends which they never honestly seek are the great hindrance to the attainment of those ends, and that whoever has the attainment really at heart must expect a war of extermination with all such confederacies.

Thus far as to the political effects of civilization. Its moral effects, which as yet we have only glanced at, demand further elucidation. They may be considered under two heads—the direct influence of civilization itself upon individual character, and the moral effects produced by the insignificance into which the individual falls in comparison with the masses.

One of the effects of a high state of civilization upon character is a relaxation of individual energy, or rather the concentration of it within the narrow sphere of the individual's money-getting pursuits. As civilization advances, every person becomes dependent for more and more of what most nearly concerns him, not upon his own exertions, but upon the general arrangements of society. In a rude state, each man's personal security, the protection of his family, his property, his liberty itself, depend greatly upon his bodily strength and his mental energy or cunning: in a civilized state, all this is secured to him by causes extrinsic to himself. The growing mildness of manners is a protection to him against much that he was before exposed to; while, for the remainder, he may rely with constantly increasing assurance upon the soldier, the policeman, and the judge, and (where the efficiency or purity of those instruments, as is usually the case, lags behind the general march of civilization) upon the advancing strength of public opinion. There remain, as inducements to call forth the energy of character, the desire of wealth or of personal aggrandizement, the passion of philanthropy, and the love of active virtue. But the objects to which these various feelings point are matters of choice, not of necessity; nor do the feelings act with any thing like equal force upon all minds. The only one of them which can be considered as any thing like universal is the desire of wealth; and wealth being, in the case of the majority, the most accessible means of gratifying all their other desires, nearly the whole of the energy of character which exists in highly civilized societies concentrates itself on the pursuit of that object. In the case, however, of the most influential classes—those whose energies, if they had them, might be exercised on the greatest scale and with the most considerable result—the desire of wealth is already sufficiently satisfied to render them averse to suffer pain or incur much voluntary labor for the sake of any further increase. The same classes also enjoy, from their station alone, a high degree of personal consideration. Except the high offices of the state, there is hardly any thing to tempt the ambition of men in their circumstances. Those offices, when a great nobleman could have them for asking for, and keep them with less trouble than he could manage his private estate, were, no doubt, desirable enough possessions for such persons; but when they become posts of labor, vexation, and anxiety, and, besides, cannot be had without paying the price of some previous toil, experience shows, that, among men unaccustomed to sacrifice their amusements and their ease, the number upon whom these high offices operate as incentives to activity, or in whom they call forth any vigor of character, is extremely limited. Thus it happens, that in highly civilized countries, and particularly among ourselves, the energies of the middle classes are almost confined to money-getting, and those of the higher classes are nearly extinct.

There is another circumstance to which we may trace much both of the good and of the bad qualities which distinguish our civilization from the rudeness of former times. One of the effects of civilization (not to say one of the ingredients in it) is, that the spectacle, and even the very idea, of pain, is kept more and more out of the sight of those classes who enjoy in their fulness the benefits of civilization. The state of perpetual personal conflict, rendered necessary by the circumstances of former times, and from which it was hardly possible for any person, in whatever rank of society, to be exempt, necessarily habituated every one to the spectacle of harshness, rudeness, and violence, to the struggle of one indomitable will against another, and to the alternate suffering and infliction of pain. These things, consequently, were not as revolting even to the best and most actively benevolent men of former days as they are to our own; and we find the recorded conduct of those men frequently such as would be universally considered very unfeeling in a person of our own day. They, however, thought less of the infliction of pain, because they thought less of pain altogether. When we read of actions of the Greeks and Romans, or of our own ancestors, denoting callousness to human suffering, we must not think that those who committed these actions were as cruel as we must become before we could do the like. The pain which they inflicted they were in the habit of voluntarily undergoing from slight causes: it did not appear to them as great an evil as it appears, and as it really is, to us; nor did it in any way degrade their minds. In our own time, the necessity of personal collision between one person and another is, comparatively speaking, amost at an end. All those necessary portions of the business of society which oblige any person to be the immediate agent or ocular witness of the infliction of pain are delegated by common consent to peculiar and narrow classes—to the judge, the soldier, the surgeon, the butcher, and the executioner. To most people in easy circumstances, any pain, except that inflicted upon the body by accident or disease, and upon the mind by the inevitable sorrows of life, is rather a thing known of than actually experienced. This is much more emphatically true in the more refined classes, and as refinement advances; for it is in avoiding the presence, not only of actual pain, but of whatever suggests offensive or disagreeable ideas, that a great part of refinement consists. We may remark, too, that this is possible only by a perfection of mechanical arrangements impracticable in any but a high state of civilization. Now, most kinds of pain and annoyance appear much more unendurable to those who have little experience of them than to those who have much. The consequence is, that, compared with former times, there is in the more opulent classes of modern civilized communities much more of the amiable and humane, and much less of the heroic. The heroic essentially consists in being ready, for a worthy object, to do and to suffer, but especially to do, what is painful or disagreeable; and whoever does not early learn to be capable of this will never be a great character. There has crept over the refined classes, over the whole class of gentlemen in England, a moral effeminacy, an inaptitude for every kind of struggle. They shrink from all effort, from every thing which is troublesome and disagreeable. The same causes which render them sluggish and unenterprising, make them, it is true, for the most part, stoical under inevitable evils. But heroism is an active, not a passive quality; and when it is necessary not to bear pain, but to seek it, little needs be expected from the men of the present day. They cannot undergo labor, they cannot brook ridicule, they cannot brave evil tongues: they have not hardihood to say an unpleasant thing to any one whom they are in the habit of seeing, or to face, even with a nation at their back, the coldness of some little coterie which surrounds them. This torpidity and cowardice, as a general characteristic, is new in the world; but (modified by the different temperaments of different nations) it is a natural consequence of the progress of civilization, and will continue until met by a system of cultivation adapted to counteract it.

If the source of great virtues thus dries up, great vices are placed, no doubt, under considerable restraint. The *régime* of public opinion is adverse to at least the indecorous vices; and as that restraining power gains strength, and certain classes or individuals cease to possess a virtual exemption from it, the change is highly favorable to the outward decencies of life. Nor can it be denied, that the diffusion of even such knowledge as civilization naturally brings has no slight tendency to rectify, though it be but partially, the standard of public opinion; to undermine many of those prejudices and superstitions which made mankind hate each other for things not really odious; to make them take a juster measure of the tendencies of actions, and weigh more correctly the evidence on which they condemn or applaud their fellow-creatures; to make, in short, their approbation direct itself more correctly to good actions, and their disapprobation to bad. What are the limits to this natural improvement in public opinion, when there is no other sort of cultivation going on than that which is the accompaniment of civilization, we need not at present inquire. It is enough that within those limits there is an extensive range; that as much improvement in the general understanding, softening of the feelings, and decay of pernicious errors, as naturally attends the progress of wealth and the spread of reading, suffices to render the judgment of the public upon actions and persons, so far as evidence is before them, much more discriminating and correct.

But here presents itself another ramification of the effects of civilization, which it has often surprised us to find so little attended to. The individual becomes so lost in the crowd, that, though he depends more and more upon opinion, he is apt to depend less and less upon well-grounded opinion—upon the opinion of those who know him. An established character becomes at once more difficult to gain, and more easily to be dispensed with.

It is in a small society, where everybody knows everybody, that public opinion, so far as well directed, exercises its most salutary influence. Take the case of a tradesman in a small country town. To every one of his customers he is long and accurately known: their opinion of him has been formed after repeated trials: if he could deceive them once, he cannot hope to go on deceiving them, in the quality of his goods: he has no other customers to look for if he loses these; while, if his goods are really what they profess to be, he may hope, among so few competitors, that this also will be known and recognized, and that he will acquire the character, individually and professionally, which his conduct entitles him to. Far different is the case of a man setting up in business in the crowded streets of a great city. If he trust solely to the quality of his goods, to the honesty and faithfulness with which he performs what he undertakes, he may remain ten years without a customer: be he ever so honest, he is driven to cry out on the housetops that his wares are the best of wares, past, present, and to come; while if he proclaim this, however false, with sufficient loudness to excite the curiosity of passers-by, and can give his commodities "a gloss, a salable look," not easily to be seen through at a superficial glance, he may drive a thriving trade, though no customer ever enter his shop twice. There has been much complaint of late years of growth, both in the world of trade and in that of intellect, of quackery, and especially of puffing: but nobody seems to have remarked that these are the inevitable fruits of immense competition; of a state of society, where any voice, not pitched in an exaggerated key, is lost in the hubbub. Success, in so crowded a field, depends, not upon what a person is, but upon what he seems: mere marketable qualities become the object instead of substantial ones, and a man's labor and capital are expended less in doing any thing than in persuading other people that he has done it. Our own age has seen this evil brought to its consummation. Quackery there always was; but it once was a test of the absence of sterling qualities: there was a proverb, that good wine needed no bush. It is our own age which has seen the honest dealer driven to quackery by hard necessity, and the certainty of being undersold by the dishonest. For the first time, arts for attracting public attention form a necessary part of the qualifications even of the deserving; and skill in these goes farther than any other quality towards insuring success. The same intensity of competition drives the trading public more and more to play high for success; to throw for all or nothing; and this, together with the difficulty of sure calculations in a field of commerce so widely extended, renders bankruptcy no longer disgraceful, because no longer an almost certain presumption either of dishonesty or imprudence: the discredit which it still incurs belongs to it, alas! mainly as an indication of poverty. Thus public opinion loses another of those simple criteria of desert, which, and which alone, it is capable of correctly applying; and the very cause, which has rendered it omnipotent in the gross, weakens the precision and force with which its judgment is brought home to individuals.

It is not solely on the private virtues that this growing insignificance of the individual in the mass is productive of mischief. It corrupts the very fountain of the improvement of public opinion itself; it corrupts public teaching; it weakens the influence of the more cultivated few over the many. Literature has suffered more than any other human production by the common disease. When there were few books, and when few read at all save those who had been accustomed to read the best authors, books were written with the well-grounded expectation that they would be read carefully, and, if they deserved it, would be read often. A book of sterling merit, when it came out, was sure to be heard of, and might hope to be read, by the whole reading class: it might succeed by its real excellences, though not got up to strike at once; and, even if so got up, unless it had the support of genuine merit, it fell into oblivion. The rewards were then for him who wrote *well*, not *much*; for the laborious and learned, not the crude and ill-informed writer. But now the case is reversed. "This is a reading age; and, precisely because it is so reading an age, any book which is the result of profound meditation is perhaps less likely to be duly and profitably read than at a former period. The world reads too much and too quickly to read well. When books were few, to get through one was a work of time and labor: what was written with thought was read with thought, and with a desire to extract from it as much of the materials of knowledge as possible. But when almost every person who can spell, can and will write, what is to be done? It is difficult to know what to read, except by reading every thing; and so much of the world's business is now transacted through the press, that it is necessary to know what is printed, if we desire to know what is going on. Opinion weighs with so vast a weight in the balance of events, that ideas of no value in themselves are of importance from the mere circumstance that they *are* ideas, and have a *bonâ fide* existence as such anywhere out of Bedlam. (The world, in consequence, gorges itself with intellectual food; and, in order to swallow the more, *bolts* it.) Nothing is now read slowly, or twice over. Books are run through with no less rapidity, and scarcely leave a more durable impression, than a newspaper-article. It is from this, among other causes, that so few books are produced of any value. The lioness in the fable boasted, that, though she produced only one at a birth, that one was a lion; but if each lion only counted for one, and each leveret for one, the advantage would all be on the side of the hare. When every unit is individually weak, it is only multitude that tells. What wonder that the newspapers should carry all before them? A book produces hardly a greater effect than an article, and there can be three hundred and sixty-five of these in one year. He, therefore, who should and would write a book, and write it in the proper manner of writing a book, now dashes down his first hasty thoughts, or what he mistakes for thoughts, in a periodical. And the public is in the predicament of an indolent man, who cannot bring himself to apply his mind vigorously to his own affairs, and over whom, therefore, not he who speaks most wisely, but he who speaks most frequently, obtains the influence."[4]

Hence we see that literature is becoming more and more ephemeral: books, of any solidity, are almost gone by; even reviews are not now considered sufficiently light: the attention cannot sustain itself on any serious subject, even for the space of a review-article. In the more attractive kinds of literature, novels and magazines, though the demand has so greatly increased, the supply has so outstripped it, that even a novel is seldom a lucrative speculation. It is only under circumstances of rare attraction that a bookseller will now give any thing to an author for copyright. As the difficulties of success thus progressively increase, all other ends are more and more sacrificed for the attainment of it: literature becomes more and more a mere reflection of the current sentiments, and has almost entirely abandoned its mission as an enlightener and improver of them.

There are now in this country, we may say, but two modes left in which an individual mind can hope to produce much direct effect upon the minds and destinies of his countrymen generally—as a member of Parliament, or an editor of a London newspaper. In both these capacities, much may still be done by an individual; because, while the power of the collective body is very great, the number of participants in it does not admit of much increase. One of these monopolies will be opened to competition when the newspaper-stamp is taken off; whereby the importance of the newspaper-press in the aggregate, considered as the voice of public opinion, will be increased, and the influence of any one writer in helping to form that opinion necessarily diminished. This we might regret, did we not remember to what ends that influence is now used, and is sure to be so while newspapers are a mere investment of capital for the sake of mercantile profit.

Is there, then, no remedy? Are the decay of individual energy, the weakening of the influence of superior minds over the multitude, the growth of charlatanerie, and the diminished efficacy of public opinion as a restraining power—are these the price we necessarily pay for the benefits of civilization? And can they only be avoided by checking the diffusion of knowledge, discouraging the spirit of combina-

4. From a paper by the author [Mill's note].

tion, prohibiting improvements in the arts of life, and repressing the further increase of wealth and of production? Assuredly not. Those advantages which civilization cannot give—which in its uncorrected influence it has even a tendency to destroy—may yet co-exist with civilization; and it is only when joined to civilization that they can produce their fairest fruits. All that we are in danger of losing we may preserve, all that we have lost we may regain, and bring to a perfection hitherto unknown; but not by slumbering, and leaving things to themselves, no more than by ridiculously trying our strength against their irresistible tendencies: only by establishing counter-tendencies, which may combine with those tendencies, and modify them.

The evils are, that the individual is lost and becomes impotent in the crowd, and that individual character itself becomes relaxed and enervated. For the first evil, the remedy is, greater and more perfect combination among individuals; for the second, national institutions of education, and forms of polity calculated to invigorate the individual character.

The former of these desiderata, as its attainment depends upon a change in the habits of society itself, can only be realized by degrees, as the necessity becomes felt; but circumstances are even now, to a certain extent, forcing it on. In Great Britain especially (which so far surpasses the rest of the Old World in the extent and rapidity of the accumulation of wealth), the fall of profits, consequent upon the vast increase of population and capital, is rapidly extinguishing the class of small dealers and small producers, from the impossibility of living on their diminished profits; and is throwing business of all kinds more and more into the hands of large capitalists, whether these be rich individuals, or joint-stock companies formed by the aggregation of many small capitals. We are not among those who believe that this progress is tending to the complete extinction of competition, or that the entire productive resources of the country will, within any assignable number of ages, if ever, be administered by, and for the benefit of, a general association of the whole community. But we believe that the multiplication of competitors in all branches of business and in all professions—which renders it more and more difficult to obtain success by merit alone, more and more easy to obtain it by plausible pretence—will find a limiting principle in the progress of the spirit of co-operation; that, in every over-crowded department, there will arise a tendency among individuals so to unite their labor or their capital, that the purchaser or employer will have to choose, not among innumerable individuals, but among a few groups. Competition will be as active as ever; but the number of competitors will be brought within manageable bounds.

Such a spirit of co-operation is most of all wanted among the intellectual classes and professions. The amount of human labor, and labor of the most precious kind, now wasted, and wasted too, in the cruelest manner, for want of combination, is incalculable. What a spectacle, for instance, does the medical profession present! One successful practitioner burthened with more work than mortal man can perform, and which he performs so summarily, that it were often better let alone: in the surrounding streets, twenty unhappy men, each of whom has been as laboriously and expensively trained as he has to do the very same thing, and is possibly as well qualified, wasting their capabilities, and starving for want of work. Under better arrangements, these twenty would form a corps of subalterns, marshaled under their more successful leader; who (granting him to be really the ablest physician of the set, and not merely the most successful impostor) is wasting time in physicking people for headaches and heartburns, which he might with better economy of mankind's resources turn over to his subordinates, while he employed his maturer powers and greater experience in studying and treating those more obscure and difficult cases upon which science has not yet thrown sufficient light, and to which ordinary knowledge and abilities would not be adequate. By such means, every person's capacities would be turned to account; and, the highest minds being kept for the highest things, these would make progress, while ordinary occasions would be no losers.

But it is in literature, above all, that a change of this sort is of most pressing urgency. There the system of individual competition has fairly worked itself out, and things can hardly continue much longer as they are. Literature is a province of exertion, upon which more, of the first value to human nature, depends, than upon any other; a province in which the highest and most valuable order of works—those which most contribute to form the opinions and shape the characters of subsequent ages—are, more than in any other class of productions, placed beyond the possibility of appreciation by those who form the bulk of the purchasers in the book-market; insomuch that, even in ages when these were a far less numerous and more select class than now, it was an admitted point, that the only success which writers of the first order could look to was the verdict of posterity. That verdict could, in those times, be confidently expected by whoever was worthy of it: for the good judges, though few in number, were sure to read every work of merit which appeared; and, as the recollection of one book was not in those days immediately obliterated by a hundred others, they remembered it, and kept alive the knowledge of it to subsequent ages. But in our day, from the immense multitude of writers (which is now not less remarkable than the multitude of readers), and from the manner in which the people of this age are obliged to read, it is difficult, for what does not strike during its novelty, to strike at all: a book either misses fire altogether, or is so read as to make no permanent impression; and the good equally with the worthless are forgotten by the next day.

For this there is no remedy, while the public have no guidance beyond booksellers' advertisements, and the ill-considered and hasty criticisms of newspapers and small periodicals, to direct them in distinguishing what is not worth reading from what is. The resource must in time be some organized co-operation among the leading intellects of the age, whereby works of first-rate merit, of whatever class, and of whatever tendency in point of opinion, might come forth, with the stamp on them, from the first, of the approval of those whose names would carry authority. There are many causes why we must wait long for such a combination; but (with enormous defects both in plan and in execution) the Society for the Diffusion of Useful Knowledge was as considerable a step towards it as could be expected in the present state of men's minds, and in a first attempt. Literature has had in this country two ages: it must now have a third. The age of patronage, as Johnson a century ago proclaimed, is gone. The age of booksellers, it has been proclaimed by Mr. Carlyle, has well nigh died out. In the first, there was nothing intrinsically base; nor, in the second, any thing inherently independent and liberal. Each has done great things: both have had their day. The time is perhaps coming, when authors, as a collective guild, will be their own patrons and their own booksellers.

* * *

With regard to the changes, in forms of polity and social arrangements, which, in addition to reforms in education, we conceive to be required for regenerating the character of the higher classes—to express them even summarily would require a long discourse. But the general idea from which they all emanate may be stated briefly. Civilization has brought about a degree of security and fixity in the possession of all advantages once acquired, which has rendered it possible for a rich man to lead the life of a Sybarite, and nevertheless enjoy throughout life a degree of power and consideration which could formerly be earned or retained only by personal activity. We cannot undo what civilization has done, and again stimulate the energy of the higher classes by insecurity of property, or danger of life or limb. The only adventitious motive it is in the power of society to hold out is reputation and consequence; and of this as much use as possible should be made for the encouragement of desert. The main thing which social changes can do for the improvement of the higher classes—and it is what the progress of democracy is insensibly but certainly accomplishing—is gradually to put an end to every kind of unearned distinction, and let the only road open to honor and ascendency be that of personal qualities.

QUESTIONS

1. What is the function of Mill's initial definition of civilization? Outline the major parts of his essay. Which parts are devoted to analysis of conditions, which to criticism of opinions, which to proposals for improvement?

2. At the outset Mill describes the conditions of life in a savage community. Does he seem closely familiar with life as savages live it? If an anthropologist were to prove him wrong about savage societies, what would be the impact on his argument?

3. Mill attributes the weakness of savage communities to the "same cause which prevented the lions and tigers from long ago extirpating the race of men—incapacity of cooperation" (p. 456). What view of social change does this comparison suggest?

4. At various points Mill makes it clear that he thinks the changes he describes are inevitable and irresistible. Does he indicate what the cause of the changes is? What ideas about society are implicit in his approach to these changes?

5. Discussing the future, Mill makes some optimistic predictions about the progresss of a spirit of cooperation. Looking at American society today, would you say that his predictions about competition have come true? Was his optimism justified?

6. Accepting the student world that you know as a civilization, describe the signs of the times. Will you want to follow Mill's organizational plan?

EDMUND WILSON
Books of Etiquette and Emily Post

Professor Arthur M. Schlesinger, the Harvard historian, has written an entertaining little treatise called *Learning How to Behave: A Historical Study of American Etiquette Books.* It is curious and rather instructive to look at the development of the United States from the point of view of the literature of etiquette. The first manuals derived from Europe and emphasized deference to rank to the point of, in one case, admonishing the young: "If thy superior be relating a story, say not, 'I have heard it before.' . . . If he tell it not right, snigger not"; but after the Revolution, and especially after the advent of Jackson, the object became not to define class differences but to provide a set of prescriptions which would show anyone how to become a gentleman. The Southerners had, however, based their practice on seventeenth-century guides which helped the planter "to model his life on that of the English landed gentry" and "provided a fairly consistent chart of behavior . . . in emulation of the ancient ideals of Christian chivalry"; and they continued to follow this code. In the period after the Civil War, when the big fortunes were being made, a fresh crop of volumes appeared which had the purpose of orienting the newly rich among the refinements and complications of calling cards and formal dinners. There was an average of five such a year, and this continued through to 1945.

The two greatest publishing successes in the department of etiquette date from the beginning of the nineteen-twenties. At this time, a Miss Lillian Eichler, an advertising copywriter, then eighteen and just out of high school, sold thousands of copies of an *Encyclopedia of Etiquette* by means of a series of advertisements with the caption "What's Wrong with This Picture?" But the book—which had been written in 1901—was by that time, it seems, obsolete (Mr. Schlesinger does not tell us in what respect), for it was returned by "droves of dissatisfied customers." The publisher then proposed to Miss Eichler that she should herself do an up-to-date book, and the result was *The Book of Etiquette*, which between 1921 and 1945 sold over a million copies. In 1922, Emily Post brought out her *Etiquette*, which by 1945 had sold more than two-thirds of a million.

An examination of these two manuals reveals fundamental differences between them and suggests that they have been appealing to two rather different publics. Miss Eichler is practical and comfortable (her book is now frankly called *Today's Etiquette*). She tells you how to teach the children table manners and how to give a dinner without servants. She makes rough tabulations of vintage wines and supplies reliable recipes for half-a-dozen well-known cocktails; she recommends, in a chapter on *The Nature and Meaning of Culture*, that one "read more than one kind of literature: not mystery stories alone, nor light fiction alone," and she lists "nine painters of undisputed glory, with whose work every person of culture should be at least familiar." The precepts are mostly appropriate for anyone of moderate income, and the whole tone is non-invidious. She makes social life sound easy and jolly. But Mrs. Post is another affair. I had had no conception of her extraordinary book till I looked into it recently, fell under its spell and read it almost through. Mrs. Post is not merely the author of a comprehensive textbook on manners: she is a considerable imaginative writer, and her book has some of the excitement of a novel. It has also the snob-appeal which is evidently an important factor in the success of a Marquand or a Galsworthy. (I should explain that the edition I read was the third printing, of 1922.)

Mrs. Post has produced a world which has its characters, its atmosphere, its drama, I was reminded, after reading *Etiquette*, of the late Scott Fitzgerald's once telling me that he had looked into Emily Post and been inspired with the idea of a play in which all the motivations should consist of trying to do the right thing. The element of dramatic conflict would be produced by setting people at cross-purposes through stalemates of good form, from which the only possible rescue would be through the intervention of some bounder as *deus ex machina* to put an end to the sufferings of the gentle-folk who had been paralyzed by Mrs. Post's principles. (There are actually novels by Howells, and even by Henry James, which very nearly fulfill this formula.) For it is true that Mrs. Post has supplied all the materials for such a drama. Her ideal gentleman-clubman and her ideal feminine house guest—described in little essays like the "characters" of La Bruyère or the *Spectator*—are models which can never deviate, and thoroughly priggish figures which would lend themselves to satirical comedy. The "considerate guest," in particular, who is always perfectly sweet to everyone and always wants to do what the others are doing, who pretends to like children and dogs and lets them "climb over her" though she loathes them, could easily be shown as a menace from whom the party would have to be saved by Mrs. Post's hideous villain: "The Guest No One Invites Again."

But Mrs. Post, in providing illustrations, has also invented types that have names, personalities and histories, and that are threaded, like the characters of Proust, in and out all through her book. These figures were originally intended merely as convenient dummies to stand in the places of hosts and guests when she was showing how the right kind of entertaining might be done on various scales by people on different income levels; but they have taken such a hold on the author that they have gratuitously been developed to exemplify, like the groups in Proust, a variety of social milieux. They do, however, all belong to Society, and the author, unlike Miss Eichler, always assumes that the reader wants to belong to Society, too.

At the top of Mrs. Post's structure, from the point of view of a wealth which is combined with "social credentials," stand the Worldlys of Great Estates (run by their butler Hastings) and the Gildings of Golden Hall. The Worldlys are a little difficult, they are constrained by the expensive habits and the inflated self-importance of the rich; but the Gildings are more human and always fun. Of Golden Hall, Mrs. Post writes: "The house is a palace, the grounds are a park. There is not only a long wing of magnificent guest rooms in the house, occupied by young girls or important older people, but there is also a guest annex, a separate building designed and run like the most luxurious country club. . . . Perfectly equipped Turkish and Russian baths in charge of the best Swedish masseur and masseuse procurable . . . a glass-roofed and enclosed riding ring—not big enough for games of polo, but big enough to practise in winter," etc. It was after a party at Golden Hall that Mrs. Toplofty, Bobo Gilding's great-aunt, exclaimed, "How are any of us ever going to amuse any one after *this?* I feel like doing my guest rooms up in moth balls." Bobo Gilding (whose nickname is incidentally explained in a section intended to discourage what Mrs. Post calls conversational "door-slammers": "As for the name 'Bobo,' it's asinine." "Oh, it's just one of those children's names that stick sometimes for life." "Perfect rot. Ought to be called by his name.")—Bobo Gilding, on his side, does not care for his aunt's rather pompous parties, since "entering a drawing-room [for Bobo] was more suggestive of the daily afternoon tea ordeal of his early nursery days than a voluntary act of pleasure." And Mrs. Gilding (who was Lucy Wellborn) "did not care much to go either if none of her particular men friends were to be there. Little she cared to dance the cotillion with old Colonel Bluffington or to go to supper with that odious Hector Newman." Yet old Mrs. Toplofty is by no means dull, for, finding herself once at dinner "next to a man she quite openly despised, [she] said to him with apparent placidity, 'I shall not talk to you—because I don't care to. But for the sake of the hostess I shall say my multiplication tables. Twice one are two, twice two are four—' and she continued on through the tables, making him alternate them with her. As soon as she politely could, she turned to her other companion."

Lucy Gilding "smokes like a furnace and is miserable unless she can play bridge for high stakes." At her wedding, the bridesmaids were dressed "in deep shades of burnt orange and yellow, wood colored slippers and stockings, skirts that shaded from brown through orange to yellow; yellow leghorn hats trimmed with jonquils, and jonquil bouquets"; and the affair was a great success for everybody except a "distinguished uncle," with whom Mrs. Post frankly sympathizes, who declared: "I did not think it was lovely at all. Every one of the bridesmaids was so powdered and painted that there was not a sweet or fresh face among them."

The Gildings' especial friends are rich young people like the Lovejoys and the Gailys, rich bachelors like Jim Smartlington and Clubwin Doe (the former of whom was elected "with little difficulty" to Clubwin Doe's club, at the same time that young Breezy was kept out by two men who "disliked his 'manner' "). But there are also, in the higher brackets, Mr. and Mrs. Kindhart. Mrs. Kindhart, unlike Mrs. Worldly, "talks to everyone, everywhere and always." Her "position is as good as Mrs. Worldly's every bit, but perhaps she can be more relaxed." It is the Kindharts who try to be helpful at the catastrophic "bungled dinner" which is given by "you," the reader—the evening when the fire smokes and Mrs. Toplofty issues orders that the logs are to be thrown out into the yard: when the Swedish maid says "Dinner's all ready!" instead of "Dinner is served" and deals the plates out like cards and then stacks them; when the clear soup turns out a "greasy-looking brown" and the hollandaise sauce "a curdled yellow mess"—the evening after which Mrs. Toplofty, Clubwin Doe and the Worldlys and the Gildings, all of whom you invited together, will, as you well know, be telling their friends: "Whatever you do, don't dine with the Newweds unless you eat your dinner before you go, and wear black glasses so no sight can offend you." On that occasion, Mr. Kindhart is the only guest who tries to eat the soup, and Mrs. Kindhart says to you gently: "Cheer up, little girl, it doesn't really matter"—making you know for the first time "to the full how terrible the situation is." (The other guests, on this unfortunate occasion, seem to have fallen a little short of the qualities of delicacy and grace which the author has elsewhere ascribed to the truly well bred.) It was the Kindharts who gave the houseparty at informal Mountain Summit Camp which inspires Mrs. Post to one of her most memorable chapters—that party at which Mr. Kindhart points out after lunch to the guests "a dozen guides who are waiting at the boat-house" and "a small swimming pool which can be warmed artificially" for those who find the lake too cold, but at which the Worldlys strike a false note, for Mr. Worldly insists on bringing his valet, though he well knows that this was not expected, and Mrs. Worldly, at the long pine lunch-table, "looks at her napkin ring as though it were an insect"—till Mrs. Kindhart smiles and says: "I'm sorry, but I told you 'it was roughing it.' "

And then there are the Littlehouses (Mrs. Littlehouse was Sally Titherington), who, when you visit them, may "press you into service as auxiliary nurse, gardener or chauffeur," but whose "personality" is "such that there is scarcely a day in the week when the motors of the most popular of the younger set are not parked at the Littlehouse door." And, on the fringes, such occasional guests as Grace Smalltalk, who *did* write to Mrs. Norman an admirable bread-and-butter letter, and the boring Professor Bugge, who was rather a social problem till he was seated by a clever hostess next to Mrs. Entomoid. In a somewhat different category, not frowned on but not included in the Eastern set, are Mr. and Mrs. Spendeasy Western and Mr. and Mrs. Jameson Greatlake, of 24 Michigan Avenue, Chicago.

But Mrs. Post's real hero and heroine are Mr. and Mrs. Oldname. Mrs. Oldname is "*une dame élégante*"—because, as Mrs. Post tells us, there is no English word to "express the individuality of beautiful taste combined with personal dignity and grace which gives to a perfect costume an inimitable air of distinction." Her tact is unfailing and consummate: to a lady going in to dinner, she will say quietly: "Mr. Traveler, who is sitting next to you at the table, has just come back from two years alone with the cannibals." And "how does Mrs. Oldname walk? One might answer by describing how Pavlova dances. Her body is perfectly balanced, she holds herself straight, and yet nothing suggests a ramrod. She takes steps of medium length, and, like all people who move and dance well, walks from the hip, not the knee. On no account does she swing her arms, nor does she rest a hand on her hip! Nor, when walking, does she wave her hands about in gesticulation." One of the most telling of the little episodes with which Mrs. Post's commentary is interspersed is her account of a visit to the Oldnames, which has the title *The Small House of Perfection*. "A great friend of the Oldnames, but not a man who went at all into society, or considered whether people had position or not, was invited with his new wife—a woman from another State and of much wealth and discernment—to stay over a weekend at Brook Meadows." She asks her husband what sort of clothes to take, and he tells her that he has never seen Mrs. Oldname "dressed up a bit." The wife wonders whether to pack her cerise satin. The husband thinks it "much too handsome," but the wife decides to put it in. They drive up to a low, white shingled house, and the visitor notices that the flowers bordering the old-fashioned brick walk are "all of one color, all in perfect bloom." She knew no inexperienced gardener produced that apparently simple approach to a door that has been chosen as frontispiece in more than one book on Colonial architecture. The door was opened by a maid in a silver gray taffeta dress, with organdie collar, cuffs and apron, white stockings and silver buckles on black slippers, and the guest saw a quaint hall and vista of rooms that at first sight might easily be thought 'simple' by an inexpert appraiser." Mrs. Oldname herself was electrifying to the visitor of wealth from another State. To describe her as "simple," exclaims Mrs. Post, "is about as apt as to call a pearl 'simple' because it doesn't dazzle; nor was there an article in the apparently simple living-room that would be refused if it were offered to a museum." The furniture, the appointments, the other guests are filled in with glowing rapture. "That night the bride wore her cerise dress to one of the smartest dinners she ever went down to"; and when later she is alone with her husband she bursts out: "Why in the name of goodness didn't you tell me the truth about these people?" The husband misunderstands: I told you it was a little house—it was you who insisted on bringing that red dress. I told you it was much too handsome!" "Handsome!" she cries in tears. "I don't own anything half good enough to compare with the least article in this house. That 'simple' little woman, as you call her, would, I think, almost make a queen seem provincial! And as for her clothes, they are priceless—just as everything is in this little gem of a house. Why, the window curtains are as fine as the best things in my trousseau."

There is only one instance on record of anybody's scoring off the Oldnames. Mrs. Oldname had hanging in her dining-room a portrait of a Colonial officer, to which she was rather attached. One day, however, "an art critic, whose knowledge was better than his manners, blurted out, 'Will you please tell me why you have that dreadful thing in this otherwise perfect room?' Mrs. Oldname, somewhat taken aback, answered rather wonderingly: 'Is it dreadful?—Really? I have a feeling of affection for him and his dog!" The critic was merciless. 'If you call a cotton-flannel effigy a dog! And as for the figure, it is equally false and lifeless! It is amazing how anyone with your taste can bear looking at it!' In spite of his rudeness, Mrs. Old-name saw that what he said was quite true, but not until the fact had been pointed out to her. Gradually she grew to dislike the poor officer so much that he was finally relegated to the attic." It will be noted that, though the art critic carried his point, he was still guilty of a grave breach of manners.

The latest edition of Emily Post omits, as she says on the jacket, "certain non-essential customs and old-fashioned ideas," and aims to accommodate itself to the habits of later decades—including even those of the war and post-war young people—when formalities have been going by the board. The chapter, for example, which in the 1922 edition is called *The Chaperon and Other Conventions* is now headed *The Vanished Chaperon and Other Lost Conventions*. But the book is still dominated by the prestige of the Oldnames and the Gildings. Their prestige for Mrs. Post may finally have the effect of making some of her readers sympathetic toward the characters who are awful examples: the Upstarts, Mr. and Mrs. Unsuitable and that touching Mr. Richan Vulgar, who crossed the Atlantic four times a year in order to meet the smart people on shipboard and who, by capturing an innocent celebrity, attracted for a time to his table the Smartlys, the Wellborns and the Lovejoys, only to lose them every one when they found out what he was really like and took to eating their meals on deck. (The story of Mr. Richan Vulgar has been dropped from the new edition, as have also, the Unsuitables and the Upstarts, but a pathetic Miss Nobackground has appeared.) One feels, in fact, something like sadism in the whole approach of Mrs. Post. She likes to humiliate. She cannot tell us how charming Miss Wellborn is or how perfect is Mrs. Oldname's taste without putting in a little incident to show us this polish or grace making somebody else uncomfortable. Mrs. Post's popularity, I think, is partly due to precisely this.

It is obvious that the Gildings and the Oldnames do not them-selves need Mrs. Post's book of etiquette; and that the ordinary amiable American, to whom Miss Eichler addresses herself, does not necessarily need to hear about either Great Estates or the Small House of Perfection. But there are people who want to believe in the existence of a social Olympus and who find here the satisfaction that is somehow derived at once from imagining the enjoyment of glamour and power and from immolating oneself before them—since the reader is let in on the lives of the dwellers in these privileged places but is constantly being reminded how desperately he should have to watch his step if he were ever admitted among them.

What you get in Emily Post, for all her concessions to the age's vulgarization, is a crude version of the social ideal to which the mass of Americans aspired after the Civil War: an ideal that was costly and glossy, smart, self-conscious and a little disgusting in a period when even Mrs. Oldname reflected the lavish Gildings in stimulating her visitors to realize that the clothes she wore were "priceless" and her tableware and furniture museum pieces. Today this ideal must be fading with the money that kept it up, but, such as it is, a great many people must still enjoy reading about it. The publishers of Mrs. Post's *Etiquette* have announced that it has sold fifty thousand copies since the beginning of this year: its biggest sale in a decade.

QUESTIONS

1. What is the implied definition of etiquette or manners that is illustrated in Emily Post?
2. What is the implied purpose of manners? Do Mrs. Post's principles in fact serve this purpose?
3. How would Wilson's definition of manners differ from Mrs. Post's? Point to passages in which Wilson gives his own views directly or indirectly. How does he manage to convey his attitude with a minimum of direct comment?
4. Why does Wilson begin and end his essay with references to history? Why does he include a brief account of Miss Eichler's book?
5. If Mrs. Post reflects the standards and customs of an age that is now past, how can the popularity of her book today be explained?
6. What are the main differences between the Kindharts and the Oldnames? The Oldnames are said to be Mrs. Post's "real hero and heroine." Which family does Wilson prefer? Why?
7. Wilson refers to Mrs. Post's "Guest No One Invites Again" but does not quote any description of him. Making whatever inferences you can from the passages that Wilson does quote, write a description of this guest.
8. Write a brief essay discussing to what extent the observance of good manners conflicts with or hampers the expression of individuality.

MARGARET MEAD
Each Family in a Home of Its Own[1]

The belief that every family should have a home of its own seems like a truism to which almost every American would assent without further thought. Most Americans also accept the fact that we have a housing shortage as the consequences of a failure to build in the thirties and during World War II, and of discrepancies between housing costs and wages that should somehow be reconciled. But it is important to realize that the word "family" has come to mean fewer and fewer people, the number of families has steadily increased, and so the need for housing units as distinguished from living-space has also increased by leaps and bounds. Although Southern Senators may occasionally argue against some piece of legislation for women, claiming that women's place is in the home, most legislators yield, at least nominally, to the question, "Whose home?" Women's place in the United States is no longer in the home, and her exclusion from a right that has been hers in most societies is part of our belief that every family should have its own home—with only one woman in it. Furthermore, each family should consist only of a husband, a wife, and minor children.

All other forms of living are seen as having great disadvantages. A mother-son combination is classified as bad for the son, and a failure to break the silver cord; it will spoil his life. A father-daughter household is not as disapproved, but if the girl appears marriageable, then the father may be condemned and the daughter urged to bestir herself. Brother-and-sister households, such a common refuge of the genteel poor in other ages, are also frowned upon, even where one is widowed and has children. Somebody will be said to be sacrified to somebody else in such an arrangement. Unmarried children who are self-supporting shouldn't be clinging to the home; they should get out and get married and start homes of their own. Nor should the elderly parents of married children live in their children's homes, certainly not if they are both alive to be "company for each other," and not unless absolutely necessary when only one survives. The rigorousness of the American belief that in-laws, especially mothers-in-law, are ruinous to marriages takes little account of the loneliness of elderly people. We respect them when they "make their own lives," without, however, any social arrangements that make it possible for them to do so. The two exceptions to the insistence on the inferiority, and indeed genuine undesirability,

---

1. A chapter from the fourth part, "The Two Sexes in Contemporary America," of *Male and Female*, 1949.

of any other form of living-arrangement than the biological family with young or no children, are the cases of two unmarried women living together and of the divorced or widowed woman with some children who returns to the home of some relative, often an unmarried sister, or a father.[2] The proper attitude towards a woman with children to support whose husband is dead, or who is divorced, is to hope that she will marry again, and that the present living-arrangement is merely temporary. Children need a man in the home to bring them up, and are to be pitied if they haven't got a father. Grandfathers and uncles are not thought of as really good substitutes. As for the households in which two unmarried women live together, they are still regarded with a tolerance that includes some of the last century's pity and absolution from blame of the woman who did not marry, but this is markedly decreasing. Young women to-day who work and share a household have to draw heavily on the housing situation or considerations of economy to justify their continuing such an arrangement. There will be doubts, perhaps fears, that at least the chances of marriage, for one if not both, are being compromised by the arrangement. Group living for men is only really tolerated in college dormitories, in armies, and in work-camps, highly patterned situations where either men are assumed to be too young to marry or their wives cannot accompany them. Men who keep house together have to fend off very heavy social doubts as to their heterosexuality. The ethics that informs all these various social disapprovals, which is expressed in private upbraiding of the one who is assumed to be selfish and attempts to rouse the one who is assumed to be suffering, is the firm American belief that one of the most heinous sins is to limit other people's emotional freedom to live the good life. As the good life is defined as marriage, obviously any living-arrangement is wrong that may make any marriageable individual forgo marriage, and to benefit from such an arrangement is selfish and exploitive.

All of these attitudes and preferences add up to a world in which one should either be married, with a home of one's own, or live alone, eating in restaurants, reading all night in bed, seeing the same movies twice, dependent upon endless daily plans and initiative for companionship. Against such a background it is not surprising that Americans see one of the principal values in marriage as companionship, for we are a gregarious people, needing the presence of others to give us a full sense of ourselves. Nowhere in childhood or youth is there any training or any practice in self-sufficient isolation. Everything that a child does quietly by itself is suspect. "He is so

2. In 1947 one family in ten did not maintain a separate home. Of these, 2,500,000 were married couples with or without children; that is, individuals who are culturally entitled to feel that their happiness is as seriously endangered as their health would be during a famine. Three-quarters of a million were parent-child groups (nearly all mother-and-child groups) [Mead's note].

quiet he must be up to mischief." Day-dreaming is frowned upon. People who would rather stay at home with a good book than go out with friends get poor scores on personality quizzes. Even simple sensuous pleasures, such as reading in the bath-tub on Sunday morning, are regarded as pretty self-indulgent and antisocial. Most time spent alone could be spent better if spent with others, and time and money are valuables that ought to be spent in the best way possible. The child goes from a home in which the whole family share a living-room to a school in which he studies and plays in groups, through an adolescence in which any night when he doesn't have to study he feels left out if he hasn't a date, to an adulthood in which any break in ready companionship is felt as almost unbearable. In his empty room he turns on the radio as soon as he enters, to dispel the silence. "Silence," says a generation brought up to study in groups with a radio blaring over their heads, "is embarrassing." Which is another way of saying that when one is left alone with oneself, the question "What have you done to deserve being alone?" is almost inevitable, for children who are watched if they seek isolation are also as punishment sent out of the room or to bed.

> And if you doubt what things I say,
> Suppose you make the test;
> Suppose when you've been bad someday
> And up to bed are sent away
> From mother and the rest—
> Suppose you ask, "Who has been bad?"
> And then you'll hear what's true;
> For the wind will moan in its ruefullest tone:
> "Yooooooooo!
> "Yooooooooo!
> "Yooooooooo!"[3]

Self-sought loneliness and involuntary loneliness are both unattractive and suspect. The more popular and loved one is, the more sought-after, the more selfish it becomes to sit at home with a good book, and so make at least one other person involuntarily unhappy. Good-sportsmanship, which has shifted much of its meaning in America from its traditional English content, includes never refusing to do something labelled as fun if one or more other people ask you to, on such grounds as being tired, fed-up, or even needing to study, or write letters, or mend one's stockings. Critics of Americans' need for the reassurance of other people's company often neglect to stress that in a culture like ours universally acknowledged needs also imply universal duties, and that if every one is defined as lonely when he is alone, then it is obviously every one's duty to be with some one else. So children have to have "some one to play with," adolescents have to have dates, and adults have to marry and have a home of their own.

3. From Eugene Field's "The Night Wind."

Assured companionship and parenthood thus become the two socially desirable values that cannot be obtained outside marriage.
Almost every other human need that has historically been met in the
home can now be met outside it: restaurants serve food; comics,
movies, and radio provide amusement, news, and gossip; there are
laundries and dry-cleaners and places that mend one's socks and
store one's winter coat, wash one's hair and manicure one's nails and
shine one's shoes. For sex satisfaction it is no longer necessary to
choose between marriage and prostitution; for most of those without religious scruples sex is available on a friendly and amateur basis
and without responsibility. The automobile has made it even unnecessary for one of a pair of temporary sex partners to have an apartment. Entertaining can be done in a hotel or at a club. When one
is sick, one goes to a hospital, and when one dies, one can be buried
quite professionally from an undertaking establishment. A telephone service will answer one's telephone, and a shopping service do
one's shopping. The old needs of food, shelter, sex, and recreation
are all efficiently met outside the home—and yet more people are
married to-day than ever before in the country's recorded history.

Marriage is a state towards which young Americans are propelled,
and within which American women, educated to be energetic and
active, try to live out the desires that have been both encouraged
and muffled in them as children. Although there are other cultures
in which women dominate the home more, America is conspicuous
for the extent to which women have set the style of the home. This
may be referred to a variety of background events: to the way in
which the realm of the aesthetic was left to women during pioneer
days, to the emphasis on work for every one which meant that men
were too tired to spend much of their effort on the home; and, very
importantly, to the division of labour among non-English-speaking
immigrants. When immigrants came to this country, the husband
set to work to make a living, the wife to find out how to live, and
this division between making a living and a way of life, one as man's
field, the other as woman's, has been intensified. Our patterns of
urban life, with its highly developed transportation systems which
mean that fewer and fewer men ever come home to lunch, are also
one of the supporting factors in the situation. As more schools are
consolidated and the distance from home is increased, and as school-
lunches develop, the home with school-age children is deserted all
day long, while Mother is free to study the magazines and rearrange the living-room or her knowledge of world peace or the community's school system, in between answering the telephone, waiting for the laundry-man, and doing the next errand.

So it falls to the lot of women to design the way of life of the
family, consulting her husband on major issues only, simply because
that is her job. Into it, during the early days of marriage and mother-

hood she pours all the energy that comes from a healthy well-fed active childhood. If she has had a good education and is trained for some outside work, or even possibly for a career, even more if she was successful before marriage, there is likely to be an extra bit of emphasis in the way she manages her home and her children, in her insistence on what a good mother and what a good wife she is. Sometimes she can even say frankly: "Yes, I know my child is old enough to go to school alone, but I still take her. After all, that is my justification for staying home." More often, without any articulate comment on her doubt as to whether home-making really is a full-time job, she simply puts more effort into her complex day. Here the same standards apply that apply to her husband: like him, she also must succeed, must make good, must meet higher and higher standards.

When we analyze the task of home-making in the United States to-day, in the home that is celebrated in the pages of the women's magazines and assumed in the carefully unspecific radio serials, we find some very curious contradictions. The well-equipped home—towards which all the advertisements are pointed—is a home in which everything can be done more quickly and more effortlessly, clothes get white in no time, irons press almost without your noticing it, the extra attachment on the vacuum cleaner will even brush the backs of your books, the new silver-polish keeps your silver looking like new. In fact, the American woman, and the American woman's husband, who does not escape the advertisements even if he misses the radio serials, are told how fortunate, modern, and leisurely she can be—if she simply equips her house properly. There really seems to have been a period—back in the twenties, when domestic servants were still relatively available—when a married woman who had a goodly supply of gadgets, and at least one servant, did get quite a little time to play bridge. Her image lingers on in the avid comments of professional women over fifty who still see the home-maker as having a wicked amount of leisure—especially when contrasted with the life led by the woman who must both work and discharge all the duties of the home-maker, as so many American women do, not by choice but by necessity. There was a time also when in the first fine flush of laundries and bakeries, milk deliveries and canned goods, ready-made clothes and dry-cleaning, it did look as if American life was being enormously simplified. A vacuum cleaner was a great addition to a home that kept the standards of a carpet-sweeper and a broom, laundries were a godsend to a household whose routine of sheet-changing was geared to the old-fashioned wash-tub, and bakeries to homes in which the making of bread had dominated one whole day. But just as our new medical palliatives are creating new vulnerabilities and new disease states, so the new equipment has led not to more leisure, more time to play with the baby, more time to curl up and read by an open fire, or to help with the PTA, but has merely combined with other trends in making the life of the American home-maker not easier, but more exacting. Most urban-living women do not realize that, as the Bryn Mawr report shows, housekeeping activities consumed 60.55 hours a week in a typical farm family, 78.35 in urban households in cities under 100,000, and 80.57 in households in cities of over 100,000. This was in pre-war days, and in a world that has been moving steadily towards a forty-hour week on the job.

Perhaps the most significant word in family relationships that has been invented for a very long time is the word "sitter"—the extra person who must come into the family and sit whenever the two parents go out of it together. The modern wife and mother lives alone, with a husband who comes home in the evening, and children, who as little children are on her hands twenty-four hours out of twenty-four, in a house that she is expected to run with the efficiency of a factory—for hasn't she a washing-machine and a vacuum cleaner?—and from which a great number of the compensations that once went with being a home-maker have been removed. Except in rural areas, she no longer produces, in the sense of preserving and pickling and canning. She has no orgies of house-cleaning twice a year. She doesn't give the sort of party where she is admired because of the heaps of food that she has ostentatiously prepared, but instead she is admired just in proportion to the way she "looks as if it had taken her no time at all." As our factories move toward the ideal of eliminating human labor, our home ideals have paralleled them; the successful home-maker to-day should always look as if she had neither done any work nor would have to do any; she should produce a finished effect effortlessly, even if she has to spend all day Saturday rehearsing the way in which she will serve an effortless Sunday-morning breakfast. The creativity that is expected of her is a creativity of management of an assembly-line, not of materials lovingly fashioned into food and clothes for children. She shops, she markets, she chooses, she transports, she integrates, she co-ordinates, she fits little bits of time together so as "to get through the week," and her proudest boast often has to be "It was a good week. Nothing went wrong."

The average young American woman is very cheerful over these tasks. They are a drain on her nervous energy rather than on her physical strength, time-consuming rather than back-breaking; in her incredibly clean and polished home, her kitchen where the handle of the egg-beater matches the step-ladder in color, she moves lightly, producing the miracle dishes that will make her husband and children happy and strong. Two things mar her happiness, however: the fear that even though she never has any time, she is not perhaps doing a full-time job, and the fact that although she, like her brother, was taught that the right to choose a job is every American's sacred right, she doesn't feel that she chose this one. She chose wifehood and motherhood, but she did not necessarily choose to "keep house." That, in the phrasing of contemporary America, is thrust upon her becaue she is a woman; it is not a full status to be proudly chosen, but a duty that one cannot avoid and still find happiness in marriage. Women who have jobs ask her what she is doing and she says, "Nothing," or, "Just keeping house." Eighty hours a week of work, a sitter perhaps one evening a week, great loneliness as she rushes through the work that no other woman now shares, with an eye on the children as they play, hurrying so as to look "fresh and rested" when her husband comes home.

As we have narrowed the home, excluded from it the grandmother, the unmarried sister, the unmarried daughter, and—as part of the same process of repudiating any sharing of a home with another adult—the domestic servant has vanished, we have multiplied the number of homes in which the whole life of the family has to be integrated each day, meals cooked, lunches packed, children bathed, doors locked, dogs walked, cats put out, food ordered, washing-machines set in motion, flowers sent to the sick, birthday-cakes baked, pocket-money sorted, mechanical refrigerators defrosted. Where one large pot of coffee once served a household of ten or twelve, there are three or four small pots to be made and watched and washed and polished. Each home has been reduced to the bare essentials—to barer essentials than most primitive people would consider possible. Only one woman's hands to feed the baby, answer the telephone, turn off the gas under the pot that is boiling over, soothe the older child who has broken a toy, and open both doors at once. She is a nutritionist, a child psychologist, an engineer, a production manager, an expert buyer, all in one. Her husband sees her as free to plan her own time, and envies her; she sees him as having regular hours, and envies him. To the degree to which they also see each other as the same kind of people, with the same tastes and the same preferences, each is to a degree dissatisfied and inclined to be impatient with the other's discontent.

It is not new in history that men and women have misunderstood each other's rôles or envied each other, but the significant aspect of the American scene is that there is a discrepancy between the way we bring up boys and girls—each to choose both a job and a marriage partner—and then stylize housekeeping as a price the girl pays without stylizing the job as the price the boy pays. Men are trained to want a job in a mill, or a mine, on a farm, in an office, on a newspaper, or on a ship as a sign of their maleness, their success, and to want a wife and children to crown that success; but women to-day are not given the same clear career-line—to want an apartment, or a semi-detached house, or a farm-house, or a walk-up, or some other kind of home, as their job. The American woman wants a husband, yes, children, yes, a home of her own—yes indeed, it's intolerable to live with other people! But housekeeping—she isn't sure she wouldn't rather "do something" after she gets married. A great proportion of men would like a different job—to have at least better pay, or higher status, or different working-conditions— but they are not asked to face the seeming discrepancy between being reared for a choice and reared to think that success matters, and also that love matters and that every one should marry, and yet not be able to feel that the mate one chooses and the job one does after marriage are independent. It is as if a man were to make a set of plans for his life—to be an accountant, or a lawyer, or a pilot —and then have to add, "Unless of course, I marry." "Why?" you ask. "Because then I'll have to be a farmer. It's better for the children, you know."

It is not that we have found any good substitute for the association between home-making and motherhood. Good nurseries and schools can put children into good settings for many hours a day, settings that are often better than the small family where two bitter little rivals may otherwise spend hours quarreling and traumatizing each other. Freezers and frozen-food services and pressure cookers make it possible to prepare meals without long hours beside a watched pot. Hospitals do care for the very ill. But the task of integrating the lives of little children, even with the help of nursery-schools, kindergartens, and play-grounds, remains a full-time charge on some woman's time. If one woman leaves the home to work, part time or full time, another woman must replace her unless the children are to suffer. The nursery-school is no answer for the child with a cold, or the child who has been exposed to some contagious disease that it has not contracted. American women have become steadily more independent, more enterprising, more efficient, less willing to be merely part of some on-going operation, more insistent that when they do paid work, they work on a strictly professional basis, with part of their personality only, and that when they keep house they must be completely in control. But the price of this autonomy has risen also. It is almost as if the pioneer dream, which led Europeans of all sorts of backgrounds to become the independent American farmer, who could turn his hand to anything—and which survives today in the perennial nostalgia for a chicken-farm, or a business where one is one's own boss—had been transferred to the women, who live it out in their homes, but without the full pleasure of feeling that this is the job as well as the husband, the routine as well as the children, that they chose.

The intensity with which the American woman with children tends to her task of home-making includes innumerable excursions out of the home, as consumer, as transportation officer of the family, as responsible citizen who must protect the environment in which her children grow up by working for better schools, better play-grounds, better public-health regulations. To the old puritan vigour of the pioneer woman is now added a recognition that the modern isolated home, just because it is so isolated, is also terribly dependent upon the community. The functions that no one woman in a home by herself can possibly discharge must somehow be organized in the community around her, and even so, mothers cannot get sick. When they do, there are no adequate ordinary social ways of meeting this major emergency in the lives of their children. But however actively a married woman with small children takes responsibility for community work, still her life is centered in, her time filled by, her home, but principally by the children. She may importune her husband to take her out, she may complain loudly of the loneliness and the boredom of housework, but she does not complain that she has nothing to do.

It is all the harder for the mother of adolescent children when the break comes, when the children leave home for school or jobs and her task is over. Every social pressure to which she is subjected tells her that she should not spoil her children's lives, that she should let them lead their own lives, that she should make them independent and self-sufficient. Yet the more faithfully she obeys these injunctions, the more she is working herself out of a job. Some day, while she is still a young woman, she will have to face a breakfast-table with only one face across it, her husband's, and she will be alone, quite alone, in a home of their own. She is out of a job; her main justification, the work for which she "gave up everything," is gone, and yet there are still two, possibly three, meals a day to get, the door to be answered, the house to be cleaned. But there are only dishes for two and floors do not need to be polished so often when there are no children's feet to track them up. She isn't completely out of a job, but she is on the shelf, kicked upstairs, given one of those placebos by which large organizations whose employees have tenure try to disguise from the employee who is still too young to be retired the fact that he ought to be. This domestic crisis is of course much more difficult if it occurs at and is reinforced by the hormonal instability and emotional fears that surround the menopause, and combine unjustified fear of the loss of physical desire with the necessary recognition of the end of reproductivity. For married American women who have had children, the fear of loss of attractiveness and the fear of becoming emotionally unstable outweigh worries about the end of reproductivity, for they have had the one or two or three children that validate their marriages and, at least consciously, do not want more.

Meanwhile the father has been facing difficulties of his own. His rôle in the maturation of his children, especially in the maturation of his son, is to be the friendly ally of the boy, to help him cut free from his mother's apron-strings. To the extent that he sympathizes with and facilitates his son's growing desires for a job and a girl, he is a good father. He must pooh-pooh the mother's anxieties, back the boy up in minor escapades, be fraternally understanding. But to the extent that he does this he runs several risks. He relives, at least in imagination, his own budding freedom as a young adult, the freedom that he traded in so young, so willingly, for the continuous unremitting work that has kept his marriage going. Remembering, he may begin to feel that he has never really lived, that he settled down too early. This feeling may be all the stronger if it comes at a time when he realizes that further advancement in job or profession is unlikely. As long as the gradient of his life was rising, he was spurred on by the great rewards that Americans find in success. But now it will rise no further, he will instead in many cases have to work simply to hold his place, a dispiriting thought. Helping his son escape from his mother further identifies his wife for him as one from whom he has, after all, never properly escaped himself into the pleasant byways of irresponsible dalliance. Seeing his wife through his son's eyes, and through the eyes of his son's friends, he discovers a new impatience with her, as the representative of finished, self-satisfied achievement. Here he is, only in middle age, and his life is over—no new love, no new fields to conquer, only emptiness ahead. So while he is not out of a job— indeed he may often be at the height of his work-strength—the very nature of the life-cycle in America is such that he feels like an old man. He may have to fight very hard to resist the impulse to break away from it all, and he may develop serious health disturbances and die prematurely.

Superficially, the problem that faces the middle-aged couple in the home of their own is that the mother's main life-task is done while she is strong and well, and she must now find some other channel for her energies and still keep her life adjusted to the habits and needs of a husband who has lived terribly closely with her in that little self-contained home, while that husband's life-task is still going full tilt. But because of the great emphasis on Youth, because Youth is the period to which both sexes look back and age holds so few rewards, both face a deeper crisis of disappointment. The crisis may be further intensified if there are deaths of aged parents to be faced, with all the complications of the disposition of a surviving parent, long months of illness, sales of houses and furniture, all of which exacerbate the conflict about growing older. Every step of this process is made more acute by the insistence that each married couple should be self-sufficient, because many such couples have forgotten how. Yet they cannot look forward to combined homes with their married children, or with their widowed or unmarried siblings. Deeply dependent upon each other in every way, they have often become so just to the extent that the marriage is a good marriage. They have become so much like a single person that, like most individuals in America, they feel the need of others to complete themselves, to reassure them that they are good, to rid them of the self-searching that comes from being left alone and the self-reproach that attends condemning others to aloneness.

There are emerging solutions to this crisis when the children leave home. Some couples attempt a last child, for which there are even affectionate slang phrases—"little postscript," "little frost blossom" —that change the tone of the old folk-phrase "change-of-life baby." To have such a child is one way of facing the extent to which the woman's life in that home, and the marriage itself, has centered on the children. The most familiar solution is for women to make much of the independence for which they have openly yearned during the time they were tied down and go in for some active voluntary work, or even go back to the work they did before they were married. But in this event they face new hazards, especially if they have lived successfully through the instabilities of the menopause. Free of their major previous responsibilities, with twenty good years ahead of them, such women may start out on a gradient that rises steeply as they become involved in community activities or the delights of a job from which they have had a long vacation. And as it is the gradient that matters so much in America, their enthusiastic new spurt may contrast sharply with their husbands' unhappy acceptance of a plateau. A daughter's marriage and permitted absorption in grandchildren may mute the wife's energetic attitude towards her new activities, but that involves a severe problem for the husband who has to face the fact that he is a grandfather. In a country that gives so few rewards to age, who wants to be a grandfather? The woman of his unlicensed day-dreams is still a slim girl in her teens, now younger than his married daughter, who with each step that she takes towards maturity puts him more definitely out of the running.

Increasingly, the more aware middle-aged couples are treating this period seriously, assaying their personal as well as their material resources, and directing their plans not towards some dim and unhoped-for retirement, but towards the next twenty years. To the extent that both are able to re-plan their lives together, they make of the crisis a step forward rather than a step back. It is probable that society will recognize this period as a period in which professional counselling is needed as much as in adolescence. For each married couple alone in a home of their own is exposed to pressures and difficulties unknown in differently organized societies. And expressive of the shifting cycle of responsibility, the young married sons and daughters sit in their own small homes and try to decide what to do about Father and Mother. This is a question that is not answered by their all taking a house together, but by finding the parents something they can be interested in. Ideally, they will read-just their lives, live independently of their children except for grave emergencies, act as sitters, which means they go in as their children go out, and finally retire to a cottage in Florida, where their children piously hope they will have a lot of friends of their own age.

JANE JACOBS
Sidewalk Ballet[1]

Under the seeming disorder of the old city, wherever the old city is working successfully, is a marvelous order for maintaining the safety of the streets and the freedom of the city. It is a complex order. Its essence is intricacy of sidewalk use, bringing with it a constant succession of eyes. This order is all composed of move-ment and change, and although it is life, not art, we may fancifully call it the art form of the city and liken it to the dance—not to a simple-minded precision dance with everyone kicking up at the same time, twirling in unison, and bowing off en masse, but to an intricate ballet in which the individual dancers and ensembles all have distinctive parts which miraculously reinforce each other and compose an orderly whole. The ballet of the good city sidewalk never repeats itself from place to place, and in any one place is always replete with new improvisations.

The stretch of Hudson Street where I live is each day the scene of an intricate sidewalk ballet. I make my own first entrance into it a little after eight when I put out the garbage can, surely a prosaic occupation, but I enjoy my part, my little clang, as the droves of junior high school students walk by the center of the stage drop-ping candy wrappers. (How do they eat so much candy so early in the morning?)

While I sweep up the wrappers I watch the other rituals of morning: Mr. Halpert unlocking the laundry's handcart from its mooring to a cellar door, Joe Cornacchia's son-in-law stacking out the empty crates from the delicatessen, the barber bringing out his sidewalk folding chair, Mr. Goldstein arranging the coils of wire which proclaim the hardware store is open, the wife of the tene-ment's superintendent depositing her chunky three-year-old with a toy mandolin on the stoop, the vantage point from which he is learning the English his mother cannot speak. Now the primary children, heading for St. Luke's, dribble through to the south; the

1. From Chapter 2 of *The Death and Life of Great American Cities,* 1961.

children for St. Veronica's cross, heading to the west, and the children for P.S. 41, heading toward the east. Two new entrances are being made from the wings: well-dressed and even elegant women and men with briefcases emerge from doorways and side streets. Most of these are heading for the bus and subways, but some hover on the curbs, stopping taxis which have miraculously appeared at the right moment, for the taxis are part of a wider morning ritual: having dropped passengers from midtown in the downtown financial district, they are now bringing downtowners up to midtown. Simultaneously, numbers of women in housedresses have emerged and as they crisscross with one another they pause for quick conversations that sound with either laughter or joint indignation, never, it seems, anything between. It is time for me to hurry to work too, and I exchange my ritual farewell with Mr. Lofaro, the short, thick-bodied, white-aproned fruit man who stands outside his doorway a little up the street, his arms folded, his feet planted, looking solid as earth itself. We nod; we each glance quickly up and down the street, then look back to each other and smile. We have done this many a morning for more than ten years, and we both know what it means: All is well.

The heart-of-the-day ballet I seldom see, because part of the nature of it is that working people who live there, like me, are mostly gone, filling the roles of strangers on other sidewalks. But from days off, I know enough of it to know that it becomes more and more intricate. Longshoremen who are not working that day gather at the White Horse or the Ideal or the International for beer and conversation. The executives and business lunchers from the industries just to the west throng the Dorgene restaurant and the Lion's Head coffee house; meat-market workers and communications scientists fill the bakery lunchroom. Character dancers come on, a strange old man with strings of old shoes over his shoulders, motor-scooter riders with big beards and girl friends who bounce on the back of the scooters and wear their hair long in front of their faces as well as behind, drunks who follow the advice of the Hat Council and are always turned out in hats, but not hats the Council would approve. Mr. Lacey, the locksmith, shuts up his shop for a while and goes to exchange the time of day with Mr. Slube at the cigar store. Mr. Koochagian, the tailor, waters the luxuriant jungle of plants in his window, gives them a critical look from the outside, accepts a compliment on them from two passers-by, fingers the leaves on the plane tree in front of our house with a thoughtful gardener's appraisal, and crosses the street for a bite at the Ideal where he can keep an eye on customers and wigwag across the message that he is coming. The baby carriages come out, and clusters of everyone from toddlers with dolls to teen-agers with homework gather at the stoops.

When I get home after work, the ballet is reaching its crescendo. This is the time of roller skates and stilts and tricycles, and games in the lee of the stoop with bottletops and plastic cowboys; this is the time of bundles and packages, zigzagging from the drug store to the fruit stand and back over to the butcher's; this is the time when teen-agers, all dressed up, are pausing to ask if their slips show or their collars look right; this is the time when beautiful girls get out of MG's; this is the time when the fire engines go through; this is the time when anybody you know around Hudson Street will go by.

As darkness thickens and Mr. Halpert moors the laundry cart to the cellar door again, the ballet goes on under lights, eddying back and forth but intensifying at the bright spotlight pools of Joe's sidewalk pizza dispensary, the bars, the delicatessen, the restaurant, and the drug store. The night workers stop now at the delicatessen, to pick up salami and a container of milk. Things have settled down for the evening but the street and its ballet have not come to a stop.

I know the deep night ballet and its seasons best from waking long after midnight to tend a baby and, sitting in the dark, seeing the shadows and hearing the sounds of the party conversation and, about three in the morning, singing, very good singing. Sometimes there is sharpness and anger or sad, sad weeping, or a flurry of search for a string of beads broken. One night a young man came roaring along, bellowing terrible language at two girls whom he had apparently picked up and who were disappointing him. Doors opened, a wary semicircle formed around him, not too close, until the police came. Out came the heads, too, along Hudson Street, offering opinion, "Drunk . . . Crazy . . . A wild kid from the suburbs."[2]

Deep in the night, I am almost unaware how many people are on the street unless something calls them together, like the bagpipe. Who the piper was and why he favored our street I have no idea. The bagpipe just skirled out in the February night, and as if it were a signal the random, dwindled movements of the sidewalk took on direction. Swiftly, quietly, almost magically a little crowd was there, a crowd that evolved into a circle with a Highland fling inside it. The crowd could be seen on the shadowy sidewalk, the dancers could be seen, but the bagpiper himself was almost invisible because his bravura was all in his music. He was a very little man in a plain brown overcoat. When he finished and vanished, the dancers and watchers applauded, and applause came from the galleries too, half a dozen of the hundred windows on Hudson Street. Then the windows closed, and the little crowd dissolved

2. He turned out to be a wild kid from the suburbs. Sometimes, on Hudson Street, we are tempted to believe the suburbs must be a difficult place to bring up children [Jacobs' note].

into the random movements of the night street.

The strangers on Hudson Street, the allies whose eyes help us natives keep the peace of the street, are so many that they always seem to be different people from one day to the next. That does not matter. Whether they are so many always-different people as they seem to be, I do not know. Likely they are. When Jimmy Rogan fell through a plate-glass window (he was separating some scuffling friends) and almost lost his arm, a stranger in an old T shirt emerged from the Ideal bar, swiftly applied an expert tourniquet, and, according to the hospital's emergency staff, saved Jimmy's life. Nobody remembered seeing the man before and no one has seen him since. The hospital was called in this way: a woman sitting on the steps next to the accident ran over to the bus stop, wordlessly snatched the dime from the hand of a stranger who was waiting with his fifteen-cent fare ready, and raced into the Ideal's phone booth. The stranger raced after her to offer the nickel too. Nobody remembered seeing him before, and no one has seen him since. When you see the same stranger three or four times on Hudson Street, you begin to nod. This is almost getting to be an acquaintance, a public acquaintance, of course.

I have made the daily ballet of Hudson Street sound more frenetic than it is, because writing it telescopes it. In real life, it is not that way. In real life, to be sure, something is always going on, the ballet is never at a halt, but the general effect is peaceful and the general tenor even leisurely. People who know well such animated city streets will know how it is. I am afraid people who do not will always have it a little wrong in their head—like the old prints of rhinoceroses made from travelers' descriptions of rhinoceroses.

On Hudson Street, the same as in the North End of Boston or in any other animated neighborhoods of great cities, we are not innately more competent at keeping the sidewalks safe than are the people who try to live off the hostile truce of Turf in a blind-eyed city. We are the lucky possessors of a city order that makes it relatively simple to keep the peace because there are plenty of eyes on the street. But there is nothing simple about that order itself, or the bewildering number of components that go into it. Most of those components are specialized in one way or another. They unite in their joint effect upon the sidewalk, which is not specialized in the least. That is its strength.

ERIC HOFFER
The Role of the Undesirables

In the winter of 1934, I spent several weeks in a federal transient camp in California. These camps were originally established by Governor Rolph in the early days of the Depression to care for the single homeless unemployed of the state. In 1934 the federal government took charge of the camps for a time, and it was then that I first heard of them.

How I happened to get into one of the camps is soon told. Like thousands of migrant agricultural workers in California I then followed the crops from one part of the state to the other. Early in 1934 I arrived in the town of El Centro, in the Imperial Valley. I had been given a free ride on a truck from San Diego, and it was midnight when the truck driver dropped me on the outskirts of El Centro. I spread my bedroll by the side of the road and went to sleep. I had hardly dozed off when the rattle of a motorcycle drilled itself into my head and a policeman was bending over me saying, "Roll up, Mister." It looked as though I was in for something; it happened now and then that the police got overzealous and rounded up the freight trains. But this time the cop had no such thought. He said, "Better go over to the federal shelter and get yourself a bed and maybe some breakfast." He directed me to the place.

I found a large hall, obviously a former garage, dimly lit, and packed with cots. A concert of heavy breathing shook the thick air. In a small office near the door, I was registered by a middle-aged clerk. He informed me that this was the "receiving shelter" where I would get one night's lodging and breakfast. The meal was served in the camp nearby. Those who wished to stay on, he said, had to enroll in the camp. He then gave me three blankets and excused himself for not having a vacant cot. I spread the blankets on the cement floor and went to sleep.

I awoke with dawn amid a chorus of coughing, throat-clearing, the sound of running water, and the intermittent flushing of toilets in the back of the hall. There were about fifty of us, all colors and ages, all of us more or less ragged and soiled. The clerk handed out tickets for breakfast, and we filed out to the camp located several blocks away, near the railroad tracks.

From the outside the camp looked like a cross between a factory and a prison. A high fence of wire enclosed it, and inside were three large sheds and a huge boiler topped by a pillar of black smoke. Men in blue shirts and dungarees were strolling across the sandy yard. A ship's bell in front of one of the buildings announced breakfast. The regular camp members—there was a long line of them—ate first. Then we filed in through the gate, handing our tickets to the guard.

It was a good, plentiful meal. After breakfast our crowd dispersed. I heard some say that the camps in the northern part of the state were better, that they were going to catch a northbound freight. I decided to try this camp in El Centro.

My motives in enrolling were not crystal clear. I wanted to clean up. There were shower baths in the camp and wash tubs and plenty of soap. Of course I could have bathed and washed my clothes in one of the irrigation ditches, but here in the camp I had a chance to rest, get the wrinkles out of my belly, and clean up at leisure. In short, it was the easiest way out.

A brief interview at the camp office and a physical examination were all the formalities for enrollment.

There were some two hundred men in the camp. They were the kind I had worked and traveled with for years. I even saw familiar faces—men I had worked with in orchards and fields. Yet my predominant feeling was one of strangeness. It was my first experience of life in intimate contact with a crowd. For it is one thing to work and travel with a gang, and quite another thing to eat, sleep, and spend the greater part of the day cheek by jowl with two hundred men.

I found myself speculating on a variety of subjects: the reasons for their chronic bellyaching and beefing—it was more a ritual than the expression of a grievance; the amazing orderliness of the men; the comic seriousness with which they took their games of cards, checkers, and dominoes; the weird manner of reasoning one overheard now and then. Why, I kept wondering, were these men within the enclosure of a federal transient camp? Were they people temporarily hard up? Would jobs solve all their difficulties? Were we indeed like the people outside?

Up to then I was not aware of being one of a specific species of humanity. I had considered myself simply a human being—not particularly good or bad, and on the whole harmless. The people I worked and traveled with I knew as Americans and Mexicans, whites and Negroes, Northerners and Southerners, etc. It did not occur to me that we were a group possessed of peculiar traits, and that there was something—innate or acquired—in our makeup which made us adopt a particular mode of existence.

It was a slight thing that started me on a new track.

I got to talking to a mild-looking, elderly fellow. I liked his soft speech and pleasant manner. We swapped trivial experiences. Then he suggested a game of checkers. As we started to arrange the pieces on the board, I was startled by the sight of his crippled right hand. I had not noticed it before. Half of it was chopped off lengthwise, so that the horny stump with its three fingers looked like a hen's leg. I was mortified that I had not noticed the hand until he dangled it, so to speak, before my eyes. It was, perhaps, to bolster my shaken confidence in my powers of observation that I now began paying close attention to the hands of the people around me. The result was astounding. It seemed that every other man had had his hand mangled. There was a man with one arm. Some men limped. One young, good-looking fellow had a wooden leg. It was as though the majority of the men had escaped the snapping teeth of a machine and left part of themselves behind.

It was, I knew, an exaggerated impression. But I began counting the cripples as the men lined up in the yard at mealtime. I found thirty (out of two hundred) crippled either in arms or legs. I immediately sensed where the counting would land me. The simile preceded the statistical deduction: we in the camp were a human junk pile.

I began evaluating my fellow tramps as human material, and for the first time in my life I became face-conscious. There were some good faces, particularly among the young. Several of the middle-aged and the old looked healthy and well preserved. But the damaged and decayed faces were in the majority. I saw faces that were wrinkled, or bloated, or raw as the surface of a peeled plum. Some of the noses were purple and swollen, some broken, some pitted with enlarged pores. There were many toothless mouths (I counted seventy-eight). I noticed eyes that were blurred, faded, opaque, or bloodshot. I was struck by the fact that the old men, even the very old, showed their age mainly in the face. Their bodies were still slender and erect. One little man over sixty years of age looked a mere boy when seen from behind. The shriveled face joined to a boyish body made a startling sight.

My diffidence had now vanished. I was getting to know everybody in the camp. They were a friendly and talkative lot. Before many weeks I knew some essential fact about practically everyone.

And I was continually counting. Of the two hundred men in the camp there were approximately as follows:

Cripples	30
Confirmed drunkards	60
Old men (55 and over)	50
Youths under twenty	10
Men with chronic diseases, heart, asthma, TB	12
Mildly insane	4
Constitutionally lazy	6
Fugitives from justice	4
Apparently normal	70

(The numbers do not tally up to two hundred since some of the men were counted twice or even thrice—as cripples and old, or as old and confirmed drunks, etc.)

In other words: less than half the camp inmates (seventy normal, plus ten youths) were unemployed workers whose difficulties would be at an end once jobs were available. The rest (60 per cent) had handicaps in addition to unemployment.

I also counted fifty war veterans, and eighty skilled workers representing sixteen trades. All the men (including those with chronic diseases) were able to work. The one-armed man was a wizard with the shovel.

I did not attempt any definite measurement of character and intelligence. But it seemed to me that the intelligence of the men in the camp was certainly not below the average. And as to character, I found much forbearance and genuine good humor. I never came across one instance of real viciousness. Yet, on the whole, one would hardly say that these men were possessed of strong characters. Resistance, whether to one's appetites or to the ways of the world, is a chief factor in the shaping of character; and the average tramp is, more or less, a slave of his few appetites. He generally takes the easiest way out.

The connection between our makeup and our mode of existence as migrant workers presented itself now with some clarity.

The majority of us were incapable of holding onto a steady job. We lacked self-discipline and the ability to endure monotonous, leaden hours. We were probably misfits from the very beginning. Our contact with a steady job was not unlike a collision. Some of us were maimed, some got frightened and ran away, and some took to drink. We inevitably drifted in the direction of least resistance—the open road. The life of a migrant worker is varied and demands only a minimum of self-discipline. We were now in one of the drainage ditches of ordered society. We could not keep a footing in the ranks of respectability and were washed into the slough of our present existence.

Yet, I mused, there must be in this world a task with an appeal so strong that were we to have a taste of it we would hold on and be rid for good of our restlessness.

My stay in the camp lasted about four weeks. Then I found a haying job not far from town, and finally, in April, when the hot winds began blowing, I shouldered my bedroll and took the highway to San Bernardino.

It was the next morning, after I had got a lift to Indio by truck, that a new idea began to take hold of me. The highway out of Indio leads through waving date groves, fragrant grapefruit orchards, and lush alfalfa fields; then, abruptly, passes into a desert of white sand. The sharp line between garden and desert is very striking. The turning of white sand into garden seemed to me an act of magic. This, I thought, was a job one would jump at—even the men in the transient camps. They had the skill and ability of the average American. But their energies, I felt, could be quickened only by a task that was spectacular, that had in it something of the miraculous. The pioneer task of making the desert flower would certainly fill the bill.

Tramps as pioneers? It seemed absurd. Every man and child in California knows that the pioneers had been giants, men of boundless courage and indomitable spirit. However, as I strode on across the white sand, I kept mulling the idea over.

Who were the pioneers? Who were the men who left their homes and went into the wilderness? A man rarely leaves a soft spot and goes deliberately in search of hardship and privation. People become attached to the places they live in; they drive roots. A change of habitat is a painful act of uprooting. A man who has made good and has a standing in his community stays put. The successful businessmen, farmers, and workers usually stayed where they were. Who then left for the wilderness and the unknown? Obviously those who had not made good: men who went broke or never amounted to much; men who though possessed of abilities were too impulsive to stand the daily grind; men who were slaves of their appetites—drunkards, gamblers, and woman-chasers; outcasts—fugitives from justice and ex-jailbirds. There were no doubt some who went in search of health—men suffering with TB, asthma, heart trouble. Finally there was a sprinkling of young and middle-aged in search of adventure.

All these people craved change, some probably actuated by the naïve belief that a change in place brings with it a change in luck. Many wanted to go to a place where they were not known and there make a new beginning. Certainly they did not go out deliberately in search of hard work and suffering. If in the end they shouldered enormous tasks, endured unspeakable hardships, and accomplished the impossible, it was because they had to. They became men of action on the run. They acquired strength and skill in the inescapable struggle for existence. It was a question of do or die. And once they tasted the joy of achievement, they craved for more.

Clearly the same types of people which now swelled the ranks of migratory workers and tramps had probably in former times made up the bulk of the pioneers. As a group the pioneers were probably as unlike the present-day "native sons"—their descendants—as one could well imagine. Indeed, were there to be today a new influx of typical pioneers, twin brothers of the forty-niners only in a modern garb, the citizens of California would consider it a menace to health, wealth, and morals.

With few exceptions, this seems to be the case in the settlement of all new countries. Ex-convicts were the vanguard in the settling of Australia. Exiles and convicts settled Siberia. In this country, a large portion of our earlier and later settlers were failures, fugitives, and felons. The exceptions seemed to be those who were motivated by religious fervor, such as the Pilgrim Fathers and the Mormons.

Although quite logical, this train of thought seemed to me then a wonderful joke. In my exhilaration I was eating up the road in long strides, and I reached the oasis of Elim in what seemed almost no time. A passing empty truck picked me up just then and we thundered through Banning and Beaumont, all the way to Riverside. From there I walked the seven miles to San Bernardino.

Somehow, this discovery of a family likeness between tramps and pioneers took a firm hold on my mind. For years afterward it kept intertwining itself with a mass of observations which on the face of them had no relation to either tramps or pioneers. And it moved me to speculate on subjects in which, up to then, I had no real interest, and of which I knew very little.

I talked with several old-timers—one of them over eighty and a native son—in Sacramento, Placerville, Auburn, and Fresno. It was not easy, at first, to obtain the information I was after. I could not make my questions specific enough. "What kind of people were the early settlers and miners?" I asked. They were a hard-working, tough lot, I was told. They drank, fought, gambled, and wenched. They were big-hearted, grasping, profane, and God-fearing. They wallowed in luxury, or lived on next to nothing with equal ease. They were the salt of the earth.

Still it was not clear what manner of people they were.

If I asked what they looked like, I was told of whiskers, broad-brimmed hats, high boots, shirts of many colors, sun-tanned faces, horny hands. Finally I asked: "What group of people in present-day California most closely resembles the pioneers?" The answer, usually after some hesitation, was invariably the same: "The Okies and the fruit tramps."

I tried also to evaluate the tramps as potential pioneers by watching them in action. I saw them fell timber, clear firebreaks, build rock walls, put up barracks, build dams and roads, handle steam shovels, bulldozers, tractors, and concrete mixers. I saw them put in a hard day's work after a night of steady drinking. They sweated and growled, but they did the work. I saw the tramps elevated to positions of authority as foremen and superintendents. Then I could notice a remarkable physical transformation: a seamed face gradually smoothed out and the skin showed a healthy hue: an indifferent mouth became firm and expressive; dull eyes cleared and brightened; voices actually changed; there was even an apparent increase in stature. In almost no time these promoted tramps looked as if they had been on top all their lives. Yet sooner or later

I would meet up with them again in a railroad yard, on some skid
row, or in the fields—tramps again. It was usually the same story:
they got drunk or lost their temper and were fired, or they got fed
up with the steady job and quit. Usually, when a tramp becomes a
foreman, he is careful in his treatment of the tramps under him; he
knows the day of reckoning is never far off.

In short, it was not difficult to visualize the tramps as pioneers. I
reflected that if they were to find themselves in a singlehanded
life-and-death struggle with nature, they would undoubtedly display
persistence. For the pressure of responsibility and the heat of battle
steel a character. The inadaptable would perish, and those who
survived would be the equal of the successful pioneers.

I also considered the few instances of pioneering engineered
from above—that is to say, by settlers possessed of lavish means,
who were classed with the best where they came from. In these
instances, it seemed to me, the resulting social structure was inevitably precarious. For pioneering deluxe usually results in a plantation society, made up of large landowners and peon labor, either
native or imported. Very often there is a racial cleavage between
the two. The colonizing activities of the Teutonic barons in the
Baltic, the Hungarian nobles in Transylvania, the English in Ireland, the planters in our South, and the present-day plantation
societies in Kenya and other British and Dutch colonies are cases in
point. Whatever their merits, they are characterized by poor adaptability. They are likely eventually to be broken up either by a peon
revolution or by an influx of typical pioneers—who are usually of
the same race or nation as the landowners. The adjustment is not
necessarily implemented by war. Even our old South, had it not
been for the complication of secession, might eventually have
attained stability without war: namely, by the activity of its own
poor whites or by an influx of the indigent from other states.

There is in us a tendency to judge a race, a nation, or an organization by its least worthy members. The tendency is manifestly perverse and unfair; yet it has some justification. For the quality and
destiny of a nation is determined to a considerable extent by the
nature and potentialities of its inferior elements. The inert mass of
a nation is in its middle section. The industrious, decent, well-
to-do, and satisfied middle classes—whether in cities or on the
land—are worked upon and shaped by minorities at both extremes:
the best and the worst.

The superior individual, whether in politics, business, industry,
science, literature, or religion, undoubtedly plays a major role in the
shaping of a nation. But so do the individuals at the other extreme:
the poor, the outcasts, the misfits, and those who are in the grip of
some overpowering passion. The importance of these inferior elements as formative factors lies in the readiness with which they are

swayed in any direction. This peculiarity is due to their inclination to take risks ("not giving a damn") and their propensity for united action. They crave to merge their drab, wasted lives into something grand and complete. Thus they are the first and most fervent adherents of new religions, political upheavals, patriotic hysteria, gangs, and mass rushes to new lands.

And the quality of a nation—its innermost worth—is made manifest by its dregs as they rise to the top: by how brave they are, how humane, how orderly, how skilled, how generous, how independent or servile; by the bounds they will not transgress in their dealings with man's soul, with truth, and with honor.

The average American of today bristles with indignation when he is told that his country was built, largely, by hordes of undesirables from Europe. Yet, far from being derogatory, this statement, if true, should be a cause for rejoicing, should fortify our pride in the stock from which we have sprung.

This vast continent with its towns, farms, factories, dams, aqueducts, docks, railroads, highways, powerhouses, schools, and parks is the handiwork of common folk from the Old World, where for centuries men of their kind had been as beasts of burden, the property of their masters—kings, nobles, and priests—and with no will and no aspirations of their own. When on rare occasions one of the lowly had reached the top in Europe he had kept the pattern intact and, if anything, tightened the screws. The stuffy little corporal from Corsica harnessed the lusty forces released by the French Revolution to a gilded state coach, and could think of nothing grander than mixing his blood with that of the Hapsburg masters and establishing a new dynasty. In our day a bricklayer in Italy, a house painter in Germany, and a shoemaker's son in Russia have made themselves masters of their nations; and what they did was to re-establish and reinforce the old pattern.

Only here, in America, were the common folk of the Old World given a chance to show what they could do on their own, without a master to push and order them about. History contrived an earthshaking joke when it lifted by the nape of the neck lowly peasants, shopkeepers, laborers, paupers, jailbirds, and drunks from the midst of Europe, dumped them on a vast, virgin continent and said: "Go to it; it is yours!"

And the lowly were not awed by the magnitude of the task. A hunger for action, pent up for centuries, found an outlet. They went to it with ax, pick, shovel, plow, and rifle; on foot, on horse, in wagons, and on flatboats. They went to it praying, howling, singing, brawling, drinking, and fighting. Make way for the people! This is how I read the statement that this country was built by hordes of undesirables from the Old World.

Small wonder that we in this country have a deeply ingrained faith in human regeneration. We believe that, given a chance, even the degraded and the apparently worthless are capable of constructive work and great deeds. It is a faith founded on experience, not on some idealistic theory. And no matter what some anthropologists, sociologists, and geneticists may tell us, we shall go on believing that man, unlike other forms of life, is not a captive of his past—of his heredity and habits—but is possessed of infinite plasticity, and his potentialities for good and for evil are never wholly exhausted.

QUESTIONS

The following poem by Carl Sandburg speaks about "undesirables"—"rabble," "vagabonds," "hungry men." What other words might Sandburg have used for the "undesirables"? What effect do the words he uses create? Compare the terms used by Sandburg and Hoffer and determine the ways in which their words suggest similar or different attitudes toward these people.

Now the stone house on the lake front is finished and the
    workmen are beginning the fence.
The palings are made of iron bars with steel points that can
    stab the life out of any man who falls on them.
As a fence, it is a masterpiece, and will shut off the
    rabble and all vagabonds and hungry men and all
    wandering children looking for a place to play.
Passing through the bars and over the steel points will go
    nothing except Death and the Rain and To-morrow.
                  —Carl Sandburg, "A Fence"

WILLIAM O. DOUGLAS
The Six Poorest of Us[1]

The poverty of the Lurs is due partly to erosion. In Kurdistan to the north are mountain ranges practically devoid of trees; for miles and miles there is nothing but high, rolling grassland. From Kermanshah on south into Luristan one finds willow and juniper in the draws and oak on the slopes. The oaks do not form thick forests, but scattered clumps such as one sees in southwestern New Mexico and southeastern Arizona. Few are full-grown. Continuous cutting for centuries has resulted in trees that are mere bushy shoots from roots of monarchs that once commanded the range.

The grass has been so thinned by grazing that now one must take several steps between clumps. Only the thistles seem to have flourished. They stand four and five feet high in the ravines—coarse,

1. A chapter from *Strange Lands and Friendly People*, 1951.

spiny stems topped by round, blue blossoms almost as big as an orange. The scene reminded me of some overgrazed areas of our own in Oregon and Colorado.

Quick runoffs of rain and of snow water leave harsh gullies. Floods come in the spring with a mad rush, carrying topsoil with them. The water necessary for irrigation is wasted. The soil in the bottom lands is still rich, but it lacks water. Flood control and irrigation projects are needed. Protection of the ranges against overgrazing, and protection of the forests against cutting are also needed. The latter are as effective for storage of water as man-made dams. But in Luristan none of these conservation measures is in force. The wasting of resources goes on endlessly. Each year the earth is further depleted; each year the pinch of poverty is greater.

Flood control, irrigation projects, and conservation, though critical, are not the whole answer. Landownership and illiteracy are also at the bottom of the economic problems of the Lurs.

The Sagavands are often described in the chronicles of Persia as notorious highwaymen. One would not recognize them as such today. One Porsartib is their khan. Porsartib owns all the land. It lies at the head of a wide valley, fifty miles south and east of Khorramabad. There is scant water for the fields. The mountains that rim the valley on the east and west provide little moisture, except harsh runoffs in the spring. These mountains within the memory of residents of this valley were once green with oak and juniper. Now they are barren.

The tribe is sedentary—permanently settled in thirty-six villages. The menfolk gathered in a village by the road to greet me. They were in rags and tatters; their clothes more threadbare than one saw in our breadlines during the great depression. They stood huddled together, like the sheep they tend, but they held their heads with a pride despite generations of suffering and privation. These men inherited their tenancy. The entire tribe of forty-two thousand people works for Porsartib, paying one-third of the crop to him as rent. They are bound to him by debt as well. It is not extortionate debt; but it is eternal—advances to buy grain during severe winters; loans to meet the recurring emergencies of impoverished people.

Practically all the Sagavands are illiterate. Hence they have no method of escape from the system that holds them tight. Scientific agriculture, cheap means of financing, efficient methods of marketing are unknown to them. They plow with a stick pulled by a cow; they fertilize with night soil; they burn their best fertilizer—cow manure—since that is the only fuel supply they have; they reap grain with a hand sickle; they thrash it by having cows or donkeys pull a drag over it; they separate the grain from the chaff by tossing the straw in the air. This was their fathers' method. And it is likely it will be their sons'. In all the thirty-six villages there are only three schools; and these go only through the fourth grade.

There is no doctor in the entire area. Midwives with primitive methods attend to births; the umbilical cord is cut with a knife from the field. There are no medicines, no first-aid facilities. I talked with a tall, thin man with dark, deep-set eyes about the problem of medical care.

"Suppose you get a pain in your stomach, one that makes you double up. What do you do?"

He answered in a solemn voice. "If God wills it, I live."

More or less the same conditions exist among the other tribes of Lurs in this valley—the Dalvands and the Biranavands.

One August night I sat up late talking with Rustam Bahador, the khan of the Tulabi tribe, located farther to the north. Rustam Bahador owns not only the land; he owns every mud hut, every outhouse, every corral and barn in the area. He talked of the greatness of the Lurs and of their past, of the enduring qualities of his people. He emphasized the richness of their land. But this khan—rich and powerful though he is—is not leading his people out of the wilderness of ignorance and disease. I saw the villages that he owns. They have the mark of squalor on them. They have the fecal odor of the Middle East. There is no sanitation; the wells are not protected; no one is waging a campaign against flies.

Rustam Bahador—talkative, gregarious, friendly—occupies today a strong position of authority and leadership. But, like most leadership in the Middle East, it is irresponsible. He did not seem to be interested in or know anything about the central problems of agricultural production—seed selection, crossbreeding, fertilizers, irrigation, methods of plowing and cultivation, crop rotation, harvesting and thrashing. This Tulabi khan has the virtue of being a resident landlord. But the land and people he commands are merely perquisites of a feudal position.

There are not many landlords in all Persia who have a broad vision and a sense of social responsibility: Abdol Hossein Tavakoli, of Kermanshah, is one; Seyid Zia-Ed-Din of Tehran (former Prime Minister of Persia) is another. But these men are the exceptions.

One day I visited the Direkvan, Baharvand, Mir Baharvand and Papi (pronounced poppy) tribes. As I approached each village or settlement, the tribesmen tried to make a sacrifice in my honor. The Lurs are mostly too poor to kill a steer, even if they owned one; the sacrifice they usually tendered was a sheep. One day I managed to forestall it at five different places. On the sixth stop, when I visited the Papi tribe, several men had a steer tied about the ankles, preparatory to the sacrifice, and were trying to throw it. We stopped them. Beyond them, however, was another group who had four sheep in the middle of the road, ready for the sacrifice. They cut the throat of one before we had time to object. Its bright red blood streaked across the path and Ahmad Khan, their warm-hearted, friendly chief, stepped forward to greet me. And when he grasped me by the hand he put in poetic words the ultimate expression of Persian hospitality: "*Ghadam rouyeh tchashm*"—"You may walk on my eyes."

His encampment was high on slopes of the Zagros Mountains, west of Khorramabad, a thousand feet or so below Noozhian, an eight-thousand-foot pass over the range.

We sat on exquisite Persian rugs in his oblong tent of black woolen cloth. An orchestra stood on the open side of the tent. Dances went on as we sipped tea and ate melons, apples, and grapes. After a while four men seated themselves before us and played soft music. One played a long, bowl-like violin; one a flute; two played drums with their hands. And as they played they sang one of the most haunting melodies I have heard. There were seemingly endless verses ending with

> My sweetheart is Kattaneh
> I love Kattaneh
> My sweetheart is Kattaneh
> I love her dearly.

The tenderest of love songs came out of the rags and misery of the Papis. The words came almost in whispers; there was pathos in the voices; each singer poured out his heart; one middle-aged drummer had tears in his eyes. There was more than sadness in their voices; there was supplication too. It was the cry of desperately lonely people for love and affection.

Kattaneh was more than a woman; she was a symbol of justice and mercy. All in this Papi environment that met the eye spelled poverty and suffering. The music rose above the surroundings; it was an avenue of escape from the misery of this life.

The melody has haunted me through all my travels. Goatherds in the high Himalayas of India, the miserable laborers in the date orchards of Iraq, workers in the factories of Isfahan—all these conveyed the same message through their eyes. It was a plea for love—for charity and kindness; a plea which, long neglected, turns into an orgasm of hate and revenge, producing revolution and terror.

After the singing, Ahmad Khan served lunch. There were skewers of liver, kidney, chicken, and lamb done over charcoal. They were perfectly turned by a genial male chef and removed from the fire at the peak of their flavor. We stripped the meat off with our fingers; and as we ate, the crowd of ragged human beings standing before the tent moved closer. They were so marked with poverty—their faces as well as their wretched clothes—that I felt a sharp twinge of conscience.

These morsels of rich food were drawn from the larders of the poor.

This feast was tendered by the poorest of the poor—a meal the like of which they themselves had never eaten.

And as I sat, I thought of the Lurs who had died of starvation the previous winter.

And these were the people who were giving me the feast!

Not far from where I sat nine hundred Lurs out of a village of five thousand had starved to death only eight months before. The central government at last had distributed wheat; but in one village fifteen Lurs were so emaciated they died of starvation after the wheat arrived. And in the spring of this present year the Lurs in some of the villages I had visited had been so weak they could not stand for more than five minutes at a time.

I could eat no more. I motioned to two youngsters who stood in front of me to come near. They had sunken eyes and hollow cheeks. I handed first one, then the other a skewer of meat. They stripped off the delicate morsels and bolted them down. And the whole circle of hungry people moved politely nearer.

I asked my interpreter, Shahbaz, to call up at random six men among these peasants. They stood in front of me, their hands nervously twisting their gray felt skull caps. Turning to the first one I asked, "What is your name?"

"Abbas."

"What land do you own?"

"None."

"What land do you work?"

"None."

"What property do you own?"

"Four calves, ten sheep." (Skinny animals, grazed on barren tribal land.)

"How large a family do you support?"

"Five people."

I asked the other five similar questions.

Abdul. Owned no land, worked no land, owned six cows and fifteen sheep, supported a family of ten.

Emani. Owned no land; worked no land; owned four calves and twenty sheep; supported a family of two.

Hossein. Owned no land; rented wheat land from a merchant in Khorramabad and got as his share 20 per cent of the crop which last year was three hundred pounds; owned four cows and thirty sheep; supported a family of five.

Ali. Owned no land; rented wheat land from a merchant in Khorramabad and got as his share 20 per cent of the crop which last year was two hundred pounds of wheat; owned six cows and forty sheep; supported a family of two.

Taghi. Owned no land; worked no land; owned two cows and twenty sheep; supported a family of four.

I will never forget their faces. They were simple men, anxious to speak the truth, caught in a mire of poverty and squalor from which they knew not how to escape. They were eager to pour out their hearts. Their eyes searched mine, as if to obtain a promise of a new future. When I ended the conversation and turned away, the expectation and hope that had filled their faces vanished. They stood before me, ragged victims of despair.

While my questioning was going on, the elders of the tribe seated themselves on the far side of the tent. When I finished, one of them arose and came over to me. What he said was perhaps intended to save face, perhaps designed to relieve my embarrassment. He bowed graciously and then stated, "It was God's will that you should have picked the six poorest of us."

GEORGE BERNARD SHAW
The Gospel of St. Andrew Undershaft[1]

In the millionaire Undershaft I have represented a man who has become intellectually and spiritually as well as practically conscious of the irresistible natural truth which we all abhor and repudiate: to wit, that the greatest of our evils, and the worst of our crimes is poverty, and that our first duty to which every other consideration should be sacrificed, is not to be poor. "Poor but honest." "the respectable poor," and such phrases are as intolerable and as immoral as "drunken but amiable," "fraudulent but a good after-dinner speaker," "splendidly criminal," or the like. Security, the chief pretense of civilization, cannot exist where the worst of dangers, the danger of poverty, hangs over everyone's head, and where the alleged protection of our persons from violence is only an accidental result of the existence of a police force whose real business is to force the poor man to see his children starve whilst idle people overfeed pet dogs with the money that might feed and clothe them.

It is exceedingly difficult to make people realize that an evil is an evil. For instance, we seize a man and deliberately do him a malicious injury: say, imprison him for years. One would not suppose that it needed any exceptional clearness of wit to recognize in this an act of diabolical cruelty. But in England such a recognition provokes a stare of surprise, followed by an explanation that the outrage is punishment or justice or something else that is all right, or perhaps by a heated attempt to argue that we should all be robbed and

1. From the preface to his play, *Major Barbara*, 1905.

murdered in our beds if such stupid villainies as sentences of imprisonment were not committed daily. It is useless to argue that even if this were true, which it is not, the alternative to adding crimes of our own to the crimes from which we suffer is not helpless submission. Chickenpox is an evil; but if I were to declare that we must either submit to it or else repress it sternly by seizing everyone who suffers from it and punishing them by inoculation with smallpox, I should be laughed at; for though nobody could deny that the result would be to prevent chickenpox to some extent by making people avoid it much more carefully, and to effect a further apparent prevention by making them conceal it very anxiously, yet people would have sense enough to see that the deliberate propagation of smallpox was a creation of evil, and must therefore be ruled out in favor of purely humane and hygienic measures. Yet in the precisely parallel case of a man breaking into my house and stealing my wife's diamonds I am expected as a matter of course to steal ten years of his life, torturing him all the time. If he tries to defeat that monstrous retaliation by shooting me, my survivors hang him. The net result suggested by the police statistics is that we inflict atrocious injuries on the burglars we catch in order to make the rest take effectual precautions against detection; so that instead of saving our wives' diamonds from burglary we only greatly decrease our chances of ever getting them back, and increase our chances of being shot by the robber if we are unlucky enough to disturb him at his work.

But the thoughtless wickedness with which we scatter sentences of imprisonment, torture in the solitary cell and on the plank bed, and flogging, on moral invalids and energetic rebels, is as nothing compared to the silly levity with which we tolerate poverty as if it were either a wholesome tonic for lazy people or else a virtue to be embraced as St. Francis embraced it. If a man is indolent, let him be poor. If he is drunken, let him be poor. If he is not a gentleman, let him be poor. If he is addicted to the fine arts or to pure science instead of to trade and finance, let him be poor. If he chooses to spend his urban eighteen shillings a week or his agricultural thirteen shillings a week on his beer and his family instead of saving it up for his old age, let him be poor. Let nothing be done for "the undeserving": let him be poor. Serve him right! Also—somewhat inconsistently—blessed are the poor!

Now what does this Let Him Be Poor mean? It means let him be weak. Let him be ignorant. Let him become a nucleus of disease. Let him be a standing exhibition and example of ugliness and dirt. Let him have rickety children. Let him be cheap and let him drag his fellows down to his own price by selling himself to do their work. Let his habitations turn our cities into poisonous congeries of slums. Let his daughters infect our young men with the diseases of

the streets, and his sons revenge him by turning the nation's manhood into scrofula, cowardice, cruelty, hypocrisy, political imbecility
and all the other fruits of oppression and malnutrition. Let the
undeserving become still less deserving; and let the deserving lay up
for himself, not treasures in heaven, but horrors in hell upon earth.
This being so, is it really wise to let him be poor? Would he not do
ten times less harm as a prosperous burglar, incendiary, ravisher
or murderer, to the utmost limits of humanity's comparatively negligible impulses in these directions? Suppose we were to abolish all
penalties for such activities, and decide that poverty is the one thing
we will not tolerate—that every adult with less than, say, £365 a
year, shall be painlessly but inexorably killed, and every hungry half-
naked child forcibly fattened and clothed, would not that be an
enormous improvement on our existing system, which has already
destroyed so many civilizations, and is visibly destroying ours in the
same way?

Is there any radicle of such legislation in our parliamentary system? Well, there are two measures just sprouting in the political
soil, which may conceivably grow to something valuable. One is the
institution of a Legal Minimum Wage. The other, Old Age Pensions. But there is a better plan than either of these. Some time
ago I mentioned the subject of Universal Old Age Pensions to my
fellow Socialist Cobden-Sanderson, famous as an artist-craftsman in
bookbinding and printing. "Why not Universal Pensions for Life?"
said Cobden-Sanderson. In saying this, he solved the industrial problem at a stroke. At present we say callously to each citizen "If you
want money, earn it" as if his having or not having it were a matter
that concerned himself alone. We do not even secure for him the
opportunity of earning it: on the contrary, we allow our industry
to be organized in open dependence on the maintenance of "a reserve
army of unemployed" for the sake of "elasticity." The sensible
course would be Cobden-Sanderson's: that is, to give every man
enough to live well on, so as to guarantee the community against the
possibility of a case of the malignant disease of poverty, and then
(necessarily) to see that he earned it.

Undershaft, the hero of Major Barbara, is simply a man who,
having grasped the fact that poverty is a crime, knows that when
society offered him the alternative of poverty or a lucrative trade in
death and destruction,[2] it offered him, not a choice between opulent
villainy and humble virtue, but between energetic enterprise and
cowardly infamy. His conduct stands the Kantian test, which Peter
Shirley's does not.[3] Peter Shirley is what we call the honest poor
man. Undershaft is what we call the wicked rich one: Shirley is

2. Undershaft was a munitions manufacturer.
3. The Kantian test is to act only as
you would have all others act in similar
circumstances. Peter Shirley is an unemployed old man in the soup kitchen
whose conscience was shaped by social-
protest theories.

Lazarus, Undershaft Dives. Well, the misery of the world is due to the fact that the great mass of men act and believe as Peter Shirley acts and believes. If they acted and believed as Undershaft acts and believes, the immediate result would be a revolution of incalculable beneficence. To be wealthy, says Undershaft, is with me a point of honor for which I am prepared to kill at the risk of my own life. This preparedness is, as he says, the final test of sincerity. Like Froissart's medieval hero, who saw that "to rob and pill was a good life" he is not the dupe of that public sentiment against killing which is propagated and endowed by people who would otherwise be killed themselves, or of the mouth-honor paid to poverty and obedience by rich and insubordinate do-nothings who want to rob the poor without courage and command them without superiority. Froissart's knight, in placing the achievement of a good life before all the other duties—which indeed are not duties at all when they conflict with it, but plain wickednesses—behaved bravely, admirably, and, in the final analysis, public-spiritedly. Medieval society, on the other hand, behaved very badly indeed in organizing itself so stupidly that a good life could be achieved by robbing and pilling. If the knight's contemporaries had been all as resolute as he, robbing and pilling would have been the shortest way to the gallows, just as, if we were all as resolute and clearsighted as Undershaft, an attempt to live by means of what is called "an independent income" would be the shortest way to the lethal chamber. But as, thanks to our political imbecility and personal cowardice (fruits of poverty, both), the best imitation of a good life now procurable is life on an independent income, all sensible people aim at securing such an income, and are, of course, careful to legalize and moralize both it and all the actions and sentiments which lead to it and support it as an institution. What else can they do? They know, of course, that they are rich because others are poor. But they cannot help that: it is for the poor to repudiate poverty when they have had enough of it. The thing can be done easily enough: the demonstrations to the contrary made by the economists, jurists, moralists and sentimentalists hired by the rich to defend them, or even doing the work gratuitously out of sheer folly and abjectness, impose only on those who want to be imposed on.

The reason why the independent income-tax payers are not solid in defence of their position is that since we are not medieval rovers through a sparsely populated country, the poverty of those we rob prevents our having the good life for which we sacrifice them. Rich men or aristocrats with a developed sense of life—men like Ruskin and William Morris and Kropotkin—have enormous social appetites and very fastidious personal ones. They are not content with handsome houses: they want handsome cities. They are not content with bediamonded wives and blooming daughters: they complain because the charwoman is badly dressed, because the laundress smells of gin, because the sempstress is anemic, because every man they meet is not a friend and every woman not a romance. They turn up their noses at their neighbors' drains, and are made ill by the architecture of their neighbors' houses. Trade patterns made to suit vulgar people do not please them (and they can get nothing else): they cannot sleep nor sit at ease upon "slaughtered" cabinet makers' furniture. The very air is not good enough for them: there is too much factory smoke in it. They even demand abstract conditions: justice, honor, a noble moral atmosphere, a mystic nexus to replace the cash nexus. Finally they declare that though to rob and pill with your own hand on horseback and in steel coat may have been a good life, to rob and pill by the hands of the policeman, the bailiff, and the soldier, and to underpay them meanly for doing it, is not a good life, but rather fatal to all possibility of even a tolerable one. They call on the poor to revolt, and, finding the poor shocked at their ungentlemenliness, despairingly revile the proletariat for its "damned wantlessness" (*verdammte Bedürfnislosigkeit*).

So far, however, their attack on society has lacked simplicity. The poor do not share their tastes nor understand their art-criticisms. They do not want the simple life, nor the esthetic life; on the contrary, they want very much to wallow in all the costly vulgarities from which the elect souls among the rich turn away with loathing. It is by surfeit and not by abstinence that they will be cured of their hankering after unwholesome sweets. What they do dislike and despise and are ashamed of is poverty. To ask them to fight for the difference between the Christmas number of the Illustrated London News and the Kelmscott Chaucer is silly: they prefer the News. The difference between a stockbroker's cheap and dirty starched white shirt and collar and the comparatively costly and carefully dyed blue shirt of William Morris is a difference so disgraceful to Morris in their eyes that if they fought on the subject at all, they would fight in defence of the starch. "Cease to be slaves, in order that you may become cranks" is not a very inspiring call to arms; nor is it really improved by substituting saints for cranks. Both terms denote men of genius; and the common man does not want to live the life of a man of genius: he would much rather live the life of a pet collie if that were the only alternative. But he does want more money. Whatever else he may be vague about, he is clear about that. He may or may not prefer Major Barbara to the Drury Lane pantomime; but he always prefers five hundred pounds to five hundred shillings.

Now to deplore this preference as sordid, and teach children that it is sinful to desire money, is to strain towards the extreme possible limit of impudence in lying and corruption in hypocrisy

The universal regard for money is the one hopeful fact in our civilization, the one sound spot in our social conscience. Money is the most important thing in the world. It represents health, strength, honor, generosity and beauty as conspicuously and undeniably as the want of it represents illness, weakness, disgrace, meanness and ugliness. Not the least of its virtues is that it destroys base people as certainly as it fortifies and dignifies noble people. It is only when it is cheapened to worthlessness for some and made impossibly dear to others, that it becomes a curse. In short, it is a curse only in such foolish social conditions that life itself is a curse. For the two things are inseparable: money is the counter that enables life to be distributed socially: it *is* life as truly as sovereigns and bank notes are money. The first duty of every citizen is to insist on having money on reasonable terms; and this demand is not complied with by giving four men three shillings each for ten or twelve hours' drudgery and one man a thousand pounds for nothing. The crying need of the nation is not for better morals, cheaper bread, temperance, liberty, culture, redemption of fallen sisters and erring brothers, nor the grace, love and fellowship of the Trinity, but simply for enough money. And the evil to be attacked is not sin, suffering, greed, priestcraft, kingcraft, demagogy, monopoly, ignorance, drink, war, pestilence, nor any other of the scapegoats which reformers sacrifice, but simply poverty.

QUESTIONS

1. Cite some examples of Shaw's deliberately outrageous manner in his first paragraph. Does he ever modify this extreme manner?
2. In the second paragraph he speaks of two cases as "precisely parallel": what premise must he assume in order to say this? How vital is this assertion to his main line of argument? What is his central assertion?
3. Explain the definition of money as life which appears in the last paragraph.
4. Outline in more neutral words and phrases than Shaw's a more conventional approach to his argument.
5. Who are Shaw's controversial antagonists? In what way is his controversial manner suited to these antagonists?

RUSSELL BAKER

Ben Was Swell, but He's Out

Old saws are wearing out. Take the case of "The devil finds work for idle hands to do." As recently as fifteen years ago when a mother caught a son loafing around the pornography rack at the corner drugstore, she could take him by the ear and lead him home to wash the windows, with the perfectly satisfactory explanation that "The devil finds work for idle hands to do."

Nowadays, the world is different. With the march of automation, idleness is becoming the national occupation and sociologists will speak sternly to mothers who oppose it. Since ever-expanding idleness is the goal of the American economy, it is unpatriotic to mention it in the same breath with Beelzebub.

The goal now is to rehabilitate idleness, and the first step in every rehabilitation program is a name change. During World War I, when Germany became the enemy, the Hunnish sauerkraut was restored to respectability by being renamed "liberty cabbage." In the same way, ugly satanic old idleness is now rechristened "leisure."

Leisure sounds ever so much more decent than idleness. It sounds like something that the uptown set might go in for enthusiastically. Idleness was an evil to be fought by placing such weapons as window-washing rags and lawnmowers in the hands of the indolent young. Leisure is merely another typical American problem to be solved by a nexus of committees, study groups, and Congressional investigations.

Now, if a boy loafs around the pornography rack, it is merely because he has a "leisure-time problem." The solution is not to put him to work—the machines have most of the jobs well in hand—but to encourage him to take up the oboe or start a bee colony. In this way, we say, he uses his leisure "creatively."

The notion of creative leisure is mostly nonsense, of course. The sin that a boy may stumble into by keeping company with oboe players or going to bee-keepers' conventions is considerable, especially if his interest in oboes or bees is only a substitute for loafing around the drugstore.

The American economic system must, nevertheless, be justified. And so, if a boy follows the oboe path to sin, his parents are no longer permitted to blame it all on Satan; instead, the parents are indicted for failing to find a creative solution to the leisure-time problem.

There are many other pieces of ancient wisdom that have turned obsolete under the bizarre new American prosperity. Take "A penny saved is a penny earned." Sound enough in Franklin's day perhaps, but clearly subversive in 1965.

The first economic duty to every citizen today is to consume. To keep the economy booming we must consume with our cash, consume with our credit cards, consume with our charge accounts and then go to the bank to borrow the means to consume again.

It is obvious that if people began acting on the theory that "A penny saved is a penny earned," production would fall, unemployment would rise, salaries would be cut and the country would stagnate. Nowadays, the homily should read, "A penny spent is not good enough."

Then there is the collapse of "A stitch in time saves nine." To maintain even the present unsatisfactory level of employment, it is absolutely imperative that we never settle for the timely one-stitch job when a bit of dallying can make work for nine additional stitchers.

As we have seen in too many industries, the nine stitchers thrown out of work either go on relief—which reduces the timely stitcher's take-home pay—or turn in desperation to braining the smug stitch-in-time takers for their entire pay envelopes. In this type of economy, the canny stitcher takes his stitch too late.

And, of course, there is old "Early to bed and early to rise makes a man healthy, wealthy, and wise." Taken literally, this advice would now be disastrous.

In the first place, rising early would immediately raise the leisure-time problem to unmanageable proportions. The safest of all leisure-time activities is sleep, and the fellow who rolls out at cock's crow to work on his oboe is going to be thoroughly sated with leisure by breakfast time.

What's more, early rising tends to make a man reflect on the absurdity of his life. In this mood, he may very well realize that his way of life is insane and decide to change it by saving a penny, thereby triggering an economic catastrophe.

Very likely he will go to the office feeling energetic and healthy and, before he can stop himself, take a stitch in time, thus causing unemployment, raising his taxes, and increasing crime. "Early to bed and early to rise" has had its day.

So, apparently, has Benjamin Franklin.

JAMES AGEE
Cotton[1]

Cotton is only one among several crops and among many labors: and all these other crops and labors mean life itself. Cotton means nothing of the sort. It demands more work of a tenant family and yields less reward than all the rest. It is the reason the tenant has the means to do the rest, and to have the rest, and to live, as a tenant, at all. Aside from a few negligibilities of minor sale and barter and of out-of-season work, it is his one possible source of money, and through this fact, though his living depends far less on money than on the manipulations of immediate nature, it has a certain royalty. It is also that by which he has all else besides money. But it is also

---

1. An appendix from *Let Us Now Praise Famous Men,* 1939.

his chief contracted obligation, for which he must neglect all else as need be; and is the central leverage and symbol of his privation and of his wasted life. It is the one crop and labor which is in no possible way useful as it stands to the tenant's living; it is among all these the one which must and can be turned into money; it is among all these the one in which the landowner is not interested; and it is among all these the one of which the tenant can hope for least, and can be surest that he is being cheated, and is always to be cheated. All other tasks are incidental to it; it is constantly on everyone's mind; yet of all of them it is the work in which the tenant has least hope and least interest, and to which he must devote the most energy. Any less involved and self-contradictory attempt to understand what cotton and cotton work "means" to a tenant would, it seems to me, be false to it. It has the doubleness that all jobs have by which one stays alive and in which one's life is made a cheated ruin, and the same sprained and twilight effect on those who must work at it: but because it is only one among the many jobs by which a tenant family must stay alive, and deflects all these others, and receives still other light from their more personal need, reward, and value, its meanings are much more complex than those of most jobs: it is a strong stale magnet among many others more weak and more yielding of life and hope. In the mind of one in whom all these magnetisms are daily and habituated from his birth, these meanings are one somber mull: yet all their several forces are pulling at once, and by them the brain is quietly drawn and quartered. It seems to me it is only through such a complex of meanings that a tenant can feel, toward that crop, toward each plant in it, toward all that work, what he and all grown women too appear to feel, a particular automatism, a quiet, apathetic, and inarticulate yet deeply vindictive hatred, and at the same time utter hopelessness, and the deepest of their anxieties and of their hopes: as if the plant stood enormous in the unsteady sky fastened above them in all they do like the eyes of an overseer. To do all of the hardest work of your life in service of these drawings-apart of ambiguities; and to have all other tasks and all one's consciousness stained and drawn apart in it: I can conceive of little else which could be so inevitably destructive of the appetite for living, of the spirit, of the being, or by whatever name the centers of individuals are to be called: and this very literally: for just as there are deep chemical or electric changes in all the body under anger, or love, or fear, so there must certainly be at the center of these meanings and their directed emotions; perhaps most essentially, an incalculably somber and heavy weight and dark knotted iron of subnausea at the peak of the diaphragm, darkening and weakening the whole body and being, the literal feeling by which the words a broken heart are no longer poetic, but are merely the most accurate possible description.

Yet these things as themselves are withdrawn almost beyond visibility, and the true focus and right telling of it would be in the exact textures of each immediate task.

Of cotton farming I know almost nothing with my own eyes; the rest I have of Bud Woods. I asked enough of other people to realize that every tenant differs a little in his methods, so nothing of this can be set down as "standard" or "correct"; but the dissonances are of small detail rather than of the frame and series in the year. I respect dialects too deeply, when they are used by those who have a right to them, not to be hesitant in using them, but I have decided to use some of Woods' language here. I have decided, too, to try to use my imagination a little, as carefully as I can. I must warn you that the result is sure to be somewhat inaccurate: but it is accurate anyhow to my ignorance, which I would not wish to disguise.

From the end of the season and on through the winter the cotton and the corn stand stripped and destroyed, the cotton black and brown, the corn gray and brown and rotted gold, much more shattered, the banks of woodland bare, drenched and black, the clay dirt sombered wet or hard with a shine of iron, peaceful and exhausted; the look of trees in a once full-blown country where such a burning of war has gone there is no food left even for birds and insects, all now brought utterly quiet, and the bare homes dark with dampness, under the soft and mourning midwinter suns of autumnal days, when all glows gold yet lifeless, and under constrictions of those bitter freezings when the clay is shafted and sprilled with ice, and the aching thinly drifted snows which give the land its shape, and, above all, the long, cold, silent, inexhaustible, and dark winter rains:

In the late fall or middle February this tenant, which of the three or of the millions I do not care—a man, dressed against the wet coldness, may be seen small and dark in his prostrated fields, taking down these sometimes brittle, sometimes rotted forests of last year's crops with a club or with a cutter, putting death to bed, cleaning the land: and late in February, in fulfillment of an obligation to his landlord, he borrows a second mule and, with a two-horse plow, runs up the levees,[2] that is, the terraces, which shall preserve his land; this in a softening mild brightness and odoriferousness of presaging spring, and a rustling shearing apart of the heavy land, his mules moving in slow scarce-wakened method as of work before dawn, knowing the real year's work to be not started yet, only made ready for. It is when this is done, at about the first of March, that the actual work begins, with what is planted where, and with what grade and amount of fertilizer, determined by the landlord, who will also, if he wishes, criticize, advise, and govern at all stages of planting and

2. These farms are the width of a state and still more from the river. Is levee originally a land or a river word? It must be a river word, for terracing against erosion is recent in America. So the Mississippi has such power that men who have never seen it use its language in their work [Agee's note].

cultivation. But the physical work, and for that matter the knowledge by which he works, is the tenant's, and this is his tenth or his fortieth year's beginning of it, and it is of the tenant I want to tell.

How you break the land in the first place depends on whether you have one or two mules or can double up with another tenant for two mules. It is much better to broadcast if you can. With two mules you can count on doing it all in that most thorough way. But if you have only one mule you break what you have time for, more shallowly and, for the rest, you bed, that is, start the land.

To broadcast, to break the land broadcast: take a twister, which is about the same as a turning plow, and, heading the mule in concentrics the shape of the field, lay open as broad and deep a ribbon of the stiff dirt as the strength of the mule and of your own guidance can manage: eight wide by six deep with a single-horse plow, and twice that with a double, is doing well: the operation has the staggering and reeling yet steady quality of a small sailboat clambering a storm.

Where you have broadcast the land, you then lay out the furrows three and a half feet apart with a shovel plow; and put down fertilizer; and by four furrows with a turning plow, twist the dirt back over the fertilized furrow. But if, lacking mule power, you have still land which is not broken, and it is near time to plant, you bed the rest. There are two beddings. The first is hard bedding: breaking the hard pan between the rows.

Hard bedding: set the plow parallel to the line of (last year's) stalks and along their right, follow each row to its end and up the far side. The dirt lays open always to the right. Then set the plow close in against the stalks and go around again. The stubble is cleaned out this second time round and between each two rows is a bed of soft dirt: that is to say, the hard pan is all broken. That is the first bedding.

Then drop guano along the line where the stalks were, by machine or by horn. Few tenants use the machine; most of them either buy a horn, or make it, as Woods does. It is a long tin cone, small and low, with a wood handle, and a hole in the low end. It is held in the left hand, pointed low to the furrow, and is fed in fistfuls, in a steady rhythm, from the fertilizer sack, the incipient frock, slung heavy along the right side.

After you have strowed the gyewanner you turn the dirt back over with two plowings just as before: and that is the second bedding. Pitch the bed shallow, or you won't be able to work it right.

If you have done all this right you haven't got a blemish in all your land that is not broke: and you are ready to plant.

But just roughly, only as a matter of suggestion, compute the work that has been done so far, in ten acres of land, remembering that this is not counting in ten more acres of corn and a few minor crops: how many times has this land been retraced in the rolling-gaited guidance and tensions and whippings and orderings of plowing, and with the steadily held horn, the steady arc of the right arm and right hand fisting and opening like a heart, the heavy weight of the sack at the right side?

Broadcasting, the whole unbroken plaque slivered open in rectilinear concenters, eight inches apart and six deep if with one mule, sixteen apart and twelve deep if with two: remember how much length of line is coiled in one reel or within one phonograph record: and then each furrow, each three and a half feet, scooped open with a shovel plow: and in each row the fertilizer laid: and each row folded cleanly back in four transits of its complete length: or bedding, the first bedding in four transits of each length; and then the fertilizer: and four more transits of each length: every one of the many rows of the whole of the field gone eight times over with a plow and a ninth by hand; and only now is it ready for planting.

Planting

There are three harrs you might use but the spring-toothed harr is best. The long-toothed section harrow tears your bed to pieces; the short-toothed is better, but catches on snags and is more likely to pack the bed than loosen it. The springtooth moves lightly but incisively with a sort of knee-action sensitiveness to the modulations of the ground, and it jumps snags. You harrow just one row at a time and right behind the harrow comes the planter. The planter is rather like a tennis-court marker: a seed bin set between light wheels, with a little plow protruded from beneath it like a foot from under a hoopskirt. The little beak of the plow slits open the dirt; just at its lifted heel the seed thrills out in a spindling stream; a flat wheel flats the dirt over: a light-traveling, tender, iron sexual act entirely worthy of setting beside the die-log and the swept broad-handed arm.[3]

Depending on the moisture and the soil, it will be five days to two weeks before the cotton will show.

Cultivating begins as soon as it shows an inch.

Cultivation

Barring off: the sweepings: chopping: laying by:
The first job is barring off.
Set a five- to six-inch twister, the smallest one you have, as close

3. I am unsure of this planting machine; I did not see one there; but what Woods described to me seemed to tally with something I had seen, and not remembered with perfect clearness, from my childhood. The die-log is still used, Woods says, by some of the older-fashioned farmers and by some negroes. I'm not very clear about it either, but I am interested because according to Woods its use goes a *way* on back. My "impression" is that it's simple enough: a hollow homemade cylinder of wood with a hole in it to regulate and direct the falling stream of seed as would be more difficult by hand [Agee's note].

in against the stalks as you can get it and not damage them, as close as the breadth of a finger if you are good at it, and throw the dirt to the middle. Alongside this plow is a wide tin defender, which doesn't allow a blemish to fall on the young plants.

Then comes the first of the four sweepings. The sweeps are blunt stocks shaped a good deal like stingrays. Over their dull foreheads and broad shoulders they neither twist nor roll the dirt, but shake it from the middle to the beds on either side. For the first sweeping you still use the defender. Use a little stock, but the biggest you dare to; probably the eighteen-inch.

Next after that comes the chopping, and with this the whole family helps down through the children of eight or seven, and by helps, I mean that the family works full time at it. Chopping is a simple and hard job, and a hot one, for by now the sun, though still damp, is very strong, hot with a kind of itchy intensity that is seldom known in northern springs. The work is, simply, thinning the cotton to a stand; hills a foot to sixteen inches apart, two to four stalks to the hill. It is done with an eight to ten-inch hoeblade. You cut the cotton flush off at the ground, bent just a little above it, with a short sharp blow of the blade of which each stroke is light enough work; but multiplied into the many hundreds in each continuously added hour, it aches first the forearms, which so harden they seem to become one bone, and in time the whole spine.

The second sweeping is done with the twenty to twenty-two-inch stock you will use from now on; then comes hoeing, another job for the whole family; then you run the middles; that is, you put down soda by hand or horn or machine; soda makes the weed, guano puts on the fruit; then comes the third sweeping; and then another hoeing. The first and second sweepings you have gone pretty deep. The stuff is small and you want to give loose ground to your feed roots. The third sweeping is shallow, for the feed roots have extended themselves within danger of injury.

The fourth sweeping is so light a scraping that it is scarcely more than a ritual, like a barber's last delicate moments with his muse before he holds the mirror up to the dark side of your skull. The cotton has to be treated very carefully. By this last sweeping it is making. Break roots, or lack rain, and it is stopped dead as a hammer.

This fourth sweeping is the operation more propertly known as laying by. From now on until picking time, there is nothing more a farmer can do. Everything is up to the sky, the dirt, and the cotton itself; and in six weeks now, and while the farmer is fending off such of its enemies as he can touch, and, lacking rations money to live on, is desperately seeking and conceivably finding work, or with his family is hung as if on a hook on his front porch in the terrible leisure, the cotton is making, and his year's fate is being quietly fought out between agencies over which he has no control. And in this white midsummer, while he is thus waiting however he can, and defending what little he can, these are his enemies, and this is what the cotton is doing with its time:

Each square points up. That is to say: on twig-ends, certain of the fringed leaves point themselves into the sharp form of an infant prepuce; each square points up: and opens a flat white flower which turns pink next day, purple the next, and on the next day shrivels and falls, forced off by the growth, at the base of the bloom, of the boll. The development from square to boll consumes three weeks in the early summer, ten days in the later, longer and more intense heat. The plants are well fringed with pointed squares, and young cold bolls, by the time the crop is laid by; and the blooming keeps on all summer. The development of each boll from the size of a pea to that point where, at the size of a big walnut, it darkens and dries and its white contents silently explode it, takes five to eight weeks and is by no means ended when the picking season has begun.

And meanwhile the enemies: bitterweed, ragweed, Johnson grass; the weevil, the army worm; the slippery chances of the sky. Bitterweed is easily killed out and won't come up again. Ragweed will, with another prong every time. That weed can suck your crop to death. Johnson grass, it takes hell and scissors to control. You can't control it in the drill with your plowing. If you just cut it off with the hoe, it is high as your thumb by the next morning. The best you can do is dig up the root with the corner of your hoe, and that doesn't hold it back any too well.

There is a lot less trouble from the weevils[4] than there used to be, but not the army worms. Army worms are devils. The biggest of them get to be the size of your little finger. They eat leaves and squares and young bolls. You get only a light crop of them at first. They web up in the leaves and turn into flies, the flies lay eggs, the eggs turn into army worms by the millions and if they have got this good a start of you you can hear the sound of them eating in the whole field and it sounds like a brushfire. They are a bad menace but they are not as hard to control as the weevil. You mix arsenic poison with a sorry grade of flour and dust the plants late of an evening (afternoon) or soon of a morning (pre-morning); and the dew makes a paste of it that won't blow off.

It is only in a very unusual year that you do well with both of the most important crops, the two life mainly depends on, because they need rain and sun in such different amounts. Cotton needs a great deal less rain than corn; it is really a sun flower. If it is going to get a superflux of rain, that will best come before it is blooming; and if it has got to rain during that part of the summer

4. If I remember rightly, people never learned any successful method against him, and it is some insect, whose name and kind I forget, who holds him in check [Agee's note].

when a fairsized field is blooming a bale a day, it had best rain late in the evening when the blooms are shutting or at night, not in the morning or the mid day: for then the bloom is blared out flat; rain gets in it easy and hangs on it; it shuts wet, sours, and sticks to the boll; next morning it turns red and falls. Often the boll comes off with it. But the boll that stays on is sour and rotted and good for nothing. Or to put it the other way around, it can take just one rain at the wrong time of day at the wrong time of summer to wreck you out of a whole bale.

It is therefore not surprising that they are constant readers of the sky; that it holds not an ounce of "beauty" to them (though I know of no more magnificent skies than those of Alabama); that it is the lodestone of their deepest pieties; and that they have, also, the deep stormfear which is apparently common to all primitive peoples. Wind is as terrifying to them as cloud and lightning and thunder: and I remember how, sitting with the Woods, in an afternoon when George was away at work, and a storm was building, Mrs. Gudger and her children came hurrying three quarters of a mile beneath the blackening air to shelter among company. Gudger says: "You never can tell what's in a cloud."

Picking Season

Late in August the fields begin to whiten more rarely with late bloom and more frequently with cotton and then still thicker with cotton, a sparkling ground starlight of it, steadily bursting into more and more millions of points, all the leaves seeming shrunken smaller; quite as at night the whole frontage of the universe is more and more thoroughly printed in the increasing darkness; and the wide cloudless and tremendous light holds the earth clamped and trained as beneath a vacuum bell and burningglass; in such a brilliance that half and two thirds of the sky is painful to look into; and in this white maturing oven the enlarged bolls are streaked a rusty green, then bronze, and are split and splayed open each in a loose vomit of cotton. These split bolls are now *burrs*, hard and edged as chiseled wood, pointed nearly as thorns, spread open in three and four and five gores or cells. It is slow at first, just a few dozen scattered here and there and then a few tens of dozens, and then there is a space of two or three days in which a whole field seems to be crackling open at once, and at this time it seems natural that it must be gone into and picked, but all the more temperate and experienced tenants wait a few days longer until it will be fully worth the effort: and during this bursting of bolls and this waiting, there is a kind of quickening, as if deep under the ground, of all existence, toward a climax which cannot be delayed much longer, but which is held in the tensions of this reluctance, tightening, and delay: and this can be seen equally in long, sweeping drivings of a car between these spangling fields, and in any one of the small towns or the county seats, and in the changed eyes of any one family, a kind of tightening as of an undertow, the whole world and year lifted nearly upon its crest, and soon beginning the long chute down to winter: children, and once in a while a very young or a very old woman or man, whose work is scarcely entered upon or whose last task and climax this may be, are deeply taken with an excitement and a restlessness to begin picking, and in the towns, where it is going to mean money, the towns whose existence is for it and depends on it, and which in most times of year are sunken in sleep as at the bottom of a sea: these towns are sharpening awake; even the white hot streets of a large city are subtly changed in this season: but Gudger and his wife and Ricketts and Woods, and most of the heads of the million and a quarter families who have made this and are to do the working of taking it for their own harm and another's use, they are only a little more quiet than usual, as they might be if they were waiting for a train to come in, and keep looking at the fields, and judging them; and at length one morning (the Ricketts women are already three days advanced in ragged work), Gudger says, Well:

Well; I reckin tomorrow we'd better start to picking:

And the next morning very early, with their broad hats and great sacks and the hickory baskets, they are out, silent, their bodies all slanted, on the hill: and in every field in hundreds of miles, black and white, it is the same: and such as it is, it is a joy which scarcely touches any tenant; and is worn thin and through in half a morning, and is gone for a year.

It is simple and terrible work. Skill will help you; all the endurance you can draw up against it from the roots of your existence will be thoroughly used as fuel to it: but neither skill nor endurance can make it any easier.

Over the right shoulder you have slung a long white sack whose half length trails the ground behind. You work with both hands as fast and steadily as you can. The trick is to get the cotton between your fingertips at its very roots in the burr in all three or four or five gores at once so that it is brought out clean in one pluck. It is easy enough with one burr in perhaps ten, where the cotton is ready to fall; with the rest, the fibers are more tight and tricky. So another trick is, to learn these several different shapes of burr and resistance as nearly as possible by instinct, so there will be no second trying and delay, and none left wasted in the burr; and, too, as quickly to judge what may be too rotted and dirtied to use, and what is not yet quite ready to take: there are a lot suspended between these small uncertainties, and there should be no delay, no need to use the mind's judgement, and few mistakes. Still another trick is, between these strong pulls of efficiency, proper judgement, and maximum speed, not to hurt your fingers on the burrs any worse than you can help. You would have to try hard, to break your flesh on any one burr, whether on its sharp points or its edges; and a single raindrop is only scarcely instrumental in ironing a mountain flat; but in each plucking of the hand the fingers are searched deep in along these several sharp, hard edges. In two hours' picking the hands are just well limbered up. At the end of a week you are favoring your fingers, still in the obligation of speed. The later of the three to five times over the field, the last long weeks of the season, you might be happy if it were possible to exchange them for boils. With each of these hundreds of thousands of insertions of the hands, moreover, the fingers are brought to a small point, in an action upon every joint and tendon in the hand. I suggest that if you will try, three hundred times in succession, the following exercise: touch all five fingertips as closely as possible into one point, trying meanwhile to hold loose cotton in the palm of the hand: you will see that this can very quickly tire, cramp and deteriorate the whole instrument, and will understand how easily rheumatism can take up its strictures in just this place.

Meanwhile, too, you are working in a land of sunlight and heat which are special to just such country at just that time of year: sunlight that stands and stacks itself upon you with the serene weight of deep sea water, and heat that makes the jointed and muscled and fine-structured body glow like one indiscriminate oil; and this brilliant weight of heat is piled upon you more and more heavily in hour after hour so that it can seem you are a diving bell whose strained seams must at any moment burst, and the eyes are marked in stinging sweat, and the head, if your health is a little unstable, is gently roaring, like a private blowtorch, and less gently beating with aching blood: also the bag, which can hold a hundred pounds, is filling as it is dragged from plant to plant, four to nine burrs to a plant to be rifled swiftly, and the load shrugged along another foot or two and the white row stretched ahead to a blur and innumerably manifolded in other white rows which have not yet been touched, and younger bolls in the cleaned row behind already breaking like slow popcorn in the heat, and the sack still heavier and heavier, so that it pulls you back as a beast might rather than a mere dead weight: but it is not only this: cotton plants are low, so that in this heat and burden of the immanent sun and of the heavying sack you are dragging, you are continuously somewhat stooped over even if you are a child, and are bent very deep if you are a man or a woman. A strong back is a godsend, but not even the strongest back was built for that treatment, and there combine at the kidneys, and rill down the thighs and up the spine and athwart the shoulders the ticklish weakness of gruel or water, and an aching that is increased in geometric progressions, and at length, in the small of the spine, a literal and persistent sensation of yielding, buckling, splintering, and breakage: and all of this, even though the mercy of nature has hardened your flesh and has anesthetized your nerves and your powers of reflection and of imagination, yet reaches in time the brain and the more mirror-like nerves, and thereby is redoubled upon itself much more powerfully than before: and this is all compounded upon you during each successive hour of the day and during each successive day in a force which rest and food and sleep only partly and superficially refresh: and though, later in the season, you are relieved of the worst of the heat, it is in exchange at the last for a coolness which many pickers like even less well, since it so slows and chills the lubricant garment of sweat they work in, and seriously slows and stiffens the fingers which by then at best afford an excruciation in every touch.

The tenants' idiom has been used ad nauseam by the more unspeakable of the northern journalists but it happens to be accurate: that picking goes on each day from can to can't: sometimes, if there is a feeling of rush, the Ricketts continue it by moonlight. In the blasting heat of the rest of the season, unless there is a rush to beat a rain or to make up an almost completed wagonload, it is customary to quit work an hour and a half or even two hours in the worst part of the day and to sit or lie in the shade and possible draft of the hallway or porch asleep or dozing after dinner. This time narrows off as the weeks go by and a sense of rush and of the wish to be done with it grows on the pickers and is tightened through from the landlord. I have heard of tenants and pickers who have no rest-period and no midday meal,[5] but those I am acquainted with have it. It is of course no parallel in heartiness and variety to the proud and enormous meals which farm wives of the wheat country prepare for harvest hands, and which are so very zestfully regarded by some belated virgilians as common to what they like to call the American Scene. It is in fact the ordinary every day food, with perhaps a little less variety than in the earlier summer, hastily thrown together and heated by a woman who has hurried in exhausted from the field as few jumps as possible ahead of her family, and served in the dishes she hurriedly rinsed before she hurried out on the early morning as few jumps as possible behind them. When they are all done, she hurries through the dish washing and puts on her straw hat or her sunbonnet and goes on

5. On the big plantations, where a good deal of the picking is done by day labor and is watched over by riding bosses, all the equations of speed and unresting steadiness are of course intensified; the whole nature of the work, in the men and women and their children, is somewhat altered. Yet not so much as might at first seem. A man and his family working alone are drawn narrowly together in these weeds even within themselves, and know they are being watched: from the very first, in town, their landlords are observant of which tenants bring their cotton first to gin and of who is slow and late; also, there is nearly always, in the tenant's family, the exceedingly sharp need of cottonseed money [Agee's note].

back into the field, and they are all at it in a strung-out little bunch, the sun a bitter white on their deeply bent backs, and the sacks trailing, a slow breeze idling in the tops of the pines and hickories along the far side but the leaves of the low cotton scarcely touched in it, and the whole land, under hours of heat still to go, yet listed subtly forward toward the late end of the day. They seem very small in the field and very lonely, and the motions of their industry are so small, in range, their bodies so slowly moving, that it seems less that they are so hard at work than that they are bowed over so deeply into some fascination or grief, or are as those pilgrims of Quebec who take the great flights of stairs upon their knees, slowly, a prayer spoken in each step. Ellen lies in the white load of the cotton-basket in the shade asleep; Squinchy picks the front of his dress full and takes it to his mother; Clair Bell fills a hat time after time in great speed and with an expression of delight rushes up behind her mother and dumps the cotton on all of her she can reach and goes crazy with laughter, and her mother and the girls stop a minute and she is hugged, but they talk more among themselves than the other families, they are much more quiet than is usual to them, and Mrs. Ricketts only pauses a minute, cleaning the cotton from her skirts and her hair and putting it in her sack, and then she is bowed over deeply at work again. Woods is badly slowed by weakness and by the pain in his shoulder; he welcomes any possible excuse to stop and sometimes has to pause whether there is any excuse or not, but his wife and her mother are both strong and good pickers, so he is able to get by without a hired hand. Thomas is not old enough yet to be any use. Burt too is very young for it and works only by fits and starts; little is expected of children so small, but it is no harm what little they do; you can't learn them too young. Junior is not very quick with it at best. He will work for a while furiously hard, in jealousy of Louise, and then slacken up with sore hands and begin to bully Burt. Katy is very quick. Last summer, when she was only eight, she picked a hundred and ten pounds in a day in a race with Flora Merry Lee. This summer she has had runarounds and is losing two fingernails but she is picking steadily. Pearl Woods is big for her age and is very steadily useful. Louise is an extraordinarily steady and quick worker for her age; she can pick a hundred and fifty pounds in a day. The two Ricketts boys are all right when their papa is on hand to keep them at their work; as it is, with Ricketts at the sawmills they clown a good deal, and tease their sisters. Mrs. Gudger picks about the average for a woman, a hundred and fifty to two hundred pounds a day. She is fast with her fingers until the work exhausts her; "last half of the day I just don't see how I can keep on with it." George Gudger is a very poor picker. When he was a child he fell in the fireplace and burnt the flesh

off the flat of both hands to the bone, so that his fingers are stiff
and slow and the best he has ever done in a day is a hundred and
fifty pounds. The average for a man is nearer two hundred and
fifty. His back hurts him badly too, so he usually picks on his
knees, the way the others pick only when they are resting. Mrs.
Ricketts used to pick three hundred and three hundred and fifty
pounds in a day but sickness has slowed her to less than two hundred
now. Mrs. Ricketts is more often than not a fantast, quite without
realizing, and in all these figures they gave me there may be inaccuracy—according to general talk surrounding the Rust machine a
hundred pounds a day is good picking—but these are their own
estimates of their own abilities, on a matter in which tenants have
some pride, and that seems to me more to the point than their
accuracy. There are sometimes shifts into gayety in the picking, or
a brief excitement, a race between two of the children, or a snake
killed; or two who sit a few moments in their sweat in the shaded
clay when they have taken some water, but they say very little to
each other, for there is little to say, and are soon back to it, and
mainly, in hour upon hour, it is speechless, silent, serious, ceaseless
and lonely work along the great silence of the unshaded land, ending each day in a vast blaze of dust on the west, every leaf sharpened in long knives of shadow, the clay drawn down through red
to purple, and the leaves losing color, and the wild blind eyes of
the cotton staring in twilight, in those odors of work done and of
nature lost once more to night whose sweetness is a torture, and
in the slow, loaded walking home, whose stiff and gentle motions
are those of creatures just awakened.

The cotton is ordinarily stored in a small structure out in the
land, the cotton house; but none of these three families has one.
The Gudgers store it in one of the chambers of their barn, the
Woods on their front porch, raising planks around it, the Ricketts
in their spare room. The Ricketts children love to play in it, tumbling and diving and burying each other; sometimes, it is a sort of
treat, they are allowed to sleep in it. Rats like it too, to make
nest-es[6] in, and that draws ratsnakes. It is not around, though, for
very long at a time. Each family has a sort of archaic iron beam
scales, and when these scales have weighed out fourteen hundred
pounds of cotton it is loaded, if possible during the first of the
morning, onto the narrow and high-boarded wagon, and is taken into
Cookstown to gin.

It is a long tall deep narrow load shored in with weathered wagon-

6. Mrs. Gudger's word. Her saying of
it was "rats likes it to make nest-es in."
It is a common pluralization in the
south. There is no Cuteness in it, of
speaking by diminutives, and I wonder
whether this is not Scottish dialect, and
whether they, too, are not innocent of
the "itsybitsying" which the middle-class
literacy assumes of them. *Later.* On the
proof-sheets is the following note, which
I use with thanks: "Isn't it the Middle-
English plural? Chaucer used it for this
same word and as a usual plural ending"
[Agee's note].

sides and bulged up in a high puff above these sides, and the mule, held far over to the right of the highway to let the cars go by, steps more steadily and even more slowly than ordinary, with a look almost of pomp, dragging the hearse-shaped wagon: its iron wheels on the left grince in the slags of the highway, those on the right in clay: and high upon the load, the father at the reins, the whole of the family is sitting, if it is a small family, or if it is a large, those children whose turn it is, and perhaps the mother too. The husband is dressed in the better of his work clothes; the wife, and the children, in such as they might wear to town on Saturday, or even, some of them, to church, and the children are happy and excited, high on the soft load, and even a woman is taken with it a little, much more soberly, and even the man who is driving, has in the tightness of his jaws, and in his eyes, which meet those of any stranger with the curious challenging and protective, fearful and fierce pride a poor mother shows when her child, dressed in its best, is being curiously looked at; even he who knows best of any of them, is taken with something of the same: and there is in fact about the whole of it some raw, festal quality, some air also of solemn grandeur, this member in the inconceivably huge and slow parade of mule-drawn, crawling wagons, creaking under the weight of the year's bloodsweated and prayed-over work, on all the roads drawn in, from the utmost runners and ramifications of the slender red roads of all the south and into the southern highways, a wagon every few hundred yards, crested this with a white and this with a black family, all drawn toward those little trembling lodes which are the gins, and all and in each private and silent heart toward that climax of one more year's work which yields so little at best, and nothing so often, and worse to so many hundreds of thousands:

The gin itself, too, the wagons drawn up in line, the people waiting on each wagon, the suspendered white-shirted men on the platform, the emblematic sweep of the grand-shouldered iron beam scales cradling gently on the dark doorway their design of justice, the landlords in their shirt-sleeves at the gin or relaxed in swivels beside the decorated safes in their little offices, the heavy-muscled and bloodfaced young men in baseball caps who tumble the bales with short sharp hooks, the loafers drawn into this place to have their batteries recharged in the violence that is in process here in the bare and weedy outskirts of this bare and brutal town; all this also in its hard, slack, nearly speechless, sullen-eyed way, is dancelike and triumphal: the big blank surfaces of corrugated metal, bright and sick as gas in the sunlight, square their darkness round a shuddering racket that subsumes all easy speaking: the tenant gets his ticket and his bale number, and waits his turn in the long quiet line; the wagon ahead is emptied and moves forward lightly as the mule is cut; he cuts his own load heavily under as the gin head is hoisted; he reaches up for the suction pipe and they let it down to him; he swings and cradles its voracity down through the crest of and round and round his stack of cotton, until the last lint has leapt up from the wagon bed; and all the while the gin is working in the deafening appetites of its metals, only it is his work the gin is digesting now, and standing so close in next its flank, he is intimate with this noise of great energy, cost and mystery; and out at the rear, the tin and ghostly interior of the seed shed, against whose roof and rafters a pipe extends a steady sleet of seed and upon all whose interior surfaces and all the air a dry nightmare fleece like the false snows of Christmas movies hangs shuddering as it might in horror of its just accomplished parturition: and out in front, the last of the cotton snowlike relaxing in pulses down a slide of dark iron into the compress its pure whiteness; and a few moments merely of pressure under the floor level, the air of an off-stage strangling; and the bale is lifted like a theater organ, the presses unlatched, the numbered brass tag attached, the metal ties made fast: it hangs in the light breathing of the scales, his bale, the one he has made, and a little is slivered from it, and its weight and staple length are recorded on his ginning slip, and it is caught with the hooks and tumbled out of the way, his bale of cotton, depersonalized forever now, identical with all others, which shall be melted indistinguishably into an oblivion of fabrics, wounds, bleedings, and wars; he takes his ginning slip to his land-lord, and gets his cottonseed money, and does a little buying; and gathers his family together; and leaves town. The exodus from town is even more formal than the parade in was. It has taken almost exactly eighteen minutes to gin each bale, once the waiting was over, and each tenant has done almost exactly the same amount of business afterward, and the empty, light grinding wagons are dis-tributed along the roads in a likewise exact collaboration of time and space apart, that is, the time consumed by ginning plus busi-ness, and the space apart which, in that time, a mule traverses at his classic noctambular pace. It is as if those who were drawn in full by the sun and their own effort and sucked dry at a metal heart were restored, were sown once more at large upon the slow breadths of their country, in the precisions of some mechanic and super-human hand.

That is repeated as many times as you have picked a bale. Your field is combed over three, four or five times. The height of the ginning season in that part of the country is early October, and in that time the loaded wagons are on the road before the least crack of daylight, the waiting is endless hours, and the gin is still pulsing and beating after dark. After that comes hogkilling, and the gristing of the corn and milling of the sorghum that were planted late to come ready late; and more urgent and specific meditation of whether or not to move to another man, and of whether you are to be kept; and settlement time; and the sky descends, the air becomes like dark glass, the ground stiffens, the clay honeycombs with frost, the corn and the cotton stand stripped to the naked bone and the trees are black, the odors of pork and woodsmoke sharpen all over the country, the long dark silent sleeping rains stream down in such grieving as nothing shall ever stop, and the houses are cold, fragile drums, and the animals tremble, and the clay is one shapeless sea, and winter has shut.

QUESTIONS

1. In his first paragraph Agee personifies cotton by alluding to its royalty: what other hints of this personification appear in this paragraph? In the same paragraph he speaks of the tenants' "automatism" and the destruction of "the centers of individuals." What is he asserting about the relation between cotton and the people who raise it? What does his concluding picture of the cotton gin add to this assertion?
2. Why would Agee's piece be a valuable document for a future historian of the American South? How does it compare with Cash's historical discussion of southern society ("Reconstruction and the Southern Quandary,"pp.1131–1138)? Which of the two has the larger scope?
3. Agee offers a clear, detailed description of cotton farming, yet his language is certainly not the plain, neutral language we expect of how-to-do-it books. Examine a fairly long passage and note Agee's peculiarities of vocabulary and sentence structure. What do they suggest about the man?
4. Are contemporary, urban families as dominated by their economic function as the tenant farmers Agee describes?

WILLIAM MARCH
The Slave and the Cart Horse

A slave who had been beaten by his master came to the hut where his wife waited for him. He lay on a pallet, while the woman took a basin and filled it with water. He spoke after a time, answering the question his wife did not dare ask him: "It happened while I was working in the fields, near sunset. They had overloaded one of the cart horses, and the poor creature was hardly able to stand up. They were beating him with a whip, and although he was pulling with all his strength, he wasn't able to move the load out of the ruts in the field."

"Speak softer," said his wife. "The master might pass and hear you."

The slave lowered his voice and continued: "So I went to the master and told him that the horse couldn't carry such a load, and I asked him to take some of it off."

"Speak softer," said the woman. She bent over the slave and bathed his back with wet rags. "Speak softer. They'll whip you again if they hear what you're saying."

The slave got up and went to the door, to see that there was nobody outside; then he came and lay once more on the pallet. "I can't stand to see a horse cruelly treated. Horses always seem so helpless and pitiful to me."

When the woman spoke, her voice was so soft that it hardly carried to her husband's ears. "You did right," she said. "Horses aren't like us. They can't express themselves or stand up for their rights, and they have no way of defending themselves, like we have."

Then they looked into each others' eyes and sighed, thinking how fortunate they were and how cruelly horses were used, for no man can see his own misery clearly, and that is God's great mercy to us all.

THEODORA KROEBER

Ishi[1]

The story of Ishi begins for us early in the morning of the twenty-ninth day of August in the year 1911 and in the corral of a slaughter house. It begins with the sharp barking of dogs which roused the sleeping butchers. In the dawn light they saw a man at bay, crouching against the corral fence—Ishi.

They called off the dogs. Then, in some considerable excitement, they telephoned the sheriff in Oroville two or three miles away to say that they were holding a wild man and would he please come and take him off their hands. Sheriff and deputies arrived shortly, approaching the corral with guns at the ready. The wild man made no move to resist capture, quietly allowing himself to be handcuffed.

The sheriff, J. B. Webber, saw that the man was an Indian, and that he was at the limit of exhaustion and fear. He could learn nothing further, since his prisoner understood no English. Not knowing what to do with him, he motioned the Indian into the wagon with himself and his deputies, drove him to the county jail in Oroville, and locked him up in the cell for the insane. There, sheriff Webber reasoned, while he tried to discover something more about his captive he could at least protect him from the excited curiosity of the townspeople and the outsiders who were already pouring in from miles around to see the wild man.

The wild man was emaciated to starvation, his hair was burned

1. Prologue and Chapter I of *Ishi in Two Worlds*, 1961.

off close to his head, he was naked except for a ragged scrap of ancient covered-wagon canvas which he wore around his shoulders like a poncho. He was a man of middle height, the long bones, painfully apparent, were straight, strong, and not heavy, the skin color somewhat paler in tone than the full copper characteristic of most Indians. The black eyes were wary and guarded now, but were set wide in a broad face, the mouth was generous and agreeably molded. For the rest, the Indian's extreme fatigue and fright heightened a sensitiveness which was always there, while it masked the usual mobility and expressiveness of the features.

It should be said that the sheriff's action in locking Ishi up was neither stupid nor brutal given the circumstances. Until Sheriff Webber took the unwonted measure of keeping them out by force people filled the jail to gaze through the bars of his cell at the captive. Later, Ishi spoke with some diffidence of this, his first contact with white men. He said that he was put up in a fine house where he was kindly treated and well fed by a big chief. That he would eat nothing and drink nothing during his first days of captivity Ishi did not say. Such was the case; nor did he allow himself to sleep at first. Quite possibly it was a time of such strain and terror that he suppressed all memory of it. Or he may have felt that it was unkind to recall his suspicions which proved in the event groundless, for Ishi expected in those first days to be put to death. He knew of white men only that they were the murderers of his own people. It was natural that he should expect, once in their power, to be shot or hanged or killed by poisoning.

Meanwhile, local Indians and half-breeds as well as Mexicans and Spaniards tried to talk to the prisoner in Maidu, Wintu, and Spanish. Ishi listened patiently but uncomprehendingly, and when he spoke it was in a tongue which meant no more to the Indians there than to the whites.

The story of the capture of a wild Indian became headline news in the local valley papers, and reached the San Francisco dailies in forms more or less lurid and elaborated. The story in the *San Francisco Call* was accompanied by a picture, the first of many to come later. In another newspaper story, a Maidu Indian, Conway by name, "issued a statement" that he had conversed with the wild man. Conway's moment of publicity was brief since the wild man understood nothing of what he said.

These accounts were read by Professors Kroeber and Waterman, anthropologists at the University of California, who were at once alerted to the human drama behind the event and to its possible importance, the more particularly because it recalled to them an earlier episode on San Nicolas Island, one of the Channel Islands of the Pacific Ocean some seventy miles offshore from Santa Barbara.

In 1835, the padres of Mission Santa Barbara transferred the San

Nicolas Indians to the mainland. A few minutes after the boat, which was carrying the Indians, had put off from the island, it was found that one baby had been left behind. It is not easy to land a boat on San Nicolas; the captain decided against returning for the baby; the baby's mother jumped overboard, and was last seen swimming toward the island. Half-hearted efforts made to find her in subsequent weeks were unsuccessful: it was believed that she had drowned in the rough surf. In 1853, eighteen years later, seal hunters in the Channel waters reported seeing a woman on San Nicolas, and a boatload of men from Santa Barbara went in search of her. They found her, a last survivor of her tribe. Her baby, as well as all her people who had been removed to the Mission, had died. She lived only a few months after her "rescue" and died without anyone having been able to communicate with her, leaving to posterity this skeletal outline of her grim story, and four words which someone remembered from her lost language and recorded as she said them. It so happens that these four words identify her language as having been Shoshonean, related to Indian languages of the Los Angeles area, not to those of Santa Barbara.

Another reason for the anthropologists' particular interest in the wild man was that three years earlier, in 1908, some surveyors working a few miles north of Oroville had surprised and routed a little band of Indians. After hearing of this incident, Waterman with two guides had spent several weeks in an unsuccessful search for the Indians: the wild man of Oroville might well be one of them.

On August 31, 1911, Kroeber sent the following telegram: "Sheriff Butte County. Newspapers report capture wild Indian speaking language other tribes totally unable understand. Please confirm or deny by collect telegram and if story correct hold Indian till arrival Professor State University who will take charge and be responsible for him. Matter important account aboriginal history."

The sheriff's office must have confirmed the report promptly: Waterman took the train to Oroville the same day. That he and Kroeber correctly "guessed" Ishi's tribe and language was no *tour de force* of intuition. The guess was based on field work with Indians all up and down California; they knew that Oroville was adjacent to country which formerly belonged to the Yana Indians; presumably the strange Indian would be a Yana. He might even be from the southernmost tribe of Yana, believed to be extinct. If this were true, neither they nor anyone so far as they knew could speak his language. But if he were a Northern or Central Yana, there were files of expertly recorded vocabularies for those dialects from two old Yanas, Batwi, called Sam, and Chidaimiya, called Betty Brown.

With a copy of Batwi's and Chidaimiya's vocabularies in his pocket, Waterman arrived in Oroville where he identified himself to Sheriff Webber and was taken to visit the wild man. Waterman found a weary, badgered Indian sitting in his cell, wearing the butcher's apron he had been given at the slaughter house, courteously making what answer he could in his own language to a barrage of questions thrown at him in English, Spanish, and assorted Indian from a miscellaneous set of visitors.

Waterman sat down beside Ishi, and with his phonetically transcribed list of Northern and Central Yana words before him, began to read from it, repeating each word, pronouncing it as well as he knew how. Ishi was attentive but unresponding until, discouragingly far down the list, Waterman said *siwini* which means yellow pine, at the same time tapping the pine framework of the cot on which they sat. Recognition lighted up the Indian's face. Waterman said the magic word again; Ishi repeated it after him, correcting his pronounciation, and for the next moments the two of them banged at the wood of the cot, telling each other over and over, *siwini, siwini!*

With the difficult first sound recognition achieved, others followed. Ishi was indeed one of the lost tribe, a Yahi; in other words, he was from the southernmost Yana. Waterman was learning that the unknown Yahi dialect differed considerably but not to the point of unintelligibility from the two northern ones of his list. Together he and Ishi tried out more and more words and phrases: they were beginning to communicate. After a while Ishi ventured to ask Waterman, *I ne ma Yahi?* "Are you an Indian?" Waterman answered that he was. The hunted look left Ishi's eyes—here was a friend. He knew as well as did his friend that Waterman was not an Indian. The question was a tentative and subtle way of reassuring and being reassured, not an easy thing to do when the meaningful shared sounds are few. Between meetings with Ishi, Waterman wrote to Kroeber from Oroville:

This man [Ishi] is undoubtedly wild. He has pieces of deer thong in place of ornaments in the lobes of his ears and a wooden plug in the septum of his nose. He recognizes most of my Yana words and a fair proportion of his own seem to be identical [with mine]. Some of his, however, are either quite different or else my pronunciation of them is very bad, because he doesn't respond to them except by pointing to his ears and asking to have them repeated. "No!" *k'u'i*—it is not—is one. "Yes!" *ähä*, pleases him immensely. I think I get a few endings that don't occur in Northern Yana on nouns, for example. Phonetically, he has some of the prettiest cracked consonants I ever heard in my life. He will be a splendid informant, especially for phonetics, for he speaks very clearly. I have not communicated with him successfully enough to get his story, but what can I expect? He has a yarn to tell about his woman, who had a baby on her back and seems to have been drowned, except that he is so *cheerful* about it.

Waterman misunderstood. In the excitement and relief of

having someone to talk to, Ishi poured out confidences and recollections which Waterman could by no means comprehend even with the aid of an elaborate pantomime. Ishi's seeming pleasure was not in the recollected event, but was rather a near hysteria induced by human interchange of speech and feelings too long denied.

Waterman's letters continue:

We had a lot of conversation this morning about deer hunting and making acorn soup, but I got as far as my list of words would take me. If I am not mistaken, he's full of religion—bathing at sunrise, putting out pinches of tobacco where the lightning strikes, etc. I'll try rattlesnake on him when I got back after lunch. It was a picnic to see him open his eyes when he heard Yana from me. And he looked over my shoulder at the paper in a most mystified way. He knew at once where I got my inspiration.... We showed him some arrows last night, and we could hardly get them away from him. He showed us how he flaked the points, singed the edges of the feathering, and put on the sinew wrappings.

Even before Waterman had established a thin line of communication with Ishi, the sheriff had become convinced that his prisoner was neither insane nor dangerous. There were no charges against him; he did not properly belong in jail. The question was, what in place of the shelter of the jail was there for him? Waterman offered to take him to San Francisco. Phones and telegraph wires were kept busy for the next forty-eight hours between Oroville and San Francisco, where the University's Museum of Anthropology then was, and between the museum and Washington, D.C.

While these negotiations were going forward, the sheriff, at Waterman's suggestion, sent a deputy to Redding to find and bring back with him the old man, Batwi, to act as interpreter-companion to Ishi. Batwi came, and although he patronized Ishi outrageously, he was for the present a help. He and Ishi could communicate in Yana, not without some difficulty, but quite fully. Meanwhile, the Indian Bureau in Washington telegraphed permission for Ishi to go to the University's museum whose staff was to be responsible for him at least until there was opportunity for fuller investigation. The sheriff of Butte County was greatly relieved; he at once made out a receipt of release from the jail to the University. This remarkable document seems not to have survived the years of moving and storing in odd corners which has been the fate of the museum files and specimens.

In any case, Waterman, Batwi, and Ishi, with the release and government permission, left Oroville on Labor Day, September 4, arriving in San Francisco somewhat before midnight. There remained to Ishi four years and seven months of life, years which were to pass within the shelter of the museum walls at the Affiliated Colleges, or in the hospital next door when he was sick.

Ishi was the last wild Indian in North America, a man of Stone Age culture subjected for the first time when he was past middle age to twentieth-century culture. He was content that it should be so, participating as fully as he could in the new life. Before examining more closely those astounding few years and what one Stone Age man contributed in so short a time to our understanding of man as such, let us go back to the years of childhood, young manhood, and middle age—almost a whole lifetime. These were years spent by him without experience or understanding of a way of life other than that of a tiny fugitive band of fewer than a dozen souls at most, opposing their ancient Yahi skills and beliefs to an unknown but hostile outside world.

There came the time—months, perhaps two or three years before August, 1911—when Ishi was the only one remaining of the little band, violence from without, old age and illness from within, having brought death to the others.

Ishi's arrival at the slaughter house was the culmination of unprecedented behavior on his part. A few days earlier, without hope, indifferent whether he lived or died, he had started on an aimless trek in a more or less southerly direction which took him into country he did not know. Exhaustion was added to grief and loneliness. He lay down in the corral because he could go no farther. He was then about forty miles from home, a man without living kin or friends, a man who had probably never been beyond the borders of his own tribal territory.

Our task is to piece together all that is known of Ishi's life before that day: from his own account of it; from what was learned of it on a camping trip with him in his own home country; and from the miscellany of rumor and fact and speculation as reported by surveyors, ranchers, rangers, and other white residents of Butte and Tehama counties. It is an episodic story, incomplete, and loosely strung across lacunae of time, ignorance, and events too painful for Ishi to relive in memory.

That Ishi should have crossed the boundaries of his homeland, and continued on into the unknown, means to be sure that he had also reached and crossed certain physical and psychic limits. But to begin to understand how profoundly disturbed he must have been, we must know how aberrant such behavior was, not for Ishi the man merely, but for Ishi the Yahi. His life becomes more of a piece if we step back from it, as from the detail of a face or feature in a painting, to focus briefly on the whole of the canvas, bringing its background and pattern into perspective. To understand Ishi's values and behavior and belief, and his way of life, we must know in a broad and general way something of his heritage: the land and people of Indian California.

The stubborn and enduring land of California has changed less than its people. From an airplane the "colored counties" are seen spread out like a giant relief map. Mount Shasta looms to the north, Mount Whitney to the south; the Sierra Nevada forms a wall to the east; and beyond Whitney, where the Sierra appears to go underground, the desert takes over. There are the long interior valleys; and there are the tumbled, rough, and wooded Coast Ranges through which rivers and creeks break to the sea. Below, incredible, lies the vast and varied land, its mountains and deserts empty and mute today, while over the accessible valleys and coastal plains a congested and diverse population clusters close to a few centers like wasps around heavy-hanging nests. A constant stream of automobiles, looking from the air like lines of black ants on the march, fills the passes over the Sierra barrier, moving westward to the favored spots. The hills are empty except for lumbering operations wherever there is a good stand of trees; the mining towns of the Mother Lode and the old rancherias are shabby and deserted, or have been taken over by "summer people." The banks of rivers and creeks are empty save for sporadic invasions of fishermen; and the desert is without human occupants except for a citified overflow which follows in the wake of air-cooling installations, swimming pools, and motels.

What would an air view have revealed in the days of the gold rush? The same lines of black ants moving in the same westerly direction over the same passes, on horseback, and in covered wagons drawn by oxen, traveling more slowly than today's immigrants but with the same doggedness as these later ones, heading in part for the same centers, in part stopping in the hill country where ranches, mining camps, and saw and grist mills were scattered along streams and in the forests.

Hovering over the same land, but continuing our flight back in time, we view another trek, this one on foot or on mule and horseback, coming up from the south, northward along the rim of the sea. The time is the 'seventies of the eighteenth century, and the travelers, Spaniards pushing out of Mexico, keeping a sharp eye for a sheltered and sunny and likely spot for mission, rancheria, or presidio as they move slowly on.

If we take a last backward flight in time, the Spaniard is no longer seen. This is the time before his coming; the golden land belongs wholly and undisputedly to its native sons and daughters. No lines of black ants move over the high passes or come up from the south in this view. Indeed, we must fly low to see the narrow trails meandering beside a stream, or across country to an oak flat, or up into the hills. At first there seem to be neither houses nor people, but presently a frame with surf fish strung on it to dry on a sunny beach, a clearing in the trees, a thin blue wisp of smoke from a wood fire, serve to guide the eyes to the weathered roof of a low redwood house, to an earth-covered circular house, to a thatched house, to a brush shelter. We see an old woman tending the fire outside a house, a man spearing fish beside a stream, a half-grown boy paddling downstream in a dugout canoe. A young woman, her baby in a basket carrier on her back, gathers wild iris on a hillside; a hunter brings down a deer with bow and arrow. These people step noiselessly over the ground barefoot or in soft deerskin moccasins, and their naked or near-naked copper-colored bodies blend in semicamouflage against the colors of the earth. Such clothes as they wear, a skirt of shredded bark, a buckskin breechclout, an occasional fur or feather cape, also blend into the natural background. Their voices, whether in ordinary conversation, or in song or prayer or mourning cry, are light-toned, neither harsh nor loud.

The high mountains are empty. But people are living in the hills as far up as oak trees grow and wherever manzanita and other berries are abundant, and wherever there are deer; along fish-filled streams; and where a river flows into the sea; and on the desert Even so unlikely a place as Death Valley has men who call it home.

Back on the ground and again in the twentieth century, we turn to maps and estimates and reports to learn something more of these ancestral peoples whom we have glimpsed distantly through time.

We have seen that they lived on parts of the land which modern men do not find habitable or attractive, although at no place were their numbers large. The population of Indian California was small: over the whole of the state there were probably no more than a hundred and fifty thousand people, perhaps as many as two hundred and fifty thousand. (In 1860, ten years after the beginning of the gold rush, the white population of the state was already three hundred and ninety thousand.) There are, to be sure, estimates of the pre-conquest population of California which run higher, but the archaeological remains from village and burial sites point to numbers close to those given here. There is no evidence, as there is in the Southwest, in Mexico, in Yucatan of the Mayas, that a once much more numerous people suffered disaster and decimation. Nor do the histories, legends, myths, or stories of any California Indians speak of ancient wholesale famine as do the old as well as the modern chronicles of China and India.

These one or two hundred and fifty thousand native people constituted twenty-one known nationalities, or small nations, which were in turn further separated into subnationalities, and these again into tribes or tribelets to a total number of more than two hundred and fifty—exactly how many more can never be known because of the obliteration in modern times of whole peoples and cultures by Spaniard and Anglo-Saxon alike without record of tribal name or affiliation. Many of these subgroups were of course few in number and inhabited only a small area. Their numbers were almost unbelievably small beside the territorial and population figures for modern nations, but they were nonetheless true nations in their stubbornly individual and boundaried separateness and distinctiveness one from another.

One of these nationalities was the Yana. There were probably no more than three thousand of Ishi's people, perhaps only two thousand—not many to constitute a nation to be sure, but more people than live today along the favorite streams and on the village sites of the ancient Yana. And few in number as they were, even by California standards, the Yana followed the current pattern of culture fragmentation in being further sub-subdivided into four groups: Northern, Central, Southern, and Yahi (Ishi's group), each with its own geographic boundaries, its own dialect, and its own set of specializations and peculiarities of custom.

There were and are, for the whole of Indian North America, six great linguistic superfamilies, each made up of numbers of separate stocks or families of speech. Each family usually consists of several languages which differ so much one from another that their common origin can be determined only by comparative linguistics study; the superfamilies are even more varied than the large Indo-European stock or family with its Romance and Germanic and Slavic and Hindi divisions. Of the six superfamilies, five were represented in California, and contained among them twenty-one basic languages which were, for the most part, as mutually unintelligible as are German and French; and many of them were even more unlike than these two. But this is not yet the whole of the story, since the twenty-one languages further separated and elaborated themselves into a hundred and thirteen known dialects. These dialects varied, some of them, only so much as New Orleans English from the English of Boston; others so greatly that to know one would not make the other accessible, as with Swedish and German. Only parts of the Sudan and the island of New Guinea offer so much language variety within comparable areas. Or, to demonstrate the congestion of tongues another way, there are twice as many Indian languages on record as there are counties in California today.

We know that such extreme linguistic differentiation takes time. Spoken language is in a sense always changing, since each speaker of his tongue imprints on it his imperceptibly individual voice and accent and choice or rejection of particular words and usages, but the changing is as drops of water on the stone of fixed grammatical form. Ishi's California must indeed have been an old and long-settled land.

Remains of Dawn Man or of some Dawn-like man, his bones or his stones, are proclaimed from time to time as having been found on the Pacific slope, but if Dawn Man or any of his near relations once lived in California, they have yet to be rediscovered. California's first people so far as is presently known were American Indians, ancestors of today's Indians and in no significant way different from them. And they have been in California a long time; by our standards of mobility and compared with our brief history, immemorially long.

The Yana have probably been in northern California for three or four thousand years. There are those who would double this figure, but in the present state of knowledge three thousand years as a minimum is a tentative, conservative figure arrived at, surprisingly, by way of a recently accepted branch of language study known as glottochronology. Put simply, glottochronology is a study of the rate at which the meaning of words changes, and the inferences to be drawn from such changes. It began with analyses of old and documented languages such as Sanskrit, Anglo-Saxon, or Chinese, comparing the old language in each case with its living descendants, to find the rate of change from cognate to new terms of the same basic meaning. Rates of change studied thus far vary little one from another, and their average, used as the norm of change, is applied to comparisons of pairs of other related languages to find the time which has elapsed since their separation or first differentiation. A technique for learning the history of a language thus becomes a technique also for learning something of a people's political or culture history.

Yana belongs to the Hokan superfamily, one of the six superfamilies of North America. The glottochronology of Hokan confirms and sharpens other evidence that Hokan-speaking people were old in California. Apparently Ishi's ancestors were occupying wide stretches of the upper Sacramento Valley and its tributaries at a time when there was a single Hokan language. At some time, three or four thousand years ago, this single language fragmented into ten or a dozen separate languages within the same geographical territory and amongst the original speakers of Hokan.

There is no evidence of other people having disputed the territory and its occupation with the ancestral Hokans; it is to be presumed that they lived freely in the open valley, going up into the hills, which to Ishi were a year-round home, only seasonally in the course of following the deer from valley to hills to mountains. There must have been a wide dispersal of Hokan-speakers as part of the drama of change which resulted in the appearance of many new languages within the old Hokan mold. This may well have been the time of the greatest creative florescence of the Yana and other Hokan peoples.

After two or three thousand years, "barbarians" from outside, Wintun or others, who were by then stronger and more numerous then the older population, engaged in one of their own thrusts of history making, invaded Yana country, occupied the richer parts of it, and pushed the smaller, older population back into the hills.

We turn now to archaeology to decipher a curiously half-lit corroboration of this early Yana history. Paynes Cave on Antelope Creek and Kingsley Cave on Mill Creek, both in Ishi's own country, and some smaller village and cemetery sites closeby have been excavated and their bones and tools studied. Charred wood, bone, and other substances from these presumably old and undisturbed sites have been tested and assigned absolute as well as relative dates, within one or two hundred years of exactness, by measuring their carbon fourteen content against that of recent, similar material. This is a satisfactory dating technique, over long periods, because carbon fourteen is an unstable compound which decomposes at the rate of 50 per cent in fifty-five hundred years. This dating is supplemented by a comparison of styles and any changes in styles over time. Together, the two lines of evidence, which in this case converge reasonably, suggest that the Yana territory of Ishi's lifetime and of the gold rush era had been occupied only occasionally a thousand years ago, but continuously since then. In other words, it would seem to have been not much more than a millenium ago that the Yana surrendered their valley holdings to become truly and wholly a hill people.

But we must leave scientific measurement and historical reconstruction to its specialists, and move on, closer to Ishi's time, realizing meanwhile that it is the scientist and the historian who remind us that the pace of the ancient world was no doubt pedestrian as compared with the modern world with its lightning changes, but that wherever there is life there is change. History was being made by Ishi's ancestors and their enemies as surely as it is today: languages came into being and spread and shrank and died; peoples migrated and made a way of life which was dominant and which then receded. The telescopic view into the old world cannot be made sharp, except perhaps when we hear a momentary echo of old Hokan in Ishi's recorded voice and Yahi speech, or when we hold in our hands an "old-fashioned" stone knife whose style was abandoned for something "new" a thousand years ago. The focus may be fuzzy; it is at least a look at a world in flux and motion, never wholly static; contoured and stereoscopic, never flat; even as our own moving, changing world.

What, then, of the Digger Indians who are supposed to have

been the aborigines of California, to have spoken a guttural language, and to have managed barely to maintain a miserable existence by eating the roots which they dug from the unfriendly land with that most generic of tools, the wooden digging stick? Alas, the Diggers are a frontier legend, like the Siwash Indians of the Northwest, Siwash being a blanket term growing out of a mis-hearing of the word *sauvage*, the French trappers' designation for Indian. Nor was there a Digger language amongst all the babel of tongues.

There is another frontier legend which dies hard: that the hills and streams and valleys of California yielded a grudging and sorry living to their native sons and daughters. The Spaniards and Mexicans did not so misunderstand the golden land, in part because they were never wholly detached from the soil in thinking or occupation, and in part because California is not unlike much of Mexico and Spain. The Forty-niners, veteran contenders against mountains, high plains, and deserts, were without interest in the land as such, which appeared to them inhospitable, dry, barren. In the course of their continental trek, they had come to look upon food not as something to be grown or harvested, but as meat to be shot on the hoof, and as flour, sugar, coffee, and beans to be carried as part of one's pack and replaced in "Frisco" or Sacramento or at some other urban center.

The legend may have been prolonged in defiance of known fact through inertia, legends easily becoming habits which are hard to break, and through its usefulness in salving a not quite good conscience over the taking of land and lives. If the land was lean and the lives miserable then the wrong done was so much the less, or no wrong at all.

The term Digger continued to be used to refer to Indians other than those one knew. I have heard my grandmother, who came to Amador County to teach school in the early 1850's, and became a rancher's wife, speak affectionately and correctly of her Miwok Indian neighbors, and disapprovingly of the strange Digger Indians who from time to time used to wander in from a distance asking for work or perhaps only for food. Digger remains to this day a term of derogation, like "nigger."

Digger also defines, however crudely and inadequately, one occupation of California Indians which the Forty-niners must have seen over and over again. The Indians did no planting, being hunters, fishermen, gatherers and harvesters of grains and seeds and fruits and roots which grew wild in their natural habitat and uncultivated state—diggers if you will. The digging stick was used, customarily in the hands of women, who were forever going off into the hills or meadows for maidenhair and sword ferns, for squaw grass and pine root, for redbud and hazel, and for all the stems and plants and grasses which they wanted for making baskets. And the digging stick, as will be seen, helped them in season to get some of the fresh vegetables of which they were fond. Only the aberrant Mohaves and Yumas, who live on the Colorado River, have always been agriculturists of sorts. That is, they planted many of their food stuffs—not like the hard-working and true farmers of the Southwest: the Hopi, Zuni, and Rio Grande pueblo Indians—but like the people of ancient Egypt, by dropping the seeds of corn and beans and squash into the red ooze exposed by the seasonal flooding and retreat of the river, and allowing the crops to grow under the blazing sun with a minimum of attention from the planters. But the Colorado River Indians were different also—and fortunate—in having no Forty-niners.

We have seen that the varied land once supported separate little nations, rather like Greek city states at least in size, in enclaves of inland valley or rough hill-country or woods or desert or along streams or beside the sea. And we have seen that these village states set themselves off further one from another by a growth of language barrier. The peoples differed in physical type, some being broad and stocky with round faces, some slim and tall with high-bridged noses, but none resembled the Plains or woodland Indians. Some lived better than others, and with more leisure; some buried their dead while others practiced cremation. Customs and beliefs varied from tribelet to tribelet, but nonetheless underlying their differences was a certain characteristic "set," a profile of a life which, broadly speaking, fits all of them and fits no Indians east of the Sierra Nevada. It was anciently a different world, from the crest of the Sierra westward to the Pacific Ocean, as indeed it continues in oddly telling ways to be different today.

In some part, larger or smaller depending upon how one weighs it, the differences ancient and modern are born of the climate which is Mediterranean and subtropical. For the Indians this meant that during many months of each year outdoor living with only the lightest of shelters was comfortable, and that in most seasons they wore no clothes at all, a little front apron of bark and the ubiquitous brimless round basketry hat satisfying the requirements of modesty for a woman, while a man wore nothing at all except perhaps a deerskin breechclout. The buckskin shirt and leggings to be found to the east were not needed here and did not exist; an ample apron or skirt of buckskin for the women and grass or buckskin sandals with a wildcat or rabbit or feather cloak thrown over the shoulders when it was cold did very well for both men and women and completed their wardrobes except for beads and other ornaments, and ritual and dance regalia.

This was the area where, for whatever reason, basketry design was most elaborated, and the possibilities of baskets as utensils were most exploited to the almost total neglect of wood and pottery.

Baskets were used for carrying and for storing all sorts of food and materials; they were the only cooking utensils; and they were the trays, plates, bowls, and mugs of dining. The creative impulse found expression most usually in basketry; also in the intricate fashioning of feather capes and headdresses; and in occasional beautifully wrought obsidian knives made from a single obsidian flake. These knives, two, three, or four feet long and correspondingly heavy, were held to be sacred and reserved for ceremonial use.

The great staple food of the California Indian was acorn flour made into mush or bread. The acorn, of which some half dozen or more edible varieties were recognized, meant to Indians what rice means to Cantonese Chinese, or maize to Mexicans. After acorns came salmon, fresh or dried and in large variety; and after salmon, deer meat, again fresh or dried. Other fish were of course eaten, and game larger and smaller than deer, and for the coastal people there was added all the rich variety of seafood. Ducks and geese were much liked. Pine nuts, hazel nuts, buckeye, manzanita berries, wild raspberry, huckleberry, plum, grape, elderberry, barberry, and thimbleberry were enjoyed in season, and some of them were dried and stored. There were sage and tarweed and clarkia seeds, and a host of other seeds small and large and, in season, the earth-oven roasted roots of the camas, annis, tiger lily, and brodiaea were a welcome addition. Certain grubs and worms were roasted as delicacies; also grasshoppers as in modern Mexico. Snakes were not eaten, nor, so far as is known, were frogs.

But far deeper than food preferences and response to climate is the psychological set of the California cultures. To judge by their descendants, the ancestral California Indians who made the Far West their permanent home had found their way in the first place, and stayed on, in order to realize an ideal of a separatist and static arrangement of life. The most conspicuous feature of this life, at least to our view, is the preference for a small world intimately and minutely known, whose utmost boundaries were within reach by boat or on foot, a few days journey at most. Outside worlds were known to exist, of course. A man knew certain of his neighbors, sometimes when the neighbor's tongue had dialectic relation to his own so close that communication came readily, or sometimes when two worlds shared adjoining stretches of the same river, for example, and were similar enough in their ways to feel some identification even though they spoke different languages, as with the Yurok and Karok Indians along the Klamath River. But anything, everything that belonged within a man's own world, including its corpus of legendary event going back to the most ancient times, was better known and was more important than any person, place, or happening across the border.

By and large, no one voluntarily left his own and familiar world for a strange one. It was terrifying and dangerous to enter a community as a stranger. You were properly suspect, the inference being that your own people had put pressure on you to leave because of some crime you were guilty of. At best you would be without family or friends or influence or status, and forced to learn to speak a foreign language, if you were allowed to remain at all. There was always the chance that you would be killed, or ordered to move on.

The California Indian was, in other words, a true provincial. He was also an introvert, reserved, contemplative, and philosophical. He lived at ease with the supernatural and the mystical which were pervasive in all aspects of life. He felt no need to differentiate mystical truth from directly evidential or "material" truth, or the supernatural from the natural: one was as manifest as the other within his system of values and perceptions and beliefs. The promoter, the boaster, the aggressor, the egoist, the innovator, would have been looked at askance. The ideal was the man of restraint, dignity, rectitude, he of the Middle Way. Life proceeded within the limits of known and proper pattern from birth through death and beyond. Its repetitive rhythm was punctuated with ritual, courtship, dance, song, and feast, each established according to custom going back to the beginning of the world, an event which, along with subsequent events having to do with setting the way of life, was well known and fully recounted in the peoples' oral but elaborate and specific histories.

It was not an easy life, but it was a good one. The hunting and fishing and gathering, the endless labor of preparation of foods and hides, the making of baskets, tools, and implements and the always vexing problem of storage, required the industry and skill of both sexes and of young and old; but there was some choice and there was seasonal and ritual variety. There were lean times, but the lean like the fat times were shared with family, friends, and tribe. Life was as it had always been.

JAMES BALDWIN
Stranger in the Village

From all available evidence no black man had ever set foot in this tiny Swiss village before I came. I was told before arriving that I would probably be a "sight" for the village; I took this to mean that people of my complexion were rarely seen in Switzerland, and also that city people are always something of a "sight" outside of the city. It did not occur to me—possibly because I am an American—that there could be people anywhere who had never seen a Negro.

It is a fact that cannot be explained on the basis of the inaccessibility of the village. The village is very high, but it is only four hours from Milan and three hours from Lausanne. It is true that it is virtually unknown. Few people making plans for a holiday would elect to come here. On the other hand, the villagers are able, presumably, to come and go as they please—which they do: to another town at the foot of the mountain, with a population of approximately five thousand, the nearest place to see a movie or go to the bank. In the village there is no movie house, no bank, no library, no theater; very few radios, one jeep, one station wagon; and at the moment, one typewriter, mine, an invention which the woman next door to me here had never seen. There are about six hundred people living here, all Catholic—I conclude this from the fact that the Catholic church is open all year round, whereas the Protestant chapel, set off on a hill a little removed from the village, is open only in the summertime when the tourists arrive. There are four or five hotels, all closed now, and four or five *bistros*, of which, however, only two do any business during the winter. These two do not do a great deal, for life in the village seems to end around nine or ten o'clock. There are a few stores, butcher, baker, *épicerie*, a hardware store, and a money-changer—who cannot change travelers' checks, but must send them down to the bank, an operation which takes two or three days. There is something called the *Ballet Haus*, closed in the winter and used for God knows what, certainly not ballet, during the summer. There seems to be only one schoolhouse in the village, and this for the quite young children; I suppose this to mean that their older brothers and sisters at some point descend from these mountains in order to complete their education—possibly, again, to the town just below. The landscape is absolutely forbidding, mountains towering on all four sides, ice and snow as far as the eye can reach. In this white wilderness, men and women and children move all day, carrying washing, wood, buckets of milk or water, sometimes skiing on Sunday afternoons. All week long boys and young men are to be seen shoveling snow off the rooftops, or dragging wood down from the forest in sleds.

The village's only real attraction, which explains the tourist season, is the hot spring water. A disquietingly high proportion of these tourists are cripples, or semi-cripples, who come year after year—from other parts of Switzerland, usually—to take the waters. This lends the village, at the height of the season, a rather terrifying air of sanctity, as though it were a lesser Lourdes. There is often something beautiful, there is always something awful, in the spectacle of a person who has lost one of his faculties, a faculty he never questioned until it was gone, and who struggles to recover it. Yet people remain people, on crutches or indeed on deathbeds; and wherever I passed, the first summer I was here, among the native villagers or among the lame, a wind passed with me—of astonishment, curiosity, amusement, and outrage. That first summer I stayed two weeks and never intended to return. But I did return in the winter, to work; the village offers, obviously, no distractions whatever and has the further advantage of being extremely cheap. Now it is winter again, a year later, and I am here again. Everyone in the village knows my name, though they scarcely ever use it, knows that I come from America— though, this, apparently, they will never really believe: black men come from Africa—and everyone knows that I am the friend of the son of a woman who was born here, and that I am staying in their chalet. But I remain as much a stranger today as I was the first day I arrived, and the children shout *Neger! Neger!* as I walk along the streets.

It must be admitted that in the beginning I was far too shocked to have any real reaction. In so far as I reacted at all, I reacted by trying to be pleasant—it being a great part of the American Negro's education (long before he goes to school) that he must make people "like" him. This smile-and-the-world-smiles-with-you routine worked about as well in this situation as it had in the situation for which it was designed, which is to say that it did not work at all. No one, after all, can be liked whose human weight and complexity cannot be, or has not been, admitted. My smile was simply another unheard-of phenomenon which allowed them to see my teeth—they did not, really, see my smile and I began to think that, should I take to snarling, no one would notice any difference. All of the physical characteristics of the Negro which had caused me, in America, a very different and almost forgotten pain were nothing less than miraculous —or infernal—in the eyes of the village people. Some thought my hair was the color of tar, that it had the texture of wire, or the texture of cotton. It was jocularly suggested that I might let it all grow long and make myself a winter coat. If I sat in the sun for more than five minutes some daring creature was certain to come along and gingerly put his fingers on my hair, as though he were afraid of an electric shock, or put his hand on my hand, astonished that the color did not rub off. In all of this, in which it must be conceded there was the charm of genuine wonder and in which there were certainly no element of intentional unkindness, there was yet no suggestion that I was human: I was simply a living wonder.

I knew that they did not mean to be unkind, and I know it now; it is necessary, nevertheless, for me to repeat this to myself each time that I walk out of the chalet. The children who shout *Neger!* have no way of knowing the echoes this sound raises in me. They are brimming with good humor and the more daring swell with pride when I stop to speak with them. Just the same, there are days when I cannot pause and smile, when I have no heart to play with them; when, indeed, I mutter sourly to myself, exactly as I muttered on the streets of a city these children have never seen, when I was no bigger than these children are now: Your mother *was a nigger.* Joyce is right about history being a nightmare—but it may be the nightmare from which no one *can* awaken. People are trapped in history and history is trapped in them.

There is a custom in the village—I am told it is repeated in many villages—of "buying" African natives for the purpose of converting them to Christianity. There stands in the church all year round a small box with a slot for money, decorated with a black figurine, and into this box the villagers drop their francs. During the *carnaval* which precedes Lent, two village children have their faces blackened —out of which bloodless darkness their blue eyes shine like ice—and fantastic horsehair wigs are placed on their blond heads; thus disguised, they solicit among the villagers for money for the missionaries in Africa. Between the box in the church and the blackened children, the village "bought" last year six or eight African natives. This was reported to me with pride by the wife of one of the *bistro* owners and I was careful to express astonishment and pleasure at the solicitude shown by the village for the souls of black folks. The *bistro* owner's wife beamed with a pleasure far more genuine than my own and seemed to feel that I might now breathe more easily concerning the souls of at least six of my kinsmen.

I tried not to think of these so lately baptized kinsmen, of the price paid for them, or the peculiar price they themselves would pay, and said nothing about my father, who having taken his own conversion too literally never, at bottom, forgave the white world (which he described as heathen) for having saddled him with a Christ in whom, to judge at least from their treatment of him, they themselves no longer believed. I thought of white men arriving for the first time in an African village, strangers there, as I am a stranger here, and tried to imagine the astounded populace touching their hair and marveling at the color of their skin. But there is a great difference between being the first white man to be seen by Africans and being the first black man to be seen by whites. The white man takes the astonishment as tribute, for he arrives to conquer and to convert the natives, whose inferiority in relation to himself is not even to be questioned; whereas I, without a thought of conquest, find myself among a people whose culture controls me, has even, in a sense, created me, people who have cost me more in anguish and rage than they will ever know, who yet do not even know of my existence. The astonishment with which I might have greeted them, should they have stumbled into my African village a few hundred years ago, might have rejoiced their hearts. But the astonishment with which they greet me today can only poison mine.

And this is so despite everything I may do to feel differently, despite my friendly conversations with the *bistro* owner's wife, despite their three-year-old son who has at last become my friend, despite the *saluts* and *bonsoirs* which I exchange with people as I walk, despite the fact that I know that no individual can be taken to task for what history is doing, or has done. I say that the culture of these people controls me—but they can scarcely be held responsible for European culture. America comes out of Europe, but these people have never seen America, nor have most of them seen more of Europe than the hamlet at the foot of their mountain. Yet they move with an authority which I shall never have; and they regard me, quite rightly, not only as a stranger in their village but as a suspect late-comer, bearing no credentials, to everything they have—however unconsciously—inherited.

For this village, even were it incomparably more remote and incredibly more primitive, is the West, the West onto which I have been so strangely grafted. These people cannot be, from the point of view of power, strangers anywhere in the world; they have made the modern world, in effect, even if they do not know it. The most illiterate among them is related, in a way that I am not, to Dante, Shakespeare, Michelangelo, Aeschylus, Da Vinci, Rembrandt, and Racine; the cathedral at Chartres says something to them which it cannot say to me, as indeed would New York's Empire State Building, should anyone here ever see it. Out of their hymns and dances come Beethoven and Bach. Go back a few centuries and they are in their full glory—but I am in Africa, watching the conquerors arrive.

The rage of the disesteemed is personally fruitless, but it is also absolutely inevitable; this rage, so generally discounted, so little understood even among the people whose daily bread it is, is one of the things that makes history. Rage can only with difficulty, and never entirely, be brought under the domination of the intelligence and is therefore not susceptible to any arguments whatever. This is a fact which ordinary representatives of the *Herrenvolk*,[1] having never felt this rage and being unable to imagine, quite fail to understand. Also, rage cannot be hidden, it can only be dissembled. This dissembling deludes the thoughtless, and strengthens rage and adds, to rage, contempt. There are, no doubt, as many ways of coping with the resulting complex of tensions as there are black men in the world, but no black man can hope ever to be entirely liberated from this internal warfare—rage, dissembling, and contempt having inevitably accompanied his first realization of the power of white men. What is crucial here is that, since white men represent in the black man's world so heavy a weight, white men have for black men a reality which is far from being reciprocal; and hence all black men have

1. Master race.

toward all white men an attitude which is designed, really, either to rob the white man of the jewel of his naïveté, or else to make it cost him dear.

The black man insists, by whatever means he finds at his disposal, that the white man cease to regard him as an exotic rarity and recognize him as a human being. This is a very charged and difficult moment, for there is a great deal of will power involved in the white man's naïveté. Most people are not naturally reflective any more than they are naturally malicious, and the white man prefers to keep the black man at a certain human remove because it is easier for him thus to preserve his simplicity and avoid being called to account for crimes committed by his forefathers, or his neighbors. He is inescapably aware, nevertheless, that he is in a better position in the world than black men are, nor can he quite put to death the suspicion that he is hated by black men therefore. He does not wish to be hated, neither does he wish to change places, and at this point in his uneasiness he can scarcely avoid having recourse to those legends which white men have created about black men, the most usual effect of which is that the white man finds himself enmeshed, so to speak, in his own language which describes hell, as well as the attributes which lead one to hell, as being as black as night.

Every legend, moreover, contains its residuum of truth, and the root function of language is to control the universe by describing it. It is of quite considerable significance that black men remain, in the imagination, and in overwhelming numbers in fact, beyond the disciplines of salvation; and this despite the fact that the West has been "buying" African natives for centuries. There is, I should hazard, an instantaneous necessity to be divorced from this so visibly unsaved stranger, in whose heart, moreover, one cannot guess what dreams of vengeance are being nourished; and, at the same time, there are few things on earth more attractive than the idea of the unspeakable liberty which is allowed the unredeemed. When, beneath the black mask, a human being begins to make himself felt one cannot escape a certain awful wonder as to what kind of human being it is. What one's imagination makes of other people is dictated, of course, by the laws of one's own personality and it is one of the ironies of black-white relations that, by means of what the white man imagines the black man to be, the black man is enabled to know who the white man is.

I have said, for example, that I am as much a stranger in this village today as I was the first summer I arrived, but this is not quite true. The villagers wonder less about the texture of my hair than they did then, and wonder rather more about me. And the fact that their wonder now exists on another level is reflected in their attitudes and in their eyes. There are the children who make those delightful, hilarious, sometimes astonishingly grave overtures of friendship in the unpredictable fashion of children; other children, having been taught that the devil is a black man, scream in genuine anguish as I approach. Some of the older women never pass without a friendly greeting, never pass, indeed, if it seems that they will be able to engage me in conversation; other women look down or look away or rather contemptuously smirk. Some of the men drink with me and suggest that I learn how to ski—partly, I gather, because they cannot imagine what I would look like on skis—and want to know if I am married, and ask questions about my *métier*. But some of the men have accused *le sale nègre*—behind my back—of stealing wood and there is already in the eyes of some of them that peculiar, intent, paranoiac malevolence which one sometimes surprises in the eyes of American white men when, out walking with their Sunday girl, they see a Negro male approach.

There is a dreadful abyss between the streets of this village and the streets of the city in which I was born, between the children who shout *Neger!* today and those who shouted *Nigger!* yesterday—the abyss is experience, the American experience. The syllable hurled behind me today expresses, above all, wonder: I am a stranger here. But I am not a stranger in America and the same syllable riding on the American air expresses the war my presence has occasioned in the American soul.

For this village brings home to me this fact: that there was a day, and not really a very distant day, when Americans were scarcely Americans at all but discontented Europeans, facing a great unconquered continent and strolling, say, into a marketplace and seeing black men for the first time. The shock this spectacle afforded is suggested, surely, by the promptness with which they decided that these black men were not really men but cattle. It is true that the necessity on the part of the settlers of the New World of reconciling their moral assumptions with the fact—and the necessity—of slavery enhanced immensely the charm of this idea, and it is also true that this idea expresses, with a truly American bluntness, the attitude which to varying extents all masters have had toward all slaves.

But between all former slaves and slave-owners and the drama which begins for Americans over three hundred years ago at Jamestown, there are at least two differences to be observed. The American Negro slave could not suppose, for one thing, as slaves in past epochs had supposed and often done, that he would ever be able to wrest the power from his master's hands. This was a supposition which the modern era, which was to bring about such vast changes in the aims and dimensions of power, put to death; it only begins, in unprecedented fashion, and with dreadful implications, to be resurrected today. But even had this supposition persisted with undiminished force, the American Negro slave could not have used it to lend his condition dignity, for the reason that this supposition rests on another: that the slave in exile yet remains related to his past, has some means—if only in memory—of revering and sustaining the forms of his former life, is able, in short, to maintain his identity.

This was not the case with the American Negro slave. He is unique among the black men of the world in that his past was taken from him, almost literally, at one blow. One wonders what on earth the first slave found to say to the first dark child he bore. I am told that there are Haitians able to trace their ancestry back to African kings, but any American Negro wishing to go back so far will find his journey through time abruptly arrested by the signature on the bill of sale which served as the entrance paper for his ancestor. At the time—to say nothing of the circumstances—of the enslavement of the captive black man who was to become the American Negro, there was not the remotest possibility that he would ever take power from his master's hands. There was no reason to suppose that his situation would ever change, nor was there, shortly, anything to indicate that his situation had ever been different. It was his necessity, in the words of E. Franklin Frazier, to find a "motive for living under American culture or die." The identity of the American Negro comes out of this extreme situation, and the evolution of this identity was a source of the most intolerable anxiety in the minds and the lives of his masters.

For the history of the American Negro is unique also in this: that the question of his humanity, and of his rights therefore as a human being, became a burning one for several generations of Americans, so burning a question that it ultimately became one of those used to divide the nation. It is out of this argument that the venom of the epithet *Nigger!* is derived. It is an argument which Europe has never had, and hence Europe quite sincerely fails to understand how or why the argument arose in the first place, why its effects are frequently disastrous and always so unpredictable, why it refuses until today to be entirely settled. Europe's black possessions remained —and do remain—in Europe's colonies, at which remove they represented no threat whatever to European identity. If they posed any problem at all for the European conscience, it was a problem which remained comfortingly abstract: in effect, the black man, as a *man*, did not exist for Europe. But in America, even as a slave, he was an inescapable part of the general social fabric and no American could escape having an attitude toward him. Americans attempt until today to make an abstraction of the Negro, but the very nature of these abstractions reveals the tremendous effects the presence of the Negro has had on the American character.

When one considers the history of the Negro in America it is of the greatest importance to recognize that the moral beliefs of a person, or a people, are never really as tenuous as life—which is not moral—very often causes them to appear; these create for them a frame of reference and a necessary hope, the hope being that when life has done its worst they will be enabled to rise above themselves and to triumph over life. Life would scarcely be bearable if this hope did not exist. Again, even when the worst has been said, to betray a belief is not by any means to have put oneself beyond its power; the betrayal of a belief is not the same thing as ceasing to believe. If this were not so there would be no moral standards in the world at all. Yet one must also recognize that morality is based on ideas and that all ideas are dangerous—dangerous because ideas can only lead to action and where the action leads no man can say. And dangerous in this respect: that confronted with the impossibility of remaining faithful to one's beliefs, and the equal impossibility of becoming free of them, one can be driven to the most inhuman excesses. The ideas on which American beliefs are based are not, though Americans often seem to think so, ideas which originated in America. They came out of Europe. And the establishment of democracy on the American continent was scarcely as radical a break with the past as was the necessity, which Americans faced, of broadening this concept to include black men.

This was, literally, a hard necessity. It was impossible, for one thing, for Americans to abandon their beliefs, not only because these beliefs alone seemed able to justify the sacrifices they had endured and the blood that they had spilled, but also because these beliefs afforded them their only bulwark against a moral chaos as absolute as the physical chaos of the continent it was their destiny to conquer. But in the situation in which Americans found themselves, these beliefs threatened an idea which, whether or not one likes to think so, is the very warp and woof of the heritage of the West, the idea of white supremacy.

Americans have made themselves notorious by the shrillness and the brutality with which they have insisted on this idea, but they did not invent it; and it has escaped the world's notice that those very excesses of which Americans have been guilty imply a certain, unprecedented uneasiness over the idea's life and power, if not, indeed, the idea's validity. The idea of white supremacy rests simply on the fact that white men are the creators of civilization (the present civilization, which is the only one that matters; all previous civilizations are simply "contributions" to our own) and are therefore civilization's guardians and defenders. Thus it was impossible for Americans to accept the black man as one of themselves, for to do so was to jeopardize their status as white men. But not so to accept him was to deny his human reality, his human weight and complexity, and the strain of denying the overwhelmingly undeniable forced Americans into rationalizations so fantastic that they approached the pathological.

At the root of the American Negro problem is the necessity of the American white man to find a way of living with the Negro in order to be able to live with himself. And the history of this problem can be reduced to the means used by Americans—lynch law and law, segregation and legal acceptance, terrorization and concession —either to come to terms with this necessity, or to find a way around it, or (most usually) to find a way of doing both these things at once. The resulting spectacle, at once foolish and dreadful, led someone to make the quite accurate observation that "the Negro-in-America is a form of insanity which overtakes white men."

In this long battle, a battle by no means finished, the unforeseeable effects of which will be felt by many future generations, the white man's motive was the protection of his identity; the black man was motivated by the need to establish an identity. And despite the terrorization which the Negro in America endured and endures sporadically until today, despite the cruel and totally inescapable ambivalence of his status in his country, the battle for his identity has long ago been won. He is not a visitor to the West, but a citizen there, an American; as American as the Americans who despise him, the Americans who fear him, the Americans who love him—the Americans who became less than themselves, or rose to be greater than themselves by virtue of the fact that the challenge he represented was inescapable. He is perhaps the only black man in the world whose relationship to white men is more terrible, more subtle, and more meaningful than the relationship of bitter possessed to uncertain possessors. His survival depended, and his development depends, on his ability to turn his peculiar status in the Western world to his own advantage and, it may be, to the very great advantage of that world. It remains for him to fashion out of his experience that which will give him sustenance, and a voice.

The cathedral at Chartres, I have said, says something to the people of this village which it cannot say to me; but it is important to understand that this cathedral says something to me which it cannot say to them. Perhaps they are struck by the power of the spires, the glory of the windows; but they have known God, after all, longer than I have known him, and in a different way, and I am terrified by the slippery bottomless well to be found in the crypt, down which heretics were hurled to death, and by the obscene, inescapable gargoyles jutting out of the stone and seeming to say that God and the devil can never be divorced. I doubt that the villagers think of the devil when they face a cathedral because they have never been identified with the devil. But I must accept the status which myth, if nothing else, gives me in the West before I can hope to change the myth.

Yet, if the American Negro has arrived at his identity by virtue of the absoluteness of his estrangement from his past, American white men still nourish the illusion that there is some means of recovering the European innocence, of returning to a state in which black men do not exist. This is one of the greatest errors Americans can make. The identity they fought so hard to protect has, by virtue of that battle, undergone a change: Americans are as unlike any other white people in the world as it is possible to be. I do not think, for example, that it is too much to suggest that the American vision of the world—which allows so little reality, generally speaking, for any of the darker forces in human life, which tends until today to paint moral issues in glaring black and white—owes a great deal to the battle waged by Americans to maintain between themselves and black men a human separation which could not be bridged. It is only now beginning to be borne in on us—very faintly, it must be admitted, very slowly, and very much against our will—that this vision of the world is dangerously inaccurate, and perfectly useless. For it protects our moral high-mindedness at the terrible expense of weakening our grasp of reality. People who shut their eyes to reality simply invite their own destruction, and anyone who insists on remaining in a state of innocence long after that innocence is dead turns himself into a monster.

The time has come to realize that the interracial drama acted out on the American continent has not only created a new black man, it has created a new white man, too. No road whatever will lead Americans back to the simplicity of this European village where white men still have the luxury of looking on me as a stranger. I am not, really, a stranger any longer for any American alive. One of the things that distinguishes Americans from other people is that no other people has ever been so deeply involved in the lives of black men, and vice versa. This fact faced, with all its implications, it can be seen that the history of the American Negro problem is not merely shameful, it is also something of an achievement. For even when the worst has been said, it must also be added that the perpetual challenge posed by this problem was always, somehow, perpetually met. It is precisely this black-white experience which may prove of indispensable value to us in the world we face today. This world is white no longer, and it will never be white again.

QUESTIONS

1. *Baldwin begins with the narration of his experience in a Swiss village. At what point do you become aware that he is going to do more than tell the story of his stay in the village? What purpose does he make his experience serve?*
2. *On page 552 Baldwin says that Americans have attempted to make an abstraction of the Negro. To what degree has his purpose forced Baldwin to make an abstraction of the white man? What are the components of that abstraction?*
3. *What abstract argumentative thesis emerges from this essay? Many of the other essays in this section of the book (Hoffer,*

Shaw, Agee) deal with similarly large social questions and,
therefore, in abstractions and generalizations. What is different
about Baldwin's way of generalizing and abstracting?
4. Mill ("Civilization," pp. 453–472) is concerned about a threat to
human individuality. Does his analysis of the problem account
for the American Negro's predicament as Baldwin describes it?
5. Baldwin intimately relates the white man's language and legends
about black men to the "laws" of the white man's personality.
Bettelheim makes similar use of the myths of science fiction.
This kind of inference reveals a conviction both men share about
the nature of language; what is that conviction?
6. Describe some particular experience which raises a large social
question or shows the working of large social forces. Does
Baldwin offer any help in the problem of connecting the particular and the general?
7. Define alienation.

MARTIN LUTHER KING, JR.
Letter from Birmingham Jail[1]

MY DEAR FELLOW CLERGYMEN:

While confined here in the Birmingham city jail, I came across
your recent statement calling my present activities "unwise and
untimely." Seldom do I pause to answer criticism of my work and
ideas. If I sought to answer all the criticisms that cross my desk, my
secretaries would have little time for anything other than such correspondence in the course of the day, and I would have no time for
constructive work. But since I feel that you are men of genuine
good will and that your criticisms are sincerely set forth, I want to
try to answer your statement in what I hope will be patient and
reasonable terms.

I think I should indicate why I am here in Birmingham, since
you have been influenced by the view which argues against "outsiders coming in." I have the honor of serving as president of the
Southern Christian Leadership Conference, an organization operating in every southern state, with headquarters in Atlanta, Georgia.
We have some eighty-five affiliated organizations across the South,

1. This response to a published statement by eight fellow clergymen from
Alabama (Bishop C. C. J. Carpenter,
Bishop Joseph A. Durick, Rabbi Hilton
L. Grafman, Bishop Paul Hardin,
Bishop Holan B. Harmon, the Reverend
George M. Murray, the Reverend Edward V. Ramage and the Reverend Earl
Stallings) was composed under somewhat constricting circumstances. Begun
on the margins of the newspaper in
which the statement appeared while I
was in jail, the letter was continued
on scraps of writing paper supplied by
a friendly Negro trusty, and concluded
on a pad my attorneys were eventually
permitted to leave me. Although the
text remains in substance unaltered, I
have indulged in the author's prerogative of polishing it for publication
[King's note].

and one of them is the Alabama Christian Movement for Human Rights. Frequently we share staff, educational, and financial resources with our affiliates. Several months ago the affiliate here in Birmingham asked us to be on call to engage in a nonviolent direct-action program if such were deemed necessary. We readily consented, and when the hour came we lived up to our promise. So I, along with several members of my staff, am here because I was invited here. I am here because I have organizational ties here.

But more basically, I am in Birmingham because injustice is here. Just as the prophets of the eighth century B.C. left their villages and carried their "thus saith the Lord" far beyond the boundaries of their home towns, and just as the Apostle Paul left his village of Tarsus and carried the gospel of Jesus Christ to the far corners of the Greco-Roman world, so am I compelled to carry the gospel of freedom beyond my own home town. Like Paul, I must constantly respond to the Macedonian call for aid.

Moreover, I am cognizant of the interrelatedness of all communities and states. I cannot sit idly by in Atlanta and not be concerned about what happens in Birmingham. Injustice anywhere is a threat to justice everywhere. We are caught in an inescapable network of mutuality, tied in a single garment of destiny. Whatever affects one directly, affects all indirectly. Never again can we afford to live with the narrow, provincial "outside agitator" idea. Anyone who lives inside the United States can never be considered an outsider anywhere within its bounds.

You deplore the demonstrations taking place in Birmingham. But your statement, I am sorry to say, fails to express a similar concern for the conditions that brought about the demonstrations. I am sure that none of you would want to rest content with the superficial kind of social analysis that deals merely with effects and does not grapple with underlying causes. It is unfortunate that demonstrations are taking place in Birmingham, but it is even more unfortunate that the city's white power structure left the Negro community with no alternative.

In any nonviolent campaign there are four basic steps: collection of the facts to determine whether injustices exist; negotiation; self-purification; and direct action. We have gone through all these steps in Birmingham. There can be no gainsaying the fact that racial injustice engulfs this community. Birmingham is probably the most thoroughly segregated city in the United States. Its ugly record of brutality is widely known. Negroes have experienced grossly unjust treatment in the courts. There have been more unsolved bombings of Negro homes and churches in Birmingham than in any other city in the nation. These are the hard, brutal facts of the case. On the basis of these conditions, Negro leaders sought to negotiate with the city fathers. But the latter consistently refused to engage in good-faith negotiation.

Then, last September, came the opportunity to talk with leaders of Birmingham's economic community. In the course of the negotiations, certain promises were made by the merchants—for example, to remove the stores' humiliating racial signs. On the basis of these promises, the Reverend Fred Shuttlesworth and the leaders of the Alabama Christian Movement for Human Rights agreed to a moratorium on all demonstrations. As the weeks and months went by, we realized that we were the victims of a broken promise. A few signs, briefly removed, returned; the others remained.

As in so many past experiences, our hopes had been blasted, and the shadow of deep disappointment settled upon us. We had no alternative except to prepare for direct action, whereby we would present our very bodies as a means of laying our case before the conscience of the local and the national community. Mindful of the difficulties involved, we decided to undertake a process of self-purification. We began a series of workshops on nonviolence, and we repeatedly asked ourselves: "Are you able to accept blows without retaliating?" "Are you able to endure the ordeal of jail?" We decided to schedule our direct-action program for the Easter season, realizing that except for Christmas, this is the main shopping period of the year. Knowing that a strong economic-withdrawal program would be the by-product of direct action, we felt that this would be the best time to bring pressure to bear on the merchants for the needed change.

Then it occurred to us that Birmingham's mayoral election was coming up in March, and we speedily decided to postpone action until after election day. When we discovered that the Commissioner of Public Safety, Eugene "Bull" Connor, had piled up enough votes to be in the run-off, we decided again to postpone action until the day after the run-off so that the demonstrations could not be used to cloud the issues. Like many others, we waited to see Mr. Connor defeated, and to this end we endured postponement after postponement. Having aided in this community need, we felt that our direct-action program could be delayed no longer.

You may well ask, "Why direct action? Why sit-ins, marches, and so forth? Isn't negotiation a better path?" You are quite right in calling for negotiation. Indeed, this is the very purpose of direct action. Nonviolent direct action seeks to create such a crisis and foster such a tension that a community which has constantly refused to negotiate is forced to confront the issue. It seeks so to dramatize the issue that it can no longer be ignored. My citing the creation of tension as part of the work of the nonviolent-resister may sound rather shocking. But I must confess that I am not afraid of the word "tension." I have earnestly opposed violent tension, but there is a type of constructive, nonviolent tension which is necessary for growth. Just as Socrates felt that it was necessary to create a tension in the mind so that individuals could rise from the bondage of myths and half-truths to the unfettered realm of creative analysis and objective appraisal, so must we see the need for nonviolent gadflies to create the kind of tension in society that will help men rise from the dark depths of prejudice and racism to the majestic heights of understanding and brotherhood.

The purpose of our direct-action program is to create a situation so crisis-packed that it will inevitably open the door to negotiation. I therefore concur with you in your call for negotiation. Too long has our beloved Southland been bogged down in a tragic effort to live in monologue rather than dialogue.

One of the basic points in your statement is that the action that I and my associates have taken in Birmingham is untimely. Some have asked: "Why didn't you give the new city administration time to act?" The only answer that I can give to this query is that the new Birmingham administration must be prodded about as much as the outgoing one, before it will act. We are sadly mistaken if we feel that the election of Albert Boutwell as mayor will bring the millennium to Birmingham. While Mr. Boutwell is a much more gentle person than Mr. Connor, they are both segregationists, dedicated to maintenance of the status quo. I have hoped that Mr. Boutwell will be reasonable enough to see the futility of massive resistance to desegregation. But he will not see this without pressure from devotees of civil rights. My friends, I must say to you that we have not made a single gain in civil rights without determined legal and nonviolent pressure. Lamentably, it is an historical fact that privileged groups seldom give up their privileges voluntarily. Individuals may see the moral light and voluntarily give up their unjust posture; but, as Reinhold Niebuhr has reminded us, groups tend to be more immoral than individuals.

We know through painful experience that freedom is never voluntarily given by the oppressor; it must be demanded by the oppressed. Frankly, I have yet to engage in a direct-action campaign that was "well timed" in the view of those who have not suffered unduly from the disease of segregation. For years now I have heard the word "Wait!" It rings in the ear of every Negro with piercing familiarity. This "Wait" has almost always meant "Never." We must come to see, with one of our distinguished jurists, that "justice too long delayed is justice denied."

We have waited for more than 340 years for our constitutional and God-given rights. The nations of Asia and Africa are moving with jetlike speed toward gaining political independence, but we still creep at horse-and-buggy pace toward gaining a cup of coffee at a lunch counter. Perhaps it is easy for those who have never felt the stinging darts of segregation to say, "Wait." But when you have seen vicious mobs lynch your mothers and fathers at will and drown your sisters and brothers at whim; when you have seen hate-filled policemen curse, kick, and even kill your black brothers and sisters; when you see the vast majority of your twenty million Negro brothers smothering in an airtight cage of poverty in the midst of an affluent society; when you suddenly find your tongue twisted and your speech stammering as you seek to explain to your six-year-old daughter why she can't go to the public amusement park that has just been advertised on television, and see tears welling up in her eyes when she is told that Funtown is closed to colored children, and see ominous clouds of inferiority beginning to form in her little mental sky, and see her beginning to distort her personality by developing an unconscious bitterness toward white people; when you have to concoct an answer for a five-year-old son who is asking, "Daddy, why do white people treat colored people so mean?"; when you take a cross-country drive and find it necessary to sleep night after night in the uncomfortable corners of your automobile because no motel will accept you; when you are humiliated day in and day out by nagging signs reading "white" and "colored"; when your first name becomes "nigger," your middle name becomes "boy" (however old you are) and your last name becomes "John," and your wife and mother are never given the respected title "Mrs."; when you are harried by day and haunted by night by the fact that you are a Negro, living constantly at tiptoe stance, never quite knowing what to expect next, and are plagued with inner fears and outer resentments; when you are forever fighting a degenerating sense of "nobodiness"—then you will understand why we find it difficult to wait. There comes a time when the cup of endurance runs over, and men are no longer willing to be plunged into the abyss of despair. I hope, sirs, you can understand our legitimate and unavoidable impatience.

You express a great deal of anxiety over our willingness to break laws. This is certainly a legitimate concern. Since we so diligently urge people to obey the Supreme Court's decision of 1954 outlawing segregation in the public schools, at first glance it may seem rather paradoxical for us consciously to break laws. One may well ask: "How can you advocate breaking some laws and obeying others?" The answer lies in the fact that there are two types of laws: just and unjust. I would be the first to advocate obeying just laws. One has not only a legal but a moral responsibility to obey just laws. Conversely, one has a moral responsibility to disobey unjust laws. I would agree with St. Augustine that "an unjust law is no law at all."

Now, what is the difference between the two? How does one determine whether a law is just or unjust? A just law is a man-made code that squares with the moral law or the law of God. An unjust law is a code that is out of harmony with the moral law. To put it in the terms of St. Thomas Aquinas: An unjust law is a human law that is not rooted in eternal law and natural law. Any law that uplifts human personality is just. Any law that degrades human personality is unjust. All segregation statutes are unjust because segregation distorts the soul and damages the personality. It gives the segregator a false sense of superiority and the segregated a false sense of inferiority. Segregation, to use the terminology of the Jewish philosopher Martin Buber, substitutes an "I-it" relationship for an "I-thou" relationship and ends up relegating persons to the status of things. Hence segregation is not only politically, economically, and sociologically unsound, it is morally wrong and sinful. Paul Tillich has said that sin is separation. Is not segregation an existential expression of man's tragic separation, his awful estrangement, his terrible sinfulness? Thus it is that I can urge men to obey the 1954 decision of the Supreme Court, for it is morally right; and I can urge them to disobey segregation ordinances, for they are morally wrong.

Let us consider a more concrete example of just and unjust laws. An unjust law is a code that a numerical or power majority group compels a minority group to obey but does not make binding on itself. This is *difference* made legal. By the same token, a just law is a code that a majority compels a minority to follow and that it is willing to follow itself. This is *sameness* made legal.

Let me given another explanation. A law is unjust if it is inflicted on a minority that, as a result of being denied the right to vote, had no part in enacting or devising the law. Who can say that the legislature of Alabama which set up that state's segregation laws was democratically elected? Throughout Alabama all sorts of devious methods are used to prevent Negroes from becoming registered voters, and there are some counties in which, even though Negroes constitute a majority of the population, not a single Negro is registered. Can any law enacted under such circumstances be considered democratically structured?

Sometimes a law is just on its face and unjust in its application. For instance, I have been arrested on a charge of parading without a permit. Now, there is nothing wrong in having an ordinance which requires a permit for a parade. But such an ordinance becomes unjust when it is used to maintain segregation and to deny citizens the First-Amendment privilege of peaceful assembly and protest.

I hope you are able to see the distinction I am trying to point out. In no sense do I advocate evading or defying the law, as would the rabid segregationist. That would lead to anarchy. One who breaks an unjust law must do so openly, lovingly, and with a willingness to accept the penalty. I submit that an individual who breaks a law that conscience tells him is unjust, and who willingly accepts the penalty of imprisonment in order to arouse the conscience of the community over its injustice, is in reality expressing the highest respect for law.

Of course, there is nothing new about this kind of civil disobedience. It was evidenced sublimely in the refusal of Shadrach, Meshach, and Abednego to obey the laws of Nebuchadnezzar, on the ground that a higher moral law was at stake. It was practiced superbly by the early Christians, who were willing to face hungry lions and the excruciating pain of chopping blocks rather than submit to certain unjust laws of the Roman Empire. To a degree, academic freedom is a reality today because Socrates practiced civil disobedience. In our own nation, the Boston Tea Party represented a massive act of civil disobedience.

We should never forget that everything Adolf Hitler did in Germany was "legal" and everything the Hungarian freedom fighters did in Hungary was "illegal." It was "illegal" to aid and comfort a Jew in Hitler's Germany. Even so, I am sure that, had I lived in Germany at the time, I would have aided and comforted my Jewish brothers. If today I lived in a Communist country where certain principles dear to the Christian faith are suppressed, I would openly advocate disobeying that country's anti-religious laws.

I must make two honest confessions to you, my Christian and Jewish brothers. First, I must confess that over the past few years I have been gravely disappointed with the white moderate. I have almost reached the regrettable conclusion that the Negro's great stumbling block in his stride toward freedom is not the White Citizen's Counciler or the Ku Klux Klanner, but the white moderate, who is more devoted to "order" than to justice; who prefers a negative peace which is the absence of tension to a positive peace which is the presence of justice; who constantly says, "I agree with you in the goal you seek, but I cannot agree with your methods of direct action"; who paternalistically believes he can set the timetable for another man's freedom; who lives by a mythical concept of time and who constantly advises the Negro to wait for a "more convenient season." Shallow understanding from people of good will is more frustrating than absolute misunderstanding from people of ill will. Lukewarm acceptance is much more bewildering than outright rejection.

I had hoped that the white moderate would understand that law and order exist for the purpose of establishing justice and that when they fail in this purpose they become the dangerously structured dams that block the flow of social progress. I had hoped that the white moderate would understand that the present tension in the South is a necessary phase of the transition from an obnoxious negative peace, in which the Negro passively accepted his unjust plight, to a substantive and positive peace, in which all men will respect the dignity and worth of human personality. Actually, we who engage in nonviolent direct action are not the creators of tension. We merely bring to the surface the hidden tension that is already alive. We bring it out in the open, where it can be seen and dealt with. Like a boil that can never be cured so long as it is covered up but must be opened with all its ugliness to the natural medicines of air and light, injustice must be exposed, with all the tension its exposure creates, to the light of human conscience and the air of national opinion, before it can be cured.

In your statement you assert that our actions, even though peaceful, must be condemned because they precipitate violence. But is this a logical assertion? Isn't this like condemning a robbed man because his possession of money precipitated the evil act of robbery? Isn't this like condemning Socrates because his unswerving commitment to truth and his philosophical inquiries precipitated the act by the misguided populace in which they made him drink hemlock? Isn't this like condemning Jesus because his unique God-consciousness and never-ceasing devotion to God's will precipitated the evil act of crucifixion? We must come to see that, as the federal courts have consistently affirmed, it is wrong to urge an individual to cease his efforts to gain his basic constitutional rights because the quest may precipitate violence. Society must protect the robbed and punish the robber.

I had also hoped that the white moderate would reject the myth concerning time in relation to the struggle for freedom. I have just received a letter from a white brother in Texas. He writes: "All Christians know that the colored people will receive equal rights eventually, but it is possible that you are in too great a religious hurry. It has taken Christianity almost two thousand years to accomplish what it has. The teachings of Christ take time to come to earth." Such an attitude stems from a tragic misconception of time, from the strangely irrational notion that there is something in the very flow of time that will inevitably cure all ills. Actually, time itself is neutral; it can be used either destructively or constructively. More and more I feel that the people of ill will have used time much more effectively than have the people of good will. We will have to repent in this generation not merely for the hateful words and actions of the bad people, but for the appalling silence of the good people. Human progress never rolls in on wheels of inevitability; it comes through the tireless efforts of men willing to be co-workers with God, and without this hard work, time itself becomes an ally of the forces of social stagnation. We must use time creatively, in the knowledge that the time is always ripe to do right. Now is the time to make real the promise of democracy and transform our pending national elegy into a creative psalm of brotherhood. Now is the time to lift our national policy from the quicksand of racial injustice to the solid rock of human dignity.

You speak of our activity in Birmingham as extreme. At first I was rather disappointed that fellow clergymen would see my nonviolent efforts as those of an extremist. I began thinking about the fact that I stand in the middle of two opposing forces in the Negro community. One is a force of complacency, made up in part of Negroes who, as a result of long years of oppression, are so drained of self-respect and a sense of "somebodiness" that they have adjusted to segregation; and in part of a few middle-class Negroes who, because of a degree of academic and economic security and because in some ways they profit by segregation, have become insensitive to the problems of the masses. The other force is one of bitterness and hatred, and it comes perilously close to advocating violence. It is expressed in the various black nationalist groups that are springing up across the nation, the largest and best-known being Elijah Muhammad's Muslim movement. Nourished by the Negro's frustration over the continued existence of racial discrimination, this movement is made up of people who have lost faith in America, who have absolutely repudiated Christianity, and who have concluded that the white man is an incorrigible "devil."

I have tried to stand between these two forces, saying that we need emulate neither the "do-nothingism" of the complacent nor the hatred and despair of the black nationalist. For there is the more excellent way of love and nonviolent protest. I am grateful to God that, through the influence of the Negro church, the way of nonviolence became an integral part of our struggle.

If this philosophy had not emerged, by now many streets of the South would, I am convinced, be flowing with blood. And I am further convinced that if our white brothers dismiss as "rabble-rousers" and "outside agitators" those of us who employ nonviolent direct action, and if they refuse to support our nonviolent efforts, millions of Negroes will, out of frustration and despair, seek solace and security in black-nationalist ideologies—a development that would inevitably lead to a frightening racial nightmare.

Oppressed people cannot remain oppressed forever. The yearning for freedom eventually manifests itself, and that is what has happened to the American Negro. Something within has reminded him of his birthright of freedom, and something without has reminded him that it can be gained. Consciously or unconsciously, he has been caught up by the *Zeitgeist,* and with his black brothers of Africa and his brown and yellow brothers of Asia, South America, and the Caribbean, the United States Negro is moving with a sense of great urgency toward the promised land of racial justice. If one recognizes this vital urge that has engulfed the Negro community, one should readily understand why public demonstrations are taking place. The Negro has many pent-up resentments and latent frustrations, and he must release them. So let him march; let him make prayer pilgrimages to the city hall; let him go on freedom rides—and try to understand why he must do so. If his repressed emotions are not released in nonviolent ways, they will seek expression through violence; this is not a threat but a fact of history. So I have not said to my people, "Get rid of your discontent." Rather, I have tried to say that this normal and healthy discontent can be channeled into the creative outlet of nonviolent direct action. And now this approach is being termed extremist.

But though I was initially disappointed at being categorized as an extremist, as I continued to think about the matter I gradually gained a measure of satisfaction from the label. Was not Jesus an extremist for love: "Love your enemies, bless them that curse you, do good to them that hate you, and pray for them which despitefully use you, and persecute you." Was not Amos an extremist for justice: "Let justice roll down like waters and righteousness like an ever-flowing stream." Was not Paul an extremist for the Christian gospel: "I bear in my body the marks of the Lord Jesus." Was not Martin Luther an extremist: "Here I stand; I cannot do otherwise, so help me God." And John Bunyan: "I will stay in jail to the end of my days before I make a butchery of my conscience." And Abraham Lincoln: "This nation cannot survive half slave and half free." And Thomas Jefferson: "We hold these truths to be self-evident, that all men are created equal. . . ." So the question is not whether we will be extremists, but what kind of extremists we will be. Will we be extremists for hate or for love? Will we be extremists for the preservation of injustice or for the extension of justice? In that dramatic scene on Calvary's hill three men were crucified. We must never forget that all three were crucified for the same crime—the crime of extremism. Two were extremists for immorality, and thus fell below their environment. The other, Jesus Christ, was an extremist for love, truth, and goodness, and thereby rose above his environment. Perhaps the South, the nation, and the world are in dire need of creative extremists.

I had hoped that the white moderate would see this need. Perhaps I was too optimistic; perhaps I expected too much. I suppose I should have realized that few members of the oppressor race can understand the deep groans and passionate yearnings of the oppressed race, and still fewer have the vision to see that injustice must be rooted out by strong, persistent, and determined action. I am thankful, however, that some of our white brothers in the South have grasped the meaning of this social revolution and committed themselves to it. They are still all too few in quantity, but they are big in quality. Some—such as Ralph McGill, Lillian Smith, Harry Golden, James McBride Dabbs, Ann Braden, and

Sarah Patton Boyle—have written about our struggle in eloquent and prophetic terms. Others have marched with us down nameless streets of the South. They have languished in filthy, roach-infested jails, suffering the abuse and brutality of policemen who view them as "dirty nigger-lovers." Unlike so many of their moderate brothers and sisters, they have recognized the urgency of the moment and sensed the need for powerful "action" antidotes to combat the disease of segregation.

Let me take note of my other major disappointment. I have been so greatly disappointed with the white church and its leadership. Of course, there are some notable exceptions. I am not unmindful of the fact that each of you has taken some significant stands on this issue. I commend you, Reverend Stallings, for your Christian stand on this past Sunday, in welcoming Negroes to your worship service on a nonsegregated basis. I commend the Catholic leaders of this state for integrating Spring Hill College several years ago.

But despite these notable exceptions, I must honestly reiterate that I have been disappointed with the church. I do not say this as one of those negative critics who can always find something wrong with the church. I say this as a minister of the gospel, who loves the church; who was nurtured in its bosom; who has been sustained by its spiritual blessings and who will remain true to it as long as the cord of life shall lengthen.

When I was suddenly catapulted into the leadership of the bus protest in Montgomery, Alabama, a few years ago, I felt we would be supported by the white church. I felt that the white ministers, priests, and rabbis of the South would be among our strongest allies. Instead, some have been outright opponents, refusing to understand the freedom movement and misrepresenting its leaders; all too many others have been more cautious than courageous and have remained silent behind the anesthetizing security of stained-glass windows.

In spite of my shattered dreams, I came to Birmingham with the hope that the white religious leadership of this community would see the justice of our cause and, with deep moral concern, would serve as the channel through which our just grievances could reach the power structure. I had hoped that each of you would understand. But again I have been disappointed.

I have heard numerous southern religious leaders admonish their worshipers to comply with a desegregation decision because it is the law, but I have longed to hear white ministers declare: "Follow this decree because integration is morally right and because the Negro is your brother." In the midst of blatant injustices inflicted upon the Negro, I have watched white churchmen stand on the sideline and mouth pious irrelevancies and sanctimonious trivialities. In the midst of a mighty struggle to rid our nation of racial and economic injustice, I have heard many ministers say: "Those are social issues, with which the gospel has no real concern." And I have watched many churches commit themselves to a completely otherworldly religion which makes a strange, un-Biblical distinction between body and soul, between the sacred and the secular.

I have traveled the length and breadth of Alabama, Mississippi, and all the other southern states. On sweltering summer days and crisp autumn mornings I have looked at the South's beautiful churches with their lofty spires pointing heavenward. I have beheld the impressive outlines of her massive religious-education buildings. Over and over I have found myself asking: "What kind of people worship here? Who is their God? Where were their voices when the lips of Governor Barnett dripped with words of interposition and nullification? Where were they when Governor Wallace gave a clarion call for defiance and hatred? Where were their voices of support when bruised and weary Negro men and women decided to rise from the dark dungeons of complacency to the bright hills of creative protest?"

Yes, these questions are still in my mind. In deep disappointment I have wept over the laxity of the church. But be assured that my tears have been tears of love. There can be no deep disappointment where there is not deep love. Yes, I love the church. How could I do otherwise? I am in the rather unique position of being the son, the grandson, and the great-grandson of preachers. Yes, I see the church as the body of Christ. But, oh! How we have blemished and scarred that body through social neglect and through fear of being nonconformists.

There was a time when the church was very powerful—in the time when the early Christians rejoiced at being deemed worthy to suffer for what they believed. In those days the church was not merely a thermometer that recorded the ideas and principles of popular opinion; it was a thermostat that transformed the mores of society. Whenever the early Christians entered a town, the people in power became disturbed and immediately sought to convict the Christians for being "disturbers of the peace" and "outside agitators." But the Christians pressed on, in the conviction that they were "a colony of heaven," called to obey God rather than man. Small in number, they were big in commitment. They were too God-intoxicated to be "astronomically intimidated." By their effort and example they brought an end to such ancient evils as infanticide and gladiatorial contests.

Things are different now. So often the contemporary church is a weak, ineffectual voice with an uncertain sound. So often it is an archdefender of the status quo. Far from being disturbed by the presence of the church, the power structure of the average community is consoled by the church's silent—and often even vocal—

sanction of things as they are.

But the judgment of God is upon the church as never before. If today's church does not recapture the sacrificial spirit of the early church, it will lose its authenticity, forfeit the loyalty of millions, and be dismissed as an irrelevant social club with no meaning for the twentieth century. Every day I meet young people whose disappointment with the church has turned into outright disgust.

Perhaps I have once again been too optimistic. Is organized religion too inextricably bound to the status quo to save our nation and the world? Perhaps I must turn my faith to the inner spiritual church, the church within the church, as the true *ekklesia*[2] and the hope of the world. But again I am thankful to God that some noble souls from the ranks of organized religion have broken loose from the paralyzing chains of conformity and joined us as active partners in the struggle for freedom. They have left their secure congregations and walked the streets of Albany, Georgia, with us. They have gone down the highways of the South on tortuous rides for freedom. Yes, they have gone to jail with us. Some have been dismissed from their churches, have lost the support of their bishops and fellow ministers. But they have acted in the faith that right defeated is stronger than evil triumphant. Their witness has been the spiritual salt that has preserved the true meaning of the gospel in these troubled times. They have carved a tunnel of hope through the dark mountain of disappointment.

I hope the church as a whole will meet the challenge of this decisive hour. But even if the church does not come to the aid of justice, I have no despair about the future. I have no fear about the outcome of our struggle in Birmingham, even if our motives are at present misunderstood. We will reach the goal of freedom in Birmingham and all over the nation, because the goal of America is freedom. Abused and scorned though we may be, our destiny is tied up with America's destiny. Before the pilgrims landed at Plymouth, we were here. Before the pen of Jefferson etched the majestic words of the Declaration of Independence across the pages of history, we were here. For more than two centuries our forebears labored in this country without wages; they made cotton king; they built the homes of their masters while suffering gross injustice and shameful humiliation—and yet out of a bottomless vitality they continued to thrive and develop. If the inexpressible cruelties of slavery could not stop us, the opposition we now face will surely fail. We will win our freedom because the sacred heritage of our nation and the eternal will of God are embodied in our echoing demands.

Before closing I feel impelled to mention one other point in your statement that has troubled me profoundly. You warmly com-

2. The Greek New Testament word for the early Christian church.

mended the Birmingham police force for keeping "order" and "preventing violence." I doubt that you would have so warmly commended the police force if you had seen its dogs sinking their teeth into unarmed, nonviolent Negroes. I doubt that you would so quickly commend the policemen if you were to observe their ugly and inhumane treatment of Negroes here in the city jail; if you were to watch them push and curse old Negro women and young Negro girls; if you were to see them slap and kick old Negro men and young boys; if you were to observe them, as they did on two occasions, refuse to give us food because we wanted to sing our grace together. I cannot join you in your praise of the Birmingham police department.

It is true that the police have exercised a degree of discipline in handling the demonstrators. In this sense they have conducted themselves rather "nonviolently" in public. But for what purpose? To preserve the evil system of segregation. Over the past few years I have consistently preached that nonviolence demands that the means we use must be as pure as the ends we seek. I have tried to make clear that it is wrong to use immoral means to attain moral ends. But now I must affirm that it is just as wrong, or perhaps even more so, to use moral means to preserve immoral ends. Perhaps Mr. Connor and his policemen have been rather nonviolent in public, as was Chief Pritchett in Albany, Georgia, but they have used the moral means of nonviolence to maintain the immoral end of racial injustice. As T. S. Eliot has said, "The last temptation is the greatest treason: To do the right deed for the wrong reason."

I wish you had commended the Negro sit-inners and demonstrators of Birmingham for their sublime courage, their willingness to suffer, and their amazing discipline in the midst of great provocation. One day the South will recognize its real heroes. They will be the James Merediths, with the noble sense of purpose that enables them to face jeering and hostile mobs, and with the agonizing loneliness that characterizes the life of the pioneer. They will be old, oppressed, battered Negro women, symbolized in a seventy-two-year-old woman in Montgomery, Alabama, who rose up with a sense of dignity and with her people decided not to ride segregated buses, and who responded with ungrammatical profundity to one who inquired about her weariness: "My feets is tired, but my soul is at rest." They will be the young high school and college students, the young ministers of the gospel and a host of their elders, courageously and nonviolently sitting in at lunch counters and willingly going to jail for conscience' sake. One day the South will know that when these disinherited children of God sat down at lunch counters, they were in reality standing up for what is best in the American dream and for the most sacred values in our Judaeo-Christian heritage, thereby bringing our nation back to those great wells of democracy which were dug deep by the founding fathers in their formulation of the Constitution and the Declaration of Independence.

Never before have I written so long a letter. I'm afraid it is much too long to take your precious time. I can assure you that it would have been much shorter if I had been writing from a comfortable desk, but what else can one do when he is alone in a narrow jail cell, other than write long letters, think long thoughts, and pray long prayers?

If I have said anything in this letter that overstates the truth and indicates an unreasonable impatience, I beg you to forgive me. If I have said anything that understates the truth and indicates my having a patience that allows me to settle for anything less than brotherhood, I beg God to forgive me.

I hope this letter finds you strong in the faith. I also hope that circumstances will soon make it possible for me to meet each of you, not as an integrationist or a civil-rights leader but as a fellow clergyman and a Christian brother. Let us all hope that the dark clouds of racial prejudice will soon pass away and the deep fog of misunderstanding will be lifted from our fear-drenched communities, and in some not too distant tomorrow the radiant stars of love and brotherhood will shine over our great nation with all their scintillating beauty.

> Yours for the cause of Peace and Brotherhood,
> MARTIN LUTHER KING, JR.

MARSHALL McLUHAN

Introduction to *Understanding Media*

James Reston wrote in *The New York Times* (July 7, 1957):

> A health director...reported this week that a small mouse, which presumably had been watching television, attacked a little girl and her full-grown cat. . . . Both mouse and cat survived, and the incident is recorded here as a reminder that things seem to be changing.

After three thousand years of explosion, by means of fragmentary and mechanical technologies, the Western world is imploding. During the mechanical ages we had extended our bodies in space. Today, after more than a century of electric technology, we have extended our central nervous system itself in a global embrace, abolishing both space and time as far as our planet is concerned. Rapidly, we approach the final phase of the extensions of man—the technological simulation of consciousness, when the creative process of knowing will be collectively and corporately extended to the whole of human society, much as we have already extended our senses and our nerves by the various media. Whether the extension of consciousness, so long sought by advertisers for specific products, will be "a good thing" is a question that admits of a wide solution. There is little possibility of answering such questions about the extensions of man without considering all of them together. Any extension, whether of skin, hand, or foot, affects the whole psychic and social complex.

Some of the principal extensions, together with some of their psychic and social consequences, are studied in this book. Just how little consideration has been given to such matters in the past can be gathered from the consternation of one of the editors of this book. He noted in dismay that "seventy-five per cent of your material is new. A successful book cannot venture to be more than ten per cent new." Such a risk seems quite worth taking at the present time when the stakes are very high, and the need to understand the effects of the extensions of man becomes more urgent by the hour.

In the mechanical age now receding, many actions could be taken without too much concern. Slow movement insured that the reactions were delayed for considerable periods of time. Today the action and the reaction occur almost at the same time. We actually live mythically and integrally, as it were, but we continue to think in the old, fragmented space and time patterns of the pre-electric age.

Western man acquired from the technology of literacy the power to act without reacting. The advantages of fragmenting himself in this way are seen in the case of the surgeon who would be quite helpless if he were to become humanly involved in his operation. We acquired the art of carrying out the most dangerous social operations with complete detachment. But our detachment was a posture of noninvolvement. In the electric age, when our central nervous system is technologically extended to involve us in the whole of mankind and to incorporate the whole of mankind in us, we necessarily participate, in depth, in the consequences of our every action. It is no longer possible to adopt the aloof and dissociated role of the literate Westerner.

The Theater of the Absurd dramatizes this recent dilemma of Western man, the man of action who appears not to be involved in the action. Such is the origin and appeal of Samuel Beckett's clowns. After three thousand years of specialist explosion and of increasing specialism and alienation in the technological extensions of our bodies, our world has become compressional by dramatic reversal. As electrically contracted, the globe is no more than a village. Electric speed in bringing all social and political functions together in a sudden implosion has heightened human awareness of responsibility to an intense degree. It is this implosive factor that alters the position of the Negro, the teen-ager, and some other groups. They can no longer be *contained*, in the political sense of limited association. They are now *involved* in our lives, as we in theirs, thanks to the electric media.

This is the Age of Anxiety for the reason of the electric implosion that compels commitment and participation, quite regardless of any "point of view." The partial and specialized character of the viewpoint, however noble, will not serve at all in the electric age. At the information level the same upset has occurred with the substitution of the inclusive image for the mere viewpoint. If the nineteenth century was the age of the editorial chair, ours is the century of the psychiatrist's couch. As extension of man the chair is a specialist ablation of the posterior, a sort of ablative absolute of backside, whereas the couch extends the integral being. The psychiatrist employs the couch, since it removes the temptation to express private points of view and obviates the need to rationalize events.

The aspiration of our time for wholeness, empathy, and depth of awareness is a natural adjunct of electric technology. The age of mechanical industry that preceded us found vehement assertion of private outlook the natural mode of expression. Every culture and every age has its favorite model of perception and knowledge that it is inclined to prescribe for everybody and everything. The mark of our time is its revulsion against imposed patterns. We are suddenly eager to have things and people declare their beings totally. There is a deep faith to be found in this new attitude—a faith that concerns the ultimate harmony of all being. Such is the faith in which this book has been written. It explores the contours of our own extended beings in our technologies, seeking the principle of intelligibility in each of them. In the full confidence that it is possible to win an understanding of these forms that will bring them into orderly service, I have looked at them anew, accepting very little of the conventional wisdom concerning them. One can say of media as Robert Theobald has said of economic depressions: "There is one additional factor that has helped to control depressions, and that is a better understanding of their development." Examination of the origin and development of the individual extensions of man should be preceded by a look at some general aspects of the media, or extensions of man, beginning with the never-explained numbness that each extension brings about in the individual and society.

BENJAMIN DeMOTT
Against McLuhan

A marvy year for Marshall McLuhan, take it all in all. Tom Wolfe compared him with Darwin, Freud, and Einstein, Susan Sontag said in public she thought he was swell. London saw him as an epoch maker and intellectual frontiersman (*Encounter* and the *Times Lit Supp*), and *The New Yorker* reviewed him rapt. What is more, academe—after a period of sitting tall but silent on his bandwagon—began talking out loud about his work. (One example: a recent international convocation of savants at Southern Illinois University spent days discussing the "communications revolution" in open session—mainly in McLuhanian terms.) Success being what it is, wasps and carpers were doubtless waiting for the man a piece or two up the road. But no amount of carping could obscure the facts of his rise. Overnight the author of *Understanding Media* had emerged as Midcult's Mr. Big. And ahead of him lay a shot at mass adulation and the title of Everyman's Favorite Brain.

The secret of this ascent isn't instantly visible to casual reportorial eyes. Marshall McLuhan is no literary old pro blessed with a power base and a rich experience at name-making. An English professor for most of his working life (Wisconsin, Assumption, St. Louis), he moved on from teaching only quite recently to his present post as director of Toronto University's Center for Culture and Technology. And despite long years in the classroom, he has no credit reserves in the trade—no stretch of unheralded, scholarly labor of the kind fellow professionals pant to puff. McLuhan avoided book-writing until he was forty. His first work, *The Mechanical Bride* (1951), was an analysis of the sex-power-horsepower ploy by which two generations of ad men have sold us our annual car. (Not much there for the Modern Language Association.) And after the *Bride* appeared, the author resumed his silence as a bookman and maintained it for another full decade and more.

Nor can it be said—still on the mystery of the McLuhanian boom—that here is a case of a late-blooming stylist, somebody who had to turn fifty to turn a slick phrase. In terms of style, this flower has yet to bud. Marshall McLuhan's present reputation rests on two books—*The Gutenberg Galaxy* (1962) and *Understanding Media* (1964); both are sometimes stimulating, but neither is pretty prose. One problem is that of opacity (McLuhan's pages are dense with stoppers like "sense ratios," "interiorizations of alphabetic technology," and the like). Another is that the favored method of organization has a bit too much in common with that of an impresario squirrel. *The Gutenberg Galaxy* looks gathered, not written: a pasteup from a hundred histories of math, political theology, nationalism, and fur-trading, and from a thousand "other authorities." (Walt Whitman and Walt Whitman Rostow, Cicero and Father Ong, de Chardin and de Beauvoir, Rabelais, Riesman, and Shakespeare, the Opies, Powys, and Poe—name your hero, he surely is here.) The man's work reads for pages at a stretch like a Marboro clearance ad:

Clagett [author of *The Science of Mechanics in the Middle Ages*] presents the treatise of Nicholas of Oresme *On the Configurations of Qualities* in which Oresme says: 'Every measurable thing except numbers is conceived in the manner of continuous quantity.' This recalls us to the Greek world in which as Tobias D. Dantzig points out in his *Number: The Language of Science* (pp. 141-2): 'The attempt to apply rational arithmetic to a problem in geometry resulted in the first crisis in the history of mathematics....' Number is the dimension of tactility, as Ivins explained in *Art and Geometry* (p. 7) . . .

Furthermore, the two leading articles of this thinker's gospel can't be called easy to grasp. The first is a theory of culture which contends that communications media impose a wide range of assumptions "subliminally." (The form of the media, not the content, structures men's values, according to McLuhan; the form also determines the content of the senses and the very look of the world.) The second is an interpretation of history which claims that revolutionary transformations of media occur periodically through the ages, and that one such transformation is in progress right now. (A five-hundred-year-old "typographic and mechanical" era is ending and an "electric galaxy of events" has begun; the new "galaxy" offers experiences of simultaneity and heightened interdependence in which traditional values—privacy, independence, and so on—are engulfed.) Neither of these items is wholly lacking in interest, and McLuhan's historical chapters are often enlivened by canny, comprehensible remarks. But the key idea, to repeat—that of the centrality of *form* in the media as the determinant of social structure and individual minds—is to most men unfamiliar and abstract. An author who makes it into his dogma would ordinarily be ill-advised to brood overmuch about fame.

That Marshall McLuhan is now in position (if he chooses) to brood about nothing else owes a little to his skill with the magic of the modern. "Baby, it's what's happening" is a regularly sounded ground theme in his work. The basic language is view-mesh, circuits and data processing. Injunctions to *Think Modern!* appear on page after page. ("We still have our eyes fixed on the rearview mirror looking firmly and squarely at the job that is receding into the nineteenth-century past.") The right names, Cage, Camp,

Bond, Van Der Beek, the whole of the switched-on mob—are fingered throughout like sacred medals. The Farthest-out Art—electric landscapes, Pop Happenings, or whatever—is treated either as classic or already passé, and idols of the hour are probed intensely, like important neglected codes:

The Beatles stare at us with eloquent messages of changed sensory modes for our whole population, and yet people merely think how whimsical, how bizarre, how grotesque. The Beatles are trying to tell us by the antienvironment they present just how we have changed and in what ways.

Old times and old-timers do turn up, as indicated—especially in *The Gutenberg Galaxy*. But even they swim into the reader's ken to a definite R-and-R beat. (Who was Christopher Marlowe? The man, says McLuhan, turning dead Kit hummingly on, who "set up a national P.A. system of blank verse." Who was Heidegger? A cat who "surfboards along on the electronic wave." What were the Middle Ages? *"The Late Show* for the Renaissance.")

Among other crowd-pleasing elements in the McLuhanian equation, the author's literary persona rates a word. At some moments this writer plays Inside Dopester (I called the Kennedy-Nixon election, he announces, I knew exactly why Jack would win). At others he's simply a Scrappy Little Professorial Guy. Enemies as various as George Bernard Shaw ("he lost his nerve") and General Sarnoff ("the voice of the current somnambulism") are worked over in his books; Lewis Mumford, Arnold Toynbee, and dozens more are patronized, and English profs ("literary brahmins") come off naturally as jerks. The author also does a turn as Kitsch Cynic, mocker of Goodie-good types—and it is here that he shows his best stuff, speaking again and again with the clarity of last night's knowing cabby or this week's issue of *Time*. People who are easily shocked give him the laughing fits. ("The historian Daniel Boorstin was scandalized by the fact that celebrity in our information age was not due to a person's having done anything but simply to his being known for being well-known. Professor Parkinson is scandalized that the structure of human work now seems to be quite independent of any job to be done.") And he likes interrupting the argument to defend the innocent guilty and to lean on moralizing twerps:

So great was the audience participation in the quiz shows that the directors of the show were prosecuted as con men. Moreover, press and radio ad interests, bitter about the success of the new TV medium, were delighted to lacerate the flesh of their rivals. Of course, the riggers had been blithely unaware of the nature of their medium, and had given it the movie treatment of intense realism, instead of the softer mythic focus proper to TV. Charles Van Doren merely got clobbered as an innocent bystander, and the whole investigation elicited no insight into the nature or effects of the TV medium. Regrettably, it simply provided a field day for the earnest moralizers. A moral point of view too often serves as a substitute for understanding in technological matters.

A literary self that amounts to an amalgam of Bogie and Dr. Huer might not seem everybody's dish; but the thing obviously meets a felt need.[1]

And the same can be said about McLuhan's gamesmanly ploys as a historian. A specialist in unnoticed causes, this scholar never delves into a historical situation without emerging with "major factors" nobody quite hit on before. The handling in *Understanding Media* of the advent of philanthropy a century ago is typical of his cunning moves. Why did "even the hardiest of the rich dwindle into modest ways of timid service to mankind"? Because of the invention of the telegraph, McLuhan explains—and does not stop for questions. What is the key factor in the Southern civil-rights struggle? The internal-combustion engine. ("The real integrator or leveler of white and Negro in the South was the private car and the truck, not the expression of moral points of view.") Why were the Jews murdered by the million? Because radio came before TV. ("Had TV come first there would have been no Hitler at all.") The talent in question isn't the kind treasured by trade historians, but it is what is called provocative and universally pleasing to wits.

In the end it won't do, though, to pretend that Marshall McLuhan's secret is a matter either of mere wit or mere newsiness or mere literary self-creation. The truth is more complicated—and more painful—than that. Grasping it means facing up to the dozen different kinds of stratagem by which this author empties facts and agonies from the world he thinks of as "Now." Some of these stratagems depend on tricks of futuristic projection, displacements of present-day reality which treat desperate hopes as facts. (Write that "the real integrator of the white and Negro *was*," and you imply that the struggle has already been won.) Other tricks include sudden weird tonal abstractions—see the flip comment about TV and Hitler—deadenings of feeling and sympathy that distance holocaust and shame. Still others con the reader into a frankly theatrical view of experience, a vision that insulates him from immediacies and shows forth all life as a production or stunt. Taken singly, needless to say, none of the stratagems would rank as original, amazing, or troubling; taken in concert they have powerful and obnoxious effect. The complaint isn't that Professor McLuhan puts

1. There are occasional bad break-downs or inconsistencies in this public literary mask. McLuhan stands forth usually as a man quite unafflicted by any sense of inferiority. "I am in the position of Louis Pasteur," he tells his reader repeatedly. Yet the word *humility* comes not infrequently to his lips. For example: his address at Southern Illinois, which began with a summary of likenesses between Marshall McLuhan and Plato, ended with the assertion that "I really feel shatteringly humble." It was a sequel that left some alert listeners confused.

together a thoroughly fantastic account of the situation of contemporary man; it is that he sets himself up, speaking bluntly, as the constituted pardoner of this age—a purveyor of perfect absolution for every genuine kind of modern guilt.

Do I chide myself for trivial failings—my laxness as a parent, my sins of permissiveness, my failure to exact respect from the kids? Do I worry about rearing layabouts incapable of work or thought?—Oh but come *on*, says Marshall McLuhan, a benign forgiving face, the truth is your children are grand:

> Some people have estimated that the young person, the infant and the small child, growing up in our world today works harder than any child ever did in any previous human environment—only the work he has to perform is that of data processing. The small child in twentieth-century America does more data processing—more work—than any child in any previous culture in the history of the world.... We haven't really cottoned on to the fact that our children work furiously, processing data in an electrically structured world....

Do I feel bad about my *own* laziness, say—my own unending belt of mindlessness in front of TV? Situation comedy, secret agents, mean mockeries of domestic life.... Has my intellectual appetite gone dead? My mind turned slush?—Forget it, says this Constant Comforter. The medium is the message, and whatever you think you are doing in front of the box, the fact is you're being expanded-extended-improved. "TV has opened the doors of audile-tactile perception to the nonvisual world of spoken languages and food and the plastic arts. . . ." TV has transformed "American innocence into depth sophistication, independently of 'content'. . . ." TV has "changed our sense-lives and our mental processes. It has created a taste for all experience in *depth*. . . . And oddly enough, with the demand for the depth, goes the demand for crash-programming [in education]. Not only deeper, but further, into all knowledge has become the normal popular demand since TV."

Or am I bugged by my pointless affluence, my guilt about having fat on my hide at a time when sores of starvation are the rule for hundreds of millions elsewhere?—But don't be *silly*, says my adviser, you're being ridiculous again. You're mired in outmoded thinking, you're the victim of moldy figs. Oh, yes, we've all heard about the underdeveloped nations, the "ascent into history," the necessity of hard labor, the problems of locating resources, building factories, educating work forces, creating credit systems, and the like. But *we* know, don't we now, *we* know that we have it within us practically at this instant to do the miracle of our choice whenever we choose:

> The computer will be in a position to carry out orchestrated programming for the sensory life of entire populations. It can be pro-

grammed in terms of their total needs, not just in terms of the messages they should be hearing, but in terms of the total experience as picked up and patterned by all the senses at once. For example, if you were to write an ideal sensory program for Indonesia or some area of the world that you wanted to leapfrog across a lot of old technology, this would be possible if you knew in the first place its present sensory thresholds, and, second, if you had established what kind of sensory effect a given technology like radio or literacy had upon sensory life as a whole.

Or suppose I am simply worried about my *natural* self, my condition as part of the creation, my indecencies to the life around me that is coextensive with mine. I deface the garden, Earth, with cigarette butts, billboards, beer cans. I pollute the streams with uncycled wastes from my factory. Should I not then despise myself as a rapist?

Well, do what you like, answers Marshall McLuhan sniffishly, but you are a bit of a wag. Men may have been a bit hard on the planet in the past—but full amends are about to be made. If you'll just be patient a minute or two, you'll see us doing a kind of honor to this Little Old Earth that will more than make up for the past:

> If the planet itself has thus become the content of a new space created by its satellites, and its electronic extensions, if the planet has become the content and not the environment, then we can confidently expect to see the next few decades devoted to turning the planet into an art form. We will caress and shape and pattern every facet, every contour of this planet as if it were a work of art, just as surely as we put a new environment around it.

In sum: give it all over, is the message. Give over self-doubt, self-torment, self-hatred. Give over politics. Give over conscience. Relax, go soft and complacent, accept your subliminal perfectability. Before us, almost at hand, is a moment of revelation when it shall be shown that "we are living in a period richer" than that of Shakespeare, that our time is properly thought of as "the greatest of all human ages, whether in the arts or in the sciences." And while we are waiting, there are worthy acts to be done. We can cut ourselves off from our depressions. We can look beyond the trivia of daily life—beyond entanglements with wives and children and employers, beyond neighbors, bond issues, tax bills, and the rest. We can overcome the tired sense that there are urgent local and international issues, and learn to see the dropout, the teach-in, even the casualty himself, as part of The Greater Showbiz:

> ...we now experience simultaneously the dropout and the teach-in. The two forms are correlative. They belong together. The teach-in represents an attempt to shift education from instruction to discovery, from brainwashing students to brainwashing instructors. It is a big dramatic reversal. Vietnam, as the content of the teach-in, is a very small, misleading Red Herring. It really has nothing to do with the teach-in as such any more than with the dropout. The dropout represents a rejec-

tion of nineteenth-century technology as manifested in our educational establishments. The teach-in represents a creative effort to switch the educational process to discovery, from package to prove.

Thus will we rise to the certainty that Style and Method are all, that the visible—Vietnam or wherever—is not in any real sense *there*. And having done this we can take off absolutely, fly up from the non-world of consciousness into the broad sanctuaries of ecstasy and hope. ("The computer, in short, promises by technology a Pentecostal condition of universal understanding and unity . . . a perpetuity of collective harmony and peace.")

It is here, of course, precisely here—in the gift of oblivion—that the heart of the McLuhanian munificence is found. This writer does bestow on his reader a welcome grant of hip modernity. He stimulates in addition a voluptuous sense of mastery (to say "The Middle Ages were *The Late Show* for the Renaissance" is rather like cornering a Corvette). And whether or not the basis of his sunniness is sheer terror, his work does rank as the strongest incitement to optimism yet produced in this age. But the great gift offered is, ultimately, the release from consciousness itself. Those who accept it have clearly won a deliverance, a free way up and out.

Are they so reprehensible, it is asked? Poor men, the ignorant, the hopeless, have to buy *their* release from pushers. The Professor's enthusiasts spend less and get more. They buy a guarantee that the disorder, chaos, and misery around them are but veils and shadows, lies told by the stupid conscious mind—yet they make no sacrifice whatever of their ability to function in the workaday world. In the act of discounting their own senses and anxieties, they rise up to form an elite—men dignified by their access to the knowledge that nobody knows what's what. If they are at bottom blind devotees of the subliminal dogma, they have at least kept their self-respect.

—And in any case what *is* the compulsion to Gloomsville that makes it shameful to smile with a Happy Prof? By what laws are we obliged to speak and act always as though tragedy, endless tragedy, were the perpetual human lot? Is it really a badge of reason to hold at every hour of day and night—as Santayana claimed— "the only true dignity of man is his capacity to despise himself"?

The frustration that breathes in these questions, the boredom with canting pessimism, the thirst for a refreshening of life, the longing for an inward sense of courage—these are doubtless the deepest secrets known by our new King of Popthink, the deepest needs his elixir is designed to meet. And making light of the needs is no less inhuman than exploiting them. The best that can be done is to repeat the questions that consciousness—were there any of it left around—would probably feel bound to raise, *viz*.: How much can be said for an intellectual vision whose effect is to encourage abdication from all responsibility of mind? Or: what good is this famous McLuhanacy if it makes men drunk as it makes them bold?

QUESTIONS

1. DeMott begins his essay by recounting some of the praise McLuhan has received. Why does he do this? How does it contribute to his argument?
2. Characterize the style DeMott uses in his essay, and explain why he affects this style. What is the particular effect of his saying "A marvy year for Marshall McLuhan. . . ."? Why does he write "Susan Sontag said in public she thought he was swell"? Give other examples of this technique in the essay.
3. What specific criticism does DeMott make of McLuhan's writing and influence? How does he attempt to persuade the reader that this criticism is valid and just? What values are assumed in DeMott's attack on McLuhan?

MARSHALL McLUHAN
Preface to the Third Printing of *Understanding Media*

Jack Paar mentioned that he once had said to a young friend, "Why do you kids use 'cool' to mean 'hot'?" The friend replied, "Because you folks used up the word 'hot' before we came along." It is true that "cool" is often used nowadays to mean what used to be conveyed by "hot." Formerly a "hot argument" meant one in which people were deeply involved. On the other hand, a "cool attitude" used to mean one of detached objectivity and disinterestedness. In those days the word "disinterested" meant a noble quality of fairmindedness. Suddenly it got to mean "couldn't care less." The word "hot" has fallen into similar disuse as these deep changes of outlook have developed. But the slang term "cool" conveys a good deal besides the old idea of "hot." It indicates a kind of commitment and participation in situations that involves all of one's faculties. In that sense, one can say that automation is cool, whereas the older mechanical kinds of specialist or fragmented "jobs" are "square." The "square" person and situation are not "cool" because they manifest little of the habit of depth involvement of our faculties. The young now say, "Humor is not cool." Their favorite jokes bear this out. They ask, "What is purple and hums?" Answer, "An electric grape." "Why does it hum?" Answer, "Because it doesn't know the words." Humor is presumably not "cool" because it inclines us to laugh *at* something, instead of getting us emphatically involved *in* something. The story line is dropped from "cool" jokes and "cool" movies alike. The Bergman and Fellini movies demand far more involvement than do narrative shows. A story line encompasses a set of events much like a melodic line in music. Melody, the *melos modos,* "the road round," is a continuous, connected, and repetitive structure that is not used in the "cool" art of the Orient. The art and poetry of Zen create involvement by means of the *interval,* not by the *connection* used in the visually organized Western world. Spectator becomes artist in oriental art because he must supply all the connections.

The section on "media hot and cool" confused many reviewers of *Understanding Media* who were unable to recognize the very large structural changes in human outlook that are occurring today. Slang offers an immediate index to changing perception. Slang is based not on theories but on immediate experience. The student of media will not only value slang as a guide to changing perception, but he will also study media as bringing about new perceptual habits.

The section on "the medium is the message" can, perhaps, be clarified by pointing out that any technology gradually creates a totally new human environment. Environments are not passive wrappings but active processes. In his splendid work *Preface to Plato* (Harvard University Press, 1963), Eric Havelock contrasts the oral and written cultures of the Greeks. By Plato's time the written word had created a new environment that had begun to detribalize man. Previously the Greeks had grown up by benefit of the process of the *tribal encyclopedia.* They had memorized the poets. The poets provided specific operational wisdom for all the contingencies of life—Ann Landers in verse. With the advent of individual detribalized man, a new education was needed. Plato devised such a new program for literate men. It was based on the Ideas. With the phonetic alphabet, classified wisdom took over from the operational wisdom of Homer and Hesiod and the tribal encyclopedia. Education by classified data has been the Western program ever since.

Now, however, in the electronic age, data classification yields to pattern recognition, the key phrase at IBM. When data move instantly, classification is too fragmentary. In order to cope with data at electric speed in typical situations of "information over-load," men resort to the study of configurations, like the sailor in Edgar Allan Poe's *Maelstrom.* The drop-out situation in our schools at present has only begun to develop. The young student today grows up in an electrically configured world. It is a world not of wheels but of circuits, not of fragments but of integral patterns. The student today *lives* mythically and in depth. At school, however, he encounters a situation organized by means of classified information. The subjects are unrelated. They are visually conceived in terms of a blueprint. The student can find no possible means of involvement for himself, nor can he discover how the educational scene relates to the "mythic" world of electronically processed data and experience that he takes for granted. As one IBM executive puts it, "My children had lived several lifetimes compared to their grandparents when they began grade one."

"The medium is the message" means, in terms of the electronic age, that a totally new environment has been created. The "content" of this new environment is the old mechanized environment of the industrial age. The new environment reprocesses the old one as radically as TV is reprocessing the film. For the "content" of TV is the movie. TV is environmental and imperceptible, like all environments. We are aware only of the "content" or the old environment. When machine production was new, it gradually created an environment whose content was the old environment of agrarian life and the arts and crafts. This older environment was elevated to an art form by the new mechanical environment. The machine turned Nature into an art form. For the first time men began to regard Nature as a source of aesthetic and spiritual values. They began to marvel that earlier ages had been so unaware of the world of Nature as Art. Each new technology creates an environment that is itself regarded as corrupt and degrading. Yet the new one turns its predecessor into an art form. When writing was new, Plato transformed the old oral dialogue into an art form. When printing was new the Middle Ages became an art form. "The Elizabethan world view" was a view of the Middle Ages. And the industrial age turned the Renaissance into an art form as seen in the work of Jacob Burckhardt. Siegfried Giedion, in turn, has in the electric age taught us how to see the entire process of mechanization as an art process (*Mechanization Takes Command*).

As our proliferating technologies have created a whole series of new environments, men have become aware of the arts as "anti-environments" or "counter-environments" that provide us with the means of perceiving the environment itself. For, as Edward T. Hall has explained in *The Silent Language*, men are never aware of the ground rules of their environment systems or cultures. Today technologies and their consequent environments succeed each other so rapidly that one environment makes us aware of the next. Technologies begin to perform the function of art in making us aware of the psychic and social consequences of technology.

Art as anti-environment becomes more than ever a means of training perception and judgment. Art offered as a consumer commodity rather than as a means of training perception is as ludicrous and snobbish as always. Media study at once opens the doors of perception. And here it is that the young can do top-level research work. The teacher has only to invite the student to do as complete an inventory as possible. Any child can list the effects of the telephone or the radio or the motor car in shaping the life and work of his friends and his society. An inclusive list of media effects opens many unexpected avenues of awareness and investigation.

Edmund Bacon, of the Philadelphia town-planning commission, discovered that school children could be invaluable researchers and colleagues in the task of remaking the image of the city. We are entering the new age of education that is programmed for discovery rather than instruction. As the means of input increase, so does the need for insight or pattern recognition. The famous Hawthrone experiment, at the General Electric plant near Chicago, revealed a mysterious effect years ago. No matter how the conditions of the workers were altered, the workers did more and better work. Whether the heat and light and leisure were arranged adversely or pleasantly, the quantity and quality of output improved. The testers gloomily concluded that testing distorted the evidence. They missed the all-important fact that when the workers are permitted to join their energies to a process of learning and discovery, the increased efficiency is phenomenal.

Earlier it was mentioned how the school drop-out situation will get very much worse because of the frustration of the student need for participation in the learning process. This situation concerns also the problem of "the culturally disadvantaged child." This child exists not only in the slums but increasingly in the suburbs of the upper-income homes. The culturally disadvantaged child is the TV child. For TV has provided a new environment of low visual orientation and high involvement that makes accommodation to our older educational establishment quite difficult. One strategy of cultural response would be to raise the visual level of the TV image to enable the young student to gain access to the old visual world of the classroom and the curriculum. This would be worth trying as a temporary expedient. But TV is only one component of the electric environment of instant circuitry that has succeeded the old world of the wheel and nuts and bolts. We would be foolish not to ease our transition from the fragmented visual world of the existing educational establishment by every possible means.

The existential philosophy, as well as the Theater of the Absurd, represents anti-environments that point to the critical pressures of the new electric environment. Jean Paul Sartre, as much as Samuel Beckett and Arthur Miller, has declared the futility of blueprints and classified data and "jobs" as a way out. Even the words "escape" and "vicarious living" have dwindled from the new scene of electronic involvement. TV engineers have begun to explore the braille-like character of the TV image as a means of enabling the blind to see by having this image projected directly onto their skins. We need to use all media in this wise, to enable us to see our situation.

* * *

The power of the arts to anticipate future social and technological developments, by a generation and more, has long been recognized. In this century Ezra Pound called the artist "the antennae of the race." Art as radar acts as "an early alarm system," as it were, enabling us to discover social and psychic targets in lots of time to prepare to cope with them. This concept of the arts as prophetic, contrasts with the popular idea of them as mere self-expression. If art is an "early warning system," to use the phrase from World War II, when radar was new, art has the utmost relevance not only to media study but to the development of media controls.

When radar was new it was found necessary to eliminate the balloon system for city protection that had preceded radar. The balloons got in the way of the electric feedback of the new radar information. Such may well prove to be the case with much of our existing school curriculum, to say nothing of the generality of the arts. We can afford to use only those portions of them that enhance the perception of our technologies, and their psychic and social consequences. Art as a radar environment takes on the function of indispensable perceptual training rather than the role of a privileged diet for the elite. While the arts as radar feedback provide a dynamic and changing corporate image, their purpose may be not to enable us to change but rather to maintain an even course toward permanent goals, even amidst the most disrupting innovations. We have already discovered the futility of changing our goals as often as we change our technologies.

DIANA TRILLING

Celebrating with Dr. Leary

Although we had been told on what was presumably sound authority that the previous Tuesday evening, the opening night of Dr. Leary's scheduled series of Psychedelic Celebrations, the audience had been "tough" and that therefore on our evening too we must expect some element of danger, or at least unpleasantness, actually it would be hard to imagine a milder scene than awaited us at the Village Barn, the small theatre in Greenwich Village to which Dr. Leary's show had suddenly moved from the Village Theatre where it had originally been booked. Here, surely, was nothing for fear on the score of criminality, menace, or even bad manners. My husband and I were meeting friends. There had been confusion about the arrangements because of the change of theater, so that we arrived almost an hour before the announced curtain time. But the entrance to the Barn was already jammed—no fewer than two hundred people, probably close to three hundred, were waiting for admission and as time went on the crowd became so dense that it blocked traffic through the street. But the conduct of Dr. Leary's audience was exemplary. There was no sign of impatience about the possibility of not getting seats; no one pushed or showed any of the usual impulse to assert territorial claims. On the other hand I should scarcely describe it as a friendly gathering, and this despite the fact that most of Dr. Leary's audience was of much the same age—under thirty—and of roughly the same situation in life: middle-class dissident, above the average in education.

It was not a crowd that talked or laughed; I saw no exchange of greetings, it was even difficult to particularize couples. The group seemed to be made up of strangely isolate young people who, if they were acquainted with each other, were not concerned to further the connection. The general atmosphere was nevertheless one of virtually palpable benevolence. If one can speak of the face of a gathering, this was the face of an entire, an almost programmatic, goodwill and peaceableness—it reminded me of the mandatory calm of recent converts to Christian Science. At first I was surprised by this prevalence of benignity in young people many of whom might be assumed to be in some degree involved in the subversive world of drug-taking and who, at any rate, were all of them dressed in the rather violent contemporary uniforms of dissent, either harshly black or, at the other extreme, colorful in refusal of middle-class conformities of dress—until I reminded myself that, after all, there lies at the heart of the LSD movement as of most contemporary movements of youthful protest the conviction that it is those who accept, or at least accommodate themselves to, the values of Western society who have lost the knowledge of peace and kindliness. Then, too, LSD would seem to have a gentling effect on the personality. I have observed this curious transformation in all the young people I know who have taken the drug; even after only one or two trips they attain a sort of supra-humanity, as if they had been purged of mortal error; and as far as I can make out, this change persists. But one must be cautious with conclusions drawn only from personal observation. In our present highly-deficient state of scientific understanding of LSD, we know with certainty only that its power to work alterations on the brain is enormous: it is 5,000 times more powerful than mescaline. But the precise nature of the changes it makes and how far they extend or how long they last we do not know—which is of course why those who use it or who for whatever reason do not wish to oppose its use can persuade themselves that all warning of its danger is without scientific foundation.

We were fortunate in having reserved Press seats for the four of us by telephone, otherwise we might never have got into Dr. Leary's show. It was when I was trying to get through the lobby to pick up our tickets that I had the encounter which stays with me as summing up the peculiar quality of transcendence that characterized this audience. A young man blocked my path. I touched his shoulder to ask if I could pass. Although the situation demanded no more than politeness, he turned elaborately, looked down at me from what seemed a divine height and said, "I want you to do anything you want to do." So sublime a response surely had its reference elsewhere than where we stood. Not merely his words but the young man's smile, his bearing, were clearly pointed at some sweeter moral universe than a crowded theater lobby in Greenwich Village, New York. Yet, even at this early moment in my psychedelic evening, I knew it was a mistake to regard this young man as an extraordinary instance of elevation. It was his personal quality, not mine, that appeared to be the norm of the occasion—in a gathering like Dr. Leary's I had already come to feel cumbersomely earthbound, of a graceless and unloving species. Since my night among Dr. Leary's followers—and followers I must suppose the largest part of his audience to have been, judging not only by appearance and manner but by their conduct in the course of the performance and certainly in the question-and-answer period at the end of the ceremonies—I have seen a special LSD issue of the French magazine, *Crapouillot*, with excellent photographs of people at various stages of LSD intoxication. Some of the subjects appear to be having a grievously bad time but none of them, no matter in what agony, is without his smile of fine imperturbability, which bears about the same relation to our usual notions of self-containment that the smile of classical hysteria (*"la belle indifférence"*) bears to our usual imagination of pleasurable emotion.

Is it perhaps straining for consistency that I found in Dr. Leary's prose, written or spoken, a character not unlike that of his audience—the same imperviousness achieved at an equal cost in substantive actuality? For instance, a placard was posted in the lobby to explain the last-minute switch of Dr. Leary's show from the Village Theatre to the Village Barn. Later I copied it out:

> With regard to Dr. Leary's Psychedelic Celebration at the Village Theatre: It is with regret that Dr. Leary has discovered inequities and is experiencing financial problems with the theater. Therefore he is forced to announce that he will no longer appear at the Village Theatre. Instead, Dr. Leary will conduct a psychedelic religious celebration tonight at the Village Barn at 9:00. There will be no admission charge.

Prose like this, at once so plain and "elegant," colloquial and fine, commonplace and yet formal, almost legalistic, is compounded of entirely familiar elements of communication. Certainly it has no shock value. But when we examine it we see that although it is offered in explanation, it explains nothing; it merely seduces one into the belief that one has been addressed with a familiar cogency. And so with Dr. Leary's spoken language. It creates the illusion of coherence, it seems to proceed reasonably enough; it is only when one applies oneself to it that it eludes the grasp. Dr. Leary's impossible plausibility would not seem, however, to be consciously contrived, and in this his verbal style differs from that of more orthodox evangelists. Dr. Leary is nothing if not sincere; his language could not be less ornate or theatrical. In fact, it is precisely from its naturalness and sincerity that its hallucinatory quality derives. Much more than Dr. Leary's speech reminded me of someone like Father Divine, it put me in mind of the mother of Lee Oswald, as Jean Stafford describes her in a remarkable little book, *A Mother in History*, the transcription of a series of interviews between Miss Stafford and Mrs. Oswald. Just as in the case of Mrs. Oswald, I began to long for some stageprop or costume to assure me that this mistress of the ardently simple and utterly unconnected statement was only acting, not communicating a real-life condition, just so as I put myself to Dr. Leary's "honesty" I came to yearn for the contrivance of theater.

But, more, what particularly struck me when I came back to Dr. Leary's notice in the lobby after I had become better acquainted with his mode of discourse was its premise of innocence. It is of course its innocence that constitutes a chief appeal of Dr. Leary's doctrine to the privileged young who, perhaps because they are the offspring of a parent-generation intent on keeping no knowledge from them, now regard their elders as uniquely impure in motive and behavior. If the audience at the Village Barn was a fair sampling, and I think it was, Dr. Leary's followers are certainly not to be associated with any ordinary image we may have of juvenile delinquency. The class difference, involving as it does not only differences in education but in social assumption, significantly separates the users of LSD from the young world of street gangs and violence. The LSD phenomenon therefore represents a quite separate social problem located, I think, at that special place in society where cultural influences tend to supplant the better-understood social pressures.

Still, nothing I learned in my evening with Dr. Leary proposed the idea that because his young followers make so urgent an option for virtue and purity of motive, they have any special endowment of native goodness, or even any notable sensitivity to ugliness, or inability to sustain it. As to the first, there is no ground for the belief that behind their benevolence there do not lie the usual human angers and aggressions. As to the second, in the course of my evening at the Barn I came to suspect that if we are going to stay with the "frightened generation" explanation of the LSD phenomenon we need to be precise about what we mean. Far from suggesting any extreme vulnerability to the terrors of life, these young people seemed to me to be unduly armored—and if this is because LSD has reduced their moral alertness, then we must regard the drug as perhaps more dehumanizing than we have yet recognized. My point could not be simpler: at the most alarming moments of the evening, when Dr. Leary announced that he knew no child over the age of seven who was not on drugs, or when his coadjutor, Dr. Alpert, in response to a question about 16-, 17-, or 18-year-olds on LSD, said, "Even if they end up in a hospital or prison for a few months, it doesn't bother me," there was no slightest sign of dismay in their audience. Fearful these young people may be, like the rest of us; they have a fearsome world in which to be young. But fear can show itself in a number of ways, and defines character only by the form it takes and the ends it is made to serve. To express concern for the children of Viet Nam and yet remain unmoved by the idea of submitting 7-year-olds to hallucinogenic drugs is surely to obey the dictates of culture rather than of reliable feeling.

Dr. Leary and Dr. Alpert have both been university teachers, teaching psychologists. I daresay my own response to statements as cruelly irresponsible as these—they were casual remarks, really, spoken with an entire ease—is underscored by the importance I assign, the special importance, to their former profession. In a society as mobile as that of America, the school is more than an institution for teaching the intellectual disciplines, it is the matrix of our ongoing culture, the chief source and guardian of our personal and social morality. What the school establishes today, the home will have absorbed by tomorrow—most of the precepts of our post-Freudian family culture were first formulated in our teacher-training programs. But the problem is that it is exactly because America is so open-ended that youth is valued as it is, beyond its possible emotional and social capacities. And this means that the teacher whose task it is to instruct the young in the complexity of the conditions on which the continuing life of society depends and in the limitations imposed upon the individual by emotional and social reality must himself be able to resist the seductions of rebelliousness for its own youthful sake—which seems to be a difficult demand to make today of anyone of radical spirit and imagination. No one in American public life, certainly no one in government, has the ear of the young like their university instructors, unless it is the advanced social and literary critics, and these are often the same persons, so that if—as now is increasingly happening—the teacher is reluctant to surrender the glamor of youthful rebelliousness and to discover its own grave satisfaction in the exercise of the parental role, he leaves his students in the position of children who have been robbed of the definition they can only achieve when those who train them, and whom they naturally rebel against, have a firm authority of their own; they face emptiness, a world without boundaries. I am not suggesting that the tide of nihilism in which the young appear to be more and more caught up takes its sole or primary force from the school, but only that if anything is to be done to stem it, the salvage will have to be undertaken by the same class of people who did such a successful job of bringing the failure of modern culture to our educated consciousness. Dr. Leary was dismissed, as Dr. Alpert was too, from his Harvard post for engaging his students in his experiments with drugs, but I doubt he would have reached the young as he has were it not for his earlier professional certification.

But, at our evening in the Barn, Dr. Leary was not resting with his pedagogic function. He also made it a religious occasion, and thus drew on the shared fund of recollected church-going his audience, even his young audince, might be supposed to have brought to his celebration. (We keep it in mind, however, that Dr. Leary is under indictment for illegal possession of drugs and if he is to plead freedom of religion under the First Amendment, he does well to put public emphasis on his religious convictions.) His show our night was called "The Incarnation of Christ"; he also does an "Illumination of the Buddha." The ceremonies had been advertised on the theater rather than the religious pages of the papers, with Dr. Leary "in person" as the leading attraction. His religious purpose was nevertheless kept dominant. In addition to the film-and-dance portion of the program, itself ritualistic, there was a sermon, there were prayers by Dr. Leary, and even a moment of silent prayer on the part of the "congregation." Early in the performance Dr. Leary reminded us that while we were gathered here in New York for our religious ceremonies our opposite numbers in India were enjoying the religious ecstasy on the shores of the Ganges, and our opposite numbers in Mexico attaining their exaltation with peyote. Of ecstasy and exaltation there might actually be none, either in Dr. Leary's program or his audience, but unmistakably a spirit of devoutness permeated the auditorium. The religious emotions of Dr. Leary seemed, however, to be considerably interfered with by the strains and temptations of showmanship. And he was very tired, one saw his fatigue from the start, as soon as he took his place on the platform in the darkened hall; he might have been managing a hangover. This was a weary impresario and performer, a weary pedagogue, a weary Messiah—the multiplication and confusion of roles that Dr. Leary now assumes are his burden as the leader of a movement which even he could not have guessed would grow so fast.

We had been shown to our seats at a Press table; amusingly, not unexpectedly, a disproportionate space in this small auditorium had been set aside for those Dr. Leary might hope would give his movement still more of the publicity it has already had in such abundance. Although it was legitimate enough that we should present ourselves as members of the Press, at least for me even this means we had used to procure seats added to the self-consciousness I had felt ever since I had arrived at the hall. It is always uncomfortable to sightsee in other people's emotional universe; and after all it had come only as an afterthought, when we were already seated, that I might some time want to write about the occasion and should therefore take notes. Some days later I was to read a review of our evening in *The New York Times,* by a reporter who apparently spotted us for the tourists we were. She got us by name and described us as "initiates of the older cults of politics and psychoanalysis." We were likened—and this is uncommonly vivid reporting for the *Times*—to "atheists attending a religious ritual out of sociological interest . . . our expressions faintly tinged with boredom and distaste." Well, the sociological posture was unquestionably readiest to hand, but I am afraid I was unprotected by scientific distance from the objects of my study. I looked around the theater at this strangely subdued and isolate audience, and I was painfully aware of the chasm that stretched between the world of these young people and my own at the same age, of the difference between this dedication of theirs and the political dedication of the Marxist '30's in which I had come to maturity. We too, at their age, had pointed to the violence of those in power. My contemporaries, too, had set themselves to make a revolution in consciousness, which would make us "free." But our means had been social and political, and now the very concept of society was inoperative. But if ours had been an ideology of social involvement, not of withdrawal, this could now be no boast—it had led to a blockage of hope which could perhaps never be, certainly had not been, surmounted by a succeeding generation. And for us there had been no atomic bomb. And there had been no such limitlessness in our world, no such vacuum as now passes for the social and personal structure of life. It was not necessary to find any particular emotional vulnerability or even feelingness in Dr. Leary's followers to recognize that they had sufficient ground for confusion and despair, a good bit more even than we had had when we rejected our society as given.

The unease of my situation was much relieved as soon as Allen Ginsberg came to sit at my side, and this is surely not the least interesting aspect of the evening, that by some marvelous transmutation of things as we think them to be, the fact that Ginsberg sat next to me throughout most of the performance was more than a comfort, it provided my chief link with sanity. We had seen him entering the hall and had waved. He had come over to say hello and just then the performance began. To avoid disturbance, Ginsberg sat down at my side. His beard was by far the most lavish in this well-bearded audience; were it still not a blackest black, he should be called the good grey poet of the psychedelic movement, such is his air of venerableness and wisdom, such the authority with which he now seems vested. Time had passed—seven years, eight years?—since I had last seen him. Then, too, it had been a public evening of which I had also tried (not entirely successfully, as it turned out; but, then, one has not the right to ask self-consciousness of one's readers, only of oneself) to report the inevitable reciprocity between the observed and the observer. It was very little later that Dr. Leary mentioned, in all mildness, the presence in the hall of agents from the Narcotics Squad; for a bad instant, as I looked around me and saw no one who met the description, I supposed it might be the four of us Dr. Leary was referring to—except, of course, we had Allen Ginsberg to vouch for us, he was our security in this alien territory. Throughout the ceremonies, speaking in a low steady voice, precise, in firm pedagogic control of knowledge it pleased him to share, this former student of my husband's gave me the assurance I needed of my own identity, unchallenged, in no subtlest degree suborned. The adroitness with which Ginsberg made his aesthetic and critical removal from what was going on onstage while keeping intact his old ties of theoretical and even practical approval of the drug-taking enterprise was something of a triumph. Everything about him indeed, his weight of purpose no less than his canniness, freshly pressed upon me the importance, in the psychedelic universe as elsewhere, of the wish for fame and immortality, the most traditional impulse of the gifted. For what is it, finally, other than the force of this desire, that has sustained Ginsberg, regulated the degree of his involvement in dangerous personal experiment, urged him beyond the anonymousness implicit in the pursuit of selfhood through drugs.

Is Dr. Leary, as well, an exception to the harsh rule of self-eradication in drugs? I doubt it. Certainly drug promotion is now giving Dr. Leary a rare celebrity. And by the evidence of these religious ceremonies he courts immortality in the largest possible way by identification with immortal principles and personages. But succeed as he may in making converts to his religion, as a self he wears the pale but indelible marks of doom: you see it as soon as he takes the microphone in his hand and invites the spotlight. As a self, he has the invincible anonymousness of a television master of ceremonies, than which surely nothing could be more stricken from the immortal rolls. Dr. Leary looks to be in his mid-forties; he is tall, slim, with a suggestion of willowiness. He is, if you will, handsome, with something of the consciousness of the professional charmer, and I should suppose he is especially comfortable in his stage costume of white trousers and open-necked white shirt. The family background seems to be a little vague: apparently it was Irish Catholic, middle-Western; one reads of an Army father and that he himself went to West Point, but this is not the impression he creates—in appearance and voice he is only "sensitive" deteriorated Harvard, throwing away some considerable advantages of birth. He is fair-haired and tousled, wears a necklace, and performs in bare feet. When he takes the microphone in his hand, one feels it is a natural extension of his infatuate ego and that it will more and more become his staff and his rod, his auxiliary drug, his surrogate selfhood. As the evening wore on, with Dr. Leary up there on the platform and Allen Ginsberg at my side, I had the sense of a certain entertaining ambiguity in the relation of these two psychedelic figures. At least before friends like ourselves from an earlier period in his career Ginsberg seemed to me to make a point of his poetic pride, of his superiority to the leader, even of his superior scholarship, but I may have misread him. At any rate, in the course of the ceremonies, he several times alluded to the need for humor in dealing with the LSD subject. For the poverty of Dr. Leary's show as art he was carefully and courteously apologetic.

There was, first, the darkening of the hall and Dr. Leary's entrance into the spotlight, behind him a white and still-empty screen. From the wings of this makeshift theater came the soft strumming of a guitar, and immediately the audience was churchy-still—except that the comparison is absurd: church is where people cough and rustle and squirm and there was no coughing or rustling or squirming in the Barn, unless on the part of four unlicensed sociologists. Through the next two hours (I guess the show lasted) Dr. Leary had his audience in entire control; he could be envied by the professionals.

With his opening remarks Dr. Leary effectively formulated, if one can put it so, the incoherence through which I would try to grope for the remainder of the evening. I have a friend who shares his apartment with a painter; one day my friend's mother (this is a Jewish story) came to see him, examined the paintings on his walls and turned to her son with the question, "Who authorized these pictures?" It was the question I would have put to Dr. Leary: Who, or what, had authorized this particular conglomerate of pageant, preachment, classroom, revival meeting, dance, movie, and off-Broadway amateur night? Where had this performance come from, what was the source of its inspiration? How much was it the psychedelic experience itself that was being reproduced for us, how much an "artistic" derivation? How much was Dr. Leary improvising a gospel, and how much was he bearing witness to the accepted doctrine? Where did the play end and pedagogy begin, where did pedagogy end and the play begin? Had Dr. Leary and his co-performers recently taken LSD and was the drug thus so-to-speak present in the talk that accompanied the film, or had there been at least the intention of artistic detachment from the actual drugged state? It was reported of the movie, *Flaming Creatures*, whether accurately or not I have no way of knowing, that its actors were all of them under drugs when it was made; this one could credit from the loose automatism of their movements and their dispersed sexuality. Dr. Leary's film and the sporadic miming that took place in front of the screen and the words Dr. Leary himself spoke and those that were intoned antiphonally by the male pantomimist and a woman at the side of the stage were certainly all of them sufficiently lifeless to suggest some similar interference with normal process. Still, I realize that an actor has to be highly skilled to simulate nature unimpeded by human awkwardness What looked like blocked transmission in Dr. Leary's show may simply have been amateurishness. "You have to go out of your mind to come to your senses." "We don't pray to anyone up there but to what is inside ourselves." Even announcing his best-shaped slogans, Dr. Leary himself, and despite his naturalness and sincerity, failed to take significant shape except in a form already made iconographic by nightclub and television "personalities." The essential quality he conveyed was that of a schoolmaster acting the master of ceremonies in a school show—a good-looking, tired, essentially vulgar, still-boyish teacher, histrionic, equally pleased with his popularity with his students and with the privileges of office which he could exercise as occasion demanded.

He stayed in the spotlight, quite alone, for rather a while. I had no sense it was too long for his audience. His lecture-preachment-patter covered a general territory already well known from repeated accounts of the doctrine. What one had not been sufficiently prepared for was the vagrancy of Dr. Leary's thought, its bold (however tired), bald carelessness of the ordinary rules of reasonableness, of intelligible discourse. For the occasion of ceremony everything was spoken with the cadence of ceremony, something between a croon and a subdued exhortation. *We pray we are not hung up and that you will have a good trip* (did he mean in our next LSD session, or only metaphorically, here in the theater?). . . . *The voyage is always the same* (did he mean reliable, or was he remarking the singleness of the indicated path?). . . . *We renew and reenact the ancient myths* (this could

refer to the play, but it could also refer to the sacred journey to
which we were being urged). . . . *We pass on what we* (an editorialized Dr. Leary, psychologist?) *have learned in ten years of hard
work.* . . . *We* (Dr. Leary and his audience? Dr. Leary and others
under the influence of LSD?) *meet in our retinas, we meet on the
screen in the vibrating beams of light, also we meet in the liquid
canals of the ear; then we move within to resurrect the body, redis-
cover the timepiece of the universe: the heartbeat . . . Then we
breathe together.* . . . *You should not take a trip without a road
map.* . . . *Myths are cellular.* . . . *The myth is a blueprint.*
. . . *Tonight we invite you to relive the myth of Jesus Christ.* . . .
The resurrection of Jesus Christ has been a rough trip for all of us
(Dr. Leary and his co-authors? All of us in the 20th century who
are the inheritors of the Christian tradition?). . . .

*First we ran into Christian backlash, second the backlash from
Jews and atheists.* . . . *The Christian myth means, once there was a
man who took all the guilts, the shoulds and shouldn'ts, on his
own shoulders and wiped them out. If you experience this myth*
(before you take the drug? afterwards?) *you are free.* . . . *Go back
and free the world from good and evil.* . . . *The tolling of the bell
at Millbrook* (here the clanging of a loud bell presumably took us
to Dr. Leary's "institute") *takes us on a voyage of discovery. You
have to have a guide in the person who has been there before you:
an old witch or a frog or a hunchback. Today, your teen-age
child.* . . . *They have the key to the voyage and it always involves a
chemical tick.* (Trick?) *This is the Chalice, the Holy Communion,
and always the Last Supper: good-bye to all back there.* . . . *I welcome you in the name of the Father, the Son, and the Holy
Ghost.* . . . *Give thanks as we take the Chalice and let our thanks
ascend. Drink. This is my flesh, bone and blood.* . . . *As often as
you do this, do this in memory of me.*

Lights had now begun to flash on the screen and Dr. Leary
moved to the side of the stage. His voice rose in intensity. *Open
the naked eye, find the center!* Great circles of light appear on the
screen, and the show complicates itself:

GIRL'S VOICE: *Can you float through the universe of your body
and not lose your way?*

No one directly answers the question. Mushroom-like patterns
form on the screen. In front of the screen a man in black trousers,
bare above the waist, sways slowly, it would seem painfully, his
arms weaving and reaching in the familiar dance-idiom of tortured
quest.

GIRL'S VOICE: *What is happening?*

DR. LEARY: *Float to the center.*

MAN'S VOICE: *I am drowning in blood.* . . . *Help.* . . . *Please make it stop.* . . . *No, no, don't make it stop.*

GIRL'S VOICE: *Blood to death.* . . . *Out.* . . . *Out.* . . . *Blood to death.* . . . *Life.* . . . *Life.* . . . *Scarlet.* . . .

MAN'S VOICE: *So warm.* . . . *Drifting down.* . . . *Melting.* . . . *Breath of life.* . . .

Here my notes indicate a certain amount of groaning on the stage but not who is the sufferer. Unfortunately, I have no short-hand. But if at first I am troubled by my inability to catch every word being spoken on the stage, soon enough as I catch the drift I realize that the drift is all. It is said of LSD that it taps the unconscious in order to add to the store of the conscious: this is indeed its principal and much-vaunted value, that it is supposed to augment consciousness. But surely to call the LSD experience consciousness-enhancing is to merge two meanings of the word "consciousness"—that which we oppose to *un*consciousness and by which we mean those activities of the mind which we can take note of as they proceed, and, second, the honorific meaning, that of active and useful awareness. If one is to judge the LSD state by Dr. Leary's representation or adumbration of it in his ceremonies or by anything one has so far read of it, what happens under LSD may very well be a flooding of the mind with images or emotions from which it is otherwise closed off. But what the mind does with this new material speaks not at all of a significantly enhanced mental activity such as we usually adduce in our appreciation of awareness. The problem is, of course, an old one in aesthetics. It is not without interest that the new Coleridge scholarship demonstrates with some persuasiveness that "Kubla Khan" was not actually an opium dream and that Coleridge offered it as such only in polemic, as a defense of the role of nonreason in the writing of poetry. But it is not solely an aesthetic problem, it is also a scientific problem and a vexing one: how define what we mean by consciousness, especially in the creative process?

The dialogue between male and female voice now peters out and Dr. Leary relinquishes the spotlight so that the full attention of the audience can be focused on the screen. The pictures that appear look to me like magnified blood cells or other organic matter. Then gradually they become more complex, "social," sometimes fleetingly identifiable. Also, the background music now rises in volume, becomes more assertive—Ginsberg whispers to me, "The *Missa Luba,* a Congo version of the Catholic Mass," and obediently I hear what could perhaps be the *Kyrie Eleison;* he whispers "Verdi's *Requiem*" and, more reluctantly, I hear that as well. Without my having quite noted, the guitar has eliminated itself, been replaced by a sound-track to accompany what is apparently intended as a representation, or evocation, of the evolutionary process, a kind of psychedelic March of Time. Ginsberg mentions a word that sounds

like *Straboscopia,* which I take to derive from the same root as
Strabismus: "Med. A disorder of the eye in which the optic axes
cannot be directed to the same object because of incoordination of
the muscles of the eyeballs. . . ." In later dictionary consultation I
realize he said *Stroboscopic,* pertaining to "an instrument for
observing the successive phases of a periodic motion by means of
light periodically interrupted." But the difference is only objective.
The camera's wish to catch the speed of psychedelic imagery affects
me like a sickness of the eye. From my Press table I no longer see
Dr. Leary. I assume he is seated stage right. His voice resumes the
incantation:

*Let's return to the twentieth century and reincarnate Jesus
Christ. Let's do it every one of us right now. . . . You have to take
on all the guilt, sin, and wretchedness of the world. . . . You have
to do this for everyone so that there won't be any more. . . . Then
we're all through with the good-evil thing and you will be
reborn. . . .* All-embracing, Dr. Leary invites the police and the narcotics agents to join in the rebirth, and for the first and only time
in the evening, his audience is vocally responsive. "You're right,"
come several voices from the audience, soft, devout. My notes do
not say if Dr. Leary is now once more stage center, in full spotlight,
but I recollect him to be. The film has now run its spotty course,
from our unicellular origins to our modern metropolitan mediocrity, and we can have the sermon. Certainly it is in fullest stage
center that Dr. Leary makes his biggest pitch of the evening, inviting someone to come up from the audience on to the platform,
take off his clothes, and be nailed to the cross. *Let's look in the
bag. There are some nails here and a crown of thorns.* The audience remains unmoving. Dr. Leary is apparently not surprised, he
had expected no volunteers; one wonders, in fact, what he would
do if a too-eager listener proffered his services. He repeats: *Will
anyone volunteer to be nailed to the cross if we guarantee you there
will be no more evil in the world?* He dissipates the reverential
hush, or at least lifts it a fraction, with a prepared comment: Dr.
Leary confides to us that he had been warned that if he made such
a proposal in this setting, "four hundred and ninety-seven exhibi-
tionists, sado-masochists, and faggots would storm the platform."
There is no laughter. *No, we must not do it that way, we must do
it with our clothes on, or even our uniforms. . . . But let's do it.*

There follows the more formal sermon, wholly Dr. Leary's own
show and, like all sermons, lengthy. Its text, Dr. Leary announces,
is from William Blake *who had been in our profession a couple of
hundred years ago* (sic). . . . *He who is a fool persists in his folly*
(sic). . . . We must start a new religion, says Dr. Leary, and
start a new country. *We have been working six years*—it had been
ten, I recall, a few minutes back—*to work out a plan to turn on*

this country and this planet. . . . Starting a new religion is like start-
ing a new business. . . . Or a garden. There are inevitable
sequences. . . . A series of ordeals or tests. . . . We have no
paranoia or hostility about our opposition, it's a rough business
starting a new religion. It's a rough business but highly stylized,
more classic than baseball or football. . . .We must turn on, tune
in, and drop out. . . .Turn off your mind and go within. . . .You
need a sacrament and today it is a chemical. The chemicals we use
are ancient. . . . Treat these sacraments with the respect they
deserve. Before you turn on you must be in a state of grace. You
must look into yourself and see where you have sinned. On your
own chessboard. You are the only one who can forgive yourself.
You look in your mirror, in your retina is the history. You confess
to yourself. If you don't go to confession before you take a sacra-
ment you may writhe, suffer, call for a doctor. . . . Once you turn
on, then you tune in, show others what has been shown to you. Dr.
Leary calls on Rudi and Jackie, assistants, to come forward and testify. They have apparently helped to put the show together, now
they will help us tune in.

Dr. Leary: *Rudi, where are we now and where are we going?*

Rudi (thinking): *We are working from a core which is a circle*
of love. A very beautiful and pure thing.

Dr. Leary: *Jackie, where are we?*

Jackie (who is a girl): *We are here and happy to be here. And*
we are going from here out, to turn on the world.

Dr. Leary: *We have to work with the young, the artists, the*
underground groups for a new breakthrough. Artists change con-
sciousness and the change lasts. . . . We work to change family
life. . . . Encourage husbands and wives to take LSD together. . . . I
can't imagine a husband being turned on without wanting to turn
on his wife. I can't imagine parents being turned on without want-
ing to turn on their children. I know no child over the age of seven
who hasn't been given drugs and I know many of them. The par-
ents turn on the children.

Dr. Leary has a practiced device of irony. He echoes his outrages
of decency in the voice of outraged respectability:

Imagine turning on children!

There is a pregnant pause, and Dr. Leary recapitulates:

The psychedelic experience is one you want to share with those
you care most about. . . . Inconceivable that parents would take
LSD and not want their children to share the experience. . . .

The audience continues to be dead still: no one stamps, hisses,
rises to object. No one leaves the theater. (And no reporter, to my
knowledge, undertakes to report what we all of us at Dr. Leary's
Press tables so clearly heard.) From this point forward, the rest of

Dr. Leary's sermon is bound to be anti-climax:

We are now in a legal and political phase. . . . Several million Americans are taking LSD, more taking marijuana, for serious purposes. . . . They need an institution. . . . We are working with the courts to license small groups to take LSD. . . . After you tune in you drop out. It happens so gracefully. . . . A detachment from old ambitions and drives. . . . What we meet and work for is what you want and know is possible. . . . We need and invite your comments and questions.

The comments and questions that comprise the remainder of the program may be what Dr. Leary invites, they cannot be what he needs. But then, what speaker ever gets the questions he needs, and these were at least intended neither to provoke nor challenge. Dr. Leary fares better than most public speakers when they finish a talk and discover to whom they have been speaking and what they are thought to have said. A man rises from the audience to say that he has confronted the beast: Is this what Dr. Leary meant by confrontation with the wolf? Myself, I had heard no mention of wolves, singular or plural. I wonder if the questioner has in mind the beast one confronts in the mirror when one confesses to oneself, or merely an encounter on the psychedelic journey. Dr. Leary is perhaps himself confused. At any rate, he chooses this moment to call to the stage "his well-known colleague" Dr. Richard Alpert, recently returned from California. Together, Dr. Leary and Dr. Alpert respond to the question that has been asked by explaining the uterine recapitulation of man's long slow evolution. *Memory cards flash through your brain when you take LSD, so it doesn't fit your tidy twentieth-century mind.* I conclude from this that when you take LSD you return to the womb and relive the prenatal development.

The second questioner is a priest; he is recognized by Dr. Leary and Dr. Alpert as a friend. The priest wants to know whether after many trips you could not have the same experience without taking the drug. It is Dr. Alpert who undertakes to reply: *After a trip you get depressed by your new sense of your daily life. After enough of this, you stay high all the time because you have revised your life. . . . LSD is not a substitute for the conscious effort of digging here and now. . . . LSD is a constant reminder of our divinity. We mustn't stop because we are too busy. . . . Find someone not on LSD and find out how he and I are us.* This is the point at which I recall, with a certain syntactical confusion, the priest in Ilf and Petrov's wonderful *The Little Golden Calf* of whom the verb "befuddle" is used as an active verb of expression: "Yes," befuddled the priest—"No," befuddled the priest. But of course this was in another country. . . . The priest sits down; he is apparently satisfied with the answer that has been given him.

And now the master of ceremonies introduces Allen Ginsberg from the audience, calls him to the stage. Ginsberg rises modestly but readily—had he been forewarned?—to join the circle on the platform. While he is threading his way through the audience, Dr. Leary intersperses some remarks on electrons, heightens the scientific authority of the occasion. He also addresses himself to the subject of people killing themselves under the effects of LSD: the percentage is negligible, he assures us, and anyway, these are the people who failed to go to confession and expunge their guilts. Dr. Leary gives the nod to the next questioner.

This time the question, although manifestly not intended to give offense, does suggest criticism; it is carefully larded with apology. It seems that although the questioner himself understands the moral nature of the LSD enterprise, there are people of his acquaintance who take the drug just for kicks. Would Dr. Leary comment on this? From the other side of the theater, I have no trouble hearing the question. But Dr. Leary seems to have difficulty; he turns to his coadjutors in appeal but meeting no help he invites his interrogator to the stage. But on his way, this young man is checked by another member of the audience who rises to protest that such a question can only come from someone caught "in the game"—which is to say, someone under the influence of this-worldly, non-psychedelic, values. A moment of tension develops between the two men at the foot of the platform—it represents something of a relief amidst all this benignity—and then Allen Ginsberg intervenes: *You're taking it too seriously, keep some humor.* The questioner addresses the stage in self-defense: *But I want a successful revolution.* To which Leary responds soothingly: *Tell us why, how are we sliding back from the center?* The questioner identifies himself as an instructor in a college in South Jersey. Grievingly he explains that some of his students fail to understand the moral purpose of LSD, they take it for the sensation, they are not *serious.* (He hits the word as I have not heard a word hit since the days when the comrades would accuse each other of being *subjective.*) *And I want you to win, I want a revolution like you do.* The troubled comrade from South Jersey is at last disposed of by Dr. Alpert, judiciously: *It doesn't matter from what motive these kids of 16, 17, or 18 take LSD, if they turn on for 30 seconds the experience is so profound. Even if they end up in a hospital or prison for a few months, it doesn't bother me. . . . The confusion is the greatest kind of confusion for these kids, at any age. It opens the door and makes a mensch of them.* The audience is relieved and ready for the catharsis of humor after such unblessed controversy.

The necessary humorous relief is supplied by a Negro, a solid and comely man who rises at the rear of the hall and announces in a big resonant voice that he has only a single question to ask: *What is LSD?* Although he has produced through the hall the only titter of the evening, he meets a wall of impenetrable silence on the stage. The questioner repeats his question, once, twice, a third time. He becomes insistent: *I'm just asking a single question. I hear you all talking about LSD. What I want to know is, what is LSD?* After what seems forever—the audience is becoming restive—someone onstage has the presence of mind to answer firmly: *It is a chemical.* And the subject is closed; the questioner sits down. Dr. Leary makes a few remarks about his League for Spiritual Discovery, much in the spirit of a preacher before the plate is passed; no plate is passed, the evening has been an expense to no one. *We in the League are working, at risk, to legalize marijuana and LSD. . . It is an intimate family thing we're doing.* Allen Ginsberg steps forward and announces an anti-war rally on the following Saturday—no, not an anti-war rally, a "peaceable march, a transcendence over anger." The meeting is at an end.

There is again no elbowing or pressing as the crowd begins to leave the hall. Now, as not before the performance started, I begin to see couples, pairs of boys and girls holding hands, much as married couples leave funerals or weddings with clasped hands, bound in the intimacy of shared deep emotion. (Dr. Leary, incidentally, could not be more pious than he is about coupling: approaching the sexual subject, he speaks only of "making love to your wife.") It also becomes possible, here and there, to particularize other sightseers among the dedicated: the slowed-down man in his late thirties who wears the mark of yearning, of loneliness, of the failed artist; the dykish, tight-lipped girl who belongs at the side of the swimming-pool of a woman's "Y"; the bookkeeper, as I am certain, who stands out in the crowd for her excruciating neatness and spinsterishness not less than for her advanced years—it is she whom I overhear greeting an acquaintance: "What did you think of it? Weren't you *impressed*?" These are the wanderers between worlds.

But for the most part the audience is as one had first perceived it: young, Village but middle-class, good contemporary faces of the kind one wants to trust, the faces of people to whom intellectual leadership might be thought appropriate, except that they had made another choice and the signal of it is in their eyes. The four of us appeal to each other: Is it only the gifted who go in for this sort of thing? Are these the best, the brightest, of their generation? We of course haven't the answer, any more than we have the answer to a corollary question. How can any enlightened person of whatever age take this psychedelic leader with intellectual seriousness, assent in an ideology so barren of ideas? As we move out on to the street, away from the theater—unregenerate, we are looking for a beer—this becomes, in fact, the nub of our anxiety. For us, Dr. Leary's religious ceremony had been ridiculous when it had not been despicable, but we had been surrounded by young people of good education who not only could take Dr. Leary's drug and this celebration of it but had also somehow managed to issue to the whole subject of LSD a safe-conduct which exempted it from rational inspection, creating—or perhaps only responding to?—an atmosphere in which whoever would put it to adverse question is automatically taken to be repressive, retrograde, lacking in imagination, deficient indeed in scientific open-mindedness.

But Dr. Leary's epiphany gave rise to perhaps even bleaker thoughts than these. In the past month I had heard of four more young people, four adolescent children of friends, who had broken down as a result of LSD—two college boys and a college girl who had had to be hospitalized, a high school boy who, on the edge of psychosis, had had to be withdrawn from school. This made, so far, seven LSD casualties within my own small circle of acquaintance. Of course, some or all of them may have been predisposed to mental breakdown. And we had no figures to tell us whether they were in any way representative of what could happen to Dr. Leary's followers. This being so, how long were we to wait for the statistics to accumulate and be got in order?

For Dr. Alpert there were surely no such anxieties. "These kids" were simply casualties of the new dispensation, eggs that had to be broken to make Dr. Leary's omelette. But I could no more shrug off this concern, retreat into "scientific" or ironic detachment, than I could muster "objectivity" to meet the destruction of the young for the sake of some new Jerusalem of the political imagination. The destruction of a person's mental powers is *actual*, like hunger, poverty, death. It happens in actual life; it entails actual anguish. No, the nub of my anxiety as I left Dr. Leary's show was not that his audience could give credence to the nonsense he spoke—clever as so many of his young followers are, they have no doubt already learned to trust the LSD tale rather than its teller—but the recognition that the direction we take from our present-day assumption that the new and dissident are good in themselves, no matter what their form, may very well lose for us the basic and ordinary knowledge of human decency, including the knowledge that the human mind, even in all its weakness and error, is valuable.

QUESTIONS

1. What is the author's attitude toward and evaluation of the performance she reports? Give specific instances of how her attitude and evaluation are conveyed implicitly as well as explicitly. What standards of value underlie her comments?

2. In his essay "Civilization: Signs of the Times," Mill writes of "the decay of individual energy, the weakening of the influence of superior minds over the multitude, the growth of charlatanerie, and the diminished efficacy of public opinion as a restraining power . . ." (p. 468). Could these phrases fairly characterize Leary's performance? Give reasons for or against that view, and determine whether any of Mill's analysis is applicable to this situation.

3. What effect does the author seek by including a definition of the word Strabismus?

4. Does Leary imply something about himself in the question quoted: "Will anyone volunteer to be nailed to the cross if we guarantee there will be no more evil in the world?" (p. 596)? Is this a serious question?

5. Have you an answer for the author's question: "How can any enlightened person of whatever age take this psychedelic leader with intellectual seriousness, assent in an ideology so barren of ideas?"?

6. In the last two paragraphs a change occurs in the author's style, her approach to the subject, and manner of expressing it. Describe this change, and contrast the style here with that found throughout most of the essay. Is the change in style indicative of a change in purpose?

DANIEL P. MOYNIHAN
Nirvana Now

One of the defining qualities of the period of current history that began, roughly, with the assassination of President Kennedy has been the emergence of widespread, radical protest on the part of American youth. As it happens, this development has been congruent, and in some measure associated, with even wider protest against the current course of American foreign policy, but there is a distinction between those who differ with decisions made by the existing system, and those who reject the system itself. There is at this moment a high level of both kinds of protest, but the latter is the more singular, and almost certainly the more significant.

Following a period when college youth in particular were repeatedly accused of quiescent conformism, this development has taken the World War II generation rather by surprise. More than one college president given to deploring "the silent generation" appears in retrospect not half so bold, and considerably less prescient than he would have had his charges suppose. Never to trust anyone under thirty has become almost a first principle of prudence for academic administrators, and not a bad rule for politicians. It is yet to be seen, however, what if anything we shall learn from this surprising and unexpected development.

Of necessity, we tend to interpret present events in terms of past experience, there being, despite the efforts of the American Academy of Arts and Sciences, as yet but little future experience to guide us. I would, however, argue that we have so far been looking to misleading analogues. We have been seeing in the flamboyance of the hippies, the bitterness of the alienated college youth, the outrageousness of the New Left, little more than mutants of the old bohemianism, the never-ending conflict of generations, and perhaps the persistence of neo-Marxist radicalism. We may be wrong. Just possibly, something more important is abroad. We may be witnessing the first heresies of liberalism.

In its familiar setting heresy refers to religious views contrary to the established dogma of a church. It will seem odd to use it to describe such assertively nonreligious phenomena as the Students for a Democratic Society. Some also will object that inasmuch as the doctrines of liberalism are derived from experience, rather than right reason, there can be no final liberal view about anything, and therefore no finally heretical dissent from such views. I suggest, however, that the phenomenon of protest we observe today is more psychological than doctrinal in origin, and that to the youth of this time secular liberalism presents itself as every bit as much a system of "established and commonly received doctrine" as did Christianity, for example, when it was the legally prescribed belief of the Holy Roman Empire, or the Massachusetts Bay Colony. To be sure, the doctrines of liberalism can be elusive. It is a conviction, Learned Hand might say, that is not too sure of itself—save on the point that it is vastly to be preferred to any creed that is. Liberals are not without tracts—hardly—but tend more to look to institutions as repositories of their beliefs, liberalism being in every sense as much a *way* of doing things, as it is a set of propositions as to what is to be done. It is not without its schisms and assuredly not without its confusions. But in all its essentials of an optimistic belief in progress, in toleration, in equality, in the rule of law, and in the possibility of attaining a high and sustained measure of human happiness here on earth, liberalism is the nigh universally accepted creed of the ruling elites of the Western world. Religious faith persists, even grows. But it does so as a private matter: supernatural beliefs have almost no influence on the course of events. Secular liberalism is triumphant. Not surprisingly, then, given especially the great value liberalism places on skepticism and inquiry, liberalism itself is beginning to be questioned.

It is notorious, of course, that among the most eminent of the literary men of this century the liberal values of the larger society have been viewed with a detachment ranging from indifference to detestation. But these were men born in the nineteenth century, and raised in a world that still had, or thought it had, some options with respect to forsaking the traditionalist, hierarchical, Christian past and embracing the new creed. To these writers it had been a mistake to do so; they withheld their own assent. Thus it may have been incongruous, even perhaps unpatriotic, for a St. Louis boy such as Mr. Eliot to show such enthusiasm for the Church of England and the Royal Family, but it was not absurd. American youth today have no such option. The liberal present is the only world they know, and if it is not to their liking, as for many it is not, their only alternative is to consider how it might evolve into something new, there being no possibility of reverting to something old. What follows is very like a spiritual crisis, and in the manner of individuals and communities that have confronted such in the past, some lapse into indifference and quietism, others escape into varied forms of stabilized hysteria, while still others turn to confront doctrine itself, and in a mood of intensely felt revelation reject the very foundations of orthodoxy.

What indeed is most striking about the current surge of protest is the degree to which it reenacts in matters of style and structure the great heresies that have assailed the religious establishments of other ages. "The sun shone," Samuel Beckett writes in the opening passage of *Murphy*, "having no alternative, on the nothing new."

The forms of youthful protest at this time are many, and not all, of course, visible. But there are three clusters of behavior that are sufficiently coherent as to suggest a central tendency in each, and to offer the possibility of analogies with earlier phenomena.

The most familiar-seeming, and for that reason possibly the most deceptive of the new tendencies, is that of the New Left itself. It is familiar because it has taken a familiar form: the organization of a group defined by political objectives. Yet in truth something profoundly new may be present here, for the object of the New Left is not to capture the system but to transform it. The older radicalisms were inextricably involved with things-as-they-are, and, owing especially to Marx's view of economic determinism, they largely deprived the radical challenge to liberal capitalism of any *moral* basis: the system had a destiny that was working itself out regardless of any intentions, good or evil, on the part of mortals so innocent of the laws of economics as to suppose they, rather than things, were in the saddle. The Old Left was so utterly "materialistic" and "realistic" as to use those very terms to describe one of its defining dogmas. As Richard Blumenthal, of the Harvard Class of 1967, recently observed in the *Nation*, it is precisely this "crass materialism" that the Students for a Democratic Society reject. It is precisely the "dehumanizing" of modern society that they resent.

Society's "main and transcending" concern, Tom Hayden writes, "must be the unfolding and refinement of the moral, aesthetic and logical capacities of men in a manner that creates genuine independence." However that is to be achieved, Blumenthal adds, it is not likely to be by way of "a house in the country and a two-car garage." The movement is purposely "anti-ideological, even anti-intellectual." It is precisely that rational commitment to logic and consistency—of the kind that can lead from game theory at the RAND Corporation to the use of napalm in Vietnam—that these young persons abhor.

Of late they have set about building things called "independent power bases" among the poor (a concept one fears may have been borrowed from the Strategic Air Command), but the striking fact about the famous Port Huron Statement adopted by S.D.S. in 1962 is that it barely, and then only indirectly, touches on problems such as poverty. It is addressed exclusively to middle-class intellectuals and college students: the "people of this generation, bred in at least modest comfort, housed now in universities, looking uncomfortably to the world we inherit." The world about them was so content with material affluence as to suppose it had attained stability, where in truth there was only stagnation. The theme of the Port Huron Statement is that men must *live*, not simply exist. "Some would have us believe that Americans feel contentment amidst prosperity—but might it not better be called a glaze above deeply felt anxieties about their role in the new world?" Man, they declared, had acquired a role of consumer rather than creator. His capacity for love, for creativity, for meaningful relations with others was being lost amidst the machinery of government. S.D.S. proclaimed a social system in which men would not only share one another's fate, but participate, each one, in shaping that destiny: "We believe in generosity of a kind that imprints one's unique individual qualities in the relation to other men, and to all human activity." For such a goal the Gross National Product is indeed a crude indicator of success.

Who are these outrageous young people? I suggest to you they are Christians arrived on the scene of Second Century Rome. The quality of life of that time remains difficult to assess, not least because triumphant Christianity did so much to put an end to it. James Anthony Froude, however, in his great Victorian essay "Origen and Celsus," gives us a glimpse of that world in his reconstruction of the mind of the Epicurean Celsus, a contemporary of Marcus Aurelius, who composed a tract concerning the illogicalities and misstatements of fact in Christian doctrine of such apparent force that Origen himself undertook to refute him. The second century was not unlike the twentieth, and, leaving aside the somewhat gratuitous assumptions of Europeans that they are the Greeks of this age, let there be no doubt that we are the Romans. It was a world, Froude writes, in which "Moral good and moral evil were played with as fancies in the lecture rooms; but they were fancies merely, with no bearing on life. The one practical belief was that pleasure was pleasant. The very memory disappeared that there was any evil except bodily pain. . . ." It was a tolerant world that knew too much about itself to expect words and deeds invariably to conform. "Into the midst of this strange scene of imposture, profligacy, enthusiasm and craving for light," Froude continues, "Christianity emerged out of Palestine with its message of lofty humility."

Who were these Christians? They were first of all outrageous. They were "bad citizens, refusing public employment and avoiding service in the army; and while . . . they claimed toleration for their own creed, they had no toleration for others; every god but their own they openly called a devil. . . ." They had no temples, no altars, no images, and boasted just that. "Fathers and tutors, they say, are mad or blind, unable to understand or do any good thing, given over to vain imaginations. The weavers and cobblers only are wise, they only have the secret of life, they only can show the way to peace and happiness." Of learning they had little and cared less. Nor had they any great interest in respectable people who observed the rules of society and tried to keep it running; they cared only for the outcast and miserable. To be a sinner, they seemed to say, was the one sure way to be saved. They were altogether of a seditious and revolutionary character.

Such people were a bafflement to Celsus. If he spoke bitterly about them, he observed, it was because he was bitter. One can imagine him thinking, if not quite putting to paper: "Do they not see how precarious is the balance of things; how readily it might all be brought down?" He was every bit an admirable, reasonable man. "He considered," Froude writes, "that human affairs could be best ordered by attention and obedience to the teaching of observed facts, and that superstition, however accredited by honorable objects or apparent good effects, could only be mischievous in the long run. Sorcerers, charlatans, enthusiasts were rising thick on all sides, pretending a mission from the invisible world. Of such men and such messages Celsus and his friends were inexorable antagonists." His is the tone of the sensitive, and in ways holy, Inquisitor speaking before the trial of the Maid in Shaw's *Saint Joan*: "If you have seen what I have seen of heresy, you would not think it a light thing even in the most apparently harmless and even lovable and pious origins. Heresy begins with people who are to all appearances better than their neighbors. A gentle and pious girl, or a young man who has obeyed the command of our Lord by giving all his riches to the poor, and putting on the garb of poverty, the life of austerity, and the rule of humility and charity, may be the founder of a heresy that will wreck both Church and Empire if not ruthlessly stamped out in time." The Christians, Celsus declared, were welcome to stay and become part of the commonwealth, but if that was to be their choice, they must live by its rules. Otherwise be gone. Nothing was required that a reasonable man need find objectionable: to salute the sun, or to sing a hymn to Athene did no harm to anyone. Whatever private views one might have on the subject were one's own affair. But society had a right to allegiance.

Point by point Celsus took on Christianity. Point by point he won the intellectual argument, and lost the moral and spiritual one. For he was thinking about the world, and Christians were thinking about the soul. "Most persons," Froude notes, "would now admit that Celsus spoke with wise diffidence when he hesitated at the assumption that the universe and all that it contained was created solely for the sake of man. Origen is perfectly certain that God had no other object. Sun, moon, and stars, and earth and everything living upon it were subordinated to man. In man alone, or in reference to man, the creation had its purpose and meaning." God commanded that the world provide that which is needed by man: as he is weak there must be compassion; as he is sinful there must be the forgiveness of sins; and above all, as he is Godlike, his life must be seen as sacred. If that condition has never been achieved, neither has the Western world ever been the same since first embracing the belief that it should be. Can there be any mistaking that the New Left speaks to the rational, tolerant, reasonable society of the present with the same irrationality, intolerance and unreasonableness, but possibly also the same truth with which the absurd Christians spoke to Imperial Rome? Even Froude, professed and militant Christian, was not less a product of Imperial Britain, and in his grasp of Celsus' arguments, a certain affinity shows through. One recalls the curious moral judgments on display in his own essay, "The English in Ireland in the Eighteenth Century."

Among reasonable beings right is forever tending to make might. Inferiority of numbers is compensated by superior cohesiveness, intelligence, and daring. The better sort of men submit willingly to be governed by those who are nobler and wiser than themselves; organization creates superiority of force; and the ignorant and the selfish may be and are justly compelled for their own advantage to obey a rule which rescues them from their natural weakness. . . . And the right of a people to self-government consists and can consist in nothing but their power to defend themselves. No other definition is possible. . . . When resistance has been tried and failed—when the inequality has been proved beyond dispute by long and painful experience—the wisdom, and ultimately the duty, of the weaker party is to accept the benefits which are offered in exchange for submission.

In truth, is there not a touch of this in the liberal doctrines of the

American Empire, with its panoply of technical assistance, constitutional conventions, mutual assistance treaties and development loans, accompanied as it seems to be by the untroubled, or at least willing, use of astonishing degrees of violence to help others perceive the value of going along?

The young people of the New Left know what they want; a larger, more diffuse group can best be described as knowing what they do not want, which is what they have. These are so-called alienated students of the present generation. The psychiatrist Seymour L. Halleck recently described them as "existing in a state of chronic identity crisis. . . . [their] constant cries of 'Who am I, I don't know what I believe, I have no self' are accompanied by anxiety which while subdued is nevertheless pervasive and relentless." Affluence means nothing and the increase in personal freedom that comes with growing up is as much as anything a threat to which the individual responds with "a peculiar kind of apathy and withdrawal. . . . Having failed to develop an internalized value system which allows him to determine his direction in life, he is paralyzed when the external world removes its guidelines and restraints." Such persons, Dr. Halleck reports, will occasionally involve themselves in campus protest movements and sustain the interest for a short while, but not long, which is perhaps just as well as "When he does become involved with the activist groups he can be characterized as the most angry and irrational member of that group." Sex and drugs are outlets, but joyless ones. They have everything, but nothing works.

Have we not seen this person through history, turning away from a religion that was failing him, rejecting its laws and opting instead for standards of conduct derived wholly from internal personal resources? The object of a liberal secular society being to induce human happiness, it more or less follows that those who reject it will choose to be unhappy and evoke their spirituality in despair more than ecstasy, but *mutatis mutandis*,[1] are we not witnessing the emergence of secular antinomianism?

Not a precise, but an interesting parallel is to be seen in Sabbatianism, the mystical Jewish heresy that sprang up in the Holy Land in the seventeenth century and spread through large sections of Sephardic and then Ashkenazic Jewry. Gershom G. Scholem described this heresy in the Hilda Stich Stroock Lectures delivered in New York in 1938. Judaism faced a series of crises at this time: persecution, apostasy and, for some reason, a sudden impatience with the Lord: how long were the Jews to wander in exile? Scholem writes: "Doctrines arose which had one thing in common: That they tried to bridge the gap between the inner experience and the external reality which had ceased to function as its symbol."

---

1. "The necessary changes being made."

Sabbatai Zevi, a Cabalistic ascetic, and almost certainly a manic depressive, proclaimed himself the Messiah in Gaza in 1665, and eventually won a great following even though—and seemingly because—he went on to become an apostate! A singular quality of the man was that under the influence of his manic enthusiasms he would commit acts counter to religious law. Harmless enough at first, this practice developed among his radical followers into full-fledged antinomianism. "The Torah," the radical Sabbatians were fond of declaring, "is the seed-corn of Salvation, and just as the seed-corn must rot in the earth in order to sprout and bear fruit, the Torah must be subverted in order to appear in its true Messianic glory." This developed in time into a doctrine of the holiness of sin when committed by an elect who are fundamentally different from the crowd. It was of course a profound affront to Rabbinical Judaism, and in its extreme forms acquired a sinister cast indeed, but Scholem writes, "The religious . . . and moral nihilism of the radicals is after all only the confused and mistaken expression of their urge towards a fundamental regeneration of Jewish life, which under the historic conditions of those times could not find a normal expression." The heresy plagued Jewry for a century or more, and seems to have some influence in the rise of the openly antireligious doctrines of the French Revolution. Nathan M. Pusey has voiced his own serious doubts about "the idea that the way to advance civilization is to start over," but one cannot deny the attraction of just this view for persons who find themselves inexplicably not getting from society exactly those satisfactions society most confidently promises them.

Of course, far the most visible of the new protestants are those who do not protest at all, who simple smile, wave daffodils, cover the walls of their *quartiers* with graffiti suggesting we "Legalize Living," and wear their own variety of campaign buttons the quintessential of which demands with purest obstinacy, "Nirvana Now." These are the hippies. Lilies of the field. Bearded and sandaled, they live on air, and love and, alas, drugs. They seek not to change our society, but simply to have nothing to do with it. They are in quest of experiences wholly mystical and internal on the one hand, and tribal on the other. The modern American style of the effective individual functioning in a coherent but competitive society is not for them. Hunter S. Thompson in *The New York Times Sunday Magazine* recently reported an interview with such a young woman living in the Haight-Ashbury section of San Francisco: "I love the whole world," she said, "I am the divine mother, part of Buddha, part of God, part of everything." How did she live? "From meal to meal. I have no money, no possessions, money is beautiful only when it's flowing; when it piles up it's a hang-up. We take care of each other." Did she use drugs? Yes: "When I find myself becoming confused I drop out and take a dose of acid. It's a shortcut to reality; it throws you right into it." Did she pray? "Oh yes, I pray in the morning sun. It nourishes me with its energy so I can spread love and beauty and nourish others. I never pray *for* anything; I don't need anything. Whatever turns me on is a sacrament: LSD, sex, my bells, my colors . . . that is the holy communion, you dig?"

Perhaps not. Yet those assertions would have seemed perfectly clear and altogether admirable to a member of the Brethren of the Free Spirit (or the Spiritual Libertines), a mystical Christian heresy that permeated vast areas of medieval Europe, notably the teeming cities of Flanders and the lowlands, from the twelfth century onward almost to our time. Perhaps because its adepts lived in communities within larger polities, and never took over regions for themselves, and also, being clearly heretical, tended at most times to be more or less underground, little attention has been given the Brethren. But they appear to have significantly influenced the political, if not the religious, development of Europe.

In their mystical craving for an immediate experience of God, their antinomianism, and emphasis on ecstasy, the Brethren of the Free Spirit were not unlike the Jewish Sabbatians, or for that matter the early Christians. Indeed a certain correspondence obtains among all these movements. When they took matters to an extreme of public display, the Brethren, like those before and after them, both fascinated and horrified the orthodox. "The core of the heresy," Norman Cohn writes in *The Pursuit of the Millenium*, ". . . lay in the adept's attitude towards himself: he believed that he had attained a perfection so absolute that he was incapable of sin." Sexual promiscuity became a matter of principle, and marriage was denounced as an impure state. Eroticism and ecstasy were valued beyond all things as symbols of having achieved what was in truth a state of self-deification. In an age when wealth suddenly appeared in Europe, these heretics characteristically preached a communism of property, and chose to be utterly penniless: in Cohn's words, an elite of amoral supermen.

As with Celsus, we are forced to learn most about the views of the Brethren from denunciations by their enemies. Documents from Cromwell's England, a time when the Brethren, known as Ranters, were flourishing, leave no doubt, again in Cohn's words, that the " 'Free Spirit' really was exactly what it was said to be: a system of self-exaltation often amounting to self-deification; a pursuit of total emancipation which in practice could result in antinomianism and particularly in anarchic eroticism; often also a revolutionary social doctrine which denounced the institution of private property; and aimed at its abolition." The Quakers at first saw them as kindred spirits—and the two were often lumped together by others—but efforts at rapprochement were unavailing. The saintly George Fox came upon a group of them as fellow prisoners at Charing Cross. He proposed, we cannot doubt, that they meditate together on the love of God. They called instead for beer and tobacco. A comedy of 1651 by Samuel Sheppard describes the "Character of the roaring Ranters of these Times" in terms that are familiar to say the least:

> ...our women are all in common.
> We drink quite drunk together, share our Oaths,
> If one man's cloak be rent, all their Cloaths.

A chorus goes:

> Come away, make no delay, of mirth we are no scanters,
> Dance and sing all in a Ring, for we are Jovial Ranters

And the verses fearfully so:

> All lie down, as in a swown,
> To have a pleasing vision.
> And then rise with bared thighs,
> Who'd fear such sweet incision?

> About, about, ye Joviall rout,
> Dance antick like Hob-goblins;
> Drink and roar, and swear and whore,
> But yet no brawls or squoblings.

It is said the youth of Haight-Ashbury are not much addicted to scholarship, and they may be pardoned for giving to their service corps the name of "Diggers," after the primitivist community established near Cobham in Surrey in 1649–50. (Such folk have an instinct for agreeable settings.) But they are nonetheless mistaken. Hippies are Ranters.

Supposing all this to be so, does it matter? I believe it does. In the first place these persons matter: they number some of the fine spirits of the age. A liberal must regret the loss of belief in another as much as a decent churchman would. In the second place, these youths are trying to tell us something. It was Chesterton, surely, who described heresy as truth gone astray.

Seen in large terms, it is clear that these protests have been generated by at least three problems facing our society, each one of which can be said to arise from tendencies that are distinctively those of secular liberalism.

The first tendency is that our optimsim, belief in progress, and the possibility of achieving human happiness on earth, combined with our considerable achievement in this respect at home, have led us to an increasingly dangerous and costly effort to extend our system abroad. We are in the grip of what Reinhold Niebuhr has called "The Myth of Democratic Universality," the idea that democracy is a "universal option for all nations." The irony, of course, is that it is just because our own history has been so unique that we are led to suppose that the system that has emerged from it can be made worldwide. It is an effort doomed to fail.

No civilization has ever succeeded in doing anything of the kind, and surely none whose qualities are as historically conditioned as ours should even try. But it is not just that we shall fail: something more serious is involved. In his inaugural lecture at the London School of Economics and Political Science, Michael Oakeshott, succeeding Harold Laski, made a remark of some significance here. " . . . To try to do something which is inherently impossible," he said, "is always a corrupting enterprise." That, in a word, is what I believe has happened to us overseas. As our efforts repeatedly fall short of their pronounced goals, we begin covering up, taking short-cuts, and in desperation end up doing things we would never con-ceivably start out to do. Princes of the Church, modest sons of small-town grocers, begin proclaiming holy wars in Asia, while the man in the street acquires an appallingly troubled vision of those who protest. In the words of a Columbia student, describing the mood of a crowd watching a peace march: "War is virility; love of peace is bohemianism and quite probably a sexual perversion."

Liberals have simply got to restrain their enthusiasm for civiliz-ing others. It is their greatest weakness and ultimate arrogance. Ber-trand Russell suggests that the great Albigensian heresy, with its quest for personal holiness and cult of poverty, was due at least in part to "disappointment of the failure of the crusades." Very likely it will be the success rather than the failure of *our* crusades that will most repel youth. Nathan Glazer has suggested that this gener-ation is already marked by the belief that its government is capable of performing abhorrent deeds.

Not the least reason the American commitment to the diffusion of liberal democracy abroad has become a corrupting enterprise is that those values are not yet genuinely secure at home. This is an ugly fact we somehow never finally confront. At just those moments when we seem about to do so, something, somehow, comes along to distract us. Yet there persists in American opinion a powerful component that is illiberal, irrational, intolerant, anti-intellectual, and capable if unleashed of doing the most grievous damage to the fabric of our own society. A century of universal education has not destroyed this tendency, it has only made it more articulate. And it can drive the liberal elite to astonishing dis-tortions. During this past year we have had to begin admitting that during the height of the cold war the United States government began secretly using intelligence funds to support organizations of liberal and even left-leaning students and intellectuals. This was done out of a sincere and almost certainly sound conviction that

the activities of these groups would aid in the struggle against totalitarianism. Observe the irony: the liberals running American foreign policy were forced to resort, in effect, to corrupt practices—
totalitarian practices if you will—in order to advance liberal
causes—*because the popularly elected Congress would never dream
of doing so.* The man most commonly blamed, of course, is a
decent enough Irish Democrat from Brooklyn: his voting record is
impeccably progressive, but neither he nor his constituents share
the elite enthusiasm for intellectuals. In the explanations of it all a
note even of poignancy enters: can you imagine, writes one former
member of the intelligence establishment, trying to get the F.B.I.
to grant security clearances to the Boston Symphony Orchestra?
The problem goes beyond an affinity for Culture. We have not
been able to get rid of racism, or to secure an equal place for
Negroes in our society. (An effort in which liberals themselves have
not been unfailingly helpful: Woodrow Wilson restored segregation to federal employment policies.) And we begin to perceive
that Negroes are not immune to some of the less attractive qualities of their persecutors. We have not been able to get rid of poverty, and begin to perceive that some of our more treasured liberal
reforms may have had unanticipated consequences that may even
make it more difficult to do so. (Thus, having destroyed the power
of the working class political party organization in our cities, we
now pour millions of dollars of federal funds into projects designed
to overcome the psychic effects of "powerlessness" among the
poor.) And we have not rid ourselves of a brutal streak of violence.
If the Administration has escalated the conflict in Vietnam,
remember that the largest body of opinion in the United States
would bomb the yellow bastards into the stone age, and a solid
quarter specifically favors using the atom bomb. Cohn reports that
the Ranters really began to flourish after the execution of Charles I.

A third problem that has contributed to the rise of youthful protest is, I would suggest, that as the life of the educated elite in
America becomes more rational, more dogged of inquiry and fearless of result, the wellsprings of emotion *do* dry up, and in particular the primal sense of community begins to fade. As much for the
successful as for the failed, society becomes, in Durkheim's phrase,
"a dust of individuals." But to the rational liberal, the tribal attachments of blood and soil appear somehow unseemly and primitive.
They repress or conceal them, much as others might a particularly
lurid sexual interest. It is for this reason, I would suggest, that the
nation has had such difficulties accepting the persistence of ethni-
city and group cohesion as a fact both of domestic and of world
politics.

Thus it is possible not only to sympathize with the new protest,
but to see much that is valid in it. At the same time we are

required to note that which is dangerous. The protest movement is likely to grow rather than otherwise, for the educated middle class from which it draws its strength is growing, and will soon be the dominant American social group. Moreover, the forms of protest are likely to have a striking impact for the very reason that their object is not to redirect the system, but to disrupt it, and this is never a difficult thing to do. It is entirely possible that this disruption could bring to power the forces of the right, and this is indeed an avowed strategy. *Nach Hitler uns.*[2] As the traditional radical Tom Kahn wrote recently in *Partisan Review*, it would be silly to blame the 1966 liberal defeat in California on the New Left and the advocates of Black Power, but "it is enough to say that what they could do, they did." In some forms the rejection of existing society is merely confused, and essentially sophomoric. This winter at Harvard, for example, a document was distributed by a left group that brought to light the fact that in certain regions of Alaska community affairs are under the control of "local politicians, a control that in practice has often been responsive to local interests." At another level, it is anything but. This year, also at Harvard, when a member of the Cabinet came as an invited guest, but under arrangements that did not suit them, the students of the New Left took possession of his person. Such tactics in the early days of Fascist Italy appalled civilization. They are not less objectionable on the Harvard campus. Kahn has described the New Left as "panic disguised as moral superiority" and others have noted how that panic subtly induces a fascination with violence—the most grievous of all possible liberal heresies.

To see history as an earnest evolution from the peat bogs to John Stuart Mill, or to the 1964 Democratic platform, is a simplicity that will not much commend itself to anyone any longer. Having read Mill and having helped draft that platform, I am for one aware of greater shortcomings than, say, the former's need to read Wordsworth at the onset of middle age. But neither would I reject the theme of J. H. Plumb's new series, *The History of Human Society*, "that the condition of man now is superior to what it was." Things are better, and where they are best is in the liberal industrial democracies of the North Atlantic world. I hold these regimes to be the best accommodation to the human condition yet devised, and will demand to know of those who reject it, just what they have in mind as a replacement. By and large the central religious and philosophical traditions of the West have led us to where we are now. Some of the heresies against that tradition have helped, and some indeed have been incorporated into it. But just as many have evidenced ugly and dangerous tendencies, of which a terrible certainty about things is surely the foremost.

2. "Hitler's way for us."

The ancient Gnostics were a charming people, and there is much to be learned from their contact between the hidden, benevolent God, and the Old Testament, law-giving one. But as Scholem writes, "The term *Jewish God*, or *God of Israel*, is abusive and meant to be so. The Gnostics regarded the confusion between the two Gods, the higher, loving one, and the lower who is merely just, as a misfortune for religion. It is metaphysical antisemitism in its profoundest and most effective form which has found expression in these ideas and continues to do so." The Brethren of the Free Spirit are nothing if not a lovable folk, but Cohn notes, "They were in fact gnostics intent upon their own individual salvation; but the gnosis at which they arrived was a quasi-mystical anarchism—an affirmation of freedom so reckless and unqualified that it amounted to a total denial of every kind of restraint and limitation." They were in fact the "remote precursors" of Bakunin and of Nietzsche: "Nietzsche's Superman, in however vulgarized a form, certainly obsessed the imagination of many of the 'armed bohemians' who made the National-Socialist revolution; and many a Communist intellectual, whether he knows it or not, owes more to Bakunin than to Marx."

To protect dissent, no matter how noxious, is one thing. To be indifferent to its growth is another. Men who would undo the system may speak: but they must be answered. The less than soul stirring belief of the liberal in due process, in restraint, in the rule of law is something more than a bourgeois *apparat*:[3] it involves, I argue, the most profound perception of the nature of human society that has yet been achieved, and, precisely in its acknowledgment of the frailty of man and the persistence of sin and failure, it is in the deepest harmony with the central tradition of Judeo-Christian theology. It is not a belief to be frittered away in deference to a mystique of youth.

What we must do first of all is listen. Young people are trying to tell us something. They are probably right in much of what they say, however wrong their prescriptions for righting matters. Then we must respond. American liberalism needs to bring its commitments in balance with its resources—overseas and at home. Some years ago Robert Warshaw noted that "So much of 'official' American culture has been cheaply optimistic that we are likely almost by reflex to take pessimism as a measure of seriousness." It is just this unthinking encouragement of bloated expectation that leads young persons to compare forecast with outcome and to conclude that hypocrisy and duplicity are at work. What is asked of us is honesty: and what that requires is a great deal more rigor in matching our performance to our standards. It is now the only way to maintain the credibility of those standards.

3. "Affectation."

If we do this we shall find, of course, that there is altogether too much that is shoddy and derivative, and in a final sense dishonest, about American life. I suspect we will also find that the awareness of this fact is more diffused within the American electorate than it will have suited the mildly dissenting liberal *cognoscenti* to imagine. It is one thing to read in Richard Rovere's "Letter from Washington" in the *New Yorker* that "This city is awash with lies and deceptions . . . ." It is another to learn, as Rovere with his unmatched toughness of mind would insist, that two-thirds of the American people believe the assassination of President Kennedy to have been part of a broader conspiracy. The Catholic philosopher Michael Novak, commenting in *Commonweal* on the growing rejection of the American system by the New Left, has suggested:

> Perhaps the rumors that wealthy businessmen hired former CIA agents to assassinate Kennedy are the mythical expression of a growing perception of reality: a majority of Americans, and certainly a very wealthy and politically powerful minority, do not wish to see a further social or political revolution in America.

These are signs of danger, as much as are the rioting cities and turbulent campuses. The foundations of popular confidence in the American system are proving to be nothing like so solid and enduring as the confident liberal establishment has supposed. The ability to respond to signs of danger is the essential condition of the ability to survive. It is not too much to declare that our ability is now being tested: it is always being tested. If we respond well to these signs of danger—and if we find a meaningful role in helping to transform the system for those who now attack it—we are likely to evolve a society of considerable nobility. But the first requirement is to acknowledge that what we have so far made of our opportunity is very much less than we should have.

The story is told of the building of the great Catholic Shrine of the Immaculate Conception in Washington: generations of truck drivers, coal miners, and cleaning women contributed their pittances to the coffers of the American hierarchy which slowly amassed the fortune required to construct this most fabulous edifice. It was a building that had everything. Nothing was spared of precious metal and lustrous stone. Nothing was spared by way of design: elements of every architectural tradition in the world were skillfully incorporated in the soaring facade and billowing dome. At last it was finished, and there followed a triumphant week of procession and ceremony, chorus and sermon. Then silence fell. The next morning a child was praying in the crypt when a vision of Our Lady appeared. Smiling that most beatific of all smiles, she looked down and said, "Build a beautiful church on this site."

QUESTIONS

1. What, according to Moynihan, are the essential characteristics of liberalism? What are its weaknesses? What dangers threaten its continuance? Why is it worth preserving? How can it be preserved?
2. Moynihan asserts that the contemporary protest movements are analogous to certain historical religious heresies. What are the heresies and the analogies he draws? How does he attempt to establish the validity of these analogies? What is his purpose in proposing them?
3. Moynihan writes (p. 604): ". . . there are three clusters of behavior that are sufficiently coherent as to suggest a central tendency in each. . . ." What are these "three clusters"?
4. Is there any relationship between the "three clusters of behavior" of which Moynihan writes and his account of the perennial modes of response to spiritual crisis, in which (p. 604) "some lapse into indifference and quietism, others escape into varied forms of stabilized hysteria, while still others turn to confront doctrine itself, and in a mood of intensely felt revelation reject the very foundations of orthodoxy"? If so, with which of these responses would the author have us associate each of the "clusters of behavior"?
5. Moynihan writes that "protests have been generated by three problems facing our society, each one of which can be said to arise from tendencies that are distinctly those of secular liberalism" (p. 611). What are the three problems? Why, writing in defense of liberalism, does Moynihan include this indictment of liberalism, why expose its faults?
6. What is the point of the anecdote closing the essay?

X. J. KENNEDY

Who Killed King Kong?

The ordeal and spectacular death of King Kong, the giant ape, undoubtedly have been witnessed by more Americans than have ever seen a performance of *Hamlet*, *Iphigenia at Aulis*, or even *Tobacco Road*. Since RKO-Radio Pictures first released *King Kong*, a quarter-century has gone by; yet year after year, from prints that grow more rain-beaten, from sound tracks that grow more tinny, ticket-buyers by thousands still pursue Kong's luckless fight against the forces of technology, tabloid journalism, and the DAR. They see him chloroformed to sleep, see him whisked from his jungle isle to New York and placed on show, see him burst his chains to roam the city (lugging a frightened blonde), at last to plunge from the spire of the Empire State Building, machine-gunned by model airplanes.

Though Kong may die, one begins to think his legend unkillable. No clearer proof of his hold upon the popular imagination may be seen than what emerged one catastrophic week in March 1955, when New York WOR-TV programmed *Kong* for seven evenings in a row (a total of sixteen showings). Many a rival network vice-president must have scowled when surveys showed that *Kong*—the 1933 B-picture—had lured away fat segments of the viewing populace from such powerful competitors as Ed Sullivan, Groucho Marx and Bishop Sheen.

But even television has failed to run *King Kong* into oblivion. Coffee-in-the-lobby cinemas still show the old hunk of hokum, with the apology that in its use of composite shots and animated models the film remains technically interesting. And no other monster in movie history has won so devoted a popular audience. None of the plodding mummies, the stultified draculas, the white-coated Lugosis[1] with their shiny pinball-machine laboratories, none of the invisible stranglers, berserk robots, or menaces from Mars has ever enjoyed so many resurrections.

Why does the American public refuse to let King Kong rest in peace? It is true, I'll admit, that *Kong* outdid every monster movie before or since in sheer carnage. Producers Cooper and Schoedsack crammed into it dinosaurs, headhunters, riots, aerial battles, bullets, bombs, bloodletting. Heroine Fay Wray, whose function is mainly to scream, shuts her mouth for hardly one uninterrupted minute from first reel to last. It is also true that *Kong* is larded with good healthy sadism, for those whose joy it is to see the frantic girl dangled from cliffs and harried by pterodactyls. But it seems to me that the abiding appeal of the giant ape rests on other foundations.

Kong has, first of all, the attraction of being manlike. His simian nature gives him one huge advantage over giant ants and walking vegetables in that an audience may conceivably identify with him. Kong's appeal has the quality that established the Tarzan series as American myth—for what man doesn't secretly image himself a huge hairy howler against whom no other monster has a chance? If Tarzan recalls the ape in us, then Kong may well appeal to that great-granddaddy primordial brute from whose tribe we have all deteriorated.

Intentionally or not, the producers of *King Kong* encourage this identification by etching the character of Kong with keen sympathy. For the ape is a figure in a tradition familiar to moviegoers: the tradition of the pitiable monster. We think of Lon Chaney in the role of Quasimodo, of Karloff in the original *Frankenstein*. As we

---

1. Bela Lugosi, an actor in many horror movies.

watch the Frankenstein monster's fumbling and disastrous attempts
to befriend a flower-picking child, our sympathies are enlisted with
the monster in his impenetrable loneliness. And so with Kong. As
he roars in his chains, while barkers sell tickets to boobs who gape
at him, we perhaps feel something more deep than pathos. We begin
to sense something of the problem that engaged Eugene O'Neill in
The Hairy Ape: the dilemma of a displaced animal spirit forced
to live in a jungle built by machines.

King Kong, it is true, had special relevance in 1933. Landscapes of
the depression are glimpsed early in the film when an impresario,
seeking some desperate pretty girl to play the lead in a jungle movie,
visits souplines and a Woman's Home Mission. In Fay Wray—who's
been caught snitching an apple from a fruitstand—his search is
ended. When he gives her a big feed and a movie contract, the girl
is magic-carpeted out of the world of the National Recovery Act.
And when, in the film's climax, Kong smashes that very Third
Avenue landscape in which Fay had wandered hungry, audiences of
1933 may well have felt a personal satisfaction.

What is curious is that audiences of 1960 remain hooked. For in
the heart of urban man, one suspects, lurks the impulse to fling a
bomb. Though machines speed him to the scene of his daily grind,
though IBM comptometers ("freeing the human mind from drudgery") enable him to drudge more efficiently once he arrives, there
comes a moment when he wishes to turn upon his machines and
kick hell out of them. He wants to hurl his combination radio-
alarmclock out the bedroom window and listen to its smash. What
subway commuter wouldn't love—just for once—to see the downtown express smack head-on into the uptown local? Such a wish is
gratified in that memorable scene in *Kong* that opens with a wide-
angle shot: interior of a railway car on the Third Avenue El. Strap-
hangers are nodding, the literate refold their newspapers. Unknown
to them, Kong has torn away a section of trestle toward which the
train now speeds. The motorman spies Kong up ahead, jams on the
brakes. Passengers hurtle together like so many peas in a pail. In a
window of the car appear Kong's bloodshot eyes. Women shriek.
Kong picks up the railway car as if it were a rat, flips it to the street
and ties knots in it, or something. To any commuter the scene must
appear one of the most satisfactory pieces of celluloid ever exposed.

Yet however violent his acts, Kong remains a gentleman. Remarkable is his sense of chivalry. Whenever a fresh boa constrictor threatens Fay, Kong first sees that the lady is safely parked, then manfully thrashes her attacker. (And she, the ingrate, runs away every
time his back is turned.) Atop the Empire State Building, ignoring
his pursuers, Kong places Fay on a ledge as tenderly as if she were
a dozen eggs. He fondles her, then turns to face the Army Air
Force. And Kong is perhaps the most disinterested lover since

Cyrano: his attentions to the lady are utterly without hope of reward. After all, between a five-foot blonde and a fifty-foot ape, love can hardly be more than an intellectual flirtation. In his simian way King Kong is the hopelessly yearning lover of Petrarchan convention. His forced exit from his jungle, in chains, results directly from his single-minded pursuit of Fay. He smashes a Broadway theater when the notion enters his dull brain that the flashbulbs of photographers somehow endanger the lady. His perilous shinnying up a skyscraper to pluck Fay from her boudoir is an act of the kindliest of hearts. He's impossible to discourage even though the love of his life can't lay eyes on him without shrieking murder.

The tragedy of King Kong then, is to be the beast who at the end of the fable fails to turn into the handsome prince. This is the conviction that the scriptwriters would leave with us in the film's closing line. As Kong's corpse lies blocking traffic in the street, the enterpreneur who brought Kong to New York turns to the assembled reporters and proclaims: "That's your story, boys—it was Beauty killed the Beast!" But greater forces than those of the screaming Lady have combined to lay Kong low, if you ask me. Kong lives for a time as one of those persecuted near-animal souls bewildered in the middle of an industrial order, whose simple desires are thwarted at every turn. He climbs the Empire State Building because in all New York it's the closest thing he can find to the clifftop of his jungle isle. He dies, a pitiful dolt, and the army brass and publicity-men cackle over him. His death is the only possible outcome to as neat a tragic dilemma as you can ask for. The machine-guns do him in, while the manicured human hero (a nice clean Dartmouth boy) carries away Kong's sweetheart to the altar. O, the misery of it all. There's far more truth about upper-middle-class American life in King Kong than in the last seven dozen novels of John P. Marquand.

A Negro friend from Atlanta tells me that in movie houses in colored neighborhoods throughout the South, Kong does a constant business. They show the thing in Atlanta at least every year, presumably to the same audiences. Perhaps this popularity may simply be due to the fact that Kong is one of the most watchable movies ever constructed, but I wonder whether Negro audiences may not find some archetypical appeal in this serio-comic tale of a huge black powerful free spirit whom all the hardworking white policemen are out to kill.

Every day in the week on a screen somewhere in the world, King Kong relives his agony. Again and again he expires on the Empire State Building, as audiences of the devout assist his sacrifice. We watch him die, and by extension kill the ape within our bones, but these little deaths of ours occur in prosaic surroundings. We do not die on a tower, New York before our feet, nor do we give our lives to smash a few flying machines. It is not for us to bring to a momentary standstill the civilization in which we move. King Kong does this for us. And so we kill him again and again, in much-spliced celluloid, while the ape in us expires from day to day, obscure, in desperation.

On Literature and the Arts

W. H. AUDEN

Reading[1]

A book is a mirror: if an ass peers into it, you can't expect an apostle to look out.

C. G. LICHTENBERG

One only reads well that which one reads with some quite personal purpose. It may be to acquire some power. It can be out of hatred for the author.

PAUL VALÉRY

The interests of a writer and the interests of his readers are never the same and if, on occasion, they happen to coincide, this is a lucky accident.

In relation to a writer, most readers believe in the Double Standard: they may be unfaithful to him as often as they like, but he must never, never be unfaithful to them.

To read is to translate, for no two persons' experiences are the same. A bad reader is like a bad translator: he interprets literally when he ought to paraphrase and paraphrases when he ought to interpret literally. In learning to read well, scholarship, valuable as it is, is less important than instinct; some great scholars have been poor translators.

We often derive much profit from reading a book in a different way from that which its author intended but only (once childhood is over) if we know that we are doing so.

As readers, most of us, to some degree, are like those urchins who pencil mustaches on the faces of girls in advertisements.

1. From the prologue to *The Dyer's Hand*, 1962.

One sign that a book has literary value is that it can be read in a number of different ways. Vice versa, the proof that pornography has no literary value is, that, if one attempts to read it in any other way than as a sexual stimulus, to read it, say, as a psychological case-history of the author's sexual fantasies, one is bored to tears.

Though a work of literature can be read in a number of ways, this number is finite and can be arranged in a hierarchical order; some readings are obviously "truer" than others, some doubtful, some obviously false, and some, like reading a novel backwards, absurd. That is why, for a desert island, one would choose a good dictionary rather than the greatest literary masterpiece imaginable, for, in relation to its readers, a dictionary is absolutely passive and may legitimately be read in an infinite number of ways.

We cannot read an author for the first time in the same way that we read the latest book by an established author. In a new author, we tend to see either only his virtues or only his defects and, even if we do see both, we cannot see the relation between them. In the case of an established author, if we can still read him at all, we know that we cannot enjoy the virtues we admire in him without tolerating the defects we deplore. Moreover, our judgment of an established author is never simply an aesthetic judgment. In addition to any literary merit it may have, a new book by him has a historic interest for us as the act of a person in whom we have long been interested. He is not only a poet or a novelist; he is also a character in our biography.

A poet cannot read another poet, nor a novelist another novelist, without comparing their work to his own. His judgments as he reads are of this kind: *My God! My Great-Grandfather! My Uncle! My Enemy! My Brother! My imbecile Brother!*

In literature, vulgarity is preferable to nullity, just as grocer's port is preferable to distilled water.

Good taste is much more a matter of discrimination than of exclusion, and when good taste feels compelled to exclude, it is with regret, not with pleasure.

Pleasure is by no means an infallible critical guide, but it is the least fallible.

A child's reading is guided by pleasure, but his pleasure is undifferentiated; he cannot distinguish, for example, between aesthetic pleasure and the pleasures of learning or daydreaming. In adolescence we realize that there are different kinds of pleasure, some of which cannot be enjoyed simultaneously, but we need help from

others in defining them. Whether it be a matter of taste in food or
taste in literature, the adolescent looks for a mentor in whose
authority he can believe. He eats or reads what his mentor recommends and, inevitably, there are occasions when he has to deceive
himself a little; he has to pretend that he enjoys olives or *War and
Peace* a little more than he actually does. Between the ages of
twenty and forty we are engaged in the process of discovering who
we are, which involves learning the difference between accidental
limitations which it is our duty to outgrow and the necessary limitations of our nature beyond which we cannot trespass with impunity.
Few of us can learn this without making mistakes, without trying to
become a little more of a universal man than we are permitted to
be. It is during this period that a writer can most easily be led astray
by another writer or by some ideology. When someone between
twenty and forty says apropos of a work of art, "I know what I like,"
he is really saying "I have no taste of my own but accept the taste of
my cultural milieu," because, between twenty and forty, the surest
sign that a man has a genuine taste of his own is that he is uncertain
of it. After forty, if we have not lost our authentic selves altogether,
pleasure can again become what it was when we were children, the
proper guide to what we should read.

NORTHROP FRYE
The Keys to Dreamland[1]

* * * Suppose you're walking down the street of a North
American city. All around you is a highly artificial society, but you
don't think of it as artificial: you're so accustomed to it that you
think of it as natural. But suppose your imagination plays a little
trick on you of a kind that it often does play, and you suddenly feel
like a complete outsider, someone who's just blown in from Mars
on a flying saucer. Instantly you see how conventionalized everything is: the clothes, the shop windows, the movement of the cars
in traffic, the cropped hair and shaved faces of the men, the red
lips and blue eyelids that women put on because they want to con-
ventionalize their faces, or "look nice," as they say, which means
the same thing. All this convention is pressing toward uniformity or
likeness. To be outside the convention makes a person look queer,
or, if he's driving a car, a menace to life and limb. The only exceptions are people who have decided to conform to different conventions, like nuns or beatniks. There's clearly a strong force making
toward conformity in society, so strong that it seems to have something to do with the stability of society itself. In ordinary life even

1. Chapter 4 in *The Educated Imagination*, 1964.

the most splendid things we can think of, goodness and truth and beauty, all mean essentially what we're accustomed to. As I hinted just now in speaking of female makeup, most of our ideas of beauty are pure convention, and even truth has been defined as whatever doesn't disturb the pattern of what we already know.

When we move on to literature, we again find conventions, but this time we notice that they are conventions, because we're not so used to them. These conventions seem to have something to do with making literature as unlike life as possible. Chaucer represents people as making up stories in ten-syllable couplets. Shakespeare uses dramatic conventions, which means, for instance, that Iago has to smash Othello's marriage and dreams of future happiness and get him ready to murder his wife in a few minutes. Milton has two nudes in a garden haranguing each other in set speeches beginning with such lines as "Daughter of God and Man, immortal Eve"—Eve being Adam's daughter because she's just been extracted from his ribcase. Almost every story we read demands that we accept as fact something that we know to be nonsense: that good people always win, especially in love; that murders are complicated and ingenious puzzles to be solved by logic, and so on. It isn't only popular literature that demands this: more highbrow stories are apt to be more ironic, but irony has its conventions too. If we go further back into literature, we run into such conventions as the king's rash promise, the enraged cuckold, the cruel mistress of love poetry—never anything that we or any other time would recognize as the normal behavior of adult people, only the maddened ethics of fairyland.

Even the details of literature are equally perverse. Literature is a world where phoenixes and unicorns are quite as important as horses and dogs—and in literature some of the horses talk, like the ones in *Gulliver's Travels*. A random example is calling Shakespeare the "swan of Avon"—he was called that by Ben Jonson. The town of Stratford, Ontario, keeps swans in its river partly as a literary allusion. Poets of Shakespeare's day hated to admit that they were writing words on a page: they always insisted that they were producing music. In pastoral poetry they might be playing a flute (or more accurately an oboe), but every other kind of poetic effort was called song, with a harp, a lyre or a lute in the background, depending on how highbrow the song was. Singing suggests birds, and so for their typical songbird and emblem of themselves, the poets chose the swan, a bird that can't sing. Because it can't sing, they made up a legend that it sang once before death, when nobody was listening. But Shakespeare didn't burst into song before his death: he wrote two plays a year until he'd made enough money to retire, and spent the last five years of his life counting his take.

So however useful literature may be in improving one's imagination or vocabulary, it would be the wildest kind of pedantry to use it directly as a guide to life. Perhaps here we see one reason why the poet is not only very seldom a person one would turn to for insight into the state of the world, but often seems even more gullible and simple-minded than the rest of us. For the poet, the particular literary conventions he adopts are likely to become, for him, facts of life. If he finds that the kind of writing he's best at has a good deal to do with fairies, like Yeats, or a white goddess, like Graves, or a life-force, like Bernard Shaw, or episcopal sermons, like T. S. Eliot, or bullfights, like Hemingway, or exasperation at social hypocrisies, as with the so-called angry school, these things are apt to take on a reality for him that seems badly out of proportion to his contemporaries. His life may imitate literature in a way that may warp or even destroy his social personality, as Byron wore himself out at thirty-four with the strain of being Byronic. Life and literature, then, are both conventionalized, and of the conventions of literature about all we can say is that they don't much resemble the conditions of life. It's when two sets of conventions collide that we realize how different they are.

In fact, whenever literature gets too probable, too much like life, some self-defeating process, some mysterious law of diminishing returns, seems to set in. There's a vivid and expertly written novel by H. G. Wells called *Kipps*, about a lower-middle-class, inarticulate, very likeable Cockney, the kind of character we often find in Dickens. Kipps is carefully studied: he never says anything that a man like Kipps wouldn't say; he never sounds the "h" in home or head; nothing he does is out of line with what we expect such a person to be like. It's an admirable novel, well worth reading, and yet I have a nagging feeling that there's some inner secret in bringing him completely to life that Dickens would have and that Wells doesn't have. All right, then, what would Dickens have done? Well, one of the things that Dickens often does do is write *badly*. He might have given Kipps sentimental speeches and false heroics and all sorts of inappropriate verbiage to say; and some readers would have clucked and tut-tutted over these passages and explained to each other how bad Dickens's taste was and how uncertain his hold on character could be. Perhaps they'd be right too. But we'd have had Kipps a few times the way he'd look to himself or the way he'd sometimes wish he could be: that's part of his reality, and the effect would remain with us however much we disapproved of it. Whether I'm right about this book or not, and I'm not at all sure I am, I think my general principle is right. What we'd never see except in a book is often what we go to books to find. Whatever is completely lifelike in literature is a bit of a laboratory specimen there. To bring anything really to life in literature we can't be lifelike: we have to be literaturelike.

The same thing is true even of the use of language. We're often taught that prose is the language of ordinary speech, which is usually true in literature. But in ordinary life prose is no more the language of ordinary speech than one's Sunday suit is a bathing suit. The people who actually speak prose are highly cultivated and articulate people, who've read a good many books, and even they can speak prose only to each other. If you read the beautiful sentences of Elizabeth Bennett's conversation in *Pride and Prejudice*, you can see how in that book they give a powerfully convincing impression of a sensible and intelligent girl. But any girl who talked as coherently as that on a street car would be stared at as though she had green hair. It isn't only the difference between 1813 and 1962 that's involved either, as you'll see if you compare her speech with her mother's. The poet Emily Dickinson complained that everybody said "What?" to her, until finally she practically gave up trying to talk altogether, and confined herself to writing notes.

All this is involved with the difference between literary and other kinds of writing. If we're writing to convey information, or for any practical reason, our writing is an act of will and intention: we mean what we say, and the words we use represent that meaning directly. It's different in literature, not because the poet doesn't mean what he says too, but because his real effort is one of putting words together. What's important is not what he may have meant to say, but what words themselves say when they get fitted together. With a novelist it's rather the incidents in the story he tells that get fitted together—as D. H. Lawrence says, don't trust the novelist; trust his story. That's why so much of a writer's best writing is or seems to be involuntary. It's involuntary because the forms of literature itself are taking control of it, and these forms are what are embodied in the conventions of literature. Conventions, we see, have the same role in literature that they have in life: they impose certain patterns of order and stability on the writer. Only, if they're such different conventions, it seems clear that the order of words, or the structure of literature, is different from the social order.

The absence of any clear line of connection between literature and life comes out in the issues involved in censorship. Because of the large involuntary element in writing, works of literature can't be treated as embodiments of conscious will or intention, like people, and so no laws can be framed to control their behavior which assume a tendency to do this or an intention of doing that. Works of literature get into legal trouble because they offend some powerful religious or political interest, and this interest in its turn usually acquires or exploits the kind of social hysteria that's always revolving around sex. But it's impossible to give legal definitions of such terms as obscenity in relation to works of literature. What happens to the book depends mainly on the intelligence of the judge. If he's a sensible man we get a sensible decision; if he's an ass we get that sort of decision, but what we don't get is a legal decision, because the basis for one doesn't exist. The best we get is a precedent tending to discourage cranks and pressure groups from attacking serious books. If you read the casebook on the trial of *Lady Chatterley's Lover*, you may remember how bewildered the critics were when they were asked what the moral effect of the book would be. They weren't putting on an act: they didn't know. Novels can only be good or bad in their own categories. There's no such thing as a morally bad novel: its moral effect depends entirely on the moral quality of its reader, and nobody can predict what that will be. And if literature isn't morally bad it isn't morally good either. I suppose one reason why *Lady Chatterley's Lover* dramatized this question so vividly was that it's a rather preachy and self-conscious book: like the Sunday-school novels of my childhood, it bores me a little because it tries so hard to do me good.

So literature has no consistent connection with ordinary life, positive or negative. Here we touch on another important difference between structures of the imagination and structures of practical sense, which include the applied sciences. Imagination is certainly essential to science, applied or pure. Without a constructive power in the mind to make models of experience, get hunches and follow them out, play freely around with hypotheses, and so forth, no scientist could get anywhere. But all imaginative effort in practical fields has to meet the test of practicability, otherwise it's discarded. The imagination in literature has no such test to meet. You don't relate it directly to life or reality: you relate works of literature to each other. Whatever value there is in studying literature, cultural or practical, comes from the total body of our reading, the castle of words we've built, and keep adding new wings to all the time.

So it's natural to swing to the opposite extreme and say that literature is really a refuge or escape from life, a self-contained world like the world of the dream, a world of play or make-believe to balance the world of work. Some literature is like that, and many people tell us that they only read to get away from reality for a bit. And I've suggested myself that the sense of escape, or at least detachment, does come into everybody's literary experience. But the real point of literature can hardly be that. Think of such writers as William Faulkner or François Mauriac, their great moral dignity, the intensity and compassion that they've studied the life around them with. Or think of James Joyce, spending seven years on one book and seventeen on another, and having them ridiculed or abused or banned by the customs when they did get published. Or of the poets Rilke and Valéry, waiting patiently for years in silence until what they had to say was ready to be said. There's a deadly seriousness in all this that even the most refined theories of fantasy or make-believe won't quite cover. Still, let's go along with the idea for a bit, because we're not getting on very fast with the relation of literature of life, or what we could call the horizontal perspective of literature. That seems to block us off on all sides.

The world of literature is a world where there is no reality except that of the human imagination.We see a great deal in it that reminds us vividly of the life we know. But in that very vividness there's something unreal. We can understand this more clearly with pictures, perhaps. There are trick-pictures—*trompe l'oeil*, the French call them—where the resemblance to life is very strong. An American painter of this school played a joke on his bitchy wife by painting one of her best napkins so expertly that she grabbed at the canvas trying to pull it off. But a painting as realistic as that isn't a reality but an illusion: it has the glittering unnatural clarity of a hallucination. The real realities, so to speak, are things that don't remind us directly of our own experience, but are such things as the wrath of Achilles or the jealousy of Othello, which are bigger and more intense experiences than anything we can reach—except in our imagination, which is what we're reaching with. Sometimes, as in the happy endings of comedies, or in the ideal world of romances, we seem to be looking at a pleasanter world than we ordinarily know. Sometimes, as in tragedy and satire, we seem to be looking at a world more devoted to suffering or absurdity than we ordinarily know. In literature we always seem to be looking either up or down. It's the vertical perspective that's important, not the horizontal one that looks out to life. Of course, in the greatest works of literature we get both the up and down views, often at the same time as different aspects of one event.

There are two halves to literary experience, then. Imagination gives us both a better and a worse world than the one we usually live with, and demands that we keep looking steadily at them both. The arts follow the path of the emotions, and of the tendency of the emotions to separate the world into a half that we like and a half that we don't like. Literature is not a world of dreams, but it would be if we had only one half without the other. If we had nothing but romances and comedies with happy endings, literature would express only a wish-fulfilment dream. Some people ask why poets want to write tragedies when the world's so full of them anyway, and suggest that enjoying such things has something morbid or gloating about it. It doesn't, but it might if there were nothing else in literature.

This point is worth spending another minute on. You recall that terrible scene in *King Lear* where Gloucester's eyes are put out on the stage. That's part of a play, and a play is supposed to be enter-taining. Now in what sense can a scene like that be entertaining?

The fact that it's not really happening is certainly important. It would be degrading to watch a real blinding scene, and far more so to get any pleasure out of watching it. Consequently, the entertainment doesn't consist in its reminding us of a real blinding scene. If it did, one of the great scenes of drama would turn into a piece of repulsive pornography. We couldn't stop anyone from reacting in this way, and it certainly wouldn't cure him, much less help the public, to start blaming or censoring Shakespeare for putting sadistic ideas in his head. But a reaction of that kind has nothing to do with drama. In a dramatic scene of cruelty and hatred we're seeing cruelty and hatred, which we know are permanently real things in human life, from the point of view of the imagination. What the imagination suggests is horror, not the paralyzing sickening horror of a real blinding scene, but an exuberant horror, full of the energy of repudiation. This is as powerful a rendering as we can ever get of life as we don't want it.

So we see that there are moral standards in literature after all, even though they have nothing to do with calling the police when we see a word in a book that's more familiar in sound that in print. One of the things Gloucester says in that scene is: "I am tied to the stake, and I must stand the course." In Shakespeare's day it was a favorite sport to tie a bear to a stake and set dogs on it until they killed it. The Puritans suppressed this sport, according to Macaulay, not because it gave pain to the bear but because it gave pleasure to the spectators. Macaulay may have intended his remark to be a sneer at the Puritans, but surely if the Puritans did feel this way they were one hundred per cent right. What other reason is there for abolishing public hangings? Whatever their motives, the Puritans and Shakespeare were operating in the same direction. Literature keeps presenting the most vicious things to us as entertainment, but what is appeals to is not any pleasure in these things, but the exhilaration of standing apart from them and being able to see them for what they are because they aren't really happening. The more exposed we are to this, the less likely we are to find an unthinking pleasure in cruel or evil things. As the eighteenth century said in a fine mouth-filling phrase, literature refines our sensibilities.

The top half of literature is the world expressed by such words as sublime, inspiring, and the like, where what we feel is not detachment but absorption. This is the world of heroes and gods' and titans and Rabelaisian giants, a world of powers and passions and moments of ecstasy far greater than anything we meet outside the imagination. Such forces would not only absorb but annihilate us if they entered ordinary life, but luckily the protecting wall of the imagination is here too. As the German poet Rilke says, we adore them because they disdain to destroy us. We seem to have got quite a long way from our emotions with their division of things into "I like this" and "I don't like this." Literature gives us an experience that stretches us vertically to the heights and depths of what the human mind can conceive, to what corresponds to the conceptions of heaven and hell in religion. In this perspective what I like or don't like disappears, because there's nothing left of me as a separate person: as a reader of literature I exist only as a representative of humanity as a whole.

No matter how much experience we may gather in life, we can never in life get the dimension of experience that the imagination gives us. Only the arts and sciences can do that, and of these, only literature gives us the whole sweep and range of human imagination as it sees itself. It seems to be very difficult for many people to understand the reality and intensity of literary experience. To give an example that you may think a bit irrelevant: why have so many people managed to convince themselves that Shakespeare did not write Shakespeare's plays, when there is not an atom of evidence that anybody else did? Apparently because they feel that poetry must be written out of personal experience, and that Shakespeare didn't have enough experience of the right kind. But Shakespeare's plays weren't produced by his experience: they were produced by his imagination, and the way to develop the imagination is to read a good book or two. As for us, we can't speak or think or comprehend even our own experience except within the limits of our own power over words, and those limits have been established for us by our great writers.

Literature, then, is not a dream-world: it's two dreams, a wish-fulfillment dream and an anxiety dream, that are focused together, like a pair of glasses, and become a fully conscious vision. Art, according to Plato, is a dream for awakened minds, a work of imagination withdrawn from ordinary life, dominated by the same forces that dominate the dream, and yet giving us a perspective and dimension on reality that we don't get from any other approach to reality. So the poet and the dreamer are distinct, as Keats says. Ordinary life forms a community, and literature is among other things an art of communication, so it forms a community too. In ordinary life we fall into a private and separate subconscious every night, where we reshape the world according to a private and separate imagination. Underneath literature there's another kind of subconscious, which is social and not private, a need for forming a community around certain symbols, like the Queen and the flag, or around certain gods that represent order and stability, or becoming and change, or death and rebirth to a new life. This is the myth-making power of the human mind, which throws up and dissolves one civilization after another.

I've taken my title, "The Keys to Dreamland," from what is possibly the greatest single effort of the literary imagination in the twentieth century, Joyce's *Finnegans Wake*. In this book a man goes to sleep and falls, not into the Freudian separate or private subconscious, but into the deeper dream of man that creates and destroys his own societies. The entire book is written in the language of this dream. It's a subconscious language, mainly English, but connected by associations and puns with the eighteen or so other languages that Joyce knew. *Finnegans Wake* is not a book to read, but a book to decipher: as Joyce says, it's about a dreamer, but it's addressed to an ideal reader suffering from an ideal insomnia. The reader or critic, then, has a role complementing the poet's role. We need two powers in literature, a power to create and a power to understand.

In all our literary experience there are two kinds of response. There is the direct experience of the work itself, while we're reading a book or seeing a play, especially for the first time. This experience is uncritical, or rather pre-critical, so it's not infallible. If our experience is limited, we can be roused to enthusiasm or carried away by something that we can later see to have been second-rate or even phony. Then there is the conscious, critical response we make after we've finished reading or left the theatre, where we compare what we've experienced with other things of the same kind, and form a judgment of value and proportion on it. This critical response, with practice, gradually makes our pre-critical responses more sensitive and accurate, or improves our taste, as we say. But behind our responses to individual works, there's a bigger response to our literary experience as a whole, as a total possession.

The critic has always been called a judge of literature, which means, not that he's in a superior position to the poet, but that he ought to know something about literature, just as a judge's right to be on a bench depends on his knowledge of law. If he's up against something the size of Shakespeare, he's the one being judged. The critic's function is to interpret every work of literature in the light of all the literature he knows, to keep constantly struggling to understand what literature as a whole is about. Literature as a whole is not an aggregate of exhibits with red and blue ribbons attached to them, like a cat show, but the range of articulate human imagination as it extends from the height of imaginative heaven to the depth of imaginative hell. Literature is a human apocalypse, man's revelation to man, and criticism is not a body of adjudications, but the awareness of that revelation, the last judgment of mankind.

QUESTIONS

1. Frye uses the word "conventions" a number of times; what meanings does he appear to give the word? Why does he seek to

show that life has conventions as does literature? Are they the
same sort of conventions?

2. Early in his essay Frye makes some amusing remarks about poets
   and their ways. Is he making fun of them? If so, why? Does he
   suggest that poets are contemptible? If not, what is he trying to
   do?

3. Toward what sort of audience is Frye addressing his remarks?
   What can you tell about the audience he has in view from the
   language he chooses, and from the line of development his essay
   takes? What conception of the relationship between life and literature does Frye assume his audience might have at the outset?
   Does Frye seek to persuade his audience to adopt a certain view
   of literature, perhaps to change a previous view? What devices in
   his writing (as of tone, diction, figures of speech) are directed
   toward persuasion?

4. What ideas about literature and its relationship to life does Frye
   examine and reject? Why does he reject them? What are the
   main features of his own position? Does he set forth that position in a single thesis sentence anywhere in the essay?

5. What is Frye's view of the moral effect of art and literature?
   How does his view compare with that of Wilde ("The Decay of
   Lying," pp. 633–650)? of Krutch ("Modern Painting," pp. 710–
   716)? of Maritain ("An Essay on Art," pp. 674–684)?

OSCAR WILDE

The Decay of Lying[1]

AN OBSERVATION (A DIALOGUE)

PERSONS: *Cyril and Vivian.*
SCENE: *The library of a country house in Nottinghamshire.*

CYRIL (*coming in through the open window from the terrace*).
My dear Vivian, don't coop yourself up all day in the library. It is
a perfectly lovely afternoon. The air is exquisite. There is a mist
upon the woods, like the purple bloom upon a plum. Let us go and
lie on the grass, and smoke cigarettes, and enjoy Nature.

VIVIAN. Enjoy Nature! I am glad to say that I have entirely lost
that faculty. People tell us that Art makes us love Nature more than
we loved her before; that it reveals her secrets to us; and that after
a careful study of Corot and Constable[2] we see things in her that
had escaped our observation. My own experience is that the more
we study Art, the less we care for Nature. What Art really reveals
to us is Nature's lack of design, her curious crudities, her extraordinary monotony, her absolutely unfinished condition. Nature has

1. Portions of the essay, largely topi-   2. Landscape painters.
cal, have been excluded.

good intentions, of course, but, as Aristotle once said, she cannot carry them out. When I look at a landscape I cannot help seeing all its defects. It is fortunate for us, however, that Nature is so imperfect, as otherwise we should have had no art at all. Art is our spirited protest, our gallant attempt to teach Nature her proper place. As for the infinite variety of Nature, that is a pure myth. It is not to be found in Nature herself. It resides in the imagination, or fancy, or cultivated blindness of the man who looks at her.

CYRIL.. Well, you need not look at the landscape. You can lie on the grass and smoke and talk.

VIVIAN. But Nature is so uncomfortable. Grass is hard and lumpy and damp, and full of dreadful black insects. Why, even Morris'[3] poorest workman could make you a more comfortable seat than the whole of Nature can. Nature pales before the furniture of "the street which from Oxford has borrowed its name," as the poet you love so much once vilely phrased it. I don't complain. If Nature had been comfortable, mankind would never have invented architecture, and I prefer houses to the open air. In a house we all feel of the proper proportions. Everything is subordinated to us, fashioned for our use and our pleasure. Egotism itself, which is so necessary to a proper sense of human dignity, is entirely the result of indoor life. Out of doors one becomes abstract and impersonal. One's individuality absolutely leaves one. And then Nature is so indifferent, so unappreciative. Whenever I am walking in the park here I always feel that I am no more to her than the cattle that browse on the slope, or the burdock that blooms in the ditch. Nothing is more evident than that Nature hates Mind. Thinking is the most unhealthy thing in the world, and people die of it just as they die of any other disease. Fortunately, in England, at any rate, thought is not catching. Our splendid physique as a people is entirely due to our national stupidity. I only hope we shall be able to keep this great historic bulwark of our happiness for many years to come; but I am afraid that we are beginning to be overeducated; at least, everybody who is incapable of learning has taken to teaching —that is really what our enthusiasm for education has come to. In the meantime, you had better go back to your wearisome uncomfortable Nature, and leave me to correct my proofs.

CYRIL. Writing an article! That is not very consistent after what you have just said.

VIVIAN. Who wants to be consistent? The dullard and the doctrinaire, the tedious people who carry out their principles to the bitter end of action, to the *reductio ad absurdum* of practice. Not I. Like Emerson, I write over the door of my library the word "Whim." Besides, my article is really a most salutary and valuable

3. William Morris, nineteenth-century English poet, artist, and social theorist, sought to stimulate high standards of craftsmanship and beauty in furnishings. The allusion is to the "Morris chair," from his design.

warning. If it is attended to, there may be a new Renaissance of Art.

CYRIL. What is the subject?

VIVIAN. I intend to call it "The Decay of Lying: A Protest."

CYRIL. Lying! I should have thought that our politicians kept up that habit.

VIVIAN. I assure you that they do not. They never rise beyond the level of misrepresentation, and actually condescend to prove, to discuss, to argue. How different from the temper of the true liar, with his frank, fearless statements, his superb irresponsibility, his healthy, natural disdain of proof of any kind! After all, what is a fine lie? Simply that which is its own evidence. If a man is sufficiently unimaginative to produce evidence in support of a lie, he might just as well speak the truth at once. No, the politicians won't do. Something may, perhaps be urged on behalf of the Bar. The mantle of the Sophist has fallen on its members. Their feigned ardors and unreal rhetoric are delightful. They can make the worse appear the better cause, as though they were fresh from Leontine schools, and have been known to wrest from reluctant juries triumphant verdicts of acquittal for their clients, even when those clients, as often happens, were clearly and unmistakably innocent. But they are briefed by the prosaic, and are not ashamed to appeal to precedent. In spite of their endeavors, the truth will out. Newspapers, even, have degenerated. They may now be absolutely relied upon. One feels it as one wades through their columns. It is always the unreadable that occurs. I am afraid that there is not much to be said in favor of either the lawyer or the journalist. Besides, what I am pleading for is Lying in art. Shall I read you what I have written? It might do you a great deal of good.

CYRIL. Certainly, if you give me a cigarette. Thanks. * * *

VIVIAN. (*reading in a very clear, musical voice*). "THE DECAY OF LYING: A PROTEST. One of the chief causes that can be assigned for the curiously commonplace character of most of the literature of our age is undoubtedly the decay of Lying as an art, a science, and a social pleasure. The ancient historians gave us delightful fiction in the form of fact; the modern novelist presents us with dull facts under the guise of fiction. The Blue-Book[4] is rapidly becoming his ideal both for method and manner. He has his tedious '*document humain*,' his miserable little '*coin de la création*,'[5] into which he peers with his microscope. He is to be found at the Librarie Nationale, or at the British Museum, shamelessly reading up his subject. He has not even the courage of other people's ideas, but insists on going directly to life for everything, and ultimately, between encyclopedias and personal experience, he comes to the

---

4. A British parliamentary report, a factual document.

5. "Corner of the universe," a phrase similar to "slice of life" to characterize realism in fiction.

ground, having drawn his types from the family circle or from the weekly washerwoman, and having acquired an amount of useful information from which never, even in his most meditative moments, can he thoroughly free himself.

"The loss that results to literature in general from this false ideal of our time can hardly be over-estimated. People have a careless way of talking about a 'born liar,' just as they talk about a 'born poet.' But in both cases they are wrong. Lying and poetry are arts— arts, as Plato saw, not unconnected with each other—and they require the most careful study, the most disinterested devotion. Indeed, they have their technique, just as the more material arts of painting and sculpture have, their subtle secrets of form and color, their craft-mysteries, their deliberate artistic methods. As one knows the poet by his fine music, so one can recognize the liar by his rich rhythmic utterance, and in neither case will the casual inspiration of the moment suffice. Here, as elsewhere, practice must precede perfection. But in modern days while the fashion of writing poetry has become far too common, and should, if possible, be discouraged, the fashion of lying has almost fallen into disrepute. Many a young man starts in life with a natural gift for exaggeration which, if nurtured in congenial and sympathetic surroundings, or by the imitation of the best models, might grow into something really great and wonderful. But, as a rule, he comes to nothing. He either falls into careless habits of accuracy——"

CYRIL. My dear fellow!

VIVIAN. Please don't interrupt in the middle of a sentence. "He either falls into careless habits of accuracy, or takes to frequenting the society of the aged and the well-informed. Both things are equally fatal to his imagination, as indeed they would be fatal to the imagination of anybody, and in a short time he develops a morbid and unhealthy faculty of truth-telling, begins to verify all statements made in his presence, has no hesitation in contradicting people who are much younger than himself, and often ends by writing novels which are so like life that no one can possibly believe in their probability. This is no isolated instance that we are giving. It is simply one example out of many; and if something cannot be done to check, or at least to modify, our monstrous worship of facts, Art will become sterile, and Beauty will pass away from the land. * * *

The only real people are the people who never existed, and if a novelist is base enough to go to life for his personages he should at least pretend that they are creations, and not boast of them as copies. The justification of a character in a novel is not that other persons are what they are, but that the author is what he is. Otherwise the novel is not a work of art. * * * In point of fact, what is interesting about people in good society * * * is the mask that each one of them wears, not the reality that lies behind the mask. It is a humiliating confession, but we are all of us made out of the same stuff. In Falstaff there is something of Hamlet, in Hamlet there is not a little of Falstaff. The fat knight has his moods of melancholy, and the young prince his moments of coarse humor. Where we differ from each other is purely in accidentals: in personal appearance, tricks of habit, and the like. The more one analyzes people, the more all reasons for analysis disappear. Sooner or later one comes to that dreadful universal thing called human nature. Indeed, as any one who has ever worked among the poor knows only too well, the brotherhood of man is no mere poet's dream, it is a most depressing and humiliating reality; and if a writer insists upon analyzing the upper classes, he might just as well write of match-girls and costermongers at once." However, my dear Cyril, I will not detain you any further just here. I quite admit that modern novels have many good points. All I insist on is that as a class, they are quite unreadable. * * *

CYRIL. Do you object to modernity of form, then?

VIVIAN. Yes. It is a huge price to pay for a very poor result. Pure modernity of form is always somewhat vulgarizing. It cannot help being so. The public imagine that, because they are interested in their immediate surroundings, Art should be interested in them also, and should take them as her subject-matter. But the mere fact that they are interested in these things makes them unsuitable subjects for Art. The only beautiful things, as somebody once said, are the things that do not concern us. As long as a thing is useful or necessary to us, or affects us in any way, either for pain or for pleasure, or appeals strongly to our sympathies, or is a vital part of the environment in which we live, it is outside the proper sphere of art. To art's subject-matter we should be more or less indifferent. We should, at any rate, have no preferences, no prejudices, no partisan feelings of any kind. It is exactly because Hecuba is nothing to us that her sorrows are such an admirable motive for tragedy.[6] * * * Believe me, my dear Cyril, modernity of form and modernity of subject-matter are entirely and absolutely wrong. We have mistaken the common livery of the age for the vesture of the Muses, and spend our days in the sordid streets and hideous suburbs of our vile cities when we should be out on the hillside with Apollo. Certainly we are a degraded race, and have sold our birthright for a mess of facts.

CYRIL. There is something in what you say, and there is no doubt that whatever amusement we may find in reading a purely modern novel, we have rarely any artistic pleasure in re-reading it. And this is perhaps the best rough test of what is literature and what is not. If one cannot enjoy reading a book over and over again, there

6. *Hamlet* II. ii. 522-586.

is no use reading it at all. But what do you say about the return to Life and Nature? This is the panacea that is always being recommended to us.

VIVIAN. I will read you what I say on that subject. The passage comes later on in the article, but I may as well give it to you now:

"The popular cry of our time is 'Let us return to Life and Nature; they will recreate Art for us, and send the red blood coursing through her veins; they will shoe her feet with swiftness and make her hand strong.' But, alas! we are mistaken in our amiable and well-meaning efforts. Nature is always behind the age. And as for Life, she is the solvent that breaks up Art, the enemy that lays waste her house."

CYRIL. What do you mean by saying that Nature is always behind the age?

VIVIAN. Well, perhaps that is rather cryptic. What I mean is this. If we take Nature to mean natural simple instinct as opposed to self-conscious culture, the work produced under this influence is always old-fashioned, antiquated, and out of date. One touch of Nature may make the whole world kin, but two touches of Nature will destroy any work of Art. If, on the other hand, we regard Nature as the collection of phenomena external to man, people only discover in her what they bring to her. She has no suggestions of her own. Wordsworth went to the lakes, but he was never a lake poet. He found in stones the sermons he had already hidden there. He went moralizing about the district, but his good work was produced when he returned, not to Nature but to poetry. Poetry gave him "Laodamia," and the fine sonnets, and the great Ode, such as it is. Nature gave him "Martha Ray" and "Peter Bell," and the address to Mr. Wilkinson's spade.

CYRIL. I think that view might be questioned. I am rather inclined to believe in the "impulse from a vernal wood," though, of course, the artistic value of such an impulse depends entirely on the kind of temperament that receives it, so that the return to Nature would come to mean simply the advance to a great personality. You would agree with that, I fancy. However, proceed with your article.

VIVIAN. (reading). "Art begins with abstract decoration, with purely imaginative and pleasurable work dealing with what is unreal and nonexistent. This is the first stage. Then Life becomes fascinated with this new wonder, and asks to be admitted into the charmed circle. Art takes life as part of her rough material, recreates it, and refashions it in fresh forms, is absolutely indifferent to fact, invents, imagines, dreams, and keeps between herself and reality the impenetrable barrier of beautiful style, of decorative or ideal treatment. The third stage is when Life gets the upper hand, and drives Art out into the wilderness. This is the true decadence, and it is from this that we are now suffering.

"Take the case of the English drama. At first in the hands of the monks Dramatic Art was abstract, decorative, and mythological. Then she enlisted Life in her service, and using some of Life's external forms, she created an entirely new race of beings, whose sorrows were more terrible than any sorrow man has ever felt, whose joys were keener than lover's joys, who had the rage of the Titans and the calm of the gods, who had monstrous and marvelous sins, monstrous and marvelous virtues. To them she gave a language different from that of actual use, a language full of resonant music and sweet rhythm, made stately by solemn cadence, or made delicate by fanciful rhyme, jeweled with wonderful words, and enriched with lofty diction. She clothed her children in strange raiment and gave them masks, and at her bidding the antique world rose from its marble tomb. A new Caesar stalked through the streets of risen Rome, and with purple sail and flute-led oars another Cleopatra passed up the river to Antioch. Old myth and legend and dream took shape and substance. History was entirely re-written, and there was hardly one of the dramatists who did not recognize that the object of Art is not simple truth but complex beauty. In this they were perfectly right. Art itself is really a form of exaggeration; and selection, which is the very spirit of art, is nothing more than an intensified mode of over-emphasis.

"But Life soon shattered the perfection of the form. Even in Shakespeare we can see the beginning of the end. It shows itself by the gradual breaking up of the blank-verse in the later plays, by the predominance given to prose, and by the over-importance assigned to characterization. The passages in Shakespeare—and they are many—where the language is uncouth, vulgar, exaggerated, fantastic, obscene even, are entirely due to Life calling for an echo of her own voice, and rejecting the intervention of beautiful style, through which alone should Life be suffered to find expression. Shakespeare is not by any means a flawless artist. He is too fond of going directly to life, and borrowing life's natural utterance. He forgets that when Art surrenders her imaginative medium she surrenders everything. Goethe says, somewhere—'It is in working within limits that the master reveals himself,' and the limitation, the very condition of any art is style. However, we need not linger any longer over Shakespeare's realism. *The Tempest* is the most perfect of palinodes. All that we desired to point out was, that the magnificent work of the Elizabethan and Jacobean artists contained within itself the seeds of its own dissolution, and that, if it drew some of its strength from using life as a rough material, it drew all its weakness from using life as an artistic method. As the inevitable result of this substitution of an imitative for a creative medium, this surrender of an imaginative form, we have the modern

English melodrama. The characters in these plays talk on the stage exactly as they would talk off it; they have neither aspirations nor aspirates; they are taken directly from life and reproduce its vulgarity down to the smallest detail; they present the gait, manner, costume, and accent of real people; they would pass unnoticed in a third-class railway carriage. And yet how wearisome the plays are! They do not succeed in producing even that impression of reality at which they aim, and which is their only reason for existing. As a method, realism is a complete failure.

"What is true about the drama and the novel is no less true about those arts that we call the decorative arts. The whole history of these arts in Europe is the record of the struggle between Orientalism, with its frank rejection of imitation, its love of artistic convention, its dislike to the actual representation of any object in Nature, and our own imitative spirit. Wherever the former has been paramount, as in Byzantium, Sicily, and Spain, by actual contact, or in the rest of Europe by the influence of the Crusades, we have had beautiful and imaginative work in which the visible things of life are transmuted into artistic conventions, and the things that Life has not are invented and fashioned for her delight. But wherever we have returned to Life and Nature, our work has always become vulgar, common, and uninteresting. Modern tapestry, with its aërial effects, its elaborate perspective, its broad expanses of waste sky, its faithful and laborious realism, has no beauty whatsoever. The pictorial glass of Germany is absolutely detestable. We are beginning to weave possible carpets in England, but only because we have returned to the method and spirit of the East. Our rugs and carpets of twenty years ago, with their solemn depressing truths, their inane worship of Nature, their sordid reproductions of visible objects, have become, even to the Philistine, a source of laughter. A cultured Mahomedan once remarked to us, 'You Christians are so occupied in misinterpreting the fourth commandment that you have never thought of making an artistic application of the second.' He was perfectly right, and the whole truth of the matter is this: The proper school to learn art in is not Life but Art."

And now let me read you a passage which seems to me to settle the question very completely:

"It was not always thus. We need not say anything about the poets, for they, with the unfortunate exception of Mr. Wordsworth, have been really faithful to their high mission, and are universally recognized as being absolutely unreliable. But in the works of Herodotus, who, in spite of the shallow and ungenerous attempts of modern sciolists to verify his history, may justly be called the 'Father of Lies'; in the published speeches of Cicero and the biographies of Suetonius; in Tacitus at his best; in Pliny's *Natural History*; in Hanno's *Periplus*; in all the early chronicles; in the Lives of the Saints; in Froissart and Sir Thomas Mallory; in the travels of Marco Polo; in Olaus Magnus, and Aldrovandus, and Conrad Lycosthenes, with his magnificent *Prodigiorum et Ostentorum Chronicon*; in the autobiography of Benvenuto Cellini; in the memoirs of Casanuova; in Defoe's *History of the Plague*; in Boswell's *Life of Johnson*; in Napoleon's dispatches, and in the works of our own Carlyle, whose *French Revolution* is one of the most fascinating historical novels ever written, facts are either kept in their proper subordinate position, or else entirely excluded on the general ground of dullness. Now, everything is changed. Facts are not merely finding a footing-place in history, but they are usurping the domain of Fancy, and have invaded the kingdom of Romance. Their chilling touch is over everything. They are vulgarizing mankind. The crude commercialism of America, its materializing spirit, its indifference to the poetical side of things, and its lack of imagination and of high unattainable ideals, are entirely due to that country having adopted for its national hero a man, who, according to his own confession, was incapable of telling a lie, and it is not too much to say that the story of George Washington and the cherry-tree has done more harm, and in a shorter space of time, then any other moral tale in the whole of literature."

CYRIL. My dear boy!

VIVIAN. I assure you it is the case, and the amusing part of the whole thing is that the story of the cherry-tree is an absolute myth. However, you must not think that I am too despondent about the artistic future either of America or of our own country. Listen to this:

"That some change will take place before this century has drawn to its close we have no doubt whatsoever. Bored by the tedious and improving conversation of those who have neither the wit to exaggerate nor the genius to romance, tired of the intelligent person whose reminiscences are always based upon memory, whose statements are invariably limited by probability, and who is at any time liable to be corroborated by the merest Philistine who happens to be present, Society sooner or later must return to its lost leader, the cultured and fascinating liar. Who he was who first, without ever having gone out to the rude chase, told the wondering cavemen at sunset how he had dragged the Megatherium from the purple darkness of its jasper cave, or slain the Mammoth in single combat and brought back its giant tusks, we cannot tell, and not one of our modern anthropologists, for all their much-boasted science, has had the ordinary courage to tell us. Whatever was his name or race, he certainly was the true founder of social intercourse. For the aim of the liar is simply to charm, to delight, to give pleasure. He is the very basis of civilized society, and without him a dinner party, even at the mansions of the great, is as dull as a lecture at the Royal Society, or a debate at the Incorporated Authors, or one of Mr. Burnand's farcical comedies.

"Nor will he be welcomed by society alone. Art, breaking from the prison-house of realism, will run to greet him, and will kiss his false, beautiful lips, knowing that he alone is in possession of the great secret of all her manifestations, the secret that Truth is entirely and absolutely a matter of style; while Life—poor, probable, uninteresting human life—tired of repeating herself for the benefit of Mr. Herbert Spencer, scientific historians, and the compilers of statistics in general, will follow meekly after him, and try to reproduce, in her own simple and untutored way, some of the marvels of which he talks.

"No doubt there will always be critics who, like a certain writer in the *Saturday Review*, will gravely censure the teller of fairy tales for his defective knowledge of natural history, who will measure imaginative work by their own lack of any imaginative faculty, and will hold up their inkstained hands in horror if some honest gentleman, who has never been farther than the yew-trees of his own garden, pens a fascinating book of travels like Sir John Mandeville, or, like great Raleigh, writes a whole history of the world, without knowing anything whatsoever about the past. To excuse themselves they will try and shelter under the shield of him who made Prospero the magician, and gave him Caliban and Ariel as his servants, who heard the Tritons blowing their horns round the coral reefs of the Enchanted Isle, and the fairies singing to each other in a wood near Athens, who led the phantom kings in dim procession across the misty Scottish heath, and hid Hecate in a cave with the weird sisters. They will call upon Shakespeare— they always do—and will quote that hackneyed passage[7] about Art holding the mirror up to Nature, forgetting that this unfortunate aphorism is deliberately said by Hamlet in order to convince the bystanders of his absolute insanity in all art-matters."

CYRIL. Ahem! Another cigarette, please.

VIVIAN. My dear fellow, whatever you may say, it is merely a dramatic utterance, and no more represents Shakespeare's real views upon art than the speeches of Iago represent his real views upon morals. But let me get to the end of the passage:

"Art finds her own perfection within, and not outside of, herself. She is not to be judged by any external standard of resemblance. She is a veil, rather than a mirror. She has flowers that no forests know of, birds that no woodland possesses. She makes and unmakes many worlds, and can draw the moon from heaven with a scarlet thread. Hers are the 'forms more real than living man,' and hers the great archetypes of which things that have existence are but

7. *Hamlet* III. ii. 22-27.

unfinished copies. Nature has, in her eyes, no laws, no uniformity. She can work miracles at her will, and when she calls monsters from the deep they come. She can bid the almond tree blossom in winter, and send the snow upon the ripe cornfield. At her word the frost lays its silver finger on the burning mouth of June, and the winged lions creep out from the hollows of the Lydian hills. The dryads peer from the thicket as she passes by, and the brown fauns smile strangely at her when she comes near them. She has hawk-faced gods that worship her, and the centaurs gallop at her side."

CYRIL. I like that. I can see it. Is that the end?

VIVIAN. No. There is one more passage, but it is purely practical. It simply suggests some methods by which we could revive this lost art of Lying.

CYRIL. Well, before you read it to me, I should like to ask you a question. What do you mean by saying that life, "poor, probable, uninteresting human life," will try to reproduce the marvels of art? I can quite understand your objection to art being treated as a mirror. You think it would reduce genius to the position of a cracked looking-glass. But you don't mean to say that you seriously believe that Life imitates Art, that Life in fact is the mirror, and Art the reality?

VIVIAN. Certainly I do. Paradox though it may seem—and para-doxes are always dangerous things—it is none the less true that Life imitates art far more than Art imitates life. * * * A great artist invents a type, and Life tries to copy it, to reproduce it in a popular form, like an enterprising publisher. Neither Holbein nor Vandyck[8] found in England what they have given us. They brought their types with them, and Life with her keen imitative faculty set herself to supply the master with models. The Greeks, with their quick artistic instinct, understood this, and set in the bride's chamber the statue of Hermes or of Apollo, that she might bear children as lovely as the works of art that she looked at in her rapture or her pain. They knew that Life gains from Art not merely spirituality, depth of thought and feeling, soul-turmoil or soul-peace, but that she can form herself on the very lines and colors of art, and can reproduce the dignity of Phidias as well as the grace of Praxiteles. Hence came their objection to realism. They disliked it on purely social grounds. They felt that it inevi-tably makes people ugly, and they were perfectly right. We try to improve the conditions of the race by means of good air, free sunlight, wholesome water, and hideous bare buildings for the better housing of the lower orders. But these things merely pro-duce health, they do not produce beauty. For this, Art is required, and the true disciples of the great artist are not his studio-imitators,

8. Portrait painters.

but those who become like his works of art, be they plastic as in Greek days, or pictorial as in modern times; in a word, Life is Art's best, Art's only pupil.

As it is with the visible arts, so it is with literature. The most obvious and the vulgarest form in which this is shown is in the case of the silly boys who, after reading the adventures of Jack Sheppard or Dick Turpin, pillage the stalls of unfortunate apple-women, break into sweet-shops at night, and alarm old gentlemen who are returning home from the city by leaping out on them in suburban lanes, with black masks and unloaded revolvers. This interesting phenomenon, which always occurs after the appearance of a new edition of either of the books I have alluded to, is usually attributed to the influence of literature on the imagination. But this is a mistake. The imagination is essentially creative and always seeks for a new form. The boy-burglar is simply the inevitable result of life's imitative instinct. He is Fact, occupied as Fact usually is, with trying to reproduce Fiction, and what we see in him is repeated on an extended scale throughout the whole of life. Schopenhauer has analyzed the pessimism that characterizes modern thought, but Hamlet invented it. The world has become sad because a puppet was once melancholy. The Nihilist, that strange martyr who has no faith, who goes to the stake without enthusiasm, and dies for what he does not believe in, is a purely literary product. He was invented by Tourgénieff, and completed by Dostoieffski. Robespierre came out of the pages of Rousseau as surely as the People's Palace rose out of the *débris* of a novel.[9] Literature always anticipates life. It does not copy it, but molds it to its purpose. * * *

Life holds the mirror up to Art, and either reproduces some strange type imagined by painter or sculptor, or realizes in fact what has been dreamed in fiction. Scientifically speaking, the basis of life—the energy of life, as Aristotle would call it—is simply the desire for expression, and Art is always presenting various forms through which this expression can be attained. Life seizes on them and uses them, even if they be to her own hurt. Young men have committed suicide because Rolla did so, have died by their own hand because by his own hand Werther died.[1] Think of what we owe to the imitation of Christ, of what we owe to the imitation of Caesar.

CYRIL. The theory is certainly a very curious one, but to make it complete you must show that Nature, no less than Life, is an imitation of Art. Are you prepared to prove that?

VIVIAN. My dear fellow, I am prepared to prove anything.

9. The People's Palace was erected in Victorian London to provide a theater for the working class. Wilde claims that it was inspired by a fictional prototype just as (he asserts) the character of Robespierre, who rose to power in the French Revolution's Reign of Terror, was formed from the writings of Jean Jacques Rousseau.
1. Fictional heroes.

CYRIL. Nature follows the landscape painter then, and takes her effects from him?

VIVIAN. Certainly. Where, if not from the Impressionists, do we get those wonderful brown fogs that come creeping down our streets, blurring the gas-lamps and changing the houses into monstrous shadows? To whom, if not to them and their master, do we owe the lovely silver mists that brood over our river, and turn to faint forms of fading grace, curved bridge and swaying barge? The extraordinary change that has taken place in the climate of London during the last ten years is entirely due to this particular school of Art. You smile. Consider the matter from a scientific or a metaphysical point of view, and you will find that I am right. For what is Nature? Nature is no great mother who has borne us. She is our creation. It is in our brain that she quickens to life. Things are because we see them, and what we see, and how we see it, depends on the Arts that have influenced us. To look at a thing is very different from seeing a thing. One does not see anything until one sees its beauty. Then, and then only does it come into existence. At present, people see fogs, not because there are fogs, but because poets and painters have taught them the mysterious loveliness of such effects. There may have been fogs for centuries in London. I dare say there were. But no one saw them, and so we do not know anything about them. They did not exist until Art had invented them. Now, it must be admitted, fogs are carried to excess. They have become the mere mannerisms of a clique, and the exaggerated realism of their method gives dull people bronchitis. Where the cultured catch an effect, the uncultured catch cold. And so, let us be humane, and invite Art to turn her wonderful eyes elsewhere. She has done so already, indeed. That white quivering sunlight that one sees now in France, with its strange blotches of mauve, and its restless violet shadows, is her latest fancy, and, on the whole, Nature reproduces it quite admirably. Where she used to give us Corots and Daubignys, she gives us now exquisite Monets and entrancing Pisaros. Indeed, there are moments, rare, it is true, but still to be observed from time to time, when Nature becomes absolutely modern. Of course she is not always to be relied upon. The fact is that she is in this unfortunate position: Art creates an incomparable and unique effect, and, having done so, passes on to other things. Nature, upon the other hand, forgetting that imitation can be made the sincerest form of insult, keeps on repeating this effect until we all become absolutely wearied of it. Nobody of any real culture, for instance, ever talks nowadays about the beauty of a sunset. Sunsets are quite old-fashioned. They belong to the time when Turner was the last note in art. To admire them is a distinct sign of provincialism of temperament. Upon the other hand they go on. Yesterday evening Mrs. Arundel insisted on my going to the window, and looking at the glorious sky, as she called it. Of course I had to look at it. She is one of those absurdly pretty Philistines, to whom one can deny nothing. And what was it? It was simply a very second-rate Turner, a Turner of a bad period, with all the painter's worst faults exaggerated and over-emphasized. * * * But have I proved my theory to your satisfaction?

CYRIL. You have proved it to my dissatisfaction, which is better. But even admitting this strange imitative instinct in Life and Nature, surely you would acknowledge that Art expresses the temper of its age, the spirit of its time, the moral and social conditions that surround it, and under whose influence it is produced.

VIVIAN. Certainly not! Art never expresses anything but itself. This is the principle of my new aesthetics; and it is this, more than that vital connection between form and substance, on which Mr. Pater dwells, that makes music the type of all the arts. Of course, nations and individuals, with that healthy natural vanity which is the secret of existence, are always under the impression that it is of them that the Muses are talking, always trying to find in the calm dignity of imaginative art some mirror of their own turbid passions, always forgetting that the singer of life is not Apollo, but Marsyas.[2] Remote from reality, and with her eyes turned away from the shadows of the cave, Art reveals her own perfection, and the wondering crowd that watches the opening of the marvelous, many-petalled rose fancies that it is its own history that is being told to it, its own spirit that is finding expression in a new form. But it is not so. The highest art rejects the burden of the human spirit, and gains more from a new medium or a fresh material than she does from any enthusiasm for art, or from any great awakening of the human consciousness. She develops purely on her own lines. She is not symbolic of any age. It is the ages that are her symbols.

Even those who hold that Art is representative of time and place and people, cannot help admitting that the more imitative an art is, the less it represents to us the spirit of its age. The evil faces of the Roman emperors look out at us from the foul porphyry and spotted jasper in which the realistic artists of the day delighted to work, and we fancy that in those cruel lips and heavy sensual jaws we can find the secret of the ruin of the Empire. But it was not so. The vices of Tiberius could not destroy that supreme civilization, any more than the virtues of the Antonines could save it. It fell for other, for less interesting reasons. The sibyls and prophets of the Sistine may indeed serve to interpret for some that new birth of the emancipated spirit

2. In Greek mythology, Marsyas, presumptuously rivaling the god Apollo, was defeated by the god in a musical contest and flayed alive. Here Wilde presents Marsyas as typifying the false notion of art, and Apollo the true.

that we call the Renaissance; but what do the drunken boors and brawling peasants of Dutch art tell us about the great soul of Holland? The more abstract, the more ideal an art is, the more it reveals to us the temper of its age. If we wish to understand a nation by means of its art, let us look at its architecture or its music.

CYRIL. I quite agree with you there. The spirit of an age may be best expressed in the abstract ideal arts, for the spirit itself is abstract and ideal. Upon the other hand, for the visible aspect of an age, for its look, as the phrase goes, we must, of course, go to the arts of imitation.

VIVIAN. I don't think so. After all, what the imitative arts really give us are merely the various styles of particular artists, or of certain schools of artists. Surely you don't imagine that the people of the Middle Ages bore any resemblance at all to the figures on mediaeval stained glass, or in mediaeval stone and wood carving, or on mediaeval metal-work, or tapestries, or illuminated MSS. They were probably very ordinary-looking people with nothing grotesque, or remarkable, or fantastic in their appearance. The Middle Ages, as we know them in art, are simply a definite form of style, and there is no reason at all why an artist with this style should not be produced in the nineteenth century. No great artist ever sees things as they really are. If he did, he would cease to be an artist. * * * The fact is that we look back on the ages entirely through the medium of Art, and Art, very fortunately, has never once told us the truth.

CYRIL. But modern portraits by English painters, what of them? Surely they are like the people they pretend to represent?

VIVIAN. Quite so. They are so like them that a hundred years from now no one will believe in them. The only portraits in which one believes are portraits where there is very little of the sitter and a very great deal of the artist. Holbein's drawings of the men and women of his time impress us with a sense of their absolute reality. But this is simply because Holbein compelled life to accept his conditions, to restrain itself within his limitations, to reproduce his type, and to appear as he wished it to appear. It is style that makes us believe in a thing—nothing but style. Most of our modern portrait painters are doomed to absolute oblivion. They never paint what they see. They paint what the public sees, and the public never sees anything.

CYRIL. Well, after that, I think I should like to hear the end of your article.

VIVIAN. With pleasure. * * * "What we have to do, what at any rate it is our duty to do, is to revive this old art of Lying. Much, of course, may be done, in the way of educating the public, by amateurs in the domestic circle, at literary lunches, and at afternoon teas. But this is merely the light and graceful side of lying, such as was probably heard at Cretan dinner parties. There are many other forms. Lying for the sake of gaining some immediate personal advantage, for instance—lying with a moral purpose, as it is usually called—though of late it has been rather looked down upon, was extremely popular with the antique world. Athena laughs when Odysseus tells her 'his words of sly devising,' as Mr. William Morris phrases it, and the glory of mendacity illumines the pale brow of the stainless hero of Euripidean tragedy, and sets among the noble women of the past the young bride of one of Horace's most exquisite odes. Later on, what at first had been merely a natural instinct was elevated into a self-conscious science. Elaborate rules were laid down for the guidance of mankind, and an important school of literature grew up round the subject. Indeed, when one remembers the excellent philosophical treatise of Sanchez[3] on the whole question, one cannot help regretting that no one has ever thought of publishing a cheap and condensed edition of the works of that great casuist. A short primer, 'When to Lie and How,' if brought out in an attractive and not too expensive a form, would, no doubt, command a large sale, and would prove of real practical service to many earnest and deep-thinking people. Lying for the sake of the improvement of the young, which is the basis of home education, still lingers amongst us, and its advantages are so admirably set forth in the early books of Plato's *Republic* that it is unnecessary to dwell upon them here. It is a mode of lying for which all good mothers have peculiar capabilities, but it is capable of still further development, and has been sadly overlooked by the School Board. Lying for the sake of a monthly salary is, of course, well known in Fleet Street,[4] and the profession of a political leader-writer is not without its advantages. But it is said to be a somewhat dull occupation, and it certainly does not lead to much beyond a kind of ostentatious obscurity. The only form of lying that is absolutely beyond reproach is Lying for its own sake, and the highest development of this is, as we have already pointed out, Lying in Art. Just as those who do not love Plato more than Truth cannot pass beyond the threshold of the Academe, so those who do not love Beauty more than Truth never know the inmost shrine of Art. The solid, stolid British intellect lies in the desert sands like the Sphinx in Flaubert's marvelous tale, and fantasy, *La Chimère*, dances round it, and calls to it with her false, flute-toned voice. It may not hear her now, but surely some day, when we are all bored to death with the commonplace character of modern fiction, it will hearken to her and try to borrow her wings.

"And when that day dawns, or sunset reddens, how joyous we

3. Thomas Sanchez (1550-1610), Spanish Jesuit and moralist, whose works include treatment of the morality of equivocation.
4. The London street where most British newspapers have offices.

shall all be! Facts will be regarded as discreditable, Truth will be found mourning over her fetters, and Romance, with her temper of wonder, will return to the land. The very aspect of the world will change to our startled eyes. Out of the sea will rise Behemoth and Leviathan, and sail round the high-pooped galleys, as they do on the delightful maps of those ages when books on geography were actually readable. Dragons will wander about the waste places, and the phoenix will soar from her nest of fire into the air. We shall lay our hands upon the basilisk, and see the jewel in the toad's head. Champing his gilded oats, the Hippogriff will stand in our stalls, and over our heads will float the Blue Bird, singing of beautiful and impossible things, of things that are lovely and that never happen, of things that are not and that should be. But before this comes to pass, we must cultivate the lost art of Lying."

CYRIL. Then we must certainly cultivate it at once. But in order to avoid making any error, I want you to tell me briefly the doctrines of the new aesthetics.

VIVIAN. Briefly, then, they are these. Art never expresses anything but itself. It has an independent life, just as Thought has, and develops purely on its own lines. It is not necessarily realistic in an age of realism, nor spiritual in an age of faith. So far from being the creation of its time, it is usually in direct opposition to it, and the only history that it preserves for us is the history of its own progress. Sometimes it returns upon its footsteps, and revives some antique form, as happened in the archaistic movement of late Greek Art, and in the pre-Raphaelite movement of our own day. At other times it entirely anticipates its age, and produces in one century work that it takes another century to understand, to appreciate, and to enjoy. In no case does it reproduce its age. To pass from the art of a time to the time itself is the great mistake that all historians commit.

The second doctrine is this. All bad art comes from returning to Life and Nature, and elevating them into ideals. Life and Nature may sometimes be used as a part of Art's rough material, but before they are of any real service to art they must be translated into artistic conventions. The moment Art surrenders its imaginative medium it surrenders everything. As a method, Realism is a complete failure, and the two things that every artist should avoid are modernity of form and modernity of subject-matter. To us, who live in the nineteenth century, any century is a suitable subject for art except our own. The only beautiful things are the things that do not concern us. It is, to have the pleasure of quoting myself, exactly because Hecuba is nothing to us that her sorrows are so suitable a motive for a tragedy. Besides, it is only the modern that ever becomes old-fashioned. M. Zola sits down to give us a picture of the Second Empire. Who cares for the Second Empire now? It is out of date. Life goes faster than Realism, but Romanticism is always in front of Life.

The third doctrine is that Life imitates Art far more than Art imitates Life. This results not merely from Life's imitative instinct, but from the fact that the self-conscious aim of Life is to find expression, and that Art offers it certain beautiful forms through which it may realize that energy. It is a theory that has never been put forward before, but it is extremely fruitful, and throws an entirely new light upon the history of Art.

It follows, as a corollary from this, that external Nature also imitates Art. The only effects that she can show us are effects that we have already seen through poetry, or in paintings. This is the secret of Nature's charm, as well as the explanation of Nature's weakness.

The final revelation is that Lying, the telling of beautiful untrue things, is the proper aim of Art. But of this I think I have spoken at sufficient length. And now let us go out on the terrace, where "droops the milk-white peacock like a ghost," while the evening star "washes the dusk with silver." At twilight nature becomes a wonderfully suggestive effect, and is not without loveliness, though perhaps its chief use is to illustrate quotations from the poets. Come! We have talked long enough.

QUESTIONS

1. In "The Decay of Lying" Wilde advances a number of rather unusual ideas about Art and Nature. How does the dialogue form facilitate his task? How are the two speakers differentiated?

2. What, according to Vivian, is the real relation between Nature and Art? What proofs does he bring forward in support of his thesis? How persuasive are they? Indicate some further proofs or present the counterargument.

3. What illustrations from present-day life might Vivian give of his doctrine that Life imitates Art? What place might television and advertising, business and fashion have in his argument?

4. What objections has Vivian to realism in literature? Upon what assumptions does he hold realism to rest, and what refutation of those assumptions does he offer?

5. Vivian says of the realistic novelist that "he has not even the courage of other peoples' ideas" (p. 635). From what does the humor of his statement derive? Give other instances of Wilde's humor.

C. S. LEWIS

On Misreading by the Literary[1]

We must now consider a fault in reading which cuts right across our distinction between the literary and the unliterary. Some of the former are guilty of it and some of the latter are not.

Essentially, it involves a confusion between life and art, even a failure to allow for the existence of art at all. Its crudest form is pilloried in the old story of the backwoodsman in the gallery who shot the "villain" on the stage. We see it also in the lowest type of reader who wants sensational narrative but will not accept it unless it is offered him as "news." On a higher level it appears as the belief that all good books are good primarily because they give us knowledge, teach us "truths" about "life." Dramatists and novelists are praised as if they were doing, essentially, what used to be expected of theologians and philosophers, and the qualities which belong to their works as inventions and as designs are neglected. They are reverenced as teachers and insufficiently appreciated as artists. In a word, De Quincey's "literature of power" is treated as a species within his "literature of knowledge."[2]

We may begin by ruling out of consideration one way of treating fictions as sources of knowledge which, though not strictly literary, is pardonable at a certain age and usually transient. Between the ages of twelve and twenty nearly all of us acquired from novels, along with plenty of misinformation, a great deal of information about the world we live in: about the food, clothes, customs, and climates of various countries, the working of various professions, about methods of travel, manners, law, and political machinery. We were getting not a philosophy of life but what is called "general knowledge." In a particular case a fiction may serve this purpose for even an adult reader. An inhabitant of the cruel countries might come to grasp our principle that a man is innocent till he is proved guilty from reading our detective stories (in that sense such stories are a great proof of real civilization). But in general this use of fiction is abandoned as we grow older. The curiosities it used to satisfy have been satisfied or simply died away, or, if they survive, would now seek information from more reliable sources. That is one reason why we have less inclination to take up a new novel than we had in our youth.

Having got this special case out of the way, we may now return to the real subject.

1. Chapter 8 in *An Experiment in Criticism*, 1961.
2. See De Quincey, "Literature of Knowledge and Literature of Power," pp. 224-226.

It is obvious that some of the unliterary mistake art for an account of real life. As we have seen, those whose reading is conducted, egotistic castle-building will inevitably do so. They wish to be deceived; they want to feel that though these beautiful things have not really happened to them, yet they might. ("He might take a fancy to me like that Duke did to that factory girl in the story.") But it is equally obvious that a great many of the unliterary are not in this state at all—are indeed almost safer from it than anyone else. Try the experiment on your grocer or gardener. You cannot often try it about a book, for he has read few, but a film will do just as well for our purpose. If you complain to him about the gross improbability of its happy ending, he will very probably reply "Ah. I reckon they just put that in to wind it up like." If you complain about the dull and perfunctory love-interest which has been thrust into a story of masculine adventure, he will say "Oh well, you know, they usually got to put in a bit of that. The women like it." He knows perfectly well that the film is art, not knowledge. In a sense his very unliterariness saves him from confusing the two. He never expected the film to be anything but transitory, and not very important, entertainment; he never dreamed that any art could provide more than this. He goes to the pictures not to learn but to relax. The idea that any of his opinions about the real world could be modified by what he saw there would seem to him preposterous. Do you take him for a fool? Turn the conversation from art to life—gossip with him, bargain with him—and you will find he is as shrewd and realistic as you can wish.

Contrariwise, we find the error, in a subtle and especially insidious form, among the literary. When my pupils have talked to me about Tragedy (they have talked much less often, uncompelled, about tragedies), I have sometimes discovered a belief that it is valuable, is worth witnessing or reading, chiefly because it communicates something called the tragic "view" or "sense" or "philosophy" of "life." This content is variously described, but in the most widely diffused version it seems to consist of two propositions: (1) That great miseries result from a flaw in the principal sufferer; (2) That these miseries, pushed to the extreme, reveal to us a certain splendor in man, or even in the universe. Though the anguish is great, it is at least not sordid, meaningless, or merely depressing.

No one denies that miseries with such a cause and such a close can occur in real life. But if tragedy is taken as a comment on life in the sense that we are meant to conclude from it "This is the typical or usual, or ultimate, form of human misery," then tragedy becomes wishful moonshine. Flaws in character do cause suffering; but bombs and bayonets, cancer and polio, dictators and road hogs, fluctations in the value of money or in employment, and mere meaningless coincidence, cause a great deal more. Tribulation falls on the integrated and well adjusted and prudent as readily as on anyone else. Nor do real miseries often end with a curtain and a roll of drums "in calm of mind, all passion spent." The dying seldom make magnificent last speeches. And we who watch them die do not, I think, behave very like the minor characters in a tragic death scene. For unfortunately the play is not over. We have no *exeunt omnes*. The real story does not end: it proceeds to ringing up undertakers, paying bills, getting death certificates, finding and proving a will, answering letters of condolence. There is no grandeur and no finality. Real sorrow ends neither with a bang nor a whimper. Sometimes, after a spiritual journey like Dante's, down to the center and then, terrace by terrace, up the mountain of accepted pain, it may rise into peace—but a peace hardly less severe than itself. Sometimes it remains for life, a puddle in the mind which grows always wider, shallower, and more unwholesome. Sometimes it just peters out, as other moods do. One of these alternatives has grandeur, but not tragic grandeur. The other two—ugly, slow, bathetic, unimpressive—would be of no use at all to a dramatist. The tragedian dare not present the totality of suffering as it usually is in its uncouth mixture of agony with littleness, all the indignities and (save for pity) the uninterestingness, of grief. It would ruin his play. It would be merely dull and depressing. He selects from the reality just what his art needs; and what it needs is the exceptional. Conversely, to approach anyone in real sorrow with these ideas about tragic grandeur, to insinuate that he is now assuming that "sceptred pall," would be worse than imbecile: it would be odious.

Next to a world in which there were no sorrows we should like one where sorrows were always significant and sublime. But if we allow the "tragic view of life" to make us believe that we live in such a world, we shall be deceived. Our very eyes teach us better. Where in all nature is there anything uglier and more undignified than an adult male face blubbered and distorted with weeping? And what's behind it is not much prettier. There is no sceptre and no pall.

It seems to me undeniable, that tragedy, taken as a philosophy of life, is the most obstinate and best camouflaged of all wish-fulfillments, just because its pretensions are so apparently realistic. The claim is that it has faced the worst. The conclusion that, despite the worst, some sublimity and significance remains, is therefore as convincing as the testimony of a witness who appears to speak against his will. But the claim that it has faced the worst—at any rate the commonest sort of "worst"—is in my opinion simply false.

It is not the fault of the tragedians that this claim deceives certain readers, for the tragedians never made it. It is critics who make it. The tragedians chose for their themes stories (often grounded in the mythical and impossible) suitable to the art they practiced. Almost by definition, such stories would be atypical, striking, and in various other ways adapted to the purpose. Stories with a sublime and satisfying *finale* were chosen not because such a *finale* is characteristic of human misery, but because it is necessary to good drama.

It is probably from this view of tragedy that many young people derive the belief that tragedy is essentially "truer to life" than comedy. This seems to me wholly unfounded. Each of these forms chooses out of real life just those sorts of events it needs. The raw materials are all around us, mixed anyhow. It is selection, isolation, and patterning, not a philosophy, that makes the two sorts of play. The two products do not contradict one another any more than two nosegays plucked out of the same garden. Contradiction comes in only when we (not the dramatists) turn them into propositions such as "This is what human life is like."

It may seem odd that the same people who think comedy less true than tragedy often regard broad farce as realistic. I have often met the opinion that in turning from the *Troilus* to his *faibliaux* Chaucer was drawing nearer to reality. I think this arises from a failure to distinguish between realism of presentation and realism of content. Chaucer's farce is rich in realism of presentation; not in that of content. Criseyde and Alisoun are equally probable women, but what happens in the *Troilus* is very much more probable than what happens in the *Miller's Tale*. The world of farce is hardly less ideal than that of pastoral. It is a paradise of jokes where the wildest coincidences are accepted and where all works together to produce laughter. Real life seldom succeeds in being, and never remains for more than a few minutes, nearly as funny as a well-invented farce. That is why the people feel that they cannot acknowledge the comicality of a real situation more emphatically than by saying "It's as good as a play."

All three forms of art make the abstractions proper to them. Tragedies omit the clumsy and apparently meaningless bludgeoning of much real misfortune and the prosaic littlenesses which usually rob real sorrows of their dignity. Comedies ignore the possibility that the marriage of lovers does not always lead to permanent, nor even to perfect, happiness. Farce excludes pity for its butts in situations where, if they were real, they would deserve it. None of the three kinds is making a statement about life in general. They are all constructions: things made *out* of the stuff of real life; additions to life rather than comments on it.

At this point I must take pains not to be misunderstood. The great artist—or at all events the great literary artist—cannot be a man shallow either in his thoughts or his feelings. However improbable and abnormal a story he has chosen, it will, as we say, "come to life" in his hands. The life to which it comes will be impregnated with all the wisdom, knowledge, and experience the author has; and even more by something which I can only vaguely describe as the flavor or "feel" that actual life has for him. It is this omnipresent flavor or feel that makes bad inventions so mawkish and suffocating, and good ones so tonic. The good ones allow us temporarily to share a sort of passionate sanity. And we may also—which is less important—expect to find in them many psychological truths and profound, at least profoundly felt, reflections. But all this comes to us, and was very possibly called out of the poet, as the "spirit" (using that word in a quasi-chemical sense) of a work of art, a play. To formulate it as a philosophy, even if it were a rational philosophy, and regard the actual play as primarily a vehicle for that philosophy, is an outrage to the thing the poet has made for us.

I use the words *thing* and *made* advisedly. We have already mentioned, but not answered, the question whether a poem "should not mean but be." What guards the good reader from treating a tragedy—he will not talk much about an abstraction like "Tragedy"—as a mere vehicle for truth is his continual awareness that it not only means, but is. It is not merely *logos* (something said) but *poiema* (something made). The same is true of a novel or narrative poem. They are complex and carefully made objects. Attention to the very objects they are is our first step. To value them chiefly for reflections which they may suggest to us or morals we may draw from them, is a flagrant instance of "using" instead of "receiving."

What I mean by "objects" need not remain mysterious. One of the prime achievements in every good fiction has nothing to do with truth or philosophy or a *Weltanschauung* at all. It is the triumphant adjustment of two different kinds of order. On the one hand, the events (the mere plot) have their chronological and causal order, that which they would have in real life. On the other, all the scenes or other divisions of the work must be related to each other according to principles of design, like the masses in a picture or the passages in a symphony. Our feelings and imaginations must be led through "taste after taste, upheld with kindliest change." Contrasts (but also premonitions and echoes) between the darker and the lighter, the swifter and the slower, the simpler and the more sophisticated, must have something like a balance, but never a too perfect symmetry, so that the shape of the whole work will be felt as inevitable and satisfying. Yet this second order must never confuse the first. The transition from the "platform" to the court scene at the beginning of *Hamlet*, the placing of Aeneas' narrative in *Aeneid* ii and iii, or the darkness in the first two books of *Paradise Lost* leading to the ascent in the third, are simple illustrations. But there is yet another requisite. As little as possible must exist solely for the sake of other things. Every episode, explanation, description, dialogue—ideally every sentence—must be pleasureable and interesting for its own sake. (A fault in Conrad's *Nostromo* is that we have to read so much pseudo-history before we get to the central matter, for which alone this history exists.)

Some will discount this as "mere technique." We must certainly agree that these orderings, apart from that which they order, are worse than "mere"; they are nonentities, as shape is a nonentity apart from the body whose shape it is. But an "appreciation" of sculpture which ignored the statue's shape in favor of the sculptor's "view of life" would be self-deception. It is by the shape that it is a statue. Only because it is a statue do we come to be mentioning the sculptor's view of life at all.

It is very natural that when we have gone through the ordered movements which a great play or narrative excites in us—when we have danced that dance or enacted that ritual or submitted to that pattern—it should suggest to us many interesting reflections. We have "put on mental muscle" as a result of this activity. We may thank Shakespeare or Dante for that muscle, but we had better not father on them the philosophical or ethical use we make of it. For one thing, this use is unlikely to rise very much—it may rise a little—above our own ordinary level. Many of the comments on life which people get out of Shakespeare could have been reached by very moderate talents without his assistance. For another, it may well impede future receptions of the work itself. We may go back to it chiefly to find further confirmation for our belief that it teaches this or that, rather than for a fresh immersion in what it is. We shall be like a man poking his fire, not to boil the kettle or warm the room, but in the hope of seeing in it the same pictures he saw yesterday. And since a text is "but a cheverel glove"[3] to a determined critic—since everything can be a symbol, or an irony, or an ambiguity—we shall easily find what we want. The supreme objection to this is that which lies against the popular use of all the arts. We are so busy doing things with the work that we give it too little chance to work on us. Thus increasingly we meet only ourselves.

But one of the chief operations of art is to remove our gaze from that mirrored face, to deliver us from that solitude. When we read the "literature of knowledge" we hope, as a result, to think more correctly and clearly. In reading imaginative work, I suggest, we should be much less concerned with altering our own opinions— though this of course is sometimes their effect—than with entering fully into the opinions, and therefore also the attitudes, feelings, and total experience, of other men. Who in his ordinary senses

---

3. A kidskin glove, which can easily be turned inside out. See Shakespeare's   *Twelfth Night,* III.i.13.

would try to decide between the claims of materialism and theism by reading Lucretius and Dante? But who in his literary senses would not delightedly learn from them a great deal about what it is like to be a materialist or a theist?

In good reading there ought to be no "problem of belief." I read Lucretius and Dante at a time when (by and large) I agreed with Lucretius. I have read them since I came (by and large) to agree with Dante. I cannot find that this has much altered my experience, or at all altered my evaluation, of either. A true lover of literature should be in one way like an honest examiner, who is prepared to give the highest marks to the telling, felicitous, and well-documented exposition of views he dissents from or even abominates.

The sort of misreading I here protest against is unfortunately encouraged by the increasing importance of "English Literature" as an academic discipline. This directs to the study of literature a great many talented, ingenious, and diligent people whose real interests are not specifically literary at all. Forced to talk incessantly about books, what can they do but try to make books into the sort of things they can talk about? Hence literature becomes for them a religion, a philosophy, a school of ethics, a psychotherapy, a sociology—anything rather than a collection of works of art. Lighter works—*divertissements*—are either disparaged or misrepresented as being really far more serious than they look. But to a real lover of literature an exquisitely made *divertissement* is a very much more respectable thing than some of the "philosophies of life" which are foisted upon the great poets. For one thing, it is a good deal harder to make.

This is not to say that all critics who extract such a philosophy from their favorite novelists or poets produce work without value. Each attributes to his chosen author what he believes to be wisdom; and the sort of thing that seems to him wise will of course be determined by his own caliber. If he is a fool he will find and admire foolishness, if he is a mediocrity, platitude, in all his favorites. But if he is a profound thinker himself, what he acclaims and expounds as his author's philosophy may be well worth reading, even if it is in reality his own. We may compare him to the long succession of divines who have based edifying and eloquent sermons on some straining of their texts. The sermon, though bad exegesis, was often good homiletics in its own right.

QUESTIONS

1. *What objection does Lewis oppose to the belief that all good books are good because they give us knowledge, teach us "truths" about life? Is the objection valid? Does Lewis suppose life has no truths?*

2. What, by Lewis' account, is "the tragic view of life"? Why does he call it a wish-fulfillment? Do you agree with this judgment of the tragic view? Is the tragic view of life more realistic than the comic view? Explain.

3. Why, according to Lewis, should we consider matters of technique when we attend to a work of art or literature? Does attention to technique distract from the meaning of the work, from, for instance, the view of life it contains?

4. Lewis writes, "Many of the comments on life which people get out of Shakespeare could have been reached by very moderate talents without his assistance." Would "To thine own self be true" (from Polonius' speech in Hamlet, i.3. 55–81) be an example of Lewis' point? Does Lewis mean that Shakespeare was a rather mediocre philosopher?

5. Both Lewis and Northrop Frye ("The Keys to Dreamland," pp. 624–633) treat of literature, examining conceptions of it and assumptions about its relationship to life. Compare their approaches to the subject in relation to the audiences their respective essays appear to have in view.

RICHARD D. ALTICK
Textual Study[1]

Nobody yet knows how it happened, but happen it did: in the first American edition of Henry James's *The Ambassadors*, Chapter 29 was printed before Chapter 28. Whether or not James was somehow responsible, we do not know; he supervised the first London edition, published two months earlier in 1903, and there the chapters were in the right order. Whatever its cause, the transposition persisted in all American editions, and not until 1950 was attention called to it. In 1955 the publishers, Harper and Brothers, announced that the forthcoming reprinting of *The Ambassadors* in their Modern Classics Series would finally present the chapters in the right order. *Hubris*[2] is as sure an invitation to disaster in the publishing trade as anywhere else, and Harpers promptly had a great fall; for in the new edition, Chapter 29 once again preceded Chapter 28. After corporate prayer and fasting, Harpers sent the book back to press in 1957, and, to their relief, the chapters finally came out in the right order. But the next year the firm leased their rights to Doubleday for an Anchor paperback edition. "That edition," they wrote in their house organ in November, 1958, "has just been published and with a flourish (how well we recall *our* April, 1955, announcement) the Anchor people have proclaimed to

1. From *The Art of Literary Research*, 1963. 2. "Over-confidence."

the world that *here* is an edition of the novel with *all chapters in their proper sequence.* And you know what? They aren't."

Subsequently, to bring the story down to date, several paperback *Ambassadors* have had the chapters in correct sequence. But it would be a rash prophet who could assure the world that henceforth, without fail, Chapter 28 will precede Chapter 29.[3]

From this it appears that some errors are, in the strictest sense, incorrigible. They simply refuse to give way to truth. And the attention this bibliographical comedy attracted during its long run in the 1950's was a symptom of the times. Although scholars had long been insisting on textual accuracy, it was the new critical stress upon close reading that focused interest as never before on the very words the author wrote. To be sure, most "new critics" seemed themselves not to care whether their texts were, in fact, faithful to the last comma of the writer's intention. Many a *gaffe* could have been avoided had they—as well as critics of quite different schools—taken pains to be sure they were talking about precisely what *had* come from his pen; the late F. O. Matthiessen, for instance, conceivably would not have lavished so much admiration on what he took to be the *discordia concors*[4] of the "soiled fish" image in *White-Jacket* (Chapter XCII) had he known that "soiled" was a printer's error for the "coiled" that Melville had written.[5] But if critics, in pursuit of hidden subtleties, often failed to distinguish between the author's true intention and a casual misprint, with every passing year scholars became more conscious of the number of error-spotted versions of masterpieces that have passed down to us through the hands of careless printers and easygoing editors and, in lack of better ones, remain the texts upon which critical discussion rests. Today we realize that accurate texts are indispensable to the progress of literary study. It is futile to try to interpret and evaluate any work of art on the basis of an imperfect reproduction. Before we presume to judge an author's meaning and the artistic terms in which he conveys it, we had better be sure we have his *exact* words before us.[6]

The most bountiful case in point is Shakespeare, the textual history of whose plays is incredibly complicated. Half of them appeared in one or more quartos (small-format printings of individual plays) which preceded the first collected ("folio") edition of 1623, and the readings of which differ among themselves as well as

3. For a review of this curious story, see Leon Edel, "The Text of *The Ambassadors*," *Harvard Library Bulletin*, XIV, (1960), 453-60 [Altick's note].

4. A harmony arrived at by a combining of inharmonious elements.

5. John W. Nichol, "Melville's ' "Soiled" Fish of the Sea,' " *American Literature*, XXI (1949), 338-39 [Altick's note].

6. As M. J. C. Hodgart has observed, however ("Misquotation as Recreation," *Essays in Criticism*, III [1953], 28–38), inaccurate quotation on the part of both poets and critics sometimes has its own critical significance, representing an attempt at "creative rewriting." But the inadvertent emendations are seldom as good as the authentic originals [Altick's note].

from the folio. Moreover, we now know that even among individual copies of the same printing, which one would expect to be identical, there may be hundreds of textual variations. This discovery was made possible by the invention of the Hinman Collating Machine, an ingenious optical device which, by superimposing on a screen the images of two different copies of a printing, opened at the same page, shows up minute differences of typesetting. And besides the quartos and the four seventeenth-century folios, there have been scores of eighteenth-century and later editions whose editors have constantly introduced their own readings or emendations. For the past fifty years, an immense amount of labor has gone into straightening out all this confusion and returning as nearly as possible to what Shakespeare presumably wrote. Meanwhile ordinary readers continue to use texts which are far from authoritative; the editions most commonly used in the classroom, for instance, are based on the "Globe" text, which was prepared a century ago, long before the advent of scientific textual study.

Although for sheer prolific quantity of error and more or less capricious emendation the Shakespeare canon is probably unmatched in the history of English literature, many other classic texts have suffered the same way, beginning with the original printer's misreading of copy and continuing through subsequent misadventures in the printing house and at the nodding or overingenious editor's desk. Between 1711–12, when the *Spectator* papers were first printed, and 1868, when Henry Morley prepared what remains the best critical edition, some 3,000 corruptions worked their way into the text.[7] Except for Jane Austen, no nineteenth-century English novelist can be read in a textually reliable collected edition. Modern trade editions of Dickens, for instance, usually trace their text back to one or another of the editions published in his lifetime, not necessarily representing either the version that the first readers saw or the last version Dickens approved, and are disfigured by a generous accretion of subsequent printer's errors. American editions of nineteenth- and twentieth-century British writers are notoriously undependable, since they were often set up from uncorrected proofs or advance sheets of the British edition and suffered further indignities at the hands of American editors and printers. Hardy's American admirers, as Carl J. Weber has demonstrated with many examples, seldom read exactly what their English contemporaries did; in the Harper edition of *The Return of the Native* that was long current, a whole page was missing, and until very recently all of the American editions of *The Woodlanders* reproduced the novel's magazine text, without taking account of the

7. Donald F. Bond, "The Text of the   [Altick's note].
Spectator," SB, V (1952/3), 109–28

numerous changes Hardy had made in successive London editions.[8]

The list of great literary works which until lately have been, and in many cases still are, read in undependable texts could be extended almost indefinitely. Beginning with the second edition, the type for which was set hastily to meet an unexpected demand and was not proofread by Hawthorne, the text of *The Scarlet Letter* became more and more corrupt, until the "standard" text of 1883 contained many hundreds of variants from the first edition. Only in 1961 did the first-edition text, the only one Hawthorne corrected, become available in a modern printing.[9] David Daiches has pointed out that "in the first one-volume American edition of the collected poems of W. B. Yeats there are at least half a dozen misprints which completely change the meaning of the passages in which they occur, and in some cases critics have actually analyzed the misprinted poems unaware of the errors, and have justified and even praised the mistaken words. The printing of 'he' as 'she' at the end of the second stanza of 'Crazy Jane on the Day of Judgment' changes the meaning of the whole poem, for the poem is a dialogue and the misprint transfers a key statement to the wrong speaker." Similarly, the substitution of the sixth line for the second in another dialogue poem, "Cuchulain's Fight with the Sea," had the effect of attributing every subsequent speech to the wrong speaker.[1] But this is only one aspect—the most accidental—of the perplexity that attends a study of Yeats's texts, for he was a ceaseless reviser and his poems, even after publication, were in a constant state of flux.

The best text of *The Great Gatsby* is found in Fitzgerald's posthumous *Three Novels*. Of the seventy-five significant changes between the first edition and the latter text, thirty-eight were suggested by Fitzgerald, the rest being inserted by the publisher without his authorization—and, conversely, a number of other corrections which the novelist proposed were *not* made. Thus even the "best" text does not represent the way Fitzgerald wanted his book to read.[2]

In this highly unsatisfactory state of affairs, the textual scholar has acquired greatly enlarged importance. It is he who produces a certified copy of a literary text, so that the interpretive critic has an absolutely authentic basis for his exegesis. But to identify or reconstruct a "sound" or "pure" text is a complicated job, because the

8. "American Editions of English Authors," *Nineteenth Century English Books* (Urbana, Ill., 1952), pp. 27–50 *passim* [Altick's note].

9. It is interesting to note that some of the most authoritative texts now available are those found in paperback editions prepared by scholars for classroom use [Altick's note].

1. *Critical Approaches to Literature* (New York, 1956) pp. 332–33. See also Russell K. Alspach, "Some Textual Problems in Yeats," *SB*, IX (1957), 51–67 [Altick's note].

2. Bruce Harkness, "Bibliography and the Novelistic Fallacy," *SB*, XII (1959), 59–73 [Altick's note].

histories of individual books vary greatly and it is often hard to decide which of several available versions should be used as "copy text." The three earliest printings of the *Spectator*—the original folio sheets (contemporary newspaper format), the first collected edition (in octavo volumes), and the second (in duodecimo)— "differ widely," as Donald Bond has reported, "not only in punctuation, spelling, and capitalization, but in phrasing, in grammatical construction, and in literary style. For how many of these changes—in spelling, for example—were Steele and Addison responsible? How many were due to the style of the printinghouse, or to the care—or negligence—of the compositor?"[3] Sometimes complexity is heaped on complexity by the existence of manuscript and other versions which deviate at many points from the received printed text. The editor of John Stuart Mill's *Autobiography*, for example, must cope with at least four versions: an early manuscript draft (printed for the first time in 1961), a second draft (from which the "Columbia" text of 1924 was printed), a copy prepared for the press after Mill's death (and containing over 2,650 variants from the manuscript on which it was based), and the printed first edition of 1873.[4]

Sir Walter Greg, whose article on "The Rationale of Copy-Text" (*Studies in Bibliography*, III [1950/51], 19–36) is a *locus classicus* for modern methodology, had some preference for the earliest printed text as the most authoritative, because it was closest to the writer's manuscript. A reprint whose text has been thoroughly revised by the author, however, seemed to Greg to have at least the authority of a first edition. He concluded, therefore, that "it seems impossible to lay down any hard and fast rule as. to when an editor should take the original edition as his copy-text and when the revised reprint. All that can be said is that if the original be selected, then the author's corrections must be incorporated; and that if the reprint be selected, then the original reading must be restored when that of the reprint is due to unauthorized variation [such as a compositor's error or a publishing-house editor's "improvement"]. Thus the editor cannot escape the responsibility of distinguishing to the best of his ability the two categories."

Greg, who died in 1959 at the age of eighty-three, was one of the pioneers (R. B. McKerrow and A. W. Pollard being two noteworthy coadjutors) of the so-called "new bibliography," a British-made discipline as sophisticated, and in its own sphere as epoch-making, as the American-bred "new criticism" was to be somewhat later. Their purpose was, by reconstructing the steps by which an older author's manuscript found its way into print, to discover what vicissitudes the text may have suffered in the process.

---

3. Bond (cited earlier, in note 7), p. 112 [Altick's note].

4. Jack Stillinger, "The Text of John Stuart Mill's *Autobiography*," *Bulletin of the John Rylands Library*, XLIII (1960), 220–42 [Altick's note].

Their laboriously acquired knowledge of the conditions and practices that prevailed in the English book trade during the sixteenth
and seventeenth centuries made possible the production (by themselves and others) of editions of Renaissance literary works, most
notably the printed drama, that are closer to the authors' manuscripts than any editions which preceded them. In the last two decades or so, a new generation of editors have been turning their
attention to establishing the texts of writers since Dryden, for it
has become recognized that the corruptions in the received versions
of post-1700 literary works are as numerous, and often have as
much effect on meaning, as those which have marred the editions
of earlier writers.

Hard physical evidence, higher mathematics (the title of a basic
book in the field—another of Greg's works—is *The Calculus of
Variants*), and rigorous logical procedures dominate the bibliographical techniques that are preliminary to textual study. Although
many practitioners, including R. C. Bald and Jacob Blanck,
deny that their discipline is a "science," on the ground that
the results they obtain lack absolute certitude, their procedures are
thoroughly scientific. Success in textual study requires talents similar to those the scientist possesses: among them endless patience in
dealing with the minutiae of physical and textual differences in
books, a gift for detecting significant relationships in a seeming
chaos of fragmentary data, and the ability to re-create the often
complicated printing history of a literary work on the basis of these
technical data.

The specialized knowledge necessary to study the textual history
of printed books lies in the province of "analytical," "descriptive"
and "critical" bibliography. These are Fredson Bowers' terms. *Analytical* bibliography is the "technical investigation of the printing of
specific books, or of general printing practice, based exclusively on
the physical evidence of the books themselves"; *descriptive* bibliography involves using all the data and methods of analytic bibliography to describe the physical format (and thus the printing history) of a given book; *critical* bibliography is "the application of
the evidence of analytical bibliography . . . to textual problems
where meaning of some sort is involved."[5]

The classic guide to the field is McKerrow's *Introduction to Bibliography for Literary Students* (1927), a work whose contents
every prospective literary scholar should master, although it has
been amplified and, in a few minor details, corrected by later
research. Once one has learned from McKerrow the procedures followed in the shop that printed Shakespeare's first folio, he can
apply that knowledge to any problem in book production down to

5. "Bibliography, Pure Bibliography, (1952), 191–96 [Altick's note].
and Literary Studies," *PBSA*, XLVI

the introduction of steam printing and stereotyping in the early decades of the nineteenth century.

In all literary study there are few more absorbing topics than the hazards an author's manuscript underwent between the time he delivered it to the printer and the moment the printed and folded sheets of the book were ready for the binder. There was the form of the manuscript itself, fit to baffle any typesetter—illegible handwriting, cryptic interlineations, balloons in the margins, additional matter (inadequately indicated) on the other side of the leaf, abbreviations to be interpreted. There were the manifold accidents of typesetting—reaching into the wrong compartment (or into the right compartment into which a printer's devil had negligently put the wrong type) and consequently setting a wrong letter; the "memorial" errors attendant on trying to keep too large a phrase of the copy in mind before taking another look at the manuscript; possibly the mishearing of a word if the copy was read aloud to the compositor; distractions of every sort, including the many occasions that called for a drink or two (a newly qualified journeyman, completion of a big job, a religious or civic festival). The history of literary texts was deeply affected by what we may call the factor of the trembling hand and the blurred eyesight, as well as by all the other human conditions that conspired to produce an imperfect book: "a harassed author, a testy master printer, a stupid proofreader, a love-sick compositor, a drunken pressman, a newly-articled apprentice."[6] The wonder is not so much that early books contain so many errors, as that, given the conditions under which their type was set, they contain so few. Although many authors supposedly were indifferent to the state in which their well-chosen words finally were set before the public, from the very beginning there were occasional tense scenes in the printing house, such as the one suggested by Thomas Heywood's bitter words:

> The infinite faults escaped in my booke of *Britaines Troy*, by the negligence of the Printer, as the misquotations, mistaking of sillables, misplacing halfe lines, coining of strange and neuer heard of words. These being without number, when I would haue taken a particular account of the *Errata*, the Printer answered me, hee would not publish his own disworkemanship, but rather let his owne fault lye vpon the necke of the Author....[7]

Our knowledge of the way printers worked in the earlier centuries is still far from exhaustive, but it is steadily growing, and as it does, the assumptions on which we base our reconstruction of a book's textual history have to be revised. One recent discovery, the implications of which are unusually far-reaching, is that type was not set in consecutive page order, as one would copy a manuscript on the typewriter. Instead, Elizabethan printers were governed by

6. R. C. Bald, "Evidence and Inference in Bibliography," *English Institute Annual 1941* (New York, 1942), p. 162 [Altick's note].

7. *An Apology for Actors* (London, 1612), sig. [G4]ʳ [Altick's note].

the fact that the composed type for all the pages that would make up one side of a printed sheet had to be arranged in a certain systematic, but non-progressive, order in the frame upon which the sheet was laid to receive the inked impression of the type. Thus a compositor first set page 6, then pages 7, 5, 8, 4, 9, 3, 10, 2, 11, 1, and 12; or if two men were working, the first would set 6, 5, 4, 3, 2, and 1, in that order, while the other set 7, 8, 9, 10, 11, and 12. This system meant, of course, that the foreman had to "cast off" copy beforehand—that is, go through the manuscript or printed book and mark off as much copy as he expected to occupy each page of the new setting. The state of the copy naturally affected the precision with which this could be done. If the type were to be set from a printed book or a reasonably clean manuscript, an experienced printer could predict fairly accurately how much matter would go into a single page. But, as Charlton Hinman, who made this discovery, says, "real difficulty would probably be encountered . . . in copy very untidily made up from various sources, interlined, supplied with marginal annotations partly in verse and partly in prose, and so on"; hence, "miscalculations would be inevitable and gross inaccuracy would be more likely to occur with edited than with unedited copy." To take up slack or, on the other hand, to pack more matter into a page than had been allowed for, the typesetter resorted to various typographical or outright verbal alterations—dividing a line into two, running two lines into one, omitting a word (or line) or two, and so forth. The more evidence that is found of forced expansion and compression in response to the arbitrary space requirements imposed by casting-off, the greater the likelihood that a book was set from copy that was hard to estimate and to follow.[8]

By similar analysis of evidence, Hinman and other modern specialists have also shown how many compositors set a given book, and for which pages or formes each was responsible. It was previously known that the tragedies in the Shakespeare First Folio were set by three compositors, one of whom probably was an apprentice (each typesetter's work has its own peculiarities). But Hinman went a step further by identifying parts of *Hamlet, Othello,* and *Lear* which the apprentice seems to have composed. His work was most inexpert, requiring constant correction before printing (the signs of which are readily evident to an expert, and Hinman concluded that because of his incompetence he was not allowed to set copy from manuscript but was, instead, limited to relatively easy-to-follow printed text.[9]

The intricate reasoning by which specialists arrive at such conclusions is fascinating to watch, but the results are what count. Inferences derived from the practice of casting-off and from the habits

8. "Cast-off Copy for the First Folio of Shakespeare," *Shakespeare Quarterly,* VI (1955), 259–73 [Altick's note].

9. "The Prentice Hand in the Tragedies of the Shakespeare First Folio," *SB,* IX (1957), 3–20 [Altick's note].

and competence of individual typesetters, fitted in with various other kinds of textual evidence, are the closest we can get to establishing the nature of the copy from which a Shakespearean play was set—whether an earlier quarto (which may have been comparatively unmarked or, on the other hand, lavishly corrected), or a clean manuscript, or a much battered and amended one, or a bewildering patchwork made from two or more of these. And the nearer we come to deciding what that copy was like, the more confident can be the subsequent process of deducing, from the printed text that eventually emerged, the exact words the typesetter had before him.

The changes that have occurred in the publishing trade and printing techniques since 1800 have complicated the textual editor's task. More and more books first appeared as serials in periodicals, and often, as was true of Hardy's novels, important changes were made in the text when it was printed as a volume. Hence, the editor must meticulously compare the magazine text with that of the first and subsequent book-form editions. Again, although the invention of stereotypes tended to stabilize a text, since there was no longer any standing type to be reset every time someone thought of an alteration, the fact that successive editions were printed from the same plates does not eliminate the possibility that changes were made in those plates between printings—or the further possibility that, as one error was corrected, another was invented. The use of duplicate plates for large press runs, one set of which is corrected and the other not, as in the case of Sinclair Lewis' *Babbitt*, adds one more complexity to the textual study of modern authors.[1]

Thus far I have been talking about textual study as if it were primarily concerned with printed books and the evidence they can be made to yield about the nature of the (no longer extant) manuscript which lay before the original compositor. This kind of textual work is at present more in the scholarly limelight because of both the novelty and sophistication of its methods and the dramatic results it has produced. But textual criticism of another sort is much older: the branch that deals with the history and relationships of existing, and sometimes also of hypothetical, manuscripts. It began as long ago as the early Renaissance, with the humanists' attempts to determine, from a critical examination of codices (manuscripts), the oldest of which were still several centuries removed from the originals, the text of the books of the New Testament and of the Greek and Latin classics.

At the end of the nineteenth century, the techniques that had

1. Matthew J. Bruccoli, "Textual Variants in Sinclair Lewis's *Babbitt*," *SB*, XI (1958), 263–68 [Altick's note].

been developed in Biblical and classical studies began to be applied to English literature, especially to works written before the printing press was invented and of which, therefore, a number of manuscript copies were made. The essential problem was—and is—to establish the date and place of origin of each manuscript and thus, eventually, to construct a pedigree (technically known as a *stammbaum* or *stemma codicum*), at the top of which will stand the manuscript which presumably is closest to the lost original. Sometimes this genealogical diagram will involve hundreds of manuscripts, each with its peculiar variants of phraseology and dialect, its omissions and insertions and different placements of specific lines or passages, its obvious mistakes, and all the other idiosyncrasies that help the scholar to determine its place in the history of the author's text. Of Chaucer's *Canterbury Tales*, there are some ninety manuscripts and early printed versions, either of groups of tales or the whole sequence. An examination of the Manly-Rickert edition based on all these texts will give as impressive an idea as one could wish of the problems an editor faces as he seeks to work back through the maze of later versions to Chaucer's own words.

Needless to say, this kind of research, which ordinarily concentrates on medieval and early Renaissance texts, is not for the novice. One must be able to interpret the significance of scribal errors, dialectal variations, and other varieties of characteristic corruptions for the sake of placing each manuscript in its appropriate chronological-genealogical slot and, more important, of suggesting emendations that will clarify the meaning. In addition, an expert knowledge of paleography, the study of medieval and Renaissance handwriting, is essential. A certain amount of the requisite knowledge and technical skill can be acquired by reading, but only experience with actual manuscripts, under firm guidance, can produce a finished textual critic.

The complete textual scholar must of course be at home among both manuscripts and printed books. In some types of investigation he has to deal with only one category: a student of *Piers Plowman*, for example, has little to do with printed texts, but his hands are full enough with the sixty-odd manuscript copies that represent three different versions of the poem. An editor of Spenser, on the other hand, has only printed books to cope with. But beginning about the time of Ben Jonson, authors' manuscripts start to survive side by side with the printed texts, and these supply the indispensable basis of any authoritative edition.

In recent times, just as in earlier centuries, there have been plenty of slips and second thoughts in the interval between completion of copy for the printer and the emergence of the book from the press. Wherever possible, the textual student must examine the correspondence exchanged by the author and his publisher or editor, for the sake of whatever discussion of alterations it may contain, and the printer's proofs may provide vital evidence of the way an author's creative powers kept working even after his book was set in type. A few years ago the proof-sheets of the first eight books of Pope's translation of the *Iliad* were discovered in the Bibliothèque de l'Arsenal in Paris. Although the proofs of Books I-IV contain Pope's corrections of typographical errors only, the remainder show him painstakingly reconsidering his artistry, "from emendations of a single word to cancellations and revisions of quite long passages."[2] The corrected proofs of John Gibson Lockhart's life of Scott throw light on both his biographical craftsmanship and his desire, strengthened by advice from friends, not to give offense. As late as proof-stage Lockhart was busily touching up dialogue and description and altering the text of Scott's journals and letters so as to add consistency and vividness to the idealized conception of his father-in-law which he strove to present throughout his long biography; and at the same time he tactfully adjusted many details relating to Scott's financial transactions, and cut out numerous painful references to the novelist's mental deterioration during his final months.[3] Comparison of a set of unrevised galley proofs of Faulkner's *Sanctuary* with the printed book has revealed a striking instance of a novelist's completely changing the focus and manner of a book after type was set. In Faulkner's own words, he "tore the galleys down and rewrote the book."[4]

The contributions which textual study makes to our understanding of literature, then, are twofold. In the first place, an authoritative text may reveal the author's intentions, purged of the blemishes and misrepresentations that crept into a book after he ceased to control it. It is, in any event, a *sine qua non* for the informed criticism of a work considered solely as a finished product. Secondly, an examination of manuscripts, proofs, or successive printed versions or, in unusual cases, all three is a matchless means of watching the whole process of literary creation. Manuscripts alone are valuable enough. M. R. Ridley's analysis, in *Keats' Craftsmanship* (1933), of the heavily corrected drafts of "The Eve of St. Agnes," *Hyperion*, *Lamia*, and "To Autumn" excitingly reconstructs the working of a poet's mind as he wrote, corrected, debated, revised, struck out, restored, interlined, and in general tinkered. The DeSelincourt edition of the two texts of Wordsworth's *Prelude* (1805-6 and 1850) reveals the way the poet's intellect and sensibility both mellowed and hardened over a long

2. Norman Callan, "Pope's *Iliad*: a New Document," *RES*, n.s. IV (1953), 109–21 [Altick's note].

3. Francis Russell Hart, "Proofreading Lockhart's *Scott*: The Dynamics of Biographical Reticence," *SB*, XIV (1961), 3–22 [Altick's note].

4. Linton Massey, "Notes on the Unrevised Galleys of Faulkner's *Sanctuary*," *SB*, VIII (1956), 195–208 [Altick's note].

span of years. The Victoria and Albert Museum's rich collection of Dickens' memoranda, manuscripts, and proof sheets (including his rough working plans and passages that were discarded for lack of space) permits us to watch a great novelist at work under the new pressure of serial publication: "how he responded to and conveyed 'the feelings of the day,' what methods of work he evolved as best suited to his own genius and to the demands of monthly or weekly publication, and above all, how he [learned] to combine the 'circumspection' of preparation with the immediate and intimate relation to his readers which he valued so highly."[5] Equally valuable, for other reasons, is the comparison of successive printed texts in each of which the author has exercised his privilege of retouching. T. S. Eliot's *The Waste Land,* for instance, appeared in two periodicals (the *Criterion* and the *Dial*), then had a number of separate editions in book form (both British and American), and, in due course, was included in the poet's collected poems. The variant readings in all of Eliot's texts, as one scholar has noted, afford "added insight into recurrent phrasing and themes in the poems and plays and a stricter sense of their chronology and possible interrelationships," as well as "the alterations in phrasing which borrowings from other authors have undergone."[6]

Textual criticism is not a labor to be undertaken lightly. It is among the most demanding of all branches of literary scholarship. The technical knowledge, the infinite patience, and the reasoning powers which the ideal editor brings to his task are found combined in few men or women. And sometimes, it must be admitted, these gifts are squandered on unworthy causes; a fourth-rate example of literature does not repay the labor of a first-class editorial job, and candid critics, in such instances, can scarcely be blamed for remarking that it takes more than a meticulous determination of text to make a bad poem better. But at its best, when it enables us either to behold a work of art exactly as it left its author's pen or to watch it in the very state of "becoming," textual study has, in Fredson Bowers' words, the dignity of "an independent act of critical inquiry into the author's mind and art."[7]

Of all the literary scholars practicing today, comparatively few have either the training or the occasion to do such extensive work in textual criticism and editing as to qualify as specialists. But the exacting standards of modern textual study embody a responsibility to which everyone who deals with literary works and their history, for whatever purpose, is subject. The expert's *summum bonum* is the non-expert's working rule. Few of us may dedicate our energies

5. John Butt and Kathleen Tillotson, *Dickens at Work* (London, 1957), p. 9 [Altick's note].

6. Robert L. Beare, "Notes on the Text of T. S. Eliot: Variants from Russell Square," *SB,* IX (1957), 21–49 [Altick's note].

7. *Textual and Literary Criticism* (Cambridge, 1959), p. 17 [Altick's note].

to the patient unraveling of the knotty textual history of a work; all of us, however, have an inescapable obligation to base our scholarly and critical activity upon the most authentic text that is available and to reproduce it with the utmost fidelity in whatever we publish for the use of others.

RALPH WALDO EMERSON
An Evening of Dance[1]

I saw in Boston Fanny Elssler in the ballet of *Nathalie*. She must show, I suppose, the whole compass of her instrument, and add to her softest graces of motion or "the wisdom of her feet," the feats of the rope-dancer and tumbler; and perhaps on the whole the beauty of the exhibition is enhanced by this that is strong and strange, as when she stands erect on the extremities of her toes or on one toe, or "performs the impossible" in attitude. But the chief beauty is in the extreme grace of her movement, the variety and nature of her attitude, the winning fun and spirit of all her little coquetries, the beautiful erectness of her body, and the freedom and determination which she can so easily assume, and, what struck me much, the air of perfect sympathy with the house, and that mixture of deference and conscious superiority which puts her in perfect spirits and equality to her part. When she curtsies, her sweet and slow and prolonged salaam which descends and still descends whilst the curtain falls, until she seems to have invented new depths of grace and condescension, she earns well the profusion of bouquets of flowers which are hurled on to the stage.

As to the morals, as it is called, of this exhibition, that lies wholly with the spectator. The basis of this exhibition, like that of every human talent, is moral, is the sport and triumph of health or the virtue of organization. Her charm for the house is that she dances for them or they dance in her, not being (fault of some defect in their forms and educations) able to dance themselves. We must be expressed. Hence all the cheer and exhilaration which the spectacle imparts and the intimate property which each beholder feels in the dancer, and the joy with which he hears good anecdotes of her spirit and her benevolence. They know that such surpassing grace must rest on some occult foundations of inward harmony.

But over and above her genius for dancing are the incidental vices of this individual, her own false taste or her meretricious arts to please the groundlings and which must displease the judicious. The immorality the immoral will see; the very immoral will see that only; the pure will not heed it—for it is not obtrusive—perhaps will not see it at all. I should not think of danger to young women

1. From Emerson's *Journals*.

stepping with their father or brother out of happy and guarded parlors into this theatre to return in a few hours to the same; but I can easily suppose that it is not the safest resort for college boys who have left metaphysics, conic sections, or Tacitus to see these tripping satin slippers, and they may not forget this graceful, silvery swimmer when they have retreated again to their baccalaureate cells.

It is a great satisfaction to see the best in each kind, and as a good student of the world, I desire to let pass nothing that is excellent in its own kind unseen, unheard.

E. M. FORSTER

Not Listening to Music

Listening to music is such a muddle that one scarcely knows how to start describing it. The first point to get clear in my own case is that during the greater part of every performance I do not attend. The nice sounds make me think of something else. I wool-gather most of the time, and am surprised that others don't. Professional critics can listen to a piece as consistently and as steadily as if they were reading a chapter in a novel. This seems to me an amazing feat, and probably they only achieve it through intellectual training; that is to say, they find in the music the equivalent of a plot; they are following the ground bass or expecting the theme to re-enter in the dominant, and so on, and this keeps them on the rails. But I fly off every minute: after a bar or two I think how musical I am, or of something smart I might have said in conversation; or I wonder what the composer—dead a couple of centuries—can be feeling as the flames on the altar still flicker up; or how soon an H.E. bomb[1] would extinguish them. Not to mention more obvious distractions: the tilt of the soprano's chin or chins; the antics of the conductor, that impassioned beetle, especially when it is night time and he waves his shards; the affection of the pianist when he takes a top note with difficulty, as if he too were a soprano; the backs of the chairs; the bumps on the ceiling; the extreme physical ugliness of the audience. A classical audience is surely the plainest collection of people anywhere assembled for any common purpose; contributing my quota, I have the right to point this out. Compare us with a gang of navvies or with an office staff, and you will be appalled. This, too, distracts me.

What do I hear during the intervals when I do attend? Two sorts of music. They melt into each other all the time, and are not easy to christen, but I will call one of them "music that reminds me of

1. A high explosive.

something," and the other "music itself." I used to be very fond of music that reminded me of something, and especially fond of Wagner. With Wagner I always knew where I was; he never let the fancy roam; he ordained that one phrase should recall the ring, another the sword, another the blameless fool and so on; he was as precise in his indications as an oriental dancer. Since he is a great poet, that did not matter, but I accepted his leitmotiv system much too reverently and forced it onto other composers whom it did not suit, such as Beethoven and Franck. I thought that music must be the better for having a meaning. I think so still, but am less clear as to what "a meaning" is. In those days it was either a non-musical object, such as a sword or a blameless fool, or a non-musical emotion, such as fear, lust, or resignation. When music reminded me of something which was not music, I supposed it was getting me somewhere. "How like Monet!" I thought when listening to Debussy, and "How like Debussy!" when looking at Monet. I translated sounds into colours, saw the piccolo as apple-green, and the trumpets as scarlet. The arts were to be enriched by taking in one another's washing.

I still listen to some music this way. For instance, the slow start of Beethoven's Seventh Symphony invokes a gray-green tapestry of hunting scenes, and the slow movement of his Fourth Piano Concerto (the dialogue between piano and orchestra) reminds me of the dialogue between Orpheus and the Furies in Gluck. The climax of the first movement of the Appassionata (the "più allegro") seems to me sexual, although I can detect no sex in the Kreutzer, nor have I come across anyone who could, except Tolstoy. That disappointing work, Brahms' Violin Concerto, promises me clear skies at the opening, and only when the violin has squealed up in the air for page after page is the promise falsified. Wolf's "Ganymed" does give me sky—stratosphere beyond stratosphere. In these cases and in many others music reminds me of something non-musical, and I fancy that to do so is part of its job. Only a purist would condemn all visual parallels, all emotional labelings, all programs.

Yet there is a danger. Music that reminds does open the door to that imp of the concert hall, inattention. To think of a gray-green tapestry is not very different from thinking of the backs of the chairs. We gather a superior wool from it, still we do wool-gather, and the sounds slip by blurred. The sounds! It is for them that we come, and the closer we can get up against them the better. So I do prefer "music itself" and listen to it and for it as far as possible. In this connection, I will try to analyze a mishap that has recently overtaken the Coriolanus Overture. I used to listen to the Coriolanus for "itself," conscious when it passed of something important and agitating, but not defining further. Now I learn that Wagner, endorsed by Sir Donald Tovey, has provided it with a Program: the opening bars indicate the hero's decision to destroy the Volscii, then a sweet tune for female influence, then the dotted-quaver-restlessness of indecision. This seems indisputable, and there is no doubt that this was, or was almost, Beethoven's intention. All the same, I have lost my Coriolanus. Its largeness and freedom have gone. The exquisite sounds have been hardened like a road that has been tarred for traffic. One has to go somewhere down them, and to pass through the same domestic crisis to the same military impasse, each time the overture is played.

Music is so very queer that an amateur is bound to get muddled when writing about it. It seems to be more "real" than anything, and to survive when the rest of civilization decays. In these days I am always thinking of it with relief. It can never be ruined or nationalized. So that the music which is untrammeled and untainted by reference is obviously the best sort of music to listen to; we get nearer the center of reality. Yet though it is untainted, it is never abstract; it is not like mathematics, even when it uses them. The Goldberg Variations, the last Beethoven Sonata, the Franck Quartet, the Schumann Piano Quintet and the Fourth Symphonies of Tchaikovsky and of Brahms certainly have a message. Though what on earth is it? I shall get tied up trying to say. There's an insistence in music—expressed largely through rhythm; there's a sense that it is trying to push across at us something which is neither an esthetic pattern nor a sermon. That's what I listen for specially.

So music that is itself seems on the whole better than music that reminds. And now to end with an important point: my own performances upon the piano. These grow worse yearly, but never will I give them up. For one thing, they compel me to attend—no wool-gathering or thinking myself clever here—and they drain off all non-musical matter. For another thing, they teach me a little about construction. I see what becomes of a phrase, how it is transformed or returned, sometimes bottom upward, and get some notion of the relation of keys. Playing Beethoven, as I generally do, I grow familiar with his tricks, his impatience, his sudden softnesses, his dropping of a tragic theme one semitone, his love, when tragic, for the key of C minor, and his aversion to the key of B major. This gives me a physical approach to Beethoven which cannot be gained through the slough of "appreciation." Even when people play as badly as I do, they should continue: it will help them to listen.

QUESTIONS

1. Forster carries his discussion of listening to music through three stages. What are they? Where in the essay is each introduced? Where does Forster make it clear that the first two stages resemble each other?

2. What devices of language and attitude does Forster use to establish an informal, relaxed approach to his topic? Does he appear to be

addressing himself to a particular kind of audience? Explain.

3. What is "music itself"? By what means does Forster seek to define it?

4. Early in the essay Forster says that it seems to him an "amazing feat" that professional critics can listen to music "as consistently and steadily as if they were reading a chapter in a novel." What does this indicate as to Forster's view of the novel? Is he being ironical?

5. What does playing the piano teach Forster about listening to music? The closing paragraph, on playing and listening, suggests a similar relationship between writing and reading. Following Forster's strategy of organization, write a brief essay on "Not Reading a Novel," "Not Looking at Pictures," "Not Going to a Lecture," or "Not Studying an Assignment."

JACQUES MARITAIN

An Essay on Art

Dignity of Art

The philosophers tell us that art consists essentially, not in performing a moral act, but in making a thing, a work, in making an object with a view not to the human good of the agent, but to the exigencies and the proper good of the object to be made, and by employing ways of realization predetermined by the nature of the object in question.

Art thus appears as something foreign in itself to the sphere of the human good, almost as something inhuman, and whose exigencies nevertheless are absolute: for, needless to say, there are not two ways of making an object well, of realizing well the work one has conceived—there is but one way, and it must not be missed.

The philosophers go on to say that this making activity is principally and above all an intellectual activity. Art is a virtue of the intellect, of the practical intellect, and may be termed the virtue proper to working reason.

But then, you will say, if art is nothing other than an intellectual virtue of making, whence comes its dignity and its ascendancy among us? Why does this branch of our activity draw to it so much human sap? Why has one always and in all peoples admired the poet as much as the sage?

It may be answered first that to create, to produce something intellectually, to make an object *rationally constructed*, is something very great in the world: for man this alone is already a way of imitating God. And I am speaking here of art in general, such as the ancients understood it—in short, of art as the virtue of the artisan.

But where the maker of works especially becomes an imitator of

God, where the virtue of art approaches the nobility of things absolute and self-sufficient, is in that family of arts which by itself alone
constitutes a whole spiritual world, namely the fine arts.

There are two things to be considered here. On the one hand,
whatever the nature and the utilitarian ends of the art envisaged, it
participates by its object in something superhuman, since it has as
its object to create beauty. Is not beauty a transcendental, a property of being, one of the Divine Names? "The being of all things
derives from the Divine Beauty," says Saint Thomas. In this
respect, then, the artist imitates God, Who made the world by
communicating to it a likeness of His beauty.

> ... The architect, by the disposition he knows,
> Buildeth the structure of stone like a filter in the waters
>   of the Radiance of God,
> And giveth the whole building its sheen as to a pearl.

On the other hand, to create a work of beauty is to create a work
on which shines the radiance or the splendor, the mystery of a
form, in the metaphysical sense of this word, of a ray of intelligibility and truth, of an irradiation of the primal brilliance. And no
doubt the artist perceives this form in the created world, whether
exterior or interior: he does not discover it complete in the sole
contemplation of his creative spirit, for he is not, like God, the
cause of things. But it is his eye and his spirit that have perceived
and uncovered it; and it must itself be alive within him, must have
taken on human life in him, must live in his intelligence with an
intellectual life and in his heart and his flesh with a sensitive life,
in order for him to be able to communicate it to matter in the
work he makes.

Thus the work bears the mark of the artist; it is the offspring of
his soul and his spirit.

In this respect also human art imitates God: it realizes in the
order of intellectuality, that is to say, in the highest order of nature
(I do not speak of the order of charity, which is superior to it, being
supernatural), it realizes in act one of the fundamental aspects of
the ontological likeness of our soul with God.

For it is the aspiration and ardent desire of the intelligence, considered in the pure state, to beget a living being like unto itself.
Moreover every intelligence utters a word. "To be fertile, so as to
manifest that which one possesses within oneself, is a great perfection, and it essentially belongs to the intellectual nature."[1] Thus in
the world of pure spirits, where there is no generation, there is the
spiritual production of the mental word, in which the Angel in
knowing himself expresses himself to himself, and through which
he manifests what he knows to whomever it pleases him among the

---

1. John of Saint Thomas, *Cursus*   § 21 [Maritain's note].
Theol., I P., q. XXVII, disp. 12, a. 6,

other pure spirits. This mental word, it is true, this spiritual utterance remains a quality of the subject; it is not a substance, it is a sign. In creatures, the intellect does not succeed in producing in similitude of nature another "itself"; it does not, properly speaking, engender; it utters a word, but this word is not a son. This, however, is owing to the essentially deficient condition of the creature; intelligence itself, considered in the pure state, in its pure formal line, desires to engender, to produce, in knowing itself, something which will not be merely a likeness, a sign, an idea of the thing known, but the thing known itself existing for itself.

Only in God, only in Pure Act, is intelligence, which is then subsisting Intelligence, able to realize fully the fundamental exigencies of its nature and give birth to *another itself* substantial and personal, to a Word which is really a Son. It is only in the Holy Trinity that we see two functions coincide which everywhere else are separate, the uttering of the word and the generation of the son, that we see intelligence issue in a subsisting term, into which passes substantially the integrity of its own nature.

Well! We too, weak though our intelligence may be (it is on the lowest rung of the ladder of spirits), must participate in the nature of the intelligence. This is why, in spite of all the deficiencies peculiar to our kind, the intelligence endeavors to engender in us, it seeks to produce: and not only the interior word, the idea which remains within us, but a work at once material and spiritual, like ourselves, and in which superabounds something of our soul.

It is because of this exigency of the intelligence that there are artists among us.

And you see that to establish fully the dignity and the nobility of art, it was necessary for us to ascend to the mystery of the Trinity itself.

It must, however, be carefully observed that our works of art are very far from being able to be truly called our children. They are inanimate; they do not proceed from us *in similitudinem naturae*, they are the result of an artificial making, not of a natural generation.

But note that, accidentally and in a certain respect, there is in the work of art something that better answers the exigencies of the idea of generation: I mean that in his work the great artist is sure to put himself really, he is sure to imprint his own likeness on it; whereas, in the child, because of matter and heredity, one cannot be sure that it is the father or the mother, rather it may be some more or less desirable ancestor who comes to life again and manifests his or her likeness. The father thinks he finds himself again in his child, but it is the grandfather or the great-grandfather, or the mother-in-law, who appears. There is in the child a terrible unknown which does not exist in the work of art. And it is understandable, not that the artist should love his works more than his children, but at least that he should love them with a love almost as personal and, from a certain point of view, less anxious, and that he says in thinking of them: *"Not all of me will die."*

Gratuitousness

All these considerations show that art is *gratuitous* or disinterested as such—that is to say, that in the production of the work the virtue of art aims only at one thing: the good of the work-to-be-made, beauty to be made to shine in matter, the creating of the thing according to its own laws, independently of all the rest; and accordingly it desires that there be nothing in the work which will escape its regulation, and that it be alone in immediately ruling the work, in molding it and fashioning it.

There are many ways of failing in this "gratuitousness." One may think, for instance, that good moral intentions make up for the quality of the craft or the inspiration, and suffice to construct a work. Or else one may go so far as to adulterate the work itself, such as the rules and the determined ways of art would have it to be, by forcibly applying to it, in order to rule it, foreign elements—the desire to edify, or to disedify, not to shock the public, or to create scandal, to have "arrived" in society, or to cut a figure in the bars and cafés as an *artist* free and rare . . .

You see in what sense one must admit the doctrine of the gratuitousness of art: in the sense, namely, that the virtue of art which the artist uses, for whatever end it may be employed in other respects, aims by itself only at the perfection of the work, and suffers in the work no control which does not pass through it.

But this doctrine of, and the term, "gratuitousness," are often understood in a quite different and much more ambitious sense. They are then made to signify not only what I have just said, but also that art must enjoy *in man* and *among men* an absolute independence, that it must tolerate in the artist no human interest nor any superior law, absolutely nothing outside the pure concern for artistic making: which comes to saying that the artist must be *an artist only*—and therefore must not be a man. But if there is no man, there is no artist: in devouring the humanity, art has destroyed itself. This is what Baudelaire called *The Pagan School*: "Absorbed," he wrote, "by the fierce passion for the beautiful, the droll, the pretty, the picturesque—for there are degrees—the notions of what is proper and true disappear. The frenzied passion for art is a cancer which eats up everything else. . . . Excessive specialization of a faculty ends in nothing."

It seems to me that this erroneous conception of the gratuitousness of art can assume two special forms.

Under a first form, on the whole in opposition to romanticism, will be found the notion of gratuitousness professed by the Parnassians, then by the Symbolists and Mallarmé, and perhaps also, in a different sphere, by the friends of Max Jacob and Erik Satie (but already some of them would no longer hold to it). The content of the work of art, the matter to be fashioned, the artistic *thing*, the lyrical and intellectual materials, all this is a constraint and a burden, an impurity that must be eliminated. In short, pure art, art about nothing, by extenuation of the subject. I call this a sin of idealism with respect to the *matter* of art: in the end, a perfect constructing, with nothing to construct.

After the exasperation of sensibility provoked by impressionism, after so many noisy claims, so many marvels, evocations, swoons, and psychological thrills, this conception of gratuitousness has been a purifying and beneficent phase, because it has reminded us that the main thing in art is the *control* that the mind imposes upon matter. It is in this sense that Georges Auric very justly observed: "A *tight-rope walker and a dancer*, these are the two beings that every artist who moves me unites within him. Every new work is a tightrope stretched above an everlasting track. . . . Even today, you can see with what caution a Stravinsky and a Satie have to cross that wire which must be their only way." The fact remains that the theory of gratuitousness, understood in the sense that I have just emphasized—in a deliberately brutal manner—is false, because it forgets precisely the very matter which must be artistically ruled and the indispensable part that matter plays.

No doubt, if the matter is almost non-existent, the artist's task will be easier. But art, as has been sufficiently dinned into us, must not seek for facility. It needs opposition and constraint, the constraint of the rules and the opposition of matter. The more obstinate and rebellious the matter, the better will the art that triumphs over it realize its own end, which is to make a dominating intelligibility shine forth in the matter. André Gide put it very well: "Art is always the result of some constraint. To hold that it rises higher the freer it is, is to hold that what keeps the kite from climbing is the string to which it is attached. Kant's dove, which thought it would be able to fly better without the air that resisted its wings, fails to realize that in order for it to fly it needs the resistance of the air against which to lean its wings. . . . Art longs for liberty only in sick periods; it would like to exist easily. Each time it feels itself strong, it seeks for struggle and obstacles. It likes to burst its bonds, and therefore it prefers them tight."

But the doctrine of the gratuitousness of art can give rise to another more specious error, and this time it is Gide himself who undertakes to propose it to us. "The artist," Gide tells us, "is expected to appear after dinner. His function is not to provide food, but intoxication." And he says after Ernest Renan: "To be able to think freely, one must be certain that what one writes will be of no consequence," from which it follows that every thinker who envisages the consequences of what he writes does not think freely. And again, in a dialogue between himself and an imaginary interlocutor:

> The interlocutor—"Are you interested in moral questions?"
> Gide—"What! The very stuff of our books!"
> The interlocutor—"But what is morality, according to you?"
> Gide—"A branch of Aesthetics."

Oscar Wilde had said, pretty much in the same sense but in a more stately formula: "The highest Art rejects the burden of the human spirit."

The point is that the doctrine of gratuitousness, in reaction against exclusively moralist or apologetic or civic preoccupations regarded as "utilitarian," requires now, no longer the extenuation of the *matter* of art, as was the case a moment ago, but the elimination of any *human end* pursued. Let the artist take for the matter and stuff of his work whatever is most profound, most exalted and most vile, the moral life of man, that heart of man which is "hollow and full of filth"—and the rarest passions, and the spiritual life itself, nay, the Gospel and sanctity, anything he wishes; but in all of that an absolute prohibition, under pain of committing a sacrilege against art, against pursuing any other end than the pure delight, order, luxury, tranquillity and rapture that the soul must enjoy in the work. It is no longer art *in nothing,* as in the doctrine of gratuitousness in its first form; it is now art *for nothing,* for nothing else but itself.

The doctrine of gratuitousness in this second form is singularly specious, because it exploits and distorts something very true concerning the nature of art, and which we must take care not to overlook. It is nevertheless a very pernicious poison, which must in the long run exercise a completely sterilizing effect upon art.

Precisely because, given this or that work-to-be-made, there are strictly determined ways of realizing it, ways that depend on the pure exigencies of the work itself and that brook no liberties, the virtue of art, as I just indicated, does not allow the work to be interfered with or immediately ruled by anything other than itself. It insists that it alone shall touch the work in order to bring it into being. In short, art requires that nothing shall attain the work except *through art itself.* This is the element of truth in the doctrine of gratuitousness. Woe to the artist who is deficient with respect to this exigency of his art, a jealous and fierce exigency, as are all the exigencies of the intelligence and its virtues. Here again we can find in our art a vestige as it were of the Trinity. *The Word,* says Saint Augustine, *is in some way the art of Almighty God.* And it is through the Word that the whole of the divine work was made, *omnia per ipsum facta sunt*. It is through His Word and His art that God attains, rules, and brings into being everything He makes. In the same way it is *through his art* that the human artist must attain, rule and bring into being all his work.

But does this imply that the work depends on art alone, and not on the entire soul of the artist; that it is made by the art alone, separate, cut off from all the rest in man, and not by man the artist with all the human purposes, desires, and longings, all the human thoughts and beliefs he has in his heart, and with all the higher laws he would have himself obey? Nonsense! It is as though, under the pretext that everything was made *per verbum*, through the Divine Word, one were to say that the world was not made by the whole undivided Trinity: gratuitously, to be sure—it is the sole example of perfectly gratuitous art—and in a manner totally free from the least interested intention, but to an end nevertheless, an end which is not simply the perfection of the work to be achieved, and which is of an order superior to art—the communication of divine goodness.

The theorists of gratuitousness overlook an elementary distinction; they fail to distinguish between *art*, which, as such, has no other end than the good of the object to be made, and the *artist*, who, as a man performing an act, can have all the ends he pleases. And they overlook this common-sense distinction because they fail to take account of a more subtle distinction, the distinction between the "principal agent" and the "instrumental cause," between the workman and the instrument. Through the instrument wielded by the workman there passes an invisible and intangible activity, which causes the instrument to produce an effect nobler than itself and really to produce the whole work, but as subordinate agent. Thus the picture is wholly from the brush and wholly from the painter; there is nothing, absolutely nothing, in the picture that does not come to it from the brush, and there is nothing in it that does not come from the painter.

This distinction plays a role of capital importance in metaphysics; it alone enables us to understand how the free act of the creature is wholly of the creature, as second cause, and, if it is good, wholly of God, as first cause. God activates the will to act according to its own mode, that is to say, freely. The philosophers who do not make this distinction are forced to consider the divine action as inserting into human liberty some kind of foreign element, some kind of rival which would compromise its purity. André Gide makes a similar mistake. He does not see that the virtue of art, with all its perfection and peculiar exigencies, is an *instrument* in relation to the artist, the principal agent.

The soul of the artist, with all its human fullness, with all that it admires and all that it loves, with all the purposes of a non-artistic order—human, moral, religious—that it can pursue, is the principal cause which uses the virtue of art as an instrument; and thus the work is wholly of the soul and the will of the artist as principal cause, and wholly of his art as instrument, without his art losing any of its mastery over the matter or any of its rectitude, purity, and ingenuousness—just as our good acts are wholly from us as second cause and wholly from God as first cause, without on that account losing any of their freedom.

This does not mean that we have here a juxtaposition of two forces each pulling its own way. There is instrumental subordination of the virtue of art to the soul which acts through it. The greater the artist, the more vigorous is his art, not bowed over or bent, certainly, but erect and imperious—and the more the man succeeds in passing wholly into his work, through his art. Diminish the man in the artist, and you necessarily diminish the art itself, which is something of man. The doctrine of gratuitousness in its second form is another idealist heresy. It is no longer the *matter* of the work of art, it is the *human subject*, of whom the virtue of art is a quality, which is here disregarded.

If the artist has not taken sides in the great debate between the angels and men, if he is not convinced that he provides, together with delight, a food and not simply intoxication, his work will always remain deficient and paltry in some respects. The greatest poets, and the most disinterested ones, the most "gratuitous," had something to say to men. Is not this the case with Dante, Cervantes, Racine, Shakespeare, Goethe, Baudelaire, Dostoievsky? Whatever may be the latter's ideology, his heart is Christian; Gide, who could see in him only his own countenance, was strangely mistaken about Dostoievsky. How reasonable—need it be further remarked from this point of view?—and how little "immoralist," are the explanations Goethe gives us in *Dichtung und Wahrheit* as to the origin of *Werther!* And in *Mon coeur mis à nu,* what a tragically religious anxiety the dandyism of Baudelaire suddenly reveals to us!

Is not the art of La Fontaine an eminent example of *gratuitous* art? But as Henri Ghéon observed to Valéry, "if it were not lacking in a grain of spirituality, a touch of Christianity, the art of this maker of apologues would be the art of the *apologist*, the very type of *edifying* art."

Well and good, one will say. But suppose that La Fontaine had acquired this grain of spirituality the while remaining La Fontaine, the La Fontaine we know; in exercising his apologist's art, he would never have been consumed by the zeal for souls and the apostolate. "If Jammes and Claudel are Christian artists, it is not because of their manifest and distinctive devotion. The apostolate is never an aesthetic virtue."[2] More generally, does it not seem that the happiest conditions for the artist are conditions of peace and spiritual order within and around him, such that having, we certainly hope, his soul under control and turned towards its last end, he have however in addition to this no other concern than to reveal himself—such as he is—in his work, without giving a thought to anything else, without pursuing any particular and determined human end? Was not this precisely how the artists of the Middle Ages worked? Or in our day a Cézanne?

To this objection—which is not lacking in force, and which concedes the essential—I have two answers to give. First of all, if it is true that for the workman who in making his work pursues a particular and definite human end—for example, a Lucretius intending to spread the Epicurean system, a Virgil composing the *Georgics* to bring man-power back to the land, or even a Wagner seeking to glorify the Teutonic religion—if it is true, I say, that for such a workman the task is more difficult, the danger of giving way greater, nevertheless this danger is not insurmountable, this task is not impossible, as witness the names I just cited.

Secondly, and more importantly, those who wish to serve through their art the Truth that is Christ, do not pursue a particular human end, they pursue a divine end, an end as universal as God Himself. The more they live their faith, the more their inner life becomes spiritualized, the more deeply they are of the Church—the more they rise above the human limitations, conventions, opinions, and special interests of such or such a social group; so that, understanding better the pure spirituality and universality of God's action in souls, their art and their thought are purified of all human narrowness, in order to be henceforth directed only towards the boundless Love Who is and acts on earth as in Heaven. This is what those men cannot understand who, ignorant of everything of the Faith or deceived by too many appearances, see in zeal for souls only an effort of human domination, an attempt to serve some commercial or party interest. They do not see that those who engage as Christians, because they are Christians, in the works of the mind, are not practicing a *clerical* philosophy or a *clerical* art, or a *confessional* philosophy or a *confessional* art. In this sense there is no Catholic art or Catholic philosophy, for Catholicism is not a *particular confession*, just as it is not *a* religion: it is *the* religion, confessing the unique and omnipresent Truth. Yet their art and their philosophy are catholic, that is to say, authentically universal.

May I add that one always serves some master, and that the devil is not the least exacting overlord. In forbidding man to pursue any

2. Max Jacob, *Art Poétique*, Paris, 1922 [Maritain's note].

other end than art itself, we are, whatever we may do, positively assigning to him a last end, a God: Art in person. One binds oneself to a religion, and to a religion much more tyrannical than the true religion. One delivers oneself up to aesthetic clericalism, which is assuredly one of the most pernicious forms of clericalism.

Gide strikes me as being under constant constraint, cribbed, cabined, and confined by inexorable conventions, never free, never spontaneous; forever haunted by morality. A moral choice confronts him at every corner of the street, and he is compelled to make a decision: quick, should he escape? Escape through here! What torture!

The artist who consents to be a man, who has no fear of morality, who is not afraid at each moment of losing the flower of his ingenuousness—he it is that enjoys the true gratuitousness of art. He is what he is, without caring about what he may appear to be; he asserts if he wants to assert; he believes, he loves, he chooses, he gives himself, he follows his bent and his fancy, he recreates and amuses himself, he plays.

Of a Too Human Antinomy

Truthfully, I do not believe that it is possible outside of Catholicism to reconcile in man, without diminishing or doing violence to them, the rights of morality and the claims of intellectuality, art or science. Morality as such aims only at the good of the human being, the supreme interests of the Subject who acts; intellectuality as such aims only at the Object—what it is, if it is a question of knowing it, what it ought to be, if it is a question of making it. What a temptation for poor human nature to be faithful to one only at the expense of the other! It is true, we know, *haec oportebat facere, et illa non omittere;*[3] but how are the children of Adam to keep the balance?

Outside the Church and her divine life it is natural that moral and religious zeal turn man against the intelligence; and it is natural that zeal for art or science turn man away from the eternal laws. In one camp we have Socrates' judges, Luther, Rousseau, Tolstoy, the Anglo-Saxon pragmatists; in the other, Bruno, Bacon, the great pagans of the Renaissance, and Goethe himself, and Nietzsche.

Catholicism orders our whole life to Truth itself and to subsisting Beauty. It puts into us—above the moral virtues and the intellectual virtues—the theological virtues, and through them gives us peace. *Et ego si exaltatus fuero, omnia traham ad meipsum.*[4] Christ Crucified draws to Him all that is in man; all things are reconciled, but at the height of His heart.

Here is a religion whose moral exigencies are more elevated than

3. "This need be done, and that other not neglected."

4. "Yes, if I be lifted up, I will draw all men to me" (John xii.32).

those of any other, since the heroism of sanctity can alone fully satisfy them, and which at the same time loves and protects the intelligence more than any other. I say that this is a sign of the divinity of this religion. A superhuman virtue is necessary to assure among men the free play of art and science under the rule of the divine law and the primacy of Charity, and thus to achieve the higher reconciliation of the *moral* and the *intellectual*.

KENNETH CLARK
The Blot and the Diagram

I have been told to "look down from a high place over the whole extensive landscape of modern art." We all know how tempting high places can be, and how dangerous. I usually avoid them myself. But if I must do as I am told, I shall try to find out why modern art has taken its peculiar form, and to guess how long that form will continue.

I shall begin with Leonardo da Vinci, because although all processes are gradual, he does represent one clearly marked turning point in the history of art. Before that time, the painters intentions were quite simple; they were first of all to tell a story, secondly to make the invisible visible, and thirdly to turn a plain surface into a decorated surface. Those are all very ancient aims, going back to the earliest civilizations, or beyond; and for three hundred years painters had been instructed how to carry them out by means of a workshop tradition. Of course, there had been breaks in that tradition—in the fourth century, maybe, and towards the end of the seventh century; but broadly speaking, the artist learnt what he could about the technique of art from his master in his workshop, and then set up shop on his own and tried to do better.

As is well known, Leonardo had a different view of art. He thought that it involved both science and the pursuit of some peculiar attribute called beauty or grace. He was, by inclination, a scientist: he wanted to find out how things worked, and he believed that this knowledge could be stated mathematically. He said "Let no one who is not a mathematician read my works," and he tried to relate this belief in measurement to his belief in beauty. This involved him in two rather different lines of thought, one concerned with magic—the magic of numbers—the other with science. Ever since Pythagoras had discovered that the musical scale could be stated mathematically, by means of the length of the strings, etc., and so had thrown a bridge between intellectual analysis and sensory perception, thinkers on art had felt that it should be possible to do the same for painting. I must say that their effort had not been very rewarding; the modulus, or golden section, and the logarithmic spiral of shells are practically the only undisputed results. But Leonardo lived at a time when it was still possible to hope great things from perspective, which should not only define space, but order it harmoniously; and he also inherited a belief that ideal mathematical combinations could be derived from the proportions of the human body. This line of thought may be called the *mystique* of measurement. The other line may be called *the use* of measurement. Leonardo wished to state mathematically various facts related to the act of seeing. How do we see light passing over a sphere? What happens when objects make themselves perceptible on our retina? Both these lines of thought involved him in drawing diagrams and taking measurements, and for this reason were closely related in his mind. No painter except perhaps Piero della Francesca has tried more strenuously to find a mathematical statement of art, nor has had a greater equipment for doing so.

But Leonardo was also a man of powerful and disturbing imagination. In his notebooks, side by side with his attempts to achieve *order* by mathematics, are drawings and descriptions of the most violent scenes of *disorder* which the human mind can conceive—battles, deluges, eruptions. And he included in his treatise on painting advice on how to develop this side of the artistic faculty also. The passages in which he does so have often been quoted, but they are so incredibly foreign to the whole Renaissance idea of art, although related to a remark in Pliny,[1] that each time I read them, they give me a fresh surprise. I will, therefore, quote them again.

> I shall not refrain from including among these precepts a new and speculative idea, which although it may seem trivial and almost laughable, is none the less of great value in quickening the spirit of invention. It is this: that you should look at certain walls stained with damp or at stones of uneven color. If you have to invent some setting you will be able to see in these the likeness of divine landscapes, adorned with mountains, ruins, rocks, woods, great plains, hills and valleys in great variety; and then again you will see there battles and strange figures in violent action, expressions of faces and clothes and an infinity of things which you will be able to reduce to their complete and proper forms. In such walls the same thing happens as in the sound of bells, in whose strokes you may find every named word which you can imagine.

Later he repeats this suggestion in slightly different form, advising the painter to study not only marks on walls, but also "the embers of the fire, or clouds or mud, or other similar objects from which you will find most admirable ideas . . . because from a confusion of shapes the spirit is quickened to new inventions."

I hardly need to insist on how relevant these passages are to modern painting. Almost every morning I receive cards inviting me

1. Roman naturalist, first century A.D.

to current exhibitions, and on the cards are photographs of the works exhibited. Some of them consist of blots, some of scrawls, some look like clouds, some like embers of the fire, some are like mud—some of them are mud; a great many look like stains on walls, and one of them, I remember, consisted of actual stains on walls, photographed and framed. Leonardo's famous passage has been illustrated in every particular. And yet I doubt if he would have been satisfied with the results, because he believed that we must somehow unite the two opposite poles of our faculties. Art itself was the connection between the diagram and the blot.

Now in order to prevent the impression that I am taking advantage of a metaphor, as writers on art are often bound to do, I should explain how I am going to use these words. By "diagram" I mean a rational statement in a visible form, involving measurements, and usually done with an ulterior motive. The theorem of Pythagoras is proved by a diagram. Leonardo's drawings of light striking a sphere are diagrams; but the works of Mondrian, although made up of straight lines, are not diagrams, because they are not done in order to prove or measure some experience, but to please the eye. That they look like diagrams is due to influences which I will examine later. But diagrams can exist with no motive other than their own perfection, just as mathematical propositions can.

By "blots" I mean marks or areas which are not intended to convey information, but which, for some reason, seem pleasant and memorable to the maker, and can be accepted in the same sense by the spectator. I said that these blots were not intended to convey information, but of course they do, and that of two kinds. First, they tell us through association, about things we had forgotten; that was the function of Leonardo's stains on walls, which as he said, quickened the spirit of invention, and it can be the function of man-made blots as well; and secondly a man-made blot will tell us about the artist. Unless it is made entirely accidentally, as by spilling an inkpot, it will be a commitment. It is quite difficult to make a non-committal blot. Although the two are connected, I think we can distinguish between analogy blots and gesture blots.

Now let me try to apply this to modern art. Modern art is not a subject on which one can hope for a large measure of agreement, but I hope I may be allowed two assumptions. The first is that the kind of painting and architecture which we call, with varying inflections of the voice, "modern," is a true and vital expression of our own day; and the second assumption is that it differs radically from any art which has preceded it. Both these assumptions have been questioned. It has been said that modern art is "a racket" engineered by art dealers, who have exploited the incompetence of artists and the gullibility of patrons, that the whole thing is a kind of vast and very expensive practical joke. Well, fifty years is a long time to keep up a hoax of this kind, and during these years modern art has spread all over the free world and created a complete international style. I don't think that any honest-minded historian, whether he liked it or not, could pretend that modern art was the result of an accident or a conspiracy. The only doubt he could have would be whether it is, so to say, a long-term or a short-term movement. In the history of art there are stylistic changes which appear to develop from purely internal causes, and seem almost accidental in relation to the other circumstances of life and society. Such, for example, was the state of art in Italy (outside Venice) from about 1530 to 1600. When all is said about the religious disturbances of the time, the real cause of the Mannerist style was the domination of Michelangelo, who had both created an irresistible style and exhausted its possibilities. It needed the almost equally powerful pictorial imagination of Cara-vaggio to produce a counter-infection, which could spread from Rome to Spain and the Netherlands and prepare the way for Rembrandt. I can see nothing in the history of man's spirit to account for this episode. It seems to me to be due to an internal and specifically artistic chain of events which are easily related to one another, and comprehensible within the general framework of European art. On the other hand, there are events in the history of art which go far beyond the interaction of styles and which evidently reflect a change in the whole condition of the human spirit. Such an event took place towards the end of the fifth century, when the Hellenistic-Roman style gradually became what we call Byzantine; and again in the early thirteenth century, when the Gothic cathedrals shot up out of the ground. In each case the historian could produce a series of examples to prove that the change was inevitable. But actually, it was nothing of the sort; it was wholly unpredictable; and was part of a complete spiritual revolution.

Whether we think that modern art represents a transformation of style or a change of spirit depends to some extent on my second assumption, that it differs radically from anything which has pre-ceded it. This too has been questioned; it has been said that Léger is only a logical development of Poussin, or Mondrian of Vermeer.[2] And it is true that the element of design in each has something in common. If we pare a Poussin down to its bare bones, there are combinations of curves and cubes which are the foundations of much classical painting, and Léger had the good sense to make use of them. Similarly, in Vermeer there is a use of rectangles, large areas con-trasted with very narrow ones, and a feeling for shallow recessions, which became the preferred theme of Mondrian. But such analogies are trifling compared with the differences. Poussin was a very intelligent man who thought deeply about his art, and if anyone

2. Léger and Mondrian: French and Dutch modern painters, respectively. Poussin, French, and Vermeer, Dutch, were both seventeenth-century painters.

had suggested to him that his pictures were praiseworthy solely on account of their construction, he would have been incredulous and affronted.

So let us agree that the kind of painting and architecture which we find most representative of our times—say, the painting of Jackson Pollock and the architecture of the Lever building—is deeply different from the painting and architecture of the past; and is *not* a mere whim of fashion, but the result of a great change in our ways of thinking and feeling.

How did this great change take place and what does it mean? To begin with, I think it is related to the development upon which all industrial civilization depends, the differentiation of function. Leonardo was exceptional, almost unique in his integration of functions —the scientific and the imaginative. Yet he foreshadowed more than any other artist their disintegration, by noting and treating in isolation the diagrammatic faculty and the blot-making faculty. The average artist took the unity of these faculties for granted. They were united in Leonardo, and in lesser artists, by *interest or pleasure in the thing seen.* The external object was like a magnetic pole which drew the two faculties together. At some point the external object became a negative rather than a positive charge. Instead of drawing together the two faculties, it completely dissociated them; architecture went off in one direction with the diagram, painting went in the other direction with the blot.

This disintegration was related to a radical change in the philosophy of art. We all know that such changes, however harmless they sound when first enunciated, can have drastic consequences in the world of action. Rulers who wish to maintain the *status quo* are well advised to chop off the heads of all philosophers. What Hilaire Belloc called the "remote and ineffectual don" is more dangerous than the busy columnist with his eye on the day's news. The revolution in our ideas about the nature of painting seems to have been hatched by a don who was considered remote and ineffectual even by Oxford standards—Walter Pater. It was he (inspired, I believe, by Schopenhauer) who first propounded the idea of the aesthetic sensation, intuitively perceived.

> In its primary aspect [Pater said] a great picture has no more difficult message for us than an accidental play of sunlight and shadow for a few moments on the wall or floor; in itself, in truth, a space of such fallen light, caught, as in the colors of an Eastern carpet, but refined upon and dealt with more subtly and exquisitely than by nature itself.

It is true that his comparison with an Eastern carpet admits the possibility of "pleasant sensations" being arranged or organized; and Pater confirms this need for organization a few lines later, when he sets down his famous dictum that "all art constantly aspires towards the condition of music." He does not believe in blots uncontrolled by the conscious mind. But he is very far from the information-giving diagram.

This belief that art has its origin in our intuitive rather than our rational faculties, picturesquely asserted by Pater, was worked out historically and philosophically, in the somewhat wearisome volumes of Benedetto Croce, and owing to his authoritative tone, he is usually considered the originator of a new theory of aesthetics. It was, in fact, the reversion to a very old idea. Long before the Romantics had stressed the importance of intuition and self-expression, men had admitted the Dionysiac nature of art. But philosophers had always assumed that the frenzy of inspiration must be controlled by law and by the intellectual power of putting things into harmonious order. And this general philosophic concept of art as a combination of intuition and intellect had been supported by technical necessities. It was necessary to master certain laws and to use the intellect in order to build the Gothic cathedrals, or set up the stained glass windows of Chartres or cast the bronze doors of the Florence Baptistry. When this bracing element of craftsmanship ceased to dominate the artist's outlook, as happened soon after the time of Leonardo, new scientific disciples had to be invented to maintain the intellectual element in art. Such were perspective and anatomy. From a purely artistic point of view, they were unneccessary. The Chinese produced some of the finest landscapes ever painted, without any systematic knowledge of perspective. Greek figure sculpture reached its highest point before the study of anatomy had been systematized. But from the Renaissance onwards, painters felt that these two sciences made their art intellectually respectable. They were two ways of connecting the diagram and the blot.

In the nineteenth century, belief in art as a scientific activity declined, for a quantity of reasons. Science and technology withdrew into specialization. Voltaire's efforts to investigate the nature of heat seem to us ludicrous; Goethe's studies of botany and physics a waste of a great poet's time. In spite of their belief in inspiration, the great Romantics were aware of the impoverishment of the imagination which would take place when science had drifted out of reach, and both Shelley and Coleridge spent much time in chemical experiments. Even Turner, whose letters reveal a singular lack of analytic faculty, annotated Goethe's theories of color, and painted two pictures to demonstrate them. No good. The laws which govern the movement of the human spirit are inexorable. The enveloping assumption, within which the artist has to function, was that science was no longer approachable by any but the specialist. And gradually there grew up the idea that all intellectual activities were hostile to art.

I have mentioned the philosophic development of this view of Croce. Let me give one example of its quiet acceptance by the official mind. The British Council sends all over the world, even to Florence and Rome, exhibitions of children's art—the point of these children's pictures being that they have no instruction of any kind, and do not attempt the troublesome task of painting what they see. Well, why not, after all? The results are quite agreeable—sometimes strangely beautiful; and the therapeutic effect on the children is said to be excellent. It is like one of those small harmless heresies which we are shocked to find were the object of persecution by the Mediaeval Church. When, however, we hear admired modern painters saying that they draw their inspiration from the drawings of children and lunatics, as well as from stains on walls, we recognize that we have accomplices in a revolution.

The lawless and intuitive character of modern art is a familiar theme and certain historians have said that it is symptomatic of a decline in Western civilization. This is journalism—one of those statements that sound well to-day and nonsense to-morrow. It is obvious that the development of physical science in the last hundred years has been one of the most colossal efforts the human intellect has ever made. But I think it is also true that human beings can produce, in a given epoch, only a certain amount of creative energy, and that this is directed to different ends and different times —music in the eighteenth century is the obvious example; and I believe that the dazzling achievements of science during the last seventy years have deflected far more of those skills and endowments which go to the making of a work of art than is usually realized. To begin with, there is the sheer energy. In every molding of a Renaissance palace we are conscious of an immense intellectual energy, and it is the absence of this energy in the nineteenth-century copies of Renaissance buildings which makes them seem so dead. To find a form with the same vitality as a window molding of the Palazzo Farnese I must wait till I get back into an aeroplane, and look at the relation of the engine to the wing. That form is alive, not (as used to be said) because it is functional—many functional shapes are entirely uninteresting—but because it is animated by the breath of modern science.

The deflections from art to science are the more serious because these are not, as used to be supposed, two contrary activities, but in fact draw on many of the same capacities of the human mind. In the last resort each depends on the imagination. Artist and scientist alike are both trying to give concrete form to dimly apprehended ideas. Dr. Bronowski has put it very well: "All science is the search for unity in hidden likenesses, and the starting point is an image, because then the unity is before our mind's eye." Even if we no longer have to pretend that a group of stars looks like a plough or a bear, our scientists still depend on humanly comprehensible images, and it is striking that the valid symbols of our time, invented to

embody some scientific truth, have taken root in the popular imagination. Do those red and blue balls connected by rods really resemble
a type of atomic structure? I am too ignorant to say. I accept the
symbol just as an early Christian accepted the Fish or the Lamb,
and I find it echoed or even (it would seem) anticipated in the work
of modern artists like Kandinsky and Miró.

Finally, there is the question of popular interest and approval.
We have grown accustomed to the idea that artists can work in
solitude and incomprehension; but that was not the way things happened in the Renaissance or the seventeenth century, still less in
ancient Greece. The pictures carried through the streets by cheering
crowds, the *Te Deum* sung on completion of a public building—all
this indicates a state of opinion in which men could undertake
great works of art with a confidence quite impossible to-day. The
research scientist, on the other hand, not only has millions of
pounds worth of plant and equipment for the asking, he has
principalities and powers waiting for his conclusions. He goes to
work, as Titian once did, confident that he will succeed because the
strong tide of popular admiration is flowing with him.

But although science has absorbed so many of the functions of art
and deflected (I believe) so many potential artists, it obviously
cannot be a *substitute* for art. Its mental process may be similar,
but its ends are different. There have been three views about the
purpose of art. First that it aims simply at imitation; secondly that
it should influence human conduct; and thirdly that it should produce a kind of exalted happiness. The first view, which was
developed in ancient Greece, must be reckoned one of the outstanding failures of Greek thought. It is simply contrary to experience, because if the visual arts aimed solely at imitating things they
would be of very little importance; whereas the Greeks above all
people knew that they were important, and treated them as such.
Yet such was the prestige of Greek thought that this theory of art
was revived in the Renaissance, in an uncomfortable sort of way,
and had a remarkable recrudescence in the nineteenth century. The
second view, that art should influence conduct and opinions, is more
respectable, and held the field throughout the Middle Ages; indeed
the more we learn about the art of the past and motives of those
who commissioned it, the more important this particular aim
appears to be; it still dominated art theory in the time of Diderot.
The third view, that art should produce a kind of exalted happiness,
was invented by the Romantics at the beginning of the nineteenth
century (well, perhaps *invented* by Plotinus, but given currency by
the Romantics), and gradually gained ground until by the end of
the century it was believed in by almost all educated people. It has
held the field in Western Europe till the present day. Leaving aside
the question which of these theories is correct, let me ask which

of them is most likely to be a helpful background to art (for that is all that a theory of aesthetics can be) in an age when science has such an overwhelming domination over the human mind. The first aim must be reckoned *by itself* to be pointless, since science has now discovered so many ways of imitating appearances, which are incomparably more accurate and convincing than even the most realistic picture. Painting might defend itself against the daguerreo-type, but not against Cinerama.

The popular application of science has also, it seems to me, invalidated the second aim of art, because it is quite obvious that no picture can influence human conduct as effectively as a television advertisement. It is quite true that in totalitarian countries artists are still instructed to influence conduct. But that is either due to technical deficiencies, as in China, where in default of T.V., broad-sheets and posters are an important way of communicating with an illiterate population; or, in Russia, to a philosophic time-lag. The fact is that very few countries have had the courage to take Plato's advice and exclude works of art altogether. They have, therefore, had to invent some excuse for keeping them on, and the Russians are still using the pretext that paintings and sculpture can influence people in favor of socialist and national policies, although it must have dawned on them that these results can be obtained far more effectively by the cinema and television.

So it seems to me that of these three possible purposes of art—imitation, persuasion, or exalted pleasure—only the third still holds good in an age of science; and it must be justified very largely by the fact that it is a feeling which is absent from scientific achievements—although mathematicians have told us that it is similar to the feeling aroused by their finest calculations. We might say that in the modern world the art of painting is defensible only in so far as it is complementary to science.

We are propelled in the same direction by another achievement of modern science, the study of psychology. That peeling away of the psyche, which was formerly confined to spiritual instructors, or the great novelists, has become a commonplace of conversation. When a good, solid, external word like Duty is turned into a vague, uneasy, internal word like Guilt, one cannot expect artists to take much interest in good, solid, external objects. The artist has always been involved in the painful process of turning himself inside out, but in the past his inner convictions have been of such a kind that they can, so to say, re-form themselves round an object. But, as we have seen, even in Leonardo's time, there were certain obscure needs and patterns of the spirit, which could discover themselves only through less precise analogies—the analogies provided by stains on walls or the embers of a fire. Now, I think that in this inward-looking age, when we have become so much more aware of the vagaries of the spirit, and so respectful of the working of the unconscious, the artist is more likely to find his point of departure in analogies of this kind. They are more exciting because they, so to say, take us by surprise, like forgotten smells; and they seem to be more profound because the memories they awaken have been deeply buried in our minds. Whether Jung is right in believing that this free, undirected, illogical form of mental activity will allow us to pick up, like a magic radio station, some deep memories of our race which can be of universal interest, I do not know. The satisfaction we derive from certain combinations of shape and color does seem to be inexplicable even by the remotest analogies, and may perhaps involve inherited memories. It is not yet time for the art-historian to venture in to that mysterious jungle. I must, however, observe that our respect for the unconscious mind not only gives us an interest in analogy blots, but in what I called "gesture blots" as well. We recognize how free and forceful such a communication can be, and this aspect of art has become more important in the last ten years. An apologist of modern art has said: "What we want to know is not what the world looks like, but what we mean to each other." So the gesture blot becomes a sort of ideogram, like primitive Chinese writing. Students of Zen assure us it is a means of communication more direct and complete than anything which our analytic system can achieve. Almost 2,000 years before Leonardo looked for images in blots, Lao-tzu had written:

> The Tao is something blurred and indistinct.
> How indistinct! How blurred!
> Yet within are images,
> How blurred! How indistinct!
> Yet within are things.

I said that when the split took place between our faculties of measurement and intuition, *architecture* went off with the diagram. Of course architecture had always been involved with measurement and calculation, but we tend to forget how greatly it was also involved with the imitation of external objects. "The question to be determined," said Ruskin, "is whether architecture is a frame for the sculpture, or the sculpture an ornament of the architecture." And he came down on the first alternative. He thought that a building became architecture only in so far as it was a frame for figurative sculpture. I wonder if there is a single person alive who would agree with him. And yet Ruskin had the most sensitive eye and the keenest analytic faculty that has ever been applied to architecture. Many people disagreed with him in his own day; they thought that sculpture should be subordinate to the total design of the building. But that anything claiming to be architecture could dispense with ornament altogether never entered anyone's head till a relatively short time ago.

A purely diagrammatic architecture is only about thirty years older than a purely blottesque painting; yet it has changed the face of the world and produced in every big city a growing uniformity. Perhaps because it is a little older, perhaps because it seems to have a material justification, we have come to accept it without question. People who are still puzzled or affronted by action painting are proud of the great steel and glass boxes which have arisen so miraculously in the last ten years. And yet these two are manifestations of the same state of mind. The same difficulties of function, the same deflection from the external object, and the same triumph of science. Abstract painting and glass box architecture are related in two different ways. There is the direct relationship of style—the kind of relationship which painting and architecture had with one another in the great consistent ages of art like the 13th and 17th centuries. For modern architecture is not simply functional; at its best it has a style which is almost as definite and as arbitrary as Gothic. And this leads me back to my earlier point: that diagrams can be drawn in order to achieve some imagined perfection, similar to that of certain mathematical propositions. Thirty years after Pater's famous dictum, painters in Russia, Holland, and France began to put into practice the theory that "all art constantly aspires to the condition of music"; and curiously enough this Pythagorean mystique of measurements produced a style—the style which reached its purest expression in the Dutch painter, Mondrian. And through the influence of the Bauhaus, this became the leading style of modern architecture.

The other relationship between contemporary architecture and painting appears to be indirect and even accidental. I am thinking of the visual impact when the whole upper part of a tall glass building mirrors the clouds or the dying embers of a sunset, and so becomes a frame for a marvelous, moving Tachiste[3] picture. I do not think that future historians of art will find this accidental at all, but will see it as the culmination of a long process beginning in the Romantic period, in which, from Wordsworth and De Quincey onwards, poets and philosophers recognized the movement of clouds as the symbol of a newly discovered mental faculty.

Such, then, would be my diagnosis of the present condition of art. I must now, by special request, say what I think will happen to art in the future. I think that the state of affairs which I have called the blot and the diagram will last for a long time. Architecture will continue to be made up of glass boxes and steel grids, without ornament of any kind. Painting will continue to be subjective and arcane, an art of accident rather than rule, of stains on walls rather than of calculation, of inscape rather than of external reality.

3. A method of nonrepresentational contemporary painting which exploits the quality of freely flowing oil paint for its own sake.

This conclusion is rejected by those who believe in a social theory of art. They maintain that a living art must depend on the popular will, and that neither the blot nor the diagram is popular; and, since those who hold a social theory of art are usually Marxists, they point to Soviet Russia as a country where all my conditions obtain—differentiation of function, the domination of science and so forth—and yet what we call modern art has gained no hold. This argument does not impress me. There is of course, nothing at all in the idea that Communist doctrines inevitably produce social realism. Painting in Yugoslavia, in Poland and Hungary is in the same modern idiom as painting in the United States, and shows remarkable vitality. Whereas the official social realism of the U.S.S.R., except for a few illustrators, lacks life or conviction, and shows no evidence of representing the popular will. In fact Russian architecture has already dropped the grandiose official style, and I am told that this is now taking place in painting also. In spite of disapproval amounting to persecution, experimental painters exist and find buyers.

I doubt if the Marxists are even correct in saying that the blot and the diagram are not popular. The power, size, and splendor of, say, the Seagram building in New York makes it as much the object of pride and wonder as great architecture was in the past. And one of the remarkable things about Tachisme is the speed with which it has spread throughout the world, not only in sophisticated centers, but in small local art societies. It has become as much an international style as Gothic in the 14th and Baroque in the 17th centuries. I recently visited the exhibition of a provincial academy in the north of England, a very respectable body then celebrating its hundred and fiftieth anniversary. A few years ago it had been full of Welsh mountain landscapes, and scenes of streets and harbors, carefully delineated. Now practically every picture was in the Tachiste style, and I found that many of them were painted by the same artists, often quite elderly people, who had previously painted the mountains and streets. As works of art, they seemed to me neither better nor worse. But I could not help thinking that they must have been less trouble to do, and I reflected that the painters must have had a happy time releasing the Dionysiac elements in their natures. However, we must not be too cynical about this. I do not believe that the spread of action painting is due solely to the fact that it is easy to do. Cubism, especially synthetic Cubism, also looks easy to do, and never had this immense diffusion. It remained the style of a small élite of professional painters and specialized art lovers; whereas Tachisme has spread to fabrics, to the decoration of public buildings, to the backgrounds of television programs, to advertising of all kinds. Indeed the closest analogy to action painting is the most popular art of all—the art of jazz. The trumpeter who rises

from his seat as one possessed, and squirts out his melody like a
scarlet scrawl against a background of plangent dashes and dots, is
not as a rule performing for a small body of intellectuals.

Nevertheless, I do not think that the style of the blot and the
diagram will last forever. For one thing, I believe that the imitation
of external reality is a fundamental human instinct which is bound
to reassert itself. In his admirable book on sculpture called *Aratra
Pentelici*, Ruskin describes an experience which many of us could
confirm. "Having been always desirous," he says,

> that the education of women should begin in learning how to cook, I got
> leave, one day, for a little girl of eleven years old to exchange, much to her
> satisfaction, her schoolroom for the kitchen. But as ill fortune would have
> it, there was some pastry toward, and she was left unadvisedly in command
> of some delicately rolled paste; whereof she made no pies, but an unlimited
> quantity of cats and mice....

> Now [he continues] you may read the works of the gravest critics of
> art from end to end; but you will find, at last, they can give you no other
> true account of the spirit of sculpture than that it is an irresistible human
> instinct for the making of cats and mice, and other imitable living crea-
> tures, in such permanent form that one may play with the images at leisure.

I cannot help feeling that he was right. I am fond of works of art,
and I collect them. But I do not want to hang them on the wall
simply in order to get an electric shock every time that I pass them.
I want to hold them, and turn them round and re-hang them—in
short, to play with the images at leisure. And, putting aside what
may be no more than a personal prejudice, I rather doubt if an art
which depends solely on the first impact on our emotions is
permanently valid. When the shock is exhausted, we have nothing
to occupy our minds. And this is particularly troublesome with an
art which depends so much on the unconscious, because, as we
know from the analysis of dreams, the furniture of our unconscious
minds is even more limited, repetitive, and commonplace than that
of our conscious minds. The blots and stains of modern painting
depend ultimately on the memories of things seen, memories sunk
deep in the unconscious, overlaid, transformed, assimilated to a
physical condition, but memories none the less. *Ex nihilo nihil fit.*
It is not possible for a painter to lose contact with the visible world.

At this point the apes have provided valuable evidence. There is
no doubt that they are Tachiste painters of considerable accomplishment. I do not myself care for the work of Congo the chimp, but
Sophie, the Rotterdam gorilla, is a charming artist, whose delicate
traceries remind me of early Paul Klee. As you know, apes take
their painting seriously. The patterns they produce are not the
result of mere accident, but of intense, if short-lived, concentration,
and a lively sense of balance and space-filling. If you compare the
painting of a young ape with that of a human child of relatively the
same age, you will find that in the first, expressive, pattern-making

stage, the ape is superior. Then, automatically and inexorably the child begins to draw *things*—man, house, truck, etc. This the ape never does. Of course his Tachiste paintings are far more attractive than the child's crude conceptual outlines. But they cannot develop. They are monotonous and ultimately rather depressing.

The difference between the child and the ape does not show itself in aesthetic perception, or in physical perception of any kind, but in the child's power to form a concept. Later, as we know, he will spend his time trying to adapt his concept to the evidence of physical sensation; in that struggle lies the whole of style. But the concept —the need to draw a line round his thought—comes first. Now it is a truism that the power to form concepts is what distinguishes man from the animals; although the prophets of modern society, Freud, Jung, D. H. Lawrence, have rightly insisted on the importance of animal perceptions in balanced human personality, the concept-forming faculty has not declined in modern man. On the contrary, it is the basis of that vast scientific achievement which, as I said earlier, seems almost to have put art out of business.

Now, if the desire to represent external reality depended solely on an interest in visual sensation, I would agree that it might disappear from art and never return. But if, as the evidence of children and monkeys indicates, it depends primarily on the formation of concepts, which are then modified by visual sensation, I think it is bound to return. For I consider the human faculty of forming concepts at least as "inalienable" as "life, liberty, and the pursuit of happiness. . . ."

I am not, of course, suggesting that the imitation of external reality will ever again become what it was in European art from the mid-17th to the late 19th centuries. Such a subordination of the concept to the visual sensation was altogether exceptional in the history of art. Much of the territory won by modern painting will, I believe, be held. For example, freedom of association, the immediate passage from one association to another—which is so much a part of Picasso's painting and Henry Moore's sculpture, is something which has existed in music since Wagner and in poetry since Rimbaud and Mallarmé. (I mean existed consciously; of course it underlies all great poetry and music.) It need not be sacrificed in a return to external reality. Nor need the direct communication of intuition, through touch and an instinctive sense of materials. This I consider pure gain. In the words of my original metaphor, both the association blot and the gesture blot can remain. But they must be given more nourishment: they must be related to a fuller knowledge of the forms and structures which impress us most powerfully, and so become part of our concept of natural order. At the end of the passage in which Leonardo tells the painter that he can look for battles, landscapes, and animals in the stains on walls, he adds this caution, "But first be sure that you know all the members of all things you wish to depict, both the members of the animals and the members of landscapes, that is to say of rocks, plants, and so forth." It is because one feels in Henry Moore's sculpture this knowledge of the members of animals and plants, that his work, even at its most abstract, makes an impression on us different from that of his imitators. His figures are not merely pleasing examples of design, but seem to be a part of nature, "rolled round in Earth's diurnal course with rocks and stones and trees."

Those lines of Wordsworth lead me to the last reason why I feel that the intuitive blot and scribble may not dominate painting forever. Our belief in the whole purpose of art may change. I said earlier that we now believe it should aim at producing a kind of exalted happiness: this really means that art becomes an end in itself. Now it is an incontrovertible fact of history that the greatest art has always been *about* something, a means of communicating some truth which is assumed to be more important than the art itself. The truths which art has been able to communicate have been of a kind which could not be put in any other way. They have been ultimate truths, stated symbolically. Science has achieved its triumph precisely by disregarding such truths, by not asking unanswerable questions, but sticking to the question "how." I confess it looks to me as if we shall have to wait a long time before there is some new belief which requires expression through art rather than through statistics or equations. And until this happens, the visual arts will fall short of the greatest epochs, the ages of the Parthenon, the Sistine Ceiling, and Chartres Cathedral.

I am afraid there is nothing we can do about it. No amount of goodwill and no expenditure of money can affect that sort of change. We cannot even dimly foresee when it will happen or what form it will take. We can only be thankful for what we have got—a vigorous, popular, decorative art, complementary to our architecture and our science, somewhat monotonous, somewhat prone to charlatanism, but genuinely expressive of our time.

QUESTIONS

1. What definition does Clark give of his central metaphor, "the blot and the diagram"? Are "blot" and "diagram" the equivalents of "art" and "science"? Explain.
2. What distinction does Clark make between "analogy (or association) blot" and "gesture blot"? What importance does the distinction have for his discussion of modern painting?
3. In what ways, according to Clark, is the place of science in the modern world similar to the place occupied by science in the past? What past functions of art has science assumed? To what extent does Clark consider the situation satisfactory? What defects does he mention?

4. How does Clark show "blot" painting and "diagram" architecture to be related? Is architecture today an art or a science? How scientific is painting?
5. Clark points out that "the closest analogy to action painting is the most popular art of all—the art of jazz" (p. 695). Is there any jazz analogous to "diagram"? Explain.
6. Study closely some examples of advertising layout. To what extent do they appear influenced by "blot"? Is there influence of "diagram" in any? Are any exemplary of "blot" and "diagram" in harmony?
7. What extensions into other disciplines can be made of Clark's blot-diagram antithesis? Does it apply in literature? In psychology?
8. Why, according to Clark, will man's concept-forming nature eventually bring about a change of style in art?

LESTER D. LONGMAN
Criteria in Criticism of Contemporary Art

What we value in art today is not clear. We have systematically depreciated all the qualities which are discriminated in standard aesthetic theory as perennially desirable. Respectable critics agree fairly well in their approval of trends and general classes of objects, but are vague or negligent in considering the qualities which might sustain a work of art after interest in an approved trend or class of objects declines. As a result, it is virtually impossible to predict a critic's opinion of a particular contemporary work of art even when one knows the critic well. This is especially obvious when the artist is relatively unknown and when he can't be clearly classified.

As recently as twenty-five years ago this was not true. When we knew the critic, we knew that he would commend a work of art for its pictorial design, its technical virtuosity, its social commentary, its truth to medium, its functional utility, its humanistic insight, or some similiar virtue conceived to transcend the enthusiasms of the moment. Today, however, any clear criterion seems dogmatic. Confronted with what appears to be the only alternative, we prefer anarchy in criticism.

A major cause of this anarchy seems to be that critics no longer respect the independence of their profession. In theory, a criticism is a judicial appraisal, which is as detached and objective as possible, viewing the work from a more comprehensive perspective than that of the artist. Now, however, critics seem to be entangled with the artists themselves in a common syndrome of preoccupations and involvements. They pronounce their opinions from within the same charmed circle of shared experiences, enjoying the same emotional commitments and the same prestige of an *avant-garde* status, desiring no larger frame of reference, and using the same prejudicial or equivocal terminology. The psychology of the perpetual revolutionary holds tightly in its grip both artist and critic. Hence, neither can afford to consult tradition, consider the more permanent values, or even be unambiguous in view of the certainty of continuous change.

For the critic this is a form of abdication, a renunciation of the art of criticism. What he writes may still be interesting, just as what the artist paints may still be interesting—so long as the current mood persists; but he should be detached enough to observe that in the long run more is required of the artist than to be representative of his time, and more is required of himself than sophisticated involvement in the passions of the moment. One remembers the infatuations to which many critics succumbed in the recent past—to surrealism, to social realism, to regionalism, to cubism, etc. We bought for museums and gave prizes to the right kind of art, that which was then new and respectable. With the passage of time our enthusiasms were dissipated, and now much that was exciting while *à la mode* seems grotesquely lifeless for lack of those more permanent aesthetic values which would sustain it. A work of art is one thing, an historical artifact quite another, and the critic's function is to distinguish between them at a moment when the rest of us are lost in excited admiration of the latest vogue.

At the present time the criteria of value which seem to enjoy the highest prestige in the world of art are originality and its corollaries, contemporaneity and irrationality. They would be inadequate to define permanent aesthetic value, unless their usual connotations are greatly altered; but they point to art which we consider "vital" and "modern" and, in our zest, credulity, and infatuation with their style, we scarcely miss what we doubt could be attained in any case. And with our psychology of permanent revolution, the critic who stands aside from the enthusiasms of the day, as in any kind of revolution, finds doubt identified with black reaction: he who is not with us is against us.

Originality is the paramount value today. The term "beauty" has been abandoned, or at most restricted to one kind of aesthetic value like that of Greek art of the fifth and fourth centuries. The general quality of beauty is now designated by the term "originality," much as the surrealists deliberately extended the term "marvelous" to make it synonymous with the beautiful. This usage is bound to generate inconsistencies and non sequiturs, since in aesthetic value neither the new nor the old is inherently superior. We all recognize this in other contexts than a discussion of modern art. Why, then, in modern art does the new seem to have a built-in superiority over the old?

In part, no doubt, it results from our addiction to the religion of progress. We normally prefer new models of every product and assume the new is the better, as frequently it is in the realm of technology where progress is most conspicuous. This is especially true in America. In Rome a large exhibition of contemporary art may contain work in every style since Courbet, with no apparent feeling that older styles are disqualified because they are outmoded. It may also be due to an unconscious analogy with science, where the new is usually superior because of the cumulative character of scientific knowledge. Although there is no parallel in art to this unilinear progress in the evolution of science, in this age of science we can hardly avoid, in any area of activity, the dynamic and pervasive influence of scientific modes of thought.

Strangely enough, this admiration of the latest model is inconsistently reversed when the same critic turns to historic styles. In that case the older object is normally considered superior unless there is incontestable evidence to the contrary. An archaizing Hellenistic sculpture rises immensely in esteem and monetary value if it is proved to be Greek of the transitional period. And "improvements" to pictures introduced by later repaintings are removed, layer by layer, in order to arrive at the superior, older version. Occasionally in this process the original turns out to be rather commonplace, the improvements having been made by a more accomplished artist; nevertheless the older one is preferred. Such an inconsistency should make more obvious the elementary principle that neither the new nor the old in art is valuable artistically because of its age.

In science the new unseats the old when validated by standard procedures of experimental verifications. While there is no analogue in art to this kind of progress, we act as though new work discredits that which went before as soon as it becomes widespread. *Success* is progress. Thus, there can be no such thing as decline or retrogression in the history of art. Even in Late Minoan or West Christian art, historians condemn examples which are *retardataire*[1] in the story of that which succeeds. It is reassuring that no currently successful movement in modern art can possibly represent a general decline. Such reasoning saves us from a morbid concern about the ultimate significance of widespread contemporary styles; although we may sometimes wonder why we now relegate to museum basements much of the art of the nineteenth century, which was international in style and at the time widely approved by cultural authorities. We used to base an adverse judgment of this art on aesthetic and a-historical grounds, but could not do so if originality is beauty and success is the measure of merit. At one time sentimental naturalism was original and it soon became a very successful international style.

1. Appearing late.

In line with this reasoning, the most original artist would be the one with most imitators. We could have no other way to recognize him or to judge an artist's achievement. Thus Michelangelo's art was very original during his life time, but El Greco's would not be until nearly three hundred years after his death; and the significance of a contemporary artist with a following could not be doubted. Such a view seems over-simplified. Avoiding the complexities of aesthetic judgment, it contents itself with historic importance as an agreeably simple substitute.

The current concept of originality in art raises another kind of semantic problem. Again by analogy with science, we tend to apply the term "originality" to those cases which exhibit a new general principle which can be phrased in words, like a new scientific theory. We may coin a word ending in "ism" to designate the new concept. The aesthetic value of a given painting is then determined by the degree to which its character incorporates the values ascribed to the general principle or "ism"; and critics may be content to stop the inquiry at this point, being unaccustomed or unable to judge a work of art on grounds different from those which evaluate the class as a whole. A work of art, however, is not essentially an illustration of an idea; and its originality does not consist of mere conceptual innovation. On the contrary, one may be exceptionally original while working in any established style, for there is an infinite number of possible variations in any general style of expression, and the differential of originality between the most significant and the most negligible example is also infinite.

As historians, we recognize this on many occasions. We do not lament the similarities between Simone Martini and Duccio, Van der Weyden and the Van Eycks, the early Titian and Giorgione, Leonardo and Verrocchio. Although Luini and Gaddi could not do so, it was possible in principle for followers of Leonardo and Giotto to equal or surpass them while continuing to work in the same style. We do not reprove Rouault for imitating Gothic glass, Picasso for imitating Pompeian murals or African sculpture, or Matisse for imitating Persian art; and if David and Canova are not universally admired, it would be an error of judgment to say that it was because they imitated Hellenistic sculpture. In theory, Rembrandt might have had a follower whose work surpassed his own. Indeed, such an imitator could still arise, reviving with exciting new content the same general style, unless art be wholly conditioned by the historical context, and this our concept of originality does not permit. We accept complete historical determinism only when convenient to advocate a prejudice; at other times the complete autonomy of the artist's imagination is a more useful rationalization. The judicious position is that a stylistic revival, incorporating content with which we are concerned today, is always theoretically possible, even when it seems empirically unlikely.

Our inconsistency in believing in originality and simultaneously in historical determinism in modern art leads us to an excessive devaluation of historic art and of many traditional values. Artists and critics of modern art have little time for the Metropolitan Museum. Visiting it for serious study would be like reading a novel in a foreign language, something the average educated man does only occasionally. The greater the artist the less he should fear the weight of tradition; it is the minor artist who escapes its burden by cavalierly declaring that one cannot "revive the past." Rouault, Matisse, and Picasso have proved the value of trying. Michelangelo's generation created a great new art while believing it was engaged in reviving classical forms; and we can see now that David's generation made something new and timely in spite of its very serious intention to imitate. It is so certain that one cannot really revive the past that one need never fear to try.

The identification of originality with ideological innovation is discredited in practice by our esteem for the successive works of major artists. Should Titian have contented himself with one reclining Venus because his first version made the essential point? Or should he have avoided the subject altogether after seeing Giorgione's *Sleeping Venus*, to which he could add only a corollary? Perugino and Botticelli may have painted too many Madonnas, but was one enough? If originality is measured by innovations, Mondrian could have made his point with one painting about 1921, after which his originality could be seriously questioned. Are we misguided to buy and hang on the walls of museums the repetitious variations of an artist's major themes?

It would seem so when we note how artists strain today for the kind of originality which can be classified by a new term, and when we see them abetted in this error by the critics. An artist who strives to be himself will turn out as original as he can be, and the one who succeeds in the long view of history was certainly thinking about something else than originality while he worked. Such an observation is not likely, however, to deter the artist who is anxious to be "modern." He struggles so hard to find a new method that the methodology itself may become the content, for one paints what one is thinking about. He and his fellow artists, eyeing one another in the labor of their lonely battles, end up being eccentric in much the same way. Or he may imitate a recent innovator like Klee or Kandinsky, rather than an older one like Degas or Cézanne; it is no less imitation, but current critical opinion will illogically allow him to retain the eulogistic vocabulary of innovation in speaking about his work.

Another result of our exaltation of the original is an excessive esteem for an art that is disaffected. When every artist and critic feels obliged to become a pioneer of a new movement, they reinforce their efforts by depreciating salutary as well as moribund conventions. David was perhaps the last major artist to glorify the prevailing social ideology; thereafter the history of art is, increasingly as the generations pass in review, a history of rebels against the status quo. Admittedly, the principle of alienation from one's fellows can and has produced great artists; but it has not been the usual pattern in history and we normally (and inconsistently) commend the great painters and sculptors of all periods before the French Revolution for their achievements in faithfully symbolizing the prevailing thought of the ruling classes and intellectuals of their day. We try to explain away the inconsistency by a semantic manipulation, by claiming that the few rebels among us are the true representatives of our time—thus they are both the pioneers of a future culture and simultaneously the "true" spokesmen of the dominant culture against which they rebel.

Our inordinate emphasis on the aesthetic value of originality also leads to excessive tolerance in criticism. If the cardinal virtue of the artist is invention of the new, that of the critic must be to recognize it immediately. What can one say of a critic more reprehensible than that he did not recognize a certain original artist while he lived? Lurid examples of such failures by the distinguished critics over the past hundred years are constantly held up to ridicule to keep alive the awful moral. Who can forget what was said of the Impressionists during the 1870's? Have we overdone it, playing safe by praising every eccentric effort? I am told that in an old movie the Marx Brothers had to play the part of surgeons. They busied themselves rushing around with their tools and equipment and endlessly washing and rewashing their hands and arms clear up to the armpits. Finally someone had the courage to challenge them, saying, "Why don't you get down to business; you guys must be crazy." Whereupon Groucho replied, "That's what they said about Pasteur."

Even our extraordinary critical tolerance is no guarantee that the original artist of our time will be caught in the ample net. For in one respect it may not be ample enough. The majority of critics are expecting to find the true pioneers within the compass of styles approved by the recognized art authorities—representatives of certain art museums, editors of art magazines, certain writers on contemporary movements, and a selection of college professors—in short the representatives of official taste, the vanguard *pompiers*,[2] all of whom have entrenched interests interweaving financial and psychological commitments, and who could not easily change their minds on fundamental matters. Unfortunately, it was the same class of officials who made all the flagrant errors

2. Philistines, conventional or old-fashioned persons.

of the recent past. Will history repeat itself? Are they perhaps again united in dramatic error? If not, who are the Bouguereaus[3] of our generation, highly venerated by authorities today and destined tomorrow to be relegated to museum basements? Or have such egregious errors ceased? We claim the artists who are right are rebels and are few. Can, then, the critics who are right be the official arbiters of taste and their legions of complacent followers who uphold the *status quo*. Where are the rebel critics?

Turning now to the criterion of contemporaneity, which naturally follows from our emphasis upon originality in art, as we have noted an artist who struggles unsuccessfully to be original may be commended by critics if he works within a style of very recent vintage which the leading authorities consider truly contemporary. Many critics believe that abstract expressionism or action painting is the true mode of contemporaneity, or that some mystical determinism will force it upon the future. They proclaim certain artists superior and genuinely progressive abstractionists and others inferior and derivative. The evidence of current critical writing and statements by leading artists suggest that we ordinarily base such judgments upon spontaneous acts of intuition, whose authority rests upon eloquence and office. To believe them is an act of faith in dogma. There are high priests, each with a magic talisman of ineffable sensibility, and from the offices for which they are paid they pronounce aesthetic decrees supported by casually eloquent rationalizations. The rest of us play the game of follow the leader, with the hope that the blind are not leading the blind down a path to ultimate disillusionment and the dark laughter of another generation.

Who, in fact, is qualified to define the content of the term "contemporaneity" for our time? Historians say that the post-impressionists expressed the *Zeitgeist* of the late nineteenth century, but at that time they were scarcely known. Most critics and artists, including even Van Gogh, would have pointed to Bouguereau as typically contemporaneous. Such a view is still reasonable. Either it is no virtue to be contemporaneous, which seems likely, or it is not possible to define contemporaneity, which also seems likely. How often, on the other hand, have we heard it said that a serious artist today has the *obligation* to express our time, and that the important artists are those who do? As a result, many try to conform to what they consider the most respectable version of contemporaneity, which leads them away from those personal concerns which alone can make their art persuasive and enduring.

The current use of the term "contemporaneity" to refer to art not representative of one's time but "ahead of it," introduces

3. Adolphe-William Bouguereau was a nineteenth-century French academic painter acclaimed by the critics in his lifetime and forgotten today.

semantic confusion to promote a cause. We must question whether any artist can succeed in being contemporaneous in this sense by deliberately trying to, and whether any critic can identify the contemporaneous artist while he lives. How can either one predict what the *Zeitgeist* requires of him, or travel ahead of others over the horizon of time merely by taking thought? Such pretense demeans the critic's art, for it can be no more than special pleading disguised as prophecy, and it is irrelevant to aesthetic judgment.

If, on the other hand, to be contemporaneous means to reflect one's time in the most literal sense, then no one can avoid doing so. Everyone today, no matter how he paints or what his critical judgments may be, is reflecting our time in some aspect—Norman Rockwell and Grandma Moses no less than Picasso and Dali or Kline and Barnett Newman, and everyone in equal measure. Thus, in this case, too, the problem of aesthetic evaluation remains to be solved on other grounds.

One hears sometimes from reputable critics that representation is dead, and that it takes abstraction to express contemporaneity. It is true, of course, that those abstract artists who have made a gesture toward reviving representation have ordinarily been unable to carry it far, being content to suggest enigmatically a human figure or part thereof. To be more explicit one must be more sure of what one means to say about the nature of a human being, and must be willing to take the consequences of not being ambiguous. Very few are ready for this at present. We will know how to do it when someone does it, and then it will not look so difficult.

In principle, one might have claimed at any time in history that representation had reached its end and had said all it was capable of saying. Could Giotto's admiring followers have foreseen the images created by Michelangelo, and could Michelangelo's benumbed imitators foretell the vision of Rembrandt? It seems likely that representational forms may be eloquently significant in any age and that their potential variability is unlimited, just as there is no imaginable limit to the number and variety of forms and faces and personalities of human being themselves. Were artists and critics certain of this today many of them would be freed from the needless tensions produced by the contemporaneity complex.

Our emphasis upon originality as the central criterion of aesthetic merit encourages a corollary stress upon irrationality as a value. The surrealists seem to have left their mark upon us when they said that rational thought during the creative act may alter the result, but cannot augment the aesthetic quality of the work of art. Every serious artist knows from personal experience that this is not true. On the other hand original work cannot be produced by pure calculation, and hence cannot be fully accounted for by the critic. In this sense its value is not rational. It does not follow, however, that one can most likely produce something original by using irrational methods of working and by exploiting equivocal and enigmatic content. It is easy to see why we are intrigued by this non sequitur, in a time when the sensitive intellectual is certain of nothing except the appropriateness of uncertainty, and when he fears the creeping mechanization of life. To him, art which is systematically irrational will seem "vitally contemporaneous." The time will come, of course, when this point of view is out of date and today's paintings and sculpture will be judged by the more perennial aesthetic values. A responsible critic interested in judicial appraisals will be *avant-garde* in recognizing this now.

At the moment, however, critics of prestige imitate the artists they admire in their apotheosis of the irrational, assuming like the surrealists that rational criticism only illuminates the inconsequential and does not touch the aesthetic. If this were true, even criticism in the limited sense of "verbal equivalents expressed in poetic form" would be impossible, for one can never know the intent of the artist if it be wholly irrational. Such criticism is often met in journalistic literature, but with increasing frequency the critic is following the complete logic of his premises. He stops trying to uncover and paraphrase the intent of the artist. He writes instead a poetic arrangement of words and ideas which the work of art suggests at least to him, and which fits into and tends to complete and perfect his own notion of the spiritually contemporaneous. By implication, anyone else has an equal right to do the same, hoping that literary distinction may suffice to replace the judicial objectivity which eludes our grasp. Any question regarding the accuracy, the truth, or even the appropriateness of such "criticism" would be meaningless. Thus in criticism, as in art itself, the door is wide open to sensationalism and to anarchy. The critic, now an artist with words, inspired by objects conventionally labelled art, pours out a poem distinguished, he hopes, by originality and spiritual contemporaneity. Like the artist, he is inspired by the Dionysiac muses of mystery, magic, mysticism and enigma, of virtuosity, vitality, violence and obscurity. He, too, would be a pioneering artist and share the same motivations and prejudices. He would ride side by side with the artist upon the wave of the future. This is both safer for the moment and more fun than to stand aside and view the artist in the light of a larger perspective and more constant norms, in an effort to predict how his work will stand the test of time.

Meanwhile the *avant-garde* artist, more learned than inspired, profiting by a capacity for intellectual discrimination unusual among the artists of history, emulates the condition of the critic, painting repetitious non-verbal "criticism" of what he considers the well-established doctrines of our mass culture. His work often seems to need and indeed may have clever verbal texts, either supplied in the catalogue or volubly to the critic himself, to be passed on to eager, sympathetic artists and intellectuals in search of what is expected of them. Thus artists disarm critics by assimilating them, rendering them harmless and gaining their cooperation. And critics write poetic descriptions which are inspired by paintings, but which make no claim to genuine relevance—in other words, poetry which has not yet been painted but soon may be.

We do, of course, on occasion use terms like vitality, conviction, and sincerity to describe work which we intuitively approve. But these terms are ambiguous and mercurial. One can be meaninglessly vital; one can be as convinced of error as of truth; and one may also be sincerely insincere. Every critic must have been deluded at one time or another by the apparent vitality, sincerity, and conviction of a dedicated abstract artist. He may have questioned the artist's sense of design and been reminded that a painting which seems well-designed by current taste is already dead, and that it is a signal virtue for a painting to have a built-in non-art quality; later it will *become* art. Did the technical inadequacy of the artist disturb him? If so, he may have forgotten that good technique is merely being able to say what one wants to say, and that each picture requires and generates its own technique; otherwise it couldn't be original enough to merit our attention. Was the content apparently vacuous? Perhaps he failed to understand its private symbolism and cosmic import. The artist is able to explain at length with indubitable sincerity and conviction. A tolerant critic in such a case may fear to chance an error.

How disillusioning, then, if one discovers later that the artist had been deceiving himself, that he admits to having been an opportunist with one eye on the dealer's prejudice, or that of the museum director, the exhibition jury, or art editor—all of whom expect the sincere artist to work in a variation on an approved manner—to be original, but not too original. In art, the *avant-garde* artist may be a typical "organization man." He may sincerely misunderstand his own motives, conforming to prevailing official taste with the utmost conviction. And, at the same time, for years he may employ the eulogistic vocabulary of individualism and freedom of expression to describe his principles and his work. The critic is in no position to illuminate his true condition for, unlike the psychoanalyst, he shares the same couch with the artist.

Our confusion in criticism is also compounded by our indulgence in semantic transformations, by which terms lose their pristine meaning through a process of intentional forfeiture. Our purpose is to rationalize our prejudices, as when a tyranny claims to be another form of democracy, or slavery is pronounced a form of freedom after the yoke ceases to be felt about the neck. Thus, both terms are rendered useless if we accept the partial truth that abstraction is but another form of representation, or vice versa. "Humanism" is surely broad enough when used to designate those works of art which interpret the condition of man; it becomes useless if extended to designate, as well, all works which manifest the condition of the artist who made them.

Even the term "irrational" may be destroyed by extention, as when we equate it with the accidental. To say that creative art is irrational in nature is not to admit that it is accidental, even though at times a quality is found by accident. Jumping to this conclusion, however, dadaistic artists in large numbers endeavor to create art by contriving accidents and critics are prepared to judge it good if the accidents are fortunate. In the process, art becomes anonymous and the values once attributed to self-expression are lost. It follows, too, that art cannot in any sense be taught, although we still get paid for going through the motions. And, finally, the respectability of this art of anonymity justifies the serious consideration which we give to paintings made by chimpanzees and parrots, to whom as to humans fortunate accidents may happen.

Because in most artistic excellence there is an element of originality, we let the part stand for the whole and equate these terms to the detriment of both. Because in originality there is an element of the irrational we often equate these terms, and all that is irrational becomes original. Because in the irrational there may be an element of the accidental—at least there is no evident casual determinism at work—we equate these terms. And thus, at length, the beautiful in art becomes the accidental; and to be consistent we are obliged to hang the work of a chimpanzee or parrot and consider it for prizes—except when the authorities announce in advance that the exhibition is open only to humans for reasons of space limitations. One beholds this state of affairs as did the peasant who looked for the first time at a camel and said: "It isn't true." And one is reminded of Verdi's reputed remark: "Let us return to old times and that will be progress." It undoubtedly would be although, of course, this is not enough to ask in an age of restless vitality and rich endowment.

We need to re-examine the adequacy of the criteria of originality, contemporaneity, and irrationality by which we judge the merits of contemporary art. We need to stop misusing terms for the purpose of advocacy. And the critic needs to divorce himself from the enticing world of involvements, enthusiasms, and commitments enjoyed by the artist, in order that he may repair his damaged vocabulary, view the scene from a larger and more enduring perspective, and revive his power to make judicial appraisals based upon clear and independent reasoning.

QUESTIONS

1. Outline Longman's essay. What is his thesis concerning the criteria prevailing in contemporary art criticism? Concerning the role of the art critic? What criteria does he discuss, and in what order? Which criterion is dominant? What is Longman's main argumentative strategy in presenting his case against the validity or adequacy of these criteria?
2. What causes, in Longman's view, help bring about the great value placed upon originality in art? Which of these involve a transference of ideas from other phenomena to art? Which such transferences does Longman consider faulty? What distinction does he draw between new work in science and new work in art?
3. What specific inconsistencies does Longman point to as incurred by the criterion of originality? What results from the application of this criterion does Longman specially deprecate? What does the anecdote about the Marx Brothers illustrate?
4. Why does Longman object to "contemporaneity" as a criterion for art? What confusions does the term entail? How is it used as a term of advocacy, to promote a cause?
5. Does Longman deny that irrationality is a component in art? Explain.
6. "In art, the avant-garde artist may be a typical 'organization man' " (p. 708). Explain Longman's meaning.
7. What relationships does Longman indicate between aberrancies in contemporary art criticism and other characteristics of modern life?
8. Both Longman and Clark ("The Blot and the Diagram," p. 696) mention painting by chimpanzees. Compare their attitudes toward the phenomenon and what it signifies.
9. Does Longman's essay constitute an attack upon modern art? Explain.

JOSEPH WOOD KRUTCH
Modern Painting

I am, I hope, not insensitive to any of the arts. I have spent happy hours in museums, and I listen with pleasure to Bach, Mozart, and Beethoven. But I have more confidence in my ability to understand what is said in words than I have in my understanding of anything that dispenses with them. Such opinions as I hold concerning modern music or modern painting are as tentative as those I once expressed in these pages[1] about modern architecture.

Nevertheless, as I said on that occasion, it is one of the privileges of the essayist to hold forth on subjects he doesn't know much about. Because he does not pretend to any expertness, those who

1. "If You Don't Mind My Saying So," Mr. Krutch's regular column in *The American Scholar.*

know better than he what he is talking about need be no more than mildly exasperated. His misconceptions may give valuable hints to those who would set him right. If he didn't expose his obtuseness, his would-be mentors wouldn't know so well just what the misconceptions are and how they arose. An honest philistinism is easier to educate than the conscious or unconscious hypocrisy of those who admire whatever they are told that they should.

In the case of modern painting, the very fact that I can take pleasure in some of the works of yesterday's *avant-garde* but little in that of my own day suggests, even to me, that I may be merely the victim of a cultural lag. But there is no use in pretending that I am delighted by what delights me not, and I find that much serious criticism of the most recent painting is no help. Those who write it are talking over my head; they just don't start far enough back.

For instance, I read in the *Nation* that what a certain painter I had never heard of had accomplished during the war might be summarized as "an unstructured painterliness—neither expressionist nor surrealist in character, and therefore out of keeping with available alternatives." Shortly after the war "he followed through with an intimation of the picture facade as its own reason for being, preferring a unitary sensation, by being irregularly blotted out by masses that kept on pushing at, and disappearing past, the perimeters. Executed on a vastness of scale quite unprecedented in easel painting (which he was in any event attacking), these paintings sidestep drawing and the illusion of spatial recession without ever giving the impression of evasiveness. The result was a sense of the picture surface—now extraordinarily flattened—as a kind of wall whereby constricted elements no longer had any exclusive formal relationship with one another."

When I read things like that my first impulse is to exclaim, "If that young man expresses himself in terms too deep for me..."[2] But then I realize the possibility that the words do say something to those whose visual perceptions are better trained than mine. I am at best a second grader, still struggling with the multiplication table, who has wandered into a seminar at the Institute for Advanced Studies.

When, therefore, I happened to see an advertisement of the Book-of-the-Month Club explaining that the Metropolitan Museum of Art had been persuaded to prepare a twelve-part seminar on art, which could be subscribed to for "only $60," I had the feeling that this might very well be getting down to my level. The advertisement was adorned by reproductions of two contrasting pictures: one of the Metropolitan's own "Storm" (or "Paul and

2. " * * * Why, what a most particularly deep young man that deep young man must be." So the aesthete Bunthorne sings admiringly of himself in Gilbert and Sullivan's *Patience*.

Virginia") by Pierre Cot, and the other of a swirling abstraction.
"Which of these is a good painting?" demanded the headline. My
immediate answer "Neither." And I was not too much discouraged
by the fact that I was pretty sure this was not the right answer.

I think I know at least some of the reasons why "The Storm" is
not one of the great masterpieces—even though some supposedly
competent expert must have once paid a whopping price for it. On
the other hand, I had not the slightest idea why the abstraction
was good or even just not quite as bad as the supposedly horrid
example facing it.

I confess that I did not subscribe to the seminars. But I did
borrow a set from an acquaintance who had done so, and I must
report that I did understand what the Metropolitan people were
saying as I had not understood the *Nation* critic. But I was not by
any means wholly convinced. Many years ago I read Roger Fry on
"Significant Form" and the terrible-tempered Albert Barnes on *The
Art in Painting*. I found nothing in the Metropolitan seminar that
was not this doctrine somewhat updated, and I was no more convinced than I had been by the earlier critics that what they were
talking about was indeed the only thing in painting worth talking
about, or that significant form by itself (if that is possible) was as
good as, if not better than, classical paintings in which equally significant form had been imposed upon subject matters themselves
interesting or moving in one way or another. In that problem lies
the real crux of the matter. Granted that "composition," "significant form," or whatever you want to call it is a *sine qua non* of
great painting, is it also the one thing necessary? Is it *the* art in
painting or only *an* art in painting? My mentors from the Metropolitan are by no means fanatical. They never themselves insist that
subject matter, or the communication of an emotion in connection
with it, is irrelevant in judging a picture. But unless my memory
fails me, they never really face the question of the extent to which
the painter who abandons the suggestion of a subject matter is to
that extent lesser than one who at the same time tells a story,
reveals a character, or communicates an attitude.

The hopeful student is confronted at the very beginning with
what seems to me this unanswered question. He is warned that
"Whistler's Mother" was called by the artist "Arrangement in Grey
and Black"—and let that be a lesson to you. You may think that
your enjoyment of the picture derives from its "appealing likeness
of the author's mother and from sentimental associations with old
age," but "the *real* [italics in the original] subject is something
else . . . We may ask whether the picture would be just as effective
if we omitted the subject altogether . . . the abstract school of contemporary painting argues that subject matter is only something
that gets in the way. It confuses the issue—the issue being pure

expression by means of color, texture, line, and shape existing in their own right and representing nothing at all."

Throughout the course, stress is laid again and again on the comparison between two seemingly very different pictures said to be similar, although I don't think they are ever said to be identical. For instance, Vermeer's "The Artist and His Studio" is compared with Picasso's "The Studio." "Picasso," I am told, "had sacrificed . . . the interest inherent in the objects comprising the picture . . . the fascination and variety of natural textures . . . the harmonies of flowing light, the satisfaction of building solid forms out of light and shape. What has he gained? . . . Complete freedom to manipulate the forms of his picture . . . The abstractionist would argue that the enjoyment of a picture like Picasso's 'The Studio' is more intense because it is purer than the enjoyment we take in Vermeer."

Is "purer" the right adjective? Is it purer or merely thinner? To me the answer is quite plain and the same as that given to the proponents of pure poetry who argued that poetry is essentially only sound so that the most beautiful single line in French literature is Racine's "*La fille de Minos et de Pasiphaé*," not because the genealogy of Phèdre was interesting but just because the sound of the words is delightful. The sound of "O frabjous day! Callooh! Callay!" is also delightful but I don't think it as good as, for instance, "No spring, nor summer beauty hath such grace,/ As I have seen in one autumnal face."

It is all very well to say that two pictures as different as those by Vermeer and Picasso are somewhat similar in composition and that to this extent they produce a somewhat similar effect. But to say that the total experience of the two is not vastly different is, so it seems to me, pure nonsense and so is the statement that the two experiences are equally rich.

The author of the seminar session just quoted seems himself to think so when he writes: "But we also contend that a painting is a projection of the personality of the man who painted it, and a statement of the philosophy of the age that produced it."

If that is true, then the painter who claims to be "painting nothing but paint" is either a very deficient painter or is, perhaps without knowing it, projecting his personality and making a statement of a philosophy of the age that produced it. He is doing that just as truly and just as inevitably as Whistler was doing more than an arrangement in black and grey. And if that also is true, then the way to understand what is most meaningful and significant in any modern painting is to ask what it is that the painter, consciously or not, is revealing about his personality and about the age that finds his philosophy and his personality congenial.

At least that much seems often to be admitted by admiring critics of certain painters not fully abstract but who seem to be interested primarily in pure form. Take, for instance, the case of Ferdinand Léger and his reduction of the whole visible world, including human beings, to what looks like mechanical drawings. Are they examples of pure form meaning nothing but themselves? Certainly they are not always so considered by admirers. When the painter died in 1955 the distinguished critic André Chastel wrote:

> From 1910 on, his views of cities with smoke-like zinc, his country scenes inspired as if by a woodchopper, his still lifes made as if of metal, clearly showed what always remained his inspiration: the maximum hardening of a world of objects, which he made firmer and more articulate than they are in reality. Sacrifice of color and nuance was total and line was defined with severity and a well-meaning aggressiveness, projecting his violent, cold Norman temperament. This revolution he consecrated himself to seemed rather simple—the exaltation of the machine age, which after 1920 dominated the western world.

To me it seems equally plain that even those who profess to paint nothing but paint are in fact doing a great deal more because they would not find anything of the sort to be the real aim of painting unless they had certain attitudes toward nature, toward society, and toward man. What that attitude is cannot, I think, be very well defined without recourse to two words that I hate to use because they have become so fashionable and are so loosely tossed about. What these painters are expressing is the alienation of the existentialist. They no longer represent anything in the external world because they no longer believe that the world that exists outside of man in any way shares or supports human aspirations and values or has any meaning for him. They are determined, like the existential moralist, to go it alone. They do not believe that in nature there is anything inherently beautiful, just as the existentialist moralizer refuses to believe that there is any suggestion of moral values in the external universe. The great literature and painting of the past have almost invariably been founded upon assumptions the exact opposite of these. They expressed man's attempt to find beauty and meaning in an external world from which he was not alienated because he believed that both his aesthetic and his moral sense corresponded to something outside himself.

Salvador Dali (whom, in general, I do not greatly admire) once made the remark that Picasso's greatness consisted in the fact that he had destroyed one by one all the historical styles of painting. I am not sure that there is not something in that remark, and if there is, then it suggests that in many important respects Picasso is much like the workers in several branches of literature whose aim is to destroy the novel with the antinovel, the theater with the antitheater, and philosophy by philosophies that consist, like logical positivism and linguistic analysis, in a refusal to philosophize. They are all determined, as the surrealist André Breton once said he was, to "wring the neck of literature."

Having now convinced myself of all these things, I will crawl farther out on a limb and confess that I have often wondered if the new styles created by modern painters—pointillism, cubism, surrealism, and the mechanism of Léger (to say nothing of op and pop)—ought not be regarded as gimmicks rather than actual styles. And to my own great astonishment I have discovered that Picasso himself believes, or did once believe, exactly that.

The luxurious French monthly *Jardin des Arts* published (March 1964) a long and laudatory article on Picasso in the course of which it cited "a text of Picasso on himself" which had been reproduced at various times but most recently in a periodical called *Le Spectacle du Monde* (November 1962). I translate as follows:

When I was young I was possessed by the religion of great art. But, as the years passed, I realized that art as one conceived it up to the end of the 1880's was, from then on, dying, condemned, and finished and that the pretended artistic activity of today, despite all its superabundance, was nothing but a manifestation of its agony . . . Despite appearances our contemporaries have given their heart to the machine, to scientific discovery, to wealth, to the control of natural forces, and of the world . . . From that moment when art became no longer the food of the superior, the artist was able to exteriorize his talent in various sorts of experiments, in new formulae, in all kinds of caprices and fantasies, and in all the varieties of intellectual charlatanism . . .

As for me, from cubism on I have satisfied these gentlemen [rich people who are looking for something extravagant] and the critics also with all the many bizarre notions which have come into my head and the less they understood the more they admired them . . . Today, as you know, I am famous and rich. But when I am alone with my soul, I haven't the courage to consider myself as an artist. In the great and ancient sense of that word, Greco, Titian, Rembrandt, and Goya were great painters. I am only the entertainer of a public which understands its age.

Chirico is another modern painter who has said something very much like this. But enough of quotations. And to me it seems that Picasso said all that I have been trying to say, namely, that a picture somehow involved with the world of reality outside man is more valuable than one that has nothing to say about anything except the painter himself. What he calls painters "in the great and ancient sense of that word" were able to be such only because they were not alienated existentialists.

QUESTIONS

1. *Indicate particular details that show what Krutch suggests to be the proper business of an essayist.*

2. What is this essay's thesis? What assumptions underlie the thesis?
3. What relationship does Krutch see between modern painting and "the philosophy of the age"? How does he attempt to demonstrate, or illustrate, that relationship? Is this view persuasive? Why, or why not?
4. Does Krutch assume that his audience is disposed at the outset to think of modern painting very much as he does, or very differently? to think as he does in some particulars, and not in others? Show, by specific details of his manner, what attitudes he seems to expect, what responses he anticipates.
5. Why does Krutch quote (p. 711) a passage he has read about a certain painter? What can be learned from the quotation? Would it help to know the identity of the painter? Why doesn't Krutch name him?
6. What effect does Krutch achieve by referring twice, in two separate connections, to Picasso?

HENRI BERGSON

The Comic in General; the Comic Element in Forms and Movements[1]

What does laughter mean? What is the basal element in the laughable? What common ground can we find between the grimace of a merry-andrew,[2] a play upon words, an equivocal situation in a burlesque and a scene of high comedy? What method of distillation will yield us invariably the same essence from which so many different products borrow either their obtrusive odor or their delicate perfume? The greatest of thinkers, from Aristotle downwards, have tackled this little problem, which has a knack of baffling every effort, of slipping away and escaping only to bob up again, a pert challenge flung at philosophic speculation.

Our excuse for attacking the problem in our turn must lie in the fact that we shall not aim at imprisoning the comic spirit within a definition. We regard it, above all, as a living thing. However trivial it may be, we shall treat it with the respect due to life. We shall confine ourselves to watching it grow and expand. Passing by imperceptible gradations from one form to another, it will be seen to achieve the strangest metamorphoses. We shall disdain nothing we have seen. Maybe we may gain from this prolonged contact, for the matter of that, something more flexible than an abstract definition—a practical, intimate acquaintance, such as springs from a long companionship. And maybe we may also find that, unintentionally, we have made an acquaintance that is useful.

1. From the opening section of Bergson's essay "Laughter."
2. A clown.

For the comic spirit has a logic of its own, even in its wildest eccentricities. It has a method in its madness. It dreams, I admit, but it conjures up in its dreams visions that are at once accepted and understood by the whole of a social group. Can it then fail to throw light for us on the way that human imagination works, and more particularly social, collective, and popular imagination? Begotten of real life and akin to art, should it not also have something of its own to tell us about art and life?

At the outset we shall put forward three observations which we look upon as fundamental. They have less bearing on the actually comic than on the field within which it must be sought.

I

The first point to which attention should be called is that the comic does not exist outside the pale of what is strictly *human*. A landscape may be beautiful, charming and sublime, or insignificant and ugly; it will never be laughable. You may laugh at an animal, but only because you have detected in it some human attitude or expression. You may laugh at a hat, but what you are making fun of, in this case, is not the piece of felt or straw, but the shape that men have given it—the human caprice whose mold it has assumed. It is strange that so important a fact, and such a simple one too, has not attracted to a greater degree the attention of philosophers. Several have defined man as "an animal which laughs." They might equally well have defined him as an animal which is laughed at; for if any other animal, or some lifeless object, produces the same effect, it is always because of some resemblance to man, of the stamp he gives it or the use he puts it to.

Here I would point out, as a symptom equally worthy of notice, the *absence of feeling* which usually accompanies laughter. It seems as though the comic could not produce its disturbing effect unless it fell, so to say, on the surface of a soul that is thoroughly calm and unruffled. Indifference is its natural environment, for laughter has no greater foe than emotion. I do not mean that we could not laugh at a person who inspires us with pity, for instance, or even with affection, but in such a case we must, for the moment, put our affection out of court and impose silence upon our pity. In a society composed of pure intelligences there would probably be no more tears, though perhaps there would still be laughter; whereas highly emotional souls, in tune and unison with life, in whom every event would be sentimentally prolonged and re-echoed, would neither know nor understand laughter. Try, for a moment, to become interested in everything that is being said and done; act, in imagination, with those who act, and feel with those who feel; in a word, give your sympathy its widest expansion: as though at the touch of a fairy wand you will see the flimsiest of objects assume importance, and a gloomy hue spread over everything. Now step aside, look upon life as a disinterested spectator: many a drama will turn into a comedy. It is enough for us to stop our ears to the sound of music in a room, where dancing is going on, for the dancers at once to appear ridiculous. How many human actions would stand a similar test? Should we not see many of them suddenly pass from grave to gay, on isolating them from the accompanying music of sentiment? To produce the whole of its effect, then, the comic demands something like a momentary anesthesia of the heart. Its appeal is to intelligence, pure and simple.

This intelligence, however, must always remain in touch with other intelligences. And here is the third fact to which attention should be drawn. You would hardly appreciate the comic if you felt yourself isolated from others. Laughter appears to stand in need of an echo. Listen to it carefully: it is not an articulate, clear, well-defined sound; it is something which would fain be prolonged by reverberating from one to another, something beginning with a crash, to continue in successive rumblings, like thunder in a mountain. Still, this reverberation cannot go on for ever. It can travel within as wide a circle as you please: the circle remains, none the less, a closed one. Our laughter is always the laughter of a group. It may, perchance, have happened to you, when seated in a railway carriage or at *table d'hôte*, to hear travelers relating to one another stories which must have been comic to them, for they laughed heartily. Had you been one of their company, you would have laughed like them, but, as you were not, you had no desire whatever to do so. A man who was once asked why he did not weep at a sermon when everybody else was shedding tears replied: "I don't belong to the parish!" What that man thought of tears would be still more true of laughter. However spontaneous it seems, laughter always implies a kind of secret freemasonry, or even complicity, with other laughers, real or imaginary. How often has it been said that the fuller the theatre, the more uncontrolled the laughter of the audience! On the other hand, how often has the remark been made that many comic effects are incapable of translation from one language to another, because they refer to the customs and ideas of a particular social group! It is through not understanding the importance of this double fact that the comic has been looked upon as a mere curiosity in which the mind finds amusement, and laughter itself as a strange, isolated phenomenon, without any bearing on the rest of human activity. Hence those definitions which tend to make the comic into an abstract relation between ideas: "an intellectual contrast," "a patent absurdity," etc., definitions which, even were they really suitable to every form of the comic, would not in the least explain why the comic makes us laugh. How, indeed, should it come about that this particular logical relation, as soon as it is perceived, contracts, expands and shakes our limbs, whilst all other relations leave the body un-affected? It is not from this point of view that we shall approach the problem. To understand laughter, we must put it back into its natural environment, which is society, and above all must we deter-mine the utility of its functions, which is a social one. Such, let us say at once, will be the leading idea of all our investigations. Laughter must answer to certain requirements of life in common. It must have a *social* signification.

Let us clearly mark the point towards which our three preliminary observations are converging. The comic will come into being, it appears, whenever a group of men concentrate their attention on one of their number, imposing silence on their emotions and calling into play nothing but their intelligence. What, now, is the particu-lar point on which their attention will have to be concentrated, and what will here be the function of intelligence? To reply to these questions will be at once to come to closer grips with the problem. But here a few examples have become indispensable.

II

A man, running along the street, stumbles and falls; the passers-by burst out laughing. They would not laugh at him, I imagine, could they suppose that the whim had suddenly seized him to sit down on the ground. They laugh because his sitting down is invol-untary. Consequently, it is not his sudden change of attitude that raises a laugh, but rather the involuntary element in this change—his clumsiness, in fact. Perhaps there was a stone on the road. He should have altered his pace or avoided the obstacle. Instead of that, through lack of elasticity, through absentmindedness and a kind of physical obstinacy, *as a result, in fact, of rigidity or of momentum*, the muscles continued to perform the same movement when the circumstances of the case called for something else. That is the reason of the man's fall, and also of the people's laughter.

Now, take the case of a person who attends to the petty occupa-tions of his everyday life with mathematical precision. The objects around him, however, have all been tampered with by a mischievous wag, the result being that when he dips his pen into the inkstand he draws it out all covered with mud, when he fancies he is sitting down on a solid chair he finds himself sprawling on the floor, in a word his actions are all topsy-turvy or mere beating the air, while in every case the effect is invariably one of momentum. Habit has given the impulse: what was wanted was to check the movement or deflect it. He did nothing of the sort, but continued like a machine in the same straight line. The victim, then, of a practical joke is in a position similar to that of a runner who falls—he is comic for the same reason. The laughable element in both cases consists of a certain *mechanical inelasticity*, just where one would expect to find the wideawake adaptability and the living pliableness of a human being. The only difference in the two cases is that the former happened of itself, whilst the latter was obtained artificially. In the first instance, the passer-by does nothing but look on, but in the second the mischievous wag intervenes.

All the same, in both cases the result has been brought about by an external circumstance. The comic is therefore accidental: it remains, so to speak, in superficial contact with the person. How is it to penetrate within? The necessary conditions will be fulfilled when mechanical rigidity no longer requires for its manifestation a stumbling-block which either the hazard of circumstance or human knavery has set in its way, but extracts by natural processes, from its own store, an inexhaustible series of opportunities for externally revealing its presence. Suppose, then, we imagine a mind always thinking of what it has just done and never of what it is doing, like a song which lags behind its accompaniment. Let us try to picture to ourselves a certain inborn lack of elasticity of both senses and intelligence, which brings it to pass that we continue to see what is no longer visible, to hear what is no longer audible, to say what is no longer to the point: in short, to adapt ourselves to a past and therefore imaginary situation, when we ought to be shaping our conduct in accordance with the reality which is present. This time the comic will take up its abode in the person himself; it is the person who will supply it with everything—matter and form, cause and opportunity. Is it then surprising that the absentminded individual—for this is the character we have just been describing—has usually fired the imagination of comic authors? When La Bruyère[3] came across this particular type, he realized, on analyzing it, that he had got hold of a recipe for the wholesale manufacture of comic effects. As a matter of fact he overdid it, and gave us far too lengthy and detailed a description of *Ménalque*, coming back to his subject, dwelling and expatiating on it beyond all bounds. The very facility of the subject fascinated him. Absentmindedness, indeed, is not perhaps the actual fountain-head of the comic, but surely it is contiguous to a certain stream of facts and fancies which flows straight from the fountain-head. It is situated, so to say, on one of the great natural watersheds of laughter.

Now, the effect of absentmindedness may gather strength in its turn. There is a general law, the first example of which we have just encountered, and which we will formulate in the following terms: when a certain comic effect has its origin in a certain cause, the more natural we regard the cause to be, the more comic shall we find the effect. Even now we laugh at absentmindedness when presented to us as a simple fact. Still more laughable will be the absentmindedness we have seen springing up and growing before

3. Seventeenth-century French moralist, a writer of "characters"; his *Ménalque* describes the absent-minded man.

our very eyes, with whose origin we are acquainted and whose life-history we can reconstruct. To choose a definite example: suppose a man has taken to reading nothing but romances of love and chivalry. Attracted and fascinated by his heroes, his thoughts and intentions gradually turn more and more towards them, till one fine day we find him walking among us like a somnambulist. His actions are distractions. But then his distractions can be traced back to a definite, positive cause. They are no longer cases of *absence* of mind, pure and simple; they find their explanation in the *presence* of the individual in quite definite, though imaginary, surroundings. Doubtless a fall is always a fall, but it is one thing to tumble into a well because you were looking anywhere but in front of you, it is quite another thing to fall into it because you were intent upon a star. It was certainly a star at which Don Quixote was gazing. How profound is the comic element in the over-romantic, Utopian bent of mind! And yet, if you reintroduce the idea of absentmindedness, which acts as a go-between you will see this profound comic element uniting with the most superficial type. Yes, indeed, these whimsical wild enthusiasts, these madmen who are yet so strangely reasonable, excite us to laugher by playing on the same chords within ourselves, by setting in motion the same inner mechanism, as does the victim of a practical joke or the passer-by who slips down in the street. They, too, are runners who fall and simple souls who are being hoaxed—runners after the ideal who stumble over realities, child-like dreamers for whom life delights to lie in wait. But, above all, they are past-masters in absentmindedness, with this superiority over their fellows that their absentmindedness is systematic and organized around one central idea, and that their mishaps are also quite coherent, thanks to the inexorable logic which reality applies to the correction of dreams, so that they kindle in those around them, by a series of cumulative effects, a hilarity capable of unlimited expansion.

Now, let us go a little further. Might not certain vices have the same relation to character that the rigidity of a fixed idea has to intellect? Whether as a moral kink or a crooked twist given to the will, vice has often the appearance of a curvature of the soul. Doubtless there are vices into which the soul plunges deeply with all its pregnant potency, which it rejuvenates and drags along with it into a moving circle of reincarnations. Those are tragic vices. But the vice capable of making us comic is, on the contrary, that which is brought from without, like a ready-made frame into which we are to step. It lends us its own rigidity instead of borrowing from us our flexibility. We do not render it more complicated; on the contrary, it simplifies us. Here, as we shall see later on in the concluding section of this study, lies the essential difference between comedy and drama. A drama, even when portraying passions or vices that bear a name, so completely incorporates them in the person that their names are forgotten, their general characteristics effaced, and we no longer think of them at all, but rather of the person in whom they are assimilated; hence, the title of a drama can seldom be anything else than a proper noun. On the other hand, many comedies have a common noun as their title: *l'Avare*, *le Joueur*, etc. Were you asked to think of a play capable of being called *le Jaloux*, for instance, you would find that *Sganarelle* or *George Dandin* would occur to your mind, but not *Othello*: *le Jaloux* could only be the title of a comedy.⁴ The reason is that, however intimately vice, when comic, is associated with persons, it none the less retains its simple, independent existence, it remains the central character, present though invisible, to which the characters in flesh and blood on the stage are attached. At times it delights in dragging them down with its own weight and making them share in its tumbles. More frequently, however, it plays on them as on an instrument or pulls the strings as though they were puppets. Look closely: you will find that the art of the comic poet consists in making us so well acquainted with the particular vice, in introducing us, the spectators, to such a degree of intimacy with it, that in the end we get hold of some of the strings of the marionette with which he is playing, and actually work them ourselves; this it is that explains part of the pleasure we feel. Here, too, it is really a kind of automatism that makes us laugh—an automatism, as we have already remarked, closely akin to mere absentmindedness. To realize this more fully, it need only be noted that a comic character is generally comic in proportion to his ignorance of himself. The comic person is unconscious. As though wearing the ring of Gyges with reverse effect, he becomes invisible to himself while remaining visible to all the world. A character in a tragedy will make no change in his conduct because he will know how it is judged by us; he may continue therein even though fully conscious of what he is and feeling keenly the horror he inspires in us. But a defect that is ridiculous, as soon as it feels itself to be so, endeavors to modify itself or at least to appear as though it did. Were Harpagon⁵ to see us laugh at his miserliness, I do not say that he would get rid of it, but he would either show it less or show it differently. Indeed, it is in this sense only that laughter "corrects men's manners." It makes us at once endeavor to appear what we ought to be, what some day we shall perhaps end in being.

It is unnecessary to carry this analysis any further. From the runner who falls to the simpleton who is hoaxed, from a state of

---

4. *L'Avare* (*The Miser*) is a play by Molière, and *le Joueur* (*The Gamester*) was the work of his successor, Jean-Francois Regnard. Molière's *Sganarelle* and *George Dandin* have jealous husbands as their chief comic figures, so that *le Jaloux* (*The Jealous Man*) would be a suitable title for either play.

5. The miser of Molière's *l'Avare*.

being hoaxed to one of absentmindedness, from absentmindedness to wild enthusiasm, from wild enthusiasm to various distortions of character and will, we have followed the line of progress along which the comic becomes more and more deeply imbedded in the person, yet without ceasing, in its subtler manifestations, to recall to us some trace of what we noticed in its grosser forms, an effect of automatism and of inelasticity. Now we can obtain a first glimpse —a distant one, it is true, and still hazy and confused—of the laughable side of human nature and of the ordinary function of laughter.

What life and society require of each of us is a constantly alert attention that discerns the outlines of the present situation, together with a certain elasticity of mind and body to enable us to adapt ourselves in consequence. *Tension* and *elasticity* are two forces, mutually complementary, which life brings into play. If these two forces are lacking in the body to any considerable extent, we have sickness and infirmity and accidents of every kind. If they are lacking in the mind, we find every degree of mental deficiency, every variety of insanity. Finally, if they are lacking in the character, we have cases of the gravest inadaptability to social life, which are the sources of misery and at times the causes of crime. Once these elements of inferiority that affect the serious side of existence are removed—and they tend to eliminate themselves in what has been called the struggle for life—the person can live, and that in common with other persons. But society asks for something more; it is not satisfied with simply living, it insists on living well. What it now has to dread is that each one of us, content with paying attention to what affects the essentials of life, will, so far as the rest is concerned, give way to the easy automatism of acquired habits. Another thing it must fear is that the members of whom it is made up, instead of aiming after an increasingly delicate adjustment of wills which will fit more and more perfectly into one another, will confine themselves to respecting simply the fundamental conditions of this adjustment: a cut-and-dried agreement among the persons will not satisfy it, it insists on a constant striving after reciprocal adaptation. Society will therefore be suspicious of all *inelasticity* of character, of mind and even of body, because it is the possible sign of a slumbering activity as well as of an activity with separatist tendencies, that inclines to swerve from the common center round which society gravitates: in short, because it is the sign of an eccentricity. And yet, society cannot intervene at this stage by material repression, since it is not affected in a material fashion. It is confronted with something that makes it uneasy, but only as a symptom—scarcely a threat, at the very most a gesture. A gesture, therefore, will be its reply. Laughter must be something of this kind, a sort of *social gesture*. By the fear which it inspires, it restrains eccentricity, keeps constantly awake and in mutual contact certain activities of a secondary order which might retire into their shell and go to sleep, and in short, softens down whatever the surface of the social body may retain of mechanical inelasticity. Laughter, then, does not belong to the province of esthetics alone, since unconsciously (and even immorally in many particular instances) it pursues a utilitarian aim of general improvement. And yet there is something esthetic about it, since the comic comes into being just when society and the individual, freed from the worry of self-preservation, begin to regard themselves as works of art. In a word, if a circle be drawn round those actions and dispositions—implied in individual or social life—to which their natural consequences bring their own penalties, there remains outside this sphere of emotion and struggle—and within a neutral zone in which man simply exposes himself to man's curiosity—a certain rigidity of body, mind and character that society would still like to get rid of in order to obtain from its members the greatest possible degree of elasticity and sociability. This rigidity is the comic, and laughter is its corrective.

Still, we must not accept this formula as a definition of the comic. It is suitable only for cases that are elementary, theoretical and perfect, in which the comic is free from all adulteration. Nor do we offer it, either, as an explanation. We prefer to make it, if you will, the *leitmotiv* which is to accompany all our explanations. We must ever keep it in mind, though without dwelling on it too much, somewhat as a skilful fencer must think of the discontinuous movements of the lesson whilst his body is given up to the continuity of the fencing-match. We will now endeavor to reconstruct the sequence of comic forms, taking up again the thread that leads from the horseplay of a clown up to the most refined effects of comedy, following this thread in its often unforeseen windings, halting at intervals to look around, and finally getting back, if possible, to the point at which the thread is dangling and where we shall perhaps find—since the comic oscillates between life and art—the general relation that art bears to life.

QUESTIONS

1. What three conditions does Bergson say are necessary to the appearance of comic effect? Does Bergson contradict himself when he says that the appeal of the comic "is to intelligence, pure and simple" but that a definition of the comic as "an abstract relation between ideas" is inadequate? Explain his point.
2. According to what principle does Bergson arrange his examples of the comic in section II of the essay? How are the examples differentiated, and what are they said to have in common?
3. What relationships exist between sections I and II of the essay?
4. What, according to Bergson, is the social function of laughter?

5. One stage of Bergson's analysis of comic effect concerns the practical joke. What considerations might inhibit laughter at this kind of joke? Compare Leacock's attitude toward the practical joke ("Humor as I See It," below).
6. Bergson refers to Don Quixote as exemplary of comic romantic idealism. But few readers consider the Don solely comic. Why not? What considerations might inhibit, or replace, laughter as romantic idealism?
7. Does Bergson's analysis explain the comic effect of animated movie cartoons, often violent and preposterous? How? What qualities of film comedy in general does Bergson's discussion illuminate?

STEPHEN LEACOCK

Humor as I See It

It is only fair that I should be allowed a few pages to myself to put down some things that I really think. Once I might have taken my pen in hand to write about humor with the confident air of an acknowledged professional.

But that time is past. Such claim as I had has been taken from me. In fact I stand unmasked. An English reviewer writing in a literary journal, the very name of which is enough to put contradiction to sleep, has said of my writing, "What is there, after all, in Professor Leacock's humor but a rather ingenious mixture of hyperbole and myosis?"

The man was right. How he stumbled upon this trade secret, I do not know. But I am willing to admit, since the truth is out, that it has long been my custom in preparing an article of a humorous nature to go down to the cellar and mix up half a gallon of myosis with a pint of hyperbole. If I want to give the article a decidedly literary character, I find it well to put in about half a pint of paresis. The whole thing is amazingly simple.

But I only mention this by way of introduction and to dispel any idea that I am conceited enough to write about humor, with the professional authority of Ella Wheeler Wilcox writing about love, or Fred Astaire talking about dancing.

All that I dare claim is that I have as much sense of humor as other people. And, oddly enough, I notice that everybody else makes this same claim. Any man will admit, if need be, that his sight is not good, or that he cannot swim, or shoots badly with a rifle, but to touch upon his sense of humor is to give him a mortal affront.

"No," said a friend of mine the other day, "I never go to Grand Opera," and then he added with an air of pride—"You see, I have absolutely no ear for music."

"You don't say so!" I exclaimed.

"None!" he went on. "I can't tell one tune from another. I don't know *Home, Sweet Home* from *God Save the King*. I can't tell whether a man is tuning a violin or playing a sonata."

He seemed to get prouder and prouder over each item of his own deficiency. He ended by saying that he had a dog at his house that had a far better ear for music than he had. As soon as his wife or any visitor started to play the piano the dog always began to howl—plaintively, he said, as if it were hurt. He himself never did this.

When he had finished I made what I thought a harmless comment.

"I suppose," I said, "that you find your sense of humor deficient in the same way: the two generally go together."

My friend was livid with rage in a moment.

"Sense of humor!" he said. "My sense of humor! Me without a sense of humor! Why, I suppose I've a keener sense of humor than any man, or any two men, in this city!"

From that he turned to bitter personal attack. He said that my sense of humor seemed to have withered altogether.

He left me, still quivering with indignation.

Personally, however, I do not mind making the admission, however damaging it may be, that there are certain forms of so-called humor, or, at least, fun, which I am quite unable to appreciate. Chief among these is that ancient thing called the Practical Joke.

"You never knew McGann, did you?" a friend of mine asked me the other day. When I said, "No, I had never known McGann," he shook his head with a sigh, and said:

"Ah, you should have known McGann. He had the greatest sense of humor of any man I ever knew—always full of jokes. I remember one night at the boarding house where we were, he stretched a string across the passageway and then rang the dinner bell. One of the boarders broke his leg. We nearly died laughing."

"Dear me!" I said. "What a humorist! Did he often do things like that?"

"Oh, yes, he was at them all the time. He used to put tar in the tomato soup, and beeswax and tin-tacks on the chairs. He was full of ideas. They seemed to come to him without any trouble."

McGann, I understand, is dead. I am not sorry for it. Indeed I think that for most of us the time has gone by when we can see the fun of putting tacks on chairs, or thistles in beds, or live snakes in people's boots.

To me it has always seemed that the very essence of good humor is that it must be without harm and without malice. I admit that there is in all of us a certain vein of the old original demoniacal humor or joy in the misfortune of another which sticks to us like our original sin. It ought not to be funny to see a man, especially a fat and pompous man, slip suddenly on a banana skin. But it is. When a skater on a pond who is describing graceful circles and showing off before the crowd, breaks through the ice and gets a ducking, everybody shouts with joy. To the original savage, the cream of the joke in such cases was found if the man who slipped broke his neck, or the man who went through the ice never came up again. I can imagine a group of prehistoric men standing round the ice-hole where he had disappeared and laughing till their sides split. If there had been such a thing as a prehistoric newspaper, the affair would have been headed up: "*Amusing Incident. Unknown Gentleman Breaks Through Ice and Is Drowned.*"

But our sense of humor under civilization has been weakened. Much of the fun of this sort of thing has been lost on us.

Children, however, still retain a large share of this primitive sense of enjoyment.

I remember once watching two little boys making snow-balls at the side of the street and getting ready a little store of them to use. As they worked there came along an old man wearing a silk hat, and belonging by appearance to the class of "jolly old gentlemen." When he saw the boys his gold spectacles gleamed with kindly enjoyment. He began waving his arms and calling, "Now, then, boys, free shot at me! free shot!" In his gaiety he had, without noticing it, edged himself over the sidewalk on to the street. An express cart collided with him and knocked him over on his back in a heap of snow. He lay there gasping and trying to get the snow off his face and spectacles. The boys gathered up their snow-balls and took a run towards him. "Free shot!" they yelled. "Soak him! Soak him!"

I repeat, however, that for me, as I suppose for most of us, it is a prime condition of humor that it must be without harm or malice, nor should it convey even incidentally any real picture of sorrow or suffering or death. There is a great deal in the humor of Scotland (I admit its general merit) which seems to me, not being a Scotchman, to sin in this respect. Take this familiar story (I quote it as something already known and not for the sake of telling it).

A Scotchman had a sister-in-law—his wife's sister—with whom he could never agree. He always objected to going anywhere with her, and in spite of his wife's entreaties always refused to do so. The wife was taken mortally ill and as she lay dying, she whispered, "John, ye'll drive Janet with you to the funeral, will ye no?".The Scotchman, after an internal struggle, answered, "Margaret, I'll do it for ye, but it'll spoil my day."

Whatever humor there may be in this is lost for me by the actual and vivid picture that it conjures up—the dying wife, the darkened room and the last whispered request.

No doubt the Scotch see things differently. That wonderful peo-

ple—whom personally I cannot too much admire—always seem to
me to prefer adversity to sunshine, to welcome the prospect of a
pretty general damnation, and to live with grim cheerfulness within
the very shadow of death. Alone among the nations they have converted the devil—under such names as Old Horny—into a familiar
acquaintance not without a certain grim charm of his own. No
doubt also there enters into their humor something of the original
barbaric attitude towards things. For a primitive people who saw
death often and at first hand, and for whom the future world was
a vivid reality, that could be *felt*, as it were, in the midnight forest
and heard in the roaring storm—for such a people it was no doubt
natural to turn the flank of terror by forcing a merry and jovial
acquaintance with the unseen world. Such a practice as a wake, and
the merrymaking about the corpse, carry us back to the twilight of
the world, with the poor savage in his bewildered misery, pretending that his dead still lived. Our funeral with its black trappings
and its elaborate ceremonies is the lineal descendant of a merrymaking. Our undertaker is, by evolution, a genial master of ceremonies, keeping things lively at the death-dance. Thus have the
ceremonies and the trappings of death been transformed in the
course of ages till the forced gaiety is gone, and the black hearse
and the gloomy mutes betoken the cold dignity of our despair.

But I fear this article is getting serious. I must apologize.

I was about to say, when I wandered from the point, that there
is another form of humor which I am also quite unable to appreciate. This is that particular form of story which may be called,
par excellence, the English Anecdote. It always deals with persons
of rank and birth, and, except for the exalted nature of the subject
itself, is, as far as I can see, absolutely pointless.

This is the kind of thing that I mean.

"His Grace the Fourth Duke of Marlborough was noted for the
open-handed hospitality which reigned at Blenheim, the family
seat, during his régime. One day on going in to luncheon it was
discovered that there were thirty guests present, whereas the table
only held covers for twenty-one. 'Oh, well,' said the Duke, not a
whit abashed, 'some of us will have to eat standing up.' Everybody,
of course, roared with laughter."

My only wonder is that they didn't kill themselves with it. A
mere roar doesn't seem enough to do justice to such a story as this.

The Duke of Wellington has been made the storm-center of
three generations of wit of this sort. In fact the typical Duke of
Wellington story had been reduced to a thin skeleton such as this:

"A young subaltern once met the Duke of Wellington coming
out of Westminster Abbey. 'Good morning, your Grace,' he said,
'rather a wet morning.' 'Yes,' said the Duke, with a very rigid bow,

'but it was a damn sight wetter, sir, on the morning of Waterloo.'
The young subaltern, rightly rebuked, hung his head."

Nor is it only the English who sin in regard to anecdotes.

One can indeed make the sweeping assertion that the telling of
stories as a mode of amusing others, ought to be kept within strict
limits. Few people realize how extremely difficult it is to tell a
story so as to reproduce the real fun of it—to "get it over" as the
actors say. The mere "facts" of a story seldom make it funny. It
needs the right words, with every word in its proper place. Here
and there, perhaps once in a hundred times, a story turns up which
needs no telling. The humor of it turns so completely on a sudden
twist or incongruity in the dénouement of it that no narrator however clumsy can altogether fumble it.

Take, for example, this well known instance—a story which, in
one form or other, everybody has heard.

"George Grossmith, the famous comedian, was once badly run
down and went to consult a doctor. It happened that the doctor,
though, like everybody else, he had often seen Grossmith on the
stage, had never seen him without his make-up and did not know
him by sight. He examined his patient, looked at his tongue, felt
his pulse and tapped his lungs. Then he shook his head. 'There's
nothing wrong with you, sir,' he said, 'except that you're run down
from overwork and worry. You need rest and amusement. Take a
night off and go and see George Grossmith at the Savoy.'

" 'Thank you,' said the patient, 'I *am* George Grossmith.' "

Let the reader please observe that I have purposely told this
story all wrongly, just as wrongly as could be, and yet there is
something left of it. Will the reader kindly look back to the beginning of it and see for himself just how it ought to be narrated
and what obvious error has been made. If he has any particle of
the artist in his make-up, he will see at once that the story ought
to begin:

"One day a very haggard and nervous-looking patient called at
the office of a fashionable doctor, etc., etc."

In other words, the chief point of the joke lies in keeping it
concealed till the moment when the patient says, "Thank you, I
am George Grossmith." But the story is such a good one that it
cannot be completely spoiled even when told wrongly. This particular anecdote has been variously told of George Grossmith, Coquelin,
Joe Jefferson, John Hare, Cyril Maude, and about sixty others. And
I have noticed that there is a certain type of man who, on hearing
this story about Grossmith, immediately tells it all back again,
putting in the name of somebody else, and goes into new fits of
laughter over it, as if the change of name made it brand new.

But few people, I repeat, realize the difficulty of reproducing a humorous or comic effect in its original spirit.

"I saw Harry Lauder last night," said Griggs, a Stock-Exchange friend of mine, as we walked up town together the other day. "He came onto the stage in kilts" (here Griggs started to chuckle) "and he had a slate under his arm" (here Griggs began to laugh quite heartily), "and he said, 'I always like to carry a slate with me' (of course he said it in Scotch, but I can't do the Scotch the way he does it) 'just in case there might be any figures I'd be wanting to put down'" (by this time Griggs was almost suffocated with laughter)—"and he took a little bit of chalk out of his pocket, and he said" (Griggs was now almost hysterical), "'I like to carry a wee bit chalk along because I find the slate is'" (Griggs was now faint with laughter), "'the slate is—is—not much good without the chalk.'"

Griggs had to stop, with his hand to his side and lean against a lamp post. "I can't, of course, do the Scotch the way Harry Lauder does it," he repeated.

Exactly. He couldn't do the Scotch and he couldn't do the rich mellow voice of Mr. Lauder and the face beaming with merriment, and the spectacles glittering with amusement, and he couldn't do the slate, nor the "wee bit chalk"—in fact he couldn't do any of it. He ought merely to have said "Harry Lauder," and leaned up against a post and laughed till he had got over it.

Yet in spite of everything, people insist on spoiling conversation by telling stories. I know nothing more dreadful at a dinner table than one of these amateur raconteurs—except perhaps, two of them. After about three stories have been told, there falls on the dinner table an uncomfortable silence, in which everybody is aware that everybody else is trying hard to think of another story, and is failing to find it. There is no peace in the gathering again till some man of firm and quiet mind turns to his neighbor and says—"But after all there is no doubt that whether we like it or not prohibition is coming." Then everybody in his heart says, Thank Heaven! and the whole tableful are happy and contented again, till one of the story tellers "thinks of another," and breaks loose.

Worst of all perhaps is the modest story teller who is haunted by the idea that one has heard his story before. He attacks you after this fashion:

"I heard a very good story the other day on the steamer going to Bermuda"—then he pauses with a certain doubt in his face—"but perhaps you've heard this?"

"No, no, I've never been to Bermuda. Go ahead."

"Well, this is a story that they tell about a man who went down to Bermuda one winter to get cured of rheumatism—but you've heard this?"

"No, no."

"Well, he had rheumatism pretty bad and he went to Bermuda to get cured of it. And so when he went into the hotel he said to the clerk at the desk—but, perhaps you know this."

"No, no, go right ahead."

"Well, he said to the clerk I want a room that looks out over the sea—but perhaps—"

Now the sensible thing to do is to stop the narrator right at this point. Say to him quietly and firmly, "Yes, I have heard that story. I always liked it ever since it came out in *Titbits* in 1878, and I read it every time I see it. Go on and tell it to me and I'll sit back with my eyes closed and enjoy it."

No doubt the story-telling habit owes much to the fact that ordinary people, quite unconsciously, rate humor very low: I mean, they underestimate the difficulty of "making humor." It would never occur to them that the thing is hard, meritorious and dignified. Because the result is gay and light, they think the process must be. Few people would realize that it is much harder to write one of Owen Seaman's "funny" poems in *Punch* than to write one of the Archbishop of Canterbury's sermons. Mark Twain's *Huckleberry Finn* is a greater work than Kant's *Critique of Pure Reason*, and Charles Dickens' creation of Mr. Pickwick did more for the elevation of the human race—I say it in all seriousness—than Cardinal Newman's *Lead, Kindly Light, Amid the Encircling Gloom*. Newman only cried out for light in the gloom of a sad world. Dickens gave it.

But the deep background that lies behind and beyond what we call humor is revealed only to the few who, by instinct or by effort, have given thought to it. The world's humor, in its best and greatest sense, is perhaps the highest product of our civilization. One thinks here not of the mere spasmodic effects of the comic artist or the blackface expert of the vaudeville show, but of the really great humor which, once or twice in a generation at best, illuminates and elevates our literature. It is no longer dependent upon the mere trick and quibble of words, or the odd and meaningless incongruities in things that strike us as "funny." Its basis lies in the deeper contrasts offered by life itself: the strange incongruity between our aspiration and our achievement, the eager and fretful anxieties of to-day that fade into nothingness to-morrow, the burning pain and the sharp sorrow that are softened in the gentle retrospect of time, till as we look back upon the course that has been traversed we pass in view the panorama of our lives, as people in old age may recall, with mingled tears and smiles, the angry quarrels of their childhood. And here, in its larger aspect, humor is blended with pathos till the two are one, and represent, as they have in every age, the mingled heritage of tears and laughter that is our lot on earth.

WILLIAM EDWARD WILSON
Madeline Among the Midshipmen

One night not long ago, I found myself remembering for the first time in years a gruff and briny old sea-dog I served under for a while in the Second World War. I had been reading the poems of Percy Bysshe Shelley, and it was the "Hymn to Intellectual Beauty" that brought my old skipper to mind.

No finer officer than this Captain, U.S.N., ever sailed the seas, I am sure, but when I knew him he was Head of the Department of English, History, and Government at the United States Naval Academy. At the Academy, the Department of E., H., and G. is appropriately known as "the Bull Department," and I was assigned to it early in the war when BuPers decided I was more expendable with a book in my hand than while conning an LST. Why the Captain was assigned to that Department I do not know, unless it was because he had once read "A Dissertation on Roast Pig."

"You ever read that thing about roast pork?" he always asked newcomers to the Department, as a test of their backgrounds in literature. "I thought it was a pretty good yarn when I was a Midshipman."

I admired the Captain. Indeed, I was grateful that he was my first skipper on shore duty, because he gave a salty atmosphere to Mahan Hall and almost justified the Academy's ironclad rule that we must think of walls as bulkheads, floors as decks, drinking fountains as scuttlebutts, and ourselves as Naval officers. Still, with all the ribbons on his broad chest, the Captain had never fought the campaign of iambic pentameter nor the battle of the synecdoche, nor had he navigated any closer to the main current of English Literature than Charles Lamb's little eddy about roast pig. It was therefore inevitable that the day he discovered Shelley in the Plebe reading assignments he blew all his stacks at once.

When he came steaming across the gangway to the Lit Deck in Mahan Hall that day, the Lit textbook in his hand and his eyes ablaze, we officers of the Lit Detail were so startled that we knocked over a half dozen chairs coming to attention.

"Ten*shun!*" shouted the Chairman of the Lit Detail, a Lieutenant, U.S.N.R., recently surfaced from the Harvard Graduate School; but we were already standing and as stiff as *rigor mortis*.

"What is *this* doing in here?" the Captain roared; and as he spoke he pounded the Lit text so hard with his fist that he knocked it out of his own hand.

The Chairman of the Lit Detail leaped to pick the book up.

"Find that fellow Shelley for me," the Captain commanded. "That thing about beauty."

Later, the Chairman of the Lit Detail said it was like looking for hay in a haystack. But he took a long shot and returned the book to the Captain opened to "Hymn to Intellectual Beauty."

The Captain scanned the page till he found the lines he wanted.

"Now, hear this!" he bellowed, and began to read to us in a high falsetto, which he obviously intended to sound effeminate but which sounded, instead, more like a bosun with laryngitis:

"Sudden, thy shadow fell on me; I shrieked and clasped my hands with ecstasy."

Snapping the book shut, the Captain then glowered at each of us in turn, as if to ferret out any concealed admiration for the lines he had read. If there was any such admiration in that complement of men, it was not exposed. The officers of the Lit Detail, every man-jack of them—and the majority held Ph.D.'s in English— looked as if they had never before heard of Percy Bysshe Shelley.

When he was satisfied with his inspection, the Captain proceeded to a pronouncement.

"That Shelley fellow was a *sissy!* Strike the poem off the reading list."

"Aye, aye, sir!" said the Chairman of the Lit Detail.

The Captain warped his majestic hull around toward the door, but there he stopped, caught in the backwash of an afterthought.

"Belay that," he said, turning to the Chairman. "Not just that thing about beauty. Strike off everything in the book by that fellow. No Shelley. Understand?"

"But, sir—" the Chairman began.

"*All* of it!" the Captain shouted. "No Shelley! Won't do for Midshipmen. Can't have them exposed to that kind of bilge." He gave his falsetto a try again. "*Shrieking* and *clasping* his hands!" But he still sounded like a bosun in sick bay. "I might have known it when I saw the fellow's name on the list. *Percy*—!"

"Please let us keep 'Ode to the West Wind,' Captain," the Chairman of the Lit Detail pleaded. "In a way, sir, it's a nautical poem. That is, it's about the weather."

The Captain shook his head.

"Won't do!" he said. 'That one too! *All* of them! After all, there's a war on. Throw them *all* out! Understand? *Shrieking* and all that bilge! *Percy*—! Percy Bysshe—! Percy *Bosh*, I say!"

So, that year at the United States Naval Academy, Nineteenth Century English Poetry was taught with no mention of Percy Bysshe Shelley. To quiet my conscience in the matter, I tried to believe that a whole class of officers in the U. S. Navy would be manlier than their comrades in Blue and Gold because they had never heard of him. At least, if they ever encountered Beauty and recognized it and *shrieked*, they would have no one to blame but themselves.

We did retain Keats in the Plebe syllabus that year, however, probably because the Captain never had the stomach for looking into "The Eve of St. Agnes" after he jettisoned Shelley. At the time, I was sure that if he had known what was going on in Madeline's bedroom on St. Agnes Eve and heard the commotion it caused in my Plebe class John Keats would have gone over the side too.

At the Naval Academy, the teaching method is somewhat different from the method practiced in most institutions of so-called higher learning. Or so it was during the war. Every Midshipman had to have a grade in the instructor's grade book for every day, and for that reason you had very little time for shilly-shallying around with superfluous things like ideas. You got each Midshipman on his feet in the course of the fifty-minute period, asked him a question that he would find it hard to answer equivocally, jotted a numerical grade in your grade book, and proceeded to the next man. According to Academy Regs, you said, "That is well," at the end of each recitation, whether all was well or not; and it was a good idea to observe this rule because, if you didn't, your Midshipman would remain standing at attention, as solemn as a ninepin, even after you had called on someone else.

When I came to "The Eve of St. Agnes" in the Lit syllabus, I was pleased to note that there were forty-two stanzas in the poem. There were twenty-one Plebes in my Lit class. That meant two stanzas per Plebe. At the rate of a minute per stanza, I would have eight minutes left over for teaching.

We cast off to a good start with Keats's poem. I gave the class the poop about the legend of St. Agnes Eve, made sure they had the word on the rivalry between Madeline's family and Porphyro's, ran them through a drill in pronouncing Porphyro as *Porphyro* and not *Proffero*, and together we convoyed that amorous young man through the "dusky galleries" of Madeline's castle and into Madeline's bedroom, where, as Keats put it, he "took covert, pleased amain." That phrase caused a little difficulty, but I persuaded my future officers and gentlemen that *Porphyro*, being himself a gentleman if not a Naval officer, only hid in a corner of Madeline's room and did not take to the covers of her sack.

Then came Madeline's turn. All innocence, but eagerness too, "St. Agnes' charméd maid" climbed the marble stairs, lighting her way with a candle, and finally hove to at the door of her room, where Porphyro was hiding.

"Then what happened?" I asked the Plebe I had brought to attention to sound off on Stanzas 23 and 24.

The Plebe hesitated, and I thought he looked puzzled. But it was hard to tell. Most Plebes looked puzzled aboard the Bull Department.

"Well, sir," he said, finally, "when Madeline opened her bedroom door, a big animal ran out."

I could not have been more startled if the Engineering Department (known as "Steam") had blown out a boiler under my classroom windows, as indeed they were in the habit of doing from time to time.

"A big *what?*" I said.

"A big animal, sir."

I tried to think of all the things cluttering Madeline's bedroom that St. Agnes Eve. There was a table covered with cloth of woven crimson, gold, and jet. There were candied apple, quince, and plum and lucent syrops, tinct with cinnamon. And of course there was Porphyro. But I could recall no animals, large or small on the loose in the girl's chamber.

"I think you must be mistaken," I said.

"It's in the book, sir," the Plebe replied, solemnly. "May I show you?"

In the Navy, if it's in the book it's so. In my place, even the Captain would have had to give that Plebe a 4.0 for the day if he proved himself right.

"Very well," I said. "Find it in the book and read it to me."

The Plebe opened his book to Stanza 23 and read the first line.

"*Out went the taper as she hurried in. . . .* That's a large tropical animal found mainly in South America, sir," he said. "I looked it up."

Five minutes later, Steam was sending over a man to ask *us* to pipe down.

The Captain never heard about this interpretation of Keats in my classroom, and at the time I was grateful. Maybe, though, it would have been all right if he had. On second thought, I believe he would have approved of Madeline's bedroom. After all, he liked animals in literature. It was only Beauty and that sort of bilge that he disapproved of.

JAMES B. GREENOUGH and
GEORGE LYMAN KITTREDGE

Language Is Poetry[1]

When we examine the dictionary of any highly developed language like English, we are impressed not only with the enormous extent of the vocabulary, but with its infinite variety. There are

---

1. Chapter 2 of *Words and Their Ways in English Speech*, 1900. Some of the authors' footnotes have been omitted.

plain words for common things (as *bread, stone, house, child, horse*) and simple physical acts (as *eat, drink, run, climb*); there are formal or dignified or poetical words for equally simple conceptions (like *residence, progeny, quaff, masticate*); there are vague words (like *thing, affair, matter, act, do*) and scientific terms of rigid exactness (like *oxygen, atmosphere, chloride, carbon, inoculate*); there are abstract terms for mental and moral qualities (as *sagacity, carelessness, probity, honor*) and adjectives describing persons who exemplify these qualities (as *sagacious, careless, honest, honorable*); there are words of a distinctly undignified character (like *chum, crank, bamboozle, blubber, bawl, fizzle*), others so dignified as to be uncommon in familiar talk (as *remunerative, emolument, eleemosynary, recalcitrant*) or so high-sounding as hardly to be allowable even in elaborate writing (as *exacerbate, cachinnation, adumbrate*), there are words which have poetical associations (as *golden, roseate, silver-tongued, gambol, soaring, eterne*), and others so prosaic that every poet avoids them (as *fry, exchequer, discount, cross-question, extra, medium, miscellaneous*); there are words so technical as to be understood by specialists only (as *electrolysis, cotyledon, ontology, quaternions*), and others so childish as to be confined to the dialect of the nursery (as *naughty, mammy, dad, dolly*.)

Frequently, too, we find a number of different words ("synonyms," we call them) for what is essentially the same idea[2]: *ask, request, beseech, pray, beg, petition, supplicate, entreat, implore, solicit, crave, importune; angry, wrathful, incensed, irritated, vexed, resentful, enraged, furious, indignant, exasperated, irate, hot, infuriated; join, unite, associate, unify, link, connect, couple, combine.*[3]

The same marvelous variety shows itself when we study the different meanings of a single word. Thus *figure* may be equally well applied to a persons's form, a polygon, a numerical sign, an elaborate drawing or picture in a book, a metaphor or simile; *energy* may be used in a general sense or in the technical language of science ("the conservation of *energy*"); *property* may be a quality, one's possessions, or (in theatrical language) a thing or utensil used in setting the stage; *character* may refer to one's personal qualities, or it may denote a mark or sign in writing or printing, or it may be colloquially used for an eccentric person.

The question is immediately suggested: Whence does a nation provide itself with this enormous mass of words, with their multi-

2. So-called synonyms almost always differ from each other in some shade of meaning, or in emphasis, or at all events in their connotations [Greenough and Kittredge's note].

3. The reader may easily multiply examples by collecting, for instance, the synonyms for *awkward, beautiful, healthy, strange, throw, go, law, sin, people, custom* [Greenough and Kittredge's note].

farious meanings so aptly differentiated as to express all the aspects of any conception that can occur to the mind of civilized man?

In the first place, no people is perfectly homogenous, and this is strikingly true of the English nation, which is "Saxon and Norman and Dane," as Tennyson wrote, and Celtic as well. Each component part of the population contributes its proportion of words, small or large, but always characteristic, and distinct in many particulars from the contributions of all the rest. Then, too, all cultivated languages have borrowed much from outside nations with whom they have come in contact in war or trade or literature. Our own language, as we shall see, has enriched itself in this way from every quarter of the globe.

The varied materials thus brought together are constantly subjected to what may be called mechanical processes of growth. Every language has its machinery of prefixes and suffixes and compounds, by means of which a single word may become the center of a considerable group of related terms: as, *true, tru-th, tru-ly, un-true, un-tru-ly, tru-th-ful, tru-th-ful-ness*, etc.

But these causes are not sufficient to explain the richness and complexity of our speech. Such a result was achieved only when this great mass of variously derived material had been subjected for centuries to the language-making instinct; that is, to the poetic faculty of man. The dictum that "all language is poetry," then, if properly understood, goes far toward answering the question with which we are concerned.

The essentially poetical or figurative character of language may easily be seen by comparing a number of passages from the poets with ordinary prosaic expressions.

When Wordsworth writes, in "Laodamia,"

> The gods approve,
> The *depth*, and not the tumult of the soul,

the imaginative power of his phrasing at once appeals to us. If, however, we compare such common expressions as "He was *deeply* moved," "*profoundly* affected," "from the *bottom* of my heart," we recognize the same figure of speech. In other words, the poetical history of Wordsworth's line goes back to that unknown time when some primitive poet, without knowing that he was talking poetry, first applied to the emotions words which in their literal sense were only applicable to the physical conception of *depth*. As time has passed, the primitive metaphor has grown so familiar that it has ceased to be a metaphor. It has become merely an ordinary meaning of a group of common words. The modern poet, perceiving the imaginative significance of this usage, elaborated the figure it embodied, phrased it anew with conscious literary art, and thus, in an instant, restored it to its full poetic rights. Similarly, we may compare with "the *tumult* of the soul," such prose expressions as "his mind was *disturbed*," "his *agitation* was painful to witness," "the *violence* of his *emotion*"—each of which, though no longer felt as figurative, embodies a metaphor precisely similar to Wordsworth's.[4] We are not at this moment concerned with the ethical or philosophical contents of Wordsworth's line, for these might have been stated, with perfect accuracy, in the plainest terms, but merely with the poetical language in which he clothed his thought.

When Banquo says to Macbeth that the witches' salutation "might yet *enkindle* him unto the crown," we perceive that *enkindle* is used metaphorically. So, also, when Macbeth declares

> I have no *spur*
> To *prick* the sides of my intent.

But we feel the figure less vividly in such a phrase as "*fired* with ambition," and in the terms *instigation* and *incentive* we are not conscious of any metaphor whatever. Yet *instigation* comes from a root which means "to goad," and *incentive* means literally "that which sets the tune" (from L. *in* and *canere*, "to sing"); so that both these words were, in their first application to "motives" or "promptings," quite as poetical as either *enkindle* or *spur*.

The ordinary processes by which words change their meanings are, then, essentially the same as the devices of poetry; or, to express the fact more accurately, the figurative language of poetry differs from the speech of common life mainly in employing fresher figures, or in revivifying those which have lost their freshness from age and constant use.

Language is fossil poetry which is constantly being worked over for the uses of speech. Our commonest words are worn-out metaphors.

Thus, *depend* is literally "to hang from" (L. *dependo*); *egregious* means "selected from the [common] herd" (L. *e*, "from," and *grex, gregis*, "herd"); *spoil* means "to strip," i.e. "to strip off the armor, etc., of a slain or defeated enemy"; *front* means "forehead" (L. *frons, frontis*); to fret is originally "to eat up," "to devour" (A.S. *fretan, for-*, "away," and *etan*, "eat")—compare "gnawing anxiety"; *precocious* means "too early ripe" (L. *praecox*, from *prae-*, "before," and *coquo*, "to cook," "to ripen"); to thrill is literally "to bore," "to pierce," and is related to *drill* (the same word is seen in *nostril*, formerly *nosethril*); *sullen* means at first "solitary" and comes (through the French) from L. *solus*, "alone," (whence our adjective *sole*).

---

4. *Disturb* is to "drive asunder in disorder," from L. *dis-*, "apart," and *turba*, "disorder," "a riotous crowd." *Agitation* comes from L. *agito*, "to drive to and fro." *Violence* is from *vis*, "force." *Emotion* is the "act of moving (one) away," "disturbance (of mind)" [Greenough and Kittredge's note].

Such illustrations might be multiplied indefinitely. Indeed, almost every word that we shall have occasion to study will serve as an example, for the processes that we are considering go on incessantly so long as a language is alive. We shall find that there is no device which we are accustomed to call poetical, no similitude so slight, no metaphor so strained or so commonplace, that language has not seized upon it to make new forms of expression as the needs of advancing thought required them. Even when the resultant words appear intensely prosaic, the processes that created them are identical with those of artistic poetry.

This important truth may be further illustrated in the growth of words from a single root.

The Indo-European family of languages (to which belong Sanskrit, Greek, Latin, English, and many other tongues) had a simple linguistic form (a "root") PET, which signified "rapid motion across the field of vision." This root is clearly seen in the Latin verb *peto*. Since such motion is produced either by *falling* or by *flying*, words with these meanings have been formed from the root PET in various languages of our family. But such motion may include also the idea of "intentional direction." Hence other words from the same root have acquired the sense of "aim," and, by the transference from actual to figurative aim, the meanings (originally metaphorical) of "seek" and "ask." All three senses, "aim," "seek," and "ask," are found in the Latin verb *peto*. Thus from this one root PET, we have, by various differentiations of meaning, such words[5] as the following:

Latin *penna*, "a means of flying," "a wing," "a feather"—whence, through the French, the English *pen*, originally applied to a quill used for writing, but now extended to other devices (steel pen, gold pen, stylographic pen, etc.).

Greek πτωσις (*ptôsis*), "a falling"—then, figuratively, "a case" in grammar (since the genitive, dative, and other so-called "oblique" cases were conceived as *falling away from* the nominative, which was fancifully called the "upright case").

im-petus, "a force of forward movement"—first literal, then figurative.

ap-petite, "a craving" (of body or mind).

re-peat, "to go back *to get* something," "to take up a thing a second time."

petition, "a seeking," "a request."

com-petition, "a seeking together"—then, especially, "rivalry" (in modern times applied especially to commercial rivalry).

petulant, "butting" (as goats do), "attacking"—then figuratively, for "ill-humored," "irritable."

Another root, PU, meant "clean," and thence came the Latin adjectives *putus*, "clean," and *purus*, "clear." From *putus* arose a verb *puto*, "to clean." In a vine-bearing country, *cleaning* is particularly "pruning," and from that idea, specially applied in surgery,

5. These words are built up by the mechanical means of word-formations developed in the various languages [Greenough and Kittredge's note].

we get *amputation*. In mercantile language "to clean up accounts" (*putare rationes*) became a common expression for "reckoning," and finally "accounts" (*rationes*) was dropped, and *puto* was used for "reckon" in general (as in *computation*). From "reckon" we pass easily to "think,"[6] and this becomes the ruling sense of *puto* (as in the adjective *putative*). From the same mercantile dialect comes *imputo*, "reckon in," "credit or charge to the account of," whence we get *imputation*. From "considering" or "turning back to observe" (cf. *re-gard*, *re-spect*, both meaning originally "to look back") we get the word *reputation*; and *deputation* is derived from another idea of "consideration carried out in *resolve*." Thus from a root signifying originally "clean," the imagination of the race, utilizing the mechanical means which the laws of derivation and composition afford, has gradually formed a group of words of the most varied meaning. Vine-dressing, surgery, mathematics, commerce, and politics are all included within this circle, and one word (*reputation*) is general enough to apply to all men.

Finally we may establish the poetical character of language by a striking and conclusive test. Literature has been attentively studied, as *literature*, for hundreds and even thousands of years. Hence there has grown up among scholars a set of technical terms —the names of the so-called "figures of speech"—which designate what are commonly regarded as the ornaments or devices that characterize the poetical style as opposed to the speech of everyday life. Yet it is easy to see that all of these "figures" are perfectly familiar in our ordinary talk. *Metaphor*, the most important of all figures, we have already considered. It occurs everywhere, and one can hardly utter a sentence without employing it. Every occupation of mankind, every subject (however remote) that engages man's attention, has furnished us with metaphorical expressions. We shall have occasion to return to this point again and again. For the present we may pass to other figures, making a selection from those comprised in the list commonly printed in works on grammar or rhetoric.

Simile is involved in the great class of English adjectives that end in *-ly*, which is an abraded form of *like*. Thus a "*manly* boy" is a boy who is "*like* a man" in certain traits of character. So *cowardly*, *ruffianly*, *saintly*, *homely* ("like home," and so "ordinary," "commonplace," with a further development of meaning in America to "hard-featured," "plain"). Still clearer cases of simile are the more recent adjectives compounded with *like*: as *childlike*, *lionlike*, *birdlike*, *homelike*, etc.

Metonymy is the figure by which a thing is designated, not by its own name, but by the name of something that resembles or

---

6. Compare the provincial use of *I reckon* for "I think," in both England and America [Greenough and Kittredge's note].

suggests it—as in Tennyson's "the bright death" for "the keen fatal knife," or Horace's *Pontica pinus* for "ship of wood from Pontus." This "figure" is so common in ordinary speech that it seldom attracts our attention. Thus we say *irons* for "fetters," *glasses* for "spectacles," or "drinking-glasses," *the knife* for "surgery," *canvas* for "sails," *style* (from L. *stilus*, a writing implement) for "manner of writing," *bilboes* for "shackles" (from *Bilbao*, in Spain, famous for its iron and steel), and so on. Many of the words thus treated are perfectly prosaic, but the process is the same as that of poetry. A man's *linen* or *flannels* are just as much metonymy as Milton's "nodding horror" for the branches of a thick and dismal forest.

Synecodoche (the part for the whole, the genus for the species, or *vice versa*) is seen in "sixty *head*" (of cattle), "fifty *sail*" (of ships), "a *bottomry* bond," "a *poll* tax," a *rumshop*, a *gin-palace*, a *cutthroat* for a "murderer," a *hangman* for an "executioner."

Antonomasia, or the use of a person's name for any one who resembles him, is very common; a *Solomon*, a *Shylock*, "a *Daniel* come to judgment," a *Maecenas*, "a regular *Nero*," "a *Roland* for an *Oliver*."

Hyperbole is natural in unstudied speech: "I beg a *thousand* pardons," "scared to *death*," "I'd give the *world* to see him." Expressions of approval and disapproval are especially affected by hyperbole ("good for nothing," "a magnificent idea"), and the language of schoolgirls is proverbially made up of it: "thanks awfully," "extravagantly fond," "tremendously angry," "immensely obliged."

Antithesis is frequent in the commonest expressions, as: "up and down," "hither and yon," "this way and that." So, "Napoleon the Little," "Prince and Peasant."

Alliteration, a favorite poetic fancy, is found in such phrases as, "tit for tat," "blind as a bat," "spick and span," "the seven senses," "neck or nothing," "rough and ready."

Onomatopoeia has given rise to such words as *whiz buzz, chickadee, bobolink*, and countless others. Many of them are humorous, and not a few are slangy.

Irony appears in "a *pretty* how-d'ye-do!" "Here's richness!" and other colloquialisms. Horace's "splendide mendax"[7] is called a poetical *oxymoron*, but such phrases as "a magnificent failure," "a beautiful imbroglio," "to swim like a stone," show the same figure—the joining of two inconsistent words to produce a peculiar rhetorical effect.

Catachresis, as it is called by the pedantic grammarians—that is, an "abuse" of language consisting in the employment of a harsh metaphor—is not peculiar to the poets. A well-known writer has ventured "He *spasmed* to him," to express the act of a boy

7. "Finely false."

making signs to another by contortion of the face. This is not likely to become good English, but it might easily become slang, and "misuses of language" quite as extraordinary have often made their way into our vocabulary. "To *jockey* a confiding partner" is an example. A *chaush* is a Turkish official interpreter; in 1609, a particular *chaush* is said to have distinguished himself by swindling a number of merchants in London; hence *chouse* for "defraud"— a sufficiently good instance of *catachresis* in its origin.

Litotes, or understatement, is found in all languages, but is heard particularly in New England provincialisms, as well as in slang. It comes partly from euphemism, and partly from caution or hesitation. Thus we have "the late unpleasantness" for the Civil War, "no conjuror" for a stupid person, "pretty well" and "so-so" for "in good health." The sarcastic *rather!* may be compared.

Periphrasis, like litotes, is a favorite means of avoiding plain language: "he came to grief," "I hope nothing will happen to him," "I am inclined to think your accounts are not very accurate," will serve as examples.

Pleonasm, or the practice of saying the same thing twice over in the same expression, is a universal characteristic of speech: as "go back again," "reared up," "go away from here," "he fell down and jumped up again." Excessive pleonasm is of course objectionable, but it is idle for the purist to object to such idiomatic phrases as those which we have just cited. They are of the very fiber of language. As well complain of "John! John!" or "no! no!" on the ground that one *John* or one *no* would suffice. The double comparative ("*most unkindest* cut of all"), formerly in good usage, is an excellent example of pleonasm.[8] The same tendency may be seen in such compounds as *inexsuperabilis*.[9]

Thus we have subjected the principle that "language is poetry" to a variety of tests. We have compared specific passages of poetry with ordinary phraseology, and have found a similar metaphorical character in both. We have observed the imaginative nature of the development of many meanings from a simple root-idea. We have recognized the existence of many so-called "figures of speech" in the commonest locutions of everyday life. We may feel certain, therefore, that the principle is a sound one, and may utilize it whenever it appears to be useful in our further study of English words.

8. Many forms which appear to be units are really instances of "double comparison." Thus *nearer* is *near* (comparative of *nigh*) with a comparative suffix *-er* added. Similarly *farther*, *nethermost*, *uppermost*, and so on. Compare the incorrect *furtherer* and *furtherest*, which are simply examples of the same tendency that have not had the fortune to gain admittance to good linguistic society [Greenough and Kittredge's note].

9. Insurmountable. Since *superabilis* and *exsuperabilis* both mean surmountable, the *ex-* is pleonastic.

QUESTIONS

1. What *several* causes contribute to the variety and complexity of language? What main principle do Greenough and Kittredge present, and in what ways do they develop and support their thesis?
2. Select a short passage of poetry and show whether the language vivifies or restores the figurative force of ordinary prosaic expressions.
3. Show whether the following group of words exemplifies the principle adumbrated in this essay: respect, suspect, inspector, expectations, spectacular.
4. Give a further example, for each class set out in the essay, of "figures of speech" in ordinary talk.
5. In their own writing Greenough and Kittredge frequently exemplify the principle they are discussing. Explain the full meaning of: "Language is fossil poetry" (p. 738); "the growth of words from a single root" (p. 739); "-ly which is an abraded form of like" (p. 740). Give further instances of the same. Should this occurrence be expected? Explain.

CHARLES L. STEVENSON
On the "Analysis" of a Work of Art

I

For the sense or senses of the term that here interest me, "analysis" refers to a familiar aspect of the criticism of the arts. Donald Tovey, for instance, is noted for his analysis of music, Roger Fry for his analysis of paintings, and William Empson for his analysis of poetry. It is characteristic of analytical criticism to avoid rhapsody and at the same time to look somewhat askance at the information provided by biography and history. Its aim, rather, is to lead us to scrutinize the work of art itself with a sensitivity to these or those details, in the hope that we shall come to discern or understand certain features of it that might otherwise escape us.

This use of the term "analysis" is for the most part fairly clear. It is not likely to be confused with the various other uses (current in chemistry, physics, mathematics, psychiatry, philosophy, and so on) that have at most a cousinly resemblance to it. But a use that is "fairly" clear is for some purposes obscure; so in the present paper I shall consider how "analysis" can be defined, and always with attention, of course, to examples drawn from criticism.

Our ordinary habits of speaking mark off a certain area within which my clarified sense or senses can be expected to lie. But this area is of a noticeable size, and within it I cannot be guided by what people do mean but must consider what they *need* to mean if the term is to be useful to them. To that extent my remarks about the meaning of "analysis" will be prescriptive rather than descriptive: they will require me to single out, from the various things that critics do under the name of "analysis," those that are important enough to deserve emphasis in a definition and to leave to one side those that are not. It is quite possible that my often implicit judgments about what is important or unimportant will not stand up under examination; but that is the risk that attends any prescriptive study of terms. To avoid the risk would be in effect to avoid the central issue.

II

I must begin with some distinctions that bear on "analysis" only indirectly but which will provide my remarks with a necessary background. In particular, I must distinguish certain sorts of *attention* and relate them to corresponding sorts of sensory *experience*. I shall want to say, for instance, that when we observe a work of art with "synoptic" attention, rather than with "dissective" attention, we get an experienced "net impression" of the work. These terms only half-suggest what I want to mean by them; but perhaps the following examples, supplemented by those that will be given in the remainder of the paper, will be sufficient to make them serve their purpose.

In listening to an orchestra we are sometimes not specifically aware of the viola part; for although the physical sounds of the violas are constantly making a difference to our auditory experience, this difference may amount to no more than an increased sense of the richness of the orchestral sonorities. On occasion, however, we may especially "listen for" the violas and as if psychologically amplify them until we hear them as a felt melodic line that stands out with a certain individuality and prominence. When we do this quite insistently, moreover, we hear far less of the other instruments; it is now they, rather than the violas, that are lost in an indefinite sense of sonority, much as though their prominence and individuality had been borrowed from them. In such a case I shall say that we are listening to the orchestra with "dissective" attention to the violas, though with the reminder that I am giving that term a special sense, letting it have some of the force of such terms as "sharp," "highly selective," and "exclusive." In general, dissective attention is directed to some one aspect (i.e., some one part or some one property) of a complex thing or event; it emphasizes this aspect in the sense that it makes our experience of it particularly definite; and with regard to all the other aspects it has just the opposite effect.

Let me contrast this with another sort of attention. When we hear an orchestra we are rarely content, as above, to single out only one of the instrumental voices; our interests are likely to be more diversified than that. We may "listen for" the contrary motion of the violas and violins, say, and at the same time follow a varied melodic line played by the flutes; and although we may notice one of these voices more than the others, it remains the case that the others do not seem entirely amorphous. Now I propose to call this "synoptic" attention. Its effect is to emphasize each of the several voices, or more generally, each of the several aspects, toward which it is directed; but the very fact that these aspects are several, rather than one, tends to limit the degree to which such an emphasis is possible. Thus the violas may yield a *somewhat* definite and individualized experience when they share synoptic attention with the violins and flutes; but all else being equal, they would yield a still more definite and individualized experience if they were (as in the preceding paragraph) the object of dissective attention.

To the extent that the distinction between dissective and synoptic attention depends on the *number* of aspects that are involved, we shall find it convenient to count "a" given aspect as several, rather than one, whenever we proportionately reduce the complexity of the example we are considering. For an orchestra we may wish, as above, to consider each instrumental voice as one aspect; but for a single unaccompanied instrument we may wish to consider its one voice as having many "smaller" aspects, one of them being its rhythmic pattern, another its dynamic pattern, and so on. So we cannot call a given manner of paying attention "dissective" or "synoptic" without considering some frame of reference, as it were, that is set up by the complexity of our example. But once the frame of reference is established—and it usually needs no explicit mention, being evident from the context—the terms will serve to classify attention in contrasting ways.

Since I shall often have occasion to speak of the *experience* that is correlated with synoptic attention (given, of course, this or that frame of reference) I shall refer to it by the term "net impression." One of my examples, then, was concerned with our auditory net impression of the violins, violas, and flutes; that is, it was concerned with an experience whose main aspects corresponded to these instruments, each aspect being at least slightly definite, prominent, and individualized. One might also say, somewhat roughly, that the example was concerned with an auditory net impression "of the orchestra"—implying, of course, not that *every* orchestral voice seemed to have its degree of definiteness, but only that *several* did.

As I need scarcely point out, when I describe the aspects of a net impression as being "slightly definite," "slightly individualized," and so forth, my terms become intelligible mainly from the examples by which I illustrate them. Further examples, drawn from the arts other than music, will be introduced as the paper proceeds; but meanwhile it should be noted that my terms stand close to various others that are more familiar in aesthetics. Mr. Stephen Pepper, for instance, would presumably say that the component aspects of my net impressions often lack a full definiteness because they are "fused," that term implying some special sort of unity in variety. And those in the Gestalt tradition would presumably say that my net impressions are wholes greater than the sum of their parts. I have no doubt that these ways of speaking point to something very important in our experience and that they frequently do so more effectively than my own way of speaking; but they are so complicated that a full examination of them, with care in defending them from possible misunderstandings, is a proper topic for an independent study. For the present, then, I shall leave them with only this passing mention. I shall use my own makeshift terms in the hope that they will proclaim their psychological innocence and will permit me to resort to a deliberate naiveté (as space insistently requires) without seeming to ascribe a similar naiveté to others.

III

Guided by the use of examples, let me now turn to the nature of aesthetic analysis. My first example, though it deals with a subtlety, will serve to introduce my main points; and perhaps it will prove to be more typical of analytical criticism than it first seems.

Mr. F. W. Bateson, in his *English Poetry and the English Language*,[1] remarks that in Tennyson's line,

> Between the loud stream and the trembling stars

there is a connection of sound that helps to "bridge" a disparity of sense. He analyzes the line—and I trust that "analyze" is an appropriate term in this context—by pointing out that " 'trembling stars' repeats five of the consonants (l, s, t, r, m) of 'loud stream'." That is to say, he discerns a partly internal alliteration, which he in some sense explains or reveals to us.

Now whatever else this example of analysis may amount to, it is evidently concerned with an interplay between various sorts of attention. If we listen to the line with virtual *in*attention to the consonants we may find that we feel no connection of sound at all. Bateson would doubtless acknowledge this but would be likely to take it as a mark of our poetic insensitivity. If we listen to the line with *dissective* attention to the consonants, however, which is what Bateson's observation invites us to do, we may find that the l, s, t, r, and m are sharply emphasized, yielding individualized and abstractable elements in our experience. But this is an extraordinary way of listening to poetry, and whatever else we may think of it we cannot suppose that Bateson or anyone else would want to recom-

1. Oxford, 1934, p. 21 [Stevenson's note].

mend it to us as a permanent habit. If we listen to the line, finally, with some form of *synoptic* attention—noticing the consonants along with the rhythm and calence of the line, say, and keeping ourselves responsive to the images that it can evoke—we shall have a still different experience. Our *net impression* of the line will now include a sense of alliteration that is not entirely without prominence (as it was with virtual inattention to the consonants) and at the same time is not sharply prominent (as it was with dissective attention to the consonants); we are likely to call it a feeling of "alliterative nuance," say, or a subtle and elusive "echoing effect." And we may presume that Bateson, like most critics, would find this experience of genuine poetic interest.

We shall get a better idea of what analysis is if, bearing these points in mind, we view Bateson's observation in a broader perspective, asking what purposes it can be expected to serve. (I am interested in the purposes that his observation *can* serve, of course, and not necessarily those that he may have explicitly had in mind.) There are here two important possibilities, the first being of special concern to poets and the second to those who wish only to appreciate poetry; so I shall discuss them in turn.

To understand the first possibility, let us suppose that a certain poet, on hearing Tennyson's line, spontaneously gets a net impression of it that includes the alliterative "echoing effect." Let us suppose further that he is interested in this effect and wants to create a similar one in a poem of his own. He may at first be puzzled, for although he can readily hear the effect he may not know what sort of words (conceived as physical sounds) will produce it. The reason for this is easily seen: the aspects of a net impression, or of any experience that is not a product of the very sharpest, dissective attention, are poor clues to their physical correlates. Now it is here that Bateson's observation, or a similar one that the poet can make for himself, is likely to be useful. Once the poet learns that the desired effect comes from repeated consonants, rather than from repeated vowels or syllable lengths, and so forth—a conclusion that he can check, in part, by temporarily examining Tennyson's line with *dissective* attention—he will have a better understanding of the resources of his medium and will have less difficulty in finding the words that he needs.

When so interpreted the example raises an informal counterpart of a question in psychophysics. It asks why our experience (here a net impression) is of a certain nature; and it is fully answered when every experience of this nature is found to be correlated, given such-and-such a psychological "set" (here a certain kind of synoptic attention) with such-and-such a physical stimulus. The poet will not be likely, of course, to conceive of the stimulus in the technical

manner of a scientist; he will think of it in terms of uttered consonants and not in terms of composite sound waves. But that is only
to repeat that his psychophysics is of an "informal" character.

Note that synoptic and dissective attention must *alternate* in this
example. Synoptic attention gives the poet the net impression that
he finds of artistic interest in its own right. Dissective attention,
which is so sharp and exclusive that it interferes with his net
impression, gives him an experience that (in this special case, at
least) has no such interest. But when he is analyzing Tennyson's
line, rather than simply enjoying it, he must even so make use of
dissective attention; for it helps him to know about the repeated
consonants and thus to learn how a certain aspect of a net impression (for those who listen synoptically) can be brought about.

I have mentioned two purposes that Bateson's example might
serve but have discussed only one of them. Let me turn to the
other, which is of concern less to poets, it will be remembered,
than to those who want only to appreciate poetry.

Suppose, then, that a certain reader (or listener) is somewhat
unresponsive to poetic language, missing much of its music, and
that he is anxious, knowing this, to hear more of it than he is now
able to hear. He must accordingly correct his virtual *in*attention to
its musical aspects, developing a form of synoptic attention that
will include them; and this in turn will require practice. It will
require practice in listening to poetry, let me repeat, and not just a
theory about poetry. And if we consider what sort of practice he
will need, we can readily see that some part of it, at least, can be
provided by analytical procedures like the one that my example
from Bateson has illustrated. Let us see more specifically how this
might be so.

When he first hears the line from Tennyson (reading it aloud to
himself, say) we may suppose that his virtual inattention to the
consonants prevents him from getting any sense of alliteration at
all. He has no difficulty, however, in checking what Bateson says,
either by reading the line very slowly, first listening for the
l-sounds, then for the *s*-sounds, and so on, or else by looking closely
at the printed consonants and inferring the presence of the spoken
ones by the rules of pronunciation. During this process he observes
with dissective attention; and his accompanying experiences of the
consonants, though no longer amorphous as before, are still, of
course, devoid of any immediate poetic interest. In fact they are
now so prominent that he may find the line *less* interesting than it
initially was. But even so, his procedure may have the indirect
effect of developing his poetic sensibilities. For if he later returns to
the line, now listening unselfconsciously, he may find that he hears
something that pleases him; he may get a net impression of the line
in which an alliterative nuance, being neither very indefinite nor

very definite, takes its place amid other aspects of his experience. His temporary use of dissective attention has had an *aftereffect* on his powers of auditory discrimination and has helped him to listen to the line, as he previously could not, with a broadened synoptic attention. His concern with analysis has afforded him the very kind of *practice* that he needed; it has provided him with a technical exercise, so to speak, for cultivating the virtuosity of his listening.

Let me contrast this version of the example with my previous one. We have seen that the previous version, in which analysis was of interest to a poet, was tantamount to a problem in psychophysics: it attempted to account for a subtle kind of experience by correlating it with its stimulus. The present version, however, in which analysis is of interest to one who wishes only to listen to poetry, has no more than an incidental connection with psychophysics. To be sure, it brings about changes in attention and experience that psychophysics would seek to explain, and it may provide evidence that has a bearing on the explanation; but its importance, so far as it contributes to the appreciation of poetry, lies not in *accounting for* a subtle kind of experience but rather in exercising one's powers of *getting* it. It eventuates not in a new conclusion about experience (save incidentally) but rather in a new experience, which our previously insensitive listener now finds accessible to him.

We can see the contrast more clearly if we ask what happens to *synoptic* attention in the two cases. For the poet, whom I have assumed to have the requisite form of it from the start, nothing happens to it. Dissective attention temporarily interrupts it, to be sure, in the course of developing a psychophysical explanation; but otherwise it leaves synoptic attention unaltered. For the reader, however, synoptic attention is in the course of being developed. The aftereffects of his dissective attention progressively enable his synoptic attention to include certain sounds that he used to ignore.

Such, then, are the two main uses of Bateson's example. The one eventuates primarily in knowledge and is of special interest to poets; and the other eventuates primarily in a new experience (coming with an altered form of attention) and is of special interest to those who listen to poetry. These interests often go together, of course; and anyone who is learning both to write poetry and to increase his sensitivity to it can use the example for both purposes at the same time.

v

I shall now generalize from what I have said, tentatively suggesting a definition of "analysis." It will not do, of course, to base the definition merely on my one example, even though it has been discussed in detail. This is likely to lead to a sense that is too narrow; and indeed, in examining further examples I shall have occasion to "stretch" my present sense into a broader one. But if we first examine this sense and later consider the general way in which this or that broadened sense can arise, we may find that we have as good an understanding of the term as the purposes of criticism or aesthetics are likely to require.

Subject to the above reservation, then, I want to suggest that anyone gives an "analysis" of a work of art[2] if and only if:

1. he is concerned with a net impression of the work—one that he thinks it will yield if it is observed with a certain kind of synoptic attention;

2. he causes certain aspects of the work to be observed with dissective attention and thus temporarily *prevents* it from yielding the net impression; and

3. he proceeds as if guided by the purpose (which he may or may not have explicitly in mind) either of (a) showing that the net impression, for those who observe synoptically, has such-and-such a factor among its physical correlates, or of (b) cultivating synoptic attention by the aftereffects of dissective attention and thus helping people to experience the net impression later on.

Note that the definition makes "analysis" refer to a process that may or may not be successful. Thus an analysis that seems useful for purpose (3a) may on occasion lead to *mis*information about the physical correlates of a net impression. And an analysis that seems useful for purpose (3b) may *fail* to make a net impression more readily experienced; or alternatively, it may make too much of this particular net impression, at the expense of some other one that is more appropriate to the work. It is convenient to speak in this way, since the success of an analysis is likely to be controversial. By keeping "analysis" as a neutral term we can more readily use it to raise a question about the success of a given example, leaving the answer for subsequent critical judgment, in the light of full discussion. Note further that analysis is not limited by my definition to net impressions that make a work seem beautiful. On occasion it may deal with those that make the work seem ugly; and a critic may analyze in the hope of showing artists how to avoid them, or in the hope of making observers sensitive to the inadequacies of the work.

Let me add a few words to guard my definition from a possible source of confusion. An analysis normally attempts to disclose unsuspected complexities; and for the present sense we may be tempted to say that the complexities are somehow secretly present in "the" experience that we have of a work of art. That is to say,

---

2. I use the term "work of art" to designate a special kind of physical object or event. Thus I do not use it, as Dewey does, to designate a "transaction" between an observer but rather to designate the art object itself. I am for the moment ignoring the complexities introduced by "repeatable" works of art (such as poems and symphonies): for my manner of dealing with their physical aspects will be evident from my paper, "On 'What is a poem?'" in the *Philosophical Review*, LXVI (1957), 329-362 [Stevenson's note].

we may suppose that the work repeatedly gives us only one determinate kind of experience—an experience whose components are only half-revealed by synoptic attention but are fully revealed, though in an analytical and piecemeal fashion, by dissective attention. In supposing this, however, we are making our conception of experience needlessly complicated. We are going back to the old view of "mental chemistry," which insisted that any experience must have a hidden complexity that exactly corresponds to the complexity of its stimulus.[3] Such a view is now pretty well outmoded, since its "hidden" complexity explains nothing that cannot be explained equally well by the stimulus alone. It is more economical, then, to take the experience attending synoptic attention (in spite of the constant stimulus) as being numerically distinct from the experience attending dissective attention; and if we do that (as I have been doing all along) we cannot say that the latter shows us the aspects of the former "as they really were." A man can, to be sure, attempt to tell us about the *felt* aspects (which are in no sense "hidden" from him, however hard they may be to name) of a complex experience; but that is not an analysis in the sense I have defined and is best referred to, in general, not as an "analysis" but rather as a "description" of experience, or as an "introspective report" about it.

The unsuspected complexity that an analysis reveals, when the term is used in my defined sense, is always concerned with the *physical* aspects of a work of art; and although these are intimately related to a certain experience (namely, a net impression), they are not themselves the aspects of this experience. They are simply the factors that can yield this experience and which sometimes do not yield it until they are first made to yield other experiences that are more definite, prominent, and individualized.

VI

I must now test my definition. That is to say, I must supplement my earlier example with some others that would normally be said to represent "analysis," making sure that my definition provides the common usage of the term with a legitimate heir. A thorough test would require me to refer to the criticism of literature, music, painting, sculpture, and so on; for I intend the definition to apply to all the arts. But since any such effort would be tedious and would end by reminding the reader of much that he can supply for himself, I shall be content to examine only a few examples, the first two being thoroughly familiar in the criticism of painting.

The example that is a paradigm, perhaps, of aesthetic analysis is

3. I am using "mental chemistry" in its broadest sense, which includes reference to views like those of James Mill no less than those of J. S. Mill. For variant senses of the term see E. G. Boring, *A History of Experimental Psychology*, 2d ed. (New York, 1950), p. 331 [Stevenson's note].

concerned with the location of the figure of Christ in Leonardo da Vinci's "The Last Supper." According to the rules of perspective, lines perpendicular to the plane of the picture must be represented as having the same vanishing point; and it has often been remarked that the figure of Christ, being placed at this vanishing point, with many lines in the background directed to it, is made to dominate the entire picture.

This is clearly an example that fits in with my definition. It deals with (1) a net impression of the picture in which the figure of Christ is felt to be dominant; and although (2) it directs dissective attention to the background in a way that is temporarily hostile to this net impression, it (3) may prove useful for either of the two purposes I have mentioned. That is to say, it may (a) show that the felt dominance of the figure of Christ has a convergence of lines as (a part of) its physical correlate; or, alternatively, it may (b) make this felt dominance become an actual experience for certain observers rather than a merely potential one—that being so because a dissective attention to the background, compensating for the *in*attention with which these observers normally look at it, may end by cultivating in them, later on, a synoptic attention of the sort that the net impression requires.

I do not wish to suggest, of course, that this example always works out successfully. When it is used in elementary schools, where it is presumably intended to serve its second purpose, it may in fact have a somewhat paralyzing effect. The children's dissective attention, instead of cultivating their later synoptic attention, may lead only to a self-conscious state of mind in which their observation of the picture is distracted by various questions and doubts. They may wonder, for instance, whether the teacher expects them to keep thinking about the perspective effect every time they see the picture and whether, in general, an appreciation of painting is always going to involve such unnatural efforts. Amid these distracting thoughts, of course, any sustained net impression of the picture becomes virtually impossible for them. So we here find, in their earliest origins, what seem to be grounds for maintaining that we murder to dissect. Actually, however, they are grounds only for a weaker and less exciting conclusion: that analysis is a method that has always to be used with caution. For if we should draw the stronger conclusion we should be blaming analysis itself for what may be no more than an unskillfully presented or untimely instance of it.

Let me now turn to a further example. In analyzing Poussin's "Ulysses Discovering Achilles" Roger Fry tries to help us discern its "rhythms" and the "exquisite rightness" of its "plastic forms;"[4] he wants to help us get a net impression of the picture in which these

---

4. *Transformations* (New York, 1956), pp. 23 ff. [Stevenson's note].

subtleties of experience are included.[5] But he proceeds indirectly: he points out that the two rooms depicted, in spite of their contrasting perspectives, are related by occasional similarities in the brightness of colors; he notes the way in which the arms of some of the figures introduce curves in the picture; he remarks that a diagonally placed figure breaks up the uniformity of the many perpendicular lines; and so on. To this extent he directs our dissective attention to the picture. This does not, of course, immediately give us a sense of its spatial rhythms or its plastic forms; but shortly afterward, when we half-forget what he has said and look at the painting with an attention that has become synoptic, it may indeed give us a sense of these qualities. We have again, then, an example of analysis in the sense I have defined. It is presumably intended to serve its second purpose but could also lend itself, with only a change in emphasis, to its first purpose as well.

Apart from testing my definition this example introduces a further point of interest: it shows how analysis can help critics to make the most of their often vague (and perhaps inevitably vague) terminology. Suppose, for instance, that Fry merely said, "Note the rhythms and plastic forms of the picture." Most of his readers would then have had a decidedly imperfect understanding of what he was talking about. But his actual procedure, which does much to reduce such a failure in communication, is to take steps toward showing them what he is talking about. He first calls attention to aspects of the picture that are more readily named and more readily located and lets these, by their effect on subsequent attention, help to yield the net impression that interests him. Once this has been done the terms "rhythm" and "plastic form" have their modest function. Anyone who eventually discerns something in the picture that these terms suggest, even though they suggest it only by a slender metaphor, will have a little more reason to suppose that he is seeing what Fry expects him to see. But when divorced from analysis these terms are likely to be too vague to be helpful.

I can put this otherwise by saying that any term like "rhythm" or "plastic form," in acquiring its reference to a property involving a net impression, depends heavily on a process akin to ostensive definition and that analysis, when used for its second purpose, is helpful in implementing this process. We have seen that dissective attention does not in itself yield a net impression; but it can "indirectly point" to one, so to speak, by helping us achieve it subse-

5. I am assuming that "rhythm" and "plastic form" (along with many other such terms) designate properties of a painting that we cannot *discern* without getting a net impression. But I am not saying that these terms serve normally to name a net impression, or any of its aspects. Rather, they name (as I see it) a *tendency* of the painting, realized under "proper" conditions of observation, to produce a net impression. I have discussed this topic further in my paper, "Interpretation and Evaluation in Asthetics," in *Philosophical Analysis*, ed. by Max Black (Ithaca, N. Y., 1950) [Stevenson's note].

quently and in that way can enable us to associate it with whatever term the critic wishes to select. Anything akin to an ostensive definition is a lengthy process, however, which for these particular terms rarely can be brought to a practical completion. Normally, then, a critic must bear in mind that he is only half-using the terms and that for the rest he is always introducing them.

VII

My defined sense of "analysis" has so far proved to be rather close, extensionally at least, to its usual sense; but I have tested it only for contexts that deal with the *formal* aspects of the arts. There are contexts of another sort which readily show that my sense is a little too narrow. It was for that reason, indeed, that I stated the definition provisionally, remarking that it would later have to be "stretched." The stretching is mainly needed to provide for an analysis of literary meanings; so let me develop my point in that special connection.

As before, I shall generalize from an example. William Empson, in discussing Macbeth's lines,

> If th' Assassination
> Could trammel up the Consequence, and catch
> With his surcease, Success . . .

says that the word "Consequence" means both "a causal result . . . and, as in 'a person of consequence,' the divinity that doth hedge a king."[6] Or to put it less succinctly, he says that "Consequence," as it occurs in this context, conveys two meanings at once: in addition to referring to the *result* of the assassination it also refers to the prestige of (Duncan's) kingship that makes the assassination difficult. Empson then goes on to find multiple meanings in various other words of the lines, his general aim being to analyze—and note that "analyze" is just the word that is needed here—the "unparalleled richness" of Shakespeare's language.

Now here it will not quite do, I think, to speak of a "dissective attention" to Shakespeare's multiple meanings, nor will it do to speak of a "synoptic attention" that yields a "net impression" of them; for that will put more burden on these terms (which have been introduced only by examples that lie nearer to seeing and hearing) than they can be expected to bear. It is on that account that my definition does not quite fit this example. There can be little doubt, however, that my three principal terms have analogues that fit the example quite closely. So to show the direction in which my definition can usefully be "stretched" I shall simply make these analogues more explicit:

Empson's examination of the lines is 'dissective' (and I use the

6. William Empson, *Seven Types of Ambiguity* (New York, 1955), p. 59. Empson mentions still a third sense of "Consequence," which I omit in order to simplify my discussion [Stevenson's note].

single quotation marks to suggest that only an analogue is in question) in that it involves a slow-motion reading, as it were, combined with a high sensitivity now to this and now to that sense of a word, each sense being separately drawn out and emphasized by the use of a synonym. This stands in contrast, of course, to an insensitive reading; but it also stands in contrast to a sensitive but 'synoptic' reading that yields a 'net impression' of meanings—that is, a reading in which the several senses are grasped at once but not altogether fully and definitely.

The richness of Shakespeare's language, as Empson uses that term, is presumably its tendency to yield complicated 'net impressions.' For we may presume that neither Empson nor anyone else, on hearing Macbeth's lines spoken in the context of the play, will be likely to get the feeling that he is understanding "Consequence" in two fully 'prominent' senses. Words that have such a subtle combination of meanings (as distinct from those used in plain puns) are likely to yield a reaction that is almost unitary. They can be called complex only because their main sense brings with it a *hint* of some supplementary sense; and although a 'synoptic' reading (or listening) keeps us from ignoring this hint, it does not make it very arresting. So any marked feeling of understanding such a word twice over arises only in a 'dissective' reading and not in a 'synoptic' reading.

We can now see that Empson's analysis (in a sense that I shall now take as intelligibly "stretched") has a point-for-point resemblance to the examples that I have previously discussed and that it can be used for much the same purposes. If it serves its first purpose it will do something to explain why Shakespeare's language so often yields a rich 'net impression.' That is to say, it will help to confirm some such generalization as this: words that impress us as having rich meanings, when read 'synoptically,' are often words that can be seen, with 'dissective' reading, to have two or more quite distinct senses. To the extent that this generalization is true, of course, it is one that a poet is likely to find of interest. Moreover, if Empson's analysis serves its second purpose, it will do something to cultivate our ability to respond to Shakespeare's language. It will provide an 'exercise' that at first, with its somewhat forced, 'dissective' reading, may stand in the way of any rich 'net impression'; but it may also help to increase our powers of reading 'synoptically' later on and thus help to make the richness of the language become apparent to us.

In discussing this example, no less than the others that I have considered, I want to leave open the question whether it represents a good piece of analysis or a bad one. If anyone thinks it is bad merely because initially it seems artificial—merely because it seems to put the two meanings of "Consequence" into excessively conspicuous frames, as it were—then I do, to be sure, wish to suggest that he should reconsider his judgment; for analysis is artificial by its very nature, and I think we can agree that it should be judged not by this transitory aspect but rather by its ultimate outcome. But if anyone should feel, having allowed for this, that Empson's analysis is bad even so—that it reads meanings into Shakespeare, making us seek more richness in his language than we should— then I do not wish to argue the matter; for my aim is only to illustrate what the term "analysis" can appropriately be taken to mean.

If my sense of "analysis" is stretched just a trifle more it will help to explain the element of paradox in some familiar remarks made by A. C. Bradley.[7] Having attempted to interpret a line from Virgil, Bradley concludes:

> What the meaning is *I* cannot say: Virgil has said it . . . Because poetry is words, we vainly fancy that some other words than its own will express its meaning. And they will do so no more—or, if you like to speak loosely, only a trifle more—than words will express the meaning of the Dresden Madonna.

This half-suggests that poetry cannot be interpreted; whereas we know better.

But we can easily accept Bradley's remarks when we remember that his own words should never have been expected to take the place of Virgil's. A paraphrase of a poetic line is always an artificial, 'dissective' paraphrase, giving us explicitly and crudely something like what the line itself can give us subtly. The paraphrase is comparable to an analysis (or, in an extended sense, is actually a step in an analysis) that serves the second of its two purposes: it is an exercise for our understanding and becomes helpful only when, having partly forgotten it, we go back to the poetic line itself with altered sensibilities.

VIII

If I were to complete my study I should have to examine the various other ways in which my defined sense of "analysis" can be stretched. I should then have to consider whether these stretched senses could be included within some more general definition of the term, or whether, alternatively, they could better be taken to exemplify new and distinct senses, all belonging to the same general family. And finally, I should have to test my conclusions by examining a great many more examples—including examples that are of interest to interpretive artists (such as actors and virtuosos), whose problems I have here neglected. But in a subject like aesthetics, whose varied needs and aims virtually force its terms to be "open in texture," an insistence on definitions is useful only when

7. *Oxford Lectures on Poetry* (London, 1941), pp. 21, 25, and 33, n. F. The last of these references indicates that Bradley might himself have been content to accept the explanation of his remarks that I am here suggesting [Stevenson's note].

developed up to a certain point and thereafter becomes academic. So having now said enough to typify what "analysis" is likely to mean, I shall assume that any remaining points can be left without explicit mention.

In concluding my paper, then, I shall simply review its main conclusions, though with an effort to emphasize more sharply their connection with a broad and much-discussed question, namely, "To what extent does criticism differ from science?" My answer to this question is far from decisive, if only because analysis presents just one of the many tasks of criticism; but I have given an answer to this extent:

At least one part of criticism—that involving an analysis used for its first purpose—is an "informal" science. It leads to conclusions about the physical factors correlated with net impressions, or about multiple meanings correlated with a sense of linguistic richness. But at least one other part of criticism—that involving analysis used for its second purpose—is quite different from a science, even though it can be guided and explained by science. It is different from it in this obvious way: instead of developing our beliefs about the arts it alters our immediate reactions to them. It facilitates new ways of responding, much as a pianist's exercises facilitate new ways of playing; and when we are acquiring these new abilities to respond we are not just doing science, any more than a pianist is doing science when he is practicing.

It is perhaps appropriate to suggest, then, that criticism goes "beyond" science not because it has a nonscientific subject matter but only because it sometimes has a noncognitive and therefore nonscientific aim. I have maintained this elsewhere in connection with topics that border on the evaluative aspects of criticism.[8] And it is interesting to see that the present, rather simpler topic, which abstracts from evaluative questions, leads to observations that bear out the same conclusion.

8. "Interpretation and Evaluation of Aesthetics"; see n. 4 [Stevenson's note].

HAROLD ZYSKIND

A Rhetorical Analysis of the Gettysburg Address

The analysis of the Gettysburg Address presented below is intended to exemplify one way of treating literary texts in undergraduate, preferably junior college, discussions. The treatment or method, roughly speaking, is generic: the meaning, structure, and purpose of the text are sought on the hypothesis that the Address is an instance of a literary genre; and the general nature of the

Address is sought on the hypothesis that its parts converge to create a unity of meaning or effect. In application to any particular text, the hypotheses need not be wholly true: they are employed to suggest a mode of analysis, not aesthetic criteria. Since such an approach seeks to recover meaning in context, it is applicable to readings in almost any field of knowledge. And, since the concern is, in equal measure, with the literary construction and the genre of a work, the approach is peculiarly relevant to the humanities.[1]

ADDRESS DELIVERED AT THE DEDICATION OF THE CEMETERY AT GETTYSBURG[2]

Four score and seven years ago our fathers brought forth on this continent, a new nation, conceived in Liberty, and dedicated to the proposition that all men are created equal.

[2.] Now we are engaged in a great Civil War, testing whether that nation, or any nation so conceived and so dedicated, can long endure. [3.] We are met on a great battlefield of that war. [4.] We have come to dedicate a portion of that field, as a final resting place for those who here gave their lives that that nation might live. [5.] It is altogether fitting and proper that we should do this.

[6.] But, in a larger sense, we cannot dedicate—we cannot consecrate—we cannot hallow—this ground. [7.] The brave men, living and dead, who struggled here, have consecrated it far above our poor power to add or detract. [8.] The world will little note, nor long remember what we say here, but it can never forget what they did here. [9.] It is for us the living, rather, to be dedicated here to the unfinished work which they who fought here have thus far so nobly advanced. [10.] It is rather for us to be here dedicated to the great task remaining before us—that from these honored dead we take increased devotion to that cause for which they gave the last full measure of devotion—that we here highly resolve that these dead shall not have died in vain—that this nation, under God, shall have a new birth of freedom—and that government of the people, by the people, for the people, shall not perish from the earth.

ABRAHAM LINCOLN

November 19, 1863

I

A generic analysis obviously depends on a particular definition of the genre in question (in this case, rhetoric) and on the principles supporting it. I do not believe it relevant to argue the principle here, however, since the defense assumed for the definition of rhetoric employed in this article is pedagogic, not philosophic. If the grounds of greatness of the Gettysburg Address were the primary consideration, perhaps a preliminary discussion of principle would be

---

1. For the role of analysis in a humanities program see Richard McKeon, "The Nature and Searching of the Humanities," *Journal of General Education*, III, No. 4 (July, 1949), 290–303. [Zyskind's note].

2. Text taken from the "final manuscript" copy appearing in William E. Barton, *Lincoln at Gettysburg* (Indianapolis: Bobbs-Merrill Co., 1930), plate facing p. 208 [Zyskind's note].

in order. But a final judgment as to its greatness is not involved necessarily in a generic analysis. The primary questions are: Does the Address belong to the genre as defined (however arbitrarily defined)? Are the meaning and purpose of the Address—is its uniqueness—in any way illuminated by an analysis of it as belonging to that genre? The latter question is predominant; only for its sake is the former one asked. In general terms, the familiar notion is used here of a rhetorical work as one designed primarily to create a certain effect on, or to persuade, a particular audience, by whatever means. The merit of the definition, for immediate purposes, is simply that it suggests specific questions to ask about the Gettysburg Address—for example, it immediately suggests an inquiry to discover the traits of the audience envisaged in the statements of Lincoln's speech. Thus, although originating in part from a more or less specific notion as to what rhetoric is (the details of this notion are at least implicit throughout the article), the analysis proceeds—and may be tested for fruitfulness—by reference to the Address itself.

This approach lends itself well to creative participation by students in class discussion. Since no great body of auxiliary or background facts is essential for an intelligent analysis within the framework of the approach, discussion need not consist of attempts by students to anticipate what is in the mind of an instructor better informed than they. In addition, of course, the approach allows for the formulation of questions whose answers require thought about the text rather than recitation from it. The discussion will go better, I believe, if the students are aware generally of the nature of the approach. Otherwise, the instructor's questions may appear to reflect his ingenuity, but they are not likely to suggest the particular and sharply limited purpose of the inquiry.

One way of helping students become clearer about a generic or analytic inquiry is to differentiate it from two other approaches closely related to it. The first kinsman is the biographer. His interests will coincide with the analyst's frequently enough so that the latter must be alert against being diverted by the kinds of biographical questions which do not concern him except incidentally. Does the Address reveal how Lincoln truly felt about the conscripted soldiers and the substitutes? Was Lincoln sincere in all that he said, or was he pretending for the occasion? These may be significant questions for politics or that kind of history called "biography." But, at best, they would be tangential to the analyst's chief emphasis. Whether an orator made a statement because he truly believed it or because he felt it expedient to pretend that he believed it, the statement remains the same. Once delivered, the speech exists. The analyst's primary interest is to discover its meaning and power, as it stands, since he views the Address in the particular compass of his approach as an artistic creation designed for some end. The biographer, on the other hand, sees the speech ultimately as a clue, a piece of evidence which may yield valuable information about the facts of Lincoln's life.

Another approach akin to the analyst's but different in emphasis is that of the geneticist, who works hand in hand with the biographer, but in rather a reverse direction. The biographer seeks to understand the forces and facts of Lincoln's life by studying the speech as evidence, while the geneticist seeks to understand the speech by studying the facts or forces in Lincoln's life as evidence. Quite properly for his interests, the geneticist discovers the historical or psychological causes which motivated Lincoln to write the Address.

One unkind and narrow geneticist explanation of Lincoln's purpose in writing the Gettysburg Address that might be presented to students as an example could run roughly as follows: In November, 1863, the month in which the speech was delivered, Lincoln was concerned about the coming presidential campaign of 1864. For his campaign to be successful, he knew he needed the support of Pennsylvania's governor, Andrew H. Curtin. At the time, however, this support was in doubt. And so, since Curtin was the chief sponsor of the national cemetery at Gettysburg and had been widely advertised as such, Lincoln therefore decided to lay aside his pressing duties at Washington and to accept the invitation to speak at the dedication ceremony, as a way of pleasing and indorsing Curtin publicly. So evident was Lincoln's purpose that he rode up to Gettysburg the day before the ceremony in the hope of seeing the governor at some of the preliminary social affairs, although Secretary of War Stanton had arranged for him to leave Washington the following day in ample time for the actual dedication. Finally, the intention of pleasing Curtin is made clear in the speech itself, for in the fifth sentence Lincoln makes a point of declaring that the ceremony—Curtin's ceremony—is altogether fitting and proper.

Whether or not this explanation were accepted, if one began to search Lincoln's letters and records in order to confirm or disprove it, he would be turning away from the chief focus of the generic analysis. The latter does seek to determine the purpose or intention of the speech. But by that is meant the aim which the words and ideas of the Address seem designed to achieve. What I am saying may be made clearer, I think, by glancing again at the fifth sentence. What one geneticist might find significant in this sentence already has been seen. If his kind of explanation of it were accepted as adequate for the analyst, the latter would be distracted from observing, for example, that the fifth sentence marks the last stage of a steady process of inward narrowing or contraction in the Address. Let us trace this process.

The first sentence opens broadly on the concepts of the continent, the nation, liberty, and equality. Then in the second sentence Lincoln narrows attention to the Civil War; then the circle contracts to the battlefield of that war; next, attention is pinpointed on that part of the battlefield which is being dedicated; and, finally, in the fifth sentence the narrowing movement from continent-nation to war to battlefield to cemetery plots ends in the statement that the dedication of this cemetery is altogether fitting and proper. The termination of the inward movement here, accompanied appropriately as it is by the matter-of-fact diction of this fifth sentence, prepares in tone and thought for the subsequent statement of the inadequacy of the ceremony. More important, since it raises the question of the fittingness of the ceremony, it creates a need, and opens the way, for the expansion and rising emphasis which begin in the sixth sentence with the words "but in a *larger* sense," and which continue until the final plea that this nation and democratic government may not perish from the earth. In this final statement Lincoln has reascended to concepts similar to those with which he began: that is, this continent, the nation, liberty, and equality of the opening are paralleled in the closing statement—though not in the same order—by the earth, this nation, freedom, and government of the people. The movement is like the shape of an hourglass, a steady contraction from broad considerations, followed by progressive expansion back to those considerations. The fifth sentence functions in diction and tone and thought as the narrow passageway connecting the two periods of the movement. There will be more to say of the fifth sentence later, but the point here is that this kind of observation about it is immediately relevant to the analyst's interest, and he should not be diverted from it by an exclusive concern with the relation between Lincoln and the governor of Pennsylvania.

I have distinguished between the approaches with perhaps excessive rigidity. Just as the sound geneticist will relate Lincoln's habits of thought and composition to the structure of the Address, so the generic analyst cannot read the Address in a vacuum of indifference to its genesis in Lincoln's mind and environment. But the emphasis in the two approaches is nonetheless distinct. The geneticist sees the speech primarily as a historical event which is to be interpreted by discovering its external causes and consequences; the analyst sees the Address primarily as a construction which may be interpreted by discovering its intrinsic causes—its aim, its structure, its assumptions about the audience, its parts and their interrelations.

II

With such an interest, the analysis[3] may begin in a preliminary

3. Among the works consulted in the preparation of this analysis was a lecture by Andrew Meyer, professor of English, Hood College. I wish here to express thanks for insights obtained from his paper [Zyskind's note].

and tentative fashion by considering the literary form or genre of the Address, since the initial conception of the form will suggest a more specific direction that questions may take. The fact that the speech is oratory and was delivered on a ceremonial occasion does not classify it automatically as rhetoric. Orton H. Carmichael says the Address will last through time—because, in his words, "Truth only is eternal."[4] He here obviously is treating the speech as political philosophy. And it is true that Lincoln speaks strongly of fundamental principles of government. One might assert, even, that the Address is history, since it lays down in the second sentence a thesis as to the historical significance of the Civil War. No law requires that the Address lie meekly in any rigorous category or that it not have value for us—like Herodotus' work—as philosophy, history, and rhetoric. But there are reasons which suggest a rhetorical analysis as primary: The Gettysburg Address assumes—it does not seek to demonstrate—the truth of the political propositions that it lays down. The listeners are presumed in advance to believe that democratic government is desirable. The same applies to the broader historical statements. No substantiation is offered. Lincoln simply asserts what the significance of the Civil War is. He apparently relies for substantiation on the audience's existing convictions rather than on the kind of evidence and interpretations observed in most histories. Lincoln's method in this regard is characteristic of rhetoric. If the aim is to create an effect on a particular audience, the relevant question for the rhetorician is not whether a proposition necessary to the argument really is true but whether the listeners believe it to be true. Consequently, what would have to be demonstrated in some fashion for the historian or scientist often is offered in rhetoric as an assumed premise, just as Lincoln's broad historical and philosophic statements are offered here. In addition, the Address has an obvious emotional pitch and makes frequent references to the audience, thus further suggesting its essentially persuasive character. Although the Address has not been shown by any means to be exclusively rhetorical, it seems clear that an inquiry into it as rhetoric should yield some insight into its meaning and aim. First, then, to the question of its rhetorical effect or aim.

The ceremonial occasion, as Lincoln expressly describes it in the speech, suggests that he sought to bestow honor on the dead of Gettysburg and all those who had fought that the Union might live. This aim is supported especially by the emphasis that Lincoln gives to the inadequacy of the ceremony in contrast to the larger and more genuine dedication of the ground achieved by the soldiers who fought there. The speech thus would be epideictic rhetoric;

4. *Lincoln's Gettysburg Address* (New   [Zyskind's note].
York: Abingdon Press, 1917), p. 113

that is, its aim would be to exhibit the deeds or memory of the fallen soldiers in such solemn and stirring manner as to excite the audience's immediate, present praise of them. Another possibility is that Lincoln's aim is deliberative; that is, that his concern is to persuade the audience to take some specified course of action represented as desirable for its future consequences. This is supported chiefly by the two final sentences, each of which begins with an injunction to the audience to devote themselves to actions on behalf of the Union's survival.

Is either of these two aims dominant over the other? Is the Address primarily epideictic or primarily deliberative, or some combination of the two? These are the questions to be posed at this point. But the analyst's ultimate aim is not to bury the Address in some neat verbal category. His primary purpose is not to label it deliberate or epideictic. Rather he tries to place it in one or both these categories because such an attempt requires him to examine the Address itself in a somewhat systematic manner. For example, since a temporal distinction is involved in the categories being considered—present honor and future action—one must look for the temporal emphases in the structure of the Address. This search leads to awareness of a quite evident pattern: first, Lincoln tells what happened eighty-seven years before; then, in the second sentence, attention turns to what is happening now; and, finally, the Address closes with reference to what must happen in the future. On this basis Part I of the speech would consist of the first sentence. Part II would move from the second into the eighth sentence, since the shift to the present is made explicit when the Civil War is introduced, and this emphasis on the present tense—in connection with the war, the battlefield, and the dedication ceremony—continues into the transitional eighth sentence. There the phrase "the world will little note" foreshadows the shift to the future which becomes dominant in the ninth and tenth sentences, as in such phrases as "that these dead shall not have died in vain" or that this nation "shall not perish from the earth."

This division by itself, however, does not help appreciably in deciding whether the Address aims at present praise or future action, for all stages of the temporal stream are represented, and not always in connection with honor or action. The division needs obviously is not concerned with the nature of time itself but with to be explored further before it becomes meaningful, for Lincoln what takes place in the temporal stream. What or who moves along it? The most apparent and constant element is the audience itself—or, rather, the speaker and audience combined, who constitute the general "we" of the Address. This "we" appears in some form at least once in every statement in the speech. Sometimes it changes to the possessive "our" or the accusative "us," but the plural pronoun in the first person still is there. A glance down the speech reveals: "our fathers"; "we are engaged"; "we are met"; "we have come"; "that we should do this"; "we cannot dedicate"; "our poor power"; and so on in each sentence through "that we here highly resolve."

Thus, whatever it is whose temporal sequence Lincoln is follow-ing, he explicitly underlines his and the listeners' roles at each stage of the sequence. From the standpoint solely of what this role of the audience is, a climactic rise is apparent from stage to stage. In Part I the phrase "our fathers" incidentally implies the audience's role as inheritors of the nation founded eighty-seven years before; the listeners here are passive beneficiaries, inactive heirs. Part II repre-sents them as engaged in a Civil War generally, but their particular role in it at the present moment is to dedicate the cemetery: the point of the dedication is what is said. The listeners are here, there-fore, mere talkers or utterers of words. Part III begins in the ninth sentence to urge them to more positive action in the future, to carry on the unfinished work, so that they now become, poten-tially, doers of deeds. Thus as the speech moves in temporal climax from past to present to future, the role ascribed to the audience moves climactically from that of receivers to speakers to doers. It may be noticed, incidentally, how complete these divisions are: just as past, present, and future cover the whole of a temporal stream, so also passivity, speech, and action cover all kinds of ex-ternal service which the listeners or any men could render to a cause.

At any rate, when the two patterns of time and the listeners' role are linked, the emphasis in the final section falls on the audience's future action; and the inquiry has shown that the solemn call to action emerges in this final section not as an appendage or after-thought but rather as the systematic culmination and climax (in time and kind of service) to the two preceding sections. The impli-cation therefore is that the epideictic elements of the speech must be subordinate to and must help achieve its deliberative aim.

To test this implication, one may examine the way in which the epideictic elements do figure in the pattern already observed. These elements are "our fathers" and the soldiers, since they are the only persons in the Address for whom there is any strong note of praise. Notice that the praise given is for the high degree of worthy action or doing which Lincoln ascribes to them. In Part I, when one barely thinks of the passive role implied for the audience, the fathers are engaged in the mighty task of bringing forth a nation. In Part II, the deeds of the soldiers— "what they did here"—are expressly contrasted with "what we say here."

Hence the pattern of the analysis must be expanded to include doers at every stage of the Address. In the first, it is our fathers who are the doers; in the second, it is the soldiers; in the third, as evident from the earlier analysis, it is the audience potentially. The connection is clear and explicit. Because in Parts I and II the deeds of the fathers and soldiers are represented to some extent epideictically as praiseworthy in contrast to the mere talk of the audience, therefore in Part III Lincoln urges the audience to act as the soldiers have acted in preserving what was achieved through action by the fathers. The dominance of the deliberative aim is therefore clear.[5]

What it might have meant for Lincoln to have made the epideictic aim dominant instead may be indicated vividly by drawing on the speech delivered on the same occasion by Edward Everett. As chief orator of that day at Gettysburg, he spoke magnificently for some two hours. Here are the concluding sentences of his speech:

"The whole earth," said Pericles, as he stood over the remains of his fellow-citizens, who had fallen in the first year of the Peloponnesian War, "the whole earth is the sepulchre of illustrious men." All time, he might have added, is the millennium of their glory. Surely I would do no injustice to the other noble achievements of the war, which have reflected such honor on both arms of the service, and have entitled the armies and the navy of the United States, their officers and men, to the warmest thanks and the richest rewards which a grateful people can pay. But they, I am sure, will join us in saying, as we bid farewell to the dust of these martyr-heroes, that wheresoever throughout the civilized world the accounts of this great warfare are read, and down to the latest periods of recorded time, in the glorious annals of our common country there will be no brighter page than that which relates The Battles of Gettysburg.[6]

Mr. Everett's eloquent concern at this point with nobility, honor, and glory has an epideictic emphasis which ought to illuminate, by contrast, the quite different end of the Gettysburg Address.

III

While the interpretation up to this point presumably is justified, there is a rather striking omission from it. No mention has been made of a usual characteristic by which a speech is recognized as deliberative. Milton's *Areopagitica*, or virtually any contemporary political speech, exemplifies this trait well. Milton wants the licensing act repealed. Consequently, he tells Parliament that the passage

5. A simple diagram of analysis up to this point would be as follows:

Part	Sentences	Time	Audience Role	Models
I	1	Past	Passivity	Action (fathers)
II	2–8	Present	Speech	Action (soldiers)
III	8/9–10	Future	Action	

[Zyskind's note]

6. *Address of the Hon. Edward Everett, at the Consecration of the National Cemetery at Gettysburg, 19th November, 1863, with the Dedicatory* *Speech of President Lincoln. . . .* (Boston: Little, Brown & Co., 1864), p. 82 [Zyskind's note].

of the act produces bad ends and that the repeal of the act will be the means for restoring truth and virtue. As in most deliberative oratory, the argument turns on the issue of means and ends, since the aim is to stimulate a course of action by showing the desirable effect which it will have.

If the Gettysburg Address is deliberative, what about its argument? This question may be explored by looking at the Address for a moment solely from the standpoint of its concern with means and ends. In the opening sentence what is important about our fathers is the end which they achieved—the founding of the nation. Then the Civil War is identified by the fact that it also has as its end the survival of that nation. The battlefield and the cemetery plot are next presented implicitly in terms of the same end, since, as Lincoln develops the narrowing process observed earlier, the Civil War's arena includes the battlefield, which, in turn, includes the plot of ground being dedicated. The connection thus established between the cemetery and the welfare of the nation is reaffirmed when Lincoln expressly describes the cemetry as the resting place for those who gave their lives that that nation might live. Accordingly, the fifth sentence may declare the ceremonial dedication altogether fitting and proper, because—and here I shall go back up the ladder from the fifth to the first sentence—the cemetery contains the dead who fought on the battlefield of the war whose end is the survival of the nation that our fathers founded. Thus these opening sentences comprise more than the narrowing movement noticed earlier; they form a unit in which the career of the Union is established and held to steadfastly by Lincoln as the one end or standard by which to understand or judge our fathers, the war, the soldiers, the cemetery, and the ceremony.

Next, one may notice how, after Stage I of the argument—i.e., the unit formed by the first five sentences—has been completed, Lincoln begins in the sixth sentence to shift his emphasis from the end of action to a consideration of the most noble and effective means. In Stage I there is no mention of the bravery of the soldiers, that is, of the way they fought, but only of the end for which they fought. Now in Stage II (sentences six, seven, eight) their bravery becomes important because it characterizes the means which they employed toward the end. Similarly, it is in this second stage that Lincoln considers the audience's poor power to add or detract, that is, the ineffectiveness of the ceremony as a means. Ostensibly, Lincoln here in Stage II of the argument is modifying and expanding his former judgment of the ceremony. It is incapable of truly dedicating the ground, because the soldier's deeds have done this more genuinely and because their deeds—not the words of the ceremony—will be memorable to the world. This contrast between words and deeds is an opposition between two kinds of means for serving the same end.

In the light, now, of the first five sentences as comprising Stage I and the next three sentences as comprising Stage II, of what is loosely called the "argument," we may summarize the grounds on which two apparently opposed judgments of the dedication ceremony are offered. Stage I judges it by the end toward which it is directed and therefore finds the ceremony, like the soldier's deeds, to be altogether fitting and proper. Stage II, however, judges the ceremony by the means employed and therefore finds it, unlike the soldier's brave deeds, to be altogether inadequate and transitory.

Thus not only has Lincoln passed judgment on the ceremony, but, in doing so, he has employed broad and basic criteria for action in any crucial period of the democratic Union's career. Even should the audience forget the particular judgment of the ceremony, Lincoln has impressed on them the principles by which they should live and act in the future—they know the right end and the most effective means. With such criteria for future action established, the way is open for the third and final stage of the argument, which begins with the ninth sentence and needs only to press the listeners with deep emotion to act according to these principles.

Lincoln does not once mar the beauty of his words or the fluency of his thought by speaking expressly of means and ends. But when in Stage III he encourages the listeners rather to be doers, like the soldiers, so that the nation may live, he is urging them to carry on the means which had been established as preferable in Stage II of the argument, for the end which had been premised as desirable in Stage I.[7]

IV

The inquiry thus far has yielded some conception of what Lincoln's speech seeks to persuade its listeners to do. It is necessary, next, to try to identify these listeners. Until one knows whom the Address seeks to arouse to action, the conception of its aim as deliberative rhetoric remains somewhat empty. Of course, there was the physical audience seated before Lincoln at the ceremony. But some of them may have been distracted at the moment of the speech—especially since the speech is so short—by a neighbor's sneezing fit. Indeed, the evidence is not at all clear as to whether Lincoln produced much of an effect of any kind on the persons seated before him. Perhaps he had in mind the newspaper readers

7. A simple diagram of the argument of the speech would be as follows:

Stage	Sentences	Judgment	Criterion
I	1-5	Ceremony fitting	End
II	6-8	Ceremony inadequate	Means
III	9-10	Therefore, act for the Union (means) (end)	

[Zyskind's note]

who would see the Address on the morning after the ceremony. Or, again, to the extent that modern readers or listeners are affected by the speech, perhaps they constitute the true audience. Such questions will have to be left chiefly to the biographer or the geneticist, who are more concerned with discovering just whom Lincoln had in mind and precisely what historical consequences the Address has had on the oratory and emotions of America. In view of the practical difficulties alone, an analysis on the undergraduate level could hardly attempt to define the audience by such research. But there is a limited kind of inquiry appropriate here which is germane to the analyst's interests. He can try to discover, from the Address, roughly the kind of persons to whom it is likely to appeal.

For example, it is quite apparent that an atheist is not a member of the envisaged audience, so far as the phrase "under God," which appears in the tenth sentence, is concerned. If we are right about Lincoln's purpose, then the phrase "under God"—like any other phrase in the Address—ought to help lead the listener toward being an active doer in the service of the nation. That fact that the nation is said to be under God will have no such effect on an atheist, and in that respect—though perhaps in no other—he will be excluded from the envisaged audience. If this line of reasoning is pursued in a more general and practicable manner, we should say that the true or envisaged audience will comprise those who have some kind of positive and favorable feelings about the Founding Fathers, this continent, liberty, equality, bravery in battle, and so on. From such a beginning one could go on to build up a more detailed picture of the sort of person to whom the speech is appealing.

Notice how broad and inclusive this audience is. Nowhere does Lincoln touch on particular issues which might tend to cut off some partisan group from his reach. Nor does he make any nice distinctions about the definition of liberty or democratic government. Whatever theoretic or even practical differences about methods may separate believers in political democracy, Lincoln chooses the terms[8] dear to all of them and appeals to the basic convictions which they have in common. Whatever disadvantages in specificity of appeal this method may entail, the audience is envisaged with a breadth that will attract nearly all persons who bring to the speech a feeling that they have a genuine attachment to American democracy.

It is not enough, however, to designate the listeners whom Lincoln is trying to reach, for Lincoln is doing more than appealing *to*

8. The orientation of this analysis may perhaps best be indicated at this point, since Lincoln's use of undefined generalities is considered here only for its persuasive qualities, whereas often such a device is praised or blamed as the declaration of true ideals or the misleading exploitation of glittering generalities, depending on whether one supports or opposes the particular rhetorician under consideration [Zyskind's note].

them. He is *using* them as part of his means of persuasion. The audience constitutes material for the skillful rhetorician as surely as words do. With perhaps a single symbol, the skillful rhetorician awakens emotions and convictions already possessed by his listeners, though perhaps vaguely or dormantly; and he then channels these emotions toward the end that he has in mind. Among the already existent feelings which Lincoln awakens and stimulates are admiration for the Founding Fathers, respect for liberty, emulation of bravery, love and veneration of God. But, having aroused this diversity of emotions and convictions, what does Lincoln do with them? By what means does he turn them to his purpose? To answer this in part, one may notice the systematic way in which Lincoln implicitly defines all the diverse objects which have emotional significance for the audience. All such objects take on meaning, for the instant of the Address, only insofar as they relate to the concept of the free nation. Our fathers, whatever else they may have done in fact, have meaning in the Address only as the founders of the nation. Bravery is here a virtue only insofar as it prompts brave deeds in the service of the nation. Liberty is defined only as a characteristic of the nation. And God, whatever other significance he may have in our lives, is represented in the Address only as the Being who stands over the nation. One could proceed thus with all the major emotional terms in the speech. The point here is that, since all these terms have meaning in the Address only as they relate to the nation, then all the emotions associated with the terms tend to be transferred to the nation. Thus all the diverse feelings and sympathies which Lincoln awakens are channeled so as to crystallize into an instant of intense devotion to the free Union in peril.

The cumulative channeling of this feeling is not interrupted by any aspect of the Address, not even by an attempt on Lincoln's part to tell how deeply moved he himself is as President. In other speeches he does not hesitate to use the pronoun "I" and thereby to represent his own character, motives, and position in a favorable light. He could have done the same in the Gettysburg Address. But he represents himself only as an indistinguishable member among those gathered to honor the dead. In representing himself in such a way, Lincoln adds emotionally to the idea that the only touchstone of importance is one's relation to the nation's survival. At the moment he is engaged, like the audience, in honoring the dead with words; therefore, he and the audience are one.

The resultant sense of unity is sustained by the Address as a whole. Lincoln, the audience, the soldiers, the Founding Fathers, even God—all are united in the Address in their concern with the same end. Though a war is in progress, nowhere does Lincoln introduce a single note of division; he forgoes all the advantages he could have gained from emotional condemnations of the unpopular Copperheads of the North or the hated slave barons of the South. Nowhere does he mention enemies, and it is obvious that "our fathers" were from Virginia as well as from New York. Whatever Lincoln may forfeit in partisan emotional appeal by this method he gains back in a sense of emotional unity.

V

A final stage in the inquiry still is necessary before it may be considered adequate. We have some notion now of Lincoln's aim and of the ideas and emotional associations that he employs to achieve this aim. But, unless the ideas and emotions are presented stirringly and appropriately, the speech will lack effectiveness. I shall not inquire thoroughly here into this topic of style or tone, for it is what is so often emphasized in "rhetorical" analysis. One may observe the biblical tone of such a word as "consecrate" and of such a phrase as "Four score and seven years ago"; this diction imparts a solemnity appropriate both to the dedication ceremony and to the larger dedication which Lincoln urges upon his audience. Or one may contrast the matter-of-fact form of the sentence—"We are met on a great battlefield of that war"—to the parallelism in the sixth sentence: ". . . we cannot dedicate—we cannot consecrate—we cannot hallow—this ground." And the symphonic progression represented by that contrast may be traced as it builds up further from that sixth sentence to the more extended climactic parallels, the solemn rhythms, and the periodic form of the final appeal in the tenth sentence.

But I prefer here to emphasize the basic metaphor that Lincoln employs for the nation, since the emotional tone is derived in such large measure from it; that is, from the figure of the nation as a single being moving through an organic life-cycle. The ideas of the speech, and the diction as well, emphasize the vicissitudes of this metaphoric cycle. Our fathers *brought forth* the nation. It was *conceived* in liberty. The war tests whether it can *endure*. The soldiers fought that it might *live*. And we must see that it has a new *birth* of freedom and *not perish* from the earth. No figure could have been more appropriate to an occasion commemorating the dead. Its appropriateness—and the religious tone set by solemn discussion of generation and death—are sustained by the characterization of the audience as the living in contrast to the dead of the battlefield, who gave their lives that the nation might live.

VI

On the day following Lincoln's delivery of the Address, he received a note from Edward Everett, who said: "I should be glad if I could flatter myself that I came as near to the central idea of the occasion in two hours as you did in two minutes."[9] What Ever-

---

9. Barton, *op. cit.*, p. 105 [Zyskind's note].

ett had in mind, perhaps, was the central point seen re-emerging successively in the various rhetorical aspects of the Address as analyzed here—that is, that the dedication ceremony and all the ideas and actions appropriate to it take on in Lincoln's address a solemn significance precisely because they are exhibited to us so skillfully and so exclusively from the perspective of their bearing on the Union in peril. As an argument, the Address establishes service to the nation as the end of action and positive deeds as the proper means. In the process of the argument a wide range of the envisaged audience's sympathies and convictions are channeled and brought to focus on the nation and the necessity for its survival. And, in style, the occasion is made the basis of a metaphor which transforms appropriate thoughts about the soldiers' deaths into a consideration of the nation's life.

In stirring his audience thus to action on behalf of the Union, Lincoln's subordination of what may be called the "logical" element to the emotional and intuitive has been evident. The argument itself sets up its criteria of means and ends in its first two stages, so that the final stage of even so brief a speech has nothing to establish—it has only to drive home emotionally the implications of these principles for the listeners' choice of future action. The emotional process is stimulated further by the sense of unity created in the audience and by the skillful evoking of a wide range of their traditional feelings. And, finally, the kind of simplicity and solemnity created by the metaphor of birth and death, by the religious diction and the climactic progressions, lends a quality of timelessness to Lincoln's statements.

Thus the deliberative aim of the Address, as it may be reformulated now in the light of the entire analysis, is not to persuade the listeners of the truth of the idea that the Union must be reborn. In a logical sense the truth of the general idea that future action is needed is largely taken for granted. The aim rather is to take this accepted general idea and sink it deeply into the feelings of the audience, fix it as an emotional experience so powerful that each listener will, at any crucial time, do what he can specifically for the future of the nation to which he is here dedicated.

QUESTIONS
1. What is the author's purpose in this essay? Does he wish to praise Lincoln's Gettysburg Address? Is he trying to urge people to read and think about it?
2. Is it the author's point that Lincoln wrote the Gettysburg Address in order to secure the political support of Governor Curtin of Pennsylvania? Why does the author include consideration of that topic in his essay?
3. Does this essay have an argument? If so, state it.

4. Make an analysis of the structure of Zyskind's essay, following his procedure in discussing the Gettysburg Address. In what specific ways does such analysis clarify the meaning and purpose of this essay?

5. Apply Zyskind's method of analysis to one of the writings in this book (e.g., White, "Once More to the Lake," pp. 89–95; Gold, "A Dog in Brooklyn, A Girl in Detroit," pp. 55–67; Lincoln, "Letter to James M. Cutts, Jr.," pp. 450–451). What does analysis of structure enable you to say about the nature of the piece? What appears to be its aim? What effect on its audience does it seek? How do answers to these questions help define or clarify its meaning?

W. K. WIMSATT
What to Say About a Poem [1]

At the outset what can we be sure of? Mainly that a poem says or means something, or ought to mean something (or ought to if we as teachers have any business with it—perhaps that is the safe minimum). The meaning of the poem may be quite obscure and difficult (rough, opaque, and resistant to first glance), or it may be smooth and easy, perhaps deceptively smooth and easy, a nice surface and seemingly transparent. For either kind of poem, the simplest, but not the least important kind of observation we can make, the simplest question we can ask, is the kind which relates to the dictionary. What does a certain word or phrase mean? We are lucky enough, I am assuming, to have a poem which contains some archaic, technical, or esoteric expression, which the class, without previous research, will not understand. If we are even luckier, the word has another, a modern, an easy and plausible meaning, which conceals the more difficult meaning. (Ambiguity, double or simultaneous meaning, our grammar instructs us, is a normal situation in poems.) In any case, we can put our question in two stages: "Are there any difficulties or questions with this stanza?" "Well, in that case, Miss Proudfit, what does the word *braw* mean?" "What does

1. This essay is a reduced version of a paper read before *The Eighth Yale Conference on the Teaching of English,* at New Haven, April 14, 1962. An introductory section, here omitted, touched on the "grammar" of criticism, the categories of theme, diction, metaphor, symbol, meter, genre, person, tone, tension, wit, irony, and the like, which theoretical effort makes available to criticism. These, I argued, are an important part of critical equipment but not necessarily the immediate idiom of practical criticism and certainly not a dictionary of the trophies which criticism can expect to bring away from its exploration of actual poems. My essay aims to consider in a less technical way how we are using the materials of language and poetry, and how we are using our own minds, when we address ourselves to the examination of a given poem, to asking questions about it, to eliciting answers from our students. In its original form, the paper was fortified by a fairly extended explication of one short poem, William Blake's "London," in his *Songs of Experience* [Wimsatt's note].

kirkward mean?" "When six braw gentlemen kirkward shall carry ye." We are lucky, I say, not simply that we have a chance to teach the class something—to earn our salary in a clear and measurable way. But of course because we hereby succeed in turning the attention of the class to the poem, to the surface, and then through the surface. They may begin to suspect the whole of this surface. They may ask a few questions of their own.

The answers to questions of the kind just noticed lie in a clean, dictionary region of meaning. This kind of meaning is definitely, definably, and provably there—some of our pupils just did not happen to be aware of it. Let us call this *explicit* meaning. I believe it is important to give this kind of meaning a name and to keep it fixed. The act of expounding this meaning also needs a name. Let us call it explanation—*explanation of the explicit*.

Obviously, our talking about the poem will not go far at this level—not much farther than our translation of Caesar or Virgil in a Latin reading class.

And so we proceed, or most often we do, to another level of commentary on the poem—not necessarily second *in order* for every teacher or for every poem, but at least early and fundamental, or in part so. This level of commentary may usefully be called *description* of a poem—not *explanation*, just *description*. There is no way of describing the weather report, except to repeat what it says—describing the weather. A poem, on the other hand, not only says something, but *is* something. "A poem," we know, "should not mean but be." And so the poem itself especially *invites* description.

The meter of a poem, for instance, is of a certain kind, with certain kinds of variations and certain relations to the syntax; one kind of word rhymes with another kind (*Aristotle* with *bottle*, in Byron; *Adam* with *madam*, in Yeats); some conspicuous repetition or refrain in a poem shows partial variations ("On the Echoing Green. . . . On the darkening Green." "Could frame thy fearful symmetry. . . . Dare frame thy fearful symmetry"). Some unusual word is repeated several times in a short poem, or a word appears in some curious position. Some image (or "symbol") or cluster of images recurs in a tragedy or is played against some other image or cluster. Shakespeare's *Hamlet*, for instance, may be described as a dramatic poem which concerns the murder of a father and a son's burden of exacting revenge. At the same time it is a work which exhibits a remarkable number and variety of images relating to the expressive arts and to the criticism of the arts—music, poetry, the theater. "That's an ill phrase, a vile phrase; 'beautified' is a vile phrase." "Speak the speech, I pray you . . . trippingly on the tongue." "Govern these ventages with your finger and thumb . . . it will discourse most eloquent music."

Description in the most direct sense moves inside the poem,

accenting the parts and showing their relations. It may also, however, look outside the poem. *Internal* and *external* are complementary. The external includes all the kinds of history in which the poem has its setting. A specially important kind of history, for example, is the literary tradition itself. The small neat squared-off quatrains of Andrew Marvell's *Horatian Ode* upon Oliver Cromwell go in a very exact way with the title and with the main statement of the poem. Both in ostensible theme and in prosody the poem is a kind of echo of Horatian alcaics in honor of Caesar Augustus. The blank verse of Milton's *Paradise Lost* and the couplets of Dryden's translation of the *Aeneid* are both attempts to find an equivalent for, or a vehicle of reference to, the hexameters of Greek and Latin epic poetry. A poem in William Blake's *Songs of Innocence* is written in simple quatrains, four rising feet or three to a line, with perhaps alternate rhymes. These are something like the stanzas of a folk ballad, but they are more like something else. A more immediate antecedent both of Blake's metric and of his vocabulary of child-like piety, virtues, and vices, hopes and fears, is the popular religious poetry of the eighteenth century, the hymns sung at the evangelical chapels, written for children by authors like Isaac Watts or Christopher Smart.

II

We can insist, then, on *description* of poems, both *internal* and *external*, as a moment of critical discourse which has its own identity and may be usefully recognized and defined. Let us hasten to add, however, that in making the effort to define this moment we are mainly concerned with setting up a platform for the accurate construction of something further.

The truth is that description of a poetic structure is never simply a report on appearances (as it might be, for instance, if the object were a painted wooden box). Description of a poetic structure is inevitably also an engagement with meanings which inhere in that structure. It is a necessary first part of the engagement with certain kinds of meaning. (*Certain kinds*—in the long run we shall want to lay some emphasis on that qualification. But for the moment the point is that there *is* meaning.) In the critic's discourse "pure description" will always have a hard time taking the "place of sense."

Perhaps we shall feel guilty of stretching the meaning of the word *meaning* slightly, but unless we are willing to leave many kinds of intimation out of our account of poetry, we shall have to say, for example, that Byron meant that criticism had fallen on evil days—and that it didn't matter very much. "Longinus o'er a bottle, Or, Every Poet his *own* Aristotle." We shall have to say, surely we shall wish to say, that Milton in the opening of his *Paradise*

Lost means, "This is the language and style of epic, the greatest kind of poetry; and this is the one theme that surpasses those of the greatest epics of antiquity." ("This"—in a sense—"is an epic to end all epics." As it did.) Alexander Pope in his *Epistle to Augustus* means, "This is a poem to the King of England which sounds curiously like the Epistle of Horace to the Emperor Augustus. Let anybody who cares or dares notice how curious it sounds." Shakespeare means that the action of *Hamlet* takes place on a stage, in a world, where relations between appearance and reality are manifold and some of them oddly warped.

Through description of poems, then, we move back to meaning—though scarcely to the same kind of meaning as that with which we were engaged in our initial and simple explanation of words. Through description, we arrive at a kind of meaning which ought to have its own special name. We can safely and usefully, I think, give it the simple name of the *implicit*. What we are doing with it had better too be given a special name. Perhaps *explication* is the best, though the harsher word *explicitation* may seem invited. The realms of the *explicit* and the *implicit* do not, of course, constitute sealed-off separate compartments. Still there will be some meanings which we can say are clearly explicit, and some which are clearly but implicit.

I believe that we ought to work to keep ourselves keenly aware of, and on occasion ought to make as clear as we can to our pupils, two things concerning the nature of *implicit* meaning. One of these is the strongly directive and selective power of such meaning—the power of the *pattern*, of the main formally controlling purpose in the well-written poem (in terms of Gestalt psychology, the principle of "closure"). It is this which is the altogether sufficient and compelling reason in many of our decisions about details of meaning which we proceed, during our discussion of the poem, to make quite explicit—though the dictionary cannot instruct us. In the third stanza of Marvell's *Garden*: "No white or red was ever seen/ So am'rous as this lovely green." How do we know that the words *white* and *red* refer to the complexions of the British ladies?—and not, for instance, to white and red roses? The word *am'rous* gives a clue. The whole implicit pattern of meaning in the poem proves it. In these lines of this poem the words can mean nothing else. In Marvell's *Ode on Cromwell*: ". . . now the *Irish* are asham'd to see themselves in one Year tam'd. . . . They can affirm his Praises best, And have, though overcome, confest How good he is, how just, And fit for highest Trust." How do we show that these words do not express simply a complacent English report, for the year 1650, on the ruthless efficiency of Cromwell in Ireland? Only by appealing to the delicately managed intimations of the whole poem. The cruder reading, which might be unavoidable in some other context, will here reveal (in the interest of a supposedly stolid historical accuracy) a strange critical indifference to the extraordinary finesse of Marvell's poetic achievement. "Proud Maisie is in the wood, Walking so early.... 'Tell me, thou bonny bird, When shall I marry me?' 'When six braw gentlemen, Kirkward shall carry ye.' " How do we prove to our freshman class, that the word *proud* does not mean in the first place—does not necessarily mean at all— conceited, unlikable, nasty, unlovable, that Maisie does not suffer a fate more or less well deserved (withered and grown old as a spinster—an example of poetic justice)? Only, I think, by appealing to the whole contour and intent of this tiny but exquisitely complete poem.

> "Who makes the bridal bed,
>   Birdie, say truly?"—
> "The gray-headed sexton
>   Who delves the grave duly.
> "The glow-worm o'er grave and stone
>   Shall light thee steady.
> The owl from the steeple sing,
>   'Welcome, proud lady.' "

The second thing concerning *implicit* meaning which I think we ought to stress is exactly its character as *implicit*—and this in reaction against certain confused modes of talk which sometimes prevail. It was a hard fight for criticism, at one time not so long past, to gain recognition of the formal and implicit at all as a kind of meaning. But that fight being in part won, perhaps a careless habit developed of talking about all sorts and levels of meaning as if they all were meaning in the same direct and simple way. And this has brought anguished bursts of protest from more sober and literal scholars. The critic seems all too gracefully and readily to move beyond mere explanation. (Being a sophisticated man, he feels perhaps the need to do relatively little of this.) He soars or plunges into descriptions of the colors and structures of the poem, with immense involvements of meaning, manifold explicitations—yet all perhaps in one level tone of confident and precise insistence, which scarcely advertises or even admits what is actually going on. The trouble with this kind of criticism is that it knows too much. Students, who of course know too little, will sometimes render back and magnify this kind of weakness in weird parodies, innocent sabotage. "I am overtired/Of the great harvest I myself desired," proclaims the man who lives on the farm with the orchard, the cellar bin, the drinking trough, and the woodchuck, in Robert Frost's *After Apple-Picking*. "This man," says the student in his homework paper, "is tired of life. He wants to go to sleep and die." This we mark with a red pencil. Then we set to work, somehow, in class, to retrieve the "symbolism." This monodrama of a tired applepicker, with the feel of the ladder rungs in his instep, bears nearly the same relation to the end of a country fair, the end of a victorious football season, of a long vacation, or of a full lifetime, as a doughnut bears to a Christmas wreath, a ferris wheel, or the rings of Saturn. *Nearly the same relation*, let us say. A poem is a kind of shape, a cunning and precise shape of words and human experience, which has something of the indeterminacy of a simpler physical shape, round or square, but which at the same time invites and justifies a very wide replication or reflection of itself in the field of our awareness.

> Till the little ones, weary,
> No more can be merry;
> The sun does descend,
> And our sports have an end.
> Round the laps of their mothers
> Many sisters and brothers,
> Like birds in their nest,
> Are ready for rest,
> And sport no more seen
> On the darkening Green.

What experience has any member of the class ever had, or what experiences can he think of or imagine, that are parallel to or concentric to that of the apple-picker? of the Echoing Green?—yet the words of the poem do not *mean* these other experiences in the same way that they mean the apples, the ladder, the man, the sport, and the green. The kind of student interpretation which I have mentioned may be described as the fallacy of the literal feedback. Proud Maisie translated into conceited Maisie may be viewed as a miniature instance of the same. And this will illustrate the close relation between the two errors of implicit reading which I have just been trying to describe. The uncontrolled reading is very often the over-explicit reading.

III

Explanation, then—of the explicit and clearly ascertainable but perhaps obscure or disguised meaning of words; *description*—of the poem's structure and parts, its shape and colors, and its historical relations; *explication*—the turning of such description as far as possible into meaning. These I believe are the teacher-critic's staple commitments—which we may sum up, if we wish, in some such generic term as *elucidation* or *interpretation*. But is this all? Is there not another activity which has been going on in our minds, almost inevitably, all this while? The activity of *appreciation*. All this time, while reading the poem so carefully, have we not also been liking it or disliking it? Admiring it or despising it? Presumably we have. And presumably we ought now to ask ourselves this further question: Is there any connection between the things we have managed so far to say about the poem and the kind of response we experience toward it? Our liking it or our disliking it? Are we inclined to try to explain why we like the poem? Do we know how to do this? More precisely: Would a statement of our liking for the poem, an act of praise or appreciation, be something different from (even though perhaps dependent upon) the things we have already been saying? Or has the appreciation already been sufficiently implied or entailed by what we have been saying?

At the first level, that of simple dictionary *explanation*, very little, we will probably say, has been implied. And very little, we will most likely say, in many of our motions at the second level, the simply *descriptive*. It is not a merit in a poem, or surely not much of a merit, that it should contain any given vocabulary, say of striking or unusual words, or even that it should have metaphors, or that it should have meter or any certain kind of meter, or rhymes, as any of these entities may be purely conceived.

But that—as we have been saying—is to put these matters of simple *explanation* and simple *description* more simply and more abstractly than they are really susceptible of being put. We pass imperceptibly and quickly beyond these matters. We are inevitably and soon caught up in the demands of *explication*—the realization of the vastly more rich and interesting implicit kinds of meaning. We are engaged with features of a poem which—given always other features too of the whole context—do tend to assert themselves as reasons for our pleasure in the poem and our admiration for it. We begin to talk about patterns of meaning; we encounter structures or forms which are radiant or resonant with meaning. Patterns and structures involve coherence (unity, coherence, and emphasis), and coherence is an aspect of truth and significance. I do not think that our evaluative intimations will often, if ever, advance to the firmness and completeness of a demonstration. Perhaps it is hardly conceivable that they should. But our discourse upon the poem will almost inevitably be charged with intimations of its value. It will be more difficult to keep out these intimations than to let them in. Critics who have announced the most resolute programs of neutrality have found this out. Take care of the weight, the color, the shape of the poem, be fair to the explanation and description, the indisputable parts of the formal explication—the appreciation will be there, and it will be difficult to avoid having expressed it.

Explicatory criticism (or explicatory evaluation) is an account of a poem which exhibits the relation between its form and its meaning. Only poems which are worth something are susceptible of this kind of account. It is something like a definition of poetry to say that whereas rhetoric—in the sense of mere persuasion or sophistic—is a kind of discourse the power of which diminishes in proportion as the artifice of it is understood or seen through; poetry, on the other hand, is a kind of discourse the power of which—or the satisfaction which we derive from it—is actually increased by an increase in our understanding of the artifice. In poetry the artifice is art. This comes close I think to the center of the aesthetic fact.

IV

One of the attempts at a standard of poetic value most often reiterated in past ages has been the doctrinal—the explicitly didactic. The aim of poetry, says the ancient Roman poet, is double, both to give pleasure and to teach some useful doctrine. You might get by with only one or the other, but it is much sounder to do both. Or, the aim of poetry is to teach some doctrine—and to do this convincingly and persuasively, by *means* of vividness and pleasure—as in effect the Elizabethan courtier and the eighteenth-century essayist would say. But in what does the pleasure consist? Why is the discourse pleasurable? Well, the aim of poetry is really to please us by means of or through the act of teaching us. The pleasure is a dramatized *moral* pleasure. Thus in effect some theories of drama in France during the seventeenth century. Or, the pleasure of poetry is a pleasure simply of tender and morally good feelings. Thus in effect the philosophers of the age of reason in England and France. And at length the date 1790 and Immanuel Kant's *Critique of Judgment*: which asserts that the end or effect of art is not teaching certainly, and not, on the other hand, pleasure in anything like a simple sensuous way—rather it is something apart, a feeling, but precisely its own kind of feeling, the aesthetic. Art is autonomous—though related symbolically to the realm of moral values.

Between the time of Immanuel Kant and our own some complications in the purity of the aesthetic view have developed. Through the romantic period and after, the poetic mind advanced pretty steadily in its own autonomous way, toward a claim to be in itself the creator of higher values—to be perhaps the only creator. Today there is nothing that the literary theorist—at least in the British and American-speaking world—will be more eager to repudiate than any hint of moral or religious didacticism, any least intimation that the poem is to measure its meaning or get its sanction from any kind of authority more abstract or more overtly legislative than itself. But on the other hand there has probably never been a generation of teachers of literature less willing to admit any lack of high seriousness, of implicit and embodied ethical content, even of normative vision in the object of their study. Despite our reiterated denials of didacticism, we live in an age, we help to make an age, of momentous claims for poetry—claims the most momentous conceivable, as they advance more and more under the sanction of an absolutely creative and autonomous visionary imagination. The visionary imagination perforce repudiates all but the tautological commitment to itself. And thus, especially when it assumes (as now it begins to do) the form of what is called the "Tragic

Vision" (not "The Vision of Tragedy"), it is the newest version of
the *Everlasting No*. Vision *per se* is the vision of itself. "Tragic
Vision" is the nearly identical vision of "Absurdity." (War-
weariness and war-horror, the developing mind and studies of a
generation that came out of the Second War and has been living in
expectation of the third may go far to explain the phenomenon,
but will not justify it.) Anti-doctrine is of course no less a didactic
energy than doctrine itself. It is the reverse of doctrine. No more
than doctrine itself, can it be located or even approached by a discussion of the relation between poetic form and poetic meaning.
Anti-doctrine is actually asserted by the poems of several English
romantic poets, and notably, it would appear, though it is difficult
to be sure, by the "prophecies" of William Blake. The idea of it
may be hence a part of these poems, though never their achieved
result or expression. Any more than an acceptable statement of
Christian doctrine is Milton's achieved expression in *Paradise Lost*,
or a statement of Aristotelian ethics is the real business of Spenser's
Faerie Queene. Today I believe no prizes are being given for even
the best doctrinal interpretation of poems. (The homiletic or para-
bolic interpretation of Shakespeare, for example, has hard going with
the reviewer.) On the other hand, it you are willing to take a part
in the exploitation of the neuroses, the misgivings, the anxieties,
the infidelities of the age—if you have talents for the attitudes of
Titanism, the graces needed by an impresario of the nuptials of
Heaven and Hell, you are likely to find yourself in some sense
rewarded. It is my own earnest conviction, and I believe it important for the critic who understands this to assert it at every opportunity, that the reward will *not* consist in the achievement of a
valid account of the relation between poetic form and poetic meaning.

ROBERT FROST

Education by Poetry: A Meditative Monologue[1]

I am going to urge nothing in my talk. I am not an advocate. I am
going to consider a matter, and commit a description. And I am
going to describe other colleges than Amherst. Or, rather say all
that is good can be taken as about Amherst; all that is bad will be
about other colleges.

I know whole colleges where all American poetry is barred—whole
colleges. I know whole colleges where all contemporary poetry is
barred.

I once heard of a minister who turned his daughter—his poetry-
writing daughter—out on the street to earn a living, because he said

1. An address given at Amherst College in 1930.

there should be no more books written; God wrote one book, and that was enough. (My friend George Russell, "Æ", has read no literature, he protests, since just before Chaucer.)

That all seems sufficiently safe, and you can say one thing for it. It takes the onus off the poetry of having to be used to teach children anything. It comes pretty hard on poetry, I sometimes think, what it has to bear in the teaching process.

Then I know whole colleges where, though they let in older poetry, they manage to bar all that is poetical in it by treating it as something other than poetry. It is not so hard to do that. Their reason I have often hunted for. It may be that these people act from a kind of modesty. Who are professors that they should attempt to deal with a thing as high and as fine as poetry? Who are *they?* There is a certain manly modesty in that.

That is the best general way of settling the problem; treat all poetry as if it were something else than poetry, as if it were syntax, language, science. Then you can even come down into the American and into the contemporary without any special risk.

There is another reason they have, and that is that they are, first and foremost in life, markers. They have the marking problem to consider. Now, I stand here a teacher of many years' experience and I have never complained of having had to mark. I had rather mark anyone for anything—for his looks, carriage, his ideas, his correctness, his exactness, anything you please—I would rather give him a mark in terms of letters, A, B, C, D, than have to use adjectives on him. We are all being marked by each other all the time, classified, ranked, put in our place, and I see no escape from that. I am no sentimentalist. You have got to mark, and you have got to mark, first of all, for accuracy, for correctness. But if I am going to give a mark, that is the least part of my marking. The hard part is the part beyond that, the part where the adventure begins.

One other way to rid the curriculum of the poetry nuisance has been considered. More merciful than the others it would neither abolish nor denature the poetry, but only turn it out to disport itself, with the plays and games—in no wise discredited, though given no credit for. Any one who liked to teach poetically could take his subject, whether English, Latin, Greek or French, out into the no-where along with the poetry. One side of a sharp line would be left to the rigorous and righteous; the other side would be assigned to the flowery where they would know what could be expected of them. Grade marks where more easily given, of course, in the courses concentrating on correctness and exactness as the only forms of honesty recognized by plain people; a general indefinite mark of X in the courses that scatter brains over taste and opinion. On inquiry I have found no teacher willing to take position on either side of the line, either among the rigors or among the flowers. No one is willing to admit that his discipline is not partly in exactness. No one is willing to admit that his discipline is not partly in taste and enthusiasm.

How shall a man go through college without having been marked for taste and judgment? What will become of him? What will his end be? He will have to take continuation courses for college graduates. He will have to go to night schools. They are having night schools now, you know, for college graduates. Why? Because they have not been educated enough to find their way around in contemporary literature. They don't know what they may safely like in the libraries and galleries. They don't know how to judge an editorial when they see one. They don't know how to judge a political campaign. They don't know when they are being fooled by a metaphor, an analogy, a parable. And metaphor is, of course, what we are talking about. Education by poetry is education by metaphor.

Suppose we stop short of imagination, initiative, enthusiasm, inspiration and originality—dread words. Suppose we don't mark in such things at all. There are still two minimal things, that we have got to take care of, taste and judgment. Americans are supposed to have more judgment than taste, but taste is there to be dealt with. That is what poetry, the only art in the colleges of arts, is there for. I for my part would not be afraid to go in for enthusiasm. There is the enthusiasm like a blinding light, or the enthusiasm of the deafening shout, the crude enthusiasm that you get uneducated by poetry, outside of poetry. It is exemplified in what I might call "sunset raving." You look westward toward the sunset, or if you get up early enough, eastward toward the sunrise, and you rave. It is oh's and ah's with you and no more.

But the enthusiasm I mean is taken through the prism of the intellect and spread on the screen in a color, all the way from hyperbole at one end—or overstatement, at one end—to understatement at the other end. It is a long strip of dark lines and many colors. Such enthusiasm is one object of all teaching in poetry. I heard wonderful things said about Virgil yesterday, and many of them seemed to me crude enthusiasm, more like a deafening shout, many of them. But one speech had range, something of overstatement, something of statement, and something of understatement. It had all the colors of an enthusiasm passed through an idea.

I would be willing to throw away everything else but that: enthusiasm tamed by metaphor. Let me rest the case there. Enthusiasm tamed to metaphor, tamed to that much of it. I do not think anybody ever knows the discreet use of metaphor, his own and other people's, the discreet handling of metaphor, unless he has been properly educated in poetry.

Poetry begins in trivial metaphors, petty metaphors, "grace" metaphors, and goes on to the profoundest thinking that we have. Poetry provides the one permissible way of saying one thing and meaning another. People say, "Why don't you say what you mean?"

We never do that, do we, being all of us too much poets. We like to talk in parables and in hints and in indirections—whether from diffidence or some other instinct.

I have wanted in late years to go further and further in making metaphor the whole of thinking. I find some one now and then to agree with me that all thinking, except mathematical thinking, is metaphorical, or all thinking except scientific thinking. The mathematical might be difficult for me to bring in, but the scientific is easy enough.

Once on a time all the Greeks were busy telling each other what the All was—or was like unto. All was three elements, air, earth, and water (we once thought it was ninety elements; now we think it is only one). All was substance, said another. All was change, said a third. But best and most fruitful was Pythagoras' comparison of the universe with number. Number of what? Number of feet, pounds, and seconds was the answer, and we had science and all that has followed in science. The metaphor has held and held, breaking down only when it came to the spiritual and psychological or the out of the way places of the physical.

The other day we had a visitor here, a noted scientist, whose latest word to the world has been that the more accurately you know where a thing is, the less accurately you are able to state how fast it is moving. You can see why that would be so, without going back to Zeno's problem of the arrow's flight. In carrying numbers into the realm of space and at the same time into the realm of time you are mixing metaphors, that is all, and you are in trouble. They won't mix. The two don't go together.

Let's take two or three more of the metaphors now in use to live by. I have just spoken of one of the new ones, a charming mixed metaphor right in the realm of higher mathematics and higher physics: that the more accurately you state where a thing is, the less accurately you will be able to tell how fast it is moving. And, of course everything is moving. Everything is an event now. Another metaphor. A thing, they say, is an event. Do you believe it is? Not quite. I believe it is almost an event. But I like the comparison of a thing with an event.

I notice another from the same quarter. "In the neighborhood of matter space is something like curved." Isn't that a good one! It seems to me that that is simply and utterly charming—to say that space is something like curved in the neighborhood of matter. "Something like."

Another amusing one is from—what is the book?—I can't say it now; but here is the metaphor. Its aim is to restore you to your ideas of free will. It wants to give you back your freedom of will. All right, here it is on a platter. You know that you can't tell by name what persons in a certain class will be dead ten years after graduation, but you can tell actuarially how many will be dead. Now, just so this scientist says of the particles of matter flying at a screen, striking a screen; you can't tell what individual particles will come, but you can say in general that a certain number will strike in a given time. It shows, you see, that the individual particle can come freely. I asked Bohr about that particularly, and he said, "Yes, it is so. It can come when it wills and as it wills; and the action of the individual particle is unpredictable. But it is not so of the action of the mass. There you can predict." He says, "That gives the individual atom its freedom, but the mass its necessity."

Another metaphor that has interested us in our time and has done all our thinking for us is the metaphor of evolution. Never mind going into the Latin word. The metaphor is simply the metaphor of the growing plant or of the growing thing. And somebody very brilliantly, quite a while ago, said that the whole universe, the whole of everything, was like unto a growing thing. That is all. I know the metaphor will break down at some point, but it has not failed everywhere. It is a very brilliant metaphor, I acknowledge, though I myself get too tired of the kind of essay that talks about the evolution of candy, we will say, or the evolution of elevators—the evolution of this, that, and the other. Everything is evolution. I emancipate myself by simply saying that I didn't get up the metaphor and so am not much interested in it.

What I am pointing out is that unless you are at home in the metaphor, unless you have had your proper poetical education in the metaphor, you are not safe anywhere. Because you are not at ease with figurative values: you don't know the metaphor in its strength and its weakness. You don't know how far you may expect to ride it and when it may break down with you. You are not safe in science; you are not safe in history. In history, for instance—to show that is the same in history as elsewhere—I heard somebody say yesterday that Aeneas was to be likened unto (those words, "likened unto"!) George Washington. He was that type of national hero, the middle-class man, not thinking of being a hero at all, bent on building the future, bent on his children, his descendants. A good metaphor, as far as it goes, and you must know how far. And then he added that Odysseus should be likened unto Theodore Roosevelt. I don't think that is so good. Someone visiting Gibbon at the point of death, said he was the same Gibbon as of old; still at his parallels.

Take the way we have been led into our present position morally, the world over. It is by a sort of metaphorical gradient. There is a kind of thinking—to speak metaphorically—there is a kind of thinking you might say was endemic in the brothel. It is always there. And every now and then in some mysterious way it becomes epidemic in the world. And how does it do so? By using all the good words that virtue has invented to maintain virtue. It uses honesty, first—frankness, sincerity—those words; picks them up, uses them. "In the name of honesty, let us see what we are." You know. And then it picks up the word joy. "Let us in the name of joy, which is the enemy of our ancestors, the Puritans . . . Let us in the name of joy, which is the enemy of the kill-joy Puritan . . . " You see. "Let us," and so on. And then, "In the name of health . . . " Health is another good word. And that is the metaphor Freudianism trades on, mental health. And the first thing we know, it has us all in up to the top knot. I suppose we may blame the artists a good deal, because they are great people to spread by metaphor. The stage too—the stage is always a good intermediary between the two worlds, the under and the upper, if I may say so without personal prejudice to the stage.

In all this, I have only been saying that the devil can quote Scripture, which simply means that the good words you have lying around the devil can use for his purposes as well as anybody else. Never mind about my morality. I am not here to urge anything. I don't care whether the world is good or bad—not on any particular day.

Let me ask you to watch a metaphor breaking down here before you.

Somebody said to me a little while ago, "It is easy enough for me to think of the universe as a machine, as a mechanism."

I said, "You mean the universe is like a machine?"

He said, "No. I think it is one . . . Well, it is like . . ."

"I think you mean the universe is like a machine."

"All right. Let it go at that."

I asked him, "Did you ever see a machine without a pedal for the foot, or a lever for the hand, or a button for the finger?"

He said "No—no."

I said, "All right. Is the universe like that?"

And he said, "No. I mean it is like a machine, only . . ."

". . . it is different from a machine," I said.

He wanted to go just that far with that metaphor and no further. And so do we all. All metaphor breaks down somewhere. That is the beauty of it. It is touch and go with the metaphor, and until you have lived with it long enough you don't know when it is going. You don't know how much you can get out of it and when it will cease to yield. It is a very living thing. It is as life itself.

I have heard this ever since I can remember, and ever since I have taught: the teacher must teach the pupil to think. I saw a teacher once going around in a great school and snapping pupils' heads with thumb and finger and saying, "Think." That was when thinking was becoming the fashion. The fashion hasn't yet quite gone out.

We still ask boys in college to think, as in the nineties, but we seldom tell them what thinking means; we seldom tell them it is just putting this and that together; it is saying one thing in terms of another. To tell them is to set their feet on the first rung of a ladder the top of which sticks through the sky.

Greatest of all attempts to say one thing in terms of another is the philosophical attempt to say matter in terms of spirit, or spirit in terms of matter, to make the final unity. That is the greatest attempt that ever failed. We stop just short there. But it is the height of poetry, the height of all thinking, the height of all poetic thinking, that attempt to say matter in terms of spirit and spirit in terms of matter. It is wrong to call anybody a materialist simply because he tries to say spirit in terms of matter, as if that were a sin. Materialism is not the attempt to say all in terms of matter. The only materialist —be he poet, teacher, scientist, politician, or statesman—is the man who gets lost in his material without a gathering metaphor to throw it into shape and order. He is the lost soul.

We ask people to think, and we don't show them what thinking is. Somebody says we don't need to show them how to think; bye and bye they will think. We will give them the forms of sentences and, if they have any ideas, then they will know how to write them. But that is preposterous. All there is to writing is having ideas. To learn to write is to learn to have ideas.

The first little metaphor . . . Take some of the trivial ones. I would rather have trivial ones of my own to live by than the big ones of other people.

I remember a boy saying, "He is the kind of person that wounds with his shield." That may be a slender one, of course. It goes a good way in character description. It has poetic grace. "He is the kind that wounds with his shield."

The shield reminds me—just to linger a minute—the shield reminds me of the inverted shield spoken of in one of the books of the *Odyssey*, the book that tells about the longest swim on record. I forget how long it lasted—several days, was it?—but at last as Odysseus came near the coast of Phoenicia, he saw it on the horizon "like an inverted shield."

There is a better metaphor in the same book. In the end Odysseus comes ashore and crawls up the beach to spend the night under a double olive tree, and it says, as in a lonely farmhouse where it is hard to get fire—I am not quoting exactly—where it is hard to start the fire again if it goes out, they cover the seeds of fire with ashes to preserve it for the night, so Odysseus covered himself with the leaves around him and went to sleep. There you have something that gives you character, something of Odysseus himself. "Seeds of fire." So Odysseus covered the seeds of fire in himself. You get the greatness of his nature.

But these are slighter metaphors than the ones we live by. They have their charm, their passing charm. They are as it were the first steps toward the great thoughts, grave thoughts, thoughts lasting to the end.

The metaphor whose manage we are best taught in poetry—that is all there is of thinking. It may not seem far for the mind to go but it is the mind's furthest. The richest accumulation of the ages is the noble metaphors we have rolled up.

I want to add one thing more that the experience of poetry is to anyone who comes close to poetry. There are two ways of coming close to poetry. One is by writing poetry. And some people think I want people to write poetry, but I don't; that is, I don't necessarily. I only want people to write poetry if they want to write poetry. I have never encouraged anybody to write poetry that did not want to write it, and I have not always encouraged those who did want to write it. That ought to be one's own funeral. It is a hard, hard life, as they say.

(I have just been to a city in the West, a city full of poets, a city they have made safe for poets. The whole city is so lovely that you do not have to write it up to make it poetry; it is ready-made for you. But, I don't know—the poetry written in that city might not seem like poetry if read outside of the city. It would be like the jokes made when you were drunk; you have to get drunk again to appreciate them.)

But as I say, there is another way to come close to poetry, fortunately, and that is in the reading of it, not as linguistics, not as history, not as anything but poetry. It is one of the hard things for a teacher to know how close a man has come in reading poetry. How do I know whether a man has come close to Keats in reading Keats? It is hard for me to know. I have lived with some boys a whole year over some of the poets and I have not felt sure whether they have come near what it was all about. One remark sometimes told me. One remark was their mark for the year; had to be—it was all I got that told me what I wanted to know. And that is enough, if it was the right remark, if it came close enough. I think a man might make twenty fool remarks if he made one good one some time in the year. His mark would depend on that good remark.

The closeness—everything depends on the closeness with which you come, and you ought to be marked for the closeness, for nothing else. And that will have to be estimated by chance remarks, not by question and answer. It is only by accident that you know some day how near a person has come.

The person who gets close enough to poetry, he is going to know more about the word *belief* than anybody else knows, even in religion nowadays. There are two or three places where we know belief outside of religion. One of them is at the age of fifteen to twenty, in our self-belief. A young man knows more about himself

than he is able to prove to anybody. He has no knowledge that anybody else will accept as knowledge. In his foreknowledge he has
something that is going to believe itself into fulfilment, into acceptance.

There is another belief like that, the belief in someone else, a
relationship of two that is going to be believed into fulfilment. That
is what we are talking about in our novels, the belief of love. And
disillusionment that the novels are full of is simply the disillusionment from disappointment in that belief. That belief can fail,
of course.

Then there is a literary belief. Every time a poem is written, every
time a short story is written, it is written not by cunning, but by
belief. The beauty, the something, the little charm of the thing to
be, is more felt than known. There is a common jest, one that always annoys me, on the writers, that they write the last end first, and
then work up to it; that they lay a train toward one sentence that they
think is pretty nice and have all fixed up to set like a trap to close with.
No, it should not be that way at all. No one who has ever come close
to the arts has failed to see the difference between things written
that way, with cunning and device, and the kind that are believed
into existence, that begin in something more felt than known. This
you can realize quite as well—not quite as well, perhaps, but nearly as
well—in reading as you can in writing. I would undertake to separate
short stories on that principle; stories that have been believed into
existence and stories that have been cunningly devised. And I could
separate the poems still more easily.

Now I think—I happen to think—that those three beliefs that I
speak of, the self-belief, the love-belief, and the art-belief, are all
closely related to the God-belief, that the belief in God is a relationship you enter into with Him to bring about the future.

There is a national belief like that, too. One feels it. I have been
where I came near getting up and walking out on the people who
thought that they had to talk against nations, against nationalism, in
order to curry favor with internationalism. Their metaphors are all
mixed up. They think that because a Frenchman and an American and
an Englishman can all sit down on the same platform and receive
honors together, it must be that there is no such thing as nations.
That kind of bad thinking springs from a source we all know. I should
want to say to anyone like that: "Look! First I want to be a person.
And I want you to be a person, and then we can be as interpersonal as
you please. We can pull each other's noses—do all sorts of things.
But, first of all, you have got to have the personality. First of all, you
have got to have the nations and then they can be as international as they please with each other."

I should like to use another metaphor on them. I want my palette,
if I am a painter, I want my palette on my thumb or on my chair,

all clean, pure, separate colors. Then I will do the mixing on the canvas. The canvas is where the work of art is, where we make the conquest. But we want the nations all separate, pure, distinct, things as separate as we can make them; and then in our thoughts, in our arts, and so on, we can do what we please about it.

But I go back. There are four beliefs that I know more about from having lived with poetry. One is the personal belief, which is a knowledge that you don't want to tell other people about because you cannot prove that you know. You are saying nothing about it till you see. The love belief, just the same, has that same shyness. It knows it cannot tell; only the outcome can tell. And the national belief we enter into socially with each other, all together, party of the first part, party of the second part, we enter into that to bring the future of the country. We cannot tell some people what it is we believe, partly, because they are too stupid to understand and partly because we are too proudly vague to explain. And anyway it has got to be fulfilled, and we are not talking until we know more, until we have something to show. And then the literary one in every work of art, not of cunning and craft, mind you, but of real art; that believing the thing into existence, saying as you go more than you even hoped you were going to be able to say, and coming with surprise to an end that you foreknew only with some sort of emotion. And then finally the relationship we enter into with God to believe the future in—to believe the hereafter in.

QUESTIONS

1. *In what way does the subtitle describe this essay? Is it rambling? Is it unified?*
2. *How can the "poetry nuisance" be gotten out of the curriculum? Does Frost think it ought to stay in? Why?*
3. *What is meant by "enthusiasm passed through an idea" and "enthusiasm tamed to metaphor" (p. 782)? What sort of metaphors does Frost use in those phrases, and what do they imply?*
4. *What does Frost mean when he says "unless you have had your proper poetical education in the metaphor, you are not safe anywhere" (p. 784)? Indicate some of the metaphors Frost examines in this essay. From what fields are they drawn? What does he say about each? Nominate some further metaphors—from politics, science, sociology, or anything else—and analyze them. To what extent are they useful? Do they have a breaking point? How might they mislead beyond the breaking point?*
5. *Frost admires a speech that has "range, something of overstatement, something of statement, and something of understatement." Is this spectrum visible in Frost's own speech? Show where and how.*

Prose Forms: Characters

[One of the oldest activities of the human mind is to give a concrete shape to an abstract idea. The legends and myths about ancient gods and heroes make concrete a whole complex of historical and cultural ideas. The symbolisms of a church, the allegory of Bunyan's The Pilgrim's Progress, and even the church or school pageant where children act the parts of "Truth" or "Friendliness"—these are all, in their various ways, illustrative of the effort significantly to relate ideas in the mind and the particular realities that the senses are familiar with in everyday experience. What it means to be a "good student" becomes clearer if Mary Brown's accomplishments are called to mind. What one learns in a sociology course about the problems of minorities in urban centers gains greater authority during field work among those groups. The specific conduct of Germany in World War II would doubtless help more than mere points of theoretical ethics to understand why the idea that "might makes right" is false and dangerous.

Although much that a man understands, or how he understands, begins in abstractions and large general ideas, his desire to communicate with another person immediately raises the necessity for points of reference to the realities of concrete experience. To make his ideas clear and forceful to an audience, he will often convey the ideas in forms of concrete particulars. Like the novelist or the dramatist, he will show, rather than tell, if what he wants to define or explain is to be communicated simply and directly. To say a certain character is vile may be clear enough if the novelist writes what in effect is an essay explaining and specifying the ideas of vileness. But how much more effective and compelling it is to create a set of circumstances in which the character shows by his speech, his behavior, his thoughts that he is unquestionably vile.

Perhaps something of this difference between showing and telling was in the mind of the Greek philosopher Theophrastus when he developed for his students a set of explicatory descriptions called Characters to pinpoint the essential characteristics of certain types of people. Theophrastus chose to show, not tell abstractly, what the several foibles of men are. Not that dealing directly with abstractions is without merit; there are many subjects—and occasions— when to do so is entirely appropriate and effective. But because the mind is specially receptive to the concrete, the ends of communication are often better served by engaging the reader's mind with

790

concrete particulars than by inviting his mind to analyze the abstract descriptively.

Once given Theophrastus' simple definition of flattery, the reader is made to realize immediately what a person must be like whose behavior represents it. From "flattery" to "flatterer" is a direct movement from a broad abstract conception to a narrower one. But Theophrastus shows the flatterer behaving in very particular ways. The reader overhears his remarks to someone whose favor he courts; his stance as he walks and talks is clearly visible; the very scene of his behavior is particularized in the number of people present, the apples and pears he buys. And yet it is not that singular person, John Jones flatterer, described to the reader; it is the essential character of any flatterer, but set out so concretely that the reader feels as if the John Jones, flatterer, whom he knows, is in the writer's mind. The universal or general idea is preserved, but its content is explored through representative particulars drawn from a common body of fact and experience shared by the writer and the reader.

In some of the characters of John Earle a critical accent is more explicit than in those of Theophrastus. In "A Young Man" Earle offers a set of specific conditions, beliefs, actions which characterize the type of the young man. But it is clear that Earle believes the conditions of youth are not particularly happy and agreeable, whether or not the youth himself realizes this. This attitude toward youth is not asserted overtly; it is apparent in the way Earle describes a characteristic, as in the matter of youth's virtue: "He is free from many vices, by being not grown to the performance, and is only more virtuous out of weakness." Exposition of the idea of "young man" moves toward a proposition about that idea; there is a subject, and a thesis. The conditions of the essay begin to be manifest.

The character conventionally concerns itself with a single idea, usually a single aspect of the moral nature of men. The writer's intent is to define that idea and to substantiate its truth through observations of concrete experience. Because it invites both its writer and its reader to attend carefully to men and their behavior, the character requires intensive powers of observation, generalization, and judgment. And because it points to, rather than analyzes, its matter, the character is brief. The form becomes, then, a singularly helpful way of forcing the writer to answer the question "What do you mean by that idea?" with a brief and definitive adjustment of abstracts and concretes. In its conception and method the character represents one of the fundamental processes that define the essay: communicating thought and experience by appealing to the deep instinct of the mind for a significant relation between ideas about experience and experience itself. Practice in writing characters gives a concrete and easily accessible shape to one's ideas, and therefore can be a model discipline for skill and effectiveness with the essay.]

JOHN EARLE: A Child

Is a man in a small letter, yet the best copy of Adam before he tasted of Eve or the apple; and he is happy whose small practice in the world can only write his character. He is nature's fresh picture newly drawn in oil, which time, and much handling, dims and defaces. His soul is yet a white paper unscribbled with observations of the world, wherewith, at length, it becomes a blurred note-book. He is purely happy because he knows no evil, nor hath made means by sin to be acquainted with misery. He arrives not at the mischief of being wise, nor endures evils to come, by foreseeing them. He kisses and loves all, and, when the smart of the rod is past, smiles on his beater. Nature and parents alike dandle him, and tice him on with a bait of sugar to a draft of wormwood. He plays yet, like a young prentice the first day, and is not come to his task of melancholy. All the language he speaks yet is tears, and they serve him well enough to express his necessity. His hardest labor is his tongue, as if he were loath to use so deceitful an organ; and he is best company with it when he can but prattle. We laugh at his foolish sports, but his game is our earnest; and his drums, rattles and hobbyhorses, but the emblems and mocking of man's business. His father hath writ him as his own little story, wherein he reads those days of his life that he cannot remember, and sighs to see what innocence he hath outlived. The elder he grows, he is a stair lower from God; and, like his first father, much worse in his breeches. He is the Christian's example, and the old man's relapse; the one imitates his pureness, and the other falls into his simplicity. Could he put off his body with his little coat, he had got eternity without a burden, and exchanged but one heaven for another.

JOHN EARLE: A Young Man

He is now out of nature's protection, though not yet able to guide himself; but let loose to the world and fortune, from which the weakness of his childhood preserved him; and now his strength exposes him. He is, indeed, just of age to be miserable, yet in his own conceit first begins to be happy; and he is happier in this imagination, and his misery not felt is less. He sees yet but the outside of the world and men, and conceives them, according to their appearing, glitter, and out of this ignorance believes them. He pursues all vanities for happiness, and enjoys them best in this fancy. His reason serves, not to curb but understand his attitude, and prosecute the motions thereof with a more eager earnestness. Himself is his own temptation, and needs not Satan, and the world will come hereafter. He leaves repentance for gray hairs, and performs it in being covetous. He is mingled with the vices of the age as the fashion and custom, with which he longs to be acquainted, and sins to better his understanding. He conceives his youth as the season of his lust, and the hour wherein he ought to be bad; and because he would not lose his time, spends it. He distastes religion as a sad thing, and is six years elder for a thought of heaven. He scorns and fears, and yet hopes for old age, but dares not imagine it with wrinkles. He loves and hates with the same inflammation, and when the heat is over is cool alike to friends and enemies. His friendship is seldom so steadfast, but that lust, drink or anger may overturn it. He offers you his blood to-day in kindness, and is ready to take yours to-morrow. He does seldom any thing which he wishes not to do again, and is only wise after a misfortune. He suffers much for his knowledge, and a great deal of folly it is makes him a wise man. He is free from many vices, by being not grown to the performance, and is only more virtuous out of weakness. Every action is his danger, and every man his ambush. He is a ship without pilot or tackling, and only good fortune may steer him. If he scape this age, he has scaped a tempest, and may live to be a man.

JOHN EARLE: A Plausible Man

Is one that would fain run an even path in the world, and jut against no man. His endeavor is not to offend, and his aim the general opinion. His conversation is a kind of continued compliment, and his life a practice of manners. The relation he bears to others, a kind of fashionable respect, not friendship but friendliness, which is equal to all and general, and his kindnesses seldom exceed courtesies. He loves not deeper mutualities, because he would not take sides, nor hazard himself on displeasures, which he principally avoids. At your first acquaintance with him he is exceedingly kind and friendly, and at your twentieth meeting after but friendly still. He has an excellent command over his patience and tongue, especially the last, which he accommodates always to the times and persons, and speaks seldom what is sincere, but what is civil. He is one that uses all companies, drinks all healths, and is reasonable cool in all religions. He considers who are friends to the company, and speaks well where he is sure to hear of it again. He can listen to a foolish discourse with an applausive attention, and conceal his laughter at nonsense. Silly men much honor and esteem him, because by his fair reasoning with them as with men of understanding, he puts them into an erroneous opinion of themselves, and makes them forwarder thereafter to their own discovery. He is one rather well thought on than beloved, and that love he has is more of whole companies together than any one in particular. Men gratify him notwithstanding with a good report, and whatever vices he has besides, yet having no enemies, he is sure to be an honest fellow.

JOHN EARLE: A Coward

Is the man that is commonly most fierce against the coward, and laboring to take off this suspicion from himself; for the opinion of valor is a good protection to those that dare not use it. No man is valianter than he is in civil company, and where he thinks no danger may come on it, and is the readiest man to fall upon a drawer and those that must not strike again: wonderful exceptious and choleric where he sees men are loth to give him occasion, and you cannot pacify him better than by quarreling with him. The hotter you grow, the more temperate man is he; he protests he always honored you, and the more you rail upon him, the more he honors you, and you threaten him at last into a very honest quiet man. The sight of a sword wounds him more sensibly than the stroke, for before that come he is dead already. Every man is his master that dare beat him, and every man dares that knows him. And he that dare do this is the only man can do much with him; for his friend he cares not for, as a man that carries no such terror as his enemy, which for this cause only is more potent with him of the two: and men fall out with him of purpose to get courtesies from him, and be bribed again to a reconcilement. A man in whom no secret can be bound up, for the apprehension of each danger loosens him, and makes him bewray both the room and it. He is a Christian merely for fear of hell-fire; and if any religion could fright him more, would be of that.

THOMAS FULLER: The Harlot

The Harlot is one that herself is both merchant and merchandise, which she selleth for profit, and hath pleasure given her into the bargain, and yet remains a great loser. To describe her is very difficult; it being hard to draw those to the life, who never sit still: she is so various in her humors and mutable, it is almost impossible to character her in fixed posture; yea, indeed, some cunning harlots are not discernible from honest women. Solomon saith, "She wipeth her mouth"; and who can distinguish betwixt that which was never foul, and that which is cleanly wiped?

THEOPHRASTUS: The Flatterer

Flattery is a cringing sort of conduct that aims to promote the advantage of the flatterer. The flatterer is the kind of man who, as he walks with an acquaintance, says: "Behold! how the people gaze at you! There is not a man in the city who enjoys so much notice as yourself. Yesterday your praises were the talk of the Porch. While above thirty men were sitting there together and the conversation fell upon the topic: 'Who is our noblest citizen?' they all began and ended with your name." As the flatterer goes on talking in this strain he picks a speck of lint from his hero's cloak; or if the wind has lodged a bit of straw in his locks, he plucks it off and says laughingly, "See you? Because I have not been with you these two days, your beard is turned gray. And yet if any man has a beard that is black for his years, it is you."

While his patron speaks, he bids the rest be silent. He sounds his praises in his hearing and after the patron's speech gives the cue for applause by "Bravo!" If the patron makes a stale jest, the flatterer laughs and stuffs his sleeve into his mouth as though he could not contain himself.

If they meet people on the street, he asks them to wait until the master passes. He buys apples and pears, carries them to his hero's house and gives them to the children, and in the presence of the father, who is looking on, he kisses them, exclaiming: "Bairns of a worthy sire!" When the patron buys a pair of shoes, the flatterer observes: "The foot is of a finer pattern than the boot"; if he calls on a friend, the flatterer trips on ahead and says: "*You* are to have the honor of his visit"; and then turns back with, "I have announced you." Of course he can run and do the errands at the market in a twinkle.

Amongst guests at a banquet he is the first to praise the wine and, doing it ample justice, he observes: "What a fine cuisine you have!" He takes a bit from the board and exclaims: "What a dainty morsel this is!" Then he inquires whether his friend is chilly, asks if he would like a wrap put over his shoulders, and whether he shall throw one about him. With these words he bends over and whispers in his ear. While his talk is directed to the rest, his eye is fixed on his patron. In the theatre he takes the cushions from the page and himself adjusts them for the comfort of the master. Of his hero's house he says: "It is well built"; of his farm: "It is well tilled"; and of his portrait: "It is a speaking image."

SÖREN KIERKEGAARD: The Knight of Faith

I candidly admit that in my practice I have not found any reliable example of the knight of faith, though I would not therefore deny that every second man may be such an example. I have been trying, however, for several years to get on the track of this, and all in vain. People commonly travel around the world to see rivers and mountains, new stars, birds of rare plumage, queerly deformed fishes, ridiculous breeds of men—they abandon themselves to the bestial stupor which gapes at existence, and they think they have seen something. This does not interest me. But if I knew where there was such a knight of faith, I would make a pilgrimage to him on foot, for this prodigy interests me absolutely. I would not let go of him for an instant, every moment I would watch to see how he managed to make the movements, I would regard myself as secured for life, and would divide my time between looking at him and practicing the exercises myself, and thus would spend all my time admiring him. As was said, I have not found any such person, but I can well think him. Here he is. Acquaintance made, I am introduced to him. The moment I set eyes on him I instantly push him from me, I myself leap backwards, I clasp my hands and say half aloud, "Good Lord, is this the man? Is it really he? Why, he looks like a tax collector!" However, it is the man after all. I draw closer to him, watching his least movements to see whether there might not be visible a little heterogeneous fractional telegraphic message from the infinite, a glance, a look, a gesture, a note of sadness, a smile, which betrayed the infinite in its heterogeneity with the finite. No! I examine his figure from tip to toe to see if there might not be a cranny through which the infinite was peeping. No! He is solid through and through. His tread? It is vigorous, belonging entirely to finiteness; no smartly dressed townsman who walks out to Fresberg on a Sunday afternoon treads the ground more firmly, he belongs entirely to the world, no Philistine more so. One can discover nothing of that aloof and superior nature whereby one recognizes the knight of the infinite. He takes delight in everything, and whenever one sees him taking part in a particular pleasure, he does it with the persistence which is the mark of the earthly man whose soul is absorbed in such things. He tends to his work. So when one looks at him one might suppose that he was a clerk who had lost his soul in an intricate system of bookkeeping, so precise is he. He takes a holiday on Sunday. He goes to church. No heavenly glance or any other token of the incommensurable betrays him; if one did not know him, it would be impossible to distinguish him from the rest of the congregation, for his healthy and vigorous hymn singing proves at the most that he has a good chest. In the afternoon he walks to the forest. He takes delight in everything he sees, in the human swarm, in the new omnibuses, in the water of the Sound; when one meets him on the Beach Road one might suppose he was a shopkeeper taking his fling, that's just the way he disports himself, for he is not a poet, and I have sought in vain to detect in him the poetic incommensurability. Toward evening he walks home, his gait is as indefatigable as that of the postman. On his way he reflects that his wife has surely a special little warm dish prepared for him, e.g. a calf's head roasted, garnished with vegetables. If he were to meet a man like-minded, he could continue as far as East Gate to discourse with him about that dish, with a passion befitting a hotel chef. As it happens, he hasn't four pence to his name, and yet he fully and firmly believes that his wife has that dainty dish for him. If she had it, it would then be an invidious sight for superior people and an inspiring one for the plain man, to see him eat; for his appetite is greater than Esau's. His wife hasn't it—strangely enough, it is quite the same to him. On the way he comes past a building site and runs across another man. They talk together for a moment. In the twinkling of an eye he erects a new building, he has at his disposition all the powers necessary for it. The stranger leaves him with the thought that he certainly was a capitalist, while my admired knight thinks, "Yes, if the money were needed, I dare say I could get it." He lounges at an open window and looks out on the square on which he lives; he is interested in everything that goes on, in a rat which slips under the curb, in the children's play, and this with the nonchalance of a girl of sixteen. And yet he is no genius, for in vain I have sought in him the incommensurability of genius. In the evening he smokes his pipe; to look at him one would swear that it was the grocer over the way vegetating in the twilight. He lives as carefree as a ne'er-do-well, and yet he buys up the acceptable time at the dearest price, for he does not do the least thing except by virtue of the absurd. And yet, and yet—actually I could become dubious over it, for envy if for no other reason—this man has made and every instant is making the movements of infinity. With infinite resignation he has drained the cup of life's profound sadness, he knows the bliss of the infinite, he senses the pain of renouncing everything, the dearest things he possesses in the world, and yet finiteness tastes to him just as good as to one who never knew anything higher, for his continuance in the finite did not bear a trace of the cowed and fearful spirit produced by the process of training; and yet he has the sense of security in enjoying it, as though the finite life were the surest thing of all. And yet, and yet the whole earthly form he exhibits is a new creation by virtue of the absurd. He resigned everything infinitely, and then he grasped everything again by virtue of the absurd. He constantly makes the movements of infinity, but he does this with such correctness and assurance that he constantly gets the finite out of it, and there is not a second when one has a notion of anything else. It is supposed to be the most difficult task for a dancer to leap into a definite posture in such a way that there is not a second when he is grasping after the posture, but by the leap itself he stands fixed in that posture. Perhaps no dancer can do it—that is what this knight does. Most people live dejectedly in wordly sorrow and joy; they are the ones who sit along the wall and do not join in the dance. The knights of infinity are dancers and possess elevation. They make the movements upward, and fall down again; and this too is no mean pastime, nor ungraceful to behold. But whenever they fall down they are not able at once to assume the posture, they vacillate an instant, and this vacillation shows that after all they are strangers in the world. This is more or less strikingly evident in proportion to the art they possess, but even the most artistic knights cannot altogether conceal this vacillation. One need not look at them when they are up in the air, but only the instant they touch or have touched the ground—then one recognizes them. But to be able to fall down in such a way that the same second it looks as if one were standing and walking, to transform the leap of life into a walk, absolutely to express the sublime in the pedestrian—that only the knight of faith can do—and this is the one and only prodigy.

LA ROCHEFOUCAULD: Self Portrait

I am of medium build, broad and well-proportioned. My complexion is dark, but fairly uniform; my forehead is high and reasonably wide, my eyes are black, small, deep-set, with brows that though black and thick are well-formed. I find it hard to give a proper description of my nose, for it is neither flat, nor aquiline, nor thick, nor pointed—or so at least it seems to me. All I can say is that it is on the large rather than the small side, and that it is perhaps a trifle too long. I have a big mouth and my lips, which are usually rather red, are neither well nor ill shaped. My teeth are white and passably regular. In the old days I used to be told that I had too much chin: I have just felt it, and also looked in the glass to see if this is so, and I really cannot say whether it is true or not. As for the shape of my face, it is either squarish or oval: I should find it hard to be sure which. My hair is black, curls naturally, and is sufficiently long and thick for me to be able to claim a fine head of hair. My expression has something of gloom and also of pride to it: this has led most people to assume that I am contemptuous of them, though no assumption could be further from the truth. I move with ease and perhaps slightly too much, to the extent that I gesticulate a great deal when talking. That is my frank opinion of my appearance, and it will be found, I think, that this description is not far removed from the truth. I shall be equally honest in the remaining part of this self portrait; for I have studied myself enough to know myself well, and I have both sufficient self-assurance to be able to speak openly of those good qualities I may possess and enough sincerity to admit to my defects.

In the first place, my prevailing humor may be described as melancholic, to the extent that in these last three or four years I have hardly been known to laugh more than three or four times. Nevertheless it seems to me that my melancholia would be sufficiently bearable and gentle were it derived solely from my temperament: but I have been afflicted with so many extraneous causes for sadness, which have so filled my imagination and preoccupied my mind, that I usually sit in silence, lost in thought, or when I do speak it is in an abstracted fashion. I am extremely reserved with strangers, and I am not even very open with most of the people whom I know. This is a defect, as I am well aware, and I shall spare no pains to rid myself of it: but since my somewhat gloomy expression tends to make me appear even more reserved than I actually am, and since it is not within our power to alter a disagreeable appearance which is due to nature's arrangement of our features, I fear that though I may correct the internal causes of the impression I make, the displeasing external marks of this failing will remain with me, do what I may.

I am witty, and I do not blush to say so; why put up any pretence in the matter? Endless shilly-shallyings and apologetics before stating one's advantages seem to me to smack of vanity hidden beneath a show of modesty: it is a very skillful means of persuading others to think even more highly of oneself than one allegedly wishes them to do. For myself I have no desire that I should be thought finer than I say I am, nor better tempered than I paint myself as being, nor wittier and cleverer than my own description of myself. So, once again, I have wit, but it is tainted with melancholy: for though I can express myself well, have a useful memory and can think without confusion, I am nevertheless so preoccupied with my own chagrins that I often, in fact, put my meaning across rather badly.

One of the pleasures I value most highly is well-bred conversation; I like it to be serious, and to deal largely with moral questions. Nevertheless I am quite able to appreciate flippancy as well; and if I do not often myself make remarks intended to raise a laugh, it is not at all that I do not enjoy a well-turned witticism, and I find those amusing interchanges, at which certain relaxed and quick minds are so adept, highly entertaining.

I write well in prose and also in verse; and if I were to attach more importance to the glory that comes from such accomplishments I believe that I could, with a little effort, achieve quite a considerable reputation as a writer. I like reading, my favorite books being those which help to form the mind and fortify the soul. Above all, I derive an extreme satisfaction from reading aloud, with a clever companion; for when so doing one will be constantly reflecting upon the written word; and the reflections thus made constitute the most agreeable sort of conversation in the world, and the most useful.

When my opinion is asked I am a fairly good judge of works in verse or in prose; but I am inclined to express my views on them somewhat too freely. Another mistake I make is my tendency to be over-fastidious and too harsh in my criticism. It does not distress me when others argue, and I will even on occasion join in quite voluntarily; but I usually advance my own opinions with undue heat; and when the wrong cause is being upheld against me, I will sometimes become so passionate an advocate of reason as to grow well-nigh unreasonable myself.

My sentiments are virtuous, my intentions good, and so great is my desire to be a perfect gentleman and honorable man-of-the-world that my friends can cause me no greater pleasure than by frankly pointing out to me when I am at fault. Those persons who know me fairly well, and who have been good enough on occasion to advise me in this fashion, will admit that I have always listened to them with the utmost gratification and with all the humility of mind that can be desired.

All my passions are rather gentle and well under my control: I have hardly ever been observed in a temper, and I have never hated anyone. This does not mean that I am incapable of exacting vengeance, particularly if I have been offended in a matter that touches my honor and which I therefore cannot ignore. On the contrary, I am sure that my sense of duty towards myself will, at such times, so well replace the emotion of hatred that in my search for vengeance I will display even greater energy than other men.

I am not troubled by ambition. There are few things which frighten me, death least of any. I am scarcely susceptible to pity, and would wish not to feel it at all. On the other hand there are no lengths to which I will not go in order to alleviate the afflictions of others; and I really believe that in such cases one should do everything, even to the extent of showing a great deal of compassion for them in their misfortunes; but I also believe that one should be satisfied with the display and avoid, most carefully, the true feeling. For pity is an emotion which is quite useless in a well-formed soul;

it serves only to enfeeble the heart; and it should be left to the common people who, since they never behave according to the dictates of reason, must be stirred by emotion.

I am fond of my friends, so fond of them that I should not hesitate for a moment if it were a question of sacrificing my interests for theirs; I am tolerant, will patiently endure their bad moods, and will readily make excuses for them. But I am not particularly demonstrative as a friend, nor am I much put out if I do not see them for considerable periods of time.

I am by nature poorly endowed with curiosity concerning most of those matters which others find of such absorbing interest. I am very discreet and have less difficulty than most in keeping a secret that has been entrusted to me. I am extremely reliable: I never break my word, no matter what the results of keeping it may be, and that is a rule of conduct to which I have adhered with the utmost rigor throughout my whole life.

With women I am meticulously polite, and I do not believe that I have ever behaved, in the presence of a woman, in such a way as to cause her distress. When they have good minds, I prefer their conversation to that of men; their talk has a sort of gentleness which is never to be met with in ours, and, apart from that, it seems to me that they can express themselves more neatly and can give a pleasanter turn to what they say.

As for love, in the past I have gone in for it a little: at present I do so no longer, although I am still young. I have given up flirting, and it is a source of astonishment to me that so many honest people should still indulge in it.

I have the greatest respect for fine passions, which are the mark of great souls; and although the disquiet they engender is in some ways antagonistic to strict wisdom, they are so easily linked to the most austere virtues that I do not believe they can be justly condemned. Knowing well all the delicacy and strength of great passion, I do believe that should I myself ever fall in love, it will be in this manner; but being made the way I am, I very much doubt whether this knowledge of mine will ever be transferred from the head to the heart.

CARDINAL DE RETZ: Portrait of La Rochefoucauld

There has always been something of the indefinable about M. de la Rochefoucauld. Since his childhood he has wanted to take a hand in intrigue, but though he has been unconcerned with the little deals—which have never been his weakness—he has been ignorant of the big ones—which, from another point of view, have not been his strength. He was never capable of any business, though I know not why, for he has qualities which in any other man would have compensated for those he lacks. His vision was not broad enough and he did not even see in its entirety what was within his range, but his good sense—very good in abstract speculation—together with his mildness and winning manners, which are admirable, ought to have compensated for his lack of insight more than it has. He has always lacked resolution, but indeed I do not know how to account for this lack. It could not have come from his imagination, which is nothing less than lively. I cannot attribute it to sterility of judgment; for, although he has not shown it strikingly in action, he has a good fund of reason: we see the effects of that irresolution even though we do not know its cause. He has never been warlike, although he was very much the soldier. He has never, unaided, been a good courtier, although he always intended to be. He has never been a good party member, although he has been pledged to a party all his life. That air of embarrassment and diffidence that you see in him in civil life became in public affairs an air of defensiveness: he always felt he needed it. All this, plus the fact that his *Maxims* do not show enough faith in virtue and that his practice has always been to try to extricate himself from affairs with as much eagerness as he entered into them, makes me conclude that he would have done much better to know himself truly and confine himself to passing (as he could have) for the most polished courtier to appear in his age.

LA ROCHEFOUCAULD: Portrait of the Cardinal de Retz

Paul de Gondi, Cardinal de Retz, has an abundance of grandeur and intellectual breadth, and more the show of courage than true courage. He has an extraordinary memory; more vigor than good breeding in his speech; a quick temper but pliancy and weakness in enduring the complaints and reproaches of his friends; little real piety but some semblance of religion. He appears ambitious without being so; his vanity and his advisers have made him undertake great things—almost all of them inappropriate to his calling. He has stirred up great disorders in the State, without forming any plan for taking advantage of them; and rather than declaring himself the enemy of Cardinal Mazarin in order to take over his place, he thought only of frightening him and of flattering his vanity with being his opponent. He nonetheless knew how to profit cleverly from public misfortunes to make himself cardinal; he endured his imprisonment with firmness and owed his liberty to his hardihood alone. During several years sloth sustained him gloriously in the obscurity of a wandering and retired existence. He preserved the archbishopric of Paris against the power of Cardinal Mazarin; but after the death of this minister of state he gave up his position without realizing what he was doing and without seizing that opportunity to forward his own interests and those of his friends. He took part in several conclaves and his conduct always increased his reputation. His natural bent is idleness; he works, nonetheless, with dispatch on affairs which are urgent and he rests with unconcern when they have been taken care of. He has great presence of mind and he knows so well how to turn to his advantage the opportunities that chance offers him that it seems as if he had foreseen and wished for them. He loves to tell stories of extraordinary adventures and dazzle any who will listen to him: often his imagination supplies more than his memory. Most of his good qualities are counterfeit and his skill in making his faults appear in a good light has contributed most to his reputation. He is insensitive to hatred and to affection, whatever pains he has taken to appear concerned with one or the other; he is incapable of envy or avarice, whether through virtue or through lassitude. He has borrowed more from his friends than a private individual could expect to repay; he savored the vanity of finding so much credit and of undertaking to discharge his debts. He has neither taste nor refinement; he is amused by everything and pleased by nothing; he skillfully avoids letting others realize that all his knowledge is superficial. His recent retirement is the most dazzling and the most false action of his life; it is a sacrifice which he makes to his pride under the pretext of piety: he quits the court, where he cannot find a place, and withdraws from the world, which withdraws from him.

ANTHONY ASHLEY COOPER,
FIRST EARL OF SHAFTESBURY: Henry Hastings

Mr. Hastings, by his quality, being the son, brother, and uncle to the Earls of Huntingdon, and his way of living, had the first place amongst us. He was peradventure an original in our age, or rather the copy of our nobility in ancient days in hunting and not warlike times: he was low, very strong and very active, of a reddish flaxen hair, his clothes always green cloth, and never all worth when new five pounds. His house was perfectly of the old fashion, in the midst of a large park well stocked with deer, and near the house rabbits to serve his kitchen, many fish ponds, and great store of wood and timber; a bowling green in it, long but narrow, full of high ridges, it being never leveled since it was ploughed; they used round sand bowls, and it had a banqueting house like a stand, a large one built in a tree. He kept all manner of sport-hounds that ran buck, fox, hare, otter, and badger, and hawks long and short winged; he had all sorts of nets for fishing; he had a walk in the New Forest and the manor of Christ Church. This last supplied him with red deer, sea and river fish; and indeed all his neighbors' grounds and royalties were free to him, who bestowed all his time in such sports, but what he borrowed to caress his neighbors' wives and daughters, there being not a woman in all his walks of the degree of a yeoman's wife or under, and under the age of forty, but it was extremely her fault if he were not intimately acquainted with her. This made him very popular, always speaking kindly to the husband, brother, or father, who was to boot very welcome to his house whenever he came; there he found beef pudding and small beer in great plenty, a house not so neatly kept as to shame him or his dirty shoes, the great hall strewed with marrow bones, full of hawks' perches, hounds, spaniels, and terriers, the upper sides of the hall hung with the fox skins of this and the last year's skinning, here and there a polecat intermixed, guns and keepers' and huntsmen's poles in abundance. The parlor was a large long room, as properly furnished; in a great hearth paved with brick lay some terriers and the choicest hounds and spaniels; seldom but two of the great chairs had litters of young cats in them, which were not to be disturbed, he having always three or four attending him at dinner, and a little white round stick of fourteen inches long lying by his trencher that he might defend such meat as he had no mind to part with to them. The windows, which were very large, served for places to lay his arrows, crossbows, stonebows, and other such like accoutrements; the corners of the room full of the best chose hunting and hawking poles; an oyster-table at the lower end, which was of constant use twice a day all the year round, for he never failed to eat oysters before dinner and supper through all seasons: the neighboring town of Poole supplied him with them. The upper part of this room had two small tables and a desk, on the one side of which was a church Bible, on the other the Book of Martyrs; on the tables were hawks' hoods, bells, and such like, two or three old green hats with their crowns thrust in so as to hold ten or a dozen eggs, which were of a pheasant kind of poultry he took much care of and fed himself; tables, dice, cards, and boxes were not wanting. In the hole of the desk were store of tobacco pipes that had been used. On one side of this end of the room was the door of a closet, wherein stood the strong beer and the wine, which never came thence but in single glasses, that being the rule of the house exactly observed, for he never exceeded in drink or permitted it. On the other side was a door into an old chapel not used for devotion; the pulpit, as the safest place, was never wanting of a cold chine of beef, pasty of venison, gammon of bacon, or great apple pie with thick crust extremely baked. His table cost him not much, though it was very good to eat at, his sports supplying all but beef and mutton, except Friday, when he had the best sea-fish he could get, and was the day that his neighbors of best quality most visited him. He never wanted a London pudding, and always sung it in with "my part lies therein-a." He drank a glass of wine or two at meals, very often syrup of gilliflower in his sack, and had always a tun glass without feet stood by him holding a pint of small beer, which he often stirred with a great sprig of rosemary. He was well natured, but soon angry, calling his servants bastard and cuckoldy knaves, in one of which he often spoke truth to his own knowledge, and sometimes in both, though of the same man. He lived to a hundred, never lost his eyesight, but always writ and read without spectacles, and got to horse without help. Until past fourscore he rode to the death of a stag as well as any.

DONALD PEARCE: Rosalie[1]

Life among the peasants of Belgium has been extremely pleasant; in fact, delightful. The platoon is quartered in a bar, but I—thank God—am in the farmhouse, where I occcupy the spare bedroom and can observe what goes on inside this beehive. The day begins at 4:30 A.M. At that time I can hear Rosalie, the fifty-year-old woman who runs this little farm, padding to and fro in soft slippers doing I know not what to the stove, the dishes, the kitchen, and the pantry. By the time I get up, a couple of hours later, the cows have been attended to, breakfast prepared, the washing hung out, apples peeled, eggs collected, and other unseen tasks performed. Rosalie waves me to the kitchen table; and, though the gruel is curiously sour, I must eat, for she has made it especially for me and has filled it full of her best grains and buttermilk. She nods, smacks her lips, smiles her head, in vicarious delight, with every spoonful I take. I smile and grunt right back, and lately I have meant it, for the flavor of the stuff begins to grow on you.

I've watched Rosalie for days now, and have not once seen her idle. Her day is geared to the minute hand of the kitchen clock, and neither she or it ever stops. Her whole life must have been spent in continuous activity, or rather service, and it has bent her over. Inactivity is obviously immoral to her. If there is no big task to hand, like kneading huge quantities of dough (on her knees, by the stove), she polishes the stove-lifter, waxes the table top, scrubs the doorstep, shines the windows. She is constantly cleaning. Yet she hasn't the faintest idea of real sanitation. A primitive cleanliness is all that she understands. She scrubs the floor each day with

1. From *Journal of a War*, 1965.

boiling water, but the hands that have wrung out the mop plunge themselves tirelessly and deep into the heavy dough. She scalds the dishes and then dries them with a dirty cloth. She cleans the forks with a far-from-immaculate apron. She wears herself out. She has done so for at least forty years, and now she can no longer walk upright, but moves bent over, hustling here and there from one corner of the room to another, led by a momentary fixed idea rather than a plan of work. The salt is at the opposite end of the kitchen from the pepper, the butter from the milk, but she always returns them to these disparate places in the scuttling darkness of her low-beamed kitchen.

Her brother Raymond, who is a widower, is about Rosalie's age. He sits by the stove most of the day, warming his back and soaking his lame foot in water. He does little work, and probably never has; his foot is only sprained from a fall. Work has never bent him over, or any of the other men I see in this district. They are like dwindled feudal lords, and the women are their uncomplaining serfs. Girls of fourteen do hard barnyard work, or labor in the fields all day long. They will all be Rosalies at last, you can see it coming. They carry pails of milk or water suspended at their sides from yokes that fit over their shoulders, haul baskets of potatoes, and only stop pulling up acres of mangels for half an hour for lunch. Boys of the same age work much less, ride bicycles most of the time, and in the evenings talk to the soldiers in the taverns.

Rosalie is strictly religious. Her day begins with matins and closes with an evening prayer. She prays silently and like a statue before and after each meal. On all the walls of the rooms she has pinned up religious pictures which she has cut from calendars or magazines. Here and there are sacred mottoes and phrases, done in *petit-point* and set in little frames above doorways. Mantelpieces are laden with metal crucifixes and silver figures of saints and angels in a variety of attitudes. By candlelight, these effigies gleam softly along the walls like peering eyes. Rosalie lifts them, straining upwards with apparent tenderness, and dusts off the spots on which they stand, and puts them softly back. There are two before which she blesses herself.

At night, perhaps ten of the men from the platoon gather in the kitchen. We sit around a big table, the top of which is never completely dry because Rosalie scrubs it three times every day, and in the glow of the single candle we raise a great deal of noise and laughter, eat huge helpings of creamed potatoes, and gulp down cognac. In the background, quite in the shadows, four or five visitors sit smoking their pipes beside the stove, and watch our party. Rosalie peels a peck or more of potatoes while we are there, never looking down as she works and never breaking a single peel; they lie in a great curling pile at her feet, like a pile of carpenter's shavings.

We get noisier and noisier, and Rosalie peels faster and faster, till her fingers fairly flicker and her hair comes loose in wisps about her forehead. We stand beside the stove in a large dim group, and everybody tries to talk Flemish to the visitors. They offer us cigars, we give them cigarettes, and the place so fills with smoke that there is a bright halo around the candle. When we fail to understand them, which is usually, they shout at us as if we were deaf, poking their whiskered faces near our ears.

We sing a song or two, and prepare to leave. Rosalie sees each one out, guiding them through the cluster of wooden shoes near the door; they look like a fleet of little tied-up gondolas. Then the visitors leave, indicating to me with their hands beside their cheeks that they are going to go to bed. Rosalie makes me some hot milk, washes the dishes in a nearly dark corner, and starts to mix some applesauce, at which she can still be heard working long after I have gone to bed. I read a French newspaper by candlelight and listen to stray aircraft carrying bombs or supplies to the front. It is a deep and comfortable bed, and I never wake up all night.

On Ethics

LA ROCHEFOUCAULD

Bravery and Cowardice

Perfect bravery and total cowardice are two extremes only rarely to be met. Between them lies a vast territory where will be found every variation and degree of courage. These are as diverse as are men's faces or their feelings. There are soldiers who will readily risk their lives early in the engagement, but who will lose heart later in the day. There are others who are satisfied when they have upheld their honor in the eyes of the world, and who will scarcely advance beyond this. Some are not uniformly masters of their fears: some are susceptible to the contagion of panic: others advance to the attack because they dare not stay behind. There are men who, becoming gradually accustomed to smaller perils, are reinforced in their courage and enabled to confront greater ones. Some are brave with a sword, but frightened by musket fire; others can face bullets but fear steel. All these various forms of courage have this in common: that whereas darkness increases fear, it also hides both good and bad deeds, so that a soldier has greater opportunities for caution by night. There is another aspect of self-protection which is of more general application: no man is ever as totally brave as he would be, were he quite certain of surviving the day. The fear of death, in fact, diminishes valor.

ROBERT LYND

On Not Being a Philosopher

"Have you read Epictetus lately?" "No, not lately." "Oh, you ought to read him. Tommy's been reading him for the first time, and is fearfully excited." I caught this scrap of dialogue from the next table in the lounge of an hotel. I became interested, curious, for I had never read Epictetus, though I had often looked at his works on the shelf—perhaps I had even quoted him—and I wondered if here at last was the book of wisdom that I had been looking for at intervals ever since I was at school. Never have I lost my early faith that wisdom is to be found somewhere in a book—to be picked up as easily as a shell from the sand. I desire wisdom as keenly as Solomon did, but it must be wisdom that can be obtained with very little effort—wisdom that can be caught almost by infection. I have no time or energy for the laborious quest of philosophy. I wish the philosophers to perform the laborious quest and, at the end of it, to feed me with the fruits of their labors; just as I get eggs from the farmer, apples from the fruit-grower, medicines from the chemist, so do I expect the philosopher to provide me with wisdom at the cost of a few shillings. That is why at one time I read Emerson and, at another, Marcus Aurelius. To read them, I hoped, was to become wise by reading. But I did not become wise. I agreed with them while I read them, but, when I had finished reading, I was still much the same man that I had been before, incapable of concentrating on the things on which they said I should concentrate or of not being indifferent to the things to which they said I should not be indifferent. Still, I have never lost faith in books, believing that somewhere printed matter exists from which I shall be able to absorb philosophy and strength of character while smoking in an armchair. It was in this mood that I took down Epictetus after hearing the conversation in the hotel lounge.

I read him, I confess, with considerable excitement. He is the kind of philosopher I like, not treating life as if at its finest it were an argument conducted in difficult jargon, but discussing, among other things, how men should behave in the affairs of ordinary life. Also, I agreed with nearly everything he said. Indifference to pain, death, poverty—yes, that is eminently desirable. Not to be troubled about anything over which one has no control, whether the oppression of tyrants or the peril of earthquakes—on the necessity of this also, Epictetus and I are as one. Yet, close as is the resemblance between our opinions, I could not help feeling, as I read, that Epictetus was wise in holding his opinions and that I, though holding the same opinions, was far from wise. For, indeed, though I held the same opinions for purposes of theory, I could not entertain them for a moment for purposes of conduct. Death, pain, and poverty are to me very real evils, except when I am in an armchair reading a book by a philosopher. If an earthquake happened while I was reading a book of philosophy, I should forget the book of philosophy and think only of the earthquake and how to avoid tumbling walls and chimneys. This, though I am the staunchest possible admirer of Socrates, Pliny, and people of that sort. Sound though I am as an armchair philosopher, at a crisis I find that both the spirit and the flesh are weak.

Even in the small things of life I cannot comfort myself like a philosopher of the school of Epictetus. Thus, for example, when he advises us how to "eat acceptably to the gods" and bids us to this end to be patient even under the most incompetent service at our meals, he commends a spiritual attitude of which my nature is incapable. "When you have asked for warm water," he says, "and the slave does not heed you; or if he does heed you but brings tepid water; or if he is not even to be found in the house, then to refrain from anger and not to explode, is not this acceptable to the gods? . . . Do you not remember over whom you rule—that they are kinsmen, that they are brothers by nature, and they are the offspring of Zeus?" That is all perfectly true, and I should like very much to be a man who could sit in a restaurant, smiling patiently and philosophically while the waiter brought all the wrong things or forgot to bring anything at all. But in point of fact bad waiting irritates me. I dislike having to ask three times for the wine-list. I am annoyed when, after a quarter of an hour's delay, I am told that there is no celery. It is true that I do not make a scene on such occasions. I have not enough courage for that. I am as sparing of objurgations as a philosopher, but I suspect that the scowling spirit within me must show itself in my features. Certainly, I do not think of telling myself: "This waiter is my kinsman; he is the off-spring of Zeus." Besides, even if he were, why should the offspring of Zeus wait so badly? Epictetus never dined at the ——— Restaurant. And yet his patience might have served him even there. If so, what a difference between Epictetus and me! And, if I cannot achieve his imperturbability in so small affairs as I have mentioned, what hope is there of my being able to play the philosopher in presence of tyrants and earthquakes?

Again, when Epictetus expresses his opinions on material posses-sions and counsels us to be so indifferent to them that we should not object to their being stolen, I agree with him in theory and yet in practice I know I should be unable to obey him. There is nothing more certain than that a man whose happiness depends on his pos-sessions is not happy. I am sure a wise man can be happy on a pit-tance. Not that happiness should be the aim of life, according to Epictetus or myself. But Epictetus at least holds up an ideal of imperturbability, and he assures us that we shall achieve this if we care so little for material things that it does not matter to us whether somebody steals them or not. "Stop admiring your clothes," he bids us, "and you are not angry at the man who steals them." And he goes on persuasively concerning the thief: "*He* does not know where-in the true good of man consists, but fancies that it consists in having fine clothes, the very same fancy that you also entertain. Shall he not come, then, and carry them off?" Yes, logically I suppose he should, and yet I cannot feel so at the moment at which I find that a guest at a party has taken my new hat and left his old one in its place. It gives me no comfort to say to myself: "*He* does not know wherein the true good of man consists, but fancies that it consists in having my hat." Nor should I dream of attempting to console a guest at a party in my own house with such philosophy in similar circumstances. It is very irritating to lose a new hat. It is very irritating to lose anything at all, especially if one thinks it has been taken on purpose. I feel that I could imitate Epictetus if I lived in a world in which nothing happened. But in a world in which things disappear through loss, theft, and "pinching," and in which bad meals are served by bad waiters in many of the restaurants, and a thousand other disagreeable things happen, an ordinary man might as well set out to climb the Himalayas in walking shoes as attempt to live the life of a philosopher at all hours.

In spite of this, however, most of us cannot help believing that the philosophers were right—right when they proclaimed, amid all their differences, that most of the things we bother about are not worth bothering about. It is easier to believe that oneself is a fool than that Socrates was a fool, and yet, if he was not right, he must have been the greatest fool who ever lived. The truth is, nearly everybody is agreed that such men as Socrates and Epictetus were right in their indifference to external things. Even men earning £10,000 a year and working for more would admit this. Yet, while admitting it, most of us would be alarmed if one of our dearest friends began to put the philosophy of Epictetus into practice too literally. What we regard as wisdom in Epictetus we should look on as insanity in an acquaintance. Or, perhaps, not in an acquaintance, but at least in a near relation. I am sure that if I became as indifferent to money and comfort and all external things as Epictetus, and reasoned in his fashion with a happy smile about property and thieves, my relations would become more perturbed than if I became a successful company promoter with the most materialistic philosophy conceivable. Think, for example, of the reasoning of Epictetus over the thief who stole his iron lamp:

He bought a lamp for a very high price; for a lamp he became a thief, for a lamp he became faithless, for a lamp he became bestial. This is what seemed to him to be profitable!

The reasoning is sound, yet neither individually nor as a society do we live in that contempt of property on which it is based. A few saints do, but even they are at first a cause of great concern to their friends. When the world is normally cheerful and comfortable, we hold the paradoxical belief that the philosophers were wise men, but that we should be fools to imitate them. We are convinced that, while philosophers are worth reading, material things are worth bothering about. It is as though we enjoyed wisdom as a spectacle— a delightful spectacle on a stage which it would be unseemly for the audience to attempt to invade. Were the Greeks and the Romans made differently? Did the admirers of Socrates and Epictetus really attempt to become philosophers, or were they like ourselves, hopeful of achieving wisdom, not by practice but through a magic potion administered by a wiser man than they? To become wise without effort—by listening to a voice, by reading a book—it is at once the most exciting and the most soothing of dreams. In such a dream I took down Epictetus. And, behold, it was only a dream.

QUESTIONS

1. What relation to his audience does Lynd seek to establish? How does he achieve it?
2. What is funny about Lynd's juxtaposing the advice of Epictetus with his own feelings about restaurant service? Are there other instances of a similar effect in the essay? Is the resulting tone sardonic? Cynical? Contemptuous of philosophy?
3. Lynd in his closing paragraph (p. 811) writes, "we hold the paradoxical belief that the philosophers were wise men, but that we should be fools to imitate them." Does he seek to explain the paradox? Can you offer an explanation for it? What is the significance of the "when" clause in the earlier part of that sentence?
4. Lynd in his opening paragraph (p. 809) writes, "Still, I have never lost faith in books, believing that somewhere printed matter exists from which I shall be able to absorb philosophy and strength of character while smoking in an armchair." In the light of the whole essay, how is that statement to be taken?
5. To what degree does Lynd's essay exhibit the ideal of imperturbability he admires in philosophy? Explain.
6. Is there some pursuit, activity, ideal that you admire but do not seek to practice? Write an essay explaining your attitude.

SAMUEL JOHNSON
On Self-love and Indolence[1]

—*Steriles transmisimus annos,*
Haec aevi mihi prima dies, haec limina vitae.
STAT. [I. 362]

—Our barren years are past;
Be this of life the first, of sloth the last.
ELPHINSTON

No weakness of the human mind has more frequently incurred animadversion, than the negligence with which men overlook their own faults, however flagrant, and the easiness with which they pardon them, however frequently repeated.

It seems generally believed, that, as the eye cannot see itself, the mind has no faculties by which it can contemplate its own state, and that therefore we have not means of becoming acquainted with our real characters; an opinion which, like innumerable other postulates, an inquirer finds himself inclined to admit upon very little evidence, because it affords a ready solution of many difficulties. It will explain why the greatest abilities frequently fail to promote the happiness of those who possess them; why those who can distinguish with the utmost nicety the boundaries of vice and virtue, suffer them to be confounded in their own conduct; why the active and vigilant resign their affairs implicitly to the management of others; and why the cautious and fearful make hourly approaches toward ruin, without one sigh of solicitude or struggle for escape.

When a position teems thus with commodious consequences, who can without regret confess it to be false? Yet it is certain that declaimers have indulged a disposition to describe the dominion of the passions as extended beyond the limits that nature assigned. Self-love is often rather arrogant than blind; it does not hide our faults from ourselves, but persuades us that they escape the notice of others, and disposes us to resent censures lest we would confess them to be just. We are secretly conscious of defects and vices which we hope to conceal from the public eye, and please ourselves with innumerable impostures, by which, in reality, no body is deceived.

In proof of the dimness of our internal sight, or the general inability of man to determine rightly concerning his own character, it is common to urge the success of the most absurd and incredible flattery, and the resentment always raised by advice, however soft, benevolent, and reasonable. But flattery, if its operation be nearly examined, will be found to owe its acceptance not to our ignorance but knowledge of our failures, and to delight us rather as it consoles

1. *The Rambler*, No. 15, Tuesday, September 10, 1751.

our wants than displays our possessions. He that shall solicit the favor of his patron by praising him for qualities which he can find in himself, will be defeated by the more daring panegyrist who enriches him with adscititious excellence. Just praise is only a debt, but flattery is a present. The acknowledgment of those virtues on which conscience congratulates us, is a tribute that we can at any time exact with confidence, but the celebration of those which we only feign, or desire without any vigorous endeavors to attain them, is received as a confession of sovereignty over regions never conquered, as a favorable decision of disputable claims, and is more welcome as it is more gratuitous.

Advice is offensive, not because it lays us open to unexpected regret, or convicts us of any fault which had escaped our notice, but because it shows us that we are known to others as well as to ourselves; and the officious monitor is persecuted with hatred, not because his accusation is false, but because he assumes that superiority which we are not willing to grant him, and has dared to detect what we desired to conceal.

For this reason advice is commonly ineffectual. If those who follow the call of their desires, without inquiry whither they are going, had deviated ignorantly from the paths of wisdom, and were rushing upon dangers unforeseen, they would readily listen to information that recalls them from their errors, and catch the first alarm by which destruction or infamy is denounced. Few that wander in the wrong way mistake it for the right; they only find it more smooth and flowery, and indulge their own choice rather than approve it: therefore few are persuaded to quit it by admonition or reproof, since it impresses no new conviction, nor confers any powers of action or resistance. He that is gravely informed how soon profusion will annihilate his fortune, hears with little advantage what he knew before, and catches at the next occasion of expense, because advice has no force to suppress his vanity. He that is told how certainly intemperance will hurry him to the grave, runs with his usual speed to a new course of luxury, because his reason is not invigorated, nor his appetite weakened.

The mischief of flattery is, not that it persuades any man that he is what he is not, but that it suppresses the influence of honest ambition, by raising an opinion that honor may be gained without the toil of merit; and the benefit of advice arises commonly, not from any new light imparted to the mind, but from the discovery which it affords of the publick suffrages. He that could withstand conscience, is frighted at infamy, and shame prevails where reason was defeated.

As we all know our own faults, and know them commonly with many aggravations which human perspicacity cannot discover, there is, perhaps, no man, however hardened by impudence or dissipated by levity, sheltered by hypocrisy, or blasted by disgrace, who does not intend some time to review his conduct, and to regulate the remainder of his life by the laws of virtue. New temptations indeed attack him, new invitations are offered by pleasure and interest, and the hour of reformation is always delayed; every delay gives vice another opportunity of fortifying itself by habit; and the change of manners, though sincerely intended and rationally planned, is referred to the time when some craving passion shall be fully gratified, or some powerful allurement cease its importunity.

Thus procrastination is accumulated on procrastination, and one impediment succeeds another, till age shatters our resolution, or death intercepts the project of amendment. Such is often the end of salutary purposes, after they have long delighted the imagination, and appeased that disquiet which every mind feels from known misconduct, when the attention is not diverted by business or by pleasure.

Nothing surely can be more unworthy of a reasonable nature, than to continue in a state so opposite to real happiness, as that all the peace of solitude and felicity of meditation, must arise from resolutions of forsaking it. Yet the world will often afford examples of men, who pass months and years in a continual war with their own convictions, and are daily dragged by habit or betrayed by passion into practices, which they closed and opened their eyes with purposes to avoid; purposes which, though settled on conviction, the first impulse of momentary desire totally overthrows.

The influence of custom is indeed such that to conquer it will require the utmost efforts of fortitude and virtue, nor can I think any man more worthy of veneration and renown, than those who have burst the shackles of habitual vice. This victory however has different degrees of glory as of difficulty; it is more heroic as the objects of guilty gratification are more familiar, and the recurrence of solicitation more frequent. He that from experience of the folly of ambition resigns his offices, may set himself free at once from temptation to squander his life in courts, because he cannot regain his former station. He who is enslaved by an amorous passion, may quit his tyrant in disgust, and absence will without the help of reason overcome by degrees the desire of returning. But those appetites to which every place affords their proper object, and which require no preparatory measures or gradual advances, are more tenaciously adhesive; the wish is so near the enjoyment, that compliance often precedes consideration, and before the powers of reason can be summoned, the time for employing them is past.

Indolence is therefore one of the vices from which those whom it once infects are seldom reformed. Every other species of luxury operates upon some appetite that is quickly satiated, and requires some concurrence of art or accident which every place will not supply; but the desire of ease acts equally at all hours, and the longer it is indulged in the more increased. To do nothing is in every man's power; we can never want an opportunity of omitting duties. The lapse to indolence is soft and imperceptible, because it is only a mere cessation of activity; but the return to diligence is difficult, because it implies a change from rest to motion, from privation to reality.

> —*Facilis descensus Averni:*
> *Noctes atque dies patet atri janua Ditis:*
> *Sed revocare gradum, superasque evadere ad auras,*
> *Hoc opus, hic labor est.—*
>
> [VIR. *Aeneid* VI. 126]

> The gates of *Hell* are open night and day;
> Smooth the descent, and easy is the way:
> But, to return, and view the chearful skies;
> In this, the task and mighty labour lies.
>
> **DRYDEN**

Of this vice, as of all others, every man who indulges it is conscious; we all know our own state, if we could be induced to consider it; and it might perhaps be useful to the conquest of all these ensnarers of the mind, if at certain stated days life was reviewed. Many things necessary are omitted, because we vainly imagine that they may be always performed, and what cannot be done without pain will for ever be delayed if the time of doing it be left unsettled. No corruption is great but by long negligence, which can scarcely prevail in a mind regularly and frequently awakened by periodical remorse. He that thus breaks his life into parts, will find in himself a desire to distinguish every stage of his existence by some improvement, and delight himself with the approach of the day of recollection, as of the time which is to begin a new series of virtue and felicity.

W. H. AUDEN
Pride[1]

He who despises himself, nevertheless esteems himself as a self-despiser. (NIETZSCHE.) A vain person is always vain *about* something. He overestimates the importance of some quality or exaggerates the degree to which he possesses it, but the quality has some real importance and he does possess it to some degree. The fantasy of overestimation or exaggeration makes the vain person comic, but the fact that he cannot be vain about nothing makes his vanity a venial sin, because it is always open to correction by appeal to objective fact.

A proud person, on the other hand, is not proud *of* anything, he *is* proud, he exists proudly. Pride is neither comic nor venial, but the most mortal of all sins because, lacking any basis in concrete particulars, it is both incorrigible and absolute: one cannot be more or less proud, only proud or humble.

Thus, if a painter tries to portray the Seven Deadly Sins, his experience will furnish him readily enough with images symbolic of Gluttony, Lust, Sloth, Anger, Avarice, and Envy, for all these are qualities of a person's relations to others and the world, but no experience can provide an image of Pride, for the relation it qualifies is the subjective relation of a person to himself. In the seventh frame, therefore, the painter can only place, in lieu of a canvas, a mirror.

1. From "Hic et Ille" (This and That), in *The Dyer's Hand*, 1962.

JOHN DONNE
Tentation

After wee have parled with a tentation,[1] debating whether we should embrace it or no, and entertain'd some discourse with it, though some tendernesse, some remorse, make us turn our back upon it, and depart a little from it, yet the arrow overtakes us; some *reclinations*, some *retrospects* we have, a little of *Lot's wife*[2] is in us, a little *sociablenesse*, and *conversation*, a little point of *honour*, not to be false to former promises, a little *false gratitude*, and thankfulnesse, in respect of former obligations, a little of the *compassion* and *charity* of Hell, that another should not be miserable, for want of *us*, a little of this, which is but the good nature of the *Devill*, arrests us, stops us, fixes us, till the arrow, the tentation

1. Parleyed, spoken with a temptation.
2. Fleeing from the burning Sodom, she looked back upon the city. Genesis xix. 17-26.

shoot us in the back, even when wee had a purpose of departing from that sin, and kils us over again.

QUESTIONS

1. Analyze this single-sentence passage, determining its syntax. What are the subject, predicate, and object? How many main or independent clauses are there? Which clauses and phrases are modifiers?
2. What metaphors does Donne use?
3. Taking syntax and metaphorical content together, indicate the effects Donne achieves in this sentence. Does it convey a sense of motion, speedy or lingering? What scene or scenes are pictured? What use is made of the sense of touch? How does the presentation of physical sensation work to convey Donne's statement about the operation of temptation?

JAMES THURBER
The Bear Who Let It Alone

In the words of the Far West there once lived a brown bear who could take it or let it alone. He would go into a bar where they sold mead, a fermented drink made of honey, and he would have just two drinks. Then he would put some money on the bar and say, "See what the bears in the back room will have," and he would go home. But finally he took to drinking by himself most of the day. He would reel home at night, kick over the umbrella stand, knock down the bridge lamps, and ram his elbows through the windows. Then he would collapse on the floor and lie there until he went to sleep. His wife was greatly distressed and his children were very frightened.

At length the bear saw the error of his ways and began to reform. In the end he became a famous teetotaller and a persistent temperance lecturer. He would tell everybody that came to his house about the awful effects of drink, and he would boast about how strong and well he had become since he gave up touching the stuff. To demonstrate this, he would stand on his head and on his hands and he would turn cartwheels in the house, kicking over the umbrella stand, knocking down the bridge lamps, and ramming his elbows through the windows. Then he would lie down on the floor, tired by his healthful exercise, and go to sleep. His wife was greatly distressed and his children were very frightened.

Moral: You might as well fall flat on your face as lean over too far backward.

WILLIAM JAMES
Letter to Peg[1]

Villa Luise
Bad-Nauheim, May 26, 1900

DARLING PEG—Your letter came last night and explained sufficiently the cause of your long silence. You have evidently been in
a bad state of spirits again, and dissatisfied with your environment;
and I judge that you have been still more dissatisfied with the inner
state of trying to consume your own smoke, and grin and bear it,
so as to carry out your mother's behests made after the time when
you scared us so by your inexplicable tragic outcries in those earlier
letters. Well! I believe you have been trying to do the manly thing
under difficult circumstances, but one learns only gradually to do
the *best* thing; and the best thing for you would be to write at least
weekly, if only a post-card, and say just how things are going. If you
are in bad spirits, there is no harm whatever in communicating that
fact, and defining the character of it, or describing it as exactly as
you like. The bad thing is to pour out the *contents* of one's bad
spirits on others and leave them with it, as it were, on their hands,
as if it was for them to do something about it. That was what you
did in your other letter which alarmed us so, for your shrieks of
anguish were so excessive, and so unexplained by anything you told us
in the way of facts, that we didn't know but what you had suddenly
gone crazy. That is the *worst* sort of thing you can do. The middle
sort of thing is what you do this time—namely, keep silent for more
than a fortnight, and when you do write, still write rather mysteriously about your sorrows, not being quite open enough.

Now, my dear little girl, you have come to an age when the inward
life develops and when some people (and on the whole those who
have most of a destiny) find that all is not a bed of roses. Among
other things there will be waves of terrible sadness, which last sometimes for days; and dissatisfaction with one's self, and irritation at
others, and anger at circumstances and stony insensibility, etc., etc.,
which taken together form a melancholy. Now, painful as it is, this
is sent to us for an enlightenment. It always passes off, and we learn
about life from it, and we ought to learn a great many good things
if we react on it rightly. [*From margin.*] (For instance, you learn how
good a thing your home is, and your country, and your brothers,
and you may learn to be more considerate of other people, who,
you now learn, may have their inner weaknesses and sufferings, too.)

---

1. Peg is James' thirteen-year-old
daughter who was then living with family friends in England and experiencing
some home-sickness.

Many persons take a kind of sickly delight in hugging it; and some sentimental ones may even be proud of it, as showing a fine sorrowful kind of sensibility. Such persons make a regular habit of the luxury of woe. That is the worst possible reaction on it. It is usually a sort of disease, when we get it strong, arising from the organism having generated some poison in the blood; and we mustn't submit to it an hour longer than we can help, but jump at every chance to attend to anything cheerful or comic or take part in anything active that will divert us from our mean, pining inward state of feeling. When it passes off, as I said, we know more than we did before. And we must try to make it last as short a time as possible. The worst of it often is that, while we are in it, we don't *want* to get out of it. We hate it, and yet we prefer staying in it—that is a part of the disease. If we find ourselves like that, we must make ourselves do something different, go with people, speak cheerfully, set ourselves to some hard work, make ourselves sweat, etc.; and that is the good way of reacting that makes of us a valuable character. The disease makes you think of *yourself* all the time; and the way out of it is to keep as busy as we can thinking of *things* and of *other people* —no matter what's the matter with our self.

I have no doubt you are doing as well as you know how, darling little Peg; but we have to learn everything, and I also have no doubt that you'll manage it better and better if you ever have any more of it, and soon it will fade away, simply leaving you with more experience. The great thing for you *now*, I should suppose, would be to enter as friendlily as possible into the interest of the Clarke children. If you like them, or acted as if you liked them, you needn't trouble about the question of whether they like you or not. They probably will, fast enough; and if they don't, it will be their funeral, not yours. But this is a great lecture, so I will stop. The great thing about it is that it is all true.

QUESTIONS

1. What distinction does James intend between pouring out "the contents of one's bad spirits" and "communicating that fact, and defining the character of it, or describing it as exactly as you like"? Why does he advise against the one and encourage the other?

2. James says we can learn a great many good things if we react rightly to an experience of melancholy. What things does he mention? What other things might be learned?

FRANCIS BACON
Of Simulation and Dissimulation

Dissimulation is but a faint kind of policy or wisdom; for it asketh a strong wit and a strong heart to know when to tell truth, and to do it. Therefore it is the weaker sort of politics[1] that are the great dissemblers.

Tacitus saith, *Livia sorted well with the arts of her husband and dissimulation of her son;* attributing arts or policy to Augustus, and dissimulation to Tiberius. And again, when Mucianus encourageth Vespasian to take arms against Vitellius, he saith, *We rise not against the piercing judgment of Augustus, nor the extreme caution or closeness of Tiberius.*[2] These properties, of arts or policy and dissimulation or closeness, are indeed habits and faculties several, and to be distinguished. For if a man have that penetration of judgment as he can discern what things are to be laid open, and what to be secreted, and what to be shewed at half lights, and to whom and when, (which indeed are arts of state and arts of life, as Tacitus well calleth them), to him a habit of dissimulation is a hinderance and a poorness. But if a man cannot obtain to that judgment, then it is left to him generally to be close, and a dissembler. For where a man cannot choose or vary in particulars, there it is good to take the safest and wariest way in general; like the going softly, by one that cannot well see. Certainly the ablest men that ever were have had all an openness and frankness of dealing; and a name of certainty and veracity; but then they were like horses well managed; for they could tell passing well when to stop or turn; and at such times when they thought the case indeed required dissimulation, if then they used it, it came to pass that the former opinion spread abroad of their good faith and clearness of dealing made them almost invisible.

There be three degrees of this hiding and veiling of a man's self. The first, Closeness, Reservation, and Secrecy; when a man leaveth himself without observation, or without hold to be taken, what he is. The second, Dissimulation, in the negative; when a man lets fall signs and arguments, that he is not that he is. And the third, Simulation, in the affirmative; when a man industriously and expressly feigns and pretends to be that he is not.

For the first of these, Secrecy; it is indeed the virtue of a confessor.[3] And assuredly the secret man heareth many confessions. For

---

1. Politicians.

2. The Roman historian Tacitus here speaks of the plottings of Livia, wife of the emperor Augustus Caesar and mother of his successor Tiberius; and of the Roman official Mucianus, who in 69 A.D. supported Vespasian in his successful struggle against Vitellius to gain the imperial throne.

3. One to whom confession is made.

who will open himself to a blab or babbler? But if a man be thought secret, it inviteth discovery; as the more close air sucketh in the more open; and as in confession the revealing is not for worldly use, but for the ease of a man's heart, so secret men come to the knowledge of many things in that kind; while men rather discharge their minds than impart their minds. In few words, mysteries are due to secrecy. Besides (to say truth) nakedness is uncomely, as well in mind as body; and it addeth no small reverence to men's manners and actions, if they be not altogether open. As for talkers and futile persons, they are commonly vain and credulous withal. For he that talketh what he knoweth, will also talk what he knoweth not. Therefore set it down, *that an habit of secrecy is both politic and moral.* And in this part, it is good that a man's face give his tongue leave to speak. For the discovery of a man's self by the tracts of his countenance is a great weakness and betraying; by how much it is many times more marked and believed than a man's words.

For the second, which is Dissimulation; it followeth many times upon secrecy by a necessity; so that he that will be secret must be a dissembler in some degree. For men are too cunning to suffer a man to keep an indifferent carriage between both, and to be secret, without swaying the balance on either side. They will so beset a man with questions, and draw him on, and pick it out of him, that, without an absurd silence, he must shew an inclination one way; or if he do not, they will gather as much by his silence as by his speech. As for equivocations, or oraculous speeches, they cannot hold out for long. So that no man can be secret, except he give himself a little scope of dissimulation; which is, as it were, but the skirts or train of secrecy.

But for the third degree, which is Simulation and false profession; that I hold more culpable, and less politic; except it be in great and rare matters. And therefore a general custom of simulation (which is this last degree) is a vice, rising either of a natural falseness or fearfulness, or of a mind that hath some main faults, which because a man must needs disguise, it maketh him practice simulation in other things, lest his hand should be out of ure.[4]

The great advantages of simulation and dissimulation are three. First, to lay asleep opposition, and to surprise. For where a man's intentions are published, it is an alarum to call up all that are against them. The second is, to reserve to a man's self a fair retreat. For if a man engage himself by a manifest declaration, he must go through or take a fall. The third is, the better to discover the mind of another. For to him that opens himself men will hardly shew themselves adverse; but will (fair) let him go on, and turn their freedom of speech to freedom of thought. And therefore it is a good shrewd proverb of the Spaniard, *Tell a lie and find a troth.* As if

4. Practice.

there were no way of discovery but by simulation. There be also three disadvantages, to set it even. The first, that simulation and dissimulation commonly carry with them a shew of fearfulness, which in any business doth spoil the feathers of round flying up to the mark.[5] The second, that it puzzleth and perplexeth the conceits of many, that perhaps would otherwise co-operate with him; and makes a man walk almost alone to his own ends. The third and greatest is, that it depriveth a man of one of the most principal instruments for action; which is trust and belief. The best composition and temperature is to have openness in fame and opinion; secrecy in habit; dissimulation in seasonable use; and a power to feign, if there be no remedy.

5. Conceptions, thoughts.

QUESTIONS

1. Explain Bacon's distinction, drawn in the first two paragraphs, between dissembling, on the one hand, and, on the other, arts and policy. How does this opening prepare the way for the remainder of the essay?
2. How is the word "dissimulation" as used in the third paragraph and thereafter to be distinguished from its use in the first two paragraphs?
3. What are the three degrees of hiding of a man's self? According to what principles does Bacon arrange these degrees? What accounts for his according unequal amounts of space to the exposition of them?
4. Make a close analysis of Bacon's closing paragraph, indicating the ways Bacon achieves symmetry, balance. How does that effect contribute to his tone and purpose? What elements in the paragraph offset a mere symmetry?
5. In what connection and to what purpose does Bacon use the following expressions? Explain the image or allusion in each:
   a. "like the going softly, by one that cannot well see" (p. 821)
   b. "like horses well managed; for they could tell passing well when to stop or turn" (p. 821)
   c. "as the more close air sucketh in the more open" (p. 822)
   d. "it is good that a man's face give his tongue leave to speak" (p. 822)
   e. "he must go through or take a fall" (p. 822)
   f. "fearfulness, which in any business doth spoil the feathers of round flying up to the mark" (p. 823)
6. Bacon would allow "simulation and false profession" in "great and rare matters." Would you? Give an example of such matters. Write a brief essay explaining your position.
7. What view of the world underlies Bacon's essay? Write an essay showing what Bacon's assumptions about the world seem to be. Be careful to show how you draw upon the essay to find out Bacon's assumptions.

STEPHEN POTTER
The Game Itself[1]

"East wind dhu blëow
En-tout-cas dhu gëow."
ESSEX SAYING

Some Basic Plays

"How to win Games Without Being Able to Play Them." Reduced to the simplest terms, that is the formula, and the student must not at first try flights too far away from this basic thought.

To begin with, let him, say, carry on the "flurry" motive. Let him aim at tension. Let him, for instance, invent some "train which he would rather like to catch if the game was over by then," but "doesn't want to hurry."

Sportsmanship Play

Remember the slogan: "THE GOOD GAMESMAN IS THE GOOD SPORTSMAN." The use of sportsmanship is, of course, most important. In general, with the athletic but stupid player, ex-rowing or ex-boxing, perhaps, who is going to take it out of you, by God, if he suspects you of being unsporting, extreme sportingness is the thing, and the instant waiving of any rule which works in your favor is the procedure.

On the other hand, playing against the introvert crusty cynical type, remember that sportingness will be wasted on him. There must be no unsportingness on your part, of course; but a keen knowledge of little-known rules and penalties will cause him to feel he is being beaten at his own game. (See under "Croquet, rulesmanship in.")

When questioned about the etiquette of gamesmanship—so important for the young player—I talk about Fidgets. If your adversary is nervy, and put off by the mannerisms of his opponent, it is unsporting, and therefore not gamesmanship, to go in, e.g., for a loud noseblow, say, at billiards, or to chalk your cue squeakingly, when he is either making or considering a shot.

On the other hand, a basic play, in perfect order, can be achieved by, say, whistling fidgetingly *while playing yourself*. And I once converted two down into two up when playing golf against P. Beard,

---

1. Chapter III of *The Theory and Practice of Gamesmanship or the Art of Winning Games Without Actually Cheating*, 1947.

known also as the leader of an orchestra, by constantly whistling a phrase from the Dorabella Variation with one note—always the same note—wrong.[2]

A good general attack can be made by talking to your opponent about his own job, in the character of the kind of man who always tries to know more about your own profession than you know yourself.

Playing-For-Fun Play

The good gamesman, like the good sportsman, never plays for large sums of money. But something can usually be made out of the situation if your opponent expresses a wish to play for the "usual half-crown," or a wish not to do so. It is obviously easy for the gamesman to make his opponent feel awkward by countering his suggestion that they should play for stakes with a frank, "Come, let's play for the fun of the game." Alternatively, if your opponent refuses your offer to play for half a crown here is a neat counter:

LAYMAN: Half a crown on it? No, I'm not particularly anxious to play for money. What *is* the point? If one starts worrying about the pennies...

GAMESMAN: Exactly. If money is important to you, much better not.

LAYMAN: But I meant——

GAMESMAN (*friendly*): Of course.

Nice Chapmanship

A bitter subject which may be introduced here revolves round the huge question of nice chapmanship and its uses. (I refuse to use the hideous neologism "nicemanship" which I see much in evidence lately.)

Here is the general principle: that Being a Nice Chap in *certain circumstances* is valuable when playing against extremely young, public schooly players who are genuinely nice. A train of thought can be started in their minds to the effect that "it would be rather a rotten trick to beat old G. by too much." Thereby that fatal "letting up" is inaugurated which can be the undoing of so many fine players. R. Lodge, at sixty-five, always said that he had never been beaten, in a key match, by any decently brought up boy under twenty-five, and that he would always "feel 'em out of their phizzes."

---

2. It may be worth recalling that Elgar himself, when playing croquet against fellow-musicians, made use of the Horn *motiv* from the *Ring*:

He would whistle this correctly except for the second note, substituting for A some inappropriate variant, often a slightly flattened D sharp, *sliding* up to it, from the opening note of the phrase:

A voice from the past indeed. Yet have any of our modern experts in the music ploy really improved on this phrase, devised before Gamesmanship was formulated or even described? [Potter's note.]

Audience Play

Nice chapmanship is, of course, closely associated with sportsmanship, especially in its relation to the question of playing or not playing to the audience. There is obviously some value in a good hearty "Have it again" early in the game (of darts, for instance), or the lawn tennis ball slammed into the net after the doubtful decision, especially if this is done so that your opponent can see through the ploy[3] but the onlookers cannot.

But the experienced gamesman knows that if he is playing to a small audience he must make up his mind whether he is going to play *to* the audience, or whether he is going to retire behind an impersonal mask of modesty.

In general, the rule holds—LET YOUR ATTITUDE BE THE ANTITHESIS OF YOUR OPPONENT's; and let your manner of emphasizing this different attitude put him in the wrong.

For example, if your opponent is a great showman, assume (e.g., at snooker) an air of modesty anonymity; be appreciative, even, of his antics; then quietly play your shot, so that the audience begins to say, "I prefer G.'s game. He gets on with it, anyhow."

Per contra, when in play against a dour opponent, who studiously avoids all reaction to the audience, implying that "this is a match"— *then*, by all means be the "chap who doesn't care a damn" . . . though "Of course—sh!—old L. is taking this devilish seriously so I must keep a straight face."

(There is some danger of counter-gamesmanship here. The layman, if he is wise, will pursue his poker-faced policy and you may find your assumption of ill-suppressed gaiety wearing thin. I have myself experienced a partial paralysis in this situation.)

So much for some of the principal general ploys. Now for some common technical phrases.

Ruggership and Ruggership Counter-Play

Under the heading of "Ruggership" comes all that great interplay of suggestion summarized in the phrase "Of course, this isn't my game," with the implication that "this game is rather an amusing game, but not grand, dangerous and classical like my game . . ." If "my game" is rugger or polo or tennis (see under "Tennis players, how to press home advantage of, over lawn tennis players"), then very good work can be done with this gambit.

But it has severe weaknesses, and a promising gamesman in his second year may be able to counter with some such simple enquiry as this:

COUNTER-GAMESMAN (*with interest*): When did you *last play* rugger?
GAMESMAN: Oh! How long since actually playing? I wonder....I was talking to Leggers the other day——

---

3. Sub-plays, or individual maneuvers of a gambit, are usually referred to as "ploys." It is not known why this is [Potter's note].

COUNTER-GAMESMAN: Yes, but how long is it since you played yourself? I mean what date, roughly, was it when you last held a ball in your hand?

GAMESMAN (*hard-pressed*): 1913.

COUNTER-GAMESMAN: A bit of a time. But that, I imagine, is one of the grand things about rugger. If you've ever kicked a rugger ball, at a prep school or home club, you feel that you're a rugger player for the rest of your life.

Much exaggerated praise has been churned out in honor of gamesmanship and its part in the building of the British character. Still, if we study the records, they do reveal not a little of courage in the overcoming of apparently hopeless odds. I am thinking, of course, of G. Tearle—not the actor, but the croquet-player. And, indeed, some of the prettiest effects of gamesmanship are to be seen when an expert in, say, croquet, plays golf, it may be, off the same handicap, against a real expert in, say, rugger—a man who really has played rugger, twice capped for England. The rugger man certainly starts with a tremendous advantage. His name is a legend, his game is glorious. Croquet is considered, by the lay world, to be piddling. The two meet on the common ground of golf; and even golf, to the rugger man, is considered fairly piddling. Yet I have seen Tearle not only break down this view *but reverse it*, so that in the end the Rugger international would sometimes even be heard claiming that he came from croquet people, but that his character "was not suited to the game."

Tearle by long practice actually made capital out of croquet. And let me add that Tearle's triumph demonstrates once again that it is in these long-drawn-out reversal tactics that training and the proper diet stand you in such good stead.

Counterpoint

This phrase, now used exclusively in music, originally stood for Number Three of the general Principles of Gamesmanship. "PLAY AGAINST YOUR OPPONENT'S TEMPO." This is one of the oldest of gambits and is now almost entirely used in the form "My Slow to your Fast." E.g., at billiards, or snooker, or golf especially, against a player who makes a great deal of "wanting to get on with the game," the technique is (1) to agree (Jeffreys always adds here "as long as we don't hurry on the shot"); (2) to hold things up by fifteen to twenty disguised pauses. Peg-top tees for golf were introduced by Samuel in '33 for this use. The technique is to tee the ball, frame up for the shot, and then at the last moment stop, pretend to push the peg a little further in or pull it a little further out, and then start all over again. At the next hole vary this with Samuel's "Golden Perfecto" peg tee, made in such a way that the ball, after sitting still in the cup for two to three seconds, rolls off. (Fig. 1.)

Through the green, the usual procedure is to frame up for the shot and then decide on another club at the last moment.

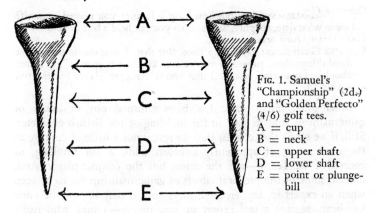

Fig. 1. Samuel's "Championship" (2d.) and "Golden Perfecto" (4/6) golf tees.
A = cup
B = neck
C = upper shaft
D = lower shaft
E = point or plunge-bill

NOTE—*Do not attempt to irritate partner by spending too long looking for your lost ball.* This is unsporting. But good gamesmanship which is also very good sportsmanship can be practiced if the gamesman makes a great and irritatingly prolonged parade of spending extra time looking for his *opponent's* ball.

At billiards, the custom of arranging to be summoned to the telephone on fake calls, so as to break your opponent's concentration, is out of date now and interesting only as a reminder of the days when "couriers" were paid to gallop up to the old billiard halls for the same purpose. In snooker, the usual practice is to walk quickly up to the table, squat half down on the haunches to look at sight-lines, move to the other end of the table to look at sight-lines of balls which may come in to play later on in the break which you are supposed to be planning. Decide on the shot. Frame up for it, and then at the last moment see some obvious red shot which you had "missed," and which your opponent and everybody else will have noticed before you moved to the table, and which they know is the shot you are going to play in the end anyhow.

For chess tempos see "Chess, tempi."

"My To-morrow's Match"

In a Key Friendly, or any individual match which you are particularly anxious to win, the best general approach (Rule IV) is the expression of anxiety *to play to-day, because of the match to-morrow.* Construct a story that you are playing A. J. du C. Masterman.[4] Or perhaps the name should be A. C. Swinburne (your opponent will feel he has vaguely heard of this name). Go on to say (if the game is golf)—"Do you mind if I practice using my Number One iron to-day"—(no need to use it or even have one)—"as I want to know whether to take it to-morrow?" Take one practice shot after having picked up your ball, at a lost hole. Seek the advice of oppo-

4. Names impress according to the square of their initials [Potter's note].

nent. Ask him "What *he* would do if he found himself playing against a *really* long driver, like A. C. Swinburne."

Game Leg (Also Known as "Crocked Ankle Play," or "Gamesman's Leg"[5])

"Limpmanship," as it used to be called, or the exact use of minor injury, not only for the purpose of getting out of, but for actually winning difficult contests, is certainly as old as the mediaeval tourneys, the knightly combats, of ancient chivalry. Yet, nowadays, no device is more clumsily used, no gambit more often muffed. "I hope I shall be able to give you a game," says the middle-aged golfer to his young opponent, turning his head from side to side and hunching up his shoulders. "My back was a bit seized up yesterday . . . this wind." How wretchedly weak. "O.K. My youth *versus* your age," says the young counter-gamesman to himself, and rubs this thought in with a variety of subsequent slanting references: "You ought to take it easy, for a week or two," etc. No, if use the hackneyed ankle gambit you must, let the injury be the result of a campaign in one of the wars, or a quixotic attempt to stop a runaway horse, at least.

But, here as so often, it is the *reply*, the counter, wherein the ploy of the gamesman can be used to best effect. Indeed, there is nothing prettier than the right use of an opponent's injury. There is the refusal to be put off even if the injury is genuine. There is the adoption of a game which, though apparently ignoring and indeed even favoring your opponent's disability, will yet benefit you in the end. In their own different ways, the "Two F's," Frier and Frith-Morteroy, were the greatest masters of the art of "Countering the Crock." No one who heard them will ever forget their apologies for sending a short one to the man with the twisted ankle, their excuses for the accidental lob in the sun against an opponent with sensitive eyes. But the Frith-Morteroy counter, though not for beginners, has more of grace, and needs more of explanation. Let it be lawn tennis—Frith's game. Frith against "Novice Gamesman," we will call him.

Novice Gamesman is limping slightly. "Hopes he can give F.-M. a game, but his rugger knee has just been prodded back into place by old Coutts of Welbeck Street." Right. F.-M. is full of sympathy. F.-M. sends not a single short one. In fact he does nothing whatever. His supporters become anxious—and then—during, say, the *first* game of the *second* set, while they are changing sides Frith is heard to say (on arriving at point K—see Fig. 2) "Ooo!" sharply.

Novice Gamesman: What's that?
Frith-Morteroy: Nothing. Nothing. I thought——
N. G. (*further away*): What did you say?
F.-M.: Nothing.

5. Usually shortened now into "Game Leg" [Potter's note].

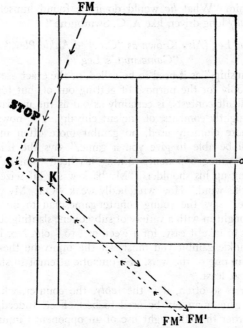

FIG. 2. Diagram of tennis court to show Frith-Morteroy's path of changing, and the position S from which he makes his "echo" attack, in Morteroy Counter Game Leg play. Point K on the line FM-FM¹ is the position from which the demi-cry is made. At point S, on the line FM², the full cry is made. "Stop" marks the usual position for the actual verbal interchange or "parlette."

The game continues. But at that next cross over, Frith says "Ow!" (point S, Fig. 2). He pauses a minute, and stands as if lost in thought.

N. G.: What's up?
F.-M.: Nothing. Half a moment.
N. G.: Something wrong?
F.-M. (*rubs his chest with his knuckles*): No. No. It's only the old pump.
N. G.: Pump?
F.-M.: Yes. The ancient ticker.
N. G.: What—heart?
F.-M.: I'm supposed not to be using it full out at the moment. Only a temporary thing.
N. G.: Good Lord.
F.-M.: It's all right now!
N. G.: Good.
F.-M.: Couple of crocks!
N. G.: Well. Shall we get on?

"*Couple* of crocks." Observe the triple thrust against the Novice Gamesman. (1) Frith establishes the fact that he, also, labors under a handicap; (2) the atmosphere which Novice Gamesman has built up with so much restraint, but so much labor—the suggestion of silent suffering—is the precise climate in which Frith is now going to prosper, and (3)—most important of all—Frith has won the gamesmanship part of the contest already, set and match, by sportingly waiting, say twenty-five minutes, before revealing his own somewhat worse disability. Novice Gamesman having mentioned his rugger knee—a stale type of infliction anyhow—is made to look a fool and a fusser. More, he is made to look unsporting.

I believe it is true to say that once Frith-Morteroy had achieved this position, he was never known to lose a game. He made a special study of it—and I believe much of his spare time was spent reading the medical books on the subject of minor cardiac weaknesses.

Jack Rivers Opening

After this most successful of basic plays, may I dare to end this chapter with a very simple but favorite gambit of my own?

I call it the Jack Rivers Opening. I have written elsewhere of the sporting-unsporting approach, always to be revered as the parent of modern gamesman play. But if sporting-unsporting is vaguely regarded as a thing of the past, the gamesman knows that it is a habit of thought still rooted in many British players.

Perhaps the most difficult type for the gamesman to beat is the man who indulges in pure play. He gets down to it, he gets on with it, he plays each shot according to its merits, and his own powers, without a trace of exhibitionism, and no by-play whatever. In golf, croquet or ping-pong—golf especially—he is liable to wear you down by playing the "old aunty" type of game.

My only counter to this, which some have praised, is to invent, early in the game or before it has started, an imaginary character called "Jack Rivers." I speak of his charm, his good looks, his fine war record and his talent for games—and, "by the way, he is a first-class pianist as well." Then, a little later: "I like Jack Rivers's game," I say. "He doesn't care a damn whether he wins or loses so long as he has a good match."

Some such rubbish as this, although at first it may not be effective, often wears down the most successfully cautious opponent, *if the method is given time to soak in.* Allow your opponent to achieve a small lead, perhaps, by his stone-walling methods; and the chances are that—even if he has only been hearing about Jack Rivers for thirty minutes—he will begin to think: "Well, perhaps I am being a bit of a stick-in-the-mud." He feels an irrational desire to play up to what appears to be your ideal of a good fellow. After all, he remembers, hadn't he been once chaffed for breaking a window with a cricketball when he was on holiday at Whitby? He himself was a bit mad once. Soon he is throwing away point after point by adopting a happy-go-lucky, hit-or-miss method which doesn't suit his game in the least.

Meanwhile *you* begin to play with pawky steadiness, and screen this fact by redoubling your references to Jack Rivers. You talk of the way in which Jack, too, loved to open his shoulders for a mighty smite, landing him in trouble as often as not; but the glorious thing about him was that he didn't care two hoots for that . . . and so long as he had a good smack, and a good game . . ., etc.

So much for the Principal Plays, in gamesmanship. Now for the other gambits which must be brought into play as the game progresses.

ERNEST HEMINGWAY

Bullfighting[1]

The bullfight is not a sport in the Anglo-Saxon sense of the word, that is, it is not an equal contest or an attempt at an equal contest between a bull and a man. Rather it is a tragedy; the death of the bull, which is played, more or less well, by the bull and the man involved and in which there is danger for the man but certain death for the animal. This danger to the man can be increased by the bullfighter at will in the measure in which he works close to the bull's horns. Keeping within the rules for bullfighting on foot in a closed ring formulated by years of experience, which, if known and followed, permit a man to perform certain actions with a bull without being caught by the bull's horns, the bullfighter may, by decreasing his distance from the bull's horns, depend more and more on his own reflexes and judgment of that distance to protect him from the points. This danger of goring, which the man creates voluntarily, can be changed to certainty of being caught and tossed by the bull if the man, through ignorance, slowness, torpidness, blind folly, or momentary grogginess breaks any of these fundamental rules for the execution of the different suertes. Everything that is done by the man in the ring is called a "suerte." It is the easiest term to use as it is short. It means act, but the word act has, in English, a connotation of the theatre that makes its use confusing.

People seeing their first bullfight say, "But the bulls are so stupid. They always go for the cape and not for the man."

The bull only goes for the percale of the cape or for the scarlet serge of the muleta[2] if the man makes him and so handles the cloth that the bull sees it rather than the man. Therefore to really start to see bullfights a spectator should go to the novilladas or

---

1. Chapter 2 in *Death in the After-noon*, 1932.
2. A small cloth attached to a short tapered stick and used by a matador during the final passes leading to the kill.

apprentice fights. There the bulls do not always go for the cloth because the bullfighters are learning before your eyes the rules of bullfighting and they do not always remember or know the proper terrain to take and how to keep the bull after the lure and away from the man. It is one thing to know the rules in principle and another to remember them as they are needed when facing an animal that is seeking to kill you, and the spectator who wants to see men tossed and gored rather than judge the manner in which the bulls are dominated should go to a novillada before he sees a corrida de toros or complete bullfight. It should be a good thing for him to see a novillada first anyway if he wants to learn about technique, since the employment of knowledge that we call by that bastard name is always most visible in its imperfection. At a novillada the spectator may see the mistakes of the bullfighters, and the penalties that these mistakes carry. He will learn something too about the state of training or lack of training of the men and the effect this has on their courage.

One time in Madrid I remember we went to a novillada in the middle of the summer on a very hot Sunday when every one who could afford it had left the city for the beaches of the north or the mountains and the bullfight was not advertised to start until six o'clock in the evening, to see six Tovar bulls killed by three aspirant matadors who have all since failed in their profession. We sat in the first row behind the wooden barrier and when the first bull came out it was clear that Domingo Hernandorena, a short, thick-ankled, graceless Basque with a pale face who looked nervous and incompletely fed in a cheap rented suit, if he was to kill this bull would either make a fool of himself or be gored. Hernandorena could not control the nervousness of his feet. He wanted to stand quietly and play the bull with the cape with a slow movement of his arms, but when he tried to stand still as the bull charged his feet jumped away in short, nervous jerks. His feet were obviously not under his personal control and his effort to be statuesque while his feet jittered him away out of danger was very funny to the crowd. It was funny to them because many of them knew that was how their own feet would behave if they saw the horns coming toward them, and as always, they resented any one else being in there in the ring, making money, who had the same physical defects which barred them, the spectators, from that supposedly highly paid way of making a living. In their turn the other two matadors were very fancy with the cape and Hernandorena's nervous jerking was even worse after their performance. He had not been in the ring with a bull for over a year and he was altogether unable to control his nervousness. When the banderillas were in and it was time for him to go out with the red cloth and the sword to prepare the bull for killing and to kill, the crowd which had applauded ironically at every nervous move he had made knew something very funny would happen. Below us, as he took the muleta and the sword and rinsed his mouth out with water I could see the muscles of his cheeks twitching. The bull stood against the barrier watching him. Hernandorena could not trust his legs to carry him slowly toward the bull. He knew there was only one way he could stay in one place in the ring. He ran out toward the bull, and ten yards in front of him dropped to both knees on the sand. In that position he was safe from ridicule. He spread the red cloth with his sword and jerked himself forward on his knees toward the bull. The bull was watching the man and the triangle of red cloth, his ears pointed, his eyes fixed, and Hernandorena knee-ed himself a yard closer and shook the cloth. The bull's tail rose, his head lowered and he charged and, as he reached the man, Hernandorena rose solidly from his knees into the air, swung over like a bundle, his legs in all directions now, and then dropped to the ground. The bull looked for him, found a wide-spread moving cape held by another bullfighter instead, charged it, and Hernandorena stood up with sand on his white face and looked for his sword and the cloth. As he stood up I saw the heavy, soiled gray silk of his rented trousers open cleanly and deeply to show the thigh bone from the hip almost to the knee. He saw it too and looked very surprised and put his hand on it while people jumped over the barrier and ran toward him to carry him to the infirmary. The technical error that he had committed was in not keeping the red cloth of the muleta between himself and the bull until the charge; then at the moment of jurisdiction as it is called, when the bull's lowered head reaches the cloth, swaying back while he held the cloth, spread by the stick and the sword, far enough forward so that the bull following it would be clear of his body. It was a simple technical error.

That night at the café I heard no word of sympathy for him. He was ignorant, he was torpid, and he was out of training. Why did he insist on being a bullfighter? Why did he go down on both knees? Because he was a coward, they said. The knees are for cowards. If he was a coward why did he insist on being a bullfighter? There was no natural sympathy for uncontrollable nervousness because he was a paid public performer. It was preferable that he be gored rather than run from the bull. To be gored was honorable; they would have sympathized with him had he been caught in one of his nervous uncontrollable jerky retreats, which, although they mocked, they knew were from lack of training, rather than for him to have gone down on his knees. Because the hardest thing when frightened by the bull is to control the feet and let the bull come, and any attempt to control the feet was honorable even though they jeered at it because it looked ridiculous. But when he went on both knees, without the technique to fight from that position; the technique that Marcial Lalanda, the most scientific of living bull-fighters, has, and which alone makes that position honorable; then Hernandorena admitted his nervousness. To show his nervousness was not shameful; only to admit it. When, lacking the technique and thereby admitting his inability to control his feet, the matador went down on both knees before the bull the crowd had no more sympathy with him than with a suicide.

For myself, not being a bullfighter, and being much interested in suicides, the problem was one of depiction and waking in the night I tried to remember what it was that seemed just out of my remembering and that was the thing that I had really seen and, finally, remembering all around, I got it. When he stood up, his face white and dirty and the silk of his breeches opened from waist to knee, it was the dirtiness of the rented breeches, the dirtiness of his slit underwear, and the clean, clean, unbearably clean whiteness of the thigh bone that I had seen, and it was that which was important.

At the novilladas, too, besides the study of technique, and the consequences of its lack you have a chance to learn about the manner of dealing with defective bulls since bulls which cannot be used in a formal bullfight because of some obvious defect are killed in the apprentice fights. Nearly all bulls develop defects in the course of any fight which must be corrected by the bullfighter, but in the novillada these defects, those of vision for instance, are many times obvious at the start and so the manner of their correcting, or the result of their not being corrected, is apparent.

The formal bullfight is a tragedy, not a sport, and the bull is certain to be killed. If the matador cannot kill him and, at the end of the allotted fifteen minutes for the preparation and killing, the bull is led and herded out of the ring alive by steers to dishonor the killer, he must, by law, be killed in the corrals. It is one hundred to one against the matador de toros or formally invested bull-fighter being killed unless he is inexperienced, ignorant, out of training or too old and heavy on his feet. But the matador, if he knows his profession, can increase the amount of the danger of death that he runs exactly as much as he wishes. He should, however, increase this danger, *within the rules provided for his protection.* In other words it is to his credit if he does something that he knows how to do in a highly dangerous but still geo-metrically possible manner. It is to his discredit if he runs danger through ignorance, through disregard of the fundamental rules, through physical or mental slowness, or through blind folly.

The matador must dominate the bulls by knowledge and science. In the measure in which this domination is accomplished with grace will it be beautiful to watch. Strength is of little use to him except at the actual moment of killing. Once some one asked Rafael Gomez, "El Gallo," nearing fifty years old, a gypsy, brother of Jose Gomez, "Gallito," and the last living member of the great family of gypsy bullfighters of that name, what physical exercise he, Gallo, took to keep his strength up for bullfighting.

"Strength," Gallo said. "What do I want with strength, man? The bull weighs half a ton. Should I take exercises for strength to match him? Let the bull have the strength."

If the bulls were allowed to increase their knowledge as the bull-fighter does and if those bulls which are not killed in the alloted fifteen minutes in the ring were not afterwards killed in the corrals but were allowed to be fought again they would kill all the bull-fighters, if the bullfighters fought them according to the rules. Bull-fighting is based on the fact that it is the first meeting between the wild animal and a dismounted man. This is the fundamental premise of modern bullfighting; that the bull has never been in the ring before. In the early days of bullfighting bulls were allowed to be fought which had been in the ring before and so many men were killed in the bull ring that on November 20, 1567, Pope Pius the Fifth issued a Papal edict excommunicating all Christian princes who should permit bullfights in their countries and denying Christian burial to any person killed in the bull ring. The Church only agreed to tolerate bullfighting, which continued steadily in Spain in spite of the edict, when it was agreed that the bulls should only appear once in the ring.

You would think then that it would make of bullfighting a true sport, rather than merely a tragic spectacle, if bulls that had been in the ring were allowed to reappear. I have seen such bulls fought, in violation of the law, in provincial towns in improvised arenas made by blocking the entrances to the public square with piled-up carts in the illegal capeas, or town-square bullfights with used bulls. The aspirant bullfighters, who have no financial backing, get their first experience in capeas. It is a sport, a very savage and primitive sport, and for the most part a truly amateur one. I am afraid however due to the danger of death it involves it would never have much success among the amateur sportsmen of America and England who play games. We, in games, are not fascinated by death, its nearness and its avoidance. We are fascinated by victory and we replace the avoidance of death by the avoidance of defeat. It is a very nice symbolism but it takes more cojones to be a sportsman when death is a closer party to the game. The bull in the capeas is rarely killed. This should appeal to sports-men who are lovers of animals. The town is usually too poor to afford to pay for the killing of the bull and none of the aspirant bullfighters has enough money to buy a sword or he would not have chosen to serve his apprenticeship in the capeas. This would afford an opportunity for the man who is a wealthy sportsman, for he could afford to pay for the bull and buy himself a sword as well.

However, due to the mechanics of a bull's mental development the used bull does not make a brilliant spectacle. After his first charge or so he will stand quite still and will only charge if he is certain of getting the man or boy who is tempting him with a cape. When there is a crowd and the bull charges into it he will pick one man out and follow him, no matter how he may dodge, run and twist until he gets him and tosses him. If the tips of the bull's horns have been blunted this chasing and tossing is good fun to see for a little while. No one has to go in with the bull who does not want to, although of course many who want to very little go in to show their courage. It is very exciting for those who are down in the square, that is one test of a true amateur sport, whether it is more enjoyable to player than to spectator (as soon as it becomes enjoyable enough to the spectator for the charging of admission to be profitable the sport contains the germ of professionalism), and the smallest evidence of coolness or composure brings immediate applause. But when the bull's horns are sharp-pointed it is a disturbing spectacle. The men and boys try cape work with sacks, blouses, and old capes on the bull just as they do when his horns have been blunted; the only difference is that when the bull catches them and tosses them they are liable to come off the horn with wounds no local surgeon can cope with. One bull which was a great favorite in the capeas of the province of Valencia killed sixteen men and boys and badly wounded over sixty in a career of five years. The people who go into these capeas do so sometimes as aspirant professionals to get free experience with bulls but most often as amateurs, purely for sport, for the immediate excitement, and it is very great excitement; and for the retrospective pleasure, of having shown their contempt for death on a hot day in their own town square. Many go in from pride, hoping that they will be brave. Many find they are not brave at all; but at least they went in. There is absolutely nothing for them to gain except the inner satisfaction of having been in the ring with a bull; itself a thing that any one who has done it will always remember. It is a strange feeling to have an animal come toward you consciously seeking to kill you, his eyes open looking at you, and see the oncoming of the lowered horn that he intends to kill you with. It gives enough of a sensation so that there are always men willing to go into the capeas for the pride of having experienced it and the pleasure of having tried some bullfighting maneuver with a real bull although the actual pleasure at the time may not be great. Sometimes the bull is killed if the town has the money to afford it, or if the populace gets out of control; every one swarming on him at once with knives, daggers, butcher knives, and rocks; a man perhaps between his horns, being swung up and down, another flying through the air, surely several holding his tail, a swarm of choppers, thrusters and stabbers pushing into him, laying on him or cutting up at him until he sways and goes down. All amateur or group killing is a very barbarous, messy, though exciting business and is a long way from the ritual of the formal bullfight.

The bull which killed the sixteen and wounded the sixty was killed in a very odd way. One of those he had killed was a gypsy boy of about fourteen. Afterward the boy's brother and sister followed the bull around hoping perhaps to have a chance to assassinate him when he was loaded in his cage after a capea. That was difficult since, being a very highly valued performer, the bull was carefully taken care of. They followed him around for two years, not attempting anything, simply turning up wherever the bull was used. When the capeas were again abolished, they are always being abolished and reabolished, by government order, the bull's owner decided to send him to the slaughterhouse in Valencia, for the bull was getting on in years anyway. The two gypsies were at the slaughterhouse and the young man asked permission, since the bull had killed his brother, to kill the bull. This was granted and he started in by digging out both the bull's eyes while the bull was in his cage, and spitting carefully into the sockets, then after killing him by severing the spinal marrow between the neck vertebrae with a dagger, he experienced some difficulty in this, he asked permission to cut off the bull's testicles, which being granted, he and his sister built a small fire at the edge of the dusty street outside the slaughterhouse and roasted the two glands on sticks and when they were done, ate them. They then turned their backs on the slaughterhouse and went away along the road and out of town.

ERNEST van den HAAG
Is Pornography a Cause of Crime?

Whether pornography should be treated as a crime is largely a moral question. In her book *On Iniquity*, Pamela Hansford Johnson was more concerned with a factual and logical question: Is pornography a cause of crime? She became inclined to think so as she reported (scantily) and reflected (impressionistically) on the "Moors" trial in which Ian Brady and Myra Hindley were found guilty of having murdered an adolescent boy (Evans) and of having abused, tortured, and murdered a little girl aged ten and a boy twelve years old. The bodies of the child victims were found in the moors nearby. The motive was sexual gratification: the pair compelled the children to pose for obscene pictures and made a recording of the terrified screams, the sobs and pitiful pleas for mercy of ten-year-old Lesley Ann Downey as they tortured her to death. In 1966, a court in Chester sentenced the couple to life imprisonment, the severest penalty available.

Although continuing her longstanding opposition to the death penalty, Lady Snow felt uneasy: the outcome of the trial was "aesthetically" disappointing—it did not produce a catharsis. The parents of the dead children (and possibly the community generally) probably were not relieved either by learning that English law now compels them to feed, house, and protect the murderers as long as they live. (The death penalty may have drawbacks but life imprisonment has no fewer.)

Miss Johnson briefly asks whether the murderers might be insane but finds no reason to think so. Neither did the defense. (Both defendants testified rationally, if not very credibly.) In the U.S. insanity might have been pleaded more easily: many American judges and psychiatrists are convinced that people are born good and that wicked acts are sufficient proof that the perpetrators were sick (preferably driven into sickness by society). These psychiatrists and judges transform "sickness" from an independently testable clinical category into the morally necessary cause of all wicked acts. Therefore, the perpetrators of outrageous acts are made sick by definition. Thus, a factual category is transformed into a (rather dubious) moral category unfalsifiable by evidence, yet withdrawn from philosophical scrutiny by being disguised as a scientific (clinical) finding. Psychiatry becomes a normative pseudo-science; and the administration of justice an odd way of providing therapy.

Unfortunately Miss Johnson's reporting tells us more about her reactions to the proceedings, and to the defendants, than about their personalities. Perhaps it is because she is so honestly puzzled about behavior so alien to her that she wonders whether it was Brady's reading which transformed the benevolent utilitarianism so familiar to her—it does not occur to her to question it—into the malevolent utilitarianism which Brady used to rationalize his actions.

Brady had a library almost exclusively concerned with sex and sadism. The works of the Marquis de Sade were prominent and Brady thought of himself as a disciple of his philosophy.

It is here that the issue is joined. Did Brady read what he read because he was what he was? (Might he even have gratified his pre-existing disposition more often by action without the vicarious satisfaction yielded by his reading?) Or, conversely, did Brady become what he became because of his reading? In short, was the reading the effect or the cause?[1] Posed in this way, the question can be (and has been) endlessly debated. But if it is formulated more reasonably, a tentative answer can be given.

Obviously not all readers of de Sade become sadists; nor do all non-readers lead blameless lives. It follows that reading de Sade is not sufficient to become a sadist, nor necessary. It does not follow that reading him has no effect, or that the effect cannot be, at times, decisive either in initiating an inclination leading to acts, or in precipitating acts when the inclination exists.[2] The possibility of sadism is in all of us. Various external conditions may lead us to sadistic actions, or to mere fantasies, or to repudiation of either. Reading of the fantasies of others may lead to actions no less than other external stimuli. From the fact that not all readers of the Bible become Christians or act as such, and that some non-readers do, few people would conclude that the Bible has no influence. Or (to avoid the issue of "grace"): not all readers of Marx become Marxists, but some do; some non-readers might have become socialists anyway. Are we to say that Marx had no influence?

How can literate persons accept Jimmy Walker's famous dictum, "No girl was ever seduced by a book"? Dante's view expressed by Francesca, that she and Paolo were seduced by a book (*galeotto fu il libro e chi lo scrisse*)[3] is certainly more realistic. Actions are influenced by ideas; even emotions—such as love or hate—are often shaped by ideas and ideal models. Else why write about

1. Mr. J. W. Lambert knows that "the appetites of people like Brady are formed long before any books . . . can have influenced them. Their appetites will lead them to literature not *vice versa.*" Unfortunately Mr. Lambert does not disclose the source of his knowledge. If he has evidence why not disclose it? Or is he pronouncing a dogma? That the opposite case has not been proven is, he surely knows, not proof of his contention. At any rate the issue is not so much "appetites"—these are common enough although usually unconscious—but their translation into action. This translation can plausibly be fostered by literary, moral, or social support. I think it has been [van den Haag's note].

2. Certainly Mr. Kenneth Allsop's argument that "vile deeds originated" with non-readers of sadistic books as well, is irrelevant as an argument against eliminating *one* of the possible causes of "vile deeds." So is his remarkable argument that "a far greater number of children are killed by the motor car each year," or "by aerial bombardment." I am against traffic accidents and wars but I do not see why their occurrence argues for not

controlling homicidal literature (or for it not being homicidal). Oddly enough, the fact that we have not found expedient means of preventing traffic accidents or wars has not persuaded Messrs. Lambert and Allsop to come out in favor of either; nor do they favor giving up attempts to control them. Yet they both argue as though their belief that no reasonable way of distinguishing and controlling sadistic literature can be found—quite unrealistic in my opinion—shows the undesirability or unnecessariness of attempting to control it. Of course, it merely shows the difficulties facing (possibly the inexpediency of) an enterprise that remains desirable. It is surely easier to get rid of, and as a first step to prohibit, sadistic literature, than to abolish wars and traffic accidents. Although prohibition will not prevent all distribution it will reduce it and deprive it of social approval. The advantage of this must be weighed against likely disadvantages. I find no such pondering in the intemperate, fustian *ex cathedra* rhetoric of Messrs. Lambert and Allsop [van den Haag's note].

3. "A betrayer was that book and he who wrote it."

them, or about anything? The desire for sex may inhere in us. But when and how to gratify it, what actions are morally permissible and what actions are not, whether and when to seduce (or be seduced) and how, whether and when to rape, or torture, or kill—these decisions are influenced by culture and milieu, in turn certainly influenced by literature—quite apart from its direct influence on individuals.

Of course it is hard to trace the direct causes of any individual act, and to say whether it would have occurred without the book that, however indirectly, suggested it. The possible causes cannot be isolated from each other and their role in any action is difficult to assess. But this hardly argues that books have no influence. It is odd (as well as wrong) to defend the freedom of literature by pretending that it has no influence. The influence of books varies from case to case; it can contribute to the formation of dispositions (given the individual potential for the disposition) or can precipitate the action, once the disposition has been formed for whatever reasons—just as LSD may precipitate a psychotic episode when there is a disposition. Since a book hardly ever can be the only influence, or be influential in isolation—it is always a person with previous experiences and preexisting disposition who is being influenced—its precise quantitative role in causation is hard to trace. But the conclusion that it has *no role* is logically unwarranted and empirically implausible. Nor can one argue reasonably that something else would necessarily have taken the place of books among the causes of action. The drug addict might have become an alcoholic—but not necessarily.

It is strange that the criminal rampage of, say, a deprived Negro in the U.S.A. is easily ascribed to his deprivation. We are told that we are guilty of failing to remedy it, and thus of his acts (and that he is not). But why are we not guilty then of failing to restrict literature, no less logically connected with the rampage of the sadist who read it? In neither case can a direct causal connection be established, or such matters as disposition discounted. In both cases, a causal connection of some sort seems quite likely.

Unless one objects to pornography *per se*, these reflections apply only to sadistic pornography, or to literature that invites nonconsensual sexual acts. However, I believe that pornography nearly always leads to sadistic pornography. By definition, pornography deindividualizes and dehumanizes sexual acts; by eliminating all the contexts it reduces people simply to bearers of impersonal sensations of pleasure and pain. This dehumanization eliminates the empathy that restrains us ultimately from sadism and nonconsensual acts. The cliché language and the stereotyped situations, the characters not characterized except sexually, are defining characteristics of pornography: the pornographer avoids distraction from the masturbatory fantasy by avoiding art and humanity. Art may "cancel lust" (as Santayana thought) or sublimate it. The pornographer wants to desublimate it. Those who resort to such fantasies habitually are people who are ungratified by others (for endogenous or external reasons). They seek gratification in using others, in inflicting pain (sometimes in suffering it) at least in their fantasy. In this respect, *The Story of O*, which, itself pornographic, also depicts the (rather self-defeating) outcome of pornographic fantasy, is paradigmatic.

In a sense, pornographic and finally sadistic literature is anti-human. Were it directed against a specific human group—*e.g.* Jews or Negroes—the same libertarian ideologues who now oppose censorship might advocate it. Should we find a little Negro or Jewish girl tortured to death and her death agony taped by her murderers, and should we find the murderers imbued with sadistic anti-Semitic or anti-Negro literature—certainly most liberals would advocate that the circulation of such literature be prohibited. But why should humanity as such be less protected than any of the specific groups that compose it? That the hate articulated is directed against people in general rather than against only Jews or Negroes makes it no less dangerous; on the contrary: it makes it as dangerous to more people.

I do not foresee a social organization which can avoid resentments in individuals or sadistic wishes and fantasies. But we could do better in controlling them by, among other things, censoring the literature that by offering models and rationalizations fosters their growth and precipitates them into action.

But shouldn't an adult be able to control himself and read without enacting what he knows to be wrong or, at least, illegal? Perhaps he should. But we are not dealing with a homogeneous group called grown-ups (nor is it possible in the American modern environment to limit anything to adults; children and adolescents are not supervised enough—and the authority of their supervisors has been absent far too long—to make that possible). Too many grown-ups are far from the self-restrained healthy type envisaged by democratic theory. They may easily be given a last, or first, push by the literature I would like to see restricted.

Now, if that literature had literary value, we would have to weigh its loss against the importance of avoiding the deleterious influence it may have. We may even be ready to sacrifice some probable victims for the sake of this literary value. But pornographic "literature" is without literary value. It is printed but it is not literature. Hence there is nothing to be lost by restricting it and there possibly is something to be gained—the lives of the victims who are spared.

There remains the problem of distinguishing pornography from literature. I am convinced that our presumed inability to do so is largely a pretended inability and often pretended in bad faith. But how do you determine what is to be censored? "Lewdness" and "prurience" are matters of opinion; so, therefore, is censorship. Because the power of the censor cannot but be used arbitrarily, by relying on one opinion or another, it endangers the freedom of literature, ultimately of all expression, no less than the license of pornography. Isn't this too high a price to pay?

I don't think we have to pay this price. And, I know of no historical instance where censorship of pornography has endangered freedom in other areas. (The converse does occur, but is irrelevant. Communism or Nazism restricts freedom and *thereupon* censors pornography.) Anyway, a definition of pornography which distinguishes it from literature is neither so nearly impossible a task as some lawyers make it, nor as different from other legal distinctions as they presume. And if we can distinguish pornography from literature we can censor one without restricting the other.

Several extrinsic and intrinsic qualities set pornography apart. The extrinsic qualities are: (1) the intention of the author (or painter, comedian, actor, photographer, editor—or anyone who communicates); (2) the use made of his work—the means used to advertise and sell it, the context created for it; (3) the actual effect on the consumer.

1. If pornographic intention is admitted or proved by testimony and circumstances, there is no problem. If doubtful, intention must be tested by the intrinsic qualities of the work.

2. Regardless of the author's intent his work may be advertised or sold by stressing its (actual or putative) prurient appeal. By itself this justifies action against the seller only. Yet, although sales tactics are neither sufficient nor necessary to establish the prurient appeal of what is sold, they can be relevant: the image created by the seller may well fuse with the object of which it is an image and have effects on the consumer. Advertisers often claim they achieve this fusion. Sometimes they can—when the object lends itself to it.

3. The actual effect on the consumer—whether "prurient interest" is or is not aroused—depends on the work, its presentation, and the character of the consumer. A work not intended to be pornographic may nonetheless awaken lust, or have lewd effects; and one intended to do so may fail. Censors must consult not only their own reactions but rely on testimony about probable and prevailing reactions and standards. Pornography, to be such, must be likely to have a prurient or lewd effect. But this effect alone, though necessary, is not sufficient. However, together the three extrinsic qualities certainly are. Any two of them seem quite enough.

These qualities suffice to characterize "hard-core" pornography, which is "hard-core" precisely because it has at least two of these extrinsic qualities—and not much else to confuse matters. But what about works which cannot be classified by means of their extrinsic qualities alone—where effect or intention are mixed, or doubtful? Such works can be dealt with only by exploring the intrinsic qualities which make pornography pornographic.

Characteristically, pornography, while dreary and repulsive to one part of the normal (more usual) personality, is also seductive to another: it severs sex from its human context (the Id from Ego and Super-ego), reduces the world to orifices and organs, the action to their combinations.

The pornographic reduction of life to varieties of sex is but the spinning out of pre-adolescent fantasies which reject the burdens of reality and individuation, of conflict, commitment, thought, consideration, and love, of regarding others as more than objects—a burden which becomes heavier and less avoidable in adolescence. Thus in fantasy a return to the pure libidinal pleasure principle is achieved—and fantasy may regress to even more infantile fears and wishes: people are literally devoured, tortured, mutilated, and altogether dehumanized. (Such fantasies are acted out—*e.g.* in concentration camps—whenever authority fails to control, or supports, the impulses it usually helps to repress.)

So much for the content of pornography. It has one aim only: to arouse the reader's lust so that, by sharing the fantasy manufactured for him, he may attain a vicarious sexual experience. Pornography is intended to produce this experience, unlike literature, which aims at the contemplation of experience, at the revelation of its significance. Revelation too is an experience—but one which helps understand and enlarge the possibilities and complexities of the human career—whereas pornography narrows and simplifies them till they are reduced to a series of more or less sophisticated but anonymous (therefore monotonous) sensations.

It is impossible, of course, to serve pornography pure. The vicarious experience must occur through the medium of words, and be depicted in a setting that permits the suspension of disbelief. Yet aesthetic merit would be distracting. To avoid this, pornographers use well-worn and inconspicuous clichés and conventions which do not encumber the libidinous purpose. These qualities are intrinsic to pornography and distinguish it from literature.

Some lawyers argue that the perception of the intrinsic qualities of pornography in any work depends on literary criticism and is, therefore, a matter of opinion. It seems odd, though, that, in a legal context, serious critics themselves often behave as though they believed criticism to be a matter of opinion. Why be a critic—and teach in universities—if it involves no more than uttering capricious and arbitrary opinions? And if criticism cannot tell pornography from literature what can it tell us? Of course critics may disagree; so do other witnesses, including psychiatrists and handwriting experts. The decision is up to the court; the literary witnesses only have the obligation to testify truthfully as to what is or is not pornography.

Some of the critics who claim that they cannot make the distinction do not wish to because they regard pornography as legitimate; others fear that censorship of pornography may be extended to literature. Whatever the merits of such views, they do not justify testifying that the distinction cannot be made. A witness is not entitled to deny that he saw what he did see, simply to save the accused from a punishment he dislikes. A critic who is really incapable of distinguishing pornography from literature certainly has no business being one; a critic who is capable of making the distinction has no business testifying that he is not.

Impulsively, I am against both censors and pornographers—but even more am I against one without the other; if you are for either you should be for both. On reflection, I am: both are wanted and they call for each other, as toreros and bulls do, or hunters and game.

Censorship is no less possible nor less needed than pornography. If we indulge pornography, and do not allow censorship to restrict it, our society at best will become ever more coarse, brutal, anxious, indifferent, de-individualized, hedonistic; at worst its ethos will disintegrate altogether.

The self-restrained and controlled individual may exist and function in an environment which fosters reasonable conduct—but few such individuals will be created, and they will function less well in an environment where they receive little social support, where sadistic acts are openly held up as models and sadistic fantasies are sold to any purchaser. To be sure, a virtuous man will not commit adultery. But a wise wife will avoid situations where the possibility is alluring and the opportunity available. Why must society lead its members into temptation and then punish them when they do what they were tempted to do?

QUESTIONS

1. Upon what argumentative method does van den Haag place his primary reliance? How does he face up to the hard question of determining pornography's effect?
2. How does van den Haag define pornography? How does he distinguish it from literature? Would Lawrence ("Morality and the Novel," pp. 846–851) agree with his distinction?
3. In a reply to van den Haag, J. W. Lambert says: "Twice Mr.

van den Haag quite unnecessarily shows his cloven hoof—when making, as it happens, perfectly valid points: 'Were it [sadistic pornography] directed against specific human groups—e.g., Jews or Negroes—certainly most liberals would advocate that the circulation of such literature be prohibited.' He is quite right, of course, and this is one of the problems which champions of freedom are almost surely going to have to face in the near future. But the way he has chosen to phrase the observation makes it into an attack on liberal attitudes of mind rather than a strictly relevant comment on the subject under discussion. Again, 'Too many grown-ups,' he writes, 'are far from the self-restrained, healthy type envisaged by democratic theory.' Perfectly true, but the way in which he has chosen to frame the remark turns it into a sneer at democratic values." Is Lambert right? Lambert further says that the way van den Haag argues his case makes him appear to be a "muddle-headed authoritarian"; does it?

D. H. LAWRENCE
Morality and the Novel

The business of art is to reveal the relation between man and his circumambient universe, at the living moment. As mankind is always struggling in the toils of old relationships, art is always ahead of the "times," which themselves are always far in the rear of the living moment.

When Van Gogh paints sunflowers, he reveals, or achieves, the vivid relation between himself, as man, and the sunflower, as sunflower, at that quick moment of time. His painting does not represent the sunflower itself. We shall never know what the sunflower itself is. And the camera will *visualize* the sunflower far more perfectly than Van Gogh can.

The vision on the canvas is a third thing, utterly intangible and inexplicable, the offspring of the sunflower itself and Van Gogh himself. The vision on the canvas is forever incommensurable with the canvas, or the paint, or Van Gogh as a human organism, or the sunflower as a botanical organism. You cannot weigh nor measure nor even describe the vision on the canvas. It exists, to tell the truth, only in the much-debated fourth dimension. In dimensional space it has no existence.

It is a revelation of the perfected relation, at a certain moment, between a man and a sunflower. It is neither man-in-the-mirror nor flower-in-the-mirror, neither is it above or below or across anything. It is between everything, in the fourth dimension.

And this perfected relation between man and his circumambient universe is life itself, for mankind. It has the fourth-dimensional quality of eternity and perfection. Yet it is momentaneous.

Man and the sunflower both pass away from the moment, in the process of forming a new relationship. The relation between all things changes from day to day, in a subtle stealth of change. Hence art, which reveals or attains to another perfect relationship, will be forever new.

At the same time, that which exists in the non-dimensional space of pure relationship is deathless, lifeless, and eternal. That is, it gives us the *feeling* of being beyond life or death. We say an Assyrian lion or an Eyptian hawk's head "lives." What we really mean is that it is beyond life, and therefore beyond death. It gives us that feeling. And there is something inside us which must also be beyond life and beyond death, since that "feeling" which we get from an Assyrian lion or an Egyptian hawk's head is so infinitely precious to us. As the evening star, that spark of pure relation between night and day, has been precious to man since time began.

If we think about it, we find that our life *consists in* this achieving of a pure relationship between ourselves and the living universe about us. This is how I "save my soul" by accomplishing a pure relationship between me and another person, me and other people, me and a nation, me and a race of men, me and the animals, me and the trees or flowers, me and the earth, me and the skies and sun and stars, me and the moon: an infinity of pure relations, big and little, like the stars of the sky: that makes our eternity, for each one of us, me and the timber I am sawing, the lines of force I follow; me and dough I knead for bread, me and the very motion with which I write, me and the bit of gold I have got. This, if we knew it, is our life and our eternity: the subtle, perfected relation between me and my whole circumambient universe.

And morality is that delicate, forever trembling and changing *balance* between me and my circumambient universe, which precedes and accompanies a true relatedness.

Now here we see the beauty and the great value of the novel. Philosophy, religion, science, they are all of them busy nailing things down, to get a stable equilibrium. Religion, with its nailed-down One God, who says *Thou shalt, Thou shan't,* and hammers home every time; philosophy, with its fixed ideas; science with its "laws": they, all of them, all the time, want to nail us onto some tree or other.

But the novel, no. The novel is the highest example of subtle inter-relatedness that man has discovered. Everything is true in its own time, place, circumstance, and untrue outside of its own place, circumstance. If you try to nail anything down, in the novel, either it kills the novel, or the novel gets up and walks away with the nail.

Morality in the novel is the trembling instability of the balance. When the novelist puts his thumb in the scale, to pull down the balance to his own predilection, that is immorality.

The modern novel tends to become more and more immoral, as the novelist tends to press his thumb heavier and heavier in the pan: either on the side of love, pure love: or on the side of licentious "freedom."

The novel is not, as a rule, immoral because the novelist has any dominant *idea*, or *purpose*. The immorality lies in the novelist's helpless, unconscious predilection. Love is a great emotion. But if you set out to write a novel, and you yourself are in the throes of the great predilection for love, love as the supreme, the only emotion worth living for, then you will write an immoral novel.

Because no emotion is supreme, or exclusively worth living for. *All* emotions go to the achieving of a living relationship between a human being and the other human being or creature or thing he becomes purely related to. All emotions, including love and hate, and rage and tenderness, go to the adjusting of the oscillating, unestablished balance between two people who amount to anything. If the novelist puts his thumb in the pan, for love, tenderness, sweetness, peace, then he commits an immoral act: he *prevents* the possibility of a pure relationship, a pure relatedness, the only thing that matters: and he makes inevitable the horrible reaction, when he lets his thumb go, towards hate and brutality, cruelty and destruction.

Life is so made that opposites sway about a trembling center of balance. The sins of the fathers are visited on the children. If the fathers drag down the balance on the side of love, peace, and production, then in the third or fourth generation the balance will swing back violently to hate, rage, and destruction. We must balance as we go.

And of all the art forms, the novel most of all demands the trembling and oscillating of the balance. The "sweet" novel is more falsified, and therefore more immoral, than the blood-and-thunder novel.

The same with the smart and smudgily cynical novel, which says it doesn't matter what you do, because one thing is as good as another, anyhow, and prostitution is just as much "life" as anything else.

This misses the point entirely. A thing isn't life just because somebody does it. This the artist ought to know perfectly well. The ordinary bank clerk buying himself a new straw hat isn't "life" at all: it is just existence, quite all right, like everyday dinners: but not "life."

By life, we mean something that gleams, that has the fourth-dimensional quality. If the bank clerk feels really piquant about his hat, if he establishes a lively relation with it, and goes out of the shop with the new straw on his head, a changed man, be-aureoled, then that is life.

The same with the prostitute. If a man establishes a living relation to her, if only for one moment, then it is life. But if it
doesn't: if it is just money and function, then it is not life, but sor-
didness, and a betrayal of living.

If a novel reveals true and vivid relationships, it is a moral work,
no matter what the relationships may consist in. If the novelist
honors the relationship in itself, it will be a great novel.

But there are so many relationships which are not real. When
the man in *Crime and Punishment* murders the old woman for sixpence, although it is *actual* enough, it is never quite real. The balance between the murderer and the old woman is gone entirely; it
is only a mess. It is actuality, but it is not "life," in the living
sense.

The popular novel, on the other hand, dishes up a *réchauffé*[1]
of old relationships: *If Winter Comes*. And old relationships dished
up are likewise immoral. Even a magnificent painter like Raphael
does nothing more than dress up in gorgeous new dresses relationships which have already been experienced. And this gives a glut-
tonous kind of pleasure of the mass: a voluptuousness, a wallowing.
For centuries, men say of their voluptuously ideal woman: "She is
a Raphael Madonna." And women are only just learning to take it
as an insult.

A new relation, a new relatedness hurts somewhat in the attaining; and will always hurt. So life will always hurt. Because real voluptuousness lies in re-acting old relationships, and at the best, getting an alcoholic sort of pleasure out of it, slightly depraving.

Each time we strive to a new relation, with anyone or anything,
it is bound to hurt somewhat. Because it means the struggle with
and the displacing of old connections, and this is never pleasant.
And moreover, between living things at least, an adjustment means
also a fight, for each party, inevitably, must "seek its own" in the
other, and be denied. When, in the parties, each of them seeks his
own, her own, absolutely, then it is a fight to the death. And this is
true of the thing called "passion." On the other hand, when, of the
two parties, one yields utterly to the other, this is called sacrifice,
and it also means death. So the Constant Nymph[2] died of her
eighteen months of constancy.

It isn't the nature of nymphs to be constant. She should have
been constant in her nymphhood. And it is unmanly to accept sacrifices. He should have abided by his own manhood.

There is, however, the third thing, which is neither sacrifice nor
fight to the death: when each seeks only the true relatedness to the

---

1. Warmed-over meal.
2. The title character in a novel by
Margaret Kennedy. She dies shortly
after she goes off with the man to
whom she had been true although he
had married another girl.

other. Each must be true to himself, herself, his own manhood, her own womanhood, and let the relationship work out of itself. This means courage above all things: and then discipline. Courage to accept the life-thrust from within oneself, and from the other person. Discipline, not to exceed oneself any more than one can help. Courage, when one has exceeded oneself, to accept the fact and not whine about it.

Obviously, to read a really new novel will *always* hurt, to some extent. There will always be resistance. The same with new pictures, new music. You may judge of their reality by the fact that they do arouse a certain resistance, and compel, at length, a certain acquiescence.

The great relationship, for humanity, will always be the relation between man and woman. The relation between man and man, woman and woman, parent and child, will always be subsidiary.

And the relation between man and woman will change forever, and will forever be the new central clue to human life. It is the *relation itself* which is the quick and the central clue to life, not the man, nor the woman, nor the children that result from the relationship, as a contingency.

It is no use thinking you can put a stamp on the relation between man and woman, to keep it in the *status quo*. You can't. You might as well try to put a stamp on the rainbow or the rain.

As for the bond of love, better put it off when it galls. It is an absurdity, to say that men and women *must* love. Men and women will be forever subtly and changingly related to one another; no need to yoke them with any "bond" at all. The only morality is to have man true to his manhood, woman to her womanhood, and let the relationship form of itself, in all honor. For it is, to each, *life itself*.

If we are going to be moral, let us refrain from driving pegs through anything, either through each other or through the third thing, the relationship, which is forever the ghost of both of us. Every sacrificial crucifixion needs five pegs, four short ones and a long one, each one an abomination. But when you try to nail down the relationship itself, and write over it *Love* instead of *This is the King of the Jews*, then you can go on putting in nails forever. Even Jesus called it the Holy Ghost, to show you that you can't lay salt on its tail.

The novel is a perfect medium for revealing to us the changing rainbow of our living relationships. The novel can help us to live, as nothing else can: no didactic Scripture, anyhow. If the novelist keeps his thumb out of the pan.

But when the novelist *has* his thumb in the pan, the novel becomes an unparalleled perverter of men and women. To be compared only, perhaps to that great mischief of sentimental hymns, like "Lead, Kindly Light," which have helped to rot the marrow in the bones of the present generation.

QUESTIONS

1. Lawrence writes sentence fragments, and, when speaking of the insubstantiality of the Holy Ghost, he says that "you can't lay salt on its tail." A writer like that is not going to approve of fancy phrases; yet he often refers to the "circumambient universe." What does that mean? Is it a fancy phrase? Would his fourth dimension, the dimension "between," have the same value if his universe were not "circumambient"?
2. What is "life" according to Lawrence? How does he go about defining it?
3. Why is it that, according to Lawrence, a novelist's advocacy of love and peace would be immoral?
4. Lawrence places the highest value on the relation between man and woman and says that the morality which governs it derives from "manhood" and "womanhood." Do "manhood" and "womanhood" exist in human beings, the circumambient universe, or in between? How does this idea of Lawrence's compare with Erikson's mutuality (pp. 874–875)?

RICHARD M. HARE

Philosophy, Ethics, and Racial Discrimination[1]

I will start with a brief and general classification, with examples, of arguments that might be used by people when faced with conflicts between races. I do not hope to make this classification very profound or complete; for I am aiming only to produce instances of the chief sorts of argument that are of logical interest. I shall start with arguments concerned with matters of fact; and I shall subdivide these into those concerned with genuine matters of fact, and those concerned with questions which look like questions of fact but turn out not to be. I shall then consider various moral arguments which could still go on even when the facts are agreed. I hope that this classification will be of some philosophical interest, as shedding light on the relation between facts and moral judgments.

First, then, genuine questions of fact. In this class, we may mention first questions about the actual characteristics of different races. And these can be subdivided into (1) questions about their capabilities; (2) questions about their moral and other propensities; and (3) questions about what it is like to *be* a member of such and such a race in such and such a situation.

1. From Chapter 11 in *Freedom and Reason*.

1. *The capabilities of different races.* It is sometimes said that black people are incapable of self-government, or of leadership (political or otherwise), or of acquiring an advanced education, or even certain practical skills. Now, if these allegations were true, it would have an effect on some moral arguments; for obviously it is no use maintaining that black people *ought* to be allowed to exercise self-government if they *cannot* do so; and it is no use saying that they ought to be made foremen, if they cannot do the job of foremen. The "argument from incapability" is not always put in this extreme form. Sometimes it is said merely that black people, though they *can* acquire these capabilities, cannot acquire them to the same degree and are therefore bound to remain inferior to white people in these respects. It is not at all clear that the weaker form of the thesis has the consequences for moral arguments which follow from the stronger form. For example, black people might not be able to govern themselves according to the standards which are said to be observed in Westminster: but this would not be an argument against the view that they ought to be allowed to govern themselves in whatever way they can. Alternatively, it may be said that black people, though they may become capable of governing themselves, etc., at some date in the distant future, are not capable of doing so now. This, if admitted, would have an important bearing on some moral questions, but not the same bearing as either of the other two theses mentioned.

2. *The moral and other propensities of races.* It is sometimes said that members of a certain race inherit, either genetically or culturally, defects of character which might make it right to treat them differently from other races. The Jews have often been a target for such accusations; and it has also been alleged from time to time that Orientals of certain races are less truthful or less trustworthy than Englishmen claim to be. If these arrogant-sounding accusations were established, they would have some bearing on moral arguments; but how powerful it was would depend on the particular defect that existed. One would also, if the defect was inherited culturally and not genetically, have to consider to what extent the cultural and social factors causing the perpetuation of the defect were the fault of the members of the race itself, and to what extent they were the result of the actions of other races—e.g., the persecution of the Jews.

These two kinds of factual arguments are not such as can be established or refuted by philosophical reasoning. They have to be shown to be true or false by the means appropriate to the examination of alleged facts of these kinds—i.e., by the objective study of history and, in appropriate cases, by social or psychological surveys and experiments. The sincerity of people who make these kinds of allegation can, indeed, be put to the proof by seeing whether they are willing to submit to these objective tests.

3. *What it is like to be a member of a certain race.* Another type of factual argument which may be adduced in moral disputes about race relations is concerned with the effect of certain sorts of treatment upon the happiness, etc., of the members of a certain race. Thus, it has sometimes been maintained that to use black people as slaves, or in conditions resembling slavery, is not cruel in the same way as it would be to use white people as slaves, because black people do not have the same sensibilities as white. An extreme form of this argument is the doctrine that blacks are like animals, or (it has sometimes even been said) actually *are* animals—though this is really a spurious factual argument and will be treated later. It is certainly true that if working on a farm in conditions similar to those of an ox on the same farm were no more a cause of unhappiness to a Bantu than to an ox, certain moral arguments against treating the Bantu in this way would not be available.

Now there are difficulties in assessing this kind of factual argument which there are not in the cases of the first two kinds mentioned. For there are notorious philosophical obstacles to verifying propositions about the feelings of other people. We can, however, sidestep these difficulties by saying that the difficulty of knowing what it feels like to be a Bantu is, at any rate, nothing like so great as that of knowing what it feels like to be an ox; and that the difficulty is one of the same kind as, and greater only in degree than, that of knowing what it is like to be James, my twin brother. The practical, as opposed to the philosophical, difficulty of knowing what it feels like to be a Bantu on a farm is to be got over by a closer and more sympathetic acquaintance with individual Bantus on farms. I shall not resume until later the question of why it is relevant to moral arguments to know what it feels like to be a Bantu.

One other more particular type of factual argument needs to be mentioned; it is not coordinate with the first three, but is a way of applying one or more of them to actual situations. It is sometimes said that if certain racial policies are pursued, the results will be so and so—with the implication that these results ought to be avoided at all costs, and that therefore the policy ought to be rejected. For example, it may be argued that if the pass laws are repealed, there will be no check on subversive activities by members of the subject race, and that all sorts of violence will then break out, leading eventually to a breakdown of ordered government. Or it may be argued that if the color bar is at all relaxed, miscegenation will result (it being taken for granted that this would be an unspeakable evil). These arguments are simply examples of a type of argument which is exceedingly common in morals, and might, indeed, be said to be a constituent in any moral argument. It is of the form "If you do *this* in *these* circumstances, what you will be doing is to bring about *these* consequences." The effect of such an argument is to show what, *in concreto,* the person will be doing if he does what he is proposing. In racial contexts such arguments often depend on arguments of the type already considered: e.g., it has sometimes been said that if Jews are allowed to do business without restriction, they will, because of their moral and other propensities, soon get a stranglehold on the economy of some country and use it against the interests of non-Jews, and it was sometimes said that if Indians were allowed a greater share in the government of India, there would be, because of their incompetence and corruptibility, a breakdown of the high standards of administration maintained by the (British-staffed) Indian Civil Service. If such hypothetical predictions had been correct, then the further question would have arisen of whether the states of affairs predicted were worse than the states of affairs which would come into being if alternative policies were pursued. But, subject to this proviso, this is a perfectly legitimate argument in morals, if the premises are true. That is to say, it is quite in order to try to show that the facts are such that if a certain policy is pursued then a certain moral principle will be observed or infringed; and the argument then shifts to questions of moral principle.

Let us now turn from genuine factual arguments to spurious ones. These are forthcoming from both parties to most racial questions; they are not the monopoly of those of whose policies liberals disapprove. However, I shall start with arguments which are put forward by people of whose policies the majority of my readers will disapprove; I shall thus, perhaps, the more easily display the fallaciousness of the arguments; and then I shall turn to some similar arguments, just as lacking in cogency, which are used by those who are on the angels' side.

Suppose that a Nazi argues that he has a right to persecute members of non-Germanic races because there is something in the hereditary makeup (in the "blood," he might say) of the Germanic races which gives them a natural superiority over other races and a right to make them their subjects. This looks at first sight very like some perfectly good factual arguments that we mentioned earlier; we have the statement that the facts are such that a certain moral principle applies. But the argument suffers from two fatal weaknesses. In the first place, no determinate criterion is given for discovering whether this factor is present in the heredity or blood of any particular person. No empirical tests are offered for determining the truth of the assertion that members of Germanic races actually have this mark of natural superiority to members of other races. So the argument rests on statements of "fact" whose truth is in principle not ascertainable; and therefore we can never know whether the premises of the argument, or its conclusion, are true. We do not need to be logical positivists to reject this sort of argument; but if anyone does accept some kind of verification theory of meaning, he will go further, and say that the premises of such arguments are not merely untestable but meaningless. Into this question I shall not go, merely remarking that here is an instance where a seemingly quite abstract philosophical controversy has a direct application to practical questions.

In the second place, even if the premises of these arguments were all right, the users of them have not told us *why* the moral conclusions follow from the premises. In order that the presence of this blood-factor in Germans should justify their domination of other races, it has to be the case that the factor confers a right to dominate; and it is hard to see why this should be so. Even if it could be proved by experiment that whenever the blood of a German has a certain chemical added to it it turns purple, and that this is so with the blood of no other race, it is not thereby established that any moral consequences follow from this. We shall have to postpone further consideration of this question until we have come back to the general question of the place of factual premises in moral arguments.

As further examples of this type of spurious factual argument, we may mention the argument that Christians may persecute Jews, because certain Jews said on a famous occasion "His blood be upon us and upon our children",[2] and the argument that white people may make black people their subjects, because black people are the descendants of Ham, and it says in the Bible that Noah cursed the descendants of Ham because Ham had looked at Noah's naked body when Noah was in a drunken stupor.[3] In both cases there is no conceivable way of discovering whether an individual Jew or Bantu who is being maltreated is really the descendant of Ham, or of a member of the crowd outside Pilate's palace; and, even if they were, it is not in the least clear why this should justify their maltreatment.

Let us now consider some examples of arguments suffering from these same two defects which are often used by more respectable people. It is often said that white people ought to treat black people better because they are their brothers; or because they are, like whites, children of God. As before, no criterion is stated for determining whether an individual member of some other race is or is not my "brother," in the extended sense, or whether he is or is not a child of God; if two people were arguing about whether the natives of a certain territory were or were not children of God, it is entirely unclear by what tests they could ever settle their argument.

2. Matthew xxvii.25 [Hare's note].   3. Genesis ix.25 [Hare's note].

We cannot, indeed, deny the value of these forms of expression as metaphors; but what we need to do is to find out what they are metaphors for, and whether propositions expressed in terms of them are, when put unmetaphorically, true.

Secondly, even if it could be established beyond doubt that a certain man was my "brother," or that he was a "child of God," it is not clear why it follows that I ought to treat him in a certain way. What moral principles are the basis of my duties even to my real brothers, or to the children of my human father? Admittedly, if we agree, as most of us do, that we have certain duties to our real brothers, then these duties must have as their ground *something* about the relation "being a brother of." It would need to be elucidated what this something is—for until this is done we shall not know what is the principle involved. Has it, for example, something to do with common nurture, and does it therefore extend to foster-brothers? Or has it something to do with common parenthood, and if so do both parents have to be the same or only one? If we could answer these questions, we should then know the precise features of brothers which we think to be the grounds of our duties towards them. It would then become a question whether black people, who are our brothers only in an extended sense, possess, in common with our real brothers, those features which are the grounds of our duties to our real brothers. And it is, to say the least, rather unlikely that this would prove to be the case.

* * *

There are the same sort of difficulties with the expression "child of God." It is not obvious *a priori* that we ought to treat fellow-children of God in certain ways. We require, presumably, the general premise that God's will ought to be done, and the particular premise that God wills his children to treat one another in certain ways. Well-known philosophical problems arise concerning both these premises; but there is not room to discuss them here.

We may notice, lastly in this class of arguments, one which can be shown to possess the same defects as these ones, but which nevertheless enjoys a certain philosophical respectability, and which is therefore worth examining in more detail. This is the argument that we ought to treat blacks in certain ways because they are *people*. Now it must be said at the start that this argument is in fact an attempted shortcut; it is perfectly possible, given that blacks are people, and given also certain other assumptions, to reason cogently that they ought to be treated in the same way as other people. This I shall later attempt to show. But the argument is nevertheless worthless as it stands, since it suffers from the same defects as I have already exposed. In order to turn it into a cogent piece of reasoning, we have to bring out into the open certain concealed steps in the argument and certain suppressed assumptions; and the complaint to be made against those who use this kind of argument is not that they arrive at wrong conclusions, but that they bury the really important and interesting factors in the arguments, and thus conceal from us some very fundamental features of moral arguments and of moral discourse in general. It is only by understanding these fundamental features that the arguments can be seen to be cogent. The shortcut proposed has thus to be condemned for two reasons: it gets to a desirable conclusion by a fallacious mode of reasoning which could also be used to justify the most damnable conclusions; and, by seeming to offer an easy way to this desirable conclusion, it encourages us to leave off our study of moral philosophy when it has reached only a very superficial level. As it stands, the inference from "X is a person" to "I ought to be kind to X" is logically no better than that from "X is a non-Aryan" to "I ought to put X in the gas-chamber."

In order to understand this, let us first notice that the "people" argument suffers from the same defects as the "brothers" and "children of God" arguments. No criterion is offered for determining whether something is a person or not. Is it sufficient to be a live member of the human species? It does not seem to follow from the fact that a black person is a live member of the human species that I ought to treat him in any particular way. So if we have *this* determinate criterion for being called a person, no moral conclusion seems to follow from the fact that someone is a person. The same will be the case whatever determinate criterion we are given. For example, it may be said that someone is a person if he has the power of rational choice. But it will still not be obvious why a human being who has this power ought to be allowed to exercise this choice as much as possible, for no grounds have been given for this contention.

Suppose, in general, that there is a determinate criterion for deciding whether a given being is a person or not. It will then require establishing that we ought to treat such a being in one way rather than in another. Faced with this challenge, a defender of this type of argument might make his principle indubitable by making it analytic. He might say that by establishing that X is a person one has established that X ought to be treated as a person; and that this is analytic, because "as a person" means merely "as a person ought to be treated." But though it is, certainly, analytic that people ought to be treated as people ought to be treated, the question is, how ought people to be treated?

One way that might be suggested for getting out of this difficulty is to write into the notion of a person some moral content. By calling a being a person we should then imply, as part of what we are saying, that he ought to be treated in a certain way. This will validate the step from "X is a person" to "X ought to be treated in a certain way." But now we are left without a determinate and morally neutral criterion for finding out whether he *is* a person. In order to be sure that he is a person, we shall first have to satisfy ourselves that he ought to be treated in a certain way, and no basis has yet been established for making this moral judgment.

Having dealt with a number of arguments which are unsatisfactory, and with others which are incomplete, in that they appeal to antecedent moral principles, we come now to the constructive part of this chapter.

Let us ask, first, why it is that we think what I have called factual arguments to be relevant to moral questions. Why did I say that certain factual arguments (for example about the predictable results of certain policies) were perfectly admissible; and why, on the other hand, do we have this strange phenomenon of Nazis and others inventing obviously spurious factual arguments in order to justify their actions morally? Why not just get on with the job of exterminating the Jews? What need is supplied by the bogus claim that Germans have some special element in their heredity which distinguishes them from other men? Or why does it make a difference to the moral argument that a certain policy would have a certain result? It looks as if facts (or some sorts of facts) are held to be relevant to moral arguments; so much so that if one has not got any genuine facts one invents some make-believe ones. But why is this? In short, what is the bearing of facts on moral arguments? This is one of the central problems of moral philosophy.

An obvious, and so far as it goes true, but incomplete, answer to the question "Why are facts relevant to moral arguments?" is this: moral judgments have to be *about something*; and it is the facts of the case which determine what we are judging. Thus, when we are asking moral questions about a proposed action, it is relevant to know what the person would be doing who did the action; for, if we do not know this, we literally shall not know what we are talking about.

I say that this answer is incomplete for two reasons. The first is that it does not explain why we think some facts, and not others, relevant to moral arguments. The second is that it does not explain why it makes a difference if it is a *moral* argument. If I were deciding just what *to do*, without any thought of what I *ought* to do, it would still be important to me to know *what* I should be doing if I did so and so. We shall see that these two incompletenesses are related to each other.

There are some philosophers who can see only one possible way in which facts might have relevance in moral arguments. This is by there being some logical link, holding in virtue of the meanings of words, between factual premises and moral conclusions. Now I do not think that there is any such link. And because these philosophers have eyes only for this sort of relevance, they think that if I deny the possibility of such a link, I am committed to holding that facts are not relevant to moral arguments; and this would be an absurd position. But what I have been maintaining is that facts are relevant to moral arguments, but not in the way that these people think.

Facts are relevant to moral arguments because they make a difference between cases which would otherwise be similar. Let us illustrate this by considering again why the Nazis set so much store by the claim that there is something in the blood of Germans which differentiates them from other races. The explanation is that they were proposing to treat other races in a markedly different way from Germans, and wanted a reason why they *ought* to do this. A Nazi might say, as he contemplated the Jews that he was just driving into the gas-chamber, "These men look just as I would look if I were starved and naked like them; they have the same feelings and aspirations, and there is, apparently, no other relevant difference between them and myself or my German friends. And I would not think it right to treat a German in this way. But there is something that makes a difference; although Germans and Jews are often indistinguishable to the naked eye, there is this all-important thing about them, that they lack that factor in their heredity which true Germans have, and which entitles Germans to send them to the gas-chamber." Put thus crudely, the argument sounds grotesque; yet something of the sort undoubtedly lies behind many claims of racial superiority. And this parody of moral thinking, just because it is a parody of moral thinking, illustrates extremely well the role which even bogus facts can play in moral arguments—even bad ones. This argument of the Nazis is pretending to be like a perfectly good moral argument, and thus shows us something about what a good moral argument would be like.

The point is this: it is part of the meanings of the moral words that we are logically prohibited from making different moral judgments about two cases, when we cannot adduce any difference between the cases which is the ground for the difference in moral judgments. This is one way of stating the requirement of universalizability which is fundamental to all moral reasoning. Since the Nazi cannot justify his different treatment of Germans and Jews without adducing some difference between their cases, he invents a difference

Other participants in race conflicts are more fortunate: they do not have to invent anything; the difference is there, for all to see, in the color of their victims' skins. This is why it seems so much easier to justify racial discrimination when there is a color difference than when there is not. But even less obvious differences than those of color will serve if they have to. What is important to the would-be discriminator is that there should be *some* qualitative difference (i.e. not merely a numerical difference) between the class of people whom he wishes to oppress, exploit, or persecute and those whom he does not. Some of us remember how, at school, the wearing of shoes of a different pattern was enough to mark out some poor boy for maltreatment.

These caricatures of moral reasoning teach us something about the real thing. It is indeed required that, to justify different treatment of people, qualitative differences have to be produced between them or between their actions or circumstances. We try to justify our singular moral judgments by producing principles involved in them: one may or ought to do such and such a *kind* of thing in such and such a *kind* of situation to people of a certain *kind*.

Now these examples of spurious moral reasoning are parodies. The question which next arises, therefore, is, How do we distinguish the parody from its original? If we do not think that it is an adequate justification for discriminating against a person that his skin is black, how would we distinguish those features of the man or his situation which do justify different treatment from those which do not? There seems at first sight to be no formal difference between saying "It is right to kill him because his skin is black" and saying "It is right to kill him because he has killed another man." Some people regard both of these as good reasons; some, neither; and some, one but not the other. We have therefore to ask, can moral philosophy point out any means of distinguishing between good and bad reasons of this sort; or, in other words, between relevant differences, such as really do justify discrimination, and those which are not relevant? Have we any reason for saying that black skin is not relevant, but being a murderer is?

There are those who try to answer this question in the following way. They take a look at the kind of differences that people *do* call morally relevant; and they make a list of them, reduce them if they can to some sort of system, and then say that we *mean* by "morally relevant difference" just these differences and no others, and *mean* by "morality" just that system of evaluations which takes these, and no other, differences into account. There are many objections to this procedure; I will here mention just two. First, how do we know that we could not get a different list if we did the investigation in South Africa or Soviet Russia or ancient Sparta? Secondly, to make such a list does not explain anything; we want to know what leads to things getting put on the list or left off it. The proponents of this view do not seem to have gone far enough in their search for an explanation.

Now, if the argument of this book is correct, we can in fact go a good deal further, by a step which is really no different in principle from one which we took a moment ago. We saw that it follows from the meanings of the moral terms that if different moral judgments are made, relevant differences must be adduced; and we saw that this was a version of the requirement of universalizability.

In order to illustrate this use again, let us suppose that we are having an argument with a man who maintains that a black skin, by itself, is a sufficient ground for discriminating against its possessor. We tell him, and he, being a credulous person, believes, the following story. The Soviet Institute of Race Relations (which is a much more enterprising and scientific body than its Western counterparts) has just succeeded in breeding a new kind of bacillus, which Soviet agents are at this very moment broadcasting in areas of racial conflict throughout the world. This bacillus is very catching, and the symptom of the disease which it induces is that, if the patient's skin was white, it turns permanently black, and vice versa. Now when the person with whom we are arguing has absorbed the implications of this story, we ask him whether he still thinks that skin-color by itself is a sufficient ground for moral discrimination. It is unlikely that he will go on saying that it is; for then he will have to say that if he catches the disease the former blacks who have also had it will have acquired the right to oppress *him*, and all his formerly white friends.

What do we learn from this simple piece of science fiction? What we have got our opponent to do by this innocent deception is to perform an intellectual operation which, if he had really been wanting to reason morally, he would have performed without the deception. This operation is to consider the hypothetical case in which he himself has lost the quality which he said was a sufficient ground for discrimination, and his present victims have gained it—and to consider this hypothetical case as if it were actual. There are two stages in the process of universalization. The first is passed when we have found a universal principle, not containing proper names or other singular terms, from which the moral judgment which we want to make follows, given the facts of our particular situation. This stage is comparatively easy to pass, even for the proponent of the most scandalous moral views. It is passed, for example, by adducing the principle that it is all right for black people to be oppressed by white people. But the next stage is more difficult. It is necessary, not merely that this principle should be produced, but that the person who produces it should actually hold it. It is necessary not merely to *quote* a maxim, but (in Kantian language) to *will* it to be a universal law. It is here that prescriptivity, the second main logical feature of moral judgments, makes its most decisive appearance. For willing it to be a universal law involves willing it to apply even when the roles played by the parties are reversed. And this test will be failed by all maxims or principles which look attractive to oppressors and persecutors on the first test. It will indeed be found that, if we apply these two tests, both founded on the logical, formal features of moral terms, we shall be able to sort out, in the field of race relations at least, the grounds of discrimination which we are really prepared to count as morally relevant from those which we are not.

From this satisfactory conclusion, however, there is, as we have seen, a way of escape for the sufficiently determined racialist. It remains to illustrate, in terms of the present example, what price he has to pay for his escape. Let us suppose that there is a racialist the mainspring of whose racialism is a horror of miscegenation; and let us suppose that the source of this horror is not any belief about the consequences, social or biological, of miscegenation. That is to say, he is not moved by alleged facts about the weakening of the human stock by mating between people of different colors, or about the unsatisfactory life lived by people of mixed descent, or by anything of that kind. If these were his grounds, we could argue with him in a scientific way, trying to show that the offspring of mixed marriages are just as likely to be vigorous and intelligent as those of other marriages; or that any bad social effects of miscegenation would be removed if *he* and people like him abandoned their attempts to enforce a color bar. Let us suppose, however, that his grounds are not these, but simply a horror of the very idea of a black man mating with a white woman. This cannot be touched by any scientific or factual argument of the sort described. And it may well be true that, if miscegenation is to be prevented, it is necessary to have a rigid color bar; and that if this is enforced, and leads to resentment, other repressive measures will be necessary for the maintenance of public order, and thus we shall have the whole apparatus of racial repression. If this is true, then it will be hard for us to argue with this man. He detests miscegenation so much that he is prepared to live in a police state in order to avoid it.

And he must be prepared for more than this. He must, if he is going to universalize his moral judgments, be prepared that he himself should not merely live in a police state, but live in it in the same conditions as he is now prepared to make the blacks live in—conditions which are getting steadily worse. He must be prepared that *he* should be subject to arbitrary arrest and maltreatment just on grounds of skin color, and to butchery if he tries, in collaboration with his fellows, to protest.

Now it may be that there are people so fanatical as to be prepared for all these things in order to avoid miscegenation. But they are surely very few. The repression happens because these few people have on their side a multitude of other people who are not prepared at all to suffer thus, but who have not really thought through the argument. They think, perhaps, that all will be well without too much repression; or that blacks do not mind being treated like this as much as whites would; or that there is a scientific basis for belief in racial superiority—or some of the many other things that racialists tend to believe. All these beliefs can perhaps be refuted severally by scientists and others without any help from the philosopher; but they are apt, collectively, to form an amalgam in the minds of racialists which makes into allies of the fanatic many people who are not, in themselves, in the least fanatical. The contribution of the philosopher is to take this amalgam apart, deposit such beliefs as are open to scientific refutation in the in-trays of the scientists, and, when the scientists have dealt with them, exhibit the prescriptive remainder of racialism for what it is—something that fanatics may hold but which the bulk of a people—even a people as hard-pressed as the white South Africans—never will.

We are now in a position to explain why, in spite of the inadequacy of an argument which we mentioned earlier, it *is* morally relevant that blacks are people. Saying that they are people is saying that they are like us in certain respects. It is not clear yet in *what* respects; this will be found to vary from case to case, as we shall see. But the principle of this argument from the fact that blacks are people can now be exposed as follows. If a black man whom I am contemplating maltreating has, as I have every reason to suppose that he has, certain characteristics in common with myself—if, to use an example from an earlier century, it causes him great suffering if he and his wife are separated and sent as slaves to different countries—then I can reason as follows. I am not prepared in general to accept the maxim that it is all right for people to separate husbands from wives for commercial gain, for this would be committing myself to the judgment that it would be all right for somebody to do this to me if he were in a position to do so. But can I say that it is all right to do this to blacks? The answer must be "No," for if I envisage myself becoming a black, but retaining my other characteristics, and in particular the characteristic of being attached to my wife, I am not (since I am not a fanatic for the liberty of commerce) prepared to accept a maxim which permits people to do this to me.

On the other hand, if we take the example of the murderer mentioned above, the position is altered. I may very well be prepared to prescribe that, if I commit a murder, I should be hanged. In actual fact I am not for I am not a supporter of capital punishment—for reasons which are irrelevant to the present argument. But let us, in order to avoid this difficulty, substitute "put in prison" for "hanged" or "killed." I am prepared to prescribe that if I commit a murder I should be put in prison: and my reasons are utilitarian ones. But reasons of this sort are not available to racialists. Thus we see why it is thought not to be relevant that the man is black, but is thought to be relevant that a man is a murderer. More important, we see why it is thought to be relevant that a slave loves his wife. The duties which we acknowledge towards people are not derived from the "essence of man" or from any philosophical mystifications of that sort; they are acknowledged because we say "There, but for my good fortune, go I. That man is like me in important respects; in particular, the same things as cause me to suffer cause him to suffer therefore, unless I am prepared to accept a maxim which would permit me to be treated like him were I to acquire a black skin (which I am not), I cannot say that it is all right for me to treat him thus."

This line of reasoning also helps to explain why we recognize certain duties. towards both men and animals, but certain others towards men only. For example, nobody would be thought to be oppressing animals because he did not allow them self-government; but, on the other hand, it is generally thought to be wrong to torture animals for fun. Now why is it that we do not acknowledge a duty to accord animals self-government? It is simply because we think that there is a real and relevant difference between men and animals in this respect. We can say "If I were turned into an animal, I should stop having any desire for political liberty, and therefore the lack of it would be no hardship to me." It is possible to say this even of men in certain stages of development. Nobody thinks that children ought to have complete political liberty; and most people recognize that it would be foolish to introduce the more advanced kinds of political liberty all at once in backward countries, where people have not got to the stage of wanting it, and would not know what to do with it if they got it. So this mode of reasoning allows us to make the many distinctions that are necessary in assessing our obligations towards different *kinds* of people, and indeed of sentient beings. In all cases the principle is the same—am I prepared to accept a maxim which would allow this to be done to me, were I in the position of this man or animal, and capable of having only the experiences, desires, etc., of him or it?

It may be objected that not all people will follow this mode of reasoning which I have been suggesting. Those who indulged in bear-baiting did not reason: "If we were bears we should suffer horribly if treated thus; therefore we cannot accept any maxim which permits bears to be treated thus; therefore we cannot say that it is all right to treat bears thus." And no doubt there are some white South Africans (a few) who will be quite unmoved by being told that they are causing the Bantu to suffer. It seems that I am required to say what has gone wrong in such cases.

A number of different things may have gone wrong. The commonest is what we call insensitivity or lack of imagination. The bear-baiter does not really imagine what it is like to be a bear. If he did, he would think and act differently. Another way of putting this is to say that these people are not paying attention to the relevant similarities between themselves and their victims. If we like to revert to the metaphor, having understood what it stands for, the bear-baiter is not thinking of the bear as his brother—or even cousin.

It is also possible that, though fully aware of what they are doing to their victims, they are not reasoning morally about it. That is to say, they are not asking themselves whether they can universalize their prescriptions; though they may make play with the moral *words* which they have heard other people use, they are not, in their own thinking, using these words according to the logical rules which are implicit in their meaning. And there are other possibilities, too numerous to mention here.

It may be asked: What is to be done about this? Can the philosopher, in particular, do anything about it? When South African believers in white supremacy read this book, will they at once hasten to repeal the pass laws and make the blacks their political equals? This is highly unlikely; and in any case they will not read the book. To get people to think morally it is not sufficient to tell them how to do it; it is necessary also to induce in them the wish to do it. And this is not the province of the philosopher. It is more likely that enlightened politicians, journalists, radio commentators, preachers, novelists, and all those who have an influence on public opinion will gradually effect a change for the better—given that events do not overtake them. Perhaps people in areas of racial conflict can be, in the end, brought to think of the resemblances between themselves and members of other races as morally relevant, and of the differences as morally irrelevant. Perhaps, even, they may learn to cultivate their imaginations. But this much can be claimed for philosophy, that it is sometimes easier to bring something about if we understand clearly what it is we are trying to do.

QUESTIONS

1. Hare's discussion is full of heavily explicit transitions and "signposts" ("Having dealt with . . . we come. . . ."; "We are now in a position. . . ."); are they justifiable?
2. What is Hare's objection to the argument that whites "ought to treat blacks in certain ways because they are people"?
3. What moral function would Hare assign to the novel as Lawrence conceives of it (pp. 846–851)? Is it likely that they would conceive of it similarly?

4. Are there other applications of Hare's analysis, i.e., in questions relating to war, drugs, sexual relationships?
5. According to Hare, what is the function of the philosopher in matters of ethics? In "The Golden Rule in the Light of New Insight," (pp. 866–883) Erikson writes from a psychoanalytic perspective; is his golden rule significantly different from Hare's universalizability?

ERIK H. ERIKSON

The Golden Rule in the Light of New Insight[1]

When a lecture is announced one does not usually expect the title to foretell very much about the content. But it must be rare, indeed, that a title is as opaque as the one on your invitation to this lecture: for it does not specify the field from which new insight is to come and throw new light on the old principle of the Golden Rule. You took a chance, then, in coming, and now that I have been introduced as a psychoanalyst, you must feel that you have taken a double chance.

Let me tell you, therefore, how I came upon our subject. In Harvard College, I teach a course, "The Human Life Cycle." There (since I am by experience primarily a clinician) we begin by considering those aggravated *crises* which mark each stage of life and are known to psychiatry as potentially pathogenic. But we proceed to discuss the potential *strengths* which each stage contributes to human maturity. In either case, so psychiatric experience and the observation of healthy children tell us, much depends on the interplay of generations in which human strength can be revitalized or human weakness perseverated "into the second and third generation." But this leads us to the role of the individual in the sequence of generations, and thus to that evolved order which your scriptures call *Lokasangraha*—the "maintenance of the world" (in Professor Radhakrishnan's translation). Through the study of case-histories and of life-histories we psychoanalysts have begun to discern certain fateful and certain fruitful patterns of interaction in those most concrete categories (parent and child, man and woman, teacher and pupil) which carry the burden of maintenance from generation to generation. The implication of our insights for ethics had preoccupied me before I came here; and, as you will well understand, a few months of animated discussion in India have by no means disabused me from such concerns. I have, therefore, chosen to tell you where I stand in my teaching, in the hope of learning more from you in further discussion.

1. An address given in India at the University of Delhi.

My base line is the Golden Rule, which advocates that one should do (or not do) to another what one wishes to be (or not to be) done by. Systematic students of ethics often indicate a certain disdain for this all-too-primitive ancestor of more logical principles; and Bernard Shaw found the rule an easy target: don't do to another what you would like to be done by, he warned, because his tastes may differ from yours. Yet this rule has marked a mysterious meeting ground between ancient peoples separated by oceans and eras, and has provided a hidden theme in the most memorable sayings of many thinkers.

The Golden Rule obviously concerns itself with one of the very basic paradoxes of human existence. Each man calls his own a separate body, a self-conscious individuality, a personal awareness of the cosmos, and a certain death; and yet he shares this world as a *reality* also perceived and judged by others and as an *actuality* within which he must commit himself to ceaseless interaction. This is acknowledged in your scriptures as the principle of Karma.

To identify self-interest and the interest of other selves, the Rule alternately employs the method of warning, "Do *not* as you would *not* be done by," and of exhortation, "Do, as you *would* be done by." For psychological appeal, some versions rely on a minimum of *egotistic prudence,* while others demand a maximum of *altruistic sympathy.* It must be admitted that the formula, "Do not to others what if done to you would cause you pain," does not presuppose much more than the mental level of the small child who desists from pinching when it gets pinched in return. More mature insight is assumed in the saying, "No one is a believer until he loves for his brother what he loves for himself." Of all the versions, however, none commit us as unconditionally as the Upanishad's, "he who sees all beings in his own self and his own self in all beings," and the Christian injunction, "love thy neighbor as thyself." They even suggest a true love and a true knowledge of ourselves. Freud, of course, took this Christian maxim deftly apart as altogether illusory, thus denying with the irony of the enlightenment what a maxim really is—and what (as I hope to show) his method may really stand for.

I will not (I could not) trace the versions of the Rule to various world religions. No doubt in English translation all of them have become somewhat assimilated to Biblical versions. Yet the basic formula seems to be universal, and it re-appears in an astonishing number of the most revered sayings of our civilization, from St. Francis' prayer to Kant's moral imperative and Lincoln's simple political creed: "As I would not be slave, I would not be master."

The variations of the Rule have, of course, provided material for many a discussion of ethics weighting the soundness of the logic implied and measuring the degree of ethical nobility reached in each. My field of inquiry, the clinical study of the human life cycle, suggests that I desist from arguing logical merit or spiritual worth and instead distinguish *variations in moral and ethical sensitivity* in accordance with stages in the development of human conscience.

The dictionary, our first refuge from ambiguity, in this case only confounds it: morals and ethics are defined as synonyms *and* antonyms of each other. In other words, they are the same, with a difference—a difference which I intend to emphasize. For it is clear that he who knows what is legal or illegal and what is moral or immoral has not necessarily learned thereby what is ethical. Highly moralistic people can do unethical things, while an ethical man's involvement in immoral doings becomes by inner necessity an occasion for tragedy.

I would propose that we consider *moral rules* of conduct to be based on a fear of *threats* to be forestalled. These may be outer threats of abandonment, punishment and public exposure, or a threatening inner sense of guilt, of shame or of isolation. In either case, the rationale for obeying a rule may not be too clear; it is the threat that counts. In contrast, I would consider *ethical rules* to be based on *ideals* to be striven for with a high degree of rational assent and with a ready consent to a formulated good, a definition of perfection, and some promise of self-realization. This differentiation may not agree with all existing definitions, but it is substantiated by the observation of human development. Here, then, is my first proposition: the moral and the ethical sense are different in their psychological dynamics, because the moral sense develops on an earlier, more immature level. This does not mean that the moral sense could be skipped, as it were. On the contrary, all that exists layer upon layer in an adult's mind has developed step by step in the growing child's, and all the major steps in the comprehension of what is considered good behavior in one's cultural universe are—for better and for worse—related to different stages in individual maturation. But they are all necessary to one another.

The response to a moral tone of voice develops early, and many an adult is startled when inadvertently he makes an infant cry, because his voice has conveyed more disapproval than he intended to. Yet, the small child, so limited to the intensity of the moment, somehow must learn the boundaries marked by "don'ts." Here, cultures have a certain leeway in underscoring the goodness of one who does not transgress or the evilness of one who does. But the conclusion is unavoidable that children can be made to feel evil, and that adults continue to project evil on one another and on their children far beyond the verdict of rational judgment. Mark Twain once characterized man as "the animal that blushes."

Psychoanalytic obervation first established the psychological basis of a fact which Eastern thinkers have always known, namely, that the radical division into good and bad can be *the* sickness of the mind. It has traced the moral scruples and excesses of the adult to the childhood stages in which guilt and shame are ready to be aroused and are easily exploited. It has named and studied the "super-ego" which hovers over the ego as the inner perpetuation of the child's subordination to the restraining will of his elders. The voice of the super-ego is not always cruel and derisive, but it is ever ready to become so whenever the precarious balance which we call a good conscience is upset, at which times the secret weapons of this inner governor are revealed: the brand of shame and the bite of conscience. We who deal with the consequences in individual neuroses and in collective irrationality must ask ourselves whether excessive guilt and excessive shame are "caused" or merely accentuated by the pressure of parental and communal methods, by the threat of loss of affection, of corporal punishment, of public shaming. Or are they by now a proclivity for self-alienation which has become a part—and, to some extent, a necessary part—of man's evolutionary heritage?

All we know for certain is that the moral proclivity in man does not develop without the establishment of some chronic self-doubt and some truly terrible—even if largely submerged—rage against anybody and anything that reinforces such doubt. The "lowest" in man is thus apt to reappear in the guise of the "highest." Irrational and pre-rational combinations of goodness, doubt, and rage can re-emerge in the adult in those malignant forms of righteousness and prejudice which we may call *moralism*. In the name of high moral principles all the vindictiveness of derision, of torture, and of mass extinction can be employed. One surely must come to the conclusion that the Golden Rule was meant to protect man not only against his enemy's open attacks, but also against his friend's righteousness.

Lest this view, in spite of the evidence of history, seem too "clinical," we turn to the writings of the evolutionists who in the last few decades have joined psychoanalysis in recognizing the super-ego as an evolutionary fact—and danger. The *developmental* principle is thus joined by an *evolutionary* one. Waddington[2] even goes so far as to say that super-ego rigidity may be an overspecialization in the human race, like the excessive body armor of the late dinosaurs. In a less grandiose comparison he likens the super-ego to "the finicky adaptation of certain parasites which fits them to live only on one host animal." In recommending his book, *The Ethical Animal*, I must admit that his terminology contradicts mine. He calls the awakening of morality in childhood a proclivity for "ethicizing,"

2. C. H. Waddington, *The Ethical Animal*, London: Allen and Unwin, 1960 [Erikson's note].

whereas I would prefer to call it moralizing. As do many animal psychologists, he dwells on analogies between the very young child and the young animal instead of comparing, as I think we must, the young animal with the pre-adult human, including the adolescent.

In fact, I must introduce here an amendment to my first, my "developmental" proposition, for between the development in childhood of man's *moral* proclivity and that of his *ethical* powers in adulthood, adolescence intervenes when he perceives the universal good in *ideological* terms. The imagery of steps in development, of course, is useful only where it is to be suggested that one item precedes another in such a way that the earlier one is necessary to the later ones and that each later one is of a higher order.

This "epigenetic" principle, according to which the constituent parts of a ground plan develop during successive stages, will be immediately familiar to you. For in the traditional Hindu concept of the life cycle the four intrinsic goals of life (Dharma, the orders that define virtue; Artha, the powers of the actual; Kama, the joys of libidinal abandon; and Moksha, the peace of deliverance) come to their successive and mutual perfection during the four stages, the ashramas of the apprentice, the householder, the hermit, and the ascetic. These stages are divided from each other by sharp turns of direction; yet, each depends on the previous one, and whatever perfection is possible depends on them all.

I would not be able to discuss the relation of these two foursomes to each other, nor ready to compare this ideal conception to our epigenetic views of the life cycle. But the affinities of the two conceptions are apparent, and at least the ideological indoctrination of the apprentice, the Brahmacharya, and the ethical one of the Grihasta, the householder, correspond to the developmental categories suggested here.

No wonder; for it is the joint development of cognitive and emotional powers paired with appropriate social learning which enables the individual to realize the potentialities of a stage. Thus youth becomes ready—if often only after a severe bout with moralistic regression—to envisage the more universal principles of a highest human good. The adolescent learns to grasp the flux of time, to anticipate the future in a coherent way, to perceive ideas and to assent to ideals, to take—in short—an *ideological* position for which the younger child is cognitively not prepared. In adolescence, then, an ethical view is approximated, but it remains susceptible to an alternation of impulsive judgment and odd rationalization. It is, then, as true for adolescence as it is for childhood that man's way stations to maturity can become fixed, can become premature end stations, or stations for future regression.

The moral sense, in its perfections and its perversions, has been an intrinsic part of man's *evolution*, while the sense of ideological rejuvenation has pervaded his *revolutions*, both with prophetic idealism and with destructive fanaticism. Adolescent man, in all his sensitivity to the ideal, is easily exploited by promises of counterfeit millennia, easily taken in by the promise of a new and arrogantly exclusive identity.

The *true* ethical sense of the young adult, finally, encompasses and goes beyond moral restraint and ideal vision, while insisting on concrete commitments to those intimate relationships and work associations by which man can hope to share a lifetime of productivity and competence. But young adulthood engenders its own dangers. It adds to the moralist's righteousness, the *territorial defensiveness* of one who has appropriated and staked out his earthly claim and who seeks eternal security in the super-identity of organizations. Thus, what the Golden Rule at its highest has attempted to make all-inclusive, tribes and nations, castes and classes, moralities and ideologies have consistently made exclusive again—proudly, superstitiously, and viciously denying the status of reciprocal ethics to those "outside."

If I have so far underscored the malignant potentials of man's slow maturation, I have done so not in order to dwell on a kind of dogmatic pessimism which can emerge all too easily from clinical preoccupation and often leads only to anxious avoidances. I know that man's moral, ideological, and ethical propensities can find, and have found on occasion, a sublime integration, in individuals and in groups who were both tolerant and firm, both flexible and strong, both wise and obedient. Above all, men have always shown a dim knowledge of their better potentialities by paying homage to those purest leaders who taught the simplest and most inclusive rules for an undivided mankind. I will have a word to say later about Gandhi's continued "presence" in India. But men have also persistently betrayed them, on what passed for moral or ideological grounds, even as they are now preparing a potential betrayal of the human heritage on scientific and technological grounds in the name of that which is considered good merely because it can be made to work—no matter where it leads. No longer do we have license to emphasize either the "positive" or the "negative" in man. Step for step, they go together: moralism with moral obedience, fanaticism with ideological devotion, and rigid conservatism with adult ethics.

Man's socio-genetic evolution is about to reach a crisis in the full sense of the word, a crossroads offering one path to fatality, and one to recovery and further growth. Artful perverter of joy and keen exploiter of strength, man is the animal that has learned to survive "in a fashion," to multiply without food for the multitudes, to grow up healthily without reaching personal maturity, to live well but without purpose, to invent ingeniously without aim, and to kill grandiosely without need. But the processes of socio-genetic evolution also seem to promise a new humanism, the acceptance by man—as an evolved product as well as a producer, and a self-conscious tool of further evolution—of the obligation to be guided in his planned actions and his chosen self-restraints by his knowledge and his insights. In this endeavor, then, it may be of a certain importance to learn to understand and to master the differences between infantile morality, adolescent ideology and adult ethics. Each is necessary to the next, but each is effective only if they eventually combine in that wisdom which, as Waddington puts it, "fulfills sufficiently the function of mediating evolutionary advance."

At the point, however, when one is about to end an argument with a global injunction of what we *must* do, it is well to remember Blake's admonition that the common good readily becomes the topic of "the scoundrel, the hypocrite, and the flatterer"; and that he who would do some good must do so in "minute particulars." And indeed, I have so far spoken only of the developmental and the evolutionary principle, according to which the propensity for ethics grows in the individual as part of an adaptation roughly laid down by evolution. Yet, to grow in the individual, ethics must be generated and regenerated in and by the sequence of generations— again, a matter fully grasped and systematized, some will say stereotyped, in the Hindu tradition. I must now make more explicit what our insights tell us about this process.

Let me make an altogether new start here. Let us look at scientific man in his dealings with animals and let us assume (this is not a strange assumption in India) that animals, too, may have a place close to the "other" included in the Rule. The psychologists among you know Professor Harry Harlow's studies on the development of what he calls affection in monkeys.[3] He did some exquisite experimental and photographic work attempting, in the life of laboratory monkeys, to "control the mother variable." He took monkeys from their mothers within a few hours after birth, isolated them and left them with "mothers" made out of wire, metal, wood, and terry cloth. A rubber nipple somewhere in their middles emitted piped-in milk, and the whole contraption was wired for body warmth. All the "variables" of this mother situation were controlled: the amount of rocking, the temperature of the "skin," and the exact incline of the maternal body necessary to make a scared monkey feel safe and comfortable. Years ago, when this method was presented as a study of the development of affection in monkeys, the clinician could not help wondering whether the small animals' obvious

3. H. F. Harlow and M. K. Harlow, "A Study of Animal Affection," *The Journal of the American Museum of* *Natural History*, Vol. 70, No. 10, 1961 [Erikson's note].

attachment to this contraption was really *monkey* affection or a fetishist addiction to inanimate objects. And, indeed, while these laboratory-reared monkeys became healthier and healthier, and much more easily trained in technical know-how than the inferior animals brought up by mere monkey mothers, they became at the end what Harlow calls "psychotics." They sit passively, they stare vacantly, and some do a terrifying thing: when poked they bite themselves and tear at their own flesh until the blood flows. They have not learned to experience "the other," whether as mother, mate, child—or enemy. Only a tiny minority of the females produced offspring, and only one of them made an attempt to nurse hers. But science remains a wonderful thing. Now that we have succeeded in producing "psychotic" monkeys experimentally, we can convince ourselves that we have at last given scientific support to the theory that severely disturbed mother-child relationships "cause" human psychosis.

This is a long story; but it speaks for Professor Harlow's methods that what they demonstrate is unforgettable. At the same time, they lead us to that borderline where we recognize that the scientific approach toward living beings must be with concepts and methods adequate to the study of ongoing life, not of selective extinction. I have put it this way: one can study the nature of things by doing something *to* them, but one can really learn something about the essential nature of living beings only by doing something *with* them or *for* them. This, of course, is the principle of clinical science. It does not deny that one can learn by dissecting the dead, or that animal or man can be motivated to lend circumscribed parts of themselves to an experimental procedure. But for the study of those central transactions which are the carriers of socio-genetic evolution, and for which we must take responsibility in the future, the chosen unit of observation must be the generation, not the individual. Whether an individual animal or human being has partaken of the stuff of life can only be tested by the kind of observation which includes his ability to transmit life—in some essential form—to the next generation.

One remembers here the work of Konrad Lorenz, and the kind of "inter-living" research which he and others have developed, making—in principle—the life cycle of certain selected animals part of the same environment in which the observer lives his own life cycle, studying his own role as well as theirs and taking his chances with what his ingenuity can discern in a setting of sophisticated naturalist inquiry. One remembers also Elsa the lioness, a foundling who was brought up in the Adamson household in Kenya. There the mother variable was not controlled, it was in control. Mrs. Adamson and her husband even felt responsible for putting grown-up Elsa back among the lions and succeeded in sending her back to the bush, where she mated and had cubs, and yet came back from time to time (accompanied by her cubs) to visit her human foster parents. In our context, we cannot fail to wonder about the built-in "moral" sense that made Elsa respond—and respond in very critical situations, indeed—to the words, "No, Elsa, no," *if* the words came from human beings she trusted. Yet, even with this built-in "moral" response, and with a lasting trust in her foster parents (which she transmitted to her wild cubs) she was able to live as a wild lion. Her mate, however, never appeared; he apparently was not too curious about her folks.

The point of this and similar stories is that our habitual relationship to what we call beasts in nature and "instinctive" or "instinctual" beastliness in ourselves may be highly distorted by thousands of years of superstition, and that there may be resources for peace even in our "animal nature" if we will only learn to nurture nature, as well as to master it. Today, we can teach a monkey, in the very words of the Bible, to "eat the flesh of his own arm," even as we can permit "erring leaders" to make of all mankind the "fuel of the fire." Yet, it seems equally plausible that we can also let our children grow up to lead "the calf and the young lion and the fatling together"—in nature and in their own nature.

To recognize one of man's prime resources, however, we must trace back his individual development to his *pre-moral* days, his infancy. His earliest social experimentation at that time leads to a certain ratio of basic trust and basic mistrust—a ratio which, if favorable, establishes the fundamental human strength: hope. This over-all attitude emerges as the newborn organism reaches out to its caretakers and as they bring to it what we will now discuss as *mutuality*. The failure of basic trust and of mutuality has been recognized in psychiatry as the most far-reaching failure, undercutting all development. We know how tragic and deeply pathogenic its absence can be in children and parents who cannot arouse and cannot respond. It is my further proposition, then, that all moral, ideological, and ethical propensities depend on this early experience of mutuality.

I would call mutuality a relationship in which partners depend on each other for the development of their respective strengths. A baby's first responses can be seen as part of an actuality consisting of many details of mutual arousal and response. While the baby initially smiles at a mere configuration resembling the human face, the adult cannot help smiling back, filled with expectations of a "recognition" which he needs to secure from the new being as surely as it needs him. The fact is that the mutuality of adult and baby is the original source of hope, the basic ingredient of all effective as well as ethical human action. As far back as 1895, Freud, in his first outline of a "Psychology for Neurologists," confronts the "helpless" newborn infant with a "help-rich" ("*hil-freich*") adult, and postulates that their mutual understanding is "the primal source of all moral motives."[4] Should we, then, endow the Golden Rule with a principle of mutuality, replacing the reciprocity of both prudence and sympathy?

Here we must add the observation that a parent dealing with a child will be strengthened in *his* vitality, in *his* sense of identity, and in *his* readiness for ethical action by the very ministrations by means of which he secures to the child vitality, future identity, and eventual readiness for ethical action.

But we should avoid making a new Utopia out of the "mother-child relationship." The paradise of early childhood must be abandoned—a fact which man has as yet not learned to accept. The earliest mutuality is only a beginning and leads to more complicated encounters, as both the child and his interaction with a widening circle of persons grow more complicated. I need only point out that the second basic set of vital strengths in childhood (following trust and hope) is autonomy and will, and it must be clear that a situation in which the child's willfulness faces the adult's will is a different proposition from that of the mutuality of instilling hope. Yet, any adult who has managed to train a child's will must admit—for better or for worse—that he has learned much about himself and about will that he never knew before, something which cannot be learned in any other way. Thus each growing individual's developing strength "dovetails" with the strengths of an increasing number of persons arranged about him in the formalized orders of family, school, community and society. But orders and rules are kept alive only by those "virtues" of which Shakespeare says (in what appears to me to be *his* passionate version of the Rule) that they, "shining upon others heat them and they retort that heat again to the first giver."

One more proposition must be added to the developmental and to the generational one, and to that of mutuality. It is implied in the term "activate," and I would call it the principle of *active choice*. It is, I think, most venerably expressed in St. Francis's prayer: "Grant that I may not so much seek to be consoled as to console; to be understood, as to understand; to be loved as to love; for it is in giving that we receive." Such commitment to an initiative in love is, of course, contained in the admonition to "love thy neighbor." I think that we can recognize in these words a psychological verity, namely, that only he who approaches an encounter in a (consciously and unconsciously) active and giving attitude, rather than in a demanding and dependent one, will be able to make of that encounter what it can become.

4. Sigmund Freud, *The Origins of Psychoanalysis: Letters to Wilhelm Fliess, Drafts and Notes: 1887-1902*, edited by Marie Bonaparte, Anna Freud and Ernst Kris, New York: Basic Books, 1954 [Erikson's note].

With these considerations in mind, then, I will try to formulate my understanding of the Golden Rule. I have been reluctant to come to this point; it has taken thousands of years and many linguistic acrobatics to translate this Rule from one era to another and from one language into another, and at best one can only confound it again, in a somewhat different way.

I would advocate a general orientation which has its center in whatever activity or activities gives man the feeling, as William James put it, of being "most deeply and intensely active and alive." In this, so James promises, each one will find his "real me"; but, I would now add, he will also acquire the experience that *truly worthwhile acts enhance a mutuality between the doer and the other—a mutuality which strengthens the doer even as it strengthens the other.* Thus, the "doer" and "the other" are partners in one deed. Seen in the light of human development, this means that the doer is activated in whatever strength is *appropriate to his age, stage, and condition,* even as he activates in the other the strength appropriate to *his* age, stage, and condition. Understood this way, the Rule would say that it is best to do to another what will strengthen you even as it will strengthen him—that is, what will develop his best potentials even as it develops your own.

This variation of the Rule is obvious enough when applied to the relation of parent and child. But does the uniqueness of their respective positions, which has served as our model so far, have any significant analogies in other situations in which uniqueness depends on a divided function?

To return to particulars, I will attempt to apply my amendment to the diversity of function in the two sexes. I have not dwelled so far on this most usual subject of a psychoanalytic discourse, sexuality. So much of this otherwise absorbing aspect of life has, in recent years, become stereotyped in theoretical discussion. Among the terminological culprits to be blamed for this sorry fact is the psychoanalytic term "love object." For this word "object" in Freud's theory has been taken too literally by many of his friends and by most of his enemies—and moralistic critics do delight in misrepresenting a man's transitory formulations as his ultimate "values." The fact is that Freud, on purely conceptual grounds, and on the basis of the scientific language of his laboratory days, pointed out that drive energies have "objects." But he certainly never advocated that men or women should treat one another as objects on which to live out their sexual idiosyncrasies.

Instead, his central theory of genitality which combines strivings of sexuality and of love points to one of those basic mutualities in which *a partner's potency and potentialities are activated even as he activates the other's potency and potentialities.* Freud's theory implies that a man will be more a man to the extent to which he makes a woman more a woman—and vice versa—because only two uniquely different beings can enhance their respective uniqueness for one another. A "genital" person in Freud's sense is thus more apt to act in accordance with Kant's version of the Golden Rule, in that he would so act as to treat humanity "whether in his person or in another, always as an end, and never as only a means." What Freud added to the ethical principle, however, is a methodology which opens to our inquiry and to our influence the powerhouse of inner forces. For they provide the shining heat for our strengths— and the smoldering smoke of our weaknesses.

I cannot leave the subject of the two sexes without a word on the uniqueness of women. One may well question whether or not the Rule in its oldest form tacitly meant to include women as partners in the golden deal. Today's study of lives still leaves quite obscure the place of women in what is most relevant in the male image of man. True, women are being granted *equality* of political rights, and the recognition of a certain *sameness* in mental and moral equipment. But what they have not begun to earn, partially because they have not cared to ask for it, is the *equal right to be effectively unique*, and to use hard-won rights in the service of what they uniquely represent in human evolution. The West has much to learn, for example, from the unimpaired womanliness of India's modern women. But there is today a universal sense of the emergence of a new feminism as part of a more inclusive humanism. This coincides with a growing conviction—highly ambivalent, to be sure—that the future of mankind cannot depend on men alone and may well depend on the fate of a "mother variable" uncontrolled by technological man. The resistance to such a consideration always comes from men and women who are mortally afraid that by emphasizing what is unique one may tend to re-emphasize what is unequal. And, indeed, the study of life histories confirms a far-reaching sameness in men and women insofar as they express the mathematical architecture of the universe, the organization of logical thought, and the structure of language. But such a study also suggests that while boys and girls can think and act and talk alike, they naturally do not experience their bodies (and thus the world) alike. I have attempted to demonstrate this by pointing to sex differences in the structuralization of space in the play of children.[5] But I assume that a uniqueness of either sex will be granted without proof, and that the "difference" acclaimed by the much-quoted Frenchman is not considered only a matter of anatomical appointments for mutual sexual enjoyment, but a psychobiological differ-

5. Erik H. Erikson, "Sex Differences in the Play Constructions of Pre-Adolescents," in *Discussions in Child Development*, World Health Organization, Vol. III, New York: International Universities Press, 1958. See also "Reflections on Womanhood," *Daedalus*, Spring 1964 [Erikson's note].

ence central to two great modes of life, the *paternal* and the *maternal* modes. The amended Golden Rule suggests that one sex enhances the uniqueness of the other; it also implies that each, to be really unique, depends on a mutuality with an equally unique partner.

From the most intimate human encounters we now turn to a professional, and yet relatively intimate, one: that between healer and patient. There is a very real and specific inequality in the relationship of doctor and patient in their roles of knower and known, helper and sufferer, practitioner of life and victim of disease and death. For this reason medical people have their own and unique professional oath and strive to live up to a universal ideal of "the doctor." Yet the practice of the healing arts permits extreme types of practitioners, from the absolute authoritarian over homes and clinics to the harassed servant of demanding mankind, from the sadist of mere proficiency, to the effusive lover of all (well, almost all) of his patients. Here, too, Freud has thrown intimate and original light on the workings of a unique relationship. His letters to his friend and mentor Fliess illustrate the singular experience which made him recognize in his patients what he called "transference"—that is, the patient's wish to exploit sickness and treatment for infantile and regressive ends. But more, Freud, recognized a "countertransference" in the healer's motivation to exploit the patient's transference and to dominate or serve, possess or love him to the disadvantage of his true function. He made systematic insight into transference *and* countertransference part of the training of the psychoanalytic practitioner.

I would think that all of the motivations necessarily entering so vast and so intricate a field could be reconciled in a Golden Rule amended to include a mutuality of divided function. Each specialty and each technique in its own way permits the medical man to *develop as a practitioner, and as a person, even as the patient is cured as a patient, and as a person.* For a real cure transcends the transitory state of patienthood. It is an experience which enables the cured patient to develop and to transmit to home and neighborhood an attitude toward health which is one of the most essential ingredients of an ethical outlook.

Beyond this, can the healing arts and sciences contribute to a new ethical outlook? This question always recurs in psychoanalysis and is usually disposed of with Freud's original answer that the psychoanalyst represents the ethics of scientific truth only and is committed to studying ethics (or morality) in a scientific way. Beyond this, he leaves *Weltanschauungen* (ethical world views) to others.

It seems to me, however, that the clinical arts and sciences, while employing the scientific method, are not defined by it or limited by it. The healer is commited to a highest good, the preservation of life and the furtherance of well-being—the "maintenance of life." He need not prove scientifically that these are, in fact, the highest good; rather, he is precommitted to this basic proposition while investigating what can be verified by scientific means. This, I think, is the meaning of the Hippocratic oath, which subordinates all medical method to a humanist ethic. True, a man can separate his personal, his professional, and his scientific ethics, seeking fulfillment of idiosyncratic needs in personal life, the welfare of others in his profession, and truths independent of personal preference or service in his research. However, there are psychological limits to the multiplicity of values a man can live by, and, in the end, not only the practitioner, but also his patient and his research, depend on a certain unification in him of temperament, intellect, and ethics. This unification clearly characterizes great doctors.

While it is true, then, that as scientists we must study ethics objectively, we are, as professional individuals, committed to a unification of personality, training, and conviction which alone will help us to do our work adequately. At the same time, as transient members of the human race, we must record the truest meaning of which the fallible methods of our era and the accidental circumstances of our existence have made us aware. In this sense, there is (and always has been) not only an ethics governing clinical work, and a clinical approach to the study of ethics, but also a contribution to ethics of the healing orientation. The healer, furthermore, has now committed himself to prevention on a large scale, and he cannot evade the problem of assuring ethical vitality to all lives saved from undernourishment, morbidity, and early mortality. Man's technical ability and social resolve to prevent accidental conception makes every child conceived a subject of universal responsibility.

As I approach my conclusion, let me again change my focus and devote a few minutes to a matter political and economic as well as ethical: Gandhi's "Rule."

In Ahmedabad I had occasion to visit Gandhi's ashram[6] across the Sabarmati River; and it was not long before I realized that in Ahmedabad a hallowed and yet eminently concrete event had occurred which perfectly exemplifies everything I am trying to say. I refer, of course, to Gandhi's leadership in the lockout and strike of the mill-workers in 1918, and his first fast in a public cause. This event is well known in the history of industrial relations the world over, and vaguely known to all educated Indians. Yet, I believe that only in Ahmedabad, among surviving witnesses and living institutions, can one fathom the "presence" of that event as a lastingly

6. Holy retreat.

successful "experiment" in local industrial relations, influential in Indian politics, and, above all, representing a new type of encounter in divided human functions. The details of the strike and of the settlement need not concern us here. As usual, it began as a matter of wages. Nor can I take time to indicate the limited political and economic applicability of the Ahmedabad experiment to other industrial areas in and beyond India. What interests us here is the fact that Gandhi, from the moment of his entry into the struggle, considered it an occasion not for maximum reciprocal coercion resulting in the usual compromise, but as an opportunity for all—the workers, the owners, and himself—"to rise from the present conditions."

The utopian quality of the principles on which he determined to focus can only be grasped by one who can visualize the squalor of the workmen's living conditions, the latent panic in the ranks of the paternalistic millowners (beset by worries of British competition), and Gandhi's then as yet relative inexperience in handling the masses of India. The shadows of defeat, violence, and corruption hovered over every one of the "lofty" words which I am about to quote. But to Gandhi, any worthwhile struggle must "transform the inner life of the people." Gandhi spoke to the workers daily under the famous Babul Tree outside the medieval Shahpur Gate. He had studied their desperate condition, yet he urged them to ignore the threats and the promises of the millowners who in the obstinate fashion of all "haves" feared the anarchic insolence and violence of the "have nots." He knew that they feared him, too, for they had indicated that they might even accept his terms if only he would promise to leave and to stay away forever. But he settled down to prove that a just man could "secure the good of the workers while safeguarding the good of the employers"—the two opposing sides being represented by a sister and a brother, Anasuyabehn and Ambalal Sarabhai. Under the Babul Tree Gandhi announced the principle which somehow corresponds to our amended Rule: "*That line of action is alone justice which does not harm either party to a dispute.*" By harm he meant—and his daily announcements leave no doubt of this—an inseparable combination of economic disadvantage, social indignity, loss of self-esteem, and latent vengeance.

Neither side found it easy to grasp this principle. When the workers began to weaken, Gandhi suddenly declared a fast. Some of his friends, he admitted, considered this "foolish, unmanly, or worse"; and some were deeply distressed. But, "I wanted to show you," he said to the workers, "that I was not playing with you." He was, as we would say, in dead earnest, and this fact, then as later, immediately raised an issue of local conscience to national significance. In daily appeals, Gandhi stressed variously those basic inner strengths without which no issue has "virtue," namely, will with justice, purpose with discipline, respect for work of any kind, and truthfulness. But he knew, and he said so, that these masses of illiterate men and women, newly arrived from the villages and already exposed to proletarization, did not have the moral strength or the social solidarity to adhere to principle without strong leadership. "You have yet to learn how and when to take an oath," he told them. The oath, the dead earnestness, then, was as yet the leader's privilege and commitment. In the end the matter was settled, not without a few Gandhian compromises to save face all around, but with a true acceptance of the settlement originally proposed by Gandhi.

I do not claim to understand the complex motivations and curious turns of Gandhi's mind—some contradicting Western rigidity in matters of principle, and some, I assume, strange to Indian observers, as well. I can also see in Gandhi's actions a paternalism which may now be "dated." But his monumental simplicity and total involvement in the "experiment" made both workers and owners revere him. And he himself said with humorous awe, "I have never come across such a fight." For, indeed both sides had matured in a way that lifted labor relations in Ahmedabad to a new and lasting level. Let me quote only the fact that, in 1950, the Ahmedabad Textile Labor Organization accounted for only a twentieth of India's union membership, but for eighty per cent of its welfare expenditures.

Such a singular historical event, then, reveals something essential in human strength, in traditional Indian strength, and in the power of Gandhi's own personal transformation at the time. To me, the miracle of the Ahmedabad experiment has been not only its lasting success and its tenacity during those days of anarchic violence which after the great partition broke down so many dams of solidarity, but above all, the spirit which points beyond the event.

And now a final word on what is, and will be for a long time to come, the sinister horizon of the world in which we all study and work: the international situation. Here, too, we cannot afford to live for long with a division of personal, professional, and political ethics—a division endangering the very life which our professions have vowed to keep intact, and thus cutting through the very fiber of our personal existence. Only in our time, and in our very generation, have we come, with traumatic suddenness, to be conscious of what was self-evident all along, namely, that in all of previous history the Rule, in whatever form, has comfortably coexisted with warfare. A warrior, all armored and spiked and set to do to another what he fully expected the other to be ready to do to him, saw no ethical contradiction between the Rule and his military ideology.

He could, in fact, grant to his adversary a respect which he hoped to earn in return. This tenuous coexistence of ethics and warfare may outlive itself in our time. Even the military mind may well come to fear for its historical identity, as boundless slaughter replaces tactical warfare. What is there, even for a "fighting man," in the Golden Rule of the Nuclear Age, which seems to say, "Do not unto others—unless you are sure you can do them in as totally as they can do you in"?

One wonders, however, whether this deadlock in international morals can be broken by the most courageous protest, the most incisive interpretation, or the most prophetic warning—a warning of catastrophe so all-consuming that most men must ignore it, as they ignore their own death and have learned to ignore the monotonous prediction of hell. It seems, instead that only an ethical orientation, a direction for vigorous cooperation, can free today's energies from their bondage in armed defensiveness. We live at a time in which—with all the species-wide destruction possible—we can think for the first time of a species-wide identity, of a truly universal ethics, such as has been prepared in the world religions, in humanism, and by some philosophers. Ethics, however, cannot be fabricated. They can only emerge from an informed and inspired search for a more inclusive human identity, which a new technology and a new world image make possible as well as mandatory. But again, all I can offer you here is another variation of the theme. What has been said about the relationships of parent and child, of man and woman, and of doctor and patient, may have some application to the relationship of nations to each other. Nations today are by definition units at different stages of political, technological, and economic transformation. Under these conditions, it is all too easy for overdeveloped nations to believe that nations, too, should treat one another with a superior educative or clinical attitude. The point of what I have to say, however, is not underscored inequality, but respected uniqueness within historical differences. Insofar as a nation thinks of itself as a collective individual, then, it may well learn to visualize its task as that of maintaining mutuality in international relations. For the only alternative to armed competition seems to be the effort to *activate in the historical partner what will strengthen him in his historical development even as it strengthens the actor in his own development— toward a common future identity.* Only thus can we find a common denominator in the rapid change of technology and history and transcend the dangerous imagery of victory and defeat, of subjugation and exploitation which is the heritage of a fragmented past.

Does this sound utopian? I think, on the contrary, that all of what I have said is already known in many ways, is being expressed in many languages, and practiced on many levels. At our historical moment it becomes clear in a most practical way that the doer of the Golden Rule, and he who is done by, is the same man, *is* man.

Men of clinical background, however, must not lose sight of a dimension which I have taken for granted here. While the Golden Rule in its classical versions prods man to strive *consciously* for a highest good and to avoid mutual harm with a sharpened awareness, our insights assume an *unconscious* substratum of ethical strength and, at the same time, unconscious arsenals of destructive rage. The last century has traumatically expanded man's awareness of unconscious motivations stemming from his animal ancestry, from his economic history, and from his inner estrangements. It has also created (in all these respects) methods of productive self-analysis. These I consider the pragmatic Western version of that universal trend toward self-scrutiny which once reached such heights in Asian tradition. It will be the task of the next generation everywhere to begin to integrate new and old methods of self-awareness with the minute particulars of universal technical proficiency.

It does not seem easy to speak of ethical subjects without indulging in some moralizing. As an antidote I will conclude with the Talmudic version of the Rule. Rabbi Hillel once was asked by an unbeliever to tell the whole of the Torah while he stood on one foot. I do not know whether he meant to answer the request or to remark on its condition when he said: "What is hateful to yourself, do not to your fellow man. That is the whole of the Torah and the rest is but commentary." At any rate, he did not add: "Act accordingly." He said: "Go and learn it."

QUESTIONS

1. At times Erikson implies that he is digressing, and he certainly does cover a wide range of topics. How tightly is his talk organized? Can it be outlined?
2. Erikson distinguishes three stages of growth—moral, ideological, and ethical. What are the significant characteristics of each, and how do they relate to one another? What does Erikson mean by "evolution"?
3. How might Erikson regard Samuel Johnson's conviction that man is a free agent (p. 931), or Thucydides' conception of human nature as self-seeking and anarchic (p. 1163)?
4. How might Erikson regard Milgram's procedure as he reports it in "A Behavioral Study of Obedience" (pp. 413–427)?
5. Compare Erikson's application of the golden rule with Hare's idea of "universalizability" (p. 859). What are the differences? Are the differences due to the differences in perspective because one is a psychoanalyst and the other a philosopher?

6. Bruno Bettelheim said that liberals, the press, and teachers who failed to assert their authority all shared some blame for denying superego models to the young, particularly to the poor and disadvantaged: "There's no doubt about the underlying violence with which we are born. Whether we are going to have violence depends to a very large degree on how we develop the superego and controls of the coming generation." Would Erikson agree? Can you think of ways in which superego models are denied? Does a man in authority have to be unusually good himself to serve as a satisfactory model?

EDWARD SHILS

The Sanctity of Life

To persons who are not murderers, concentration camp administrators or dreamers of sadistic fantasies, the inviolability of human life seems to be so self-evident that it might appear pointless to enquire about it. It is embarrassing as well because, once raised, it seems to commit us to beliefs we do not wish to espouse. Yet because of a conjunction of circumstances, it is worthwhile to discuss it.

One of these circumstances is the decline of Christian belief about the place of man in the divine scheme and the consequent diminution of its adduction as a criterion in the judgment of the worth and permissibility of human actions. As long as it was believed that man was created and had been assigned a destiny by God, it seemed evident that man's life was a sacred entity. It was sacred because man was a manifestation of the source and plan of the universe; for that reason his biological vitality and his soul (or mind) were not to be subjected to the transforming manipulations of other men. The cognitive content of Christian doctrine, and above all the grandiose Christian symbolization of man's origin and destiny, have lost much of their appeal. Large sections of contemporary Western societies, particularly the highly educated, do not, by and large, believe in the immortality of the soul. They probably do not believe in a soul at all. (Some of them even allege that they do not believe in the existence of mind.) If there is no God, no divine creation, no immortality of the soul, no redemption, why should man's life be regarded with any more reverence than we regard the lives of wild and domestic animals which we hunt and eat, or pets which we breed and cherish?

Another of the epochal circumstances which has caused us to raise the question is the advancement of the life sciences and the technological possibilities based on them. Physiological knowledge has been in the process of growth for three centuries but in recent decades its progress has become much more fundamental. (The advance is to some extent a function of the great improvement in instrumental technology.) Surgery is also old but it has become vastly more daring in its undertakings and proficient in its accomplishments in recent decades. The life sciences seem on the verge of an efflorescence like that through which the physical sciences passed during the first half of the present century. They are beginning to attract talents—of the quality and in large numbers—such as physics attracted in its recent very great period. As a result, life scientists and physicians and surgeons are acquiring the knowledge and the capacities to intervene purposefully and effectively in the course of the life of individuals and of the reproduction of generations such as they have never possessed before.

Alongside of these heightened powers of observation of the human organism and intervention in its vital processes, the powers of observing—of seeing and hearing—and of reaching into the social behavior of human beings, have also increased correspondingly. These latter developments are in part functions of technological improvement: in part they are functions of greater curiosity—greater sympathy and more scientific detachment—and an aspiration for a more far-reaching surveillance and control, which are thought to be called for by the larger size of the corporate bodies into which so much of modern society is organized. Once again, the potentiality of the technology and the power of those who are its masters give rise to almost shapeless apprehension.

We live also in an epoch in which one of the most famous countries, Germany, not particularly de-Christianized as compared with the other countries of the modern world, participated in the deliberate murder of numerous millions of persons of alien ethnic stocks. Mankind was accustomed to the destruction of lives by war incidental to the pursuit of military ends, and by murder by individuals out of powerfully passionate and transient impulses. The Nazi destruction was, however, so unprecedented in its scale, organization, persistence, and "rationality" that many sensitive persons have come to feel that we live unsteadily suspended over an abyss of unlimited murderousness. Another memorial of this epoch is the dropping of the two nuclear bombs at the end of the Second World War. Each of these destroyed more human lives than any other single and separate action performed by a small number of men had ever done before. The nuclear weapons were made possible by the scientific research done in the present century by some of the greatest minds of human history.

The fading of Christian belief and the plausible confidence of the biomedical sciences, acting jointly with our awareness of the

destructive capacities of sadism served by large-scale organization—
which was also occasionally justified by the invocation of pseudo-
scientific genetic doctrines and which was attended by some alleged
medical experiments—and of genuinely outstanding scientific genius in the service of, or utilized for, military purposes in the atomic
bomb, have raised a fundamental question. How is the human race
as we have known it, with all its deficiencies, to be protected from
the murderous and manipulative wickedness of some of its members and the scientific and technological genius of others?

Each of these major factors working alone would have raised
questions about the grounds on which one man's life or individuality may be interfered with, changed or discontinued, and the factors which might extend or restrict such acts of intervention. Their
coincidence renders it desirable to consider the whole problem
more closely. This is why we ask the questions as to whether life is
sacred, and as to how far morality permits and how far the law
should allow us to intervene in reproduction, the course of life, and
the constitution of individuality and privacy.

Despite the diminution of theological belief among the educated, many persons, including the educated, experience a sense of
abhorrence in the face of the new or prospective capacities of geneticists, neurosurgeons, psychiatrists, psychologists, and electronics
engineers to intervene in what has hitherto been regarded largely as
given by man's ancestry and his "natural" cognitive and moral
powers. The loosening of the hold of ancestry, the circumvention
of normal sexual intercourse as a pre-condition of procreation, the
modification of memory, temperament, and sensory experience, all
produce an effect of shock in many persons. The shock is not just
the shock of surprise in the presence of novelty. It seems to possess
elements of a deep abhorrence or revulsion. We see it in the struggles of courts and lawyers to cope with these new facts of human
existence. We see it in the responses of those who still accept the
Christian view of man, and we see it amongst the agnostic humanists who think that their view of the world is entirely secular and
utilitarian. But when it comes to the formulation of an intellectually coherent and acceptable justification of the sense of abhorrence, there seem to be difficulties.

Why do so many persons experience this vague and sometimes
passionate revulsion at the thought of a deliberate modification of
the genetic determinants of the life of a human being—or of the
modification of the personality by a neurosurgical operation—or of
the observation and recording of a conversation which is believed
by the participants to be held away from the awareness of anyone
except themselves? Can this revulsion be explained by a persisting
commitment to the doctrine that man is a creature of a divine act

and that it is not for man himself to undertake to form or modify the highest of God's creatures? This explanation is reasonable for those who are believing Christians or Jews.

What about those who experience this abhorrence but who are, as far as they know, not subscribers to the view that man is God's creature, that his soul is a part of a divine scheme and that it does not fall within man's proper jurisdiction to tamper with it? One interpretation of this response is that the latter are the victims, unwitting to be sure, of the religious conception of man, even though they themselves do not believe in any religion. The tree of religious belief has been felled but the roots are still in their minds. Their revulsion might be interpreted as nothing but a vestigial feeling left over from beliefs to which they no longer accord validity.

It is quite possible that there is some truth in this interpretation but I doubt whether it is really the whole truth. If it is wholly true, then the ground in reason for the revulsion disintegrates. The revulsion which many people feel in contemplation of the prospect of human intervention in the chain which binds us to our ancestry, in the constitution of our individuality, and in the islands of privacy which surround individuality, would appear then to be no more than a prejudice, utterly irrational and unjustifiable by rational argument.

I myself do not share this latter view either of the motivation of those who feel the revulsion against the manipulation of life and individuality or of the rationality of the grounds in principle for being morally distrustful or repelled by these activities which I will refer to as "contrived intervention." It seems to me that the apprehension about the intervention of medical, psychological, and electronic technology has an even deeper source in human existence than is to be found in Christian theology. The source of the revulsion or apprehension is deeper than the culture of Christianity and its doctrine was enabled to maintain its long prosperity and to become so effective because it was able to conform for so many centuries to a deeper, proto-religious "natural metaphysic." Cultural traditions play a great part in sustaining the sense of revulsion but they themselves would not go on if they were not continuously impelled by this "natural metaphysic."

Human beings do have a conception of the "normal" or the "natural" and it is not simply a function of what is statistically the most frequent or a product of indoctrination although both play a part in forming its content and maintaining it. Much of this conception of the "normal" or the "natural" centers on heterosexuality, lineage ties, and the integrity of the human organism and its memory.

Such developments as the transplantation of organs, the implan-

tation of substitute organs made from inorganic materials, the instigation and control of human reproductive processes independently
of sexual intercourse (artificial inovulation and insemination), the
prospective modification of genetic constitution, the modification
of personality qualities by pre-frontal lobotomy, electrical-shock
therapy, the transformation of memory by electronic devices or
chemical substances, the pharmaceutical transformation of the
senses and the imagination, etc., all generate in different ways
among a variety of persons some apprehension about the dangers of
deviation from the "normal" or the "natural" which are obscurely
intimated by these increased powers. These apprehensions are not
just vestiges of archaic theological traditions. They are direct
responses to sacrilege.

The response is accentuated by the fact that these very possibilities are greeted by numerous persons with great enthusiasm. Those
who are put off by these new possibilities, who shudder at the sight
or thought of this new Promethean aspiration to do things which
lay hitherto beyond human powers, are further alarmed by the
enthusiasts. There is a more widespread anxiety about the moral
status of these interventions and about the institutional controls
which would restrict their uses for diabolical purposes and which
would seek to develop legal rules and institutions adequate to deal
with new conceptions or criteria of death, parenthood, etc.

Indeed it is often the unqualified enthusiasm of the proponents
and prophets of "contrived intervention" which disturbs and alarms
those who would have misgivings enough about the new possibilities without having to confront the enthusiasts. It must however be
acknowledged that the enthusiasts stand in a great tradition. The
improvement of the physical quality of life, the aspiration for a life
without pain or unhappiness, the improvement in human powers
and the pleasure in the exercise of the powers of knowing and constructing—the prizing of these accomplishments is part of our most
valuable traditions. Yet there are probably also some motives which
are less worthy—aspirations to omnipotence, desires to manipulate
the individuality and to intrude on the privacy of human beings
and therewith to enjoy the experience of their degradation.

These latter motives, to the extent that they are thought to exist,
reinforce the apprehensions about Prometheanism. It should be
remembered however that Prometheus was a benefactor of the
human race who suffered because he sought to displace the gods by
diffusing their powers among men. Those who stand uneasily apart
from the recent biomedical and technological advances might not
believe that there are certain kinds of knowledge which belong only
to God; they are not, however, confident about the wisdom or the
self-restraint of man in dealing with the sanctity of life and in re-

specting the "natural" or the "normal" in which that sacredness is incorporated.

Obviously, these conceptions have been influenced by Christian culture but they are not simply left-over fragments from a Christianity which has begun to recede.

The chief feature of the proto-religious, "natural metaphysic" is the affirmation that life *is* sacred. It is believed to be sacred not because it is a manifestation of a transcendent creator from whom life comes: it is believed to be sacred because it is life. The idea of sacredness is generated by the primordial experience of being alive, of experiencing the elemental sensation of vitality and of fearing its extinction. Man stands in awe before his own vitality, the vitality of his lineage and of his species. He stands in awe before the natural order in which that vitality is maintained. The sense of awe is the attribution of sanctity, and all else which man feels to be sacred derives its sanctity because it controls or embraces that sacred vitality of the individual, the lineage and the species.

The fear of the extinction of vitality, of one's own organism, of the species, and of one's own lineage, testifies to a primordial attachment to an elemental fact. What is at work here is not merely the attachment of the individual human organism which experiences and appreciates its own vitality; it is also an appreciation of the continuity of the vitality of one's own breed and progeny, unborn and unknown, the vitality of the territorial and civil community of which one is a member, and of the vitality of the species. Within this context, these are thought to be "normal" or "natural" modes of embodiment of the vital. When we speak of the sanctity of life, it is of these forms of life that we speak.

To say that the idea of the sacred is at bottom the appreciation of vitality requires some explanation—because it seems to be so contradictory to the usual idea which asserts that the sacred lies outside and beyond both the individual organic and the collective carriers of vitality. It is often asserted that these are sacred because they are infused or touched or generated by transcendent sacred powers. My own view is that the transcendent sacred is a construction which the human mind itself has adduced, to account for and to place in a necessary order the primordial experience of the actual embodiment of vitality to which it attributes sacredness. The transcendent sacred is valued because to it are imputed the powers which are thought to have generated, which maintain, enhance, and protect human vitality. The ultimate laws which govern human vitality and its manifestations—whether they be the laws of the physical and organic universe disclosed by scientific research, whether they be the properties of divinity disclosed by revelation, the study of sacred books and theological analysis, or the laws of society disclosed and promulgated by research, reason, and authority—possess their property of sacredness or sanctity because they are believed to govern, underlie, account for, guide, and control human vitality. They possess sanctity, or rather have it attributed to them, because they explain why life—and the universe which is its frame and ground, and society which enfolds and contains it—exists and because they control its movement, whether they do so through the laws of the universe of physical and organic nature or in the form of the laws of society in general or of a particular society.

If man did not prize his own vitality, the sacred and its vast symbolic elaboration into cosmogonies and theologies would not exist. It has been created and has held dominion over so many human beings through much of the course of history because of the need to place in an order of power and justice the vicissitudes of human vitality. If life were not viewed and experienced as sacred, then nothing else could be sacred. This is true of societies which are regarded as increasingly secular as well as of those which for their entire history have lived with a powerful admixture of traditional religious belief and practice.

If human beings attribute sacredness to human life, why do so many human beings destroy life, and condone its destruction? Why are they so apparently indifferent to the lives of their fellow men?

Rulers until well into modern times in most parts of the world, and even now in many, have been and are largely indifferent to the vital condition of their subjects and countrymen. Generals have often thrown away the lives of large numbers of their soldiers. Churches and states have persecuted and destroyed lives. Governmental authorities have destroyed those who have, in fact or symbolically, endangered the political and social order.

Often those who deny the sanctity of particular individual lives do so on behalf of institutions which they themselves regard as sacred. Moreover, the incumbents of the institutional roles to which sacredness is attributed frequently regard their own sanctity as having overriding rights *vis-à-vis* other claimants to sanctity. States and churches which regard themselves as possessing sanctity do not find it difficult to disregard or deny the sanctity of the lives of particular individuals, while believing themselves still committed to the sanctity of life as such.

But it is not just the custodians of collective sanctity who infringe on the sanctity of individual lives. Murders by private citizens are common to say the least; multitudes are killed inadvertently by careless or incompetent motor-car drivers; human lives are abbreviated by man-made pollution of the air. Violent hatred and sheer indifference show that the sense of the sanctity of life is often faint and feeble. It is clear that the sense of the sanctity of individual life is not in exclusive possession of the field of forces which control human life.

Nonetheless, the occurrence of war, murder, capital punishment, torture, and indifference to human suffering no more invalidates the hypothesis of the widespread affirmation of the sanctity of life than the fact of suicide annuls the proposition of the near universality of the individual's appreciation of his own vitality and its continuance. The real problem is how to explain the coexistence of these two contradictory tendencies.

Sensitivity to the sacred is unequally distributed among the members of any given society. It is also intermittent in its operation and of uneven intensity in the extent to which it attributes sacredness to different individuals and collectivities. Some lives are regarded as more sacred than other lives. (This is true with respect to both the sanctity of the vitality of the individual and to the various forms and symbols of transcendent powers in which the sacredness of life is objectified.) There is a gradation of "sanctity" moving from the individual outward—first through his kinship and affectional attachments, then local, national, class, ethnic group, and culture, becoming more attenuated and patchier as it reaches into other countries, continents, and races. Just as the personal affections diminish as they radiate outward, so the sense of identity constituted by a sense of shared sanctity also diminishes—although it has far greater radiative capacity than personal affection. Is there a point of disjunction in the downward curve of attribution of sanctity? There seems to be such a point where it is thought that primordial or genetic affinity ends or becomes very thin. There is less concern for the lives of those outside the presumptive genetic network of which we regard ourselves as a part. Tribe, caste, ethnic group, nationality, and national state—the boundaries of these groups are the points of disjunction, beyond which human life is less sacred than it is within.

Yet much destruction of life takes place within primordial groups and in civil communities. Members of families are cruel to each other and a substantial proportion of all murders occurs within families. There is in fact no situation in which the acknowledgement of the sanctity of life is guaranteed.

Indeed, in the very fact of its sanctity lies some part of the danger to which it is exposed. Sanctity calls forth sacrilegious dispositions. The affirmation of vitality arouses an impulse to destroy it. (Conversely, the awareness of these destructive, desecrating impulses calls forth a protective reaffirmation of the sanctity of life, and one which is indeed often fused with destructive impulses of its own—as in the case of capital punishment for murder and treason.)

Detachment, the absence of a sense of affinity, makes injury and destruction easier—although there is a total sense of disaffinity only at the psychopathological margins. Thus in most cases of destruction there is probably some element of a sense of affinity, and some sense of the sacredness of life, which is overpowered by fear and hatred and sacrilegious impulses.

All that I have been saying so far is descriptive. The question still remains: is human life really sacred? My answer is that it is, self-evidently. We participate in it through our own membership in the species, through our own humanity. The sacredness of life is given by our being alive. Its sacredness is a primary experience and the fact that many human beings act contrarily, or do not apprehend it, does not change it. The fact that many people tell lies, and the fact that scientific truths cannot be appreciated except by those who have been trained to appreciate them, do not make scientific propositions any less truthful nor do they abolish the intrinsic value of scientific truth.

But even if my affirmation is affirmed, our problems are still far from solution. The proposition that life is sacred is no more than a guiding principle. The forms of human life that are sacred are however so variegated, so often in tension with each other, and so resistant to being placed on a clear-cut scale of degrees of sacredness, that infinitely difficult problems still remain in deciding what is permissible or intolerable.

I should like therefore to examine some of the major modes of "contrived intervention" in the light of the building principle.

I should state at the outset that, although I am not an enthusiast for "contrived intervention," and in fact am distrustful of those who envisage an entirely new and wholly better humanity in consequence of the development of the life sciences and certain types of biomedical and other technologies, I do not regard the problem, at least as it appears at present, as really very worrying. To begin at the simplest levels, we have always accepted the surgery which excises a diseased and dispensable organ, such as a gall bladder or even a lung. We have always accepted the surgery which replaced a nonfunctioning or diseased part of the body by an artificial substitute such as a false tooth or a wooden leg. Does the introduction of a plastic aorta represent a qualitative change from a porcelain tooth? Is it more of a deformation of individuality? Clearly not. Blood transfusions, too, have been accepted even though they go further than the other types of surgery by the introduction of substances from the body of another human being. This would appear to verge on the infringement of individuality. But the fact is that the introduction of blood or a kidney from another human being, living or dead, works, to the extent that it works at all, only if the organism asserts its systemic coherence and integrates the foreign element into itself. A kidney and blood are alien substances but the organism remains an organism and assimilates them into its biological system or individuality. Hence, I do not think that the vitality of the individual human organism is infringed by such interventions. The organism as a whole retains its coherence and its continuity, and its vitality is in fact extended and reinvigorated. Surgical technology as it is working today, or is likely to work in the future, does not infringe on the sanctity of life. Rather the opposite: it affirms the sanctity of life by extending and enhancing vitality and it offers no affront to individuality. It raises no moral problems beyond those which medical practice has always had to face.[1]

Since such "reconstructions" are not undertaken without the consent of the patient and/or the responsible members of his or her family, ethically and logically the situation is the same here as in all medical treatment. The physician is the expert who proposes courses of action but it is not within his powers—given the traditional pattern of medical belief and practice[2]—to impose a given course of action indifferent to the will and assent of the patient or his legitimate custodian.

Additional considerations arise when we come to artificial insemination (AID), artificial inovulation, and "genetic engineering." "Genetic engineering" and artificial human inovulation are at present only prospects, and the former is not even a near one: they are not yet real issues. It is, however, appropriate to discuss them because they are at the center of the apprehensions which are aroused by other forms of contrived intervention. They affect not the vitality of the living human being but rather the process of procreation and the continuity of the lineage.

AID does, and artificial inovulation and genetic engineering would, intrude into and disrupt the lineage; they provide a "descendant" who is not in a direct genetic line with his ancestors. Of course there have always been variant forms of adoption which

1. Of course these technological operations which require extremely scarce skills and resources almost always require decisions with moral overtones as to whether they should be undertaken and on whom among the possible beneficiaries. And this does place a responsibility for a moral decision on a physician or surgeon, just as the choice of men to be sent out on a dangerous patrol involves an officer in a moral choice as to whose life should be preserved and whose should be endangered or destroyed. The affirmation of the sanctity of life as such does not remove moral dilemmas given by the diversity of the forms of life, the existence of other values, and the ineluctible fact of scarcity [Shils's note].

2. The development of experimental techniques in medical research raises grave issues. Medical research workers sometimes proceed in disregard of these issues but within the medical profession itself there is serious scrutiny and criticism of this disregard. Much information and deep reflection on the whole problem are to be found in the writings of Dr. Henry Beecher of the Massachusetts General Hospital [Shils's note].

introduced a genetically alien element into the lineage, but they have been marginal or superficial in the depth of their entry into the process. The new or prospective forms of intervention penetrate into the center of the process and they therewith affront the primordial sentiment of the sacredness of the stream of life passed down through membership in a common physiological substance. They create a human being who lacks the genetic continuity with the line of descent of those who take him (or her) as a child.[3]

The genetic manipulator or the artificial inseminator or inovulator is not a member of the lineage; like the organism he helps into existence he too stands outside the stream of primordial continuity. His motives might be sacrilegious; they might with equal likelihood be benevolent or he might be profoundly neutral, concerned only with the efficient performance of an assigned and accepted task. But unless it becomes possible to produce a fetus and bring it to human life outside a human uterus, the process cannot be carried out without the consent of the woman who is to bear the child. The situation is therefore identical in this respect to the situation which obtains traditionally between patient and physician. The physician does not do what the patient does not agree to allow him to do.[4] It is true that the sanctity of the lineage, which is derivative from the sanctity of life, is infringed by these procedures.

Yet I do not think that the matter must be taken tragically. Like religious sensitivity, the sense of the sacredness of lineage is unevenly distributed among human beings. Most human beings possess it: some to a very high degree and others possess it only slightly. Some persons even react against it violently. There are certainly numerous parents who do not care about their children. There are numerous children who do not care about their parents. There are numerous human beings who do not care about their ancestry. For them, what to many of us appears to be an act of impiety is utterly neutral. Within rather wide limits, we accept that impiety as permissible, even though it is not admirable. There is no reason why such persons should not be permitted to act on the basis of this "lineage-neutrality."

One of the great developments of modern society, and one which many people think—quite rightly—represents a tremendous step forward in human progress, has been the diminution in the

3. It is impossible for me to say whether this lack of a sense of genetic continuity with "parents" would result in damage to the individuals who would be or are created by this process. The attitudes of adopted children to the discovery of the fact that their "parents" are not really their parents should be studied. But even if it were found that the discovery that foster parents are not real parents has a traumatic affect, that still might not outweigh the advantages of adoption, in view of the available alternatives [Shils's note].

4. The problem is somewhat complicated by whether the husband knows and consents to the artificial insemination or inovulation. But whatever the laws of adultery, they take a stand on problems of identical character [Shils's note].

weight attributed to lineage as a criterion by which to estimate the value of a human being. The decline in aristocracy and the shrinkage of the realm and power of hereditary monarchy are expressions of the decline of the importance attributed to lineage. The heightened appreciation of individuality, the enhanced evaluation of individual achievement, the growth of civility—the high evaluation of the *individual's* membership in the civil community and of his rights as an individual which come from living under a common authority in a contiguous and bounded territory, the idea of the "career open to talents" and of the corresponding principle of equality of individual opportunity—all attest to the attenuation of "lineage-consciousness" in the advanced societies of modern times. We are living in an epoch in which the center of gravity of the sanctity of life has been displaced from the sanctity of the lineage of genetically linked individual lives to the individuality of discrete human organisms. I do not think that we can have it both ways, and of the two I myself value more highly the emphasis which has become predominant in the modern age.

Furthermore I doubt whether any artificial inovulation will be practiced on a large scale. It seems very unlikely that the sense of sanctity of lineage will die out to such an extent that very large numbers of men and women would wish to resort to contrived intervention to provide them with offspring. But there will surely be some who, like those who adopt children, will be willing to have children who are not of their own genetic line. Hence, once it becomes possible, it will surely occur. If it is to occur, it is most important that it should be done under morally legitimate auspices, for good reasons and with the agreement of the "parents" who agree *irrevocably* to treat the product as their own legitimate offspring with full rights as such and with the fullest protection of the law.

The same may be said of "genetic engineering," if and when that becomes possible. If mature adults, who wish to reduce the probability of the occurrence of clearly hereditary physical and mental defects in their offspring and descendants, seek the aid of a "genetic engineer" to attain this end, I see no more objection to it than I see to the recourse of afflicted persons to the more conventional types of medical therapy. Their respect for the past of their lineage should be balanced by a concern for its future and for the vital quality of the individual members of its temporal extension.

Once more we see that the sanctity of human life is an equivocal criterion. The value which it prizes takes a variety of forms, not all of which are in all ways harmonious with each other. But where it unambiguously affirms the vitality and individuality of the living, and the persistence of a lineage into the future, "genetic engineering" seems to me to be quite acceptable.

Observance of the sacredness of the lineage is not to be coercively imposed any more than observance of the ritual of any particular religion. If there are persons whose feelings about the sacredness of the lineage are not intense, and they have good reasons such as concern for the health of their prospective offspring, there are no grounds for denying them the right to discontinue certain components of their genetic line. "Negative eugenics" which involves forbearance to many where the union would bring forth with high probability organically impaired offspring is surely compatible with an appreciation of the sanctity of life. It is even required by that appreciation. The same may be said of "genetic engineering." "Genetic engineering" will probably not even involve a complete break in the line.

After all it is not illegal, even if it is not "natural," to remain celibate and to bring one's lineage to extinction. There should, correspondingly, be no legal or moral grounds for denying such persons the right to disaffiliate their offspring, partially or wholly, from their lineage. As in regular medical and surgical practice, the protection of morally legitimate auspices, good reasons, and a completely voluntary decision on the part of the persons immediately involved must be observed.

As regards the sanctity of life itself, the biological-technological innovations we have been considering do not diminish life. They improve it. They do not constrict it, rather they enlarge it as far as individual human beings are concerned. It is certainly true that they would intervene, prospectively, at points where it was—and still is—impossible to intervene. But except for the disruption of lineage, they do nothing other than increase and enlarge the vitality of oncoming generations.

Conceivably they could do worse. They might produce a new species of monsters, less intelligent and more destructive than the present species. They might engender a species more sickly, more subject to ailments of every kind, unviable and unworthy. There is fear that they might, but I do not regard this fear as well-founded. Pharmacists could poison the human race; conspiracies of physicians and pharmacists could, even with their present technology, do extraordinary harm to humanity. Surgeons could do the same. At present they do not, and do not intend to do so. Why do they not exploit their present powers? The answer seems almost self-evident. They stand in reverence of life. They are horrified by the possibility of destruction: or they would be horrified if they thought of the possibilities. Of course there could be the "mad physicians" whom science fiction brings before us, and there have been the wicked and sadistic physicians who conducted "experiments" in the Nazi concentration camps. There is, however, no reason to expect these cases to become uncontrollably frequent as long as a civil society endures, as long as the civil authorities are reasonably humane and alert, and as long as the present ethical traditions of the medical and scientific professions endure.

It is possible, of course, that greater potentialities for evil in the future will prove more tempting than the present more limited potentialities. It is also possible that medical education, because of the greatly increased numbers with which it will have to deal in the future, will be less successful than it is at present in training into the new members of the profession that ethos which at present sustains the general appreciation of the sanctity of life.

What about the possibility of certain medically unqualified scientists evading the controls which might be quite effective in the medical profession itself? On this point I see no reason why the law should not be able to proceed against these persons as it proceeds at present against those who practice medicine without the necessary qualifications, or who, having the qualifications, behave in a clearly unethical and professionally pernicious manner.

Thus far we have discussed the prolongation or "creation" of life. But what about its annihilation through abortion and euthanasia? Are such actions morally permissible from a standpoint which regards life as sacred? I have little doubt about the former, considerable doubt about the latter.

My reasons are as follows. The postulate of the sanctity of life refers to three forms of life: (1) the life of the lineage; (2) the life of the human organism; and (3) the life of the individual human being, as the individuality constituted by self-consciousness, as a discrete entity possessing self-consciousness and the capacity for pyschic "self-locomotion" (*i.e.*, capacity for perception, the amalgamation and ordering of perceptions, memory, intentions, and choice).

A fetus, for most of the period of gestation, does not qualify for the sanctity which is attributed to life. It is still organically part of the mother; it has still not begun to learn, and by virtue of that it has not yet begun on the path to individuality. It is not yet an individual life—it is part of the life of the mother. It is not, it is true, a part in the same way as a limb or an internal organ are parts of a living human organism, but it also is not yet a discrete separate human organism beginning to remember, to discriminate, to intend. An infant is on the path to the development of individuality, which is more than biological uniqueness. A fetus is at a much earlier stage on the path on which actual birth is the decisive turning.

There are many good reasons to regret abortion or the necessity for it—effective contraception would be much more satisfactory—but I think that for our purposes it should be said that the principle of the sanctity of life of the individual as an individual, or the life of the lineage as the lineage of separate organisms, is not infringed or affronted by abortion in the earlier stages of pregnancy.

When we come to euthanasia of monsters or extreme idiots, the matter seems to me to be much more difficult because in the first place we are dealing with separate discrete human organisms which might possess some modicum of individuality. If we affirm the principle of the sanctity of life, euthanasia in marginal, and even in the extreme cases of idiocy or monstrosity, is repugnant. I am reluctant to see it embodied in laws which authorize it but would have much sympathy for a flexible attitude in the courts.

At the other end of the life-span, where there is a certainly dying person in great pain, with not even the slightest probability of recovery, and where individuality has ceased totally to exist, euthanasia is again repugnant. It might, however, be morally permissible. In some respects the fact of scarcity of medical resources permits a solution which approximates, but is not identical with, euthanasia, namely suspension of effort to keep the organism alive. The argument against the authorization of euthanasia seems to me to rest less in the nature of the action itself and more in the deficiencies of our knowledge in assessing the absence or cessation of individuality—itself so ambiguous as to defy clear definition—and in our distrust of the wisdom and generosity of men.

The sanctity of individuality is a variant form of the sanctity of life. The ambiguities of the ideas of individuality and "normality" or "naturalness" hamper our judgment when we consider another form of "contrived intervention" and when we attempt to do justice to the abhorrence which many persons experience when confronted with certain developments in psychiatric, neurosurgical, and psychological technology.

At the same time, the aversion against the taking of narcotics, the administration of hallucinogenic drugs, the use of devices for stimulating subliminal perception, and for secretly observing and recording occurrences in the private sphere seems to me an aversion against the infringement on individuality. It arises from an anxiety lest the individual be made into something other than he "is." It is a fear that the particularly individuated and differentiated current of life which exists in the individual human organism will be tampered with, damaged, or extinguished. It is not that the individuality of particular individual human beings is always taken as given and final, and is not regarded as subject to certain legitimate, although not always effective, modes of influence. The guidance and formation of character through education and domestic discipline, and the depressive and stunting effects of poverty and maltreatment, and the transformation of sensibility and mental powers through alcohol and sedative drugs are all widely, although unequally, accepted. The stimulation of the imagination through literature and drama are accepted but not the pharmacological stimulation of the imagination; the deadening of impulse through poverty and loneliness are also accepted—although decreasingly so—but not the deadening of sensibility through narcotics. The heightening of the power of the senses of vision, touch, taste, through training are accepted but not their heightening through drugs.

Some of these acceptances are functions of the compellingness of the inevitable or at least of the apparently unchangeable. Some of the acceptance is also a function of insensitivity, of an insufficient sympathy with the state of mind of others. But it is also a function of a conception of "normality." It is the product of a metaphysical belief in a pre-established and inviolable pattern of individuality which may coexist with certain externally introduced influences but not with others. Those with which coexistence is not possible are the deliberate ones, those which are contrived and which do not arise from the course of "normal" interaction. It is the elements of deliberation and cognition beyond a "normal" range which renders abhorrent the administration of drugs to the self or the manipulation of conduct by experimental means not understood by the participant-subject of the experiment.

The concept of "normality" presupposes an "essential form" in which individuality exists. Slow and imperceptible processes of change or influence are not regarded as repugnant to this conception of normality because they are not seen as "abnormal" or "unnatural" and because they do not obviously impinge on individuality. Changing oneself deliberately by the exertion of internal moral resources, or by the adduction of certain external allegedly "sacred" influences of moral and religious guidance, is all right. The anonymous influence of one's class on one's moral and cultural attitudes is also regarded as all right; religious conversion is all right. They are regarded as all right because they take place in a medium of an "essential form" of human interaction, in friendship, in work, in worship, etc., which is taken as given. Much of the content of this "essential form" may be accounted for by the statistical frequency and consequent conventional normativeness of the practices in question. But the frequency and conventionality might themselves be to some extent a function of their possession of the property of "essential form." They occur frequently because they are thought to be "normal." This "essential form" or "normality" is very vaguely conceived and it permits a fairly wide range of acceptable variation.

But one of the things it excludes is the absolutely complete dominion of one human being over another human being. And by complete dominion is meant the loss or renunciation of all individ-

ual autonomy by the dominated person. Autonomy, thus understood, is what the individual would be if left alone to the extent
that he is by his kinship group, his working colleagues, his neighbors, and his rulers. There is often not much of him left over after
this, but what is left over is his temperament and his memory of
his own individual past. When these are taken away from him by
"contrived intervention," or even by his cooperation, other persons
who do not participate in the complete dominion experience a sensation of abhorrence.

Under what conditions is the modification of temperament and
individuality by "contrived intervention" permissible?

It is certainly not permissible as a satisfaction of the curiosity of
psychologists who wish to see how far the personality is modifiable
by pharmaceutical or neurosurgical means. It is obviously not permissible for political purposes such as the maintenance of public
order or for the protection of the unchallenged dominion of the
rulers of society or any particular organization within society. Is it
permissible for therapeutic ends? I see no argument against this as
long as the usual safeguards practiced by the medical profession are
observed, *i.e.*, as long as the informed consent of the patient, or of
his kinsmen who are morally responsible for him, is given. Where
an individual has already lost such individuality as he once possessed, and where the therapeutic technique offers a reasonable
probability of the restoration to him of some parts of his previous
individuality, it seems to me to be morally unexceptionable.

The protection which the sanctity of individuality must possess
depends in part on the strength of the ethics of the medical profession and on the formation of a comparable ethical outlook among
psychologists, social workers, and related professions. It thus
depends on the moral vigilance and responsibility of the universities, and particularly of those who are in charge of training in medicine, psychology, and social work. It depends also on the vigilance
of legislators and the courts in the implementation of strict prohibition on attempts to modify individuality by persons without adequate professional qualifications. It depends thus on public opinion.

This brief examination of the range and limits of what is permissible in "contrived intervention" brings us back to where we began.
Without a widespread affirmation of the sanctity of life, and of the
variant forms of the sanctity of life such as the sanctity of individuality, as a basic and guiding principle of social life, we will be hopelessly adrift. The crisis is not yet fully upon us because the techniques of "contrived intervention" are not yet as elaborate or as
secure as they are likely to be in the future. When they do develop
more fully and effectively, the temptations to exploit the powers
which they will offer to those in whom the sense of the sanctity of

human life and of human individuality is weak or perverted will be strong—undoubtedly stronger than they are now.

The situation will surely not be made easier by the ambiguity and the inherent tensions and contradictions of the idea of the sanctity of life. By its very structure this fundamental moral principle cannot provide an absolutely unambiguous guide which will indicate infallibly what is permissible and what is not permissible in any particular case. Nonetheless, it is the only ultimate foundation for the protection against sadism in its more crude and brutal forms or in the more refined form of "scientific curiosity."

For those who accept the traditional Christian view of man and accept its theological postulates, there is no difficulty in the way of their affirmation of the sanctity of life, although its application will of course often present them with dilemmas which are inherent in the idea itself. For those who no longer accept the traditional Christian view, the acceptance of the idea of the sanctity of life might well encounter intellectual obstacles. I myself find no such obstacles, and I do not think that there are any such in the conception of sanctity which I have put forward here.

From my point of view, the task of our generation and those immediately following is not so much the re-establishment of a Christianity which is shorn of its historical and mythological accretions. Rather it is the rediscovery of what it was that for so long gave such persuasive power to Christianity. This powerful impulse became, in our culture, so intimately fused with Christian doctrine and belief that when, as has happened in the past one hundred and fifty years, Christianity has become in varying degrees unacceptable, the prior and impelling belief in the sanctity of man's life and personality also seemed to lose its acceptability. But the powerful impulse still remains and that is why the proto-religion, the "natural metaphysic" of the sanctity of life, must be intellectually rehabilitated and rendered acceptable.

PETER B. MEDAWAR

Science and the Sanctity of Life

I do not intend to deny that the advances of science may sometimes have consequences that endanger, if not life itself, then the quality of life or our self-respect as human beings (for it is in this wider sense that I think "sanctity" should be construed). Nor shall I waste time by defending science as a whole or scientists generally against a change of inner or essential malevolence. The Wicked Scientist is not to be taken seriously: Dr. Strangelove, Dr. Moreau, Dr. Moriarty, Dr. Mabuse, Dr. Frankenstein (an honorary degree, this), and the rest of them are puppets of Gothic fiction. Scientists, on the whole, are amiable and well-meaning creatures. There must be very few wicked scientists. There are, however, plenty of wicked philosophers, wicked priests, and wicked politicians.

One of the gravest charges ever made against science is that biology has now put it into our power to corrupt both the body and the mind of man. By scientific means (the charge runs) we can now breed different kinds and different races—different models, almost—of human beings, degrading some, making aristocrats of others, adapting others still to special purposes: treating them in fact like dogs, for this is how we *have* treated dogs. Or again: science now makes it possible to dominate and control the thought of human beings—to improve them, perhaps, if that should be our purpose, but more often to enslave or to corrupt with evil teaching.

But these things have always been possible. At any time in the past 5,000 years it would have been within our power to embark on a program of selecting and culling human beings and raising breeds as different from one another as toy poodles and Pekinese are from St. Bernards and Great Danes. In a genetic sense the empirical arts of the breeder are just as applicable to human beings as to horses—more easily applicable, in fact, for human beings are highly *evolvable* animals, a property they owe partly to an open and uncomplicated breeding system, which allows them a glorious range of inborn diversity and therefore a tremendous evolutionary potential; and partly to their lack of physical specializations (in the sense in which anteaters and woodpeckers and indeed dogs are specialized), a property which gives human beings a sort of amateur status among animals. And it has always been possible to pervert or corrupt human beings by coercion, propaganda, or evil indoctrination. Science has not yet improved these methods, nor have scientists used them. They have, however, been used to great effect by politicians, philosophers, and priests.

The mischief that science may do grows just as often out of trying to do good—as, for example, improving the yield of soil is intended to do good—as out of actions intended to be destructive. The reason is simple enough: however hard we try, we do not and sometimes cannot foresee all the distant consequences of scientific innovation. No one clearly foresaw that the widespread use of antibiotics might bring about an evolution of organisms resistant to their action. No one could have predicted that x-irradiation was a possible cause of cancer. No one could have foreseen the speed and scale with which advances in medicine and public health would create a problem of overpopulation that threatens to undo much of what medical science has worked for. (Thirty years ago the talk was all of how the people of the Western world were reproducing themselves too slowly to make good the wastage of mortality; we heard tell of a "Twilight of Parenthood," and wondered rather fearfully where it all would end.) But somehow or other we shall get round all these problems, for everyone of them is soluble, even the population problem, and even though its solution is obstructed above all else by the bigotry of some of our fellow men.

I choose from medicine and medical biology one or two concrete examples of how advances in science threaten or seem to threaten the sanctity of human life. Many of these threats, of course, are in no sense distinctively medical, though they are often loosely classified as such. They are merely medical contexts for far more pervasive dangers. One of them is our increasing state of dependence on medical services and the medical industries. What would become of the diabetic if the supplies of insulin dried up, or of the victims of Addison's disease deprived of synthetic steroids? Questions of this kind might be asked of every service society provides. In a complex society we all depend upon and sustain each other, for transport, communications, food, goods, shelter, protection and a hundred other things. The medical industries will not break down all by themselves, and if they do break down it will be only one episode of a far greater disaster.

The same goes for the economic burden imposed by illness in any community that takes some collective responsibility for the health of its citizens. All shared burdens have a cost which is to a greater or lesser degree shared between us: education, pensions, social welfare, legal aid and every other social service, including government.

We are getting nearer what is distinctively medical when we ask ourselves about the economics, logistics, and morality of keeping people alive by medical intervention and medical devices. At present it is the cost and complexity of the operation, and the shortage of machines and organs, that denies a kidney graft or an artificial kidney to anyone mortally in need of it. The limiting factors are thus still economic and logistic. But what about the morality of keeping people alive by these heroic medical contrivances? I do not think it is possible to give any answer that is universally valid or that, if it were valid, would remain so for more than a very few years. Medical contrivances extend all the way from pills and plasters and bottles of tonic to complex mechanical prostheses, which will one day include mechanical hearts. At what point shall we say we are wantonly interfering with Nature and prolonging life beyond what is proper and humane?

In practice the answer we give is founded not upon abstract moralizing but upon a certain natural sense of the fitness of things, a feeling that is shared by most kind and reasonable people even if we cannot define it in philosophically defensible or legally accountable terms. It is only at international conferences that we tend to adopt the convention that people behave like idiots unless acting upon clear and well turned instructions to behave sensibly. There is in fact no general formula or smooth form of words we can appeal to when in perplexity.

Moreover, our sense of what is fit and proper is not something fixed, as if it were inborn and instinctual. It changes as our experience grows, as our understanding deepens and as we enlarge our grasp of possibilities—just as living religions and laws change, and social structures and family relationships.

I feel that our sense of what is right and just is already beginning to be offended by the idea of taking great exertions to keep alive grossly deformed or monstrous newborn children, particularly if their deformities of body or mind arise from major defects of the genetic apparatus. There are in fact scientific reasons for changing an opinion that might have seemed just and reasonable a hundred years ago.

Everybody takes it for granted, because it is so obviously true, that a married couple will have children of very different kinds and constitutions on different occasions. But the traditional opinion, which most of us are still unconsciously guided by, is that the child conceived on any one occasion is the unique and necessary product of that occasion: *that* child would have been conceived, we tend to think, or no child at all. This interpretation is quite false, but human dignity and security clamor for it. A child sometimes wonderingly acknowledges that he would never have been born at all if his mother and father had not chanced to meet and fall in love and marry. He does not realize that, instead of conceiving him, his parents might have conceived any one of a hundred thousand other children, all unlike each other and unlike himself. Only over the past 100 years has it come to be realized that the child conceived on any one occasion belongs to a vast cohort of Possible Children, any one of whom might have been conceived and born if a different spermatozoon had chanced to fertilize the mother's egg cell—and the egg cell itself is only one of very many. It is a matter of luck then, a sort of genetic lottery. And sometimes it is cruelly bad luck—some terrible genetic conjunction, perhaps, which once in ten or twenty thousand times will bring together a matching pair of damaging recessive genes. Such a misfortune, being the outcome of a random process, is, considered in isolation, completely and essentially pointless. It is not even strictly true to say that a particular inborn abnormality must have lain within the genetic potentiality of the parents, for the malignant gene may have arisen *de novo* by mutation. The whole process is unhallowed—is, in the older sense of that word, profane.

I am saying that if we feel ourselves under a moral obligation to make every possible exertion to keep a monstrous embryo or new-born child alive *because* it is in some sense the naturally intended—and therefore the unique and privileged—product of its parents' union at the moment of its conception, then we are making an elementary and cruel blunder: for it is *luck* that determines which one child is in fact conceived out of the cohort of Possible Children that might have been conceived by those two parents on that occasion. I am not using the word "luck" of conception as such, nor of the processes of embryonic and fetal growth, nor indeed in any sense that derogates from the wonder and awe in which we hold processes of great complexity and natural beauty which we do not fully understand; I am simply using it in its proper sense and proper place.[1]

This train of thought leads me directly to Eugenics—"the science," to quote its founder, Francis Galton, "which deals with all the influences that improve the inborn qualities of a race; also with those that develop them to the utmost advantage." Because the upper and lower boundaries of an individual's capability and performance are set by his genetic makeup, it is clear that if eugenic policies were to be ill-founded or mistakenly applied they could offer a most terrible threat to the sanctity and dignity of human life. This threat I shall now examine.

Eugenics is traditionally subdivided into Positive and Negative Eugenics. Positive Eugenics has to do with attempts to improve human beings by genetic policies, particularly policies founded upon selective or directed breeding. Negative Eugenics has the lesser ambition of attempting to eradicate as many as possible of our inborn imperfections. The distinction is useful and pragmatically valid for the following reasons. Defects of the genetic constitution (such as those which manifest themselves as mongolism, hemophilia, galactosemia, phenylketonuria, and a hundred other hereditary abnormalities) have a much simpler genetic basis than desirable characteristics like beauty, high physical performance, intelligence, or fertility. This is almost self-evident. All geneticists believe that "fitness" in its most general sense depends on a nicely balanced coordination and interaction of genetic factors, itself the product of laborious and long drawn out evolutionary adjustment. It is inconceivable, indeed self-contradictory, that an animal should evolve into the possession of some complex pattern of interaction between genes that made it inefficient, undesirable, or unfit—*i.e.*, *less* well adapted to the prevailing circumstances. Likewise a motor car will run badly for any one of a multitude of particular and spe-

1. There are, perhaps, very weighty legal and social reasons why even tragically deformed children should be kept alive (for who is to decide? and where do we draw the line?), but these are outside my terms o reference [Medawar's note].

cial reasons, but runs well because of the harmonious mechanical interactions made possible by a sound and economically viable design.

Negative eugenics is a more manageable and understandable enterprise than positive eugenics. Nevertheless, many well-meaning people believe that, with the knowledge and skills already available to us, and within the framework of a society that upholds the rights of individuals, it is possible in principle to raise a superior kind of human being by a controlled or "recommended" scheme of mating and by regulating the number of children each couple should be allowed or encouraged to have. If stock-breeders can do it, the argument runs, why should not we?—for who can deny that domesticated animals have been improved by deliberate human intervention?

I think this argument is unsound for a lesser and for a more important reason.

1. Domesticated animals have not been "improved" in the sense in which we should use that word of human beings. They have not enjoyed an all-round improvement, for some special characteristics or faculties have been so far as possible "fixed" without special regard to and sometimes at the expense of others. Tameness and docility are most easily achieved at the expense of intelligence, but that does not matter if what we are interested in is, say, the quality and yield of wool.

2. The ambition of the stock-breeder in the past, though he did not realize it, was twofold: not merely to achieve a predictably uniform product by artificial selection, but also to establish an internal genetic uniformity (homozygosity) in respect of the characters under selection to make sure that the stock would "breed true"—for it would be a disaster if characters selected over many generations were to be irrevocably lost or mixed up in a hybrid progeny. The older stock-breeder believed that uniformity and breeding true were characteristics that necessarily went together, whereas we now know that they can be separately achieved. And he expected his product to fulfill two quite distinct functions which we now know to be separable, and often better separated: on the one hand, to be in themselves the favored stock and the top performers—the Super-sheep or Super-mice—and, on the other hand, to be the parents of the next generation of that stock. It is rather as if Rolls-Royces, in addition to being an end product of manufacture, had to be so designed as to give rise to Rolls-Royce progeny.

It is just as well these older views are mistaken, for with naturally outbreeding populations such as our own, genetic uniformity, arrived at and maintained by selective inbreeding, is a highly artificial state of affairs with many inherent and ineradicable disadvantages.

Stock-breeders, under genetic guidance, are now therefore inclining more and more towards a policy of deliberate and nicely calculated cross-breeding. In the simplest case, two partially inbred and internally uniform stocks are raised and perpetuated to provide two uniform lineages of parents, but the eugenic goal, the marketable end-product or high performer, is the progeny of a cross between members of the two parental stocks. Being of hybrid make-up, the progeny do not breed true, and are not in fact bred from; they can be likened to a manufactured end-product; but they can be uniformly reproduced at will by crossing the two parental stocks. Many more sophisticated regimens of cross-breeding have been adopted or attempted, but the innovation of principle is the same. (1) the end products are all like each other and are faithfully reproducible, but are not bred from because they do not breed true: the organisms that represent the eugenic goal have been relieved of the responsibility of reproducing themselves. And (2) the end products, though uniform in the sense of being like each other, are to a large extent hybrid—heterozygous as opposed to homozygous—in genetic composition.

The practices of stock-breeders can therefore no longer be used to support the argument that a policy of positive eugenics is applicable in principle to human beings in a society respecting the rights of individuals. The genetic manufacture of supermen by a policy of cross-breeding between two or more parental stocks is unacceptable today, and the idea that it might one day become acceptable is unacceptable also.

A deep fallacy does in fact eat into the theoretical foundations of positive eugenics and that older conception of stock-breeding out of which it grew. The fallacy was to suppose that the *product* of evolution, *i.e.*, the outcome of an episode of evolutionary change, was a new and improved genetic formula (genotype) which conferred a higher degree of adaptedness on the individuals that possessed it. This improved formula, representing a new and more successful solution of the problems of remaining alive in a hostile environment, was thought to be shared by nearly all members of the newly evolved population, and to be stable except insofar as further evolution might cause it to change again. Moreover, the population would have to be predominantly homozygous in respect of the genetic factors entering into the new formula, for otherwise the individuals possessing it would not breed true to type, and everything natural selection had won would be squandered in succeeding generations.

Most geneticists think this view mistaken. It is *populations* that evolve, not the lineages and pedigrees of old-fashioned evolutionary "family trees," and the end product of an evolutionary episode is not a new genetic formula enjoyed by a group of similar individuals, but a new spectrum of genotypes, a new pattern of genetic inequality, definable only in terms of the population as a whole. Naturally outbreeding populations are not genetically uniform, even to a first approximation. They are persistently and obstinately diverse in respect of nearly all constitutional characters which have been studied deeply enough to say for certain whether they are uniform or not. It is the *population* that breeds true, not its individual members. The progeny of a given population are themselves a population with the same pattern of genetic makeup as their parents—except insofar as evolutionary or selective forces may have altered it. Nor should we think of uniformity as a desirable state of affairs which *we* can achieve even if nature, unaided, cannot. It is inherently undesirable, for a great many reasons.

The goal of positive eugenics, in its older form, cannot be achieved, and I feel that eugenic policy must be confined (paraphrasing Karl Popper) to *piecemeal genetic engineering.* That is just what Negative Eugenics amounts to; and now, rather than to deal in generalities, I should like to consider a concrete eugenic problem and discuss the morality of one of its possible solutions.

Some "inborn" defects—some defects that are the direct consequence of an individual's genetic makeup as it was fixed at the moment of conception—are said to be of *recessive* determination. By a recessive defect is meant one that is caused by, to put it crudely, a "bad" gene that must be present in both the gametes that unite to form a fertilized egg, *i.e.,* in both spermatozoon and egg cell, not just in one or the other. If the bad gene *is* present in only one of the gametes, the individual that grows out of its fusion with the other is said to be a *carrier* (technically, a heterozygote).

Recessive defects are individually rather rare—their frequency is of the order of one in ten thousand—but collectively they are most important. Among them are, for example, phenylketonuria, a congenital inability to handle a certain dietary constituent, the amino acid phenylalanine, a constituent of many proteins; galactosemia, another inborn biochemical deficiency, the victims of which cannot cope metabolically with galactose, an immediate derivative of milk sugar; and, more common than either, fibrocystic disease of the pancreas, believed to be the symptom of a generalized disorder of mucus-secreting cells. All three are caused by particular single genetic defects; but their secondary consequences are manifold and deep-seated. The phenylketonuric baby is on the way to becoming an imbecile. The victim of galactosemia may become blind through cataract and be mentally retarded.

Contrary to popular superstition, many congenital ailments can be prevented or, if not prevented, cured. But in this context prevention and cure have very special meanings.

The phenylketonuric or galactosemic child may be protected from the consequences of his genetic lesion by keeping him on a diet free from phenylalanine in the one case or lactose in the other. This is a most unnatural proceeding, and much easier said than done, but I take it no one would be prepared to argue that it was an unwarrantable interference with the workings of providence. It is not a cure in the usual medical sense because it neither removes nor repairs the underlying congenital deficiency. What it does is to create around the patient a special little world, a microcosm free from phenylalanine or galactose as the case may be, in which the genetic deficiency cannot express itself outwardly.

Now consider the underlying morality of prevention.

We can prevent phenylketonuria by preventing the genetic conjunction responsible for it in the first instance, *i.e.*, by preventing the coming together of an egg cell and a sperm each carrying that same one harmful recessive gene. All but a very small proportion of overt phenylketonurics are the children of parents who are both carriers—carriers, you remember, being the people who inherited the gene from one only of the two gametes that fused at their conception. Carriers greatly outnumber the overtly afflicted. When two carriers of the same gene marry and bear children, one quarter of their children (on the average) will be normal, one quarter will be afflicted, and one half will be carriers like themselves. We shall accomplish our purpose, therefore, if, having identified the carriers—another thing easier said than done, but it *can* be done and in an increasing number of recessive disorders—we try to discourage them from *marrying each other* by pointing out the likely consequences if they do so. The arithmetic of this is not very alarming. In a typical recessive disease, about one marriage in every five or ten thousand would be discouraged or warned against, and each disappointed party would have between fifty and a hundred other mates to choose from.

If this policy were to be carried out, the overt incidence of disease like phenylketonuria, in which carriers can be identified, would fall almost to zero between one generation and the next.

Nevertheless the first reaction to such a proposal may be one of outrage. Here is medical officiousness planning yet another insult to human dignity, yet another deprivation of the rights of man. First it was vaccination and then fluoride; if now people are not to be allowed to marry whom they please, why not make a clean job of it and overthrow the Crown or the U.S. Constitution?

But reflect for a moment. What is being suggested is that a certain small proportion of marriages should be discouraged for genetic reasons, to do our best to avoid bringing into the world children who are biochemically crippled. In all cultures marriages are already prohibited for genetic reasons—the prohibition, for example, of certain degrees of inbreeding (the exact degree varies from one culture or religion to another). It is difficult to see why the prohibition should have arisen to some extent independently in different cultures unless it grew out of the common observation that abnormalities are more common in the children of marriages between close relatives than in children generally. Thus the prohibition of marriage for genetic reasons has an immemorial authority behind it. As to the violation of human dignity entailed by performing tests on engaged couples that are no more complex or offensive than blood tests, let me say only this: if anyone thinks or has ever thought that religion, wealth, or color are matters that may properly be taken into account when deciding whether or not a certain marriage is a suitable one, then let him not dare to suggest that the genetic welfare of human beings should not be given equal weight.

I think myself that engaged couples should themselves decide, and I am pretty certain they would be guided by the thought of the welfare of their future children. When it came to be learned about twenty years ago that marriages between Rhesus-positive men and Rhesus-negative women might lead to the birth of children afflicted by hemolytic disease, a number of young couples are said to have ended their engagements—needlessly, in most cases, because the dangers were overestimated through not being understood. But that is evidence enough that young people marrying today are not likely to take a stand upon some hypothetical right to give birth to defective children if, by taking thought, they can do otherwise.

The problems I have been discussing illustrate very clearly the way in which scientific evidence bears upon decisions that are not, of course, in themselves scientific. If the termination of a pregnancy is now in question, scientific evidence may tell us that the chances of a defective birth are 100 per cent, 50 per cent, 25 per cent, or perhaps unascertainable. The evidence is highly relevant to the decision, but the decision itself is not a scientific one, and I see no reason why scientists as such should be specially qualified to make it. The contribution of science is to have enlarged beyond all former bounds the evidence we must take account of before forming our opinions. Today's opinions may not be the same as yesterday's, because they are based on fuller or better evidence. We should quite often have occasion to say "I used to think that once, but now I have come to hold a rather different opinion." People who never say as much are either ineffectual or dangerous.

We all nowadays give too much thought to the material blessings or evils that science has brought with it, and too little to its power to liberate us from the confinements of ignorance and superstition.

It may be that the greatest liberation of thought ever achieved by the scientific revolution was to have given mankind the expectation of a future in this world. The idea that the world has a virtually indeterminate future is comparatively new. Much of the philosophic speculation of three hundred years ago was oppressed by the thought that the world had run its course and was coming shortly to an end. "I was borne in the last age of the World," said John Donne, giving it as the "ordinarily received" opinion that the world had thrice two thousand years to run between its creation and the Second Coming. According to Archbishop Ussher's chronology more than five-and-a-half of those six thousand years had gone by already.

No empirical evidence challenged this dark opinion. There were no new worlds to conquer, for the world was known to be spherical and therefore finite; certainly it was not all known, but the full extent of what was *not* known was known. Outer space did not put into people's minds then, as it does into ours now, the idea of a tremendous endeavor just beginning.

Moreover life itself seemed changeless. The world a man saw about him in adult life was much the same as it had been in his own childhood, and he had no reason to think it would change in his own or his children's lifetime. We need not wonder that the promise of the next world was held out to believers as an inducement to put up with the incompleteness and inner pointlessness of this one: the present world was only a staging post on the way to better things. There was a certain awful topicality about Thomas Burnet's description of the world in flames at the end of its long journey from "a dark chaos to a bright star," for the end of the world might indeed come at any time. And Thomas Browne warned us against the folly and extravagance of raising monuments and tombs intended to last for many centuries. We are living in The Setting Part of Time, he told us: *the Great Mutations of the World are acted: it is too late to be ambitious.*

Science has now made it the ordinarily received opinion that the world has a future reaching beyond the most distant frontiers of the imagination—and that is perhaps why, in spite of all his faults, so many scientists still count Francis Bacon their first and greatest spokesman: we may yet build a New Atlantis. The point is that when Thomas Burnet exhorted us to become Adventurers for Another World, *he* meant the next world—but we mean this one.

DONALD HALL

A Hundred Thousand Straightened Nails

When I was growing up, I spent every summer helping out on my grandparents' farm. My grandfather was a great storyteller and told me anecdotes to go with every face whose portrait hung in the farmhouse gallery, those long rows of silhouettes, daguerreotypes, tinted photographs and snapshots which my grandmother kept in the parlor and the sitting room. The portraits had names which I recognized on headstones when we visited graveyards. Though I loved the bright flowery borders and the white paint of the farmhouse, and though I loved our haying in the dry heat of the fields, I was always aware that New Hampshire was more dead than alive. Walking in the dense woods, I learned to be careful not to fall into the cellar holes.

If I was morbid, it was not my grandfather's fault. He was interested only in lively stories about the dead, and he lived so completely in the dramatic scenes of his memory that everything was continually present to him. My grandmother was occasionally elegiac, but not enough to influence me. When I was nine I saw my Great-Aunt Nannie, blind and insane, dying for one long summer on a cot in the parlor, yet my own lamentation for the dead and the past had begun even earlier. Many of my grandfather's stories were symptoms, to me and not to him, of the decay of New Hampshire; a story might include a meadow where the farm boys had played baseball, or a wood through which a railroad had once run.

I found myself, too, taking some of the characters in his stories at a value different from his. So many of them lived a half-life, a life of casual waste. He often talked about Washington Woodward, who was a cousin of ours. I knew Washington well, yet my image of him was a mixture of what I had observed and what my grandfather had told me. The whole farm was composed of things which Washington had made or at least repaired, so there was no end of devices to remind my grandfather of a story about him. Most of them were funny, for Washington was eccentric, yet after I had finished laughing, even perhaps when I lay in bed at night and thought over what had happened in the day, the final effect of the stories was not comic. I turned Washington into a sign of the dying place. I loved him, and I could feel his affection for me. Yet when I thought of the disease that afflicted New Hampshire, I knew that my grandfather's face was the exception to disease. The face of sickness was the mouth and moving beard, the ingenious futility of Washington Woodward.

This was a paradox, for Washington hated corruption and spied it everywhere like a prophet. Yet unlike a prophet he retired from corruption to the hills, meditated it, and never returned to denounce it. He bought a few acres high up New Canada Road, on Ragged Mountain, in 1895. He lived there alone, with few forays into the world, for the more than fifty years until he died.

I have seen pictures of him, in the farmhouse gallery, taken when he was a young man. He was short and muscular of body, handsome and stern, with a full black mustache over a downcurved mouth. I remembered him only as old, for even in my first memories he must have been sixty. The image I retained had him bent nearly double from the waist, with quick bright eyes and his mouth jiggling his beard in an incessant monotone.

When Washington was young, my grandfather told me, he was already the misanthrope who would exile himself. He had been the youngest of eleven children in a family related to my grandmother. His father, everyone admits, was lazy and mean. Their house burned down, and the children were boarded with various relatives. Washington was only six but already embittered and even surly when he came to live with the Kenestons. My grandmother was a baby. He stayed until he was twelve, and he always looked back to those years as a golden age; my grandmother's family was the great exception to the misanthropic rule. To my grandmother, he was an older brother; when she nursed him during illnesses late in his life, she was remembering someone who had been kind to her when she was as dependent as he had become.

He would never have left the Keneston house of his own will. When Washington was twelve, his father drove into the farmyard on his broken-down wagon and called for him until he came out of the barn where he had been wandering with little Katie. Washington knew the sort of man his father was, but he knew that sons obeyed fathers. When he had reached the wagon his father told him to lift a hundred-pound sack of grain out onto the ground, and then back into the wagon again. When he did it without straining, his father said, "You're big enough to work. Get packed up. You're coming home."

Washington ran away four years later and set up on his own as a hired hand and an odd-jobber. He was a hard worker and skillful. The best thing about him was his pride in good work. By the time he was twenty-five, he had repaired or built everything but a locomotive. Give him a forge and some scraps of old iron, my grandfather said, and he could make a locomotive too. I knew him to shoe a horse, install plumbing, dig a well, make a gun, build a road, lay a dry stone wall, do the foundation and frame of a house, invent a new kind of trap for beavers, manufacture his own shotgun shells, grind knives and turn a baseball bat on a lathe. The bat was made out of rock maple, and so heavy that I could barely lift it to my shoulders when he made it for my thirteenth birthday. The trouble was that he was incredibly slow. He was not interested in your problems, but in the problems of the job itself. He didn't care if it took him five weeks to shingle an outhouse that plumbing was going to outmode in a year. This was one outhouse that would *stay* shingled, although the shingles might protect only the spiders and the mother cat.

His slowness cost him money, but money did not matter to him. He did not even call it an abomination like drinking, cardplaying, smoking, swearing, lipstick and dancing; he simply did not think of it. He needed no more for supper than bread and milk. Did anyone else? If he didn't care about money, he cared about people sticking to their word; he cared about honor, whether it concerned his pay or the hour at which he was to finish a job. Once a deacon of the church asked Washington to fix the rickety wheels of a carriage. Washington told him it would be four dollars, and he spent six full days at the forge strengthening the wheels and adding supports until the axles would have carried five tons of hay, much less the deacon and his thin wife. But the deacon said, when the carriage was delivered, that four dollars was too much, and that three dollars was what the job was worth. Washington refused to take anything, and he never sat in his pew again, for if deacons cheated, churches were corrupt. He read his Bible by himself.

During all his years of solitude, he was extraordinarily sociable whenever he saw his family, as if the taciturnity he had assumed with his solitude was unnatural. He stored up, alone in his shack, acres of volubility which the sight of a relative discovered. If I remarked to him that an apple he had given me was a good apple, he might say, "Well, I remember; that apple came from the tree by the woodchuck hole in the northeast corner that leans toward the south; though it don't lean too much; down in that patch there; it's from a splice, that branch is, from a big tree, high as a house, on John Wentworth's land; his orchard behind his cowbarn beside the saphouse; well, the tree, old John Wentworth's been dead twenty years' tree, was always a good one for apples, big and meaty with plenty of juice to them; and one summer about 1919, no, 1920 I guess, I was working up to John's; I was fixing some sap pails had leaks and I shingled the icehouse, the back of it, where you couldn't see from the road but it was about gone; I'd done the front before and I told him the back would need doing; I was there as much as two months, ten weeks I guess; and it come apple time while I was there, and I helped him picking and he come up here and helped me; and I had my few trees up here, not so many as now, not half so many, as I reckon it, and one time I was mending a water pipe that fed the horse trough, it had come loose, and John didn't have no more solder, so I had to come all the way back to the shop; and as I was going I stopped to look at the tree, the big one, and I thought about asking John if I could splice off a limb as part pay; well, I never did get back that day because I saw a deer in the peas when I got here. . . . " And then he would tell how he waited for the deer and shot him, and what he had done with the pelt, and what John Wentworth had said to him when he asked for the limb, and how he had spliced it to his own tree, and on and on until, if the body had been strong enough, Washington would have talked out the whole contents of his mind. Scratch him anywhere and you touched his autobiography. Any detail was sufficiently relevant if it kept the tongue moving and the silence broken. My grandfather's many memories, on the other hand, were separated into stories with just enough irrelevant material of the past to keep them circumstantial; they had form, and you knew when he had come to a stopping point. Washington was a talking machine capable of producing the recall of every sensation, every motive, of a lifetime; and all the objects of his world could serve him like Proust's *madeleine*.[1]

It was not the past that interested him, but talking. If he had known about contemporary politics, he would have been willing to use it as his pretext for speech; but in the pursuit of independence he had cut himself off from everything but his daily sensations. The talking was the same when he was young and when he was old. When we visited him at his shack, he would invariably trot alongside the car or buggy as we left, jogging a hundred yards farther with the story he couldn't end. My mother remembers from her girlhood, and I from twenty-five years later, how my grandparents would go to bed while he was talking, and how he would drone on for hours in the dark. When he was old and sick, he would talk in his chair in the kitchen while they read in the living room. Sometimes he would laugh a little and pause, as he reached a brief resting space in his unfinishable monologue. My grandmother learned to say, "Is that so?" whenever there was a pause. My grandfather swore that she could do it in her sleep.

Washington always wore the same costume in the years I knew him. The only thing that ever differed about his appearance was his beard, for he shaved in the summer and let his hair grow for warmth in the winter. He wore heavy brown overalls, patched and stitched, and a lighter brown workshirt stitched so extensively that the cloth had nearly vanished under the coarse stitches; over these he wore a light, nondescript workcoat, and in winter a thick, ancient overcoat with safety pins instead of buttons. He often spent his evenings sewing by the light of a candle until his eyes hurt.

Washington had built his shack on the slope of Ragged Mountain

---

1. A small rich cake, the taste of which sets off a flood of memories of his childhood and early life in the mind of the hero of Proust's novel *Remembrance of Things Past*.

on the western, downward side of New Canada Road, two miles up from U.S. 3 by the road, but half a mile as the crow flies. He had a small pasture for cattle, a hen yard, geese wandering loose, a good orchard of various apple trees and other northern fruits, and at various times he kept pigs, goats, ducks and a dog. His shack was small, and it had grown smaller inside every year. Layers of things saved grew inward from the walls until Washington could barely move inside it. A tiny path among the boxes and animal pelts led from the door to a cross path from an iron stove to a Morris chair. Washington slept upright in the chair every night.

If he found a board in a ditch as he walked home from the day's work, and if the board had a bent nail in it, he would hammer the nail out of the board with a rock and take it home. If the board would make kindling or if it was strong enough to build with, he would take it along too. He would straighten the nail with a hammer on the anvil at his lean-to shop and put it in a box with other nails of the same dimensions. He might have to move a dozen other boxes to find the right one, but he would know where it was. It wasn't that he was a miser, because he cared nothing for the money he saved by collecting used nails. And when he died he did not, like the misers reported in the newspapers, leave a hundred thousand dollars in the back of a mirror; he left a hundred thousand straightened nails. He saved the nails because it was a sin to allow good material to go to waste. Everyone knows the story about the box of pieces of string, found in an old attic, labeled "String too short to be saved."

Besides nails, Washington kept a complete line of hardware and parts: clasps, hinges, brackets, braces, hoe handles, axe heads and spare rungs for ladders. He also saved elk, moose, bear, beaver, fox and deer pelts. On the wall beside the door were his rifle and shotgun and boxes of shells and cartridges. He was a good shot and a patient hunter. Until he was old he shot a big buck every year and ate nothing but venison until the bones were bare. Once a year, in the early fall, he had my grandmother bake him a woodchuck in her big oven. Only when his legs were so bad that he did not dare to wait out an animal, for fear that he would not be able to move after being still, did the woodchucks and hedgehogs manage to eat his peas and his apples and in this way avenge their ancestors.

He ate one kind of food exclusively until he finished his supply of it. Often it would be nothing but oatmeal for a week. Again he would buy two dozen loaves of stale bread and eat nothing else until the last moldy crust was gone. I remember him eating his way through a case of corn flakes; and when the woodchucks had eaten his garden, one winter, he ate a case of canned peas. It was no principle with him, but simply the easiest thing to do. When he was old and sick, living a winter in the rocking chair in my grandmother's kitchen beside Christopher, the canary, he bought his own food and kept it separately, in a cardboard box beside him. At this time he had a run on graham crackers. He did not eat on any schedule, and sometimes my grandparents would wake up in the middle of the night to hear him gumming a cracker, his false teeth lost in the darkness of a Mason jar.

When he was younger he must have been nearly self-sufficient. For much of each year he would refuse outside jobs from anyone, unless my grandfather particularly needed a mowing machine fixed or a scythe handle made when the store was out of them. And often he wouldn't take any money from my grandfather, although my grandmother would try to pay him in disguise with shirts and canned vegetables and pies. To pay the taxes on his land he worked a few days a year on the county road gang, repairing the dirt roads that laced the hills and connected the back farms with the main road in the valley. For clothing he had his gifts, and I know that he once made himself a coat out of fur he had trapped. For food he had all the game he shot, and he kept potatoes and apples and carrots and turnips in a lean-to (the food covered with burlap a foot thick to keep it from freezing) beside his shack, and he canned on his small stove dozens of jars of peas, tomatoes, corn and wax beans.

When he took an outside job or made a little money by peddling patent medicines like Quaker Oil or Rawleigh's Salve, he might buy himself a candy bar or five postcards or a pad of paper, or he might give it away. When my mother and her sister were at college, they sometimes had a letter from Washington with a nickel carefully wrapped inside. The patent medicines were before my time, and my grandfather told me about them. Washington would occasionally fill a large basket with his vials and jars, cut himself a walking stick, and set out to peddle on the back roads. He would sleep in barns, barter for his food, and return after a week with a pocketful of change. A room on the second floor of the farmhouse was always full of cases marked in the trade name of a cough syrup or a tonic. Everyone in the family sniffed up drops of Quaker Oil to stop sneezing, or ate a few drops on a lump of sugar for coughing.

Washington worked hard at tending his trees and garden and animals, and when he was through with his chores he invented more work for himself. He spent considerable time and energy at what I could only call his hobby. He moved big rocks. His ingenuity, which was always providing him with the creation of new, usually trivial tools (tools which took him four days to make and which simplified a fifteen-minute job), invented a massive instrument of three tall pine logs and an arrangement of pulleys. It looked like the tripod of a camera, but the camera would have been as big as a Model A. By means of this engine, he was able to move huge rocks; I don't know how he moved the whole contraption after the rock was lifted, though when I was a boy I must have heard detailed descriptions of a hundred rock-moves. (I was another who learned to shut the door between his ears and his brain.) He moved any rock for whose displacement he could find an excuse: small boulders that obstructed his fields; rocks near the house whose appearance offended him; rocks beside the road into which a car might sometime, possibly, crash; rocks, even, in the way of other people's cows in other people's pastures. When he was old and couldn't use the machine any more, it weathered beside the front door of his shack, and when he died someone took it away for the pine.

It was the cows he was thinking of, not the farmers, when he moved rocks in a pasture. However seriously he meant it, he often indicated that, except for his family and one or two others, humanity was morally inferior to animals; at least to the animals which were, like his family, his own creatures. He had developed a gorgeous line of cattle, out of a combination of devotion and shrewd trading. It was when I knew him that he had Phoebe, the last beast that he truly loved. Phoebe was a Holstein, a prodigy among milkers and the only cow in the world who thought she was a collie dog. Treated like a house pet from birth, she acted like one with Washington. She came frisking to him when he called her, romped with him, and all but whined when she couldn't follow him into the shack and curl her great bulk at his feet. Washington fed her apples and peas in the pod while he ate stale bread. She slept on the other side of a plank wall from him, so that he could hear any irregularity in her breathing. He washed her every day. When she was old and lame, Washington invented a rig like his rock-mover to help her stand or lie down. He nursed her when she was sick, and he was caressing her when she died.

My grandfather told me about an earlier pet, Old Duke the ox. Washington taught Old Duke to shake hands and roll over. He made a cart and a sled which Old Duke could pull, and it would take him a whole forenoon to drive the two and a half miles from his shack to the farmhouse. The only time Washington ever showed romantic interest in a woman was when a young girl named Esther Dodge helped out at the farm one harvest. Washington paid court by asking Esther, a pretty red-cheeked country girl as my mother remembers her, to go for a ride behind Old Duke. Esther would only go if the girls, my ten-year-old mother and her younger sister Caroline, could come along, and they giggled all the way.

When Washington was seventy-eight, Anson Buck found him in a coma one morning when he came to deliver a package on his R.F.D. route. Anson carried him into the back seat and drove fourteen miles to the hospital at Franklin, where they operated. When he recovered, he went back to his shack. One day the following December, my grandmother made some mince pies and decided to send one to Wash. She flagged down a young lumberman as he passed by in his blue 1934 Chevrolet and asked him to leave it off on his way up New Canada to work. He was back almost as soon as he left, saying, "He's looney. Old Wash is looney." After Great-Aunt Nannie, no such announcement was liable to surprise my grandmother. She called "Yoo-hoo" to the barn and told my grandfather what had happened. The lumberman drove them to the shack.

They found Washington sitting on the floor of his cabin between his sleeping chair and his cold stove, which my grandfather said hadn't been lit all night. Washington didn't seem to notice that they were there but kept on talking as they had heard him talk before they entered. What he said was incoherent at first, but they could tell that it was about building a road, about white hogs and about two ladies. He allowed himself to be helped over the thick snow into the Model A and driven back to the house.

Washington told his story for many days, over and over, until my grandparents finally understood its sequence. My grandfather told me all about it the next summer. The night before he was found, Wash said, he took a walk to look at a timber lot of my grandfather's north of his shack. (His legs were so bad that he never walked any farther than his well that winter; the timber was three-quarters of a mile away.) When he got there he saw a whole crowd of people working, though it was nearly dark, and they were cutting a big new road. They had bulldozers, which were white, and a big herd of white horses. He walked up to some of the people and tried to talk to them, but they acted as if they couldn't see him, and they were jabbering in a language he couldn't make out, but it wasn't Canuck. He walked away from the crowd and climbed a little rise, and when he looked down on the other side of the rise to a cleared field he saw about a hundred hogs, all pure white. In front of them were the biggest sow and the biggest boar he had ever seen, both pure white, and they were mating. Washington started to walk down the hill and he stubbed his boot on the nose of a horse that was sticking up through the snow. He and the horse fell in the snow, down and down, until the people lifted them up on the huge piece of chicken wire that was underneath the snow. Then two women among the people took him back to his cabin and stayed there all night with him. He watched, all night long, the tips of their hats against the background of starlight from the cracks in the cabin walls. Though he asked them questions, they never answered.

The doctor came and listened to Washington and gave him morphine. When he woke up he seemed fine except that he kept on with his story. My grandfather told him that there was no road going into his timber lot, and Washington was only indignant. After a week he began to ask visitors about the road, and they all told him there wasn't any, and he stopped telling the story. In the spring he paid a boy with a flivver to drive him past the place so that he could see with his own eyes.

He never had delusions again. Perhaps he had left his cabin for water and had fallen in the snow when his legs failed him. Perhaps he had crawled for an hour in pain through all that whiteness back to his shack where he had talked to the boxes all night. By April he was back at his cabin again, and that summer he was eighty years old.

He died in a state nursing home. My grandfather and I went to see him a month before he died, and his cheeks were flushed above the white beard, and his eyes shone while he performed his monologue. He joked with us and showed us the sores on his legs. He displayed me to his nurses and to the silent old men in the room with him. It was a little like all the other times I had met him, yet seeing him ready to die I was all the more impressed by the waste of him —the energy, the ingenuity, the strength to do what he wanted— as he lay frail and bearded in a nightgown provided by the legislature. The waste that he hated, I thought, was through him like blood in his veins. He had saved nails and wasted life. He had lived alone, but if he was a hermit he was neither religious nor philosophical. His fanaticisms, which might have been creative, were as petulant as his break from the church. I felt that he was intelligent, or it would not have mattered, but I had no evidence to support my conviction. His only vision was a delusion of white hogs. He worked hard all his life at being himself, but there were no principles to examine when his life was over. It was as if there had been a moral skeleton which had lacked the flesh of the intellect and the blood of experience. The life that he could recall totally was not worth recalling; it was a box of string too short to be saved.

Standing beside him in the nursing home, I saw ahead for one moment into the residue, five years from then, of Washington Woodward's life: the shack has caved in and his straightened nails have rusted into the dirt of Ragged Mountain; though the rocks stay where he moved them, no one knows how they got there; his animals are dead and their descendants have made bad connections; his apple trees produce small and sour fruits; the best built hayracks rot under rotting sheds; in New Hampshire the frost tumbles the cleverest wall; those who knew him best are dead or dying, and his gestures have assumed the final waste of irrelevance.

THOMAS BABINGTON MACAULAY

Boswell[1]

The Life of Johnson is assuredly a great, a very great work. Homer is not more decidedly the first of heroic poets, Shakespeare is not more decidedly the first of dramatists, Demosthenes is not more decidedly the first of orators, than Boswell is the first of biographers. He has no second. He has distanced all his competitors so decidedly that it is not worth while to place them. Eclipse is first, and the rest nowhere.

We are not sure that there is in the whole history of the human intellect so strange a phenomenon as this book. Many of the greatest men that ever lived have written biography. Boswell was one of the smallest men that ever lived, and he has beaten them all. He was, if we are to give any credit to his own account or to the united testimony of all who knew him, a man of the meanest and feeblest intellect. Johnson described him as a fellow who had missed his only chance of immortality by not having been alive when the Dunciad was written. Beauclerk used his name as a proverbial expression for a bore. He was the laughing-stock of the whole of that brilliant society which has owed to him the greater part of its fame. He was always laying himself at the feet of some eminent man, and begging to be spit upon and trampled upon. He was always earning some ridiculous nickname, and then "binding it as a crown unto him," not merely in metaphor, but literally. He exhibited himself, at the Shakespeare Jubilee, to all the crowd which filled Stratford-on-Avon, with a placard round his hat bearing the inscription of Corsica Boswell.[2] In his Tour he proclaimed to all the world that at Edinburgh he was known by the appellation of Paoli Boswell. Servile and impertinent, shallow and pedantic, a bigot and a sot, bloated with family pride, and eternally blustering about the dignity of a born gentleman, yet stooping to be a tale-bearer, an eavesdropper, a common butt in the taverns of London, so curious to know everybody who was talked about, that, Tory and high Churchman as he was, he maneuvered, we have been told, for an introduction to Tom Paine, so vain of the most childish distinctions, that when he had been to court, he drove to the office where his book was printing without changing his clothes, and summoned all the printer's devils to admire his new ruffles and sword; such was this man, and such he was content and proud to be. Everything which another man would

---

1. From a review of Croker's edition (1831) of Boswell's *Life of Johnson*.

2. Boswell traveled on the Continent in 1765-1766 and was introduced to General Paoli, leader of the resistance to French power in Corsica. Boswell sympathized with the Corsican cause and paraded his sentiments.

have hidden, everything the publication of which would have made another man hang himself, was matter of gay and clamorous exultation to his weak and diseased mind. What silly things he said, what bitter retorts he provoked, how at one place he was troubled with evil presentiments which came to nothing, how at another place, on waking from a drunken doze, he read the prayerbook and took a hair of the dog that had bitten him, how he went to see men hanged and came away maudlin, how he added five hundred pounds to the fortune of one of his babies because she was not scared at Johnson's ugly face, how he was frightened out of his wits at sea, and how the sailors quieted him as they would have quieted a child, how tipsy he was at Lady Cork's one evening and how much his merriment annoyed the ladies, how impertinent he was to the Duchess of Argyle and with what stately contempt she put down his impertinence, how Colonel Macleod sneered to his face at his impudent obtrusiveness, how his father and the very wife of his bosom laughed and fretted at his fooleries, all these things he proclaimed to all the world, as if they had been subjects for pride and ostentatious rejoicing. All the caprices of his temper, all the illusions of his vanity, all his hypochondriac whimsies, all his castles in the air, he displayed with a cool self-complacency, a perfect unconsciousness that he was making a fool of himself, to which it is impossible to find a parallel in the whole history of mankind. He has used many people ill; but assuredly he has used nobody so ill as himself.

That such a man should have written one of the best books in the world is strange enough. But this is not all. Many persons who have conducted themselves foolishly in active life, and whose conversation has indicated no superior powers of mind, have left us valuable works. Goldsmith was very justly described by one of his contemporaries as an inspired idiot, and by another as a being

> Who wrote like an angel, and talked like poor Poll.

La Fontaine was in society a mere simpleton. His blunders would not come in amiss among the stories of Hierocles.[3] But these men attained literary eminence in spite of their weaknesses. Boswell attained it by reason of his weaknesses. If he had not been a great fool, he would never have been a great writer. Without all the qualities which made him the jest and the torment of those among whom he lived, without the officiousness, the inquisitiveness, the effrontery, the toad-eating,[4] the insensibility to all reproof, he never could have produced so excellent a book. He was a slave, proud of his servitude, a Paul Pry, convinced that his own curiosity and garrulity were virtues, an unsafe companion who never scrupled to repay the most liberal hospitality by the basest violation of confidence, a man without delicacy, without shame, without sense enough to know when

3. A fourth-century Roman versifier, author of *Facetiae (Jests)*.

4. Obsequiousness, servile flattery.

he was hurting the feelings of others or when he was exposing himself to derision; and because he was all this, he has, in an important department of literature,[5] immeasurably surpassed such writers as Tacitus, Clarendon, Alfieri, and his own idol Johnson.

Of the talents which ordinarily raise men to eminence as writers, Boswell had absolutely none. There is not in all his books a single remark of his own on literature, politics, religion, or society, which is not either commonplace or absurd. His dissertations on hereditary gentility, on the slave-trade, and on the entailing of landed estates, may serve as examples. To say that these passages are sophistical would be to pay them an extravagant compliment. They have no pretence to argument, or even to meaning. He has reported innumerable observations made by himself in the course of conversation. Of those observations we do not remember one which is above the intellectual capacity of a boy of fifteen. He has printed many of his own letters, and in these letters he is always ranting or twaddling. Logic, eloquence, wit, taste, all those things which are generally considered as making a book valuable, were utterly wanting to him. He had, indeed, a quick observation and a retentive memory. These qualities, if he had been a man of sense and virtue, would scarcely of themselves have sufficed to make him conspicuous; but, because he was a dunce, a parasite, and a coxcomb, they have made him immortal.

Those parts of his book which, considered abstractedly, are most utterly worthless, are delightful when we read them as illustrations of the character of the writer. Bad in themselves, they are good dramatically, like the nonsense of Justice Shallow, the clipped English of Dr. Caius, or the misplaced consonants of Fluellen.[6] Of all confessors, Boswell is the most candid. Other men who have pretended to lay open their own hearts, Rousseau, for example, and Lord Byron, have evidently written with a constant view to effect, and are to be then most distrusted when they seem to be most sincere. There is scarcely any man who would not rather accuse himself of great crimes and of dark and tempestuous passions than proclaim all his little vanities and wild fancies. It would be easier to find a person who would avow actions like those of Caesar Borgia or Danton, than one who would publish a daydream like those of Alnaschar and Malvolio.[7] Those weaknesses which most men keep covered up in the most secret places of the mind, not to be disclosed to the eye of friendship or of love, were precisely the weaknesses which Boswell paraded before all the world. He was perfectly frank, because the weakness of his understanding and the tumult of his spirits pre-

5. Biography.
6. Comic characters in Shakespeare's *Henry IV Part Two*, *The Merry Wives of Windsor*, and *Henry V*, respectively.
7. Caesar Borgia was a Renaissance prince, infamous for treachery and cruel- ty, and Danton was a leader in the Terror during the French Revolution. Malvolio, a character in Shakespeare's *Twelfth Night*, and Alnaschar, a figure in the *Arabian Nights*, are both noted for foolish vanity and ludicrous fantasies.

vented him from knowing when he made himself ridiculous. His book resembles nothing so much as the conversation of the inmates of the Palace of Truth.

His fame is great; and it will, we have no doubt, be lasting, but it is fame of a peculiar kind, and indeed marvelously resembles infamy. We remember no other case in which the world has made so great a distinction between a book and its author. In general, the book and the author are considered as one. To admire the book is to admire the author. The case of Boswell is an exception, we think the only exception, to this rule. His work is universally allowed to be interesting, instructive, eminently original: yet it has brought him nothing but contempt. All the world reads it: all the world delights in it: yet we do not remember ever to have read or ever to have heard any expression of respect and admiration for the man to whom we owe so much instruction and amusement. While edition after edition of his book was coming forth, his son, as Mr. Croker tells us, was ashamed of it, and hated to hear it mentioned. This feeling was natural and reasonable. Sir Alexander saw that, in proportion to the celebrity of the work, was the degradation of the author. The very editors of this unfortunate gentleman's books have forgotten their allegiance, and, like those Puritan casuists who took arms by the authority of the king against his person, have attacked the writer while doing homage to the writings. Mr. Croker, for example, has published two thousand five hundred notes on the life of Johnson, and yet scarcely ever mentions the biographer whose performance he has taken such pains to illustrate without some expression of contempt.

An ill-natured man Boswell certainly was not. Yet the malignity of the most malignant satirist could scarcely cut deeper than his thoughtless loquacity. Having himself no sensibility to derision and contempt, he took it for granted that all others were equally callous. He was not ashamed to exhibit himself to the whole world as a common spy, a common tattler, a humble companion without the excuse of poverty, and to tell a hundred stories of his own pertness and folly, and of the insults which his pertness and folly brought upon him. It was natural that he should show little discretion in cases in which the feelings or the honor of others might be concerned. No man, surely, ever published such stories respecting persons whom he professed to love and revere. He would infallibly have made his hero as contemptible as he has made himself, had not his hero really possessed some moral and intellectual qualities of a very high order. The best proof that Johnson was really an extraordinary man is that his character, instead of being degraded, has, on the whole, been decidedly raised by a work in which all his vices and weaknesses are exposed more unsparingly than they ever were exposed by

Churchill or by Kenrick.[8]

8. The one a satiric poet and the other an irritable scholar, contemporaries of Johnson who attacked him in verse and biography.

QUESTIONS

1. In what ways does Macaulay use contrast, antithesis, to carry out his characterization of Boswell? What major contrast is central to the sketch, its organizing principle? With what other writers is Boswell compared, and to what purposes? To what extent and in what particular ways does antithesis appear in the construction of the paragraphs?
2. Indicate several instances of repetition of sentence structure. What effects does Macaulay seek with such repetition? How does he vary from it, and with what results?
3. What, according to Macaulay, are the defects in Boswell's personal character that contribute to the excellence of his writing?
4. What particulars of Macaulay's characterization are discernible in these two extracts from Boswell's Life of Johnson:

The heterogeneous composition of human nature was remarkably exemplified in Johnson. His liberality in giving his money to persons in distress was extraordinary. Yet there lurked about him a propensity to paltry saving. One day I owned to him that "I was occasionally troubled with a fit of *narrowness*." "Why, sir," said he, "so am I. *But I do not tell it.*" He has now and then borrowed a shilling of me; and when I asked for it again, seemed to be rather out of humor. A droll little circumstance once occurred: As if he meant to reprimand my minute exactness as a creditor, he thus addressed me—"Boswell, lend me sixpence—*not to be repaid.*"

I have no minute of any interview with Johnson till Thursday, May 15th, when I find what follows:

BOSWELL. "I wish much to be in Parliament, sir." JOHNSON. "Why, sir, unless you come resolved to support any administration, you would be the worse for being in Parliament, because you would be obliged to live more expensively." BOSWELL. "Perhaps, sir, I should be the less happy for being in Parliament. I never would sell my vote, and I should be vexed if things went wrong." JOHNSON. "That's cant, sir. It would not vex you more in the house than in the gallery; public affairs vex no man." BOSWELL. "Have not they vexed yourself a little, sir? Have not you been vexed by all the turbulence of this reign, and by that absurd vote in the House of Commons, 'That the influence of the Crown has increased, is increasing, and ought to be diminished?' " JOHNSON. "Sir, I have never slept an hour less nor eat an ounce less meat. I would have knocked the factious dogs on the head, to be sure; but I was not vexed." BOSWELL. "I declare, sir, upon my honor, I did imagine I was vexed, and took a pride in it; but it was, perhaps, cant; for I own I neither ate less nor slept less." JOHNSON. "My dear friend, clear your mind of cant. You may talk as other people do; you may say to a man, 'Sir, I am your most humble servant.' You are not his most humble servant. You may say, 'These are bad times; it is a melancholy thing to be reserved to such times.' You don't mind the times. You tell a man, 'I am sorry you had such bad weather the last day of your journey, and were so much wet.' You don't care sixpence whether he is wet or dry. You may *talk* in this manner; it is a mode of talking in society; but don't *think* foolishly."

WALTER JACKSON BATE
A Life of Allegory[1]

It is Johnson from the age of about fifty-five, in 1764, to his death twenty years later, of whom Boswell could say, near the beginning of his biography, that his "character . . . nay his figure and manner, are, I believe, more generally known than those of almost any man." This is also the Johnson who passed into legend during the century after his death. For perhaps the most engaging group of memoirs in literary history have Johnson in his later years as their subject. Of them, those of Mrs. Thrale, Fanny Burney, and especially Boswell, together contain records of direct conversation richer and more complete than those for any man before the twentieth century. Boswell's great *Life* has the additional attraction of providing, as does no other biography or memoir, a panorama of the social and intellectual life of its age. Aside from the range of topics discussed, some of the most remarkable men of the period appear directly, like characters in a drama. For the company in which Johnson appears includes such men as Edmund Burke, Sir Joshua Reynolds, Oliver Goldsmith, and David Garrick; and, to a less degree, Adam Smith and Edward Gibbon. The famous Club founded in 1764, originally composed of nine members, had expanded to thirty-five after Johnson's death. It is doubtful whether any similar group has had so distinguished a membership.

But if Johnson's character and manner at the time of his death were "more generally known than those of almost any man" the principal reason is Johnson himself. It is not a series of happy accidents that the accounts of Johnson's conversation during these years are unrivaled in their vitality and completeness. He said even "the most common things," as Thomas Tyers wrote, "in the *newest* manner." Johnson's habitual power of phrase, and the ready range of his knowledge, stimulated the desire of Boswell and others to record what he said. To this was joined the strong personal appeal he made to so many different people, even those unacquainted with the struggles of his earlier life. Boswell's unrivaled art has only

1. Chapter 9 in *The Achievement of Samuel Johnson*, 1955.

recently begun to be understood. Still, the ultimate greatness of Boswell's *Life*, as Mr. Tinker has said, is really Johnson, who is "not merely the subject, but in the last analysis the author too." Yet the very vividness with which Johnson's conversation is recorded proved so attractive that during the nineteenth century it drew attention from his work to his life, and to his life principally in his later years. Hence the common picture of him enthroned in a tavern or at the home of the Thrales. Also the recorded remarks of Johnson naturally tend to be the sort that would be remembered and written down. The enormous charity of Johnson is stressed by Boswell and others, and examples of it appear repeatedly. But Johnson's wit and occasionally abrupt remarks were naturally more quotable. Particularly when edged with exasperation, they have lingered picturesquely in the minds of Boswell's readers; and one finds a widespread assumption that his talk was always thus. When, after an argument, a rather dense acquaintance stated, "I do not *understand* that," Johnson replied, "I have furnished you with an argument. I am not obliged to furnish you with an *understanding*." And there are the even more irritable replies in Mrs. Thrale's *Anecdotes*. Abominating, as he did, loose talk about the ease of being content and happy in a world of misery, he became heated when a friend pushed the matter by suddenly stating that "his wife's sister was *really* happy, and called upon the lady to confirm his assertion." When she did so "somewhat roundly," and with a pert superiority, Johnson exploded:

"If your sister-in-law is really the contented being she professes herself ... her life gives the lie to every research of humanity; for she is happy without health, without beauty, without money, and without understanding." [When Mrs. Thrale later] expressed something of the horror I felt, "The same stupidity (said he) which prompted her to extol a felicity she never felt, hindered her from feeling what shocks you ... I tell you, the woman is ugly, and sickly, and foolish, and poor; and would it not make a man *hang* himself to hear such a creature say, it was happy."[2]

Often painfully ill, and, particularly in his last years, forcing himself out into company in a healthy attempt to get his mind on other subjects than himself, the temptation to make such testy remarks was naturally strong. Though Boswell and others remind us of the physical and mental pain Johnson was often suffering, this context is easily forgotten. Instead, the remarks start out from the page and are then coalesced with others of a similar sort. When further joined with the various oddities of manner mentioned by Boswell, Mrs. Thrale, Miss Reynolds, and others, they could produce, especially for the nineteenth century, a caricature of fascinating grotesqueness. Macaulay's famous essay is the classic example:

2. Piozzi, *Anecdotes, J.M.*, I, 335 [Bate's note].

"The old philosopher is still among us, in the brown coat with the metal buttons and the shirt which ought to, be at wash, blinking puffing, rolling his head, drumming with his fingers, tearing his meat like a tiger, and swallowing his tea in oceans."

By its very success and vividness, then, Boswell's portrait of Johnson has often tempted readers to substitute it for Johnson himself. The hardy persistence of the nineteenth-century legend of Johnson illustrates the danger of building wholly on Boswell, particularly if this fires one to do some additional decoration. Still, Boswell's *Life* is not only the most fascinating but, for the later years, the most truthful of biographies. Without a doubt, he was able, in reworking his notes, to achieve the authentic tone of Johnson. There is the same ready imagery that we find in his written prose: "Learning among the Scotch is like bread in a besieged town: every man gets a little, but no man gets a full meal." "A woman's preaching is like a dog standing on its hind legs. It is not done well, but we are surprised to find it done at all." There is the same common-sense seizing of essentials, the same habitual and sharp distinctions, in even the smallest matters. Speaking of Mrs. Elizabeth Montagu's *Essay on Shakespeare*, Reynolds states, " 'I think that essay does her honor': JOHNSON. Yes, Sir; it does *her* honor, but it would do nobody else honor. I have, indeed, not read it all. But when I take up the end of a web, and find it packthread, I do not expect, by looking further, to find it embroidery.' " Later: " 'Mrs. Montagu has dropped me. Now, Sir, there are people whom one should very well like to *drop*, but would not wish to be *dropped by*.' " Thomas Newton's *Dissertations on the Prophecies*, said Dr. Adams, " 'is his great work': JOHNSON. 'Why, Sir, it is *Tom's* great work; but how far it is great, or how much of it is *Tom's* are other questions.' " And there are the engaging, quite unexpected touches, heightened by Johnson's own amused self-awareness of his temptation to "talk for victory." Doubtless expecting an elaborate defense, Boswell once asked: "can you trace the cause of your antipathy to the Scotch?" But the reply was simply, " 'I *can not*, Sir': BOSWELL. 'Old Mr. Sheridan says, it is because they sold out Charles the First.' JOHNSON. 'Then, Sir, *old Mr. Sheridan has found out a very good reason.*' "

To recount the last twenty years of Johnson's life is indeed to quote from Boswell. The uniqueness of a work often appears in the extent to which it resists summary. The quality of Johnson's talk, as of his writing, is lost by summary: it can only be quoted. And so impressive and copious are the recorded conversations of these years that any narration of this period of his life—or even an attempt to analyze it topically—inevitably gives up and relapses into an anthology of selected quotations. The appeal of Johnson's talk is to be found in the union of strength, quickness, and range. The desperate clutch upward from the dark welter of his own subjective feelings gives urgency and impetus to his expressions. But to stop here is to stumble into the fallacy of interpreting genius by compensation. For the need to order experience does not by itself explain the final order achieved. Simultaneously accompanying it is the uncanny readiness of mind, whatever the occasion: in the brilliant defense Johnson dictated for the escaped Negro pleading his liberty in the Scottish courts; or in the eighteen-line birthday poem extemporized at Mrs. Thrale's request—in which the lines all rhyme with "five," and the rhyme-words are arranged alphabetically. It appears even in mere grumbling: Boswell asks whether Bishop Burnet did not give " 'a good Life of Rochester.' JOHNSON. 'We have a good *Death*: there is not much *Life* ' "; "BOSWELL. 'Is not the Giant's Causeway worth seeing?' JOHNSON 'Worth seeing, yes; but not worth *going* to see' "; " 'I mentioned there was not half a guinea's worth of pleasure in seeing [the new amusement-center, the "Pantheon"]. JOHNSON. 'But, Sir, there is half a guinea's worth of inferiority to other people in *not* having seen it.' " As for range, he could repeat *verbatim*, as we have noted, whole pages he had lightly skimmed, from the entire body of known literature at the time, and yet arouse admiration by his discussion of mechanics before the Society of Arts and Manufacturers. The inventor, Richard Arkwright, thought him "the only person who, on a first view, understood the principle and powers of his most complicated piece of machinery"—the spinning-jenny.[3] "Last night," Boswell records in the *Tour to the Hebrides*, Johnson "gave us an account of the whole process of tanning, and of the nature of milk and the various operations upon it, as making whey, etc."; and then Boswell tells that, before the company, he successfully tried out Johnson on the intricacies of what he thought would be as "far out of the way of a philosopher and poet" as he could think of at the moment—"the trade of a butcher." Earlier, there were the talks with the officers at Fort George on granulating gunpowder—where Johnson later felt he had spoken too "ostentatiously." "He this morning gave us all the operation of coining, and at night . . . the operation of brewing spirits." Mrs. Thrale tells of his talk with her daughter's dancing-master about dancing, "which the man protested, at the close of the discourse, the Doctor knew more of than himself." As he grew older, he became more consciously deliberate in his effort to avoid the easy gossip and routine anecdotes that serve as the mainstay of most conversation: to avoid "stagnation" by the constant incursion of "new images" and "new topics." And on one of the rare occasions when he spoke favorably of any quality in himself, he admitted to Boswell:

3. George Steevens, *Anecdotes, J.M.,* II, 325 [Bate's note].

"I value myself upon this, that there is *nothing of the old man in my conversation.* I am now sixty-eight, and I have no more of it than at twenty-eight. . . . Mrs. Thrale's mother said of me what flattered me much. A clergyman was complaining of want of society in the country . . . and said, 'They talk of *runts;*' (that is, young cows). 'Sir, (said Mrs. Salusbury) Mr. Johnson would learn to talk of runts.' . . . He added, 'I think myself a very polite man.' "[4]

Certainly the years from 1766 to about 1781, when he was seventy-two, brought Johnson more happiness than he had ever had. From Monday night through Friday he commonly stayed with the Thrales at Streatham, and spent the weekends, as Mrs. Thrale said, with "his numerous family in Fleet Street . . . treating them with the same, or perhaps more ceremonious civility, than he would have done by as many people of fashion . . ." There were the frequent trips to Lichfield, and the visits with Dr. Adams at Oxford and Dr. Taylor at Ashbourne. At sixty-four, he took the exacting, at times even dangerous, tour with Boswell through Scotland and the Hebrides (1773), recounted in his *Journey to the Western Islands* (1775) and Boswell's *Tour to the Hebrides* (1785). With the Thrales he traveled to both North Wales (1774) and France (1775). During the thirteen years after 1765, when the edition of Shakespeare appeared, he wrote very little. Except for the prefaces, dedications, and other contributions he made for friends and others who needed help, there are only the *Journey to the Western Islands* and the political pamphlets—*The False Alarm* (1770), the *Falkland's Islands* pamphlet (1771), *The Patriot* (1774), and *Taxation no Tyranny* (1775)—which he wrote with a fraction of his mind and in no time at all. But there is little of the lacerating sense of guilt about indolence, and the fright at month-long states of helpless languor that he felt before and after his work on Shakespeare. We may think of the precept he keeps quoting from Robert Burton's *Anatomy of Melancholy:* "Be not solitary, be not idle." If, so far as writing is concerned, he was idle, he was certainly not solitary. One of the most frequently recurring words in Johnson's work is the verb "fill." It appears in many psychological contexts: "*filling* the time" alternating with "*wearing out* the day"; "*filling* the imagination"; "*filling* the mind." To some extent, these years were now "filled"; and though they seem long, because of the timeless figure of Johnson that emerges from the recorded conversations, they were only a decade and a half. It is, indeed, a relief approaching comic catharsis to find him so satisfied, at least temporarily, that he can lapse from self-struggle into a moment of complacency. This may explain the diverting appeal of an incident recorded by Miss Reynolds. It is so altogether unusual and unexpected. For Johnson's harshness with his friends came from uneasi-

4. *Tour to the Hebrides*, pp. 208-9,   Boswell, *Life*, III, 337 [Bate's note].
175; Piozzi, *Anecdotes, J.M.*, I, 212;

ness: the "loud explosions," as Boswell said, were "guns of distress"; and afterward he was far from pleased with himself. On this occasion he spoke so roughly to Mrs. Thrale that, after the ladies withdrew, one of them expressed indignation. But Mrs. Thrale said no more than

> "Oh! Dear good man!" . . . [the other] Lady took the first opportunity of communicating it to him, repeating her own animadversion. . . . He seem'd much *delighted* with this intelligence, and sometime after, as he was lying back in his Chair, seeming to be half asleep, but more evidently musing on this pleasing incident, he repeated in a loud whisper, "*Oh! Dear good man!*"[5]

More frequent, however, was the sudden and impulsive sense of shame, sometimes appearing as an irritable admission when he was pressed—"I am sorry for it. I'll make it up to you *twenty different ways*, as you please"—but at other times as genuine contriteness. A remark often quoted is the reply to the rather foolish question of Mrs. Thrale's nephew, "Would you advise me to marry?"—"I would advise no man to marry, Sir . . . who is not likely to propagate understanding." But the sequel is rarely cited. Johnson, who had left the room, suddenly returned, said Mrs. Thrale, "and drawing his chair among us, with altered looks and a softened voice . . . insensibly led the conversation to the subject of marriage," and talked so effectively "that no one ever recollected the offense, except to rejoice in its consequences."[6]

Indeed, the history of Johnson's later years may be partly described as a self-enforced, often pathetic, attempt to cultivate habitual good nature and overcome the strong aggressiveness his bitter life and sensitive pride made inevitable. He once despondently admitted to Mr. Thrale that he had never even "sought to please till past thirty years old, considering the matter as hopeless." Long after most people's characters have set like plaster, Johnson continued to try to remake his own. His constant belief that one can be a "free agent," that it is never impossible to gain "superiority over habits" and remold one's character, underlies his insistent assertion that "All good humor and complaisance is *acquired*." Indeed, in his eagerness to maintain this, he was sometimes led to violate the ideal of the "art of pleasing" he had in mind. When a clergyman, at the house of Sir Joshua Reynolds, said that " after forty-five a man did not improve," "I *differ* with you," interrupted Johnson, roused to unusual antagonism: "A man *may* improve, and"—he unfairly added—"you *yourself* have great room for improvement." The "nice people," said Mrs. Thrale, who could only dine at a certain time, who "cannot bear to be waked at an unusual hour, or miss a stated meal," "found no mercy" from John-

---

5. Frances Reynolds, *Recollections*, *J.M., II*, 273 [Bate's note].

6. Piozzi, *Anecdotes, J.M.*, I, 213-14 [Bate's note].

son: "*He* had no such prejudices . . . 'Delicacy does not surely consist (says he) in *impossibility to be pleased*.'" And there is the almost comic outburst in the *Tour to the Hebrides* for the cause of "good humor." In order to avoid liquor, Johnson had long taken to lemonade. When Boswell proposed carrying lemons so that lemonade would be sure to be available, Johnson became angry. "I do not wish to be thought that *feeble man who cannot do without anything*. Sir, it is very bad manners to carry provisions to any man's house, as if he could not entertain you."[7] Repeatedly, said Reynolds, he was "the first to seek after a reconciliation." His aggressive habit of "talking for victory" on any side of a question also lay uneasily on his conscience. So habitually did he regard conversation as a contest that he once let slip the remark, when he was quite ill, that he was glad Edmund Burke was not present—he "calls forth all my powers. Were I to see Burke now, it would kill me." Increasingly, Johnson tried not to interrupt others; he even felt he could say he was unusually "attentive when others are speaking." The habit, which all his friends noted, of never beginning a conversation, but waiting till others spoke—even if it meant, as at Dr. Burney's famous evening party, sitting all evening without saying a word—is obviously a result of this deliberate attempt not to obtrude himself on the company. Indeed, all the stock characteristics associated with the legendary Johnson can easily be matched by resolutions and efforts to overcome them. The compulsive tics, the touching of posts, the St. Vitus' dance, have their counterpart in his often-expressed dislike of gesticulation and his resolutions, in the *Prayers and Meditations*, "to avoid all Singularity." The often playful pushing of his Tory prejudices is matched by the disarming admissions that he did not really much care. Like all his attempts to operate by principle, there is a certain desperation in the effort to cultivate "good nature" and "the state of being pleased." It reminds one a little of the stories of the feats of physical strength that he performed even when old and ill: Johnson climbing high trees, or plunging into the stream and swimming when the current was said to be dangerous; his riding to hounds "fifty miles on end sometimes," as Mrs. Thrale said, and then violently jumping over a cabriolet stool when Mr. Thrale had done the same thing to show he was not tired.[8]

The attempt to turn outward, to attain "good humor"—a "state of *being* pleased"—was, in a sense, Johnson's most difficult task in his later years. There are always so many more reasons, as he said, for rejecting than embracing; and few lives could have been more justified in ending in such an habitually negative state. Against this

7. Boswell, *Life*, IV, 431; Piozzi, *Anecdotes, J.M.*, I, 328-9; *Tour to the Hebrides*, p. 50 [Bate's note].
8. Frances Reynolds, *Recollections*;

H. D. Best, *Personal and Literary Memorials*; and Piozzi, *Anecdotes, J.M.*, II, 277-8, 391; I, 150, 287-8 [Bate's note].

temptation is to be put his clairvoyant realization, even in his darkest years, that such an end is destructive of everything; that outgoing concern and vital, receptive emotion must be preserved at all costs. "He loved the poor," said Mrs. Thrale,

as I never yet saw any one else do, with an earnest desire to make them happy.—What signifies, says some one, giving halfpence to common beggars? They only lay it out in gin or tobacco. "*And why should they be denied such sweeteners of their existence* (says Johnson)? It is surely very savage to refuse them every possible avenue to pleasure, reckoned too coarse for our own acceptance. *Life is a pill which none of us can bear to swallow without gilding.* ⁑ ⁑ ."[9]

And this same compassion he learned to extend to others in very different circumstances, though few men would have had more excuse for not doing so. Even when he was pressed by the most bitter poverty, his essays in the *Rambler* were weighted with a close and feeling knowledge of the acid of the boredom, self-dissatisfaction, and pain that can eat into any condition of life, however wealthy. Again, no one valued active and thoughtful conversation more than Johnson. No one, indeed, has more exemplified it. Yet when Boswell complained that at a sumptuous dinner there was "not one sentence of conversation worthy of being remembered," and asked, "Why then meet at table?" Johnson could say, "Why, to eat and drink together, *to promote kindness*," and then add—with sympathy, but no approval—that "perhaps this is better done when there is no solid conversation; for when there is, people differ in opinion, and get into bad humor, or some of the company, who are not capable of such conversation, are left out, and feel themselves uneasy." Again, as a young man eager for intelligent talk, he could disparage anyone who would "shuffle cards and rattle dice from noon to midnight without tracing any new idea in his mind." But he was now "sorry I have not learnt to play at cards": in its own way, it somewhat "*generates kindness* and consolidates society." So with all other things except positive evils like envy and malice. "A man," as he said during the Scottish tour, "grows better-humored as he grows older, by experience. He learns to think himself of no consequence and little things of little importance; and so he becomes more patient, and better pleased." Two days before his death, he asserted that he was "ready now to call a man *a good man*, upon easier terms than I was formerly." Often this growing charity was to wrestle against some of his strongest inclinations. We may think, for example, of his struggle all his life against the temptation to drink, of his complete abstinence from it for years at a time, of his natural attempts to buttress his resolution by attacks on drinking, and of his frequent, self-defensive outbursts—"I will argue with you no more," as he roared to Reynolds when they were debating the advantages of drink; "you are too

9. Piozzi, *Anecdotes*, *J.M.*, I, 204-5 [Bate's note].

far gone." But when Mrs. Williams, as he thought, spoke too lightly of drink, and said, "I wonder what pleasure men can take in making *beasts* of themselves," Johnson, whose pity could now extend to what he could least commend, retorted, "*I* wonder, Madam, that you have not penetration enough to see the strong inducement of this excess; for he who makes a *beast* of himself gets rid of the *pain of being a man*."[1]

The result of this enlarging and deepening of sympathy, this readiness to share, is to strengthen the moral premises that underlie Johnson's great writing on life and literature. In a different way, it may also be seen, with quick personal application, in his own daily life. One aspect is the engaging delight in comedy that fifty-five years of mental misery and physical pain could never destroy. There is Miss Reynolds' charming story of Johnson's race with the young lady in Devonshire who boasted she could outrun any of the company. "Madam," he cried out, "you cannot outrun me":

> The lady at first had the advantage; but Dr. Johnson happening to have slippers on much too small for his feet, kicked them off up into the air, and ran . . . leaving the lady far behind him, and . . . returned, leading her by the hand, with looks of high exultation and delight.[2]

This is the Johnson—never sufficiently stressed—who gleefully climbed a high tree when an elderly gentleman pointed to it and boasted he had often climbed it as a boy and "thought nothing of it": the Johnson who rolled exuberantly down a long hill; who, in a gloomy place in Scotland, said Boswell, playfully "diverted himself with trying to frighten me," and later put on a Scottish "war-bonnet," and strutted about the room; and who, one morning, said Boswell,

> called me to his bedside . . . and to my astonishment he *took off* Lady Macdonald leaning forward with a hand on each cheek and her mouth open—quite insipidity on a monument . . . To see a beauty represented by Mr. Johnson was excessively high. I told him it was a masterpiece and that he *must have studied it much*. "*Ay*," said he.[3]

A week before this, he had visited a Scottish minister, Alexander Grant. Grant never forgot the occasion. Years afterward he was to tell others of the incident, which occurred on a solemn Scottish Sunday. Johnson spoke of the trip of his friend, Sir Joseph Banks, to Australia, where Banks discovered "an extraordinary animal called the *kangaroo*." The appearance and habits of the animal were so singular that, "in order to render his description more vivid," Johnson rose from his chair and

> volunteered an imitation of the animal. The company stared . . . nothing could be more ludicrous than the appearance of a tall, heavy, grave-

1. Rev. Percival Stockdale, *Anec-dotes, J.M.*, II, 333 [Bate's note].
2. Frances Reynolds, *Recollections*, *J.M.*, II, 278 [Bate's note].
3. *Tour to the Hebrides*, pp. 84, 314, 121 [Bate's note].

looking man, like Dr. Johnson, standing up to mimic the shape and motions of a kangaroo. He stood erect, *put out his hands like feelers*, and, gathering up the tails of his huge brown coat so as to resemble the pouch of the animal, *made two or three vigorous bounds across the room!*[4]

In 1778, Johnson, now approaching seventy, began writing the *Lives of the English Poets* (1779-1781). A group of forty booksellers joined together to publish a large collection of the *Works of the English Poets* spanning the century from about 1660 to 1760, excluding whatever poets were still alive. The publishers appointed a committee to ask Johnson to write what finally amounted to fifty-two biographical prefaces, one for each poet, indicating that he could name his own terms. Johnson agreed, gave much more than was expected, and took virtually nothing. For it is understatement to say that most of the *Lives* turned out to be far from mere biographical prefaces. As for money, Johnson asked for £200. He might easily, as Edmund Malone believed, have asked for £1500. After Johnson's death, Arthur Murphy received £300 for his comparatively short *Essay on the Life and Genius of Samuel Johnson.* Years before, after Johnson had finished the *Dictionary*, Sir John Hawkins, speaking of the forthcoming edition of Shakespeare, said, "Now you have finished your *Dictionary*, I suppose you will labor your present work *con amore.*" Johnson answered, "No, Sir, nothing excites a man to write but necessity." Certainly, Johnson always needed some external incentive to write. Simply because it had been a task for so long, the whole process of writing had become inevitably associated with need and effort; and in such cases, as he himself said, "an habitual dislike" gradually steals over one's approach to an occupation. On the other hand, Boswell is probably justified in believing that he gave "less attention to profit from his labors than any man to whom literature has been a profession." The *Prayers and Meditations* record the completion of the *Lives of the Poets* in March 1781—written "in my usual way, dilatorily and hastily, unwilling to work, and working with vigor and haste." But the haste mattered less now than ever before. Drawing on his own copious memory, often dealing with writers at whom he had hardly glanced for many years, these volumes are not only a landmark in the history of criticism. They are also the finest example of one of the great English prose-styles.

Characteristically, Johnson took no initiative in his last great work. He had no particular "theory" of literary biography in mind. He simply wrote the requested prefaces in so superior a way that, in the process of doing so, he "gave to the British nation," as the editor of the 1825 edition said, "a new style of biography"—of biography, that is, extensively filled with specifically literary criti-

4. P. 98n. Cf. Sir W. R. Brain, "Dr. Johnson and the Kangaroo," *Es-* *says and Studies for the English Association* (1951), pp. 112-17 [Bate's note].

cism of the man's works and general attainment. Seventy years were to pass before another critic, Sainte-Beuve, could focus on so many individual writers in so penetrating a way. And if Sainte-Beuve brings to bear on the personal character of his subjects the more subtle psychological knowledge of his own day, he does not equal Johnson in his critical grasp of particular works of literature or of specific problems of form and style. Least of all did Johnson plan or edit the *Works of the English Poets*; and he was later to protest to the publishers that the edition should be "very impudently called mine." One of the quaint ironies of literary history is the frequent impression during the nineteenth century that the period of the poets represented was determined by Johnson himself, and that their achievement represents his *beau ideal* of what poetry should be. The irony is heightened by the fact that this impression was especially current among critics or historians who possessed at most a fraction of Johnson's *verbatim* knowledge of English poetry before the period covered by the *Lives*. From one point of view, the entire *Lives of the Poets* may be called a conscientious study of English poetry after what Johnson himself called its "golden age." The sympathy and consideration he brings to bear is a tribute to his own ability to think by principle. Johnson's strong attraction to the works of the "giants before the flood," and to the "larger *genres*" (especially the tragic drama and the epic), and his sense of the subsiding power of imagery and "strength of thought" in poetry after 1660, all furnished strong temptations to follow a theory of "decline"—a theory by no means uncommon in eighteenth-century England. But to surrender to such a temptation was to fold one's hands before historical determinism, and deny what Johnson most prized as a moral premise: the ability of man to remain a "free agent" and to determine within limits his own destiny. There is consequently the effort to see this period sympathetically for what it is. The situation is analogous to what we should hope to find in any fair critical treatment of the past century and a half. To few critics of the present day—to still fewer two centuries hence—is our own era likely to appear as one of the supreme triumphs of poetic genius. Yet any honest survey of its achievement must not only include the large vision, the constant remembrance of other achievements, the lack of narrow partisanship which Johnson possessed. It must also retain the same active interest in whatever recent or contemporary genius can produce.

Now begins the period to which sympathetic students of Johnson's life have always found themselves, as they grow older, recurring with a certain awe. "There are few things not purely evil," as Johnson wrote in the last issue of the *Idler*, "of which we can say, without some emotion of uneasiness, *this is the last*. . . . The secret horror of the last is *inseparable from a thinking being*, whose life is limited, and to whom death is dreadful." Nor is there anything morbid in this solemn fascination with the final three and a half years of Johnson's life. The appeal resides in the indomitable courage with which Johnson, during this long death-agony, faced the literal tearing from him of the few "sweeteners of existence" that he had so precariously acquired. The happy life at the taverns and at Streatham, even the quarreling inmates of his house are gone. In their place are the scenes of the dying and lonely Johnson: of Johnson back in 1779 weeping at the grave of Garrick, and bidding farewell to Streatham in 1782, the year after Thrale's death; Johnson alone in the house in London, wracked with four fatal diseases, sitting up in pain all night and coughing, and fighting energetically to turn outward to new interests. The last few years were the final or acid test of his ability—against a temperament almost impossibly obdurate—to transmute objective and moral awareness into concrete and daily life.

Beneath the note in the *Prayers and Meditations* that mentions the finish of the *Lives of the Poets* is a restrained account of the death of Henry Thrale, in April 1781, and of Johnson looking "for the last time upon the face that for fifteen years had never been turned upon me but with respect or benignity." Within another year and a half, the comfort and gaiety of Streatham were lost to him; the place was closed down. Moreover, Mrs. Thrale—who had been much younger than her husband—became interested in an Italian musician, Gabriel Piozzi, and later married him. Johnson's own bleak dwelling, to which he now had to return, was meanwhile emptying. Mr. Levet died not long after Mr. Thrale. Mrs. Williams was gravely ill. Johnson's letters—he had typically always disliked writing them—refer only briefly to the "cheerless solitude" in which he now found himself. Suddenly, in June 1783, he awoke early in the morning to find that he had a paralytic stroke. He wrote to a neighbor:

DEAR SIR,
It has pleased GOD, this morning, to deprive me of the powers of speech; and as I do not know but that it may be his further good pleasure to deprive me soon of my senses, I request you will on the receipt of this note, come to me, and act for me, as the exigencies of my case may require.
I am,
Sincerely yours,
SAM. JOHNSON.

Two days later, he wrote to Mrs. Thrale, describing the stroke: "I was alarmed, and prayed to GOD, that however he might afflict my body, he would spare my understanding. This prayer, that I might try the integrity of my faculties, I made in Latin verse. The lines were not very good, but *I knew them not to be very good.*"[5] His powers of speech returned. But his heart was meanwhile failing, and produced a dropsy so extreme that the water began to invade his lungs—ten quarts being drained from his body at one time. Other ailments quickly followed, and then Mrs. Williams suddenly died. If he could admit to Bennet Langton that he now lived in a "habitation vacant and desolate," he could also, in the same letter, state that "Disease produces much *selfishness.* A man in pain is *looking after ease. . . .*" Quite naturally, Johnson's lifelong, almost pathological fear of death now became constant. A vivid sense of guilt alternated with horror at possible annihilation. For many years, said Arthur Murphy, Johnson—in those fits of absence of mind to which he was liable—might be heard muttering to himself the speech from *Measure for Measure:*

> Ay, but to die and go we know not where;
> To lie in cold obstruction and to rot . . .[6]

But the result is nothing like the virtual collapse of twenty years before, with its almost hopeless fear of madness. The startling insertions in the *Prayers and Meditations* keep recurring in one's thought of Johnson now: "I try because reformation is necessary and *despair is criminal . . . I will not despair.* Help me, help me, O my God." To recount these last years in detail is to see a courage rising in direct proportion as the need becomes higher. The courage is, indeed, one of protest—"I will be *conquered,*" as he said to Dr. Burney, "I will not capitulate"—and it is crossed with frantic snatches at hope. But in general this last struggle of an heroic life against extinction may be described as an exemplification of the great statement of William the Silent, in the black days of Holland: "It is not necessary to hope in order to undertake, or to succeed in order to persevere."

With a final effort of will, Johnson tried, even in his last two months, to "find *new topics of merriment,* or *new incitements to curiosity.*" "Life," he wrote now, "is very short and very uncertain; let us spend it as well as we can." "The first talk of the sick," he reminded himself, "is commonly of *themselves.*" And his own talk was very different. Partly because he was so often alone, he now read more persistently than he had since the age of eighteen. In order to supplement the Literary Club, he also started its pitiable shadow, the little "Essex-Head Club." Though he was so ill that he had to rest four times between the inn and his lodgings, Fanny Burney, in the same week, could say that he was "in most excellent good humor and spirits," though she had little notion of the

5. Boswell, *Life,* IV, 228–30 [Bate's note].

6. *Essay on the Life and Genius of Samuel Johnson, J.M.* II, 439 [Bate's note].

upsurge of will behind this active and outgoing Johnson. In his farewell to Boswell, he sprang away from the carriage "with a kind of pathetic briskness." Boswell, shortly afterward, wrote complaining of melancholy. Johnson's reply is typical. For he quotes a remark of Sir William Temple he had read long ago, now recurring to him when harassed by a solitude, fear, and perhaps physical pain beyond Boswell's own experience: *"Be well,"* he wrote, *"when you are not ill, and pleased when you are not angry."*[7]

As he lay dying the last week, and the heart-disease that finally killed him had produced a dropsy that spread from his breast to his feet, he turned on the surgeon who refused to make further incisions: "Deeper, deeper, *I want length of life,* and you are afraid of giving me pain, which I do not value." He grasped a pair of scissors, and after the physicians were gone, awkwardly stabbed himself in three places, hoping to drain the accumulated water, but succeeded only in letting unnecessary blood. In one of the most moving passages in the *Life of Johnson,* Boswell compares Johnson's mind to a gladiator in the Coliseum meeting the beasts as they emerge from the center of the arena, and driving them back to their dens. It is a fitting comparison. Among Johnson's last words are those recorded by Sir John Hawkins: *"Iam Moriturus"*—"I who am now about to die." Uttered almost in delirium, they seem to echo the ancient salutation of the Roman gladiators to Caesar.

After his death on 13 December 1784, two acquaintances dropped by—Seward and Hoole—who were never to forget *"the most awful sight* of Dr. Johnson *laid out on his bed, without life!"*[8] The finish of the lifelong achievement of Johnson struck home in the same way to almost everyone acquainted with him. Especially to those who knew of Johnson walking the muddy roads to Birmingham and the school at Market-Bosworth, leaving Lichfield with the tragedy of *Irene* in his pocket, tossing off the Parliamentary Debates in a garret, and trudging the streets of London all night; who knew at least a little of what underlay the *Dictionary,* the moral essays, and the *Preface to Shakespeare*—who had seen something of the Johnson that rolled down the hills, imitated the kangaroo, and sat in the bed with the handkerchief atop his head, exclaiming "O brave we!"—the complete evaporation of this enormous capacity for life seemed hardly credible. The reaction of one of them is typical: "He has made a chasm, which not only nothing can fill up, but which *nothing has a tendency to fill up.*—Johnson is dead.—Let us go to the next best:—*There is nobody;*—no man can be said to put you in mind of Johnson."[9]

There is a suggestive distinction of William James between the

7. Boswell, *Life,* IV, 364, 379, 253-4, 339, 379 [Bate's note].

8. John Hoole, *Narrative,* and Hawkins, *Life, J.M.,* II, 160, 134 [Bate's note].

9. Boswell, *Life,* IV, 420-21 [Bate's note].

"once-born," who are naturally serene and harmoniously integrated, and the "second-born," who attain fulfillment only precariously, after prolonged self-struggle and despair. The life of Johnson, of course, is almost a prototype or *exemplum* of the latter. But the universality of its force is to be found in the fact that all human attainment is, to some extent, "second-born." The moral of its struggle is the freedom of the human spirit, however adverse the circumstances, to evolve its own destiny. It is this as much as anything else that increasingly leads us to think of Johnson almost as an allegorical figure, like Valiant-for-truth in *The Pilgrim's Progress*. But fortunately Johnson was also one of the supreme writers of English prose; and both the struggle and the final achievement are written in large and graphic outline throughout his own work. To Johnson as to few others we may apply Keats's remark about Shakespeare—that he "led a life of Allegory: his works are the comments on it."

EDITH HAMILTON
Xenophon[1]

To turn from Thucydides to Xenophon is a pleasant, but surprising, experience. The lives of the two men overlapped, although Xenophon was much the younger. Both were Athenians and soldiers; both lived through the war and saw the defeat of Athens.[2] Yet they inhabited different worlds; worlds so different, they seem to have no connection with each other. Thucydides' world was a place racked and ruined and disintegrated by war, where hope was gone and happiness was unimaginable. Xenophon's was a cheerful place with many nice people in it and many agreeable ways of passing the time. There was hunting, for instance. He writes a charming essay about it: of the delights of the early start, in winter over the snow, to track the hare with hounds as keen for the chase as their masters; in spring "when the fields are so full of wildflowers, the scent for the dogs is poor"; or a deer may be the quarry, first-rate sport; or a wild boar, dangerous, but delightfully exciting. Such rewards, too, as the hunter has: he keeps strong and young far longer than other men; he is braver, and even more trustworthy—although why that should be our author does not trouble to explain. A hunting man just is better than one who does not hunt and that is all there is to it. Ask any fox-hunting squire in English literature. Hunting is a good, healthy, honest pleasure, and a young man is lucky if he takes to it. It will save him from city vices and incline

1. Chapter 10 in *The Greek Way*, 1930. The preceding chapter deals with Thucydides.   2. Sparta conquered Athens in 404 B.C., after twenty-seven years of war.

him to love virtue.

At what period in Thucydides' history were the Athenians going a hunting, one wonders. Did that man of tragic vision ever watch a hunt? Did he ever listen to stories about the size of the boar that had been killed? Was he ever at a dinner-party where any stories were told over the wine? The imagination fails before the attempt to put him there, even if Socrates had been a guest as he was at a dinner Xenophon went to and reported. It followed more closely, we must suppose, the fashion of the day for such parties than did Plato's famous supper at Agathon's house, where conversation was the only entertainment. Agathon's guests were the elite of Athens and wanted lofty discourse for their diversion. The guests at Xenophon's dinner, except for himself and Socrates, were ordinary people who would quickly have been bored by the speeches in the *Symposium*. But no one could possibly have been bored at the party Xenophon describes. It was from first to last a most enjoyable occasion. There was some good talk at the table, of course—Socrates would see to that; and now and then the discourse turned to matters sober enough to have engaged even Thucydides' attention. But for the most part, it was lighthearted as befitted a good dinner. There was a great deal of laughter when, for instance, Socrates defended his flat nose as being preferable to a straight one, and when a man newly married refused the onions. There was music, too, and Socrates obliged with a song, to the delighted amusement of the others. A pleasant interlude was afforded by a happy boy, and Xenophon's description reveals his power of keen observation and quick sympathy. The lad had been invited to come with his father, a great honor, but he had just won the chief contest for boys at the principal Athenian festival. He sat beside his father, regarded very kindly by the company. They tried to draw him out, but he was too shy to speak a word until someone asked him what he was most proud of, and someone else cried, "Oh, his victory, of course." At this he blushed and blurted out, "No—I'm not." All were delighted to have him finally say something and they encouraged him. "No? Of what are you proudest, then?" "Of my father," he said, and pressed closer to him. It is an attractive picture of Athenian boyhood in the brilliant, corrupt city where Thucydides could find nothing good.

As was usual, entertainment had been provided for the guests. A girl did some diverting and surprising feats. The best turn was when she danced and kept twelve hoops whirling in the air, catching and throwing them in perfect time with the music. Watching her with great attention Socrates declared that he was forced to conclude, "Not only from this girl, my friends, but from other things, too, that a woman's talent is not at all inferior to a man's." A pleasant thing to know, he added, if any of them wanted to teach something to his wife. A murmur passed around the table: "Xanthippe"; and one of the company ventured, "Why do not you, then, teach good temper to yours?" "Because," Socrates retorted, "my great aim in life is to get on well with people, and I chose Xanthippe because I knew if I could get on with her I could with anyone." The explanation was unanimously voted satisfactory.

A little desultory talk followed that finally turned upon exercise, and Socrates said, to the intense delight of all, that he danced every morning in order to reduce. "It's true," one of the others broke in. "I found him doing it and I thought he'd gone mad. But he talked to me and I tell you he convinced me. When I went home—will you believe it? I did not dance; I don't know how; but I waved my arms about." There was a general outcry, "O, Socrates, let us see you, too."

By this time the dancing girl was turning somersaults and leaping headfirst into a circle formed by swords. This displeased Socrates. "No doubt it is a wonderful performance," he conceded. "But pleasure? In watching a lovely young creature exposing herself to to danger like that? I don't find it agreeable." The others agreed, and a pantomime between the girl and her partner, a graceful boy, was quickly substituted: "The Rescue of the Forsaken Ariadne by Bacchus." It was performed to admiration. Not a word was spoken by the two actors, but such was their skill that by gestures and dancing they expressed all the events and emotions of the story with perfect clarity to the spectators. "They seemed not actors who had learned their parts, but veritable lovers." With that the party broke up, Socrates walking home with the nice boy and his father. Of himself Xenophon says nothing throughout the essay except at the very beginning when he explains that he was one of the guests and decided to give an account of the dinner because he thought what honorable and virtuous men did in their hours of amusement had its importance. One can only regret that so few Greek writers agreed with him.

Another pleasant picture he gives of domestic Athens has an interest not only as a period piece but because it shows a glimpse of that person so elusive in all periods, the woman of ancient Greece. A man lately married talks about his wife. She was not yet fifteen, he says, and had been admirably brought up "to see as little, and hear as little, and ask as few questions as possible." The young husband had the delightful prospect of inscribing on this blank page whatever he chose. There was no doubt in his mind what he should start with. "Of course," Xenophon reports him as saying, "I had to give her time to grow used to me; but when we had reached a point where we could talk easily together, I told her she had great responsibilities. I took up with her what I expected of her as a housekeeper. She said wonderingly, 'But my mother told me I was of no consequence, only you. All I had to do, she said, was to be sensible and careful.' " Her husband was quick to seize the cue. Kindly but weightily he explained to the young thing that her life henceforth was to be a perpetual exercise in carefulness and good sense. She would have to keep stock of everything brought into the house; oversee all the work that went on; superintend the spinning, the weaving, the making of clothes; train the new servants and nurse the sick. At this point the girl's spirits seem to have risen a little for she murmured that she thought she would like to take care of sick people. But her husband kept steadily on. Of course she would stay indoors. He himself enjoyed starting the day with a long ride into the country—very healthful as well as very pleasant. But for a woman to be roaming abroad was most discreditable. However, she could get plenty of exercise, at the loom, or making beds, or supervising the maids. Kneading bread was said to be as good exercise as one could find. All that sort of thing would improve her health and help her complexion—very important in keeping herself attractive to her husband. Artificial substitutes were no good: husbands always knew when their wives painted, and they never liked it; white and red stuff on the face was disgusting when a man was aware of it, as a husband must be. The essay ends happily with the declaration, "Ever since, my wife has done in all respects just as I taught her."

It is as hard to fit the dutiful young wife and the happily important husband and their immaculate household into Thucydides' Athens as it is to put Thucydides himself at the table beside Socrates watching the girl with the hoops. There is no use trying to make a composite picture out of Xenophon and Thucydides. The only result would be to lose the truth on each side. Thucydides' truth was immeasurably more profound. In life's uneasy panorama he could discover unchanging verities. He could probe to the depths in the never varying evils of human nature. In Sparta's victory over Athens he saw what the decision of war was worth as a test of values, and that war would forever decide matters of highest importance to the world if men continued to be governed by greed and the passion for power. What he knew was truth indeed, with no shadow of turning and inexpressibly sad.

But Xenophon's truths were true, too. There were pleasant parties and well-ordered homes and nice lads and jolly hunters in war-wracked Greece. History never takes account of such pleasantries, but they have their importance. The Greek world would have gone insane if Thucydides' picture had been all-inclusive. Of course, Xenophon's mind was on an altogether lower level. Eternal truths were not in his line. The average man in Periclean Athens can be seen through Xenophon's eyes as he cannot be through Thucydides' or Plato's. In Xenophon there are no dark, greed-ridden schemers such as Thucydides saw in Athens; neither are there any Platonic idealists. The people in his books are ordinary, pleasant folk, not given to extremes in any direction and convincingly real, just as Xenophon himself is. Here is a picture he draws of one of them:

> He said that he had long realized that "unless we know what we ought to do and try our best to do it God has decided that we have no right to be prosperous. If we are wise and do take pains he makes some of us prosperous, although not all. So to start with, I reverence him and then do all I can to be worthy when I pray to be given health and strength of body and the respect of the Athenians and the affection of my friends and an increase of wealth—with honor, and safety in war—with honor."

These eminently sensible aspirations strike a true Greek note. The man who uttered them and the man who recorded them were typical Athenian gentlemen. What Xenophon was comes through clearly in his writings—a man of good will and good sense, kindly, honest, pious; intelligent, too, interested in ideas, not the purely speculative kind, rather those that could be made to work toward some rational, practical good. His friends were like him, they were representative Athenians of the better sort.

In another way, too, Xenophon represented his times. His life shows the widely separated interests and varied occupations which made the Periclean Athenians different from other men. As a young man he came to Athens from his father's estate in Attica, to be educated out of country ways; he joined the circle around Socrates, where young and old alike were, as Plato puts it, "possessed and maddened with the passion for knowledge," or, as he himself states, "wanting to become good and fine men and learn their duty to their family, their servants, their friends and their country." The Socrates he listened to did not, like Plato's Socrates, discourse upon "the glorious sights of justice and wisdom and truth the enraptured soul beholds, shining in pure light," or anything like that. This Socrates was a soberly thinking man, distinguished for common sense, and in Xenophon's record of him, the *Memorabilia*, what he chiefly does for his young friends is to give them practical advice on how to manage their affairs. A budding officer is told the way to make his men efficient soldiers; a conscientious lad, burdened with many female relatives, is shown how they can be taught to support themselves, and so on, while Xenophon listens entranced by such serviceable wisdom. How long Xenophon lived this delightful life of conversation is not known, but he was still young when he left it for the very opposite kind of life, that of a soldier. He was truly a man of his times, when poets and dramatists and historians were soldiers and generals and explorers.

In his campaigns he traveled far and saw the great world. He also got enough money to live on for the rest of his days by capturing and holding for ransom a rich Persian noble. Then he went back to Greece—but to Sparta, not Athens. Curiously, although he has left in his *Anabasis* an unsurpassed picture of what the democratic ideal can accomplish, he was himself no democrat. He came of a noble family and all his life kept the convictions of his class. He always loved Sparta and distrusted Athens. Even so, in the great crisis of his life, when he and his companions faced imminent destruction, he acted like a true Athenian, who knew what freedom was and what free men could achieve. When the Ten Thousand elected him general in order to get them out of their terrible predicament, he never tried out any Spartan ideas on them. He became as democratic a leader as there could possibly be of the freest democracy conceivable. The fact that the astonishing success which resulted had no permanent effect upon his point of view should not be surprising; a converted aristocrat is a rare figure in history. Xenophon never went back to Athens; indeed, a few years after his return to Greece he was fighting on the Spartan side against her and was declared an exile. The Spartans gave him an estate in the pleasant country near Olympia, where he lived for many years, riding and hunting and farming, a model country gentleman. Here he wrote a great many books on subjects as far apart as the dinner Socrates attended and the proper management of the Athenian revenues. With two or three exceptions the writings are quite pedestrian; sensible, straightforward, clearly written, but no more. There are a few sentences, however, scattered through them which show a surprising power of thought and far-reaching vision. Although, or perhaps because, he had fought much, he believed that peace should be the aim of all states. Diplomacy, he says, is the way to settle disputes, not war. He urges Athens to use her influence to maintain peace, and he suggests making Delphi a meeting place for the nations, where they can talk out their differences. "He who conquers by force," he says, "may fancy that he can continue to do so, but the only conquests that last are when men willingly submit to those who are better than themselves. The only way really to conquer a country is through generosity." The world has not yet caught up with Xenophon.

His best book, however, the book he really lives by, is on war. It is, of course, the *Anabasis*, the "Retreat of the Ten Thousand," a great story, and of great importance for our knowledge of the Greeks. No other piece of writing gives so clear a picture of Greek individualism, that instinct which was supremely characteristic of ancient Greece and decided the course of the Greek achievement. It was the cause, or the result, as one chooses to look at it, of the Greek love for freedom. A Greek had a passion for being left free to live his life in his own way. He wanted to act by himself and think for himself. It did not come natural to him to turn to others for direction; he depended upon his own sense of what was right and true. Indeed, there was no generally acknowledged source of direction anywhere in Greece except the oracles, difficult to reach and still more difficult to understand. Athens had no authoritarian church, or state either, to formulate what a man should believe and to regulate the details of how he should live. There was no agency or institution to oppose his thinking in any way he chose on anything whatsoever. As for the state, it never entered an Athenian's head that it could interfere with his private life: that it could see, for instance, that his children were taught to be patriotic, or limit the amount of liquor he could buy, or compel him to save for his old age. Everything like that a citizen of Athens had to decide himself and take full responsibility for.

The basis of the Athenian democracy was the conviction of all democracies—that the average man can be depended upon to do his duty and to use good sense in doing it. *Trust the individual* was the avowed doctrine in Athens, and expressed or unexpressed it was common to Greece. Sparta we know as the exception, and there must have been other backwaters; nevertheless, the most reactionary Greek might at any time revert to type. It is on record that Spartan soldiers abroad shouted down an unpopular officer; threw stones at a general whose orders they did not approve; in an emergency, put down incompetent leaders and acted for themselves. Even the iron discipline of Sparta could not completely eradicate the primary Greek passion for independence. "A people ruling," says Herodotus, "—the very name of it is so beautiful." In Aeschylus' play about the defeat of the Persians at Salamis, the Persian queen asks, "Who is set over the Greeks as despots?" and the proud answer is, "They are the slaves and vassals of no man." Therefore, all Greeks believed, they conquered the slave-subjects of the Persian tyrant. Free men, independent men, were always worth inexpressibly more than men submissive and controlled.

Military authorities have never advocated this point of view, but how applicable it is to soldiers, too, is shown for all time by the *Anabasis*. The Ten Thousand got back safely after one of the most perilous marches ever undertaken just because they were not a model, disciplined army but a band of enterprising individuals.

The epic of the Retreat begins in a camp beside a little town in Asia not far from Babylon. There, more than ten thousand Greeks were gathered. They had come from different places: one of the leaders was from Thessaly; another from Boeotia; the commander-in-chief was a Spartan; on his staff was a young civilian from Athens named Xenophon. They were soldiers of fortune, a typical army of mercenaries who had gone abroad because there was no hope of employment at home. Greece was not at war for the moment. A Spartan peace was over the land. It was the summer of 401, three years after the fall of Athens.

Persia, however, was a hotbed of plots and counterplots that were bringing a revolution near. The late king's two sons were enemies, and the younger planned to take the throne from his brother. This young man was Cyrus, named for the great Cyrus, the conqueror of Babylon a hundred and fifty years earlier. His namesake is famous for one reason only: because when he marched into Persia Xenophon joined his army. If that had not happened he would be lost in the endless list of little Asiatic royalties forever fighting for no purpose of the slightest importance to the world. As it is, he lives in Xenophon's pages, gay and gallant and generous; careful for his soldiers' welfare; sharing their hardships; always first in the fighting; a great leader.

The Ten Thousand had enlisted under his banner with no clear idea of what they were to do beyond the matter of real importance, get regular pay and enough food. They earned their share of both in the next few months. They marched from the Mediterranean through sandy deserts far into Asia Minor living on the country, which generally meant a minimum of food and occasionally none at all. There was a large Asiatic contingent, a hundred thousand strong at the least, but they play very little part in the *Anabasis*. The Greeks are the real army Cyrus depends upon. As Xenophon tells the story they won the day for him when he met the king's forces. The battle of Cunaxa was a decisive victory for Cyrus. Only, he himself was dead, killed in the fighting as he struck at his brother and wounded him. With his death the reason for the expedition ceased to exist. The Asiatic forces melted away. The little Greek army was alone in the heart of Asia, in an unknown country swarming with hostile troops, with no food, no ammunition, and no notion how to get back. Soon there were no leaders either. The chief officers went to a conference with the Persians under a safe-conduct. Their return, eagerly awaited, was alarmingly delayed; and all eyes were watching for them when in the distance a man, one man all alone, was seen advancing very slowly, a Greek by his dress. They ran to meet him and caught him as he fell dying, terribly wounded. He could just gasp out that all the others were dead, assassinated by the Persians.

That was a terrible night. The Persian plan was clear. In their experience leaderless men were helpless. Kill the officers and the army would be a lot of sheep waiting to be slaughtered. The only thing wrong with the idea was that this was a Greek army.

Xenophon, all his friends dead, wandered away from the horrified camp, found a quiet spot and fell asleep. He dreamed a dream. He saw the thunderbolt of Zeus fall on his home and a great light shine forth, and he awoke with the absolute conviction that Zeus had chosen him to save the army. On fire with enthusiasm, he called a council of the under officers who had not gone to the conference.

There, young and a civilian, he stood up and addressed them, hardened veterans all. He told them to throw off despair and "show some superiority to misfortune." He reminded them that they were Greeks, not to be cowed by mere Asiatics. Something of his own fire was communicated to them. He even got them laughing. One man who stubbornly objected to everything and would talk only of their desperate case, Xenophon advised reducing to the ranks and using to carry baggage; he would make an excellent mule, he told his appreciative audience. They elected him unanimously to lead the rear, and then had the general assembly sounded so that he could address the soldiers. He gave them a rousing talk. Things were black and might seem hopeless to others, but they were Greeks, free men, living in free states, born of free ancestors. The enemy they had to face were slaves, ruled by despots, ignorant of the very idea of freedom. "They think we are defeated because our officers are dead and our good old general Clearchus. But we will show them that they have turned us all into generals. Instead of one Clearchus they have ten thousand Clearchuses against them." He won them over and that very morning the ten thousand generals started the march back.

They had only enemies around them, not one man they could trust as a guide, and there were no maps in those days and no compasses. One thing only they were sure of: they could not go back by the way they had come. Wherever they had passed the food was exhausted. They were forced to turn northward and follow the course of the rivers up to the mountains where the Tigris and the Euphrates rise, through what is to-day the wilds of Kurdistan and the highlands of Georgia and Armenia, all inhabited by savage mountain tribes. These were their only source of provisions. If they could not conquer their strongholds and get at their stores they would starve. Mountain warfare of the most desperate character awaited them, waged by an enemy who knew every foot of the country, who watched for them on the heights above narrow valleys and rolled masses of rocks down on them, whose sharpshooters attacked them hidden in thickets on the opposite bank of some torrential icy river while the Greeks searched desperately for a ford. As they advanced ever higher into the hills, they found bitter cold and deep snow, and their equipment was designed for the Arabian desert.

Probably anyone to-day considering their plight would conclude that their only chance of safety would lie in maintaining strict discipline, abiding by their excellent military tradition, and obeying their leaders implicitly. The chief leaders, however, were dead; mountain fighting against savages was not a part of their military tradition; above all, being Greeks, they did not incline to blind obedience in desperate circumstances. In point of fact, the situation which confronted them could be met only by throwing away the rules and regulations that had been drilled into them. What they needed was to draw upon all the intelligence and power of initiative every man of them possessed.

They were merely a band of mercenaries, but they were Greek mercenaries and the average of intelligence was high. The question of discipline among ten thousand generals would otherwise certainly have been serious and might well have proved fatal, but, no less than our westward-faring pioneer ancestors who resembled them, they understood the necessity of acting together. Not a soldier but knew what it would mean to have disorder added to the perils they faced. Their discipline was a voluntary product, but it worked. When the covered wagons made their way across America any leader that arose did so by virtue of superior ability, which men in danger always follow willingly. The leaders of the Ten Thousand got their posts in the same way. The army was keen to perceive a man's quality and before long the young civilian Xenophon was practically in command.

Each man, however, had a share in the responsibility. Once when Xenophon sent out a reconnoitering force to find a pass through the mountains, he told them, "Every one of you is the leader." At any crisis an assembly was held, the situation explained and full discussion invited. "Whoever has a better plan, let him speak. Our aim is the safety of all and that is the concern of all." The case was argued back and forth, then put to the vote and the majority decided. Incompetent leaders were brought to trial. The whole army sat as judges and acquitted or punished. It reads like a caricature, but there has never been a better vindication of the average man when he is up against it. The ten thousand judges, which the ten thousand generals turned into on occasion, never, so far as Xenophon's record goes, passed an unjust sentence. On one occasion Xenophon was called to account for striking a soldier. " 'I own that I did so,' he said. 'I told him to carry to camp a wounded man, but I found him burying him still alive. I have struck others, too, half-frozen men who were sinking down in the snow to die, worn-out men lagging behind where the enemy might catch them. A blow would often make them get up and hasten. Those I have given offense to now accuse me. But those I have helped, in battle, on the march, in cold, in sickness, none of them speak up. They do not remember. And yet surely it is better—and happier, too— to remember a man's good deeds than his evil deeds.' Upon this," the narrative goes on, "the assembly, calling the past to mind, rose up and Xenophon was acquitted."

This completely disarming speech for the defense shows how well Xenophon knew the way to manage men. There is wounded feeling in his words, but no anger, no resentment, above all, no self-righteousness. Those listening were convinced by his frankness of his honesty; reminded, without a suggestion of boasting, how great his services had been; and given to understand that far from claiming to be faultless, he appealed to them only to remember his deserts as well as his mistakes. He understood his audience and the qualities a leader must have, at least any leader who would lead Greeks. In a book he wrote on the education of the great Cyrus he draws a picture of the ideal general which, absurd as it is when applied to an Oriental monarch, shows to perfection the Greek idea of the one method that will make men who are worth anything independent, self-reliant men, willing to follow another man. "The leader," he writes, "must himself believe that willing obedience always beats forced obedience, and that he can get this only by really knowing what should be done. Thus he can secure obedience from his men because he can convince them that he knows best, precisely as a good doctor makes his patients obey him. Also he must be ready to suffer more hardships than he asks of his soldiers, more fatigue, greater extremes of heat and cold. 'No one,' Cyrus always said, 'can be a good officer who does not undergo more than those he commands.' " However that may be, it is certain that the inexperienced civilian Xenophon was could have won over the Ten Thousand in no other way. He was able to convince them that he knew best and they gave up their own ideas and followed him willingly.

He showed them too that even if they made him their leader, it was share and share alike between him and the army. On one occasion when he was riding up from his post in the rear to consult with the van, and the snow was deep and the marching hard, a soldier cried to him, "Oh, it's easy enough for you on horseback." Xenophon leaped from his horse, flung the man aside and marched in his place.

Always, no matter how desperate things seemed, the initiative which only free men can be counted on to develop got them through. They abandoned their baggage by common consent and threw away their loot. "We will make the enemy carry our baggage for us," they said. "When we have conquered them we can take what we want." Early in the march they were terribly harassed by the Persian cavalry because they had none of their own. The men of Rhodes could throw with their slings twice as far as the Persians. They set them on baggage mules, directed them to aim at the riders, but spare their mounts and bring them back, and from that time on the Persians kept them in horses. If they needed ammunition they sent bowmen who could shoot farther than the foe to draw down showers of arrows that fell short and could be easily collected. One way or another they forced the Persians into service. When they got to the hills they discarded the tactics they had been trained in. They gave up the solid line, the only formation they knew, and the army advanced by columns, sometimes far apart. It was merely common sense in the rough broken country, but that virtue belongs peculiarly to men acting for themselves. The disciplined military mind has never been distinguished for it.

So, always cold and sometimes freezing, always hungry and sometimes starving, and always, always fighting, they held their own. No one by now had any clear idea where in the world they were. One day, Xenophon, riding in the rear, putting his horse up a steep hill, heard a great noise in front. A tumult was carried back to him by the wind, loud cries and shouting. An ambush, he thought, and calling to the others to follow at full speed, he drove his horse forward. No enemy was on the hilltop; only the Greeks. They were standing, all faced the same way, with tears running down their faces, their arms stretched out to what they saw before them. The shouting swelled into a great roar, "The sea! The sea!"

They were home at last. The sea was home to a Greek. It was the middle of January. They had left Cunaxa on the seventh of September. In four months they had marched well on to two thousand miles in circumstances never surpassed before or since for hardship and danger.

The *Anabasis* is the story of the Greeks in miniature. Ten thousand men, fiercely independent by nature, in a situation where they were a law unto themselves, showed that they were pre-eminently able to work together and proved what miracles of achievement willing co-operation can bring to pass. The Greek state, at any rate the Athenian state, which we know best, showed the same. What brought the Greeks safely back from Asia was precisely what made Athens great. The Athenian was a law unto himself, but his dominant instinct to stand alone was counterbalanced by his sense of overwhelming obligation to serve the state. This was his own spontaneous reaction to the facts of his life, nothing imposed upon him from outside. The city was his defense in a hostile world, his security, his pride, too, the guarantee to all of his worth as an Athenian.

Plato said that men could find their true moral development only in service to the city. The Athenian was saved from looking at his life as a private affair. Our word "idiot" comes from the Greek name for the man who took no share in public matters. Pericles in the funeral oration reported by Thucydides says:

> We are a free democracy, but we are obedient. We obey the laws, more especially those which protect the oppressed, and the unwritten laws whose transgression brings acknowledged shame. We do not allow absorption in our own affairs to interfere with participation in the city's. We differ from other states in regarding the man who holds aloof from public life as useless, yet we yield to none in independence of spirit and complete self-reliance.

This happy balance was maintained for a very brief period. No doubt at its best it was as imperfect as the working out of every lofty idea in human terms is bound to be. Even so, it was the foundation of the Greek achievement. The creed of democracy, spiritual and political liberty for all, and each man a willing servant of the state, was the conception which underlay the highest reach of Greek genius. It was fatally weakened by the race for money and power in the Periclean age; the Peloponnesian War destroyed it and Greece lost it forever. Nevertheless, the ideal of free individuals unified by a spontaneous service to the common life was left as a possession to the world, never to be forgotten.

QUESTIONS

1. Hamilton's account of Xenophon has two main parts, a description of his life and writings in Greece and of his conduct during the Persian campaign. How does the characterization of Xenophon in Greece prepare for or illuminate his actions as commander of the Ten Thousand? What qualities in Xenophon are emphasized in this portrayal? Show some of the details selected to point up Xenophon's character.

2. What contrasts does Hamilton draw between the attitudes and interests of Xenophon and Thucydides? What implications for the writing and study of history are there in these contrasts? Compare your conclusions with E. H. Carr's discussion of the nature of historical fact ("The Historian and His Facts," pp. 1198–1215).

3. What does Xenophon's description of the dinner party indicate of the life of ancient Greece? Which details seem peculiar to that time and place? Which appear perennial, details that might be matched in accounts of comparable dinner parties at any time or place?

4. Does the account Xenophon gives of Socrates accord with that given by Plato? To what extent can the two accounts be reconciled?

5. In the closing paragraph of his essay "On Not Being a Philosopher" (p. 808), Lynd asks some questions about the attitude of the Greeks toward their philosophers. What answers does the account Xenophon gives of himself and other young men in the company of Socrates provide?

6. In what ways does Hamilton demonstrate that the Greek ideal of liberty combined personal independence with willing service to the state, to the common good? Compare Santayana's account, "Classic Liberty" (pp. 1433–1435).

7. Write an account of an incident in your own experience (comparable to Xenophon's dinner party) as if you were going to include it in a history of your own time. Take into account the results of your thinking about Questions 2 and 3, above.

On Government

JAMES THURBER

The Rabbits Who Caused All the Trouble

Within the memory of the youngest child there was a family of rabbits who lived near a pack of wolves. The wolves announced that they did not like the way the rabbits were living. (The wolves were crazy about the way they themselves were living, because it was the only way to live.) One night several wolves were killed in an earthquake and this was blamed on the rabbits, for it is well known that rabbits pound on the ground with their hind legs and cause earthquakes. On another night one of the wolves was killed by a bolt of lightning and this was also blamed on the rabbits, for it is well known that lettuce-eaters cause lightning. The wolves threatened to civilize the rabbits if they didn't behave, and the rabbits decided to run away to a desert island. But the other animals, who lived at a great distance, shamed them, saying, "You must stay where you are and be brave. This is no world for escapists. If the wolves attack you, we will come to your aid, in all probability." So the rabbits continued to live near the wolves and one day there was a terrible flood which drowned a great many wolves. This was blamed on the rabbits, for it is well known that carrot-nibblers with long ears cause floods. The wolves descended on the rabbits, for their own good, and imprisoned them in a dark cave, for their own protection.

When nothing was heard about the rabbits for some weeks, the other animals demanded to know what had happened to them. The wolves replied that the rabbits had been eaten and since they had been eaten the affair was a purely internal matter. But the other animals warned that they might possibly unite against the

wolves unless some reason was given for the destruction of the rabbits. So the wolves gave them one. "They were trying to escape," said the wolves, "and, as you know, this is no world for escapists."
Moral: Run, don't walk, to the nearest desert island.

NICCOLÒ MACHIAVELLI
The Morals of the Prince[1]

On Things for Which Men, and Particularly Princes, Are Praised or Blamed

We now have left to consider what should be the manners and attitudes of a prince toward his subjects and his friends. As I know that many have written on this subject I feel that I may be held presumptuous in what I have to say, if in my comments I do not follow the lines laid down by others. Since, however, it has been my intention to write something which may be of use to the understanding reader, it has seemed wiser to me to follow the real truth of the matter rather than what we imagine it to be. For imagination has created many principalities and republics that have never been seen or known to have any real existence, for how we live is so different from how we ought to live that he who studies what ought to be done rather than what is done will learn the way to his downfall rather than to his preservation. A man striving in every way to be good will meet his ruin among the great number who are not good. Hence it is necessary for a prince, if he wishes to remain in power, to learn how not to be good and to use his knowledge or refrain from using it as he may need.

Putting aside then the things imagined as pertaining to a prince and considering those that really do, I will say that all men, and particularly princes because of their prominence, when comment is made of them, are noted as having some characteristics deserving either praise or blame. One is accounted liberal, another stingy, to use a Tuscan term—for in our speech avaricious (*avaro*) is applied to such as are desirous of acquiring by rapine whereas stingy (*misero*) is the term used for those who are reluctant to part with their own—one is considered bountiful, another rapacious; one cruel, another tender-hearted; one false to his word, another trustworthy; one effeminate and pusillanimous, another wild and spirited; one humane, another haughty; one lascivious, another chaste; one a man of integrity and another sly; one tough and another pliant; one serious and another frivolous; one religious and another skeptical, and so on. Everyone will agree, I know, that it would be a most praiseworthy thing if all the qualities accounted as good

1. Chapters 15-18 of *The Prince*.

in the above enumeration were found in a Prince. But since they cannot be so possessed nor observed because of human conditions which do not allow of it, what is necessary for the prince is to be prudent enough to escape the infamy of such vices as would result in the loss of his state; as for the others which would not have that effect, he must guard himself from them as far as possible but if he cannot, he may overlook them as being of less importance. Further, he should have no concern about incurring the infamy of such vices without which the preservation of his state would be difficult. For, if the matter be well considered, it will be seen that some habits which appear virtuous, if adopted would signify ruin, and others that seem vices lead to security and the well-being of a prince.

Generosity and Meanness

To begin then with the first characteristic set forth above, I will say that it would be well always to be considered generous, yet generosity used in such a way as not to bring you honor does you harm, for if it is practiced virtuously and as it is meant to be practiced it will not be publicly known and you will not lose the name of being just the opposite of generous. Hence to preserve the reputation of being generous among your friends you must not neglect any kind of lavish display, yet a prince of this sort will consume all his property in such gestures and, if he wishes to preserve his reputation for generosity, he will be forced to levy heavy taxes on his subjects and turn to fiscal measures and do everything possible to get money. Thus he will begin to be regarded with hatred by his subjects and should he become poor he will be held in scant esteem; having by his prodigality given offense to many and rewarded only a few, he will suffer at the first hint of adversity, and the first danger will be critical for him. Yet when he realizes this and tries to reform he will immediately get the name of being a miser. So a prince, as he is unable to adopt the virtue of generosity without danger to himself, must, if he is a wise man, accept with indifference the name of miser. For with the passage of time he will be regarded as increasingly generous when it is seen that, by virtue of his parsimony, his income suffices for him to defend himself in wartime and undertake his enterprises without heavily taxing his people. For in that way he practices generosity towards all from whom he refrains from taking money, who are many, and stinginess only toward those from whom he withholds gifts, who are few.

In our times we have seen great things accomplished only by such as have had the name of misers; all others have come to naught. Pope Julius made use of his reputation for generosity to make himself Pope but later, in order to carry on his war against the King of France, he made no effort to maintain it; and he has waged a great number of wars without having had recourse to heavy taxation because his persistent parsimony has made up for the extra expenses. The present King of Spain, had he had any reputation for generosity, would never have carried through to victory so many enterprises.

A prince then, if he wishes not to rob his subjects but to be able to defend himself and not to become poor and despised nor to be obliged to become rapacious, must consider it a matter of small importance to incur the name of miser, for this is one of the vices which keep him on his throne. Some may say Caesar through generosity won his way to the purple, and others either through being generous or being accounted so have risen to the highest ranks. But I will answer by pointing out that either you are already a prince or you are on the way to becoming one and in the first case generosity is harmful while in the second it is very necessary to be considered open-handed. Caesar was seeking to arrive at the domination of Rome but if he had survived after reaching his goal and had not moderated his lavishness he would certainly have destroyed the empire.

It might also be objected that there have been many princes, accomplishing great things with their armies, who have been acclaimed for their generosity. To which I would answer that the prince either spends his own (or his subjects') money or that of others; in the first case he must be very sparing but in the second he should overlook no aspect of open-handedness. So the prince who leads his armies and lives on looting and extortion and booty, thus handling the wealth of others, must indeed have this quality of generosity for otherwise his soldiers will not follow him. You can be very free with wealth not belonging to yourself or your subjects, in the fashion of Cyrus, Caesar, or Alexander, for spending what belongs to others rather enhances your reputation than detracts from it; it is only spending your own wealth that is dangerous. There is nothing that consumes itself as does prodigality; even as you practice it you lose the faculty of practicing it and either you become poor and despicable or, in order to escape poverty, rapacious and unpopular. And among the things a prince must guard against is precisely the danger of becoming an object either of contempt or of hatred. Generosity leads you to both these evils, wherefore it is wiser to accept the name of miserly, since the reproach it brings is without hatred, than to seek a reputation for generosity and thus perforce acquire the name of rapacious, which breeds hatred as well as infamy.

Cruelty and Clemency and Whether It Is Better to Be Loved or Feared

Now to continue with the list of characteristics. It should be the desire of every prince to be considered merciful and not cruel, yet he should take care not to make poor use of his clemency. Cesare Borgia was regarded as cruel, yet his cruelty reorganized Romagna and united it in peace and loyalty. Indeed, if we reflect, we shall see that this man was more merciful than the Florentines who, to avoid the charge of cruelty, allowed Pistoia to be destroyed.[2] A prince should care nothing for the accusation of cruelty so long as he keeps his subjects united and loyal; by making a very few examples he can be more truly merciful than those who through too much tender-heartedness allow disorders to arise whence come killings and rapine. For these offend an entire community, while the few executions ordered by the prince affect only a few individuals. For a new prince above all it is impossible not to earn a reputation for cruelty since new states are full of dangers. Virgil indeed has Dido apologize for the inhumanity of her rule because it is new, in the words:

> *Res dura et regni novitas me talia cogunt*
> *Moliri et late fines custode tueri.*[3]

Nevertheless a prince should not be too ready to listen to tale-bearers nor to act on suspicion, nor should he allow himself to be easily frightened. He should proceed with a mixture of prudence and humanity in such a way as not to be made incautious by over-confidence nor yet intolerable by excessive mistrust.

Here the question arises; whether it is better to be loved than feared or feared than loved. The answer is that it would be desirable to be both but, since that is difficult, it is much safer to be feared than to be loved, if one must choose. For on men in general this observation may be made: they are ungrateful, fickle, and deceitful, eager to avoid dangers, and avid for gain, and while you are useful to them they are all with you, offering you their blood, their property, their lives, and their sons so long as danger is remote, as we noted above, but when it approaches they turn on you. Any prince, trusting only in their words and having no other preparations made, will fall to his ruin, for friendships that are bought at a price and not by greatness and nobility of soul are paid for indeed, but they are not owned and cannot be called upon in time of need. Men have less hesitation in offending a man who is loved than one who is feared, for love is held by a bond of obligation which, as men are wicked, is broken whenever personal advantage suggests it, but fear is accompanied by the dread of punishment which never relaxes.

Yet a prince should make himself feared in such a way that, if he does not thereby merit love, at least he may escape odium, for being feared and not hated may well go together. And indeed the prince may attain this end if he but respect the property and the

---

2. By unchecked rioting between opposing factions (1502).

3. ". . . my cruel fate / And doubts attending an unsettled state / Force me to guard my coast from foreign foes" — DRYDEN.

women of his subjects and citizens. And if it should become necessary to seek the death of someone, he should find a proper justification and a public cause, and above all he should keep his hands off another's property, for men forget more readily the death of their father than the loss of their patrimony. Besides, pretexts for seizing property are never lacking, and when a prince begins to live by means of rapine he will always find some excuse for plundering others, and conversely pretexts for execution are rarer and are more quickly exhausted.

A prince at the head of his armies and with a vast number of soldiers under his command should give not the slightest heed if he is esteemed cruel, for without such a reputation he will not be able to keep his army united and ready for action. Among the marvelous things told of Hannibal is that, having a vast army under his command made up of all kinds and races of men and waging war far from his own country, he never allowed any dissension to arise either as between the troops and their leaders or among the troops themselves, and this both in times of good fortune and bad. This could only have come about through his most inhuman cruelty which, taken in conjunction with his great valor, kept him always an object of respect and terror in the eyes of his soldiers. And without the cruelty his other characteristics would not have achieved this effect. Thoughtless writers have admired his actions and at the same time deplored the cruelty which was the basis of them. As evidence of the truth of our statement that his other virtues would have been insufficient let us examine the case of Scipio, an extraordinary leader not only in his own day but for all recorded history. His army in Spain revolted and for no other reason than because of his kind-heartedness, which had allowed more license to his soldiery than military discipline properly permits. His policy was attacked in the Senate by Fabius Maximus, who called him a corrupter of the Roman arms. When the Locrians had been mishandled by one of his lieutenants, his easy-going nature prevented him from avenging them or disciplining his officer, and it was apropos of this incident that one of the senators remarked, wishing to find an excuse for him, that there were many men who knew better how to avoid error themselves than to correct it in others. This characteristic of Scipio would have clouded his fame and glory had he continued in authority, but as he lived under the government of the Senate, its harmful aspect was hidden and it reflected credit on him.

Hence, on the subject of being loved or feared I will conclude that since love depends on the subjects, but the prince has it in his own hands to create fear, a wise prince will rely on what is his own, remembering at the same time that he must avoid arousing hatred, as we have said.

In What Manner Princes Should Keep Their Word

How laudable it is for a prince to keep his word and govern his actions by integrity rather than trickery will be understood by all. Nonetheless we have in our times seen great things accomplished by many princes who have thought little of keeping their promises and have known the art of mystifying the minds of men. Such princes have won out over those whose actions were based on fidelity to their word.

It must be understood that there are two ways of fighting, one with laws and the other with arms. The first is the way of men, the second is the style of beasts, but since very often the first does not suffice it is necessary to turn to the second. Therefore a prince must know how to play the beast as well as the man. This lesson was taught allegorically by the ancient writers who related that Achilles and many other princes were brought up by Chiron the Centaur, who took them under his discipline. The clear significance of this half-man and half-beast preceptorship is that a prince must know how to use either of these two natures and that one without the other has no enduring strength. Now since the prince must make use of the characteristics of beasts he should choose those of the fox and the lion, though the lion cannot defend himself against snares and the fox is helpless against wolves. One must be a fox in avoiding traps and a lion in frightening wolves. Such as choose simply the rôle of a lion do not rightly understand the matter. Hence a wise leader cannot and should not keep his word when keeping it is not to his advantage or when the reasons that made him give it are no longer valid. If men were good, this would not be a good precept, but since they are wicked and will not keep faith with you, you are not bound to keep faith with them.

A prince has never lacked legitimate reasons to justify his breach of faith. We could give countless recent examples and show how any number of peace treaties or promises have been broken and rendered meaningless by the faithlessness of princes, and how success has fallen to the one who best knows how to counterfeit the fox. But it is necessary to know how to disguise this nature well and how to pretend and dissemble. Men are so simple and so ready to follow the needs of the moment that the deceiver will always find some one to deceive. Of recent examples I shall mention one. Alexander VI did nothing but deceive and never thought of anything else and always found some occasion for it. Never was there a man more convincing in his asseverations nor more willing to offer the most solemn oaths nor less likely to observe them. Yet his deceptions were always successful for he was an expert in this field.

So a prince need not have all the aforementioned good qualities, but it is most essential that he appear to have them. Indeed, I should go so far as to say that having them and always practising them is harmful, while seeming to have them is useful. It is good to appear clement, trustworthy, humane, religious, and honest, and also to be so, but always with the mind so disposed that, when the occasion arises not to be so, you can become the opposite. It must be understood that a prince and particularly a new prince cannot practise all the virtues for which men are accounted good, for the necessity of preserving the state often compels him to take actions which are opposed to loyalty, charity, humanity, and religion. Hence he must have a spirit ready to adapt itself as the varying winds of fortune command him. As I have said, so far as he is able, a prince should stick to the path of good but, if the necessity arises, he should know how to follow evil.

A prince must take great care that no word ever passes his lips that is not full of the above mentioned five good qualities, and he must seem to all who see and hear him a model of piety, loyalty, integrity, humanity, and religion. Nothing is more necessary than to seem to possess this last quality, for men in general judge more by the eye than the hand, as all can see but few can feel. Everyone sees what you seem to be, few experience what you really are and these few do not dare to set themselves up against the opinion of the majority supported by the majesty of the state. In the actions of all men and especially princes, where there is no court of appeal, the end is all that counts. Let a prince then concern himself with the acquisition or the maintenance of a state; the means employed will always be considered honorable and praised by all, for the mass of mankind is always swayed by appearances and by the outcome of an enterprise. And in the world there is only the mass, for the few find their place only when the majority has no base of support.

DESIDERIUS ERASMUS
The Arts of Peace[1]

Although the writers of antiquity divided the whole theory of state government into two sections, war and peace, the first and most important objective is the instruction of the prince in the matter of ruling wisely during times of peace, in which he should strive his utmost to preclude any future need for the science of war. In this matter it seems best that the prince should first know his own kingdom. This knowledge is best gained from a study of geography and history and from frequent visits through his provinces and cities. Let him first be eager to learn the location of his districts and cities, with their beginnings, their nature, institutions, customs,

---

1. From *The Education of a Christian Prince.*

laws, annals, and privileges. No one can heal the body until he is thoroughly conversant with it. No one can properly till a field which he does not understand. To be sure, the tyrant takes great care in such matters, but it is the spirit, not the act, which singles out the good prince. The physician studies the functions of the body so as to be more adept in healing it; the poisoning assassin, to more surely end it! Next, the prince should love the land over which he rules just as a farmer loves the fields of his ancestors or as a good man feels affection toward his household. He should make it his especial interest to hand it over to his successor, whosoever he may be, better than he received it. If he has any children, devotion toward them should urge him on; if he has no family, he should be guided by devotion to his country; and he should always keep kindled the flame of love for his subjects. He should consider his kingdom as a great body of which he is the most outstanding member and remember that they who have entrusted all their fortunes and their very safety to the good faith of one man are deserving of consideration. He should keep constantly in mind the example of those rulers to whom the welfare of their people was dearer than their own lives; for it is obviously impossible for a prince to do violence to the state without injuring himself.

In the second place the prince will see to it that he is loved by his subjects in return, but in such a way that his authority is no less strong among them. There are some who are so stupid as to strive to win good will for themselves by incantations and magic rings, when there is no charm more efficacious than good character itself; nothing can be more lovable than that, for, as this is a real and immortal good, so it brings a man true and undying good will. The best formula is this: let him love, who would be loved, so that he may attach his subjects to him as God has won the peoples of the world to Himself by His goodness.

They are also wrong who win the hearts of the masses by largesses, feasts, and gross indulgence. It is true that some popular favor, instead of affection, is gained by these means, but it is neither genuine nor permanent. In the meanwhile the greed of the populace is developed, which, as happens, after it has reached large proportions thinks nothing is enough. Then there is an uprising, unless complete satisfaction is made to their demands. By this means your people are not won, but corrupted. And so by this means the average prince is accustomed to win his way into the hearts of the people after the fashion of these foolish husbands who beguile their wives with blandishments, gifts, and complaisance, instead of winning their love by their character and good actions. So at length it comes about that they are not loved; instead of a thrifty and well mannered wife they have a haughty and intractable one; instead of an obedient spouse they find one who is quarrelsome and rebellious. Or take the case of those unhappy women who desperately try to arouse love in their husbands' hearts by giving them drugs, with the result that they have madmen instead of sane lovers.

The wife should first learn the ways and means of loving her husband and then let him show himself worthy of her love. And so with the people—let them become accustomed to the best, and let the prince be the source of the best things. Those who begin to love through reason, love long.

In the first place, then, he who would be loved by his people should show himself a prince worthy of love; after that it will do some good to consider how best he may win his way into their hearts. The prince should do this first so that the best men may have the highest regard for him and that he may be accepted by those who are lauded by all. They are the men he should have for his close friends; they are the ones for his counselors; they are the ones on whom he should bestow his honors and whom he should allow to have the greatest influence with him. By this means everyone will come to have an excellent opinion of the prince, who is the source of all good will. I have known some princes who were not really evil themselves who incurred the hatred of the people for no other reason than that they granted too much liberty to those whom universal public sentiment condemned. The people judged the character of the prince by these other men.

For my part, I should like to see the prince born and raised among those people whom he is destined to rule, because friendship is created and confirmed most when the source of good will is in nature itself. The common people shun and hate even good qualities which they are unknown to them, while evils which are familiar are sometimes loved. This matter at hand has a twofold advantage to offer, for the prince will be more kindly disposed toward his subjects and certainly more ready to regard them as his own. The people on their part will feel more kindness in their hearts and be more willing to recognize his position as prince. For this reason I am especially opposed to the accepted [idea of] alliances of the princes with foreign, particularly with distant, nations.

The ties of birth and country and a mutual spirit of understanding, as it were, have a great deal to do with establishing a feeling of good will. A goodly part of this feeling must of necessity be lost if mixed marriages confuse that native and inborn spirit. But when nature has laid a foundation of mutual affection, then it should be developed and strengthened by every other means. When the opposite situation is presented, then even greater energy must be employed to secure this feeling of good will by mutual obligations and a character worthy of commendation. In marriage, the wife at first yields entirely to the husband, and he makes a few concessions to her and indulges her whims until, as they come really to know one another, a firm bond unites them; so it should be in the case of a prince selected from a foreign country. Mithridates learned the languages of all the peoples over whom he ruled, and they were said to be twenty in number. Alexander the Great, however barbarous the peoples with whom he was dealing, at once used to imitate their ways and customs and by this method subtly worked himself into their good graces. Alcibiades has been praised for the same thing. Nothing so alienates the affections of his people from a prince as for him to take great pleasure in living abroad, because then they seem to be neglected by him to whom they wish to be most important. The result of this is that the people feel that they are not paying taxes to a prince (since the moneys are spent elsewhere and totally lost as far as they are concerned) but that they are casting spoils to foreigners. Lastly, there is nothing more harmful and disastrous to a country, nor more dangerous for a prince, than visits to far-away places, especially if these visits are prolonged; for it was this, according to the opinion of everyone, that took Philip from us and injured his kingdom no less than the war with the Gelrii, which was dragged out for so many years. The king bee is hedged about in the midst of the swarm and does not fly out and away. The heart is situated in the very middle of the body. Just so should a prince always be found among his own people.

There are two factors, as Aristotle tells us in his *Politics*, which have played the greatest roles in the overthrow of empires. They are hatred and contempt. Good will is the opposite of hatred; respected authority, of contempt. Therefore it will be the duty of the prince to study the best way to win the former and avoid the latter. Hatred is kindled by an ugly temper, by violence, insulting language, sourness of character, meanness, and greediness; it is more easily aroused than allayed. A good prince must therefore use every caution to prevent any possibility of losing the affections of his subjects. You may take my word that whoever loses the favor of his people is thereby stripped of a great safeguard. On the other hand, the affections of the populace are won by those characteristics which, in general, are farthest removed from tyranny. They are clemency, affability, fairness, courtesy, and kindliness. This last is a spur to duty, especially if they who have been of good service to the state, see that they will be rewarded at the hands of the prince. Clemency inspires to better efforts those who are aware of their faults, while forgiveness extends hope to those who are now eager to make recompense by virtuous conduct for the shortcomings of their earlier life and provides the steadfast with a happy reflection on human nature. Courtesy everywhere engenders love—or at least assuages hatred. This quality in a great prince is by far the most pleasing to the masses.

Contempt is most likely to spring from a penchant for the worldly pleasures of lust, for excessive drinking and eating, and for fools and clowns—in other words, for folly and idleness. Authority is gained by the following varied characteristics: in the first place wisdom, then integrity, self-restraint, seriousness, and alertness. These are the things by which a prince should commend himself, if he would be respected in his authority over his subjects. Some have the absurd idea that if they make the greatest confusion possible by their appearance, and dress with pompous display, they must be held in high esteem among their subjects. Who thinks a prince great just because he is adorned with gold and precious stones? Everyone knows he has as many as he wants. But in the meanwhile what else does the prince expose except the misfortunes of his people, who are supporting his extravagance to their great cost? And now lastly, what else does such a prince sow among his people, if not the seeds of all crime? Let the good prince be reared in such a manner and [continue to] live in such a manner that from the example of his life all the others (nobles and commoners alike) may take the model of frugality and temperance. Let him so conduct himself in the privacy of his home as not to be caught unawares by the sudden entrance of anyone. And in public it is unseemly for a prince to be seen anywhere, unless always in connection with something that will benefit the people as a whole. The real character of the prince is revealed by his speech rather than by his dress. Every word that is dropped from the lips of the prince is scattered wide among the masses. He should exercise the greatest care to see that whatever he says bears the stamp of [genuine] worth and evidences a mind becoming a good prince.

Aristotle's advice on this subject should not be overlooked. He says that a prince who would escape incurring the hatred of his people and would foster their affection for him should delegate to others the odious duties and keep for himself the tasks which will be sure to win favor. Thereby a great portion of any unpopularity will be diverted upon those who carry out the administration, and especially will it be so if these men are unpopular with the people on other grounds as well. In the matter of benefits, however, the genuine thanks redound to the prince alone. I should like to add also that gratitude for a favor will be returned twofold if it is given quickly, with no hesitation, spontaneously, and with a few words of friendly commendation. If anything must be refused, refusal should be affable and without offense. If it is necessary to impose a punishment, some slight diminution of the penalty prescribed by law should be made, and the sentence should be carried out as if the prince were being forced [to act] against his own desires.

It is not enough for the prince to keep his own character pure and uncorrupted for his state. He must give no less serious attention, in so far as he can, to see that every member of his household

—his nobles, his friends, his ministers, and his magistrates—follows his example. They are one with the prince, and any hatred that is aroused by their vicious acts rebounds upon the prince himself. But, someone will say, this supervision is extremely difficult to accomplish. It will be easy enough if the prince is careful to admit only the best men into his household, and if he makes them understand that the prince is most pleased by that which is best for the people. Otherwise it too often turns out that, due to the disregard of the prince in these matters or even his connivance in them, the most criminal men (hiding under cover of the prince) force a tyranny upon the people, and while they appear to be carrying out the affairs of the prince, they are doing the greatest harm to his good name. What is more, the condition of the state is more bearable when the prince himself is wicked than when he has evil friends; we manage to bear up under a single tyrant. Somehow or other the people can sate the greed of one man without difficulty: it is not a matter of great effort to satisfy the wild desires of just one man or to appease the vicious fierceness of a single individual, but to content so many tyrants is a heavy burden. The prince should avoid every novel idea in so far as he is capable of doing so; for even if conditions are bettered thereby, the very innovation is a stumbling block. The establishment of a state, the unwritten laws of a city, or the old legal code are never changed without great confusion. Therefore, if there is anything of this sort that can be endured, it should not be changed but should either be tolerated or happily diverted to a better function. As a last resort, if there is some absolutely unbearable condition, the change should be made, but [only] gradually and by a practiced hand.

The end which the prince sets for himself is of the greatest consequence, for if he shows little wisdom in its selection he must of necessity be wrong in all his plans. The cardinal principle of a good prince should be not only to preserve the present prosperity of the state but to pass it on more prosperous than when he received it. To use the jargon of the Peripatetics, there are three kinds of "good"—that of the mind, that of the body, and the external good. The prince must be careful not to evaluate them in reverse order and judge the good fortune of his state mainly by the external good, for these latter conditions should only be judged good in so far as they relate to the good of the mind and of the body; that is, in a word, the prince should consider his subjects to be most fortunate not if they are very wealthy or in excellent bodily health but if they are most honorable and self-controlled, if they have as little taste for greed and quarreling as could be hoped for, and if they are not at all factious but live in complete accord with one another. He must also beware of being deceived by the false names of the fairest things, for in this deception lies the fountainhead from which spring practically all the evils that abound in the world. It is no true state of happiness in which the people are given over to idleness and wasteful extravagance, any more than it is true liberty for everyone to be allowed to do as he pleases. Neither is it a state of servitude to live according to the letter of just laws. Nor is that a peaceful state in which the populace bows to every whim of the prince; but rather is it peaceful when it obeys good laws and a prince who has a keen regard for the authority of the laws. Equity does not lie in giving everyone the same reward, the same rights, the same honor; as a matter of fact, that is sometimes a mark of the greatest unfairness.

A prince who is about to assume control of the state must be advised at once that the main hope of a state lies in the proper education of its youth. This Xenophon wisely taught in his *Cyropaedia*. Pliable youth is amenable to any system of training. Therefore the greatest care should be exercised over public and private schools and over the education of the girls, so that the children may be placed under the best and most trustworthy instructors and may learn the teachings of Christ and that good literature which is beneficial to the state. As a result of this scheme of things, there will be no need for many laws or punishments, for the people will of their own free will follow the course of right.

Education exerts such a powerful influence, as Plato says, that a man who has been trained in the right develops into a sort of divine creature, while on the other hand, a person who has received a perverted training degenerates into a monstrous sort of savage beast. Nothing is of more importance to a prince than to have the best possible subjects.

The first effort, then, is to get them accustomed to the best influences, because any music has a soothing effect to the accustomed ear, and there is nothing harder than to rid people of those traits which have become second nature to them through habit. None of those tasks will be too difficult if the prince himself adheres to the best manners. It is the essence of tyranny, or rather trickery, to treat the common citizen as animal trainers are accustomed to treat a savage beast: first they carefully study the way in which these creatures are quieted or aroused, and then they anger them or quiet them at their pleasure. This Plato has painstakingly pointed out. Such a course is an abuse of the emotions of the masses and is no help to them. However, if the people prove intractable and rebel against what is good for them, then you must bide your time and gradually lead them over to your end, either by some subterfuge or by some helpful pretence. This works just as wine does, for when that is first taken it has no effect, but when it has gradually flowed through every vein it captivates the whole man and holds him in its power.

If sometimes the whirling course of events and public opinion beat the prince from his course, and he is forced to obey the [exigencies of the] time, yet he must not cease his efforts as long as he is able to renew his fight, and what he has not accomplished by one method he should try to effect by another.

QUESTIONS

1. Early in the essay Erasmus analogizes the relation of prince to people to that of a physician to the body, a farmer to a field, a husband to a wife. Why does he develop this last analogy more fully than the others and use it again later? How does his use of analogy differ from Winthrop's (pp. 967–970)?
2. On page 964 Erasmus lists the "varied characteristics" by which authority is gained. Why does he put wisdom "in the first place"? Is there any significance to the order in which he places the other characteristics?
3. Erasmus says that "the real character of the prince is revealed by his speech rather than by his dress." Would this be equally true of people other than princes? How can both speech and dress reveal character?
4. Compare Erasmus' ideal prince with Machiavelli's. What is the significance of the title, "The Arts of Peace"?
5. Is the advice to "avoid every novel idea" (p. 965) sound? To what does "novelty" apply in this context? How would Erasmus counter the charge that such a policy might lead to stagnation and corruption in government?
6. Why does Erasmus find it necessary to qualify so carefully what he means by "prosperity" (p. 965)? How does his definition differ from more commonly accepted ones today?
7. "Equity does not lie in giving everyone the same reward, the same rights, the same honor; as a matter of fact, that is sometimes a mark of the greatest unfairness" (p. 966). How does this implied definition of "equity" jibe with the statement in the Declaration of Independence that "all men are created equal" and "are endowed by their Creator with certain unalienable Rights" (pp. 996–999)?
8. How far do leading political figures today correspond to Erasmus' ideal prince?

JOHN WINTHROP

Speech to the General Court[1]

I suppose something may be expected from me, upon this charge that is befallen me, which moves me to speak now to you; yet I intend not to intermeddle in the proceedings of the court, or with

1. Winthrop, who had been found innocent of exceeding his authority as a magistrate, gave this speech to the General Court of Massachusetts Bay Colony on July 3, 1645.

any of the persons concerned therein. Only I bless God, that I see
an issue of this troublesome business. I also acknowledge the justice
of the court, and, for mine own part, I am well satisfied, I was
publicly charged, and I am publicly and legally acquitted, which is
all I did expect or desire. And though this be sufficient for my
justification before men, yet not so before the God, who hath seen
so much amiss in my dispensations (and even in this affair) as
calls me to be humble. For to be publicly and criminally charged in
this court, is matter of humiliation, (and I desire to make a right
use of it) notwithstanding I be thus acquitted. If her father had spit
in her face, (saith the Lord concerning Miriam), should she not
have been ashamed seven days?[2] Shame had lien upon her, whatever
the occasion had been. I am unwilling to stay you from your urgent
affairs, yet give me leave (upon this special occasion) to speak a
little more to this assembly. It may be of some good use, to inform
and rectify the judgments of some of the people, and may prevent
such distempers as have arisen amongst us. The great questions
that have troubled the country, are about the authority of the
magistrates and the liberty of the people. It is yourselves who
have called us to this office, and being called by you, we have our
authority from God, in way of an ordinance, such as hath the
image of God eminently stamped upon it, the contempt and violation whereof hath been vindicated with examples of divine vengeance, I entreat you to consider, that when you choose magistrates,
you take them from among yourselves, men subject to like passions
as you are. Therefore when you see infirmities in us, you should
reflect upon your own, and that would make you bear the more
with us, and not be severe censurers of the failings of your magistrates, when you have continual experience of the like infirmities
in yourselves and others. We account him a good servant, who
breaks not his covenant. The covenant between you and us is the
oath you have taken of us, which is to this purpose, that we shall
govern you and judge your causes by the rules of God's laws and
our own, according to our best skill. When you agree with a workman to build you a ship or house, etc., he undertakes as well for
his skill as for his faithfulness, for it is his profession, and you pay
him for both. But when you call one to be a magistrate, he doth not
profess nor undertake to have sufficient skill for that office, nor
can you furnish him with gifts, etc., therefore you must run the
hazard of his skill and ability. But if he fail in faithfulness, which
by his oath he is bound unto, that he must answer for. If it fall out
that the case be clear to common apprehension, and the rule clear
also, if he transgress here, the error is not in the skill, but in the
evil of the will: it must be required of him. But if the case be
doubtful, or the rule doubtful, to men of such understanding and

2. See Numbers xii. 1-15.

parts as your magistrates are, if your magistrates should err here, yourselves must bear it.

For the other point concerning liberty, I observe a great mistake in the country about that. There is a twofold liberty, natural (I mean as our nature is now corrupt) and civil or federal. The first is common to man with beasts and other creatures. By this, man, as he stands in relation to man simply, hath liberty to do what he lists; it is a liberty to evil as well as to good. This liberty is incompatible and inconsistent with authority, and cannot endure the least restraint of the most just authority. The exercise and maintaining of this liberty makes men grow more evil, and in time to be worse than brute beasts: *omnes sumus licentia deteriores*.[3] This is that great enemy of truth and peace, that wild beast, which all the ordinances of God are bent against, to restrain and subdue it. The other kind of liberty I call civil or federal, it may also be termed moral, in reference to the covenant between God and man, in the moral law, and the politic covenants and constitutions, amongst men themselves. This liberty is the proper end and object of authority, and cannot subsist without it; and it is a liberty to that only which is good, just, and honest. This liberty you are to stand for, with the hazard (not only of your goods, but) of your lives, if need be. Whatsoever crosseth this, is not authority, but a distemper thereof. This liberty is maintained and exercised in a way of subjection to authority; it is of the same kind of liberty wherewith Christ hath made us free. The woman's own choice makes such a man her husband; yet being so chosen, he is her lord, and she is to be subject to him, yet in a way of liberty, not of bondage and a true wife accounts her subjection her honor and freedom, and would not think her condition safe and free, but in her subjection to her husband's authority. Such is the liberty of the church under the authority of Christ, her king and husband; his yoke is so easy and sweet to her as a bride's ornaments; and if through forwardness or wantonness, etc., she shake it off, at any time, she is at no rest in her spirit, until she take it up again; and whether her lord smiles upon her, and embraceth her in his arms, or whether he frowns, or rebukes, or smites her, she apprehends the sweetness of his love in all, and is refreshed, supported, and instructed by every such dispensation of his authority over her. On the other side, ye know who they are that complain of this yoke and say, let us break their bands, etc., we will not have this man to rule over us. Even so, brethren, it will be between you and your magistrates. If you stand for your natural corrupt liberties, and will do what is good in your own eyes, you will not endure the least weight of authority, but will murmur, and oppose, and be always striving to shake off that yoke; but if you will be satisfied to enjoy such civil and lawful liberties, such as

3. "We all become meaner through selfish liberty."

Christ allows you, then will you quietly and cheerfully submit unto that authority which is set over you, in all the administrations of it, for your good. Wherein, if we fail at any time, we hope we shall be willing (by God's assistance) to hearken to good advice from any of you, or in any other way of God; so shall your liberties be preserved, in upholding the honor and power of authority amongst you.

QUESTIONS

1. What is Winthrop's distinction between "skill" and "will"? What connection has this with the two kinds of liberty he discusses?
2. Does Winthrop use the two extended analogies of the workman and the marriage partners in the same way and for the same purpose? Explain.
3. In what ways might Lincoln's definition of liberty (p. 999) be considered a refinement of Winthrop's?

ABRAHAM LINCOLN
Second Inaugural Address

At this second appearing to take the oath of the presidential office, there is less occasion for an extended address than there was at the first. Then a statement, somewhat in detail, of a course to be pursued, seemed fitting and proper. Now, at the expiration of four years, during which public declarations have been constantly called forth on every point and phase of the great contest which still absorbs the attention, and engrosses the energies of the nation, little that is new could be presented. The progress of our arms, upon which all else chiefly depends, is as well known to the public as to myself; and it is, I trust, reasonably satisfactory and encouraging to all. With high hope for the future, no prediction in regard to it is ventured.

On the occasion corresponding to this four years ago, all thoughts were anxiously directed to an impending civil war. All dreaded it— all sought to avert it. While the inaugural address was being delivered from this place, devoted altogether to *saving* the Union without war, insurgent agents were in the city seeking to *destroy* it without war—seeking to dissolve the Union, and divide effects, by negotiation. Both parties deprecated war; but one of them would *make* war rather than let the nation survive; and the other would *accept* war rather than let it perish. And the war came.

One-eighth of the whole population were colored slaves, not distributed generally over the Union, but localized in the Southern part of it. These slaves constituted a peculiar and powerful interest.

All knew that this interest was, somehow, the cause of the war. To strengthen, perpetuate, and extend this interest was the object for which the insurgents would rend the Union, even by war; while the government claimed no right to do more than to restrict the territorial enlargement of it. Neither party expected for the war, the magnitude, or the duration, which it has already attained. Neither anticipated that the *cause* of the conflict might cease with, or even before, the conflict itself should cease. Each looked for an easier triumph, and a result less fundamental and astounding. Both read the same Bible, and pray to the same God; and each invokes His aid against the other. It may seem strange that any men should dare to ask a just God's assistance in wringing their bread from the sweat of other men's faces[1]; but let us judge not that we be not judged.[2] The prayers of both could not be answered; that of neither has been answered fully. The Almighty has His own purposes. "Woe unto the world because of offenses! for it must needs be that offenses come; but woe to that man by whom the offense cometh!"[3] If we shall suppose that American slavery is one of those offenses which, in the providence of God, must needs come, but which, having continued through His appointed time, He now wills to remove, and that He gives to both North and South, this terrible war, as the woe due to those by whom the offense came, shall we discern therein any departure from those divine attributes which the believers in a Living God always ascribe to Him? Fondly do we hope—fervently do we pray—that this mighty scourge of war may speedily pass away. Yet, if God wills that it continue, until all the wealth piled by the bondman's two hundred and fifty years of unrequited toil shall be sunk, and until every drop of blood drawn with the lash, shall be paid by another drawn with the sword, as was said three thousand years ago, so still it must be said "the judgments of the Lord are true and righteous altogether."[4]

With malice toward none; with charity for all; with firmness in the right, as God gives us to see the right, let us strive on to finish the work we are in; to bind up the nation's wounds; to care for him who shall have borne the battle, and for his widow, and his orphan —to do all which may achieve and cherish a just, and a lasting peace, among ourselves, and with all nations.

1. See Genesis iii. 19.
2. See Matthew vii. 1.
3. See Matthew xviii. 7.
4. See Psalms xix. 9.

JONATHAN SWIFT
A Modest Proposal

FOR PREVENTING THE CHILDREN OF POOR PEOPLE IN IRELAND FROM BEING A BURDEN TO THEIR PARENTS OR COUNTRY, AND FOR MAKING THEM BENEFICIAL TO THE PUBLIC

It is a melancholy object to those who walk through this great town or travel in the country, when they see the streets, the roads, and cabin doors, crowded with beggars of the female-sex, followed by three, four, or six children, all in rags and importuning every passenger for an alms. These mothers, instead of being able to work for their honest livelihood, are forced to employ all their time in strolling to beg sustenance for their helpless infants, who, as they grow up, either turn thieves for want of work, or leave their dear native country to fight for the Pretender in Spain, or sell themselves to the Barbadoes.[1]

I think it is agreed by all parties that this prodigious number of children in the arms, or on the backs, or at the heels of their mothers, and frequently of their fathers, is in the present deplorable state of the kingdom a very great additional grievance; and therefore whoever could find out a fair, cheap, and easy method of making these children sound, useful members of the commonwealth would deserve so well of the public as to have his statue set up for a preserver of the nation.

But my intention is very far from being confined to provide only for the children of professed beggars; it is of a much greater extent, and shall take in the whole number of infants at a certain age who are born of parents in effect as little able to support them as those who demand our charity in the streets.

As to my own part, having turned my thoughts for many years upon this important subject, and maturely weighed the several schemes of other projectors, I have always found them grossly mistaken in their computation. It is true, a child just dropped from its dam may be supported by her milk for a solar year, with little other nourishment; at most not above the value of two shillings, which the mother may certainly get, or the value in scraps, by her lawful occupation of begging; and it is exactly at one year old that I propose to provide for them in such a manner as instead of being a charge upon their parents or the parish, or wanting food and raiment for the rest of their lives, they shall on the contrary contribute to the feeding, and partly to the clothing, of many thousands.

There is likewise another great advantage in my scheme, that it

---

1. That is, bind themselves to work for a period of years, in order to pay for their transportation to a colony.

will prevent those voluntary abortions, and that horrid practice of women murdering their bastard children, alas, too frequent among us, sacrificing the poor innocent babes, I doubt, more to avoid the expense than the shame, which would move tears and pity in the most savage and inhuman breast.

The number of souls in this kingdom being usually reckoned one million and a half, of these I calculate there may be about two hundred thousand couple whose wives are breeders; from which number I subtract thirty thousand couples who are able to maintain their own children, although I apprehend there cannot be so many under the present distresses of the kingdom; but this being granted, there will remain an hundred and seventy thousand breeders. I again subtract fifty thousand for those women who miscarry, or whose children die by accident or disease within the year. There only remain an hundred and twenty thousand children of poor parents annually born. The question therefore is, how this number shall be reared and provided for, which, as I have already said, under the present situation of affairs, is utterly impossible by all the methods hitherto proposed. For we can neither employ them in handicraft or agriculture; we neither build houses (I mean in the country) nor cultivate land. They can very seldom pick up a livelihood by stealing till they arrive at six years old, except where they are of towardly parts; although I confess they learn the rudiments much earlier, during which time they can however be looked upon only as probationers, as I have been informed by a principal gentleman in the county of Cavan, who protested to me that he never knew above one or two instances under the age of six, even in a part of the kingdom so renowned for the quickest proficiency in that art.

I am assured by our merchants that a boy or a girl before twelve years old is no salable commodity; and even when they come to this age they will not yield above three pounds, or three pounds and half a crown at most on the Exchange; which cannot turn to account either to the parents or the kingdom, the charge of nutriment and rags having been at least four times that value.

I shall now therefore humbly propose my own thoughts, which I hope will not be liable to the least objection.

I have been assured by a very knowing American of my acquaintance in London, that a young healthy child well nursed is at a year old a most delicious, nourishing, and wholesome food, whether stewed, roasted, baked, or boiled; and I make no doubt that it will equally serve in a fricassee or a ragout.

I do therefore humbly offer it to public consideration that of the hundred and twenty thousand children, already computed, twenty thousand may be reserved for breed, whereof only one fourth part to be males, which is more than we allow to sheep, black cattle, or swine; and my reason is that these children are seldom the fruits of marriage, a circumstance not much regarded by our savages, therefore one male will be sufficient to serve four females. That the remaining hundred thousand may at a year old be offered in sale to the persons of quality and fortune through the kingdom, always advising the mother to let them suck plentifully in the last month, so as to render them plump and fat for a good table. A child will make two dishes at an entertainment for friends; and when the family dines alone, the fore or hind quarter will make a reasonable dish, and seasoned with a little pepper or salt will be very good boiled on the fourth day, especially in winter.

I have reckoned upon a medium that a child just born will weigh twelve pounds, and in a solar year if tolerably nursed increaseth to twenty-eight pounds.

I grant this food will be somewhat dear, and therefore very proper for landlords, who, as they have already devoured most of the parents, seem to have the best title to the children.

Infant's flesh will be in season throughout the year, but more plentiful in March, and a little before and after. For we are told by a grave author, an eminent French physician,[2] that fish being a prolific diet, there are more children born in Roman Catholic countries about nine months after Lent than at any other season; therefore, reckoning a year after Lent, the markets will be more glutted than usual, because the number of popish infants is at least three to one in this kingdom; and therefore it will have one other collateral advantage, by lessening the number of Papists among us.

I have already computed the charge of nursing a beggar's child (in which list I reckon all cottagers, laborers, and four fifths of the farmers) to be about two shillings per annum, rags included; and I believe no gentleman would repine to give ten shillings for the carcass of a good fat child, which, as I have said, will make four dishes of excellent nutritive meat, when he hath only some particular friend or his own family to dine with him. Thus the squire will learn to be a good landlord, and grow popular among the tenants; the mother will have eight shillings net profit, and be fit for work till she produces another child.

Those who are more thrifty (as I must confess the times require) may flay the carcass; the skin of which artificially dressed will make admirable gloves for ladies, and summer boots for fine gentlemen.

As to our city of Dublin, shambles may be appointed for this purpose in the most convenient parts of it, and butchers we may be assured will not be wanting; although I rather recommend buying the children alive, and dressing them hot from the knife as we do roasting pigs.

A very worthy person, a true lover of his country, and whose

2. Rabelais.

virtues I highly esteem, was lately pleased in discoursing on this matter to offer a refinement upon my scheme. He said that many gentlemen of this kingdom, having of late destroyed their deer, he conceived that the want of venison might be well supplied by the bodies of young lads and maidens, not exceeding fourteen years of age nor under twelve, so great a number of both sexes in every county being now ready to starve for want of work and service; and these to be disposed of by their parents, if alive, or otherwise by their nearest relations. But with due deference to so excellent a friend and so deserving a patriot, I cannot be altogether in his sentiments; for as to the males, my American acquaintance assured me from frequent experience that their flesh was generally tough and lean, like that of our schoolboys, by continual exercise, and their taste disagreeable; and to fatten them would not answer the charge. Then as to the females, it would, I think with humble submission, be a loss to the public, because they soon would become breeders themselves: and besides, it is not improbable that some scrupulous people might be apt to censure such a practice (although indeed very unjustly) as a little bordering upon cruelty; which, I confess, hath always been with me the strongest objection against any project, how well soever intended.

But in order to justify my friend, he confessed that this expedient was put into his head by the famous Psalmanazar, a native of the island Formosa, who came from thence to London above twenty years ago, and in conversation told my friend that in his country when any young person happened to be put to death, the executioner sold the carcass to persons of quality as a prime dainty; and that in his time the body of a plump girl of fifteen, who was crucified for an attempt to poison the emperor, was sold to his Imperial Majesty's prime minister of state, and other great mandarins of the court, in joints from the gibbet, at four hundred crowns. Neither indeed can I deny that if the same use were made of several plump young girls in this town, who without one single groat to their fortunes cannot stir abroad without a chair, and appear at the playhouse and assemblies in foreign fineries which they never will pay for, the kingdom would not be the worse.

Some persons of a desponding spirit are in great concern about that vast number of poor people who are aged, diseased, or maimed, and I have been desired to employ my thoughts what course may be taken to ease the nation of so grievous an encumbrance. But I am not in the least pain upon that matter, because it is very well known that they are every day dying and rotting by cold and famine, and filth and vermin, as fast as can be reasonably expected. And as to the younger laborers, they are now in almost as hopeful a condition. They cannot get work, and consequently pine away for want of nourishment to a degree that if at any time they are accidentally hired to common labor, they have not strength to perform it; and thus the country and themselves are happily delivered from the evils to come.

I have too long digressed, and therefore shall return to my subject. I think the advantages by the proposal which I have made are obvious and many, as well as of the highest importance.

For first, as I have already observed, it would greatly lessen the number of Papists, with whom we are yearly overrun, being the principal breeders of the nation as well as our most dangerous enemies; and who stay at home on purpose to deliver the kingdom to the Pretender, hoping to take their advantage by the absence of so many good Protestants, who have chosen rather to leave their country than to stay at home and pay tithes against their conscience to an Episcopal curate.

Secondly, the poorer tenants will have something valuable of their own, which by law may be made liable to distress, and help to pay their landlord's rent, their corn and cattle being already seized and money a thing unknown.

Thirdly, whereas the maintenance of an hundred thousand children, from two years old and upwards, cannot be computed at less than ten shillings a piece per annum, the nation's stock will be thereby increased fifty thousand pounds per annum, besides the profit of a new dish introduced to the tables of all gentlemen of fortune in the kingdom who have any refinement in taste. And the money will circulate among ourselves, the goods being entirely of our own growth and manufacture.

Fourthly, the constant breeders, besides the gain of eight shillings sterling per annum by the sale of their children, will be rid of the charge of maintaining them after the first year.

Fifthly, this food would likewise bring great custom to taverns, where the vintners will certainly be so prudent as to procure the best receipts for dressing it to perfection, and consequently have their houses frequented by all the fine gentlemen, who justly value themselves upon their knowledge in good eating; and a skillful cook, who understands how to oblige his guests, will contrive to make it as expensive as they please.

Sixthly, this would be a great inducement to marriage, which all wise nations have either encouraged by rewards or enforced by laws and penalties. It would increase the care and tenderness of mothers toward their children, when they were sure of a settlement for life to the poor babes, provided in some sort by the public, to their annual profit instead of expense. We should see an honest emulation among the married women, which of them could bring the fattest child to the market. Men would become as fond of their wives during the time of their pregnancy as they are now of their mares in foal, their cows in calf, or sows when they are ready to farrow;

nor offer to beat or kick them (as is too frequent a practice) for fear of a miscarriage.

Many other advantages might be enumerated. For instance, the addition of some thousand carcasses in our exportation of barreled beef, the propagation of swine's flesh, and improvement in the art of making good bacon, so much wanted among us by the great destruction of pigs, too frequent at our tables, which are no way comparable in taste or magnificence to a well-grown, fat, yearling child, which roasted whole will make a considerable figure at a lord mayor's feast or any other public entertainment. But this and many others I omit, being studious of brevity.

Supposing that one thousand families in this city would be constant customers for infants' flesh, besides others who might have it at merry meetings, particularly weddings and christenings, I compute that Dublin would take off annually about twenty thousand carcasses, and the rest of the kingdom (where probably they will be sold somewhat cheaper) the remaining eighty thousand.

I can think of no one objection that will possibly be raised against this proposal, unless it should be urged that the number of people will be thereby much lessened in the kingdom. This I freely own, and it was indeed one principal design in offering it to the world. I desire the reader will observe, that I calculate my remedy for this one individual kingdom of Ireland and for no other that ever was, is, or I think ever can be upon earth. Therefore let no man talk to me of other expedients: of taxing our absentees at five shillings a pound: of using neither clothes nor household furniture except what is of our own growth and manufacture: of utterly rejecting the materials and instruments that promote foreign luxury: of curing the expensiveness of pride, vanity, idleness, and gaming in our women: of introducing a vein of parsimony, prudence, and temperance: of learning to love our country, in the want of which we differ even from Laplanders and the inhabitants of Topinamboo[3]: of quitting our animosities and factions, nor acting any longer like the Jews, who were murdering one another at the very moment their city was taken: of being a little cautious not to sell our country and conscience for nothing: of teaching landlords to have at least one degree of mercy toward their tenants: lastly, of putting a spirit of honesty, industry, and skill into our shopkeepers; who, if a resolution could now be taken to buy only our native goods, would immediately unite to cheat and exact upon us in the price, the measure, and the goodness, nor could ever yet be brought to make one fair proposal of just dealing, though often and earnestly invited to it.[4]

Therefore I repeat, let no man talk to me of these and the like

3. A district in Brazil.
4. Swift himself has made these various proposals in previous works.

expedients, till he hath at least some glimpse of hope that there will ever be some hearty and sincere attempt to put them in practice.

But as to myself, having been wearied out for many years with offering vain, idle, visionary thoughts, and at length utterly despairing of success, I fortunately fell upon this proposal, which, as it is wholly new, so it hath something solid and real, of no expense and little trouble, full in our own power, and whereby we can incur no danger in disobliging England. For this kind of commodity will not bear exportation, the flesh being of too tender a consistence to admit a long continuance in salt, although perhaps I could name a country which would be glad to eat up our whole nation without it.

After all, I am not so violently bent upon my own opinion as to reject any offer proposed by wise men, which shall be found equally innocent, cheap, easy, and effectual. But before something of that kind shall be advanced in contradiction to my scheme, and offering a better, I desire the author or authors will be pleased maturely to consider two points. First, as things now stand, how they will be able to find food and raiment for an hundred thousand useless mouths and backs. And secondly, there being a round million of creatures in human figure throughout this kingdom, whose sole subsistence put into a common stock would leave them in debt two millions of pounds sterling, adding those who are beggars by profession to the bulk of farmers, cottagers, and laborers, with their wives and children who are beggars in effect; I desire those politicians who dislike my overture, and may perhaps be so bold to attempt an answer, that they will first ask the parents of these mortals whether they would not at this day think it a great happiness to have been sold for food at a year old in the manner I prescribe, and thereby have avoided such a perpetual scene of misfortunes as they have since gone through by the oppression of landlords, the impossibility of paying rent without money or trade, the want of common sustenance, with neither house nor clothes to cover them from the inclemencies of the weather, and the most inevitable prospect of entailing the like or greater miseries upon their breed forever.

I profess, in the sincerity of my heart, that I have not the least personal interest in endeavoring to promote this necessary work, having no other motive than the public good of my country, by advancing our trade, providing for infants, relieving the poor, and giving some pleasure to the rich. I have no children by which I can propose to get a single penny; the youngest being nine years old, and my wife past childbearing.

QUESTIONS

1. This essay has been called one of the best examples of sustained irony in the English language. Irony is difficult to handle because

there is always the danger that the reader will miss the irony and take what is said literally. What does Swift do to try to prevent this? In answering this question, consider such matters as these: Is the first sentence of the essay ironic? At what point do you begin to suspect that Swift is using irony? What further evidence accumulates to make you certain that Swift is being ironic?

2. What is the speaker like? How are his views and character different from Swift's? Is the character of the speaker consistent? What is the purpose of the essay's final sentence?

3. Why does Swift use such phrases as "just dropt from its dam," "whose wives are breeders," "one fourth part to be males"?

4. Does the essay shock you? Was it Swift's purpose to shock you?

5. What is the main target of Swift's attack? What subsidiary targets are there? Does Swift offer any serious solutions for the problems and conditions he is describing?

6. What devices of argument, apart from the use of irony, does Swift use that could be successfully applied to other subjects?

7. Compare Swift's methods of drawing in or engaging his audience to Coffin's ("What Crucified Christ?" pp. 1464–1479).

CLARENCE DARROW

Address to the Prisoners in the Cook County Jail[1]

If I looked at jails and crimes and prisoners in the way the ordinary person does, I should not speak on this subject to you. The reason I talk to you on the question of crime, its cause and cure, is that I really do not in the least believe in crime. There is no such thing as a crime as the word is generally understood. I do not believe there is any sort of distinction between the real moral conditions of the people in and out of jail. One is just as good as the other. The people here can no more help being here than the people outside can avoid being outside. I do not believe that people are in jail because they deserve to be. They are in jail simply because they cannot avoid it on account of circumstances which are entirely beyond their control and for which they are in no way responsible.

I suppose a great many people on the outside would say I was doing you harm if they should hear what I say to you this afternoon, but you cannot be hurt a great deal anyway, so it will not

1. The warden of the Cook County Jail in Chicago, who knew Darrow as a criminologist, lawyer, and writer, invited him to speak before the inmates of the jail in 1902. Darrow's friends felt that the talk was inappropriate for its audience, but Darrow defended himself in the introduction to the lecture, which he had printed in pamphlet form: "Realizing the force of the suggestion that the truth should not be spoken to all people, I have caused these remarks to be printed on rather good paper and in a somewhat expensive form. In this way the truth does not become cheap and vulgar, and is only placed before those whose intelligence and affluence will prevent their being influenced by it." The pamphlet sold for five cents.

matter. Good people outside would say that I was really teaching you things that were calculated to injure society, but it's worth while now and then to hear something different from what you ordinarily get from preachers and the like. These will tell you that you should be good and then you will get rich and be happy. Of course we know that people do not get rich by being good, and that is the reason why so many of you people try to get rich some other way, only you do not understand how to do it quite as well as the fellow outside.

There are people who think that everything in this world is an accident. But really there is no such thing as an accident. A great many folks admit that many of the people in jail ought to be there, and many who are outside ought to be in. I think none of them ought to be here. There ought to be no jails; and if it were not for the fact that the people on the outside are so grasping and heartless in their dealings with the people on the inside, there would be no such institution as jails.

I do not want you to believe that I think all you people here are angels. I do not think that. You are people of all kinds, all of you doing the best you can—and that is evidently not very well. You are people of all kinds and conditions and under all circumstances. In one sense everybody is equally good and equally bad. We all do the best we can under the circumstances. But as to the exact things for which you are sent here, some of you are guilty and did the particular act because you needed the money. Some of you did it because you are in the habit of doing it, and some of you because you are born to it, and it comes to be as natural as it does, for instance, for me to be good.

Most of you probably have nothing against me, and most of you would treat me the same way as any other person would, probably better than some of the people on the outside would treat me, because you think I believe in you and they know I do not believe in them. While you would not have the least thing against me in the world, you might pick my pockets. I do not think all of you would, but I think some of you would. You would not have anything against me, but that's your profession, a few of you. Some of the rest of you, if my doors were unlocked, might come in if you saw anything you wanted—not out of any malice to me, but because that is your trade. There is no doubt there are quite a number of people in this jail who would pick my pockets. And still I know this—that when I get outside pretty nearly everybody picks my pocket. There may be some of you who would hold up a man on the street, if you did not happen to have something else to do, and needed the money; but when I want to light my house or my office the gas company holds me up. They charge me one dollar for something that is worth twenty-five cents. Still all these people are good people; they are pillars of society and support the churches, and they are respectable.

When I ride on the streetcars I am held up—I pay five cents for a ride that is worth two and a half cents, simply because a body of men have bribed the city council and the legislature, so that all the rest of us have to pay tribute to them.

If I do not want to fall into the clutches of the gas trust and choose to burn oil instead of gas, then good Mr. Rockefeller holds me up, and he uses a certain portion of his money to build universities and support churches which are engaged in telling us how to be good.

Some of you are here for obtaining property under false pretenses—yet I pick up a great Sunday paper and read the advertisements of a merchant prince—"Shirtwaists for 39 cents, marked down from $3.00."

When I read the advertisements in the paper I see they are all lies. When I want to get out and find a place to stand anywhere on the face of the earth, I find that it has all been taken up long ago before I came here, and before you came here, and somebody says, "Get off, swim into the lake, fly into the air; go anywhere, but get off." That is because these people have the police and they have the jails and the judges and the lawyers and the soldiers and all the rest of them to take care of the earth and drive everybody off that comes in their way.

A great many people will tell you that all this is true, but that it does not excuse you. These facts do not excuse some fellow who reaches into my pocket and takes out a five-dollar bill. The fact that the gas company bribes the members of the legislature from year to year, and fixes the law, so that all you people are compelled to be "fleeced" whenever you deal with them; the fact that the streetcar companies and the gas companies have control of the streets; and the fact that the landlords own all the earth—this, they say, has nothing to do with you.

Let us see whether there is any connection between the crimes of the respectable classes and your presence in the jail. Many of you people are in jail because you have really committed burglary; many of you, because you have stolen something. In the meaning of the law, you have taken some other person's property. Some of you have entered a store and carried off a pair of shoes because you did not have the price. Possibly some of you have committed murder. I cannot tell what all of you did. There are a great many people here who have done some of these things who really do not know themselves why they did them. I think I know why you did them—every one of you; you did these things because you were bound to do them. It looked to you at the time as if you had a chance to do them or not, as you saw fit; but still, after all, you had no choice.

There may be people here who had some money in their pockets and who still went out and got some more money in a way society forbids. Now, you may not yourselves see exactly why it was you did this thing, but if you look at the question deeply enough and carefully enough you will see that there were circumstances that drove you to do exactly the thing which you did. You could not help it any more than we outside can help taking the positions that we take. The reformers who tell you to be good and you will be happy, and the people on the outside who have property to protect—they think that the only way to do it is by building jails and locking you up in cells on weekdays and praying for you Sundays.

I think that all of this has nothing whatever to do with right conduct. I think it is very easily seen what has to do with right conduct. Some so-called criminals—and I will use this word because it is handy, it means nothing to me—I speak of the criminals who get caught as distinguished from the criminals who catch them—some of these so-called criminals are in jail for their first offenses, but nine tenths of you are in jail because you did not have a good lawyer and, of course, you did not have a good lawyer because you did not have enough money to pay a good lawyer. There is no very great danger of a rich man going to jail.

Some of you may be here for the first time. If we would open the doors and let you out, and leave the laws as they are today, some of you would be back tomorrow. This is about as good a place as you can get anyway. There are many people here who are so in the habit of coming that they would not know where else to go. There are people who are born with the tendency to break into jail every chance they get, and they cannot avoid it. You cannot figure out your life and see why it was, but still there is a reason for it; and if we were all wise and knew all the facts, we could figure it out.

In the first place, there are a good many more people who go to jail in the wintertime than in summer. Why is this? Is it because people are more wicked in winter? No, it is because the coal trust begins to get in its grip in the winter. A few gentlemen take possession of the coal, and unless the people will pay seven or eight dollars a ton for something that is worth three dollars, they will have to freeze. Then there is nothing to do but to break into jail, and so there are many more in jail in the winter than in summer. It costs more for gas in the winter because the nights are longer, and people go to jail to save gas bills. The jails are electric-lighted. You may not know it, but these economic laws are working all the time, whether we know it or do not know it.

There are more people who go to jail in hard times than in good times—few people, comparatively, go to jail except when they are hard up. They go to jail because they have no other place to go. They may not know why, but it is true all the same. People are not more wicked in hard times. That is not the reason. The fact is true all over the world that in hard times more people go to jail than in good times, and in winter more people go to jail than in summer. Of course it is pretty hard times for people who go to jail at any time. The people who go to jail are almost always poor people— people who have no other place to live, first and last. When times are hard, then you find large numbers of people who go to jail who would not otherwise be in jail.

Long ago, Mr. Buckle,[2] who was a great philosopher and historian, collected facts, and he showed that the number of people who are arrested increased just as the price of food increased. When they put up the price of gas ten cents a thousand, I do not know who will go to jail, but I do know that a certain number of people will go. When the meat combine raises the price of beef, I do not know who is going to jail, but I know that a large number of people are bound to go. Whenever the Standard Oil Company raises the price of oil, I know that a certain number of girls who are seamstresses, and who work night after night long hours for somebody else, will be compelled to go out on the streets and ply another trade, and I know that Mr. Rockefeller and his associates are responsible and not the poor girls in the jails.

First and last, people are sent to jail because they are poor. Sometimes, as I say, you may not need money at the particular time, but you wish to have thrifty forehanded habits, and do not always wait until you are in absolute want. Some of you people are perhaps plying the trade, the profession, which is called burglary. No man in his right senses will go into a strange house in the dead of night and prowl around with a dark lantern through unfamiliar rooms and take chances of his life, if he has plenty of the good things of the world in his own home. You would not take any such chances as that. If a man had clothes in his clothes-press and beefsteak in his pantry and money in the bank, he would not navigate around nights in houses where he knows nothing about the premises whatever. It always requires experience and education for this profession, and people who fit themselves for it are no more to blame than I am for being a lawyer. A man would not hold up another man on the street if he had plenty of money in his own pocket. He might do it if he had one dollar or two dollars, but he wouldn't if he had as much money as Mr. Rockefeller has. Mr. Rockefeller has a great deal better hold-up game than that.

The more that is taken from the poor by the rich, who have the chance to take it, the more poor people there are who are com-

2. Henry Thomas Buckle (1821-1862), British historian and author of a *History of Civilization*, who was attacked during his lifetime by conservatives for his "radical" views of history.

pelled to resort to these means for a livelihood. They may not understand it, they may not think so at once, but after all they are driven into that line of employment.

There is a bill before the legislature of this state to punish kidnaping children with death. We have wise members of the legislature. They know the gas trust when they see it and they always see it—they can furnish light enough to be seen; and this legislature thinks it is going to stop kidnaping children by making a law punishing kidnapers of children with death. I don't believe in kidnaping children, but the legislature is all wrong. Kidnaping children is not a crime, it is a profession. It has been developed with the times. It has been developed with our modern industrial conditions. There are many ways of making money—many new ways that our ancestors knew nothing about. Our ancestors knew nothing about a billion-dollar trust; and here comes some poor fellow who has no other trade and he discovers the profession of kidnaping children.

This crime is born, not because people are bad; people don't kidnap other people's children because they want the children or because they are devilish, but because they see a chance to get some money out of it. You cannot cure this crime by passing a law punishing by death kidnapers of children. There is one way to cure it. There is one way to cure all these offenses, and that is to give the people a chance to live. There is no other way, and there never was any other way since the world began; and the world is so blind and stupid that it will not see. If every man and woman and child in the world had a chance to make a decent, fair, honest living, there would be no jails and no lawyers and no courts. There might be some persons here or there with some peculiar formation of their brain, like Rockefeller, who would do these things simply to be doing them; but they would be very, very few, and those should be sent to a hospital and treated, and not sent to jail; and they would entirely disappear in the second generation, or at least in the third generation.

I am not talking pure theory. I will just give you two or three illustrations.

The English people once punished criminals by sending them away. They would load them on a ship and export them to Australia. England was owned by lords and nobles and rich people. They owned the whole earth over there, and the other people had to stay in the streets. They could not get a decent living. They used to take their criminals and send them to Australia—I mean the class of criminals who got caught. When these criminals got over there, and nobody else had come, they had the whole continent to run over, and so they could raise sheep and furnish their own meat, which is easier than stealing it. These criminals then became decent, respectable people because they had a chance to live. They did not commit any crimes. They were just like the English people who sent them there, only better. And in the second generation the descendants of those criminals were as good and respectable a class of people as there were on the face of the earth, and then they began building churches and jails themselves.

A portion of this country was settled in the same way, landing prisoners down on the southern coast; but when they got here and had a whole continent to run over and plenty of chances to make a living, they became respectable citizens, making their own living just like any other citizen in the world. But finally the descendants of the English aristocracy who sent the people over to Australia found out they were getting rich, and so they went over to get possession of the earth as they always do, and they organized land syndicates and got control of the land and ores, and then they had just as many criminals in Australia as they did in England. It was not because the world had grown bad; it was because the earth had been taken away from the people.

Some of you people have lived in the country. It's prettier than it is here. And if you have ever lived on a farm you understand that if you put a lot of cattle in a field, when the pasture is short they will jump over the fence; but put them in a good field where there is plenty of pasture, and they will be law-abiding cattle to the end of time. The human animal is just like the rest of the animals, only a little more so. The same thing that governs in the one governs in the other.

Everybody makes his living along the lines of least resistance. A wise man who comes into a country early sees a great undeveloped land. For instance, our rich men twenty-five years ago saw that Chicago was small and knew a lot of people would come here and settle, and they readily saw that if they had all the land around here it would be worth a good deal, so they grabbed the land. You cannot be a landlord because somebody has got it all. You must find some other calling. In England and Ireland and Scotland less than five per cent own all the land there is, and the people are bound to stay there on any kind of terms the landlords give. They must live the best they can, so they develop all these various professions—burglary, picking pockets, and the like.

Again, people find all sorts of ways of getting rich. These are diseases like everything else. You look at people getting rich, organizing trusts and making a million dollars, and somebody gets the disease and he starts out. He catches it just as a man catches the mumps or the measles; he is not to blame, it is in the air. You will find men speculating beyond their means, because the mania of money-getting is taking possession of them. It is simply a disease—nothing more, nothing less. You cannot avoid catching it; but the fellows who have control of the earth have the advantage of you. See what the law is: when these men get control of things, they make the laws. They do not make the laws to protect anybody; courts are not instruments of justice. When your case gets into court it will make little difference whether you are guilty or innocent, but it's better if you have a smart lawyer. And you cannot have a smart lawyer unless you have money. First and last it's a question of money. Those men who own the earth make the laws to protect what they have. They fix up a sort of fence or pen around what they have, and they fix the law so the fellow on the outside cannot get in. The laws are really organized for the protection of the men who rule the world. They were never organized or enforced to do justice. We have no system for doing justice, not the slightest in the world.

Let me illustrate: Take the poorest person in this room. If the community had provided a system of doing justice, the poorest person in this room would have as good a lawyer as the richest, would he not? When you went into court you would have just as long a trial and just as fair a trial as the richest person in Chicago. Your case would not be tried in fifteen or twenty minutes, whereas it would take fifteen days to get through with a rich man's case.

Then if you were rich and were beaten, your case would be taken to the Appellate Court. A poor man cannot take his case to the Appellate Court; he has not the price. And then to the Supreme Court. And if he were beaten there he might perhaps go to the United States Supreme Court. And he might die of old age before he got into jail. If you are poor, it's a quick job. You are almost known to be guilty, else you would not be there. Why should anyone be in the criminal court if he were not guilty? He would not be there if he could be anywhere else. The officials have no time to look after all these cases. The people who are on the outside, who are running banks and building churches and making jails, they have no time to examine 600 or 700 prisoners each year to see whether they are guilty or innocent. If the courts were organized to promote justice the people would elect somebody to defend all these criminals, somebody as smart as the prosecutor—and give him as many detectives and as many assistants to help, and pay as much money to defend you as to prosecute you. We have a very able man for state's attorney, and he has many assistants, detectives, and policemen without end, and judges to hear the cases—everything handy.

Most all of our criminal code consists in offenses against property. People are sent to jail because they have committed a crime against property. It is of very little consequence whether one hundred people more or less go to jail who ought not to go—you must protect property, because in this world property is of more importance than anything else.

How is it done? These people who have property fix it so they can protect what they have. When somebody commits a crime it does not follow that he has done something that is morally wrong. The man on the outside who has committed no crime may have done something. For instance: to take all the coal in the United States and raise the price two dollars or three dollars when there is no need of it, and thus kill thousands of babies and send thousands of people to the poorhouse and tens of thousands to jail, as is done every year in the United States—this is a greater crime than all the people in our jails ever committed; but the law does not punish it. Why? Because the fellows who control the earth make the laws. If you and I had the making of the laws, the first thing we would do would be to punish the fellow who gets control of the earth. Nature put this coal in the ground for me as well as for them and nature made the prairies up here to raise wheat for me as well as for them, and then the great railroad companies came along and fenced it up.

Most all of the crimes for which we are punished are property crimes. There are a few personal crimes, like murder—but they are very few. The crimes committed are mostly those against property. If this punishment is right the criminals must have a lot of property. How much money is there is this crowd? And yet you are all here for crimes against property. The people up and down the Lake Shore[3] have not committed crime; still they have so much property they don't know what to do with it. It is perfectly plain why these people have not committed crimes against property; they make the laws and therefore do not need to break them. And in order for you to get some property you are obliged to break the rules of the game. I don't know but what some of you may have had a very nice chance to get rich by carrying a hod for one dollar a day, twelve hours. Instead of taking that nice, easy profession, you are a burglar. If you had been given a chance to be a banker you would rather follow that. Some of you may have had a chance to work as a switchman on a railroad where you know, according to statistics, that you cannot live and keep all your limbs more than seven years, and you can get fifty dollars or seventy-five dollars a month for taking your lives in your hands; and instead of taking that lucrative position you chose to be a sneak thief, or something like that. Some of you made that sort of choice. I don't know which I would take if I was reduced to this choice. I have an easier choice.

I will guarantee to take from this jail, or any jail in the world, five hundred men who have been the worst criminals and lawbreakers who ever got into jail, and I will go down to our lowest streets and take five hundred of the most abandoned prostitutes, and go out somewhere where there is plenty of land, and will give them a

3. The fashionable and expensive section of Chicago along Lake Michigan.

chance to make a living, and they will be as good people as the average in the community.

There is a remedy for the sort of condition we see here. The world never finds it out, or when it does find it out it does not enforce it. You may pass a law punishing every person with death for burglary, and it will make no difference. Men will commit it just the same. In England there was a time when one hundred different offenses were punishable with death, and it made no difference. The English people strangely found out that so fast as they repealed the severe penalties and so fast as they did away with punishing men by death, crime decreased instead of increased; that the smaller the penalty the fewer the crimes.

Hanging men in our county jails does not prevent murder. It makes murderers.

And this has been the history of the world. It's easy to see how to do away with what we call crime. It is not so easy to do it. I will tell you how to do it. It can be done by giving the people a chance to live—by destroying special privileges. So long as big criminals can get the coal fields, so long as the big criminals have control of the city council and get the public streets for streetcars and gas rights—this is bound to send thousands of poor people to jail. So long as men are allowed to monopolize all the earth, and compel others to live on such terms as these men see fit to make, then you are bound to get into jail.

The only way in the world to abolish crime and criminals is to abolish the big ones and the little ones together. Make fair conditions of life. Give men a chance to live. Abolish the right of private ownership of land, abolish monopoly, make the world partners in production, partners in the good things of life. Nobody would steal if he could get something of his own some easier way. Nobody will commit burglary when he has a house full. No girl will go out on the streets when she has a comfortable place at home. The man who owns a sweatshop or a department store may not be to blame himself for the condition of his girls, but when he pays them five dollars, three dollars, and two dollars a week, I wonder where he thinks they will get the rest of their money to live. The only way to cure these conditions is by equality. There should be no jails. They do not accomplish what they pretend to accomplish. If you would wipe them out there would be no more criminals than now. They terrorize nobody. They are a blot upon any civilization, and a jail is an evidence of the lack of charity of the people on the outside who make the jails and fill them with the victims of their greed.

QUESTIONS

1. What is Darrow's central thesis? What relationship does he see between the nature of a government or a society and the action of the individual?

2. One of the prisoners that Darrow addressed is said to have commented that the speech was "too radical." What might Darrow say this shows about his audience and their society?

3. Remembering that Darrow is a lawyer writing in 1902 and Martin Luther King, Jr. ("Letter from Birmingham Jail," pp. 556–570) a minister writing in 1963,

   a. compare the two pieces with respect to the writers, the occasions, and the audiences; and

   b. discuss whether segregation represents for King the things that property does for Darrow. (How far do their ideas on justice, minorities, and laws coincide? What possibilities for action by the individual does each see?)

4. Compare Darrow's views on poverty with those expressed by Shaw in "The Gospel of St. Andrew Undershaft" (pp. 508–513).

JOHN DOS PASSOS

Fighting Bob[1]

La Follette was born in the town limits of Primrose; he worked on a farm in Dane County, Wisconsin, until he was nineteen.

At the university of Wisconsin he worked his way through. He wanted to be an actor, studied elocution and Robert Ingersoll and Shakespeare and Burke;

(who will ever explain the influence of Shakespeare in the last century, Marc Antony over Caesar's bier, Othello to the Venetian Senate and Polonius, everywhere Polonius?)

riding home in a buggy after commencement he was Booth and Wilkes writing the Junius papers and Daniel Webster and Ingersoll defying God and the togaed great grave and incorruptible as statues magnificently spouting through the capitoline centuries;

he was the star debater in his class,

and won an interstate debate with an oration on the character of Iago.

He went to work in a law office and ran for district attorney. His schoolfriends canvassed the county riding round evenings. He bucked the machine and won the election.

It was the revolt of the young man against the state republican machine

and Boss Keyes the postmaster in Madison who ran the county was so surprised he about fell out of his chair.

That gave La Follette a salary to marry on. He was twenty-five years old.

Four years later he ran for congress; the university was with him

1. From *The 42nd Parallel* (1930).

again; he was the youngsters' candidate. When he was elected he was the youngest representative in the house

He was introduced round Washington by Philetus Sawyer the Wisconsin lumber king who was used to stacking and selling politicians the way he stacked and sold cordwood.

He was a Republican and he'd bucked the machine. Now they thought they had him. No man could stay honest in Washington.

Booth[2] played Shakespeare in Baltimore that winter. Booth never would go to Washington on account of the bitter memory of his brother. Bob La Follette and his wife went to every performance.

In the parlor of the Plankinton Hotel in Milwaukee during the state fair, Boss Sawyer the lumber king tried to bribe him to influence his brother-in-law who was presiding judge over the prosecution of the Republican state treasurer;

Bob La Follette walked out of the hotel in a white rage. From that time it was war without quarter with the Republican machine in Wisconsin until he was elected governor and wrecked the Republican machine;

this was the tenyears war that left Wisconsin the model state where the voters, orderloving Germans and Finns, Scandinavians fond of their own opinion, learned to use the new leverage, direct primaries, referendum and recall.

La Follette taxed the railroads

John C. Payne[3] said to a group of politicians in the lobby of the Ebbitt House in Washington "La Follette's a damn fool if he thinks he can buck a railroad with five thousand miles of continuous track, he'll find he's mistaken . . . We'll take care of him when the time comes."

But when the time came the farmers of Wisconsin and the young lawyers and doctors and businessmen just out of school

took care of him

and elected him governor three times

and then to the United States Senate,

where he worked all his life making long speeches full of statistics, struggling to save democratic government, to make a farmers' and small businessmen's commonwealth, lonely with his back to the wall, fighting corruption and big business and high finance and trusts and combinations of combinations and the miasmic lethargy of Washington.

2. Edwin Booth, brother of Lincoln's assassin.

3. Apparently a slip for Henry C. Payne, lobbyist for the St. Paul road and packing interests. The incident is chronicled by Belle Case La Follette and Fola La Follette in their *Robert M. La Follette* (New York, 1953), Vol. I, p. 82.

He was one of "the little group of wilful men expressing no opinion but their own"

who stood out against Woodrow Wilson's armed ship bill that made war with Germany certain; they called it a filibuster but it was six men with nerve straining to hold back a crazy steamroller with their bare hands;

the press pumped hatred into its readers against La Follette, the traitor,

they burned him in effigy in Illinois;

in Wheeling they refused to let him speak.

In nineteen twentyfour La Follette ran for president and without money or political machine rolled up four and a half million votes

but he was a sick man, incessant work and the breathed out air of committee rooms and legislative chambers choked him

and the dirty smell of politicians,

and he died,

an orator haranguing from the capitol of a lost republic;

but we will remember

how he sat firm in March nineteen seventeen while Woodrow Wilson was being inaugurated for the second time, and for three days held the vast machine at deadlock.[4] They wouldn't let him speak; the galleries glared hatred at him; the senate was a lynching party,

a stumpy man with a lined face, one leg stuck out in the aisle and his arms folded and a chewed cigar in the corner of his mouth

and an undelivered speech on his desk,

a wilful man expressing no opinion but his own.

4. President Wilson submitted the Armed-ship bill to the 64th Congress only a few days before its automatic termination on March 4, 1917. The bill would have enabled the President to sup-ply merchant ships with defensive arms. La Follette saw the bill as leading the U.S. into World War I and was instrumental in preventing it from coming to a vote.

QUESTIONS

1. What has guided Dos Passos in his selection of the particular things about La Follette that he includes? Why, for example, does he gives illustrations of La Follette's interest in Shakespeare?
2. What were the chief influences in La Follette's education?
3. Why does Dos Passos devote so little space to La Follette's Senate career?
4. What connotations would usually attach to the phrase "the little group of wilful men expressing no opinion but their own"? What is its effect in the context in which Dos Passos places it?
5. What impression of La Follette does Dos Passos wish to create? Write a brief sketch of La Follette using only the information given by Dos Passos, but attempting to create a different impression.

THOMAS JEFFERSON

Original Draft of the Declaration of Independence

A DECLARATION OF THE REPRESENTATIVES OF THE UNITED STATES OF AMERICA, IN GENERAL CONGRESS ASSEMBLED.

When in the course of human events it becomes necessary for a people to advance from that subordination in which they have hitherto remained, & to assume among the powers of the earth the equal & independant station to which the laws of nature & of nature's god entitle them, a decent respect to the opinions of mankind requires that they should declare the causes which impel them to the change.

We hold these truths to be sacred & undeniable; that all men are created equal & independant, that from that equal creation they derive rights inherent & inalienable, among which are the preservation of life, & liberty, & the spirit of happiness; that to secure these ends, governments are instituted among men, deriving their just powers from the consent of the governed; that whenever any form of government shall become destructive of these ends, it is the right of the people to alter or to abolish it, & to institute new government, laying it's foundation on such principles & organising it's powers in such form, as to them shall seem most likely to effect their safety & happiness. prudence indeed will dictate that governments long established should not be changed for light & transient causes: and accordingly all experience hath shewn that mankind are more disposed to suffer while evils are sufferable, than to right themselves by abolishing the forms to which they are accustomed. but when a long train of abuses & usurpations, begun at a distinguished period, & pursuing invariably the same object, evinces a design to subject them to arbitrary power, it is their right, it is their duty, to throw off such government & to provide new guards for their future security. such has been the patient sufferance of these colonies; & such is now the necessity which constrains them to expunge their former systems of government. the history of his present majesty, is a history of unremitting injuries and usurpations, among which no one fact stands single or solitary to contradict the uniform tenor of the rest, all of which have in direct object the establishment of an absolute tyranny over these states. to prove this, let facts be submited to a candid world, for the truth of which we pledge a faith yet unsullied by falsehood.

he has refused his assent to laws the most wholesome and necessary for the public good:

he has forbidden his governors to pass laws of immediate & pressing importance, unless suspended in their operation till his assent should be obtained; and when so suspended, he has neglected utterly to attend to them.

he has refused to pass other laws for the accommodation of large districts of people unless those people would relinquish the right of representation, a right inestimable to them, & formidable to tyrants alone:[1]

he has dissolved Representative houses repeatedly & continually, for opposing with manly firmness his invasions on the rights of the people:

he has refused for a long space of time to cause others to be elected, whereby the legislative powers, incapable of annihilation, have returned to the people at large for their exercise, the state remaining in the mean time exposed to all the dangers of invasion from without, &, convulsions within:

he has suffered the administration of justice totally to cease in some of these colonies, refusing his assent to laws for establishing judiciary powers:

he has made our judges dependant on his will alone, for the tenure of their offices, and amount of their salaries:

he has erected a multitude of new offices by a self-assumed power, & sent hither swarms of officers to harrass our people & eat out their substance:

he has kept among us in times of peace standing armies & ships of war:

he has affected to render the military, independent of & superior to the civil power:

he has combined with others to subject us to a jurisdiction foreign to our constitutions and unacknoledged by our laws; giving his assent to their pretended acts of legislation, for quartering large bodies of armed troops among us;

for protecting them by a mock-trial from punishment for any murders they should commit on the inhabitants of these states;

for cutting off our trade with all parts of the world;

for imposing taxes on us without our consent;

for depriving us of the benefits of trial by jury

he has endeavored to prevent the population of these states; for that purpose obstructing the laws for naturalization of foreigners; refusing to pass others to encourage their migrations hither; & raising the conditions of new appropriations of lands;

1. At this point in the manuscript a strip containing the following clause is inserted: "He called together legislative bodies at places unusual, unco[mfortable, & distant from] the depository of their public records for the sole purpose of fatiguing [them into compliance] with his measures:" Missing parts in the Library of Congress text are supplied from the copy made by Jefferson for George Wythe. This copy is in the New York Public Library. The fact that this passage was omitted from John Adams's transcript suggests that it was not a part of Jefferson's original rough draft.

> for transporting us beyond seas to be tried for pretended offences:
>
> for taking away our charters & altering fundamentally the forms of our governments;
>
> for suspending our own legislatures & declaring themselves invested with power to legislate for us in all cases whatsoever:

he has abdicated government here, withdrawing his governors, & declaring us out of his allegiance & protection:

he has plundered our seas, ravaged our coasts, burnt our towns & destroyed the lives of our people:

he is at this time transporting large armies of foreign mercenaries to compleat the works of death, desolation & tyranny, already begun with circumstances of cruelty & perfidy unworthy the head of a civilized nation:

he has endeavored to bring on the inhabitants of our frontiers the merciless Indian savages, whose known rule of warfare is an undistinguished destruction of all ages, sexes, & conditions of existence:

he has incited treasonable insurrections of our fellow-citizens, with the allurements of forfeiture & confiscation of our property:

he has waged cruel war against human nature itself, violating it's most sacred rights of life & liberty in the persons of a distant people who never offended him, captivating & carrying them into slavery in another hemisphere, or to incur miserable death in their transportion thither. this piratical warfare, the opprobrium of *infidel* powers, is the warfare of the CHRISTIAN king of Great Britain. determined to keep open a market where MEN should be bought & sold; he has prostituted his negative for suppressing every legislative attempt to prohibit or to restrain this execrable commerce: and that this assemblage of horrors might want no fact of distinguished die, he is now exciting those very people to rise in arms among us, and to purchase that liberty of which *he* has deprived them, by murdering the people upon whom *he* also obtruded them; thus paying off former crimes committed against the *liberties* of one people, with crimes which he urges them to commit against the *lives* of another.

in every stage of these oppressions we have petitioned for redress in the most humble terms; our repeated petitions have been answered by repeated injury. a prince whose character is thus marked by every act which may define a tyrant, is unfit to be the ruler of a people who mean to be free. future ages will scarce believe that the hardiness of one man, adventured within the short compass of twelve years only, on so many acts of tyranny without a mask, over a people fostered & fixed in principles of liberty.

Nor have we been wanting in attentions to our British brethren. we have warned them from time to time of attempts by their legislature to extend a jurisdiction over these our states. we have reminded them of the circumstances of our emigration & settlement here, no one of which could warrant so strange a pretension: that these were effected at the expence of our own blood & treasure, unassisted by the wealth or the strength of Great Britain: that in constituting indeed our several forms of government, we had adopted one common king, thereby laying a foundation for perpetual league & amity with them; but that submission to their [Parliament, was no Part of our Constitution, nor ever in Idea, if History may be][2] credited: and we appealed to their native justice & magnanimity, as to the ties of our common kindred to disavow these usurpations which were likely to interrupt our correspondence & connection. they too have been deaf to the voice of justice & of consanguinity, & when occasions have been given them, by the regular course of their laws, of removing from their councils the disturbers of our harmony, they have by their free election re-established them in power. at this very time too they are permitting their chief magistrate to send over not only soldiers of our common blood, but Scotch & foreign mercenaries to invade & deluge us in blood. these facts have given the last stab to agonizing affection, and manly spirit bids us to renounce for ever these unfeeling brethren. we must endeavor to forget our former love for them, and to hold them as we hold the rest of mankind, enemies in war, in peace friends. we might have been a free & a great people together; but a communication of grandeur & of freedom it seems is below their dignity. be it so, since they will have it: the road to glory & happiness is open to us too; we will climb it in a separate state, and acquiesce in the necessity which pronounces our everlasting Adieu!

We therefore the representatives of the United States of America in General Congress assembled do, in the name & by authority of the good people of these states, reject and renounce all allegiance & subjection to the kings of Great Britain & all others who may hereafter claim by, through, or under them; we utterly dissolve & break off all political connection which may have heretofore subsisted between us & the people or parliament of Great Britain; and finally we do assert and declare these colonies to be free and independant states, and that as free & independant states they shall hereafter have power to levy war, conclude peace, contract alliances, establish commerce, & to do all other acts and things which independant states may of right do. And for the support of this declaration we mutually pledge to each other our lives, our fortunes, & our sacred honour.

2. An illegible passage is supplied from John Adams' transcription.

THOMAS JEFFERSON and OTHERS
The Declaration of Independence

IN CONGRESS, JULY 4, 1776
THE UNANIMOUS DECLARATION OF THE
THIRTEEN UNITED STATES OF AMERICA

When in the Course of human events it becomes necessary for one people to dissolve the political bands which have connected them with another, and to assume among the powers of the earth, the separate and equal station to which the Laws of Nature and of Nature's God entitle them, a decent respect to the opinions of mankind requires that they should declare the causes which impel them to the separation.

We hold these truths to be self-evident, that all men are created equal, that they are endowed by their Creator with certain unalienable Rights, that among these are Life, Liberty and the pursuit of Happiness. That to secure these rights, Governments are instituted among Men, deriving their just powers from the consent of the governed, That whenever any Form of Government becomes destructive of these ends, it is the Right of the People to alter or to abolish it, and to institute new Government, laying its foundation on such principles and organizing its powers in such form, as to them shall seem most likely to affect their Safety and Happiness. Prudence, indeed, will dictate that Governments long established should not be changed for light and transient causes; and accordingly all experience hath shewn that mankind are more disposed to suffer, while evils are sufferable, than to right themselves by abolishing the forms to which they are accustomed. But when a long train of abuses and usurpations, pursuing invariably the same Object evinces a design to reduce them under absolute Despotism, it is their right, it is their duty, to throw off such Government, and to provide new Guards for their future security. Such has been the patient sufferance of these Colonies; and such is now the necessity which constrains them to alter their former Systems of Government. The history of the present King of Great Britain is a history of repeated injuries and usurpations, all having in direct object the establishment of an absolute Tyranny over these States. To prove this, let Facts be submitted to a candid world.

He has refused his Assent to Laws, the most wholesome and necessary for the public good.

He has forbidden his Governors to pass laws of immediate and pressing importance, unless suspended in their operation till his Assent should be obtained; and when so suspended, he has utterly neglected to attend to them.

He has refused to pass other Laws for the accommodation of large districts of people, unless those people would relinquish the right of Representation in the Legislature, a right inestimable to them and formidable to tyrants only.

He has called together legislative bodies at places unusual, uncomfortable, and distant from the depository of their Public Records, for the sole purpose of fatiguing them into compliance with his measures.

He has dissolved Representative Houses repeatedly, for opposing with manly firmness his invasions on the rights of the people.

He has refused for a long time, after such dissolutions, to cause others to be elected; whereby the Legislative Powers, incapable of Annihilation, have returned to the People at large for their exercise; the State remaining in the mean time exposed to all the dangers of invasion from without, and convulsions within.

He has endeavored to prevent the population of these States; for that purpose obstructing the Laws for Naturalization of For eigners; refusing to pass others to encourage their migration hither, and raising the conditions of new Appropriations of Lands.

He has obstructed the Administration of Justice, by refusing his Assent to Laws for establishing Judiciary Powers.

He has made Judges dependent on his Will alone, for the tenure of their offices, and the amount and payment of their salaries.

He has erected a multitude of New Offices, and sent hither swarms of Officers to harass our people, and eat out their substance.

He has kept among us, in times of peace, Standing Armies without the Consent of our legislatures.

He has affected to render the Military independent of and superior to the Civil Power.

He has combined with others to subject us to a jurisdiction foreign to our constitution, and unacknowledged by our laws; giving his Assent to their Acts of pretended Legislation: For quartering large bodies of armed troops among us: For protecting them, by a mock Trial, from punishment for any Murders which they should commit on the Inhabitants of these States: For cutting off our Trade with all parts of the world: For imposing Taxes on us without our Consent: For depriving us in many cases, of the benefits of Trial by Jury; For transporting us beyond Seas to be tried for pretended offenses: for abolishing the free System of English Laws in a neighboring Province, establishing therein an Arbitrary government, and enlarging its Boundaries so as to render it at once an example and fit instrument for introducing the same absolute rule into these Colonies: For taking away our Charters, abolishing our most valuable Laws and altering fundamentally the Forms of our Governments: For suspending our own Legislatures, and declaring themselves invested with power to legislate for us in all cases whatsoever.

He has abdicated Government here, by declaring us out of his Protection and waging War against us.

He has plundered our seas, ravaged our Coasts, burnt our towns, and destroyed the lives of our people.

He is at this time transporting large Armies of foreign Mercenaries to complete the works of death, desolation and tyranny, already begun with circumstances of Cruelty & Perfidy scarcely paralleled in the most barbarous ages, and totally unworthy the Head of a civilized nation.

He has constrained our fellow Citizens taken Captive on the high Seas to bear Arms against their Country, to become the executioners of their friends and Brethren, or to fall themselves by their Hands.

He has excited domestic insurrections amongst us, and has endeavored to bring on the inhabitants of our frontiers, the merciless Indian Savages, whose known rule of warfare, is an undistinguished destruction of all ages, sexes, and conditions.

In every stage of these Oppressions We have Petitioned for Redress in the most humble terms: Our repeated Petitions have been answered only by repeated injury. A Prince, whose character is thus marked by every act which may define a Tyrant, is unfit to be the ruler of a free people.

Nor have We been wanting in attention to our British brethren. We have warned them from time to time of attempts by their legislature to extend an unwarrantable jurisdiction over us. We have reminded them of the circumstances of our emigration and settlement here. We have appealed to their native justice and magnanimity, and we have conjured them by the ties of our common kindred to disavow these usurpations, which would inevitably interrupt our connections and correspondence. They too have been deaf to the voice of justice and of consanguinity. We must, therefore, acquiesce in the necessity, which denounces our Separation, and hold them, as we hold the rest of mankind, Enemies in War, in Peace Friends.

We, THEREFORE, the Representatives of the UNITED STATES OF AMERICA, in General Congress, Assembled, appealing to the Supreme Judge of the world for the rectitude of our intentions, do, in the Name, and by Authority of the good People of these Colonies, solemnly publish and declare, That these United Colonies are, and of Right ought to be FREE AND INDEPENDENT STATES; that they are Absolved from all Allegiance to the British Crown, and that all political connection between them and the State of Great Britain, is and ought to be totally dissolved; and that as Free and Independent States, they have full Power to levy War, conclude Peace, contract Alliances, establish Commerce, and to do all other Acts and Things which Independent States may of right do. And for the

support of this Declaration, with a firm reliance on the protection
of Divine Providence, we mutually pledge to each other our Lives, our
Fortunes, and our sacred Honor.

QUESTIONS

1. The Declaration of Independence was addressed to several audiences: the king of Great Britain, the people of Great Britain, the
   people of America, and the world at large. Show ways in which
   the final draft was adapted for its several audiences.
2. Examine the second paragraph of each version closely. How have
   the revisions in the final version increased its effectiveness over
   the first draft?
3. The Declaration has often been called a classic example of deductive argument: setting up general statements, relating particular cases to them, and drawing conclusions. Trace this pattern
   through the document, noting the way each part is developed.
   Would the document have been as effective if the long middle
   part had either come first or been left out entirely? Explain.
4. Find the key terms and phrases of the Declaration (such as "these
   truths . . . self-evident," "created equal," "unalienable rights,"
   and so on) and determine how fully they are defined by the
   contexts in which they occur. Why are no formal definitions given
   for them?
5. The signers of the Declaration appeal both to general principles
   and to factual evidence in presenting their case. Which of the
   appeals to principle could still legitimately be made today by a
   nation eager to achieve independence? In other words, how far
   does the Declaration reflect unique events of history and how far
   does it reflect universal aspirations and ideals?

ABRAHAM LINCOLN
Liberty[1]

The world has never had a good definition of the word liberty,
and the American people, just now, are much in want of one. We
all declare for liberty; but in using the same *word* we do not all
mean the same *thing*. With some the word liberty may mean for
each man to do as he pleases with himself, and the product of his
labor; while with others the same word may mean for some men
to do as they please with other men, and the product of other
men's labor. Here are two, not only different, but incompatible
things, called by the same name—liberty. And it follows that each
of the things is, by the respective parties, called by two different
and incompatible names—liberty and tyranny.

The shepherd drives the wolf from the sheep's throat, for which

1. From an address at the Sanitary Fair, Baltimore, Maryland, April 18, 1864.

the sheep thanks the shepherd as a *liberator*, while the wolf denounces him for the same act as the destroyer of liberty, especially as the sheep was a black one. Plainly the sheep and the wolf are not agreed upon a definition of the word liberty; and precisely the same difference prevails today among us human creatures, even in the North, and all professing to love liberty. Hence we behold the processes by which thousands are daily passing from under the yoke of bondage, hailed by some as the advance of liberty, and bewailed by others as the destruction of all liberty. Recently, as it seems, the people of Maryland have been doing something to define liberty; and thanks to them that, in what they have done, the wolf's dictionary has been repudiated.

QUESTIONS

1. How does the analogy of the sheep and the wolf in the second paragraph correspond to the two conceptions of liberty Lincoln has given in the first paragraph? How exact is the analogy?
2. How does the choice of that particular analogy reveal Lincoln's own attitude toward liberty? What connotations do we usually associate with the wolf who attacks the sheep?
3. How is Lincoln's definition of liberty applicable to the situation he talks about in his Second Inaugural Address?
4. Compare Lincoln's use of figurative language here with E. B. White's (below). What are the significant similarities and differences?

E. B. WHITE

Democracy

July 3, 1943

We received a letter from the Writers' War Board the other day asking for a statement on "The Meaning of Democracy." It presumably is our duty to comply with such a request, and it is certainly our pleasure.

Surely the Board knows what democracy is. It is the line that forms on the right. It is the don't in don't shove. It is the hole in the stuffed shirt through which the sawdust slowly trickles; it is the dent in the high hat. Democracy is the recurrent suspicion that more than half of the people are right more than half of the time. It is the feeling of privacy in the voting booths, the feeling of communion in the libraries, the feeling of vitality everywhere. Democracy is a letter to the editor. Democracy is the score at the beginning of the ninth. It is an idea which hasn't been disproved yet, a song the words of which have not gone bad. It's the mustard on the hot dog and the cream in the rationed coffee. Democracy is a request from a War Board, in the middle of a morning in the middle of a war, wanting to know what democracy is.

QUESTIONS

1. White's piece is dated July 3, 1943, the middle of World War II. How did the occasion shape what White says about democracy?

2. Look up "democracy" in a standard desk dictionary. Of the several meanings given, which one best applies to Becker's definition (below)? Does more than one apply to White's?

3. How does Becker's language (in the essay following) differ from White's? What does the difference suggest about the purposes and audiences of the two men?

4. Translate White's definition into non-metaphorical language. (For example, "It is the line that forms on the right" might be translated by "It has no special privileges.") Determine what is lost in the translation, or, in other words, what White has gained by using figurative language.

CARL BECKER

Democracy[1]

Democracy, like liberty or science or progress, is a word with which we are all so familiar that we rarely take the trouble to ask what we mean by it. It is a term, as the devotees of semantics say, which has no "referent"—there is no precise or palpable thing or object which we all think of when the word is pronounced. On the contrary, it is a word which connotes different things to different people, a kind of conceptual Gladstone bag which, with a little manipulation, can be made to accommodate almost any collection of social facts we may wish to carry about in it. In it we can as easily pack a dictatorship as any other form of government. We have only to stretch the concept to include any form of government supported by a majority of the people, for whatever reasons and by whatever means of expressing assent, and before we know it the empire of Napoleon, the Soviet regime of Stalin, and the Fascist systems of Mussolini and Hitler are all safely in the bag. But if this is what we mean by democracy, then virtually all forms of government are democratic, since virtually all governments, except in times of revolution, rest upon the explicit or implicit consent of the people. In order to discuss democracy intelligently it will be necessary, therefore, to define it, to attach to the word a sufficiently precise meaning to avoid the confusion which is not infrequently

1. From Lecture I, "The Ideal," in *Modern Democracy*, 1941.

the chief result of such discussions.

All human institutions, we are told, have their ideal forms laid away in heaven, and we do not need to be told that the actual institutions conform but indifferently to these ideal counterparts. It would be possible then to define democracy either in terms of the ideal or in terms of the real form—to define it as government of the people, by the people, for the people; or to define it as government of the people, by the politicians, for whatever pressure groups can get their interests taken care of. But as a historian I am naturally disposed to be satisfied with the meaning which, in the history of politics, men have commonly attributed to the word—a meaning, needless to say, which derives partly from the experience and partly from the aspirations of mankind. So regarded, the term democracy refers primarily to a form of government, and it has always meant government by the many as opposed to government by the one—government by the people as opposed to government by a tyrant, a dictator, or an absolute monarch. This is the most general meaning of the word as men have commonly understood it.

In this antithesis there are, however, certain implications, always tacitly understood, which give a more precise meaning to the term. Peisistratus, for example, was supported by a majority of the people, but his government was never regarded as a democracy for all that. Caesar's power derived from a popular mandate, conveyed through established republican forms, but that did not make his government any the less a dictatorship. Napoleon called his government a democratic empire, but no one, least of all Napoleon himself, doubted that he had destroyed the last vestiges of the democratic republic. Since the Greeks first used the term, the essential test of democratic government has always been this: the source of political authority must be and remain in the people and not in the ruler. A democratic government has always meant one in which the citizens, or a sufficient number of them to represent more or less effectively the common will, freely act from time to time, and according to established forms, to appoint or recall the magistrates and to enact or revoke the laws by which the community is governed. This I take to be the meaning which history has impressed upon the term democracy as a form of government.

CECIL S. EMDEN
"The People"[1]

It has been remarked, with great authority, that "the 'people' is so indeterminate an expression that its use, let alone its abuse,

1. Appendix I in *The People and the Constitution*, 1933.

obscures almost all political discussions."[2] An even more absolute indictment is that of Disraeli,[3] who once said that, as a political expression, "the people" is "sheer nonsense." He regarded it as belonging rather to the realm of natural history than to that of politics.[4] It was, however, only a few years after making these observations that Disraeli introduced a Bill into the House of Commons "to amend the representation of the people," without perhaps considering whether the term "people" in the title of the Bill referred to the electorate or the whole population.

The ambiguities of the present day are fewer than they were before democracy had become a generally accepted principle. Now that the qualification for the franchise is practically that of being an adult, many embarrassments in the use of the expression are removed. Nevertheless the mention of one or two incidents illustrative of earlier ambiguities will help to point the contrast between the past and the present.

Discrimination between the whole population of a State and what used to be known as the commonalty, populace, or masses had its counterpart in the terminology of many centuries ago. The Romans drew a distinction between the class which comprised the whole of the citizens and the class which comprised the citizens without the patricians; and separate words were adopted to describe those two classes. Equivalent expressions have recurred in European countries during medieval times. The result of these early complexities was that, when the introduction of democratic government raised problems requiring the use of accurate terms, the significance of "the people" was found to be uncertain.

Only a little more than a hundred years ago, Canning protested against members of Parliament speaking of "the people" in contradistinction to the whole of the citizens. He regarded the people as incomplete without the aristocracy and gentry. Nowadays this protest would hardly be necessary, since the aristocracy and gentry are so diminished as a political force that it is extremely unlikely that it would occur to anyone to exclude them. The decrease in the old class distinction has, in fact, largely helped to dissipate opportunities for confusion in meaning.

2. A. F. Pollard, *Evolution of Parliament*, 2nd ed., p. 343 [Emden's note].

3. The men referred to throughout this essay are, in order of appearance: Benjamin Disraeli, first Earl of Beaconsfield (1804–1881), British statesman, writer, and prime minister; George Canning (1770–1827), British statesman and prime minister; Jonathan Swift (1667–1745), Irish-born English satirist and author of several political pamphlets as well as of *Gulliver's Travels*; Daniel Defoe (1659?–1731), author of political essays as well as of works of fiction; Henry Fox, first Baron Holland (1705–1774), British statesman; Edmund Burke (1729–1797), British statesman and orator; Henry Peter Brougham, Baron Brougham and Vaux (1778–1868), Scottish jurist; Emanuel Joseph Siéyès, Abbé Sieyès (1748–1836), French revolutionist and statesman; and James Bryce, Viscount Bryce (1838–1922), British jurist, statesman, and historian.

4. *The Spirit of Whiggism* (1836); cf. a speech by him in 1866 in which he characterized "the people" as "a mere indiscriminate multitude" (183 *Parl. Deb.*, 3 s., 103); and see his articles in the *Morning Post* for 26 Aug. and 2 Sept. 1835 [Emden's note].

Before democratic government had become firmly established, politicians of various shades of opinion used the expression "the people" to describe the class which they wished to be regarded as dominant. The expression was applied to some large portion of the nation which was not sovereign in fact, but to which, in the opinion of the user, sovereignty ought to be transferred or secured.[5] At the beginning of the eighteenth century, for instance, Swift and Defoe both contended that political rights should be confined to freeholders. Swift asserted that "law in a free country is, or ought to be, the determination of those who have property in land"; and Defoe, in speaking of the "right of the People," thus qualified his remarks: "I would be understood of the freeholders, for all the other inhabitants live upon sufferance, . . . and have no title to their living in England, other than as servants."

Henry Fox, in the middle of the eighteenth century, is reported as having observed in the House of Commons that, "when we talk of people with regard to elections, we ought to think only of those of the better sort." The report is not unimpeachable; but, if Fox did not use these precise words, it is undeniable that they may be taken as a characteristic exposition of the views of his kind.[6]

Towards the end of his career, Burke indulged in a mathematical estimate of that section of the inhabitants which was capable of dealing intelligently with political questions. This body he regarded as truly entitled to the description of "the people." "I have often endeavored," he said, "to compute and to class those who, in any political view, are to be called the people. . . . In England and Scotland, I compute that those of adult age, not declining in life, of tolerable leisure for such discussions, and of some means of information, more or less, and who are above menial dependence (or what virtually is such) may amount to about four hundred thousand."[7] The chief point of interest in this passage is not, perhaps, in the figure estimated by Burke, but rather in the acceptance of the qualification of intelligence as that which entitled citizens to play a part in politics.

It became more apparent in the early nineteenth century that the claim to political predominance could no longer be put forward on behalf of landowners or of aristocrats in the narrow sense of that expression. It was advanced on behalf of the more instructed, or, as Canning described them, "that sound and sober majority of the nation—that bulk and body of the community which are truly and legitimately the people." Brougham, in the earlier part of his career, was impressed by "the necessity in the present times of looking more than formerly may have been essential to the body of the people out of doors, meaning by people the well-informed and

---

5. John Austin, *A Plea for the Constitution*, p. 10 n. [Emden's note].
6. 12 *Parl. Hist.* 463 [Emden's note].

7. *First Letter on Regicide Peace* [Emden's note].

weighty parts of the community."[8] Later in his career, when speaking in support of the great Reform Bill in 1831, his interpretation was a little different. When discussing the attitude of the people towards the Bill, he said: "I do not mean the populace—the mob: I have never bowed to them, though I never have testified any unbecoming contempt of them. . . . But, if there is a mob, there is the people also. I speak now of the middle classes—of those hundreds of thousands of respectable persons—the most numerous, and by far the most wealthy of the community."[9]

At the time of the first Reform Bill, the expression "the people" was generally used to describe what were then known as the lower classes, as well as the middle classes; but, as a result of the enlargement of the franchise effected by recent statutes, it is impossible for there to be more than two opinions at the present day regarding the meaning to be given to the expression. Either it means all the inhabitants, or it means the electorate. The latter is the meaning adopted by the *New English Dictionary*, where, under the sub-head "politics," "the people" is defined as "the whole body of enfranchised or qualified citizens, considered as the source of power; especially in a democratic State, the electorate." If this definition is accepted, some other term will be required to designate the inhabitants as a whole, regarded as a class having political rights, even though these rights be passive rather than active.

The distinction between these two meanings was emphasized in a peculiar way by Siéyès at the beginning of the French Revolution in 1789. He was the first person to draw attention in explicit terms to a division into active and passive citizens. The former he described as having political rights, the latter as having merely natural rights. "All the inhabitants of a country," he said, "should enjoy therein the rights of a passive citizen; all have a right to the protection of their persons, their property, their liberty, and so on; but all have not the right to take part in the formation of public authority; all are not active citizens."[1]

At the present day the preponderance, among adults, of active over passive citizens in this country is large. The existence of the latter class does not raise any important problems. It is no longer necessary, as it was two hundred years ago, for liberal-minded per-

8. Cf. A. Aspinall, *Lord Brougham and the Whig Party*, p. 82 [Emden's note].
9. 8 *Parl. Deb.*, 3 s., 251. Peel, voicing the Conservative interpretation of "the people," denied that the expression, as used in the Bill, corresponded with the earlier meaning, namely "the great corporate bodies, and those great classes of the community to whom the franchise was intrusted" (5 *Parl. Deb.*. 3 s., 114-15). On another occasion in 1831 Peel criticized his opponents for talking of the people as if they were to be numbered by heads and for forgetting the influence of wealth and education (3 *Parl. Deb.*, 3 s., 1774) [Emden's note].
1. Aulard, *French Revolution* (translation), vol. i, p. 181. Although Siéyès drew fresh attention to the distinction between the two kinds of rights, their existence had given rise to discussion in England many years earlier. See, for instance, passages in the preface of the famous tract *Fura Populi Anglicani* (1701) and *The Craftsman*, 6 July 1734 [Emden's note].

sons to make protests on behalf of large sections of the inhabitants, who have no direct representation and no efficient means of making their views known on public matters of seeking redress in respect of general grievances. But the one remaining ambiguity in the use of the expression "the people" is sometimes liable to cause inconvenience. Bryce, in his monumental work on *Modern Democracies*, asked: "Does it [the term 'people'] in any given country cover, or ought it to cover, the whole population or only those who are legally citizens, i.e., entitled to share in the government by expressing their mind and will on public questions?"[2] And he did not seem to supply an answer to that question.

One way of evading the difficulty would be to use the term "electorate," clumsy though it is, to designate the enfranchised and to use the term "people" to refer to the whole population. Speeches of statesmen and even writings of political scientists frequently contain references to "the nation," "the community," "the public," and "the country," as alternatives to the terms already mentioned. But one expression is often as good as another; and it is only occasionally that exact terminology is requisite.

2. Vol. i, p. 162 [Emden's note].

WALTER LIPPMANN
The Indispensable Opposition

Were they pressed hard enough, most men would probably confess that political freedom—that is to say, the right to speak freely and to act in opposition—is a noble ideal rather than a practical necessity. As the case for freedom is generally put today, the argument lends itself to this feeling. It is made to appear that, whereas each man claims his freedom as a matter of right, the freedom he accords to other men is a matter of toleration. Thus, the defense of freedom of opinion tends to rest not on its substantial, beneficial, and indispensable consequences, but on a somewhat eccentric, a rather vaguely benevolent, attachment to an abstraction.

It is all very well to say with Voltaire, "I wholly disapprove of what you say, but will defend to the death your right to say it," but as a matter of fact most men will not defend to the death the rights of other men: if they disapprove sufficiently what other men say, they will somehow suppress those men if they can.

So, if this is the best that can be said for liberty of opinion, that a man must tolerate his opponents because everyone has a "right" to say what he pleases, then we shall find that liberty of opinion is a luxury, safe only in pleasant times when men can be tolerant because they are not deeply and vitally concerned.

Yet actually, as a matter of historic fact, there is a much stronger foundation for the great constitutional right of freedom of speech, and as a matter of practical human experience there is a much more compelling reason for cultivating the habits of free men. We take, it seems to me, a naïvely self-righteous view when we argue as if the right of our opponents to speak were something that we protect because we are magnanimous, noble, and unselfish. The compelling reason why, if liberty of opinion did not exist, we should have to invent it, why it will eventually have to be restored in all civilized countries where it is now suppressed, is that we must protect the right of our opponents to speak because we must hear what they have to say.

We miss the whole point when we imagine that we tolerate the freedom of our political opponents as we tolerate a howling baby next door, as we put up with the blasts from our neighbor's radio because we are too peaceable to heave a brick through the window. If this were all there is to freedom of opinion, that we are too good-natured or too timid to do anything about our opponents and our critics except to let them talk, it would be difficult to say whether we are tolerant because we are magnanimous or because we are lazy, because we have strong principles or because we lack serious convictions, whether we have the hospitality of an inquiring mind or the indifference of an empty mind. And so, if we truly wish to understand why freedom is necessary in a civilized society, we must begin by realizing that, because freedom of discussion improves our own opinions, the liberties of other men are our own vital necessity.

We are much closer to the essence of the matter, not when we quote Voltaire, but when we go to the doctor and pay him to ask us the most embarrassing questions and to prescribe the most disagreeable diet. When we pay the doctor to exercise complete freedom of speech about the cause and cure of our stomachache, we do not look upon ourselves as tolerant and magnanimous, and worthy to be admired by ourselves. We have enough common sense to know that if we threaten to put the doctor in jail because we do not like the diagnosis and the prescription it will be unpleasant for the doctor, to be sure, but equally unpleasant for our own stomach-ache. That is why even the most ferocious dictator would rather be treated by a doctor who was free to think and speak the truth than by his own Minister of Propaganda. For there is a point, the point at which things really matter, where the freedom of others is no longer a question of their right but of our own need.

The point at which we recognize this need is much higher in some men than in others. The totalitarian rulers think they do not need the freedom of an opposition: they exile, imprison, or shoot their opponents. We have concluded on the basis of practical experience, which goes back to Magna Carta and beyond, that we need the opposition. We pay the opposition salaries out of the public treasury.

In so far as the usual apology for freedom of speech ignores this experience, it becomes abstract and eccentric rather than concrete and human. The emphasis is generally put on the right to speak, as if all that mattered were that the doctor should be free to go out into the park and explain to the vacant air why I have a stomach-ache. Surely that is a miserable caricature of the great civic right which men have bled and died for. What really matters is that the doctor should tell *me* what ails me, that I should listen to him; that if I do not like what he says I should be free to call in another doctor; and that then the first doctor should have to listen to the second doctor; and that out of all the speaking and listening, the give-and-take of opinions, the truth should be arrived at.

This is the creative principle of freedom of speech, not that it is a system for the tolerating of error, but that it is a system for finding the truth. It may not produce the truth, or the whole truth all the time, or often, or in some cases ever. But if the truth can be found, there is no other system which will normally and habitually find so much truth. Until we have thoroughly understood this principle, we shall not know why we must value our liberty, or how we can protect and develop it.

Let us apply this principle to the system of public speech in a totalitarian state. We may, without any serious falsification, picture a condition of affairs in which the mass of the people are being addressed through one broadcasting system by one man and his chosen subordinates. The orators speak. The audience listens but cannot and dare not speak back. It is a system of one-way communication; the opinions of the rulers are broadcast outwardly to the mass of the people. But nothing comes back to the rulers from the people except the cheers; nothing returns in the way of knowledge of forgotten facts, hidden feelings, neglected truths, and practical suggestions.

But even a dictator cannot govern by his own one-way inspiration alone. In practice, therefore, the totalitarian rulers get back the reports of the secret police and of their party henchmen down among the crowd. If these reports are competent, the rulers may manage to remain in touch with public sentiment. Yet that is not enough to know what the audience feels. The rulers have also to make great decisions that have enormous consequences, and here their system provides virtually no help from the give-and-take of opinion in the nation. So they must either rely on their own intuition, which cannot be permanently and continually inspired, or, if they are intelligent despots, encourage their trusted advisers and their technicians to speak and debate freely in their presence.

On the walls of the houses of Italian peasants one may see

inscribed in large letters the legend, "Mussolini is always right." But if that legend is taken seriously by Italian ambassadors, by the Italian General Staff, and by the Ministry of Finance, then all one can say is heaven help Mussolini, heaven help Italy, and the new Emperor of Ethiopia.

For at some point, even in a totalitarian state, it is indispensable that there should exist the freedom of opinion which causes opposing opinions to be debated. As time goes on, that is less and less easy under a despotism; critical discussion disappears as the internal opposition is liquidated in favor of men who think and feel alike. That is why the early successes of despots, of Napoleon I and of Napoleon III, have usually been followed by an irreparable mistake. For in listening only to his yes men—the others being in exile or in concentration camps, or terrified—the despot shuts himself off from the truth that no man can dispense with.

We know all this well enough when we contemplate the dictatorships. But when we try to picture our own system, by way of contrast, what picture do we have in our minds? It is, is it not, that anyone may stand up on his own soapbox and say anything he pleases, like the individuals in Kipling's poem[1] who sit each in his separate star and draw the Thing as they see it for the God of Things as they are. Kipling, perhaps, could do this, since he was a poet. But the ordinary mortal isolated on his separate star will have an hallucination, and a citizenry declaiming from separate soapboxes will poison the air with hot and nonsensical confusion.

If the democratic alternative to the totalitarian one-way broadcasts is a row of separate soapboxes, than I submit that the alternative is unworkable, is unreasonable, and is humanly unattractive. It is above all a false alternative. It is not true that liberty has developed among civilized men when anyone is free to set up a soapbox, is free to hire a hall where he may expound his opinions to those who are willing to listen. On the contrary, freedom of speech is established to achieve its essential purpose only when different opinions are expounded in the same hall to the same audience.

For, while the right to talk may be the beginning of freedom, the necessity of listening is what makes the right important. Even in Russia and Germany a man may still stand in an open field and speak his mind. What matters is not the utterance of opinions. What matters is the confrontation of opinions in debate. No man can care profoundly that every fool should say what he likes. Nothing has been accomplished if the wisest man proclaims his wisdom in the middle of the Sahara Desert. This is the shadow. We have the substance of liberty when the fool is compelled to listen to the wise man and learn; when the wise man is compelled to take account

1. "L'Envoi."

of the fool, and to instruct him; when the wise man can increase
his wisdom by hearing the judgment of his peers.

That is why civilized men must cherish liberty—as a means of
promoting the discovery of truth. So we must not fix our whole
attention on the right of anyone to hire his own hall, to rent his
own broadcasting station, to distribute his own pamphlets. These
rights are incidental; and though they must be preserved, they can
be preserved only by regarding them as incidental, as auxiliary
to the substance of liberty that must be cherished and cultivated.

Freedom of speech is best conceived, therefore, by having in mind
the picture of a place like the American Congress, an assembly
where opposing views are represented, where ideas are not merely
uttered but debated, or the British Parliament, where men who
are free to speak are also compelled to answer. We may picture the
true condition of freedom as existing in a place like a court of law,
where witnesses testify and are cross-examined, where the lawyer
argues against the opposing lawyer before the same judge and in
the presence of one jury. We may picture freedom as existing in
a forum where the speaker must respond to questions; in a gathering
of scientists where the data, the hypothesis, and the conclusion are
submitted to men competent to judge them; in a reputable newspaper which not only will publish the opinions of those who disagree but will re-examine its own opinion in the light of what
they say.

Thus the essence of freedom of opinion is not in mere toleration
as such, but in the debate which toleration provides: it is not in
the venting of opinion, but in the confrontation of opinion. That
this is the practical substance can readily be understood when we
remember how differently we feel and act about the censorship
and regulation of opinion purveyed by different media of communication. We find then that, in so far as the medium makes difficult
the confrontation of opinion in debate, we are driven towards censorship and regulation.

There is, for example, the whispering campaign, the circulation of
anonymous rumors by men who cannot be compelled to prove what
they say. They put the utmost strain on our tolerance, and there
are few who do not rejoice when the anonymous slanderer is caught,
exposed, and punished. At a higher level there is the moving picture, a most powerful medium for conveying ideas, but a medium
which does not permit debate. A moving picture cannot be answered effectively by another moving picture; in all free countries
there is some censorship of the movies, and there would be more
if the producers did not recognize their limitations by avoiding
political controversy. There is then the radio. Here debate is difficult: it is not easy to make sure that the speaker is being answered
in the presence of the same audience. Inevitably, there is some regu-

lation of the radio.

When we reach the newspaper press, the opportunity for debate is so considerable that discontent cannot grow to the point where under normal conditions there is any disposition to regulate the press. But when newspapers abuse their power by injuring people who have no means of replying, a disposition to regulate the press appears. When we arrive at Congress we find that, because the membership of the House is so large, full debate is impracticable. So there are restrictive rules. On the other hand, in the Senate, where the conditions of full debate exist, there is almost absolute freedom of speech.

This shows us that the preservation and development of freedom of opinion are not only a matter of adhering to abstract legal rights, but also, and very urgently, a matter of organizing and arranging sufficient debate. Once we have a firm hold on the central principle, there are many practical conclusions to be drawn. We then realize that the defense of freedom of opinion consists primarily in perfecting the opportunity for an adequate give-and-take of opinion; it consists also in regulating the freedom of those revolutionists who cannot or will not permit or maintain debate when it does not suit their purposes.

We must insist that free oratory is only the beginning of free speech; it is not the end, but a means to an end. The end is to find the truth. The practical justification of civil liberty is not that self-expression is one of the rights of man. It is that the examination of opinion is one of the necessities of man. For experience tells us that it is only when freedom of opinion becomes the compulsion to debate that the seed which our fathers planted has produced its fruit. When that is understood, freedom will be cherished not because it is a vent for our opinions but because it is the surest method of correcting them.

The unexamined life, said Socrates, is unfit to be lived by man. This is the virtue of liberty, and the ground on which we may best justify our belief in it, that it tolerates error in order to serve the truth. When men are brought face to face with their opponents, forced to listen and learn and mend their ideas, they cease to be children and savages and begin to live like civilized men. Then only is freedom a reality, when men may voice their opinions because they must examine their opinions.

The only reason for dwelling on all this is that if we are to preserve democracy we must understand its principles. And the principle which distinguishes it from all other forms of government is that in a democracy the opposition not only is tolerated as constitutional but must be maintained because it is in fact indispensable.

The democratic system cannot be operated without effective

opposition. For, in making the great experiment of governing people by consent rather than by coercion, it is not sufficient that the party in power should have a majority. It is just as necessary that the party in power should never outrage the minority. That means that it must listen to the minority and be moved by the criticisms of the minority. That means that its measures must take account of the minority's objections, and that in administering measures it must remember that the minority may become the majority.

The opposition is indispensable. A good statesman, like any other sensible human being, always learns more from his opponents than from his fervent supporters. For his supporters will push him to disaster unless his opponents show him where the dangers are. So if he is wise he will often pray to be delivered from his friends, because they will ruin him. But, though it hurts, he ought also to pray never to be left without opponents; for they keep him on the path of reason and good sense.

The national unity of a free people depends upon a sufficiently even balance of political power to make it impracticable for the administration to be arbitrary and for the opposition to be revolutionary and irreconcilable. Where that balance no longer exists, democracy perishes. For unless all the citizens of a state are forced by circumstances to compromise, unless they feel that they can affect policy but that no one can wholly dominate it, unless by habit and necessity they have to give and take, freedom cannot be maintained.

QUESTIONS

1. What is Lippmann's reason for dividing the essay into three parts? What is the purpose of the third part?
2. What is the importance of Lippmann's distinction between "free oratory" and "free speech" (p.1011)?
3. What does Lippmann mean when he says that the point at which we recognize the need for the freedom of others "is much higher in some men than in others" (p.1007)? Does this assertion in any way weaken his argument?
4. Why has Lippmann discussed motion pictures but not literature (p.1010)? How sound is his view that the motion picture is "a medium which does not permit debate"? Does literature permit debate?
5. What does Lippmann mean by his statement that "the usual apology for freedom of speech . . . becomes abstract and eccentric rather than concrete and human" (p.1008)? Why has he chosen these particular words to contrast the "usual apology" with his own view? Is his argument "concrete and human"?
6. Thurber's rabbits (p. 953) listened to their opposition—that is, "the other animals, who lived at a great distance"—and were annihilated. Does Thurber's fable suggest any necessary qualification for Lippmann's thesis concerning the value of the opposition? Explain.

7. *Lippmann's essay was written before the term "brainwashing" was in common use. If he were writing the essay today, how might he take account of this term?*

JAMES MADISON
The Merits of a Republic[1]

To the People of the State of New York

Among the numerous advantages promised by a well-constructed Union, none deserves to be more accurately developed than its tendency to break and control the violence of faction. The friend of popular governments never finds himself so much alarmed for their character and fate, as when he contemplates their propensity to this dangerous vice. He will not fail, therefore, to set a due value on any plan which, without violating the principles to which he is attached, provides a proper cure for it. The instability, injustice, and confusion introduced into the public councils have, in truth, been the mortal diseases under which popular governments have everywhere perished; as they continue to be the favorite and fruitful topics from which the adversaries to liberty derive their most specious declamations. The valuable improvements made by the American constitutions on the popular models, both ancient and modern, cannot certainly be too much admired; but it would be an unwarrantable partiality, to contend that they have as effectually obviated the danger on this side, as was wished and expected. Complaints are everywhere heard from our most considerate and virtuous citizens, equally the friends of public and private faith, and of public and personal liberty, that our governments are too unstable, that the public good is disregarded in the conflicts of rival parties, and that measures are too often decided, not according to the rules of justice and the rights of the minor party, but by the superior force of an interested and overbearing majority. However anxiously we may wish that these complaints had no foundation, the evidence of known facts will not permit us to deny that they are in some degree true. It will be found, indeed, on a candid review of our situation, that some of the distresses under which we labor have been erroneously charged on the operation of our governments; but it will be found, at the same time, that other causes will not alone account for many of our heaviest misfortunes; and, particularly, for that prevailing and increasing distrust of public engagements, and alarm for private rights, which are echoed from one end of the continent to the other. These must be chiefly, if not wholly, effects of the unsteadiness and injustice with which a factious spirit has tainted our public administrations.

1. From *The Federalist*, No. 10.

By a faction, I understand a number of citizens, whether amounting to a majority or minority of the whole, who are united and actuated by some common impulse of passion, or of interest, adverse to the rights of other citizens, or to the permanent and aggregate interests of the community.

There are two methods of curing the mischiefs of faction: the one, by removing its causes; the other, by controlling its effects.

There are again two methods of removing the causes of faction: the one, by destroying the liberty which is essential to its existence; the other, by giving to every citizen the same opinions, the same passions, and the same interests.

It could never be more truly said than of the first remedy, that it was worse than the disease. Liberty is to faction what air is to fire, an ailment without which it instantly expires. But it could not be less folly to abolish liberty, which is essential to political life, because it nourishes faction, than it would be to wish the annihilation of air, which is essential to animal life, because it imparts to fire its destructive agency.

The second expedient is as impracticable as the first would be unwise. As long as the reason of man continues fallible, and he is at liberty to exercise it, different opinions will be formed. As long as the connection subsists between his reason and his self-love, his opinions and his passions will have a reciprocal influence on each other; and the former will be objects to which the latter will attach themselves. The diversity in the faculties of men, from which the rights of property originate, is not less an insuperable obstacle to a uniformity of interests. The protection of these faculties is the first object of government. From the protection of different and unequal faculties of acquiring property, the possession of different degrees and kinds of property immediately results; and from the influence of these on the sentiments and views of the respective proprietors, ensues a division of the society into different interests and parties.

The latent causes of faction are thus sown in the nature of man; and we see them everywhere brought into different degrees of activity, according to the different circumstances of civil society. A zeal for different opinions concerning religion, concerning government, and many other points, as well of speculation as of practice; an attachment to different leaders ambitiously contending for preeminence and power; or to persons of other descriptions whose fortunes have been interesting to the human passions, have, in turn, divided mankind into parties, inflamed them with mutual animosity, and rendered them much more disposed to vex and oppress each other than to co-operate for their common good. So strong is this propensity of mankind to fall into mutual animosities, that where no substantial occasion presents itself, the most frivolous and fanciful distinctions have been sufficient to kindle their unfriendly passions and excite their most violent conflicts. But the most common and durable source of factions has been the various and unequal distribution of property. Those who hold and those who are without property have ever formed distinct interests in society. Those who are creditors, and those who are debtors, fall under a like discrimination. A landed interest, a manufacturing interest, a mercantile interest, a moneyed interest, with many lesser interests, grow up of necessity in civilized nations, and divide them into different classes, actuated by different sentiments and views. The regulation of these various and interfering interests forms the principal task of modern legislation, and involves the spirit of party and faction in the necessary and ordinary operations of the government.

No man is allowed to be a judge in his own cause, because his interest would certainly bias his judgment, and, not improbably, corrupt his integrity. With equal, nay with greater reason, a body of men are unfit to be both judges and parties at the same time; yet what are many of the most important acts of legislation, but so many judicial determinations, not indeed concerning the rights of single persons, but concerning the rights of large bodies of citizens? And what are the different classes of legislators but advocates and parties to the causes which they determine? Is a law proposed concerning private debts? It is a question to which the creditors are parties on one side and the debtors on the other. Justice ought to hold the balance between them. Yet the parties are, and must be, themselves the judges; and the most numerous party, or, in other words, the most powerful faction must be expected to prevail. Shall domestic manufactures be encouraged, and in what degree, by restrictions on foreign manufactures? are questions which would be differently decided by the landed and the manufacturing classes, and probably by neither with a sole regard to justice and the public good. The apportionment of taxes on the various descriptions of property is an act which seems to require the most exact impartiality; yet there is, perhaps, no legislative act in which greater opportunity and temptation are given to a predominant party to trample on the rules of justice. Every shilling with which they overburden the inferior number, is a shilling saved to their own pockets.

It is in vain to say that enlightened statesmen will be able to adjust these clashing interests, and render them all subservient to the public good. Enlightened statesmen will not always be at the helm. Nor, in many cases, can such an adjustment be made at all without taking into view indirect and remote considerations, which will rarely prevail over the immediate interest which one party may find in disregarding the rights of another or the good of the whole.

The inference to which we are brought is, that the *causes* of faction cannot be removed, and that relief is only to be sought in the means of controlling its *effects*.

If a faction consists of less than a majority, relief is supplied by the republican principle, which enables the majority to defeat its sinister views by regular vote. It may clog the administration, it may convulse the society; but it will be unable to execute and mask its violence under the forms of the Constitution. When a majority is included in a faction, the form of popular government, on the other hand, enables it to sacrifice to its ruling passion or interest both the public good and the rights of other citizens. To secure the public good and private rights against the danger of such a faction, and at the same time to preserve the spirit and the form of popular government, is then the great object to which our inquiries are directed. Let me add that it is the great desideratum by which this form of government can be rescued from the opprobrium under which it has so long labored, and be recommended to the esteem and adoption of mankind.

By what means is this object attainable? Evidently by one of two only. Either the existence of the same passion or interest in a majority at the same time must be prevented, or the majority, having such coexistent passion or interest, must be rendered, by their number and local situation, unable to concert and carry into effect schemes of oppression. If the impulse and the opportunity be suffered to coincide, we well know that neither moral nor religious motives can be relied on as an adequate control. They are not found to be such on the injustice and violence of individuals, and lose their efficacy in proportion to the number combined together, that is, in proportion as their efficacy becomes needful.

From this view of the subject it may be concluded that a pure democracy, by which I mean a society consisting of a small number of citizens, who assemble and administer the government in person, can admit of no cure for the mischiefs of faction. A common passion or interest will, in almost every case, be felt by a majority of the whole; a communication and concert result from the form of government itself; and there is nothing to check the inducements to sacrifice the weaker party or an obnoxious individual. Hence it is that such democracies have ever been spectacles of turbulence and contention; have ever been found incompatible with personal security or the rights of property; and have in general been as short in their lives as they have been violent in their deaths. Theoretic politicians, who have patronized this species of government, have erroneously supposed that by reducing mankind to a perfect equality in their political rights, they would, at the same time, be perfectly equalized and assimilated in their possessions, their opinions, and their passions.

A republic, by which I mean a government in which the scheme of representation takes place, opens a different prospect, and promises the cure for which we are seeking. Let us examine the points in which it varies from pure democracy, and we shall comprehend both the nature of the cure and the efficacy which it must derive from the Union.

The two great points of difference between a democracy and a republic are: first, the delegation of the government, in the latter, to a small number of citizens elected by the rest; secondly, the greater number of citizens, and greater sphere of country, over which the latter may be extended.

The effect of the first difference is, on the one hand, to refine and enlarge the public views, by passing them through the medium of a chosen body of citizens, whose wisdom may be best discern the true interest of their country, and whose patriotism and love of justice will be least likely to sacrifice it to temporary or partial considerations. Under such a regulation, it may well happen that the public voice, pronounced by the representatives of the people, will be more consonant to the public good than if pronounced by the people themselves, convened for the purpose. On the other hand, the effect may be inverted. Men of factious tempers, of local prejudices, or of sinister designs, may, by intrigue, by corruption, or by other means, first obtain the suffrages, and then betray the interests, of the people. The question resulting is, whether small or extensive republics are more favorable to the election of proper guardians of the public weal; and it is clearly decided in favor of the latter by two obvious considerations:

In the first place, it is to be remarked that, however small the republic may be, the representatives must be raised to a certain number, in order to guard against the cabals of a few; and that, however large it may be, they must be limited to a certain number, in order to guard against the confusion of a multitude. Hence, the number of representatives in the two cases not being in proportion to that of the two constituents, and being proportionally greater in the small republic, it follows that, if the proportion of fit characters be not less in the large than in the small republic, the former will present a greater option, and consequently a greater probability of a fit choice.

In the next place, as each representative will be chosen by a greater number of citizens in the large than in the small republic, it will be more difficult for unworthy candidates to practise with success the vicious arts by which elections are too often carried; and the suffrages of the people being more free, will be more likely to centre in men who possess the most attractive merit and the most diffusive and established characters.

It must be confessed that in this, as in most other cases, there is a mean, on both sides of which inconveniences will be found to lie. By enlarging too much the number of electors, you render the representative too little acquainted with all their local circumstances and lesser interests; as by reducing it too much, you render him unduly attached to these, and too little fit to comprehend and pursue great and national objects. The federal Constitution forms a happy combination in this respect; the great and aggregate interests being referred to the national, the local and particularly to the State legislatures.

The other point of difference is, the greater number of citizens and extent of territory which may be brought within the compass of republican than of democratic government; and it is this circumstance principally which renders factious combinations less to be dreaded in the former than in the latter. The smaller the society, the fewer probably will be the distinct parties and interests composing it; the fewer the distinct parties and interests, the more frequently will a majority be found of the same party; and the smaller the number of individuals composing a majority, and the smaller the compass within which they are placed, the more easily will they concert and execute their plans of oppression. Extend the sphere, and you take in a greater variety of parties and interests; you make it less probable that a majority of the whole will have a common motive to invade the rights of other citizens; or if such a common motive exists, it will be more difficult for all who feel it to discover their own strength, and to act in unison with each other. Besides other impediments, it may be remarked that, where there is a consciousness of unjust or dishonorable purposes, communication is always checked by distrust in proportion to the number whose concurrence is necessary.

Hence, it clearly appears, that the same advantage which a republic has over a democracy, in controlling the effects of faction, is enjoyed by a large over a small republic,—is enjoyed by the Union over the States composing it. Does the advantage consist in the substitution of representatives whose enlightened views and virtuous sentiments render them superior to local prejudices and to schemes of injustice? It will not be denied that the representation of the Union will be most likely to possess these requisite endowments. Does it consist in the greater security afforded by a greater variety of parties, against the event of any one party being able to outnumber and oppress the rest? In an equal degree does the increased variety of parties comprised within the Union, increase this security. Does it, in fine, consist in the greater obstacles opposed to the concert and accomplishment of the secret wishes of an unjust and interested majority? Here, again, the extent of the Union gives it the most palpable advantage.

The influence of factious leaders may kindle a flame within their particular States, but will be unable to spread a general conflagration through the other States. A religious sect may degenerate into a political faction in a part of the Confederacy; but the variety of sects dispersed over the entire face of it must secure the national councils against any danger from that source. A rage for paper money, for an abolition of debts, for an equal division of property, or for any other improper or wicked project, will be less apt to pervade the whole body of the Union than a particular member of it; in the same proportion as such a malady is more likely to taint a particular county or district, than an entire State.

In the extent and proper structure of the Union, therefore, we behold a republican remedy for the diseases most incident to republican government. And according to the degree of pleasure and pride we feel in being republicans, ought to be our zeal in cherishing the spirit and supporting the character of Federalists.

QUESTIONS

1. Outline Madison's essay. What does the structure of the essay suggest about Madison's purpose? What has guided him in the order in which he treats his major points? Has he left out any important considerations?
2. This piece has sometimes been titled "The Control of Faction." Is the present title preferable? Explain.
3. Does Madison seem to view his audience as hostile, skeptical, neutral, or sympathetic? Explain.
4. Examine Madison's definition of "faction." What would happen if one or another of the clauses in the definition were left out?
5. What is the relationship between Madison's definition of faction and his distinction between a democracy and a republic?
6. Discuss the relative merits of a democracy and a republic. What is the place of factions in each form of government?
7. Compare Madison's view of the role of minorities with Lippmann's in "The Indispensable Opposition" (pp. 1006–1013).

MORTIMER J. ADLER

The Future of Democracy: A Swan Song

The last great book in political theory—a work that stands in the line of Plato, Aristotle, Aquinas, Marsilius, Hobbes, Spinoza, Montesquieu, Locke, Rousseau, Kant, and Hegel—was published in 1861, a little more than a hundred years ago. John Stuart Mill's *Representative Government* has, in addition to its intrinsic greatness, the distinction of being the first major work in political philosophy which, addressing itself, as is appropriate to a treatise in political philosophy, to the question of the ideally best form of government, answers that question by a fully reasoned and critically cautious defense of the proposition that democracy is, of all forms of government, the only one that is perfectly just—the ideal polity.

At the time that Mill wrote *Representative Government*, democracy in his sense of the term—constitutional government with universal suffrage operating through elected representatives—did not exist anywhere in the world. Republics there were and constitutional monarchies, but all of them were oligarchies of one type or another: the ruling class—the enfranchised citizenry in the republics or the citizenry and the nobility in the constitutional monarchies—comprised only a small fraction of the population. The rest were disfranchised subjects or slaves.

Nor had democracy, in Mill's sense, ever existed in the whole of the historic past. From the beginnings of constitutional government in the city-states of Greece right down to Mill's day and beyond that into the twentieth century, the republics which went furthest in the direction of popular government were all oligarchies, in which "the people"—the constituents of the government, the enfranchised citizens—formed a privileged ruling class, rising above the subjects and slaves who formed the rest, usually the majority, of the population. In the Athens of Pericles, where what Aristotle would have regarded as an extreme form of democracy prevailed for a short time, the citizens numbered 30,000 or less in a population of 120,000.

We should certainly not allow ourselves to be distracted or confused by the fact that the Greeks invented the name "democracy" and used it, either invidiously for mob rule as Plato did or descriptively as Aristotle did for a form of government which, as contrasted with oligarchy, set a much lower property qualification for citizenship and public office. The democracies of the ancient world differed from the oligarchies only in the degree to which participation in government was restricted by property qualifications for citizenship and public office—which could result, as it did in the case of Athens, in the difference between a democracy of 30,000 and an oligarchy of 500. However significant that difference must have seemed to the 30,000, it could hardly have had any meaning for the 90,000 disfranchised human beings who, in Aristotle's terms, were useful parts of the political community, but not members of it.

We have no reason to complain about how the Greeks used the word "democracy," but it is disingenuous, to say the least, for contemporary writers to use it as a synonym for "popular government," and then make that term applicable to any form of government in which some portion of the population—the few, the many, or even all except infants, idiots, and criminals—participate somehow in the political life of the community. By that use of the term, anything other than an absolute monarchy is a democracy in some degree, more or less, according to the proportion of the population that forms "the people"—the ruling class. According to such usage, "democracy" in Mill's sense of the term is merely the limiting case in the spectrum of popular governments, the case in which the people is co-extensive with the population, excepting only those who, as Mill says, are disqualified by their own default. We are then compelled to say that the Greek oligarchies were simply "less democratic" than the Greek democracies; and that modern democracies became more and more democratic as the working classes and finally women were granted suffrage. It would take the semantic sophistication of a six-year-old to recognize that this is a use of words calculated to obscure problems and issues rather than to clarify them.

It can be said, of course, as it has been, that democracy in Mill's sense represents an ideal which, through the course of history, diverse forms of constitutional government have been approaching in various degrees; and hence, to whatever extent they are popular—to whatever extent "the people" is an appreciable fraction of the population—they are entitled to be called "democratic" by virtue of their tending to approximate the ideal. But to say this is worse than confusing. While it may be poetically true to describe the course of history as tending toward democracy as the political ideal, it is simply and factually false to attribute that tendency to our ancestors as if it were the manifestation of a conscious intention on their part. Democracy, in Mill's sense, was not the ideal to which the past aspired and toward which it strove by political revolutions or reforms. With the possible and qualified exception of Kant, no political philosopher before Mill ever argued for the inherent or natural and equal right of every human being to be a citizen actively participating in the government of his or her community; none regarded it as an ideal; none, in fact, even contemplated the possibility of a genuinely universal suffrage.

In the sphere of political action, as distinct from that of political thought, Mill did have some predecessors, such as Colonel Rainborough and Sir John Wildman among the Levellers in Cromwell's army;[1] Mr. Sanford and Mr. Ross in the New York Constitutional Convention of 1821;[2] Robert Owen in the formation of the community at New Lanark[3] and similar communities elsewhere. But even in the sphere of practical politics, Mill is the first to advocate the enfranchisement of women and hence the first to conceive universal suffrage as including the other half of the population.

1. The Levellers were a "radical" group in Cromwell's army during the British Civil War who believed in the natural rights of man and wished to make all men politically equal.

2. The Constitution adopted in 1822 extended the franchise in New York, virtually ending the property qualification for all white male voters.

3. Robert Owen (1771–1858), British industrialist and socialist reformer, purchased, with his partners, New Lanark Mills, near Glasgow, Scotland in 1799. Here he instituted numerous social and educational benefits for the workers, believing that labor was the natural standard of value.

The prior uses of the term "democracy," both descriptive and denigrative, should not prevent us from perceiving what is genuinely novel in the political conception for which Mill appropriated that term. (1) It involves an adequate appreciation of the full extent to which universal suffrage should be carried on the grounds of a right to participate in government, a right inherent in every human being. Hence, (2) it regards constitutional government with truly universal suffrage as the only completely just form of government—the ideal polity.

In what follows, I shall be exclusively concerned with this new conception which, under any other name, would be exactly the same. Since no other name, nearly as appropriate, is available, I shall use "democracy" in Mill's sense of the term, hoping that the reader will remember why, *when the term is used in that sense,* nothing prior in theory or practice can be called "democracy" or "democratic." Anyone, of course, is privileged to use words as he pleases, but that privilege does not justify obfuscation or confusion in their use.

My main purpose in this paper is to consider the question: Under current and future conditions, is democracy possible? Is government by the people *practicable* in the world as it is today and as it is likely to become? Or to state this still another way: *Can* the people participate through suffrage in the government of a modern state?

There is, of course, a prior question: *Should* they? *Should* all human beings, as a matter of right and duty, actively participate in the political affairs of their community. If political democracy is not, as a matter of right and justice, the ideal polity, then why waste time concerning ourselves about its practical feasibility?

One might also ask, Do the people—or most people—really *want* to participate in government, or would they, as a matter of fact, rather concern themselves exclusively with their private affairs while someone else takes care of the business of government? This question is, in a sense, a subordinate part of the question about whether democracy is practically feasible; for certainly one major obstacle to its being effectively practiced would be a general indifference to political affairs on the part of most people. That indifference, if it exists, would have to be overcome by education or other means if democracy is to become effectively operative.

Let us return to the primary question: Is democracy the ideal polity—the most just, the only completely just, form of government? I share Mill's affirmative answer to this question. My explication of the answer, which I cannot attribute wholly to Mill, can be briefly stated as follows:

There are three principles or elements of political justice. (1)

Government is just if it acts to serve the common good and general welfare of the community and not the private or special interests of those who happen to wield political power. By this principle, tyrannical government, exploiting the ruled in the interests of the rulers, is unjust; and, by this same principle, a benevolent despotism can be to some extent just.

(2) Government is just if it is duly constituted; that is, if it derives its powers from the consent of the governed. The powers of government are then *de jure* powers, and not simply *de facto*: we have a government of laws instead of a government of men. By this principle, constitutional governments of all types have an element of justice lacked by all absolute governments; by this criterion, an absolute monarchy, however benevolent the despotism, is unjust.

(3) Government is just if it secures the rights inherent in the governed, *i.e.*, the natural, and hence the equal, rights which belong to men as men. Among these rights is the right to liberty, and of the several freedoms to which every man has a natural right, one is political liberty—the freedom possessed by those who have some voice in the making of the laws under which they live. When political liberty is thus understood, only men who are citizens with suffrage enjoy political liberty. The unenfranchised are subjects who may be ruled paternalistically or benevolently for their own good, but who are also unjustly treated insofar as they are deprived of a natural human right. By this principle, every constitutional oligarchy is unjust, and only a constitutional democracy is just.

The last of these three principles is the critical one, the one that is essential to democracy. With the exception of tyranny, other forms of government may have certain aspects of justice, but only democracy, in addition to being constitutional government and government for the common good, has the justice which derives from granting every man the right to participate in his own government. This right needs a word or two more of explanation.

Like every natural right, this one is rooted in the nature of man. Its authenticity rests on the truth of the proposition that man is by nature a political animal. To affirm this proposition is to say that *all* men, not just some men, should be *constituents* of the government under which they live and so should be governed only with their own *consent*, and that in addition, they should be citizens with *suffrage* and be thus empowered to *participate* in their own government. (I have italicized all the crucial words in the statement of the proposition's meaning.)

It was Aristotle, of course, who said that man is by nature a political animal, but he himself denied one of the crucial elements in the proposition's meaning when he also said that some men are by nature slaves; for to assert that some men have natures which fit them only for slavery (*i.e.*, naturally incapable of participating in government) directly contradicts the proposition that all men are by nature political (*i.e.*, fit to participate in government.)

To accommodate modern ears, let me translate Aristotle's remarks about natural slavery into the proposition that some men are intended by nature (*i.e.*, by their endowments at birth) to be governed for their own good and for their own good should be deprived of any voice in their own government. If this proposition is true, then political democracy could hardly claim to be the ideal polity. It has no special justice in excess of that possessed by a constitutional oligarchy, administered for the benefit of those subject to its rule. In fact, it might even be said to involve a certain injustice, insofar as it gives political power to those who *should not* have it—all those who are not by nature fit for suffrage. In short, *only if all men are by nature political animals*—only if all are naturally endowed to live as free or self-governing men—do all have the right to be enfranchised citizens and the duty to participate in government. Only then is democracy, of all forms of government, supremely just.

This is not the place to argue the truth of the central proposition or of its contradictory. But we ought to spend a moment considering what the best form of government would be *if only some men are by nature political animals*. Would the "some" be a small or a large proportion of the population? Would they be the few or the many? Undoubtedly, the few. These, then, should comprise a political elite, a corps of officials, a professional bureaucracy that should govern the people at large for their own good. So far we have a benevolent despotism; but if we now add (1) that the government should be duly constituted (*i.e.*, should be constitutional or limited rather than absolute—a government of laws) and, (2) that, except for the political distinction between the official ruling class and the rest of the people, an equality of social and economic conditions should prevail (*i.e.*, all men should equally share in the general welfare that the government aims to promote), and (3) that the government should safeguard, equally, the private rights and liberties of each individual or family, then what we come out with is the kind of government recommended by certain commentators on the present political scene; *e.g.*, Bertrand de Jouvenel, with a fondness for Gaullism, or Walter Lippmann, with nostalgia for Platonism.

Such a form of government can appropriate to itself the name "democracy" by appealing to Tocqueville's[4] sociological rather than political conception of democracy as a society in which a general equality of conditions prevails. Equality of conditions can, as Tocqueville recognized, tend toward completely centralized totalitarian government, more oppressive than any ancient despotism;

4. Alexis Charles Henri Maurice Clérel de Tocqueville (1805–1859), French statesman and author of *Democracy in America*.

but if a community retains the limitations and checks of constitutional government, and if the general welfare that is promoted by the government includes the protection of the private rights and liberties of the people, then, perhaps, it does deserve to be called, as De Jouvenel calls it, a "social democracy." But it is not a political democracy; for while the community enjoys government *of* and *for* the people, government *by* the people has been replaced by the rule of a professional bureaucracy (which, it is hoped, comprise the few who are by nature competent to govern).

A "social democracy," thus conceived, might very well be the best—the most just—form of government *if it were true that only some men are by nature political animals.* But if the contradictory proposition is true—*if all are*—then it involves the same essential injustice that is to be found in any benevolent despotism. As Mill helps us to see, what is pernicious about the idea of the good and wise despot—in all the forms that it has taken from Plato to De Gaulle—is not the myth that any one man or any few actually have the superior qualities that merit putting the government entirely in their hands; the point is rather that, granted such men can be found, letting them rule, with wisdom and benevolence, reduces the rest of the population to a perpetual childhood, their political natures stunted rather than developed. By the standards of wisdom, efficiency, or competence in government, political democracy may not compare with the excellence in government that can be achieved by a specially qualified bureaucracy; but if all men deserve political liberty because they have a right to a voice in their own government, then government by the people must be preserved against all the tendencies now at work in the opposite direction—and for one reason and one alone, its superior justice.

The question remains: Can it be preserved?

In the hundred years since Mill wrote *Representative Government*, a small number of political democracies have come into existence for the first time in history, most of them since the turn of the century and most of them in Europe or North America. This is not to say that the ideal polity has been actually and fully realized on earth in our time. Far from it! What came into existence in our time were the legal enactments—the constitutional provisions or amendments—which established the form of democratic government in a small number of political communities. But in most cases—most notably, perhaps, in the United States—the discrepancy between democracy on paper and democracy in practice was vast at the beginning and has nowhere yet become negligible.

If significant inequality of conditions, if educational deficiencies, if the obstinate persistence of privileged minorities, on the one hand, and the failure to eradicate underprivileged minorities, on the other, prevent the effective operation of democratic institutions, then the full realization of democracy still belongs to the future, even in the politically most advanced countries. Nevertheless, one might have been cautiously optimistic twenty years ago, as I was, in thinking that the future belonged to democracy, that the general direction of change in the conditions of human life promised not only the legal institution of democracy where it did not yet exist, but also a slow and steady progress toward its fuller realization in practice wherever it did exist. It looked as if Tocqueville were right in thinking that "an aristocracy cannot again be founded in the world" and that "the nations of our time cannot prevent the conditions of men from becoming equal"; and therefore right in predicting that "the gradual development of equality of conditions" is inevitable.

It looked, in other words, as if all of Mill's fears about "the infirmities and dangers to which representative government is liable" would gradually be made groundless by the social and economic changes that have been taking place since his day. While advocating the extension of the suffrage to the laboring classes (because it was clearly unjust "to withhold from anyone, unless for the prevention of greater evils, the ordinary privilege of having his voice reckoned in the disposal of affairs in which he has the same interest as other people"), he feared that the enfranchised masses would exercise their new-found power in their own factional interests and tyrannically subjugate the upper-class minorities to their will. He also feared that the judgment of the uneducated would prevail, by sheer weight of numbers, over the judgment of their betters to the detriment of the community as a whole.

The marked inequality of conditions which, in Mill's day, separated the working masses from the upper class and brought them into a sharp conflict of factional interests led Mill, the proponent of democracy, to have the same fears about it that led others to oppose it. And, let it be said in passing, that the remedies—proportional representation and plural voting—which Mill proposed as ways of safeguarding democracy from its own deficiencies would as effectively have nullified democracy in practice, if they had been carried out, as the devices proposed by James Madison or John Calhoun to prevent the will of the numerical majority from prevailing. To be in favor of universal suffrage (which makes the ruling class co-extensive with the population) while at the same time wishing somehow to undercut the rule of the majority, is as self-contradictory as being for and against democracy at the same time.

This is not to say that the problems which concerned Mill were not genuine in his time. These problems—especially the problem of factions (the age-old conflict between the haves and the have-nots) and the problem of an educated electorate—can be solved, not in the way that Mill, or Madison, or Calhoun, proposed, but only through the development of a general equality of conditions, which, by gradually substituting a classless society of haves for a class-divided one, tends to reduce and ultimately to eliminate the conflict of economic factions; and which also, by gradually giving all equal access to schooling and enough free time for leisure and learning in adult life, enables every educable human being (*i.e.*, all except the incurable feeble-minded or insane) to become educated to the point where he can be as good a citizen—as sensible in the exercise of his suffrage—as anyone else.

All men are not equally intelligent at birth; nor will all ever become equally wise or virtuous through the development of their minds and characters; but these ineradicable inequalities in human beings do not in themselves undermine the democratic proposition that all normal men are educable enough to become good citizens. To think otherwise is to revert to the aristocratic proposition that some men are so superior to others in natural endowment that they alone are educable to the extent required for participation in government. I am not saying that the problem of producing a sufficiently educated electorate (when it is co-extensive with the population of the community) has yet been solved. It certainly has not been, and we are still a long way from solving it. I am only saying that the changes which have taken place since Mill's day— especially the technological advances which have brought affluence and ample opportunity for learning and leisure in their wake—give us more hope that it can be solved than he could possibly have summoned to support his wavering democratic convictions.

Herein lies one of the paradoxes of the present situation. The same technological advances which have created relatively affluent societies for the first time in history, and without which it would have been impossible to effect all the social and economic reforms that have tended to create a greater equality of conditions, are now made the basis for despair about the feasibility of democratic government. Again and again, in discussions conducted by the Center for the Study of Democratic Institutions, for instance, it has been said that government by the people is no longer possible, because, in our technologically advanced societies, the problems of government have become so complex that neither the people themselves nor their elected representatives in congress or parliament can contribute to their intelligent solution. It has been suggested that, if not now, then certainly in the foreseeable future, decision-making will have to be taken over by computers and by the experts who know how to program them.

Government by the people may have been a feasible polity in ancient Athens when the *few* who constituted the citizenry met in the agora and debated questions of policy which they could understand and think about in terms of the relatively simple state of facts with which they were generally acquainted. It may even have made some sense in certain countries during the eighteenth and nineteenth centuries, when the significant citizenry were still a very small portion of the population and when their elected representatives in congress or parliament could still have understood the questions they debated and have had some command over the facts relevant to reaching decisions. But now that the citizenry is, in effect, the whole population—now that, at last, we have constitutional democracy with universal suffrage—most of the basic questions which confront a twentieth-century government can no longer be intelligently debated, much less decided, by the public at large or even by representative assemblies.

There are other sources for the current despair about the feasibility of democratic government—if that is really taken to mean participation in government by the whole population through voting and through other ways of expressing their views on public policy, either directly or by pressure on their representatives. One is the ever-increasing size of the population and the intricately complicated and ever-changing conditions under which the enlarged population now lives and struggles to form a community. Another is a series of studies of the voting process, made in recent years by social scientists, which tends to confirm the worst suspicions of antidemocrats concerning the folly of supposing that the voters pay any attention whatsoever to the real public issues involved in an election when, in fact, they merely express their emotions or their prejudices at the polls. Still another is a mathematical analysis of voting which leads to the conclusion that the principle of majority rule does not work when the voters are presented with more than two alternatives.

One could go on, either to spell out in detail the sources of despair about democracy or to add many others of similar vein, but that is not necessary in order for us to face the fact that today the prevailing opinion among the learned—the professional students of sociology and politics—is that a realistic approach to the process of government leads to the conclusion that the ideal of democracy, as Mill envisioned it, is simply a misleading myth. Even if democracy were ideal in terms of the principles of justice(a matter which most of the learned no longer deign to discuss, or else dismiss as the kind of loose talk in which only philosophers indulge), it does not now have and probably never can have any reality in the world of things as they are.

Since I am only a philosopher—and also a relatively ignorant man with regard to the current state of learning in the behavioral and social sciences—I cannot assess the validity of the conclusion just stated in terms of the evidence or considerations on which it is based. Such questions as: *Does democracy now actually exist to any degree?* or *Under present and future conditions, is the realization of democracy highly improbable?* are questions of fact. I do not know the answers to these questions; and, being a philosopher, I suspect that no one else does either. I also doubt, as any philosopher would, that such questions can be answered demonstratively. The answers to them always remain in the sphere of opinion and are always likely to be subject to reasonable differences of opinion in the light of all the evidence that can be gathered.

Confronted with the opinion about democracy that is now prevalent among the learned, at least among those of realistic persuasion, a philosopher is impelled to ask questions.

Let me begin by assuming the truth of the realistic denial in its most extreme form; *i.e.*, let us assume the *impossibility* of government by the people in any sense which tends to realize, in some degree, the ideal of democracy. What then?

First, must we not conclude that the ideal is a purely visionary utopian one, not based on men or conditions as they are? For if it were a practicable ideal, based on things as they are, then how could it be impossible of realization—in the strict sense of impossible? Those who thus eliminate democracy as a practicable ideal must therefore be asked whether they have any genuinely practicable (*i.e.*, actually realizable) political ideal to substitute for it. If they say no, they must be further asked whether the reason is that they reject normative political thinking entirely and so refuse to take the question seriously. In that case I, as a philosopher, have no interest in questioning them any further. But if they concede the possibility of sensible and reasonable talk about good and bad forms of government, and hence are seriously concerned with thinking about the best of all possible (*i.e.*, realizable) forms, then they should either have some alternative to democracy as the ideal polity or be in search of one. In either case, they must be asked to state the standard, principle, or norm in terms of which they would propose a particular form of government as best, or better than some other. Justice? Wisdom? Efficiency? Strength? If they appeal to any standard other than justice, or do not include justice among the principles to which they appeal, I must remind them that democracy is said to be the best form of government only in terms of justice, not in terms of wisdom, efficiency, strength, or any other criterion; and so they have failed to find a substitute for democracy. If they then reply that justice is totally irrelevant to the goodness of government, I either have no more questions to ask them or too many to set forth here.

Let me turn next to a milder form of the current despair about democracy—to the view that the difficulties in the way of realizing it are now very great and, the way things are going, are likely to become even greater in the future. Let us assume that this is true. However great they are or are likely to become, they cannot be regarded as insurmountable; for that would throw us back to the extreme position that government by the people is impossible. Here we have only two main questions to ask.

The first is addressed to those who are so deeply impressed—and claim to be so sorely distressed—by all the difficulties which now loom up and stand in the way of making democracy work, especially the difficulty that arises from the complexity of the problems which governments now face, a complexity that seems to place them beyond the competence so far manifested by the electorate or by representative assemblies, or any degree of competence that might reasonably be expected of them in the near future. I must, in passing, warn our friends not to overstate this difficulty lest it become insurmountable and we be once more thrown back to the extreme view that democracy is impossible. If they heed this warning and continue to concede that democracy is practicable, however difficult putting it into practice may be, then I would like to ask them whether they also concede that it is the ideal polity. My question, I must remind them, is not about democracy in *any* sense of that term, but about democracy as defined: constitutional government with genuinely universal suffrage, operating through elections and elected representatives, with majority rule, and under conditions of social and economic as well as political equality. Do they regard democracy thus defined as the ideal polity, and if they do, do they hold it up as the ideal by reference to principles of justice?

If they answer this compound question with a double affirmative, then there is only one further question to ask. Let me assume that they take the view that the difficulties confronting democracy—if not now then certainly in the future—are likely to be so great that, even if they are not, absolutely speaking, insurmountable, we may nevertheless be unable to overcome them in any really satisfactory manner. Hence, they may say, we should prepare ourselves for this eventuality by thinking of a second-best form of government, one which, while less just, would be more workable because it would get around the difficulties now besetting democracy. What shape would that take?

I do not know whether there is more than one possible answer to this question; but I do know, and have already mentioned (see page 1025), one alternative to democracy that is espoused by those who wish to discard government by the people while retaining government of and for the people. I am even willing to concede that if political democracy should prove to be impossible, then so-called social democracy may very well be a second-best. But I am not yet willing to yield—and I see nothing in the contemporary discussion of the difficulties of democracy which requires me to yield—on the proposition that all men are by nature political. I must, therefore, repeat what I said earlier; namely, that, men being what they are, "social democracy" is a poor second-best, for it imposes upon the many who are disfranchised the essential injustice which characterizes any benevolent despotism. Hence, until—as nearly as possible demonstrably—insurmountable difficulties force us to surrender all hope in democracy and for its future, we should be loath to settle for anything less than the best form of government that befits the nature of man.

Until then, the only course for us to follow—with courage and intelligence—is the one outlined by Robert M. Hutchins[5] in a recently published conversation in which he engaged with Joseph P. Lyford on the subject of man the political animal.

Summing up, Mr. Hutchins said, "The Center [The Center for the Study of Democratic Institutions] is committed to constitutional democracy. Its reasons lie in the nature of man. Man is a political animal. It is unjust to deprive him of his political life." He then went on to say in conclusion:

The task of those who are committed to political democracy is to discover how democracy can work in a technical, bureaucratic society in which all problems appear to be beyond the reach, to say nothing of the grasp, of the citizen. The task calls for more than haphazard thoughts and random discussions and the dusting off of ancient but irrelevant slogans. It requires a prodigious effort of the best minds everywhere to restore the dialogue that is the basis of the political community. Above all, the effort calls for faith that, whatever the defects of our society, self-government can and must endure because it is the only form of rule consistent with the nature of man.

5. Robert M. Hutchins (1899–   ), American educator and Director of the Center for the Study of Democratic Institutions. Adler's essay originally appeared in *Humanistic Education and Western Civilization*, 1954, a volume of essays honoring Hutchins.

QUESTIONS

1. Why does Adler feel it necessary to devote so much space to defining and distinguishing between the different meanings of democracy? In what ways do the definitions contribute to the development of his thesis?

2. For what reasons does Adler praise Mill? Why does he feel that Mill has relevance for us today? What questions does he feel are implicit in Mill's discussion?

3. Does the paragraph on page 1027 beginning "Government by the people . . ." represent Adler's view or someone else's? How can one tell?

4. Adler distinguishes between questions of fact and questions of opinion. What is the difference between the two? He also speaks of the philosopher's questions. What is characteristic of such questions?

5. Why doesn't Adler discuss more fully "the proposition that all men are by nature political"? How might a fuller discussion of this contribute to the essay?
6. Does Adler's conclusion follow from the rest of the essay? Is it consistent with the title? Explain.
7. Would the essay be better without the last three paragraphs? Explain.

D. H. LAWRENCE

The Spirit of Place[1]

We like to think of the old-fashioned American classics as children's books. Just childishness, on our part.

The old American art-speech contains an alien quality, which belongs to the American continent and to nowhere else. But, of course, so long as we insist on reading the books as children's tales, we miss all that.

One wonders what the proper highbrow Romans of the third and fourth or later centuries read into the strange utterances of Lucretius or Apuleius or Tertullian, Augustine or Athanasius. The uncanny voice of Iberian Spain, the weirdness of old Carthage, the passion of Libya and North Africa; you may bet the proper old Romans never heard these at all.[2] They read old Latin inference over the top of it, as we read old European inference over the top of Poe or Hawthorne.

It is hard to hear a new voice, as hard as it is to listen to an unknown language. We just don't listen. There is a new voice in the old American classics. The world has declined to hear it, and has blabbed about children's stories.

Why? Out of fear. The world fears a new experience more than it fears anything. Because a new experience displaces so many old experiences. And it is like trying to use muscles that have perhaps never been used, or that have been going stiff for ages. It hurts horribly.

The world doesn't fear a new idea. It can pigeonhole any idea. But it can't pigeonhole a real new experience. It can only dodge. The world is a great dodger, and the Americans the greatest. Because they dodge their own very selves.

There is a new feeling in the old American books, far more than there is in the modern American books, which are pretty empty of any feeling, and proud of it. There is a "different" feeling in the old American classics. It is the shifting over from the old psyche to

1. Chapter 1 in *Studies in Classic American Literature*, 1923.
2. The writers Lawrence names were out of the main stream of Roman literature, being associated with outlying regions of the Roman world and representing new literary directions in their works.

something new, a displacement. And displacements hurt. This hurts. So we try to tie it up, like a cut finger. Put a rag around it.

It is a cut, too. Cutting away the old emotions and consciousness. Don't ask what is left.

Art-speech is the only truth. An artist is usually a damned liar, but his art, if it be art, will tell you the truth of his day. And that is all that matters. Away with eternal truth. Truth lives from day to day, and the marvelous Plato of yesterday is chiefly bosh today.

The old American artists were hopeless liars. But they were artists, in spite of themselves. Which is more than you can say of most living practitioners.

And you can please yourself, when you read *The Scarlet Letter*, whether you accept what that sugary, blue-eyed little darling of a Hawthorne has to say for himself, false as all darlings are, or whether you read the impeccable truth of his art-speech.

The curious thing about art-speech is that it prevaricates so terribly, I mean it tells such lies. I suppose because we always all the time tell ourselves lies. And out of a pattern of lies art weaves the truth. Like Dostoevsky posing as a sort of Jesus, but most truthfully revealing himself all the while as a little horror.

Truly art is a sort of subterfuge. But thank God for it, we can see through the subterfuge if we choose. Art has two great functions. First, it provides an emotional experience. And then, if we have the courage of our own feelings, it becomes a mine of practical truth. We have had the feelings *ad nauseam*. But we've never dared dig the actual truth out of them, the truth that concerns us, whether it concerns our grandchildren or not.

The artist usually sets out—or used to—to point a moral and adorn a tale. The tale, however, points the other way, as a rule. Two blankly opposing morals, the artist's and the tale's. Never trust the artist. Trust the tale. The proper function of a critic is to save the tale from the artist who created it.

Now we know our business in these studies: saving the American tale from the American artist.

Let us look at this American artist first. How did he ever get to America, to start with? Why isn't he a European still, like his father before him?

Now listen to me, don't listen to him. He'll tell you the lie you expect. Which is partly your fault for expecting it.

He didn't come in search of freedom of worship. England had more freedom of worship in the year 1700 than America had. Won by Englishmen who wanted freedom, and so stopped at home and fought for it. And got it. Freedom of worship. Read the history of New England during the first century of its existence.

Freedom anyhow? The land of the free! This the land of the free! Why, if I say anything that displeases them, the free mob will lynch me, and that's my freedom. Free? Why I have never been in any country where the individual has such an abject fear of his fellow countrymen. Because, as I say, they are free to lynch him the moment he shows he is not one of them.

No, no, if you're so fond of the truth about Queen Victoria, try a little about yourself.

Those Pilgrim Fathers and their successors never came here for freedom of worship. What did they set up when they got here? Freedom, would you call it?

They didn't come for freedom. Or if they did, they sadly went back on themselves.

All right then, what did they come for? For lots of reasons. Perhaps least of all in search of freedom of any sort: positive freedom, that is.

They came largely to get *away*—that most simple of motives. To get away. Away from what? In the long run, away from themselves. Away from everything. That's why most people have come to America, and still do come. To get away from everything they are and have been.

"Henceforth be masterless."

Which is all very well, but it isn't freedom. Rather the reverse. A hopeless sort of constraint. It is never freedom till you find something you really *positively want to be.* And people in America have always been shouting about the things they are *not.* Unless of course they are millionaires, made or in the making.

And after all there is a positive side to the movement. All that vast flood of human life that has flowed over the Atlantic in ships from Europe to America has not flowed over simply on a tide of revulsion from Europe and from the confinements of the European ways of life. This revulsion was, and still is, I believe, the prime motive in emigration. But there was some cause, even for the revulsion.

It seems as if at times man had a frenzy for getting away from any control of any sort. In Europe the old Christianity was the real master. The Church and the true aristocracy bore the responsibility for the working out of the Christian ideals: a little irregularly, maybe, but responsible nevertheless.

Mastery, kingship, fatherhood had their power destroyed at the time of the Renaissance.

And it was precisely at this moment that the great drift over the Atlantic started. What were men drifting away from? The old authority of Europe? Were they breaking the bonds of authority, and escaping to a new more absolute unrestrainedness? Maybe. But there was more to it.

Liberty is all very well, but men cannot live without masters. There is always a master. And men either live in glad obedience to the master they believe in, or they live in a frictional opposition to the master they wish to undermine. In America this frictional opposition has been the vital factor. It has given the Yankee his kick. Only the continual influx of more servile Europeans has provided America with an obedient laboring class. The true obedience never outlasting the first generation.

But there sits the old master, over in Europe. Like a parent. Somewhere deep in every American heart lies a rebellion against the old parenthood of Europe. Yet no American feels he has completely escaped its mastery. Hence the slow, smoldering patience of American opposition. The slow, smoldering, corrosive obedience to the old master Europe, the unwilling subject, the unremitting opposition.

Whatever else you are, be masterless.

> Ca Ca Caliban
> Get a new master, be a new man.[3]

Escaped slaves, we might say, people the republics of Liberia or Haiti. Liberia enough! Are we to look at America in the same way? A vast republic of escaped slaves. When you consider the hordes from eastern Europe, you might well say it: a vast republic of escaped slaves. But one dare not say this of the Pilgrim Fathers, and the great old body of idealist Americans, the modern Americans tortured with thought. A vast republic of escaped slaves. Look out, America! And a minority of earnest, self-tortured people.

The masterless.

> Ca Ca Caliban
> Get a new master, be a new man.

What did the Pilgrim Fathers come for, then, when they came so gruesomely over the black sea? Oh, it was in a black spirit. A black revulsion from Europe, from the old authority of Europe, from kings and bishops and popes. And more. When you look into it, more. They were black, masterful men, they wanted something else. No kings, no bishops maybe. Even no God Almighty. But also, no more of this new "humanity" which followed the Renaissance. None of this new liberty which was to be so pretty in Europe. Something grimmer, by no means free-and-easy.

America has never been easy, and is not easy today. Americans have always been at a certain tension. Their liberty is a thing of sheer will, sheer tension: a liberty of THOU SHALT NOT. And it has been so from the first. The land of THOU SHALT NOT. Only the first commandment is: THOU SHALT NOT PRESUME TO BE A MASTER. Hence democracy.

---

3. Lawrence quotes loosely from Shakespeare's *The Tempest* (II. ii. 188–189). The next line reads: "Freedom, heyday! Heyday, freedom! Freedom, heyday, freedom!" Caliban, the half-human monster, has gotten drunk and is declaring his freedom from Prospero, the magician.

"We are the masterless." That is what the American Eagle shrieks. It's a Hen-Eagle.

The Spaniards refused the post-Renaissance liberty of Europe. And the Spaniards filled most of America. The Yankees, too, refused, refused the post-Renaissance humanism of Europe. First and foremost, they hated masters. But under that, they hated the flowing ease of humor in Europe. At the bottom of the American soul was always a dark suspense, at the bottom of the Spanish-American soul the same. And this dark suspense hated and hates the old European spontaneity, watches it collapse with satisfaction.

Every continent has its own great spirit of place. Every people is polarized in some particular locality, which is home, the homeland. Different places on the face of the earth have different vital effluence, different vibration, different chemical exhalation, different polarity with different stars: call it what you like. But the spirit of place is a great reality. The Nile valley produced not only the corn, but the terrific religions of Egypt. China produces the Chinese, and will go on doing so. The Chinese in San Francisco will in time cease to be Chinese, for America is a great melting pot.

There was a tremendous polarity in Italy, in the city of Rome. And this seems to have died. For even places die. The Island of Great Britain had a wonderful terrestrial magnetism or polarity of its own, which made the British people. For the moment, this polarity seems to be breaking. Can England die? And what if England dies?

Men are less free than they imagine; ah, far less free. The freest are perhaps least free.

Men are free when they are in a living homeland, not when they are straying and breaking away. Men are free when they are obeying some deep, inward voice of religious belief. Obeying from within. Men are free when they belong to a living, organic, *believing* community, active in fulfilling some unfulfilled, perhaps unrealized purpose. Not when they are escaping to some wild west. The most unfree souls go west, and shout of freedom. Men are freest when they are most unconscious of freedom. The shout is a rattling of chains, always was.

Men are not free when they are doing just what they like. The moment you can do just what you like, there is nothing you care about doing. Men are only free when they are doing what the deepest self likes.

And there is getting down to the deepest self! It takes some diving.

Because the deepest self is way down, and the conscious self is an obstinate monkey. But of one thing we may be sure. If one wants to be free, one has to give up the illusion of doing what one likes, and seek what IT wishes done.

But before you can do what IT likes, you must first break the spell of the old mastery, the old IT.

Perhaps at the Renaissance, when kingship and fatherhood fell, Europe drifted into a very dangerous half-truth: of liberty and equality. Perhaps the men who went to America felt this, and so repudiated the old world altogether. Went one better than Europe. Liberty in America has meant so far the breaking away from *all* dominion. The true liberty will only begin when Americans discover IT, and proceed possibly to fulfill IT. IT being the deepest *whole* self of man, the self in its wholeness, not idealistic halfness.

That's why the Pilgrim Fathers came to America, then; and that's why we come. Driven by IT. We cannot see that invisible winds carry us, as they carry swarms of locusts, that invisible magnetism brings us as it brings the migrating birds to their unfore-known goal. But it is so. We are not the marvelous choosers and deciders we think we are. IT chooses for us, and decides for us. Unless of course we are just escaped slaves, vulgarly cocksure of our ready-made destiny. But if we are living people, in touch with the source, IT drives us and decides us. We are free only so long as we obey. When we run counter, and think we will do as we like, we just flee around like Orestes pursued by the Eumenides.[4]

And still, when the great day begins, when Americans have at last discovered America and their own wholeness, still there will be the vast number of escaped slaves to reckon with, those who have no cocksure, ready-made destinies.

Which will win in America, the escaped slaves, or the new whole men?

The real American day hasn't begun yet. Or at least, not yet sunrise. So far it has been the false dawn. That is, in the progressive American consciousness there has been the one dominant desire, to do away with the old thing. Do away with masters, exalt the will of the people. The will of the people being nothing but a figment, the exalting doesn't count for much. So, in the name of the will of the people, get rid of masters. When you have got rid of masters, you are left with this mere phrase of the will of the people. Then you pause and bethink yourself, and try to recover your own wholeness.

So much for the conscious American motive, and for democracy over here. Democracy in America is just the tool with which the old mastery of Europe, the European spirit, is undermined. Europe destroyed, potentially, American democracy will evaporate. America will begin.

American consciousness has so far been a false dawn. The negative ideal of democracy. But underneath, and contrary to this open

4. In Greek mythology Orestes was pursued by the Eumenides or Furies (avenging goddesses) for killing his mother, Clytemnestra, who had killed his father, Agamemnon.

ideal, the first hints and revelations of IT. IT, the American whole soul.

You have got to pull the democratic and idealistic clothes off American utterance, and see what you can of the dusky body of IT underneath.

"Henceforth be masterless."

Henceforth be mastered.

QUESTIONS

1. By what means does Lawrence try to overcome his audience's probable disagreement with his views? How persuasive is he? Explain.
2. Compare Lawrence's definition of liberty with Lincoln's (p. 999).
3. On page 1036 Lawrence speaks of "the deepest self." Does the "IT" in the following sentences refer to "the deepest self" alone? Explain whether the discussion of "IT" changes or expands the meaning conveyed by the term "the deepest self."

PAUL A. FREUND

5-to-4: Are the Justices Really Objective?[1]

The recurrence of 5-to-4 decisions of the Supreme Court raises once again the question whether the judicial process is really objective in resolving important issues of constitutional law.

Given a constitutional text written in plain and, for the most part, nontechnical English, how are we to explain the sharp divergence of views in applying the Constitution to an undisputed set of facts? Is there no explanation except that the judges are free to impose their personal social beliefs on the country in the name of the Constitution?

The first thing to observe is that constitutional guarantees like due process of law, freedom of speech, press, and assembly, and equal protection of the laws do not supply ready-made answers to concrete, changing, and unforeseen problems as those problems arise in life. Moreover, various constitutional guarantees may point in opposite directions. Criminal trials are to be fair, and the press is to be free; how then do we decide whether the news media may or may not publish distorted and sensational accounts of a criminal suspect or a trial in progress?

Working with mandates so deliberately spacious and sometimes ambiguous as these, the wonder may well be that there is as much

1. This essay first appeared in *The Boston Globe* in 1967.

agreement as we actually find among the judges in their resolution of the controversies before them. For the dramatic dissents that capture public attention should not obscure the very substantial measure of common ground among the judges. One of the recent 5-to-4 decisions that captured public attention was the case of the civil rights demonstrators who were convicted for refusing to leave the courtyard of a jail. Justice Black's majority opinion was widely regarded as a significant retreat by the court from its previous positions.[2] Actually, all the members of the court would clearly have agreed that a demonstration in the gallery of a legislative hall could be punished without any infringement of freedom of speech or assembly. By the same token, there would have been agreement that a peaceful demonstration in the public park would have been immune from prosecution. Thus the precise and narrow issue was whether a demonstration in the courtyard of a jail was more like that in a legislative hall or in a public park. It is hardly astonishing that an answer is not to be found in the constitutional text.

Granted that the cleavages may not be as wide or as deep as the rhetoric of the opinions might suggest, the question still remains: how are we to account for the differences that do exist, except in terms of willful and unconstrained predilection? When Justice Cardozo had to describe the judicial process, he referred to several ingredients that enter into a decision; the most important, in his view, were logic, history, and social utility. The real problem is how they shall be mixed in order to reach a satisfying conclusion. When this kind of question was put to Justice Frankfurter, he was fond of quoting the reply of Velázquez to a lady who asked him how he mixed his paints. "Madame," he said, "I mix them with taste."

Two recent examples will illustrate how judges have to mix their ingredients with judgment as artists mix theirs with taste.

The Supreme Court ruled in another 5-to-4 decision that Georgia might elect its governor by vote of the Legislature after a popular election produced no majority for any candidate. The dissenters argued that this result was repugnant to the principle of the reapportionment cases, the equality of weight to each person's vote, since the Legislature might select for governor a candidate who would not prevail in a runoff.

On the other hand, Justice Black for the majority reasoned that Georgia could regard the popular vote as having exhausted itself and a new kind of election as having been substituted in which each legislator was free to vote his own choice. Both opinions were

2. In the decision referred to (Adderley v. Florida), the majority held that some places, such as courtrooms, were not appropriate for demonstrations and that hence the state had the right to prosecute. This represented a retreat from previous decisions, since it placed limits on places where free speech and assembly could be exercised.

perfectly logical; they simply differed in the premises from which they started. The dissent regarded the whole selection process as a unit, while the majority looked on it as two separate processes. In choosing between these premises, the dissent would have extended the majoritarian philosophy of the reapportionment cases. Speaking for the court, Justice Black gave controlling weight to the long history of the legislative role in the election of a governor in Georgia, a role dating back to the state constitution of 1824. Both positions were rationally defensible. What would be indefensible is a judicial decision motivated by a personal preference for candidate Maddox or candidate Callaway.

The other illustration involves the validity of a poll tax as a condition of voting in state elections. Here the court ruled the condition on the suffrage to be a violation of equal protection of the laws. Justice Black, dissenting, relied heavily on the long history of the poll tax in relation to voting rights, reflecting a tolerable judgment that the privilege of voting might be made to rest on a financial stake of the voter in his government.

But the majority were not persuaded by the weight of this history, in view of marked changes in the sharing of tax burdens and in our general outlook on the relevance of poverty to the rights of citizenship. There is no suggestion that Justice Black is personally more enamored of the poll tax than are his colleagues.

The upshot is that judges are constrained but not wholly so, and are free but by no means completely at large. This ought not to be so surprising when we recall that even scientists, who are thought to be engaged in an exact discipline, differ sharply when they reach frontier questions. On the same evidence and with the same principles of reasoning one astronomer will maintain the "big-bang" view of the cosmos and another the "steady-state" theory. So, also, will one philosopher maintain a theory of freedom of the will and another of determinism.

The judges, like the scientists and the philosophers, may see the same phenomenon in different lights, with different predictions of what will in time satisfy thoughtful minds. The pursuit of justice, after all, is not necessarily easier than the pursuit of truth.

FELIX FRANKFURTER
Haley v. Ohio[1]

[In this case, Justice Frankfurter cast the deciding vote to help form the necessary majority for reversing a conviction in a state court because of the methods used by the police in securing the confession on which it was based. His opinion explaining why he did so illustrates dramatically the extent to which it continues to be true that whether a conviction will be upset depends on the way the Justices see the circumstances in the particular case.

Arrested on Friday evening for the murder of a storekeeper, Haley, a fifteen-year-old Negro, was questioned for five hours during the night, without counsel or family being present, and was not brought before a magistrate until Tuesday. His mother was not allowed to see him until Thursday. Said Justice William O. Douglas for the Court: "A 15-year-old lad, questioned through the dead of night by relays of police, is a ready victim of the inquisition. Mature men possibly might stand the ordeal from midnight to 5 A.M. But we cannot believe that a lad of tender years is a match for the police in such a contest. He needs counsel and support if he is not to become the victim first of fear, then of panic. He needs someone on whom to lean lest the overpowering presence of the law, as he knows it, crush him. No friend stood at the side of this 15-year-old boy as the police, working in relays, questioned him hour after hour, from midnight until dawn. No lawyer stood guard to make sure that the police went so far and no farther, to see to it that they stopped short of the point where he became the victim of coercion." Chief Justice Vinson and Justices Reed, Jackson, and Burton dissented.

Mr. Justice Frankfurter's concurring opinion said in part:]

In a recent series of cases, beginning with *Brown* v. *Mississippi*, 297 U.S. 278, the Court has set aside convictions coming here from State courts because they were based on confessions admitted under circumstances that offended the requirements of the "due process" exacted from the States by the Fourteenth Amendment. If the rationale of those cases ruled this, we would dispose of it *per curiam*[2] with the mere citation of the cases. They do not rule it. Since at best this Court's reversal of a State court's conviction for want of due process always involves a delicate exercise of power and since there is sharp division as to the propriety of its exercise in this case, I deem it appropriate to state as explicitly as possible why, although I have doubts and difficulties, I cannot support affirmance of the conviction.

The doubts and difficulties derive from the very nature of the problem before us. They arise frequently when this Court is obliged to give definiteness to "the vague contours" of Due Process or, to

---

1. *Haley* v. *Ohio*, 332 U.S. 596, 601 (1948). From *The Constitutional World of Mr. Justice Frankfurter*, ed. Samuel J. Konefsky. The introductory note is by Mr. Konefsky.

2. "Through the court"—that is, by a decision rendered without elaborate discussion.

change the figure, to spin judgment upon State action out of that gossamer concept. Subtle and even elusive as its criteria are, we cannot escape that duty of judicial review. The nature of the duty, however, makes it especially important to be humble in exercising it. Humility in this context means an alert self-scrutiny so as to avoid infusing into the vagueness of a Constitutional command one's merely private notions. Like other mortals, judges, though unaware, may be in the grip of prepossessions. The only way to relax such a grip, the only way to avoid finding in the Constitution the personal bias one has placed in it, is to explore the influences that have shaped one's unanalyzed views in order to lay bare prepossessions.

A lifetime's preoccupation with criminal justice, as prosecutor, defender of civil liberties and scientific student, naturally leaves one with views. Thus, I disbelieve in capital punishment. But as a judge I could not impose the views of the very few States who through bitter experience have abolished capital punishment upon all the other States, by finding that "due process" proscribes it. Again, I do not believe that even capital offenses by boys of fifteen should be dealt with according to the conventional criminal procedure. It would, however, be bald judicial usurpation to hold that States violate the Constitution in subjecting minors like Haley to such a procedure. If a State, consistently with the Fourteenth Amendment, may try a boy of fifteen charged with murder by the ordinary criminal procedure, I cannot say that such a youth is never capable of that free choice of action which, in the eyes of the law, makes a confession "voluntary."

But whether a confession of a lad of fifteen is "voluntary" and as such admissible, or "coerced" and thus wanting in due process, is not a matter of mathematical determination. Essentially it invites psychological judgment—a psychological judgment that reflects deep, even if inarticulate, feelings of our society. Judges must divine that feeling as best they can from all the relevant evidence and light which they can bring to bear for a confident judgment of such an issue, and with every endeavor to detach themselves from their merely private views. . . .

While the issue thus formulated appears vague and impalpable, it cannot be too often repeated that the limitations which the Due Process Clause of the Fourteenth Amendment placed upon the methods by which the States may prosecute for crime cannot be more narrowly conceived. This Court must give the freest possible scope to States in the choice of their methods of criminal procedure. But these procedures cannot include methods that may fairly be deemed to be in conflict with deeply rooted feelings of the community. . . . Of course this is a most difficult test to apply, but apply it we must, warily, and from case to case.

This brings me to the precise issue on the record before us.

Suspecting a fifteen-year-old boy of complicity in murder resulting from attempted robbery, at about midnight the police took him from his home to police headquarters. There he was questioned for about five hours by at least five police officers who interrogated in relays of two or more. About five o'clock in the morning this procedure culminated in what the police regarded as a confession, whereupon it was formally reduced to writing. During the course of the interrogation the boy was not advised that he was not obliged to talk, that it was his right if he chose to say not a word, nor that he was entitled to have the benefit of counsel or the help of his family. Bearing upon the safeguards of these rights, the Chief of Police admitted that while he knew that the boy "had a right to remain mute and not answer any questions" he did not know that it was the duty of the police to apprise him of that fact. Unquestionably, during this whole period he was held incommunicado. Only after the nightlong questioning had resulted in disclosures satisfactory to the police and as such to be documented, was there read to the boy a clause giving the conventional formula about his constitutional right to make or withhold a statement and stating that if he makes it, he makes it of his "own free will." Do these uncontested facts justify a State court in finding that the boy's confession was "voluntary," or do the circumstances by their very nature preclude a finding that a deliberate and responsible choice was exercised by the boy in the confession that came at the end of five hours' questioning?

The answer, as has already been intimated, depends on an evaluation of psychological factors, or, more accurately stated, upon the pervasive feeling of society regarding such psychological factors. Unfortunately, we cannot draw upon any formulated expression of the existence of such feeling. Nor are there available experts on such matters to guide the judicial judgment. Our Constitutional system makes it the Court's duty to interpret those feelings of society to which the Due Process Clause gives legal protection. Because of their inherent vagueness the tests by which we are to be guided are most unsatisfactory, but such as they are we must apply them.

The Ohio courts have in effect denied that the very nature of the circumstances of the boy's confession precludes a finding that it was voluntary. Their denial carries great weight, of course. It requires much to be overborne. But it does not end the matter. Against it we have the judgment that comes from judicial experience with the conduct of criminal trials as they pass in review before this Court. An impressive series of cases in this and other courts admonishes of the temptations to abuse of police endeavors to secure confessions from suspects, through protracted questioning, carried on in secrecy, with the inevitable disquietude and fears police interrogations naturally engender in individuals questioned while held incommunicado, without the aid of counsel and unprotected by the safeguards of a judicial inquiry. Disinterested zeal for the public good does not assure either wisdom or right in the methods it pursues. A report of President Hoover's National Commission on Law Observance and Enforcement gave proof of the fact, unfortunately, that these potentialities of abuse were not the imaginings of mawkish sentimentality, nor their tolerance desirable or necessary for a stern policy against crime. Legislation throughout the country reflects a similar belief that detention for purposes of eliciting confessions through secret, persistent, long-continued interrogation violates sentiments deeply embedded in the feelings of our people. . . .

It is suggested that Haley's guilt could easily have been established without the confession elicited by the sweating process of the night's secret interrogation. But this only affords one more proof that in guarding against misuse of the law enforcement process the effective detection of crime and the prosecution of criminals are furthered and not hampered. Such constitutional restraints of decency derive from reliance upon the resources of intelligence in dealing with crime and discourage the too easy temptations of unimaginative crude force, even when such force is not brutally employed. . . .

It would disregard standards that we cherish as part of our faith in the strength and well-being of a rational, civilized society to hold that a confession is "voluntary" simply because the confession is the product of a sentient choice. "Conduct under duress involves a choice," . . . and conduct devoid of physical pressure but not leaving a free exercise of choice is the product of duress as much so as choice reflecting physical constraint.

Unhappily we have neither physical nor intellectual weights and measures by which judicial judgment can determine when pressures in securing a confession reach the coercive intensity that calls for the exclusion of a statement so secured. Of course, the police meant to exercise pressure upon Haley to make him talk. That was the very purpose of their procedure. In concluding that the pressures that were exerted in this case to make a lad of fifteen talk when the Constitution gives him the right to keep silent, and when the situation was so contrived that appreciation of his rights and thereby the means of asserting them were effectively withheld from him by the police, I do not believe I express a merely personal bias against such a procedure. Such a finding, I believe, reflects those fundamental notions of fairness and justice in the determination of guilt or innocence which lie embedded in the feelings of the American people and are enshrined in the Due Process Clause of the Fourteenth Amendment. To remove the inductment to resort to such methods this Court has repeatedly denied use of the fruits of illicit methods.

Accordingly, I think Haley's confession should have been excluded and the conviction based upon it should not stand.

QUESTIONS

1. Why does Frankfurter have "doubts and difficulties" in taking the stand he does? What specific facts in the case weighed most heavily with him when he arrived at his opinion?
2. How does Frankfurter distinguish between a "Constitutional command" and "one's merely private notions"?
3. What definition of "voluntary" does Frankfurter give? How does he develop it?
4. Frankfurter nowhere gives a formal definition of "due process." What can be deduced about that concept from his use of the term?
5. What does Frankfurter mean by the "deeply rooted feelings of the community"? What other examples of such feelings might be given?

TALBOT SMITH

Salmon *v.* Bagley Laundry Company[1]

[Mrs. Salmon was employed by the defendant laundry, her job being to feed clothes into a mangle and to fold them when they came out.

On the day in question, Mrs. Salmon began work at 8:00 A.M. and worked until the morning rest period which began at 9:20 A.M. She and other employees then went to a nearby restaurant where she had coffee. On returning from the restaurant and on ascending the step outside the front door of the laundry, which step was on the laundry's premises, she slipped and injured her left wrist.

Prior to the plaintiff's injury, a contract had been negotiated by her union, providing for the ten-minute rest period in the morning and another in the afternoon. During these times employees were permitted to leave the laundry for a coffee-break. When the coffee-break period arrived, a whistle would blow and the employees could go out for coffee or take care of other personal wants. No deduction of wages was made during the period. Prior to the inauguration of the ten-minute rest period under the contract, the employees were permitted, at their own discretion, but with the consent of the employer, to go out of the laundry to get coffee and sandwiches, as the laundry did not provide such facilities. The main purpose in selecting a particular time for the rest period, was to eliminate the previous confusion arising from departure from the laundry by employees at irregular periods.

The application by Mrs. Salmon for workmen's compensation for her injuries sustained in the manner above described was granted by Workmen's Compensation Commission, which said: "It is our opinion that plain-

1. 344 Mich. 471 (1955).

tiff sustained an accidental injury while performing an act which was beneficial to her employer, incident to and within the ambit of her employment and conclusive of the proposition that her injury arose out of and in the course of her employment." The defendant employer and its insurance company appealed from the workmen's compensation award for Mrs. Salmon. A majority of the (Michigan) Supreme Court reversed the Workmen's Compensation Commission. Justice Smith dissented.

The majority held that the basic question was whether Mrs. Salmon's injuries arose out of and in the course of her employment. The court went on to say: "The right to control or direct an employee is an essential element in determining whether the relationship of employer and employee exists." The court concluded that in the case of Mrs. Salmon, the right to control the actions or activities of the employees during the noon hour lunch period or coffee-break was absent. In the instant case plaintiff had the option of leaving the laundry for coffee or remaining within the building for a rest period. During this period her employer had no control over her actions, nor can it be said that she was actively engaged in rendering a service to her employer. The fact that she was paid during this 10-minute interval has no bearing upon whether her injury arose out of and during the course of her employment. During this period plaintiff was exercising a privilege common to all employees of the defendant company. The facts in this case do not warrant a finding that her injury arose out of and during the course of her employment. Excerpts from Justice Smith's dissent follow:]

. . . The fundamental issue posed by this simple case is so sweeping that we may be justified in casting a glance backward before we begin to appraise the present. It was the combination of the mechanization of industry and the development of the corporate device which brought together large masses of people and great pools of capital. As a result, we have been showered with blessings of a material nature. But it must never be forgotten that there is a poor relation in the back room, a tragic by-product of our progress, the injured worker, sometimes grotesque, sometimes severely crippled. His number is appalling. Somers' recent treatise *Workmen's Compensation* contains in readily available form the summaries, respecting disabling work injuries, of the United States Bureau of Labor Statistics, expressed by the authors in the following language (p. 2):

Another way of putting it would be that one American worker will have been killed or crippled every three minutes. Another will have been injured every 11 seconds.

Multiply the daily casualty list by the 260 days which constitute an average American work year and you arrive at the annual human toll which modern industry exacts: about 16,000 fatalities, 91,000 permanent disabilities—of which some 1600 are "total" such as paraplegia, broken backs, blindness, or double amputations, the others representing loss, or loss of use of, an arm, a leg, an eye, a finger or part thereof—and nearly two million temporary disabilities.

What have we done about this injured worker? It is clear what we have done. First of all, we no longer shoulder him aside and leave him to his own devices. Rejected also is the theory of the handout. What we have given him is called "compensation," which, though modest, was to be certain and speedy, and the reason we gave it was because of widespread dissatisfaction with the application of common-law tort theories to the injuries of workmen. The common law, in truth, was almost helpless to meet the challenge of the industrial age. "To speak of the common-law personal injury action as a remedy for the problem was to jest with serious subjects, to give a stone to one who asks for bread," said the supreme court of Wisconsin in *Borgnis* v. *Falk Company,* 147 Wis. 327, 348. Why was the common law helpless in this situation? Largely because the courts looked to tort concepts, developed in strikingly dissimilar situations, for precedent. At the risk of oversimplifying a most complex matter we observe that fault and negligence, in the ordinary tort law sought to be applied by the early courts, were personal. How, then, could the employer be forced to answer for the injury? He (as distinguished from the early master who worked shoulder to shoulder with his apprentice and servant) usually was not even in the plant at the time of the injury. . . .

The atmosphere, in brief, was one of sorrow and frustration. The industrial revolution had arrived and with it had come mechanization. But the machine was as contemptuous of human flesh as it was of impersonal steel. The face of the courts was turned, turned by what was thought to be precedent and *stare decisis.*[1] Our sons cried out.

Our answer was given in the form of the great workmen's compensation acts, humanitarian measures which, all courts agree, are to be construed liberally (e.g., *Adkins* v. *Rives Plating Corp.,* 338 Mich. 265) to accomplish their healing mission of solace and relief . . .

. . . How is it possible, under an act passed "to ameliorate a social condition—not to define a situation or fix a liability by adherence to the old common law," an act to be construed both reasonably and liberally, how is it possible that the laundress before us, injured on the employer's premises during the working day, in an activity sanctioned by contract and paid for by her employer, can find herself without recovery? In reply we are told that the employer lacked "control" over her at the time she was hurt.

From whence comes this requirement of "control"? There is nothing in the act fixing liability in such terms. It comes from the law of torts. It is blood brother to contributory negligence, assumption of risk, the fellow-servant rule[2] and the other tort concepts which were utilized so effectively in the common-law courts to bar employees' recovery; so effectively, in fact, that this act was

1. "To stand by decided matters"; the policy of judge and lawyers to "follow precedent."

2. The rule exempting an employer from liability for injuries suffered by an employee if these were caused by the negligence of another employee (the first employee's fellow servant).

passed in response to peremptory and overwhelming public demand. I cannot agree that we should import this tort concept into this great remedial statute. It is foreign to the purposes of the act. . . .

Consider the application of the control test to the facts before us. The claimant, when she came to work that morning, was concededly an employee. As such, in the normal situation, and we find nothing in this record to indicate otherwise, she comes to work when the employer says to come. She goes when he says to go. She stops at his command. She performs her routine tasks as he directs them to be performed. If her work is unsatisfactory, or business is "slack" she is free, even requested, to seek employment elsewhere. She is dependent, economically, upon her wage, and she earns it from her employer by doing his bidding. In all of this I find complete control, if we require such. Now, when did this control cease? When she went for coffee? (Even the mechanics of the coffee break, as we gather them from the record, demonstrate the plenary control exercised. A whistle blew. Production stopped. The machines were shut down. The front door was thrown open [in the winter] and those who wished went for coffee. Another whistle, the doors were closed, and the rest period was at a close. I have difficulty in saying that all of this is not control. Even from whistle to whistle there is at least a smell of control.)

To repeat, there was indisputably an employment relation until the coffee whistle blew. All tests, even control, could lead only to such conclusion. Was this employment relation suspended at the blast of the whistle because of lack of "control"?

If so, it is well to observe that we have, throughout the working day, not continuous employment, but a checkerboard of legal relationships. The workman comes to his job. At that point he is an employee. He turns from the lathe to blow his nose. Plainly the board of directors does not "control" this operation. He is no longer an employee. He returns to the work assigned. Once again he is an employee. He goes to the toilet. He returns. He takes the coffee break. Again, he loses his employment status.

I must reject the checkerboard resulting from the application of the control concept. It must be apparent that the answer to our problem is not to be found in the ancient and dubious concept of control, lifted from the law of torts . . .

. . . The act provides, very simply, that injuries suffered in the course of employment be recompensed . . . Do, then, the words "course of employment" include the coffee break described?

The question can, consistently with the purpose of the act, as described in *Mackin* v. *Detroit Timken Axle Company*, be answered only in the affirmative. The manufacture of the product involves a series of casualties and deaths. The cost of the product must bear the burden, thus spreading the burden among the consumers rather than concentrating it on the helpless family unit involved. The words "course of employment" in our act include the coffee break simply because the product, which must shoulder the burdens of injuries in its manufacture, is made by a human being. He brings to his work all of his human characteristics, his frailties as well as his virtues. We cannot, either actually or legally, make the precise excisions of the surgeon. We cannot remove from him, and put to work for his employer, only his strength. His strength goes hand in hand with his temper. It is impossible for us to employ only the grace and charm of the female worker. We hire as well her lively curiosity. We collect these people by the hundreds, even thousands, and we put them to work, sometimes amid noise and vibration, sometimes in smoke and steam. They get tired. They get hungry. They get thirsty. They have to go to the toilet. The day wears on and tempers grow short. Relief is sought in horseplay. Trips to the water cooler and coffee urn grow in number and duration. This is the course of employment. "Course of employment" is not a sterile form of words. It is descriptive of life in the industrial age. These human deviations from the course of the automaton do not suspend the employer-employee relationship. They are not departures from employment, but the very substance of it. They are the inevitable concomitants of the working relationship and conditions which produce the product. Its cost must reflect the fatigue, the irritations, and sometimes the blood that went into it. It is here that we find the explanation for the horseplay cases, the curiosity cases, and the assault cases. Such problems will cease with the arrival of automation.

I take it to be clear, then, that the course of employment of a human being . . . includes not only his repetitive acts at the machine to which he is assigned, but includes, as well, his ministrations to his human needs. . . .

Here, then, is the reason for the compensation award: His injury was suffered during his working day while he was doing a natural thing, a thing which an employee, while working, might reasonably do. The fundamental inquiry is whether or not the act in question, either because of its nature, or local custom, or contractual provision, is reasonably to be regarded as part of the on-the-job activities of the human being involved, a part of his normal and reasonable sphere of activities. If so, it takes place "in the course of his employment." . . .

Prose Forms: Apothegms

[At the beginning of Bacon's essay "Of Truth," jesting Pilate asks, "What is truth?" and does not stay for an answer. Perhaps Pilate asked in jest because he thought the question foolish; perhaps because he thought an answer impossible. Something of Pilate's skepticism is in most of us, but something too of a belief that there is truth, even if—as the history of philosophy teaches us—determining its nature may be enormously difficult. We readily assume some things to be true even if we hesitate to say what ultimately is Truth.

The test of truth most often is an appeal to the observed facts of experience. The observation of experience yields knowledge; the generalized statement of that knowledge yields a concept of the experience; the concise, descriptive form in which that concept is expressed we call variously, apothegm, proverb, maxim, or aphorism. Thus Sir James Mackintosh can speak of apothegms as "the condensed good sense of nations," because the apothegm conveys the distilled observations of men about their own persistent conduct. To hear the familiar "Absence makes the heart grow fonder" is to be reminded of a general truth which you and the world acknowledge. It does not matter that the equally familiar "Out of sight, out of mind" seems to contradict the other saying; both are true but applicable to different situations. Both statements are immediately recognizable as true and neither requires to be argued for, representing as they do the collective experience of mankind intelligently observed.

Not everyone is as astute an observer as the writer of apothegms and maxims, of course, but everyone is presumably capable of perceiving their rightness. What we perceive first is the facts to which the saying applies. When Franklin says "An empty bag cannot stand upright" (in 1740 he obviously had in mind a cloth bag), we acknowledge that this is the condition of the empty bag—and of ourselves when we are empty. Or when La Rochefoucauld says "We are all strong enough to endure the misfortunes of others," he too observes a condition that exists among men.

Many aphoristic assertions claim their validity primarily in descriptive terms. But the descriptive "is" in most apothegms and maxims is joined to a normative "ought" and the sayings therefore convey admonitions about and judgments of the conditions they describe.

"Waste not, want not" is a simple illustration of this use of fact to admonish. Mark Twain assumes as observed fact the value of illusions, and goes on to offer a warning: "Don't part with your illusions. When they are gone you may still exist, but you have ceased to live." The condition of "ought" need not always be admonitory; it may be the implied judgment in La Rochefoucauld's assertion that "It is the habit of mediocre minds to condemn all that is beyond their grasp." The judgment is explicit in Franklin's "Fish and visitors stink in three days." And Bierce's definitions of ordinary words are not specifications of meanings in the way of ordinary dictionaries, but critical concepts of the experiences to which the words point.

"Wisdom" or "good sense," then, is the heart of the apothegm or maxim, the conjunction of "is" and "ought" in an assertion of universal truth. Unlike ordinary assertions of fact or opinion usually concerned with particular rather than universal experience, the wise saying is complete in its brevity. Before the ordinary assertion is allowed to hold, we require that the assumptions on which it rests, the implications it carries, the critical concepts and terms it contains, be examined closely and explored or justified. If someone says that the modern college student wants most to succeed materially in life, we want to be satisfied about what constitutes "modern," which college students (and where) are referred to, what else is involved in the comparative "most," what specifically is meant by "materially." But the apothegm assumes facts widely known and accepted, and in its judgments invokes values or attitudes readily intelligible to the great majority. It is the truth as most men experience it.

In a sense, every writer's concern is ultimately with truth. Certainly the essayist is directly concerned, in his definition and ordering of ideas, to say what is true and, somehow, to say it "new." Much of what he says is of the nature of assertion about particular experience; he must therefore be at pains to handle such matters as assumptions and logical proofs carefully and deliberately. But he cannot always be starting from scratch, not daring to assume anything, trusting no certain knowledge or experience or beliefs held in common with his fellows. Careful he must be, but also aware that available to him, in addition to methods of logical analysis and proof, rules of evidence, and the other means to effective exposition, is the whole memory and record of the vast experience of the race contained in a people's apothegms and aphorisms. In them is a treasury of truths useful to many demands of clarity and precision. And in them, too, is a valuable lesson in the way a significantly large body of experience— direct, in a person's day-to-day encounters; indirect, in his study of all forms of history—can be observed, conceptualized, and then expressed in an economy of language brief in form, comprehensive in meaning, and satisfyingly true.]

W. H. AUDEN: Apothegms

Some books are undeservedly forgotten; none are undeservedly remembered.

You do not educate a person's palate by telling him that what he has been in the habit of eating—watery, overboiled cabbage, let us say—is disgusting, but by persuading him to try a dish of vegetables which have been properly cooked. With some people, it is true, you seem to get quicker results by telling them—"Only vulgar people like overcooked cabbage; the best people like cabbage as the Chinese cook it"—but the results are less likely to be lasting.

No poet or novelist wishes he were the only one who ever lived, but most of them wish they were the only one alive, and quite a number fondly believe their wish has been granted.

The integrity of a writer is more threatened by appeals to his social conscience, his political or religious convictions, than by appeals to his cupidity. It is morally less confusing to be goosed by a traveling salesman than by a bishop.

Only a minor talent can be a perfect gentleman; a major talent is always more than a bit of a cad. Hence the importance of minor writers—as teachers of good manners. Now and again, an exquisite minor work can make a master feel thoroughly ashamed of himself.

Narcissus does not fall in love with his reflection because it is beautiful, but because it is *his*. If it were his beauty that enthralled him he would be set free in a few years by its fading.

"After all," sighed Narcissus the hunchback, "on *me* it looks good."

Our sufferings and weaknesses, in so far as they are personal, *our* sufferings, *our* weaknesses, are of no literary interest whatsoever. They are only interesting in so far as we can see them as typical of the human condition. A suffering, a weakness, which cannot be expressed as an aphorism should not be mentioned.

The same rules apply to self-examination as apply to confession to a priest: *be brief, be blunt, be gone*. Be brief, be blunt, forget. The scrupuland is a nasty specimen.

In a state of panic, a man runs round in circles by himself. In a state of joy, he links hands with others and they dance round in a circle together.

A sense of humor develops in a society to the degree that its members are simultaneously conscious of being each a unique person and of being all in common subjection to unalterable laws.

Among those whom I like or admire, I can find no common denominator, but among those whom I love, I can: all of them make me laugh.

If Homer had tried reading the *Iliad* to the gods on Olympus, they would either have started to fidget and presently asked if he hadn't got something a little lighter, or, taking it as a comic poem, would have roared with laughter or possibly, even, reacting like ourselves to a tear-jerking movie, have poured pleasing tears.

AMBROSE BIERCE: *from* The Devil's Dictionary

abdication, *n.* An act whereby a sovereign attests his sense of the high temperature of the throne.

abscond, *v.i.* To "move in a mysterious way," commonly with the property of another.

absent, *adj.* Peculiarly exposed to the tooth of detraction; vilified; hopelessly in the wrong; superseded in the consideration and affection of another.

accident, *n.* An inevitable occurrence due to the action of immutable natural laws.

accordion, *n.* An instrument in harmony with the sentiments of an assassin.

achievement, *n.* The death of endeavor and the birth of disgust.

admiration, *n.* Our polite recognition of another's resemblance to ourselves.

alone, *adj.* In bad company.

applause, *n.* The echo of a platitude.

ardor, *n.* The quality that distinguishes love without knowledge.

bore, *n.* A person who talks when you wish him to listen.

cemetery, *n.* An isolated suburban spot where mourners match lies, poets write at a target and stone-cutters spell for a wager. The inscription following will serve to illustrate the success attained in these Olympian games:

> His virtues were so conspicuous that his enemies, unable to overlook them, denied them, and his friends, to whose loose lives they were a rebuke, represented them as vices. They are here commemorated by his family, who shared them.

childhood, *n.* The period of human life intermediate between the idiocy of infancy and the folly of youth—two removes from the sin of manhood and three from the remorse of age.

Christian, *n.* One who believes that the New Testament is a divinely inspired book admirably suited to the spiritual needs of his neighbor. One who follows the teachings of Christ in so far as they are not inconsistent with a life of sin.

compulsion, *n.* The eloquence of power.

congratulation, *n.* The civility of envy.

conservative, *n.* A statesman who is enamored of existing evils, as distinguished from the Liberal, who wishes to replace them with others.

consult, *v.t.* To seek another's approval of a course already decided on.

contempt, *n.* The feeling of a prudent man for an enemy who is too formidable safely to be opposed.

coward, *n.* One who in a perilous emergency thinks with his legs.

debauchee, *n.* One who has so earnestly pursued pleasure that he has had the misfortune to overtake it.

destiny, *n.* A tyrant's authority for crime and a fool's excuse for failure.

diplomacy, *n.* The patriotic art of lying for one's country.

distance, *n.* The only thing that the rich are willing for the poor to call theirs and keep.

duty, *n.* That which sternly impels us in the direction of profit, along the line of desire.

education, *n.* That which discloses to the wise and disguises from the foolish their lack of understanding.

erudition, *n.* Dust shaken out of a book into an empty skull.

extinction, *n.* The raw material out of which theology created the future state.

faith, *n.* Belief without evidence in what is told by one who speaks without knowledge, of things without parallel.

genealogy, *n.* An account of one's descent from an ancestor who did not particularly care to trace his own.

ghost, *n.* The outward and visible sign of an inward fear.

habit, *n.* A shackle for the free.

heaven, *n.* A place where the wicked cease from troubling you with talk of their personal affairs, and the good listen with attention while you expound your own.

historian, *n.* A broad-gauge gossip.

hope, *n.* Desire and expectation rolled into one.

hypocrite, *n.* One who, professing virtues that he does not respect, secures the advantage of seeming to be what he despises.

impiety, *n.* Your irreverence toward my deity.

impunity, *n.* Wealth.

language, *n.* The music with which we charm the serpents guarding another's treasure.

logic, *n.* The art of thinking and reasoning in strict accordance with the limitations and incapacities of the human misunderstanding. The basic of logic is the syllogism, consisting of a major and a minor premise and a conclusion—thus:

Major Premise: Sixty men can do a piece of work sixty times as quickly as one man.

Minor Premise: One man can dig a post-hole in sixty seconds; therefore—

Conclusion: Sixty men can dig a post-hole in one second.

This may be called the syllogism arithmetical, in which, by combining logic and mathematics, we obtain a double certainty and are twice blessed.

love, *n.* A temporary insanity curable by marriage or by removal of the patient from the influences under which he incurred the disorder. This disease, like *caries* and many other ailments, is prevalent only among civilized races living under artificial conditions; barbarous nations breathing pure air and eating simple food enjoy immunity from its ravages. It is sometimes fatal, but more frequently to the physician than to the patient.

miracle, *n.* An act or event out of the order of nature and unaccountable, as beating a normal hand of four kings and an ace with four aces and a king.

monkey, *n.* An arboreal animal which makes itself at home in genealogical trees.

mouth, *n.* In man, the gateway to the soul; in woman, the outlet of the heart.

non-combatant, *n.* A dead Quaker.

platitude, *n.* The fundamental element and special glory of popular literature. A thought that snores in words that smoke. The wisdom of a million fools in the diction of a dullard. A fossil sentiment in artificial rock. A moral without the fable. All that is mortal of a departed truth. A demi-tasse of milk-and-morality. The Pope's-nose of a featherless peacock. A jelly-fish withering on the shore of the sea of thought. The cackle surviving the egg. A dessicated epigram.

pray, *v.* To ask that the laws of the universe be annulled in behalf of a single petitioner confessedly unworthy.

presidency, *n.* The greased pig in the field game of American politics.

prude, *n.* A bawd hiding behind the back of her demeanor.

rapacity, *n.* Providence without industry. The thrift of power.

reason, *v.i.* To weigh probabilities in the scales of desire.

religion, *n.* A daughter of Hope and Fear, explaining to Ignorance the nature of the Unknowable.

resolute, *adj.* Obstinate in a course that we approve.

retaliation, *n.* The natural rock upon which is reared the Temple of Law.

saint, *n.* A dead sinner revised and edited.

The Duchess of Orleans relates that the irreverent old calumniator, Marshal Villeroi, who in his youth had known St. Francis de Sales, said, on hearing him called saint: "I am delighted to hear that Monsieur de Sales is a saint. He was fond of saying indelicate things, and used to cheat at cards. In other respects he was a perfect gentleman, though a fool."

valor, *n.* A soldierly compound of vanity, duty and the gambler's hope:

> "Why have you halted?" roared the commander of a division at Chickamauga, who had ordered a charge; "move forward, sir, at once."
> "General," said the commander of the delinquent brigade, "I am persuaded that any further display of valor by my troops will bring them into collision with the enemy."

WILLIAM BLAKE: Proverbs of Hell

In seed time learn, in harvest teach, in winter enjoy.
Drive your cart and your plough over the bones of the dead.
The road of excess leads to the palace of wisdom.
Prudence is a rich, ugly old maid courted by Incapacity.
He who desires but acts not, breeds pestilence.
The cut worm forgives the plough.
Dip him in the river who loves water.
A fool sees not the same tree that a wise man sees.
He whose face gives no light, shall never become a star.
Eternity is in love with the productions of time.
The busy bee has no time for sorrow.
The hours of folly are measur'd by the clock; but of wisdom, no clock can measure.
All wholesome food is caught without a net or a trap.
Bring out number, weight, and measure in a year of dearth.
No bird soars too high, if he soars with his own wings.
A dead body revenges not injuries.
The most sublime act is to set another before you.
If the fool would persist in his folly he would become wise.
Folly is the cloak of knavery.
Shame is Pride's cloak.
Prisons are built with stones of Law, brothels with bricks of Religion.
The pride of the peacock is the glory of God.
The lust of the goat is the bounty of God.
The wrath of the lion is the wisdom of God.
The nakedness of woman is the work of God.
Excess of sorrow laughs. Excess of joy weeps.
The roaring of lions, the howling of wolves, the raging of the stormy sea, and the destructive sword are portions of eternity too great for the eye of man.
The fox condemns the trap, not himself.
Joys impregnate. Sorrows bring forth.

Let man wear the fell of the lion, woman the fleece of the sheep.

The bird a nest, the spider a web, man friendship.

The selfish, smiling fool, and the sullen, frowning fool shall be both thought wise, that they may be a rod.

What is now proved was once only imagin'd.

The rat, the mouse, the fox, the rabbit watch the roots; the lion, the tiger, the horse, the elephant watch the fruits.

The cistern contains: the fountain overflows.

One thought fills immensity.

Always be ready to speak your mind, and a base man will avoid you.

Everything possible to be believ'd is an image of truth.

The eagle never lost so much time as when he submitted to learn of the crow.

The fox provides for himself; but God provides for the lion.

Think in the morning. Act in the noon. Eat in the evening. Sleep in the night.

He who has suffer'd you to impose on him, knows you.

As the plough follows words, so God rewards prayers.

The tigers of wrath are wiser than the horses of instruction.

Expect poison from the standing water.

You never know what is enough unless you know what is more than enough.

Listen to the fool's reproach! it is a kingly title!

The eyes of fire, the nostrils of air, the mouth of water, the beard of earth.

The weak in courage is strong in cunning.

The apple tree never asks the beech how he shall grow; nor the lion, the horse, how he shall take his prey.

The thankful receiver bears a plentiful harvest.

If others had not been foolish, we should be so.

The soul of sweet delight can never be defil'd.

When thou seest an eagle, thou seest a portion of Genius; lift up thy head!

As the caterpillar chooses the fairest leaves to lay her eggs on, so the priest lays his curse on the fairest joys.

To create a little flower is the labor of ages.

Damn braces. Bless relaxes.

The best wine is the oldest, the best water the newest.

Prayers plough not! Praises reap not!

Joys laugh not! Sorrows weep not!

The head Sublime, the heart Pathos, the genitals Beauty, the hands and feet Proportion.

As the air to a bird or the sea to a fish, so is contempt to the contemptible.

The crow wish'd everything was black, the owl that everything was white.

Exuberance is Beauty.

If the lion was advised by the fox, he would be cunning.

Improvement makes straight roads; but the crooked roads without improvement are roads of Genius.

Sooner murder an infant in its cradle than nurse unacted desires.

Where man is not, nature is barren.

Truth can never be told so as to be understood, and not be believ'd.

Enough! or Too much.

SAMUEL L. CLEMENS: *from* Pudd'nhead Wilson's Calendars

Training is everything. The peach was once a bitter almond; cauliflower is nothing but cabbage with a college education.

As to the Adjective: when in doubt, strike it out.

Noise proves nothing. Often a hen who has merely laid an egg cackles as if she had laid an asteroid.

Everything human is pathetic. The secret source of Humor itself is not joy but sorrow. There is no humor in heaven.

We should be careful to get out of an experience only the wisdom that is in it—and stop there; lest we be like the cat that sits down on a hot stove-lid. She will never sit down on a hot stove-lid again, and that is well; but also she will never sit down on a cold one any more.

Truth is stranger than Fiction, but it is because Fiction is obliged to stick to possibilities; Truth isn't.

Man is the Only Animal that blushes. Or needs to.

When people do not respect us we are sharply offended; yet deep down in his private heart no man much respects himself.

There are several good protections against temptations but the surest is cowardice.

It takes your enemy and your friend, working together, to hurt you to the heart, the one to slander you and the other to get the news to you.

Let me make the superstitions of a nation and I care not who makes its laws or its songs either.

True irreverence is disrespect for another man's god.

Don't part with your illusions. When they are gone you may still exist but you have ceased to live.

Every one is a moon and has a dark side which he never shows to anybody.

BENJAMIN FRANKLIN: *from* Poor Richard's Almanack

Light purse, heavy heart.   1733
He's a fool that makes his doctor his heir.
Love well, whip well.
Hunger never saw bad bread.
Fools make feasts, and wise men eat 'em.
He that lies down with dogs, shall rise up with fleas.
He is ill clothed, who is bare of virtue.
There is no little enemy.

Without justice courage is weak..   1734
Where there's marriage without love, there will be love without
marriage.
Do good to thy friend to keep him, to thy enemy to gain him.
He that cannot obey, cannot command.
Marry your son when you will, but your daughter when you can.

Approve not of him who commends all you say.   1735
Necessity never made a good bargain.
Be slow in chusing a friend, slower in changing.
Three may keep a secret, if two of them are dead.
Deny self for self's sake.
To be humble to superiors is duty, to equals courtesy, to inferiors
nobleness.

Fish and visitors stink in three days.   1736
Do not do that which you would not have known.
Bargaining has neither friends nor relations.
Now I've a sheep and a cow, every body bids me good morrow.
God helps them that help themselves.
He that speaks much, is much mistaken.
God heals, and the doctor takes the fees.

There are no ugly loves, nor handsome prisons.   1737
Three good meals a day is bad living.

Who has deceiv'd thee so oft as thyself?   1738
Read much, but not many books.
Let thy vices die before thee.

He that falls in love with himself, will have no rivals.   1739
Sin is not hurtful because it is forbidden, but it is forbidden because it's hurtful.

An empty bag cannot stand upright.   1740

Learn of the skilful: he that teaches himself, hath a fool for his master.   1741

Death takes no bribes.   1742

An old man in a house is a good sign.   1744
Fear God, and your enemies will fear you.

He's a fool that cannot conceal his wisdom.   1745
Many complain of their memory, few of their judgment.

When the well's dry, we know the worth of water.   1746
The sting of a reproach is the truth of it.

Write injuries in dust, benefits in marble.   1747

Nine men in *ten* are suicides.   1749
A man in a passion rides a mad horse.

He is a governor that governs his passions, and he is a servant that serves them.   1750
Sorrow is good for nothing but sin.

Calamity and prosperity are the touchstones of integrity.   1752
Generous minds are all of kin.

Haste makes waste.   1753

The doors of wisdom are never shut.   1755

The way to be safe, is never to be secure.   1757

WILLIAM HAZLITT: *from* Characteristics

1. Of all virtues, magnanimity is the rarest. There are a hundred persons of merit for one who willingly acknowledges it in another.

13. Some people tell us all the harm—others as carefully conceal all the good they hear of us.

15. The silence of a friend commonly amounts to treachery. His not daring to say anything in our behalf implies a tacit censure.

23. Envy is a littleness of soul, which cannot see beyond a certain point, and if it does not occupy the whole space, feels itself excluded.

27. Those who are the most distrustful of themselves, are the most envious of others; as the most weak and cowardly are the most revengeful.

38. The wish is often "father to the thought"; but we are quite as apt to believe what we dread as what we hope.

46. We like characters and actions which we do not approve. There are amiable vices and obnoxious virtues, on the mere principle that our sympathy with a person who yields to obvious impulses (however prejudicial) is itself agreeable, while to sympathize with exercises of self-denial or fortitude, is a painful effort. Virtue costs the spectator, as well as the performer, something. We are touched by the immediate motives of actions, we judge of them by the consequences. We like a convivial character better than an abstemious one, because the idea of conviviality in the first instance is pleasanter than that of sobriety. For the same reason, we prefer generosity to justice, because the imagination lends itself more easily to an ebullition of feeling, than to the suppression of it on remote and abstract principles; and we like a good-natured fool, or even knave better than the severe professors of wisdom and morality. Cato, Brutus, etc. are characters to admire and applaud, rather than to love or imitate.

57. The surest way to make ourselves agreeable to others is by seeming to think them so. If we appear fully sensible of their good qualities, they will not complain of the want of them in us.

59. Silence is one great art of conversation. He is not a fool who knows when to hold his tongue; and a person may gain credit for sense, eloquence, wit, who merely says nothing to lessen the opinion which others have of these qualities in themselves.

61. A man who is always defending his friends from the most trifling charges, will be apt to make other people their enemies.

64. We do not like our friends the worse because they sometimes give us an opportunity to rail at them heartily. Their faults reconcile us to their virtues. Indeed, we never have much esteem or regard, except for those that we can afford to speak our minds of freely; whose follies vex us in proportion to our anxiety for their welfare, and who have plenty of redeeming points about them to balance their defects. When we "spy abuses" of this kind, it is a wiser and more generous proceeding to give vent to our impatience and ill-humor, than to brood over it, and let it, by sinking into our minds, poison the very sources of our goodwill.

85. The public have neither shame nor gratitude.

89. It is wonderful how soon men acquire talents for offices of trust and importance. The higher the situation, the higher the opinion it gives us of ourselves; and as is our confidence, so is our capacity. We *assume* an equality with circumstances.

105. The error in the reasonings of Mandeville, Rochefoucauld, and others, is this: they first find out that there is something mixed in the motives of all our actions, and they then proceed to argue, that they must all arise from one motive, *viz.* self-love. They make

the exception the rule. It would be easy to reverse the argument, and prove that our most selfish actions are disinterested. There is honor among thieves. Robbers, murderers, etc. do not commit those actions, from a pleasure in pure villainy, or for their own benefit only, but from a mistaken regard to the welfare or good opinion of those with whom they are immediately connected.

115. We do not hate those who injure us, if they do not at the same time wound our self-love. We can forgive any one sooner than those who lower us in our own opinion. It is no wonder, therefore, that we as often dislike others for their virtues as for their vices. We naturally hate whatever makes us despise ourselves.

127. We as often repent the good we have done as the ill.

131. The fear of punishment may be necessary to the suppression of vice; but it also suspends the finer motives to virtue.

134. Vulgar prejudices are those which arise out of accident, ignorance, or authority. Natural prejudices are those which arise out of the constitution of the human mind itself.

138. Most codes of morality proceed on a supposition of *Original Sin*; as if the only object was to coerce the headstrong propensities to vice, and there were no natural disposition to good in the mind, which it was possible to improve, refine, and cultivate.

139. This *negative* system of virtue leads to a very low style of moral sentiment. It is as if the highest excellence in a picture was to avoid gross defects in drawing; or in writing, instances of bad grammar. It ought surely to be our aim in virtue, as well as in other things, "to snatch a grace beyond the reach of art."

142. When the imagination is continually led to the brink of vice by a system of terror and denunciations, people fling themselves over the precipice from the mere dread of falling.

145. Honesty is one part of eloquence. We persuade others by being in earnest ourselves.

LA ROCHEFOUCAULD: *from* Maxims

Our virtues are mostly but vices in disguise.

14. Men not only forget benefits received and injuries endured; they even come to dislike those to whom they are indebted, while ceasing to hate those others who have done them harm. Diligence in returning good for good, and in exacting vengeance for evil, comes to be a sort of servitude which we do not readily accept.

19. We are all strong enough to endure the misfortunes of others.

20. The steadiness of the wise man is only the art of keeping his agitations locked within his breast.

25. Firmer virtues are required to support good fortune than bad.

28. Jealousy is, in its way, both fair and reasonable, since its intention is to preserve for ourselves something which is ours, or which we believe to be ours; envy, on the other hand, is a frenzy which cannot endure contemplating the possessions of others.

31. Were we faultless, we would not derive such satisfaction from remarking the faults of others.

38. Our promises are made in hope, and kept in fear.

50. A man convinced of his own merit will accept misfortune as an honor, for thus can he persuade others, as well as himself, that he is a worthy target for the arrows of fate.

56. To achieve a position in the world a man will do his utmost to appear already arrived.

59. There is no accident so disastrous that a clever man cannot derive some profit from it: nor any so fortunate that a fool cannot turn it to his disadvantage.

62. Sincerity comes from an open heart. It is exceedingly rare; what usually passes for sincerity is only an artful pretense designed to win the confidence of others.

67. Grace is to the body what sense is to the mind.

71. When two people have ceased to love, the memory that remains is almost always one of shame.

72. Love, to judge by most of its effects, is closer to hatred than to friendship.

75. Love, like fire, needs constant motion; when it ceases to hope, or to fear, love dies.

78. For most men the love of justice is only the fear of suffering injustice.

79. For a man who lacks self-confidence, silence is the wisest course.

83. What men have called friendship is only a social arrangement, a mutual adjustment of interests, an interchange of services given and received; it is, in sum, simply a business from which those involved purpose to derive a steady profit for their own self-love.

89. Everyone complains of his memory, none of his judgment.

90. In daily life our faults are frequently more pleasant than our good qualities.

93. Old people love to give good advice: it compensates them for their inability nowadays to set a bad example.

119. We are so accustomed to adopting a mask before others that we end by being unable to recognize ourselves.

122. If we master our passions it is due to their weakness, not our strength.

133. The only good copies are those which point the absurdity of bad originals.

134. We are never so ridiculous through what we are as through

what we pretend to be.

138. We would rather speak ill of ourselves than not at all.

144. We do not like to give praise, and we never do so without reasons of self-interest. Praise is a cunning, concealed and delicate form of flattery which, in different ways, gratifies both the giver and the receiver; the one accepts it as the reward for merit; the other bestows it to display his sense of justice and his powers of discernment.

146. We usually only praise that we may be praised.

149. The refusal to accept praise is the desire to be praised twice over.

150. The wish to deserve the praise we receive strengthens our virtues; and praise bestowed upon wit, courage and beauty contributes to their increase.

160. Splendid though an action may be, it should not be regarded as great unless it be the effect of a great design.

167. Avarice, more than open-handedness, is the opposite of economy.

170. When a man's behavior is straightforward, sincere and honest it is hard to be sure whether this is due to rectitude or cleverness.

176. In love there are two sorts of constancy: the one comes from the perpetual discovery of new delights in the beloved: the other, from the self-esteem which we derive from our own fidelity.

180. Our repentance is less a regret for the evil we have done than a precaution against the evil that may be done to us.

185. Evil, like good, has its heroes.

186. Not all who have vices are contemptible: all without a trace of virtue are.

190. Only great men are marked with great faults.

192. When our vices depart from us, we flatter ourselves that it is we who have rid ourselves of them.

200. Virtue would not go so far did vanity not keep her company.

205. Virtue, in women, is often love of reputation and fondness for tranquillity.

216. Perfect valor is to behave, without witnesses, as one would act were all the world watching.

218. Hypocrisy is the tribute that vice pays to virtue.

230. Nothing is as contagious as example, and we never perform an outstandingly good or evil action without its producing others of its sort. We copy goodness in the spirit of emulation, and wickedness owing to the malignity of our nature which shame holds in check until example sets it free.

237. No man should be praised for his goodness if he lacks the strength to be bad: in such cases goodness is usually only the effect of indolence or impotence of will.

259. The pleasure of love is in loving: and there is more joy in the passion one feels than in that which one inspires.

264. Pity is often only the sentiment of our own misfortunes felt in the ills of others. It is a clever pre-science of the evil times upon which we may fall. We help others in order to ensure their help in similar circumstances; and the kindnesses we do them are, if the truth were told, only acts of charity towards ourselves invested against the future.

276. Absence diminishes small loves and increases great ones, as the wind blows out the candle and blows up the bonfire.

277. Women frequently believe themselves to be in love even when they are not: the pursuit of an intrigue, the stimulus of gallantry, the natural inclination towards the joys of being loved, and the difficulty of refusal, all these combine to tell them that their passions are aroused when in fact it is but their coquetry at play.

375. It is the habit of mediocre minds to condemn all that is beyond their grasp.

376. True friendship destroys envy, as true love puts an end to coquetry.

378. We give advice but we do not inspire behavior.

392. One should treat one's fate as one does one's health; enjoy it when it is good, be patient with it when it is poorly, and never attempt any drastic cure save as an ultimate resort.

399. There is a form of eminence which is quite independent of our fate; it is an air which distinguishes us from our fellow men and makes us appear destined for great things; it is the value which we imperceptibly attach to ourselves; it is the quality which wins us the deference of others; more than birth, honours or even merit, it gives us ascendancy.

417. In love, the person who recovers first recovers best.

423. Few people know how to be old.

467. Vanity leads us to act against our inclinations more often than does reason.

479. Only people who are strong can be truly gentle: what normally passes for gentleness is mere weakness, which quickly turns sour.

483. Vanity, rather than malice, is the usual source of slander.

540. Hope and fear are inseparable. There is no hope without fear, nor any fear without hope.

576. We always discover, in the misfortunes of our dearest friends, something not altogether displeasing.

597. No man can be sure of his own courage until he has stared danger in the face.

617. How can we expect another to keep our secret, if we cannot keep it ourself?

BLAISE PASCAL: *from* Pensées

Weariness. Nothing is so insufferable to man as to be completely at rest, without passions, without business, without diversion, without study. He then feels his nothingness, his forlornness, his insufficiency, his dependence, his weakness, his emptiness. There will immediately arise from the depth of his heart weariness, gloom, sadness, fretfulness, vexation, despair.

Diversion. As men are not able to fight against death, misery, ignorance, they have taken it into their heads, in order to be happy, not to think of them at all.

The great and the humble have the same misfortunes, the same griefs, the same passions; but the one is at the top of the wheel, and the other near the center, and so less disturbed by the same revolutions.

Children are astonished to see their comrades respected.

I can well conceive a man without hands, feet, head (for it is only experience which teaches us that the head is more necessary than feet). But I cannot conceive man without thought; he would be a stone or a brute.

The strength of a man's virtue must not be measured by his efforts, but by his ordinary life.

Man is neither angel nor brute, and the unfortunate thing is that he who would act the angel acts the brute.

All the principles of skeptics, stoics, atheists, etc., are true. But their conclusions are false, because the opposite principles are also true.

If it is an extraordinary blindness to live without investigating what we are, it is a terrible one to live an evil life, while believing in God.

Experience makes us see an enormous difference between piety and goodness.

GEORGE BERNARD SHAW: *from* The Revolutionist's Handbook (*in* Man and Superman)

Democracy

If the lesser mind could measure the greater as a footrule can measure a pyramid, there would be finality in universal suffrage. As it is, the political problem remains unsolved.

Democracy substitutes selection by the incompetent many for appointment by the corrupt few.

Democratic republics can no more dispense with national idols than monarchies with public functionaries.

Government presents only one problem: the discovery of a trustworthy anthropometric method.

Liberty and Equality

He who confuses political liberty with freedom and political equality with similarity has never thought for five minutes about either.

Nothing can be unconditional: consequently nothing can be free.

Liberty means responsibility. That is why most men dread it.

The duke inquires contemptuously whether his gamekeeper is the equal of the Astronomer Royal; but he insists that they shall both be hanged equally if they murder him.

The notion that the colonel need be a better man than the private is as confused as the notion that the keystone need be stronger than the coping stone.

Where equality is undisputed, so also is subordination.

Equality is fundamental in every department of social organization.

The relation of superior to inferior excludes good manners.

Education

When a man teaches something he does not know to somebody else who has no aptitude for it, and gives him a certificate of proficiency, the latter has completed the education of a gentleman.

A fool's brain digests philosophy into folly, science into superstition, and art into pedantry. Hence University education.

The best brought-up children are those who have seen their parents as they are. Hypocrisy is not the parent's first duty.

The vilest abortionist is he who attempts to mould a child's character.

At the University every great treatise is postponed until its author attains impartial judgment and perfect knowledge. If a horse could wait as long for its shoes and would pay for them in advance, our blacksmiths would all be college dons.

He who can, does. He who cannot, teaches.

A learned man is an idler who kills time with study. Beware of his false knowledge: it is more dangerous than ignorance.

Activity is the only road to knowledge.

Every fool believes what his teachers tell him, and calls his credulity science or morality as confidently as his father called it divine revelation.

No man fully capable of his own language ever masters another.

No man can be a pure specialist without being in the strict sense an idiot.

Do not give your children moral and religious instruction unless you are quite sure they will not take it too seriously. Better be the mother of Henri Quatre and Nell Gwynne than of Robespierre and Queen Mary Tudor.

Virtues and Vices

No specific virtue or vice in a man implies the existence of any other specific virtue or vice in him, however closely the imagination may associate them.

Virtue consists, not in abstaining from vice, but in not desiring it.

Self-denial is not a virtue: it is only the effect of prudence on rascality.

Obedience simulates subordination as fear of the police simulates honesty.

Disobedience, the rarest and most courageous of the virtues, is seldom distinguished from neglect, the laziest and commonest of the vices.

Vice is waste of life. Poverty, obedience, and celibacy are the canonical vices.

Economy is the art of making the most of life.

The love of economy is the root of all virtue.

Greatness

Greatness is only one of the sensations of littleness.

In heaven an angel is nobody in particular.

Greatness is the secular name for Divinity: both mean simply what lies beyond us.

If a great man could make us understand him, we should hang him.

We admit that when the divinity we worshipped made itself visible and comprehensible we crucified it.

To a mathematician the eleventh means only a single unit: to the bushman who cannot count further than his ten fingers it is an incalculable myriad.

The difference between the shallowest routineer and the deepest thinker appears, to the latter, trifling; to the former, infinite.

In a stupid nation the man of genius becomes a god: everybody worships him and nobody does his will.

The Perfect Gentleman

The fatal reservation of the gentleman is that he sacrifices everything to his honor except his gentility.

A gentleman of our days is one who has money enough to do what every fool would do if he could afford it: that is, consume without producing.

The true diagnostic of modern gentility is parasitism.

No elaboration of physical or moral accomplishment can atone for the sin of parasitism.

A modern gentleman is necessarily the enemy of his country. Even in war he does not fight to defend it, but to prevent his power of preying on it from passing to a foreigner. Such combatants are patriots in the same sense as two dogs fighting for a bone are lovers of animals.

The North American Indian was a type of the sportsman warrior gentleman. The Periclean Athenian was a type of the intellectually and artistically cultivated gentleman. Both were political failures. The modern gentleman, without the hardihood of the one or the culture of the other, has the appetite of both put together. He will not succeed where they failed.

He who believes in education, criminal law, and sport, needs only property to make him a perfect modern gentleman.

Gambling

The most popular method of distributing wealth is the method of the roulette table.

The roulette table pays nobody except him that keeps it. Nevertheless a passion for gaming is common, though a passion for keeping roulette tables is unknown.

Gambling promises the poor what Property performs for the rich: that is why the bishops dare not denounce it fundamentally.

On History

THOMAS JEFFERSON

George Washington[1]

I think I knew General Washington intimately and thoroughly; and were I called on to delineate his character, it should be in terms like these.

His mind was great and powerful, without being of the very first order; his penetration strong, though not so acute as that of a Newton, Bacon, or Locke; and as far as he saw, no judgment was ever sounder. It was slow in operation, being little aided by invention or imagination, but sure in conclusion. Hence the common remark of his officers, of the advantage he derived from councils of war, where hearing all suggestions, he selected whatever was best; and certainly no general ever planned his battles more judiciously. But if deranged during the course of the action, if any member of his plan was dislocated by sudden circumstances, he was slow in re-adjustment. The consequence was, that he often failed in the field, and rarely against an enemy in station, as at Boston and York. He was incapable of fear, meeting personal dangers with the calmest unconcern. Perhaps the strongest feature in his character was prudence, never acting until every circumstance, every consideration, was maturely weighed; refraining if he saw a doubt, but, when once decided, going through with his purpose, whatever obstacles opposed. His integrity was most pure, his justice the most inflexible I have ever known, no motives of interest or consanguinity, of friendship or hatred, being able to bias his decision. He was, indeed, in every sense of the words, a wise, a good, and a great man. His temper was naturally irritable and high toned; but reflection and

1. From a letter written in 1814 to a Doctor Jones, who was writing a history and wanted to know about Washington's role in the Federalist-Republican controversy.

resolution had obtained a firm and habitual ascendency over it. If ever, however, it broke its bonds, he was most tremendous in his wrath. In his expenses he was honorable, but exact; liberal in contributions to whatever promised utility; but frowning and unyielding on all visionary projects, and all unworthy calls on his charity. His heart was not warm in its affections; but he exactly calculated every man's value, and gave him a solid esteem proportioned to it. His person, you know, was fine, his stature exactly what one would wish, his deportment easy, erect and noble; the best horseman of his age, and the most graceful figure that could be seen on horseback. Although in the circle of his friends, where he might be unreserved with safety, he took a free share in conversation, his colloquial talents were not above mediocrity, possessing neither copiousness of ideas, nor fluency of words. In public, when called on for a sudden opinion, he was unready, short and embarrassed. Yet he wrote readily, rather diffusely, in an easy and correct style. This he had acquired by conversation with the world, for his education was merely reading, writing and common arithmetic, to which he added surveying at a later day. His time was employed in action chiefly, reading little, and that only in agriculture and English history. His correspondence became necessarily extensive, and, with journalizing his agricultural proceedings, occupied most of his leisure hours within doors. On the whole, his character was, in its mass, perfect, in nothing bad, in few points indifferent; and it may truly be said, that never did nature and fortune combine more perfectly to make a man great, and to place him in the same constellation with whatever worthies have meritied from man an everlasting remembrance. For his was the singular destiny and merit, of leading the armies of his country successfully through an arduous war, for the establishment of its independence; of conducting its councils through the birth of a government, new in its forms and principles, until it had settled down into a quiet and orderly train; and of scrupulously obeying the laws through the whole of his career, civil and military, of which the history of the world furnishes no other example.

* * * I am satisfied the great body of republicans think of him as I do. We were, indeed, dissatisfied with him on his ratification of the British treaty. But this was short lived. We knew his honesty, the wiles with which he was encompassed, and that age had already begun to relax the firmness of his purposes; and I am convinced he is more deeply seated in the love and gratitude of the republicans, than in the Pharisaical homage of the federal monarchists. For he was no monarchist from preference of his judgment. The soundness of that gave him correct views of the rights of man, and his severe justice devoted him to them. He has often declared to me that he considered our new Constitution as an experiment on the practicability of republican government, and with what dose of liberty man could be trusted for his own good; that he was determined the experiment should have a fair trial, and would lose the last drop of his blood in support of it. And these declarations he repeated to me the oftener and more pointedly, because he knew my suspicions of Colonel Hamilton's views, and probably had heard from him the same declarations which I had, to wit, "that the British constitution, with its unequal representation, corruption and other existing abuses, was the most perfect government which had ever been established on earth, and that a reformation of those abuses would make it an impracticable government." I do believe that General Washington had not a firm confidence in the durability of our government. He was naturally distrustful of men, and inclined to gloomy apprehensions; and I was ever persuaded that a belief that we must at length end in something like a British constitution, had some weight in his adoption of the ceremonies of levees, birthdays, pompous meetings with Congress, and other forms of the same character, calculated to prepare us gradually for a change which he believed possible, and to let it come on with as little shock as might be to the public mind.

These are my opinions of General Washington which I would vouch at the judgment seat of God, having been formed on an acquaintance of thirty years. I served with him in the Virginia legislature from 1769 to the Revolutionary war, and again, a short time in Congress, until he left us to take command of the army. During the war and after it we corresponded occasionally, and in the four years of my continuance in the office of Secretary of State, our intercourse was daily, confidential and cordial. After I retired from that office, great and malignant pains were taken by our federal monarchists, and not entirely without effect, to make him view me as a theorist, holding French principles of government, which would lead infallibly to licentiousness and anarchy. And to this he listened the more easily, from my known disapprobation of the British treaty. I never saw him afterwards, or these malignant insinuations should have been dissipated before his just judgment, as mists before the sun. I felt on his death, with my countrymen, that "verily a great man hath fallen this day in Israel."

BARBARA TUCHMAN

Lord Salisbury[1]

The last government in the Western world to possess all the attributes of aristocracy in working condition took office in England in June of 1895. Great Britain was at the zenith of empire when

1. Chapter I of *The Proud Tower*, 1966.

the Conservatives won the General Election of that year, and the Cabinet they formed was her superb and resplendent image. Its members represented the greater landowners of the country who had been accustomed to govern for generations. As its superior citizens they felt they owed a duty to the State to guard its interests and manage its affairs. They governed from duty, heritage, and habit—and, as they saw it, from right.

The Prime Minister was a Marquess and lineal descendant of the father and son who had been chief ministers to Queen Elizabeth and James I. The Secretary for War was another Marquess who traced his inferior title of Baron back to the year 1181, whose great-grandfather had been Prime Minister under George III and whose grandfather had served in six cabinets under three reigns. The Lord President of the Council was a Duke who owned 186,000 acres in eleven counties, whose ancestors had served in government since the Fourteenth Century, who had himself served thirty-four years in the House of Commons and three times refused to be Prime Minister. The Secretary for India was the son of another Duke whose family seat was received in 1315 by grant from Robert the Bruce and who had four sons serving in Parliament at the same time. The President of the Local Government Board was a pre-eminent country squire who had a Duke for brother-in-law, a Marquess for son-in-law, an ancestor who had been Lord Mayor of London in the reign of Charles II, and who had himself been a Member of Parliament for twenty-seven years. The Lord Chancellor bore a family name brought to England by a Norman follower of William the Conqueror and maintained thereafter over eight centuries without a title. The Lord Lieutenant for Ireland was an Earl, a grandnephew of the Duke of Wellington and a hereditary trustee of the British Museum. The Cabinet also included a Viscount, three Barons, and two Baronets. Of its six commoners, one was a director of the Bank of England, one was a squire whose family had represented the same county in Parliament since the Sixteenth Century, one—who acted as Leader of the House of Commons—was the Prime Minister's nephew and inheritor of a Scottish fortune of £4,000,000, and one, a notable and disturbing cuckoo in the nest, was a Birmingham manufacturer widely regarded as the most successful man in England.

Besides riches, rank, broad acres, and ancient lineage, the new Government also possessed, to the regret of the Liberal Opposition and in the words of one of them, "an almost embarrassing wealth of talent and capacity." Secure in authority, resting comfortably on their electoral majority in the House of Commons and on a permanent majority in the House of Lords, of whom four-fifths were Conservatives, they were in a position, admitted the same opponent, "of unassailable strength."

Enriching their ranks were the Whig aristocrats who had seceded from the Liberal party in 1886 rather than accept Mr. Gladstone's[2] insistence on Home Rule for Ireland. They were for the most part great landowners who, like their natural brothers the Tories, regarded union with Ireland as sacrosanct. Led by the Duke of Devonshire, the Marquess of Lansdowne, and Mr. Joseph Chamberlain, they had remained independent until 1895, when they joined with the Conservative party, and the two groups emerged as the Unionist party, in recognition of the policy that had brought them together. With the exception of Mr. Chamberlain, this coalition represented that class in whose blood, training, and practice over the centuries, landowning and governing had been inseparable. Ever since Saxon chieftains met to advise the King in the first national assembly, the landowners of England had been sending members to Parliament and performing the duties of High Sheriff, Justice of the Peace, and Lord Lieutenant of the Militia in their own counties. They had learned the practice of government from the possession of great estates, and they undertook to manage the affairs of the nation as inevitably and unquestionably as beavers build a dam. It was their ordained role and natural task.

But it was threatened. By a rising rumble of protest from below, by the Radicals of the Opposition who talked about taxing unearned increment on land, by Home Rulers who wanted to detach the Irish island from which so much English income came, by Trade Unionists who talked of Labor representation in Parliament and demanded the legal right to strike and otherwise interfere with the free play of economic forces, by Socialists who wanted to nationalize property and Anarchists who wanted to abolish it, by upstart nations and strange challenges from abroad. The rumble was distant, but it spoke with one voice that said Change, and those whose business was government could not help but hear.

Planted firmly across the path of change, operating warily, shrewdly yet with passionate conviction in defense of the existing order, was a peer who was Chancelor of Oxford University for life, had twice held the India Office, twice the Foreign Office, and was now Prime Minister for the third time. He was Robert Arthur Talbot Gascoyne-Cecil, Lord Salisbury, ninth Earl and third Marquess of his line.

Lord Salisbury was both the epitome of his class and uncharacteristic of it—except insofar as the freedom to be different was a class characteristic. He was six feet four inches tall, and as a young man had been thin, ungainly, stooping, and shortsighted, with hair unusually black for an Englishman. Now sixty-five, his youthful lankiness had turned to bulk, his shoulders had grown massive and

2. William Gladstone, Prime Minister in 1886, defeated in the general   election of that year.

more stooped than ever, and his heavy bald head with full curly gray beard rested on them as if weighted down. Melancholy, intensely intellectual, subject to sleepwalking and fits of depression which he called "nerve storms," caustic, tactless, absent-minded, bored by society and fond of solitude, with a penetrating, skeptical, questioning mind, he had been called the Hamlet of English politics. He was above the conventions and refused to live in Downing Street.[3] His devotion was to religion, his interest in science. In his own home he attended private chapel every morning before breakfast, and had fitted up a chemical laboratory where he conducted solitary experiments. He harnessed the river at Hatfield for an electric power plant on his estate and strung up along the old beams of his home one of England's first electric light systems, at which his family threw cushions when the wires sparked and sputtered while they went on talking and arguing, a customary occupation of the Cecils.

Lord Salisbury cared nothing for sport and little for people. His aloofness was enhanced by shortsightedness so intense that he once failed to recognize a member of his own Cabinet, and once, his own butler. At the close of the Boer War he picked up a signed photograph of King Edward and, gazing at it pensively, remarked, "Poor Buller [referring to the Commander-in-Chief at the start of the war], what a mess he made of it." On another occasion he was seen in prolonged military conversation with a minor peer under the impression that he was talking to Field Marshal Lord Roberts.

For the upper-class Englishman's alter ego, most intimate companion and constant preoccupation, his horse, Lord Salisbury had no more regard. Riding was to him purely a means of locomotion to which the horse was "a necessary but extremely inconvenient adjunct." Nor was he addicted to shooting. When Parliament rose he did not go north to slaughter grouse upon the moors or stalk deer in Scottish forests, and when protocol required his attendance upon royalty at Balmoral, he would not go for walks and "positively refused," wrote Queen Victoria's Private Secretary, Sir Henry Ponsonby, "to admire the prospect or the deer." Ponsonby was told to have his room in the dismal castle kept "warm"—a minimum temperature of sixty degrees. Otherwise he retired for his holidays to France, where he owned a villa at Beaulieu on the Riviera and where he could exercise his fluent French and lose himself in *The Count of Monte Cristo*, the only book, he once told Dumas *fils*,[4] which allowed him to forget politics.

His acquaintance with games was confined to tennis, but when elderly he invented his own form of exercise, which consisted in

3. No. 10 Downing Street is by tradition the residence of the Prime Minister.

4. Alexandre Dumas *fils* ("son"), himself a well-known writer, was the son of the author of *The Count of Monte Cristo*, Alexandre Dumas *père* ("father").

riding a tricycle through St. James's Park in the early mornings or along paths cemented for the purpose in the park of his estate at Hatfield. Wearing for the occasion a kind of sombrero hat and a short sleeveless cloak with a hole in the middle in which he resembled a monk, he would be accompanied by a young coachman to push him up the hills. At the downhill slopes, the young man would be told to "jump on behind," and the Prime Minister, with the coachman's hands on his shoulders, would roll away, cloak flying and pedals whirring.

Hatfield, twenty miles north of London in Hertfordshire, had been the home of the Cecils for nearly three hundred years since James I had given it, in 1607, to his Prime Minister, Robert Cecil, first Earl of Salisbury, in exchange for a house of Cecil's to which the King had taken a fancy. It was the royal residence where Queen Elizabeth had spent her childhood and where, on receiving news of her accession, she held her first council, to swear in William Cecil, Lord Burghley, as her Chief Secretary of State. Its Long Gallery, with intricately carved paneled walls and gold-leaf ceiling, was 180 feet in length. The Marble Hall, named for the black and white marble floor, glowed like a jewel case with painted and gilded ceiling and Brussels tapestries. The red King James Drawing Room was hung with full-length family portraits by Romney and Reynolds and Lawrence. The library was lined from floor to gallery and ceiling with 10,000 volumes bound in leather and vellum. In other rooms were kept the Casket Letters of Mary Queen of Scots, suits of armor taken from men of the Spanish Armada, the cradle of the beheaded King, Charles I, and presentation portraits of James I and George III. Outside were yew hedges clipped in the form of crenelated battlements, and the gardens, of which Pepys[5] wrote that he never saw "so good flowers, nor so great gooseberries as big as nutmegs." Over the entrance hall hung flags captured at Waterloo and presented to Hatfield by the Duke of Wellington, who was a constant visitor and devoted admirer of the Prime Minister's mother, the second Marchioness. In her honor Wellington wore the hunt coat of the Hatfield Hounds when he was on campaign. The first Marchioness was painted by Sir Joshua Reynolds and hunted till the day she died at eighty-five, when, half-blind and strapped to the saddle, she was accompanied by a groom who would shout, when her horse approached a fence, "Jump, dammit, my Lady, jump!"

It was this exceptional person who reinvigorated the Cecil blood, which after Burghley and his son, had produced no further examples of superior mentality. Rather, the general mediocrity of succeeding generations had been varied only, according to a later Cecil,

5. Samuel Pepys, seventeenth-century government official, whose *Diary* (1660–69) affords an intimate and detailed account of his own affairs and of the life of his time.

by instances of "quite exceptional stupidity." But the second Marquess proved a vigorous and able man with a strong sense of public duty who served in several mid-century Tory cabinets. His second son, another Robert Cecil, was the Prime Minister of 1895. He in turn produced five sons who were to distinguish themselves. One became a general, one a bishop, one a minister of state, one M.P. for Oxford, and one, through service to the government, won a peerage in his own right. "In human beings as in horses," Lord Birkenhead was moved to comment on the Cecil record, "there is something to be said for the hereditary principle."

At Oxford in 1850 the contemporaries of young Robert Cecil agreed that he would end as Prime Minister either because or in spite of his remorselessly uncompromising opinions. Throughout life he never bothered to restrain them. His youthful speeches were remarkable for their virulence and insolence; he was not, said Disraeli,[6] "a man who measures his phrases." A "salisbury" became a synonym for a political imprudence. He once compared the Irish in their incapacity for self-government to Hottentots and spoke of an Indian candidate for Parliament as "that black man." In the opinion of Lord Morley his speeches were always a pleasure to read because "they were sure to contain one blazing indiscretion which it is a delight to remember." Whether these were altogether accidental is open to question for though Lord Salisbury delivered his speeches without notes, they were worked out in his head beforehand and emerged clear and perfect in sentence structure. In that time the art of oratory was considered part of the equipment of a statesman and anyone reading from a written speech would have been regarded as pitiable. When Lord Salisbury spoke, "every sentence," said a fellow member, "seemed as essential, as articulate, as vital to the argument as the members of his body to an athlete."

Appearing in public before an audience about whom he cared nothing, Salisbury was awkward; but in the Upper House, where he addressed his equals, he was perfectly and strikingly at home. He spoke sonorously, with an occasional change of tone to icy mockery or withering sarcasm. When a recently ennobled Whig took the floor to lecture the House of Lords in high-flown and solemn Whig sentiments, Salisbury asked a neighbor who the speaker was and on hearing the whispered identification, replied perfectly audibly, "I thought he was dead." When he listened to others he could become easily bored, revealed by a telltale wagging of his leg which seemed to one observer to be saying, "When will all this be over?" Or sometimes, raising his heels off the floor, he would set up a sustained quivering of his knees and legs which could last for half an hour at a time. At home, when made restless by visitors, it shook

6. Benjamin Disraeli, Earl of Beaconsfield, Prime Minister 1868 and 1874–80.

the floor and made the furniture rattle, and in the House his colleagues on the front bench complained it made them seasick. If his legs were at rest his long fingers would be in motion, incessantly twisting and turning a paper knife or beating a tattoo on his knee or on the arm of his chair.

He never dined out and rarely entertained beyond one or two political receptions at his town house in Arlington Street and an occasional garden party at Hatfield. He avoided the Carlton, official club of the Conservatives, in favor of the Junior Carlton, where a special luncheon table was set aside for him alone and the library was hung with huge placards inscribed silence. He worked from breakfast to one in the morning, returning to his desk after dinner as if he were beginning a new day. His clothes were drab and often untidy. He wore trousers and waistcoat of a dismal gray under a broadcloth frock coat grown shiny. But though careless in dress, he was particular about the trimming of his beard and carefully directed operations in the barber's chair, indicating "just a little more off here" while "artist and subject gazed fixedly in the mirror to judge the result."

Despite his rough tongue and sarcasms, Salisbury exerted a personal charm upon close colleagues and equals which, as one of them said, "was no small asset in the conduct of affairs." He gave detailed attention to party affairs and even sacrificed his exclusiveness for their sake. Once he astonished everyone by accepting an invitation to the traditional dinner for party supporters given by the Leader of the House of Commons. He asked to be given in advance biographical details about each guest. At the dinner the Prime Minister charmed his neighbor at table, a well-known agriculturist, with his expert knowledge of crop rotation and stock-breeding, chatted amiably afterward with every guest in turn, and before leaving, beckoned to his Private Secretary, saying "I think I have done them all, but there was someone I have not identified who, you said, made mustard."

Mr. Gladstone, though in political philosophy his bitterest antagonist, acknowledged him "a great gentleman in private society." In private life he was delightful and sympathetic and a complete contrast to his public self. In public acclaim, Salisbury was uninterested, for—since the populace was uninstructed—its opinions, as far as he was concerned, were worthless. He ignored the public and neither possessed nor tried to cultivate the personal touch that makes a political leader a recognizable personality to the man in the street and earns him a nickname like "Pam" or "Dizzy" or the "Grand Old Man." Not in the press, not even in *Punch*, was Lord Salisbury ever called anything but Lord Salisbury. He made no attempt to conceal his dislike for mobs of all kinds, "not excluding the House of Commons." After moving to the Lords, he never returned to the Commons to listen to its debates from the Peers'

Gallery or chat with members in the Lobby, and if compelled to allude to them in his own House, would use a tone of airy contempt, to the amusement of visitors from the Commons who came to hear him. But this was merely an outward pose designed to underline his deep inner sense of the patrician. He was not rank-conscious; he was indifferent to honors or any other form of recognition. It was simply that as a Cecil, and a superior one, he was born with a consciousness in his bones and brain cells of ability to rule and saw no reason to make any concessions of this prescriptive right to anyone whatever.

Having entered the House of Commons in the customary manner for peers' sons, from a family-controlled borough in an uncontested election at the age of twenty-three, and, during his fifteen years in the House of Commons, having been returned unopposed five times from the same borough, and having for the last twenty-seven years sat in the House of Lords, he had little personal experience of vote-getting. He regarded himself not as responsible *to* the people but as responsible *for* them. They were in his care. What reverence he felt for anyone was directed not down but up—to the monarchy. He revered Queen Victoria, who was some ten years his senior, both as her subject and, with chivalry toward her womanhood, as a man. For her he softened his brusqueness even if at Balmoral he could not conceal his boredom.

She in turn visited him at Hatfield and had the greatest confidence in him, giving him, as she told Bishop Carpenter, "if not the highest, an equal place with the highest among her ministers," not excepting Disraeli. Salisbury, who was "bad on his legs at any time," was the only man she ever asked to sit down. Unalike in every quality of mind except in their strong sense of rulership, the tiny old Queen and the tall, heavy, aging Prime Minister felt for each other mutual respect and regard.

In unimportant matters of state as in dress, Salisbury was inclined to be casual. Once when two clergymen with similar names were candidates for a vacant bishopric, he appointed the one not recommended by the Archbishop of Canterbury, and this being sorrowfully drawn to his attention, he said, "Oh, I daresay he will do just as well." He reserved high seriousness for serious matters only, and the most serious to him was the maintenance of aristocratic influence and executive power, not for its own sake, but because he believed it to be the only element capable of holding the nation united against the rising forces of democracy which he saw "splitting it into a bundle of unfriendly and distrustful fragments."

Class war and irreligion were to him the greatest evils and for this reason he detested Socialism, less for its menace to property than for its preaching of class war and its basis in materialism, which meant to him a denial of spiritual values. He did not deny the need of social reforms, but believed they could be achieved through the interplay and mutual pressures of existing parties. The Workmen's Compensation Act, for one, making employers liable for work-sustained injuries, though denounced by some of his party as interference with private enterprise, was introduced and passed with his support in 1897.

He fought all proposals designed to increase the political power of the masses. When still a younger son, and not expecting to succeed to the title, he had formulated his political philosophy in a series of some thirty articles which were published in the *Quarterly Review* in the early 1860's, when he was in his thirties. Against the growing demand at that time for a new Reform law to extend the suffrage, Lord Robert Cecil, as he then was, had declared it to be the business of the Conservative party to preserve the rights and privileges of the propertied class as the "single bulwark" against the weight of numbers. To extend the suffrage would be, as he saw it, to give the working classes not merely a voice in Parliament but a preponderating one that would give to "mere numbers a power they ought not to have." He deplored the Liberals' adulation of the working class "as if they were different from other Englishmen" when in fact the only difference was that they had less education and property and "in proportion as the property is small the danger of misusing the franchise is great." He believed the workings of democracy to be dangerous to liberty, for under democracy "passion is not the exception but the rule" and it was "perfectly impossible" to commend a farsighted passionless policy to "men whose minds are unused to thought and undisciplined to study." To widen the suffrage among the poor while increasing taxes upon the rich would end, he wrote, in a complete divorce of power from responsibility; "the rich would pay all the taxes and the poor make all the laws."

He did not believe in political equality. There was the multitude, he said, and there were "natural" leaders. "Always wealth, in some countries birth, in all countries intellectual power and culture mark out the man to whom, in a healthy state of feeling, a community looks to undertake its government." These men had the leisure for it and the fortune, "so that the struggles for ambition are not defiled by the taint of sordid greed. . . . They are the aristocracy of a country in the original and best sense of the word. . . . The important point is, that the rulers of a country should be taken from among them," and as a class they should retain that "political preponderance to which they have every right that superior fitness can confer."

So sincere and certain was his conviction of that "superior fitness" that in 1867 when the Tory Government espoused the Second Reform Bill, which doubled the electorate and enfranchised

workingmen in the towns, Salisbury at thirty-seven flung away Cabinet office within a year of first achieving it rather than be party to
what he considered a betrayal and surrender of Conservative principles. His party's reversal, engineered by Disraeli in a neat enterprise
both to "dish the Whigs" and to meet political realities, was
regarded with abhorrence by Lord Cranborne (as Lord Robert
Cecil had then become, his elder brother having died in 1865).
Though it might ruin his career he resigned as Secretary for India
and in a bitter and serious speech spoke out in the House against
the policy of the party's leaders, Lord Derby and Mr. Disraeli. He
begged the members not to do for political advantage what would
ultimately destroy them as a class. "The wealth, the intelligence,
the energy of the community, all that has given you that power
which makes you so proud of your nation and which makes the
deliberations of this House so important, will be numerically absolutely overmatched." Issues would arise in which the interests of
employers and employed would clash and could only be decided by
political force, "and in that conflict of political force you are pit-
ting an overwhelming number of employed against a hopeless
minority of employers." The outcome would "reduce to political
insignificance and extinction the classes which have hitherto contributed so much to the greatness and prosperity of their country."

A year later, on his father's death, he entered the House of Lords
as third Marquess of Salisbury. In 1895, after the passage of nearly
thirty years, his principles had not shifted an inch. With no belief
in change as improvement, nor faith in the future over the present,
he dedicated himself with "grim acidity" to preserving the existing
order. Believing that "rank, without the power of which it was originally the symbol, was a sham," he was determined, while he lived
and governed England, to resist further attack on the power of that
class of which rank was still the visible symbol. Watchful of
approaching enemies, he stood against the coming age. The pressures of democracy encircled, but had not yet closed in around, the
figure whom Lord Curzon described as "that strange, powerful,
inscrutable, brilliant, obstructive deadweight at the top."

QUESTIONS

1. This is a description of a man whose views most people today
   would regard as outmoded or reprehensible. What does the
   author do to make the description sympathetic?
2. The wealth of anecdote certainly enlivens the description; does it
   serve any historical purpose?
3. What is Lord Salisbury's attitude toward "birth"? What is the
   author's attitude?
4. To what extent would Salisbury's aristocratic attitude toward
   property be shared by a Marxist like Deutscher (pp. 1145–1158)?

NATHANIEL HAWTHORNE
Abraham Lincoln[1]

Of course, there was one other personage, in the class of statesmen, whom I should have been truly mortified to leave Washington without seeing; since (temporarily, at least, and by force of circumstances) he was the man of men. But a private grief had built up a barrier about him, impeding the customary free intercourse of Americans with their chief magistrate; so that I might have come away without a glimpse of his very remarkable physiognomy, save for a semi-official opportunity of which I was glad to take advantage. The fact is, we were invited to annex ourselves, as supernumeraries, to a deputation that was about to wait upon the President, from a Massachusetts whip factory, with a present of a splendid whip.

Our immediate party consisted only of four or five (including Major Ben Perley Poore, with his note-book and pencil), but we were joined by several other persons, who seemed to have been lounging about the precincts of the White House, under the spacious porch, or within the hall, and who swarmed in with us to take the chances of a presentation. Nine o'clock had been appointed as the time for receiving the deputation, and we were punctual to the moment; but not so the President, who sent us word that he was eating his breakfast, and would come as soon as he could. His appetite, we were glad to think, must have been a pretty fair one; for we waited about half an hour in one of the antechambers, and then were ushered into a reception-room, in one corner of which sat the Secretaries of War and of the Treasury, expecting, like ourselves, the termination of the Presidential breakfast. During this interval there were several new additions to our group, one or two of whom were in a working-garb, so that we formed a very miscellaneous collection of people, mostly unknown to each other, and without any common sponsor, but all with an equal right to look our head servant in the face.

By and by there was a little stir on the staircase and in the passage-way, and in lounged a tall, loose-jointed figure, of an exaggerated Yankee port and demeanor, whom (as being about the homeliest man I ever saw, yet by no means repulsive or disagreeable) it was impossible not to recognize as Uncle Abe.

Unquestionably, Western man though he be, and Kentuckian by birth, President Lincoln is the essential representative of all Yankees, and the veritable specimen, physically, of what the world seems determined to regard as our characteristic qualities. It is the

1. From an article in *The Atlantic Monthly*, July, 1862.

strangest and yet the fittest thing in the jumble of human vicissitudes, that he, out of so many millions, unlooked for, unselected by any intelligible process that could be based upon his genuine qualities, unknown to those who chose him, and unsuspected of what endowments may adapt him for his tremendous responsibility, should have found the way open for him to fling his lank personality into the chair of state—where, I presume, it was his first impulse to throw his legs on the council-table, and tell the Cabinet Ministers a story. There is no describing his lengthy awkwardness, nor the uncouthness of his movement; and yet it seemed as if I had been in the habit of seeing him daily, and had shaken hands with him a thousand times in some village street; so true was he to the aspect of the pattern American, though with a certain extravagance which, possibly, I exaggerated still further by the delighted eagerness with which I took it in. If put to guess his calling and livelihood, I should have taken him for a country school-master as soon as anything else. He was dressed in a rusty black frock coat and pantaloons, unbrushed, and worn so faithfully that the suit had adapted itself to the curves and angularities of his figure, and had grown to be an outer skin of the man. His hair was black, still unmixed with gray, stiff, somewhat bushy, and had apparently been acquainted with neither brush nor comb that morning, after the disarrangement of the pillow; and as to a nightcap, Uncle Abe probably knows nothing of such effeminacies. His complexion is dark and sallow, betokening, I fear, a insalubrious atmosphere around the White House; he has thick black eyebrows and an impending brow; his nose is large, and the lines about his mouth are very strongly defined.

The whole physiognomy is as coarse a one as you would meet anywhere in the length and breadth of the States; but, withal, it is redeemed, illuminated, softened, and brightened by a kindly though serious look out of his eyes, and an expression of homely sagacity, that seems weighted with rich results of village experience. A great deal of native sense; no bookish cultivation, no refinement; honest at heart, and thoroughly so, and yet, in some sort, sly—at least, endowed with a sort of tact and wisdom that are akin to craft, and would impel him, I think, to take an antagonist in flank, rather than to make a bull-run at him right in front. But, on the whole, I like this sallow, queer, sagacious visage, with the homely human sympathies that warmed it; and, for my small share in the matter, would as lief have Uncle Abe for a ruler as any man whom it would have been practicable to put in his place.

Immediately on his entrance the President accosted our member of Congress, who had us in charge, and, with a comical twist of his face, made some jocular remark about the length of his breakfast. He then greeted us all round, not waiting for an introduction, but shaking and squeezing everybody's hand with the utmost cordiality, whether the individual's name was announced to him or not. His manner towards us was wholly without pretence, but yet had a kind of natural dignity, quite sufficient to keep the forwardest of us from clapping him on the shoulder and asking him for a story. A mutual acquaintance being established, our leader took the whip out of its case, and began to read the address of presentation. The whip was an exceedingly long one, its handle wrought in ivory (by some artist in the Massachusetts State Prison, I believe), and ornamented with a medallion of the President, and other equally beautiful devices; and along its whole length there was a succession of golden bands and ferrules. The address was shorter than the whip, but equally well made, consisting chiefly of an explanatory description of these artistic designs, and closing with a hint that the gift was a suggestive and emblematic one, and that the President would recognize the use to which such an instrument should be put.

This suggestion gave Uncle Abe rather a delicate task in his reply, because, slight as the matter seemed, it apparently called for some declaration, or intimation, or faint foreshadowing of policy in reference to the conduct of the war, and the final treatment of the Rebels. But the President's Yankee aptness and not-to-be-caughtness stood him in good stead, and he jerked or wiggled himself out of the dilemma with an uncouth dexterity that was entirely in character; although, without his gesticulation of eye and mouth—and especially the flourish of the whip, with which he imagined himself touching up a pair of fat horses—I doubt whether his words would be worth recording, even if I could remember them. The gist of the reply was, that he accepted the whip as an emblem of peace, not punishment; and, this great affair over, we retired out of the presence in high good humor, only regretting that we could not have seen the President sit down and fold up his legs (which is said to be a most extraordinary spectacle), or have heard him tell one of those delectable stories for which he is so celebrated. A good many of them are afloat upon the common talk of Washington, and are certainly the aptest, pithiest, and funniest little things imaginable; though, to be sure, they smack of the frontier freedom, and would not always bear repetition in a drawing-room, or on the immaculate page of the *Atlantic*.[2]

Good Heavens! what liberties have I been taking with one of the potentates of the earth, and the man on whose conduct more important consequences depend than on that of any other historical person-

2. This passage was one of those omitted from the article as originally published, and the following note was appended to explain the omission, which had been indicated by a line of points: "We are compelled to omit two or three pages, in which the author describes the interview, and gives his idea of the personal appearance and deportment of the President. The sketch appears to have been written in a benign spirit, and perhaps conveys a not inaccurate impression of its august subject; but it lacks *reverence*, and it pains us to see a gentleman of ripe age, and who has spent years under the corrective influence of foreign institutions, falling into the characteristic and most ominous fault of Young America."

age of the century! But with whom is an American citizen entitled to take a liberty, if not with his own chief magistrate? However, lest the above allusions to President Lincoln's little peculiarities (already well known to the country and to the world) should be misinterpreted, I deem it proper to say a word or two in regard to him, of unfeigned respect and measurable confidence. He is evidently a man of keen faculties, and, what is still more to the purpose, of powerful character. As to his integrity, the people have that intuition of it which is never deceived. Before he actually entered upon his great office, and for a considerable time afterwards, there is no reason to suppose that he adequately estimated the gigantic task about to be imposed on him, or, at least, had any distinct idea how it was to be managed; and I presume there may have been more than one veteran politician who proposed to himself to take the power out of President Lincoln's hands into his own, leaving our honest friend only the public responsibility for the good or ill success of the career. The extremely imperfect development of his statesmanly qualities, at that period, may have justified such designs. But the President is teachable by events, and has now spent a year in a very arduous course of education; he has a flexible mind, capable of much expansion, and convertible towards far loftier studies and activities than those of his early life; and if he came to Washington a backwoods humorist, he has already transformed himself into as good a statesman (to speak moderately) as his prime minister.[3]

3. Presumably the Secretary of State, William H. Seward.

QUESTIONS

1. In one sentence summarize Hawthorne's attitude toward Lincoln in the first seven paragraphs.
2. What is the basic pattern of the opening sentence of the fifth paragraph? Find other examples of this pattern. What is their total impact on Hawthorne's description?
3. In his final paragraph Hawthorne seeks to prevent misunderstanding by stressing his respect for and confidence in Lincoln. Is there anything in the paragraph which runs counter to that expression? To what effect?
4. In the footnote to the seventh paragraph the editor of The Atlantic Monthly explains his omission of the first seven paragraphs. On the evidence of this statement what sort of a person does the editor seem to be? Is there anything in the omitted paragraphs that would tend to justify his decision? Is the full description superior to the last paragraph printed alone? Explain.
5. Describe someone you know with a strong personality that has contrasting characteristics.

DOUGLAS SOUTHALL FREEMAN

Over the River[1]

Every soldier had been hoping "Old Jack's" return would not be far distant. Tuesday morning, May 5, after Jackson had agreed that "all things work together for good," he welcomed Chaplain Lacy, who arrived at 10 o'clock to conduct bedside worship and to give the General the satisfacton of discussing religion. Jackson asked that Lacy come every morning at the same hour, but he had made up his mind that he ought not to gratify his wish of having Lacy go with him to Ashland. He explained to the chaplain: "It would be setting an example of self-gratification to the troops, and you had better stay at your post of duty. I have always tried to set the troops a good example."[2] Meantime, he could enjoy to the limit of his strength the privilege of Lieutenant Smith, who was of his same Presbyterian faith and was minded to the ministry.

That morning or the next, Jackson took occasion to expound one of his favorite views—that the Bible supplied rules for every action of life. He had contended many times that if an army rested on the Sabbath, it could cover more ground in a given week than if it marched all seven days. Now he argued that the Bible was rich in lessons for each exigency of a soldier's life. For instance—and he turned to Smith with a smile, "Can you tell me where the Bible gives Generals a model for their official reports of battles?"

Smith answered that he never had consulted Holy Writ to find examples of battle reports.

"Nevertheless," Jackson insisted, "there are such: and excellent models, too." He went on: "Look, for instance, at the narrative of Joshua's battle with the Amalekites; there you have one. It had clearness, brevity, fairness, modesty; and it traces the victory to its right source, the blessing of God."[3] Lee's battle, as well as Joshua's, came in for discussion, but not with any excited concern that day on the part of the wounded man. When someone told him that Hooker had entrenched North of Chancellorsville and seemed to be

1. From "Promotion for Rodes and for Jackson," Chapter XXXVI of *Lee's Lieutenants*, Vol. II, 1943.

In his notes Freeman uses short or cue titles, as follows: *Cooke's Jackson* for J. E. Cooke, *Stonewall Jackson, A Military Biography* (edition of 1866); *Dabney* for R. L. Dabney, *Life and Campaigns of Lieut.-Gen. Thomas J. Jackson;* Mrs. *Jackson* for Mary Anna Jackson, *Memoirs of Stonewall Jackson; McGuire* for Hunter H. McGuire and George L. Christian, *The Confederate Cause and Conduct in the War between the States; Owen* for W. M.

Owen, *In Camp and Battle with the Washington Artillery of New Orleans; O. R.* for *Official Records of the Union and Confederate Armies; Pendleton* for Susan P. Lee, *Memoirs of William Nelson Pendleton; R. E. Lee* for D. S. Freeman, *R. E. Lee.*

2. *Pendleton,* 271 [This and all the other footnotes are Freeman's].

3. This and the references in these pages to other phases of Jackson's religious experience at this time, merely are paraphrased from *Dabney,* 715 ff. Joshua's battle with the Amalekites is described in *Exodus* xvii, 8 ff.

inviting attack there, comment was brief: "That is bad; very bad."[4]
Beyond that, Jackson expressed no doubt of the result. As hopefully
as the day began, it ended, but to the accompaniment of a hard,
chilling rain.[5]

Light rain was falling on the morning of the 6th when, in the
Wilderness North of Chancellorsville, the pickets sent back word
that the enemy, whom Lee intended that day to attack, had crossed
during the night to the north side of the Rappahannock. If anything
of this was said to Jackson, there is no record of his observations. He
passed that day, Wednesday, as he had spent Tuesday with no
symptoms of other involvement, and with some delectable discourse
on theology. Did Dr. McGuire suppose, Jackson asked, that the
sufferers of the New Testament, who had received the healing touch
of Jesus, ever were afflicted afterward with the same disease? Mc-
Guire had no opinion. Jackson was firm in his conviction that one
healed by the Saviour of any malady never would suffer from it again.
"Oh, for infinite power!" Jackson exclaimed.

For a time he was silent, and then he asked of Smith, "Where
were the headquarters of Christianity after the crucifixion?"

Smith could answer that as readily as he could describe the road
to Yerby's or tell a stranger how to get to Moss Neck. Jerusalem,
said Smith, remained for a time the chief seat of the church; but after
the dispersion of the disciples, by reason of persecution, the Christians had no home city until they established Antioch, Iconium,
Rome and Alexandria as centers of influence.

That was fair enough as answer for most men, but the wounded
Cromwell of the South, a military realist, would not have it so:
"Why do you say, 'centers of influence'? Is not 'headquarters' a
better term?" That reiterated, he urged Smith to proceed with the
account of the manner in which those cities had become headquarters of the faith.

Smith hesitated to deliver to a wounded soldier a discourse on
church history, and before he answered, he looked inquiringly at
McGuire. An encouraging nod was assurance that Jackson might be
helped, rather than hurt by learning more about the divisional headquarters of Christendom. Smith must have thanked inwardly his
instructors and his good memory, because he was able without hesitation or vagueness to explain, in the approving words of Dr. Dabney,
"how the Apostles were directed by Divine Providence, seemingly,
to plant their most flourishing churches, at an early period, in these
great cities, which were rendered by their political, commercial and
ethnical relations, 'headquarters' of influence for the whole civilized
world."[6]

Jackson was loath to have the explanation end without supporting

4. *Dabney,* 715.
5. *Hotchkiss' MS Diary,* 187.

6. *Dabney,* 720.

topographical data. He wanted, especially, to know where Iconium was, and he bade Smith "get the map" and point out the place to him, just as Jed. Hotchkiss, a year before, had made clear to him, after some effort, that Fisher's Gap and Swift Run Gap were *not* the same pass.

Smith deferentially suggested that perhaps no map at hand would show Iconium. "Yes, sir," Jackson corrected, "you will find it in the atlas which is in my old trunk." To satisfy his chief, Smith is said to have examined the trunk[7] and, when he did not find the atlas, to have asked if it might be in Jackson's portable desk. "Yes," said Jackson, "you are right, I left it in my desk," and he mentioned the shelf, but by this time his attention was lagging. Exhaustion was creeping over him. "Mr. Smith," he said, once more the General, "I wish you would examine into that matter . . . and report to me."[8]

Despite weariness at the end, this theological meat helped to make a day of consistent and encouraging gain. Ere its close, Chaplain Lacy went to Army Headquarters to request the detail of Dr. S. B. Morrison of Early's Division, who had been the General's family physician and was, besides, a kinsman of Mrs. Jackson's. He would be an excellent medical counsellor and a relief chief nurse in the place of Dr. McGuire, who could not endure much longer his vigils at the bedside.

With word that Dr. Morrison would be sent as soon as practicable, Lacy in due time returned. The chaplain brought also a thoughtful message from General Lee: "Give [General Jackson] my affectionate regards, and tell him to make haste and get well, and come back to me as soon as he can. He has lost his left arm; but I have lost my right arm."[9] This, of course, was gratifying to Jackson and was perhaps the most pleasant incident of the day.[1]

That night, Wednesday, May 6, Dr. McGuire was so weary that instead of trying to stay awake by the General's side, he decided he would sleep on a couch in Jackson's room and would leave the patient in the care of Jim. The General's body servant, who was sponsor of many picturesque stories about his master, was devoted to Jackson and was quite competent to act as assistant nurse. With Dr. McGuire on the couch and Jim silent in the chair, Jackson went to sleep without difficulty.

About 1:00 A.M. Thursday, May 7, the General was awakened by nausea. As quietly as he could, be aroused Jim and told the Negro

7. The text follows Dabney, but W. N. Pendleton, in an order of Apr. 15, 1863, for a reduction in the baggage of officers, remarked: "General Jackson takes no trunk himself, and allows none in his Corps" (*Owen*, 210).

8. *Dabney*, 720-21. There is some doubt concerning the time of this curious incident, but the 6th, rather than the 8th, seems the more probable date.

9. *Dabney*, 716.

1. *Dabney*, 715; *Hotchkiss' MS Diary*, 187.

to get a wet towel and to apply it to his stomach. Jim was vaguely conscious that this was the wrong thing to do. Might he not wake Dr. McGuire and ask him? Jackson refused: The doctor had been very tired; let him sleep; get the towel. Obediently Jim went out, wet a towel thoroughly in cold water, and helped in applying it to the General's stomach.

The cold and the dampness did no good. Paroxysms in the right side were added to the nausea. Moment by moment, pain increased until it almost passed endurance. The General's frame was shaken but his resolution was firm: he would not wake the sleeping surgeon if he could endure till morning. Soon Jackson observed, though without panic, that the pain was sharpened every time he drew breath. Agonizing as that was, he held out until the gray of dawn and the first stir out of doors. Then he had to permit Jim to awaken McGuire.

In a moment the tall young physician with his long face and his understanding eye was by the bedside. He listened intently to the General's breathing and he examined the painful area of the chest. All too readily, McGuire became convinced of what the patient himself may have suspected: Jackson was developing pneumonia.

Hope and planning and confident expectation now were halted. Instead of an early removal to Ashland, a peaceful convalescence at Lexington and a prompt return to the head of the Second Corps, there must be a sterner battle there in the cottage at Chandlers'. If it was won, Chancellorsville was a double victory. Were the battle lost—were it possible, even, to think that Jackson might not recover —then the North would be repaid for all the boys who had been slain or maimed there in the Wilderness of Spotsylvania, where the burnt forest still smoked and the dead lay unburied.

Jackson was not afraid. He did not believe pneumonia would kill him. Judgment, confidence, faith, ambition—something had convinced him that he had more work to do. Attack, then, the disease that was assailing him! Preliminary to cupping, which would bring more blood to the affected member, Jackson was given morphia.

This of course made him less sensitive to his pain but it threw him quickly into a stupor. From that hour, the personality of Jackson, as his officers knew it, seemed in a haze, obscured, uncertain. He began to mutter and occasionally he used connected sentences, but it was difficult to tell whether he was rational or was babbling. His attendants disagreed, at least in retrospect, regarding his consciousness at particular moments. What seemed to one auditor the expression of clear religious faith seemed to another hearer the uncontrolled expression of the formal words the General had loved and learned. In the first offthrust of reason, he seemed to be carried back again to the attack on Hooker's right. "Major Pendleton," he exclaimed, "send in and see if there is higher ground back of Chancellorsville."[2]

About noon, when the doctors had done what they could for him, he asked for a glass of lemonade. This, after some whispering and considerable delay, was brought him by Smith. The General sipped it and then said quickly: "You did not mix this, it is too. sweet; take it back."

He was correct in saying that Smith had not prepared the beverage, but had he known by whose anxious hands it had been prepared, he would have been less critical. Soon he was aware of another presence in the room. There by his bed, white-faced but composed, was his wife. He stirred himself to greet her and he found words to express his thankfulness that she had come, but so deeply was he under his opiate that he dropped off again quickly. When she spoke or ministered to him he was able to show by smile or glance that he knew her. At length, looking steadfastly at her he observed the emotion she was trying to conceal. With an effort, but seemingly in full command of his faculties, he said, "My darling, you must cheer up and not wear a long face. I love cheerfulness and brightness in a sickroom."[3]

Had he known all she had endured, he would have been proud that she held back her tears. On Sunday morning, May 3, after family worship at Dr. Hoge's home in Richmond, she had been told as gently as possible that the evening before her husband had been wounded severely but, it was hoped, not dangerously. Her instant wish, of course, was to hasten to him. That was impossible. North of Richmond, railway service was suspended because of Stoneman's raid; private travel over more than forty-five miles of road was dangerous until the Federal cavalry were driven back. Communication by telegraph and by mail was uncertain. It was Tuesday before Mrs. Jackson's brother Joseph, who left the General Sunday, got to Richmond and told her the circumstances of the wounding and of the operation.

This report increased her solicitude. She begged to be permitted to start immediately and to take her chances of eluding the enemy; but she received word that the railroad company expected at any

2. *Dabney*, 715. In *Pendleton*, 271, on the authority of Chaplain Lacy, Jackson is quoted as saying: "I must find out whether there is high ground between Chancellorsville and the river.... Push up the columns.... Hasten the columns. ... Pendleton, you take charge of that. ... Where's Pendleton? ... Tell him to push up the columns." It is necessary to give warning that Jackson's delirious and semi-conscious remarks during his illness did not have anything that approximated the order and the dramatic quality assigned them in some of the contemporary accounts. Mrs. Jackson, *op. cit.*, 451, undoubtedly stated the fact correctly when she said: "From the time I reached him he was too ill to notice or talk much, and he lay most of the time in a semi-conscious state; but when aroused, he recognized those about him and consciousness would return."

3. *Mrs. Jackson*, 451. From noon, Thursday, May 7, Mrs. Jackson, though she wrote years afterward, is the fullest authority on the General's illness. She made some errors, confused certain events and omitted a few incidents, but she did not yield to the temptation, as more than one of the other first-hand authorities did, of "dressing up" every occurrence in the sickroom.

time to reopen the line to Guiney's. Thursday, this was done. The she started on the first passenger train that left Richmond.

As soon as she arrived, she sensed danger. All that could be said for her encouragement by the staff officer who met her was that the General was doing "pretty well." When she reached the house, Mrs. Chandler greeted her with womanly understanding and invited her to rest there until the surgeons, who were then "dressing the General's wounds" were ready for her to see her husband.

Mrs. Jackson could not sit still. She went out on the long porch[4] and walked up and down and waited, as it seemed to her, for hours.

At length she noticed men digging in the family graveyard at no great distance from the house. As she watched, she saw them bring to the surface a coffin which was being exhumed for shipment elsewhere. Horrified, Mrs. Jackson asked whose was the body. It was, she was told, that of General Paxton, of whose death she had not heard. A scene of 1861 flashed over her: "My husband's own neighbor and friend! and I knew the young wife, and remembered how I had seen her weeping bitterly as she watched his departure from her in those first days of the war, when all our hearts were well-nigh bursting with foreboding and dread. Now the cruel war had done its worst for *her*, and she was left widowed, and her children fatherless."[5] No wonder, when Mrs. Jackson was assigned the task of preparing her husband's lemonade, as a means of occupying her unhappy mind, she spoiled it with too much sugar![6]

He was trying to tell her something else: "I know you would gladly give your life for me, but I am perfectly resigned. Do not be sad; I hope I *may* yet recover. Pray for me, but always remember in your prayers to use the petition, 'Thy will be done.'"[7] Although he dozed off again then, every time he opened his eyes and saw her, he would murmur, "My darling . . . . you are very much loved" or "You are one of the most precious little wives in the world."[8] He seemed able to look at her and to speak to her without emotional strain, but more than once, when she asked, "Shall I bring in the baby for you to see?" he answered, "Not yet; wait till I feel better." The last time he had seen the child, spring was coming to the valley of the Massaponax and the peach trees had been blooming.

About 2:00 P.M., Dr. Samuel B. Morrison arrived and came at once to the General. As the surgeon leaned over him, Jackson opened his eyes, recognized Morrison, smiled and said simply: "That's an old, familiar face."[9] Morrison and McGuire now held a consultation and decided that if Mrs. Jackson was to be gratified in her wish to attend the General, she must have some capable, cheerful friend to help with the baby, who had not yet been weaned. Mrs. Jackson

4. Which was on the level of the basement—*Mrs. Pendleton's MS Statement.*
5. *Mrs. Jackson,* 449-50.
6. *Dabney,* 716-17.

7. *McGuire,* 227.
8. *Mrs. Jackson,* 451.
9. *Dabney,* 717; *Mrs. Jackson,* 453.

agreed to this and asked that Mrs. Moses D. Hoge of Richmond be asked to come. For their own part, the surgeons determined that they could call from the capital its most distinguished authority on pneumonia, Dr. David Tucker. To summon him and to escort Mrs. Hoge to Guiney's, Lieutenant Smith was sent to the city on the next train.[1] Mrs. Hoge was one of the wisest of women and would strengthen the young wife.

Jackson all the while seemed half asleep, half delirious. He continued able to rouse himself when called but he had to ask Mrs. Jackson to speak distinctly, so that he could hear every word.[2] When left alone, his mind would turn to the battlefield. More than once he seemed to be thinking of his troops as weary at the end of a long conflict. He wanted the commissary at hand, wanted the soldiers fed."Tell Major Hawks to send forward provisions to the men." The name stuck in his mind . . . . "Major Hawks . . . Major Hawks" he muttered.[3]

Despite his delirium, the doctors did not feel discouraged. When the cool evening closed in rain,[4] they could not dispute the nature and progress of the malady, but they believed he was holding his own against it. There were some reasons for thinking him better,[5] though these may have been nothing more than the effect of the opiates the surgeons continued to administer. At bedtime, Morrison took his seat by Jackson to watch and to give the medicines. The doctor had little to do. Jackson lay in stupor but kept a grip on himself. Once, during the night, when the doctor offered him a draught and asked, "Will you take this, General?" Jackson seemed almost to reprimand with a terse answer—"Do your duty!" As Morrison paused, uncertain what Jackson meant, the General said again, "Do your duty!"[6]

Friday, May 8, the anniversary of the Battle of McDowell, dawned cool and misty.[7] Among the camps, there was profound concern. For the first time, men seriously were asking. Was "Old Jack" in danger? How could the Army do without him? For a year, a rounded year that very day, his name had been the symbol of victory. Others had failed or had fallen; he had defied rout and death. Many who had seen him in battle, those blue eyes ablaze, had shared Dick Taylor's belief that the bullet which could kill "Stonewall" never had been moulded. The enemy had not struck him down; his own troops had; and if they, even they, had not been able to slay him, could pneumonia? Veterans of the old Army of the Valley, in particular, argued and wondered or feared and prayed. In the name of all of them General Lee was to speak when he said, "Surely,

1. *Dabney*, 717-18.
2. *Mrs. Jackson*, 451.
3. *Mrs. Jackson*, 452; *Dabney*, 719. Again it must be noted that these remarks cannot be given their proper sequence, but apparently they were spoken on Thursday and not, as usually stated, on Sunday.
4. *Hotchkiss' MS Diary*, 189.
5. *McGuire*, 227.
6. *Dabney*, 718-19.
7. *Hotchkiss' MS Diary*, 189.

General Jackson must recover; God will not take him from us, now that we need him so much."[8]

In the cottage at Chandlers', that Friday, some of the surgeons were not so sure. Dr. Tucker had not yet arrived from Richmond, but Surgeons Breckinridge and Smith, men of high repute in the Army Medical Corps, had come at Dr. McGuire's request for consultation. These three and Dr. Morrison made as thorough an examination as Jackson's condition allowed. The wounds appeared to be doing well. Although the discharge had diminished, healing was continuing. Pain in the side no longer was troubling the patient.

The ominous condition was his difficult breathing and his great exhaustion. Of his sense of weakness, Jackson spoke; but when Dr. Breckinridge expressed hope that a blister would help, Jackson voiced his own confidence in that treatment and maintained that he would get well.[9] Later in the day, Dr. Morrison had to express a fear that the disease might not be overcome. To this, Jackson listened without emotion, and then, rallying his mind and tongue, he said deliberately: "I am not afraid to die; I am willing to abide by the will of my Heavenly Father. But I do not believe that I shall die at this time; I am persuaded the Almighty has yet a work for me to perform."[1] The General demanded that Dr. McGuire be summoned to pass on Dr. Morrison's opinion; and even after his own Medical Director admitted doubt concerning the outcome, Jackson still insisted that he would recover. He had a restless night, but he did not appear to be shaken in his confidence that he would beat his new adversary.

Out of doors, the brightest day of a changeable May week was Saturday, the 9th.[2] It found Jackson's breathing apparently less difficult and his pain diminished. His weakness manifestly was worse.[3] He still observed intermittently what was going on in his sick room, and he noticed dimly that to the intelligent faces of the doctors around his bed, another had been added—that of David Tucker, the Richmond authority on pneumonia, who at length had arrived. Jackson did not remark at the moment how many consultants had been summoned. Later in the day he said slowly to McGuire: "I see from the number of physicians that you think my condition dangerous, but I thank God, if it is His will, that I am ready to go."[4] Ready though he was, he still was determined to fight for recovery. He asked to see his baby and, when she came, he beamed at her in no spirit of farewell. With his splinted hand, which the child did not seem to fear, he caressed her. "Little comforter . . . little comforter," he murmured.[5]

8. *Cf.* 2 *R. E. Lee,* 562. This remark was made Sunday, May 10.

9. *McGuire,* 227.

1. These sentences are put in quotations because Dr. Dabney, *op. cit.,* 719, insisted that Jackson used "precisely these words." Further, Dr. Dabney insisted that Jackson distinguished with care and purpose between "my Heavenly Father," when speaking of his own relationship to God, and "the Almighty" when he referred to the divine plan.

2. *Hotchkiss' MS Diary,* 189.

3. *Dabney,* 721; *McGuire,* 227.

4. *McGuire,* 227.

5. *Ibid.*

In the afternoon, he bade his attendants summon Chaplain Lacy. At the time, the lungs of Jackson were so nearly filled that his breathing was difficult again. Such respiration as he had was shallow and cruelly fast. For these reasons, Mrs. Jackson and the physicians tried to dissuade him from conversing with Lacy. The General would not be balked. He must see the Chaplain. It was important. His attendants yielded. Tucker Lacy came in as if for another of the theological discussions in which Jackson delighted. This time the General had a more practical question of religion: Was Lacy working to promote Sunday observance by the Army in the manner previously enjoined on him? Lacy was able to report that he was. Jackson was pleased and relieved, but as the subject was one regarding which he had positive convictions, he tried to explain them once again, slowly and painfully, to the Chaplain.[6] When Lacy at length arose, he offered to remain with the General on the Sabbath Day; but Jackson insisted that Lacy go to second corps headquarters and preach, as usual, to the soldiers.[7]

Evening came, clear and warm. A week before, at that very hour, Jackson had been driving furiously through the Wilderness and, looking backward at the sunset skies, he had wished for an hour more of daylight.[8] Now, what was it he desired as he lay there and lifted his arm above his head again, in his familiar gesture, and shut his eyes and seemed to pray?[9] Was it for another day of life—for recovery—for opportunity, with blazing batteries and the cheering line of his veterans, to drive Hooker into the river? He talked more of battle than of anything else and he commanded and exhorted— "Order A. P. Hill to prepare for action . . . Pass the infantry to the front."[1] Most of his other words were confused or unintelligible.

Now, again, into the deepening silence, came the voice of Mrs. Jackson: Might she read to him some of the Psalms of consolation? He shook his head vaguely; he was suffering too much, he said, to be able to listen. No sooner had he spoken than his disciplined conscience stirred and smote him even in his stupor. Would he not heed the Psalms, the Word of God? "Yes," he corrected himself, "we must never refuse that." He managed to add briefly: "Get the Bible and read them."

She brought the book and in her soft voice read. He tried to fix his attention on the promises of the Most High but he grew weary. "Sing to me," he said presently, and when she asked what she should sing, he bade her choose the most spiritual of the hymns. The brave woman thus far had endured the emotional strain but she was afraid to trust her voice alone on the hymns beloved by the man she loved. Her brother Joseph—the Lieutenant Morrison who had been with Jackson in the Wilderness—was there at the cottage.

6. *Mrs. Jackson*, 453; *Dabney*, 721.
7. *Mrs. Jackson*, 453.
8. *Cooke's Jackson*, 419.

9. *McGuire*, 227, with no certainty concerning the hour this occurred.
1. See *supra*, p. 671, n. 119.

Would he help her? He came. She got the hymn book. Together in the dim light of the room, brother and sister sat by the bed and sang . . . to the ominous accompaniment of Jackson's wild breathing.

"Sing, 'Shew Pity, Lord,' " Jackson gasped.

They knew what he wanted—Dr. Watts's rendering of part of the Fifty-first Psalm, which was marked "A penitent pleading for pardon"—

> Shew pity, Lord; O Lord, forgive;
> Let a repenting rebel live;
> Are not thy mercies large and free?
> May not a sinner trust in thee?[2]

Doubtless, as it was written, they sang it through its sixth and last verse:

> Yet save a trembling sinner, Lord,
> Whose hope, still hov'ring round thy word,
> Would light on some sweet promise there,
> Some sure support against despair.

"The singing," Mrs. Jackson said afterward, "had a quieting effect, and he seemed to rest in perfect peace."[3] When Dr. Morrison hinted again, later in the evening, that the end might not be far distant, the spirit of the soldier asserted itself once more. "I don't think so," said Jackson; "I think I will be better by morning."[4]

Determined as he was to fight on, he lost ground as the night passed and, half conscious, he seemed to get no relief except from cold sponging of his face and forehead.[5] As he appeared to be sinking steadily, one of the physicians tried to get him to take a drink of brandy. Jackson tasted it but refused to do more. "It tastes like fire," he said, "and cannot do me any good."[6]

The soft spring night ended at last in warmth and promise of sunshine.[7] It was the 10th of May. Two years ago that day at Harpers Ferry, when he was a Colonel of Virginia Volunteers, he had named as Surgeon the man who now was leaning over him. Orders had been issued also, May 10, 1861, for regimental commanders to superintend the drill of their regiments. Captains had been directed to inspect their companies before marching them to dress parade.[8]

Jackson's mind then had been intent on training the superb raw manpower he had. Plans he had been maturing to increase the artillery of his command.[9] A year later, May 10, 1862, as a Major General in the Provisional Army of the Confederacy, he had been in pursuit of Milroy after the action at McDowell, and he had been writing Ewell: "My troops are in advance. Should circumstances justify it, I will try, through God's blessing, to get in Banks'

2. In Winchell's *Watts,* this is assigned the tunes German, Bath and Limehouse; but Dr. Dabney, *op cit.,* 722, stated that it was sung to the tune Old Hundred.

3. *Mrs. Jackson,* 473.

4. *Dabney,* 719.
5. *Dabney,* 722.
6. *Mrs. Jackson,* 454.
7. *Hotchkiss' MS Diary.*
8. *Calendar Confederate Papers,* 286.
9. *O. R.,* 2, 823-24.

rear . . . "[1] In Richmond, on the 10th of May, 1862, there had been rejoicing over the brief telegram he had sent on the 9th to the Adjutant General: "God blessed our arms with victory at McDowell yesterday."[2] Was all that ended now—McDowell, Front Royal, Winchester, Cross Keys, Port Republic, Cedar Mountain, Groveton, Harpers Ferry—those battles of his own and all those he had fought with Lee? It was Sunday; was the day to witness the last contest? In his mind there was contention—muttered references again to A. P. Hill, orders to Major Hawks, directions for the battle.

Mrs. Jackson slipped out of the room. If he observed her departure, he said nothing. Breathing hard, he lay there and said nothing. Jim sat drowsily by. One of the surgeons helplessly watched. Minutes passed in silence. Presently, as the morning light grew brighter, Mrs. Jackson came back. The others left the chamber. Alone, she sat down by him. On her face were the marks of an emotional battle, but he was calm. Long before, he had told her that he did not fear to die but that he hoped he would "have a few hours' preparation before entering into the presence of his Maker and Redeemer." Now she felt she had to discharge the hard, hard duty that remark imposed.

Her voice came to him on the border of the far country. He stirred in evidence that he heard it but at first he could not arouse himself. She was talking to him: "Do you know the doctors say, you must very soon be in Heaven?"

He said nothing. She repeated it, and added: "Do you not feel willing to acquiesce in God's allotment, if He wills you to go today?"

Again she had to ask him the same question. Slowly the words and their import sank into his mind. He opened his eyes and looked at her. "I prefer it," he said slowly and with much difficulty. If he could focus his eyes to see her expression, he must have noticed that she seemed uncertain whether he was babbling or knew what he was saying. More carefully he framed the syllables: "I prefer it."

"Well," she said, incredibly keeping her self-control, "before this day closes, you will be with the blessed Saviour in His glory."

He steadied himself for the effort of speech and said deliberately, "I will be an infinite gainer to be translated."[3]

She talked with him further and asked his wishes about many things, but she could not hold his attention.[4] Nor did he appear to be convinced that his end actually was at hand. The man who had beaten off all the foe's attacks at Groveton was not of the spirit to believe that even the Last Enemy could rout him.

1. *O. R.*, 12, pt. 3, p. 386.
2. *O. R.*, 12, pt. 1, p. 470.
3. *Dabney*, 722-23.
4. Mrs. Jackson wrote as if all the wishes expressed by Jackson were voiced in a single interview which occurred in the early morning. Dr. McGuire mentioned a second conversation at 11 A.M.

The sole way to reconcile the difference between Mrs. Jackson's account and the earlier narrative of Dr. McGuire is to assume that Mrs. Jackson forgot, after thirty years, that she had the second and longer conversation with her husband later in the morning.

After Mrs. Jackson conversed with him, the surgeons must have made their examinations, but they did not attempt to dress his wounds. He was disturbed as little as possible. About 11 A.M.—the day continued warm and beautiful—he was aroused again by Mrs. Jackson. This time she was kneeling by his bed and was telling him again that before the sun went down he would be in Heaven. Often, in battle, he had met on their way to the rear unnerved men who had told of calamity and death at the front. He had rebuked them; he could not fail now to chide even her. Full consciousness seemed to return. Clearly he said: "Oh, no! you are frightened, my child; death is not so near; I may yet get well."

With this she threw herself on the bed and in a flood of tears told him that the doctors said there was no hope for him. He listened and seemed to reflect, and then he asked her to call Dr. McGuire.

Almost on the instant, the man who so often had come to his campfire to report the wounded and the dead, was at his command. "Doctor," said Jackson, still distinctly, "Anna informs me that you have told her that I am to die today; is it so?"

As gently and as sympathetically as was possible, McGuire replied that medicine had done its utmost.

Again Jackson seemed to ponder. He turned his eyes from McGuire's face to the ceiling and gazed upward for a few moments. In battle, when orders were well executed or some shining deed was performed, he often would say, "Good, good"; but now he thought the orders of Higher Command had been given, his response was stronger: "Very good; very good; it is all right."[5] With that he turned to the weeping woman and tried to comfort her. Much he had to tell her, he said, but he was too weak.[6] After a struggle, she undertook to inquire what he desired for himself and for her and the baby? Should she go back to her father when it was all over? she asked.

"You have a kind and good father," he said, scarcely conscious, "but there is no one so kind and good as your Heavenly Father."[7]

Where did he wish to be buried?

He did not seem to be interested. "Charlotte," she understood him to say, and she inquired again. "Charlottesville," he said half consciously.

There was no reason for that, no association other than that of names. She prompted him: Did he wish to be buried in Lexington? "Yes," he answered, "in Lexington, and in my own plot," but he spoke of it casually, as if it scarcely mattered.[8]

In accordance with the customs of the day, it seemed proper that

5. *McGuire*, 228.
6. *Ibid.*
7. It is possible that he made this remark in the first conversation of the morning with Mrs. Jackson, cf. *McGuire*, 227-28, but the probabilities would seem to favor the discussion of all the family arrangements at one time.
8. *Mrs. Jackson*, 456. Dabney said, *op. cit.*, 723, "his tune expressed rather acquiescence than lively interest."

he say farewell to his child. Mrs. Hoge accordingly brought in the baby, with the nurse. Jackson recognized the child at once and seemed far more pleased to see her than to talk of funerary details. His face, now emaciated and strangely ascetic in appearance, lighted up with a smile. "Little darling," he said, . . . "sweet one!" The baby smiled back and did not seem in any way frightened. She alone, of all the company, was the embodiment of life without knowledge or fear of death. Through the fog of morphia and weakness he played with her and called her endearing names until he sank back into the unconscious.[9]

When next he aroused, "Sandie" Pendleton in his martial gray was standing by his bed—"Sandie" who had so much of his unvoiced affection and soldierly admiration. The presence of the young soldier brought Jackson back for an instant to a world of camps and sinning soldiers. "Who is preaching at headquarters today?" he asked. Pendleton told him that Lacy was,[1] but he thoughtfully refrained from reminding Jackson that the Chaplain was there by the General's own forgotten order. Jackson was gratified that the men were to hear so eminent a preacher. Still more was Jackson pleased when "Sandie" told him that the whole army was praying for him. "Thank God," he murmured, "they are very kind . . ." Presently he spoke again. "It is the Lord's Day . . . . My wish is fulfilled. I have always desired to die on Sunday."[2]

"Sandie" went out to weep and not to weep alone. Everyone was in tears. The faithful Jim was overwhelmed. Not one of the doctors, looking at Jackson and listening to the struggle for breath, dared hope that the General could live even till night, but Dr. McGuire thought he should stimulate Jackson with some brandy. The next time the man on the bed seemed conscious, McGuire asked him to drink from the glass. Jackson shook his head: "It will only delay my departure, and do no good; I want to preserve my mind, if possible, to the last."[3] Once more he slipped back into the land of far and near, where faces change instantly and scenes melt one into another. He murmured again, gave orders, sat at mess with his staff, was back in Lexington with his little family, was fighting, was praying.

From another world came presently the voice of McGuire, with kindly but solemn warning that the sands were running low. It was 1:30: Jackson might not have more than two hours to live.

Feebly but firmly the assurance was given: "Very good; it is all right!"[4]

More there was in the same mutter—Hill, Hawks, orders to the infantry—and then a long, long silence, such a silence as might

9. *Mrs. Jackson*, 456.
1. Lacy's text that day was, "And we know that all things work together for good. . . ." *Romans* viii, 28. *Hotchkiss'*

MS Diary, 189.
2. *McGuire*, 228.
3. *McGuire*, 228.
4. *McGuire*, 228.

have come that May night the previous year when he had pushed the Stonewall Brigade forward toward Winchester and had halted and heard only the breath of his companions, and then had seen the fire of the Federal sharpshooters run along the hillside. Great events had been impending then. Long marches and hard battles and wide streams had been ahead. Now . . . the clock striking three, the spring sunshine in the room, the rustle of new leaves in the breeze, peace and the end of a Sabbath Day's journey. Fifteen minutes more; breathing now was in the very throat; and then from the bed, clearly, quietly, cheerfully. "Let us cross over the river, and rest under the shade of the trees."[5]

5. *McGuire, 229.* In this final quotation, McGuire's words are followed. The verb is "cross" over the river. Many of the early authorities insisted that the verb was "pass."

HENRY DAVID THOREAU
The Battle of the Ants[1]

One day when I went out to my wood-pile, or rather my pile of stumps, I observed two large ants, the one red, the other much larger, nearly half an inch long, and black, fiercely contending with one another. Having once got hold they never let go, but struggled and wrestled and rolled on the chips incessantly. Looking farther, I was surprised to find that the chips were covered with such combatants, that it was not a *duellum,* but a *bellum,* a war between two races of ants, the red always pitted against the black, and frequently two red ones to one black. The legions of these Myrmidons covered all the hills and vales in my wood-yard, and the ground was already strewn with the dead and dying, both red and black. It was the only battle which I have ever witnessed, the only battle-field I ever trod while the battle was raging; internecine war; the red republicans on the one hand, and the black imperialists on the other. On every side they were engaged in deadly combat, yet without any noise that I could hear, and human soldiers never fought so resolutely. I watched a couple that were fast locked in each other's embraces, in a little sunny valley amid the chips, now at noonday prepared to fight till the sun went down, or life went out. The smaller red champion had fastened himself like a vice to his adversary's front, and through all the tumblings on that field never for an instant ceased to gnaw at one of his feelers near the root, having already caused the other to go by the board; while the stronger black one dashed him from side to side, and, as I saw on looking nearer, had already divested him of several of his members. They fought with more pertinacity than bulldogs. Neither manifested the least disposi-

1. From "Brute Neighbors," Chapter XII of *Walden.*

tion to retreat. It was evident that their battle-cry was "Conquer or die." In the meanwhile there came along a single red ant on the hillside of this valley, evidently full of excitement, who either had despatched his foe, or had not yet taken part in the battle; probably the latter, for he had lost none of his limbs; whose mother had charged him to return with his shield or upon it. Or perchance he was some Achilles, who had nourished his wrath apart, and had now come to avenge or rescue his Patroclus.[2] He saw this unequal combat from afar—for the blacks were nearly twice the size of the red—he drew near with rapid pace till he stood on his guard within half an inch of the combatants; then, watching his opportunity, he sprang upon the black warrior, and commenced his operations near the root of his right fore leg, leaving the foe to select among his own members; and so there were three united for life, as if a new kind of attraction had been invented which put all other locks and cements to shame. I should not have wondered by this time to find that they had their respective musical bands stationed on some eminent chip, and playing their national airs the while, to excite the slow and cheer the dying combatants. I was myself excited somewhat even as if they had been men. The more you think of it, the less the difference. And certainly there is not the fight recorded in Concord history, at least, if in the history of America, that will bear a moment's comparison with this, whether for the numbers engaged in it, or for the patriotism and heroism displayed. For numbers and for carnage it was an Austerlitz or Dresden.[3] Concord Fight! Two killed on the patriots' side, and Luther Blanchard wounded! Why here every ant was a Buttrick—"Fire! for God's sake fire!"—and thousands shared the fate of Davis and Hosmer. There was not one hireling there. I have no doubt that it was a principle they fought for, as much as our ancestors, and not to avoid a three-penny tax on their tea; and the results of this battle will be as important and memorable to those whom it concerns as those of the battle of Bunker Hill, at least.

I took up the chip on which the three I have particularly described were struggling, carried into my house, and placed it under a tumbler on my window-sill, in order to see the issue. Holding a microscope to the first-mentioned red ant, I saw that, though he was assiduously gnawing at the near fore leg of his enemy, having severed his remaining feeler, his own breast was all torn away, exposing what vitals he had there to the jaws of the black warrior, whose breastplate was apparently too thick for him to pierce; and the dark carbuncles of the sufferer's eyes shone with ferocity such as war only could excite. They struggled half an hour longer under the tumbler, and when I looked again the black soldier had severed the heads of his foes from their bodies, and the still living heads were hanging on

2. A Greek warrior in the *Iliad*, whose death Achilles avenges.
3. Bloody Napoleonic victories.

either side of him like ghastly trophies at his saddle-bow, still apparently as firmly fastened as ever, and he was endeavoring with feeble struggles, being without feelers, and with only the remnant of a leg, and I know not how many other wounds, to divest himself of them; which at length, after half an hour more, he accomplished. I raised the glass, and he went off over the window-sill in that crippled state. Whether he finally survived that combat, and spent the remainder of his days in some Hôtel des Invalides, I do not know; but I thought that his industry would not be worth much thereafter. I never learned which party was victorious, nor the cause of the war, but I felt for the rest of that day as if I had my feelings excited and harrowed by witnessing the struggle, the ferocity and carnage, of a human battle before my door.

Kirby and Spence tell us that the battles of ants have long been celebrated and the date of them recorded, though they say that Huber[4] is the only modern author who appears to have witnessed them. "Aeneas Sylvius," say they, "after giving a very circumstantial account of one contested with great obstinacy by a great and small species on the trunk of a pear tree," adds that " 'this action was fought in the pontificate of Eugenius the Fourth, in the presence of Nicholas Pistoriensis, an eminent lawyer, who related the whole history of the battle with the greatest fidelity.' A similar engagement between great and small ants is recorded by Olaus Magnus, in which the small ones, being victorious, are said to have buried the bodies of their own soldiers, but left those of their giant enemies a prey to the birds. This event happened previous to the expulsion of the tyrant Christiern the Second from Sweden." The battle which I witnessed took place in the Presidency of Polk, five years before the passage of Webster's Fugitive-Slave Bill.

4. Kirby and Spence were nineteenth-century American entomologists; Huber was a great Swiss entomologist.

QUESTIONS FOR STUDY, DISCUSSION, AND WRITING

1. Thoreau uses the Latin word bellum to describe the struggle of the ants and he quickly follows this with a reference to the Myrmidons of Achilles. What comparison is implicit here? Find further examples of it. This passage comes from a chapter entitled "Brute Neighbors"; how does this comparison amplify the meaning of that title?
2. Thoreau obviously joins the lower form of life—the ant—with man. Does this reflect what Bury (pp. 1170–1181) Darwin-istic or genetic approach to history?
4. Describe the life, or part of the life, of an animal so that, while remaining faithful to the facts as you understand them, your description opens outward as do those of Thoreau, Stewart ("Vulture Country," pp. 1361–1368), and Ardrey ("From Territory To Nation," pp. 1335–1348) and speaks not only of the animal but of man, society, or nature.

JAMES ANTHONY FROUDE
Defeat of the Armada[1]

In the gallery at Madrid there is a picture, painted by Titian, representing the Genius of Spain coming to the delivery of the afflicted Bride of Christ. Titian was dead, but the temper of the age survived, and in the study of that great picture you will see the spirit in which the Spanish nation had set out for the conquest of England. The scene is the seashore. The Church a naked Andromeda,[2] with disheveled hair, fastened to the trunk of an ancient disbranched tree. The cross lies at her feet, the cup overturned, the serpents of heresy biting at her from behind with uplifted crests. Coming on before a leading breeze is the sea monster, the Moslem fleet, eager for their prey; while in front is Perseus, the Genius of Spain, banner in hand, with the legions of the faithful laying not raiment before him, but shield and helmet, the apparel of war for the Lady of Nations to clothe herself with strength and smite her foes.

In the Armada the crusading enthusiasm had reached its point and focus. England was the stake to which the Virgin, the daughter of Sion,[3] was bound in captivity. Perseus had come at last in the person of the Duke of Medina Sidonia, and with him all that was best and brightest in the countrymen of Cervantes, to break her bonds and replace her on her throne. They had sailed into the channel in pious hope, with the blessed banner waving over their heads.

To be the executor of the decrees of Providence is a lofty ambition, but men in a state of high emotion overlook the precautions which are not to be dispensed with even on the sublimest of errands. Don Quixote, when he set out to redress the wrongs of humanity, forgot that a change of linen might be necessary and that he must take money with him to pay his hotel bills. Philip II, in sending the Armada to England, and confident in supernatural protection, imagined an unresisted triumphal procession. He forgot that contractors might be rascals, that water four months in the casks in a hot climate turned putrid, and that putrid water would poison his ships' companies, though his crews were companies of angels. He forgot that the servants of the evil one might fight for their mistress after all, and that he must send adequate supplies of powder, and, worst forgetfulness of all, that a great naval expedition required a leader who understood his business. Perseus, in the shape of the Duke of Medina Sidonia, after a week of disastrous battles, found

---

1. From *English Seamen in the XVIth Century*.
2. In Greek mythology Andromeda was a maiden rescued by Perseus from a sea-serpent.
3. The hill in Jerusalem on which the temple was built.

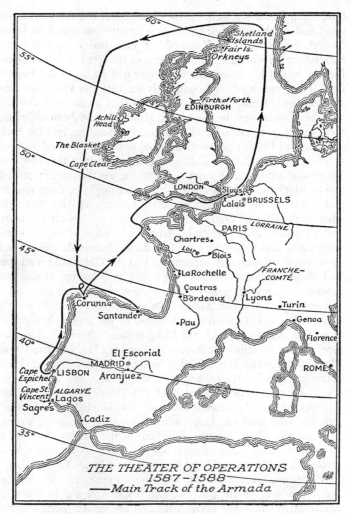

THE THEATER OF OPERATIONS
1587–1588
——Main Track of the Armada

himself at the end of it in an exposed roadstead, where he ought never to have been, nine-tenths of his provisions thrown overboard as unfit for food, his ammunition exhausted by the unforeseen demands upon it, the seamen and soldiers harassed and dispirited, officers the whole week without sleep, and the enemy, who had hunted him from Plymouth to Calais, anchored within half a league of him.

Still, after all his misadventures, he had brought the fleet, if not to the North Foreland, yet within a few miles of it, and to outward appearance not materially injured. Two of the galleons had been taken; a third, the *Santa Aña*, had strayed; and his galleys had left

him, being found too weak for the channel sea; but the great armament had reached its destination substantially uninjured so far as
English eyes could see. Hundreds of men had been killed and
hundreds more wounded, and the spirit of the rest had been shaken.
But the loss of life could only be conjectured on board the English
fleet. The English admiral could only see that the Duke was now
in touch with Parma.[4] Parma, they knew, had an army at Dunkirk
with him, which was to cross to England. He had been collecting
men, barges, and transports all the winter and spring, and the backward state of Parma's preparations could not be anticipated, still less
relied upon. The Calais anchorage was unsafe; but at that season of
the year, especially after a wet summer, the weather usually settled;
and to attack the Spaniards in a French port might be dangerous for
many reasons. It was uncertain after the day of the Barricades
whether the Duke of Guise or Henry of Valois was master of France,
and a violation of the neutrality laws might easily at that moment
bring Guise and France into the field on the Spaniards' side. It was,
no doubt, with some such expectation that the Duke and his advisers
had chosen Calais as the point at which to bring up. It was now
Saturday, the 7th of August. The governor of the town came off in
the evening to the *San Martin*. He expressed surprise to see the
Spanish fleet in so exposed a position, but he was profuse in his offers
of service. Anything which the Duke required should be provided,
especially every facility for communicating with Dunkirk and Parma.
The Duke thanked him, said that he supposed Parma to be already
embarked with his troops, ready for the passage, and that his own
stay in the roads would be but brief. On Monday morning at latest
he expected that the attempt to cross would be made. The governor
took his leave, and the Duke, relieved from his anxieties, was left
to a peaceful night. He was disturbed on the Sunday morning by
an express from Parma informing him that, so far from being
embarked, the army could not be ready for a fortnight. The barges
were not in condition for sea. The troops were in camp. The arms
and stores were on the quays at Dunkirk. As for the fly-boats and
ammunition which the Duke had asked for, he had none to spare.
He had himself looked to be supplied from the Armada. He promised
to use his best expedition, but the Duke, meanwhile, must see to
the safety of the fleet.

Unwelcome news to a harassed landsman thrust into the position
of an admiral and eager to be rid of his responsibilities. If by evil
fortune the northwester should come down upon him, with the
shoals and sandbanks close under his lee, he would be in a bad
way. Nor was the view behind him calculated for comfort. There lay
the enemy almost within gunshot, who, though scarcely more than
half his numbers, had hunted him like a pack of bloodhounds, and,

---

4. The Duke of Parma, Spanish governor in the Netherlands.

worse than all, in double strength; for the Thames squadron—three Queen's ships and thirty London adventurers—under Lord H. Seymour and Sir John Hawkins, had crossed in the night. There they were between him and Cape Grisnez, and the reinforcements meant plainly enough that mischief was in the wind.

After a week so trying the Spanish crews would have been glad of a Sunday's rest if they could have had it; but the rough handling which they had gone through had thrown everything into disorder. The sick and wounded had to be cared for, torn rigging looked to, splintered timbers mended, decks scoured, and guns and arms cleaned up and put to rights. And so it was that no rest could be allowed; so much had to be done, and so busy was every one, that the usual rations were not served out and the Sunday was kept as a fast. In the afternoon the stewards went ashore for fresh meat and vegetables. They came back with their boats loaded, and the prospect seemed a little less gloomy. Suddenly, as the Duke and a group of officers were watching the English fleet from the *San Martin's* poop deck, a small smart pinnace, carrying a gun in her bow, shot out from Howard's lines, bore down on the *San Martin*, sailed round her, sending in a shot or two as she passed, and went off unhurt. The Spanish officers could not help admiring such airy impertinence. Hugo de Monçada sent a ball after the pinnace, which went through her mainsail, but did no damage, and the pinnace again disappeared behind the English ships.

So a Spanish officer describes the scene. The English story says nothing of the pinnace; but she doubtless came and went as the Spaniard says, and for sufficient purpose. The English, too, were in straits, though the Duke did not dream of it. You will remember that the last supplies which the Queen had allowed to the fleet had been issued in the middle of June. They were to serve for a month, and the contractors were forbidden to prepare more. The Queen had clung to her hope that her differences with Philip were to be settled by the Commission at Ostend; and she feared that if Drake and Howard were too well furnished they would venture some fresh rash stroke on the coast of Spain, which might mar the negotiations. Their month's provisions had been stretched to serve for six weeks, and when the Armada appeared but two full days' rations remained. On these they had fought their way up Channel. Something had been brought out by private exertion on the Dorsetshire coast, and Seymour had, perhaps, brought a little more. But they were still in extremity. The contractors had warned the Government that they could provide nothing without notice, and notice had not been given. The adventurers were in better state, having been equipped by private owners. But the Queen's ships in a day or two more must either go home or their crews would be starving. They had been on reduced rations for near two months. Worse than that, they were still poisoned by the sour beer. The Queen had changed her mind so often, now ordering the fleet to prepare for sea, then recalling her instructions and paying off the men, that those whom Howard had with him had been enlisted in haste, had come on board as they were, and their clothes were hanging in rags on them. The fighting and the sight of the flying Spaniards were meat and drink, and clothing too, and had made them careless of all else. There was no fear of mutiny; but there was a limit to the toughest endurance. If the Armada was left undisturbed a long struggle might be still before them. The enemy would recover from its flurry, and Parma would come out from Dunkirk. To attack them directly in French waters might lead to perilous complications, while delay meant famine. The Spanish fleet had to be started from the roads in some way. Done it must be, and done immediately.

Then, on that same Sunday afternoon a memorable council of war was held in the *Ark's* main cabin. Howard, Drake, Seymour, Hawkins, Martin Frobisher, and two or three others met to consult, knowing that on them at that moment the liberties of England were depending. Their resolution was taken promptly. There was no time for talk. After nightfall a strong flood tide would be setting up along shore to the Spanish anchorage. They would try what could be done with fire ships, and the excursion of the pinnace, which was taken for bravado, was probably for a survey of the Armada's exact position. Meantime eight useless vessels were coated with pitch—hulls, spars, and rigging. Pitch was poured on the decks and over the sides, and parties were told off to steer them to their destination and then fire and leave them.

The hours stole on, and twilight passed into dark. The night was without a moon. The Duke paced his deck late with uneasy sense of danger. He observed lights moving up and down the English lines, and imagining that the *endemoniada gente*—the infernal devils— might be up to mischief, ordered a sharp look-out. A faint westerly air was curling the water, and towards midnight the watchers on board the galleons made out dimly several ships which seemed to be drifting down upon them. Their experience since the action off Plymouth had been so strange and unlooked for that anything unintelligible which the English did was alarming.

The phantom forms drew nearer, and were almost among them when they broke into a blaze from water-line to truck, and the two fleets were seen by the lurid light of the conflagration; the anchorage, the walls and windows of Calais, and the sea shining red as far as eye could reach, as if the ocean itself was burning. Among the dangers which they might have to encounter, English fireworks had been especially dreaded by the Spaniards. Fire ships—a fit device of heretics—had worked havoc among the Spanish troops, when the bridge was blown up, at Antwerp. They imagined that similar infernal machines were approaching the Armada. A capable commander would have sent a few launches to grapple the burning hulks, which of course were now deserted, and tow them out of harm's way. Spanish sailors were not cowards, and would not have flinched from duty because it might be dangerous; but the Duke and Diego Florez lost their heads again. A signal gun from the *San Martin* ordered the whole fleet to slip their cables and stand out to sea.

Orders given in panic are doubly unwise, for they spread the terror in which they originate. The danger from the fire ships was chiefly from the effect on the imagination, for they appear to have drifted by and done no real injury. And it speaks well for the seamanship and courage of the Spaniards that they were able, crowded together as they were, at midnight and in sudden alarm to set their canvas and clear out without running into one another. They buoyed their cables, expecting to return for them at daylight, and with only a single accident, to be mentioned directly, they executed successfully a really difficult maneuver.

The Duke was delighted with himself. The fire ships burned harmlessly out. He had baffled the inventions of the *endemoniada gente*. He brought up a league outside the harbour, and supposed that the whole Armada had done the same. Unluckily for himself, he found it at daylight divided into two bodies. The *San Martin* with forty of the best appointed of the galleons were riding together at their anchors. The rest, two thirds of the whole, having no second anchors ready, and inexperienced in Channel tides and currents, had been lying to. The west wind was blowing up. Without seeing where they were going they had drifted to leeward, and were two leagues off, towards Gravelines, dangerously near the shore. The Duke was too ignorant to realise the full peril of his situation. He signaled to them to return and rejoin him. As the wind and tide stood it was impossible. He proposed to follow them. The pilots told him that if he did the whole fleet might be lost on the banks. Towards the land the look of things was not more encouraging.

One accident only had happened the night before. The *Capitana* galleass, with Don Hugo de Monçada and eight hundred men on board, had fouled her helm in a cable in getting under way and had become unmanageable. The galley slaves disobeyed orders, or else Don Hugo was as incompetent as his commander-in-chief. The galleass had gone on the sands, and as the tide ebbed had fallen over on her side. Howard, seeing her condition, had followed her in the *Ark* with four or five other of the Queen's ships, and was furiously attacking her with his boats, careless of neutrality laws. Howard's theory was, as he said, to pluck the feathers one by one from the Spaniard's wing, and here was a feather worth picking up. The galleass was the most splendid vessel of her kind afloat, Don Hugo one of the greatest of Spanish grandees.

Howard was making a double mistake. He took the galleass at last after three hours' fighting. Don Hugo was killed by a musket ball. The vessel was plundered, and Howard's men took possession, meaning to carry her away when the tide rose. The French authorities ordered him off, threatening to fire upon him; and after wasting the forenoon, he was obliged at last to leave her where she lay. Worse than this, he had lost three precious hours, and had lost along with them, in the opinion of the Prince of Parma, the honors of the great day.

Drake and Hawkins knew better than to waste time plucking single feathers. The fire ships had been more effective than they could have dared to hope. The enemy was broken up. The Duke was shorn of half his strength, and the Lord had delivered him into their hand. He had got under way, still signaling wildly, and uncertain in which direction to turn. His uncertainties were ended for him by seeing Drake bear down upon him with the whole English fleet, save those which were loitering about the galleass. The English had now the advantage of numbers. The superiority of their guns he knew already, and their greater speed allowed him no hope to escape a battle. Forty ships alone were left to him to defend the banner of the crusade and the honor of Castile; but those forty were the largest and most powerfully armed and manned that he had, and on board them were Oquendo, De Leyva, Recalde, Bretandona, the best officers in the Spanish navy next to the lost Don Pedro.

It was now or never for England. The scene of the action which was to decide the future of Europe was between Calais and Dunkirk, a few miles off shore, and within sight of Parma's camp. There was no more maneuvering for the weather-gage, no more fighting at long range. Drake dashed straight upon his prey as the falcon swoops upon its quarry. A chance had fallen to him which might never return; not for the vain distinction of carrying prizes into English ports, not for the ray of honor which would fall on him if he could carry off the sacred banner itself and hang it in the Abbey at Westminster, but a chance so to handle the Armada that it should never be seen again in English waters, and deal such a blow on Philip that the Spanish Empire should reel with it. The English ships had the same superiority over the galleons which steamers have now over sailing vessels. They had twice the speed; they could lie two points nearer to the wind. Sweeping round them at cable's length, crowding them in one upon the other, yet never once giving them a chance to grapple, they hurled in their cataracts of round shot. Short as was the powder supply, there was no sparing it that morning. The hours went on, and still the battle raged, if battle it could be called where the blows were all dealt on one side and the suffering was all on the other. Never on sea or land did the Spaniards show themselves worthier of their great name than on that day. But from the first they could do nothing. It was said afterwards in Spain that the Duke showed the white feather, that he charged his pilot to keep him out of harm's way, that he shut himself up in his cabin, buried in woolpacks, and so on. The Duke had faults enough, but poltroonery was not one of them. He, who till he entered the English Channel had never been in action on sea or land, found himself, as he said, in the midst of the most furious engagement recorded in the history of the world. As to being out of harm's way, the standard at his masthead drew the hottest of the fire upon him. The *San Martin's* timbers were of oak and a foot thick, but the shot, he said, went through them enough to shatter a rock. Her deck was a slaughterhouse; half his company were killed or wounded, and no more would have been heard or seen of the *San Martin* or her commander had not Oquendo and De Leyva pushed in to the rescue and enabled him to creep away under their cover. He himself saw nothing more of the action after this. The smoke, he said, was so thick that he could make out nothing, even from his masthead. But all round it was but a repetition of the same scene. The Spanish shot flew high, as before, above the low English hulls, and they were themselves helpless butts to the English guns. And it is noticeable and supremely creditable to them that not a single galleon struck her colors. One of them, after a long duel with an Englishman, was on the point of sinking. An English officer, admiring the courage which the Spaniards had shown, ran out upon his bowsprit, told them that they had done all which became men, and urged them to surrender and save their lives. For answer they cursed the English as cowards and chickens because they refused to close. The officer was shot. His fall brought a last broadside on them, which finished the work. They went down, and the water closed over them. Rather death to the soldiers of the Cross than surrender to a heretic.

The deadly hail rained on. In some ships blood was seen streaming out of the scupper-holes. Yet there was no yielding; all ranks showed equal heroism. The priests went up and down in the midst of the carnage, holding the crucifix before the eyes of the dying. At midday Howard came up to claim a second share in a victory which was no longer doubtful. Towards the afternoon the Spanish fire slackened. Their powder was gone, and they could make no return to the cannonade which was still overwhelming them. They admitted freely afterwards that if the attack had been continued but two hours more they must all have struck or gone ashore. But the English magazines were empty also; the last cartridge was shot away, and the battle ended from mere inability to keep it up. It had been fought on both sides with peculiar determination. In the English there was the accumulated resentment of thirty years of menace to their country and their creed, with the enemy in tangible shape at last to be caught and grappled with; in the Spanish, the sense that if their cause had not brought them the help they looked for from above, the honor and faith of Castile should not suffer in their hands.

It was over. The English drew off, regretting that their thrifty mistress had limited their means of fighting for her, and so obliged them to leave their work half done. When the cannon ceased the wind rose, the smoke rolled away, and in the level light of the sunset they could see the results of the action.

A galleon in Recalde's squadron was sinking with all hands. The *San Philip* and the *San Matteo* were drifting dismasted towards the Dutch coast, where they were afterwards wrecked. Those which were left with canvas still showing were crawling slowly after their comrades who had not been engaged, the spars and rigging so cut up that they could scarce bear their sails. The loss of life could only be conjectured, but it had been obviously terrible. The nor'-wester was blowing up and was pressing the wounded ships upon the shoals, from which, if it held, it seemed impossible in their crippled state they would be able to work off.

In this condition Drake left them for the night, not to rest, but from any quarter to collect, if he could, more food and powder. The snake had been scotched, but not killed. More than half the great fleet were far away, untouched by shot, perhaps able to fight a second battle if they recovered heart. To follow, to drive them on the banks if the wind held, or into the North Sea, anywhere so that he left them no chance of joining hands with Parma again, and to use the time before they had rallied from his blows, that was the present necessity. His own poor fellows were famished and in rags; but neither he nor they had leisure to think of themselves. There was but one thought in the whole of them, to be again in chase of the flying foe. Howard was resolute as Drake. All that was possible was swiftly done. Seymour and the Thames squadron were to stay in the straits and watch Parma. From every obtainable source food and powder were collected for the rest—far short in both ways of what ought to have been, but, as Drake said, "we were resolved to put on a brag and go on as if we needed nothing." Before dawn the admiral and he were again off on the chase.

The brag was unneeded. What man could do had been done, and the rest was left to the elements. Never again could Spanish seamen be brought to face the English guns with Medina Sidonia to lead them. They had a fool at their head. The Invisible Powers in whom they had been taught to trust had deserted them. Their confidence was gone and their spirit broken. Drearily the morning broke on the Duke and his consorts the day after the battle. The Armada had collected in the night. The nor'-wester had freshened to a gale, and they were labouring heavily along, making fatal leeway towards the shoals.

It was St. Lawrence's Day, Philip's patron saint, whose shoulder-bone he had lately added to the treasures of the Escurial; but St. Lawrence was as heedless as St. Dominic. The *San Martin* had but six fathoms under her. Those nearer to the land signaled five, and right before them they could see the brown foam of the breakers curling over the sands, while on their weather-beam, a mile distant and clinging to them like the shadow of death, were the English ships which had pursued them from Plymouth like the dogs of the Furies. The Spanish sailors and soldiers had been without food since the evening when they anchored at Calais. All Sunday they had been at work, no rest allowed them to eat. On the Sunday night they had been stirred out of their sleep by the fire ships. Monday they had been fighting, and Monday night committing their dead to the sea. Now they seemed advancing directly upon inevitable destruction. As the wind stood there was still room for them to wear and thus escape the banks, but they would then have to face the enemy, who seemed only refraining from attacking them because while they continued on their present course the winds and waves would finish the work without help from man. Recalde, De Leyva, Oquendo, and other officers were sent for to the *San Martin* to consult. Oquendo came last. "Ah, Señor Oquendo," said the Duke as the heroic Biscayan stepped on board, "que haremos?" (what shall we do?) "Let your Excellency bid load the guns again," was Oquendo's gallant answer. It could not be. De Leyva himself said that the men would not fight the English again. Florez advised surrender. The Duke wavered. It was said that a boat was actually lowered to go off to Howard and make terms, and that Oquendo swore that if the boat left the *San Martin* on such an errand he would fling Florez into the sea. Oquendo's advice would have, perhaps, been the safest if the Duke could have taken it. There were still seventy ships in the Armada little hurt. The English were "bragging," as Drake said, and in no condition themselves for another serious engagement. But the temper of the entire fleet made a courageous course impossible. There was but one Oquendo. Discipline was gone. The soldiers in their desperation had taken the command out of the hands of the seamen. Officers and men alike abandoned hope, and, with no human prospect of salvation left to them, they flung themselves on their knees upon the decks and prayed the Almighty to have pity on them. But two weeks were gone since they had knelt on those same decks on the first sight of the English shore to thank Him for having brought them so far on an enterprise so glorious. Two weeks; and what weeks! Wrecked, torn by cannon shot, ten thousand of them dead or dying—for this was the estimated loss by battle—the survivors could now but pray to be delivered from a miserable death by the elements. In cyclones the wind often changes suddenly back from north-west to west, from west to south. At that moment, as if in answer to their petition, one of these sudden shifts of wind saved them from the immediate peril. The gale backed round to S.S.W., and ceased to press them on the shoals. They could ease their sheets, draw off into open water, and steer a course up the middle of the North Sea.

So only that they went north, Drake was content to leave them unmolested. Once away into the high latitudes they might go where they would. Neither Howard nor he, in the low state of their own magazines, desired any unnecessary fighting. If the Armada turned back they must close with it. If it held its present course they must follow it till they could be assured it would communicate no more for that summer with the Prince of Parma. Drake thought they would perhaps make for the Baltic or some port in Norway. They would meet no hospitable reception from either Swedes or Danes, but they would probably try. One only imminent danger remained to be provided against. If they turned into the Forth, it was still possible for the Spaniards to redeem their defeat, and even yet shake Elizabeth's throne. Among the many plans which had been formed for the invasion of England, a landing in Scotland had long been the favorite. Guise had always preferred Scotland when it was intended that Guise should be the leader. Santa Cruz had been in close correspondence with Guise on this very subject, and many officers in the Armada must have been acquainted with Santa Cruz's views. The Scotch Catholic nobles were still savage at Mary Stuart's execution and had the Armada anchored in Leith Roads with twenty thousand men, half a million ducats, and a Santa Cruz at its head, it might have kindled a blaze at that moment from John o'Groat's Land to the Border.[5]

But no such purpose occurred to the Duke of Medina Sidonia. He probably knew nothing at all of Scotland or its parties. Among the many deficiencies which he had pleaded to Philip as unfitting him for the command, he had said that Santa Cruz had acquaintances among the English and Scotch peers. He had himself none. The small information which he had of anything did not go beyond his orange gardens and his tunny fishing. His chief merit was that he was conscious of his incapacity; and, detesting a service into which he had been fooled by a hysterical nun, his only anxiety was to carry home the still considerable fleet which had been trusted to him without further loss. Beyond Scotland and the Scotch isles there was the open ocean, and in the open ocean there were no sandbanks and no English guns. Thus, with all sail set he went on before the wind. Drake and Howard attended him till they had seen him past the Forth, and knew then that there was no more to fear. It was time to see to the wants of their own poor fellows, who had endured so patiently and fought so magnificently. On the 13th of August they

5. From the north of Scotland to the English border.

saw the last of the Armada, turned back, and made their way to the Thames.

But the story has yet to be told of the final fate of the great "enterprise of England" (the "empresa de Inglaterra"), the object of so many prayers, on which the hopes of the Catholic world had been so long and passionately fixed. It had been ostentatiously a religious crusade. The preparations had been attended with peculiar solemnities. In the eyes of the faithful it was to be the execution of Divine justice on a wicked princess and a wicked people. In the eyes of millions whose convictions were less decided it was an appeal to God's judgment to decide between the Reformation and the Pope. There was an appropriateness, therefore, if due to accident, that other causes besides the action of man should have combined in its overthrow.

The Spaniards were experienced sailors; a voyage round the Orkneys and round Ireland to Spain might be tedious, but at that season of the year need not have seemed either dangerous or difficult. On inquiry, however, it was found that the condition of the fleet was seriously alarming. The provisions placed on board at Lisbon had been found unfit for food, and almost all had been thrown into the sea. The fresh stores taken in at Corunna had been consumed, and it was found that at the present rate there would be nothing left in a fortnight. Worse than all, the water-casks refilled there had been carelessly stowed. They had been shot through in the fighting and were empty; while of clothing or other comforts for the cold regions which they were entering no thought had been taken. The mules and horses were flung overboard and Scotch smacks, which had followed the retreating fleet, reported that they had sailed for miles through floating carcasses.

The rations were reduced for each man to a daily half-pound of biscuit, a pint of water, and a pint of wine. Thus, sick and hungry, the wounded left to the care of a medical officer, who went from ship to ship, the subjects of so many prayers were left to encounter the climate of the North Atlantic. The Duke blamed all but himself; he hanged one poor captain for neglect of orders, and would have hanged another had he dared; but his authority was gone. They passed the Orkneys in a single body. They then parted, it was said in a fog; but each commander had to look out for himself and his men. In many ships water must be had somewhere, or they would die. The *San Martin*, with sixty consorts, went north to the sixtieth parallel. From that height the pilots promised to take them down clear of the coast. The wind still clung to the west, each day blowing harder than the last. When they braced round to it their wounded spars gave way. Their rigging parted. With the greatest difficulty they made at last sufficient offing, and rolled down somehow out of sight of land, dipping their yards in the enormous seas. Of the rest, one or two went down among the Western Isles and became wrecks there, their crews, or part of them, making their way through Scotland to Flanders. Others went north to Shetland or the Faroe Islands. Between thirty or forty were tempted in upon the Irish coasts. There were Irishmen in the fleet, who must have told them that they would find the water there for which they were perishing, safe harbors, and a friendly Catholic people; and they found either harbors which they could not reach or sea-washed sands and reefs. They were all wrecked at various places between Donegal and the Blaskets. Something like eight thousand half-drowned wretches struggled on shore alive. Many were gentlemen, richly dressed, with velvet coats, gold chains, and rings. The common sailors and soldiers had been paid their wages before they started, and each had a bag of ducats lashed to his waist when he landed through the surf. The wild Irish of the coast, tempted by the booty, knocked unknown numbers of them on the head with their battle-axes, or stripped them naked and left them to die of the cold. On one long sand strip in Sligo an English officer counted eleven hundred bodies, and he heard that there were as many more a few miles distant.

The better educated of the Ulster chiefs, the O'Rourke and O'Donnell, hurried down to stop the butchery and spare Ireland the shame of murdering helpless Catholic friends. Many—how many cannot be said—found protection in their castles. But even so it seemed as if some inexorable fate pursued all who had sailed in that doomed expedition. Alonzo de Leyva, with half a hundred young Spanish nobles of high rank who were under his special charge, made his way in a galleass into Killibeg. He was himself disabled in landing. O'Donnell received and took care of him and his companions. After remaining in O'Donnell's castle for a month he recovered. The weather appeared to mend. The galleass was patched up, and De Leyva ventured an attempt to make his way in her to Scotland. He had passed the worst danger, and Scotland was almost in sight; but fate would have its victims. The galleass struck a rock off Dunluce and went to pieces, and Don Alonzo and the princely youths who had sailed with him were washed ashore all dead, to find an unmarked grave in Antrim.

Most pitiful of all was the fate of those who fell into the hands of the English garrisons in Galway and Mayo. Galleons had found their way into Galway Bay—one of them had reached Galway itself—the crews half dead with famine and offering a cask of wine for a cask of water. The Galway townsmen were human, and tried to feed and care for them. Most were too far gone to be revived, and died of exhaustion. Some might have recovered, but recovered they would be a danger to the State. The English in the West of

Ireland were but a handful in the midst of a sullen, half conquered population. The ashes of the Desmond rebellion were still
smoking, and Dr. Sanders and his Legatine Commission were
fresh in immediate memory. The defeat of the Armada in the
Channel could only have been vaguely heard of. All that English
officers could have accurately known must have been that an enormous expedition had been sent to England by Philip to restore the
Pope; and Spaniards, they found, were landing in thousands in the
midst of them with arms and money; distressed for the moment,
but sure, if allowed time to get their strength again, to set
Connaught in a blaze. They had no fortresses to hold so many
prisoners, no means of feeding them, no men to spare to escort
them to Dublin. They were responsible to the Queen's Government
for the safety of the country. The Spaniards had not come on any
errand of mercy to her or hers. The stern order went out to kill
them all wherever they might be found, and two thousand or more
were shot, hanged, or put to the sword. Dreadful! Yes, but war itself
is dreadful and has its own necessities.

The sixty ships which had followed the *San Martin* succeeded
at last in getting round Cape Clear, but in a condition scarcely
less miserable than that of their companions who had perished in
Ireland. Half their companions died—died of untended wounds,
hunger, thirst, and famine fever. The survivors were moving skele-
tons, more shadows and ghosts than living men, with scarce strength
left them to draw a rope or handle a tiller. In some ships there
was no water for fourteen days. The weather in the lower latitudes
lost part of its violence, or not one of them would have seen Spain
again. As it was they drifted on outside Scilly and into the Bay of
Biscay, and in the second week of September they dropped in one
by one. Recalde, with better success than the rest, made Corunna.
The Duke, not knowing where he was, found himself in sight of
Corunna also. The crew of the *San Martin* were prostrate, and
could not work her in. They signaled for help, but none came, and
they dropped away to leeward to Bilboa. Oquendo had fallen off
still farther to Santander, and the rest of the sixty arrived in the
following days at one or other of the Biscay ports. On board them,
of the thirty thousand who had left those shores but two months
before in high hope and passionate enthusiasm, nine thousand only
came back alive—if alive they could be called. It is touching to
read in a letter from Bilboa of their joy at warm Spanish sun, the
sight of the grapes on the white walls, and the taste of fresh home
bread and water again. But it came too late to save them, and those
whose bodies might have rallied died of broken hearts and disappointed dreams. Santa Cruz's old companions could not survive the
ruin of the Spanish navy. Recalde died two days after he landed at
Bilboa. Santander was Oquendo's home. He had a wife and chil-

dren there, but he refused to see them, turned his face to the wall, and died too. The common seamen and soldiers were too weak to help themselves. They had to be left on board the poisoned ships till hospitals could be prepared to take them in. The authorities of Church and State did all that men could do; but the case was past help, and before September was out all but a few hundred needed no further care.

Philip, it must be said for him, spared nothing to relieve the misery. The widows and orphans were pensioned by the State. The stroke which had fallen was received with a dignified submission to the inscrutable purposes of Heaven. Diego Florez escaped with a brief imprisonment at Burgos. None else were punished for faults which lay chiefly in the King's own presumption in imagining himself the instrument of Providence.

The Duke thought himself more sinned against than sinning. He did not die, like Recalde or Oquendo, seeing no occasion for it. He flung down his command and retired to his palace at St. Lucan; and so far was Philip from resenting the loss of the Armada on its commander, that he continued him in his governorship of Cadiz, where Essex found him seven years later, and where he ran from Essex as he had run from Drake.

The Spaniards made no attempt to conceal the greatness of their defeat. Unwilling to allow that the Upper Powers had been against them, they set it frankly down to the superior fighting powers of the English.

The English themselves, the Prince of Parma said, were modest in their victory. They thought little of their own gallantry. To them the defeat and destruction of the Spanish fleet was a declaration of the Almighty in the cause of their country and the Protestant faith. Both sides had appealed to Heaven, and Heaven had spoken.

It was the turn of the tide. The wave of the reconquest of the Netherlands ebbed from that moment. Parma took no more towns from the Hollanders. The Catholic peers and gentlemen of England, who had held aloof from the Established Church, waiting *ad illud tempus* for a religious revolution, accepted the verdict of Providence. They discovered that in Anglicanism they could keep the faith of their fathers, yet remain in communion with their Protestant fellow-countrymen, use the same liturgy, and pray in the same temples. For the first time since Elizabeth's father broke the bonds of Rome the English became a united nation, joined in loyal enthusiasm for the Queen, and were satisfied that thenceforward no Italian priest should tithe or toll in her dominions.

But all that, and all that went with it, the passing from Spain to England of the sceptre of the seas, must be left to other lectures, or other lecturers who have more years before them than I. My own theme has been the poor Protestant adventurers who fought through that perilous week in the English Channel and saved their country and their country's liberty.

QUESTIONS

1. *In his last sentence Froude says that his theme has been the English seamen. Yet in these climactic pages he has paid much more direct attention to the Spanish seamen. How does this emphasis develop his theme?*

2. *Froude's emphasis on the Spaniards gives him the opportunity to stress their confidence in providence and, therefore, the disappointment of that confidence. What larger issues does he thus introduce into his narrative of the battle? What is the tide that turns in the next to last paragraph?*

3. *Froude's approach to his theme has the potential disadvantage of encouraging partisan or nationalistic disparagement of the Spanish efforts. How does he guard against this?*

4. *Does Froude anywhere endorse English Anglicanism as superior to defeated Spanish Catholicism?*

W. H. LEWIS

The Galleys of France

Until the coming of the concentration camp, the galley held an undisputed pre-eminence as the darkest blot on Western civilization; a galley, said a poetic observer shudderingly, would cast a shadow in the blackest midnight. In the seventeenth century, the great age of the galleys, the particularly bad reputation of those of Louis XIV is fortuitous; all the Mediterranean powers possessed galleys, and the brutalities practiced on those of other powers were often more horrible than anything that would have been tolerated in the French service. And the galleys can enter a strong plea in condonation of their existence, namely, that the convict existed for the galley, not the galley for the convict. The navies of the seventeenth century had to conform to the limited strategic and tactical plan imposed upon them by their two possible propellants, wind and oar; and in consequence the galley, with its perpetual mobility, was the important fast technical unit of a Mediterranean navy. Until the coming of steam the galley, under many conditions of weather, was the fastest thing afloat on the inland sea; it composed to a considerable extent the scouting division of the fleet. In light airs the galleys, and only the galleys, could protect the coast against the Barbary pirate or hunt him down in the open sea; in a fleet action the galley was the only thing which could remove a damaged capital ship from its place in the line of battle; in amphibious operations its shallow draft made it the ideal landing craft, whilst its main armament could engage closer inshore than that of the lightest vessels of the fleet proper. The galley was in fact indispensable.

The experiment of propelling galleys by free men hired for the oar had been tried and had failed; the commanders concerned had reported that with such a bank neither the speed nor the endurance essential could be obtained. Only the whip, with the threat of worse brutalities in reserve, could send the long, lean, cranky craft into action at the requisite speed. Given the necessity for the galley on the one hand, and a country swarming with criminals on the other, the *galérien* was the obvious, indeed the only, solution, the cheap fuel so callously expended in driving these fast ships.

Who was the typical *galérien*? The society of the bench fell into five distinct classes: Turks, bought by the French Government for the service, deserters, salt smugglers, genuine criminals, and, after 1685, Huguenots, the first category being definitely the least badly treated, and the last on the whole the worst. Even before the coming of the Huguenot, the *galériens* were by no means, as is often supposed, drawn exclusively from the dregs of France; at the battle of Genoa in 1638 the galley *La Cardinale* was saved by the exertions of a convict, the Chevalier de Margaillet, who was doing time for the rape of his niece; when Mlle de Scudéry was at Marseilles in 1644 she noticed that *galériens* of good social standing were allowed a considerable degree of liberty, and in their spare hours were to be met in the best *salons* of the town; in 1670 Mme de Sévigné is assured by the General of the Galleys that her protégé Valcroissant, a *galérien*, is "living as he pleases, ashore in Marseilles, and without chains." The conductor of the orchestra of the galley *La Palme* had been a performer in the private band of Louis XIV, had thrown up his post in a fit of pique, enlisted, and then deserted. And there were many other similar cases. In the earlier part of the reign the *galérien* is dumb, we catch a glimpse of him only from the outside, or at best we look down from the poop on his crowded misery.

"We went to visit the galleys," writes Evelyn in 1644. "The Captaine of the Galley Royal gave us a most courteous entertainment in his Cabine, the slaves in the interim playing both loud and soft musiq very rarely. Then he show'd us how he commanded their motions with a nod and his whistle, making them row out. The spectacle was to me new and strange, to see so many hundreds of miserably naked persons, having their heads shaven close and having only high red bonnets and payre of coarse canvas drawers, their whole backs and leggs naked and made fast to their seats about their middles and leggs in couples, and all commanded in a trice by an imperious and cruell seaman. . . . I was amaz'd to contemplate how these miserable catyfs lie in their galley crouded together, yet there is hardly one but had some occupation by which, as leisure and calms permitted, they gat some little money. Their rising and falling back at their oare is a miserable spectacle, and the noise of their chaines with the roaring of the beaten waters has something of strange and fearefull to one unaccustomed to it. They are rul'd and chastiz'd by strokes on their backs and soles of their feete on the least disorder and without the least humanity; yet they are cherefull and full of knavery."

With the Revocation of the Edict of Nantes in 1685 the bench becomes vocal, a light shines into the sinister interior of the galley. From letters of Huguenot convicts, and the memoirs of such as survived to write them after their release in 1712, we are able to piece together a tolerably accurate account of the *galérien's* life. Bad though the story is, it is not wholly bad; its somber texture is shot through with gleams of humanity, almost of kindliness, for the officers were often less brutal than the system which they administered.

Once condemned to the galleys, the convict was consigned to the nearest jail where he might spend a considerable time in almost any variety and degree of comfort or suffering whilst awaiting the order for his transfer to the chain assembly-point—Lille for the galleys of Dunkirk, Paris for those of Marseilles. Their hands bound, and with an escort of provost's archers, the sad little groups tramped the country roads which converged on their last land prison. A Huguenot merchant, who was condemned in 1701 for trying to escape from France, has left us a description of the chain assembly-prison at Lille—a large room in St. Peter's tower, so dark that day was but darkness made visible, without fire or candle, a little broken straw, innumerable rats and mice, and the society of thirty of the most depraved scoundrels in France. . . . But for our Huguenot there was temporary deliverance in sight. The prison of Lille was under the orders of the Grand Provost of Flanders, a distant connection of a relation of the prisoner's: a tenuous lifeline enough we may think nowadays, who know nothing of the immense solidarity of seventeenth-century relationship. At any rate, the claim was instantly recognized by the Provost to the extent of moving his relation and a chosen companion into a comfortable bed-sitting-room, with every alleviation of their lot which money could provide; nor did his assistance end there, for, having delayed their departure until the last draft, he then had them carried in carts behind the chain to Dunkirk. Marolles, another Huguenot, who in 1686 found himself in La Tournelle, the Paris assembly-point, has a grimmer story to tell; after complaining of the "filthiness and execrable blasphemies" to which he is subjected, he goes on "We lie 53 of us in a place which is not above 30 feet in length and 9 in breadth. There lies on the right side of me a sick peasant, with his head to my feet and his feet to my head. There is scarce one among us who does not envy the condition of several dogs and horses"; and the conclusion of his letter to his wife is worthy to be written in letters of gold—"When I reflect on the merciful providence of God towards me, I am ravished with admiration and do evidently discover the secret steps of Providence which hath formed me from my youth after a requisite manner to bear what I suffer."

At last the almost-wished-for day came when the chain started on its long march to the Mediterranean; the weather was cold and frosty, but the convicts, weakened by ill-usage and burdened by their chains, sweated on the march. Charenton was reached in the evening, and at nine o'clock the convicts were ordered into the courtyard of an inn and made to strip naked—ostensibly to search their clothing for contraband, actually to steal from them their few poor remaining comforts. For two hours they stood naked in the frost, and when ordered to move were incapable of doing so, though "the bull's sinew whips fell like hail." As a result of the search eighteen of the convicts died during the night. And so the ghastly march continued under the lash of the archers. At night the convicts were locked in stables, where the luckiest or the strongest proceeded to bury themselves in the dung to keep warm, after dining off the "King's Bread"—literally the king's bread, 1½ lb. of it to each man. By day the trail of blood left on the road would deceive travelers into thinking there was a convoy of wine carts in front of them. It may be objected that it was, at the lowest, the king's fuel which was being wasted by this brutality: why were there not regulations for getting it to Marseilles in consumable condition? There were, but petty officialdom, our old friend the white Babu,[1] was active then as now, and the capitation grant had been cut to a figure at which it cost more to bring a prisoner alive to Marseilles in the hospital van than to let him die by the roadside: and the result was that of every five who set out, only four reached the coast, and of those four one had to be sent to the galley hospital. If he was fortunate or unfortunate enough to reach port alive, the *galérien* was sent to the depot galley where he could make himself acquainted with the layout of his future home.

The galley was in essence an open boat with makeshift accommodation and storage space. We may picture it as having about it a suggestion of the English canal barge—long for its beam, with a freeboard of only three feet, and much smaller than one would gather from the pictures; about a hundred and forty feet long. Forward was a forecastle on which was mounted the ship's main armament, and aft of the forecastle a halfdeck over the rower's space, which provided accommodation for the 120 marines. One mast was stepped through the forecastle right forward, and the other amidships: each mast carried a large lateen sail. Below the forecastle were some cubbyholes and storerooms. Fore and aft beneath the halfdeck, and the complete length of the ship, ran the gangway from which the petty officers stimulated the exertions of the rowers. Aft was a poop, below which was a small cabin for the captain, and below the captain's cabin were storerooms. The position

1. In Anglo-Indian use, *Babu* (a Hindu title equivalent to *Mr.*) refers disparagingly to a native clerk who has learned to write English and acquired a smattering of English culture.

of the other accommodations is not very clear—latrines, *Calle* or hold, where the marines slept, ship's kitchen, "tavern" or wet canteen, a speculation of the chief petty officer: and I am inclined to suspect from various accounts that the interior layout of all galleys was not uniform. When these small craft were in commission there would be a complement of over 400 souls on board, and such was the overcrowding that even the captain's cabin was common to all officers except at night: for "the cabin" was in fact the only real accommodation in the ship.

Soon after their arrival at the depot galley the convicts would be assembled, stripped, sorted into gangs of five, and drawn for by lot by the *Comites* of the various galleys needing reinforcements. Each five men, arbitrarily selected for physical reasons, were now entered into the closest of life partnerships, *La Vogue:*[2] rarely again to eat, sleep, or work apart, to be literally in close contact with each other until the end of their days. They had ceased to be men, they had become "an oar," one of fifty such oars carried by a galley.

But if they reached the port at the turn of the year, their rowing days were still three months ahead of them; the galleys, stripped to their hulls, would be emerging from their winter hibernation to face another commission. In this case the work in front of them was only one degree less arduous than that of the oar. No officers would yet have appeared on board, though a junior or two might be living ashore in the town. The seniors would be at Paris or Versailles, and the ships in the hands of the *Comites* and their *Sous-Comites*. The dictionary, I see, translates *Comite* "boatswain," which is misleading, for there never was, thank God, an English version of the word. The *Comite* was the chief slave-driver, the man with *nerf de boeuf* or bull-sinew whip. The first, indeed the only, qualification for a *Comite* was brutality; though even *Comites* varied, and the anonymous Huguenot whom I have already quoted found in his *Comite* a protector and almost a friend. We must not think too savagely of the *Comite*; only the exceptional man revolts against the abuses to which he has been brought up, and the *Comite*, had he been steam-minded, would have seen in himself nothing more than a chief engineer—half-speed ahead, one uses one's cane on the rowers' backs: full ahead one substitutes for the cane the bull-sinew whip. *Et voilà tout.*[3] The galley in the early spring was a mere shell, there being little on board but the ballast, and fitting out began by removing this from the hold and washing it on the quayside. The lightened galley was then careened, scraped, and recoated with pitch. Then came the overhaul of the cables, anchors, rigging, sails, and the repair of the awnings, the last an important feature in the interior economy of the galley. Lastly, the guns, masts, ammunition, and a thousand and one other

2. "The Rowing." 3. "And that is all."

things must be carried down from the arsenal and stowed on board. About April, or later if the season was a bad one, the order would come from Versailles for the galleys to put to sea.

Life on board when the galley was at sea was a sort of Hell's picnic, for there was really no accommodation for anyone. For the convicts, there was, of course, no question of sleep; the petty officers did the best they could on the forecastle head, the soldiers huddled into the hold, or under the deck awning if the weather was fine, and even the officers had no sleeping place except on their camp chairs under the poop awning. And so crank[4] were the ships that, to avoid risk of capsizing, the awnings could only be spread in the finest weather. Cooking facilities were primitive, and, as no one ever washed, the ship crawled with vermin from stem to stern. From below came the constant clank of chains, the crack of whips on bare flesh, screams of pain, and savage growls. At each oar all five men must rise as one at each stroke, push the eighteen-feet oar forward, dip it in the water, and pull with all their force, dropping into a sitting position at the end of each stroke. "One would not think," says a Huguenot convict, "that it was possible to keep it up for half an hour, and yet I have rowed full out for twenty-four hours without pausing for a single moment." On these occasions the rowers were fed on biscuit soaked in wine, thrust into their mouths by the *Comites* as they rowed. Those who died, or even who fainted at their posts, were cut adrift from the bench and flung overboard without further ceremony. But such a peak of suffering was never attained except in the heat of an action; had it been normal so to abuse the rowers, the whole criminal and Huguenot populations of France combined would soon have proved insufficient to keep the galleys in commission. In normal cruising, sail was set whenever possible, or, if there was no wind, only each alternate oar was pulled, so that each bench rested for 1 ½ hours in every three. Not all *galériens* were rowers; in each ship a few privileged men, who were usually Huguenots, would be employed as storekeepers, stewards, cooks, and the like. The only pleasant feature of this sorry story is the almost overt sympathy shown in most cases by Roman Catholic officers and *Comites* to the Huguenots; it was the comfortably lodged mission priests ashore in Marseilles and Dunkirk who were always on the lookout to make the Huguenots' lives harder, not the men who had to work with them. There were even cases in which something that might be called friendship sprang up between the captains and their convict secretaries and servants. Even the convicts proper, the criminal convicts, pitied and respected the Huguenots: and never failed, we are told, to address a Huguenot as *Monsieur* and pull off their bonnets when speaking to one.

4. Crank-sided; easily tipped.

In 1709 the hero of "Willington's" narrative[5] reached the haven of secretary to de Langeron, captain of his galley, and for the first time in eight years found himself freed from his chains, newly clothed, and allowed to grow his hair, with a corner of the store-room to sleep in: nay, more, "the captain ordered his steward to serve me a dish from his table at each meal, with a bottle of wine a day. . . . I was honored and respected by the officers, loved and cherished by my captain." This same de Langeron was prepared to take considerable risks for his Huguenots, though himself, of course, a Roman Catholic; when the search gun was fired from the flagship it was his duty to have each Huguenot instantly seized and searched for Protestant devotional books; but de Langeron would remark on hearing the gun to his steward—"My friend, the cock has crowed." The steward ran forward with the news, and the *Comites* would look the other way before beginning their search whilst each Huguenot handed over his Bible to the Turkish head-man of his oar. How real was the risk that de Langeron ran may be gauged by the case of Marolles's neighbour at the oar in 1686, "a dragoon officer whose name was Bonvalet, a very mild and discreet man," who was there for life for having connived at the escape of a Huguenot woman of quality from France. Marolles, too, after the horrors of his journey from Paris to Marseilles, ultimately fell on his feet when posted to the galley *Magnifique.*

"I live at present all alone," he writes, "they bring me food from abroad (i.e. from the town) and I am furnished with wine in the galley for nothing, and with some of the King's bread. . . . I am treated with civility by all on board the galley, seeing that the officers visit me . . . we have the honestest *patron* of all the galleys. He treats me with all manner of civility and respect, and he hath promised me that when it is cold he will let me lie in his cabin."

The privilege of getting food from ashore was a considerable one, for the diet of the *galériens* was, as might be imagined, spare. At eight in the morning an allowance of biscuit was issued for the day, "of which indeed they have enough, and pretty good." The only other meal was a soup made of beans or peas, with salad oil, at ten in the morning, to which when at sea there was added two-thirds of a pint of wine, morning and evening. Even during the campaigning season a galley spent much more time in port than at sea, and when in Marseilles or Dunkirk life was less hard for all concerned. Food was obtainable from the town, even by convicts, all of whom had some trade, and at night it was possible to sleep. Easily dismantled tables were erected over the convicts' benches for the officers and petty officers, on which they placed their beds, and each table became a sort of light tent by the aid of stuff curtains hung from a line fore and aft. It was then that a convict began to

5. See first item in Bibliography.

appreciate the privilege of rowing on the *Comite's* own bench, if such was his good fortune; for the *Comite's* table was built over that bench in port, and his men fed well on the leavings of his table: to say nothing of the prestige accruing from the enjoyment of the great man's conversation in his unbuttoned hours. "He was," says our anonymous authority of his *Comite*, "the cruelest man on duty I ever saw, but off duty very reasonable and filled with judicious thoughts."

After the galleys came into port in the autumn and had been laid up for the winter, the life of the convict became almost endurable. To begin with, the officers, sailors, and marines were billeted ashore, and there was much more elbow room, a general spreading out; beds were improvised in the bottom of the ship, and a huge cover on battens was pulled over the open deck, converting the ship into a sort of giant camping punt. Marolles on *La Fierce* found himself the possessor of one of the "two little cabins at the head of the galley. This favor was procured me by a young officer whom I teach algebra. . . . I have bought coals, which are very dear, and I make a little fire in our apartment." *La Fierce* must, however, have been a slack galley, for another convict, while commenting on the comparative comfort of winter quarters, adds that the chief drawback is that no fire is ever allowed in a galley in any circumstances.

Not only was the winter a time of comparative freedom, it was also the *galérien's* commercial harvest during which he earned the money for his *menus plaisirs*.[6] Every *galérien* had a trade; if he had no manual dexterity he knitted stockings; if he refused to learn to knit stockings he was flogged every day until he did. But it was only the lowest class of *galérien*, the submerged tenth, that knitted stockings; tailors, wig-makers, clock-menders, almost every trade was represented in the average galley. A week ashore was allowed by an ordinance of 1630 to the convicts of each galley in rotation, during which time they might freely peddle their wares and services through the town. Some were itinerant musicians and did well at the taverns, others hawked quack remedies, others set up stalls on the quay, others had good wig-making connections, and all stole whatever they could lay their hands upon. For there was at least one advantage in being a *galérien*: there was no extradition from the galleys for any crime whatsoever: the criminal law had washed its hands of the man sent to the galleys. To be sure he might be flogged on board for a theft or a murder if the necessary social pressure could be brought to bear on his captain, but he could not be claimed by a magistrate for even the most flagrant crime. Hence the hideous scenes in Marseilles during the great plague under the

6. "Pocket money."

Regency, when a more than usually fatuous minister inaugurated the brilliant scheme of releasing the *galériens* to help nurse the sick and dispose of the dead.

In addition to what may be somewhat loosely described as their honest tradesmen, the galleys supplied Marseilles and Dunkirk during the winter months with a plentiful infusion of swindlers of every type: apparently without the naval authorities concerning themselves about the matter. The light-fingered gentlemen in fetters who wanted change for a crown and kept both crown and change: forgers of wills, marriage certificates, and leave passes for soldiers: dealers in the seals of towns, bishoprics, corporations, and private gentlemen: renovators and adapters of legal instruments— there was no need to look far in the port for skilled professional assistance in any fraud you might be planning. Indeed, Huguenots apart, the only tolerably honest men in the galleys were the Turks, who confined themselves to a safe conservative business as receivers of stolen goods.

Such in brief outline was the life of the galleys. There is a tendency, purely English, I suspect, to assume that because a man is ill treated, he must be a good fellow; in our indignation against the whole system, we unconsciously draw a false picture of the *galérien*, on whom we need in fact waste no sympathy. The seventeenth-century criminal is not a sympathetic object, and his Huguenot fellows have left ample record of the horrors and atrocities which he boasted of having perpetrated. Whether the system made the criminal or the criminal made the system it is here irrelevant to inquire. It is all over now. The tumult and the shouting dies, the galley in all its gilded splendor and hidden misery has followed the age it symbolizes into oblivion. No more will French criminals "write on the water with a pen eighteen feet long." New horrors have displaced the old, but at least the bloody chapter of the oared navies is closed for ever.

References

The Memoirs of a Protestant condemned to the Galleys of France for his Religion, Written by himself, &c., Griffiths and Dilly, London, 1758. Translated by "James Willington" (O. Goldsmith).

Histoire de La Marine Française, vol. v., Charles de La Roncière, Paris, 1934.

Madeleine de Scudéry, Dorothy MacDougall, London, 1938.

Mme. de Sévigné, *Lettres*, edit. Aimé Martin, Paris, 6 vols., 1876.

Evelyn's *Diary*, date 7 October 1644.

An History of the Sufferings of Mr. Lewis de Marolles and Mr. Isaac Le Fevre upon the Revocation, &c., J. Priestley, LL.D., F.R.S., Birmingham, 1738.

The Seventeenth Century, Jacques Boulenger, Heinemann, 1920.

Apostle of Charity, Theodore Maynard, Allen & Unwin Ltd., 1940.

Monsieur Vincent, Aumônier des Galères, Henri Lavedan, Paris, 1928.

FRANCIS PARKMAN

La Salle Begins Anew, 1681[1]

HIS CONSTANCY—HIS PLANS—HIS SAVAGE ALLIES—HE BECOMES
SNOW-BLIND—NEGOTIATIONS—GRAND COUNCIL—LA SALLE'S ORATORY
—MEETING WITH TONTY—PREPARATION—DEPARTURE

In tracing the adventures of Tonty and the rovings of Hennepin, we have lost sight of La Salle, the pivot of the enterprise. Returning from the desolation and horror in the valley of the Illinois, he had spent the winter at Fort Miami, on the St. Joseph, by the borders of Lake Michigan. Here he might have brooded on the redoubled ruin that had befallen him: the desponding friends, the exulting foes; the wasted energies, the crushing load of debt, the stormy past, the black and lowering future. But his mind was of a different temper. He had no thought but to grapple with adversity, and out of the fragments of his ruin to build up the fabric of success.

He would not recoil; but he modified his plans to meet the new contingency. His white enemies had found, or rather, perhaps, had made, a savage ally in the Iroquois. Their incursions must be stopped, or his enterprise would come to nought; and he thought he saw the means by which this new danger could be converted into a source of strength. The tribes of the West, threatened by the common enemy, might be taught to forget their mutual animosities, and join in a defensive league, with La Salle at its head. They might be colonized around his fort in the valley of the Illinois, where, in the shadow of the French flag, and with the aid of French allies, they could hold the Iroquois in check, and acquire in some measure the arts of a settled life. The Franciscan friars could teach them the Faith; and La Salle and his associates could supply them with goods, in exchange for the vast harvest of furs which their hunters could gather in these boundless wilds. Meanwhile, he would seek out the mouth of the Mississippi; and the furs gathered at his colony in the Illinois would then find a ready passage to the markets of the world. Thus might this ancient slaughter-field of warring savages be redeemed to civilization and Christianity; and a stable settlement, half-feudal, half-commercial, grow up in the heart of the western wilderness. This plan was but a part of the original scheme of his enterprise, adapted to new and unexpected circumstances; and he now set himself to its execution with his usual vigor, joined to an address that, when dealing with Indians, never failed him.

1. This and the following selection are Chapters 19 and 20 of *La Salle and the Discovery of the Great West*.

There were allies close at hand. Near Fort Miami were the huts of twenty-five or thirty savages, exiles from their homes, and strangers in this western world. Several of the English colonies, from Virginia to Maine, had of late years been harassed by Indian wars; and the Puritans of New England, above all, had been scourged by the deadly outbreak of King Philip's war. Those engaged in it had paid a bitter price for their brief triumphs. A band of refugees, chiefly Abenakis and Mohegans, driven from their native seats, had roamed into these distant wilds, and were wintering in the friendly neighborhood of the French. La Salle soon won them over to his interests. One of their number was the Mohegan hunter, who for two years had faithfully followed his fortunes, and who had been four years in the West. He is described as a prudent and discreet young man, in whom La Salle had great confidence, and who could make himself understood in several western languages, belonging, like his own, to the great Algonquin tongue. This devoted henchman proved an efficient mediator with his countrymen. The New England Indians, with one voice, promised to follow La Salle, asking no recompense but to call him their chief, and yield to him the love and admiration which he rarely failed to command from this hero-worshipping race.

New allies soon appeared. A Shawanoe chief from the valley of the Ohio, whose following embraced a hundred and fifty warriors, came to ask the protection of the French against the all-destroying Iroquois. "The Shawanoes are too distant," was La Salle's reply; "but let them come to me at the Illinois, and they shall be safe." The chief promised to join him in the autumn, at Fort Miami, with all his band. But, more important than all, the consent and cooperation of the Illinois must be gained; and the Miamis, their neighbors, and of late their enemies, must be taught the folly of their league with the Iroquois, and the necessity of joining in the new confederation. Of late, they had been made to see the perfidy of their dangerous allies. A band of the Iroquois, returning from the slaughter of the Tamaroa Illinois, had met and murdered a band of Miamis on the Ohio, and had not only refused satisfaction, but had entrenched themselves in three rude forts of trees and brushwood in the heart of the Miami country. The moment was favorable for negotiating; but, first, La Salle wished to open a communication with the Illinois, some of whom had begun to return to the country they had abandoned. With this view, and also, it seems, to procure provisions, he set out on the first of March, with his lieutenant, La Forest, and fifteen men.

The country was sheeted in snow, and the party journeyed on snow-shoes; but, when they reached the open prairies, the white expanse glared in the sun with so dazzling a brightness that La Salle and several of the men became snow-blind. They stopped and encamped under the edge of a forest; and here La Salle remained in darkness for three days, suffering extreme pain. Meanwhile, he sent forward La Forest, and most of the men, keeping with him his old attendant Hunaut. Going out in quest of pine-leaves—a decoction of which was supposed to be useful in cases of snow-blindness—this man discovered the fresh tracks of Indians, followed them, and found a camp of Outagamies, or Foxes, from the neighborhood of Green Bay. From them he heard welcome news. They told him that Tonty was safe among the Pottawattamies, and that Hennepin had passed through their country on his return from among the Sioux.

A thaw took place; the snow melted rapidly; the rivers were opened; the blind men began to recover; and, launching the canoes which they had dragged after them, the party pursued their way by water. They soon met a band of Illinois. La Salle gave them presents, condoled with them on their losses, and urged them to make peace and alliance with the Miamis. Thus, he said, they could set the Iroquois at defiance; for he himself, with his Frenchmen and his Indian friends, would make his abode among them, supply them with goods, and aid them to defend themselves. They listened, well pleased, promised to carry his message to their countrymen, and furnished him with a large supply of corn. Meanwhile, he had rejoined La Forest, whom he now sent to Michillimackinac to await Tonty, and tell him to remain there till he, La Salle, should arrive.

Having thus accomplished the objects of his journey, he returned to Fort Miami, whence he soon after ascended the St. Joseph to the village of the Miami Indians, on the portage, at the head of the Kankakee. Here he found unwelcome guests. These were three Iroquois warriors, who had been for some time in the place, and who, as he was told, had demeaned themselves with the insolence of conquerors, and spoken of the French with the utmost contempt. He hastened to confront them, rebuked and menaced them, and told them that now, when he was present, they dared not repeat the calumnies which they had uttered in his absence. They stood abashed and confounded, and during the following night secretly left the town and fled. The effect was prodigious on the minds of the Miamis, when they saw that La Salle, backed by ten Frenchmen, could command from their arrogant visitors a respect which they, with their hundreds of warriors had wholly failed to inspire. Here at the outset, was an augury full of promise for the approaching negotiations.

There were other strangers in the town—a band of eastern Indians, more numerous than those who had wintered at the fort. The greater number were from Rhode Island, including, probably, some of King Philip's warriors; others were from New York, and others again from Virginia. La Salle called them to a council, promised them a new home in the West, under the protection of the Great King, with rich lands, an abundance of game, and French traders to supply them with the goods which they had once received from the English. Let them but help him to make peace between the Miamis and the Illinois, and he would insure for them a future of prosperity and safety. They listened with open ears, and promised their aid in the work of peace.

On the next morning, the Miamis were called to a grand council. It was held in the lodge of their chief, from which the mats were removed, that the crowd without might hear what was said. La Salle rose and harangued the concourse. Few men were so skilled in the arts of forest rhetoric and diplomacy. After the Indian mode, he was, to follow his chroniclers, "the greatest orator in North America." He began with a gift of tobacco, to clear the brains of his auditory; next, for he had brought a canoe-load of presents to support his eloquence, he gave them cloth to cover their dead, coats to dress them, hatchets to build a grand scaffold in their honor, and beads, bells, and trinkets of all sorts, to decorate their relatives at a grand funeral feast. All this was mere metaphor. The living, while appropriating the gifts to their own use, were pleased at the compliment offered to their dead; and their delight redoubled as the orator proceeded. One of their great chiefs had lately been killed; and La Salle, after a eulogy of the departed, declared that he would now raise him to life again; that is, that he would assume his name and give support to his squaws and children. This flattering announcement drew forth an outburst of applause; and when, to confirm his words, his attendants placed before them a huge pile of coats, shirts, and hunting-knives, the whole assembly exploded in yelps of admiration.

Now came the climax of the harangue, introduced by a farther present of six guns.

"He who is my master, and the master of all this country, is a mighty chief, feared by the whole world; but he loves peace, and the words of his lips are for good alone. He is called the King of France, and he is the mightiest among the chiefs beyond the great water. His goodness reaches even to your dead, and his subjects come among you to raise them up to life. But it is his will to preserve the life he has given: it is his will that you should obey his laws, and make no war without the leave of Onontio, who commands in his name at Quebec, and who loves all the nations alike, because such is the will of the Great King. You ought, then, to live at peace with your neighbors, and above all with the Illinois. You have had causes of quarrel with them; but their defeat has avenged you. Though they are still strong, they wish to make peace with you. Be content with the glory of having obliged them to ask for it. You have an interest in preserving them; since, if the Iroquois destroy them, they will next destroy you. Let us all obey the Great King, and live together in peace, under his protection. Be of my mind, and use these guns that I have given you, not to make war, but only to hunt and to defend yourselves."

So saying, he gave two belts of wampum to confirm his words; and the assembly dissolved. On the following day, the chiefs again convoked it, and made their reply in form. It was all that La Salle could have wished. "The Illinois is our brother, because he is the son of our Father, the Great King." "We make you the master to our beaver and our lands, of our minds and our bodies." "We cannot wonder that our brothers from the East wish to live with you. We should have wished so too, if we had known what a blessing it is to be the children of the Great King." The rest of this auspicious day was passed in feasts and dances, in which La Salle and his Frenchmen all bore part. His new scheme was hopefully begun. It remained to achieve the enterprise, twice defeated, of the discovery of the mouth of the Mississippi, that vital condition of his triumph, without which all other success was meaningless and vain.

To this end, he must return to Canada, appease his creditors, and collect his scattered resources. Towards the end of May, he set out in canoes from Fort Miami, and reached Michillimackinac after a prosperous voyage. Here, to his great joy, he found Tonty and Zenobe Membré, who had lately arrived from Green Bay. The meeting was one at which even his stoic nature must have melted. Each had for the other a tale of disaster; but, when La Salle recounted the long succession of his reverses, it was with the tranquil tone and cheerful look of one who relates the incidents of an ordinary journey. Membré looked on him with admiration. "Any one else," he says, "would have thrown up his hand and abandoned the enterprise; but, far from this, with a firmness and constancy that never had its equal, I saw him more resolved than ever to continue his work and push forward his discovery."

Without loss of time, they embarked together for Fort Frontenac, paddled their canoes a thousand miles, and safely reached their destination. Here, in this third beginning of his enterprise, La Salle found himself beset with embarrassments. Not only was he burdened with the fruitless costs of his two former efforts, but the heavy debts which he had incurred in building and maintaining Fort Frontenac had not been wholly paid. The fort and the seigniory were already deeply mortgaged; yet, through the influence of Count Frontenac, the assistance of his secretary, Barrois, a consummate man of business, and the support of a wealthy relative, he found means to appease his creditors and even to gain fresh advances. To this end, however, he was forced to part with a portion of his monopolies. Having first made his will at Montreal, in favor of a cousin who had befriended him, he mustered his men, and once more set forth, resolved to trust no more to agents, but to lead on his followers, in a united body, under his own personal command.

At the beginning of autumn, he was at Toronto, where the long and difficult portage to Lake Simcoe detained him a fortnight. He spent a part of it in writing an account of what had lately occurred to a correspondent in France, and he closes his letter thus: "This is all I can tell you this year. I have a hundred things to write, but you could not believe how hard it is to do it among Indians. The canoes and their lading must be got over the portage, and I must speak to them continually, and bear all their importunity, or else they will do nothing I want. I hope to write more at leisure next year, and tell you the end of this business, which I hope will turn out well: for I have M. de Tonty, who is full of zeal; thirty Frenchmen, all good men, without reckoning such as I cannot trust; and more than a hundred Indians, some of them Shawanoes, and others from New England, all of whom know how to use guns."

It was October before he reached Lake Huron. Day after day, and week after week, the heavy-laden canoes crept on along the lonely wilderness shores, by the monotonous ranks of bristling moss-bearded firs; lake and forest, forest and lake; a dreary scene haunted with yet more dreary memories—disasters, sorrows, and deferred hopes; time, strength, and wealth spent in vain; a ruinous past and a doubtful future; slander, obloquy, and hate. With unmoved heart, the patient voyager held his course, and drew up his canoes at last on the beach at Fort Miami.

W. J. CASH

Reconstruction and the Southern Quandary[1]

It had been obvious from the first, of course, that the South's most pressing internal need was for money. To get money, then, it had turned with absorbing passion to the extension of the only practice which, in its experience, had yielded it: the cultivation of cotton. In the years from 1875 to 1890 it would double its annual production of the staple; and in the next decade it would triple it. But so far from affording the expected relief, cotton, always fickle and dangerous, was developing now into a Fata Morgana, the pursuit of which was actually bearing the South deeper and deeper into trouble.

To grasp the fact here in its fullness, we have to notice first just where and how this increase in production was achieved. Some little part of it is explained by the opening of new lands westward of the

---

1. From "Of Quandary—and the Birth of a Dream," Chapter 2 of *The Mind of the South*, 1941.

limit reached by the plantation in the days before the war. Possibly a greater part is accounted for by the adoption here and there of more intensive methods on the old plantation lands. But the greatest part represented the calling into use of those old lands which in the antebellum South had been adjudged as of no worth for the growing of the fiber; the progressive passage of the culture into the fringes, the contained areas, and the upland borders of the original plantation country; the lands, that is, of the yeoman farmers and, to a large extent, of the poor whites.

But these lands, you will recall, were relatively, and often absolutely, poor lands. And cotton is a voracious plant. To grow it here at all would require fertilizers, and in growing quantities. Moreover, the conversion of the yeomen and the poor whites to cotton culture meant that, in greater or less measure, they ceased to be self-sufficient in food; they no longer produced provender enough at home to take care of themselves and their animals from crop to crop, and must, therefore, somehow manage to secure it from outside.

To this it is to be added also that cotton had long ago begun to exhaust even those plantation lands which had once seemed so eternally fecund; and that now perhaps the greater part of them were demanding fertilization almost as necessitously as those of the very poor whites. And on these plantation units, with from twenty-five to five hundred human mouths and half a dozen to a hundred mules to be fed from crop to crop, plantation units which had never been even remotely self-sufficient in this respect and which were still less so as time went on, the amount of aliment which had to be got from without was staggering.

But in the nature of the case virtually none of the farmers and none of the poor whites were in any position to finance for themselves these needs. Having to have fertilizers and food, they had to have credit. Nor was the condition of at least nine out of every ten planters any better. The financing of the plantation had always been too much for the individual planter. Even in the happiest days before the Civil War, all but the wealthiest and the most thrifty had been dependent upon the services of the cotton factor, a sort of combination banker, merchant, and sales agent located in the central markets for the staple.

Now, however, to make the circle complete, most of these great factors were bankrupt. And with them had disappeared also the whole credit machinery of the Old South. Of the few banks the region had been able to show, there was scarcely a single solvent one left. And nowhere were there sufficient aggregations of capital to set up a proper banking system anew.

To meet this situation, then, to provide the credit which had to be found, to set the farmers and the poor whites up at cotton farming, to relieve the paralysis of the plantations, there sprang into existence one of the worst systems ever developed: that of the supply merchants.

From one standpoint this system may be said to have been most admirably contrived, for it brought the available resources of the South to focus on the purpose with great effectiveness. Under it practically every man who could lay hands on from a few hundred to a few thousand dollars and persuade the wholesale houses in the North to extend him credit was soon or late borne almost irresistibly by the prospect of its rewards into establishing shop and holding himself out to supply guano and bread to two or three, a dozen, or a hundred of his neighbors, according to his resources. So thoroughly were such poor hoards of mobile capital as could be found in the South captured for the end that by the 1800's almost every crossroad was provided with at least one such banker-merchant, and every village had from two to half a score. Thus the necessary credit was achieved, as it could not, perhaps, have been achieved in any other manner.

The evil thing was the price which had to be paid. Virtual monopolists in relation to their own particular groups of clients (for though they were numerous, they were nevertheless not numerous enough, for a long time at any rate, for competition to be of any considerable importance), these new masters of Southern economics were not slow to see that it was in their power to exact whatever rate of payment they pleased. Moreover, they themselves were subjected to harsh terms by the Yankee dealers, and the risks they took were great. And so they fastened upon the unfortunate Southern cotton-grower terms which are almost without a parallel for rigor. Specifically, what he had to submit to in order to get credit from this source was the following: first, he gave a mortgage on the projected crop; next, he usually, if not strictly always, gave a mortgage on the land on which the crop was to be grown—often on all his lands and chattels—and finally, he undertook to pay charges which, what with "time prices," interest rates, and so on, commonly averaged in most districts from 40 per cent to 80 per cent.

In sum, the growing of cotton in the South was saddled with a crushing burden, with such a burden as no agricultural product could be expected to bear and still afford a decent return for the producer.

But this is as yet only half the tale. Despite this handicap, the South might still have had some hope in cotton; if only the price of the fiber had held up to the high levels prevailing in the first decade after the war. But of course it didn't. The swift extension we have been looking at speedily brought on a condition bordering upon, and often falling into, a glut in the world market. As early as 1878 the price had dropped to ten cents. And in the next twenty years, the general trend was fatally downward, until in 1898 it plunged to below five cents—the lowest level in history. For all the period from the late 1870's to the early 1900's there was not a year in which the average return per acre was more than fifteen dollars; and there were years in which the return for great areas of the South was hardly more than half that.

The sociological and psychological consequences of this situation were varied and far-reaching. But the first thing we have to observe is that it brings us fully into that major change at which I have glanced already: the turning back of the South on the road to aristocracy, and the beginning of decay, in planter and the superior sort of yeoman, of the actual content of the pattern at the same time when the legend of its full and inalienable inheritance was being finally elaborated.

For here, you see, was created a world in which the hard, energetic, horse-trading type of man was remorselessly indicated for survival— even more remorselessly, indeed, than in the old days when the plantation was flinging out over the backcountry, and land-speculation and wildcat finance were the prevailing order. To have any fair chance of coping with the new exigencies, that is, these Southerners were almost irresistibly summoned back upon the old backcountry heritage which had been progressively falling out of view in the last decades prior to the war.

All the elaborately built-up pattern of leisure and hedonistic *drift*; all the slow, cool, gracious and graceful gesturing of movement —which, if it had never been generally and fully established in sober reality, had nevertheless subsisted as an ideal and a tendency—was plainly marked out for abandonment as incompatible with success. And along with it, the vague largeness of outlook which was so essentially a part of the same aristocratic complex; the *magnanimity* in the old-fashioned sense of the word, with its contempt for mere money-grubbing, and its positive pride in a certain looseness of attention to affairs, in scorn for thrifty detail; the careless tolerance of inefficiency and humane aversion for the role of harsh taskmaster, which had gone so far by 1858 that Olmsted estimated that, on some plantations, a Negro did no more than a third of the work done by a hired farm-hand in New York State.

To make certain of getting the last penny of the possible returns with the fewest possible hands and the least expenditure of labor costs, and to make these meager returns perform the feat of meeting all the charges I have indicated, paying taxes, allowing for the replacement of draft animals every five or six years, maintaining the necessary equipment, and leaving something over to provide for his own family: such was the goal imperatively laid down by circumstances for the man of any considerable holdings.

And so he must give himself to business with a single-minded devotion which had not been the fashion in his country since the days when his sires wrested the earth from the forest with ax and brawn. More, if he were the greater sort of yeoman or the lesser sort of planter, then, always in the first case and very often in the latter, he must himself, along with all his sons, set hand to the plow. And whether his status was great or small, he must generally be out of bed before sun-up, pounding on the doors of his tenants, routing them out from the oldest crone to the child just able to toddle, and hurrying them into the field while the dawn was still only a promise in the east. And having got them there, he must stand over them all day, lashing them with his tongue (and sometimes with the whip itself; for, especially in the deeper South, its use on the Negro was far from having disappeared with the formal disestablishment of slavery), until darkness made further effort impossible.

But this was no more, perhaps, than barely to penetrate the essential shell of aristocracy. There was that here which went deeper and struck into the core of the gentlemanly ideal.

For even after the Southern landowner had complied with the conditions I recite, his troubles were often a long way from being solved. In many instances he was still short of the achievement of bare survival on any terms. And in what was perhaps the majority of cases, he came unavoidably to some such impasse as this: that either he was going to have to deny his children the toys they clamored for at Christmas; to turn a deaf ear to the pleas of his womenfolk for a new coat for winter, a new hat at Easter, a new piano for the parlor, a new coat of paint for the drab nakedness of the house, and, almost certainly, to son Will's ambition to go to college; to resign himself and his family to an unending prospect of accumulating shabbiness and frustrated desire—in many and many a case, indeed, actually to seeing himself reduced to sending his children to school barefoot or all but barefoot in winter, and even to setting his daughters to work in the fields like those of any European peasant or any black man— or he was going to have to trade in the need of his neighbor and to stint and cheat his laborers, the tenants and the sharecroppers.

One might have thought at first glance that the latter could hardly be done. Merely to feed and clothe and house them after any decent standard, and to make that add up to the whole of that portion of their product to which they were legally entitled—there was little room for the profits of skulduggery in this; for so it was likely to turn out naturally, and in the hands of the most honest and generous of men. But that phrase: "any decent standard," is an exceedingly elastic one, of course. And if the standard here was already the standard inherited from slavery, still, given the will, it could be made leaner yet.

The old monotonous, pellagra-and-rickets-breeding diet had at least been abundant? Strip it rigidly to fatback, molasses, and cornbread, dole it out with an ever stingier hand, and particularly in winter when there was no work to be done in the fields; blind your eyes to peaked faces, seal up your ears to hungry whines. New houses must be built now and then? Abandon altogether the standard of the old slave-cabin (which had been at best both solid and more or less tight), and take up in its place the poor white standard at its worst: upend green-pine clapboards into a flimsy box—clapboards which, drying and shrinking, would leave wide slits in the wall for slashing wind and wet. But even a nigger had to have a suit of over-alls once in a while? Not at all: put him in guano-sacking and meal-bagging instead. And as for shoes—why, the damn rascal had a pair year before last; if he was fool enough to wear them every day, let him go without.

Add that, under the prevailing system, the landowner commonly had all sales of the product, all settlements, the entire financing and bookkeeping of the unit, entirely in his hands; that he had usually to deal only with the most abject ignorance in his dependents; that his power was inevitably such that he could easily cow or crush any recalcitrant into submission—and the picture is finished.

Few peoples can ever have been confronted with a crueler dilemma than were these planters and labor-employing yeomen of the South. And for none, surely, has the pressure against the maintenance of honor and *noblesse oblige*—the temptation to let go of aristocratic values and fall back to more primitive and brutal standards—been more tremendous.

But let us take care to see the result here in perspective. I must not seem to suggest universal and head-long retreat, any uniform and sudden emptying out of the stuff of aristocracy from the South.

So far as that great body of men on whom the complex had never been able to stamp itself save superficially and secondarily—those men in whom it had always been impotent against the old horse-trading instinct and the hard core of the *nouveau*—so far as these were concerned, the process, indeed, tended to be comparatively rapid and simple. Faced with the logic of circumstances, they did not tarry long in coming to terms with it, in making themselves as hard as their individual situations ordained. And some of the worst of them even began before long (without in the least mitigating their asser-tion of and their belief in their gentility, and often without even putting aside the old naïve habit of noble profession) to find positive delight in the exercise, positive pride in the reputation, of their hardness.

But elsewhere: To begin with, there were those long-realized aristocrats whom I have called the Virginians—a group which, though it does not entirely fit within the frame I have set up here, may, for practical purposes, be treated just as though it did. Typi-cally, they neither could nor would meet the demands of the times. There were men within the fold, certainly, who could and did meet them in their entirety and at their worst. There were, again, individuals of unusual latent energy, who, while holding more or less fast to the better part of their heritage, managed to ride triumphantly through by sheer force. And to this it must be added also that there was in evidence from an early time some normal human tendency (which we shall see emerging more sharply later on) on the part of the young and more malleable to move toward adaptation: some tendency toward immediate and direct decay.

But typically, as I say, they were too firmly bound within their pattern, were at once too soft and too fine. Decay, as it came to them, came rather obliquely than directly; came, for long at least, and ironically, not so much through any even partial surrender to the demands made upon them as through the inevitable consequences of their failure and their refusal thus to surrender. Many of them fell into bankruptcy and found themselves reduced, like their forerunners for whom the cotton frontier of old had been too much, to keeping school or inn. And if the majority survived, they commonly survived to a steadily declining estate.

And flowing with and out of this came terror, defeatism, apathy, the will to escape. A growing inclination to withdraw themselves altogether from the struggle, from a world grown too dangerous; to shut away the present and abandon the future; here to flee to the inglorious asylum of a political sinecure, as likely as not created expressly for the case; there to retreat behind their own barred gates and hold commerce with none save the members of their own caste. A growing tendency to dissociate their standards wholly from reality, and convert them from living principles of action into mere eidolons.[2]

But it is not only the Virginians with whom we have to do. Of the *nouveaux* of the Old South, not a few were so far gone in the dawdling habit, so far removed from the nimble diligence of their sires, that they also could not encounter the requirements of the hour and went much the same way taken by their models.

And beyond these were hundreds of others: the flower of those planters and yeomen in whom the notions of aristocracy had fallen on the immensely receptive ground of the old native integrity and decency; hundreds of others who, able and consenting (however reluctantly) to put away languor and ease, to accommodate themselves to the reigning exigencies in every humane and honorable respect, yet, to their everlasting glory, set their faces against them on the inhumane and dishonorable side.

Some of them simply refused to compromise at all: not only would not stint and cheat their dependents, but even clung to the better part of magnanimity; managed somehow to reconcile the

---

2. Plato's word for the material appearances of the absolutes (cf. Bacon's term, "*idols of the mind*").

assiduous practice of thrift with the maintenance of the old liberal-
handed spirit toward the available means; and, in a word, declined
to make themselves stingy or mean or petty in any fashion whatever.
They wore their patches, they carried lean jowls, they denied themselves and their families, and, if must be, they paid the penalty of
economic ruin or decay (and, for all their superior energy, it was so
in many a case) with high pride, unflinching and undismayed.

And if, under the law of averages for human nature, the majority
of even the better sort did inevitably compromise, then they
compromised by iotas and jots—fell back by inches. They compromised no more than was required if they were to avoid extinction.
And they did it with reluctance and with genuine grief. They fought
valiantly to hold on to the essence of the heritage and strove
earnestly to keep alive and potent in their increasingly restless sons
a notion of honor distinctly bearing the aristocratic impress, and
not altogether without success.

Yet, when all this is said—by token of it, in truth—the central
fact stands fast: slowly here, rapidly there, more superficially in the
one case, more fundamentally in another, directly or indirectly, the
South was slipping back from the gains it had made: was receding
avoidlessly and forever from the aristocratic goal of the *ancien
régime*. And the old primary, simple, back-country heritage of the
vast body of Southerners was swinging continuously up from the
obscurity which had sometime engulfed it, toward the mastery of
the field again.

On the more superficial side, the change wrote itself unmistakably in the final extinction, along in the early 1890's (at a time,
that is, when general violence and, in certain ways at least, the
romantic spirit were rolling up to new heights), of the formal duel;
the universal enactment of laws against it.

And on the more important side, it wrote itself just as decisively
in a gathering tendency toward a more ruthless enunciation, even
by good men, of the old brutal individualistic doctrine—which yet
was never felt as conflicting with humane profession and notions of
paternalistic right and duty—that every man was, in economics at
any rate, absolutely responsible for himself, and that whatever he
got in this world was exactly what he deserved.

QUESTIONS

1. Describe the working of the cotton economy according to Cash.
   What is its relevance to his thesis?
2. How does Cash move from economics to morality?
3. What does each of the four last paragraphs add to the summary
   description of this large social change?
4. How might Freeman's "Over the River," (pp.1086–1099) be seen
   as a happy combination of aristocratic values and back-country
   heritage?

SAMUEL CLEMENS

A Scrap of Curious History

Marion City, on the Mississippi River, in the State of Missouri—a village; time, 1845. La Bourboule-les-Bains, France—a village; time, the end of June, 1894. I was in the one village in that early time; I am in the other now. These times and places are sufficiently wide apart, yet today I have the strange sense of being thrust back into that Missourian village and of reliving certain stirring days that I lived there so long ago.

Last Saturday night the life of the President of the French Republic was taken by an Italian assassin. Last night a mob surrounded our hotel, shouting, howling, singing the "Marseillaise," and pelting our windows with sticks and stones; for we have Italian waiters, and the mob demanded that they be turned out of the house instantly—to be drubbed, and then driven out of the village. Everybody in the hotel remained up until far into the night, and experienced the several kinds of terror which one reads about in books which tell of night attacks by Indians and by French mobs: the growing roar of the oncoming crowd; the arrival, with rain of stones and crash of glass; the withdrawal to rearrange plans—followed by a silence ominous, threatening, and harder to bear than even the active siege and the noise. The landlord and the two village policemen stood their ground, and at last the mob was persuaded to go away and leave our Italians in peace. Today four of the ringleaders have been sentenced to heavy punishment of a public sort—and are become local heroes, by consequence.

That is the very mistake which was at first made in the Missourian village half a century ago. The mistake was repeated and repeated—just as France is doing in these latter months.

In our village we had our Ravochals, our Henrys, our Vaillants; and in a humble way our Cesario—I hope I have spelled this name wrong. Fifty years ago we passed through, in all essentials, what France has been passing through during the past two or three years, in the matter of periodical frights, horrors, and shudderings.

In several details the parallels are quaintly exact. In that day, for a man to speak out openly and proclaim himself an enemy of negro slavery was simply to proclaim himself a madman. For he was blaspheming against the holiest thing known to a Missourian, and could *not* be in his right mind. For a man to proclaim himself an anarchist in France, three years ago, was to proclaim himself a madman—he could not be in his right mind.

Now the original old first blasphemer against any institution profoundly venerated by a community is quite sure to be in earnest; his followers and imitators may be humbugs and self-seekers, but he himself is sincere—his heart is in his protest.

Robert Hardy was our first *abolitionist*—awful name! He was a journeyman cooper, and worked in the big cooper-shop belonging to the great pork-packing establishment which was Marion City's chief pride and sole source of prosperity. He was a New Englander, a stranger. And, being a stranger, he was of course regarded as an inferior person—for that has been human nature from Adam down—and of course, also, he was made to feel unwelcome, for this is the ancient law with man and the other animals. Hardy was thirty years old, and a bachelor; pale, given to reverie and reading. He was reserved, and seemed to prefer the isolation which had fallen to his lot. He was treated to many side remarks by his fellows, but as he did not resent them it was decided that he was a coward.

All of a sudden he proclaimed himself an abolitionist—straight out and publicly! He said that negro slavery was a crime, an infamy. For a moment the town was paralyzed with astonishment; then it broke into a fury of rage and swarmed toward the cooper-shop to lynch Hardy. But the Methodist minister made a powerful speech to them and stayed their hands. He proved to them that Hardy was insane and not responsible for his words; that no man *could* be sane and utter such words.

So Hardy was saved. Being insane, he was allowed to go on talking. He was found to be good entertainment. Several nights running he made abolition speeches in the open air, and all the town flocked to hear and laugh. He implored them to believe him sane and sincere, and have pity on the poor slaves, and take measures for the restoration of their stolen rights, or in no long time blood would flow—blood, blood, rivers of blood!

It was great fun. But all of a sudden the aspect of things changed. A slave came flying from Palmyra, the county seat, a few miles back, and was about to escape in a canoe to Illinois and freedom in the dull twilight of the approaching dawn, when the town constable seized him. Hardy happened along and tried to rescue the negro; there was a struggle, and the constable did not come out of it alive. Hardy crossed the river with the negro, and then came back to give himself up. All this took time, for the Mississippi is not a French brook, like the Seine, the Loire, and those other rivulets, but is a real river nearly a mile wide. The town was on hand in force by now, but the Methodist preacher and the sheriff had already made arrangements in the interest of order; so Hardy was surrounded by a strong guard and safely conveyed to the village calaboose in spite of all the effort of the mob to get hold of him. The reader will have begun to perceive that this Methodist minister was a prompt man; a prompt man, with active hands and a good headpiece. Williams was his name—Damon Williams; Damon Williams in public, Damnation Williams in private, because he was so powerful on that theme and so frequent.

The excitement was prodigious. The constable was the first man who had ever been killed in the town. The event was by long odds the most imposing in the town's history. It lifted the humble village into sudden importance; its name was in everybody's mouth for twenty miles around. And so was the name of Robert Hardy—Robert Hardy, the stranger, the despised. In a day he was become the person of most consequence in the region, the only person talked about. As to those other coopers, they found their position curiously changed—they were important people, or unimportant, now, in proportion as to how large or how small had been their intercourse with the new celebrity. The two or three who had really been on a sort of familiar footing with him found themselves objects of admiring interest with the public and of envy with their shopmates.

The village weekly journal had lately gone into new hands. The new man was an enterprising fellow, and he made the most of the tragedy. He issued an extra. Then he put up posters promising to devote his whole paper to matters connected with the great event—there would be a full and intensely interesting biography of the murderer, and even a portrait of him. He was as good as his word. He carved the portrait himself, on the back of a wooden type—and a terror it was to look at. It made a great commotion, for this was the first time the village paper had ever contained a picture. The village was very proud. The output of the paper was ten times as great as it had ever been before, yet every copy was sold.

When the trial came on, people came from all the farms around, and from Hannibal, and Quincy, and even from Keokuk; and the courthouse could hold only a fraction of the crowd that applied for admission. The trial was published in the village paper, with fresh and still more trying pictures of the accused.

Hardy was convicted, and hanged—a mistake. People came from miles around to see the hanging; they brought cakes and cider, also the women and children, and made a picnic of the matter. It was the largest crowd the village had ever seen. The rope that hanged Hardy was eagerly bought up, in inch samples, for everybody wanted a memento of the memorable event.

Martyrdom gilded with notoriety has its fascinations. Within one week afterward four young lightweights in the village proclaimed themselves abolitionists! In life Hardy had not been able to make a convert; everybody laughed at him; but nobody could laugh at his legacy. The four swaggered around with their slouch hats pulled down over their faces, and hinted darkly at awful possibilities. The people were troubled and afraid, and showed it. And they were stunned, too; they could not understand it. "Abolitionist" had always been a term of shame and horror; yet here were four young men who were not only not ashamed to bear that name, but were grimly proud of it. Respectable young men they were, too—of good families, and brought up in the church. Ed Smith, the printer's apprentice, nineteen, had been the head Sunday school boy, and had once recited three thousand Bible verses without making a break. Dick Savage, twenty, the baker's apprentice; Will Joyce, twenty-two, journeyman blacksmith; and Henry Taylor, twenty-four, tobacco-stemmer—were the other three. They were all of a sentimental cast; they were all romance readers; they all wrote poetry, such as it was; they were all vain and foolish; but they had never before been suspected of having anything bad in them.

They withdrew from society, and grew more and more mysterious and dreadful. They presently achieved the distinction of being denounced by names from the pulpit—which made an immense stir! This was grandeur, this was fame. They were envied by all the other young fellows now. This was natural. Their company grew—grew alarmingly. They took a name. It was a secret name, and was divulged to no outsider; publicly they were simply the abolitionists. They had pass words, grips, and signs; they had secret meetings; their initiations were conducted with gloomy pomps and ceremonies, at midnight.

They always spoke of Hardy as "the Martyr," and every little while they moved through the principal street in procession—at midnight, black-robed, masked, to the measured tap of the solemn drum—on pilgrimage to the Martyr's grave, where they went through with some majestic fooleries and swore vengeance upon his murderers. They gave previous notice of the pilgrimage by small posters, and warned everybody to keep indoors and darken all houses along the route, and leave the road empty. These warnings were obeyed, for there was a skull and crossbones at the top of the poster.

When this kind of thing had been going on about eight weeks, a quite natural thing happened. A few men of character and grit woke up out of the nightmare of fear which had been stupefying their faculties, and began to discharge scorn and scoffings at themselves and the community for enduring this child's play; and at the same time they proposed to end it straightway. Everybody felt an uplift; life was breathed into their dead spirits; their courage rose and they began to feel like men aagain. This was on a Saturday. All day the new feeling grew and strengthened; it grew with a rush; it brought inspiration and cheer with it. Midnight saw a united community, full of zeal and pluck, and with a clearly defined and welcome piece of work in front of it. The best organizer and strongest and bitterest talker on that great Saturday was the Presbyterian clergyman who had denounced the original four from his pulpit—Rev. Hiram Fletcher—and he promised to use his pulpit in the public interest again now. On the morrow he had revelations to make, he said—secrets of the dreadful society.

But the revelations were never made. At half past two in the morning the dead silence of the village was broken by a crashing explosion, and the town patrol saw the preacher's house spring in a wreck of whirling fragments into the sky. The preacher was killed, together with a negro woman, his only slave and servant.

The town was paralyzed again, and with reason. To struggle against a visible enemy is a thing worth while, and there is a plenty of men who stand always ready to undertake it; but to struggle against an invisible one—an invisible one who sneaks in and does his awful work in the dark and leaves no trace—that is another matter. That is a thing to make the bravest tremble and hold back.

The cowed populace were afraid to go to the funeral. The man who was to have had a packed church to hear him expose and denounce the common enemy had but a handful to see him buried. The coroner's jury had brought in a verdict of "death by the visitation of God," for no witness came forward; if any existed they prudently kept out of the way. Nobody seemed sorry. Nobody wanted to see the terrible secret society provoked into the commission of further outrages. Everybody wanted the tragedy hushed up, ignored, forgotten, if possible.

And so there was a bitter surprise and an unwelcome one when Will Joyce, the blacksmith's journeyman, came out and proclaimed himself the assassin! Plainly he was not minded to be robbed of his glory. He made his proclamation, and stuck to it. Stuck to it, and insisted upon a trial. Here was an ominous thing; here was a new and peculiarly formidable terror, for a motive was revealed here which society could not hope to deal with successfully—*vanity*, thirst for notoriety. If men were going to kill for notoriety's sake, and to win the glory of newspaper renown, a big trial, and a showy execution, what possible invention of man could discourage or deter them? The town was in a sort of panic; it did not know what to do.

However, the grand jury had to take hold of the matter—it had no choice. It brought in a true bill, and presently the case went to the county court. The trial was a fine sensation. The prisoner was the principal witness for the prosecution. He gave a full account of the assassination; he furnished even the minutest particulars: how he deposited his keg of powder and laid his train—from the house to such-and-such a spot; how George Ronalds and Henry Hart came along just then, smoking, and he borrowed Hart's cigar and fired the train with it, shouting, "Down with all slave-tyrants!" and how Hart and Ronalds made no effort to capture him, but ran away, and had never come forward to testify yet.

But they had to testify now, and they did—and pitiful it was to see how reluctant they were, and how scared. The crowded house listened to Joyce's fearful tale with a profound and breathless interest, and in a deep hush which was not broken till he broke it himself, in concluding, with a roaring repetition of his "Death to all slave-tyrants!"—which came so unexpectedly and so startlingly that it made every one present catch his breath and gasp.

The trial was put in the paper, with biography and large portrait, with other slanderous and insane pictures, and the edition sold beyond imagination.

The execution of Joyce was a fine and picturesque thing. It drew a vast crowd. Good places in trees and seats on rail fences sold for half a dollar apiece; lemonade- and gingerbread-stands had great prosperity. Joyce recited a furious and fantastic and denunciatory speech on the scaffold which had imposing passages of schoolboy eloquence in it, and gave him a reputation on the spot as an orator, and the name, later, in the society's records, of the "Martyr Orator." He went to his death breathing slaughter and charging his society to "avenge his murder." If he knew anything of human nature he knew that to plenty of young fellows present in that great crowd he was a grand hero—and enviably situated.

He was hanged. It was a mistake. Within a month from his death the society which he had honored had twenty new members, some of them earnest, determined men. They did not court distinction in the same way, but they celebrated his martyrdom. The crime which had been obscure and despised had become lofty and glorified.

Such things were happening all over the country. Wild-brained martyrdom was succeeded by uprising and organization. Then, in natural order, followed riot, insurrection, and the wrack and restitutions of war. It was bound to come, and it would naturally come in that way. It has been the manner of reform since the beginning of the world.

QUESTIONS

1. Is Clemens an abolitionist? What, in this essay, is an abolitionist?
2. Why does Clemens regard sentencing the ringleaders of the French mob as mistaken? What course of action would he presumably advise? What social or political arrangements would be necessary to make that course of action possible?

ISAAC DEUTSCHER
The Unfinished Revolution[1]

Coming to the end of this survey of the Soviet half-century we ought to return to the questions with which we began: Has the Russian revolution fulfilled the hopes it has aroused? And what is its significance for our age and generation? I wish I were able to answer the first of these questions with a plain and emphatic yes, and conclude my remarks on a properly triumphal note. Unfortunately, this I cannot do. Yet, a disheartened and pessimistic conclusion would not be justified either. This is still in more than one sense an unfinished revolution. Its record is anything but plain. It is compounded of failure and success, of hope frustrated and hope fulfilled—and who can measure the hopes against one another? Where are the scales on which could be weighed the accomplishments and the frustrations of so great an epoch, and their mutual proportions established? What is evident is the immensity and the unexpected character of both the success and the failure, their interdependence and their glaring contrasts. One is reminded of Hegel's dictum, which has not yet dated, that "history is not the realm of happiness"; that "periods of happiness are its empty pages," for "although there is no lack of satisfaction in history, satisfaction which comes from the realization of great purposes surpassing any particular interest, this is not the same as what is usually described as happiness." Certainly these fifty years do not belong among history's empty pages.

"Russia is a big ship destined for big sailing," this was the poet Alexander Blok's famous phrase, in which we sense the undertone of intense national pride. A Russian looking at the record of this half-century with the eyes of the nationalist, one who sees the revolution as a purely Russian event, would have good reasons to feel even prouder. Russia is now a bigger ship still, out on a much bigger course. In terms of sheer national power—and many people the world over still think in these terms—the balance sheet is to the Soviet Union absolutely satisfactory. Our statesmen and politicians cannot consider it otherwise than with envy. Yet it seems to me that few Russians of this generation contemplate it with undisturbed exultation. Many are conscious of the fact that October 1917 was not a purely Russian event; and even those who are not do not necessarily see national power as history's *ultima ratio*.[2] Most Russians seem aware of the miseries as well as the grandeur

1. Chapter VI, "Conclusions and Prospects," of *The Unfinished Revolution*, 1967. We have preferred the book title to the original chapter title as more informative.
2. "Final argument."

of this epoch. They watch the extraordinary impetus of their economic expansion, the rising stacks of huge and ultramodern factories, the growing networks of schools and educational establishments, the feats of Soviet technology, the space flights, the impressive extension of all social services and so on; and they have a sense of the vitality and *élan* of their nation. But they know, too, that for most of them daily life is still a grinding drudgery, which mocks the splendors of one of the world's super-Powers.

To give one indication: Despite the immense scale of housing construction, the average dwelling space per person is still only six square yards. In view of the prevailing inequality this means that for many it is only five or four yards, or even less. The average is still what it was at the end of the Stalin era. This is not surprising if one recalls that in the last fifteen years alone the mass of town dwellers has grown by as much as the entire population of the British Isles. However, such statistics offer little relief or consolation to people who suffer from the desperate overcrowding; and although the situation is bound to improve gradually, the amelioration will be long in coming. The disproportion between effort and results exemplified by housing is characteristic of many aspects of Soviet life. In all too many fields the Soviet Union has had to run very fast, indeed to engage in a breathless race, only to find that it is still standing in the same place.

Western travelers, struck by the Russians' intense, almost obsessive, preoccupation with material things and with the comforts of life, often speak on this account about the "Americanization" of the Soviet mentality. Yet the background to this preoccupation is obviously different. In the United States the whole "way of life" and the dominant ideology encourage the preoccupation with material possessions, while commercial advertising works furiously to excite it constantly so as to induce or sustain artificial consumer demand and prevent overproduction. The Soviet craving for material goods reflects decades of underproduction and underconsumption, weariness with want and privation, and a popular feeling that these can at last be overcome. This popular mood compels the rulers to take greater care than they have been accustomed to take of popular needs and to satisfy them; to this extent it is a progressive factor helping to modernize and civilize the national standard, and "style," of living. But as the Soviet way of life is not geared to individual accumulation of wealth, the "Americanization" is superficial and in all probability characteristic only of the present phase of slow transition from scarcity to abundance.

The spiritual and the political life of the Soviet Union is also variously affected by the grandeur and the miseries of this half-century. Compared with the realm of dread and terror the Soviet Union was, say, fifteen years ago, it is now almost a land of freedom. Gone are the concentration camps of old, whose inmates died like flies, without knowing what they had been punished for. Gone is the all-pervading fear that had atomized the nation, making every man and woman afraid of communicating even with a friend or a relative, and turning the Soviet Union into a country virtually inaccessible to the foreigner. The nation is recovering its mind and speech. The process is slow. It is not easy for people to shed habits they had formed during decades of monolithic discipline. All the same, the change is remarkable. Soviet periodicals are nowadays astir with all sorts of dramatic, though often muffled, controversies; and ordinary people are not greatly inhibited in expressing their genuine political thoughts and feelings to complete strangers, even to tourists from hostile countries, whose inquisitiveness is not always innocuous. Yet the Soviet citizen often frets at the relatively mild bureaucratic tutelage under which he lives as he never fretted at Stalin's despotism. He feels that his spiritual freedom, too, is restricted to something like his miserable six square yards. It is one of the sublime features of the human character that men are not satisfied with what they have achieved, especially when their attainments are dubious or consist of half-gains. Such discontent is the driving force of progress. But it may also become, as it sometimes does in the Soviet Union, a source of frustration and even of sterile cynicism.

In their political life also the Russians all too often feel that they have run fast to keep in the same place. The half-freedom the Soviet Union has won since Stalin's days can indeed be even more excruciating than complete and hermetic tyranny. Recent Soviet writings, some published in the U.S.S.R., others abroad, have expressed the mortification that arises from this state of affairs, the morose pessimism it sometimes breeds, and even something like the mood of "Waiting-for-Godot." But, here again, similarities between Soviet and Western phenomena may be deceptive. The despair which permeates quite a few recent Soviet works of literature is rarely inspired by any metaphysical sense of the "absurdity of the human condition." More often than not it expresses, allusively or otherwise, a kind of baffled anger over the outrageous abnormities of Soviet political life, especially over the ambiguities of the official de-Stalinization. The spirit of these writings is more active, satirical, and militant than that which has produced recent Western variations on the old theme of *vanitas vanitatum et vanitas omnia.*[3]

The failure of the official de-Stalinization is at the heart of the malaise. It is more than a decade now since, at the Twentieth Congress, Khrushchev exposed Stalin's misdeeds. That act could make sense only if it had been the prelude to a genuine clarification of

3. "Vanity of vanities, and all is vanity" (Ecclesiastes i.2).

the many issues raised by it and to an open nationwide debate on the legacy of the Stalin era. This has not been the case. Khrushchev and the ruling group at large were eager not to open the debate but to prevent it. They intended the prologue to be also the epilogue of the de-Stalinization. Circumstances compelled them to initiate the process; this had become an imperative necessity of national life. Since the protagonists and even the followers of all anti-Stalinist oppositions had been exterminated, only men of Stalin's entourage were left to inaugurate the de-Stalinization. But the task was uncongenial to them; it went against the grain of their mental habits and interests. They could carry it out only halfheartedly and perfunctorily. They lifted a corner of the curtain over the Stalin era, but could not raise the whole curtain. And so the moral crisis, opened up by Khrushchev's revelations, remains unresolved. His disclosures caused relief and shock, confusion and shame, bewilderment and cynicism. It was a relief for the nation to be freed from the incubus of Stalinism; but it was a shock to realize how heavily the incubus had weighed down the whole body politic. Of course, many a family had suffered from the Stalinist terror and had known it in detail; but only now were they allowed to catch for the first time an overall glimpse of it, to glance at its true national dimensions. Yet this fleeting glimpse by itself was confusing. And it was a grievous humiliation to be reminded how helplessly the nation had succumbed to the terror, and how meekly it had endured it. Finally, nothing but bewilderment and cynicism could result from the fact that the grim disclosures had been made by Stalin's abettors and accessories, who, having revealed the huge skeleton in their cupboard, at once slammed the door on it and would say no more.

The issue has been too grave and fateful to be treated like this, especially in view of its close bearing on current politics. The official de-Stalinization created new cleavages and aggravated old ones. "Liberals" and "radicals," "right wing" and "left wing" communists could not but press for an uninhibited national settling of accounts with the Stalin era and a complete break with it. Crypto-Stalinists, entrenched in the bureaucracy, have been anxious to save as much as possible of the Stalinist method of government and of the Stalin legend. Outside the bureaucracy, especially among the workers, quite a few people have been so antagonized by the hypocrisy of the official de-Stalinization, that they have been almost reconverted to the Stalin cult, or want to hear no more of it, and would rather see the whole issue buried once and for all.

At the back of the divisions there is the fact that Soviet society does not know itself and is intensely conscious of this. The history of this half-century is a closed book even to the Soviet intelligentsia. Like someone who had long been struck with amnesia and only begins to recover, the nation not knowing its recent past does not understand its present. Decades of Stalinist falsification have induced the collective amnesia; and the half-truths with which the Twentieth Congress initiated the process of recovery are blocking its progress. But sooner or later the Soviet Union must take stock of this half-century, if its political consciousness is to develop and crystallize in new and positive forms.

This is a situation of especial interest to historians and political theorists; it offers a rare, perhaps a unique, example of the close interdependence of history, politics, and social consciousness. Historians often argue whether an awareness of the past contributes at all to the wisdom of statesmen and to the political intelligence of ordinary people. Some believe it does; others take the view Heine once expressed in the aphorism that history teaches us that it teaches nothing. In class society political thinking, governed by class or group interest, benefits from the study of the past only within the limits required or permitted by interest. Even the historian's views are conditioned by social background and political circumstances. Normally, "the ideas of the ruling class" tend to be "the ruling ideas of an epoch." In some epochs those ideas favor a more or less objective study of history, and political thinking gains thereby; in others they act as powerful inhibiting factors. Whatever the case, no ruling group and no society, if it is only a little more than half-civilized, can function without possessing some form of historical consciousness satisfactory to itself, without a consciousness giving most members of the ruling group and of society at large the conviction that their view of the past, especially of the recent past, is not just a tissue of falsehoods, but that it corresponds to real facts and occurrences. No ruling group can live by cynicism alone. Statesmen, leaders, and ordinary people alike need to have the subjective feeling that what they stand for is morally right; and what is morally right cannot rest on historical distortions or forgeries. And although distortions and even plain forgeries have entered into the thinking of every nation, their very effectiveness depends on whether the nation concerned accepts them as truth.

In the Soviet Union the moral crisis of the post-Stalin years consists of a profound disturbance of the nation's historical and political consciousness. Since the Twentieth Congress, people have been aware how much of what they once believed was made up of forgeries and myths. They want to learn the truth but are denied access to it. Their rulers have told them that virtually the whole record of the revolution has been falsified; but they have not thrown open the true record. To give again only a few instances: the last great scandal of the Stalin era, the so-called Doctors' Plot, has been officially denounced on the ground that the plot was a concoction. But whose concoction was it? Was Stalin alone responsible for it? And what purpose was it to serve? These questions are still unanswered. Khrushchev has suggested that the Soviet Union might not have suffered the huge losses inflicted on it in the last war had it not been for Stalin's errors and miscalculations. Yet those "errors" have not become the subject of an open debate. The Nazi-Soviet Pact of 1939 is, officially, still taboo. The people have been told about the horrors of the concentration camps and about the frame-ups and forced confessions by means of which the Great Purges had been staged. But the victims of the Purges, apart from a few exceptions, have not been rehabilitated. No one knows just how many people were deported to the camps; how many died; how many were massacred; and how many survived. A similar conspiracy of silence surrounds the circumstances of the forcible collectivization. Every one of these questions has been raised; none has been answered. Even in this jubilee year most of the leaders of 1917 remain "unpersons"; the names of most members of the Central Committee who directed the October rising are still unmentionable. People are asked to celebrate the great anniversary, but they cannot read a single trustworthy account of the events they are celebrating. (Nor can they get hold of any history of the civil war.) The ideological edifice of Stalinism has been exploded; but, with its foundations shattered, its roof blown off, and its walls charred and threatening to come down with a crash, the structure still stands; and the people are required to live in it.

Opening this series of lectures I alluded to the blessings and curses of the continuity of the Soviet regime. We have dwelt on the blessings; now we see the curses as well. Sheltered by continuity, the irrational aspects of the revolution survive and endure together with the rational ones. Can they be separated from one another? It is clearly in the Soviet Union's vital interest that it should overcome the irrationalities and release its creative powers from their grip. The present incongruous combination breeds intense disillusionment; and because of this the miseries of the revolution may, in the eyes of the people, come to overshadow its grandeur. When this happened in past revolutions the result was restoration. But although restoration was a tremendous setback, indeed a tragedy, to the nation that succumbed to it, it had its redeeming feature: it demonstrated to a people disillusioned with the revolution how inacceptable the reactionary alternative was. Returned Bourbons and Stuarts taught the people much better than Puritans, Jacobins, or Bonapartists could, that there was no way back to the past; that the basic work of the revolution was irreversible; and that it must be saved for the future. Unwittingly, the restoration thus rehabilitated the revolution, or at least its essential and rational accomplishments.

In the Soviet Union, we know, the revolution has survived all possible agents of restoration. Yet it seems to be burdened with a mass of accumulated disillusionment and even despair that in other historical circumstances might have been the driving force of a restoration. At times the Soviet Union appears to be fraught with the moral-psychological potentiality of restoration that cannot become a political actuality. Much of the record of these fifty years is utterly discredited in the eyes of the people; and no returned Romanovs are going to rehabilitate it. The revolution must rehabilitate itself, by its own efforts.

Soviet society cannot reconcile itself for much longer to remaining a mere object of history and being dependent on the whims of autocrats or the arbitrary decisions of oligarchies. It needs to regain the sense of being its own master. It needs to obtain control over its governments and to transform the State, which has so long towered above society, into an instrument of the nation's democratically expressed will and interest. It needs, in the first instance, to reestablish fredom of expression and association. This is a modest aspiration compared with the ideal of a classless and stateless society; and it is paradoxical that the Soviet people should now have to strive for those elementary liberties which once figured in all bourgeois liberal programs, programs which Marxism rightly subjected to its ruthless criticism.

In a post-capitalist society, however, freedom of expression and association has to perform a function radically different from that which it has performed in capitalism. It need hardly be stressed here how essential that freedom has been to progress even under capitalism. Yet, in bourgeois society it can be a formal freedom only. Prevailing property relations render it so, for the possessing classes exercise an almost monopolistic control over nearly all the means of opinion formation. The working classes and their intellectual mouthpieces manage to get hold of, at best, marginal facilities for social and political self-expression. Society, being itself controlled by property, cannot effectively control the State. All the more generously is it allowed to indulge in the illusion that it does so, unless keeping up the illusion causes the bourgeoisie too much embarrassment and expense. In a society like the Soviet, freedom of expression and association cannot have so formal and illusory a character: either it is real, or it does not exist at all. The power of property having been destroyed, only the State, that is, the bureaucracy, dominates society; and its domination is based solely on the suppression of the people's liberty to criticize and oppose. Capitalism could afford to enfranchise the working classes, for it could rely on its economic mechanism to keep them in subjection; the bourgeoisie maintains its social preponderance even when it exercises no political power. In post-capitalist society no automatic economic mechanism keeps the masses in subjection; it is sheer political force that does it. True, the bureaucracy derives part of its strength from the uncontrolled commanding position it holds in the economy; but it holds that too by means of political force. Without that force it cannot maintain its social supremacy; and any form of democratic control deprives it of its force. Hence the new meaning and function of the freedom of expression and association. In other words, capitalism has been able to battle against its class enemies from many economic, political, and cultural lines of defense, with much scope for retreat and maneuver. A post-capitalist bureaucratic dictatorship has far less scope: its first, its political line of defense, is its last. No wonder that it holds that line with all the tenacity it can muster.

The post-capitalist relationship between State and society is far less simple, however, than some ultraradical critics imagine. There can, in my view, be no question of any so-called abolition of bureaucracy. Bureaucracy, like the State itself, cannot be simply obliterated. The existence of expert and professional groups of civil servants, administrators, and managers is part and parcel of a necessary social division of labor which reflects wide discrepancies and cleavages between various skills and degrees of education, between skilled and unskilled labor, and, more fundamentally, between brain and brawn. These discrepancies and cleavages are diminishing; and their reduction foreshadows a time when they may become socially so insignificant that State and bureaucracy may indeed wither away. But this is still a relatively remote prospect. What seems possible in the near future is that society should be able to retrieve its civil liberties and establish political control over the State. In striving for this the Soviet people are not just reenacting one of the old battles that bourgeois liberalism had fought against absolutism; they are rather following up their own great struggle of 1917.

The outcome will, of course, greatly depend on events in the outside world. The tremendous, and to us still obscure, upheaval in China must affect the Soviet Union as well. Insofar as it loosens up or upsets one post-revolutionary bureaucratic-monolithic structure and releases popular forces, rising from the depth of society, for spontaneous political action, the Chinese example may stimulate similar processes across the Soviet border. China is undoubtedly in some respects more progressive than the Soviet Union, if only because she was able to learn from Russia's experience and avoid some of the latter's erratic drifts and blunders; and she has been less affected by bureaucratic ossification. On the other hand, China's economic and social structure is primitive and backward; and Maoism carries, in its rituals and cults, the dead weight of that backwardness. Consequently, the lessons it sets out to teach the world have all too often little or no relevance to the problems of more highly developed societies; and even when Maoism has something positive to offer, it usually does it in so rigidly orthodox a manner and in such archaic forms that the positive content is all too easily overlooked. And when the Maoists try to galvanize the Stalinist cult, they merely shock and antagonize all forward-looking elements in the U.S.S.R. But perhaps the Russo-Chinese conflict may drive home one important lesson, namely, that arrogant bureaucratic oligarchies, incorrigible in their national narrowmindedness and egoism, cannot be expected to work out any rational solution of this or any other conflict, still less can they lay stable foundations for a socialist commonwealth of peoples.

Events in the West will contribute even more decisively, for good or evil, to the further internal evolution of the Soviet Union. We may leave aside here the frequently discussed and more obvious, diplomatic and military aspects of the problem: it is evident enough what severe restrictions the cold war and the international arms race place on the growth of welfare and the enlargement of liberty in the U.S.S.R. More fundamental and difficult is the issue of the stalemate in the class struggle, the makings of which were examined earlier. Is this stalemate going to last? Or is it only a fleeting moment of equilibrium? The view that it is going to last has gained much ground recently among Western political theorists and historians; many are inclined to consider it as the final outcome of the contest between capitalism and socialism. (No doubt this opinion has its adherents in the Soviet Union and eastern Europe as well.) The argument is conducted on various social-economic and historical levels.

The social structures of the U.S.S.R. and the U.S.A., it is pointed out, have, from their opposite starting points, evolved and moved towards one another so closely that their differences are increasingly irrelevant and the similarities are decisive. Among others, Professor John Kenneth Galbraith expounds this idea in his Reith Lectures. He speaks emphatically about the "convergence of structure in countries with advanced industrial organization" and surveys the main points of the convergence in American society. There is the supremacy of the managerial elements; the divorce of management from ownership; the continuous concentration of industrial power and the extension of the scales of its operation; the withering away of *laissez faire* and of the market; the growing economic role of the State; and, consequently, the inescapable necessity of planning, which is needed not merely to prevent slumps and depressions, but to maintain normal social efficiency. "We have seen," says Professor Galbraith, "that industrial technology has an imperative that transcends ideology." Pricking some current Western misconceptions about "the revival of a market economy in the U.S.S.R.," Professor Galbraith remarks: "There is no tendency for the Soviet and the Western systems to convergence by the return of the Soviet system to the market. Both have outgrown that. What exists is a perceptible and very important convergence to the same form of planning under the growing authority of the business firm." In this presentation the "convergence" appears to occur not so much halfway between the two systems, as just within the boundaries of socialism, and the picture is not one of stalemate, but rather of a diagonal resulting from the parallelogram of capitalist and socialist pressures.[4]

Historians find a precedent for this situation in the struggle between Reformation and Counter-Reformation. Professor Butterfield, one of the early exponents of this analogy, points out that at the outset of their conflict both Protestantism and Catholicism aspired to total victory; but that, having reached a deadlock, they were compelled to seek mutual accommodation, to "co-exist peacefully" and content themselves with their respective "zones of influence" in Western Christianity.[5] In the meantime, their initial ideological antagonism had been whittled down by a process of mutual assimilation: the Church of Rome enhanced its strength by absorbing elements of Protestantism; while Protestantism, growing dogmatic and sectarian, lost much of its attraction and came to resemble its adversary. The stalemate was thus unbreakable and final; so is the deadlock between the opposed ideologies of our time—on this point the arguments of our historians and of the political or economic theorists converge.

The historical analogy, convincing though it is in some points, has its faults and flaws. As such analogies often do, it overlooks basic differences between historic epochs. In the age of the Reformation, Western society was fragmented into a multitude of feudal, semi-feudal, post-feudal, pre-capitalist, and early capitalist principalities. The Protestant consciousness played its prominent part in the formation of the nation-state; but the nation-state set the outer limits to its unifying tendencies. The reunification of Western Christianity under the aegis of one Church was an historic impossibility. In contrast to this, the technological basis of modern society, its structure and its conflicts, are international or even universal in character; they tend towards international or universal solutions. And there are the unprecedented dangers threatening our biological existence. These, above all, press for the unification of mankind, which cannot be achieved without an integrating principle of social organization.

4. The quotations are from Professor Galbraith's Reith Lectures as published in *The Listener* (15 December 1966) [Deutscher's note].

5. H. Butterfield, *International Conflict in the Twentieth Century, A Christian View* (London 1960), pp. 61-78.

My criticism of Professor Butterfield's analogy does not detract from the soundness of his courageous pleas for an international *détente* which he addressed to American audiences in the 1950s [Deutscher's note].

Protestantism and Catholicism confronted one another primarily in ideological terms; but in the background there was the great conflict between rising capitalism and declining feudalism. This was by no means brought to a halt by the ideological-religious stalemate. The division of spheres between Reformation and Counter-Reformation corresponded, very broadly, to a division between the two social systems and to a temporary equilibrium between them. As the contest between the feudal and the bourgeois ways of life went on, it assumed new ideological forms. The more mature bourgeois consciousness of the eighteenth century expressed itself not in religious but in secularist ideologies, philosophical and political. The stalemate between Protestantism and Catholicism was perpetuated on a margin of history, as it were; for all practical historical purposes, in effective social and political action, it was transcended. Not only did the social conflict not congeal with the religious divisions, but it was fought out to the end. After all, capitalism achieved total victory in Europe. It did so by a wide variety of means and methods, by revolutions from below and revolutions from above, and after many temporary deadlocks and partial defeats. Thus even in the terms of this analogy it seems at least premature to conclude that the present ideological stalemate between East and West brings to a close the historic confrontation between capitalism and socialism. The forms and ideological expressions of the antagonism may and must vary; but it does not follow that the momentum of the conflict is spent or diminished. Incidentally, the story of the Reformation offers many a warning against hasty conclusions about ideological deadlocks. When one is told that a hundred and twenty years have passed since the *Communist Manifesto* without a victorious socialist revolution in the West, one thinks willy-nilly of the many "premature" starts the Reformation made and of the protracted manner in which its ideology and movement took shape. More than a century lay between Hus and Luther; and yet another century separated Luther from the Puritan revolution.

But has not the Marxist analysis of society, and have not the universal aspirations of the Russian revolution, been invalidated by the mutual assimilation of the opposed social systems? A degree of assimilation is undeniable; and it is due to the supranational leveling impact of modern technology and to the logic of any major confrontation which imposes identical or similar methods of action on the contestants. The changes in the structure of Western, especially American, society are striking indeed. But when we look at them closely, what do we see? The deepening divorce of management from property, the importance of the managerial elements, the concentration of capital, the ever more elaborate division of labor within any huge corporation and between the corporations;

the withering away of the market and *laissez faire*; the increase in the economic weight of the State; and the technological and the economic necessity of planning—all these are in fact manifestations of that socialization of the productive process which, according to Marxism, develops in capitalism. Indeed the socialization has now been immensely accelerated. In the description of a process which Marx gave in *Das Kapital*, he very clearly foreshadowed precisely these developments and trends that seem so novel and revolutionary to Western analysts. Has not Professor Galbraith described to us something with which we are, or should be, familiar, namely, the rapid growth of the "embryo of socialism within the womb of capitalism"? The embryo is evidently getting bigger and bigger. Should we therefore conclude that there is no longer any need for the act of birth? The Marxist will reflect over the paradox that while in Russia the midwife of revolution intervened before the embryo had had the time to mature, in the West the embryo may well have grown overmature; and the consequences may become extremely dangerous to the social organism.

The fact is that, regardless of all Keynesian innovations, our productive process, so magnificently socialized in many respects, is not yet socially controlled. Property, no matter how much it is divorced from management, still controls the economy. The shareholder's profit is still its regulating motive, subject only to the needs of militarism and of the worldwide struggle against communism. In any case, our economy and social existence remain anarchic and irrational. The anarchy may not show itself in periodic deep slumps and depressions, although, on a longer view, even this is not certain. European capitalism, within its smaller compass, knew, after the Franco-Prussian war of 1870, a similar and even more prolonged prosperity, undisturbed by deep slumps; and this led Edward Bernstein and his fellow revisionists to conclude that events had given the lie to the Marxist analysis and prognostication. Soon thereafter, however, the economy was shaken by convulsions more violent than ever, and mankind was ushered into the epoch of world wars and revolutions.

Nothing would be more welcome, especially to the Marxist, than the knowledge that capitalist property relations have become so irrelevant in Western society that they no longer hinder it in organizing rationally its productive forces and creative powers. Yet the test of this is whether our society can control and marshal its resources and energies for constructive purposes and for its own general welfare; and whether it can organize and plan them internationally as well as nationally. Until now our society has failed this test. Our governments have forestalled slumps and depressions by planning for destruction and death rather than for life and welfare. Not for nothing do our economists, financial experts, and jobbers speculate gloomily on what would happen to the Western economy if, for instance, the American Administration were not to spend nearly 80 billion dollars on armament in one year. Among all the dark images of declining capitalism ever drawn by Marxists, not a single one was as black and apocalyptic as the picture that reality is producing. About sixty years ago Rosa Luxemburg predicted that one day militarism would become *the* driving force of the capitalist economy; but even her forecast pales before the facts.

This is why the message of 1917 remains valid for the world at large. The present ideological deadlock and the social status quo can hardly serve as the basis either for the solution of the problems of our epoch or even for mankind's survival. Of course, it would be the ultimate disaster if the nuclear super-Powers were to treat the social status quo as their plaything and if either of them tried to alter it by force of arms. In this sense the peaceful coexistence of East and West is a paramount historic necessity. But the social status quo cannot be perpetuated. Karl Marx speaking about stalemates in past class struggles notes that they usually ended "in the common ruin of the contending classes." A stalemate indefinitely prolonged, and guaranteed by a perpetual balance of nuclear deterrents, is sure to lead the contending classes and nations to their common and ultimate ruin. Humanity needs unity for its sheer survival; where can it find it if not in socialism? And great though the Russian and the Chinese revolutions loom in the perspective of our century, Western initiative is still essential for the further progress of socialism.

Hegel once remarked that "world history moves from the East to the West" and that "Europe represents the close of world history," whereas Asia was only its beginning. This arrogant view was inspired by Hegel's belief that the Reformation and the Prussian State were the culmination of mankind's spiritual development; yet many people in the West, worshipers of neither State nor Church, believed until recently that world history had indeed found its final abode in the West, and that the East, having nothing significant to contribute, could only be its object. We know better. We have seen how vigorously history has moved back to the East. However, we need not assume that it ends there and that the West will forever go on speaking in its present conservative voice and contribute to the annals of socialism only a few more empty pages. Socialism has still some decisive revolutionary acts to perform in the West as well as in the East; and nowhere will history come to a close. The East has been the first to give effect to the great principle of a new social organization, the principle originally conceived in the West. Fifty years of Soviet history tell us what stupendous progress a backward nation has achieved by applying that principle, even in the most adverse conditions. By this alone these years point to the

limitless new horizons that Western society can open to itself and
to the world if only it frees itself from its conservative fetishes. In
this sense the Russian revolution still confronts the West with a
grave and challenging *tua res agitur*.[6]

6. "Your welfare is at stake."

THUCYDIDES

The Corcyraean Revolution[1]

The Athenian commander Nicostratus, the son of Diitrephes,
came up from Naupactus with a force of twelve ships and 500
Messenian hoplites.[2] His aim was to arrange a settlement, and he
persuaded the two parties to agree among themselves to bring to
trial ten men who had been chiefly responsible (and who immediately went into hiding); the rest were to come to terms with each
other and live in peace, and the whole state was to conclude an
offensive and defensive alliance with Athens.

Having made this settlement, Nicostratus was on the point of
sailing away, but the leaders of the democratic party persuaded him
to leave behind five of his ships to act as a check on any movement
which their opponents might make, while they themselves would
man five of their own ships and send them with him. Nicostratus
agreed, and the democratic leaders put down the names of their
enemies for service in the ships. Those who were called up, however, fearing that they would be sent off to Athens, seated themselves as suppliants in the temple of the Dioscuri. Nicostratus
offered them guarantees and spoke reassuringly to them, but his
words had no effect. The democratic party then armed themselves
on the pretext that these men could not be sincere in their intentions if they felt doubtful about sailing with Nicostratus. They
seized their opponents' arms out of their houses, and would have
put to death some of them whom they found there, if they had not
been prevented by Nicostratus. The rest of the oligarchical party,
seeing what was happening, took up their positions as suppliants in
the temple of Hera. There were at least 400 of them. The democrats, fearing that they might do something violent, persuaded
them to rise, took them across to the island in front of the temple,
and had provisions sent out to them there.

At this stage in the revolution, four or five days after the men

1. From Book III of *The Peloponnesian War*. This war (431–404 B.C.),
fought between the Athenians (the
compatriots of Thucydides) and the
Spartans ("the Peloponnesians"), produced political divisions in the smaller
Greek cities. In the section preceding
the excerpt given here, Thucydides tells
how the democratic party in Corcyra,
intending an alliance with Athens, put
down an attempted coup by the oligarchical party, sympathetic to Sparta.

2. Infantrymen.

had been taken across to the island, the Peloponnesian ships arrived from Cyllene, where they had been stationed since their return from Ionia. There were fifty-three of them, commanded, as before, by Alcidas, though now Brasidas sailed with him as his adviser. This fleet came to anchor in the harbor of Sybota on the mainland, and at daybreak set out for Corcyra.

The Corcyraeans were now in a state of the utmost confusion, alarmed both at what was happening inside their city and at the approach of the enemy fleet. They immediately got ready sixty ships and sent them straight out against the enemy, as soon as they were manned, neglecting the advice of the Athenians, which was to let them sail out first and then come out in support of them later with all their ships together. As the Corcyraean ships approached the enemy in this disorganized way, two of them immediately deserted, in other ships the crews were fighting among themselves, and no sort of order was kept in anything. The Peloponnesians observed the confusion in which they were, set aside twenty of their ships to meet the Corcyraeans, and put all the rest of their fleet against the twelve Athenian ships, among which were the *Salaminia* and the *Paralus*.

The Corcyraeans, in their part of the battle, were soon in difficulties, since they were making their attacks inefficiently and in small detachments. The Athenians, afraid of the numbers of the enemy and of the risk of encirclement, did not commit themselves to a general engagement and did not even charge the fleet opposed to them in the center. Instead they fell upon its wing where they sank one ship. After this the Peloponnesians formed their ships up in a circle and the Athenians rowed round them, trying to create confusion among them. Seeing this, and fearing a repetition of what had happened at Naupactus, the other Peloponnesians, who had been dealing with the Corcyraeans, came up in support, and then the whole Peloponnesian fleet together bore down on the Athenians, who now began to back water and to retire in front of them. They carried out the maneuver in their own good time, wishing to give the Corcyraean ships the fullest opportunity to escape first by keeping the enemy facing them in battle formation. So the fighting went, and it continued until sunset.

The Corcyraeans now feared that the enemy would follow up their victory by sailing against the city, or rescuing the men from the island, or by taking some other bold step. So they brought the men back again from the island to the temple of Hera, and put the defenses of the city in order. The Peloponnesians, however, in spite of their victory on the sea, did not risk sailing against the town, but sailed back to their original station on the mainland, taking with them the thirteen Corcyraean ships which they had captured. Nor were they any the more disposed to sail against the city on the next day, although the Corcyraeans were thoroughly disorganized and in a state of panic, and although Brasidas is said to have urged Alcidas to do so. Brasidas, however, was overruled, and the Peloponnesians merely made a landing on the headland of Leukimme and laid waste the country.

Meanwhile the democratic party in Corcyra were still terrified at the prospect of an attack by the enemy fleet. They entered into negotiations with the suppliants and with others of their party with a view to saving the city, and they persuaded some of them to go on board the ships. Thus they succeeded in manning thirty ships to meet the expected attack.

The Peloponnesians, however, having spent the time up till midday in laying waste the land, sailed away again, and about nightfall were informed by fire signals that a fleet of sixty Athenian ships was approaching from the direction of Leucas. This fleet, which was under the command of Eurymedon, the son of Thucles, had been sent out by the Athenians when they heard that the revolution had broken out and that Alcidas's fleet was about to sail for Corcyra. Thus the Peloponnesians set off by night, at once and in a hurry, for home, sailing close in to the shore. They hauled their ships across the isthmus of Leucas, so as to avoid being seen rounding the point, and so they got away.

When the Corcyraeans realized that the Athenian fleet was approaching and that their enemies had gone, they brought the Messenians, who had previously been outside the walls, into the city and ordered the fleet which they had manned to sail round into the Hyllaic harbor. While it was doing so, they seized upon all their enemies whom they could find and put them to death. They then dealt with those whom they had persuaded to go on board the ships, killing them as they landed. Next they went to the temple of Hera and persuaded about fifty of the suppliants there to submit to a trial. They then condemned every one of them to death. Seeing what was happening, most of the other suppliants, who had refused to be tried, killed each other there in the temple; some hanged themselves on the trees, and others found various other means of committing suicide. During the seven days that Eurymedon stayed there with his sixty ships, the Corcyraeans continued to massacre those of their own citizens whom they considered to be their enemies. Their victims were accused of conspiring to overthrow the democracy, but in fact men were often killed on grounds of personal hatred or else by their debtors because of the money that they owed. There was death in every shape and form. And, as usually happens in such situations, people went to every extreme and beyond it. There were fathers who killed their sons; men were dragged from the temples or butchered on the very altars; some were actually walled up in the temple of Dionysus and died there.

So savage was the progress of this revolution, and it seemed all the more so because it was one of the first which had broken out.

Later, of course, practically the whole of the Hellenic world was convulsed, with rival parties in every state—democratic leaders trying to bring in the Athenians, and oligarchs trying to bring in the Spartans. In peacetime there would have been no excuse and no desire for calling them in, but in time of war, when each party could always count upon an alliance which would do harm to its opponents and at the same time strengthen its own position, it became a natural thing for anyone who wanted a change of government to call in help from outside. In the various cities these revolutions were the cause of many calamities—as happens and always will happen while human nature is what it is, though there may be different degrees of savagery, and, as different circumstances arise, the general rules will admit of some variety. In times of peace and prosperity cities and individuals alike follow higher standards, because they are not forced into a situation where they have to do what they do not want to do. But war is a stern teacher; in depriving them of the power of easily satisfying their daily wants, it brings most people's minds down to the level of their actual circumstances.

So revolutions broke out in city after city, and in places where the revolutions occurred late the knowledge of what had happened previously in other places caused still new extravagances of revolutionary zeal, expressed by an elaboration in the methods of seizing power and by unheard-of atrocities in revenge. To fit in with the change of events, words, too, had to change their usual meanings. What used to be described as a thoughtless act of aggression was now regarded as the courage one would expect to find in a party member; to think of the future and wait was merely another way of saying one was a coward; any idea of moderation was just an attempt to disguise one's unmanly character; ability to understand a question from all sides meant that one was totally unfitted for action. Fanatical enthusiasm was the mark of a real man, and to plot against an enemy behind his back was perfectly legitimate self-defense. Anyone who held violent opinions could always be trusted, and anyone who objected to them became a suspect. To plot successfully was a sign of intelligence, but it was still cleverer to see that a plot was hatching. If one attempted to provide against having to do either, one was disrupting the unity of the party and acting out of fear of the opposition. In short, it was equally praiseworthy to get one's blow in first against someone who was going to do wrong, and to denounce someone who had no intention of doing any wrong at all. Family relations were a weaker tie than party membership, since party members were more ready to go to any extreme for any reason whatever. These parties were not formed to enjoy the benefits of the established laws, but to acquire power by overthrowing the existing regime; and the members of these parties felt confidence in each other not because of any fellowship in a religious communion, but because they were partners in crime. If an opponent made a reasonable speech, the party in power, so far from giving it a generous reception, took every precaution to see that it had no practical effect.

Revenge was more important than self-preservation. And if pacts of mutual security were made, they were entered into by the two parties only in order to meet some temporary difficulty, and remained in force only so long as there was no other weapon available. When the chance came, the one who first seized it boldly, catching his enemy off his guard, enjoyed a revenge that was all the sweeter from having been taken, not openly, but because of a breach of faith. It was safer that way, it was considered, and at the same time a victory won by treachery gave one a title for superior intelligence. And indeed most people are more ready to call villainy cleverness than simple-mindedness honesty. They are proud of the first quality and ashamed of the second.

Love of power, operating through greed and through personal ambition, was the cause of all these evils. To this must be added the violent fanaticism which came into play once the struggle had broken out. Leaders of parties in the cities had programs which appeared admirable—on one side political equality for the masses, on the other the safe and sound government of the aristocracy—but in professing to serve the public interest they were seeking to win the prizes for themselves. In their struggles for ascendancy nothing was barred; terrible indeed were the actions to which they committed themselves, and in taking revenge they went farther still. Here they were deterred neither by the claims of justice nor by the interests of the state; their one standard was the pleasure of their own party at that particular moment, and so, either by means of condemning their enemies on an illegal vote or by violently usurping power over them, they were always ready to satisfy the hatreds of the hour. Thus neither side had any use for conscientious motives; more interest was shown in those who could produce attractive arguments to justify some disgraceful action. As for the citizens who held moderate views, they were destroyed by both the extreme parties, either for not taking part in the struggle or in envy at the possibility that they might survive.

As the result of these revolutions, there was a general deterioration of character throughout the Greek world. The simple way of looking at things, which is so much the mark of a noble nature, was regarded as a ridiculous quality and soon ceased to exist. Society had become divided into two ideologically hostile camps, and each side viewed the other with suspicion. As for ending this state of affairs, no guarantee could be given that would be trusted, no oath sworn that people would fear to break; everyone had come to the conclusion that it was hopeless to expect a permanent settlement and so, instead of being able to feel confident in others, they devoted their energies to providing against being injured themselves. As a rule those who were least remarkable for intelligence showed the greater powers of survival. Such people recognized their own deficiencies and the superior intelligence of their opponents; fearing that they might lose a debate or find themselves outmaneuvered in intrigue by their quick-witted enemies, they boldly launched straight into action; while their opponents, overconfident in the belief that they would see what was happening in advance, and not thinking it necessary to seize by force what they could secure by policy, were the more easily destroyed because they were off their guard.

Certainly it was in Corcyra that there occurred the first examples of the breakdown of law and order. There was the revenge taken in their hour of triumph by those who had in the past been arrogantly oppressed instead of wisely governed; there were the wicked resolutions taken by those who, particularly under the pressure of misfortune, wished to escape from their usual poverty and coveted the property of their neighbors; there were the savage and pitiless actions into which men were carried not so much for the sake of gain as because they were swept away into an internecine struggle by their ungovernable passions. Then, with the ordinary conventions of civilized life thrown into confusion, human nature, always ready to offend even where laws exist, showed itself proudly in its true colors, as something incapable of controlling passion, insubordinate to the idea of justice, the enemy to anything superior to itself; for, if it had not been for the pernicious power of envy, men would not so have exalted vengeance above innocence and profit above justice. Indeed, it is true that in these acts of revenge on others men take it upon themselves to begin the process of repealing those general laws of humanity which are there to give a hope of salvation to all who are in distress, instead of leaving those laws in existence, remembering that there may come a time when they, too, will be in danger and will need their protection.

QUESTIONS

1. Thucydides describes the dissolution of a functioning community at Corcyra; what are the key features of this dissolution? What is most shocking to Thucydides?
2. What does Thucydides see as the basis for a society's moral code or ethical system? What is the biggest threat to this code or system?
3. On p. 1162 Thucydides describes the effect of the revolution on the meaning of words. Compare his idea of the relation between words and reality with that of Whorf (pp. 149–160).
4. How accurate is Thucydides' general assessment of "human nature"? Can such an issue be settled by appeals to facts?

HANNAH ARENDT
Denmark and the Jews[1]

At the Wannsee Conference,[2] Martin Luther, of the Foreign Office, warned of great difficulties in the Scandinavian countries, notably in Norway and Denmark. (Sweden was never occupied, and Finland, though in the war on the side of the Axis, was one country the Nazis never even approached on the Jewish question. This surprising exception of Finland, with some two thousand Jews, may have been due to Hitler's great esteem for the Finns, whom perhaps he did not want to subject to threats and humiliating blackmail.) Luther proposed postponing evacuations from Scandinavia for the time being, and as far as Denmark was concerned, this really went without saying, since the country retained its independent government, and was respected as a neutral state, until the fall of 1943, although it, along with Norway, had been invaded by the German Army in April, 1940. There existed no Fascist or Nazi movement in Denmark worth mentioning, and therefore no collaborators. In Norway, however, the Germans had been able to find enthusiastic supporters; indeed, Vidkun Quisling, leader of the pro-Nazi and anti-Semitic Norwegian party, gave his name to what later became known as a "quisling government." The bulk of Norway's seventeen hundred Jews were stateless, refugees from Germany; they were seized and interned in a few lightning operations in October and November, 1942. When Eichmann's office ordered their deportation to Auschwitz, some of Quisling's own men resigned their government posts. This may not have come as a surprise to Mr. Luther and the Foreign Office, but what was much more serious, and certainly totally unexpected, was that Sweden immediately offered asylum, and even Swedish nationality, to all who were persecuted. Dr. Ernst von Weizsäcker, Undersecretary of State of the Foreign Office, who received the proposal, refused to discuss it, but the offer helped nevertheless. It is always relatively easy to get out of a country illegally, whereas it is nearly impossible to enter the place of refuge without permission and to dodge the immigration authorities. Hence, about nine hundred people, slightly more than half of the small Norwegian community, could be smuggled into Sweden.

It was in Denmark, however, that the Germans found out how fully justified the Foreign Offices's apprehensions had been. The story of the Danish Jews is *sui generis*, and the behavior of the Danish people and their government was unique among all the

1. From "Deportations from Western Europe—France, Belgium, Holland, Denmark, Italy," Chapter X of *Eich-mann in Jerusalem*, 1963.
2. A meeting of German officials on "the Jewish question."

countries in Europe—whether occupied, or a partner of the Axis, or neutral and truly independent. One is tempted to recommend the story as required reading in political science for all students who wish to learn something about the enormous power potential inherent in non-violent action and in resistance to an opponent possessing vastly superior means of violence. To be sure, a few other countries in Europe lacked proper "understanding of the Jewish question," and actually a majority of them were opposed to "radical" and "final" solutions. Like Denmark, Sweden, Italy, and Bulgaria proved to be nearly immune to anti-Semitism, but of the three that were in the German sphere of influence, only the Danes dared speak out on the subject to their German masters. Italy and Bulgaria sabotaged German orders and indulged in a complicated game of double-dealing and double-crossing, saving their Jews by a tour de force of sheer ingenuity, but they never contested the policy as such. That was totally different from what the Danes did. When the Germans approached them rather cautiously about intro-ducing the yellow badge, they were simply told that the King would be the first to wear it, and the Danish government officials were careful to point out that anti-Jewish measures of any sort would cause their own immediate resignation. It was decisive in this whole matter that the Germans did not even succeed in introducing the vitally important distinction between native Danes of Jewish origin, of whom there were about sixty-four hundred, and the fourteen hundred German Jewish refugees who had found asylum in the country prior to the war and who now had been declared stateless by the German government. This refusal must have surprised the Germans no end, since it appeared so "illogical" for a government to protect people to whom it had categorically denied naturalization and even permission to work. (Legally, the prewar situation of refugees in Denmark was not unlike that in France, except that the general corruption in the Third Republic's civil services enabled a few of them to obtain naturalization papers, through bribes or "connections," and most refugees in France could work illegally, without a permit. But Denmark, like Switzerland, was no country *pour se débrouiller*[3].) The Danes, however, explained to the German officials that because the stateless refugees were no longer German citizens, the Nazis could not claim them without Danish assent. This was one of the few cases in which statelessness turned out to be an asset, although it was of course not statelessness per se that saved the Jews but, on the contrary, the fact that the Danish govern-ment had decided to protect them. Thus, none of the preparatory moves, so important for the bureaucracy of murder, could be carried out, and operations were postponed until the fall of 1943.

What happened then was truly amazing; compared with what

3. For wangling—using bribery to circumvent bureaucratic regulations.

took place in other European countries, everything went topsy-tur-
vey. In August, 1943—after the German offensive in Russia had
failed, the Afrika Korps had surrendered in Tunisia, and the Allies
had invaded Italy—the Swedish government canceled its 1940
agreement with Germany which had permitted German troops
the right to pass through the country. Thereupon, the Danish workers decided that they could help a bit in hurrying things up; riots
broke out in Danish shipyards, where the dock workers refused to
repair German ships and then went on strike. The German military
commander proclaimed a state of emergency and imposed martial
law, and Himmler thought this was the right moment to tackle the
Jewish question, whose "solution" was long overdue. What he did
not reckon with was that—quite apart from Danish resistance—the
German officials who had been living in the country for years were
no longer the same. Not only did General von Hannecken, the
military commander, refuse to put troops at the disposal of the
Reich plenipotentiary, Dr. Werner Best; the special S.S. units
(*Einsatz-kommandos*) employed in Denmark very frequently
objected to "the measures they were ordered to carry out by the
central agencies"—according to Best's testimony at Nuremberg.
And Best himself, an old Gestapo man and former legal adviser to
Heydrich, author of a then famous book on the police, who had
worked for the military government in Paris to the entire satisfaction
of his superiors, could no longer be trusted, although it is doubtful
that Berlin ever learned the extent of his unreliability. Still, it was
clear from the beginning that things were not going well, and
Eichmann's office sent one of its best men to Denmark—Rolf
Günther, whom no one had ever accused of not possessing the
required "ruthless toughness." Günther made no impression on his
colleagues in Copenhagen, and now von Hannecken refused even to
issue a decree requiring all Jews to report for work.

Best went to Berlin and obtained a promise that all Jews from
Denmark would be sent to Theresienstadt[4] regardless of their category—a very important concession, from the Nazis' point of view.
The night of October 1 was set for their seizure and immediate
departure—ships were ready in the harbor—and since neither the
Danes nor the Jews nor the German troops stationed in Denmark
could be relied on to help, police units arrived from Germany for a
door-to-door search. At the last moment, Best told them that they
were not permitted to break into apartments, because the Danish
police might then interfere, and they were not supposed to fight it
out with the Danes. Hence they could seize only those Jews who
voluntarily opened their doors. They found exactly 477 people, out
of a total of more then 7,800, at home and willing to let them in.
A few days before the date of doom, a German shipping agent,

4. A camp for certain classes of prisoners who were to receive special treatment.

Georg F. Duckwitz, having probably been tipped off by Best himself, had revealed the whole plan to Danish government officials,
who, in turn, had hurriedly informed the heads of the Jewish community. They, in marked contrast to Jewish leaders in other
countries, had then communicated the news openly in the synagogues on the occasion of the New Year services. The Jews had just
time enough to leave their apartments and go into hiding, which
was very easy in Denmark, because, in the words of the judgment,
"all sections of the Danish people, from the King down to simple
citizens," stood ready to receive them.

They might have remained in hiding until the end of the war if
the Danes had not been blessed with Sweden as a neighbor. It
seemed reasonable to ship the Jews to Sweden, and this was done
with the help of the Danish fishing fleet. The cost of transportation
for people without means—about a hundred dollars per person—
was paid largely by wealthy Danish citizens, and that was perhaps
the most astounding feat of all, since this was a time when Jews
were paying for their own deportation, when the rich among them
were paying fortunes for exit permits (in Holland, Slovakia, and,
later, in Hungary) either by bribing the local authorities or by negotiating "legally" with the S.S., who accepted only hard currency
and sold exit permits, in Holland, to the tune of five or ten thousand
dollars per person. Even in places where Jews met with genuine
sympathy and a sincere willingness to help, they had to pay for it,
and the chances poor people had of escaping were nil.

It took the better part of October to ferry all the Jews across the
five to fifteen miles of water that separates Denmark from
Sweden. The Swedes received 5,919 refugees, of whom at least 1,000
were of German origin, 1,310 were half-Jews, and 686 were non-
Jews married to Jews. (Almost half the Danish Jews seem to have
remained in the country and survived the war in hiding.) The
non-Danish Jews were better off than ever before, they all received
permission to work. The few hundred Jews whom the German police
had been able to arrest were shipped to Theresienstadt. They were
old or poor people, who either had not received the news in time
or had not been able to comprehend its meaning. In the ghetto,
they enjoyed greater privileges than any other group because of the
never-ending "fuss" made about them by Danish institutions and
private persons. Forty-eight persons died, a figure that was not
particularly high, in view of the average age of the group. When
everything was over, it was the considered opinion of Eichmann that
"for various reasons the action against the Jews in Denmark has
been a failure," whereas the curious Dr. Best declared that "the
objective of the operation was not to seize a great number of Jews
but to clean Denmark of Jews, and this objective has now been
achieved."

Politically and psychologically, the most interesting aspect of this incident is perhaps the role played by the German authorities in Denmark, their obvious sabotage of orders from Berlin. It is the only case we know of in which the Nazis met with *open* native resistance, and the result seems to have been that those exposed to it changed their minds. They themselves apparently no longer looked upon the extermination of a whole people as a matter of course. They had met resistance based on principle, and their "toughness" had melted like butter in the sun, they had even been able to show a few timid beginnings of genuine courage. That the ideal of "toughness," except, perhaps, for a few half-demented brutes, was nothing but a myth of self-deception, concealing a ruthless desire for conformity at any price, was clearly revealed at the Nuremberg Trials, where the defendants accused and betrayed each other and assured the world that they "had always been against it" or claimed, as Eichmann was to do, that their best qualities had been "abused" by their superiors. (In Jerusalem, he accused "those in power" of having abused his "obedience." "The subject of a good government is lucky, the subject of a bad government is unlucky. I had no luck.") The atmosphere had changed, and although most of them must have known that they were doomed, not a single one of them had the guts to defend the Nazi ideology. Werner Best claimed at Nuremberg that he had played a complicated double role and that it was thanks to him that the Danish officials had been warned of the impending catastrophe; documentary evidence showed, on the contrary, that he himself had proposed the Danish operation in Berlin, but he explained that this was all part of the game. He was extradited to Denmark and there condemned to death, but he appealed the sentence, with surprising results; because of "new evidence," his sentence was commuted to five years in prison, from which he was released soon afterward. He must have been able to prove to the satisfaction of the Danish court that he really had done his best.

JOHN STEINBECK

Battle Scene

You can't see much of a battle. Those paintings reproduced in history books which show long lines of advancing troops, close massed, and being received by massed defending troops, are either idealized or else times and battles have changed. The account in the morning papers of the battle of yesterday was not seen by the correspondent, but was put together from reports.

What the correspondent really saw was dust and the nasty burst of shells, low bushes and slit trenches. He lay on his stomach, if he had any sense, and watched ants crawling among the little sticks on the sand dune, and his nose was so close to the ants that their progress was interfered with by it.

Then he saw an advance. Not straight lines of men marching into cannon fire, but little groups scuttling like crabs from bits of cover to other cover, while the high chatter of machine guns sounded, and the deep proom of shellfire.

Perhaps the correspondent scuttled with them and hit the ground again. His report will be of battle plan and tactics, of taken ground or lost terrain, of attack and counterattack. But these are some of the things he probably really saw:

He might have seen the splash of dirt and dust that is a shell burst, and a small Italian girl in the street with her stomach blown out, and he might have seen an American soldier standing over a twitching body, crying. He probably saw many dead mules, lying on their sides, reduced to pulp. He saw the wreckage of houses, with torn beds hanging like shreds out of the spilled hole in a plaster wall. There were red carts and the stalled vehicles of refugees who did not get away.

The stretcher-bearers come back from the lines, walking in off step, so that the burden will not be jounced too much, and the blood dripping from the canvas, brother and enemy in the stretchers, so long as they are hurt. And the walking wounded coming back with shattered arms and bandaged heads, the walking wounded struggling painfully to the rear.

He would have smelled the sharp cordite in the air and the hot reek of blood if the going has been rough. The burning odor of dust will be in his nose and the stench of men and animals killed yesterday and the day before. Then a whole building is blown up and an earthy, sour smell comes from its walls. He will smell his own sweat and the accumulated sweat of an army. When his throat is dry he will drink warm water from his canteen, which tastes of disinfectant.

While the correspondent is writing for you of advances and retreats, his skin will be raw from the woolen clothes he has not taken off for three days, and his feet will be hot and dirty and swollen from not having taken off his shoes for days. He will itch from last night's mosquito bites and from today's sand-fly bites. Perhaps he will have a little sand-fly fever, so that his head pulses and a red rim comes into his vision. His head may ache from the heat and his eyes burn with the dust. The knee that was sprained when he leaped ashore will grow stiff and painful, but it is no wound and cannot be treated.

"The 5th Army advanced two kilometers," he will write, while the lines of trucks churn the road to deep dust and truck drivers hunch over their wheels. And off to the right the burial squads are scooping slits in the sandy earth. Their charges lie huddled on the ground and before they are laid in the sand, the second of the two dog tags is detached so that you know that that man with that army serial number is dead and out of it.

These are the things he sees while he writes of tactics and strategy and names generals and in print decorates heroes. He takes a heavily waxed box from his pocket. That is his dinner. Inside there are two little packets of hard cake which have the flavor of dog biscuits. There is a tin can of cheese and a roll of vitamin-charged candy, an envelope of lemon powder to make the canteen water taste less bad and a tiny package of four cigarettes.

That is dinner, and it will keep him moving for several more hours and keep his stomach working and his heart pumping. And if the line has advanced beyond him while he eats, dirty, buglike children will sidle up to him cringing and sniffling, their noses ringed with flies, and these children will whine for one of the hard biscuits and some of the vitamin candy. They will cry for candy: "Caramela—caramela—caramela—O.K., O.K., shank you, good-by." And if he gives the candy to one, the ground will spew up more dirty, buglike children, and they will scream shrilly, "Caramela—caramela." The correspondent will get the communiqué and will write your morning dispatch on his creaking, dust-filled portable, "General Clark's 5th Army advanced two kilometers against heavy artillery fire yesterday."

J. B. BURY
Darwinism and History

1. Evolution, and the principles associated with the Darwinian theory, could not fail to exert a considerable influence on the studies connected with the history of civilized man. The speculations which are known as "philosophy of history," as well as the sciences of anthropology, ethnography, and sociology (sciences which though they stand on their own feet are for the historian auxiliary), have been deeply affected by these principles. Historiographers, indeed, have with few exceptions made little attempt to apply them; but the growth of historical study in the nineteenth century has been determined and characterized by the same general principle, which has underlain the simultaneous developments of the study of nature, namely the *genetic* idea. The "historical" conception of nature, which has produced the history of the solar system, the story of the earth, the genealogies of telluric organisms, and has revolutionized natural science, belongs to the same order of thought as the conception of

human history as a continuous, genetic, causal process—a conception which has revolutionized historical research and made it scientific. Before proceeding to consider the application of evolutional principles, it will be pertinent to notice the rise of this new view.

2. With the Greeks and Romans history had been either a descriptive record or had been written in practical interests. The most eminent of the ancient historians were pragmatical; that is, they regarded history as an instructress in statesmanship, or in the art of war, or in morals. Their records reached back such a short way, their experience was so brief, that they never attained to the conception of continuous process, or realized the significance of time; and they never viewed the history of human societies as a phenomenon to be investigated for its own sake. In the middle ages there was still less chance of the emergence of the ideas of progress and development. Such notions were excluded by the fundamental doctrines of the dominant religion which bounded and bound men's minds. As the course of history was held to be determined from hour to hour by the arbitrary will of an extra-cosmic person, there could be no self-contained causal development, only a dispensation imposed from without. And as it was believed that the world was within no great distance from the end of this dispensation, there was no motive to take much interest in understanding the temporal, which was to be only temporary.

The intellectual movements of the fifteenth and sixteenth centuries prepared the way for a new conception, but it did not emerge immediately. The historians of the Renaissance period simply reverted to the ancient pragmatical view. For Machiavelli, exactly as for Thucydides and Polybius, the use of studying history was instruction in the art of politics. The Renaissance itself was the appearance of a new culture, different from anything that had gone before; but at the time men were not conscious of this; they saw clearly that the traditions of classical antiquity had been lost for a long period, and they were seeking to revive them, but otherwise they did not perceive that the world had moved, and that their own spirit, culture, and conditions were entirely unlike those of the thirteenth century. It was hardly till the seventeenth century that the presence of a new age, as different from the middle ages as from the ages of Greece and Rome, was fully realized. It was then that the triple division of ancient, medieval, and modern was first applied to the history of western civilization. Whatever objections may be urged against this division, which has now become almost a category of thought, it marks a most significant advance in man's view of his own past. He has become conscious of the immense changes in civilization which have come about slowly in the course of time, and history confronts him with a new aspect. He has to explain how those changes have been produced, how the transformations were effected. The appearance of this problem was almost simultaneous with the rise of rationalism, and the great historians and thinkers of the eighteenth century, such as Montesquieu, Voltaire, Gibbon, attempted to explain the movement of civilization by purely natural causes. These brilliant writers prepared the way for the genetic history of the following century. But in the spirit of the *Aufklärung*, that eighteenth-century Enlightenment to which they belonged, they were concerned to judge all phenomena before the tribunal of reason; and the apotheosis of "reason" tended to foster a certain superior *a priori* attitude, which was not favorable to objective treatment and was incompatible with a "historical sense." Moreover the traditions of pragmatical historiography had by no means disappeared.

3. In the first quarter of the nineteenth century the meaning of genetic history was fully realized. "Genetic" perhaps is as good a word as can be found for the conception which in this century was applied to so many branches of knowledge in the spheres both of nature and of mind. It does not commit us to the doctrine proper of evolution, nor yet to any teleological hypothesis such as is implied in "progress." For history it meant that the present condition of the human race is simply and strictly the result of a causal series (or set of causal series)—a continuous succession of changes, where each state arises causally out of the preceding; and that the business of historians is to trace this genetic process, to explain each change, and ultimately to grasp the complete development of the life of humanity. Three influential writers, who appeared at this stage and helped to initiate a new period of research, may specially be mentioned. Ranke in 1824 definitely repudiated the pragmatical view which ascribes to history the duties of an instructress, and with no less decision renounced the function, assumed by the historians of the *Aufklärung*, to judge the past; it was his business, he said, merely to show how things really happened. Niebuhr was already working in the same spirit and did more than any other writer to establish the principle that historical transactions must be related to the ideas and conditions of their age. Savigny about the same time founded the "historical school" of law. He sought to show that law was not the creation of an enlightened will, but grew out of custom and was developed by a series of adaptations and rejections, thus applying the conception of evolution. He helped to diffuse the notion that all the institutions of a society or a nation are as closely inter-connected as the parts of a living organism.

4. The conception of the history of man as a causal development meant the elevation of historical inquiry to the dignity of a science. Just as the study of bees cannot become scientific so long as the student's interest in them is only to procure honey or to derive moral lessons from the labors of "the little busy bee," so the history of human societies cannot become the object of pure scientific inves-

tigation so long as man estimates its value in pragmatical scales. Nor can it become a science until it is conceived as lying entirely within a sphere in which the law of cause and effect has unreserved and unrestricted dominion. On the other hand, once history is envisaged as a causal process, which contains within itself the explanation of the development of man from his primitive state to the point which he has reached, such a process necessarily becomes the object of scientific investigation and the interest in it is scientific curiosity.

At the same time, the instruments were sharpened and refined. Here Wolf, a philologist with historical instinct, was a pioneer. His *Prolegomena to Homer* (1795) announced new modes of attack. Historical investigation was soon transformed by the elaboration of new methods.

5. "Progress" involves a judgment of value, which is not involved in the conception of history as a genetic process. It is also an idea distinct from that of evolution. Nevertheless it is closely related to the ideas which revolutionized history at the beginning of the last century; it swam into men's ken simultaneously; and it helped effectively to establish the notion of history as a continuous process and to emphasize the significance of time. Passing over earlier anticipations, I may point to a *Discours* of Turgot (1750), where history is presented as a process in which "the total mass of the human race" "marches continually though sometimes slowly to an ever increasing perfection." That is a clear statement of the conception which Turgot's friend Condorcet elaborated in the famous work, published in 1795,[1] *Esquisse d'un tableau historique des progrés de l'esprit humain.*[2] This work first treated with explicit fullness the idea to which a leading role was to fall in the ideology of the nineteenth century. Condorcet's book reflects the triumphs of the *Tiers état*,[3] whose growing importance had also inspired Turgot; it was the political changes in the eighteenth century which led to the doctrine, emphatically formulated by Condorcet, that the masses are the most important element in the historical process. I dwell on this because, though Condorcet had no idea of evolution, the predominant importance of the masses was the assumption which made it possible to apply evolutional principles to history. And it enabled Condorcet himself to maintain that the history of civilization, a progress still far from being complete, was a development conditioned by general laws.

6. The assimilation of society to an organism, which was a governing notion in the school of Savigny, and the conception of progress, combined to produce the idea of an organic development, in which the historian has to determine the central principle or leading character. This is illustrated by the apotheosis of democracy in Tocqueville's

---

1. Written in 1793 in prison before he took poison [Bury's note].
2. *Sketch for a Historical Picture of the Progress of the Human Mind.*

3. Third estate, representatives of the common people in the prerevolutionary Estates-General.

Démocratie en Amérique, where the theory is maintained that "the gradual and progressive development of equality is at once the past and the future of the history of men." The same two principles are combined in the doctrine of Spencer (who held that society is an organism, though he also contemplated its being what he calls a "super-organic aggregate"),[4] that social evolution is a progressive change from militarism to industrialism.

7. The idea of development assumed another form in the speculations of German idealism. Hegel conceived the successive periods of history as corresponding to the ascending phases or ideas in the self-evolution of his Absolute Being. His *Lectures on the Philosophy of History* were published in 1837 after his death. His philosophy had a considerable effect, direct and indirect, on the treatment of history by historians, and although he was superficial and unscientific himself in dealing with historical phenomena, he contributed much towards making the idea of historical development familiar. Ranke was influenced, if not by Hegel himself, at least by the Idealistic philosophies of which Hegel's was the greatest. He was inclined to conceive the stages in the process of history as marked by incarnations, as it were, of ideas, and sometimes speaks as if the ideas were independent forces, with hands and feet. But while Hegel determined his ideas by *a priori* logic, Ranke obtained his by induction—by a strict investigation of the phenomena; so that he was scientific in his method and work, and was influenced by Hegelian prepossessions only in the kind of significance which he was disposed to ascribe to his results. It is to be noted that the theory of Hegel implied a judgment of value; the movement was a progress towards perfection.

8. In France, Comte approached the subject from a different side, and exercised, outside Germany, a far wider influence than Hegel. The 4th volume of his *Cours de philosophie positive*, which appeared in 1839, created sociology and treated history as a part of this new science, namely as "social dynamics." Comte sought the key for unfolding historical development, in what he called the social-psychological point of view, and he worked out the two ideas which had been enunciated by Condorcet: that the historian's attention should be directed not, as hitherto, principally to eminent individuals, but to the collective behavior of the masses, as being the most important element in the process; and that, as in nature, so in history, there are general laws, necessary and constant, which condition the development. The two points are intimately connected, for it is only

---

4. A society presents suggestive analogies with an organism, but it certainly is not an organism, and sociologists who draw inferences from the assumption of its organic nature must fall into error. A vital organism and a society are radically distinguished by the fact that the individual components of the former, namely the cells, are morphologically as well as functionally differentiated, whereas the individuals which compose a society are morphologically homogeneous and only functionally differentiated. The resemblances and the differences are worked out in E. de Majewski's striking book, *La Science de la Civilisation*, Paris, 1908 [Bury's note].

when the masses are moved into the foreground that regularity, uniformity, and law can be conceived as applicable. To determine the social-psychological laws which have controlled the development is, according to Comte, the task of sociologists and historians.

9. The hypothesis of general laws operative in history was carried further in a book which appeared in England twenty years later and exercised an influence in Europe far beyond its intrinsic merit, Buckle's *History of Civilization in England* (1857-61). Buckle owed much to Comte, and followed him, or rather outdid him, in regarding intellect as the most important factor conditioning the upward development of man, so that progress, according to him, consisted in the victory of the intellectual over the moral laws.

10. The tendency of Comte and Buckle to assimilate history to the sciences of nature by reducing it to general "laws," derived stimulus and plausibility from the vista offered by the study of statistics, in which the Belgian Quetelet, whose book *Sur l'homme* appeared in 1835, discerned endless possibilities. The astonishing uniformities which statistical inquiry disclosed led to the belief that it was only a question of collecting a sufficient amount of statistical material, to enable us to predict how a given social group will act in a particular case. Bourdeau, a disciple of this school, looks forward to the time when historical science will become entirely quantitative. The actions of prominent individuals, which are generally considered to have altered or determined the course of things, are obviously not amenable to statistical computation or explicable by general laws. Thinkers like Buckle sought to minimize their importance or explain them away.

11. These indications may suffice to show that the new efforts to interpret history which marked the first half of the nineteenth century were governed by conceptions closely related to those which were current in the field of natural science and which resulted in the doctrine of evolution. The genetic principle, progressive development, general laws, the significance of time, the conception of society as an organic aggregate, the metaphysical theory of history as the self-evolution of spirit—all these ideas show that historical inquiry had been advancing independently on somewhat parallel lines to the sciences of nature. It was necessary to bring this out in order to appreciate the influence of Darwinism.

12. In the course of the dozen years which elapsed between the appearances of *The Origin of Species*[5] (observe that the first volume of Buckle's work was published just two years before) and of *The Descent of Man* (1871), the hypothesis of Lamarck that man is the co-descendant with other species of some lower extinct form was admitted to have been raised to the rank of an established fact by

5. 1859 [Bury's note].

most thinkers whose brains were not working under the constraint of theological authority.

One important effect of the discovery of this fact (I am not speaking now of the Darwinian explanation) was to assign to history a definite place in the coordinated whole of knowledge, and relate it more closely to other sciences. It had indeed a defined logical place in systems such as Hegel's and Comte's; but Darwinism certified its standing convincingly and without more ado. The prevailing doctrine that man was created *ex abrupto* had placed history in an isolated position, disconnected with the sciences of nature. Anthropology, which deals with the animal *anthropos*, now comes into line with zoology, and brings it into relation with history.[6] Man's condition at the present day is the result of a series of transformations, going back to the most primitive phase of society, which is the ideal (unattainable) beginning of history. But that beginning had emerged without any breach of continuity from a development which carries us back to a quadrimane ancestor, still further back (according to Darwin's conjecture) to a marine animal of the ascidian type, and then through remoter periods to the lowest form of organism. It is essential in this theory that though links have been lost there was no break in the gradual development; and this conception of a continuous progress in the evolution of life, resulting in the appearance of uncivilized Anthropos, helped to reinforce, and increase a belief in, the conception of the history of civilized Anthropos as itself also a continuous progressive development.

13. Thus the diffusion of the Darwinian theory of the origin of man, by emphasizing the idea of continuity and breaking down the barriers between the human and animal kingdoms, has had an important effect in establishing the position of history among the sciences which deal with telluric development. The perspective of history is merged in a larger perspective of development. As one of the objects of biology is to find the exact steps in the genealogy of man from the lowest organic form, so the scope of history is to determine the stages in the unique causal series from the most rudimentary to the present state of human civilization.

It is to be observed that the interest in historical research implied by this conception need not be that of Comte. In the Positive Philosophy history is part of sociology; the interest in it is to discover

6. It is to be observed that history is (not only different in scope but) not coextensive with anthropology *in time*. For it deals only with the development of man in societies, whereas anthropology includes in its definition the proto-anthropic period when *anthropos* was still non-social, whether he lived in herds like the chimpanzee, or alone like the male ourang-outang. (It has been well shown by Majewski that congregations—herds, flocks, packs, etc.—of animals are not *societies;* the characteristic of a society is differentiation of function. Bee hives, ant hills, may be called quasi-societies; but in their case the classes which perform distinct functions are morphologically different.) [Bury's note].

the sociological laws. In the view of which I have just spoken, history is permitted to be an end in itself; the reconstruction of the genetic process is an independent interest. For the purpose of the reconstruction, sociology, as well as physical geography, biology, psychology, is necessary; the sociologist and the historian play into each other's hands; but the object of the former is to establish generalizations; the aim of the latter is to trace in detail a singular causal sequence.

14. The success of the evolutional theory helped to discredit the assumption or at least the invocation of transcendent causes. Philosophically of course it is compatible with theism, but historians have for the most part desisted from invoking the naive conception of a "god in history" to explain historical movements. A historian may be a theist; but, so far as his work is concerned, this particular belief is otiose. Otherwise indeed (as was remarked above) history could not be a science; for with a *deus ex machina* who can be brought on the stage to solve difficulties scientific treatment is a farce. The transcendent element had appeared in a more subtle form through the influence of German philosophy. I noticed how Ranke is prone to refer to ideas as if they were transcendent existences manifesting themselves in the successive movements of history. It is intelligible to speak of certain ideas as controlling, in a given period—for instance, the idea of nationality; but from the scientific point of view, such ideas have no existence outside the minds of individuals and are purely psychical forces; and a historical "idea," if it does not exist in this form, is merely a way of expressing a synthesis of the historian himself.

15. From the more general influence of Darwinism on the place of history in the system of human knowledge, we may turn to the influence of the principles and methods by which Darwin explained development. It had been recognized even by ancient writers (such as Aristotle and Polybius) that physical circumstances (geography, climate) were factors conditioning the character and history of a race or society. In the sixteenth century Bodin emphasized these factors, and many subsequent writers took them into account. The investigations of Darwin, which brought them into the foreground, naturally promoted attempts to discover in them the chief key to the growth of civilization. Comte had expressly denounced the notion that the biological methods of Lamarck could be applied to social man. Buckle had taken account of natural influences, but had relegated them to a secondary plane, compared with psychological factors. But the Darwinian theory made it tempting to explain the development of civilization in terms of "adaptation to environment," "struggle for existence," "natural selection," "survival of the fittest," etc.[7]

7. Recently O. Seeck has applied these principles to the decline of Graeco-Roman civilization in his *Untergang* *der antiken Welt,* 2 vols., Berlin, 1895, 1901 [Bury's note].

The operation of these principles cannot be denied. Man is still an animal, subject to zoological as well as mechanical laws. The dark influence of heredity continues to be effective; and psychical development had [has?] begun in lower organic forms—perhaps with life itself. The organic and the social struggles for existence are manifestations of the same principle. Environment and climatic influence must be called in to explain not only the differentiation of the great racial sections of humanity, but also the varieties within these sub-species and, it may be, the assimilation of distinct varieties. Ritter's *Anthropogeography* has opened a useful line of research. But on the other hand, it is urged that, in explaining the course of history, these principles do not take us very far, and that it is chiefly for the primitive ultra-prehistoric period that they can account for human development. It may be said that, so far as concerns the actions and movements of men which are the subject of recorded history, physical environment has ceased to act mechanically, and in order to affect their actions must affect their wills first; and that this psychical character of the causal relations substantially alters the problem. The development of human societies, it may be argued, derives a completely new character from the dominance of the conscious psychical element, creating as it does new conditions (inventions, social institutions, etc.) which limit and counteract the operation of natural selection, and control and modify the influence of physical environment. Most thinkers agree now that the chief clues to the growth of civilization must be sought in the psychological sphere. Imitation, for instance, is a principle which is probably more significant for the explanation of human development than natural selection. Darwin himself was conscious that his principles had only a very restricted application in this sphere, as is evident from his cautious and tentative remarks in the 5th chapter of his *Descent of Man*. He applied natural selection to the growth of the intellectual faculties and of the fundamental social instincts, and also to the differentiation of the great races or "sub-species" (Caucasian, African, etc.) which differ in anthropological character.[8]

16. But if it is admitted that the governing factors which concern the student of social development are of the psychical order, the preliminary success of natural science in explaining organic evolution by general principles encouraged sociologists to hope that social evolution could be explained on general principles also. The idea of Condorcet, Buckle, and others, that history could be assimilated to the

---

8. Darwinian formulae may be suggestive by way of analogy. For instance, it is characteristic of social advance that a multitude of inventions, schemes and plans are framed which are never carried out, similar to, or designed for the same end as, an invention or plan which is actually adopted because it has chanced to suit the particular conditions of the hour (just as the works accomplished by an individual statesman, artist or savant are usually only a residue of the numerous projects conceived by his brain). This process in which so much abortive production occurs is analogous to elimination by natural selection [Bury's note].

natural sciences was powerfully reinforced, and the notion that the actual historical process, and every social movement involved in it, can be accounted for by sociological generalizations, so-called "laws," is still entertained by many, in one form or another. Dissentients from this view do not deny that the generalizations at which the sociologist arrives by the comparative method, by the analysis of social factors, and by psychological deduction may be an aid to the historian; but they deny that such uniformities are laws or contain an explanation of the phenomena. They can point to the element of chance coincidence. This element must have played a part in the events of organic evolution, but it has probably in a larger measure helped to determine events in social evolution. The collision of two unconnected sequences may be fraught with great results. The sudden death of a leader or a marriage without issue, to take simple cases, has again and again led to permanent political consequences. More emphasis is laid on the decisive actions of individuals, which cannot be reduced under generalizations and which deflect the course of events. If the significance of the individual will had been exaggerated to the neglect of the collective activity of the social aggregate before Condorcet, his doctrine tended to eliminate as unimportant the roles of prominent men, and by means of this elimination it was possible to found sociology. But it may be urged that it is patent on the face of history that its course has constantly been shaped and modified by the wills of individuals,[9] which are by no means always the expression of the collective will; and that the appearance of such personalities at the given moments is not a necessary outcome of the conditions and cannot be deduced. Nor is there any proof that, if such and such an individual had not been born, some one else would have arisen to do what he did. In some cases there is no reason to think that what happened need ever have come to pass. In other cases it seems evident that the actual change was inevitable, but in default of the man who initiated and guided it, it might have been postponed, and, postponed or not, might have borne a different cachet. I may illustrate by an instance which has just come under my notice. Modern painting was founded by Giotto, and the Italian expedition of Charles VIII, near the close of the sixteenth century, introduced into France the fashion of imitating Italian painters. But for Giotto and Charles VIII, French painting might have been very different. It may be said that "if Giotto had not appeared, some other great initiator would have played a role analogous to his, and that without Charles VIII there would have been the commerce with Italy, which in the long run would have sufficed to place France in relation with

---

9. We can ignore here the metaphysical question of freewill and determinism. For the character of the individual's brain depends in any case on ante-natal accidents and coincidences, and so it may be said that the role of individuals ultimately depends on chance—the accidental coincidence of independent sequences [Bury's note].

Italian artists. But the equivalent of Giotto might have been deferred for a century and probably would have been different; and commercial relations would have required ages to produce the *rayonnement imitatif* of Italian art in France, which the expedition of the royal adventurer provoked in a few years."[1] Instances furnished by political history are simply endless. Can we conjecture how events would have moved if the son of Philip of Macedon had been an incompetent? The aggressive action of Prussia which astonished Europe in 1740 determined the subsequent history of Germany; but that action was anything but inevitable; it depended entirely on the personality of Frederic the Great.

Hence it may be argued that the action of individual wills is a determining and disturbing factor, too significant and effective to allow history to be grasped by sociological formulae. The types and general forms of development which the sociologist attempts to disengage can only assist the historian in understanding the actual course of events. It is in the special domains of economic history and *Kulturgeschichte* which have come to the front in modern times that generalization is most fruitful, but even in these it may be contended that it furnishes only partial explanations.

17. The truth is that Darwinism itself offers the best illustration of the insufficiency of general laws to account for historical development. The part played by coincidence, and the part played by individuals—limited by, and related to general social conditions—render it impossible to deduce the course of the past history of man or to predict the future. But it is just the same with organic development. Darwin (or any other zoologist) could not deduce the actual course of evolution from general principles. Given an organism and its environment, he could not show that it must evolve into a more complex organism of a definite predetermined type; knowing what it has evolved into, he could attempt to discover and assign the determining causes. General principles do not account for a particular sequence; they embody necessary conditions; but there is a chapter of accidents too. It is the same in the case of history.

* * *

20. The men engaged in special historical researches—which have been pursued unremittingly for a century past, according to scientific methods of investigating evidence (initiated by Wolf, Niebuhr, Ranke)—have for the most part worked on the assumptions of genetic history or at least followed in the footsteps of those who fully grasped the genetic point of view. But their aim has been to collect and sift evidence, and determine particular facts; comparatively few have given serious thought to the lines of research and the speculations which have been considered in this paper. They

---

1. I have taken this example from G. Tarde's *La logique sociale* (p. 403), Paris, 1904, where it is used for quite a different purpose [Bury's note].

have been reasonably shy of compromising their work by applying theories which are still much debated and immature. But historiography cannot permanently evade the questions raised by these theories. One may venture to say that no historical change or transformation will be fully understood until it is explained how social environment acted on the individual components of the society (both immediately and by heredity), and how the individuals reacted upon their environment. The problem is psychical, but it is analogous to the main problem of the biologist.

QUESTIONS

1. What is the genetic idea of history? What does the last paragraph add to the definition given at the outset?
2. At the end of his first paragraph Bury sets forth a two-part organization—"applications of evolutional principles" and "rise of this view." Where is the point of transition between the two parts? How does he subdivide the first part? What is the central problem which concerns him in the second part?
3. Several times Bury defines the genetic idea of history by referring to another, antithetical idea of history. What name does he give the antithetical idea? What other names would be appropriate?
4. Carr's essay (p.1198) was written a half-century later on more or less the same subject as Bury. Does Carr feel the same antithesis between these two ideas of history? What historical generalization about the writing of history would explain your answer to this question?
5. Would Beadle (pp. 1280–1295) agree with Bury that the problem he defines for the historian "is analogous to the main problem of the biologist"?

VIRGINIA WOOLF

The New Biography

"The aim of biography," said Sir Sidney Lee, who had perhaps read and written more lives than any man of his time, "is the truthful transmission of personality," and no single sentence could more neatly split up into two parts the whole problem of biography as it presents itself to us today. On the one hand there is truth; on the other there is personality. And if we think of truth as something of granite-like solidity and of personality as something of rainbow-like intangibility and reflect that the aim of biography is to weld these two into one seamless whole, we shall admit that the problem is a stiff one and that we need not wonder if biographers have for the most part failed to solve it.

For the truth of which Sir Sidney speaks, the truth which biography demands, is truth in its hardest, most obdurate form; it is truth as truth is to be found in the British Museum; it is truth out of which all vapor of falsehood has been pressed by the weight of research. Only when truth had been thus established did Sir Sidney Lee use it in the building of his monument; and no one can be so foolish as to deny that the piles he raised of such hard facts, whether one is called Shakespeare or King Edward the Seventh, are worthy of all our respect. For there is a virtue in truth; it has an almost mystic power. Like radium, it seems able to give off forever and ever grains of energy, atoms of light. It stimulates the mind, which is endowed with a curious susceptibility in this direction as no fiction, however artful or highly colored, can stimulate it. Truth being thus efficacious and supreme, we can only explain the fact that Sir Sidney's life of Shakespeare is dull, and that his life of Edward the Seventh is unreadable, by supposing that though both are stuffed with truth, he failed to choose those truths which transmit personality. For in order that the light of personality may shine through, facts must be manipulated; some must be brightened; others shaded; yet, in the process, they must never lose their integrity. And it is obvious that it is easier to obey these precepts by considering that the true life of your subject shows itself in action which is evident rather than in that inner life of thought and emotion which meanders darkly and obscurely through the hidden channels of the soul. Hence, in the old days, the biographer chose the easier path. A life, even when it was lived by a divine, was a series of exploits. The biographer, whether he was Izaak Walton or Mrs. Hutchinson or that unknown writer who is often so surprisingly eloquent on tombstones and memorial tablets, told a tale of battle and victory. With their stately phrasing and their deliberate artistic purpose, such records transmit personality with a formal sincerity which is perfectly satisfactory of its kind. And so, perhaps, biography might have pursued its way, draping the robes decorously over the recumbent figures of the dead, had there not arisen toward the end of the eighteenth century one of those curious men of genius who seem able to break up the stiffness into which the company has fallen by speaking in his natural voice. So Boswell spoke. So we hear booming out from Boswell's page the voice of Samuel Johnson. "No, sir; stark insensibility," we hear him say. Once we have heard those words we are aware that there is an incalculable presence among us which will go on ringing and reverberating in widening circles however times may change and ourselves. All the draperies and decencies of biography fall to the ground. We can no longer maintain that life consists in actions only or in works. It consists in personality. Something has been liberated beside which all else seems cold and colorless. We are freed from a servitude which is now seen to be intolerable. No longer need we pass solemnly and stiffly from camp to council chamber. We may sit, even with the great and good, over the table and talk.

Through the influence of Boswell, presumably, biography all through the nineteenth century concerned itself as much with the lives of the sedentary as with the lives of the active. It sought painstakingly and devotedly to express not only the outer life of work and activity but the inner life of emotion and thought. The uneventful lives of poets and painters were written out as lengthily as the lives of soldiers and statesmen. But the Victorian biography was a parti-colored, hybrid, monstrous birth. For though truth of fact was observed as scrupulously as Boswell observed it, the personality which Boswell's genius set free was hampered and distorted. The convention which Boswell had destroyed settled again, only in a different form, upon biographers who lacked his art. Where the Mrs. Hutchinsons and the Izaak Waltons had wished to prove that their heroes were prodigies of courage and learning the Victorian biographer was dominated by the idea of goodness. Noble, upright, chaste, severe; it is thus that the Victorian worthies are presented to us. The figure is almost always above life size in top hat and frock coat, and the manner of presentation becomes increasingly clumsy and laborious. For lives which no longer express themselves in action take shape in innumerable words. The conscientious biographer may not tell a fine tale with a flourish, but must toil through endless labyrinths and embarrass himself with countless documents. In the end he produces an amorphous mass, a life of Tennyson, or of Gladstone, in which we go seeking disconsolately for voice or laughter, for curse or anger, for any trace that this fossil was once a living man. Often, indeed, we bring back some invaluable trophy, for Victorian biographies are laden with truth; but always we rummage among them with a sense of the prodigious waste, of the artistic wrongheadedness of such a method.

With the twentieth century, however, a change came over biography, as it came over fiction and poetry. The first and most visible sign of it was the difference in size. In the first twenty years of the new century biographies must have lost half their weight. Mr. Strachey compressed four stout Victorians into one slim volume; M. Maurois boiled the usual two volumes of a Shelley life into one little book the size of a novel. But the diminution of size was only the outward token of an inward change. The point of view had completely altered. If we open one of the new school of biographies its bareness, its emptiness makes us at once aware that the author's relation to his subject is different. He is no longer the serious and sympathetic companion, toiling even slavishly in the footsteps of his hero. Whether friend or enemy, admiring or critical, he is an equal. In any case, he preserves his freedom and his right to independent judgment. Moreover, he does not think himself con-

strained to follow every step of the way. Raised upon a little eminence which his independence has made for him, he sees his subject
spread about him. He chooses; he synthesizes; in short, he has
ceased to be the chronicler; he has become an artist.

Few books illustrate the new attitude to biography better than
Some People, by Harold Nicolson. In his biographies of Tennyson
and of Byron Mr. Nicolson followed the path which had been
already trodden by Mr. Strachey and others. Here he has taken a
step on his own initiative. For here he has devised a method of
writing about people and about himself as though they were at
once real and imaginary. He has succeeded remarkably, if not
entirely, in making the best of both worlds. *Some People* is not
fiction because it has the substance, the reality of truth. It is not
biography because it has the freedom, the artistry of fiction. And if
we try to discover how he has won the liberty which enables him to
present us with these extremely amusing pages we must in the first
place credit him with having had the courage to rid himself of a
mountain of illusion. An English diplomat is offered all the bribes
which usually induce people to swallow humbug in large doses with
composure. If Mr. Nicolson wrote about Lord Curzon it should
have been solemnly. If he mentioned the Foreign Office it should
have been respectfully. His tone toward the world of Bognors and
Whitehall should have been friendly but devout. But thanks to a
number of influences and people, among whom one might mention
Max Beerbohm and Voltaire, the attitude of the bribed and docile
official has been blown to atoms. Mr. Nicolson laughs. He laughs at
Lord Curzon; he laughs at the Foreign Office; he laughs at himself.
And since his laughter is the laughter of the intelligence it has the
effect of making us take the people he laughs at seriously. The
figure of Lord Curzon concealed behind the figure of a drunken
valet is touched off with merriment and irreverence; yet of all the
studies of Lord Curzon which have been written since his death
none makes us think more kindly of that preposterous but, it
appears, extremely human man.

So it would seem as if one of the great advantages of the new
school to which Mr. Nicolson belongs is the lack of pose, humbug,
solemnity. They approach their bigwigs fearlessly. They have no
fixed scheme of the universe, no standard of courage or morality to
which they insist that he shall conform. The man himself is the
supreme object of their curiosity. Further, and it is this chiefly
which has so reduced the bulk of biography, they maintain that the
man himself, the pith and essence of his character, shows itself to
the observant eye in the tone of a voice, the turn of a head, some
little phrase or anecdote picked up in passing. Thus in two subtle
phrases, in one passage of brilliant description, whole chapters of
the Victorian volume are synthesized and summed up. *Some Peo-*

ple is full of examples of this new phase of the biographer's art. Mr. Nicolson wants to describe a governess and he tells us that she had a drop at the end of her nose and made him salute the quarterdeck. He wants to describe Lord Curzon, and he makes him lose his trousers and recite "Tears, Idle Tears." He does not cumber himself with a single fact about them. He waits till they have said or done something characteristic, and then he pounces on it with glee. But, though he waits with an intention of pouncing which might well make his victims uneasy if they guessed it, he lays suspicion by appearing himself in his own proper person in no flattering light. He has a scrubby dinner jacket, he tells us; a pink bumptious face, curly hair, and a curly nose. He is as much the subject of his own irony and observation as they are. He lies in wait for his own absurdities as artfully as for theirs. Indeed, by the end of the book we realize that the figure which has been most completely and most subtly displayed is that of the author. Each of the supposed subjects holds up in his or her small bright diminishing mirror a different reflection of Harold Nicolson. And though the figure thus revealed is not noble or impressive or shown in a very heroic attitude, it is for these very reasons extremely like a real human being. It is thus, he would seem to say, in the mirrors of our friends, that we chiefly live.

To have contrived this effect is a triumph not of skill only, but of those positive qualities which we are likely to treat as if they were negative—freedom from pose, from sentimentality, from illusion. And the victory is definite enough to leave us asking what territory it has won for the art of biography. Mr. Nicolson has proved that one can use many of the devices of fiction in dealing with real life. He has shown that a little fiction mixed with fact can be made to transmit personality very effectively. But some objections or qualifications suggest themselves. Undoubtedly the figures in *Some People* are all rather below life size. The irony with which they are treated, though it has its tenderness, stunts their growth. It dreads nothing more than that one of these little beings should grow up and becomes serious or perhaps tragic. And, again, they never occupy the stage for more than a few brief moments. They do not want to be looked at very closely. They have not a great deal to show us. Mr. Nicolson makes us feel, in short, that he is playing with very dangerous elements. An incautious movement and the book will be blown sky high. He is trying to mix the truth of real life and the truth of fiction. He can only do it by using no more than a pinch of either. For though both truths are genuine, they are antagonistic; let them meet and they destroy each other. Even here, where the imagination is not deeply engaged, when we find people whom we know to be real like Lord Oxford or Lady Colefax, mingling with Miss Plimsoll and Marstock, whose reality we doubt, the one casts suspicion upon the other. Let it be fact, one feels, or let it be fiction; the imagination will not serve under two masters simultaneously.

And here we again approach the difficulty which, for all his ingenuity, the biographer still has to face. Truth of fact and truth of fiction are incompatible; yet he is now more than ever urged to combine them. For it would seem that the life which is increasingly real to us is the fictitious life; it dwells in the personality rather than in the act. Each of us is more Hamlet, Prince of Denmark, than he is John Smith of the Corn Exchange. Thus, the biographer's imagination is always being stimulated to use the novelist's art of arrangement, suggestion, dramatic effect to expound the private life. Yet if he carries the use of fiction too far, so that he disregards the truth, or can only introduce it with incongruity, he loses both worlds; he has neither the freedom of fiction nor the substance of fact. Boswell's astonishing power over us is based largely upon his obstinate veracity, so that we have implicit belief in what he tells us. When Johnson says "No, sir; stark insensibility," the voice has a ring in it because we have been told, soberly and prosaically, a few pages earlier, that Johnson "was entered a Commoner of Pembroke, on the 31st of October, 1728, being then in his nineteenth year." We are in the world of brick and pavement; of birth, marriage, and death; of Acts of Parliament; of Pitt and Burke and Sir Joshua Reynolds. Whether this is a more real world than the world of Bohemia and Hamlet and Macbeth we doubt; but the mixture of the two is abhorrent.

Be that as it may we can assure ourselves by a very simple experiment that the days of Victorian biography are over. Consider one's own life; pass under review a few years that one has actually lived. Conceive how Lord Morley would have expounded them; how Sir Sidney Lee would have documented them; how strangely all that has been most real in them would have slipped through their fingers. Nor can we name the biographer whose art is subtle and bold enough to present that queer amalgamation of dream and reality, that perpetual marriage of granite and rainbow. His method still remains to be discovered. But Mr. Nicolson with his mixture of biography and autobiography, of fact and fiction, of Lord Curzon's trousers and Miss Plimsoll's nose, waves his hand airily in a possible direction.

WILLIAM B. WILLCOX
The Excitement of Historical Research

Research in history, as in other fields, is hard work. It has its high moments, as teaching does, but exacts a much heavier price in drudgery and monotony. Why, then, are so many university teachers of history also researchers? Although they have many motives, the one that seems to me the strongest is curiosity. If the historian were asked why he wants to tackle a particular research problem, he might well answer in the often quoted words of a British mountaineer, when asked a generation ago why he wanted to tackle Everest: "because it's there." The problem is there, and its mere existence is a challenge. The historian, like the mountaineer, must of course decide which of many challenges will be worth his time and effort; and here he has little information to guide him. His decision, for all the hard thought that goes into it, rests essentially on hunch. He cannot predict the size of his problem, or the extent to which it will be soluble, or the value of solving it. But uncertainty is the spice of research. Exploration means reaching into the unknown, and the explorer who knows in advance what he will find is not an explorer.

An aspect of the past may appear from a distance picayune, and prove on investigation to be quite the contrary. Take for example the way in which work horses were harnessed in Merovingian times, a subject that scarcely appears calculated to fire the imagination. But appearance is deceptive. From earliest times until the Dark Ages, research disclosed, the power of the horse to pull a wagon or plough had been limited by his harness, which pressed upon his windpipe; the harder he pulled, the smaller his air supply and the less his strength. In the Merovingian period some unknown genius designed a new kind of harness that put the strain on the horse's shoulders; the animal was then free to breathe, and his efficiency went up. A mere rearrangement of leather straps augmented the basic source of power on the land, increased agricultural productivity, and so contributed to the slow beginnings of medieval civilization.

This example suggests a number of points about the nature of research. One, already mentioned, is that the importance of a problem cannot be predicted in advance. A second is that the problem is almost never tidily solved: some questions, such as the identity of the man who designed the new harness, remain unanswered for lack of evidence. A third is that the subject under investigation has no inherent limits, and must be limited arbitrarily. The investigator in this case establishes that increased horsepower was a factor in raising agricultural yield; his next logical step is to consider what other factors were at work, how they were interrelated, and for how long they operated—in other words to explore the whole economic history of the Dark and Middle Ages. This is too large a field for intensive research. Somewhere a line must be drawn, but where?

The line does not draw itself, for history is all of a piece. Studying a particular fragment of it out of context falsifies the nature of the fragment, and studying the entire context is impossible. Between the two extremes the researcher must find his own mean, by setting such limits as his interests and sense of feasibility suggest; but these limits are his own. They are not determined by any logic inherent in his problem, and they are likely to change as his investigation progresses and grows toward an end that he may never have anticipated. Take for illustration my own experience. It is with a narrow area of history, but one that I believe contains pitfalls and surprises that are not essentially different from those in many other areas.

The Clements Library of the University of Michigan has a large collection of manuscripts relating to the British side of the War of Independence. When I came to the University years ago, I knew next to nothing about the war; but the wealth of the Clements material, and the fact that no one else had explored it, were a challenge. From that mass of documents a subject or subjects for research would surely emerge. What form the research would eventually take was unimportant; all that mattered was to begin. I was like an archeologist who confronts a site, knowing approximately when it was inhabited but nothing more, and who cannot tell whether he will find disconnected fragments or the integrated complex of a city.

The more I learned about the British military effort in America, the subject with which most of the manuscripts deal, the more insistently one question obtruded itself: how did Britain manage to lose the war? She began it with many advantages—uncontested sea power, troops that were better than the American and generals that were at least no worse, a government that for all its muddleheadedness knew more than the Continental Congress did about how to conduct a war. Even French intervention in 1778 was not conclusive, and by the summer of 1781 the issue was still apparently hanging in the balance. Then the British suddenly blundered through to defeat at Yorktown, a failure that seemed to be anything but predetermined. What factors, then, brought it about?

The question in its entirety was too large, too ramified, for manuscript research. Such diverse factors were involved as American and French planning, the political weakness of Lord North's administration, the enormous logistic difficulties that confronted the bureaucrats of Whitehall; and these factors, along with many others of equal importance, I could not explore on my own. I had to depend on the often meager findings of those who had already explored them, and limit my search for original material to that which bore on the British war effort in America itself. This was both an arbitrary and a necessary limitation.

Even when the field was so narrowly circumscribed, however, it proved to be too broad for productive research. Such matters as the organization of the British army and navy, the details of tactics and logistics, and the administrative routine that engrossed the attention of headquarters should all have been grist for my mill. I knew nothing about them, however, and digging out the requisite information would have meant years of tedious work. I consequently restricted myself still further, to those factors that clearly affected the strategic planning of the British high command. I was no longer asking why Britain lost the war, but why her principal officers in America contributed as much to losing it as they patently did. Even though a definitive answer was impossible, the question was small enough to be explored. Such a partial study of the losers' side of the war could not be expected to produce dramatic results. It might, however, at least modify accepted views of the conflict as a whole.

Historical research rarely does more. In most cases it leaves the accepted views intact, but suggests their inadequacy by introducing alongside them some ingredient that they do not cover. Any subsequent interpretation of the events in question, if it is to include this new ingredient, must be a more complex synthesis than its predecessors, and hence may be expected to approximate more nearly the infinite complexity of the events themselves. The aim of historical research is not to upset the scholarly applecart, in short, but to go on adding to the number of apples in it, until someone is forced to design a bigger cart.

My own research soon produced a kind of apple that I had not anticipated. British strategic planning in America turned out to be not a single problem but two distinct problems, which had for their focus the two successive commanders in chief of the army, Sir William Howe (1775-78) and Sir Henry Clinton (1778-82). The two men were poles apart, but each in his way was an enigma; and the strategy of each was inseparable from his personality. To pursue my quest I had to become in some degree a biographer, and I had to decide which general to concentrate upon. The choice was obvious. Howe served for four years and then disappeared from the scene in 1778, and few of his papers have been preserved. Clinton served for seven years, as second in command under Howe and then as commander in chief, and few of his papers have been lost; they fill almost three hundred volumes in the Clements Library. A study of

Sir Henry would cover the whole British side of the war, and could be amply documented.

Another consideration strengthened the case for focusing on Clinton. I had already discovered that one of Britain's serious difficulties in America was the feuding that went on between her senior officers, and that as an instigator of feuds Clinton towered head and shoulders over all his fellows. The record of his altercations is fantastic, and their effect on the war was incalculable. When he was commander in chief, to take the major example, he was progressively on worse and worse terms with his opposite number in the navy and with his second in command, Lord Cornwallis, until by the summer of 1781 these two quarrels had paralyzed cooperation between the two services and disrupted the army command. Sir Henry was not solely to blame, for the officers with whom he tangled were no models of tact. But they did get on reasonably well with most other men most of the time, whereas he kept their animosity at fever pitch for months and even years on end. By doing so he helped to ruin his own career and lose the war for Britain.

Clinton thus became the focus of my inquiry. He offered an approach, in biographical and manageable terms, to the otherwise unwieldy problem of why the British failed. A biography, furthermore, might do more than merely exhume an obscure general: it could be a case study of personality as a causal factor in history. For Sir Henry was in himself a cause of Britain's defeat—not the sole or even the major cause, but one that was significant, that had not been seriously studied before, and for which the evidence was voluminous. It is obvious that great men, when they have power in moments of crisis, help to mold events. It is perhaps less obvious that in the same circumstances little men do the same, for the very reason that they are little: they fail to meet the demands that the crisis makes upon them, and their failure contributes to the outcome. Louis XVI's shortcomings, for example, affected the course of the French Revolution. Clinton's shortcomings affected the course of the American, in less important but equally real ways; and I set myself to define and evaluate those ways as best I could.

Although my field of inquiry was established and its limits apparently set, I soon discovered that research can develop as unpredictably as if it had a life of its own. Clinton's role in the war could not be defined, much less evaluated, without a clear understanding of why he behaved as he did; and some significant aspects of his behavior proved to be beyond my comprehension. His inveterate feuding, which time after time defeated his own best interests as well as those of the service, was only one case in point. Another was his ambivalence about sticking to his post: for more than four years he tried unsuccessfully to resign; and then, when he had permission and good reason to quit, he clung to the command as if his life depended on it—and at the same time refused to exert the authority that it gave him. He was the rationalist *par excellence* in some areas, such as military planning; in others he behaved with an irrationality that I could not understand.

These contrasting sides of his character came out in his handling of evidence. He left behind him lengthy memoirs of his campaigns, the only general on either side who did. In most of what he wrote he adhered scrupulously to the facts, insofar as they can be established from other sources; but at rare moments he took off into fantasy. The most striking example has to do with the British disaster at Yorktown. In his account of that campaign, written not long afterward and intended for publication, Sir Henry asserted that the government had ordered him not to interfere with Lord Cornwallis, but to support the Earl and his army in Virginia. To prove this assertion Clinton cited the specific words of the command that he said he had received from the King's Minister in Whitehall. Here was what looked like established fact, and for years historians accepted it as such.

Sir Henry's behavior during the actual campaign, however, suggested that he had received no such order. Until the eve of Yorktown he tried to interfere in Virginia, by withdrawing troops from there to New York; and neither his words nor his actions indicated that he was flouting a royal command. Where, furthermore, was the original command to be found? It was not in any letter from the Minister that Clinton kept among his papers (and this letter, of all others, he might have been expected to keep), or in the Minister's copies of his outgoing dispatches. This negative discovery posed a nice question: when is a fact in history not a fact? The Minister *may* have issued the order, which *may* be in a letter that is not extant or has not yet come to light; no amount of historical research can prove that a document never existed, and that a quotation from that document is false. But in this case the probability is overwhelming that Clinton, looking back on the campaign, manufactured out of whole cloth a command from his King.

Sir Henry, if so, was not merely misremembering the past, as other men have done, in a way that cleared him of blame for what had happened; he was introducing into the record a specific and cardinal charge against the government. He was also planning to publish the charge at a time when those whom he accused were still alive to refute him. If the accusation was false, in other words, he was planning to gamble his reputation on a foolishly palpable lie. Everything else that I knew of the man convinced me that he was neither a gambler nor a fool nor a liar. The only tenable explanation, therefore, was that he believed what he said—and what all the evidence indicated was untrue. Here was an impasse: either I was deceived in thinking that Sir Henry had fabricated his claim, or in some way that defied analysis he had deceived himself into thinking that his fabrication was fact.

The second alternative seemed much the more likely. I had already observed in Clinton a habit of self-deception, and I assumed that this episode was an extreme example of it. He was patently unaware that his quarrels, and his refusal to give up or exert the authority of his position, defeated his own best interests; he asserted instead that he had sound reason for what I was convinced was unreasonable conduct, just as he believed that he had received what I was convinced was a nonexistent royal command. His conscious self seemed to have put out a smoke screen of rationalization, behind which he acted from motives so far below consciousness that he could not even discern them, let alone understand them.

I could dimly discern, but was no more able to understand than he had been, for the historian is trained to hunt for motivation within the broad limits of the rational. He assumes that men acted from what by his as well as their lights was rational cause, and that if he has sufficient information he can formulate a highly probable conjecture about what the cause was. His psychological insight amounts to the application of common sense, and he is helpless when the men with whom he is dealing did not behave sensibly. He is not equipped to make even a conjecture about motives that were irrational and hence unconscious. If he does conjecture, with nothing to go on, he is indulging in mere guesswork. If instead he labels behavior as odd or aberrant and leaves it at that, he is confessing failure, because the whole purpose of this kind of research is to uncover the wellsprings of conduct.

The historical discipline as applied to biography has inherent limitations, which I was discovering by bumping into them. Just when my inquiry was far enough advanced to be exciting, it was unexpectedly demanding analytic tools that I could not provide. To continue the quest I had to have help, and I had the great good fortune to get it from Professor Frederick Wyatt, chief of the Psychological Clinic of the University of Michigan, a colleague with psychoanalytic training and a humanist's interest in history. We collaborated for a number of years on the puzzle of Clinton's behavior, in an effort to discover whether teamwork between our two disciplines could produce a fuller understanding of an historical figure than either discipline could produce alone.

We hoped to arrive at a theory of Clinton's personality that was plausible by our different canons and broad enough to include the irrational as well as rational aspects of his conduct. Our evidence would not, we knew, permit us to build a theory that was not merely plausible but demonstrable; evidence in history, as in psychotherapy, is almost never so obliging. The most we could expect was to resolve the apparent contradictions in the evidence we had, by bringing all of it together into a single, consistent pattern of behavior. This pattern would be our theory, and it would "solve" the problem in the sense that it would establish a relationship between what had seemed to be disparate sides of Sir Henry's character.

Our methodological difficulties were considerable, and for me they were educational. My colleague, like any psychotherapist, wanted to probe into Clinton's childhood, a subject about which the manuscripts were almost silent. The little that they did tell us, Wyatt insisted, should be compared with the norms of child-rearing in aristocratic families of the time; what were those norms? Again I did not know, or know where to find out; I was learning how fragmentary is a specialist's information about his period. We were forced to abandon this line of inquiry and try another—to examine the adult Clinton, about whom we had abundant information, in search of grounds for inference about Clinton the child.

Here we made progress. Sir Henry as a middle-aged general manifested—in his quarreling, his refusal to resign, his illusion that the government had been to blame for Yorktown—a form of behavior that is familiar to the modern clinical psychologist. It was the behavior now recognized as typical of the man who has never outgrown his childhood conflict with his parents, particularly with his father. The unresolved conflict endures: the child as adult longs to exercise paternal authority himself, and at the same time dreads to exercise it because he is trespassing on his father's preserve. Sir Henry showed the symptoms of this conflict so clearly and fully that we did not need to know the childhood roots of the conflict itself; we could assume their existence. What mattered to us was not the cause but the result—the consistency with which the adult Clinton continued to act out his difficulties with parents who by then had long been dead. To certain situations he responded, not sensibly, but with an almost predictable regularity; and his way of responding indicated an ambivalence that he could neither recognize nor control.

The consistency provided us with a pattern, or theory, that satisfied the requirements with which we had begun. How it satisfied them cannot be explained in brief compass, but we found that virtually all the irrational aspects of Sir Henry's behavior could be related to his basic internal struggle about exercising authority. Elements in his character that had hitherto seemed to me irreconcilable, because some were highly effective and others were self-defeating, fitted together as parts of a whole; and a man who had looked like a bundle of anomalies became a coherent person. We do not yet claim to have resolved every contradiction, to know Sir

Henry through and through; such a claim would be ridiculous. But we do believe that he has become intelligible enough to us to permit an evaluation of the role he played.

This has been a long illustration, and what does it illustrate? In the first place, that historical research is fluid, especially in its early stages. The inquirer begins with unknown material and no idea of what will come out of it. Even when some salient questions emerge to provide him a focus, it is not yet precise; considerations of time and his own interests, as much as of the material itself, determine how his problem develops. After it seems to have taken final shape (as when I decided on a biographical study of Clinton), new and unexpected questions can change the shape again. This evolutionary process may not come to an end of itself; and in that case the researcher, unless he wants to spend his life on one subject, must choose the moment for calling a halt.

My experience illustrates, in the second place, the problem of selecting evidence. On the one hand no project, however ambitiously designed, can embrace all the available and relevant data; arbitrary limits must be set, and even within them much relevant material receives only cursory treatment. On the other hand, once these limits are demarcated, no amount of digging will unearth all the data that the researcher wants; some areas about which he is curious, such as Clinton's childhood, remain obscure and conjectural. Research involves a series of choices, to emphasize this and neglect that, to go on digging or to stop; and few of the choices are logically satisfying. The specialist is not, as the old cliché would have it, one who learns more and more about less and less. He is one who is able to work out his own criteria for finishing a particular job, and to make his choices accordingly.

I have tried to illustrate, in the third place, the elusive quality of evidence. Historical "facts" are not facts in the sense that they can be empirically verified; they are merely the testimony of one or more observers about what happened. All testimony is suspect, because it depends upon whether the person giving it was in a position to know, whether he was calm or intelligent or objective enough to report accurately, and so on. Some "facts" such as dates—when the Declaration of Independence was signed, or when the firing stopped at Yorktown—can be established beyond reasonable doubt because many observers agree. But these are the historian's rudimentary data, which are about as important to him as the multiplication table is to a mathematician. The more significant data are those that bear on what people did and why they did it, and here the difficulties arise.

Even what people did can rarely be determined with complete assurance. The famous nineteenth-century German historian, Ranke, believed that the past can be reconstructed as it actually was, *wie es eigentlich gewesen*. Most historians today would disagree, because they recognize that they will never know enough, however profuse their evidence. A case in point is Clinton's role in the Yorktown campaign. We know a great deal about it, but we cannot know for sure whether the government curtailed his authority and therefore his responsibility. The evidence is *almost* conclusive. Yet, as long as it is not entirely so, a marginal chance remains that this fragment of the past was in actual fact quite different from what we think it was.

When the historian moves from considering people's actions to considering their motives for acting, he must become even more tentative. The reason lies not only in the nature of his evidence but also in human nature; for about motivation, of the living as much as of the dead, opinions always differ. Listen to a group of reporters today discussing what impels President Johnson or General de Gaulle to a given line of action, and you will hear as many interpretations as there are interpreters; or try to explain precisely why a friend reached an important decision, and see how many of his other friends will agree with you. When our contemporaries' reasons for acting as they do are controversial, sometimes even mysterious, to those about them, it would be surprising if the motives of historical figures were easier to penetrate.

The best evidence about the nature of motivation in a man long dead is what was said about him at the time. Most of what was said was not written down, and much of what was written down has not survived; mere chance selects for the historian a small fraction of the original evidence, and with this fraction he must work. It consists in comments, which are sure to be hard to interpret, on the behavior of the man in question. Comments that he made on himself are valuable, but have a built-in bias. Contemporaries' comments are also biased, and in conflicting ways: no two observers, in the past as in the present, who look at the same person see the same person. Clinton, for instance, changes slightly when he is viewed through the eyes of each of his few friends and admirers, and greatly when viewed through those of his numerous enemies; the motives that these men perceived in him run the gamut from whole-souled concentration on winning the war to pride, vanity, and a love for the fleshpots of power. The historian must move cautiously through testimony that is colored by the likes and dislikes of those who created it, and must weigh and evaluate, select and discard, to reach an opinion of his own. He can at most hope that that opinion, though fallible, will be better informed and more dispassionate than those of the men who provide him with his data.

All this may sound as if historical research were merely a system of guesswork, which might be defined, like the famous definition of logic, as "an organized method of going wrong with confidence."

There is, however, another side to the coin. If the historian does not know the truth about the past—and he certainly does not—he should have a better approximation of the truth than contemporaries had. They were imprisoned in their time as we are in ours, and they could not fully grasp the significance of what was happening before their eyes; they were also imprisoned in space, and could not grasp the significance of distant events. Take Clinton for illustration. He never spoke of the American Revolution because he did not know that there was one; he could not see the rebellion as revolutionary. Neither could he see the far-away troubles in Whitehall that impeded the war effort; he believed that the government was willfully neglecting him. The historian does not wear such blinders but has a broad perspective, and it reveals to him developments in time and space that were hidden from the men with whom he is dealing. He can never be entirely sure of what they did, let alone of why they did it; yet he can have a deeper understanding than they had.

Understanding, which comes in part from the historian's remoteness in time, comes also from the nature of his concern with the past. That concern is a blend of involvement and detachment, and the first is harder to achieve than the second. Involvement means using his imagination to become engaged with the people he is studying, so that as far as he can he sees through their eyes and views their controversies as they viewed them. He rarely takes sides, if only because he sees both sides at once; but the issues and the protagonists are almost as real to him as those of his own day. Unless he can achieve this feat of imagination, can enter into his period even while he is remote from it, his perspective upon it may be worse than useless. Suppose, for instance, that he is utterly incapable of imagining himself into another era; he must then impose upon it, *faute de mieux*, the presuppositions, values, and standards of judgment of his own society. These are certain to be inapplicable, and any conclusions to which they lead him are certain to be askew.

Detachment without involvement, in such an extreme case, leads the historian to distort the past by fitting it to the measure of his present, much as Procrustes distorted guests by fitting them to the measure of his bed. But involvement without detachment can also lead to distortion, although of a different kind; and here the biographer is in particular danger. No man, the saying goes, is a hero to his valet; neither should any man be a hero to his biographer, who ought to know him as well as the valet does. The man's foibles and complexities, virtues and shortcomings, should become so familiar to the biographer that he sees his subject not primarily as great or small but as alive, a person in his own right. When a biographer succumbs instead to hero-worship (or, more rarely, the inverted form that might be called villain-worship), his involvement has triumphed over his detachment. Where he should have assessed the evidence in its entirety, with all its shadings from white to black, he has selected in a way to bring out only the whites or blacks; and the resultant picture has the unreality of the oversimplified. This is the art of the cartoonist, not of the historian.

Research is not the only way to discover how to blend detachment with involvement; a few historians understand their discipline by instinct. Most, however, acquire understanding through research. They learn that they cannot work their way laboriously into a period without discarding many of their twentieth-century preconceptions and modifying the others. The more ambiguities and pitfalls they find in their evidence, the more gaps in their knowledge of what they thought were familiar events, the more complexities in the process of causation, the safer they are from the temptation to treat the past in Procrustean fashion. They remain objective, but experience teaches them to be cautious and tentative in their conclusions. The thundering ultimates of a Spengler or a Toynbee are not for them.

Exploring the past is a never-ending activity. The historian in each generation hunts for new evidence and reinterprets existing evidence, to provide fresh details and a fresh perspective. However stimulating the perspective may be at the moment; it will not remain indefinitely fresh; it is based on incomplete and conflicting data, and is likely to contain at most a kernel of lasting value. Few of the questions that the data raise can be settled once and for all, either because the evidence is lacking or because the questions are too large in their implications. Any segment of history, no matter how narrowly defined in time and space, is set in a context that is limitless and therefore cannot be entirely known. Although each researcher hopes to know a little more of it, to throw a little more light on the mystery of why a particular set of men acted as they did, he realizes that the mystery will remain, and that for all his efforts he will find only a partial approximation of truth.

Yet he cannot let the mystery alone, and involvement with it brings its own reward. His research may be narrow in scope, transient in value, riddled with unanswerable questions; it is still inherently exciting. It has no scale: any problem offers as sure an approach as any other to the underlying historical process, and demands the researcher's full powers of analysis and empathy. In his analytic function he is the rationalist, perhaps even the scientist. In his empathic function he is the artist, and it is research as art that redeems the drudgery of data-gathering.

This form of art is as exigent as any other. It requires its practitioner to enter into the past, to meet people who are very much alive yet different from him in ways that he can imperfectly apprehend, to view them objectively for what they were, and then to portray them in all their vitality. This is so large an assignment that his reach, he knows, will exceed his grasp; and why should it not? Just as the subject matter of research fascinates him because he will never be able to do it full justice, so does the art of research. The requirements of that art are too stringent for his comfort: they deny him the illusion that he has nothing more to learn, and keep him always reaching for what he cannot quite grasp. His own particular creativity is therefore at full stretch, and that is perhaps as near to pure joy as an academic can come.

EDWARD HALLETT CARR

The Historian and His Facts[1]

What is history? Lest anyone think the question meaningless or superfluous, I will take as my text two passages relating respectively to the first and second incarnations of *The Cambridge Modern History*. Here is Acton in his report of October 1896 to the Syndics of the Cambridge University Press on the work which he had undertaken to edit:

It is a unique opportunity of recording, in the way most useful to the greatest number, the fullness of the knowledge which the nineteenth century is about to bequeath.... By the judicious division of labor we should be able to do it, and to bring home to every man the last document, and the ripest conclusions of international research.

Ultimate history we cannot have in this generation; but we can dispose of conventional history, and show the point we have reached on the road from one to the other, now that all information is within reach, and every problem has become capable of solution.[2]

And almost exactly sixty years later Professor Sir George Clark, in his general introduction to the second *Cambridge Modern History*, commented on this belief of Acton and his collaborators that it would one day be possible to produce "ultimate history," and went on:

Historians of a later generation do not look forward to any such prospect. They expect their work to be superseded again and again. They consider that knowledge of the past has come down through one or more human minds, has been "processed" by them, and therefore cannot consist of elemental and impersonal atoms which nothing can alter.... The exploration seems to be endless, and some impatient scholars take refuge in scepticism, or at least in the doctrine that, since all historical judgments involve persons

1. Chapter I of *What is History?*, 1961.
2. *The Cambridge Modern History: Its Origin, Authorship and Production* (Cambridge University Press, 1907), pp. 10-12 [This and the following footnotes are Carr's].

and points of view, one is as good as another and there is no "objective" historical truth.[3]

Where the pundits contradict each other so flagrantly the field is open to enquiry. I hope that I am sufficiently up-to-date to recognize that anything written in the 1890's must be nonsense. But I am not yet advanced enough to be committed to the view that anything written in the 1950's necessarily makes sense, Indeed, it may already have occurred to you that this enquiry is liable to stray into something even broader than the nature of history. The clash between Acton and Sir George Clark is a reflection of the change in our total outlook on society over the interval between these two pronouncements. Acton speaks out of the positive belief, the clear-eyed self-confidence of the later Victorian age; Sir George Clark echoes the bewilderment and distracted scepticism of the beat generation. When we attempt to answer the question, What is history?, our answer, consciously or unconsciously, reflects our own position in time, and forms part of our answer to the broader question, what view we take of the society in which we live. I have no fear that my subject may, on closer inspection, seem trivial. I am afraid only that I may seem presumptuous to have broached a question so vast and so important.

The nineteenth century was a great age for facts. "What I want," said Mr. Gradgrind in *Hard Times*, "is Facts. . . . Facts alone are wanted in life." Nineteenth-century historians on the whole agreed with him. When Ranke in the 1830's, in legitimate protest against moralizing history, remarked that the task of the historian was "simply to show how it really was [*wie es eigentlich gewesen*]" this not very profound aphorism had an astonishing success. Three generations of German, British, and even French historians marched into battle intoning the magic words, "*Wie es eigentlich gewesen*" like an incantation—designed, like most incantations, to save them from the tiresome obligation to think for themselves. The Positivists, anxious to stake out their claim for history as a science, contributed the weight of their influence to this cult of facts. First ascertain the facts, said the positivists, then draw your conclusions from them. In Great Britain, this view of history fitted in perfectly with the empiricist tradition which was the dominant strain in British philosophy from Locke to Bertrand Russell. The empirical theory of knowledge presupposes a complete separation between subject and object. Facts, like sense-impressions, impinge on the observer from outside, and are independent. of his consciousness. The process of reception is passive: having received the data, he then acts on them. *The Shorter Oxford English Dictionary*, a useful but tendentious work of the empirical school, clearly marks

3. *The New Cambridge Modern History*, I (Cambridge University Press, 1957), pp. xxiv-xxv.

the separateness of the two processes by defining a fact as "a datum of experience as distinct from conclusions." This is what may be called the common-sense view of history. History consists of a corpus of ascertained facts. The facts are available to the historian in documents, inscriptions, and so on, like fish on the fishmonger's slab. The historian collects them, takes them home, and cooks and serves them in whatever style appeals to him. Acton, whose culinary tastes were austere, wanted them served plain. In his letter of instructions to contributors to the first *Cambridge Modern History* he announced the requirement "that our Waterloo must be one that satisfies French and English, German and Dutch alike; that nobody can tell, without examining the list of authors where the Bishop of Oxford laid down the pen, and whether Fairbairn or Gasquet, Liebermann or Harrison took it up."[4] Even Sir George Clark, critical as he was of Acton's attitude, himself contrasted the "hard core of facts" in history with the "surrounding pulp of disputable interpretation"[5]—forgetting perhaps that the pulpy part of the fruit is more rewarding than the hard core. First get your facts straight, then plunge at your peril into the shifting sands of interpretation—that is the ultimate wisdom of the empirical, common-sense school of history. It recalls the favorite dictum of the great liberal journalist C. P. Scott: "Facts are sacred, opinion is free."

Now this clearly will not do. I shall not embark on a philosophical discussion of the nature of our knowledge of the past. Let us assume for present purposes that the fact that Caesar crossed the Rubicon and the fact that there is a table in the middle of the room are facts of the same or of a comparable order, that both these facts enter our consciousness in the same or in a comparable manner, and that both have the same objective character in relation to the person who knows them. But, even on this bold and not very plausible assumption, our argument at once runs into the difficulty that not all facts about the past are historical facts, or are treated as such by the historian. What is the criterion which distinguishes the facts of history from other facts about the past?

What is a historical fact? This is a crucial question into which we must look a little more closely. According to the common-sense view, there are certain basic facts which are the same for all historians and which form, so to speak, the backbone of history—the fact, for example, that the Battle of Hastings was fought in 1066. But this view calls for two observations. In the first place, it is not with facts like these that the historian is primarily concerned. It is no doubt important to know that the great battle was fought in 1066 and not in 1065 or 1067, and that it was fought at Hastings and not at Eastbourne or Brighton. The historian must

---

4. Acton: *Lectures on Modern History* (London: Macmillan & Co., 1906), p. 318.   5. Quoted in *The Listener* (June 19, 1952), p. 992.

not get these things wrong. But when points of this kind are raised, I am reminded of Housman's remark that "accuracy is a duty, not a virtue."[6] To praise a historian for his accuracy is like praising an architect for using well-seasoned timber or properly mixed concrete in his building. It is a necessary condition of his work, but not his essential function. It is precisely for matters of this kind that the historian is entitled to rely on what have been called the "auxiliary sciences" of history—archaeology, epigraphy, numismatics, chronology, and so forth. The historian is not required to have the special skills which enable the expert to determine the origin and period of a fragment of pottery or marble, or decipher an obscure inscription, or to make the elaborate astronomical calculations necessary to establish a precise date. These so-called basic facts which are the same for all historians commonly belong to the category of the raw materials of the historian rather than of history itself. The second observation is that the necessity to establish these basic facts rests not on any quality in the facts themselves, but on an *a priori* decision of the historian. In spite of C. P. Scott's motto, every journalist knows today that the most effective way to influence opinion is by the selection and arrangement of the appropriate facts. It used to be said that facts speak for themselves. This is, of course, untrue. The facts speak only when the historian calls on them: It is he who decides to which facts to give the floor, and in what order or context. It was, I think, one of Pirandello's characters who said that a fact is like a sack—it won't stand up till you've put something in it. The only reason why we are interested to know that the battle was fought at Hastings in 1066 is that historians regard it as a major historical event. It is the historian who has decided for his own reasons that Caesar's crossing of that petty stream, the Rubicon, is a fact of history, whereas the crossing of the Rubicon by millions of other people before or since interests nobody at all. The fact that you arrived in this building half an hour ago on foot, or on a bicycle, or in a car, is just as much a fact about the past as the fact that Caesar crossed the Rubicon. But it will probably be ignored by historians. Professor Talcott Parsons once called science "a selective system of cognitive orientations to reality."[7] It might perhaps have been put more simply. But history is, among other things, that. The historian is necessarily selective. The belief in a hard core of historical facts existing objectively and independently of the interpretation of the historian is a preposterous fallacy, but one which it is very hard to eradicate.

Let us take a look at the process by which a mere fact about

6. M. Manilius: *Astronomicon: Liber Primus*, 2nd ed. (Cambridge University Press, 1937), p. 87.

7. Talcott Parsons and Edward A. Shils: *Toward a General Theory of Action*, 3rd ed. (Cambridge, Mass.: Harvard University Press, 1954), p. 167.

the past is transformed into a fact of history. At Stalybridge Wakes in 1850, a vendor of gingerbread, as the result of some petty dispute, was deliberately kicked to death by an angry mob. Is this a fact of history? A year ago I should unhesitatingly have said "no." It was recorded by an eyewitness in some little-known memoirs;[8] but I had never seen it judged worthy of mention by any historian. A year ago Dr. Kitson Clark cited it in his Ford lectures in Oxford.[9] Does this make it into a historical fact? Not, I think, yet. Its present status, I suggest, is that it has been proposed for membership of the select club of historical facts. It now awaits a seconder and sponsors. It may be that in the course of the next few years we shall see this fact appearing first in footnotes, then in the text, of articles and books about nineteenth-century England, and that in twenty or thirty years' time it may be a well established historical fact. Alternatively, nobody may take it up, in which case it will relapse into the limbo of unhistorical facts about the past from which Dr. Kitson Clark has gallantly attempted to rescue it. What will decide which of these two things will happen? It will depend, I think, on whether the thesis or interpretation in support of which Dr. Kitson Clark cited this incident is accepted by other historians as valid and significant. Its status as a historical fact will turn on a question of interpretation. This element of interpretation enters into every fact of history.

May I be allowed a personal reminiscence? When I studied ancient history in this university many years ago, I had as a special subject "Greece in the period of the Persian Wars." I collected fifteen or twenty volumes on my shelves and took it for granted that there, recorded in these volumes, I had all the facts relating to my subject. Let us assume—it was very nearly true—that those volumes contained all the facts about it that were then known, or could be known. It never occurred to me to enquire by what accident or process of attrition that minute selection of facts, out of all the myriad facts that must have once been known to somebody, had survived to become *the* facts of history. I suspect that even today one of the fascinations of ancient and mediaeval history is that it gives us the illusion of having all the facts at our disposal within a manageable compass: the nagging distinction between the facts of history and other facts about the past vanishes because the few known facts are all facts of history. As Bury, who had worked in both periods, said "the records of ancient and mediaeval history are starred with lacunae."[1] History has been called an enormous jig-saw with a lot of missing parts. But the main trouble does not consist of the lacunae. Our picture of Greece in the fifth

---

8. Lord George Sanger: *Seventy Years a Showman* (London: J. M. Dent & Sons, 1926), pp. 188-9.

9. These will shortly be published under the title *The Making of Victorian England.*

1. John Bagnell Bury: *Selected Essays* (Cambridge University Press, 1930, p. 52.)

century B.C. is defective not primarily because so many of the bits have been accidentally lost, but because it is, by and large, the picture formed by a tiny group of people in the city of Athens. We know a lot about what fifth-century Greece looked like to an Athenian citizen; but hardly anything about what it looked like to a Spartan, a Corinthian, or a Theban—not to mention a Persian, or a slave or other non-citizen resident in Athens. Our picture has been preselected and predetermined for us, not so much by accident as by people who were consciously or unconsciously imbued with a particular view and thought the facts which supported that view worth preserving. In the same way, when I read in a modern history of the Middle Ages that the people of the Middle Ages were deeply concerned with religion, I wonder how we know this, and whether it is true. What we know as the facts of mediaeval history have almost all been selected for us by generations of chroniclers who were professionally occupied in the theory and practice of religion, and who therefore thought it supremely important, and recorded everything relating to it, and not much else. The picture of the Russian peasant as devoutly religious was destroyed by the revolution of 1917. The picture of mediaeval man as devoutly religious, whether true or not, is indestructible, because nearly all the known facts about him were preselected for us by people who believed it, and wanted others to believe it, and a mass of other facts, in which we might possibly have found evidence to the contrary, has been lost beyond recall. The dead hand of vanished generations of historians, scribes, and chroniclers has determined beyond the possibility of appeal the pattern of the past. "The history we read," writes Professor Barraclough, himself trained as a mediaevalist, "though based on facts, is, strictly speaking, not factual at all, but a series of accepted judgments."[2]

But let us turn to the different, but equally grave, plight of the modern historian. The ancient or mediaeval historian may be grateful for the vast winnowing process which, over the years, has put at his disposal a manageable corpus of historical facts. As Lytton Strachey said in his mischievous way, "ignorance is the first requisite of the historian, ignorance which simplifies and clarifies, which selects and omits."[3] When I am tempted, as I sometimes am, to envy the extreme competence of colleagues engaged in writing ancient or mediaeval history, I find consolation in the reflection that they are so competent mainly because they are so ignorant of their subject. The modern historian enjoys none of the advantages of this built-in ignorance. He must cultivate this necessary ignorance for himself—the more so the nearer he comes to his own times. He has the dual task of discovering the few significant facts and turn-

2. Geoffrey Barraclough: *History in a Changing World* (London; Basil Blackwell & Mott, 1955), p. 14.

3. Lytton Strachey: Preface to *Eminent Victorians*.

ing them into facts of history, and of discarding the many insignificant facts as unhistorical. But this is the very converse of the nineteenth-century heresy that history consists of the compilation of a maximum number of irrefutable and objective facts. Anyone who succumbs to this heresy will either have to give up history as a bad job, and take to stamp-collecting or some other form of antiquarianism, or end in a madhouse. It is this heresy, which during the past hundred years has had such devastating effects on the modern historian, producing in Germany, in Great Britain, and in the United States a vast and growing mass of dry-as-dust factual histories, of minutely specialized monographs, of would-be historians knowing more and more about less and less, sunk without trace in an ocean of facts. It was, I suspect, this heresy—rather than the alleged conflict between liberal and Catholic loyalties—which frustrated Acton as a historian. In an early essay he said of his teacher Döllinger: "He would not write with imperfect materials, and to him the materials were always imperfect."[4] Acton was surely here pronouncing an anticipatory verdict on himself, on that strange phenomenon of a historian whom many would regard as the most distinguished occupant the Regius Chair of Modern History in this university has ever had—but who wrote no history. And Acton wrote his own epitaph in the introductory note to the first volume of the *Cambridge Modern History*, published just after his death, when he lamented that the requirements pressing on the historian "threaten to turn him from a man of letters into the compiler of an encyclopedia."[5] Something had gone wrong. What had gone wrong was the belief in this untiring and unending accumulation of hard facts as the foundation of history, the belief that facts speak for themselves and that we cannot have too many facts, a belief at that time so unquestioning that few historians then thought it necessary—and some still think it unnecessary today—to ask themselves the question: What is history?

The nineteenth-century fetishism of facts was completed and justified by a fetishism of documents. The documents were the Ark of the Covenant in the temple of facts. The reverent historian approached them with bowed head and spoke of them in awed tones. If you find it in the documents, it is so. But what, when we get down to it, do these documents—the decrees, the treaties, the rent-rolls, the blue books, the official correspondence, the private letters and diaries—tell us? No document can tell us more than what the author of the document thought—what he thought had happened, what he thought ought to happen or would happen,

4. Quoted in George P. Gooch: *History and Historians in the Nineteenth Century* (London: Longmans, Green & Company, 1952), p. 385. Later Acton said of Döllinger that "it was given him to form his philosophy of history on the largest induction ever available to man" (*History of Freedom and Other Essays* [London: Macmillan & Co., 1907], p. 435).
5. *The Cambridge Modern History*, I (1902), p. 4.

or perhaps only what he wanted others to think he thought, or even only what he himself thought he thought. None of this means anything until the historian has got to work on it and deciphered it. The facts, whether found in documents or not, have still to be processed by the historian before he can make any use of them: the use he makes of them is, if I may put it that way, the processing process.

Let me illustrate what I am trying to say by an example which I happen to know well. When Gustav Stresemann, the Foreign Minister of the Weimar Republic, died in 1929, he left behind him an enormous mass—300 boxes full—of papers, official, semi-official, and private, nearly all relating to the six years of his tenure of office as Foreign Minister. His friends and relatives naturally thought that a monument should be raised to the memory of so great a man. His faithful secretary Bernhardt got to work; and within three years there appeared three massive volumes, of some 600 pages each, of selected documents from the 300 boxes, with the impressive title *Stresemanns Vermächtnis*.[6] In the ordinary way the documents themselves would have moldered away in some cellar or attic and disappeared for ever; or perhaps in a hundred years or so some curious scholar would have come upon them and set out to compare them with Bernhardt's text. What happened was far more dramatic. In 1945 the documents fell into the hands of the British and the American governments, who photographed the lot and put the photostats at the disposal of scholars in the Public Record Office in London and in the National Archives in Washington, so that, if we have sufficient patience and curiosity, we can discover exactly what Bernhardt did. What he did was neither very unusual nor very shocking. When Stresemann died, his Western policy seemed to have been crowned with a series of brilliant successes—Locarno, the admission of Germany to the League of Nations, the Dawes and Young plans and the American loans, the withdrawal of allied occupation armies from the Rhineland. This seemed the important and rewarding part of Stresemann's foreign policy; and it was not unnatural that it should have been over-represented in Bernhardt's selection of documents. Stresemann's Eastern policy, on the other hand, his relations with the Soviet Union, seemed to have led nowhere in particular; and, since masses of documents about negotiations which yielded only trivial results were not very interesting and added nothing to Stresemann's reputation, the process of selection could be more rigorous. Stresemann in fact devoted a far more constant and anxious attention to relations with the Soviet Union, and they played a far larger part in his foreign policy as a whole, than the reader of the Bernhardt selection would surmise. But the Bernhardt volumes compare

6. *Stresemann's Legacy.*

favorably, I suspect, with many published collections of documents on which the ordinary historian implicitly relies.

This is not the end of my story. Shortly after the publication of Bernhardt's volumes, Hitler came into power. Stresemann's name was consigned to oblivion in Germany, and the volumes disappeared from circulation: many, perhaps most, of the copies must have been destroyed. Today *Stresemanns Vermächtnis* is a rather rare book. But in the West Stresemann's reputation stood high. In 1935 an English publisher brought out an abbreviated translation of Bernhardt's work—a selection from Bernhardt's selection; perhaps one third of the original was omitted. Sutton, a well-known translator from the German, did his job competently and well. The English version, he explained in the preface, was "slightly condensed, but only by the omission of a certain amount of what, it was felt, was more ephemeral matter . . . of little interest to English readers or students."[7] This again is natural enough. But the result is that Stresemann's Eastern policy, already under-represented in Bernhardt, recedes still further from view, and the Soviet Union appears in Sutton's volumes merely as an occasional and rather unwelcome intruder in Stresemann's predominantly Western foreign policy. Yet it is safe to say that, for all except a few specialists, Sutton and not Bernhardt—and still less the documents themselves—represents for the Western world the authentic voice of Stresemann. Had the documents perished in 1945 in the bombing, and had the remaining Bernhardt volumes disappeared, the authenticity and authority of Sutton would never have been questioned. Many printed collections of documents gratefully accepted by historians in default of the originals rest on no securer basis than this.

But I want to carry the story one step further. Let us forget about Bernhardt and Sutton, and be thankful that we can, if we choose, consult the authentic papers of a leading participant in some important events in recent European history. What do the papers tell us? Among other things they contain records of some hundreds of Stresemann's conversations with the Soviet ambassador in Berlin and of a score or so with Chicherin.[8] These records have one feature in common. They depict Stresemann as having the lion's share of the conversations and reveal his arguments as invariably well put and cogent, while those of his partner are for the most part scanty, confused, and unconvincing. This is a familiar characteristic of all records of diplomatic conversations. The documents do not tell us what happened, but only what Stresemann thought had happened. It was not Sutton or Bernhardt, but Stresemann himself, who started the process of selection. And, if we had, say, Chicherin's records of these same conversations, we should still learn from

7. *Gustav Stresemann: His Diaries, Letters, and Papers* (London: Macmillan & Co.; 1935), I.

8. Soviet foreign minister 1918-28 [Editor's note].

them only what Chicherin thought, and what really happened would still have to be reconstructed in the mind of the historian. Of course, facts and documents are essential to the historian. But do not make a fetish of them. They do not by themselves constitute history; they provide in themselves no ready-made answer to this tiresome question: What is history?

At this point I should like to say a few words on the question of why nineteenth-century historians were generally indifferent to the philosophy of history. The term was invented by Voltaire, and has since been used in different senses; but I shall take it to mean, if I use it at all, our answer to the question: What is history? The nineteenth century was, for the intellectuals of Western Europe, a comfortable period exuding confidence and optimism. The facts were on the whole satisfactory; and the inclination to ask and answer awkward questions about them was correspondingly weak. Ranke piously believed that divine providence would take care of the meaning of history if he took care of the facts; and Burckhardt with a more modern touch of cynicism observed that "we are not initiated into the purposes of the eternal wisdom." Professor Butterfield as late as 1931 noted with apparent satisfaction that "historians have reflected little upon the nature of things and even the nature of their own subject."[9] But my predecessor in these lectures, Dr. A. L. Rowse, more justly critical, wrote of Sir Winston Churchill's *The World Crisis*—his book about the First World War— that, while it matched Trotsky's *History of the Russian Revolution* in personality, vividness, and vitality, it was inferior in one respect: it had "no philosophy of history behind it."[1] British historians refused to be drawn, not because they believed that history had no meaning, but because they believed that its meaning was implicit and self-evident. The liberal nineteenth-century view of history had a close affinity with the economic doctrine of *laissez-faire*—also the product of a serene and self-confident outlook on the world. Let everyone get on with his particular job, and the hidden hand would take care of the universal harmony. The facts of history were themselves a demonstration of the supreme fact of a beneficent and apparently infinite progress towards higher things. This was the age of innocence, and historians walked in the Garden of Eden, without a scrap of philosophy to cover them, naked and unashamed before the god of history. Since then, we have known Sin and experienced a Fall; and those historians who today pretend to dispense with a philosophy of history are merely trying, vainly and self-consciously, like members of a nudist colony, to recreate the Garden of Eden in their garden suburb. Today the awkward question can no longer be evaded. * * *

9. Herbert Butterfield: *The Whig Interpretation of History* (London: George Bell & Sons, 1931), p. 67.

1. Alfred L. Rowse: *The End of an Epoch* (London: Macmillan & Co., 1947), pp. 282-3.

During the past fifty years a good deal of serious work has been done on the question: What is history? It was from Germany, the country which was to do so much to upset the comfortable reign of nineteenth-century liberalism, that the first challenge came in the 1880's and 1890's to the doctrine of the primacy and autonomy of facts in history. The philosophers who made the challenge are now little more than names: Dilthey is the only one of them who has recently received some belated recognition in Great Britain. Before the turn of the century, prosperity and confidence were still too great in this country for any attention to be paid to heretics who attacked the cult of facts. But early in the new century, the torch passed to Italy, where Croce began to propound a philosophy of history which obviously owed much to German masters. All history is "contemporary history," declared Croce,[2] meaning that history consists essentially in seeing the past through the eyes of the present and in the light of its problems, and that the main work of the historian is not to record, but to evaluate; for, if he does not evaluate, how can he know what is worth recording? In 1910 the American philosopher, Carl Becker, argued in deliberately provocative language that "the facts of history do not exist for any historian till he creates them."[3] These challenges were for the moment little noticed. It was only after 1920 that Croce began to have a considerable vogue in France and Great Britain. This was not perhaps because Croce was a subtler thinker or a better stylist than his German predecessors, but because, after the First World War, the facts seemed to smile on us less propitiously than in the years before 1914, and we were therefore more accessible to a philosophy which sought to diminish their prestige. Croce was an important influence on the Oxford philosopher and historian Collingwood, the only British thinker in the present century who has made a serious contribution to the philosophy of history. He did not live to write the systematic treatise he had planned; but his published and unpublished papers on the subject were collected after his death in a volume entitled *The Idea of History*, which appeared in 1945.

The views of Collingwood can be summarized as follows. The philosophy of history is concerned neither with "the past by itself" nor with "the historian's thought about it by itself," but with "the two things in their mutual relations." (This dictum reflects the two current meanings of the word "history"—the enquiry conducted by the historian and the series of past events into which he enquires.) "The past which a historian studies is not a dead past, but a past which in some sense is still living in the present." But a past act

---

2. The context of this celebrated aphorism is as follows: "The practical requirements which underlie every historical judgment give to all history the character of 'contemporary history,' because, however remote in time events thus recounted may seem to be, the history in reality refers to present needs and present situations wherein those events vibrate" (Benedetto Croce: *History as the Story of Liberty* [London: George Allen & Unwin, 1941], p. 19).

3. *Atlantic Monthly* (October 1928), p. 528.

is dead, *i.e.* meaningless to the historian, unless he can understand the thought that lay behind it. Hence "all history is the history of thought," and "history is the re-enactment in the historian's mind of the thought whose history he is studying." The reconstitution of the past in the historian's mind is dependent on empirical evidence. But it is not in itself an empirical process, and cannot consist in a mere recital of facts. On the contrary, the process of reconstitution governs the selection and interpretation of the facts: this, indeed, is what makes them historical facts. "History," says Professor Oakeshott, who on this point stands near to Collingwood, "is the historian's experience. It is 'made' by nobody save the historian: to write history is the only way of making it."[4]

This searching critique, though it may call for some serious reservations, brings to light certain neglected truths.

In the first place, the facts of history never come to us "pure," since they do not and cannot exist in a pure form: they are always refracted through the mind of the recorder. It follows that when we take up a work of history, our first concern should be not with the facts which it contains but with the historian who wrote it. Let me take as an example the great historian in whose honor and in whose name these lectures were founded. Trevelyan, as he tells us in his autobiography, was "brought up at home on a somewhat exuberantly Whig tradition"[5]; and he would not, I hope, disclaim the title if I described him as the last and not the least of the great English liberal historians of the Whig tradition. It is not for nothing that he traces back his family tree, through the great Whig historian George Otto Trevelyan, to Macaulay, incomparably the greatest of the Whig historians. Dr. Trevelyan's finest and maturest work *England under Queen Anne* was written against that background, and will yield its full meaning and significance to the reader only when read against that background. The author, indeed, leaves the reader with no excuse for failing to do so. For if, following the technique of connoisseurs of detective novels, you read the end first, you will find on the last few pages of the third volume the best summary known to me of what is nowadays called the Whig interpretation of history; and you will see that what Trevelyan is trying to do is to investigate the origin and development of the Whig tradition, and to roof it fairly and squarely in the years after the death of its founder, William III. Though this is not, perhaps, the only conceivable interpretation of the events of Queen Anne's reign, it is a valid and, in Trevelyan's hands, a fruitful interpretation. But, in order to appreciate it at its full value, you have to understand what the historian is doing. For if, as Collingwood says, the historian must re-enact in thought what has gone on in the mind of

4. Michael Oakeshott: *Experience and Its Modes* (Cambridge University Press, 1933), p. 99.

5. G. M. Trevelyan: *An Autobiography* (London: Longmans, Green & Company, 1949), p. 11.

his *dramatis personae*, so the reader in his turn must re-enact what goes on in the mind of the historian. Study the historian before you begin to study the facts. This is, after all, not very abstruse. It is what is already done by the intelligent undergraduate who, when recommended to read a work by that great scholar Jones of St. Jude's, goes round to a friend at St. Jude's to ask what sort of chap Jones is, and what bees he has in his bonnet. When you read a work of history, always listen out for the buzzing. If you can detect none, either you are tone deaf or your historian is a dull dog. The facts are really not at all like fish on the fishmonger's slab. They are like fish swimming about in a vast and sometimes inaccessible ocean; and what the historian catches will depend partly on chance, but mainly on what part of the ocean he chooses to fish in and what tackle he chooses to use—these two factors being, of course, determined by the kind of fish he wants to catch. By and large, the historian will get the kind of facts he wants. History means interpretation. Indeed, if, standing Sir George Clark on his head, I were to call history "a hard core of interpretation surrounded by a pulp of disputable facts," my statement would, no doubt, be one-sided and misleading, but no more so, I venture to think, than the original dictum.

The second point is the more familiar one of the historian's need of imaginative understanding for the minds of the people with whom he is dealing, for the thought behind their acts: I say "imaginative understanding," not "sympathy," lest sympathy should be supposed to imply agreement. The nineteenth century was weak in mediaeval history, because it was too much repelled by the superstitious beliefs of the Middle Ages and by the barbarities which they inspired, to have any imaginative understanding of mediaeval people. Or take Burckhardt's censorious remark about the Thirty Years' War: "It is scandalous for a creed, no matter whether it is Catholic or Protestant, to place its salvation above the integrity of the nation."[6] It was extremely difficult for a nineteenth-century liberal historian, brought up to believe that it is right and praiseworthy to kill in defense of one's country, but wicked and wrongheaded to kill in defense of one's religion, to enter into the state of mind of those who fought the Thirty Years' War. This difficulty is particularly acute in the field in which I am now working. Much of what has been written in English-speaking countries in the last ten years about the Soviet Union, and in the Soviet Union about the English-speaking countries, has been vitiated by this inability to achieve even the most elementary measure of imaginative understanding of what goes on in the mind of the other party, so that the words and actions of the other are always made to appear malign,

6. Jacob Burckhardt: *Judgments on History and Historians* (London: S. J.   Reginald Saunders & Company, 1958), p. 179.

senseless, or hypocritical. History cannot be written unless the historian can achieve some kind of contact with the mind of those about whom he is writing.

The third point is that we can view the past, and achieve our understanding of the past, only through the eyes of the present. The historian is of his own age, and is bound to it by the conditions of human existence. The very words which he uses—words like democracy, empire, war, revolution—have current connotations from which he cannot divorce them. Ancient historians have taken to using words like *polis* and *plebs* in the original, just in order to show that they have not fallen into this trap. This does not help them. They, too, live in the present, and cannot cheat themselves into the past by using unfamiliar or obsolete words, any more than they would become better Greek or Roman historians if they delivered their lectures in a *chlamys* or a *toga*. The names by which successive French historians have described the Parisian crowds which played so prominent a role in the French revolution—*les sans-culottes, le peuple, la canaille, les bras-nus*—are all, for those who know the rules of the game, manifestos of a political affiliation and of a particular interpretation. Yet the historian is obliged to choose: the use of language forbids him to be neutral. Nor is it a matter of words alone. Over the past hundred years the changed balance of power in Europe has reversed the attitude of British historians to Frederick the Great. The changed balance of power within the Christian churches between Catholicism and Protestantism has profoundly altered their attitude to such figures as Loyola, Luther, and Cromwell. It requires only a superficial knowledge of the work of French historians of the last forty years on the French revolution to recognize how deeply it has been affected by the Russian revolution of 1917. The historian belongs not to the past but to the present. Professor Trevor-Roper tells us that the historian "ought to love the past."[7] This is a dubious injunction. To love the past may easily be an expression of the nostalgic romanticism of old men and old societies, a symptom of loss of faith and interest in the present or future.[8] Cliché for *cliché*, I should prefer the one about freeing oneself from "the dead hand of the past." The function of the historian is neither to love the past nor to emancipate himself from the past, but to master and understand it as the key to the understanding of the present.

If, however, these are some of the sights of what I may call the Collingwood view of history, it is time to consider some of the dangers. The emphasis on the role of the historian in the making of

---

7. Introduction to Burckhardt: *Judgments on History and Historians*, p. 17.

8. Compare Nietzsche's view of history: "To old age belongs the old man's business of looking back and casting up his accounts, of seeking consolation in the memories of the past, in historical culture" (*Thoughts Out of Season* [London: Macmillan & Co., 1909], II, pp. 65-6).

history tends, if pressed to its logical conclusion, to rule out any objective history at all: history is what the historian makes. Collingwood seems indeed, at one moment, in an unpublished note quoted by his editor, to have reached this conclusion:

> St. Augustine looked at history from the point of view of the early Christian; Tillemont, from that of a seventeenth-century Frenchman; Gibbon, from that of an eighteenth-century Englishman; Mommsen, from that of a nineteenth-century German. There is no point in asking which was the right point of view. Each was the only one possible for the man who adopted it.[9]

This amounts to total scepticism, like Froude's remark that history is "a child's box of letters with which we can spell any word we please."[1] Collingwood, in his reaction against "scissors-and-paste history," against the view of history as a mere compilation of facts, comes perilously near to treating history as something spun out of the human brain, and leads back to the conclusion referred to by Sir George Clark in the passage which I quoted earlier, that "there is no 'objective' historical truth." In place of the theory that history has no meaning, we are offered here the theory of an infinity of meanings, none any more right than any other—which comes to much the same thing. The second theory is surely as untenable as the first. It does not follow that, because a mountain appears to take on different shapes from different angles of vision, it has objectively either no shape at all or an infinity of shapes. It does not follow that, because interpretation plays a necessary part in establishing the facts of history, and because no existing interpretation is wholly objective, one interpretation is as good as another, and the facts of history are in principle not amenable to objective interpretation. I shall have to consider at a later stage what exactly is meant by objectivity in history.

But a still greater danger lurks in the Collingwood hypothesis. If the historian necessarily looks at his period of history through the eyes of his own time, and studies the problems of the past as a key to those of the present, will he not fall into a purely pragmatic view of the facts, and maintain that the criterion of a right interpretation is its suitability to some present purpose? On this hypothesis, the facts of history are nothing, interpretation is everything. Nietzsche had already enunciated the principle: "The falseness of an opinion is not for us any objection to it. . . . The question is how far it is life-furthering, life-preserving, species-preserving, perhaps species-creating."[2] The American pragmatists moved, less explicitly and less wholeheartedly, along the same line. Knowledge is knowledge for some purpose. The validity of the knowledge depends on the validity of the purpose. But, even where no such theory has been

9. Robin G. Collingwood: *The Idea of History* (London: Oxford University Press; 1946), p. xii.

1. James Anthony Froude: *Short Studies on Great Subjects* (1894), I, p. 21.

2. Nietzsche: *Beyond Good and Evil*, Chapter 1.

professed, the practice has often been no less disquieting. In my own field of study, I have seen too many examples of extravagant interpretation riding roughshod over facts, not to be impressed with the reality of this danger. It is not surprising that perusal of some of the more extreme products of Soviet and anti-Soviet schools of historiography should sometimes breed a certain nostalgia for that illusory nineteenth-century heaven of purely factual history.

How then, in the middle of the twentieth century, are we to define the obligation of the historian to his facts? I trust that I have spent a sufficient number of hours in recent years chasing and perusing documents, and stuffing my historical narrative with properly footnoted facts, to escape the imputation of treating facts and documents too cavalierly. The duty of the historian to respect his facts is not exhausted by the obligation to see that his facts are accurate. He must seek to bring into the picture all known or knowable facts relevant, in one sense or another, to the theme on which he is engaged and to the interpretation proposed. If he seeks to depict the Victorian Englishman as a moral and rational being, he must not forget what happened at Stalybridge Wakes in 1850. But this, in turn, does not mean that he can eliminate interpretation, which is the life-blood of history. Laymen—that is to say, non-academic friends or friends from other academic disciplines—sometimes ask me how the historian goes to work when he writes history. The commonest assumption appears to be that the historian divides his work into two sharply distinguishable phases or periods. First, he spends a long preliminary period reading his source and filling his notebooks with facts: then, when this is over, he puts away his sources, takes out his notebooks, and writes his book from beginning to end. This is to me an unconvincing and unplausible picture. For myself, as soon as I have got going on a few of what I take to be the capital sources, the itch becomes too strong and I begin to write— not necessarily at the beginning, but somewhere, anywhere. Thereafter, reading and writing go on simultaneously. The writing is added to, subtracted from, re-shaped, cancelled, as I go on reading. The reading is guided and directed and made fruitful by the writing: the more I write, the more I know what I am looking for, the better I understand the significance and relevance of what I find. Some historians probably do all this preliminary writing in their head without using pen, paper, or typewriter, just as some people play chess in their heads without recourse to board and chess-men: this is a talent which I envy, but cannot emulate. But I am convinced that, for any historian worth the name, the two processes of what economists call "input" and "output" go on simultaneously and are, in practice, parts of a single process. If you try to separate them, or to give one priority over the other, you fall into one of two heresies. Either you write scissors-and-paste history without meaning or significance; or you write propaganda or historical fiction, and merely use facts of the past to embroider a kind of writing which has nothing to do with history.

Our examination of the relation of the historian to the facts of history finds us, therefore, in an apparently precarious situation, navigating delicately between the Scylla of an untenable theory of history as an objective compilation of facts, of the unqualified primacy of fact over interpretation, and the Charybdis of an equally untenable theory of history as the subjective product of the mind of the historian who establishes the facts of history and masters them through the process of interpretation, between a view of history having the center of gravity in the past and the view having the center of gravity in the present. But our situation is less precarious than it seems. We shall encounter the same dichotomy of fact and interpretation again in these lectures in other guises—the particular and the general, the empirical and the theoretical, the objective and the subjective. The predicament of the historian is a reflection of the nature of man. Man, except perhaps in earliest infancy and in extreme old age, is not totally involved in his environment and unconditionally subject to it. On the other hand, he is never totally independent of it and its unconditional master. The relation of man to his environment is the relation of the historian to his theme. The historian is neither the humble slave, nor the tyrannical master, of his facts. The relation between the historian and his facts is one of equality, of give-and-take. As any working historian knows, if he stops to reflect what he is doing as he thinks and writes, the historian is engaged on a continuous process of molding his facts to his interpretation and his interpretation to his facts. It is impossible to assign primacy to one over the other.

The historian starts with the provisional selection of facts and a provisional interpretation in the light of which that selection has been made—by others as well as by himself. As he works, both the interpretation and the selection and ordering of facts undergo subtle and perhaps partly unconscious changes through the reciprocal action of one or the other. And this reciprocal action also involves reciprocity between present and past, since the historian is part of the present and the facts belong to the past. The historian and the facts of history are necessary to one another. The historian without his facts is rootless and futile; the facts without their historian are dead and meaningless. My first answer therefore to the question, What is history?, is that it is a continuous process of interaction between the historian and his facts, an unending dialogue between the present and the past.

QUESTIONS

1. Carr begins with a question but does not answer it until the last sentence. What are the main steps of the discussion leading to his answer? The answer takes the form of a definition: which is the most important of the defining words?

2. In what sense is Steinbeck (p.1168) "saying the same thing" as Carr? What are the differences? What are the advantages of each man's approach to historical fact?

3. In his discussion of the facts of history, Carr distinguishes between a "mere fact about the past" and a "fact of history." Into which category should the following go? (a) Stonewall Jackson's lemonade (p. 1090); (b) Bruno Bettelheim's encounter with the infirmary guard (pp. 53–55).

4. Carr says, "the facts of history never come to us 'pure,' since they do not and cannot exist in a pure form: they are always refracted through the mind of the recorder" (p.1209). Freeman (pp.1086–1099) records facts which do not seem central to his subject. What are some of these facts? It would follow from Carr's statement that if such facts are refracted, their refraction might tell something about the nature of the refracting medium, the historian's mind, his interests and convictions. What do the peripheral facts he records reveal about Freeman?

5. If you were commissioned to write a history of the semester or of a particular group during the semester, what would be your most important "facts of history"?

On Science

C. D. BROAD

Bacon and the Experimental Method[1]

I will begin by giving you a very brief sketch of Bacon's life, so
that you may have some idea of the kind of man that he was and
the society in which he moved. He was born at York House,
Strand, London, in January 1561, i.e., about two years after Queen
Elizabeth came to the throne. His father was Nicholas Bacon, who
held the office of Lord Keeper; and his mother was Anne Cook,
whose father had been tutor to Edward VI. So we may say that
Bacon's family belonged to the higher ranks of the civil service.
Bacon was a very bright precocious boy, and Queen Elizabeth used
to enjoy talking to him. He was sent to Cambridge as an undergraduate of Trinity College at the extremely early age of thirteen,
and he left two years later. He then took up the study and practice
of law, which became his profession. The Queen employed him
much in legal and political business, but she seems not to have
really liked him or trusted him, and he held no important office
under her reign. After the accession of James I in 1603 Bacon's
advancement was rapid, for the King greatly admired him. He
became Lord Keeper, Lord Chancellor, and in 1620 Viscount St.
Albans. He was now a very wealthy man, but a tragedy was
approaching. He had always been careless with money and extravagant in his mode of life, and he had followed the common practice
of his day in taking presents from suitors, though he always
asserted that he had not allowed this to influence his legal judgments. However that may be, he was tried on a charge of corruption, pleaded guilty, was condemned, and had to pay a fine of
£40,000 (an immense sum in those days), lost his office, and was

1. Chapter IV of *A Short History of Science*.

banished from the court. This happened in 1621. Bacon lived on for another five years, a broken man. He died in April 1626. His last illness is said to have been caused by his getting out of his carriage in freezingly cold weather in order to try the experiment of stuffing the carcass of a fowl with snow to test the preservative effects of a low temperature.

Though Bacon was an able, and up to a point successful, lawyer and politician, his heart was not in that work. His one fundamental interest was to discover and propagate a general method by which men might gain scientific knowledge of the ultimate laws and structure of matter, and might thus acquire ever-increasing practical control over nature. He saw that, in order to collect the data from which the laws of nature were to be extracted by his methods, a huge organization of research would be needed. Vast numbers of men and women, at various levels, would have to be employed, and expensive buildings and apparatus would be required. All this would be very costly. The only hope of getting adequate supplies of money and sufficient authority and prestige to start and continue such a scheme was for Bacon himself to become a rich and prominent man and for him to persuade the King and powerful noblemen and churchmen to back it. In order to do this he must be ready to turn a blind eye to their vices and follies, to humor their whims, and to play upon their weaknesses by flattery. Bacon was nothing if not thorough, and he analyzed and practiced with his usual acuteness and assiduity the arts of worldly success. I believe that, like many other clever idealistic men, he started by seeking wealth and power wholly, or at any rate mainly, as a means to a high impersonal end, but gradually slipped into pursuing them for their own sake. I suspect also that, as often happens with such men, *he* was not quite so clever, and those whom he used and despised were not quite so stupid, as he imagined, and that he was seen through and distrusted much more than he realized.

If we are to appreciate Bacon's originality, farsightedness and breadth of vision and to be fair to his limitations and mistakes, we must see him against the background of the science of his own day and not against that of ours. The fundamental science of dynamics, for instance, did not exist. It was founded during Bacon's lifetime by Galileo (1564–1642), who also invented the telescope and noted with it the spots on the sun and the irregularities on the moon's surface. In astronomy it was still generally held that the earth is the fixed center of the universe, and that the sun and the planets revolved about it, the latter in complicated epicyclic orbits. The discovery of the three fundamental laws of planetary motion was made in Bacon's lifetime by Kepler (1571–1630). It was not until long after Bacon's death that Newton provided the first example of a scientific theory on the grand scale and in the modern sense, by explaining those laws and correlating them with the phenomena of falling bodies through his hypothesis of universal gravitation. Bacon's older contemporary Gilbert (1540–1603) had discovered some elementary facts about natural magnets, but the existence of electricity was unknown and its connection with magnetism was unsuspected. Chemistry, as a science and not a mere set of recipes, did not come into existence for another hundred and fifty years. Learned men commonly accepted without question the Aristotelian theory that earthly bodies are composed of the four elements, earth, air, fire, and water, and that heavenly bodies are fundamentally different, being composed of a superior fifth element, called the *quintessence*.

Corresponding to this lack of scientific knowledge was a lack of power over nature. The only available devices for obtaining mechanical energy were clockwork, waterwheels, and windmills. All land transport was on foot or by horse, and all water transport by rowing or sailing. Men were constantly at the mercy of local and seasonal food shortages and gluts, and were periodically decimated by epidemics, whose causes they did not understand and which they had no rational means of combating. Bacon was impressed by this impotence and its evil consequences, and he could not be expected to foresee, what we have learned since, that men can bring even greater evils upon themselves by abusing the power which science gives them than they suffered when they were powerless in face of natural forces.

Now Bacon was completely convinced that the ignorance of nature and the consequent lack of power over nature, which had prevailed from the earliest times up to his day, were by no means inevitable. They sprang, not from any fundamental imperfection in the human mind, nor from lawlessness or inextricable complexity in nature, but simply and solely from the use of a wrong method. He felt sure that he knew the right method, and that, if only this could be substituted and applied on a large enough scale, there was no limit to the possible growth of human knowledge and human power over nature. Looking back after the event, we can see that he was right, and we may be tempted to think that it was obvious. But it was not in the least obvious at the time; it was, on the contrary, a most remarkable feat of insight and an act of rational faith in the face of present appearances and past experience.

What was wrong with the methods in use up to Bacon's time? The fundamental defects, as Bacon clearly saw, were the following. In the first place there was an almost complete divorce between theory, observation and experiment, and practical application. Plenty of experiments of a kind had been done, and a certain number of disconnected empirical rules or recipes had been discovered. But the experiments were made in the main by men like alchemists and quack-salvers. These were often, though by no means always, charlatans or half-crazy enthusiasts. But, even when they were honest and sensible men, they did their experiments with some immediate practical end in view, such as turning lead into gold or discovering a universal medicine for all diseases. They were not guided by any general theory; they did not seek to discover the all-pervading laws and the minute structure of matter; and they worked in isolation from each other, keeping their results secret rather than pooling them. Bacon valued science both as an end in itself and for the immense power over nature which he believed that it could give. He thought that the failure of contemporary physics to have any useful practical applications was a sign that it was on the wrong track. But he was firmly convinced that it is fatal for scientists to work shortsightedly at the solution of this or that particular problem. Let them concentrate, he thought, on discovering by suitably designed experiments and appropriate reasoning the fundamental laws and structure of nature. Then, and only then, could they make innumerable practical applications with complete certainty of success. Anyone who reflects on how our modern applications of electromagnetism, of chemistry, and of medicine depend respectively on the theoretical work of Faraday and Maxwell, of Dalton and Avogadro, and of Pasteur, will see how right Bacon was in this.

The second defect which Bacon found in the science of his time was on the theoretical side. During the twelfth century, when Europe had reawakened from barbarism and men had again begun to take a scientific interest in external nature, it happened that the works on physics of the Greek philosopher Aristotle were rediscovered. It happened also that the greatest and most influential thinker of the Middle Ages, St. Thomas Aquinas (1226-1274), became an enthusiastic disciple and advocate of Aristotle. Now St. Thomas was a daring innovator who had to face strong opposition. But Aristotle's physics and logic were so much better than anything else available at the time, and St. Thomas was so much abler than his opponents, that the Aristotelian methods and concepts scored a complete triumph. Thenceforth they were accepted uncritically and handed down from one generation to another. Scientists decided all questions, not by investigating the observable facts, but by appealing to the infallible authority of Aristotle, just as present-day Communists appeal to that of Marx, and Engels and Lenin. Now this would have been disastrous, even if Aristotle's physics had been sound. But although he was a very great man, his strength lay in natural history and in certain branches of deductive logic. He was no mathematician, and his theories of physics and astronomy were much inferior to those of certain other Greek philosophers.

Bacon rightly accused the learned men of his time of accepting on authority sweeping general principles, which Aristotle himself had reached by hasty and uncritical generalization from a few rather superficial observations. Using these as premises, they proceeded to deduce conclusions about nature and to hold elaborate wrangles with each other by means of Aristotle's favorite form of reasoning, which is called the "syllogism." The following argument is an example of a valid syllogism: All metals are good conductors of heat, and all good conductors of electricity are metals; therefore all good conductors of electricity are good conductors of heat. Some arguments in syllogistic form are valid and others are not. Aristotle formulated the rules for distinguishing between valid and invalid syllogistic arguments. That was a very considerable achievement, but, to put it familiarly, it rather "went to his head," and made him overestimate the importance of the syllogism. What he failed to do was to suggest any method for establishing generalizations, like "all metals are good conductors of heat," which are needed as premises before any syllogistic argument can get started.

Bacon saw that syllogistic reasoning, however well it may be adapted for tripping up an opponent in the law courts or in Parliament, is utterly useless for discovering the laws of nature and for applying them to the solution of practical problems. What was wanted was a method by which we could slowly and cautiously rise from observed facts to wider and deeper generalizations, testing every such generalization at each stage by deliberately looking out for possible exceptions to it, and rejecting or modifying it if we actually found such exceptions.

That process is called "induction." Of course, as Bacon quite well knew, men have always been practicing it to a certain extent in an unconscious and unsystematic way. What Bacon did was to abstract and exhibit the general principles of such reasoning, so that in future men might perform it consciously with a full knowledge of what they were doing. Perhaps his greatest service here was to show the importance of testing every generalization by devising and performing experiments which would refute it if the result turned out in a certain way, and would confirm it if the result turned out in a certain other way.

Bacon realized that every man inherits or acquires certain mental kinks, of which he is generally quite unaware. These tend to lead us astray in our thinking, and we need to be put on our guard against them. Bacon calls these kinks by the quaint name of "Idols." Besides the tendency to accept on authority the dogmas of some prominent person or sect, which Bacon calls "Idols of the Theater," he enumerates three others. "Idols of the Tribe" are certain unfortunate mental tendencies common to the whole human race: for instance, the tendency to notice facts which support one's beliefs and fall in with one's wishes, and to ignore or pervert those which do not. Then there are "Idols of the Market Place." These arise from the fact that many words and phrases embody the false beliefs and inaccurate observations of our remote ancestors, and are thus, so to speak, crystallized errors which we swallow unconsciously. Lastly, there are "Idols of the Cave." These are sources of error or bias which are peculiar to each individual, depending on his particular temperament and the special circumstances of his upbringing.

It is time for me to bring this chapter about Bacon to an end, though there is much more that I would like to tell you about him and his work. In conclusion I would say that he was not a practicing scientist, and it would be quite unfair to judge him from that point of view. His service to science was to criticize the existing bad methods, to try to formulate the methods which should be substituted for them, and to paint a glowing picture of the power which men might acquire by such means over nature. Perhaps his main defect here was his failure to see the enormously important part which mathematics was to play in the development of science. But in other respects he showed great insight and most remarkable foresight, and he clothed his thoughts in a garment of wit and wisdom which makes his writings one of the glories of English literature.

CHARLES SANDERS PEIRCE
The Fixation of Belief[1]

That which determines us, from given premises, to draw one inference rather than another, is some habit of mind, whether it be constitutional or acquired. The habit is good or otherwise, according as it produces true conclusions from true premises or not; and an inference is regarded as valid or not, without reference to the truth or falsity of its conclusion specially, but according as the habit which determines it is such as to produce true conclusions in general or not. The particular habit of mind which governs this or that inference may be formulated in a proposition whose truth depends on the validity of the inferences which the habit determines; and such a formula is called a *guiding principle* of inference. Suppose, for example, that we observe that a rotating disk of copper quickly comes to rest when placed between the poles of a magnet, and we infer that this will happen with every disk of copper. The guiding principle is, that what is true of one piece of copper is true of another. Such a guiding principle with regard to copper would be much safer than with regard to many other substances—brass, for example.

1. The first in a series of papers, "Illustrations of the Logic of Science," published by Peirce in *The Popular Science Monthly*, 1877-1878.

A book might be written to signalize all the most important of these guiding principles of reasoning. It would probably be, we must confess, of no service to a person whose thought is directed wholly to practical subjects, and whose activity moves along thoroughly-beaten paths. The problems which present themselves to such a mind are matters of routine which he has learned once for all to handle in learning his business. But let a man venture into an unfamiliar field, or where his results are not continually checked by experience, and all history shows that the most masculine intellect will ofttimes lose his orientation and waste his efforts in directions which bring him no nearer to his goal, or even carry him entirely astray. He is like a ship in the open sea, with no one on board who understands the rules of navigation. And in such a case some general study of the guiding principles of reasoning would be sure to be found useful.

The subject could hardly be treated, however, without being first limited; since almost any fact may serve as a guiding principle. But it so happens that there exists a division among facts, such that in one class are all those which are absolutely essential as guiding principles, while in the others are all which have any other interest as objects of research. This division is between those which are necessarily taken for granted in asking whether a certain conclusion follows from certain premises, and those which are not implied in that question. A moment's thought will show that a variety of facts are already assumed when the logical question is first asked. It is implied, for instance, that there are such states of mind as doubt and belief—that a passage from one to the other is possible, the object of thought remaining the same, and that this transition is subject to some rules which all minds are alike bound by. As these are facts which we must already know before we can have any clear conception of reasoning at all, it cannot be supposed to be any longer of much interest to inquire into their truth or falsity. On the other hand, it is easy to believe that those rules of reasoning which are deduced from the very idea of the process are the ones which are the most essential; and, indeed, that so long as it conforms to these it will, at least, not lead to false conclusions from true premises. In point of fact, the importance of what may be deduced from the assumptions involved in the logical question turns out to be greater than might be supposed, and this for reasons which it is difficult to exhibit at the outset. The only one which I shall here mention is, that conceptions which are really products of logical reflection, without being readily seen to be so, mingle with our ordinary thoughts, and are frequently the causes of great confusion. This is the case, for example, with the conception of quality. A quality as such is never an object of observation. We can see that a thing is blue or green, but the quality of being blue and the quality of being green are not things which we see; they are products of logical reflection. The truth is, that common-sense, or thought as it first emerges above the level of the narrowly practical, is deeply imbued with that bad logical quality to which the epithet *metaphysical* is commonly applied; and nothing can clear it up but a severe course of logic.

We generally know when we wish to ask a question and when we wish to pronounce a judgment, for there is a dissimilarity between the sensation of doubting and that of believing.

But this is not all which distinguishes doubt from belief. There is a practical difference. Our beliefs guide our desires and shape our actions. The Assassins, or followers of the Old Man of the Mountain, used to rush into death at his least command, because they believed that obedience to him would insure everlasting felicity. Had they doubted this, they would not have acted as they did. So it is with every belief, according to its degree. The feeling of believing is a more or less sure indication of there being established in our nature some habit which will determine our actions. Doubt never has such an effect.

Nor must we overlook a third point of difference. Doubt is an uneasy and dissatisfied state from which we struggle to free ourselves and pass into the state of belief; while the latter is a calm and satisfactory state which we do not wish to avoid, or to change to a belief in anything else.[2] On the contrary, we cling tenaciously, not merely to believing, but to believing just what we do believe.

Thus, both doubt and belief have positive effects upon us, though very different ones. Belief does not make us act at once, but puts us into such a condition that we shall behave in a certain way, when the occasion arises. Doubt has not the least effect of this sort, but stimulates us to action until it is destroyed. This reminds us of the irritation of a nerve and the reflex action produced thereby; while for the analogue of belief, in the nervous system, we must look to what are called nervous associations—for example, to that habit of the nerves in consequence of which the smell of a peach will make the mouth water.

The irritation of doubt causes a struggle to attain a state of belief. I shall term this struggle *inquiry*, though it must be admitted that this is sometimes not a very apt designation.

The irritation of doubt is the only immediate motive for the struggle to attain belief. It is certainly best for us that our beliefs should be such as may truly guide our actions so as to satisfy our desires; and this reflection will make us reject any belief which does not seem to have been so formed as to insure this result. But it will only do so by creating a doubt in the place of that belief.

2. I am not speaking of secondary effects occasionally produced by the interference of other impulses [Peirce's note].

With the doubt, therefore, the struggle begins, and with the cessation of doubt it ends. Hence, the sole object of inquiry is the settlement of opinion. We may fancy that this is not enough for us, and that we seek, not merely an opinion, but a true opinion. But put this fancy to the test, and it proves groundless; for as soon as a firm belief is reached we are entirely satisfied, whether the belief be true or false. And it is clear that nothing out of the sphere of our knowledge can be our object, for nothing which does not affect the mind can be the motive for a mental effort. The most that can be maintained is, that we seek for a belief that we shall *think* to be true. But we think each one of our beliefs to be true, and, indeed, it is mere tautology to say so.

That the settlement of opinion is the sole end of inquiry is a very important proposition. It sweeps away, at once, various vague and erroneous conceptions of proof. A few of these may be noticed here.

1. Some philosophers have imagined that to start an inquiry it was only necessary to utter a question or set it down upon paper, and have even recommended us to begin our studies with questioning everything! But the mere putting of a proposition into the interrogative form does not stimulate the mind to any struggle after belief. There must be a real and living doubt, and without this all discussion is idle.

2. It is a very common idea that a demonstration must rest on some ultimate and absolutely indubitable propositions. These, according to one school, are first principles of a general nature; according to another, are first sensations. But, in point of fact, an inquiry, to have that completely satisfactory result called demonstration, has only to start with propositions perfectly free from all actual doubt. If the premises are not in fact doubted at all, they cannot be more satisfactory than they are.

3. Some people seem to love to argue a point after all the world is fully convinced of it. But no further advance can be made. When doubt ceases, mental action on the subject comes to an end; and, if it did go on, it would be without a purpose.

If the settlement of opinion is the sole object of inquiry, and if belief is of the nature of a habit, why should we not attain the desired end, by taking any answer to a question which we may fancy, and constantly reiterating it to ourselves, dwelling on all which may conduce to that belief, and learning to turn with contempt and hatred from anything which might disturb it? This simple and direct method is really pursued by many men. I remember once being entreated not to read a certain newspaper lest it might change my opinion upon free-trade. "Lest I might be entrapped by its fallacies and misstatements," was the form of expression. "You are not," my friend said, "a special student of political economy. You might, therefore, easily be deceived by fallacious arguments upon the subject. You might, then, if you read this paper, be led to believe in protection. But you admit that free-trade is the true doctrine; and you do not wish to believe what is not true." I have often known this system to be deliberately adopted. Still oftener, the instinctive dislike of an undecided state of mind, exaggerated into a vague dread of doubt, makes men cling spasmodically to the views they already take. The man feels that, if he only holds to his belief without wavering, it will be entirely satisfactory. Nor can it be denied that a steady and immovable faith yields great peace of mind. It may, indeed, give rise to inconveniences, as if a man should resolutely continue to believe that fire would not burn him, or that he would be eternally damned if he received his *ingesta* otherwise than through a stomach-pump. But then the man who adopts this method will not allow that its inconveniences are greater than its advantages. He will say, "I hold steadfastly to the truth, and the truth is always wholesome." And in many cases it may very well be that the pleasure he derives from his calm faith overbalances any inconveniences resulting from its deceptive character. Thus, if it be true that death is annihilation, then the man who believes that he will certainly go straight to heaven when he dies, provided he have fulfilled certain simple observances in this life, has a cheap pleasure which will not be followed by the least disappointment. A similar consideration seems to have weight with many persons in religious topics, for we frequently hear it said, "Oh, I could not believe so-and-so, because I should be wretched if I did." When an ostrich buries its head in the sand as danger approaches, it very likely takes the happiest course. It hides the danger, and then calmly says there is no danger; and, if it feels perfectly sure there is none, why should it raise its head to see? A man may go through life, systematically keeping out of view all that might cause a change in his opinions, and if he only succeeds—basing his method, as he does, on two fundamental psychological laws—I do not see what can be said against his doing so. It would be an egotistical impertinence to object that his procedure is irrational, for that only amounts to saying that his method of settling belief is not ours. He does not propose to himself to be rational, and, indeed, will often talk with scorn of man's weak and illusive reason. So let him think as he pleases.

But this method of fixing belief, which may be called the method of tenacity, will be unable to hold its ground in practice. The social impulse is against it. The man who adopts it will find that other men think differently from him, and it will be apt to occur to him, in some saner moment, that their opinions are quite as good as his own, and this will shake his confidence in his belief. This conception, that another man's thought or sentiment may be equivalent to one's own, is a distinctly new step, and a highly important one. It arises from an impulse too strong in man to be suppressed, without danger of destroying the human species. Unless we make ourselves hermits, we shall necessarily influence each other's opinions; so that the problem becomes how to fix belief, not in the individual merely, but in the community.

Let the will of the state act, then, instead of that of the individual. Let an institution be created which shall have for its object to keep correct doctrines before the attention of the people, to reiterate them perpetually, and to teach them to the young; having at the same time power to prevent contrary doctrines from being taught, advocated, or expressed. Let all possible causes of a change of mind be removed from men's apprehensions. Let them be kept ignorant, lest they should learn of some reason to think otherwise than they do. Let their passions be enlisted, so that they may regard private and unusual opinions with hatred and horror. Then, let all men who reject the established belief be terrified into silence. Let the people turn out and tar-and-feather such men, or let inquisitions be made into the manner of thinking of suspected persons, and, when they are found guilty of forbidden beliefs, let them be subjected to some signal punishment. When complete agreement could not otherwise be reached, a general massacre of all who have not thought in a certain way has proved a very effective means of settling opinion in a country. If the power to do this be wanting, let a list of opinions be drawn up, to which no man of the least independence of thought can assent, and let the faithful be required to accept all these propositions, in order to segregate them as radically as possible from the influence of the rest of the world.

This method has, from the earliest times, been one of the chief means of upholding correct theological and political doctrines, and of preserving their universal or catholic character. In Rome, especially, it has been practiced from the days of Numa Pompilius[3] to those of Pius Nonus.[4] This is the most perfect example in history; but wherever there is a priesthood—and no religion has been without one—this method has been more or less made use of. Wherever there is an aristocracy, or a guild, or any association of a class of men whose interests depend or are supposed to depend on certain propositions, there will be inevitably found some traces of this natural product of social feeling. Cruelties always accompany this system; and when it is consistently carried out, they become atrocities of the most horrible kind in the eyes of any rational man. Nor should this occasion surprise, for the officer of a society does not feel justified in surrendering the interests of that society for the

3. The legendary second king of Rome (715-672 B.C.), supposed to be the founder of nearly all the early religious institutions of Rome.

4. Pope, 1846-1878, foe of modernism, proclaimer of the important dogma of the Immaculate Conception, first pope to be regarded infallible.

sake of mercy, as he might his own private interests. It is natural, therefore, that sympathy and fellowship should thus produce a most ruthless power.

In judging this method of fixing belief, which may be called the method of authority, we must, in the first place, allow its immeasurable mental and moral superiority to the method of tenacity. Its success is proportionately greater; and, in fact, it has over and over again worked the most majestic results. The mere structures of stone which it has caused to be put together—in Siam, for example, in Egypt, and in Europe—have many of them a sublimity hardly more than rivaled by the greatest works of Nature. And, except the geological epochs, there are no periods of time so vast as those which are measured by some of these organized faiths. If we scrutinize the matter closely, we shall find that there has not been one of their creeds which has remained always the same; yet the change is so slow as to be imperceptible during one person's life, so that individual belief remains sensibly fixed. For the mass of mankind, then, there is perhaps no better method than this. If it is their highest impulse to be intellectual slaves, then slaves they ought to remain.

But no institution can undertake to regulate opinions upon every subject. Only the most important ones can be attended to, and on the rest men's minds must be left to the action of natural causes. This imperfection will be no source of weakness so long as men are in such a state of culture that one opinion does not influence another—that is, so long as they cannot put two and two together. But in the most priestridden states some individuals will be found who are raised above that condition. These men possess a wider sort of social feeling; they see that men in other countries and in other ages have held to very different doctrines from those which they themselves have been brought up to believe; and they cannot help seeing that it is the mere accident of their having been taught as they have, and of their having been surrounded with the manners and associations they have, that has caused them to believe as they do and not far differently. And their candor cannot resist the reflection that there is no reason to rate their own views at a higher value than those of other nations and other centuries; and this gives rise to doubts in their minds.

They will further perceive that such doubts as these must exist in their minds with reference to every belief which seems to be determined by the caprice either of themselves or of those who originated the popular opinions. The willful adherence to a belief, and the arbitrary forcing of it upon others, must, therefore, both be given up, and a new method of settling opinions must be adopted, which shall not only produce an impulse to believe, but shall also decide what proposition it is which is to be believed. Let the action of natural preferences be unimpeded, then, and under their influence let men, conversing together and regarding matters in different lights, gradually develop beliefs in harmony with natural causes. This method resembles that by which conceptions of art have been brought to maturity. The most perfect example of it is to be found in the history of metaphysical philosophy. Systems of this sort have not usually rested upon any observed facts, at least not in any great degree. They have been chiefly adopted because their fundamental propositions seemed "agreeable to reason." This is an apt expression; it does not mean that which agrees with experience, but that which we find ourselves inclined to believe. Plato, for example, finds it agreeable to reason that the distances of the celestial spheres from one another should be proportional to the different lengths of strings which produce harmonious chords. Many philosophers have been led to their main conclusions by considerations like this; but this is the lowest and least developed form which the method takes, for it is clear that another man might find Kepler's theory, that the celestial spheres are proportional to the inscribed and circumscribed spheres of the different regular solids, more agreeable to *his* reason. But the shock of opinions will soon lead men to rest on preferences of a far more universal nature. Take, for example, the doctrine that man only acts selfishly—that is, from the consideration that acting in one way will afford him more pleasure than acting in another. This rests on no fact in the world, but it has had a wide acceptance as being the only reasonable theory.

This method is far more intellectual and respectable from the point of view of reason than either of the others which we have noticed. But its failure has been the most manifest. It makes of inquiry something similar to the development of taste; but taste, unfortunately, is always more or less a matter of fashion, and accordingly metaphysicians have never come to any fixed agreement, but the pendulum has swung backward and forward between a more material and a more spiritual philosophy, from the earliest times to the latest. And so from this, which has been called the *a priori* method, we are driven, in Lord Bacon's phrase, to a true induction. We have examined into this *a priori* method as something which promised to deliver our opinions from their accidental and capricious element. But development, while it is a process which eliminates the effect of some casual circumstances, only magnifies that of others. This method, therefore, does not differ in a very essential way from that of authority. The government may not have lifted its finger to influence my convictions; I may have been left outwardly quite free to choose, we will say, between monogamy and polygamy, and, appealing to my conscience only, I may have concluded that the latter practice is in itself licentious. But when I come to see that the chief obstacle to the spread of

Christianity among a people of as high culture as the Hindus has been a conviction of the immorality of our way of treating women, I cannot help seeing that, though governments do not interfere, sentiments in their development will be very greatly determined by accidental causes. Now, there are some people, among whom I must suppose that my reader is to be found, who, when they see that any belief of theirs is determined by any circumstance extraneous to the facts, will from that moment not merely admit in words that that belief is doubtful, but will experience a real doubt of it, so that it ceases to be a belief.

To satisfy our doubts, therefore, it is necessary that a method should be found by which our beliefs may be caused by nothing human, but by some external permanency—by something upon which our thinking has no effect. Some mystics imagine that they have such a method in a private inspiration from on high. But that is only a form of the method of tenacity, in which the conception of truth as something public is not yet developed. Our external permanency could not be external, in our sense, if it was restricted in its influence to one individual. It must be something which affects, or might affect, every man. And, though these affections are necessarily as various as are individual conditions, yet the method must be such that the ultimate conclusion of every man shall be the same. Such is the method of science. Its fundamental hypothesis, restated in more familiar language, is this: There are real things, whose characters are entirely independent of our opinions about them; those realities affect our senses according to regular laws, and, though our sensations are as different as our relations to the objects, yet, by taking advantage of the laws of perception, we can ascertain by reasoning how things really are, and any man, if he have sufficient experience and reason enough about it, will be led to the one true conclusion. The new conception here involved is that of reality. It may be asked how I know that there are any realities. If this hypothesis is the sole support of my method of inquiry, my method of inquiry must not be used to support my hypothesis. The reply is this: (1) If investigation cannot be regarded as proving that there are real things, it at least does not lead to a contrary conclusion; but the method and the conception on which it is based remain ever in harmony. No doubts of the method, therefore, necessarily arise from its practice, as is the case with all the others. (2) The feeling which gives rise to any method of fixing belief is a dissatisfaction at two repugnant propositions. But here already is a vague concession that there is some *one* thing to which a proposition should conform. Nobody, therefore, can really doubt that there are realities, or, if he did, doubt would not be a source of dissatisfaction. The hypothesis, therefore, is one which every mind admits. So that the social impulse does not cause me to doubt it. (3) Everybody uses the scientific method about a great many things, and only ceases to use it when he does not know how to apply it. (4) Experience of the method has not led me to doubt it, but, on the contrary, scientific investigation has had the most wonderful triumphs in the way of settling opinion. These afford the explanation of my not doubting the method or the hypothesis which it supposes; and not having any doubt, nor believing that anybody else whom I could influence has, it would be the merest babble for me to say more about it. If there be anybody with a living doubt upon the subject, let him consider it.

To describe the method of scientific investigation is the object of this series of papers. At present I have only room to notice some points of contrast between it and other methods of fixing belief.

This is the only one of the four methods which presents any distinction of a right and a wrong way. If I adopt the method of tenacity and shut myself out from all influences, whatever I think necessary to doing this is necessary according to that method. So with the method of authority: the state may try to put down heresy by means which, from a scientific point of view, seem very ill-calculated to accomplish its purposes; but the only test *on that method* is what the state thinks, so that it cannot pursue the method wrongly. So with the *a priori* method. The very essence of it is to think as one is inclined to think. All metaphysicians will be sure to do that, however they may be inclined to judge each other to be perversely wrong. The Hegelian system recognizes every natural tendency of thought as logical, although it be certain to be abolished by counter-tendencies. Hegel thinks there is a regular system in the succession of these tendencies, in consequence of which, after drifting one way and the other for a long time, opinion will at last go right. And it is true that metaphysicians get the right ideas at last; Hegel's system of Nature represents tolerably the science of that day; and one may be sure that whatever scientific investigation has put out of doubt will presently receive *a priori* demonstration on the part of the metaphysicians. But with the scientific method the case is different. I may start with known and observed facts to proceed to the unknown; and yet the rules which I follow in doing do may not be such as investigation would approve. The test of whether I am truly following the method is not an immediate appeal to my feelings and purposes, but, on the contrary, itself involves the application of the method. Hence it is that bad reasoning as well as good reasoning is possible; and this fact is the foundation of the practical side of logic.

It is not to be supposed that the first three methods of settling opinion present no advantage whatever over the scientific method. On the contrary, each has some peculiar convenience of its own. The *a priori* method is distinguished for its comfortable conclusions. It is the nature of the process to adopt whatever belief we are inclined to, and there are certain flatteries to the vanity of man which we all believe by nature, until we are awakened from our pleasing dream by some rough facts. The method of authority will always govern the mass of mankind; and those who wield the various forms of organized force in the state will never be convinced that dangerous reasoning ought not to be suppressed in some way. If liberty of speech is to be untrammeled from the grosser forms of constraint, then uniformity of opinion will be secured by a moral terrorism to which the respectability of society will give its thorough approval. Following the method of authority is the path of peace. Certain non-conformities are permitted; certain others (considered unsafe) are forbidden. These are different in different countries and in different ages; but, wherever you are, let it be known that you seriously hold a tabooed belief, and you may be perfectly sure of being treated with a cruelty less brutal but more refined than hunting you like a wolf. Thus, the greatest intellectual benefactors of mankind have never dared, and dare not now, to utter the whole of their thought; and thus a shade of *prima facie* doubt is cast upon every proposition which is considered essential to the security of society. Singularly enough, the persecution does not all come from without; but a man torments himself and is oftentimes most distressed at finding himself believing propositions which he has been brought up to regard with aversion. The peaceful and sympathetic man will, therefore, find it hard to resist the temptation to submit his opinions to authority. But most of all I admire the method of tenacity for its strength, simplicity, and directness. Men who pursue it are distinguished for their decision of character, which becomes very easy with such a mental rule. They do not waste time in trying to make up their minds what they want, but, fastening like lightning upon whatever alternative comes first, they hold to it to the end, whatever happens, without an instant's irresolution. This is one of the splendid qualities which generally accompany brilliant, unlasting success. It is impossible not to envy the man who can dismiss reason, although we know how it must turn out at last.

Such are the advantages which the other methods of settling opinion have over scientific investigation. A man should consider well of them; and then he should consider that, after all, he wishes his opinions to coincide with the fact, and that there is no reason why the results of these three methods should do so. To bring about this effect is the prerogative of the method of science. Upon such considerations he has to make his choice—a choice which is far more than the adoption of any intellectual opinion, which is one of the ruling decisions of his life, to which, when once made, he is bound to adhere. The force of habit will sometimes cause a man to hold on to old beliefs, after he is in a condition to see that they have no sound basis. But reflection upon the state of the case will overcome these habits, and he ought to allow reflection its full weight. People sometimes shrink from doing this, having an idea that beliefs are wholesome which they cannot help feeling rest on nothing. But let such persons suppose an analogous though different case from their own. Let them ask themselves what they would say to a reformed Mussulman who should hesitate to give up his old notions in regard to the relations of the sexes; or to a reformed Catholic who should still shrink from reading the Bible. Would they not say that these persons ought to consider the matter fully, and clearly understand the new doctrine, and then ought to embrace it, in its entirety? But, above all, let it be considered that what is more wholesome than any particular belief is integrity of belief, and that to avoid looking into the support of any belief from a fear that it may turn out rotten is quite as immoral as it is disadvantageous. The person who confesses that there is such a thing as truth, which is distinguished from falsehood simply by this, that if acted on it will carry us to the point we aim at and not astray, and then, though convinced of this, dares not know the truth and seeks to avoid it, is in a sorry state of mind indeed.

Yes, the other methods do have their merits: a clear logical conscience does cost something—just as any virtue, just as all that we cherish, costs us dear. But we should not desire it to be otherwise. The genius of a man's logical method should be loved and reverenced as his bride, whom he has chosen from all the world. He need not contemn the others; on the contrary, he may honor them deeply, and in doing so he only honors her the more. But she is the one that he has chosen, and he knows that he was right in making that choice. And having made it, he will work and fight for her, and will not complain that there are blows to take, hoping that there may be as many and as hard to give, and will strive to be the worthy knight and champion of her from the blaze of whose splendors he draws his inspiration and his courage.

QUESTIONS

1. Why does Peirce distinguish between doubt and belief on p. 1223?
2. What are the four methods of inquiry? Which of the four most closely describes the development of Peirce's argument?
3. Would Peirce restrict application of the method of science to the natural sciences? Would he consider as scientific Milgram's "Behavioral Study of Obedience" (pp. 413–427)? Arendt's study of "Denmark and the Jews" (pp. 1164–1168)?
4. On p. 1230 Peirce sharply distinguishes between the a priori method and the method of science. Consider Platt's discussion ("Style in Science," pp. 1250–1261); would he agree with Peirce's sharp distinction?
5. In the next-to-last paragraph the last sentence separates the

subject noun from its verb by six clauses. Does Peirce gain or lose by this? Explain.

6. *This essay says little about religion directly, yet many of Peirce's remarks implicitly convey a decided attitude toward the subject. What is that attitude, and in which passages is it most clearly conveyed?*

DONALD FLEMING

Charles Darwin, the Anaesthetic Man

Here are three voices from Victorian England.

"What do I know of tastes and fancies? What escape have I had from problems that could be demonstrated, and realities that could be grasped? If I had been stone blind; if I had groped my way by my sense of touch, and had been free, while I knew the shapes and surfaces of things, to exercise my fancy somewhat, in regard to them; I should have been a million times wiser, happier, more loving, more contented, more innocent and human in all good respects, than I am with the eyes I have."—"I never knew you were unhappy."—"I always knew it."

I became persuaded, that my love of mankind, and of excellence for its own sake, had worn itself out. For I now saw, what I had always before received with incredulity—that the habit of analysis has a tendency to wear away the feelings. I was left stranded at the commencement of my voyage, with a well-equipped ship and a rudder, but no sail. The fountains of vanity and ambition seemed to have dried up within me, as completely as those of benevolence. I frequently asked myself if I could go on living.

I have tried lately to read Shakespeare, and found it so intolerably dull that it nauseated me. I have also almost lost my taste for pictures or music. I am glad you were at the *Messiah,* but I dare say I should find my soul too dried up to appreciate it; and then I should feel very flat, for it is a horrid bore to feel as I constantly do, that I am a withered leaf for every subject except Science. The loss of these tastes is a loss of happiness. My mind seems to have become a kind of machine for grinding general laws out of large collections of facts. It sometimes makes me hate Science.

The first speaker is Louisa in Dickens' *Hard Times* of 1854.[1] The second is John Stuart Mill in his *Autobiography* of 1873, describing a crisis that he passed through in the winter of 1826-27.[2] The third is Charles Darwin in a letter of 1868 and his autobiography of 1876.[3] Most historians would say that Dickens is validated by Mill and Darwin. One might argue instead that

1. Conflated and abbreviated from Bk. I, ch. xv, and Bk. II, ch. xii. The most stimulating analysis of *Hard Times,* by which I have been greatly influenced, is by F. R. Leavis in *The Great Tradition* (London, 1948) [Fleming's note].

2. Conflated, abbreviated, and rearranged from *Autobiography,* ed. John J. Coss (New York, 1924), pp. 96-99

[Fleming's note].

3. Conflated, abbreviated, and rearranged from Francis Darwin, ed., *The Life and Letters of Charles Darwin* (London, 1887), III, 92; and *The Autobiography of Charles Darwin, 1809-1882,* ed. Nora Barlow (London, 1958), pp. 138-139 [Fleming's note].

recollections of the inner life have to be validated by art in their representative historical character. One thing is certain, when the same theme reverberates upon itself from life to art and back again, the historian had better pay attention.

The common predicament of the fictional Louisa and the real Mill and Darwin may be described as the dissociation of knowledge and sensibility; fact and affect. They know but cannot feel and are afraid to feel and fearful of not feeling—joyless, parched, and worn-out. I am tired, says the young Louisa, "I have been tired a long time" (Bk. I, ch. iii). Louisa's state of exhaustion is the product of her father Thomas Gradgrind's fact-system of education. "Facts alone are wanted in life. Plant nothing else, and root out everything else" (Bk. I, ch. i). Over against the Gradgrinds of Coketown Dickens put the orphan circus-girl Sissy Jupe, lamentably brought up on the "destructive nonsense" of *A Thousand and One Nights* and other fairy tales and predictably unable to see why she cannot have flowers on carpets for the fancy of it, where they would get crushed if real and if not real have no business being there. " 'They wouldn't crush or wither, if you please, Sir. They would be pictures of what was very pretty and pleasant, and I would fancy—' 'Ay, ay, ay. But you musn't fancy' " (Bk. I, ch. ii). Sissy is an emblem of the circus acrobats from whom she came, with their emotional abundance and immediacy of feeling and their power of taking up easy attitudes and dispensing ease to others—artists who stacked themselves up in pyramids to lift the people of Coketown clean out of the Flood of Facts. The Gradgrinds are Utilitarians, Political Economists, Statisticians; in Dickens's terrible figure, dustmen raising clouds of dust to stifle feeling. The circus people are human beings fulfilling the human condition. In the end only Sissy Jupe can nurse Louisa into humanness.

John Stuart Mill was dusty from the cradle. He was a product of the same philosophy of education that Dickens satirized in *Hard Times*, Benthamite Utilitarianism (*Autobiography*, pp. 27-36). James Mill, the father, was a man of more spacious views than Thomas Gradgrind; and more than this, he had a not merely ideal but felt aversion from pain and suffering. Religion to him was intolerable as postulating an omnipotent and benevolent god as the ground of such evil. He was, his son thought, a man of deep feelings who could not imagine they would be in short supply with anybody else. Education was needed as a bridle upon them and could never lack for a mount to rein in. For this reason it did not occur to him to make good in his education of his son the characteristic Benthamite undervaluation of poetry and imagination. Bentham himself had said, notoriously, that "all poetry is misrepresentation," to which the younger Mill enters the odd demurrer that the old man did not really mean that *poetry* was misrepresentation but merely anything at all that was "more oratorical in its character than a sum in arithmetic" (*Autobiography*, p. 78). Which clears that up. John Stuart Mill as a boy actually did read some poetry—including Pope's *Essay on Man*—but he was like his preceptors in not being able to connect this with the real business of life, to beat abuses over the head with facts. So the boy grew up, speculatively benevolent to all mankind but mainly speculative, and headed straight for deadness of the heart.

When the doldrums had come and withered him up and he had no wind to puff his sails, he tried to find help in Byron, but that was no good—"Harold and Manfred[4] had the same burden on them which I had" (*Autobiography*, p. 103). The true medicine was Wordsworth, who dealt in "states of feeling, and of thought colored by feeling, under the excitement of beauty"—"they seemed to be the very culture of the feelings, which I was in quest of" (*Autobiography*, p. 104). The lesson that Wordsworth drove home to Mill about the necessity of poetry and art as "instruments of human culture," the best means to cultivation of the "passive susceptibilities," he tried to pass on in turn to other Utilitarians, most notably the young Radical politician J. A. Roebuck, already a lover of music, painting, and Byronic poetry, but like the rest unable to see that these things had any value as "aids in the formation of character" (*Autobiography*, pp. 105-107). Cultivation of the feelings through the imagination, Roebuck told him, was "only cultivating illusions." Mill thought that underneath, Roebuck was like his own father, endowed with "quick and strong sensibilities" but "more susceptible to the painful sympathies than to the pleasurable" and seeking to deaden his feelings rather than stir them up. If what John Stuart Mill had to say in praise of poetry could give offense to Utilitarians, his mature view on the role of music would have been more alarming still: it surpassed all other arts in "exciting enthusiasm; in winding up to a high pitch those feelings of an elevated kind which are already in the character, but to which this excitement gives a glow and a fervor, which, though transitory at its utmost height, is precious for sustaining them at other times" (*Autobiography*, p. 101). This exaltation of irresponsible excitement was like ushering an obscene force out of nightmares into the hard clear daytime of Benthamism— a fund of free-floating emotional energy, unexpended and unspoken-for, mere dangerous potentiality declining to be trussed up and handed over to any determinate end. The cure that Wordsworth had commenced, Mill's only love Helen Taylor completed—a Shelley among women in feeling, he said, a veritable Mill in liberation from superstition, as he might have added, and one integral

---

4. The brooding heroes of Byron's *Childe Harold's Pilgrimage* and *Manfred*, respectively.

being, who gave proof that Mill to be a whole man would not have to give up his father's warfare upon religion and all other forms of acquiescence in the evil of the world.

I

Louisa Gradgrind and John Stuart Mill after many vain attempts passed through the door of feeling into life. Charles Darwin traced the opposite course from a carefree youth to a desiccated old age when many doors that gave upon the world of art and feeling had slammed upon him (Darwin, *Autobiography*). From the time of his mother's death when he was only eight, the young Darwin had his whole being in the immense shadow of his father—340 pounds the last time they dared to weigh him, with an almost Johnsonian force of personality to match—but the latter never tried to mold him to order or sought to impose his own conviction that religious belief was unworthy of an intelligent man. Darwin as a young man responded to this permissive environment by displaying a catholic enthusiasm for life. His chief pleasure, indeed passion, was hunting, and he got plenty of it in, the anthem in King's Chapel made him shiver with delight, he loved Raphael and Sebastian del Piombo, Handel's *Messiah* and Maria Malibran, Shakespeare and Milton, Wordsworth and Coleridge, and fine scenery into the bargain. He was bored by long stretches of his education but was always permitted to move on to something else and some other prospective career. He began by preparing to be a physician like his father, but between the tedium of the lectures and the horror of operations before chloroform, of which the memory hounded him "for many a long year," he decided to call it a bad job, and Dr. Darwin acquiesced. He himself avoided being present at surgery and could not bear the sight of blood. Their next idea was the clergy, which would never have been the father's choice for himself but anything sooner than an idle sporting life, and the son thought it would be all right if he got a country living with a continual round of hunting and natural history, punctuated by a few sermons. Dogma was no problem. All 39 Articles[5] went down smoothly. It never struck him at the time, he later wrote, "how illogical it was to say that I believed in what I could not understand and what is in fact unintelligible." That was later. On the great voyage of the *Beagle*, Darwin passed among his shipmates for naïvely religious and given to crediting the letter of the Bible in a way that was already old-fashioned. If this was mere habit, he several times in the course of the expedition felt an experiential influx of "the sublime"—"the higher feelings of wonder, admiration, and devotion," which bore irresistible testimony to God and the immortality of the soul (*Autobiography*, p. 91). Once he stood upon the summit of the Andes and surveyed the magnificent

5. The basic statement of faith for the Church of England.

prospect all around and felt "as if his nerves had become fiddle-strings, and had all taken to rapidly vibrating" (*Life and Letters,* III, 54). But he felt "most sublime" of all in the rain-forests of Brazil, corresponding to the jungle red in tooth and claw of the homekeeping Tennyson but to Darwin on the spot a source of incommunicable delight, more gorgeous even than the landscapes of Claude Lorrain—his own comparison. Under the spell of the sublime Darwin did not see the jungle as an arena of combat to be shunned by sensitive men but as an occasion for rejoicing and deep assent to the universe. The thing that made him cringe was the uneven contest between slaves and their masters. "The remembrance," his son says, "of screams, or other sounds heard in Brazil, where he was powerless to interfere with what he believed to be the torture of a slave, haunted him for years, especially at night" (*Life and Letters,* III, 200). With these deep echoes resounding through his spirit and the queer fauna of oceanic islands teasing his brain, Darwin returned to England in 1836. In the course of the next two years he thought a good deal about religion, found that he could less and less imagine any evidence that would persuade him of the truth of Christianity, and came to think that even if true it was a "damnable doctrine" for condemning to eternal punishment unbelievers like his father and elder brother (*Autobiography,* pp. 86-87). In theory, and more or less in practice, this left open the question whether Darwin might still be able to salvage some kind of theism from the ruins of his now exploded orthodoxy. He had already gone far enough in unconventionality to make his father advise him to keep any future wife in the dark.

It was pertinent advice. In the same period when he began to find revealed religion wanting, Darwin was also canvassing in the abstract whether to get married or not. One credit item for getting married ran that a wife would be something to play with and better than a dog anyhow. Marriage it was, but marriage to a commonplace woman, deeply though not illiberally religious; no Helen Taylor to energize and set him free and add her strength to his own. It is clear that in the midst of her tender care for him, Emma Darwin was not above administering the most loving possible pinpricks on the subject of religion; for Darwin did not take his father's advice but told her everything. One gets the impression that she was always checking herself bravely on the verge of lamenting her husband's unregenerate state and professing not quite to believe that he really wasn't religious and she of course was just a poor muddle-headed little woman and he musn't mind her but had he thought of *this* argument for religion (*Autobiography,* pp. 235-238). He says, in point of fact, in his autobiography of 1876, that on the whole he did still believe in a sort of God, though not the God of the Christians, when he wrote the *Origin of Species* (*Autobiography*, p. 93). Total unbelief did not come till later.

This progression from naïve faith to abandonment of religion was one of the ground-notes of his private experience, always with the added dimension of flying in the face of his wife's desires for him. They were undergoing divergent evolution. The other ground-note was his estrangement from the arts. The history of this, not the fact itself but the stages by which it was accomplished, is difficult to pin down. Darwin says in his autobiography that "up to the age of 30," which would bring him to the year of his marriage, "or beyond," he loved poetry and specifically Milton, Gray, Bryon, Wordsworth, Coleridge, Shelley, and Shakespeare (p. 138). Now for many years he had not been able to "endure" a line of poetry and Shakespeare least of all. His old taste for pictures and music had equally deserted him. "Music generally sets me thinking too energetically on what I have been at work on, instead of giving me pleasure" (p. 138). The only art works that meant anything to him in his prime were novels read aloud by his womenfolk and stipulated to have happy endings, dear lovable women in them, and no aftertaste. Of these he says with characteristic precision of speech that they were a "wonderful relief" to him (pp. 138-139). He took novels as a sedative to put his jangling nerves and churning thoughts to sleep. Great novels making great demands he did not relish. As his contemporary George Eliot went on making her tragic vision more intense and her art more powerful, she continually declined in Darwin's favor (*Life and Letters*, II, 305; III, 40).

With this falling away from great art, Darwin associated a general loss of power to feel intensely. He had experienced a decline in his fondness for fine scenery, which he says in 1876 has lasted longer than any other source of aesthetic gratification but "does not cause me the exquisite delight which it formerly did" (*Autobiography*, p. 138). Worse still, he thought he had lost the power of loving friends deeply. "Whilst I was young and strong I was capable of very warm attachments, but of late years, though I still have very friendly feelings towards many persons, I have lost the power of becoming deeply attached to anyone, not even so deeply to my good and dear friends Hooker and Huxley, as I should formerly have been" (*Autobiography*, p. 115). He took no pleasure in this stripping bare of his personality, so that the thinking machine cast off the flesh that clothed it. "The loss of these tastes is a loss of happiness, and may possibly be injurious to the intellect, and more probably to the moral character, by enfeebling the emotional part of our nature."

II

Why did Darwin experience this atrophy of the aesthetic instincts? At least once he implied that he saw himself as Blake and Wordsworth might have seen him, murdering to dissect, a type of the analytical man who set the atomizing vision of science above the integrating vision of art. "At last I fell fast asleep on the grass, and awoke with a chorus of birds singing around me, and squirrels running up the trees, and some woodpeckers laughing, and it was as pleasant and rural a scene as ever I saw, and I did not care one penny how any of the beasts or birds had been formed" (*Life and Letters*, II, 114). This was written on the only kind of vacation from science that he ever permitted himself, an occasional short visit to a hydropathic establishment to repair the "horrid state" of his stomach induced by steady work. Once he was out from under the burden of science, he could see nature whole again and recover the posture of Wordsworth. But he always buckled his burden back on and headed for the dark tunnel of ratiocination that blotted out the light of common day. He was ratifying out of his own experience the teaching of the poets, Wordsworth, Blake, and Keats, but not Shelley, that a man could not run with them and see as they did and be a scientist too—unweave the rainbow and still expect the heart to leap up at the sight. It was an antinomy that John Stuart Mill declined to be impaled upon. He knew, he said, that clouds are "vapor of water, subject to all the laws of vapors in a state of suspension," but he knew equally that they were objects of beauty lit up by the sun, not either-or but both together (*Autobiography*, p. 107).

The healing and integral nature that Mill submitted to but Darwin put from himself dwelt in the domesticated landscapes of England. As a young man Darwin had gone voyaging on the *Beagle* into some of the most untamed landscapes in the world— from the bleak arid plains of Patagonia, too dour for human comfort, to the "great wild, untidy, luxuriant hothouse" of the Brazilian forest, which overshot the mark in the opposite direction.[6] These landscapes from another world—he so describes them, as the nearest thing to visiting another planet—Darwin could never put out of mind. They stood for a quite determinate thing in his life-history; his most powerful experience of "the sublime." This old category, rendered classic by Longinus and refurbished in the eighteenth century by numerous hands, including Edmund Burke, is the most common piece of aesthetic terminology in Darwin's writings from youth into age.[7] He was still puzzling over the exact

6. *Journal of Researches into the Geology and Natural History of the various countries visited by H. M. S. Beagle* (London, 1839), pp. 590, 604 [Fleming's note].

7. On the concept of the sublime, see Marjorie Hope Nicolson, *Mountain Gloom and Mountain Glory* (Ithaca, N.Y., 1959) [Fleming's note].

signification of it and simultaneously throwing it about with abandon in the 1870's. The two things in his experience which had the most power to trigger an access of sublimity were scenic grandeur, as in mountains and forests, and great music, always epitomized for him by the *Messiah*. "I felt glad I was alone," he said, on top of the Andes, "it was like watching a thunderstorm, or hearing a chorus of the *Messiah* in full orchestra" (*Beagle*, p. 394). What did the Hallelujah Chorus and the view from the Andes have in common? What did Darwin mean by "the sublime"? He never did give a straightforward definition, but one thing is clear. The sublime was associated by Darwin with an upwelling from the depths of the spirit that appeared to set reason aside and prevail over it. This, at any rate, was in keeping with Longinus' formula that the sublime is above and beyond the mere "persuasive"— compelling assent by no logical sequence of propositions but by immediate conviction. No wonder Darwin's sublime encompassed powerful incitements to religion. Sublime scenery as he witnessed it on his voyage around the world induced in him reverence, devotion, and worship. Great art by association with scenic grandeur, scenic grandeur with religion, and all three with the sublime, became part of a single universe of experience. "The state of mind," he says, "which grand scenes formerly excited in me, and which was intimately connected with a belief in God, did not essentially differ from that which is often called the sense of sublimity" and brings to mind "the powerful though vague and similar feelings excited by music" (*Autobiography*, p. 91-92). And again: music arouses the feelings of tenderness and love "which readily pass into devotion."[8] The mature Darwin moved away from art because he was continually moving away from religion.

The mainspring of Darwin's aversion from religion is unmistakable. He saw in religion what James and John Stuart Mill saw, assent to the evil of the world and acquiescence in it. To understand the form in which Darwin chiefly apprehended evil, it is necessary to juxtapose the peculiarities of his personal situation with the character of the age he lived in. As a boy he was encouraged by his father's example to hate the sight of blood and the practice of bleeding. As a medical student in Edinburgh, he had felt a "vivid" distress in walking the wards and rushed away in horror from blundering operations. From soon after his marriage till his death more than forty years later, he was a chronic sufferer from headaches, nausea, and stomach upsets. He had always been sensitive to pain. Now he came to live with it as an evil immediately perceived from within. It was all the more an evil for the monumental circumscription of pain that was going forward in Darwin's own lifetime. This took the double form of efforts at the

8. *The Descent of Man* (London, 1871), II, 335 [Fleming's note].

mitigation or removal of pain and the pursuit of new occasions for sympathy with it. Darwin witnessed the introduction of anaesthesia and modern narcotics, the abolition of slavery and serfdom in the Western world, and the birth of organized movements for kindness to animals and children. The "blessed discovery" of chloroform, by which he had out five "grinders" at one time and hardly felt a thing, made him very happy for his children's sake (*Life and Letters*, I, 385). On the evils of slavery, always linked in his mind with the screams heard in Brazil and for ever after in his own nightmares, he was absolutely intransigent. Affection for Asa Gray did not keep him from saying plainly that people in England would never see anything to choose between North and South till the Northern cause was indissolubly bound up with abolition; and the only harsh words he is ever known to have addressed to any of his children were spoken to a son who appeared to be apologizing for the brutal conduct of the infamous Governor Eyre in Jamaica (*Life and Letters*, II, 377; III, 52-53). He was almost equally incensed about cruelty to animals, now first looming up as an unpardonable offense against civilization.

His concern for animals effected a powerful conjunction between the assault on pain and the accomplishment of Darwin's life-work. The discovery in animals of a whole new realm of objects to be felt for, sentimentalized over, and safeguarded from harm was a fundamental, and may have been a necessary, part of the environment in which the doctrine of evolution was established. It was no accident that Darwin lived in an age when Sir Edwin Landseer and Rosa Bonheur were among the most widely admired painters and the organized movement for kindness to animals got under way. It was no accident either that the people portrayed by his contemporary Dickens in *Hard Times* as having found the secret of being fully human were circus performers living on easy terms of companionability with learned dogs and horses and actually constituting with them a single economic and social unit. Darwin and all England with him, and a good deal of the rest of the civilized world besides, were conditioned as never before to accept their kinship with animals. The strategy of a man like Bishop Wilberforce, who tried to undermine the doctrine of evolution by seizing upon the postulated link to animals, could hardly have been more inept. The great apes no doubt were not very widely kept or loved in England, and it would have been better if Darwin had been able to say that men were descended from horses or dogs or better still the Monarch of the Glen,[9] but the general idea of welcoming man's poor relations into the fold of human sympathies had already pre-

9. A painting of a noble stag (1851) by Landseer, widely popular in Victorian England.

vailed. When Darwin sprang from his carriage and fiercely berated a stranger for beating a horse, he was enacting one of the principal reasons for his inevitable triumph over his critics (*Life and Letters*, II, 200).

Not surprisingly, he took an equivocal position on the one matter where the current was superficially flowing in the other direction from the awakening of tenderness: the mushrooming recourse to vivisection by scientific investigators. Darwin did not deny that, properly guarded against abuse, it had an essential role to play in physiology. That did not change the fact that the practice made him personally "sick with horror" and he could not speak too harshly of men who engaged in it out of a "mere damnable and detestable curiosity" (*Life and Letters*, II, 200-201). As a result of these profoundly divided feelings, he initially lent his countenance to the disastrous view that moderate restraints upon vivisection by Parliament would be desirable, only to find that the restraints actually imposed (in 1876) were not moderate and not desirable. Yet even in retreat from his earlier position that legislation could do some good and no harm, he was motivated by his aversion from pain. Vivisection, humanely managed by the conscience of the investigator, would have to be tolerated precisely because it might produce new "remedies for pain and disease" in men and animals alike. He would sanction even pain to put pain to flight.

The raw sensitivity to pain which made Darwin a man of his age, and the fellow-feeling with animals which helped to make him the great vindicator of evolution, afford a clue to his alienation from the best literature of his time, symbolized in his not-so-joking remark that there ought to be a law against novels with unhappy endings. The power which great tragic novels have to raise a storm in the spirit that can never be laid again—their permanent heightening of sensitivity—he could not bear but sought instead for a dampening of consciousness by literature that left no trace behind; ephemeral and conducive to repose. He was in the position of James Mill and J. A. Roebuck, who felt so deeply that they could not imagine that others would experience a dearth of feeling and for themselves wished rather to hold it in check. In the circumstances Darwin could not possibly enter into the younger Mill's vindication of art as an emotional stimulus to the unfeeling. Darwin was trying to cut down on his emotional intake; and according to his own testimony, had considerable success in weaning himself from the rich diet of his youth and learning to feel more dimly. His turning away from art was both a means to this success and a token of it. It was a token as well of the fires within him that he was conscious of having to bank down.

Intense feeling was undesirable in Darwin's own experience as

exacerbating his already keen sensitivities. It was or could be undesirable in a cosmic view as well. Therein lay a tremendous
ambiguity at the very heart of Darwin's position. Natural selection
itself proceeds by pain, suffering, frustration, and unfulfillment—
the whole gamut that failure of promise encompasses. Any good
that comes *of* it, comes *by* evil. Darwin could not deny, in fact he
had to insist, that failure was stalking the world and performing
grim labors. If the grim labors were to slacken or failure not to take
its toll, natural selection would be by so much impeded. Darwin
points in the *Descent of Man* to many dysgenic factors in civilized
life by which those who would otherwise go under in the struggle
for survival and procreation are kept afloat by the rest, often at the
direct expense of the latter: exemption of the physically inferior
from warfare, with conscription of the strongest young men to die in
battle and leave few or no heirs behind them; public assistance to
the poor; organized solicitude for the "imbecile" and "maimed";
and universal extension of medical benefits, so that to take only
one example, thousands of people who would have succumbed to
smallpox by reason of their weak constitutions have been spared to
become fathers of the race.[1] Except for the policy on conscription,
which is partly pragmatic as well as compassionate, all of these
dysgenic factors arise out of tenderness for the weak. The implication
is clear that tenderness has become a clog upon evolution. It was
not always thus. Darwin in the *Descent of Man* can be seen looking
wistfully back to some indistinct but shining age in the past, a
moment of poise between two extremes, when men had learned
to value social solidarity but had not yet confused this with tenderness for what he calls "the imbecile, the maimed, and other useless
members of society" (*Descent of Man,* I, 103). One catches a
momentary glimpse of Darwin's Wagnerian or Carlylean self peeping shyly out from under his invalid's cloak, where such things are
often most at home, and yearning for the brave old forest days
when the world was bathed in a stern but golden light and men
were faithful to comrades, obedient to leaders, and strangers to
pity. Good actions were those requiring "self-sacrifice, self-command,
and the power of endurance" to further the ends of the tribe rather
than the happiness of the individual members (*Descent of Man,*
I, 95). Darwin hints that the light that shone in other days might
come again if men would take as their object, not the furtherance
of individual happiness, but the promotion of the "general good,"
defined as "the means by which the greatest possible number of
individuals can be reared in full vigor and health, with all their

---

1. *Descent of Man,* 2d ed. (London, 1874), cited from 2-volume edition (London, 1888), I, 206-207. The entire argument, except for conscription, in 1st ed. (London, 1871), I, 167-170. Unless otherwise indicated references will be to the latter edition [Fleming"s note].

faculties perfect, under the conditions to which they are exposed" (*Descent of Man*, I, 98). But, he adds, rather delightfully, such a procedure might "perhaps require some limitation on account of political ethics."

III

Darwin remained in his central being a deeply sensitive man, shrinking back from the spectacle of pain in other creatures, and wishing to offer some alleviation. What could this consistently be for the great proponent of natural selection? One answer was to refrain from positive acts of cruelty oneself and try to get others to refrain. More profoundly, Darwin's answer consisted in his repudiation of religion. This is the animus behind his unflagging interest in the theological interpretation of his doctrines. If natural selection were to be construed, as his great friend Asa Gray in America urged, as God's instrument of continuous creation, then there was an overmastering Will in the world that pain and evil should exist, if only to some further end. They were not mere existents, they were existents willed from on high. This to the shrinking and wincing Darwin was an intolerable conception of the universe, shared by all religions alike. People kept telling him that to conjoin belief in God with belief in natural selection merely went to deepen their faith and enlarge the consolations of religion.[2] To him, a God that dwelt in natural selection would be the worst of all possible Gods. For the proprietor of the universe to have to seek for a mere preponderance of good over evil in the world that he made, which was the best that could be said for any progress attained by natural selection, was monstrous in Darwin's eyes. He did not want a *God* that had to proceed by Benthamite calculus and either did not know how or did not care enough to decree uncontaminated good. In a sense, he belonged, with the Mills, to a class of God-deniers who were yearning after a better God than God. How high their standard was in these matters can be judged from the fact that Darwin thought there was a decided over-balance of happiness as against misery among sentient beings. He expressly says that the world is on the whole a good world—for "if all the individuals of any species were habitually to suffer to an extreme degree they would neglect to propagate their kind," but we have no evidence of this (*Autobiography*, pp. 88-90). Yet much intermittent suffering does occur; and this is sufficient in Darwin's opinion to condemn the idea of an "intelligent first cause" beyond any appeal to the admittedly greater quantity of habitual happiness. Moreover, he says that even if we are willing (as he was not) to accept the traditional Christian view that all evils suffered by men

2. See, *e.g.*, Mrs. Boole to Darwin, *ca.* 1867; *Life and Letters*, III, 63-65 [Fleming's note].

can be discounted as opportunities for spiritual improvement, the pain experienced by animals would remain an unanswerable reproach to any deity that presided over it: "the number of men in the world is as nothing compared with that of all other sentient beings, and these often suffer greatly without any moral improvement. A being so powerful and so full of knowledge as a God who could create the universe, is to our finite minds omnipotent and omniscient, and it revolts our understanding to suppose that his benevolence is not unbounded, for what advantage can there be in the sufferings of millions of the lower animals throughout almost endless time?" (*Autobiography*, p. 90). After God was discarded by Darwin, the suffering of the world remained undiminished; but he rightly intuited that modern man would rather have senseless suffering than suffering warranted to be intelligible because willed from on high. Darwin gave to his fellow men the best though terrible gift and comfort that he could devise: the assurance that the evil of the world was like the world itself, brute and ungrounded and ready to be stamped by each man with his own meaning and no other.

Here Darwin was sitting in judgment upon the tradition of natural theology, which sought to confer upon the universe the character of a work of art from the hand of the Great Artist; and more than this, sought to lend a common affective tone, a unifying vision of beauty, harmony, and fostering influences, to the universal landscape, so that all partial evils were lost in a greater good. This impulse to make a willed unity of disparate elements, to fuse parts into an emotional whole, is almost diagnostic for the artist's temperament. Natural selection was precisely the denial of nature as a planned work of art and an effort to dissipate the pleasing affective tone that natural theologians tried to lend it. It would be tempting to say that Darwin turned against works of art because he had determined to smash the greatest of all. At some deep level this may have operated; but we are on safer ground if, while recognizing the profound consonance between his revulsion from art and his repudiation of natural theology, we emphasize Darwin's resolve not to be an accomplice in the evil of the world by assenting to God's dominion.

We are brought round again to Darwin's experience of the sublime and the triple conjunction in this thought of scenic grandeur, music, and religion: all standing in common for the uncontrollable motions in the spirit and cutting adrift from reason which Darwin associated with the intimations of divinity which came to him in the Brazilian forest. He had to believe for his own comfort and the comfort of others that the instruction of the sublime in behalf of religion was false. Just so, the surges of feeling that music could arouse were capable of arming men for battle, but equally without any real bearing upon the right and reason of their cause. The dominion of art, as of religion, is the dominion of the irrational. The association can be documented from both ends of Darwin's career. At twenty-nine, he spoke of getting up close to a painting and being laid open by the "peculiar smell," presumably varnish, to the "old irrational ideas" that "thrilled across me" as an undergraduate in the Fitzwilliam Museum at Cambridge.[3] Thirty-six years later, in a moment of deep revelation in the *Descent of Man*, he touched in immediate succession upon the gusts of emotion that whip through a crowd of African Negroes, the excited chattering of monkeys, and the "sensations and ideas" aroused in modern man by music, which appear "from their vagueness, yet depth, like mental reversions to the emotions and thoughts of a long-past age."[4] Communion with primitive man and subhuman relatives of man and reversion through music to the dawn of history—it is an evocation in time and place of all occasions where feeling may be expected to prevail over reason or not even encounter any reason to put to rout. Response to music, like response to religion, does not give true evidence of anything except a will toward illusion. Music "arouses dormant sentiments of which we had not conceived the possibility, and do not know the meaning; or, as Richter says, tells us of things we have not seen and shall not see."[5] We are here in the general vicinity of Bentham's dictum that art is lies and has the power to certify lies and make them pass for truth. It was among the most terrible indictments that a man like Darwin could imagine, whose most distinctive quality was an instinct for truth-telling which has hardly ever been surpassed—has there ever been another scientist who included in his great book all the arguments against it that he could think of? He could only be true to himself by resisting the access of illusion wherever it tried to creep in.

In his resolve to be one of the great Truth-Bearers, Darwin strove to perfect himself as a fact-and-dust man, more abundant in learning and insight, more generous in spirit, and more divided than Thomas Gradgrind, but endeavoring to stand for the same thing and indeed opening out cosmic vistas for application of the Gradgrind philosophy. To deal, not in apt caricatures upon historical men, but in real men of heroic stature, Darwin was a kind of

3. Entry of 12 Aug. 1838 in the unpublished Notebook "M" in Cambridge University Library. I owe this quotation to the kindness of Dr. Sydney Smith of St. Catharine's College, Cambridge [Fleming's note].

4. *Descent of Man* (London, 1888), II, 364-365. Negroes omitted in 1st ed.;

relevant passage, II, 336 [Fleming's note].

5. *Descent of Man* (London, 1871), II, 336; the entire passage, including the quotation from Richter, quoted from Herbert Spencer. Cf. footnote 6 below [Fleming's note].

successor to the seventeenth-century Puritans with their terror of the imagination. To those who would resist its wiles, the Puritans held out in compensation the prospect of a sober and godly life. Redemption they could not promise. So too with Darwin. In repelling illusion, he was taking the only compassion upon his fellow-men that he could contrive and bestowing upon them the best though somber good that their situation permitted. The chief lie of lying religion for him was that evil could have been inflicted from on high instead of simply occurring. If, by access to the sublime, he should assent to this lie, his act of charity to mankind for uncovering the harsh necessity of natural selection would fall to the ground. Love of mankind and love of the truth combined with fear of religion to make Darwin suspicious of art, a type of the anaesthetic man, both in the literal sense of "not feeling" and in the derivative sense of taking steps to repress the pain that he was capable of feeling.

IV

His own anaesthetic state was mirrored forth in his scientific view of the world. As he had cut art out of his own life, so he left it out of his evolutionary scheme for mankind in the *Descent of Man*. In his only direct confrontation with Herbert Spencer, they took diametrically opposite views on the cosmic role of music. Spencer held that music followed speech in the evolutionary sequence as an "idealized language of emotion" and has been continually reacting upon ordinary language in the form of vocal modulation to produce a kind of running "commentary of the emotions upon the propositions of the intellect."[6] Men not only understand each other, they *feel* for each other to the extent that this language of emotions is perfected. Spencer looks to the day when perfection will be attained. We may expect, he says, that the language of feelings will ultimately enable men to partake "completely" of one another's emotions. It is a prospect of universal good-will born of music and fed by music. For Darwin the role of music in the history of the world has long since been outworn.[7] He held, in direct contradiction to Spencer, that music preceded speech and gave birth to it. Once this occurred, music had outlived its cosmic function except as a means of courtship among birds. In the life of men, music is now a mere epiphenomenon, a froth on the surface of life: "neither the enjoyment not the capacity of producing musical notes are faculties of the least direct use to man in reference to his ordinary habits of life" (*Descent of Man*, II, 333). He even went on to say that this useless attribute "must be ranked among the most

6. Herbert Spencer, "The Origin and Function of Music" (1857); in *Essays, Scientific, Political, and Speculative* (New York, 1891), II, 419, 422 [Fleming's note].

7. *Descent of Man* (London, 1888), II, 355-367; slightly amended from 1st ed., II, 330-337 [Fleming's note].

mysterious" with which man is endowed. Here, in his eagerness to put down the pretensions of music, Darwin was underestimating the power of his own teaching. He had supplied a perfectly plausible account of the *emergence* of poetry, singing, dancing, and love of ornamentation, as rooted in sexual selection. He had even assigned to music in the distant past the tremendous cosmic function of generating language. What he had failed to do was to suggest of what use the fine arts might be in the present and for the long future; why in their "mysterious" way they should stubbornly endure and grow more potent instead of shrivelling up into rudimentary organs like the appendix.

Historical circumstances conspired to make Darwin's great refusal of significance to the arts less glaring. He died in 1882, before the major works of prehistoric sculpture and painting had been authenticated. Though engraved pieces of bone were being uncovered by Edouard Lartet from the early 1860's forward, Sir Charles Lyell in his *Antiquity of Man* of 1863 always meant by "work of art" an artifact; and the incredible cave paintings of Altamira, though actually discovered at the end of the '70's, were not given a clean bill of authenticity by the principal skeptic till 1902. Darwin did refer in the second and last edition of the *Descent* in 1874 to the discovery by Lartet of two flutes made of bone, but these did not have the power to project artistic expression into the very center of prehistoric life as the great mural paintings did.[8] If one could imagine a slight speeding up in the history of archaeology—which is probably excluded by the fact that the cave paintings required for their acceptance at true value precisely the steeping of an entire generation in Darwinism—Darwin would have been confronted with a grave spiritual crisis. If driven to it, he would not have been at a loss to imagine a cosmic function for art. That was the trouble. He had a solution all too ready at hand but one that would have been intolerable to him as a human being. The iron band that clamped art, sublimity, and religion together in his own experience would have meant that the obvious way to build art into his system would be to assign a powerful role to religion as a constructive force in the development of mankind. Despite one or two equivocal tributes to religion as the mainstay of morality but also superstition, the last thing that Darwin wanted to do was to attribute any lasting evolutionary significance to it.

John Stuart Mill, if he had been charged with drawing up an evolutionary scheme, would not have lain under the same inhibition. For him the arts energized indeterminately, they did not confine him to a single channel and that unwelcome, or make him "recreant" to his prior commitments, but infused these with emo-

8. *Descent of Man* (London, 1888), II, 362 [Fleming's note].

tional gratification without in any way pitching him into the arms of religion (*Autobiography*, p. 101). He was not turned about in his course but sped rejoicing on his way. That was part of what Dickens had been trying to say about Louisa Gradgrind. By openness to works and endeavors of the imagination, she would have been "wiser, happier, more loving, more contented, more innocent and human" and persuaded that life was "worth the pain and trouble of a contest." But even at the end of the book, when she had begun to be human, she continued to lead the same domestic life as before. She did not find a new calling but new courage and zest to prosecute the old. Significantly, Dickens nowhere attributes to her any yearning after religion or ultimate conversion to it. The instrument of her redemption, Sissy Jupe, is like Mill's Helen Taylor in not even proffering solicitations to conversion.

Darwin was menaced by conversion from within and without. That was the irreducible difference between him and his wife, with her discreet endeavors at bringing him around and silent dissent from his deepening unbelief; and that, above all, was the menace of art. *He* would be turned about by art, manacled to religion, and diverted from his role in history. For the humane import of the doctrine of evolution through natural selection was to lop off the Godhead and show how biological order could be generated without a divine fiat. He could only keep upon his course and be the fit author of his own revolution by burking the evolutionary significance of the arts.

It was an omission that has never been fully repaired. Only one voice since Darwin has spoken with comparable force to the biological situation of man; and though Sigmund Freud took ample account of the arts as a fundamental human activity, he failed equally with Darwin to attribute to them any desirable function in evolution. With some qualifications, he tended to regard the arts as a strategy of concealment by which men attempted to evade the truth about their own nature, to wrap it up in symbols. If Freud had believed with Eugene O'Neill and others in the healing and saving power of illusion, he might have seen in this an aid to survival and increment of fitness. On the contrary, he regarded art as being in this character regressive, a means of turning away from reality to the pleasure principle. It was his own office to make men behold the truth about themselves in its naked aspect with a steady and unflinching regard; and health of mind lay in the scrutiny. Freud could not correct the bias in Darwin. They were as one in their mistrust of the arts as fostering illusion. As their common heirs, we still lack a universally compelling vision of science and art as reenforcing each other and flourishing together, not as truth locked in battle with illusion but as clarity of intellect joined to warmth of feeling.

JOHN RADER PLATT
Style in Science

All scientists are not alike. Look at any laboratory or university science department. Professor Able is the kind of man who seizes an idea as a dog seizes a stick, all at once. As he talks you can see him stop short, with the chalk in his fingers, and then almost jump with excitement as the insight grips him. His colleague, Baker, on the other hand, is a man who comes to understand an idea as a worm might understand the same stick, digesting it a little at a time, drawing his conclusions cautiously, and tunneling slowly through it from end to end and back again.

Which of these methods is likely to make the greater contribution to science? There are drawbacks to both. Able is volatile. He may drop his idea as rapidly as he acquired it. In a short time he can race through a forest of ideas and leave all his colleagues breathless behind, including Baker. Baker is scornful of such a procedure, perhaps a little envious. He can never try so many ideas, though in the end each one he tries becomes part of him, each one tested in every aspect.

Or consider another pair of scientific minds, whose contrasted inner workings are revealed by their contrasted footnote habits.

Charlson is the one who discovers everything for himself. He dislikes reading other men's efforts because they stale the fresh springs of his thought. Though he is famous to the world, his scientific enemies are numbered by the dozens because he never bothered to look up their prior parallelisms and dim anticipations. So he left out all the references that would have been their tendril grasps on fame. Rumors of plagiarism are heard at the Society meetings.

Doctor Doggett, instead, is footnote-happy. No historical cranny is safe. He pries out the foreshadowings, the counterarguments, and the misprints. If he makes a creative contribution himself it is lost among the references, for there are more lines of footnotes than there are of text. Yet he gathers a thousand strands together and may find distant connections which pass unnoticed by other men.

Will it be Doggett or Charlson who makes the great discovery?

This is a question we could pursue through the whole academic alphabet, contrasting the syndromes and merits of the types of scientific personality. Simply as writers, one man is dull, one witty; one verbose, another terse. This man's equations lie like boulders on the page, that man's like a fog. It is amusing to see how the differences show through the attempted impersonality of scientific verbiage.

But we soon realize that the question of relative merit hinges on a more fundamental question: Is personality significant for science? We often hear the arguments for scientific determinism, which is the belief that scientific discoveries are somewhat like the measles, breaking out everywhere at once when the time is ripe. If this is so, is not one man in a given field as likely as another to make an important discovery? Does it make any difference to knowledge who invents a thing first, or what kind of mind and style he has?

If we look at some examples from the history of science with this problem in mind, I think we will see that personality does indeed make a difference. The two aspects interpenetrate. To a remarkable extent the discovery ripe to be born selects one discoverer from among the contestants, picking out the master of a line of thought and method essential to its birth. But equally remarkable is the extent to which the undetermined and peculiar stamp of his parenthood is embedded forever in the body of pure knowledge.

The evidence for scientific determinism—with its lesser emphasis on personality—is the familiar catalogue of the instances of multiple discovery. The great cases of this kind were the simultaneous and independent discovery of the calculus by Newton and Leibnitz three centuries ago, and the simultaneous Darwin and Wallace discoveries of natural selection in the last century. Hundreds of lesser examples could be listed. Each idea, with variations, is found and found again. Patent lawyers make their living from such competition.

Independent discoveries are sometimes only months or weeks apart, especially today in the fields crowded with first-rate competitors. In physics, for example, the synchrocyclotron was invented simultaneously in the United States and in Russia. Independent communications from this country and from Germany announced the current theoretical "shell model" of atomic nuclei in the very same issue of the *Physical Review*. The race for priority hinges on days, and the Saturday afternoon Letter-to-the-Editor becomes a regular event.

Such examples make scientific developments appear almost inevitable, maturing like dandelions on both sides of company fences and national ones, to the despair of Congressmen and drug houses. The reason for this is that discoveries have preconditions that must be met. Once these are met, even a non-genius may make a discovery if he is playing with the right apparatus and tries everything. To a certain extent, science is successful because it is a code of rules that enables ordinary brains with ordinary motivations to set up, one step at a time, the necessary preconditions.

Some are mechanical. Take the discoveries of electrons and of

X-rays, which occurred within two years of each other in the 1890's. Both required the application of a high voltage to a good vacuum. This in turn required the knowledge of direct current electricity, a good cheap high-voltage generator, and a good cheap vacuum pump, with an electric motor drive for convenience. All these are late-nineteenth-century items. The incandescent lamp, not a discovery but an invention, had similar preconditions; but it could be made with a lower voltage and a poorer vacuum, and so was invented a few years earlier.

This is not to say that these discoveries could have been predicted. No one foresaw that such phenomena existed. But if anything were there to be found with that apparatus, it must have been found *then*. The discoveries were made by highly competent experimenters; yet within a few years almost any intelligent student might have made them independently, while experimenters ten times as competent could scarcely have set the dates of discovery earlier by as much as two decades. In present times, the anti-proton could be predicted, and planned for at Berkeley, years in advance; and then discovered almost as soon as the apparatus was designed, finished, and turned on. We can see why one celebrated physicist said that half of his success consisted in knowing what to order and where to order it.

There are also intellectual conditions that must be met, before a discovery can be made or appreciated or understood. The brilliant idea requires intellectual groundwork and, what is equally important, a scientific community ready for the novelty. It is just as sure a recipe for failure to have the right idea fifty years too soon as five years too late. William James might have been advising young men in any science when he said: Decide what important thing will be done in the next twenty years; then do it.

Occasionally, untimely ideas do get preserved to be marveled at. In mathematics, Fermat's Last Theorem still tantalizes us; and Hamilton's Quaternions, which were thought by his contemporaries to indicate mild insanity, were simply premature by two or three generations.

Abbé Mendel, father of genetics, actually bred his sweet peas decades too soon. His contribution was finally disinterred at the time when it could be understood. Roentgen made the discovery of X-rays in a momentary lapse from a lifelong study of crystals, which was no doubt equally painstaking and inspired but is almost unremembered because it was fifty years too early. Sometimes even a short time makes a great difference in the response to a new idea. Stories persist that the equations of quantum mechanics were derived by this man or that but were rejected by editors only a year or two before Schrödinger got his version accepted and won a Nobel prize.

We may speculate on how many good scientists may have died mute, inglorious, and bitter because their work was too advanced to be understood. This is the standard defense of the ill-prepared and the crackpot. Yet the failure to recognize a brilliant man is only partly due to the stupidity or stubbornness of the scientific community; it is also partly his own fault.

For brilliance has an obligation not only to create but also to communicate. A scientist can not really go "voyaging through strange seas of thought alone." The more penetrating eye will see him to be surrounded by a cloud of witnesses. He takes from others; he gives to others. He must address the problems of his time. He must translate his thoughts into the language of his contemporaries. He must scatter them abroad for interaction. A thought which has not penetrated to other minds will die unfruitful.

As a result, the scientist can hardly be recognized posthumously, like the artist or poet. He is much less independent, much more bound to the current needs and purposes of the scientific community. His achievement of thought needs to be at the same time an achievement of communication and leadership which must be acknowledged by the group—by at least one editor!—before its intellectual viability fades away.

It is a perishable achievement. Not many of us know who first cut the trees or cleared the land beside our houses. The scientific explorer, like the wilderness explorer, exists to be superseded. Wandering at random, he finds a first, clumsy way to the new goal. The more important the goal, the greater the speed with which his path is by-passed by short-cuts, ridden over by electronic computing machines, and obliterated by the marching masses of Ph.D.'s. His hesitations, his sextant readings, the art and intuition by which he avoided this pitfall or that rabbit track—these make dull hard reading after a few years, for they apply to a world of difficulties which, because of his very efforts, has vanished and can scarcely be reconstructed. But such a man is properly contemptuous of the incoherent genius whose ravishing discoveries are too strange and vague to be communicable.

Determinism also plays a more intimate role. Not only is the time of a discovery approximately determined, it seems that the personality of the discoverer may to some extent be determined. To find America, we must have a fifteenth-century Western sea captain, uncommercial, convinced, dogged, persuasive, with delusions of grandeur—whether his name is Columbus or something else.

To see this principle in science, we must concentrate on two components of personality which I shall call method and style. By method, I mean the type of a scientist's intuition, his normally preferred method of attack. One man loves most to design and build apparatus, a glorified instrument maker. Another is a human measuring engine who can turn out more data or more precise data than anyone else. Some like to improve on other men's experiments in familiar fields, others prefer wild and novel experiments of their own at the limit of the possible. In these differences, one major axis of variation ought to be especially emphasized. It is the difference between the generally inductive and the generally deductive types of mind.

In an inductive mind, the internal monologue might go somewhat as follows: "Now here's a funny result. It doesn't fit in at all with Smollengoble's theorem! Yes, the apparatus is okay. Didn't I see last month where someone else had trouble with that theorem? But he had lower pressure. If we increased the pressure, would it go farther in the same direction?"

The general from the particular. This is the man who covers his laboratory walls with graphs of his data and squints at them every morning before he turns on his power supply, wondering if those deviations are experimental error or a real effect. There is something of this turn of mind in all of us. A talented few, like the master organic chemists, develop it until they can play their residues and hunches as a virtuoso plays the violin.

The deductive genius may be tone deaf to such music. His passion is not for the uncertain new order but for elegance and clarity in the old. At his highest pinnacle, he is the Euclid or Maxwell who stands and looks back after a period of growth and sees that a few simple postulates will unite a whole body of separate rules into a symmetrical system.

Like the inductive mind, he sees patterns, but in a different medium. Perhaps when he closes his eyes by the fire he stares into a magnificent void where the luminous theorems move and intersect and enclose each other an he leaps up shouting, "I have it! I have it!" However jumbled his desk may be, there is some distant region of the spirit where his files are clearly labeled and his papers have been written in a neat hand on one side only and are stapled into bundles with their edges straight—the great plan encompassing every particular in every pigeonhole. There is something of this, too, in all of us.

One of these minds anticipates, the other reconstructs. Inductive steps must come before deductive ones. So in each subject area there is a time when one method is most appropriate. Then it exhausts its material, at least for the moment, and recedes as the important discoveries begin to fall to another kind of mental machine. A field of knowledge has a curve of growth and a morphology, branches and stem—a beginning, a middle, and an end. Different talents are needed in the gardeners at different times. Those with a green thumb must plant, while others with a sure balance climb ladders later for the fruit.

Take the discovery of the law of gravitation. First there is visual observation and instrumentation, from the ancients to Tycho Brahe's quadrant and his tables of years of nights of measurement. Then there are the rule-makers, from the Ptolemaic astronomers to Kepler, who asked how all this would look from the nearest star and searched Tycho's tables for regularities, boiling the regularities down to his three laws of planetary motion.

Wandering in and out of the procession are the speculators— Lucretius, Copernicus—who animate the mixture with their lively controversies. At one side are the auxiliaries: Archimedes on conic sections; the navigators, defining the shape and size of the earth; Galileo, hurling balls and abstracting from them that ingenious invention, the ideal free body.

What a preparation for Newton! It might be compared to some Biblical prophecy in its visions and connections and anticipations across the milleniums. These are the shoulders of giants, with linked arms—not merely a human pyramid, but the braced and giant framework of knowledge itself.

The main line of development in scientific theory follows this sequence of work methods: observation, rule of thumb, speculation, synthesis. Naturally the methods of work are not perfectly separated in time nor even in the individual scientists. Every research man must be capable of performing all the functions in some degree—especially the speculative function—if he is to be worth his scientific salt. He may even have several highly developed talents, like Newton. This should not blind us to the big difference in the different mental processes, even such as that between the maker of the important little first syntheses—frequently an experimenter—and the maker of final grand syntheses who often shows a native distaste for the raw and original datum.

To see the historical necessity that selects these types, let us try a thought experiment on history. Consider what would have happened if the minds of Newton and Kepler had been interchanged. The slightest acquaintance with the work of either man will show that Newton's mind was not the one to unravel Tycho's data, and Kepler's was not the one to do Newton's necessary preliminary work of discovering the calculus. Not that it would have been absolutely impossible; only that it would have been slow and burdensome for either mind to try to use intuition methods like the other, and that they would have turned aside soon and wisely to more congenial discoveries.

A mature research worker needs to seek out tasks which he can undertake best with his mental gifts at his moment of history. A Maxwell in the eighteenth century could not have united electricity and magnetism but would have had to work on, let us say, astronomy, while the Franklins did the groundwork of electricity. Maxwell in the nineteenth century could and did perfect electricity but would have been lost in atomic spectra, where a Kepler kind of mind was needed. A Maxwell today might find chemistry or field-theory almost ripe for his talents, but would probably be foolish to go back to the well-plowed area of electricity unless he proposed to make a still larger synthesis, or a synthesis from a completely new point of view.

The time sequence of work methods is never perfectly clear-cut, however; in a single field the different types of talent co-exist and make simultaneous contributions. For the different types of talent need each other. Inductive and deductive, intuitive and classical, are the two halves of a pair of scissors and cut only when they are opposed. Each work method produces its own peculiar excesses which must be seen from another viewpoint before their deformity can be recognized.

The inductive mind often goes too far. Not having the advantage of the grand synthesis, it does not know where to stop. Searching for important relations, it finds unimportant ones. Experimental error may be turned into law, or clear disproof dismissed as experimental error.

Pythagoras' useful relation between the sides of triangles seems to have been associated in his own enthusiasm with the lengths of musically harmonious strings, and so with the harmonies of the universe and the music of the spheres. This goes too far, but it is not all nonsense: the lengths of harmonious strings do indeed have simple numerical ratios.

The first regularity of planets which Kepler thought he found was that they moved on spheres circumscribed and inscribed in five vast regular polyhedrons in the heavens. This is not all nonsense: the regular spacing of the orbits is a main feature of several recent cosmologies.

Such jumps "beyond Reason" need to be continuously criticized by the deductive and classical mind. Yet the inductive mind is like a sentry who must be forgiven for firing at an occasional shadow provided he always fires toward the enemy.

The sin of the deductive mind is that it derides and suppresses those inductive jumps that later prove to be right about as harshly as those that prove to be wrong. Newton rejected Huygens' and Hooke's wave theory of light which swept out Newton's own ideas a hundred years later. An esteemed critic showed that Balmer's formula, the first real regularity found in atomic spectra, must be a mathematical accident. De Broglie's paper, which contained the first germ of quantum mechanics, was widely regarded as nonsense.

Still, this conservatism has a good result. The success of an innovator is meted out in proportion to his scientific persuasiveness, his patience in amassing crucial observations, like Darwin, to show that the old faith is unjustified. It is not the moment of insight but the moment of acceptance that marks a firm step forward. Scientific growth is by conflict. The truth is found only in the heat of controversy as each man is forced to defend his thesis: the classicist his sufficiency, the innovator his necessity.

The historical counterpoint between the inductive and deductive mind is useful even in its subtler manifestations. It provides an unspectacular tension which is a major force in keeping science balanced. Each creative worker lives in a steady stream of deductive criticism—normally, in fact, self-criticism—curbing and channeling his intuitive impulses.

It is not so much that his little daily jumps and inferences must not violate "reason" as that they must satisfy more delicate canons of scientific good taste. How many readings or decimal places to take; what precautions; how ignorant or speculative to show oneself at various stages of scientific friendship; how soon to publish; and so on. A large part of the training of science students is really devoted to instilling this code of scientific manners.

The code is a balance of opposites. A man may acquire deductive good manners at the expense of some of his inductive hope, faith, and fire; fanning the fire may soften in turn the rigor of his self-criticism. Some individuals and groups try to solve the problem by separating the two processes, starting with an idea stage in which the imaginaton runs wild and free, followed by an analytical stage in which the ideas are critically selected and combined. The genius is the one who can maximize both elements and maintain at the time the fiercest productivity and the most exacting standards.

Likewise for a successful scientific group, the curbing of inductive jumps by the canons of taste must be neither too rigid nor too loose. The scissors will not cut if the blades are locked or if they are wobbly. The rigor of editors is needed to restrict the wilder flights as much as the zeal of speculators is needed to keep knowledge alive. Science cannot be fruitful where publishers indulge unready authors, wild fancies, and incompetent techniques; nor where hoary academic despots hold the seats of power and press the young men to a mold two generations old. But neither side can afford to be dogmatic, for it is only in the light of the syntheses of a succeeding generation that we can look back and be certain what was excess of speculation and what was excess of repression.

These remarks have perhaps conveyed some idea of the depth to which scientific determinism goes. A social necessity fixes not only the timing of a discovery but the work methods of the discoverer; it affects the heat of the controversies engendered, and where science is successful it sets the canons of taste which determine whether the discovery is accepted or rejected at a given stage of proof.

Nevertheless, all is not fixed. If we move about inside this framework we can now begin to see the ornaments and gargoyles added, unnecessarily and delightfully and sometimes unexpectedly, by exuberant craftsmen, shaped by personality above and beyond strict scientific need.

For one thing, each person has his own combination of fields of interest. A scientist trained in one subject often makes spectacular contributions when his novel outlook and work methods are turned into another field. Think of the special approach of Helmholtz, the physiologist turned physicist; or of Pasteur, the chemist, among the diseases.

Personality also enters through language, with its hidden assumptions. Without Newton himself, we might never have had "force" or "mass" in the equations of motion; or they might have had very different definitions and emphases. Philosophers have pulled and hauled at them for centuries; the difficulties were ineradicable, because these symbols were written from the beginning in the Newtonian equations that worked. The Father of Physics has imprinted "force" and "mass," like intellectual genes, into every cell of the physical sciences today.

Kepler, on the other hand, seems to have eschewed, largely on aesthetic grounds, the anthropomorphic concept of "force" between heavenly bodies. In this question of taste, he anticipates Einstein. If history had put the Kepler mind in the Newton body, it might have delayed the discovery of universal gravitation, which would have been difficult for Kepler—but it might have accelerated the discovery of general relativity.

Terminology is often chained to such initial biases. Franklin's choice of the arithmetic terms "positive" and "negative" to designate the two supplementary types of electricity still plagues our thinking and may have delayed who knows what happier synthesis.

The idiosyncrasies of taste and choice, of abilities and workmanship, embellish and modify a discovery. The work method is determined; the style is not. Any physical law is exhibited in many places and forms and may be found by single experiments on hundreds of compounds or by hundreds of experiments on a grain of sand. And the discoverer may be an exhibitionist, or a conservative; an equation maker, or a model maker; he may want priority, or certainty. He may succeed by testing everything to destruction, at unusual temperatures and pressures; or by exploring his materials with nothing but a beam of light. He may be guided by shrewd and almost superstitious hunches, that only fluorocarbons will give him clear-cut answers, or density-matrix methods, or Drosophila, or sweet peas.

Sometimes the effects of such variations are profound indeed. There is one instance where a vast intellectual development has been hung on the deficiencies of a single piece of apparatus. We might not believe that electrons are in atoms except for some equipment assembled in 1898 by Zeeman in Holland, with which he found that the spectrum lines of atoms were broadened and polarized by a magnetic field. This "Zeeman effect" was explained by Lorentz on the assumption that the atoms contained the newly discovered corpuscles called electrons. Later, Bohr continued to assume this in his atomic theory; and whole-electrons-in-atoms passed on into the quantum mechanics that we now use.

But meanwhile, what of the Zeeman effect? If Zeeman had had a better spectrograph or had improved his apparatus before publishing his first results, he would have reported what a college senior can discover now; that each of his broadened spectrum lines is really a complex array of many lines, with every array different. Neither Lorentz nor anyone else would then have believed that there were intact electrons, all alike, inside the atom; perhaps fractional ones would have been assumed. The Bohr atom would have been different, or impossible. Quantum mechanics as we know it might never have appeared. No doubt some other theoretical system would have been produced in its place, but by now, after fifty years, its practitioners would speak a language incomprehensible or perhaps unbelievable to our best physicists. (The scientists will not find it any easier to talk to scientists they meet from another planet than laymen will.)

If a piece of apparatus can shape a field of knowledge, a brilliant scientist may also have a great personal effect. Many of the peculiarities of modern physics seem to have this individual stamp. Bohr, de Broglie, Schrödinger, Heisenberg, Dirac—each is responsible for some aspect of the synthesis of atomic structure which is quantum mechanics. Yet their approaches are very different: Bohr with his electron-orbits in space; de Broglie with his almost mystical waves; Heisenberg with his matrices and strict operationalism; Dirac with his formalism. If we had lost one of these, it would not have affected our ability to predict experimental results, which is often said to be the aim of science; but it would have been a great loss indeed to our understanding.

And a great change. Without Bohr himself, would the earlier

ideas of an atom as a vibrating jelly have been strangely modified by some other young pseudo-Bohr in the 1910's to explain the spectra and win the day? Without the particular style of a particular man, Dirac, we might have had formalism of a sort, but probably not the chaste, terse, awful elegance that now strikes fear and admiration into the graduate students.

The work of Willard Gibbs in chemical thermodynamics may be the most individual tour de force of all. Somewhat cut off in late-nineteenth-century America from the larger body of European theoretical physicists and chemists, he evolved an unusual kind of thinking; perhaps as an island population evolves aberrant species when cut off from the mainland. His equations show no trace of the mechanical particles bombarding the walls of a box which still dominated the thought of European scientists. He produced a theory without "forces" and without imaginary models of what was happening in the box, using simply relations among the things oberved on the outside, such as temperature, pressure, and volume. And he combined these with a logical absolute, a naked and apparently vulnerable assertion about entropy.

True, this was not completely alien to contemporary style. Differential equations like his were the admired mathematical form in other areas. There had been some interest in the physical power of syllogisms; and Mach and Einstein were shortly to remove "force" from motion and from gravitation and to assert other logical absolutes. But taken together and applied to chemistry, what a change! Small wonder that nobody noticed him but Maxwell. Small wonder that the best science students still go blank and dumb, and the little philosophy major at the back of the room suddenly begins to get the right answers, when they come to this part of the course. It hurts a three-dimensional man to see temperature computed from a syllogism.

It seems probable to me that if Gibbs had lived in England or Germany this fusion of ideas might not have occurred until at least a generation later. By that time chemical thinking would have been set in another mold, and chemistry today would be a different thing.

There are many lessons, for our culture, for our teachers, and for our scientists, to be learned from examining closely the interplay of the Great Man aspect of history with the Determinist aspect. It is exhibited in the microcosm of the scientific world in a relatively simple form in which the casual intellectual strands are rather easy to trace. The general cultural or political historian might find this limited but precisely known area a good testing ground for theories of history.

I think he would conclude, as I have here, that the nature of the achievements of a large competing scientific group is determined by the group and its history, and depends little on the behavior of individual discoverers. We can almost write down equations for the speed and scope of advance in some departments of knowledge. But the pressure of scientific determinism becomes weak and random as we approach the great unitary syntheses. For they are not only discoveries. They are also artistic creations, shaped by the taste and style of a single hand.

QUESTIONS

1. What is the relation between the first seven paragraphs and the eighth? Are the first seven necessary to the argument? If not, do they serve another function? What happens in the ninth?
2. On page 1261 Platt speaks of a "competing scientific group." Find examples of competition in his essay. What sort of competition does it seem to be? What regulates it?
3. On page 1257 Platt says, "Still this conservatism has a good result." What is the good result and what has it to do with style?
4. What does Platt mean by the classicist's "sufficiency" and the innovator's "necessity" (p. 1257)?
5. While Platt never explicitly defines style, he does imply a definition. Where is the implied definition most clearly evident? Oppenheimer ("On Style," p. 187) and Whitehead ("On Style," p. 186) do give explicit definitions of style. How do they compare with Platt's implicit definition?
6. Many people talk about style (e.g., sports editors, sociologists, and, of course, fashion editors). Define style and explain its role in some nonaesthetic and nonscientific activity.

GEORGE GAMOW

Expanding Horizons[1]

The Earth and Its Neighborhood

In the early stages of human civilization, the thing that we call the universe was considered almost ridiculously small. The earth was believed to be a large flat disc floating on the surface of the world ocean which surrounded it. Below was only water as deep as one could imagine, above was the sky, the abode of the gods. The disc was large enough to hold all lands known to the geography of that time, which included the shores of the Mediterranean Sea, with the adjacent parts of Europe, Africa, and a bit of Asia. The northern rim of the Earth disc was limited by a range of high mountains, behind which the Sun hid during the night time when it was resting on the surface of the World Ocean. * * * But in

1. Chapter X of *One Two Three . . . Infinity*, 1947.

the third century before Christ there lived a man who disagreed with this simple and generally accepted picture of the world. He was the famous Greek philosopher (so they called scientists at that time) named Aristotle.

In his book *About Heaven* Aristotle expressed the theory that our Earth is actually a sphere, covered partly by land, partly by water, and surrounded by the air. He supported his point of view by many arguments which are familiar and seem trivial to us now. He indicated that the way the ships disappear behind the horizon when the hulk vanishes first and the masts seem to stick out of the water, proves that the surface of the ocean is curved, not flat. He argued that the eclipses of the moon must be due to the shadow of the Earth passing over the face of our satellite, and since this shadow is round, the Earth itself must be round too. But only very few people at that time would believe him. People could not understand how, if what he said was true, those who lived on the opposite side of the globe (the so-called antipodes; Australians to you) could walk upside down without falling off the Earth, or why the water in these parts of the world did not flow toward what they would call the blue sky.

The people at that time, you see, did not realize that the things fall down because they are attracted by the body of the Earth. For them "above" and "below" were absolute directions in space, which should be the same everywhere. The idea that "up" can become "down" and "down" become "up" if you travel halfway around the Earth must have seemed to them just as crazy as many statements of Einstein's theory of relativity seem to many people today. The fall of heavy bodies was explained not by the pull of the Earth, as we explain it now, but by the "natural tendency" of all things to move downward; and so down you go toward the blue sky if you venture to put your foot on the under part of the Earth globe! So strong was the objection and so hard the adjustment to the new ideas that in many a book published as late as the fifteenth century, almost two thousand years after Aristotle, one could find pictures showing inhabitants of the antipodes standing head down on the "underneath" of the Earth, and ridiculing the idea of its spherical shape. Probably the great Columbus himself, setting off for his journey to discover "the-other-way-round road" to India, was not completely sure of the soundness of his plan, and as a matter of fact he did not fulfill it because the American Continent got in the way. And only after the famous around-the-world sailing of Fernando de Magalhães (better known as Magellan) did the last doubt about the spherical shape of the Earth finally disappear.

When it was first realized that the Earth has the shape of a

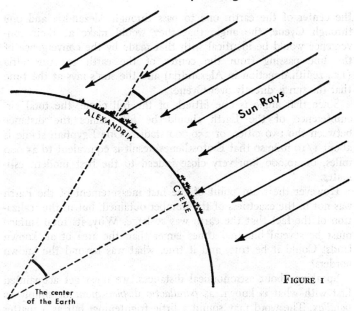

The center
of the Earth

FIGURE 1

giant sphere, it was natural to ask how large this sphere was in
comparison with the parts of the world known at that time. But
how would you measure the size of the Earth without undertaking
a round-the-world trip, which was of course out of the question
for the philosophers of ancient Greece?

Well, there is a way, and it was first seen by the famous scientist
of that time named Eratosthenes, who lived in the Greek colony
of Alexandria in Egypt during the third century B.C. He had
heard from the inhabitants of Cyene, a city on the Upper Nile
some 5000 Egyptian stadies south from Alexandria,[2] that during
the equinox the noon sun in that city stood directly overhead, so
that vertical objects threw no shadow. On the other hand
Eratosthenes knew that no such thing ever happened in Alexandria, and that on the same day the sun passes 7 degrees, or one
fiftieth of the full cycle, away from the zenith (the point directly
overhead). Assuming that the Earth is round, Eratosthenes gave
a very simple explanation of that fact, an explanation that you
can easily understand by looking at Figure 1. Indeed, since the
surface of the earth curves between the two cities, the sun rays
falling vertically in Cyene are bound to strike the earth at a certain angle in the more northerly located Alexandria. You can also
see from that figure that if two straight lines were drawn from

2. Near present location of the Aswan Dam [Gamow's note].

the center of the earth, one to pass through Alexandria and one through Cyene, the angle that they would make at their convergence would be identical with that made by the convergence of the line passing from the center of the earth to Alexandria (*i.e.*, zenith direction in Alexandria) and the sun's rays at the time that the sun is directly over Cyene.

Since that angle is one fiftieth of the full circle, the total circumference of the Earth should be fifty times the distance between the two cities, or 250,000 stadies. One Egyptian stadie is about 1/10 mile so that Eratosthenes' result is equivalent to 25,000 miles, or 40,000 km; very close indeed to the best modern estimates.

However the main point of the first measurement of the Earth was not in the exactness of the number obtained, but in the realization of the fact that the earth was *so* large. Why, its total surface must be several hundred times larger than the area of all known lands! Could it be true, and if true, what was beyond the known borders?

Speaking about astronomical distances, we must get acquainted first with what is known as *parallactic displacement* or simply as *parallax*. The word may sound a little frightening, but as a matter of fact the parallax is a very simple as well as useful thing.

We may start our acquaintance with parallax by trying to put a thread into a needle's eye. Try to do it with one eye closed, and you will find very quickly that it does not work; you will be bringing the end of the thread either too far behind the needle or stopping short in front of it. With only one eye you are unable to judge the distance to the needle and to the thread. But with two eyes open you can do it very easily, or at least learn easily how to do it. When you look at the object with two eyes, you automatically focus them both on the object. The closer the object the more you have to turn your eyes toward each other, and the muscular feeling arising from such adjustment gives you a pretty good idea about the distance.

Now if instead of looking with both eyes, you close first one and then the other, you will notice that the position of the object (the needle in this case) relative to the distant background (say, the window across the room) has changed. This effect is known as *parallactic displacement* and is certainly familiar to everybody; if you never heard about it, just try it out. * * * The farther away the object, the smaller will be its *parallactic displacement*, so that we can use it for measuring distances. Since *parallactic displacement* can be measured exactly in the degrees of the arc, this method is more precise than a simple judgment of the distance based on the muscular feeling in the eyeballs. But since the two eyes are set in our head only about three inches apart, they are not good for the estimate of distances beyond a few feet; in the case of more distant objects the axes of both eyes become almost parallel and the parallactic displacement becomes immeasurably small. In order to judge greater distances we should need to move our two eyes farther apart, thus increasing the angle of the parallactic displacement. No, no surgical operation is necessary, and the trick can be done with mirrors.

Such an arrangement was used in the Navy (before the invention of radar) to measure the distance to enemy warships during battle. It is a long tube with two mirrors (A, A') in front of each eye, and two other mirrors (B, B') at opposite ends of the tube. Looking through such a range finder you actually see with one eye from the end B and with another from the end B'. The distance between your eyes, or the so-called optical base, becomes effectively much greater, and you can estimate much longer distances. Of course, the Navy men do not rely on just the distance-feeling given by the muscles of their eyeballs. The range finders are equipped with special gadgets and dials measuring parallactic displacement with the utmost precision.

However these naval range finders, working perfectly even when the enemy ship is almost behind the horizon, would fail badly in any attempt to measure the distance even to such a comparatively near-by celestial body as the moon. In fact in order to notice the parallactic displacement of the moon in respect to the background of distant stars the optical base, that is, the distance between the two eyes must be made at least several hundred miles long. Of course it isn't necessary to arrange the optical system that would permit us to look with one eye from, say, Washington, and with another from New York, since all one has to do is to take two simultaneous photographs of the moon among the surrounding stars from these two cities. If you put this double picture in an ordinary stereoscope you will see the moon hanging in space in front of the stellar background. By measuring the photographs of the moon and the surrounding stars taken at the same instant in two different places on the surface of the Earth, astronomers have found that the parallactic displacement of the moon as it would be observed from the two opposite points of the Earth's diameter is 1° 24' 5". From this it follows that the distance to the moon equals 30.14 earth-diameters, that is, 384,403 km, or 238,857 miles.

From this distance and the observed angular diameter we find that the diameter of our satellite is about one fourth of the Earth's diameter. Its total surface is only one sixteenth of the Earth's surface, about the size of the African continent.

In a similar way one can measure the distance to the sun,

although, since the sun is much farther away, the measurements are considerably more difficult. Astronomers have found that this distance is 149,450,000 km (92,870,000 miles) or 385 times the distance to the moon. It is only because of this tremendous distance that the sun looks about the same size as the moon; actually it is much larger, its diameter being 109 times that of the Earth's diameter.

If the sun were a large pumpkin, the Earth would be a pea, the moon a poppy seed, and the Empire State Building in New York about as small as the smallest bacteria we can see through the microscope. It is worth while to remember here that at the time of ancient Greece, a progressive philosopher called Anaxagoras was punished with banishment and threatened with death for teaching that the sun was a ball of fire as big perhaps as the entire country of Greece!

In a similar way astronomers are able to estimate the distance of different planets of our system. The most distant of them, discovered only quite recently and called Pluto, is about forty times farther from the sun than the Earth; to be exact, the distance is 3,668,000,000 miles.

The Galaxy of Stars

Our next jump into space will be that from the planets to the stars, and here again the method of parallax can be used. We find, however, that even the nearest stars are so far away that at the most distant available observation points on the Earth (opposite sides of the globe) they do not show any noticeable parallactic shift in respect to the general stellar background. But we still have a way to measure these tremendous distances. If we use the dimensions of the Earth to measure the size of the Earth's orbit around the sun, why don't we use this orbit to get the distances to the stars? In other words is it not possible to notice the relative displacements of at least some of the stars by observing them from the opposite ends of the Earth's orbit? Of course it means that we have to wait half a year between the two observations, but why not?

With this idea in mind, the German astronomer Bessel started in 1838 the comparison of the relative position of stars as observed two different nights half a year apart. First he had no luck; the stars he picked up were evidently too far away to show any noticeable parallactic displacement, even with the diameter of the earth's orbit as the basis. But lo, here was the star, listed in astronomical catalogues as 61 Cygni (61st faint star in the constellation of Swan), which seemed to have been slightly off its position half a year before.

Another half a year passed and the star was again back in its old place. So it was the parallactic effect after all, and Bessel was the first man who with a yardstick stepped into the interstellar space beyond the limits of our old planetary system.

The observed annual displacement of 61 Cygni was very small indeed; only 0.6 angular seconds,[3] that is, the angle under which you would see a man 500 miles away if you could see so far at all! But astronomical instruments are very precise, and even such angles can be measured with a high degree of accuracy. From the observed parallax, and the known diameter of the Earth's orbit, Bessel calculated that his star was 103,000,000,000,000 km away, that is, 690,000 times farther away than the sun! It is rather hard to grasp the significance of that figure. In our old example, in which the sun was a pumpkin and the Earth a pea rotating around it at a distance of 20 ft., the distance of that star would correspond to 30,000 miles!

In astronomy it is customary to speak of very large distances by giving the time they could be covered by light that travels at the tremendous velocity of 300,000 km per sec. It would take light only 1/7 second to run around the Earth, slightly more than 1 second to come here from the moon, and about 8 minutes from the sun. From the star 61 Cygni, which is one of our nearest cosmic neighbors, the light travels to the Earth for about 11 years. If, because of some cosmic catastrophe the light from 61 Cygni were extinguished, or (what often happens to the stars) it were to explode in a sudden flash of fire, we should have to wait for 11 long years until the flash of the explosion, speeding through the interstellar space, and its last expiring ray finally brought to earth the latest cosmic news that a star had ceased to exist.

From the measured distance separating us from 61 Cygni, Bessel calculated that this star, appearing to us as a tiny luminous point quietly twinkling against the dark background of the night sky, is actually a giant luminous body only 30 per cent smaller and slightly less luminous than our own gorgeous sun. This was the first direct proof of the revolutionary idea first expressed by Copernicus that our sun is only one of the myriads of stars scattered at tremendous distances throughout infinite space.

Since the discovery of Bessel a great many stellar parallaxes have been measured. A few of the stars were found to be closer to us than 61 Cygni, the nearest being alpha-Centauri (the brightest star in the constellation of Centaurus), which is only 4.3 light-years away. It is very similar to our sun in its size and luminosity. Most of the stars are much farther away, so far away that even the diameter of the Earth's orbit becomes too small as the base for distance measurements.

Also the stars have been found to vary greatly in their sizes and luminosities, from shining giants such as Betelgeuse (300 light-

3. More exactly 0.600″ ± 0.06 [Gamow's note].

years away), which is about 400 times larger and 3600 times brighter than our sun, to such faint dwarfs as the so-called Van Maanen's star (13 light-years away), which is smaller than our Earth (its diameter being 75 per cent that of Earth) and about 10,000 times fainter than the sun.

We come now to the important problem of counting all existing stars. There is a popular belief, to which you also probably would subscribe, that nobody can count the stars in the sky. However, as is true of so many popular beliefs, this one is also quite wrong, at least as far as the stars visible to the naked eye are concerned. In fact, the total number of stars which may thus be seen in both hemispheres is only between 6000 and 7000, and since only one half of them are above the horizon at any one time, and since the visibility of stars close to the horizon is greatly reduced by atmospheric absorption, the number of stars which are usually visible to the naked eye on a clear moonless night is only about 2000. Thus, counting diligently at the rate of say 1 star per second, you should be able to count them all in about 1/2 hr!

If, however, you used a field binocular, you would be able to see some 50,000 additional stars, and a 2 1/2-inch telescope would reveal about 1,000,000 more. Using the famous 100-inch telescope of the Mt. Wilson Observatory in California you should be able to see about half a billion stars. Counting them at the rate of 1 star per second every day from dusk to dawn, astronomers would have to spend about a century to count them all!

But, of course, nobody has ever tried to count all the stars visible through large telescopes one by one. The total number is calculated by counting the actual stars visible in a number of areas in different parts of the sky and applying the average to the total area.

More than a century ago the famous British astronomer William Herschel, observing the stellar sky through his large self-made telescope, was struck by the fact that most of the stars that are ordinarily invisible to the naked eye appear within the faintly luminous belt cutting across the night sky and known as the Milky Way. And it is to him that the science of astronomy owes the recognition of the fact that the Milky Way is not an ordinary nebulosity or merely a belt of gas clouds spreading across space, but is actually formed from a multitude of stars that are so far away and consequently so faint that our eye cannot recognize them separately.

Using stronger and stronger telescopes we have been able to see the Milky Way as a larger and larger number of separate stars, but the main bulk of them still remains in the hazy background. It would be, however, erroneous to think that in the region of the Milky Way the stars are distributed any more densely than in any other part of the sky. It is, in fact, not the denser distribution of stars but the greater depth of stellar distribution in this direction that makes it possible to see what seems to be a larger number of stars in a given space than anywhere else in the sky. In the direction of the Milky Way the stars extend as far as the eye (strengthened by telescopes) can see, whereas in any other direction the distribution of stars does not extend to the end of visibility, and beyond them we encounter mostly the almost empty space.

Looking in the direction of the Milky Way it is as though we are looking through a deep forest where the branches of numerous trees overlap each other forming a continuous background, whereas in other directions we see patches of the empty space between the stars, as we would see the patches of the blue sky through the foliage overhead.

Thus the stellar universe, to which our sun belongs as one insignificant member, occupies a flattened area in space, extending for large distances in the plane of the Milky Way, and being comparatively thin in the direction perpendicular to it.

A more detailed study by generations of astronomers led to the conclusion that our stellar system includes about 40,000,000,000 individual stars, distributed within a lens-shaped area about 100,000 light-years in diameter and some 5000 to 10,000 light-years thick. And one result of this study comes as a slap in the face of human pride—the knowledge that our sun is not at all at the center of this giant stellar society but rather close to its outer edge.

In more scientific language the system of the Milky Way is known as the *Galaxy* (Latin of course!). The size of the Galaxy is here reduced by a factor of a hundred billion billions, though the number of points that represent separate stars are considerably fewer than forty billions, for, as one puts it, typographical reasons.

One of the most characteristic properties of the giant swarm of stars forming the galactic system is that it is in a state of rapid rotation similar to that which moves our planetary system. Just as Venus, Earth, Jupiter, and other planets move along almost circular orbits around the sun, the billions of stars forming the system of the Milky Way move around what is known as the galactic center. This center of galactic rotation is located in the direction of the constellation of Sagittarius (the Archer), and in fact if you follow the foggy shape of the Milky Way across the sky you will notice that approaching this constellation it becomes much broader, indicating that you are looking toward the central thicker part of the lens-shaped mass. (Our astronomer in Figure 3 is looking in this direction.)

What does the galactic center look like? We do not know that, since unfortunately it is screened from our sight by heavy clouds of dark interstellar material hanging in space. In fact, looking at the broadened part of the Milky Way in the region of Sagittarius[4] you would think first that the mythical celestial road branches here into two "one-way traffic lanes." But it is not an actual branching, and this impression is given simply by a dark cloud of interstellar dust and gases hanging in space right in the middle of the broadening between us and the galactic center. Thus whereas the darkness on both sides of the Milky Way is due to the background of the dark empty space, the blackness in the middle is produced by the dark opaque cloud. A few stars in the dark central patch are actually in the foreground, between us and the cloud.

It is, of course, a pity that we cannot see the mysterious galactic center around which our sun is spinning, along with billions of other stars. But in a way we know how it must look, from the observation of other stellar systems or galaxies scattered through space far beyond the outermost limit of our Milky Way. It is not some supergiant star keeping in subordination all the other members of the stellar system, as the sun reigns over the family of planets. The study of the central parts of other galaxies (which we will discuss a little later) indicates that they also consist of large multitudes of stars with the only difference that here the stars are crowded much more densely than in the outlying parts to which our sun belongs. If we think of the planetary system as an autocratic state where the Sun rules the planets, the Galaxy of stars may be likened to a kind of democracy in which some members occupy influential central places while the others have to be satisfied with more humble positions on the outskirts of their society.

As said above, all the stars including our sun rotate in giant circles around the center of the galactic system. How can this be proved, how large are the radii of these stellar orbits, and how long does it take to make a complete circuit?

All these questions were answered a few decades ago by the Dutch astronomer Oort, who applied to the sysem of stars known as the Milky Way observations very similar to those made by Copernicus in considering the planetary system.

Let us remember first Copernicus' argument. It had been observed by the ancients, the Babylonians, the Egyptians, and others, that the big planets like Saturn or Jupiter seemed to move across the sky in a rather peculiar way. They seemed to proceed along an ellipse in the way the sun does, then suddenly to stop, to back, and after a second reversal of motion, to continue their way in the original direction. In the lower part of Figure 2 we show schematically such

4. Which can be best observed on a clear night in early summer [Gamow's note].

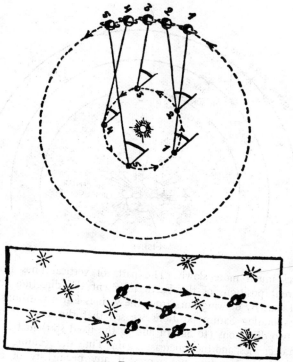

FIGURE 2

a look as described by Saturn over a period of about two years. (The period of Saturn's complete circuit is 29½ years.) Since, on account of religious prejudices that dictated the statement that our Earth is the center of the universe, all planets and the sun itself were believed to move around the Earth, the above described peculiarities of motion had to be explained by the supposition that planetary orbits have very peculiar shapes with a number of loops in them.

But Copernicus knew better, and by a stroke of genius, he explained the mysterious looping phenomenon as due to the fact that the Earth as well as all other planets move along simple circles around the Sun. This explanation of the looping effect can be easily understood after studying the schematic picture at the top of Figure 2.

The sun is in the center, the Earth (small sphere) moves along the smaller circle, and Saturn (with a ring) moves along the larger circle in the same direction as the Earth. Numbers 1, 2, 3, 4, 5 represent different positions of the Earth in the course of a year, and the corresponding positions of Saturn which, as we remember,

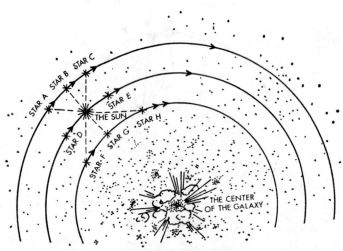

FIGURE 3

moves much more slowly. The parts of vertical lines from the different positions of the Earth represent the direction to some fixed star. By drawing lines from the various Earth positions to the corresponding Saturn positions we see that the angle formed by the two directions (to Saturn and to the fixed star) first increases, then decreases, and then increases again. Thus the seeming phenomenon of looping does not represent any peculiarity of Saturn's motion but arises from the fact that we observe this motion from different angles on the moving Earth.

The Oort argument about the rotation of the Galaxy of stars may be understood after inspection of Figure 3. Here in the lower part of the picture we see the galactic center (with dark clouds and all!) and there are plenty of stars all around it through the entire field of the figure. The three circles represent the orbits of stars at different distances from the center, the middle circle being the oribt of our sun.

Let us consider eight stars (shown with rays to distinguish them from other points), two of which are moving along the same orbit as the sun, but one slightly ahead and one slightly behind it, the others located on somewhat larger and somewhat smaller orbits as shown in the figure. We must remember that owing to the laws of gravity the outer stars have lower and the inner stars higher velocity than the stars on solar orbits (this is indicated in the figure by the arrows of different lengths).

How will the motion of these eight stars look if observed from the sun, or, what is of course the same, from the Earth? We are speaking here about the motion along the line of sight, which can be most conveniently observed by means of the so-called Doppler effect.[5] It is clear, first of all, that the two stars (marked D and E) that move along the same orbit and with the same speed as the sun will seem stationary to a solar (or terrestrial) observer. The same is true of the other two stars (B and G) located along the radius, since they move parallel to the sun, so that there is no component of velocity along the line of sight.

Now what about the stars A and C on the outer circle? Since they both move more slowly than the sun we must conclude, as clearly seen in this picture, that the star A is lagging behind, whereas the star C is being overtaken by the sun. The distance to the star A will increase while the distance to C will decrease, and the light coming from two stars must show respectively the red and violet Doppler effect. For the stars F and H on the inner circle the situation will be reversed, and we must have a violet Doppler effect for F and a red one for H.

It is assumed that the phenomenon just described could be caused only by a circular motion of the stars, and the existence of that circular motion makes it possible for us not only to prove this assumption but also to estimate the radius of stellar orbits and the velocity of stellar motion. By collecting the observational material on the observed apparent motion of stars all over the sky, Oort was able to prove that the expected phenomenon of red and violet Doppler effect really exists, thus proving beyond any doubt the rotation of the Galaxy.

In a similar way it may be demonstrated that the effect of galactic rotation will influence the apparent velocities of stars perpendicular to the line of vision. Although this component of velocity presents much larger difficulties for exact measurement (since even very great linear velocities of distant stars correspond to extremely small angular displacements on the celestial sphere) the effect was also observed by Oort and others.

The exact measurements of the Oort effect of stellar motion now make it possible to measure the orbits of stars and determine the period of rotation. Using this method of calculation it has been learned that the radius of the solar orbit having its center in Sagittarius is 30,000 light-years, that is, about two thirds the radius of the outermost orbit of the entire galactic system. The time necessary for the sun to move a complete circle around the galactic center is some 200 million years. It is a long time, of course, but

5. The difference between the frequency of sound or light waves when the wave source is in motion and when it is at rest (or in motion at a different rate) relative to the observer. Thus the pitch of a railway crossing bell is first higher, then lower, to a man in a passing train as his distance from the bell first diminishes and then increases. Similarly, light from a star rushing away from our galaxy produces a spectrum that exhibits a "red shift," or displacement toward the red end, in comparison with the spectrum the same star would produce if its distance from the earth were constant.

1274 · *George Gamow*

remembering that our stellar system is about 3 billion years old, we find that during its entire life our sun with its family of planets has made about 20 complete rotations. If, following the terminology of the terrestial year, we call the period of solar rotation "a solar year" we can say that our universe is only 20 years old. Indeed things happen slowly in the world of stars, and a solar year is quite a convenient unit for time measurements in the history of the universe!

Toward the Limits of the Unknown

As we have already mentioned above, our Galaxy is not the only isolated society of stars floating in the vast spaces of the universe. Telescope studies reveal the existence, far away in space, of many other giant groups of stars very similar to that to which our sun belongs. The nearest of them, the famous Andromeda Nebula, can be seen even by the naked eye. It appears to us as a small, faint, rather elongated nebulosity. * * * These nebulae possess a typical spiral structure; hence the name "spiral nebulae." There are many indications that our own stellar structure is similarly a spiral, but it is very difficult to determine the shape of a structure when you are inside it. As a matter of fact, our sun is most probably located at the very end of one of the spiral arms of the "Great Nebula of the Milky Way."

For a long time astronomers did not realize that the spiral nebulae are giant stellar systems similar to our Milky Way, and confused them with ordinary diffuse nebulae like that in the constellation of Orionis, which represent the large clouds of interstellar dust floating between the stars inside our Galaxy. Later, however, it was found that these foggy spiral-shaped objects are not fog at all, but are made of separate stars, which can be seen as tiny individual points when the largest magnifications are used. But they are so far away that no parallactic measurements can indicate their actual distance.

Thus it would seem at first that we had reached the limit of our means for measuring celestial distances. But no! In science, when we come to an insuperable difficulty the delay is usually only temporary; something always happens that permits us to go still farther. In this case a quite new "measuring rod" was found by the Harvard astronomer Harlow Shapley in the so-called pulsating stars or Cepheides.[6]

There are stars and stars. While most of them glow quietly in the sky, there are a few that constantly change their luminosity from bright to dim, and from dim to bright in regularly spaced cycles. The giant bodies of these stars pulsate as regularly as the heart beats,

6. So called after the star beta-Cepheus, in which the phenomenon of pulsation was first discovered [Gamow's note].

and along with this pulsation goes a periodic change of their brightness.[7] The larger the star, the longer is the period of its pulsation, just as it takes a long pendulum more time to complete its swing than a short one. The really small ones (that is, small as stars go) complete their period in the course of a few hours, whereas the real giants take years and years to go through one pulsation. Now, since the bigger stars are also the brighter, there is an apparent correlation between the period of stellar pulsation, and the average brightness of the star. This relation can be established by observing the Cepheides, which are sufficiently close to us so that their distance and consequently actual brightness may be directly measured.

If now you find a pulsating star that lies beyond the limit of parallactic measurements, all you have to do is to watch the star through the telescope and observe the time consumed by its pulsation period. Knowing the period, you will know its actual brightness, and comparing it with its apparent brightness you can tell at once how far away it is. This ingenious method was successfully used by Shapley for measuring particularly large distances within the Milky Way and has been most useful in estimating the general dimensions of our stellar system.

When Shapley applied the same method to measuring the distance to several pulsating stars found imbedded in the giant body of the Andromeda Nebula, he was in for a big surprise. The distance from the Earth to these stars, which, of course, must be the same as the distance to the Andromeda Nebula itself, turned out to be 680,000 light-years—that is, much larger than the estimated diameter of the stellar system of Milky Way. And the size of Andromeda Nebula came out only a little smaller than the size of our entire Galaxy. * * *

This discovery dealt the death blow to the earlier assumptions that the spiral nebulae are comparatively "small things" located within our Galaxy, and established them as independent galaxies of stars very similar to our own system, the Milky Way. No astronomer would now doubt that to an observer located on some small planet circling one of the billions of stars that form the Great Andromeda Nebula, our own Milky Way would look much as the Andromeda Nebula looks to us.

The further studies of these distant stellar societies, which we owe mostly to Dr. E. Hubble, the celebrated galaxy-gazer of Mt. Wilson Observatory, reveal a great many facts of great interest and importance. It was found first of all that the galaxies, which appear more numerous through a good telescope than the ordinary stars do to the naked eye, do not all have necessarily spiral form, but present

---

7. One must not confuse these pulsating stars with the so-called eclipsing variables, which actually represent systems of two stars rotating around each other and periodically eclipsing one another [Gamow's note].

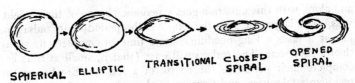

SPHERICAL   ELLIPTIC   TRANSITIONAL   CLOSED SPIRAL   OPENED SPIRAL

FIGURE 4

a great variety of different types. There are *spherical galaxies*, which look like regular discs with diffused boundaries; there are *elliptical galaxies* with different degrees of elongation. The spirals themselves differ from each other by the "tightness with which they are wound up." There are also very peculiar shapes known as "barred spirals."

It is a fact of extreme importance that all the varieties of the observed galactic shapes can be arranged in a regular sequence (Figure 4), which presumably corresponds to different stages of the evolution of these giant stellar societies.

Although we are still far from understanding the details of galactic evolution, it seems very probable that it is due to the process of progressive contraction. It is well known that when a slowly rotating spherical body of gas undergoes a steady contraction, its speed of rotation increases, and its shape becomes that of a flattened ellipsoid. At a certain stage of contraction, when the ratio of the polar radius to the equatorial radius becomes equal to 7/10, the rotating body must assume a lenticular shape with a sharp edge running along its equator. Still further contraction keeps this lenticular shape intact, but the gases forming the rotating body begin to flow away into surrounding space all along the sharp equatorial edge, leading to the formation of a thin gaseous veil in the equatorial plane.

All the above statements have been proved mathematically by the celebrated English physicist and astronomer Sir James Jeans for a rotating gas sphere, but they can also be applied without any alterations to the giant stellar clouds that we call galaxies. In fact, we can consider such a clustering of the billions of stars as a flock of gas in which the role of molecules is now played by individual stars.

In comparing the theoretical calculations of Jeans with Hubble's empirical classification of galaxies, we find that these giant stellar societies follow exactly the course or evolution described by the theory. In particular we find that the most elongated shape of elliptic nebulae is that corresponding to the radius-ratio of 7/10 (E7), and that it is the first case in which we notice a sharp equatorial edge. The spirals that develop in the later stages of evolution are apparently formed from the material ejected by the rapid rotation, although up to the present we do not have a completely satisfactory explanation of why and how these spiral forms are formed and what causes the difference between the simple and the barred spirals.

Much is still to be learned from further study of the structure, motion, and stellar content in the different parts of galactic societies of stars. A very interesting result was, for example, obtained a couple of years ago by a Mt. Wilson astronomer, W. Baade, who was able to show that, whereas the central bodies (nuclei) of spiral nebulae are formed by the same type of stars as the spherical and elliptic galaxies, the arms themselves show a rather different type of stellar population. This "spiral-arm" type of stellar population differs from the population of the central region by the presence of very hot and bright stars, the so-called "Blue Giants," which are absent in the central regions as well as in the spherical and elliptic galaxies. Since, as we shall see later, the Blue Giants most probably represent the most recently formed stars, it is reasonable to assume that the spiral arms are so to speak the breeding grounds for new stellar populations. One could imagine that a large part of the material ejected from the equatorial bulge of a contracting elliptic galaxy is formed by primordial gases that come out into the cold intergalactic space and condense into the separate large lumps of matter, which through subsequent contraction become very hot and very bright. * * * Now we must consider generally the distribution of separate galaxies through the vastness of the universe.

We must state here, first of all that the method of distance measurements based on pulsating stars, though giving excellent results when applied to quite a number of galaxies that lie in the neighborhood of our Milky Way, fails when we proceed into the depth of space, since we soon reach distances at which no separate stars may be distinguished and the galaxies look like tiny elongated nebulosities even through the strongest telescopes. Beyond this point we can rely only on the visible size, since it is fairly well established that, unlike stars, all galaxies of a given type are of about the same size. If you know that all people are of the same height, that there are no giants or dwarfs, you can always say how far a man is from you by observing his apparent size.

Using this method for estimating distances in the far-out-flung realm of galaxies, Dr. Hubble was able to prove that the galaxies are scattered more or less uniformly through space as far as the eye (fortified by the most highly powered telescope) can see. We say "more or less" because there are many cases in which the galaxies cluster in large groups containing sometimes many thousands of members, in the same way as the separate stars cluster in galaxies.

Our own galaxy, Milky Way, is apparently one member of a comparatively small group of galaxies numbering in its membership three spirals (including ours, and the Andromeda Nebula) and six elliptical and four irregular nebulae (two of which are Magellanic clouds).

However, save for such occasional clustering, the galaxies, as seen through the 100-inch telescope of the Mt. Wilson Observatory, are scattered rather uniformly through space up to a distance of 500,000,-000 light-years. The average distance between two neighboring galaxies is about 2,000,000 light-years, and the visible horizons of the universe contain about 100,000,000 individual stellar worlds!

In our old simile, in which the Empire State building was symbolized by a bacterium, the Earth by a pea, and the sun by a pumpkin, the galaxies might be represented by giant swarms of many billions of pumpkins distributed roughly within the orbit of Jupiter, separate pumpkin clusters being scattered through a spherical volume with a radius only a little smaller than the distance to the nearest star. Yes, it is very difficult to find the proper scale in cosmic distances, so that even when we scale the Earth to a pea, the size of the known universe comes out in astronomical numbers! * * *

We are now prepared to answer the fundamental question concerning the size of our universe. *Shall we consider the universe as extending into infinity and conclude that bigger and better telescopes will always reveal to the inquiring eye of an astronomer new and hitherto unexplored regions of space, or must we believe, on the contrary, that the universe occupies some very big but nevertheless finite volume, and is, at least in principle, explorable down to the last star?*

When we speak of the possibility that our universe is of "finite size," we do not mean, of couse, that somewhere at a distance of several billion light-years the explorer of space will encounter a blank wall on which is posted the notice "No trespassing."

In fact, we have seen that *space can be finite without being necessarily limited by a boundary.* It can simply curve around and "close on itself," so that a hypothetical space explorer, trying to steer his rocket ship as straight as possible will describe a geodesic line in space and come back to the point from which he started.

The situation would be, of course, quite similar to an ancient Greek explorer who travels west from his native city of Athens, and after a long journey, finds himself entering the eastern gates of the city.

And just as the curvature of the Earth's surface can be established without a trip around the world, simply by studying the geometry of only a comparatively small part of it, the question about the curvature of the three-dimensional space of the universe can be answered by similar measurements made within the range of available telescopes. One must distinguish between two kinds of curvatures: the positive one corresponding to the closed space of finite volume, and the negative one corresponding to the saddle-like opened infinite space (*cf.* Figure 5). The difference between these two types of space lies in the fact that, whereas in the *closed space* the number of uniformly scattered objects falling within a given

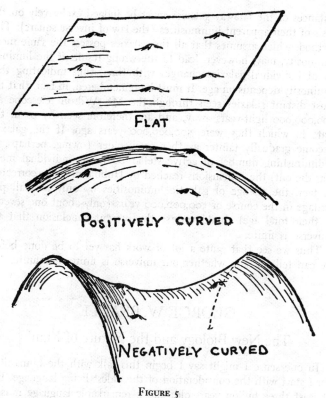

FLAT

POSITIVELY CURVED

NEGATIVELY CURVED

FIGURE 5

distance from the observer increases more slowly than the cube of that distance, the opposite is true in *opened space*.

In our universe the role of the "uniformly scattered objects" is played by the separate galaxies, so that all we have to do in order to solve the problem of the universal curvature is to count the number of individual galaxies located at different distances from us.

Such counting actually has been accomplished by Dr. Hubble, who has discovered that the *number of galaxies seems to increase somewhat more slowly than the cube of the distance, thus indicating the positive curvature and the finiteness of space*. It must be noticed, however, that the effect observed by Hubble is very small, becoming noticeable only near the very limit of the distance that it is possible to observe through the 100-inch Mt. Wilson telescope, and we can hope that the observations with the new 200-inch reflector on Palomar Mountain may throw some more light on this important problem.

Another point contributing to the uncertainty of the final answer concerning the finiteness of the universe lies in the fact that the distances of the faraway galaxies must be judged exclusively on the basis of their apparent luminosities (the law of inverse square). This method, which assumes that all the galaxies possess the same mean luminosity, may, however, lead to the wrong results if the luminosity of individual galaxies changes with time, thus indicating that luminosity depends on age. It must be remembered, in fact, that the most distant galaxies seen through the Mt. Wilson telescope are 500,000,000 light-years away, and are therefore seen by us in the state in which they were 500,000,000 years ago. If the galaxies become gradually fainter as they grow older (owing, perhaps, to a diminishing number of active stellar bodies as individual members die out) the conclusions reached by Hubble must be corrected. In fact, the change of galactic luminosities by only a small percentage in the course of 500,000,000 years (only about one seventh of their total age) would reverse the present conclusion that the universe is finite.

Thus we see that quite a lot of work has yet to be done before we can tell for sure whether our universe is finite or infinite.

GEORGE W. BEADLE

The New Biology and the Nature of Man[1]

In one sense I might say I begin this talk with the humanities, for I start with the consideration of the oldest living language. It is at least three billion years old, and a remarkable language it is. It exists only in written form, that is "written" in submicroscopic molecular code. It is remarkably simple, for it has only four letters. Each of these is one two hundred millionth of an inch across. Each is made of but five kinds of atoms—carbon, hydrogen, oxygen, nitrogen, and phosphorus—and there are only about thirty-two atoms in each letter. All the words in this language appear to be three-letter words, and there are only sixty-four of them possible. This beats Basic English by a very wide margin. Most remarkable of all, this language is the only language known to have a built-in capacity for copying itself. There is no need for secretaries, typewriters, or printing presses.

It is a language in which the specifications for all living organisms, from viruses to man, that have ever existed on earth are written.

The number of letters in the specifications for these organisms varies from five thousand letters for the specifications of the simplest

1. The Dewey F. Fagerburg Memorial Lecture, University of Michigan, 1963. The text is based on a transcript of the lecture, which was delivered informally from notes.

known virus to five billion for the specifications of man. That's over a million-fold difference. What is the name of this language? I call it DNAese, because it is contained in deoxyribose nucleic acid molecules, which we call DNA.

DNA-Deoxyribonucleic Acid

How do we know that DNA carries the specifications of the kind I have said? The answer is very simple. In viruses—some viruses at least—one can strip away all of the components except the DNA, infect a living cell of the proper kind with the DNA and reconstruct another generation of viruses. This means that whatever specifies the unique properties of the virus must be carried in the DNA. The same is true with bacteria. It is possible to take DNA molecules out of a bacterium in the purest possible form, transfer these molecules to another bacterium and alter the genetic specifications that say what the recipient bacterium is going to do. Now, viruses are known to have genes that are transmitted in essentially the same way that our genes are transmitted. Since only DNA is transmitted from generation to generation, the genes must be made of this substance. We don't know this directly in our own case, but we believe it is so in us too.

What do we want to know about the language in which these specifications are written? First of all, we would like to know how we get these specifications and how we transmit them to the next generation; for this is how we receive and transmit our biological inheritances. We want to know how these specifications are written. We want to know how they are copied. We want to know how they are translated—how it is that from these specifications we can build ourselves from a single, almost microscopic, egg cell. We want to know why it is that each of us is unique. No one of us is exactly like any other person on earth—unless we happen to be a set of identical twins or triplets. Although we have common ancestors, we differ in our specifications. How did the specifications come to differ?

Classical Genetics

First, let us talk about how we receive the specifications and how we transmit them. This you recognize immediately as classical genetics. I assume you know all about it, but I shall review it very quickly using a characteristic in man to illustrate the point. In each of us there is an enzyme, a protein, that catalyzes one of the reactions by which melanin pigment is made. Melanin is the pigment that gives color to our hair and our eyes; it is melanin in the skin that responds to light and results in our tanning. Individuals who lack this pigment are called albinos. They are comparable to pink-eyed white rabbits in that they are unable to make melanin.

Individuals unable to make melanin differ from those who make it by a single unit of their set of specifications, a unit called a gene. This particular gene comes in two forms—the form that says make a proper tyrosinase enzyme necessary for melanin synthesis and a defective form that specifies an enzyme unable to catalyze this reaction. Each of us has two representatives of this message, one from the mother, one from the father. Since the message comes in two forms, there are four possible kinds of individuals. From the mother we can get a message that says, "I can now make melanin." From the father we can get one that says the same thing. Then we are pure for the message that says, "I can now make melanin." Or from the mother we can get a positive message and from the father a negative message that says, "I can not make melanin." Because the positive message is dominant and the defective message is recessive, an individual of this kind makes melanin. Another individual may get the defective form from the mother, the active form from the father, that is, have one of each. He will also be able to make melanin. It doesn't make any difference from which parent you get the positive message. But if you get the defective message from both parents, you are pure for the message that says, "I can not make melanin." You will be an albino.

When we pass these messages on to the next generation, one or the other goes into each of the egg or sperm cells—either the one from the mother or the one from the father. If you happen to have the capability of sending both kinds of messages, half of your children will get one form, half will get the other form. And if both parents carry both messages, then it is obvious that those who get the defective form from both parents will be albinos.

I've now given you a short course in classical genetics. Essentially, that's all there is to it, except that there are perhaps a hundred thousand other similar messages that carry their parts of the total set of instructions. If you understand how one works, you understand them all. In general biology courses and courses in genetics, we make it more complicated because we don't want to be responsible for technological unemployment of geneticists. Actually, genetics is a bit more complex if you consider all of the ramifications. For example, genes come in chromosomes; and there are many messages per chromosome. They don't always stay in the same chromosome, but can cross over into the partner or homologous chromosome.

How DNA Carries Information

Now you know how hereditary messages are transmitted. Let's now consider how they are written. As I said, they are written in four "letters," which, of course, are not really letters like those of our alphabet. They are sub-units of molecules—DNA molecules.

We can represent these four different sub-units of a DNA molecule by letters of our alphabet. To illustrate, I shall use the four letters —N, E, A, T—to represent the four molecular sub-units. These units, made of five different atoms, average about thirty-two atoms per unit. Each of these units, or "letters" is about one ten-millionth of an inch across. They differ from one another in the arrangement of the atoms, not in the number of different atoms.

These DNA "letters" are arranged in long chains. One of the characteristics of this language or code is that there appears to be no spacing or punctuation between "words." It's very much simpler than ours. If I add extra letters to the sequence NEAT so that it reads NEATTNETAATNE—I have the beginning of a long message not unlike a DNA message.

In the nucleus of the egg cell from which we started development there are five billion of these "letters." If you were to take all the molecules containing the five billion units and string them end to end, they would form a chain about five feet long. But the molecules are so small in diameter that you would be unable to see the chain with the highest powered light microscope possible. The molecules can just barely be resolved with the most modern electron microscope.

How much information is contained in these five feet of DNA— in five billion units? Since there are only four letters in DNAese, to translate from it into a message of our own language would require some kind of a coding system. One system that we might use would be to have each successive three-letter unit of DNAese stand for a letter of our alphabet. If we transform the language, using the four letters NEAT, into a twenty-six letter language we might say NEA equals A, NAE equals B, and so on, until we have all twenty-six letters of the alphabet. In such a code we could take the five billion DNA "letters" of the nucleus of the egg, translate them into letters of the alphabet and then spell out a message. Since we have five billion units, and it takes three of them to make a letter of the alphabet, we'd end up with about one billion, seven hundred thousand three-letter messages or letters of our alphabet. That many letters of the alphabet will make three hundred thousand words, five letters to a word. If we write our messages in all these letters in words which average five letters, we will get sixty thousand printed pages. If we say there are six hundred pages per average volume, we will have a thousand volumes. In other words, the information in the tiny microscopic nucleus, in this sub-microscopic thread five feet long, will be the equivalent of a thousand ordinary library volumes. That is a set of genetic specifications for making one of us out of an egg cell, given a proper environment, proper raw materials, and so on.

Let's express the size of this five foot thread in another way. If it were wound back and forth, one layer thick, on the head of a pin, it would cover only about one-half of one percent of the head of the pin. That means that you could get a thousand volumes of information on half of one per cent of the head of the pin. If you covered the whole head of the pin, you would have the equivalent of two hundred thousand volumes in a monolayer so thin that you could not detect it by anything less than an electron microscope. That's pretty good miniaturization. Let's go one step further. If we took all the DNA code out of all the eggs that gave rise to all the people on earth today—say three billion people—and wound it back and forth like cordwood, how large a stack would it make? It would make a cube an eighth of an inch on a side! Since each person requires a thousand volumes to specify him genetically, this little cube an eighth of an inch on a side is the equivalent of three trillion volumes of library work. In all history since the invention of the printing press, there have been printed only about 50 million different books. In this small cube we can put the equivalent of three trillion volumes—that's 60,000 times as much as is contained in all the books ever published.

The Molecular Basis of Reproduction

The next question I'd like to ask is, how does this message copy itself? This is an interesting and important question because we know that every living system has somehow to send its specifications on to the next generation. In our case, from the time we get the specifications in the egg cell until the time we send them on to the next generation, we must copy the thousand volumes of information with every cell division. The number of cell divisions from the egg of one generation with which we started to the egg or the sperm which we send on to the next generation will vary with age and sex. It may be ten, twenty, thirty or more successive cell divisions. This means that you must copy your specifications ten, twenty, thirty or more times during your lifetime. Remember that's the equivalent of a thousand volumes with each copying. And, of course, you must not make many mistakes or the next generation won't come out right. This is the equivalent of sitting down with a typewriter and typing a thousand volumes of information and then retyping it ten to thirty times in succession. That's a lot of typing! We now know how this is done because of the work of a large number of people, climaxed by the discovery by James Dewey Watson and Francis H. C. Crick of the structure of the molecules that carry these four kinds of units. They discovered that these molecules are not simple single chains but are double parallel chains that are arranged in such a way that they carry complementary information.

Now what does this mean? Opposite every T there will be an A,

and conversely, the letter A will always have opposite it a T. The N will have opposite it an E, and the E will have opposite it an N. This means that if you know the order of the units in a four-letter segment you will know the order of its complementary chain. If I have the message TANE, I will have the double message T-A-N-E-.
Ä-T̈-Ë-N̈-

This means that this molecule has a very simple way of copying itself. It simply separates into the two single chains. Then each chain serves as a model or a template against which the individual units of new chains line up in the right order. If the molecules come apart, the TANE chain picks up the units that make an ATEN chain, and the ATEN chain picks up the units that make a TANE chain, and you have two pairs. It's as if I started with paired hands, fingers tip-to-tip; took them apart; and imagined that the left hand were to make a right hand, and the right hand were to make a left hand from separate fingers. DNA and closely related molecules are the only ones known to science that can carry out this simple kind of replication.

How do these units know how to tell their complements? How does an A know that it must pick up a T? How does an N know that it must pick up an E? The separate units are floating around in a cell in which DNA molecules are replicating. When the N in the chain comes to an E, they will fit and stick together through specific hydrogen bonding. But if the N tries to pick up any of the other three units, N, A, or T, they will not fit and, therefore, not remain in place. One chain automatically picks up the units to make a new chain. These units are free in your cells right now. And your DNA molecules in some cells are coming apart and making new complements in this simple way.

The Test of DNA Replication

Do they really replicate in this way? It's a beautiful hypothesis, so beautiful that we're almost tempted to believe it without doing any testing. But nature has a way of fooling scientists. It often finds ways of working that scientists don't think of. So obviously it's important to test this hypothesis. One way is to label DNA molecules with stable isotopes. There are eight nitrogen atoms in a typical pair of units. The total molecular weight of the pair is about 700. If we were to substitute nitrogen-15 for the normal nitrogen-14 in one pair, the molecular weight would be increased by eight. Eight in 700 is about one per cent. This would not change the size of the molecule. Therefore, it would be more dense. Now if one could find a way to separate more dense molecules from less dense ones, it would be easy to test the hypothesis. As a matter of fact, three investigators, Mathew Meselson, Frank Stahl and Jerome Vinograd, a few years ago figured out a very simple way to do this. It is very much like the way a farmer separates wheat from chaff by shaking it up in a bucket of water. The chaff floats and the wheat settles and they are, therefore, easily separated. You can do that with DNA molecules. You can separate heavy ones from light ones. It's a little more complicated than that. For one thing, it requires a $25,000 analytical ultracentrifuge instead of a bucket of water, but these days this is no problem because universities like The University of Michigan have them around.

With this method, it was possible for Meselson and Stahl to label the DNA units with nitrogen-15 and make them heavy, then to let them undergo one division in a medium in which only light nitrogen was present. The unit with heavy nitrogen comes apart and picks up light nitrogen. Of the two chains that start heavy, each will take a light partner. The new chains ought to be hybrid and intermediate in density. They are. In the next generation, the hybrid chain, the one with both heavy and light nitrogen, ought to separate into light and heavy chains. Each of these will pick up a light nitrogen partner. There will then be one hybrid chain and one completely light chain. And that, too, is found to be the case. In the next generation it is easy to figure out what happens. It does.

The Synthesis of DNA

An even more dramatic way of testing the hypothesis was used by Arthur Kornberg and his associates, now at Stanford University. They set out to see if they could make DNA molecules copy themselves in a test tube. Everyone said it was impossible—that it was so elaborate a process that no biochemist could hope to make it happen in a test tube. Kornberg set out to do it and he found out, in fact, that it was quite simple. If you take the four DNA units with two extra phosphate groups on each, under the right conditions in a test tube, and drop in molecules of double DNA, the DNA will be replicated. It will make copies of itself. Single DNA chains are even more effective in the system. There are ways of telling that the copies are like the added primer.

Even more remarkable, one can make DNA molecules without having a model. One of these is a DNA that has A-T-A-T-A-T units in one chain and the complement in the other chain, T-A-T-A-T-A. If you use such an artificial DNA as a primer, it will be copied and the copy will be like the primer. Several of Kornberg's associates, using a somewhat different approach, discovered a way of making artificial double DNA molecules in which all the units in one chain are E and all the units in the other chain are N. They were then able to use this as a primer and show that in replication more molecules like the spontaneously formed N-N-N-N are made. Ë-Ë-Ë-Ë

All of this makes if difficult to believe that the hypothesis is incorrect.

The Translation of DNA

We now come to another interesting part of the story. How do we use a simple language like this—four letters, three-letter words, and only sixty-four words—to build an organism as complex as ourselves? It sounds fantastic. If you think a bit; you see it isn't. Any set of specifications that we can write in our twenty-six letter language can be written in a language with only two symbols, dots and dashes. As a matter of fact, computer language has only two symbols, and everyone knows that with it we can write any kind of information we want. It's true that in a computer you can't normally do it with such nice short words. These nice short three-letter words are what make the language of genetics so simple and elegant.

To know how we use this information to make us, we have to understand how we translate this language. Human beings are enormously complex, being made of many thousands of kinds of molecules. The DNA specifications have somehow to say, "Make all these molecules at the right time and in the right place and put them all together in the right way." To do this, one of the first steps is the translation of the four-letter language with its three-letter words into another kind of language, perhaps the second oldest living language on earth. It may have come into existence somewhat less than three billion years ago, that is, later than DNA. Of course, no one was around to say exactly when. So mine is only a rough guess. This language is called *Proteinese* because it is written in the form of protein molecules. These are long molecules somewhat like DNA molecules in being built of sub-units. But there are twenty sub-units in protein instead of four as in DNA. These sub-units are amino acids. A typical amino acid has four or five kinds of atoms—carbon, hydrogen, oxygen, nitrogen, and, in some, sulphur. Note that they never contain phosphorus. These atoms are arranged in twenty specific ways to make the twenty units out of which we make proteins. We have some ten thousand, twenty thousand, perhaps a hundred thousand kinds of protein. These do many kinds of things. There are structural proteins. Hair is largely protein. So are fingernails. Hemoglobin, the pigment in red blood cells, is protein. All of the enzymes either are protein or contain protein. Enzymes speed up or catalyze almost all of the reactions that go on in a living system.

Let us now look at the characteristics of Proteinese as compared with DNAese. First of all, it differs in that there are twenty letters instead of four. How about the words? The words in protein are not all of the same length. They can range from perhaps hundred-letter words to thousand-letter words. How many kinds of words can you write in protein? Remember, you can write only sixty-four in DNA. But using the information in the sixty-four words of DNA, you can write twenty kinds of words that, when used in a thousand-word message, will specify a protein a thousand units long. The first unit can be any one of twenty, the second unit can be any one of twenty. So it would be twenty times twenty times twenty a thousand times. That is a number so large that for all practical purposes it is inconceivable. It is much, much larger than the total number of elementary atomic particles (electrons, protons, neutrons, and so forth) in the entire known universe. It is literally impossible to exhaust the number of combinations of words that you can make with twenty units, if they can be put together up to a thousand units long and in any proportion and in any sequence. This language, therefore, is essentially unlimited in the number of possible words.

Protein Synthesis

How do we make protein molecules with DNA units? This actually seems to be very simple. To do so we make use of another language, but fortunately it is only a dialect of the first one. How are the four letters of DNA translated into protein? If we write the four letters of DNA—N-E-A-T—we can write the complement of the DNA molecule in the dialect called RNA—ribonucleic acid. The complement of N will be an E which is almost like a DNA E. So we call it E'. E will have the complement, N'; A, the complement T'; T, the complement A'. Now, remember the letters form three-letter words. So, we have a word E'N'T' that specifies an amino acid, say amino acid number one. We can have another word N'T'A' that specifies amino acid number two.

How is an amino acid related to a DNA word? It happens in the following way. The DNA code is in the nucleus of the cell. RNA that is complementary to this code is constructed. It moves from the nucleus to the cytoplasm and there enters small microscopic structures called ribosomes. This information-carrying RNA that specifies a protein goes into the ribosome and there serves as a template to collect amino acids in the right sequence. Each of the twenty amino acids is tagged with a small segment of RNA, called transfer RNA, consisting of about eighty units. There are twenty transfer RNA's, corresponding to the twenty amino acids. Each carries a three-letter coding segment complementary to a three-letter coding segment on the template RNA. An enzymatically catalyzed reaction joins the amino acids together to form a protein molecule. This then leaves the ribosome. This is the way we make hemoglobin. You are doing this right now in your red blood cells. Interestingly enough, this process of translating the information from DNA to RNA can be done in a test tube. And the process of transferring the information from RNA to protein can also be carried out in a test tube. It is now possible to make test tube hemoglobin by following these steps. This makes it pretty clear that this is the right interpretation. That all this can be accomplished in a test tube is a remarkable achievement of modern molecular biology.

Enzymes

For what are proteins used? Let's take the protein that catalyzes the reaction by which the amino acid phenylalanine is oxidized. One oxygen atom, added in a particular place, makes the related amino acid tyrosine. We must have both of these amino acids. If we have an enzyme that says we can make tyrosine from phenylalanine, we don't have to have tyrosine in our diets. We can make the tyrosine by this reaction which is catalyzed by an enzyme which was made from a piece of DNA which we call a gene. Some people have a defective form of this enzyme and cannot catalyze the reaction by which tyrosine is made from phenylalanine. If such persons are fed normal amounts of phenylalanine, as in a usual diet, they cannot convert the phenylalanine into tyrosine. They use some of the phenylalanine for protein but the rest of it, the surplus, accumulates and indirectly posions the central nervous system. Such individuals are feeble-minded. This genetic disease is called phenylketonuria, and in English one describes it as feeble-mindedness due to inability to oxidize phenylalanine to tyrosine because of the absence of a protein. The gene that says the same thing in DNAese says so in a "sentence" of perhaps four hundred or a thousand "words."

Genetic Disease

We know of several hundred genetic diseases in man. Phenylketonuria is an interesting one. If diagnosed early, which is simple, and if an artificial diet is provided in which there is only enough phenylalanine to make protein and no excess, and if tyrosine is provided in the right amount, the individual becomes normal. The result is circumvention of a genetic disease by modern medicine. But note that this is accomplished without correcting the fundamental defect in the specifications. Such a "cured" individual will transmit defective specifications to the next generation. This creates a eugenic problem that someday society may have to be concerned about. It isn't quite as bad as it sounds because the build-up of this defect as a result of this achievement of medical science is very slow indeed. It would take many, many generations and many thousands of years before this particular disease would become frequent. On the other hand, there may someday be many genetic diseases similarly circumvented. If so, we will sooner or later have to think about what to do about them. I point out, however, that this isn't a question for science alone. It is a question for society, including scientists. One solution is simple. Persons who are of this type might be persuaded to adopt children instead of having them in a natural way. There would then be no build-up. But as I say, it is not a scientific question, and I am no more competent to advise than is any other informed citizen.

Cytoplasm

I am sure many of you are saying life can't be this simple. Of course it isn't. We have DNA specifications in the nucleus of the cell that are, so to speak, the blueprints or the recipes for making people out of egg cells. But a lot more is essential too. In addition to these specifications the egg also contains cytoplasm. And that too is specific. It must be human cytoplasm. You can't put the nucleus of a human egg into the cytoplasm of a monkey egg and get an organism. It won't work. Of course we don't do this experiment with monkeys and people, but we can do it with two kinds of frogs. We can find that the nucleus has to be in its own species of cytoplasm. Therefore, the cytoplasm is species-specific. We don't know too much about this as yet. We must leave some problems for the Ph.D. candidates of the next generation.

In addition to cytoplasm one must have food—raw materials—to make an organism as complex as one of us from an egg cell, given the proper specifications. This food must be of the right kind, in the right amount, in the right proportions and available at the right time. If these conditions are not all fulfilled, the result is nutritional disease. Each of us has consumed ten, twenty or thirty tons of food up to now, depending on age and appetite. We have used that food to make us, using a set of specifications, tearing it down with enzymes, using the pieces to construct one of us. If the specifications aren't right, or if the raw material isn't right, the individual doesn't come out right.

Mutation

Let us now turn to the last question. How do differences arise? Why am I different from other people? I have different specifications, but how did they come to be different? The answer is pretty simple. Sometimes DNA molecules make a mistake in being copied. An N unit doesn't always pick up an E unit because the hydrogen atoms that must be in the right place to make them stick together by hydrogen bonding have a way of being in alternate positions occasionally. If the hydrogen atoms happen to be in the wrong place exactly when the molecule is going to pick up its partner, the N may pick up an A instead of an E. Let's say that we have a three-letter word, TEN. The complement to that would be ANE. Now let's say that the E picks up a T instead of what it should pick up, an N. Then the complement would be ATE. Now when this ATE replicates in the next round, it is not likely to make a mistake.

The complement of ATE is TAN. By substituting an A for an E, we have now substituted the word TAN for the word TEN. That is what we call a mutation. TAN will not stand for the same amino acid as does TEN. If this change occurs in the message, there will be a wrong amino acid in the protein at a particular place. This type of change is known to happen. For example, there are forms of hemoglobin that differ by one amino acid. Sickle cell hemoglobin, which is an unfavorable kind of hemoglobin to have, differs by one amino acid at a particular place because one symbol in the DNA code was miscopied at some time in the past. This is not the only way a mutation can occur. A letter can be left out, an extra one inserted or letters can be transposed. Or there can be more complex changes like those that occur in typewriting when one gets a hand on the wrong row of keys. Sometimes an entire "chapter" may be present as an "extra." Thus in mongolian idiocy there is present in each cell an entire extra chromosome.

Breaking the Code

How do we know that the DNA words designating amino acids are three-letter words? How do scientists go about discovering this? How do we know what order of the DNA unit stands for what amino acid? That is, what is the coding relation between DNA and protein? This is like trying to decipher any code. What you do is find the equivalent of a Rosetta stone on which you have both messages written. Then, you can find out how one is related to the other. We have, so to speak, found the Rosetta stone of life that relates DNA to protein. This was done in a most interesting way. Professor Severo Ochoa at New York University found that he could make RNA molecules artificially by putting the RNA units together in a test tube under the right conditions. If you put in all A' units, you will get an RNA that has only A' in it. If you put in all T', you will get RNA made only of T'. If you put in T' and A', you will get an RNA that has T' and A'. If the T' and A' are in equal proportions, they will go together at random in equal proportions. If you put in all four DNA units, T'A'N'E', they too will go together at random.

A few years ago Marshall W. Nirenberg and J. Heinrich Matthaei of the National Institutes of Health thought of putting into the test tube system, in which they did the translation of RNA to protein, artificial RNA. When they used an artificial RNA containing only T' units, lo and behold, it did direct synthesis of a very peculiar and previously unknown protein—namely a protein made of only the one amino acid phenylalanine. This is not really a protein but a protein-like polymer called polyphenylalanine. This was a clue to breaking the code. The units had to make sense or they couldn't have made that particular protein. Whatever the coding ratio is, whether it is two-letter words, three-letter words, four-letter words, the amino acid is always the same—phenylalanine. This told Nirenberg and Matthaei that if the words are indeed three-letter words, the coding word for the amino acid phenylalanine must be T'T'T'.[2]

Now you can make a synthetic RNA in which you have T' and A'. If you put in a ratio of five times as many T' as A' and get a random association, it is easy to calculate the relative frequencies of the various possible three-letter words. Words with two T's and one A' will be relatively frequent. So will T'T'T' words. It turns out that two of the amino acids that are incorporated in the protein when this experiment is made are phenylalanine and tyrosine. The coding word for tyrosine is therefore probably two T's and an A'. But there are three possible ways to arrange the word. You put the A' first, second, or last. How do you know which way is the right way? That turns out to be simple too. Professor Ochoa found that if he started out with the one letter A', and then built up an RNA using all T' for the remaining units he got an RNA that had an A' at the end and all the rest T's, that is, ... T'T'T'T'T'T'T'A'. RNA gets synthesized from right to left; the protein gets built against it from left to right. We know this from radioactive tracers. When Ochoa used this RNA, he got a protein containing, for the most part, phenylalanine, as he should. Remember three T's equal phenylalanine. But, there was a small amount of tyrosine incorporated. It was always at the final end of the chain to be made. Obviously, if tyrosine is two T's and an A', it has to be in the arrangement, T'T'A'. By doing other experiments of this kind, it is possible to work out other code words. This is what workers have done and are doing. As a result, we know code words for nineteen of the amino acids. If you know the order of the amino acids in a protein, such as Frederick Sanger worked out for insulin, you can now come pretty close to reading the DNA message that spelled the amino acid sequence in the protein. I've simplified the story considerably but that is approximately where we are now.

It turns out that there are sixty-four words possible in DNAese, and it only takes twenty to encode the twenty amino acids. What are the other forty-four doing? For one thing, there is pretty clearly some degeneracy in the code. That means there are two or more words that encode the same amino acid. Then too, some of the words are probably used as spacers, to indicate where one protein stops and another begins. Perhaps one tells where to start reading the message. With no spaces, there must be a fixed starting point for reading the message. This kind of code is called a non-overlapping code because the letters must be read three at a time starting at a predetermined

2. The usual symbols for DNA nucle- otides are A, T, C, and G. For RNA, A, U, C, and G. I've used the ones I have so as to be able to make 20 three-letter English words [Beadle's note].

point. And it is a degenerate code because one word might stand for the same amino acid as does another word.

Three Letter Words

Now we've answered all the questions except one. How do we know that the words in this language are three-letter words? That turns out to be very simple too. And it's done this way. I have a message ANNNANATETANANTANTATETNTNAEANT, which makes some sense in terms of our own language. It says ANN NAN ATE TAN ANT etc. Crick and some of his associates took a DNA message like this that they knew made sense. Then they made mutations near the left end by adding or substracting units. If they took one letter out, the message no longer made sense. If I take the first letter away from the example given, it now reads NNN ANA TET, etc. Taking one letter out shifted the reading frame by one and scrambled the message. If you take out one letter and then put in another letter, the one you put in will compensate for the one you took out, and the message will make sense at one end, e.g., TNN NAN ATE TAN ANT etc. If you take out two letters, the message won't make sense, e.g., NNA NAT ETA etc. But, if you take out three letters, most of the message will make sense, e.g., NAN ATE TAN ANT etc. Or if you put three in the left end, the right end will retain its sense. But if you take out two or put in two, take out one or put in one, take out four or put in four, the message will not make sense. The only simple way to explain such results is to assume that the language consists of three-letter words.

Evolution

Let us now talk about evolution. These changes—taking out letters, putting them in, and rearranging them—are believed to be the basis of all organic evolution from the beginning of life on earth to the origin of man. We are of course the product of evolution and the result of many, many millions of mutations which had selective advantages. These mutations have given rise to an evolutionary sequence going back from us, if you call man the ultimate form of evolution at the present time, to simpler and simpler forms to something akin to the simplest viruses. Instead of the five billion units in the DNA of humans, the smallest viruses have only a few thousand units of DNA or RNA in their genetic specifications.

Before viruses, it is presumed that there arose spontaneously on earth in the pre-life stages, DNA or RNA molecules that were able to copy themselves. Some presumably collected protein coats that provided protection. This gave them a selective advantage. The units, out of which DNA was made, presumably came from simpler organic molecules by chemical reactions which are inevitable under favorable conditions. They, in turn, came from simpler molecules that were inorganic. These, in turn, came from the elements. We now know that all the elements are capable of coming from hydrogen by nuclear interactions that nuclear physicists know about. Hydrogen fuses to give beryllium-8, beryllium-8 captures helium nuclei and becomes carbon. And so it goes. All of this is known in principle now. If this is correct, it means that from the first postulated primitive universe of hydrogen all of evolution is possible up to man.

That sounds very mechanistic, I know. At this point, I should say it really isn't any more remarkable that there should have been created a universe of hydrogren capable of evolving into man than that there should have been created a universe already containing man. One course is as remarkable as the other. In other words the hypothesis I have advanced does not change the problem of ultimate creation one iota. In that sense, it has nothing to do with religion, which is an entirely separate matter.

Cultural Inheritance

As far as we know, we differ from all other organisms on earth in a quantitative way only. Maybe there is something we do not yet know that makes us qualitatively different from other organisms. If so, we do not know what it is. Quantitatively, however, we have a great deal that other organisms do not have. For one thing, we have a more highly developed nervous system than any other organism on earth. As a result, we have better memories. We are able to reason. Maybe other animals can reason too, but we are much better at it, there is no doubt about that. We have been able to develop a method of communication by speech. Other organisms have primitive ways of communicating by sound, but they do not have speech in the sense in which we have it. We have learned to write down messages that are equivalent to DNA. We have developed through speech and writing very effective methods of communication. These methods of communication and the ability to reason, to store information in our nervous systems, to take it out, to rearrange it, and to communicate it, make possible the evolution of a cultural inheritance, which we alone among all creatures on earth possess. This inheritance includes language, religion, music, literature, art, technology, and science.

No other organism has added this type of cultural inheritance to its biological inheritance. We accumulate our cultural inheritance individually; we transmit it to our fellow man, and we transmit it to the next generation in a cumulative fashion. Our educational institutions are engaged in the process of systematically transmitting such information to the next generation and in adding to it in a cumulative way from one generation to the next. This is in addition to and separate from our biological inheritance in its manner of accumulation, storage and transmission. As a matter of fact, we don't know how the information that we accumulate is stored in our nervous systems. This again is a problem for the next generation, and a very important one. Although we do not know how this is done, we do know that cultural inheritance cannot develop without biological inheritance through DNA—for we know our brains are made according to the specifications in DNA. The two types of inheritance are complementary.

The assumed evolutionary sequence from hydrogen to man has proceeded through a fantastic number of steps, each almost imperceptibly small. Each represents a chemical change such as the fusion of hydrogen to form helium or the modification of a DNA "letter" by a simple chemical reaction. Through science, which is a part of our cultural inheritance, we have identified many of these evolutionary steps. The humanities, too, are a part of our cultural inheritance. In this sense, the two areas are closely related. If we are to understand and appreciate our total cultural inheritance, as we believe liberally educated men and women should, we cannot reasonably disregard any of its major components.

QUESTIONS

1. *In which paragraph does Beadle set out his organizational plans? What is the plan and what principles seem to have determined it?*
2. *Which of Beadle's questions seemed hardest for him to answer? Why?*
3. *What is Beadle's implicit definition of language? Why does Beadle usually talk about writing in the passive voice?*
4. *What is the social problem created by genetic disease?*
5. *How does Beadle's conception of the relation between religion and science compare with Huxley's ("Letter to Kingsley," p. 445)? How would you account for the difference?*

JOHN LIVINGSTON LOWES

Time in the Middle Ages[1]

We live in terms of *time*. And so pervasive is that element of our consciousness that we have to stand, as it were, outside it for a moment to realize how completely it controls our lives. For we think and act perpetually, we mortals who look before and after, in relation to hours and days and weeks and months and years. Yesterday and to-morrow, next week, a month from now, a year ago, in twenty minutes—those are the terms in which, wittingly or automatically, we act and plan and think. And to orient ourselves at any moment in that streaming continuum we carry watches on our wrists, and put clocks about our houses and on our public towers, and somewhere

1. From Chapter I, "Backgrounds and Horizons," of *Geoffrey Chaucer*, 1934.

in our eye keep calendars, and scan time-tables when we would go abroad. And all this is so utterly familiar that it has ceased to be a matter of conscious thought or inference at all. And—to come to the heart of the business—unless we are mariners or woodsmen or astronomers or simple folk in lonely places, we never any longer reckon with the *sky*. Except for its bearing on the weather or upon our moods, or for contemplation of its depths of blue or fleets of white, or of the nightly splendor of its stars, we are oblivious of its influence. And therein lies the great gulf fixed between Chaucer's century and ours.

For Chaucer and his contemporaries, being likewise human, also lived in terms of time. But their calendar and time-piece was that sky through which moved immutably along predestined tracks the planets and the constellations. And no change, perhaps, wrought by the five centuries between us is more revealing of material differences than that shift of attitude towards "this brave o'erhanging firmament," the sky. And it is that change, first of all, that I wish, if I can, to make clear.

There could be, I suspect, no sharper contrast than that between the "mysterious universe" of modern science, as interpreters like Eddington and Jeans have made even laymen dimly perceive it, and the nest of closed, concentric spheres in terms of which Chaucer and his coevals thought. The structure of that universe may be stated simply enough. Its intricacies need not concern us here. About the earth, as the fixed center, revolved the spheres of the seven then known planets, of which the sun and the moon were two. Beyond these seven planetary spheres lay the sphere of the fixed stars. Beyond that in turn, and carrying along with it in its "diurnal sway" the eight spheres which lay within it, moved the *primum mobile*, a ninth sphere with which, to account for certain planetary eccentricities, the Middle Ages had supplemented the Ptolemaic system. We must think, in a word, of Chaucer's universe as geocentric— the "litel erthe," encompassed by "thilke speres thryes three."[2] As an interesting fact which we have learned, we know it; to conceive it as reality demands an exercise of the imagination. And only with that mental *volte-face* accomplished can we realize the cosmos as Chaucer thought of it.

Now the order of succession of the planetary spheres had far-reaching implications. Starting from the earth, which was their center, that succession was as follows: Moon, Mercury, Venus, Sun, Mars, Jupiter, Saturn. And implicit in that order were two fundamental consequences—the astrological status of the successive hours of the day, and the sequence of the days of the week. The two phenomena stood in intimate relation, and some apprehension of each is fundamental to an understanding of the framework of

2. "Those spheres thrice three."

conceptions within which Chaucer thought, and in terms of which he often wrote.

There were, then, in the first place—and this is strange to us—two sorts of *hours*, with both of which everybody reckoned. There were the hours from midnight to midnight, which constituted the "day natural"—the hours, that is, with which we are familiar—and these, in Chaucer's phrase, were "hours equal," or "hours of the *clock*." But there were also the hours which were reckoned from sunrise to sunset (which made up "day artificial"), and on from sunset to sunrise again. And these, which will most concern us, were termed "hours inequal," or "hours of the *planets*." And they were the hours of peculiar significance, bound up far more closely with human affairs than the "hours of the clock." It is worth, then, a moment's time to get them clear.

They were termed "inequal" for an obvious reason. For the periods between sunrise and sunset, and sunset and sunrise, respectively, change in length with the annual course of the sun, and the length of their twelfths, or hours, must of necessity change too. Between the equinoxes, then, it is clear that the inequal hours will now be longer by day than by night, now longer by night than by day. And only twice in the year, at the equinoxes, will the equal hours and the inequal hours—the hours of the clock and the hours of the planets—be identical. Moreover, each of the inequal hours (and this is of the first importance) was "ruled" by one of the seven planets, and it was as "hours of the planets" that the "hours inequal" touched most intimately human life. And that brings us at once to the days of the week, and their now almost forgotten implications. Why, to be explicit, is to-day Saturday? And why to-morrow Sunday? To answer those two questions is to arrive at one of the determining concepts of Chaucer's world.

Let me first arrange the seven planets in their order, starting (to simplify what follows) with the outermost. Their succession will then be this: Saturn, Jupiter, Mars, Sun, Venus, Mercury, Moon. Now Saturn will rule the first hour of the day which, for that reason, bears his name, and which we still call *Saturday*. Of that day Jupiter will rule the second hour, Mars the third, the Sun the fourth, Venus the fifth, Mercury the sixth, the Moon the seventh, and Saturn again, in due order, the eighth. Without carrying the computation farther around the clock it is obvious that Saturn will also rule the fifteenth and the twenty-second hours of the twenty-four which belong to his day. The twenty-third hour will then be ruled by Jupiter, the twenty-fourth by Mars, and the twenty-fifth by the Sun. But the twenty-fifth hour of one day is the first hour of the next, and accordingly the day after Saturn's day will be the Sun's day. And so, through starry compulsion, the next day after Saturday *must* be Sunday. In precisely the same fashion—accomplished most quickly by remembering that each planet must rule the twenty-second hour of its own day—the ruling planet of the first hour of each of the succeeding days may readily be found. And their order, so found, including Saturn and the Sun, is this: Saturn, Sun, Moon, Mars, Mercury, Jupiter, Venus—then Saturn again, and so on *ad libitum*. And the days of the week will accordingly be the days of the seven planets in that fixed order.

Now Saturn's day, the Sun's day, and the Moon's day are clearly recognizable in their English names of Saturday, Sunday, and Monday. But what of the remaining four—to wit, the days of Mars, Mercury, Jupiter, and Venus, which we call Tuesday, Wednesday, Thursday, and Friday? French has preserved, as also in Lundi, the planetary designations: Mardi (*Martis dies*), Mercredi (*Mercurii dies*), Jeudi (*Jovis dies*), and Vendredi (*Veneris dies*). The shift of the names in English is due to the ousting, in those four instances, of the Roman pantheon by the Germanic. Tiw, Woden, Thor, and Frig (or Freya) have usurped the seats of Mars, Mercury, Jupiter, and Venus, and given their barbarous names to the days. And in France a fourth, even more significant substitution has taken place. For the sun's day is in French *dimanche*, and *dimanche* is *dominica dies*, the Lord's day. And so between Saturn's planet and Diana's moon is memorialized, along with Mercury and Jupiter and Venus and Mars, the second Person of the Christian Trinity. The ancient world has crumbled, and its detritus has been remoulded into almost unrecognizable shapes. But half the history of Europe and of its early formative ideas is written in the nomenclature of the week. And that nomenclature depends in turn upon the succession of the planetary hours. And it was in terms of those hours that Chaucer and his contemporaries thought.

In the *Knight's Tale*, to be specific, Palamon, Emily, and Arcite go to pray, each for the granting of his own desire, to the temples respectively of Venus, Diana, and Mars. And each goes, as in due observance of ceremonial propriety he must, in the hour of the planet associated with the god to whom he prays. Palamon goes to the temple of Venus, "And *in hir houre* he walketh forth." A few lines earlier that hour has been stated in everyday terms: it was "The Sonday night, er day bigan to springe . . . Although it nere nat day by houres two"—two hours, that is, before sunrise. The day that was springing after Sunday night was Monday, and the hour of Monday's sunrise is the hour of the Moon. And the hour two hours earlier, in which Palamon walked forth, was the hour ruled by Venus, to whose temple he was on the way. And Emily and Arcite, as the tale goes on, performed their pilgrimages at similarly reckoned hours. To Chaucer and his readers all this was familiar matter of the day, as instantly comprehensible as are now to us the hours which we reckon by the clock. For us alas! it has become a theme for cumbrous exposition, because the hours of the planets have vanished, with the gods whose names they bore. All that is left of them is the time-worn and wonted sequence of the seven designations of the days.

Nothing, indeed, is more characteristic of the period in which Chaucer wrote than the strange, twisted mythology, transmogrified and confused, which emerged from the association of the planets and the gods. Not even Ovid had conceived such metamorphoses.[3] For the gods were invested with the attributes of planets, and as such became accountable for the most bizarre occurrences, and kept amazing company. Under the aegis of Mars, to take one instance only, were enrolled the butchers, hangmen, tailors, barbers, cooks, cutlers, carpenters, smiths, physicians, and apothecaries—a band about as "martial" as Falstaff's Thomas Wart and Francis Feeble.[4] And so, in "the temple of mighty Mars the rede" in the *Knight's Tale*, there were depicted, together with the "open werre" which was his by virtue of his godhead, the disastrous chances proceeding from his malign ascendancy as planet—the corpse in the bushes with cut throat, the nail driven, like Jael's, into the temple,[5] the sow eating the child in the cradle, the cook scalded in spite of his long ladle. And from among the members of what Chaucer twice calls Mars' "divisioun" there were present—together with the pick-purse, and "the smyler with the knyf under the cloke"—the barber and the butcher and the smith. And in the next paragraph Mars becomes again "this god of armes"—god of war and wicked planet inextricably interfused.

Moreover, as the day and week were conceived in terms of planetary sequence, so the year stood in intricate relation to the *stars*. The sun, with the other planets, moved annually along the vast starry track across the sky which then, as now, was called the zodiac —so called, as Chaucer lucidly explains to "litel Lowis" in the *Treatise on the Astrolabe*, because (and his etymology is sound) "*zodia* in langage of Greek sowneth [signifies] 'bestes' . . . and in the zodiak ben the twelve signes that han names of bestes." These twelve signs, as everybody knows, are Aries, Taurus, Gemini, Cancer, Leo, Virgo, Libra, Scorpio, Sagittarius, Capricornus, Aquarius, Pisces—or, to follow Chaucer's praiseworthy example and translate, Ram, Bull, Twins, Crab, Lion, Virgin, Scales, Scorpion, Archer, Goat, Water-carrier, Fishes. There they were, "eyrish bestes," as Chaucer calls them in a delightful passage that will meet us later, and along their celestial highway passed, from one sign to another, and from house to house, the seven eternal wanderers. To us who read this—though not to countless thousands even yet—the twelve

---

3. Ovid's *Metamorphoses* includes poetical renderings of myths dealing with the transformation of men and women into birds, flowers, trees, etc.

4. Recruits in Shakespeare's *Henry IV, Part 2*.
5. See Judges iv, 17-22.

constellations of the zodiac are accidental groupings, to the eye, of infinitely distant suns. To Chaucer's century they were strangely living potencies, and the earth, in the words of a greater than Chaucer, was "this huge stage . . . whereon the stars in secret influence comment." Each sign, with its constellation, had its own individual efficacy or quality—Aries, "the colerik hote signe"; Taurus, cold and dry; and so on through the other ten. Each planet likewise had its own pecular nature—Mars, like Aries, hot and dry; Venus hot and moist; and so on through the other five. And as each planet passed from sign to sign, through the agency of the successive constellations its character and influence underwent change. Chaucer in the *Astrolabe* put the matter in its simplest terms: "Whan an hot planete cometh in-to an hot signe, then encresseth his hete; and yif a planete be cold, thanne amenuseth [diminshes] his coldnesse, by-cause of the hote signe." But there was far more to it than that. For these complex planetary changes exercised a determining influence upon human beings and their affairs. Arcite behind prison bars cries out:

> Som wikke aspect or disposicioun
> Of Saturne, *by sum constellacioun,*
> Hath yeven us this.

And "the olde colde Saturnus" names the constellation:

> Myn is the prison in the derke cote...
> *Whyl I dwelle in the signe of the Leoun.*

The tragedy of Constance, as the Man of Law conceived it, comes about because Mars, at the crucial moment, was in his "derkest hous." Mars gave, on the other hand, the Wife of Bath, as she avers, her "sturdy hardinesse," because Mars, at her birth, was in the constellation Taurus, which was, in astrological terminology, her own "ascendent." And since the constellation Taurus was also the "night house" of Venus, certain other propensities which the wife displayed had been thrust upon her, as she cheerfully averred, by the temporary sojourn of Mars in Venus's house, when she was born.

But the march of the signs along the zodiac touched human life in yet another way. "Everich of thise twelve signes," Chaucer wrote again to his little Lewis, "hath respecte to a certein parcelle of the body of a man and hath it in governance; as Aries hath thyn heved, and Taurus thy nekke and thy throte. Gemini thyn armholes and thyn armes, and so forth." And at once one recalls Sir Toby Belch and Sir Andrew Aguecheek in *Twelfth Night.* "Shall we not set about some revels?" asks Sr. Andrew. "What shall we do else?" replies Sir Toby. "Were we not born under Taurus?" "Taurus!" exclaims Sir Andrews, "that's sides and heart." "No, sir," retorts Sir Toby, "it is legs and thighs." And you may still pick up, in the shops of apothecaries here and there, cheaply printed almanacs, designed to advertise quack remedies, in which the naked human figure is displayed with lines drawn from each of the pictured zodiacal signs—Ram, Bull, Crab, Scorpion—to the limbs or organs, legs, thighs, sides, or heart, which that particular sign (in Chaucerian phrase) "hath in governance." It is not only in worn stone and faded parchments that strange fragments of the elder world survive.

QUESTIONS

1. *Arrange the steps of Lowes' explanation of medieval time in a different order. Is your order superior to Lowes' or inferior? By what criteria?*
2. *When the advertising man and the engineer from the electronics laboratory become suburban gardeners, why may they have to reckon with the sky and neglect their watches and calendars?*
3. *In "Cotton" (p. 515–530) Agee describes southern tenant farmers who are certainly aware of the "inequal hours," but their awareness is no more medieval than that of the suburban gardeners. What is missing from the modern awareness?*
4. *List some ways in which the abstractions of watch and calendar (and time table) "rule" our lives. This list will be a selection from the particulars of daily life. What generalizations about our society will these particulars justify? Does our society, as focused in these generalizations, have a mythology—a set of hypothetical or typical characters going through hypothetical or typical experiences?*

LEWIS MUMFORD

The Monastery and the Clock[1]

Where did the machine first take form in modern civilization? There was plainly more than one point of origin. Our mechanical civilization represents the convergence of numerous habits, ideas, and modes of living, as well as technical instruments; and some of these were, in the beginning, directly opposed to the civilization they helped to create. But the first manifestation of the new order took place in the general picture of the world: during the first seven centuries of the machine's existence the categories of time and space underwent an extraordinary change, and no aspect of life was left untouched by this transformation. The application of quantitative methods of thought to the study of nature had its first manifestation in the regular measurement of time; and the new

1. Section two of "Cultural Preparation," Chapter I of *Technics and Civilization*, 1934.

mechanical conception of time arose in part out of the routine of the monastery. Alfred Whitehead has emphasized the importance of the scholastic belief in a universe ordered by God as one of the foundations of modern physics: but behind that belief was the presence of order in the institutions of the Church itself.

The technics of the ancient world were still carried on from Constantinople and Baghdad to Sicily and Cordova: hence the early lead taken by Salerno in the scientific and medical advances of the Middle Age. It was, however, in the monasteries of the West that the desire for order and power, other than that expressed in the military domination of weaker men, first manifested itself after the long uncertainty and bloody confusion that attended the breakdown of the Roman Empire. Within the walls of the monastery was sanctuary: under the rule of the order surprise and doubt and caprice and irregularity were put at bay. Opposed to the erratic fluctuations and pulsations of the worldly life was the iron discipline of the rule. Benedict added a seventh period to the devotions of the day, and in the seventh century, by a bull of Pope Sabinianus, it was decreed that the bells of the monastery be rung seven times in the twenty-four hours. These punctuation marks in the day were known as the canonical hours, and some means of keeping count of them and ensuring their regular repetition became necessary.

According to a now discredited legend, the first modern mechanical clock, worked by falling weights, was invented by the monk named Gerbert who afterwards became Pope Sylvester II near the close of the tenth century. This clock was probably only a water clock, one of those bequests of the ancient world either left over directly from the days of the Romans, like the water-wheel itself, or coming back again into the West through the Arabs. But the legend, as so often happens, is accurate in its implications if not in its facts. The monastery was the seat of a regular life, and an instrument for striking the hours at intervals or for reminding the bell-ringer that it was time to strike the bells, was an almost inevitable product of this life. If the mechanical clock did not appear until the cities of the thirteenth century demanded an orderly routine, the habit of order itself and the earnest regulation of time-sequences had become almost second nature in the monastery. Coulton agrees with Sombart in looking upon the Benedictines, the great working order, as perhaps the original founders of modern capitalism: their rule certainly took the curse off work and their vigorous engineering enterprises may even have robbed warfare of some of its glamor. So one is not straining the facts when one suggests that the monasteries—at one time there were 40,000 under the Benedictine rule—helped to give human enterprise the regular collective beat and rhythm of the machine; for the clock is not merely a means of keeping track of the hours, but of synchronizing the actions of men.

Was it by reason of the collective Christian desire to provide for the welfare of souls in eternity by regular prayers and devotions that time-keeping and the habits of temporal order took hold of men's minds: habits that capitalist civilization presently turned to good account? One must perhaps accept the irony of this paradox. At all events, by the thirteenth century there are definite records of mechanical clocks, and by 1370 a well-designed "modern" clock had been built by Heinrich von Wyck at Paris. Meanwhile, bell towers had come into existence, and the new clocks, if they did not have, till the fourteenth century, a dial and a hand that translated the movement of time into movement through space, at all events struck the hours. The clouds that could paralyze the sundial, the freezing that could stop the water clock on a winter night, were no longer obstacles to time-keeping: summer or winter, day or night, one was aware of the measured clank of the clock. The instrument presently spread outside the monastery; and the regular striking of the bells brought a new regularity into the life of the workman and the merchant. The bells of the clock tower almost defined urban existence. Time-keeping passed into time-serving and time-accounting and time-rationing. As this took place, Eternity ceased gradually to serve as the measure and focus of human actions.

The clock, not the steam-engine, is the key-machine of the modern industrial age. For every phase of its development the clock is both the outstanding fact and the typical symbol of the machine: even today no other machine is so ubiquitous. Here, at the very beginning of modern technics, appeared prophetically the accurate automatic machine which only after centuries of further effort, was also to prove the final consummation of this technics in every department of industrial activity. There had been power-machines, such as the water-mill, before the clock; and there had also been various kinds of automata, to awaken the wonder of the populace in the temple, or to please the idle fancy of some Moslem caliph: machines one finds illustrated in Hero and Al-Jazari. But here was a new kind of power-machine, in which the source of power and the transmission were of such a nature as to ensure the even flow of energy throughout the works and to make possible regular production and a standardized product. In its relationship to determinable quantities of energy, to standardization, to automatic action, and finally to its own special product, accurate timing, the clock has been the foremost machine in modern technics: and at each period it has remained in the lead: it marks a perfection toward which other machines aspire. The clock, moreover, served as a model for many other kinds of mechanical works, and the analysis of motion that accompanied the perfection of the clock, with the various types of gearing and transmission that were elaborated, contributed to the success of quite different kinds of machine. Smiths could have hammered thousands of suits of armor or thousands of iron cannon, wheelwrights could have shaped thousands of great water-wheels or crude gears, without inventing any of the special types of movement developed in clockwork, and without any of the accuracy of measurement and finesse of articulation that finally produced the accurate eighteenth century chronometer.

The clock, moreover, is a piece of power-machinery whose "product" is seconds and minutes: by its essential nature it dissociated time from human events and helped create the belief in an independent world of mathematically measurable sequences: the special world of science. There is relatively little foundation for this belief in common human experience: throughout the year the days are of uneven duration, and not merely does the relation between day and night steadily change, but a slight journey from East to West alters astronomical time by a certain number of minutes. In terms of the human organism itself, mechanical time is even more foreign: while human life has regularities of its own, the beat of the pulse, the breathing of the lungs, these change from hour to hour with mood and action, and in the longer span of days, time is measured not by the calendar but by the events that occupy it. The shepherd measures from the time the ewes lambed; the farmer measures back to the day of sowing or forward to the harvest: if growth has its own duration and regularities, behind it are not simply matter and motion but the facts of development: in short, history. And while mechanical time is strung out in a succession of mathematically isolated instants, organic time—what Bergson calls duration—is cumulative in its effects. Though mechanical time can, in a sense, be speeded up or run backward, like the hands of a clock or the images of a moving picture, organic time moves in only one direction—through the cycle of birth, growth, development, decay, and death—and the past that is already dead remains present in the future that has still to be born.

Around 1345, according to Thorndike, the division of hours into sixty minutes and of minutes into sixty seconds became common: it was this abstract framework of divided time that became more and more the point of reference for both action and thought, and in the effort to arrive at accuracy in this department, the astronomical exploration of the sky focused attention further upon the regular, implacable movements of the heavenly bodies through space. Early in the sixteenth century a young Nuremberg mechanic, Peter Henlein, is supposed to have created "many-wheeled watches out of small bits of iron" and by the end of the century the small domestic clock had been introduced in England and Holland. As with the motor car and the airplane, the richer classes first took over the new mechanism and popularized it: partly because they alone could afford it, partly because the new bourgeoisie were the first to discover that, as Franklin later put it, "time is money." To become "as regular as clockwork" was the bourgeois ideal, and to own a watch was for long a definite symbol of success. The increasing tempo of civilization led to a demand for greater power: and in turn power quickened the tempo.

Now, the orderly punctual life that first took shape in the monasteries is not native to mankind, although by now Western peoples are so thoroughly regimented by the clock that it is "second-nature" and they look upon its observance as a fact of nature. Many Eastern civilizations have flourished on a loose basis in time: the Hindus have in fact been so indifferent to time that they lack even an authentic chronology of the years. Only yesterday, in the midst of the industrializations of Soviet Russia, did a society come into existence to further the carrying of watches there and to propagandize the benefits of punctuality. The popularization of timekeeping, which followed the production of the cheap standardized watch, first in Geneva, then in America around the middle of the last century, was essential to a well-articulated system of transportation and production.

To keep time was once a peculiar attribute of music: it gave industrial value to the workshop song or the tattoo or the chantey of the sailors tugging at a rope. But the effect of the mechanical clock is more pervasive and strict: it presides over the day from the hour of rising to the hour of rest. When one thinks of the day as an abstract span of time, one does not go to bed with the chickens on a winter's night: one invents wicks, chimneys, lamps, gaslights, electric lamps, so as to use all the hours belonging to the day. When one thinks of time, not as a sequence of experiences, but as a collection of hours, minutes, and seconds, the habits of adding time and saving time come into existence. Time took on the character of an enclosed space: it could be divided, it could be filled up, it could even be expanded by the invention of labor-saving instruments.

Abstract time became the new medium of existence. Organic functions themselves were regulated by it: one ate, not upon feeling hungry, but when prompted by the clock: one slept, not when one was tired, but when the clock sanctioned it. A generalized time-consciousness accompanied the wider use of clocks: dissociating time from organic sequences, it became easier for the men of the Renascence to indulge the fantasy of reviving the classic past or of reliving the splendors of antique Roman civilization: the cult of history, appearing first in daily ritual, finally abstracted itself as a special discipline. In the seventeenth century journalism and periodic literature made their appearance: even in dress, following the lead of Venice as fashion-center, people altered styles every year rather than every generation.

The gain in mechanical efficiency through co-ordination and through the closer articulation of the day's events cannot be over-estimated: while this increase cannot be measured in mere horse-power, one has only to imagine its absence today to forsee the speedy disruption and eventual collapse of our entire society. The modern industrial regime could do without coal and iron and steam easier than it could do without the clock.

JAMES PACKARD
Machinable Reason: the Simpler the Better

The Binary Number System
The Binary Number System: What It Is

The celebrated philosophic axiom known as OCCAM'S RAZOR is named for William of Occam, a 14th century Nominalist. *Entia non sunt multiplicanda: Entities are not to be multiplied (beyond necessity)*. This razor served Occam both as scalpel and switch-blade, enabling him to dissect propositions and then to attack thinkers who mistook mental conveniences for necessary entities. Whatever their attitude toward intellectual delinquency, modern computer theorists find Occam's razor a useful surgical device. With it they are able to dispose of many superfluities—among them, entities in the time-honored decimal system.

We shall refer frequently to Occam's razor because this axiom expresses standards of efficiency and excellence which are pre-eminent in digital computation. We shall examine the binary system in some detail because it is perhaps the clearest example of how the most complex operations are made possible through rigor-ous manipulation of the simplest elements. This number system would have been Occam's delight, for other systems are, by com-parison, profuse if not prodigal.

Leibniz, one of the co-inventors of the calculus, can claim sole invention of the binary number system. True, a two-entity method of reckoning does appear among some primitives. One tribe of Aus-tralian aborigines reckons as follows:

Urupun	(1)
Okosa	(2)
Okosa-Urupun	(3)
Okosa-Okosa	(4)
Okosa-Okosa-Urupun	(5)
Okosa-Okosa-Okosa	(6)

From just two entities, more elaborate entities are devised by a simple additive process—which is surprisingly similar to what we shall find in digital computation. But there is a slight difference which makes all the difference between savagery and sophistication. These aborigines cannot reckon beyond 6; to them, anything from 7 to 7,000,000 is just "lots." This crude sense of number is not distinctively human: some birds and insects have demonstrated as much ability to detect slight changes in quantity.

It is unlikely that man would have learned to count if he had not been blessed with (or had not finned) fingers. Anaxagoras called man the wisest of animals because he has hands, and the observation is borne out by modern educational theories of "learning by doing." In present context, the "doing" is the ability to tick off numbers on the fingers, or to use the fingers as visual aids in conceiving, say, some property common to the number of days spent in a hunt and the number of hunters taking part in it. The Latin *digitus* meant both finger and toe, and in the vocabulary of zoologists, "digit" retains the double referent. The use in English of "digit" for the symbols 0 through 9 is evidence of the profound finger-orientation of our everyday counting system.

Why ten? After counting that far, we run out of fingers and have to start over again, beginning another cycle: Therefore 10 is the BASE, and the name of the resulting system is taken from the Latin *decimus* (tenth). The strongest early competitors of the decimal system, the quinary (base 5) and vigesimal (base 20) systems, were no less anthropomorphic. In the former, the counters restricted themselves to one hand, and in the latter they included their toes. The physiological convenience of the decimal system was perhaps reinforced by the position of base 10 in the "middle range" of psychological complexity, providing enough challenge to human mental powers but not too much. And as a system in its own right, the decimal provides a good compromise between demands for concise expression and simple structure. But otherwise it is a poor compromise: It has only two divisors (2 and 5) as against the four divisors (2, 3, 4, and 6) offered by base 12, and yet it fails to provide a prime (indivisible) base, such as 7 or 11, that would please the pure mathematician.

In his earliest published work (1666), Leibniz proposed a universal logical calculus based on arithmetical combinations of simple into complex concepts and worked out in terms of the 1 and the 0—a clear foreshadowing of his binary number system. (The name was derived from the Latin *binarius* and in turn from *bini*—"Two by two," or "two at a time.") Four years later Leibniz explained what was to be a life-long passion for subsuming the greatest possible range of subjects under the fewest possible guiding principles. He was inspired, of course, by Occam's razor, which he interpreted to mean, "The simpler a hypothesis is, the better it is." We shall see in a later section what this implied for logic; for numbering, it implied the elimination of all digits except the 1 and the 0.

Leibniz endorsed his binary system with mystical fervor, for to him it symbolized Creation, the Divinity (1) sufficing to draw all out of nothing (0) As mathematician he found conclusive advantage in its allowance for simplicity of operation and its exposure of important number relations which are obscured in other systems. These advantages could not compete with those of the decimal system, however, and the latter prevailed. Along with its lack of anthropomorphic affinity, the binary system suffered a fatal lack of compactness. The decimal number 2047 becomes 11111111111 in binary. Not many humans are comfortable with that sort of notation; but 250 years after it was elaborated, machines came along which thrived on it.

The Binary Number System: How It Works

To laymen schooled only in the decimal system, the binary system is confusing and somehow "unnatural." The assertion that $1 + 1 = 10$ rather than 2 seems subversive of other arithmetical ideas. It is less discomfiting to youngsters being taught the "New Mathematics," however, as they are warned from the outset against confusing intuitive or pictorial appeal with necessary conditions. Although their fingers continue to serve as handy calculators, the decimal is emphasized as but one of many possible bases to use in counting.

Perhaps the most familiar analogy to the binary system is the Morse code, which combines two entities (the dot and the dash) in different ways to symbolize different letters, thereby allowing for the codification of words and the transmission of verbal messages. But the two entities of the binary number system are combined positionally, in space rather than time, and unlike the dot and dash they do not represent other symbols. These digits carry as direct a reference to quantities as do those of the decimal system.

The decisive advantage of the Arabic decimal over the Roman decimal system is the positional value of digits in the former. Instead of introducing new symbols at different stages (such as the Roman X for 10 and L for 50), the Arabic adds a 1 to the digit position farthest to the left and begins a new column each time the base 10 is exhausted. Since the binary system has only two rather than ten symbols to work with, it requires many more positions to represent the same magnitude.

The following table shows the first ten numbers of the decimal and binary systems. Note that the 0 has purely positional value, and is used simply to locate the other digits in properly "weighted" columns. In this respect it serves as positional "place-holder" for both systems.

Decimal		Binary
0	=	0
1	=	1
2	=	10
3	=	11
4	=	100
5	=	101
6	=	110
7	=	111
8	=	1000
9	=	1001
10	=	1010

Thus, decimal 2 equals binary 10—which is simply 1 (the first digit in the "10") multiplied by 2 (the positional value of that first digit). We can break down binary 1010 (*reading always from right to left*) into binary 10 + binary 1000 (which equals 1 x 2 x 2 x 2, or 1 x 2^3); in decimal numbers, this is the same as adding 2 to 8. In the binary system, the power of 2 is raised (the total quantity doubled) with each move into the next column to the left, as shown here:

Power of Two		Binary Number		Decimal Number
2^0	=	1	=	1
2^1	=	10	=	2
2^2	=	100	=	4
2^3	=	1000	=	8
2^4	=	10000	=	16
2^5	=	100000	=	32
2^6	=	1000000	=	64
2^7	=	10000000	=	128
2^8	=	100000000	=	256
2^9	=	1000000000	=	512
2^{10}	=	10000000000	=	1024

Binary 11111111111 thus equals

$$1 + 2^1 + 2^2 + 2^3 + 2^4 + 2^5 + 2^6 + 2^7 + 2^8 + 2^9 + 2^{10}$$

or decimal 2047. Working the other way around and converting from decimal to binary, we find, for example, that decimal 4096 is 2^{12} or binary 1000000000000; and that decimal 100 can be broken down into $2^6 + 2^5 + 2^2$, or binary 1100100.

Addition. The simplicity of operation in the binary system is evident in these sample calculations:

10 (2)	1010 (10)	10001 (17)	111111 (63)
+ 1 (1)	+ 101 (5)	+ 10001 (17)	+ 1 (1)
11 (3)	1111 (15)	100010 (34)	1000000 (64)

The sole difficulty arises when 1 is added to 1, giving a column value of 0 with a 1 which must be carried one column to the left. As often happens in adding decimal numbers (and as is strikingly evident in the last calculation above), this can necessitate a carry-over for many successive columns.

The four sums obtained in the sample calculations are added as follows:

$$
\begin{array}{ll}
11 & (3) \\
1111 & (15) \\
100010 & (34) \\
1000000 & (64) \\
\hline
1110100 & (116)
\end{array}
$$

Two notable features emerge: the simple play between digits, and the "pile-up" of carry-overs. The carry-overs are accommodated, as we have seen, simply by adjusting column values to the left—in this instance, through four columns. As for the play between digits, the reduction to two symbols makes calculation into a kind of alternation or undulation of numerical value.

Subtraction, Multiplication, Division. In the binary number system, Occam's razor is used so skillfully that entities do not have to be multiplied at all—or divided or subtracted. All three arithmetical processes are variations on the one basic additive process.

The method of subtracting by COMPLEMENTING is known to everyone familiar with the desk or the pocket calculator. By definition, a complement is "that which fills up or completes"; therefore the complement of a number is that number which fills up or completes the cycle determined by the base. In the decimal system, for instance, the complement of 5 is 5 and the complement of 4 is 6. Now if we want to subtract 4 from 8 without departing from the additive process, we can *add* 6 to 8, obtaining 14, and can then drop the first digit to obtain 4, the desired answer. We add 6 to the larger number because it is the complement of 4, the smaller number, and consequently will make the cycle one place too large. The only "dropping" or subtracting is in restoration of the proper cycle; and this, being accounted for in advance, is conveniently formalized.

In one refinement of this technique, the *Base-Minus-1 Complement*, the same process is carried out by using the difference between the subtrahend (the quantity to be subtracted from the

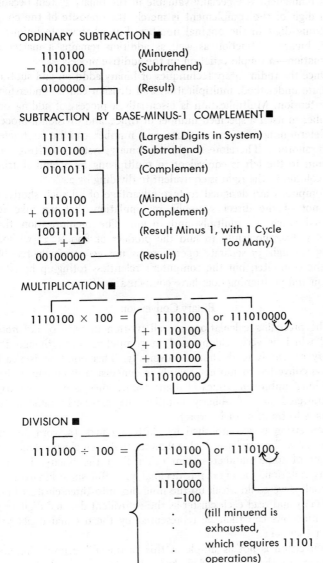

ORDINARY SUBTRACTION ■

```
  1110100        (Minuend)
− 1010100        (Subtrahend)
  0100000        (Result)
```

SUBTRACTION BY BASE-MINUS-1 COMPLEMENT■

```
  1111111        (Largest Digits in System)
  1010100        (Subtrahend)
  0101011        (Complement)

  1110100        (Minuend)
+ 0101011        (Complement)
 10011111        (Result Minus 1, with 1 Cycle
                  Too Many)
 00100000        (Result)
```

MULTIPLICATION ■

```
1110100 × 100 = ⎧    1110100 ⎫ or 111010000
                ⎨  + 1110100 ⎬
                ⎨  + 1110100 ⎬
                ⎩  + 1110100 ⎭
                   111010000
```

DIVISION ■

```
1110100 ÷ 100 = ⎧   1110100 ⎫ or 1110100
                ⎪    −100   ⎪
                ⎪   1110000 ⎪
                ⎪    −100   ⎪
                ⎨     .       (till minuend is
                ⎪     .        exhausted,
                ⎪     .        which requires 11101
                ⎪     .        operations)
                ⎩   0000000 ⎭
```

SAMPLE BINARY CALCULATIONS

minuend, or larger quantity) and the largest digits in the system. This refinement is especially valuable in the binary system because each digit of the complement is merely the opposite of the corresponding digit in the original number. But whatever technique is used, binary subtraction as well as addition remains a matter of alternation—a simple variation on the additive process.

Once the rudimentary techniques of binary addition and subtraction are understood, multiplication and division can be understood by extension. Multiplication is essentially a process of adding one number to itself a specified number of times, and division a process of determining how many times one number can be subtracted from another. Therefore, with the binary system, shifting one column to the left is equivalent to multiplying by 2, and shifting one column to the right is equivalent to dividing by 2.

Computers are designed to take advantage of all such shortcuts but not of the direct symbolic manipulation that we take for granted when we multiply and divide. The memorization that enables the schoolchild to find the product of 899 × 37 without going through 37 separate operations is not economically feasible for the computer; but the computer's relentless toting-up by alternation and positioning does have compensatory features.

Binary Conversion

The preceding calculations are all written in pure binary *notation*, which is very seldom used in computers, even though the binary *system* is used almost universally. This notation is nearly always converted to another, mainly in concession to human frailty: The long, unbroken strings of digits (sometimes as many as sixty) encountered in pure binary notation are extremely difficult for humans to transmit or interpret.

Conversion is accomplished by clustering BITS (a word derived from "BINARY DIGITS") in such a manner that each cluster stands for a digit of some number system other than the binary. In pure binary notation, 111111111 is decimal 511. But since binary 11 is decimal 7, we could break up the nine bits into three clusters (111 111 111) and read each cluster as the equivalent decimal digit (7). The nine bits can then be represented by the decimal digits 777 rather than 511.

Conversion is not as simple as this "artificial" example implies, however. In the binary-coded decimal system, each cluster must contain four bits rather than three: A cluster must be large enough to accommodate any digit within the base of the system—and decimal 8 and 9 are 1000 and 1001 in binary. Thus, decimal 9370 would have to be converted:

1001	0011	0111	000
(9)	(3)	(7)	(0)

Without some sort of modification by means of conversion, this four-bit clustering entails a good deal of waste.

Of the many available conversion techniques, the most popular is conversion into OCTAL NOTATION. The octal system uses the same rules of arithmetic as the decimal system but is built on base 8 and thus omits all 8's and 9's from its repertoire of symbols (0, 1, 2, 3, 4, 5, 6, 7, 10, 11, 12, etc.). The popularity of octal notation can be attributed to its compatibility with binary notation; since 8 is an integral power of 2, octal notation is in effect a convenient rearrangement of binary notation. And since 7 (the highest digit in the octal system) is 111 in binary, only three bits are required in each cluster (as shown in our "artificial" example). Each three-bit cluster carries a unique value and all possible clusters can be used in computation.

In the binary-coded decimal system, on the other hand, the requirement for four-bit clustering means that six clusters are built in but cannot be used. These are the equivalents for the decimal digits 11 through 16, which are *symbolically* unique but exceed the base of the system and therefore cannot be *quantitatively* unique as well. Consequently they go to waste. Four-bit clustering can be retained without waste only by resorting to the HEXIDECIMAL (base 16) system, in which six more symbols are required for the additional digits. The hexidecimal repertoire of symbols could thus run 0, 1, 2, 3, 4, 5, 6, 7, 8, 9, u, v, w, x, y, z. Once the base of the system is extended the six troublesome digits are made both symbolically and quantitatively unique, like the ten digits preceding them. A moment's reflection shows, of course, that 16 like 8 is an integral power of 2—which accounts for the compatibility of the hexidecimal and binary systems.

In brief, conversion is the rule, and the important thing in conversion is to avoid waste and the confusion which results from waste. Since the incompatibility between the decimal and binary system is intrisic, Occam's bid for parsimony is satisfied when we resort to octal representation of binary numbers—even though this "shorthand device" requires an extra step for conversion back into decimal notation. Octal representation stands as a serviceable compromise because its clustering of digits is both parsimonious and readily interpretable.

The Binary Number System: Why It Is Essential

Throughout our discussion, the critical importance of the binary number system in digital computation has been assumed. We have seen that the digital computer is essentially a counting device, and that the binary number system enables us to count discrete, successive entities in the simplest possible manner. Yet the simplicity which carries such intellectual, aesthetic, and even mystical appeal for men like Leibniz and Occam is not without its practical difficulty, as suggested by our glance at binary conversion.

No matter how thoroughly future generations are grounded in the binary system, they are unlikely to use it for calculating household budgets or for figuring the mileage between home and work. Human mental powers are not necessarily dependent on base 10 for a number system, but psychological testing indicates that some base higher than 2 is necessary—simply because our perceptual and retentive powers demand a certain conciseness of formulation. Such being the case, why not adopt a compromise number system that would suit both man and machine, doing away with the need for conversion altogether?

First, because conversion is simple enough to be mechanized along with the problem under solution. Second, because of the nature of the arithmetical process. Arithmetic is itself a logical system: It involves a few basic assumptions and a set of precise rules, and as we shall see, the binary 1 and 0 can be equated with the logical TRUE and FALSE. Third, because of the nature of the physical situation. As Claude Shannon first pointed out, the logical states of True and False can be equated with the ON and OFF states of electrical switching. In all three situations—arithmetical, logical, and physical—two entities emerge, and by manipulating them in one situation we can manipulate them symbolically in the others. Working with binary numbers thus becomes a paradigmatic operation of inexhaustible potential.

The Logical Situation

In Webster's definition, logic is "the science of formal principles of reasoning." These principles were first evolved by Parmenides, the Greek philosopher who observed a dichotomy between Being and Non-Being, proscribing the latter as humanly unthinkable and therefore false. The resultant True/False distinction underlies the whole of logic as it developed in the West.

Aristotle formalized the double-valued concept of truthfulness, working out a set of precise rules for manipulating the concept and thus providing for its application to all logical propositions. In so doing, he helped to free the propositions from total dependence on words—an invaluable service because words inevitably carry meaning other than that necessary for logical operation. By introducing quasi-aglebraic notation, Aristotle established a method through which gross semantic confusion and redundancy could be exposed.

Mathematics underwent a similar excision of verbal content in the interest of attaining symbolic exactness. As we have seen with reference to cardinal and ordinal numbers, major assumptions are implicit in the simplest counting procedures. In Euclidean geometry the assumptions are explicit: The premises and the conclusions derived from them are formulated in words. But in algebra, the ties between words and operations and between objects and symbols are cut so that the operations and symbols can be brought into closer mutual conformity. Although the result is a language of sorts, it differs from ordinary spoken language in that it has little connection with the "real world," and is restricted almost entirely to defining relationships between signs or symbols.

Modern logicians, beginning with George Boole in the mid-19th century, have furthered Aristotle's effort to divest logical operations of linguistic ties, and have worked out the operations in terms of ever purer algebraic notation. Of the 256 possible permutations set down by Aristotle, only 15 remain valid after a century of paring and scraping. In Wittgenstein's elegant verbal reduction, "If a sign is *not necessary* it is meaningless. That is the meaning of Occam's razor."

In logical systems, meaning is thus equated with necessity and becomes a property of the operation itself. If a sign "works" it is meaningful, but the resulting conclusion is not necessarily meaningful outside the operation. Logical systems are structured so as to preserve, through rigorous deduction from initial axioms, whatever truth is contained in those axioms. In fact, the main function of a logical system (as we shall see with reference to machine language—itself such a system) is to preserve the truth value of assertions throughout their conversion into different forms. Consequently, the truth of a conclusion makes sense in terms of common experience only insofar as the original assertions are commonsensical and free from mutual contradiction.

But despite the self-contained criterion implicit in all logical operations from the simplest to the most esoteric, the ultimate criterion for validity can be traced back to the True/False dichotomy observed by Parmenides and applied by Aristotle. Even the logic of probability, which works not on an opposition of value but on a scale of graded predictive value, is approached on the assumption that self-consistency is a mark of truth and self-contradiction a mark of falsity.

Therefore, in logical-algebraic contexts the two pairs of opposing entities—the 1/0 and the True/False—can be used as interchangeable parts. This was well known but had no far-reaching effects until men became aware of a third, compatible pair of entities by which they could put the other pairs to work.

The Physical Situation

With the development of electrical network theory in our own century, the affinity between the True/False logical distinction and the On/Off states of electrical switching gradually became clear—leading in 1938 to Shannon's observation that the design of computers is more a logical than an arithmetical undertaking. Although computer circuitry has advanced from electrical relays to diodes and transistors, still the mechanization of logic is best described in terms of switches because they are the most familiar devices and provide the closest approach to an ideal dichotomy.

By simplest definition switching is the connection of two points of an electrical network at controllable instants of time: Either the connection is made, the switch is closed, and the resistance approaches zero—or the switch is open, the connection is not made, and the resistance approaches infinity. The two possible physical states are discrete enough to be used as though they were absolutely discrete. And since they are conceived as pure, successive entities they can be manipulated without the error which tends to accumulate in physically continuous measurements, such as those characteristic of analog computation.

In digital computation, therefore, the physical situation is theoretically comparable to the logical and arithmetical situations. It is a system which involves a few basic assumptions and a set of precise rules. The assumptions are primarily concerned with the design of circuitry so that certain results are bound to be secured from certain built-in switching sequences. As with the 1/o and the True/False, the On/Off entities can be combined in ever more elaborate patterns with results which are reliable insofar as the rules of combination are precisely formulated and rigorously observed.

It is to attain valid predictive understanding that designers depend on Boolean algebra, for a combination of Boolean symbols can be made to correspond to a combination of physical elements in the computer: Manipulation of the symbols then corresponds to manipulation of the parts. And just as the algebraic conclusions follow logically from the previous ordering of statements, so the physical results follow logically from the previous ordering of elements. Throughout each conversion, truth value is preserved so that it can be expressed by and manipulated in the physical situation.

Thus we approach what Leibniz anticipated as "an alphabet of thoughts, or a catalogue of the highest genera," and what we have at hand is indeed "a mechanical thread of meditation."

The Logic Machine: Some Theoretical Operations

Our discussion of the binary number system was intended to convey a sense of how the simplest mode of counting can accommodate the most sophisticated modes of calculation. Similarly, this section on logical operation is intended to convey a sense of how the three pairs of entities—the 1/o, the True/False, and the On/Off—can be manipulated in digital computation so that the computer acts in effect as logic machine—as "decision maker" and "problem solver."

We will not venture into the intricacies of symbolic logic, but our sample operations will be based on one of its best known aids: the TRUTH TABLE. First used by Boole to attain greater precision in analytic thought, the truth table is a means of symbolizing truth values as they apply not to statements themselves but rather to the results of combining the statements in different ways.

In the Boolean *conjunctive operation* involving two statements we assert that the result of combining the statements is true only if *both* statements are true. If we label the first satement "A," the second statement "B," and the conclusion "C," we are in effect saying that A + B = C. Abbreviating True as "T" and False as "F," we derive this table:

A	B	C
F	F	F
T	F	F
F	T	F
T	T	T

Thus, of the four possible combinations of A and B, only the last one is true according to the rule established by our original assertion.

In the Boolean *disjunctive* operation involving two statements, we assert that the result of combining the statements is true if *either* statement is true. Here we are saying that A or B = C, and this is the table resulting:

A	B	C
F	F	F
T	F	T
F	T	T
T	T	T

Thus, of the four possible combinations of A and B, the last three are true according to the rule established by our original assertion.

[If we are tempted to go on to make assertions *within* the tables, so that A and B lose their purely symbolic status, we would do well to remember that the logical truth of a conclusion does not necessarily make sense in terms of common experience. The reader can test the disparity between operations by trying to devise simple statements for A and B which lead to common-sense conclusions for all combinations in the above tables. He will soon discover that statements compatible with one operation are not wholly compatible with the other.]

As we have noted several times earlier, the digits 1 and 0 can be equated with True and False. When the substitution is made, our two tables become:

A	B	C		A	B	C
0	0	0		0	0	0
1	0	0		1	0	1
0	1	0		0	1	1
1	1	1		1	1	1

All four combinations in the first table, which represents the conjunctive operation, can be alternatively represented by the simple switching operation shown in this schematic diagram:

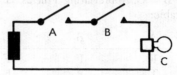

Here, A and B represent switches which can be said to carry a 0 value when they are open and a 1 value when closed; and C represents a light which is turned on when both switches are closed. The light can be said to carry a 0 value when it is off and a 1 value when it is on.

The four combinations in the second table, which represents the disjunctive operation, can be alternatively represented by a switching situation almost as simple:

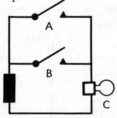

The values here remain the same, except that both switches do not have to be closed before the light is turned on: closing either one or the other will suffice.

What we have in these two diagrams are the simplest patterns of logic that can be built into computer circuitry: In the first, current will flow and an input will be registered as "True" *if and only if both switches are closed*; in the second, current will flow and "truth" will be registered *if either of the switches is closed or if both are closed*. Reverse values can be assigned, of course, since truth value refers to a change of physical state and not to any physical state in particular. Thus, closing the switches and lighting the light could be considered "False" rather than "True": This would be especially valuable in disjunctive operations, since only one of the four possible combinations is false and only this one would have to be accommodated. Parsimony is the perennial rule of thumb.

These rudimentary switching operations can be connected in ever more complicated series, allowing for the mechanization of ever more complicated logical problems. For example, simply by joining the conjunctive and disjunctive operations diagrammed above, we would be working with four switches (statements) of which *both* the first *and* second plus *either* the third *or* fourth would have to be actuated before the light would register "True." At the extremes of sophisticated computer design, there are NOR functions (negations of "or" functions) and NAND functions (which allow for alternate negation). Most computers, however, attain complete operation with the three basic functions of NOT, AND, and OR.

We gain some idea of the astounding economies made possible by two-entity modes of calculation and mechanization when we analyze the complexities introduced by a single variable and see how simply these complexities are accommodated in computer design. If there is one variable there are two possible inputs (On/Off) and four possible outputs, which are tabulated as follows:

A	f_0	f_1	f_2	f_3
O	O	1	O	1
1	O	O	1	1

"A" refers to the two input states (Off/On), and the "f's" refer to the four output functions. Note that the third function, f_2, is identical to A; that the first function, f_0, is always false; and that the fourth function, f_3, is always true. Now computer circuitry need be designed only to accommodate a change of physical state which represents a useful new condition; therefore the second function, f_3, is the only one which carries importance—and it is a simple reversal of A. Since the other three functions represent no useful new conditions, they are "trivial" and can be discarded without affecting the logical operation. Thus the four possible output functions are accommodated by just one change in physical state.

The economies are even more striking when further variables are added. For example, 16 output functions result from the addition of a second variable, and 12 of these 16 turn out to be trivial. Of the four which must be accommodated, two are simple negations of the other two, and can be accommodated by a mere reversal of current in the magnetic devices now used in nearly all computers. The complexities multiply exponentially, so that introduction of a third variable leads to 8 possible input variations and 256 possible output functions. Of these, only 16 need be accommodated—and so on.

The notable feature here and throughout computer theory is that control of the basic entities allows for maintenance of control no matter how rapid the proliferation of these entities and how intri-

cate the emerging patterns. There are myriad devices which simplify and expand the basic operations—making it possible for functions to be translated from tables into equations, for instance, and
these equations to be converted into efficient computer design—or
for charts and maps to be expressed in notation directly "decod-
able" by the computer—or for bits to express letters rather than
numbers, so that words are manipulated rather than quantities.
Although these devices are very complex, their operating principles
can always be traced back to the principles we have repeatedly
encountered: the rigorous control and manipulation of two entities
in one or more of three situations—physical, logical, arithmetical.
And the criterion of excellence remains the same for designing a
computer, for conceiving suitable problems for it to solve, or for
programming those problems. To paraphrase Leibniz's paraphrase
of Occam, "The simpler an operation, the better it is."

BERTON ROUECHÉ

A Game of Wild Indians

During the second week in August, 1946, an elderly man, a
middle-aged woman, and a boy of ten dragged themselves, singly
and painfully, into the Presbyterian Hospital, in the Washington
Heights section of Manhattan, where their trouble was unhesitatingly identified as typhoid fever. This diagnosis was soon confirmed
by laboratory analysis, and on Thursday morning, August 15th, a
report of the outbreak was dutifully telephoned to the Department
of Health. It was received and recorded there, in accordance with
the routine in all alarms of an epidemiological nature, by a clerk in
the Bureau of Preventable Diseases named Beatrice Gamso. Miss
Gamso is a low-strung woman and she has spent some thirty callous-
ing years in the Health Department, but the news gave her a turn.
She sat for an instant with her eyes on her notes. Then, steadying
herself with a practiced hand, she swung around to her typewriter
and set briskly about dispatching copies of the report to all administrative officers of the Department. Within an hour, a reliable investigator from the Bureau was on his way to Washington Heights.
He was presently followed by one of his colleagues, a Department
public-health nurse, several agents from the Bureau of Food and
Drugs, and an inspector from the Bureau of Sanitary Engineering.
  Typhoid fever was among the last of the massive pestilential
fevers to yield to the probings of medical science, but its capitu-
lation has been complete. It is wholly transparent now. Its clinical
manifestations (a distinctive rash and a tender spleen, a fiery fever
and a languid pulse, and nausea, diarrhea, and nosebleed), its cause

(a bacillus known as *Eberthella typhosa*), and its means of transmission have all been clearly established. Typhoid is invariably conveyed by food or drink contaminated with the excreta of its victims. Ordinarily, it is spread by someone who is ignorant, at least momentarily, of his morbid condition. One reason for such unawareness is that for the first several days typhoid fever tends to be disarmingly mild and indistinguishable from the countless fleeting malaises that dog the human race. Another is that nearly five per cent of the cases become typhoid carriers, continuing indefinitely to harbor a lively colony of typhoid bacilli in their systems. The existence of typhoid carriers was discovered by a group of German hygienists in 1907. Typhoid Mary Mallon, a housemaid and cook who was the stubborn cause of a total of fifty-three cases in and around New York City a generation ago, is, of course, the most celebrated of these hapless menaces. About seventy per cent, by some unexplained, physiological fortuity, are women. The names of three hundred and eighty local carriers are currently on active file in the Bureau of Preventable Diseases. They are called on regularly by public-health nurses and are permanently enjoined from any employment that involves the handling of food. More than a third of all the cases that occur here are traced to local carriers but, because of the vigilance of the Health Department, rarely to recorded carriers; new ones keep turning up. Most of the rest of the cases are of unknown or out-of-town origin. A few are attribuable to the products of polluted waters (clams and oysters and various greens).

The surveillance of carriers is one of several innovations that in little more than a generation have forced typhoid fever into an abrupt tractability throughout most of the Western world. The others include certain refinements in diagnostic technique, the institution of public-health measures requiring the chlorination of city-supplied water and proscribing the sale of unpasteurized milk, and the development of an immunizing vaccine. Since late in the nineteenth century, the local incidence of typhoid fever has dropped from five or six thousand cases a year to fewer than fifty, and it is very possible that it may soon be as rare as smallpox. Banishment has not, however, materially impaired the vigor of *Eberthella typhosa*. Typhoid fever is still a cruel and withering affliction. It is always rambunctious, generally prolonged, and often fatal. It is also one of the most explosive of communicable diseases. The month in which it is most volcanic is August.

The investigator who led the sprint to Washington Heights that August morning in 1946 was Dr. Harold T. Fuerst, an epidemiologist, and he and Dr. Ottavio J. Pellitteri, another epidemiologist, handled most of the medical inquiry. One afternoon, when I was down at the Bureau, they told me about the case. Miss Gamso sat at a desk nearby, and I noticed after a moment that she was following the conversation with rapt attention. Her interest, it turned out, was entirely understandable. Typhoid-fever investigations are frequently tedious, but they are seldom protracted. It is not unusual for a team of experienced operatives to descry the source of an outbreak in a couple of days. Some cases have been riddled in an afternoon. The root of the trouble on Washington Heights eluded detection for almost two weeks, and it is probable that but for Miss Gamso it would never have been detected at all.

"I got to Presbyterian around eleven," Dr. Fuerst told me. "I found a staff man I knew, and he led me up to the patients. It was typhoid, all right. Not that I'd doubted it, but it's routine to take a look. And they were in bad shape—too miserable to talk. One—the woman—was barely conscious. I decided to let the questioning go for the time being. At least until I'd seen their histories. A clerk in the office of the medical superintendent dug them out for me. Pretty skimpy—name, age, sex, occupation, and address, and a few clinical notations. About all I got at a glance was that they weren't members of the same family. I'd hoped, naturally, that they would be. That would have nicely limited the scope of the investigation. Then I noticed something interesting. They weren't a family, but they had a little more in common than just typhoid. For one thing, they were by way of being neighbors. One of them lived at 502 West 180th Street, another at 501 West 178th Street, and the third at 285 Audubon Avenue, just around the corner from where it runs through the five-hundred block of West 179th Street. Another thing was their surnames. They were different, but they weren't dissimilar. All three were of Armenian origin. Well, Washington Heights has an Armenian colony—very small and very clannish. I began to feel pretty good. I didn't doubt for a minute that the three of them knew each other. Quite possibly they were friends. If so, it was reasonable to suppose that they might recently have shared a meal. It wasn't very likely, of course, that they had been the only ones to share it. Ten-year-old boys don't usually go out to meals without their parents. Maybe there had been a dozen in on it. It could even have been some sort of national feast. Or a church picnic. Picnic food is an ideal breeding ground for the typhoid organism. It can't stand cooking, but it thrives in raw stuff—ice cream and mayonnaise and so on. And if a carrier had happened to have a hand in the arrangements . . . I decided we'd do well to check and see if there was an Armenian carrier on our list."

"We found one, all right," Dr. Pellitteri said. "A widow named Christos—she died a year or two ago—who lived on West 178th Street."

"To be sure, we had only three cases," Dr. Fuerst went on. "But I didn't let that bother me. I've never known an outbreak of typhoid in which everybody who was exposed got sick. There are always a certain number who escape. They either don't eat whatever it is that's contaminated or they have a natural or an acquired immunity. Moreover, the incubation period in typhoid—the time it takes for the bug to catch hold—varies with the individual. Ten days is about the average, but it can run anywhere from three to thirty. In other words, maybe we had seen only the vanguard. There might be more to come. So in the absence of anything better, the Armenian link looked pretty good. I called the Bureau and told Bill Birnkrant—he was acting director at the time—what I thought, and he seemed to think the same. He said he'd start somebody checking. I went back upstairs for another try at the patients."

"That's when the rest of us began to come into the picture," Dr. Pellitteri said. "My job was the recent social life of the Armenian colony. Ida Matthews, a public-health nurse, took the carrier angle. Neither of us had much luck. The file listed twelve carriers in Washington Heights. As I remember, the only Armenian was Mrs. Christos. At any rate, the nurse picked her first. I remember running into Miss Matthews somewhere on Audubon toward the end of that first afternoon. She told me what progress she had made. None. Mrs. Christos was old and sick, and hadn't been out of her apartment for a month. Miss Matthews said there was no reason to doubt the woman's word, as she had a good reputation at the Department—very coöperative, obeyed all the rules. Miss Matthews was feeling pretty gloomy. She'd had high hopes. Well, I knew how she felt. I'd hit nothing but dead ends myself. Our patients didn't seem to be friends. Apparently, they just knew each other. The priest at the Gregorian church in the neighborhood—Holy Cross Armenian Apostolic, on West 187th Street—knew of no recent feasts or festivals. He hadn't heard of any unusual amount of illness in the parish, either. No mysterious chills and fevers. And the Armenian doctors in the neighborhood said the same. They had seen nothing that resembled typhoid except the cases we already had. Before I gave up for the day, I even got in touch with an Armenian girl who used to work at the Department. The only thing I could think of at the moment was a check of the Armenian restaurants. When I mentioned that, she burst out laughing. It seems Armenians don't frequent Armenian restaurants. They prefer home cooking."

"I got Pellitteri's report the next morning," Dr. Fuerst said. "And Miss Matthews'. I was back at the hospital, and when I called Birnkrant, he gave me the gist of them. I can't say I was greatly surprised. To tell the truth, I was relieved. The Armenian picnic I'd hypothesized the day before would have created a real mess. Because the hospital had reported two new cases. Two women. They lived at 500 West 178th Street and 611 West 180th Street, but they weren't Armenians. One was Italian. The other was plain American. So we were right back where we started. Only, now we had five cases instead of three, and nothing to tie them together but the fact that they all lived in the same neighborhood. And had the same brand of typhoid. There are around a dozen different strains, you know, which sometimes complicates matters. About the only thing Birnkrant and I could be sure of was that the feast theory—any kind of common gathering—was out. I'd had a word with the new patients. They had never even heard of each other. So the link had to be indirect. That gave us a number of possibilities. The source of infection could be water—either drinking water or a swimming pool. Or it could be commercial ice. Or milk. Or food. Drinking water was a job for Sanitary Engineering. The others, at the moment, were up to us—meaning Pellitteri and me. They were all four conceivable. Even ice. You can find a precedent for anything and everything in the literature on typhoid. But just one was probable. That was food. Some food that is sold already prepared —like potato salad or frozen custard—or one that is usually eaten raw. All we had to do was find out what it was, and where they got it, and how it got that way. Birnkrant and I figured out the area involved. It came to roughly four square blocks. I don't know if you know that part of Washington Heights. It's no prairie. Every building is a big apartment house, and the ground floors of most are stores. At least a fourth have something to do with food."

"I was in the office when Fuerst called," Dr. Pellitteri said. "Before he hung up, I got on the phone and we made the necessary arrangements about questioning the patients and their families— who was to see who. Then I took off. I wasn't too pessimistic. The odds were against a quick answer, but you never know. It was just possible that they all bought from the same store. Well, as it happened, they did. In a way. The trouble was it wasn't one store. It was practically all of them. Fuerst had the same experience. We ended up at the office that evening with a list as long as my arm— half a dozen fruit-vegetable stands, four or five groceries, a market that sold clams, and an assortment of ice-cream parlors and confectioneries and delicatessens. Moreover, we couldn't even be sure the list included the right store. Most people have very strange memories. They forget and they imagine. You've got to assume that most of the information they give you may be either incomplete or inaccurate, or both. But there *was* a right store—we knew that. Sanitary Engineering had eliminated drinking water, and we had been able to rule out swimming and milk and ice. Only one of the group ever went swimming, all but one family had electric refrigerators, and none of them had drunk unpasteurized milk. It had to be contaminated food from a store. That much was certain."

"It was also certain that we had to have some help," Dr. Fuerst said, "Pellitteri and I could have handled a couple of stores. Or even, at a pinch, three or four. But a dozen or more—it would take us weeks. Let me give you an idea what an investigation like that involves. You don't just walk in the store and gaze around. You more or less take it apart. Every item of food that could conceivably cause trouble is examined, the physical setup is inspected for possible violations of the Sanitary Code, and all employees and their families are interviewed and specimens taken for laboratory analysis. So we needed help, and, of course, we got it. Birnkrant had a conference with the Commissioner the next morning and they talked it over, and the result was an engineer and another nurse and a fine big team from Food and Drugs. Very gratifying."

"And Miss Matthews," Dr. Pellitteri said. "We had her back again. She had finally finished with her carriers. They were all like the first. None had violated any of the rules."

"As expected," Dr. Fuerst said. "The average carrier is pretty coöperative. Well, that was Saturday. By Monday, we had made a certain amount of progress. We hadn't found anything yet, but the field was narrowing down. And all of a sudden we got a little nibble. It came from a confectionery called Pop's, on 178th Street, around noon. Pop's had been well up on our list. They sold ice cream made on the premises, and the place was a neighborhood favorite. Which meant it got a very thorough going over. But we were about ready to cross it off—everything was in good shape, including the help—when it developed that the place had just changed hands. Pop had sold out a week before, and he and his wife, who'd helped him run it, were on the way to California. Needless to say, Pop's went back on the list, and at the top. Also, somebody did some quick checking. Pop and his wife were driving, and their plan was to spend a few days with friends in Indianapolis. That gave us a chance. We called Birnkrant and he called Indianapolis—the State Health Department. They were extremely interested. Naturally. They said they'd let us know."

Dr. Fuerst lighted a cigarette. "Then we got a jolt," he said. "Several, in fact. The first was a call from the hospital. Four new cases. That brought the total up to nine. But it didn't stay there long. Tuesday night, it went to ten. I don't mind saying that set us back on our heels. Ten cases of typhoid fever in less than a week in one little corner of the city is almost unheard of in this day and age. The average annual incidence for the whole of Washington Heights is hardly half a case. That wasn't the worst of it, though. The real blow was that tenth case. I'll call him Jones. Jones didn't fit in. The four Monday cases, like the three Armenians and the Italian and the American, all lived in that one four-block area. Jones didn't. He lived on 176th Street, but way over west, almost on Riverside Drive. An entirely different neighborhood. I had a word with Jones the first thing Wednesday morning. I remember he worked for the post office. That's about all I learned. He hardly knew where he was. When I left the hospital, I called on his wife. She wasn't much help, either. She did all the family marketing, she told me, and she did it all within a block or two of home. That was that. She was very definite. On the other hand, there was Mr. Jones. He had typhoid, which doesn't just happen, and it was the same strain as all the rest. So either it was a very strange coincidence or she was too upset to think. My preference, until proved otherwise, was the latter. I found a phone, and called Birnkrant and gave him the latest news. He had some news for me. Indianapolis had called. They had located Pop and his wife and made the usual tests. The results were negative."

"I don't know which was the most discouraging," Dr. Pellitteri said. "Jones, I guess. He meant more work—a whole new string of stores to check. Pop had been ninety per cent hope. He merely aroused suspicion. He ran a popular place, he sold homemade ice cream, and when the epidemic broke, he pulled out. Or so it appeared from where we stood. It hurt to lose him. Unlikely or not, he had been a possibility—the first specific lead of any kind that we had been able to find in a week of mighty hard work. During the next few days, it began to look more and more like the last. Until Friday evening. Friday evening we got a very excited call from the laboratory. It was about a batch of specimens we had submitted that morning for analysis. One of them was positive for *E. typhosa.* The man's name doesn't matter. It didn't even then. What did matter was his occupation. He was the proprietor of a little frozen-custard shop—now extinct—that I'll call the Jupiter. The location was interesting, too. It was a trifle outside our area, but still accessible, and a nice, easy walk from the Joneses'. Food and Drugs put an embargo on the Jupiter that night. The next morning, we began to take it apart."

"I missed that," Dr. Fuerst said. "I spent Saturday at the hospital. It was quite a day. We averaged a case an hour. I'm not exaggerating. When I finally left, the count was nine. Nine brand-new cases. A couple of hours later, one more turned up. That made twenty, all told. Fortunately, that was the end. Twenty was the grand total. But, of course, we didn't know that then. There was no reason to believe they wouldn't just keep coming."

"The rest of us had the same kind of day," Dr. Pellitteri said. "Very disagreeable. There was the owner of the Jupiter—poor devil. You can imagine the state he was in. All of a sudden, he was out of business and a public menace. He didn't even know what a typhoid carrier was. He had to be calmed down and instructed. That was the beginning. It got worse. First of all, the Jupiter was as clean as a whistle. We closed it up—had to, under the circum-

stances—and embargoed the stock, but we didn't find anything.
That was peculiar. I can't explain it even now. He was either just
naturally careful or lucky. While that was going on, we went back
to the patients and questioned them again. Did they know the
Jupiter? Were they customers? Did they ever buy anything there?
We got one yes. The rest said no. Emphatically. If there had been
a few more yeses—even three or four—we might have wondered.
But they couldn't all be mistaken. So the Jupiter lead began to look
pretty wobbly. Then the laboratory finished it off. They had a type
report on the Jupiter organism. It wasn't the *E. typhosa* we were
looking for. It was one of the other strains. That may have been
some consolation to Mr. Jupiter. At least, he didn't have an
epidemic on his conscience. But it left us uncomfortably close to
the end of our rope. We had only a handful of stores still to check.
If we didn't find the answer there, we were stumped. We didn't.
We crossed off the last possibility on Tuesday morning, August 27th.
It was Number Eighty. We'd examined eighty stores and something like a thousand people, and all we had to show for it was a
new carrier."

"Well, that was something," Dr. Fuerst said. "Even if it was
beside the point. But we also had another consolation. None of the
patients had died. None was going to. They were all making excellent progress."

"That's true enough," Dr. Pellitteri said. "But we couldn't claim
much credit for that." He paused, and shifted around in his chair.
"About all we can take any credit for is Miss Gamso, here," He
smiled. "Miss Gamso saved the day. She got inspired."

Miss Gamso gave me a placid look. "I don't know about
inspired " she said. "It was more like annoyed. I heard them talking
—Dr. Birnkrant, and these two, and all the rest of them—and I
read the reports, and the days went by and they didn't seem to be
getting anywhere. That's unusual. So it was irritating. It's hard to
explain, but I got to thinking about that carrier Mrs. Christos.
There were two things about her. She lived with a son-in-law who
was a known food handler. He was a baker by trade. Also, where she
lived was right in the middle of everything—519 West 178th
Street. That's just off Audubon. And Audubon is the street where
practically all our cases did most of their shopping. Well, there
was one store in particular—a fruit-and-vegetable market called
Tony's—on almost everybody's list. The address was 261 Audubon
Avenue. Then I really got a brainstorm. It was right after lunch on
Tuesday, August 27th. I picked up the telephone and called the
bureau that registers house numbers at the Borough President's
office, and I asked them one question. Did 519 West 178th Street
and 261 Audubon Avenue happen by any chance to be the same
building? They asked me why I wanted to know. I wasn't talking,

though. I just said was it, in a nice way, and the man finally said he'd see. When he came back, I was right. They were one and the same. I was so excited I thought I'd burst. Dr. Pellitteri was sitting right where he is now. He was the first person I saw, so I marched straight over and told him. He kind of stared at me. He had the funniest expression." Miss Gamso smiled a gentle smile. "I think he thought I'd gone crazy."

"I wouldn't say that," Dr. Pellitteri said. "I'll admit, however, that I didn't quite see the connection. We'd been all over Tony's—it was almost our first stop—and there was no earthly reason to question Miss Matthews' report on Mrs. Christos. The fact that they occupied the same building was news to me. To all of us, as I recall. But what if they did? Miss Gamso thought it was significant or suspicious or something. The point escaped me. When she mentioned the son-in-law, though, I began to get a little more interested. We knew him, of course—anybody who lives with a carrier is a potential cause of trouble—and checked on him regularly. But it was just possible that since our last checkup he had become infected. That happens. And although we hadn't found him working in any of the stores, he could have come and gone a couple of weeks before we started our investigation. At any rate, it was worth looking into. Almost anything was, by then. I went up that afternoon. I walked past Tony's on the way to 519. There wasn't any doubt about their being in the same building. Tony's is gone now, like Mrs. Christos, but the way it was then, his front door was about three steps from the corner, and around the corner about three more steps was the entrance to the apartments above. The Christos flat was on the fifth floor—Apartment 53. Mrs. Christos and her son-in-law were both at home. They let me in and that's about all. I can't say they were either one delighted to see me. Or very helpful. She couldn't add anything to what she had already told Miss Matthews. The son-in-law hardly opened his mouth. His last regular job, he said, had been in January, in a cafeteria over in Astoria. Since then, he'd done nothing but odd jobs. He wouldn't say what, when, or where. I couldn't completely blame him. He was afraid that if we got to questioning any of his former employers, they'd never take him on again. When I saw how it was, I arranged for a specimen, and, for the moment, let it go at that. There was no point in getting rough until we knew for sure. I told him to sit tight. If he was positive, I'd be back in a hurry. I got the report the next day. He wasn't. He was as harmless as I am. But by then it didn't matter. By that time, it was all over. To tell the truth, I had the answer before I ever left the building."

Dr. Pellitteri shook his head. "I walked right into it," he said. "It was mostly pure luck. What happened was this. On the way out, I ran into the superintendent—an elderly woman. I was feeling two ways about the son-in-law—half sympathetic and half suspicious. It occurred to me that the superintendent might have some idea where he'd been working the past few weeks. So I stopped and asked. She was a sour old girl. She didn't know and didn't care. She had her own troubles. They were the tenants, mainly. She backed me into a corner and proceeded to unload. The children were the worst, she said—especially the boys. Always thinking up some new devilment. For example, she said, just a few weeks ago, toward the end of July, there was a gang of them up on the roof playing wild Indians. Before she could chase them off, they'd stuffed some sticks down one of the plumbing vent pipes. The result was a stoppage. The soil pipe serving one whole tier of apartments blocked and sprang a leak, and the bathroom of the bottom apartment was a nice mess. I hadn't been paying much attention until then. But at that point—Well, to put it mildly, I was fascinated. Also, I began to ask some questions. I wanted to know just what bathroom had flooded. The answer was Apartment 23. What were the other apartments in that tier? They were 33, 43, and 53. What was underneath Apartment 23? A store—Tony's Market, on the corner. Then I asked for a telephone. Birnkrant's reaction was about what you'd expect. Pretty soon, a team from Sanitary Engineering arrived. They supplied the details and the proof. Tony stored his fruits and vegetables in a big wooden walk-in refrigerator at the rear of his store. When Sanitary Engineering pulled off the top, they found the soil pipe straight overhead. The leak had been repaired almost a month before, but the sawdust insulation in the refrigerator roof was still damp from the waste that had soaked through. It wasn't Tony's fault. He hadn't known. It wasn't anybody's fault. It was just one of those things. So that was that."

"Not entirely," Dr. Fuerst said. "There was still Jones to account for. It wasn't necessary. The thing was settled. But I was curious. I had a talk with him the next day. We talked and talked. And in the end, he remembered. He was a night walker. Every evening after dinner, he went out for a walk. He walked all over Washington Heights, and usually, somewhere along the line, he stopped and bought something to eat. It was generally a piece of fruit. As I say, he finally remembered. One night, near the end of July, he was walking down Audubon and he came to a fruit stand and he bought an apple. On the way home, he ate it."

QUESTIONS

1. "*Typhoid is invariably conveyed . . .*" (*p. 1321*). *If you change invariably to all, you have the major premise of a syllogism: All typhoid is conveyed . . . victims. On August 15 the Bureau of Preventable Diseases was given a minor premise: Three people in Washington Heights have typhoid. What is the conclusion of this syllogism and how did it govern the entire investigation?*

2. What is the relation of the bureau's file of carriers to this syllogism?
3. How does Roueché's narrative correspond to the process of investigation? What is the effect of his narrative?
4. How far did methodical or systematic investigation get the bureau? What else was necessary to complete the investigation?
5. On page 1258 Platt("Style in Science") distinguishes work method from style. How could the typhoid investigation be said to show an interplay between the two?

EDWARD S. DEEVEY, JR.

Bogs

Matthew Arnold could never have expressed his feeling for Dover Beach with such words as: "The heath is calm tonight,/ The swamp is full, the moon lies fair/ Upon the peat." For the poetic geographer a bog is Gothic when it is not downright menacing, a "ghoul-haunted woodland" or a trysting place for witches. Myths of bogland are very old, and may be based on a well-founded dread of savage woodsmen; Western civilization, originating near the Mediterranean shores, has fought the forest and its denizens at every step, and has successively driven the Goth, the Pict, the Caledonian and the Seminole into dank morasses of oblivion. Today the connection between Picts and pixies, bogs and bogeys is generally forgotten. By odd coincidence, however, the bog itself offers a historical record of changing landscape and climate that leads back into those murky mists of memory. Close study suggests also that the boglands of the Northern Hemisphere may be cast to play an ominous role in changes of the earth's climate that are yet to come.

The true bog must be distinguished from the reedy marsh. Marshes form near salt water and contain mainly grasses; few trees other than mangroves can stand much salt around their roots. Bogs are found in the drier interiors of continents as well as near the ocean, but they require some rainfall—deserts have few bogs. If the rainfall is great enough and the summers are cool enough for trees to grow on the uplands of a region, bogs may be expected in the lowlands. Bogs in rainy areas may be more sodden than a tropical rain forest, but the rain water they soak up contains few salts and other nutrients. Only plants that partake sparingly of nutrients, like the shrubs and perennials of arctic barrens and cold steppes, can survive in a bog.

Upland and lowland are relative terms, and refer to the flow of water through the ground. Whenever a barrier lies athwart the flow, water is interrupted in its steady descent to the sea and may rise above the surface of the ground behind the dam. So lowlands can occur near the tops of hills. A lake of clear water formed in this way will not last long. An entering stream dumps silt into the lake, and plants growing along the water's edge add their debris. More organic material may be deposited by runoff from land above the lake, especially from swampy flats. Eventually the lake is obliterated and the mud becomes firm enough to support shrubs and then trees. Pools left in the center of the lake may be bridged by plants like the sedge or swamp loosestrife. With their aid other plants form a floating mat on which trees can grow while the water below is yet unfilled. Most bogs are probably made in this way.

The raised bog (the German *Hochmoor*) does not have to start in a lake but can form in any wet meadow. It depends on the presence of sphagnum, commonly known as peat moss. When dry, this remarkable substance resembles a sponge in its ability to take up great quantities of water by capillary action. It holds more water than absorbent cotton and so is useful as a plant mulch or even as a surgical dressing. The accumulation of dead sphagnum in a meadow forms a layer of half-decayed material, or peat, which draws ground water upward, thus permitting still more of the moss to grow on top. Where sphagnum grows in large masses, it actually raises the water table. When thoroughly wet, however, peat is as impervious to more water as dry rock. Rainwater then cannot percolate downward and runs off horizontally. The extra water eventually reaches the edge of the dome-shaped mass of sphagnum, where the peat is thinner. Thus watered at its margins, the bog grows upward and outward, and can even grow uphill. Plants other than sphagnum grow on the surface, and their remains are added to the peat. So long as the bog is growing, this debris, being water-soaked, accumulates almost unchanged. Eventually the bog reaches a size at which evaporation from the surface balances the rainfall and upward flow of ground water, and growth on the bog halts. Plant debris on the surface then decays about as fast as it accumulates, and little or no new peat forms. Material below the outer skin of the bog does not decay because oxygen cannot reach it, and plant remains—even corpses of men—do not decompose for centuries. Heather or other shrubs of the same family may grow on the stabilized surface, but few trees are to be seen. A growth of forest on a raised bog probably implies a recent change toward a drier climate.

All bogs are stores of peat with sluggish circulation. The water at the surface is poor in salts and bases, partly because much of it is rain water, and partly also because the peat absorbs dissolved matter like a chemist's Amberlite resin. In most boggy districts there is a third reason: The local rock is usually granite, which contributes almost no minerals to the ground water flowing through it. The result is that bog plants are starved for lime, phosphorus and nitrogen. The deeper the peat, the more this is true. In consequence bogs are enclaves of subarctic life; they abound in plants like black spruce, cotton grass and Labrador tea. The bogs of Cape Cod support cranberries; those of New Jersey, blueberries. Both these plants are heaths of northern lands. Even subarctic animals like the bog lemming and the olivebacked thrush may be found far south of their regular ranges, giving bogs in temperate regions a northern flavor. In a sense they were left behind as the last continental ice sheet retreated northward, taking with it the belts of tundra and taiga (spruce forest) that lay beyond its margin when it covered the present locations of New York and Chicago. Probably no area has been continuously boggy since those days, but any partly closed-in bog in the northern U.S. can be thought of, from a lemming's point of view, as tundra enclosed by taiga.

Amid the plants of the muskeg, however, are others reminiscent of the tropics. Sogginess and nitrogen deficiency are common to rain forests as well as to bogs. So a few of the hardier orchids have ventured northward to meet the Labrador tea. Insectivorous plants, mainly tropical, are also successful in bogs, since their unorthodox behavior solves the problem of nitrogen deficiency; sundews, butterwort and pitcher plants grow in bogs. The pitcher plants, in fact, go north almost to the arctic tree-line, and their rain-filled leaves serve not only as traps for unwary insects but, being enriched in nitrogen and phosphorus, form an aquatic habitat for the larvae of other insects (particularly those of midges, blowflies and mosquitoes) which can withstand the digestive enzymes in the leaves. The pitcher plant mosquito (*Wyeomyia smithii*) has followed its host northward.

Although cool, cloudy summers are essential for the existence of a raised bog, a few hot days will not destroy it, but will merely dry out its surface. A bog can then be crossed dry-shod. In damp or cooler weather it squishes underfoot like the arctic muskeg. A change in temperature or rainfall over a long period of time, however, upsets the stability of a bog. Raised bogs especially are sensitive indicators of climate. If the climate becomes moister or cooler, the bogs renew their growth both upward and outward. In drier or warmer conditions the surface will stabilize, but air will penetrate deeper into the drying peat and the zone of decay will thicken downward. If the drought is long-continued, the peat will be deeply weathered, the decay zone extending even into the older peat, and the bog will dwindle away in the sun like an ice cube.

Sensitive indicators of weather are nowhere hard to find. In tune with the variable march of the seasons, some insects emerge, some birds arrive or depart, some flowers bloom. The term of such an indicator, however, is short. Bogs exist for such long periods and respond to weather so slowly that they integrate weather into climate. Best of all, they also record it. When we cut into a bog for fuel and garden mulch, it resembles a cake of three, four, five or more layers, each marking a change in climate. At each boundary the dark, well-oxidized peat which formed, or rather weathered, when that layer was at the surface is topped by a brighter, fresher (and less combustible) peat representing renewed growth.

The episodes of rejuvenation indicated by the layers in any one bog may not mean anything important. The local water table could rise and fall for many reasons. But when all the bogs for miles around have layers formed at the same time, the implication can only be that the climate has changed repeatedly. Bright-colored layers composed of raw sphagnum peat, rich in the remains of such water plants as cotton grass, record a stage of flooding which lasted for years: the climate was cooler, and rainfall was more effective. Dark-colored, humus-rich peat—poor in recognizable fossils because of oxidation, but sometimes containing the remains of heather, birch, or alder—records a stage of stability or destruction during a run of drier, warmer summers.

This matchless record of past climates needs only a time scale to be read with assurance. The climatic chronology determined by the pollen method—according to ratios of fossilized pollen grains from different plants—is relatively coarse. Pollen is plentiful in the peat, but a pollen period is thousands of years long, covering the span of two or three bog layers. Nevertheless one point of equivalence with the pollen chronology became obvious early in the science of bogs. Before 1916, when the pollen method was founded by the great Swedish geologist Lennart von Post, C. A. Weber had noticed that one of the episodes of bog rejuvenation in northern Germany was especially well-marked and widespread. Von Post soon realized that Weber's *Grenzhorizont*[1] coincided with the beginning of his own last pollen period, the "sub-Atlantic climatic deterioration" when northern countries such as Germany and Sweden became cold and rainy. Refinements such as radiocarbon dating confirm von Post's deduction that Europe's climate took a turn for the worse about 600 B.C. The upland vegetation responded to the new conditions slowly—some plants thriving, others dying out—and the pollen count reflects this. But the bogs record a finer embroidery of moisture changes superimposed on the longer swings of temperature.

Human history has not been unrelated to these events. The decline of Greece and the rise of Rome clearly correlate with climatic change shortly after 600 B.C. The climate was somewhat better when Rome's power was at its height, but Rome's conquest of Britain was given up, in part for climatic reasons, at the time of another change, about A.D. 400. As Gibbon put it, "The masters of the fairest and most wealthy climates on the globe turned with con-

1. Boundary line.

tempt . . . from the cold and lonely heaths over which the deer of the forest were chased by a troop of naked barbarians." Since that time, or at most since 600 B.C., the extraordinary blanket-bog has crept like a glacier down the slopes of the Irish and Scottish mountains, and down the Pennines in England, overwhelming pine forests and cropland alike. Today the British Isles are very different from the sunny, forested land the Neolithic farmers knew in the third millennium B.C. Already in the Middle Bronze Age (about 1200 B.C.) the bogs were getting out of hand. Wooden tracks were laid over the increasingly squishy countryside, in an effort to keep trade routes open. Such tracks, datable by pollen, by artifacts and by radiocarbon, often turn up when British bogs are dug.

Most of Europe's forests were cut down long ago. Peat is not so good a fuel as wood, but it will burn, and the heat can be used for distilling. Fortified with peat-smoke-flavored alcohol, a man can tolerate the sight of a treeless landscape and can even come to prefer a heath to a forest. The raised bogs have been drained and dug extensively in Ireland, Scotland, Denmark, western Scandinavia, northern Germany, and to a smaller extent in Maine and New Brunswick, where wood is more plentiful. As a fuel resource the peat bogs of the world are not to be despised. George Kazakov, a Russian peat expert now living in this country, computes that there are 223 billion dry tons of peat available on earth, more than half of it in the U.S.S.R.

So large a supply of combustible carbohydrate, delicately poised between growth and destruction, can seriously affect the earth's carbon balance. The carbon-dioxide content of air has increased by 11 per cent since about 1870 and apparently is still increasing. Radiocarbon assays by Hans Suess, now of the Scripps Institution of Oceanography, prove that most of the added carbon dioxide is compounded of modern carbon. It is much too young, judging by its high radiocarbon content, to have all come from the burning of fossil fuels by industry. Fossil fuels can account for only a small portion of the increase. The rest of the new carbon dioxide must be modern, and a finger of suspicion points to bogs as the source.

The warming of the world's climate since the last century may well have set a slow fire to the peat, simply by favoring surface oxidation by soil bacteria. If the world's climate should become so warm and dry that all the peat is oxidized, about 366 billion tons of carbon dioxide would be released. This is a sixth of the amount now present in the atmosphere, and the whole reserve of carbon in land plants and animals is only 15 times as much. The estimate does not include the carbon of humus in ordinary soils which would also be oxidized if the climate changed. So it is not impossible that the carbon dioxide added to the earth's atmosphere may have come mainly from peat and humus.

Though the changes of climate and of the amount of carbon dioxide have run parallel, we cannot yet be sure which is cause and which effect. Carbon dioxide added to air causes it to absorb more heat from the sun, and it may be that the climate has become warmer because of the extra 11 per cent of "dephlogisticated air."[2] If so, we may be in for trouble. A doubling in the carbon dioxide content of the air would almost certainly warm the climate enough to cause the glaciers to melt. The added water would raise the sea level perhaps by 100 feet, drowning the largest cities of the world. It may be that before such a calamity happens, a new balance will be struck; the carbon dioxide should be dissolved in the oceans, and it is a major mystery why the extra 11 per cent has not been dissolved already. But if the added carbon dioxide does not go into the oceans, New York and London will simply have to move, and the pixies too will need new haunts, for the bogs will be thin air.

2. Here, carbon dioxide, although the usual term (drawn from eighteenth-century chemistry) was "phlogisticated air." "Phlogiston" was the hypothetical element believed to be contained in all combustible substances and liberated from them in the process of combustion. The "air" in a closed space was said to be "phlogisticated" when nothing more could be burned in it; hence gases that would not support combustion (including carbon dioxide) were "phlogisticated air." "Dephlogisticated air," on the other hand, was Priestley's term for the "air" that absorbs "phlogiston" readily and hence supports violent combustion—oxygen.

ROBERT ARDREY
From Territory to Nation[1]

The lemur did not invent the society of outward antagonism. He merely applied an ancient behavioral solution to the new primate problem of life in the light of day. To find its evolutionary origins one must go an astonishingly long way back.

Protozoa, as we all know, are one-celled creatures, and their history must date from the first billion years of emergent life. One kind of protozoa are known as slime molds. They are of the size and general appearance of a white blood cell, and they feed on bacteria such as one finds in moist soil. They divide every three or four hours, and so a population multiplies rapidly. Just about the time, however, when growing numbers have exhausted the food supply in a given area, the single-cell creatures enter the second phase of their life cycle. They begin to form societies. Around a founder cell others will bunch in a growing aggregate, clinging together until they have formed a sausage-shaped slug visible to the

1. From *The Territorial Imperative.* This is the second section of the chapter on the nation; the first section described the work of Jean-Jacques Petter in Madagascar on lemur groups unified by a common antagonism to groups on adjoining territories.

naked eye. Now this social slug of individual beings begins to behave as a single organism, and it will even move toward warmth or toward light with precision of direction. At last a portion of the community will differentiate themselves and form a stalk which they stiffen with a secretion. Then others will crawl on top of the stalk and form a sphere of cells each containing a spore, the seed of a new generation.

It sounds like something out of science fiction, but it is not. It is simply a way of life that was worked out a billion-odd years ago and that still works. How it works defies the imagination—or, more accurately, gives some slight evidence as to how little we know about living processes. One aspect, however, of the social behavior of slime molds has yielded to laboratory investigation. It is what I define as a society of outward antagonism founded on the defense of a social territory.

Investigators have been puzzling over the behavior of slime molds ever since their discovery in 1935. An American scientist began wondering if there could be some form of communication between cells. Placed in a culture dish, they distributed themselves so evenly in their first phase of life that it seemed they repelled each other. (We should call it individual distance.) Then when the time came for aggregation, it was as if a new signal went out and all obeyed. An investigator named Arndt, working in Germany, made the striking observation that the number of fruiting societies in a given area was independent of the number of individuals. In other words, if you had a thousand protozoa in an area, they might form ten groups of a hundred each. But if you had ten thousand, they would still form ten groups. The societies were somehow a function of space, not numbers.

Only recently an American biologist, John Tyler Bonner of Princeton University, has demonstrated that in a given species of slime molds, the size of the social territory is a constant. And he has proved what had been suspected for some time, that the means of social defense is a gas which repels other groups to a given distance and at the same time attracts the clan. Charcoal absorbs gas. By placing charcoal in his culture, Bonner reduced territory size so that four times as many social aggregates crowded the area.

I do not happen to know of an earlier example of the society of outward antagonism, isolated and unified by the defense of a social territory. Ants and termites do something like it. Since early in the century, when the study of social insects was in high fashion, it has been known that every colony has its own peculiar odor, and that a worker, for example, returning to the wrong colony will be smelled by guards, recognized, and instantly attacked. It was thought for a while that the difference in odor might arise from different sources of food supply. Recently, however, a colleague of Wynne-Edwards at Aberdeen, D. I. Wallis, has shown that in ant colonies the familiar, attractive odor of a social partner and the strange, repellent odor of the foreigner must at least in part be genetically determined.

We must be always wary of conclusions drawn from the ways of the social insect, since their evolutionary track lies so far from ours. But when we find a familiar behavior pattern in a common ancestral type, the protozoa, a creature so remote, so lost in the tides of animate beginnings, then an honest man must take a deep breath and ask of himself, What came first, the cart or the horse? What ultimately preceded which, body or behavior? We know today that it is a behavioral adaptation that as a rule precedes and gives selective value to bodily change. But has natural selection for two billion years chosen among increasingly complex anatomical possibilities to fulfill increasingly complex behavior patterns? Or did these complex patterns exist from the near-beginning in creatures so simple that they lacked any apparent anatomical structures to maintain them?

These are questions of philosophical note which before this inquiry closes we may perhaps be enabled to ask with sharper precision. In the meanwhile we must give our attention to a question of more immediate concern to the human circumstance: Why have students of men failed to gain from students of the animal any notion concerning the biological origins of the nation? When the true lemur, possessing nothing but the anatomical rudiments of our Eocene primate dawn, introduced a social organization which men in their time would so intricately explore, he was merely picking up a ticket written a billion or so years earlier by the brainless, nerveless, sexless, almost formless one-celled protozoa. It passes all logic to believe that if the society integrated by its outward antagonisms has a history so venerable in the transactions of animals, it could have no bearing on the passages of men. But the question, seemingly so innocent, directs an ultimate earthquake at the more inflexible structures of contemporary thought; and in all responsibility we must inform ourselves, as fully as the new biology at present permits us, concerning the implications of the social territory and the consequences which its discovery brought to the development of the territorial concept.

I have traced the ponderings of science from the days of Aristotle and Zeno down through Altum and Moffat and Howard to David Lack and his curiosity about the private territory as a reinforcement for the pair bond. In those years, however, we find few observations of any but birds. Eagles and falcons, robins and nightingales, moor hens and meadow warblers were the messengers to bring us word that between a living being and the space he occupies there is a mysterious tie beyond habit or mere familiarity. If our observations of territory were limited, it was because insects and birds, until the 1930's, were very nearly the only wild beings that man had ever studied. Territory remained a form of behavior peculiar to the ornithologist's notebook.

There were exceptions, of course. In 1912 a French psychologist published his *La Génèse des instincts*. From studies of laboratory rats Pierre Hachet-Souplet recorded a pessimistic conclusion that neither reason nor justice could ever contravene "la loi de territoire." I have in my notes no earlier speculation concerning territory and the human being. And one must wonder whether the French psychologist retained his pessimism when two years later the taxicabs of Paris headed for the Marne.[2]

There was another remarkable study of a non-bird made so early that its significance was lost. A. S. Pearse of the University of Wisconsin spent years watching that unlikely animal, the fiddler crab, in such unlikely locations as Manila Bay, the Massachusetts coast, and the flooded mangrove swamps of Colombia. He published his observations in 1913, the year after Hachet-Souplet's. Half a century later his fiddler crabs may startle us; then, lacking frame of reference, they earned small attention.

The fiddler crab is a belligerent little animal who lives on the beach and digs burrows in the sand or mud. When high tide flows, he retreats into his burrow and plugs up the opening. Pearse watched thirteen species and found the same behavior in all. Each individual lives his life near his burrow door, cleaning and scraping the sand about it. Seldom will he move more than a yard or two away, and Pearse established twelve yards as the roving limit. It is the smaller area only that he defends, however, and the fiddler will chase or fight off any intruder on his tiny estate. So vicious is his defense that if a crab is removed experimentally to any distance along a crowded beach, his return will be a harrowing affair. He must cross the territories of others, and he will be attacked by every crab along the way. The chances are better than fair that he will lose a claw, if not his life.

"Each fiddler's hand is against every man," wrote Pearse, and it is almost literally true. One claw of the fiddler is overdeveloped to huge size, sometimes a third of total body weight. This claw is called the chela. It is a brilliantly colored display object, and during the mating season, whenever a female passes, every male in the colony will stand by his burrow frantically waving his chela, often adding to the excitement by squatting and rising as he waves. Throughout the nonbreeding season, however, such diversion is lacking, and then the male fiddler crab finds other uses for his chela. David Lack concluded that fighting is what a robin likes best

2. When the Germans threatened Paris, taxicabs took French troops to the first battle of the Marne.

of all. So does the fiddler crab, but his fighting is highly formalized. Two will meet on a boundary and lock chelae precisely as two men shake hands. The object of the action is simplicity itself: by a sudden wrench to break the other crab's claw off.

Ornithology was naturally unaware of Pearse's crabs, as it was unaware of the unreasonable rats in a Paris laboratory. Interpretations of territory continued to be based entirely on the behavior of birds. And the interpretations—whether the food theory, or the dispersal of breeding pairs, or the natural selection of superior males, or reinforcement of the pair bond—all referred to the competition of individual males and in one way or another to reproduction. But then, in 1934, the American zoologist G. K. Noble brought in the fence lizard and the upsetting news that the female has a territory of her own which she defends against all comers, including males. How such behavior promoted successful reproduction was hard to say.

Many years later the way of a female lizard would be explored in sharper detail by the young Rhodesian all-around scientist C. K. Brain. In *African Genesis* I described the anthropological ingenuities which he applied to the australopithecines, the South African man-apes, and today he is curator of anthropology at South Africa's Transvaal Museum. But there was a period in Brain's career when he wearied of ancient dating, of the tools and fossil memories of small-brained proto-men, and he turned to the Kalahari desert and the chameleon. I could understand his fascination, in a way. On one of his returns from the Kalahari he showed me among other lively reptile samples a creature as upsetting to a layman as is a female proprietor to birdmen. When you looked into one ear of the deplorable creature you saw daylight coming in the other.

The young Rhodesian's confirmation of Noble's observation concerned the female of a common chameleon species who defends a solitary property against all others, female or male, with such vigor as to raise the question, How does she ever mate? By experiment Brain found the answer. The male displays by puffing out his throat. On that throat is a yellow mark which serves to make the female only worse-tempered than ever. But when the sexual season comes around, the yellow fades. She admits him to her property, and they mate. Then the yellow mark returns and she throws him out.

Brain's detailed observations were unnecessary, thirty years earlier, to lend credibility to the fence lizard. G. Kingsley Noble was curator of experimental biology at the American Museum of Natural History and his authority could not be ignored. Ponderous questions were raised for which ornithology had no answer. The female fence lizard's territorial defense most definitely did *not* reinforce a pair bond, did *not* serve to select worthy from unworthy mates, was *not* an expression of male sexual pugnacity, and could by no means be interpreted as protecting the welfare of offspring. Having laid her fertilized eggs, she would from that point on lose all interest in future generations. Then what was the selective value to the species? Brain's later demonstration showed that lizard territory could be definitely anti-sexual, since only by suspension of the behavior could mating take place.

The next non-bird man to complicate ornithology's interpretations was W. H. Burt, whose domain spread through the fields and the woodlands and the brushy river bottoms of southern Michigan, and whose castle was the University of Michigan's zoology department. Burt watched rodents: wood mice, deer mice, pine voles and lemming voles, ground squirrels and flying squirrels, chipmunks. Although he left no book about them, Burt might almost be described as the Eliot Howard[3] of the mouse world.

Rats and mice have always entered the literature of human analogy, and perhaps that is why with Burt's studies one entertains for the first time clear-cut statements of human implication. The bird inhabits the sky, and we do not tend to identify ourselves with a creature so disdainful of human limitation. Eliot Howard may have blurted to a servant girl that territory is everything; but he did not say it in public. The Michigan zoologist, however, did not hesitate to state his conviction that what was true of mice was true of men. Territory for a rodent meant security against the predator. When you live a life of marsh hawks and foxes, then the days will be fairest for those who know their homelands best.

The Muries[4] had a six-week-old deer mouse who homed two miles to the area of her nest. Burt found similar capacities in wood mice. How they got home was as inexplicable as ever, but what they did when they got there was evident. They disappeared. On its own property a small rodent knows every hole, every tunnel, every hiding place. Burt found that a wood mouse released on its own territory would vanish within twenty feet.

Security from the predator is seldom a territorial function in the lives of birds. But in the lives of rodents as in the lives of men its value is universal. One's imagination may spring to the fortified border, the castle, the drawbridge; to the walled town on an Italian hill; to the barrier of living thorns about an African kraäl; to the ancestral cave. Or it may spring no farther than to the striving market place and the quiet chair by the fire. No thoughtful observer of the territorial ways of vulnerable man could fail to recognize in them the ways of the vulnerable wood mouse. I have no doubt but that Burt in his time was accused of anthropomorphism by devotees of human uniqueness wielding vocabularies

3. A British ornithologist, author of *Territory in Bird Life*.

4. Naturalists who investigated the homing habits of deer-mice in Wyoming.

more pretentious than precise. It is an anthropomorphism to attribute to the animal the capacities of man. What Burt was stating was quite the opposite, for he was attributing to man the capacities of the animal.

W. H. Burt was one of the most significant contributors to the concept of territory, and in another field he came into conflict with his contemporaries. A chipmunk, he noted, will vigorously drive away any intruder who comes within fifty yards of her nest. But she will forage for food for a hundred yards or more beyond, ignoring there the same intruder whom she drove away from her nest's vicinity. The defended area, said Burt, is the territory; the foraging area is the home range.

The distinction between territory and range met opposition, since it minimized the economic importance of territory. As we see in instance after instance, there is an allure about the economic principle as there is about the sexual principle, for each provides simple answers: that an answer may be untrue is less formidable than that it be complicated. Fortunately for Burt's distinction, a biologist named Kenneth Gordon was at about the same time watching golden-mantled ground squirrels in the Far West. At two widely separated locations, one in Oregon, one in Colorado, their territorial behavior was identical. A proprietor would chase an intruder for about one hundred feet. But he would forage for nuts and cones to a much greater distance, and there, like the Michigan chipmunks, he would ignore the same individual whom earlier he had pursued. Burt's distinction between range and territory prevailed, and is today accepted widely in science.

While W. H. Burt brought both cleaner definitions and broader horizons to the territorial concept, his rodents and Noble's lizards thoroughly messed up those simpler interpretations drawn only from the life of birds. One principle, however, seemed to remain intact: that whatever the function territory may provide, it remains a competition between individuals and must somehow relate to individual selection. Then the American psychologist C. R. Carpenter returned from Panama with the news that howling monkeys defend as a group a social territory. The last principle was demolished. When five years later, in 1939, Noble at a symposium in Washington casually referred to a territory as "a defended area," biology leaped at the phrase. Problems of function and motivation were relegated to pigeonholes. From that day to this, biology as a whole asks but one question of a territory: is it defended? Defense defines it. Variability became the final description.

Ray Carpenter is a tall, quiet, scholarly man with a touch of Woodrow Wilson about him. And I should find it as difficult to visualize the late American President up to his armpits in an Asian swamp or ducking fecal matter showered down on him by large black belligerent monkeys in a Central American rain forest as I do this elegant academic gentleman in the bifocal glasses. Carpenter today is professor of psychology at Pennsylvania State University, and he lives in a low-flung modern house in a neighboring woodland alive with civilized squirrels and accustomed birds of soft-spoken manner. For a quarter of a century Carpenter's central preoccupation has been with university administration and the mental acrobatics of contemporary man. Yet for almost ten previous years his normal home was the jungle, his normal circle of acquaintance the jungle's temperamental citizens. A full quarter-century before Petter went to Madagascar, Carpenter went to Panama to initiate the modern study of primates in a state of nature.

At the time—and it was not so very long ago, for I must recall that I myself had already completed my formal education—there existed nowhere on earth a body of information acceptable to science which revealed the behavior of apes or monkeys in the wild. The amateur South African naturalist Eugène Marais had at the turn of the century lived for three years with a troop of baboons in the northern Transvaal, but his observations were regarded as unreliable and besides had not yet been translated from Afrikaans. Another South African, S. L. Zuckerman, had published his *Social Life of Monkeys and Apes*, and it was regarded as definitive. But according to the modern authority of K. R. L. Hall and Irven DeVore, Zuckerman's monumental study had included but a few days of experience in the field, and had otherwise been based entirely on observations in the London zoo. In large part, what science knew about the behavior of primates, that zoological family of which we are a part, had been obtained in zoos and laboratories. Under such conditions, so little did the behavior of apes and monkeys resemble our own that we came to the logical conclusion that the human way was of our own making and owed little to animal inheritance. Schools of psychology were set in motion to explain our nature in terms of the conditioned reflex. Trends in anthropology and the social sciences went their cultural or environmentalist ways. Then in 1934 Carpenter made his first return to civilization bearing under his arm a clap of thunder: our information was false.

For two years the American psychologist had been watching howling monkeys on an island in the Panama Canal's Gatun Lake. Barro Colorado Island is almost 4000 acres in extent, and at the time of Carpenter's study it was divided between twenty-eight clans, each defending a social territory and living in total hostility with its neighbors. Only three clans were so small as to include but a single mature male; in all others the males ranged from two to five and the females from two to ten. Carpenter recorded their sexual relations and the care of their young, their social organization and means of communication, and their remarkable systems of group territorial defense. The sum he published in his classic monograph *Behavior and Social Relations of the Howling Monkey.*

The first of those assumptions which his study demolished was the scientific *idée fixe*—one of such influence on the work of Sigmund Freud—that the primate is obsessed with sex and that it is sexual attraction which holds primate troops together. The assumption of a sexual obsession had offered scientific justification for the romantic tenet that love is all, for the psychological tenet that sexual energy is the fuel of the human mechanism, and for the more everyday conclusion that when you come down to it nothing matters much except fornication. The assumption that sexual attraction is the magnet drawing together the adults of a primate society had consequences even more far-reaching: Since human society is most obviously *not* held together by such a sexual magnet, then our forms of social life must be unique to man, created by man, and subject entirely to human manipulation according to our vision of human good. Anything, in a word, is possible. This is the premise of most contemporary sociology. It is also the premise that left the social sciences without other than sentimental defense against such totalitarian glimpses of the human good as fascism and communism. If anything was possible, then these were too.

The sexual assumption lies today in ruins. Mason's study of the callicebus shows the year-around integrity of the family group *except* during the sexual season. Petter's ancient lemurs, unlike most of the later monkeys and apes, retain the general mammal characteristic of seasonal heat and rut; yet their societies show an all-season solidarity. The same has been shown for the rhesus and the related Japanese monkey. Recent studies of less seasonal primates like the gorilla, the baboon, and the chimpanzee offer not a gleam of evidence to support the obsolete assumption that sex is the central preoccupation of the primate and the central force holding together his society. Yet that obsolete assumption remains today the cornerstone of most psychology, most anthropology, and very nearly all of sociology.

The assumption was, of course, rendered obsolete in 1934 by Carpenter's observations of the howling monkey. But he went further to demonstrate that it is the troop itself which is the focus of primate life. In his howler clans sexual jealousy was nonexistent. No male asserted a sexual monopoly over females, and sexual activity was an amiable entertainment in which all males shared all females. But the troop was another matter. No jealousy, neglect of young, defiance of leadership, or failure of communication could exist at the cost of the clan's welfare. Years later S. L. Washburn and Irven DeVore would record that a baboon without its troop is a dead baboon. So it was with Carpenter's howlers. On rare occasions he spotted a solitary male in the forest. But the wandering male was usually one who out of persistent conflict with his fellow males had elected to leave his clan. Someday after further persistent efforts he would join another clan, or failing, he would die alone. Few so failed. A howler without a clan is a man without a country, and what is true of men and howlers is universally true of primate species.

Finally, Carpenter's careful observations showed that the mechanism isolating and integrating the howler clan is its defense of a social territory. The territories of the callicebus, the sifaka, the black lemur are small, the borders cleanly delimited. The territories of howler clans are large, the borders vague. But clans have only to sight each other in this no man's land and total warfare breaks out. Rage shakes the forest. That rage, however, takes none but vocal expression. The howler is equipped with a voice box of dismaying dimension from which emerge cries of discouraging proportion. Black lemurs raise their voices in unison in their *cri du soir*; howler clans raise their deafening voices both morning and night as a warning against intruders. Should intrusion occur, these voices joined will be the artillery of battle. And strictly in accord with the territorial principle, the home team will always win, the visiting team will always withdraw.

The howler clan is what I should call a society of most perfect outward antagonism which has achieved a most perfect inward amity. So different from the *noyau*,[5] the biological nation spends its aggressive energies on enemies foreign, wastes none on enemies domestic. Within the howler society as within the society of the black lemur there reigns a kind of democratic tranquillity. Leadership is present, but authority is restrained. Differences of opinion are settled with a mumble and a grunt. While the female is never dominant, still her status is remarkably high. And as for offspring, they are the joint responsibility of all adults in the troop. All males, in response to a special cry, will go to the rescue of a young one who falls from a tree; all males with concerted action will defend it against the advance of a predator.

Such observations were impossible so long as we drew our conclusions from the behavior of animals in the zoo. There no natural society is possible. There no fear of the predator, no pressure of hunger, no boundary disputes with neighboring bands, not even the inconveniences of bad weather can absorb primate energy. If he seems absorbed by sex, it is simply because his captive life presents him with no other outlet for his energies. Our conclusions concerning the nature of the primate, from which we came to such

5. An animal group which bases its unity on mutual antagonism within the group.

dubious conclusions concerning the nature of man, were based on the behavior of bored, deprived, essentially neurotic animals. Carpenter presented a preliminary review of his new findings at a meeting in 1933. "You're wrong," said a dominant figure in the old biology. "I've only reported what I saw," said Carpenter. "Then you've seen wrong," said the dominant biologist.

Carpenter went back to his rain forests. In succeeding years he added major studies of that small, lithe ape, the gibbon, in Thailand, and of the rhesus monkey both in India and in a free-ranging colony which he established on an island off Puerto Rico, together with lesser studies of the red spider monkey in Panama and of that great ape, the orangutan, in Sumatra. Through the mass and variety of his experience he established standardized, objective, quantitative techniques for the difficult task of observing and recording the behavior of animals in a state of nature. In a sense he imposed the mathematics of the laboratory on the confusion of the jungle, and there are few studies made in the wild today that do not in part found their techniques on those established by Carpenter in the 1930's.

The ultimate importance of his work, of course, was less to the natural sciences than to the social sciences, less to the study of the animal than to the study of man. More recent observation might reveal primate species integrated by other than the social territory. More recent studies might reveal species in which social amity is far less perfect than is achieved by the howling monkey or the gibbon. But Carpenter's discoveries bridged the unbridged gap between man and his primate cousins, and made not only possible but compulsory a consideration of all animate life as an evolutionary whole.

What then was the impact of his discoveries on world science and world thought? The impact may be summarized briefly.

The studies were completed about 1940. When I published *African Genesis* in 1961, all were out of print, some could be obtained in specialized libraries such as those of the British Museum, several existed only as single remaining copies in a file at Carpenter's home. All since, it is pleasant to note, have been reprinted in a single volume, *Naturalistic Behavior of Nonhuman Primates*, by the Pennsylvania State University Press.

Among students of animal behavior, W. C. Allee was one who immediately grasped the whole significance of Carpenter's work, and in his article on animal sociology in the *Encyclopaedia Britannica* he discusses it at length. Little other discussion appeared, however, in reference works available to the layman.

Anyone would assume that political scientists, confronted as they are with nations and nationalism, with inspiring dreams of world federation and with the less inspiring agonies of the United

Nations, would find among their numbers at least a few crackpot souls for whom the animal's social territory carries significance. If there exists such a political scientist, then I admire him. I happen myself to be unaware that the nation as a biological expression has ever entered our lengthiest debates.

One would assume likewise that anthropology, the science of man, would have been revolutionized by Carpenter's findings. For Sir Arthur Keith, anthropology's most famous figure and one of the founders of the science, such a revolution came about. We shall return to Keith later. It is sufficient here to note that when in 1948, at the age of eighty-two, he published his masterwork, *A New Theory of Human Evolution*, he recorded that Carpenter's social territory had been a catalyst for his thinking. The book exists, however, virtually unread.

There are certain anthropologists who in the past few years have found new inspiration in ethology's investigations of animal behavior and paleontology's startling illuminations cast on the human emergence. It would be an exaggeration, though, to state that the name of C. R. Carpenter had made deep inroads on the science as a whole. In 1965, for example, the American Association of Physical Anthropologists held its annual meeting at Carpenter's home university. An official report of the conference was written by an anthropologist from the neighboring University of Pennsylvania and published in *Science*, the organ of the American Association for the Advancement of Science. Passing reference was made to the address on primate behavior delivered at the annual dinner by "Clarence S. Carpenter."

Within the specialized, developing field of ethology, of course, Carpenter's name correctly spelled traveled far. But even there something was strangely missing. When in 1960 I was completing field and reference research for my own book, I faced a mystifying absence of further material on wild primates. Niels Bolwig, the previous year, had published observations of chacma baboons drawn to the garbage pails of a camp in South Africa's Kruger Park. The conditions seemed to me artificial. A Japanese group had begun observations of semi-wild macaques frequenting traditional temple areas, but their preliminary reports had not come my way. For lack of further material I made a wrong guess or two: I underrated primate social ingenuity and presumed that he would always found his society on territory; and I overrated the probable importance of the family as his social building block.

While I was finishing my work, the vanguard of a new generation of primate students was already at theirs. Petter was in Madagascar, K. R. L. Hall in the Cape of Good Hope watching baboons, George Schaller was in the high mists of Congo volcanoes with his mountain gorillas, Jane Goodall was beginning her observations of the savannah chimpanzee near Lake Tanganyika, Adriaan Kortlandt his of forest chimpanzees lingering near a Congo plantation. The following year, too late for my book, Washburn and DeVore gave us the first of the new publications, their superb account of the social life of the baboon. But this was simply the opening wave; then came the flood: K. R. L. Hall on the patas monkey as well as the baboon, Schaller on the orangutan as well as the gorilla, Stuart A. Altmann on the rhesus in Puerto Rico, Charles H. Southwick on the rhesus in India, Stephen Gartlan as well as Brain on vervet monkeys, V. Reynolds on the forest chimp, H. Kummer and F. Kurt on the hamadryas baboon, Mason on the callicebus, Phyllis Jay on langurs, Ellefson on the gibbon in Malaya. Today, one suspects, there must be hardly a bush or a clump of vines that does not shelter a scientist, or a monkey or ape who is not busily engaged in making notes on the remarkable behavior of man.

The primate, in a scientific twinkling, became fashionable. And we may hold the legitimate suspicion, I believe, that a turn so worldwide, so spontaneous, so spectacular, has registered like a fever thermometer some change in the public temper. Monkeys and apes are the most controversial of animals, suffering as they do the misfortune of being closely related to man. And when men abruptly embrace them—it is a guess—we are seeing the first step of a rebellion, probably as yet unconscious, some first symptom of a profound dissatisfaction with all the old answers.

We shall be unwise, however, if we forget that twenty years earlier, when Ray Carpenter last emerged from the rain forest, no scientist took his place beneath the trees. He brought drama, but he played to an empty house. To believe that the sciences are rigidly objective and unswayed by the winds of intellectual fashion, of public mood, of political temper, of personal prejudice, is to go forth into the human storm clad only in trust's most innocent winding sheet. To believe that a scientist is unaffected by public disapproval, unaffected by the regard or disregard of professional colleagues, unaffected by the lack or abundance of funds for his work, is to characterize the scientist as an unperson. We, the laymen of the world, provide the milieu from which the scientist must draw his sustaining breath. You and I, we laymen, provide the freedom and the inhibitions, the receptivity and the intolerance, the affluence and the poverty, the honors and the oblivion which direct our sciences toward this goal, dissuade them from that. And it was you and I, whether we knew it or not, who in the critical year of 1940 and the decades thereafter failed to encourage our sciences to investigate further certain possibilities perhaps remote: that man and the monkey have more in common than mere anatomy; that our infant species is not as yet divorced from evolutionary processes; that nations, human as well as animal, obey the laws of the territorial imperative.

It has been an expensive failure.

QUESTIONS

1. What is the significance of the question Ardrey poses on page 1337, "What ultimately preceded which, body or behavior?" What is Ardrey's thesis and why is it significant?
2. Early in his discussion, before he sets out the implications of the slime mold's behavior, Ardrey concedes that we should be wary of drawing conclusions about humans from the behavior of non-human life. Does he maintain that diffidence throughout? Does the need for such diffidence diminish when primates are the subject of investigation?
3. Ardrey wrote plays before he turned to biological subjects, and he has been accused of letting drama intrude upon science. Assuming that personal conflict is an important element in drama, can you see anything "dramatic" about Ardrey's approach to scientific investigation? What support for such a view could he draw from Platt's essay, "Style in Science" (pp. 1250–1261)?
4. Ardrey dates our failure to encourage certain kinds of scientific investigation from the year 1940. Can you think of any historical reasons for that failure? What is the irony?

KONRAD Z. LORENZ

The Taming of the Shrew[1]

Though Nature, red in tooth and claw,
With ravine, shrieked against his creed.
TENNYSON, *In Memoriam*

All shrews are particularly difficult to keep; this is not because, as we are led proverbially to believe, they are hard to tame, but because the metabolism of these smallest of mammals is so very fast that they will die of hunger within two or three hours if the food supply fails. Since they feed exclusively on small, living animals, mostly insects, and demand, of these, considerably more than their own weight every day, they are most exacting charges. At the time of which I am writing, I had never succeeded in keeping any of the terrestrial shrews alive for any length of time; most of those that I happened to obtain had probably only been caught because they were already ill and they died almost at once. I had never succeeded in procuring a healthy specimen. Now the order Insectivora is very low in the genealogical hierarchy of mammals and is, there-

1. Chapter 9 of *King Solomon's Ring: New Light on Animal Ways*, 1952.

fore, of particular interest to the comparative ethologist. Of the whole group, there was only one representative with whose behavior I was tolerably familiar, namely the hedgehog, an extremely interesting animal of whose ethology Professor Herter of Berlin has made a very thorough study. Of the behavior of all other members of the family practically nothing is known. Since they are nocturnal and partly subterranean animals, it is nearly impossible to approach them in field observation, and the difficulty of keeping them in captivity had hitherto precluded their study in the laboratory. So the Insectivores were officially placed on my program.

First I tried to keep the common mole. It was easy to procure a healthy specimen, caught to order in the nursery gardens of my father-in-law, and I found no difficulty in keeping it alive. Immediately on its arrival, it devoured an almost incredible quantity of earthworms which, from the very first moment, it took from my hand. But, as an object of behavior study, it proved most disappointing. Certainly, it was interesting to watch its method of disappearing in the space of a few seconds under the surface of the ground, to study its astoundingly efficient use of its strong, spade-shaped fore-paws, and to feel their amazing strength when one held the little beast in one's hand. And again, it was remarkable with what surprising exactitude it located, by smell, from underground, the earthworms which I put on the surface of the soil in its terrarium. But these observations were the only benefits I derived from it. It never became any tamer and it never remained above ground any longer than it took to devour its prey; after this, it sank into the earth as a submarine sinks into the water. I soon grew tired of procuring the immense quantities of living food it required and, after a few weeks, I set it free in the garden.

It was years afterwards, on an excursion to that extraordinary lake, the Neusiedlersee, which lies on the Hungarian border of Austria, that I again thought of keeping an insectivore. This large stretch of water, though not thirty miles from Vienna, is an example of the peculiar type of lake found in the open steppes of Eastern Europe and Asia. More than thirty miles long and half as broad, its deepest parts are only about five feet deep and it is much shallower on the average. Nearly half its surface is overgrown with reeds which form an ideal habitat for all kinds of water birds. Great colonies of white, purple, and grey heron and spoonbills live among the reeds and, until a short while ago, glossy ibis were still to be found here. Greylag geese breed here in great numbers and, on the eastern, reedless shore, avocets and many other rare waders can regularly be found. On the occasion of which I am speaking, we, a dozen tired zoologists, under the experienced guidance of my friend Otto Koenig, were wending our way, slowly and painfully, through the forest of reeds. We were walking in single file, Koenig first, I second, with a few students in our wake. We literally left a wake, an inky-black one in pale grey water. In the reed forests of Lake Neusiedel, you walk knee deep in slimy, black ooze, wonderfully perfumed by sulphureted-hydrogen–producing bacteria. This mud clings tenaciously and only releases its hold on your foot with a loud, protesting plop at every step.

After a few hours of this kind of wading you discover aching muscles whose very existence you had never suspected. From the knees to the hips you are immersed in the milky, clay-colored water characteristic of the lake, which, among the reeds, is populated by myriads of extremely hungry leeches conforming to the old pharmaceutical recipe, "*Hirudines medicinales maxime affamati.*"[2] The rest of your person inhabits the upper air, which here consists of clouds of tiny mosquitoes whose bloodthirsty attacks are all the more exasperating because you require both your hands to part the dense reeds in front of you and can only slap your face at intervals. The British ornithologist who may perhaps have envied us some of our rare specimens will perceive that bird watching on Lake Neusiedel is not, after all, an entirely enviable occupation.

We were thus wending our painful way through the rushes when suddenly Koenig stopped and pointed mutely towards a pond, free from reeds, that stretched in front of us. At first, I could only see whitish water, dark blue sky and green reeds, the standard colors of Lake Neusiedel. Then, suddenly, like a cork popping up on to the surface, there appeared, in the middle of the pool, a tiny black animal, hardly bigger than a man's thumb. And for a moment I was in the rare position of a zoologist who sees a specimen and is not able to classify it, in the literal sense of the word: I did not know to which class of vertebrates the object of my gaze belonged. For the first fraction of a second I took it for the young of some diving bird of a species unknown to me. It appeared to have a beak and it swam on the water like a bird, not in it as a mammal. It swam about in narrow curves and circles, very much like a whirligig beetle, creating an extensive wedge-shaped wake, quite out of proportion to the tiny animal's size. Then a second little beast popped up from below, chased the first one with a shrill, bat-like twitter, then both dived and were gone. The whole episode had not lasted five seconds.

I stood open-mouthed, my mind racing. Koenig turned round with a broad grin, calmly detached a leech that was sticking like a leech to his wrist, wiped away the trickle of blood from the wound, slapped his cheek, thereby killing thirty-five mosquitoes, and asked, in the tone of an examiner, "What was that?" I answered as calmly as I could, "water shrews," thanking, in my heart, the leech and the mosquitoes for the respite they had given me to collect my

---

2. "In medicine, the hungriest leech is best."

thoughts. But my mind was racing on: water shrews ate fishes and frogs which were easy to procure in any quantity; water shrews were less subterranean than most other insectivores; they were the very insectivore to keep in captivity. "That's an animal I must catch and keep," I said to my friend. "That is easy," he responded. "There is a nest with young under the floor mat of my tent." I had slept that night in his tent and Koenig had not thought it worthwhile to tell me of the shrews; such things are, to him, as much a matter of course as wild little spotted crakes feeding out of his hand, or as any other wonders of his queer kingdom in the reeds.

On our return to the tent that evening, he showed me the nest. It contained eight young which, compared with their mother, who rushed away as we lifted the mat, were of enormous size. They were considerably more than half her length and must each have weighed well between a fourth and a third of their dam: that is to say, the whole litter weighed, at a very modest estimate, twice as much as the old shrew. Yet they were still quite blind and the tips of their teeth were only just visible in their rosy mouths. And two days later when I took them under my care, they were still quite unable to eat even the soft abdomens of grasshoppers, and in spite of evident greed, they chewed interminably on a soft piece of frog's meat without succeeding in detaching a morsel from it. On our journey home, I fed them on the squeezed-out insides of grasshoppers and finely minced frog's meat, a diet on which they obviously throve. Arrived home in Altenberg, I improved on this diet by preparing a food from the squeezed-out insides of mealworm larvae, with some finely chopped small, fresh fishes, worked into a sort of gravy with a little milk. They consumed large quantities of this food, and their little nest-box looked quite small in comparison with the big china bowl whose contents they emptied three times a day. All these observations raise the problem of how the female water shrew succeeds in feeding her gigantic litter. It is absolutely impossible that she should do so on milk alone. Even on a more concentrated diet my young shrews devoured the equivalent of their own weight daily and this meant nearly twice the weight of a grown shrew. Yet, at that time of their lives, young shrews could not possibly engulf a frog or a fish brought whole to them by their mother, as my charges indisputably proved. I can only think that the mother feeds her young by regurgitation of chewed food. Even thus, it is little short of miraculous that the adult female should be able to obtain enough meat to sustain herself and her voracious progeny.

When I brought them home, my young watershrews were still blind. They had not suffered from the journey and were as sleek and fat as one could wish. Their black, glossy coats were reminiscent of moles, but the white color of their underside, as well as the round, streamlined contours of their bodies, reminded me distinctly of penguins, and not, indeed, without justification: both the streamlined form and the light underside are adaptations to a life in the water. Many free-swimming animals, mammals, birds, amphibians and fishes, are silvery-white below in order to be invisible to enemies swimming in the depths. Seen from below, the shining white belly blends perfectly with the reflecting surface film of the water. It is very characteristic of these water animals that the dark dorsal and the white ventral colors do not merge gradually into each other as is the case in "counter-shaded" land animals whose coloring is calculated to make them invisible by eliminating the contrasting shade on their undersides. As in the killer whale, in dolphins, and in penguins, the white underside of the watershrew is divided from the dark upper side by a sharp line which runs, often in very decorative curves, along the animal's flank. Curiously enough, this borderline between black and white showed considerable variations in individuals and even on both sides of one animal's body. I welcomed this, since it enabled me to recognize my shrews personally.

Three days after their arrival in Altenberg my eight shrew babies opened their eyes and began, very cautiously, to explore the precincts of their nest-box. It was now time to remove them to an appropriate container, and on this question I expended much hard thinking. The enormous quantity of food they consumed and, consequently, of excrement they produced, made it impossible to keep them in an oridnary aquarium whose water, within a day, would have become a stinking brew. Adequate sanitation was imperative for particular reasons; in ducks, grebes, and all waterfowl, the plumage must be kept perfectly dry if the animal is to remain in a state of health, and the same premise may reasonably be expected to hold good of the shrew's fur. Now water which has been polluted soon turns strongly alkaline and this I knew to be very bad for the plumage of waterbirds. It causes saponification of the fat to which the feathers owe their waterproof quality, and the bird becomes thoroughly wet and is unable to stay on the water. I hold the record, as far as I know hitherto unbroken by any other birdlover, for having kept dabchicks alive and healthy in captivity for nearly two years, and even then they did not die but escaped, and may still be living. My experience with these birds proved the absolute necessity of keeping the water perfectly clean; whenever it became a little dirty I noticed their feathers beginning to get wet, a danger which they anxiously tried to counteract by constantly preening themselves. I had, therefore, to keep these little grebes in crystal clear water which was changed every day, and I rightly assumed that the same would be necessary for my water shrews.

I took a large aquarium tank, rather over a yard in length and about two feet wide. At each end of this, I placed two little tables, and weighed them down with heavy stones so that they would not float. Then I filled up the tank until the water was level with the tops of the tables. I did not at first push the tables close against the panes of the tank, which was rather narrow, for fear that the shrews might become trapped underwater in the blind alley beneath a table and drown there; this precaution, however, subsequently proved unnecessary. The water shrew which, in its natural state, swims great distances under the ice, is quite able to find its way to the open surface in much more difficult situations. The nest-box, which was placed on one of the tables, was equipped with a sliding shutter, so that I could imprison the shrews whenever the container had to be cleaned. In the morning, at the hour of general cage-cleaning, the shrews were usually at home and asleep, so that the procedure caused them no appreciable disturbance. I will admit that I take great pride in devising, by creative imagination, suitable containers for animals of which nobody, myself included, has had any previous experience, and it was particularly gratifying that the contraption described above proved so satisfactory that I never had to alter even the minutest detail.

When first my baby shrews were liberated in this container they took a very long time to explore the top of the table on which their nest-box was standing. The water's edge seemed to exert a strong attraction; they approached it ever and again, smelled the surface and seemed to feel along it with the long, fine whiskers which surround their pointed snouts like a halo and represent not only their most important organ of touch but the most important of all their sensory organs. Like other aquatic mammals, the water shrew differs from the terrestrial members of its class in that its nose, the guiding organ of the average mammal, is of no use whatsoever in its underwater hunting. The water shrew's whiskers are actively mobile like the antennae of an insect or the fingers of a blind man.

Exactly as mice and many other small rodents would do under similar conditions, the shrews interrupted their careful exploration of their new surroundings every few minutes to dash wildly back into the safe cover of their nest-box. The survival value of this peculiar behavior is evident: the animal makes sure, from time to time that it has not lost its way and that it can, at a moment's notice, retreat to the one place it knows to be safe. It was a queer spectacle to see those podgy black figures slowly and carefully whiskering their way forward and, in the next second, with lightning speed, dash back to the nest-box. Queerly enough, they did not run straight through the little door, as one would have expected, but in their wild dash for safety they jumped, one and all, first onto the roof of the box and only then, whiskering along its edge, found the opening and slipped in with a half somersault, their back turned nearly vertically downward. After many repetitions of this maneuver, they were able to find the opening without feeling for it; they "knew" perfectly its whereabouts yet still persisted in the leap onto the roof. They jumped onto it and immediately vaulted in through the door, but they never, as long as they lived, found out that the leap and vault which had become their habit was really quite unnecessary and that they could have run in directly without this extraordinary detour. We shall hear more about this dominance of path habits in the water shrew presently.

It was only on the third day, when the shrews had become thoroughly acquainted with the geography of their little rectangular island, that the largest and most enterprising of them ventured into the water. As is so often the case with mammals, birds, reptiles, and fishes, it was the largest and most handsomely colored male which played the role of leader. First he sat on the edge of the water and thrust in the fore part of his body, at the same time frantically paddling with his forelegs but still clinging with his hind ones to the board. Then he slid in, but in the next moment took fright, scampered madly across the surface very much after the manner of a frightened duckling, and jumped out onto the board at the opposite end of the tank. There he sat, excitedly grooming his belly with one hind paw, exactly as coypus and beavers do. Soon he quieted down and sat still for a moment. Then he went to the water's edge a second time, hesitated for a moment, and plunged in; diving immediately, he swam ecstatically about underwater, swerving upward and downward again, running quickly along the bottom, and finally jumping out of the water at the same place as he had first entered it.

When I first saw a water shrew swimming I was most struck by a thing which I ought to have expected but did not: at the moment of diving, the little black and white beast appears to be made of silver. Like the plumage of ducks and grebes, but quite unlike the fur of most water mammals, such as seals, otters, beavers or coypus, the fur of the water shrew remains absolutely dry under water, that is to say, it retains a thick layer of air while the animal is below the surface. In the other mammals mentioned above, it is only the short, woolly undercoat that remains dry, the superficial hair tips becoming wet, wherefore the animal looks its natural color when underwater and is superficially wet when it emerges. I was already aware of the peculiar qualities of the waterproof fur of the shrew, and, had I given it a thought, I should have known that it would look, under water, exactly like the air-retaining fur on the underside of a water beetle or on the abdomen of a water spider. Nevertheless the wonderful, transparent silver coat of the shrew was, to me, one of those delicious surprises that nature has in store for her admirers.

Another surprising detail which I only noticed when I saw my shrews in the water was that they have a fringe of stiff, erectile hairs on the outer side of their fifth toes and on the underside of their tails. These form collapsible oars and a collapsible rudder. Folded and inconspicuous as long as the animal is on dry land, they unfold the moment it enters the water and broaden the effective surface of the propelling feet and of the steering tail by a considerable area.

Like penguins, the water shrews looked rather awkward and ungainly on dry land but were transformed into objects of elegance and grace on entering the water. As long as they walked, their strongly convex underside made them look pot-bellied and reminiscent of an old, overfed dachshund. But under water, the very same protruding belly balanced harmoniously the curve of their back and gave a beautifully symmetrical streamline which, together with their silver coating and the elegance of their movements, made them a sight of entrancing beauty.

When they had all become familiar with the water, their container was one of the chief attractions that our research station had to offer to any visiting naturalists or animal lovers. Unlike all other mammals of their size, the water shrews were largely diurnal and, except in the early hours of the morning, three or four of them were constantly on the scene. It was exceedingly interesting to watch their movements upon and under the water. Like the whirligig beetle, Gyrinus, they could turn in an extremely small radius without diminishing their speed, a faculty for which the large rudder surface of the tail with its fringe of erectile hairs is evidently essential. They had two different ways of diving, either by taking a little jump as grebes or coots do and working their way down at a steep angle, or by simply lowering their snout under the surface and paddling very fast till they reached "planing speed," thus working their way downward on the principle of the inclined plane—in other words, performing the converse movement of an ascending airplane. The water shrew must expend a large amount of energy in staying down since the air contained in its fur exerts a strong pull upwards. Unless it is paddling straight downwards, a thing it rarely does, it is forced to maintain a constant minimum speed, keeping its body at a slightly downward angle in order not to float to the surface. While swimming under water the shrew seems to flatten, broadening its body in a peculiar fashion, in order to present a better planing surface to the water. I never saw my shrews try to cling by their claws to any underwater objects, as the dipper is alleged to do. When they seemed to be running along the bottom, they were really swimming close above it, but perhaps the smooth gravel on the bottom of the tank was unsuitable for holding on to and it did not occur to me then to offer them a rougher surface. They were very playful when in the water and chased one another loudly twittering on the surface, or silently in the depths.

Unlike any other mammal, but just like water birds, they could rest on the surface; this they used to do, rolling partly over and grooming themselves. Once out again, they instantly proceeded to clean their fur—one is almost tempted to say "preen" it, so similar was their behavior to that of ducks which have just left the water after a long swim.

Most interesting of all was their method of hunting under water. They came swimming along with an erratic course, darting a foot or so forward very swiftly in a straight line, then starting to gyrate in looped turns at reduced speed. While swimming straight and swiftly their whiskers were, as far as I could see, laid flat against their head, but while circling they were erect and bristled out in all directions, as they sought contact with some prey. I have no reason to believe that vision plays any part in the water shrew's hunting, except perhaps in the activation of its tactile search. My shrews may have noticed visually the presence of the live tadpoles or little fishes which I put in the tank, but in the actual hunting of its prey the animal is exclusively guided by its sense of touch, located in the wide-spreading whiskers on its snout. Certain small free-swimming species of catfish find their prey by exactly the same method. When these fishes swim fast and straight, the long feelers on their snout are depressed but, like the shrew's whiskers, are stiffly spread out when the fish becomes conscious of the proximity of potential prey; like the shrew, the fish then begins to gyrate blindly in order to establish contact with its prey. It may not even be necessary for the water shrew actually to touch its prey with one of its whiskers. Perhaps, at very close range, the water vibration caused by the movements of a small fish, a tadpole or a water insect is perceptible by those sensitive tactile organs. It is quite impossible to determine this question by mere observation, for the action is much too quick for the human eye. There is a quick turn and a snap and the shrew is already paddling shorewards with a wriggling creature in its maw.

In relation to its size, the water shrew is perhaps the most terrible predator of all vertebrate animals, and it can even vie with the invertebrates, including the murderous Dytiscus larva. It has been reported by A. E. Brehm that water shrews have killed fish more than sixty times heavier than themselves by biting out their eyes and brain. This happened only when the fish were confined in containers with no room for escape. The same story has been told to me by fishermen on Lake Neusiedel, who could not possibly have heard Brehm's report. I once offered to my shrews a large edible frog. I never did it again, nor could I bear to see out to its end the cruel scene that ensued. One of the shrews encountered the frog in the basin and instantly gave chase, repeatedly seizing hold of the creature's legs; although it was kicked off again it did not cease in its attack and finally, the frog, in desperation, jumped out of the water and onto one of the tables, where several shrews raced to the pursuer's assistance and buried their teeth in the legs and hindquarters of the wretched frog. And now, horribly, they began to eat the frog alive, beginning just where each one of them happened to have hold of it; the poor frog croaked heartrendingly, as the jaws of the shrews munched audibly in chorus. I need hardly be blamed for bringing this experiment to an abrupt and agitated end and putting the lacerated frog out of its misery. I never offered the shrews large prey again but only such as would be killed at the first bite or two. Nature can be very cruel indeed; it is not out of pity that most of the larger predatory animals kill their prey quickly. The lion has to finish off a big antelope or a buffalo very quickly indeed in order not to get hurt itself, for a beast of prey which has to hunt daily cannot afford to receive even a harmless scratch in effecting a kill; such scratches would soon add up to such an extent as to put the killer out of action. The same reason has forced the python and other large snakes to evolve a quick and really humane method of killing the well-armed mammals that are their natural prey. But where there is no danger of the victim doing damage to the killer, the latter shows no pity whatsoever. The hedgehog which, by virtue of its armor, is quite immune to the bite of a snake, regularly proceeds to eat it, beginning at the tail or in the middle of its body, and in the same way the water shrew treats its innocuous prey. But man should abstain from judging his innocently-cruel fellow creatures, for even if nature sometimes "shrieks against his creed," what pain does he himself not inflict upon the living creatures that he hunts for pleasure and not for food?

The mental qualities of the water shrew cannot be rated very high. They were quite tame and fearless of me and never tried to bite when I took them in my hand, nor did they ever try to evade it, but, like little tame rodents, they tried to dig their way out if I held them for too long in the hollow of my closed fist. Even when I took them out of their container and put them on a table or on the floor, they were by no means thrown into a panic but were quite ready to take food out of my hand and even tried actively to creep into it if they felt a longing for cover. When, in such an unwonted environment, they were shown their nest-box, they plainly showed that they knew it by sight and instantly made for it, and even pursued it with upraised heads if I moved the box along above them, just out of their reach. All in all, I really may pride myself that I have tamed the shrew, or at least one member of that family.

In their accustomed surroundings, my shrews proved to be very strict creatures of habit. I have already mentioned the remarkable conservatism with which they persevered in their unpractical way of entering their nest-box by climbing onto its roof and then vaulting, with a half turn, in through the door. Something more must be said about the unchanging tenacity with which these animals cling to their habits once they have formed them. In the water shrew, the path habits, in particular, are of a really amazing immutability; I hardly know another instance to which the saying, "As the twig is bent, so the tree is inclined," applies so literally.

In a territory unknown to it, the water shrew will never run fast except under pressure of extreme fear, and then it will run blindly along, bumping into objects and usually getting caught in a blind alley. But, unless the little animal is severely frightened, it moves, in strange surroundings, only step by step, whiskering right and left all the time and following a path that is anything but straight. Its course is determined by a hundred fortuitous factors when it walks that way for the first time. But, after a few repetitions, it is evident that the shrew recognizes the locality in which it finds itself and that it repeats, with the utmost exactitude, the movements which it performed the previous time. At the same time, it is noticeable that the animal moves along much faster whenever it is repeating what it has already learned. When placed on a path which it has already traversed a few times, the shrew starts on its way slowly, carefully whiskering. Suddenly it finds known bearings, and now rushes forward a short distance, repeating exactly every step and turn which it executed on the last occasion. Then, when it comes to a spot where it ceases to know the way by heart, it is reduced to whiskering again and to feeling its way step by step. Soon, another burst of speed follows and the same thing is repeated, bursts of speed alternating with very slow progress. In the beginning of this process of learning their way, the shrews move along at an extremely slow average rate and the little bursts of speed are few and far between. But gradually the little laps of the course which have been "learned by heart" and which can be covered quickly begin to increase in length as well as in number until they fuse and the whole course can be completed in a fast, unbroken rush.

Often, when such a path habit is almost completely formed, there still remains one particularly difficult place where the shrew always loses its bearings and has to resort to its senses of smell and touch, sniffing and whiskering vigorously to find out where the next reach of its path "joins on." Once the shrew is well settled in its path habits it is as strictly bound to them as a railway engine to its tracks and as unable to deviate from them by even a few centimeters. If it diverges from its path by so much as an inch, it is forced to stop abruptly, and laboriously regain its bearings. The same behavior can be caused experimentally by changing some small detail in the customary path of the animal. Any major alteration in the habitual path threw the shrews into complete confusion. One of their paths ran along the wall adjoining the wooden table opposite to that on which the nest box was situated. This table was weighted with two stones lying close to the panes of the tank, and the shrews, running along the wall, were accustomed to jump on and off the stones which lay right in their path. If I moved the stones out of the runway, placing both together in the middle of the table, the shrews would jump right up into the air in the place where the stone should have been; they came down with a jarring bump, were obviously disconcerted and started whiskering cautiously right and left, just as they behaved in an unknown environment. And then they did a most interesting thing: they went back the way they had come, carefully feeling their way until they had again got their bearings. Then, facing round again, they tried a second time with a rush and jumped and crashed down exactly as they had done a few seconds before. Only then did they seem to realize that the first fall had not been their own fault but was due to a change in the wonted pathway, and now they proceeded to explore the alteration, cautiously sniffing and bewhiskering the place where the stone ought to have been. This method of going back to the start, and trying again always reminded me of a small boy who, in reciting a poem, gets stuck and begins again at an earlier verse.

In rats, as in many small mammals, the process of forming a path habit, for instance in learning a maze, is very similar to that just described; but a rat is far more adaptable in its behavior and would not dream of trying to jump over a stone which was not there. The preponderance of motor habit over present perception is a most remarkable peculiarity of the water shrew. One might say that the animal actually disbelieves its senses if they report a change of environment which necessitates a sudden alteration in its motor habits. In a new environment a water shrew would be perfectly able to see a stone of that size and consequently to avoid it or to run over it in a manner well adapted to the spatial conditions; but once a habit is formed and has become ingrained, it supersedes all better knowledge. I know of no animal that is a slave to its habits in so literal a sense as the water shrew. For this animal the geometric axiom that a straight line is the shortest distance between two points simply does not hold good. To them, the shortest line is always the accustomed path and, to a certain extent, they are justified in adhering to this principle: they run with amazing speed along their pathways and arrive at their destination much sooner than they would if, by whiskering and nosing, they tried to go straight. They will keep to the wonted path, even though it winds in such a way that it crosses and recrosses itself. A rat or mouse would be quick to discover that it was making an unnecessary detour, but the water shrew is no more able to do so than is a toy train to turn off at right angles at a level crossing. In order to change its route, the water shrew must change its whole path habit, and this cannot be done at a moment's notice but gradually, over a long period of time. An unnecessary, loop-shaped detour takes weeks and weeks to become a little shorter, and after months it is not even approximately straight. The biological advantage of such a path habit is obvious: it compensates the shrew for being nearly blind and enables it to run exceedingly fast without wasting a minute on orientation. On the other hand it may, under unusual circumstances, lead the shrew to destruction. It has been reported, quite plausibly, that water shrews have broken their necks by jumping into a pond which had been recently drained. In spite of the possibility of such mishaps, it would be shortsighted if one were simply to stigmatize the water shrew as stupid because it solves the spatial problems of its daily life in quite a different way from man. On the contrary, if one thinks a little more deeply, it is very wonderful that the same result, namely a perfect orientation in space, can be brought about in two so widely divergent ways: by true observation, as we achieve it, or, as the water shrew does, by learning by heart every possible spatial contingency that may arise in a given territory.

Among themselves, my water shrews were surprisingly good-natured. Although, in their play, they would often chase each other, twittering with a great show of excitement, I never saw a serious fight between them until an unfortunate accident occurred: one morning, I forgot to reopen the little door of the nest-box after cleaning out their tank. When at last I remembered, three hours had elapsed—a very long time for the swift metabolism of such small insectivores. Upon the opening of the door, all the shrews rushed out and made a dash for the food tray. In their haste to get out, not only did they soil themselves all over but they apparently discharged, in their excitement, some sort of glandular secretion, for a strong, musk-like odor accompanied their exit from the box. Since they appeared to have incurred no damage by their three hours' fasting, I turned away from the box to occupy myself with other things. However, on nearing the container soon afterwards, I heard an unusually loud, sharp twittering and, on my hurried approach, found my eight shrews locked in deadly battle. Two were even then dying and, though I consigned them at once to separate cages, two more died in the course of the day. The real cause of this sudden and terrible battle is hard to ascertain but I cannot help suspecting that the shrews, owing to the sudden change in the usual odor, had failed to recognize each other and had fallen upon each other as they would have done upon strangers. The four survivors quietened down after a certain time and I was able to reunite them in the original container without fear of further mishap.

I kept those four remaining shrews in good health for nearly seven months and would probably have had them much longer if the assistant whom I had engaged to feed them had not forgotten to do so. I had been obliged to go to Vienna and, on my return in the late afternoon, was met by that usually reliable fellow who turned pale when he saw me, thereupon remembering that he had forgotten to feed the shrews. All four of them were alive but very weak; they ate greedily when we fed them but died nonetheless within a few hours. In other words, they showed exactly the same symptoms as the shrews which I had formerly tried to keep; this confirmed my opinion that the latter were already dying of hunger when they came into my possession.

To any advanced animal keeper who is able to set up a large tank, preferably with running water, and who can obtain a sufficient supply of small fish, tadpoles, and the like, I can recommend the water shrew as one of the most gratifying, charming, and interesting objects of care. Of course it is a somewhat exacting charge. It will eat raw chopped heart (the customary substitute for small live prey) only in the absence of something better and it cannot be fed exclusively on this diet for long periods. Moreover, really clean water is indispensable. But if these clear-cut requirements be fulfilled, the water shrew will not merely remain alive but will really thrive, nor do I exclude the possibility that it might even breed in captivity.

QUESTIONS

1. Lorenz discusses a field trip and some other matters before he reports his laboratory observations. What is the effect of this organization?
2. What features of the shrew's behavior does Lorenz select for special emphasis? What conclusions does he draw about these features?
3. Though this is mainly a report of his observations, Lorenz includes matters which are not necessary to the report of strictly controlled observation of the shrew's habits. Indicate some of the places where his discussion moves beyond strict reporting. Characterize the roles he assumes in these passages. Do these other roles or revelations of personality compromise or support his claim to being a scientist?

JOHN D. STEWART
Vulture Country

Spain is the stronghold of the vultures. There are four listed species in Europe, two common and two rare; if they are anywhere, they are in Spain. The bearded vulture and the black survive there, the Egyptian flourishes, and the great griffon swarms. The further south you go the more numerous they become, until you reach the hot grazing plains of Andalusia. There, summer and winter through, they hang in hordes in the roofless sky, for Andalusia is the vulture country.

There are three essential qualities for vulture country: a rich supply of unburied corpses, high mountains, a strong sun. Spain has the first of these, for in this sparsely populated and stony land it is not customary, or necessary, to bury dead animals. Where there are vultures in action such burial would be a self-evident waste of labor, with inferior sanitary results. Spain has mountains, too, in no part far to seek; and the summer sun is hot throughout the country. But it is hottest in Andalusia, and that is the decisive factor.

The sun, to the vulture, is not just something which makes life easier and pleasanter, a mere matter of preference. His mode of life is impossible without it. Here in Andalusia the summer sun dries up every pond and lake and almost every river. It drives the desperate frogs deep into the mud cracks and forces the storks to feed on locusts. It kills the food plants and wilts the fig trees over the heads of the panting flocks. Andalusia becomes like that part of ancient Greece, "a land where men fight for the shade of an ass."

All animals, both tame and wild, weaken in these circumstances, and the weakest go to the wall and die. The unpitying sun glares down on the corpses and speeds their putrefaction, rotting the hide and softening the sinews and the meat, to the vulture's advantage. But the sun plays a still greater part in his life. Its main and vital function, for him, is the creation of thermal currents in the atmosphere, for without these he would be helpless.

The vulture must fly high—high enough to command a wide territory, for, except at times of catastrophe, dead animals are never thick on the ground. His task is to soar to ten thousand feet, more or less, two or three times in a day, and to hang there and keep constant survey. A male griffon weighs up to sixteen pounds, so that to hoist himself up to that necessary viewpoint would call for fifty-three thousand calories, the equivalent of fifty pounds of meat. To find and eat three times his own weight in a day is clearly impossible; a short cut must be made. In the dawn of any day, in Andalusia, you may see the vulture discovering that short cut.

The eagles, buzzards, kites, and falcons are already on the wing, quartering the plain fast and low, seeking reptiles and small game. But the vulture sits on a crag and waits. He sees the sun bound up out of the sierra, and still he waits. He waits until the sun-struck rocks and the hard earth heat up and the thermal currents begin to rise. When the upstream is strong enough, he leaps out from the cliff, twists into it and without one laborious wingbeat, spirals and soars.

By the time the vulture reaches his station, a half hour later and maybe more, the sun is blazing down on the plain and betraying every detail to his telescopic eye, and the updraft is strengthening as the day approaches its zenith. His ceiling for this day is fixed by two factors. One is the strength and buoyancy of his chosen thermal, which will vary with the strength of the sun and the behavior of the upper winds. But the more important factor, for it fixes his horizontal bearings as well, is the distribution of neighboring vultures in the sky, his colleagues and competitors.

He cocks his head from side to side and checks their various positions. There they hang, dotted across the clear sky at intervals of a mile or so—at the corners of one-mile squares. Height and lateral distances all adjusted, the vulture settles, circling slowly on his invisible support, and begins his long and lonely vigil.

This griffon vulture, which I select from the four species as being by far the most prevalent and typical, is almost sure to be a male. The female rarely leaves her nest from early March, when she lays her rough white egg, until August, when her huge poult is fledged and flying. The father has to feed and carry for all three.

At first glance, from below, he appears as one great wing, ten feet from tip to tip and two feet broad. His tail is square and very short, which is all it needs to be, for there are no sharp or sudden quirks in his flight that would call for a strong rudder. His movements are premeditated, stressless, and leisurely, for his energy must be conserved at all costs and never wasted on aerobatics.

The vulture's head and neck, too, protrude very little in front of his wing plane, and this distinguishes his flight silhouette from the eagle's. His neck is, in fact, some two feet long, but since it is bare—and must be bare—he folds it back into his collar to keep it warm. His head, apart from its nakedness, is like an eagle's; his yellow claws, which never kill and rarely carry, are shorter and not so strong. His plumage is a uniform sandy color, faded and tattered by work and waiting and, perhaps, by old age. It is relieved only by his coffee-colored ruff and the broad black primary wing feathers fingering the air.

The vulture sails in silence, for no vocal signals could serve him at such a distance from his fellows. He croaks, growls, and whistles only in his family circle, and at his feasts. He circles by almost imperceptible adjustments of his wing planes, aided by slight twists of his tail. But his head is in constant and active movement. He swivels it from one side to the other, bringing each eye in turn to bear on the earth. Then he bends his neck to right or left to check on one of his neighbors to north, south, east or west.

The whole vulture network is interdependent. Each vulture can give and receive two signals or, as the scientists call them, "visual stimuli." Circling means "Nothing doing"; dropping, or its resultant hole in the sky, calls "Come here!" Like all other vultures, he rests reassured by the first and is rapidly and relentlessly drawn by the second.

It is demonstrable how, with a special density of nerve endings on his retina, the vulture can see a small animal from a great height. Many other birds—gannets, for example—have the same propensity. Their eyesight is surprising only when we compare it with the poor standards of our own. But a mystery remains: how does the bird know that the animal is dead? The sense of smell is to be ruled out straightway. It is impossible that it would operate at such a distance, even allowing for the upward current of air. Birds are not, generally, well endowed in this respect, and in the vulture's case this may be especially fortunate.

No book, no expert, could answer this question for me, and I carried it through the vulture country for years, the one tantalizing imponderable, the broken link. Then, one hot afternoon, I lay down beside an old swineherd in the shade of a cork oak on the foothills overlooking the great plan of La Janda. For fifty years, he told me, he had watched pigs on that plain—the pigs, yes, and the vultures. I put my problem to him.

The swineherd's theory is not to be proved, but it is a wise one and I shall hold it until I find a better. No, he said, it is not the white belly skin that distinguishes the dead animals. White fur may fix the vulture's eye, but it does not offer him evidence of death. All herds and flocks, said the old man, lie down together and at one time. They have their place and their hour of rest. When a vulture sees an animal lying alone and apart, he is bound to notice it. The next time he crosses, the same image strikes his eye and startles him again. Over and over again he marks it and waits and watches; but now, alerted, he watches it more closely.

The next day the animal is still there; his attention is fixed upon it now, so he circles a little lower, his eye riveted, seeking the slightest movement of limb or lung. He sees none, but he continues to wait, said the old man. It takes him two days, at least, to confirm death. He goes on circling, but lower. He becomes more engrossed, and more sure. The other vultures note his behavior and move over a little in the sky. Every time he falls, they move closer. Now he is very low. He seeks the heaving of the flanks or eye movements; he sees neither. At some point, perhaps, he receives a visual stimulus in some death sign—the protruding tongue or the wide and whitened eye. Then he falls quickly, landing heavily at a little distance from the corpse.

The swineherd and I watched the first vulture land. We watched him sidling and circling the dead goat standing erect to see better, wing tips trailing, naked neck stretched to the full, head swiveling rapidly to bring alternate eyes to bear. He hopped closer and paused, peering intently. If he could smell, even as well as we, his doubts would have been over. But he stood there, irresolute, famished yet fearful, with his bill open and his wings ready for use.

Then a big shadow swept across the brown grass, and the vulture glanced upwards. His involuntary signal had been answered, and a tall column of vultures wheeled overhead. He hopped to close quarters, stretched forward, pecked the corpse, and leapt back. He watched it for a second more; no movement. Then he croaked once, as though to bless himself, and threw himself on the body. He struck his heavy beak into the flank, flapped for balance, and thrust backwards with feet and wings to strip the hide from the ribs and belly.

Almost immediately there were eight more vultures at the corpse, and we saw that all of them sought and fought for the same place. Their aim was to penetrate, their object the viscera. Watching them thrusting their long necks deep into the belly cavity and withdrawing them befouled and bloodstained, I saw why those necks must be bare. Yes, said the swineherd, and that is the one part the vulture cannot reach to clean. His mate may clean it for him later, for pure greed, but if he had feathers there he would have maggots in them.

Now sixteen more vultures swept down, landing heavily in their haste and flap-hopping to the feast—the second square from the sky pattern. The corpse was covered, submerged in a heaving, struggling mass of broad brown wings. A new column wheeled above us, circling lower. There should be twenty-four up there, I reckoned. There were twenty-three.

The latecomers landed on nearby trees, including ours, and their weight bent thick limbs to the ground. From points four miles distant, we could expect thirty-four more, and at the height of the carnival I counted just short of one hundred birds.

A mule lasts two hours, said the old man, and an ox, three. This goat became bones in the sun in half an hour.

As the hundred fed, or hoped and waited, many more vultures circled high above, assessing the situation and the prospects and treasuring their altitude. Toward the end, when the feasters scattered and exposed the small skeleton, the watchers flapped and drifted wearily away to resume their distant stations. But they had fulfilled their function. They had marked the spot and drawn the Egyptian vultures and the kites.

Now the little Egyptian vultures landed daintily and dodged nimbly through the throng of giants. They are bare on the face and throat only, with well-feathered head and neck, and so, perforce, they are cleaner feeders. The dirty work has been done; now the long and delicate beak comes into play. The Egyptian vultures attack the skull, the large joints, and the crevices of the pelvic girdle— all parts inaccessible to the griffon's heavy beak. They extract brains, membranes, and the spinal cord, and clip out tendons and ligaments.

They dodge out through the encircling griffons with their spoils, gobble them swiftly, and dance back for more. The griffons, gorged with meat and panting in the sun, pay them scant attention.

Finally, when all but the whistling kites have left the scene, comes the great solitary bearded vulture, the fierce lammergeier. His whole head is feathered, so he despises carrion. He lives aloof from all the rest of the vulture tribe, but they serve his interests, so he keeps them within sight. The old swineherd calls him *Quebrantahuesos*— the bone smasher—and Aeschylus noted him, long ago, for the same behavior. The lammergeier seizes the largest bones, carries them high, in his claws, and drops them on the rocks. Then he swoops down and rakes out the marrow.

Like an eagle, he can kill as well as carry with his claws, and he has not the true vulture's patient, soaring habit. He attacks flocks and herds and carries off the lambs and kids and piglets. After his work has been done nothing will remain except an empty skull and some small bones, which the ants and carrion beetles pick and polish.

Our griffon, first on the scene, will not be the first to leave it. He is sure to have gorged himself with his advantage. Crop, throat, and neck distended, he squats back on his tail, with his wings spread to steady him and his beak hanging open. From time to time he chokes and belches and gags, and it is an hour, maybe, before the meat subsides in him.

When he is ready, the griffon runs and leaps across the plain, thrashing heavily with his big wings, and labors into the air. He finds a thermal, circles in it to his altitude, then slips sideways and sweeps gently across the sierra to his distant nest.

The griffon vultures are gregarious in nesting, with colonies throughout the mountains at fairly regular intervals of thirty miles. They are said to pair for life. Certainly they return every year to the same nest. In January they begin to repair the nest, a broad and battered saucer of strong branches, topped with twigs and grass. They are careless builders, and many nests have bare rock protruding in them. No attempt is made to cover it. The egg is laid in late February and incubated for forty days. The new chick is bare and blue-skinned and looks as though he might become a dragon, but soon he sprouts white down and begins to assert the characteristics of his race. In a month he is voracious, and by the end of April he will demand four pounds of meat every day. Before he is fledged he will need eight pounds. Providentially, his demands coincide with the heyday of death.

When the male vulture arrives at the nest he settles on a nearby ledge, vomits, and sorts out the result with his beak. The female helps with this assessment, feeding herself hungrily on the larger relics. Then she offers her gape and crop to her cowering, whistling infant. The chick gobbles madly. With vultures it can never be "little and often," for animals die irregularly, as they must, so the birds, young and old, must gorge to the neck when opportunity offers. That is their instinct and their nature.

A male vulture with family responsibilities cannot rest for long. Now that his load is delivered and eaten, he is likely to be the hungriest of the family. This, too, is as it should be, for the hunger sends him out and up again, however little daylight may remain, to circle in the sky until the sunset reddens the sierra.

Time was when the summer drought killed thousands of beasts every year and the floods of winter hundreds more. Nowadays there are fewer casualties, but the vultures still have a fairly constant food supply in the charnel gorges, which lie below most mountain villages.

Grazalema, Arcos, Casares, and a hundred more were built, for protection from the raiding Moors, on the edge of the precipice. All dead and dying animals, as well as all the garbage of the town, are simply pushed over the cliff and left to the birds. There is a bird in Andalusia for every class and size of refuse. From the escarpment you can watch all the scavengers of the air, soaring below you or fighting on the feast. The great black vulture may be here, the griffon and Egyptian for sure, and two kinds of kites. The cunning ravens and carrion crows wait on the outskirts, dashing in to snatch their choice. Clouds of choughs and jackdaws wheel and cry above them.

There is a new feeding ground in the unfenced highways of Andalusia. As motor traffic increases, these offer more and more dead dogs, cats, kids, pigs, and rabbits. If you are abroad at dawn, it is a common thing to run down a vulture intent on scraping a dead dog off the asphalt. Even so, with an apparently limitless population of these great birds, each looking for some thirty pounds of meat every day, one wonders how they flourish.

Their wonderful feeding system has, it seems to me, one fatal flaw. They can signal "Food here," but not how much. At the feast which I have described only some succeeded in feeding at all, and only two or three ate their fill. A majority came the distance and lost their height for little or for nothing.

In Africa, also vulture country, there is no such difficulty, for there all the game is big game, and every funeral is worth attending. It may be that some of our Andalusian vultures go there in the winter. Certainly our vulture population increases here, but that is because the vultures from further north crowd in as the heat decreases and the air currents weaken in their homelands. Fortunately, there is a seasonal food supply ready for them all, for it is the time of birth, with all its failures and fatalities. After the winter storms, too, the torrents offer up their toll of corpses. And in winter, each bird has only himself to feed. But you would not doubt, if you knew the constant panic for food which dominates him summer and winter alike, that the vulture leads a competitive and anxious life. He has strong forces for survival. It is held—and we know it to be true of eagles—that the vulture has a very long life. If this longevity is a fact, then the solitary chick each year may add up to a good replacement rate.

The nest is inaccessible, and the hen guards it constantly against the only possible natural enemy—other vultures or raptors. So the survival rate must be high as is proved by the evident increase toward saturation point.

At times, lying on my back on the plain with binoculars trained on the sky, I have seen vultures circling in two or three layers, each one high above the other. What can this mean? A hungry duplication, or triplication, hopelessly covering the same feeding ground and using the only available thermals? Or the opposite—idle and well-fed reserves standing by for surplus?

No one can tell me. But here in the vulture country there are no birds more spectacular, more fascinating to watch and to study. In time we may find out the last of their secrets. I lie on the plains and keep on watching them. And they, I know, keep on watching me.

QUESTIONS

1. On page 1362 Stewart explains the vulture's aerodynamics. What is the crucial problem and how does the bird's genetic "design" permit him to solve it?
2. The feast which is concluded on page 1366 might reasonably be taken as the climax of the essay, but in fact Stewart goes on to do more. What does his continuation add to the essay?
3. Why do the vultures keep watching Stewart and what are the implications of that last sentence?
4. Answer Question 4 on page 1101.

ALEXANDER WILSON
Ivory-Billed Woodpecker[1]

This majestic and formidable species, in strength and magnitude, stands at the head of the whole class of woodpeckers hitherto discovered. He may be called the king or chief of his tribe; and nature

---

1. From *American Ornithology*.

seems to have designed him a distinguished characteristic in the superb carmine crest and bill of polished ivory with which she has ornamented him. His eye is brilliant and daring, and his whole frame so admirably adapted for his mode of life, and method of procuring subsistence, as to impress on the mind of the examiner the most reverential ideas of the Creator. His manners have also a dignity in them superior to the common herd of woodpeckers. Trees, shrubbery, orchards, rails, fence posts, and old prostrate logs are alike interesting to those, in their humble and indefatigable search for prey; but the royal hunter now before us scorns the humility of such situations, and seeks the most towering trees of the forest; seeming particularly attached to those prodigious cypress swamps, whose crowded giant sons stretch their bare and blasted or moss-hung arms midway to the skies. In these almost inaccessible recesses, amid ruinous piles of impending timber, his trumpet-like note and loud strokes resound through the solitary savage wilds, of which he seems the sole lord and inhabitant. Wherever he frequents he leaves numerous monuments of his industry behind him. We there see enormous pine trees with cartloads of bark lying around their roots, and chips of the trunk itself in such quantities as to suggest the idea that half a dozen of axe-men had been at work there for the whole morning. The body of the tree is also disfigured with such numerous and so large excavations, that one can hardly conceive it possible for the whole to be the work of a woodpecker. With such strength, and an apparatus so powerful, what havoc might he not commit, if numerous, on the most useful of our forest trees! And yet with all these appearances, and much of vulgar prejudice against him, it may fairly be questioned whether he is at all injurious; or, at least, whether his exertions do not contribute most powerfully to the protection of our timber. Examine closely the tree where he has been at work, and you will soon perceive that it is neither from motives of mischief nor amusement that he slices off the bark, or digs his way into the trunk—for the sound and healthy tree is the least object of his attention. The diseased, infested with insects, and hastening to putrefaction, are *his* favorites; there the deadly crawling enemy have formed a lodgement between the bark and tender wood, to drink up the very vital part of the tree. It is the ravages of these vermin which the intelligent proprietor of the forest deplores, as the sole perpetrators of the destruction of his timber. Would it be believed that the larvae of an insect, or fly, no larger than a grain of rice, should silently, and in one season, destroy some thousand acres of pine trees, many of them from two to three feet in diameter, and a hundred and fifty feet high! Yet whoever passes along the high road from Georgetown to Charleston, in South Carolina, about twenty miles from the former place, can have striking and melancholy proofs of this fact. In some places the whole woods, as far as you can see around you, are dead, stripped of the bark, their wintry-looking arms and bare trunks bleaching in the sun, and tumbling in ruins before every blast, presenting a frightful picture of desolation. And yet ignorance and prejudice stubbornly persist in directing their indignation against the bird now before us, the constant and mortal enemy of these very vermin, as if the hand that probed the wound to extract its cause should be equally detested with that which inflicted it; or as if the thief-catcher should be confounded with the thief. Until some effectual preventive or more complete mode of destruction can be devised against these insects, and their larvae, I would humbly suggest the propriety of protecting, and receiving with proper feelings of gratitude, the services of this and the whole tribe of woodpeckers, letting the odium of guilt fall to its proper owners.

In looking over the accounts given of the ivory-billed woodpecker by the naturalists of Europe, I find it asserted, that it inhabits from New Jersey to Mexico. I believe, however, that few of them are ever seen to the north of Virginia, and very few of them even in that state. The first place I observed this bird at, when on my way to the south, was about twelve miles north of Wilmington in North Carolina. Having wounded it slightly in the wing, on being caught, it uttered a loudly reiterated, and most piteous note, exactly resembling the violent crying of a young child; which terrified my horse so, as nearly to have cost me my life. It was distressing to hear it. I carried it with me in the chair, under cover, to Wilmington. In passing through the streets, its affecting cries surprised everyone within hearing, particularly the females, who hurried to the doors and windows with looks of alarm and anxiety. I drove on, and, on arriving at the piazza of the hotel, where I intended to put up, the landlord came forward, and a number of other persons who happened to be there, all equally alarmed at what they heard; this was greatly increased by my asking, whether he could furnish me with accommodations for myself and my baby. The man looked blank and foolish, while the others stared with still greater astonishment. After diverting myself for a minute or two at their expense, I drew my woodpecker from under the cover, and a general laugh took place. I took him up stairs and locked him up in my room, while I went to see my horse taken care of. In less than an hour·I returned, and, on opening the door, he set up the same distressing shout, which now appeared to proceed from grief that he had been discovered in his attempts at escape. He had mounted along the side of the window, nearly as high as the ceiling, a little below which he had begun to break through. The bed was covered with large pieces of plaster; the lath was exposed for at least fifteen inches square, and a hole, large enough to admit the fist, opened to the weather-boards; so that in less than another hour he would certainly have succeeded in making his way through. I now tied a string round his leg, and, fastening it to the table, again left him. I wished to preserve his life, and had gone off in search of suitable food for him. As I reascended the stairs, I heard him again hard at work, and on entering had the mortification to perceive that he had almost entirely ruined the mahogany table to which he was fastened, and on which he had wreaked his whole vengeance. While engaged in taking a drawing, he cut me severely in several places, and, on the whole, displayed such a noble and unconquerable spirit, that I was frequently tempted to restore him to his native woods. He lived with me nearly three days, but refused all sustenance, and I witnessed his death with regret.

The head and bill of this bird is in great esteem among the southern Indians, who wear them by way of amulet or charm, as well as ornament; and, it is said, dispose of them to the northern tribes at considerable prices. An Indian believes that the head, skin, or even feathers of certain birds, confer on the wearer all the virtues or excellencies of those birds. Thus I have seen a coat made of the skins, heads, and claws of the raven; caps stuck round with heads of butcherbirds, hawks, and eagles; and as the disposition and courage of the ivory-billed woodpecker are well known to the savages, no wonder they should attach great value to it, having both beauty, and, in their estimation, distinguished merit to recommend it.

This bird is not migratory, but resident in the countries where it inhabits. In the low countries of the Carolinas it usually prefers the large timbered cypress swamps for breeding in. In the trunk of one of these trees, at a considerable height, the male and female alternately, and in conjunction, dig out a large and capacious cavity for their eggs and young. Trees thus dug out have frequently been cut down, with sometimes the eggs and young in them. This hole, according to information—for I have never seen one myself—is generally a little winding, the better to keep out the weather, and from two to five feet deep. The eggs are said to be generally four, sometimes five, as large as a pullet's, pure white, and equally thick on both ends—a description that, except in size, very nearly agrees with all the rest of our woodpeckers. The young begin to be seen abroad about the middle of June. Whether they breed more than once in the same season is uncertain.

So little attention do the people of the countries where these birds inhabit pay to the minutiae of natural history, that, generally speaking, they make no distinction between the ivory-billed and pileated woodpecker; and it was not till I showed them the two birds together that they knew of any difference. The more intelligent and observing part of the natives, however, distinguish them by the name of the large and lesser logcocks. They seldom examine them but at a distance, gunpowder being considered too precious to be thrown away on woodpeckers; nothing less than a turkey being thought worth the value of a load.

The food of this bird consists, I believe, entirely of insects and their larvae. The pileated woodpecker is suspected of sometimes tasting the Indian corn, the ivory-billed never. His common note, repeated every three or four seconds, very much resembles the tone of a trumpet, or the high note of a clarionet, and can plainly be distinguished at the distance of more than half a mile, seeming to be immediately at hand, though perhaps more than one hundred yards off. This it utters while mounting along the trunk or digging into it. At these times it has a stately and novel appearance; and the note instantly attracts the notice of a stranger. Along the borders of the Savannah river, between Savannah and Augusta, I found them very frequently; but my horse no sooner heard their trumpet-like note, than, remembering his former alarm, he became almost ungovernable.

The ivory-billed woodpecker is twenty inches long, and thirty inches in extent; the general color is black, with a considerable gloss of green when exposed to a good light; iris of the eye, vivid yellow; nostrils, covered with recumbent white hairs; forepart of the head, black; rest of the crest of a most splendid red, spotted at the bottom with white, which is only seen when the crest is erected; this long red plumage being ash-colored at its base, above that white, and ending in brilliant red; a stripe of white proceeds from a point, about half an inch below each eye, passes down each side of the neck, and along the back, where they are about an inch apart, nearly to the rump; the first five primaries are wholly black; on the next five the white spreads from the tip higher and higher to the secondaries, which are wholly white from their coverts downward. These markings, when the wings are shut, make the bird appear as if his back were white; hence he has been called by some of our naturalists the large white-backed woodpecker. The neck is long; the beak an inch broad at the base, of the color and consistence of ivory, prodigiously strong and elegantly fluted. The tail is black, tapering from the two exterior feathers, which are three inches shorter than the middle ones, and each feather has the singularity of being greatly concave below; the wing is lined with yellowish white; the legs are about an inch and a quarter long, the exterior toe about the same length, the claws exactly semicircular and remarkably powerful, the whole of a light blue or lead color. The female is about half an inch shorter, the bill rather less, and the whole plumage of the head black, glossed with green; in the other parts of the plumage, she exactly resembles the male. In the stomachs of three which I opened, I found large quantities of a species of worm called borers, two or three inches long, of a dirty cream color, with a black head; the stomach was an oblong pouch, not muscular like the gizzards of some others. The tongue was worm-shaped, and for half an inch at the tip as hard as horn, flat, pointed, of the same white color as the bill, and thickly barbed on each side.

QUESTIONS

1. Wilson reserves his description of the markings of the ivory-billed woodpecker until the end of his essay. Should these important matters of measure come at the beginning? Why or why not?
2. Wilson's opening sentence is a strong one. What commitments or concessions does it ask the reader to make?
3. Wilson wrote in the early nineteenth century. Do any of his attitudes seem quaint or old-fashioned? Is there anything in his manner of writing that seems quaint or old-fashioned?
4. Compare this account of a bird with that in Stewart's "Vulture Country" (pp. 1361–1368). What are the differences? Do the differences suggest any generalizations about changes in the study of animal life since Wilson wrote? Do these changes represent progress? If so, in what ways?
5. Compare this account of a bird with Lorenz's account of the water shrew (pp. 1348–1361). What are the similarities? What are the differences? Is Wilson's approach more like that of Lorenz or of Stewart?

Prose Forms: Parables

[When we read a short story or a novel, we are less interested in the working out of ideas than in the working out of characters and their destinies. In Dickens' *Great Expectations*, for example, Pip the hero undergoes many triumphs and defeats in his pursuit of success, only to learn finally that he has expected the wrong things, or the right things for the wrong reasons; that the great values in life are not always to be found in what the world calls success. In realizing this meaning we entertain, with Dickens, certain concepts or ideas that organize and evaluate the life in the novel, and that ultimately we apply to life generally. Ideas are there not to be exploited discursively, but to be understood as the perspective which shapes the direction of the novel and our view of its relation to life.

When ideas in their own reality are no longer the primary interest in writing, we have obviously moved from expository to other forms of prose. The shift need not be abrupt and complete, however; there is an area where the discursive interest in ideas and the narrative interest in characters and events blend. In allegory, for example, abstract ideas are personified. "Good Will" or "Peace" may be shown as a young woman, strong, confident, and benevolent in her bearing but vulnerable, through her sweet reasonableness, to the single-minded, fierce woman who is "Dissension." Our immediate interest is in their behavior as characters, but our ultimate interest is in the working out, through them, of the ideas they represent. We do not ask that the characters and events be entirely plausible in relation to actual life, as we do for the novel; we are satisfied if they are consistent with the nature of the ideas that define their vitality.

Ideas themselves have vitality, a mobile and dynamic life with a behavior of its own. The title of the familiar Negro spiritual "Sometimes I Feel Like a Motherless Child," to choose a random instance, has several kinds of "motion" as an idea. The qualitative identity of an adult's feelings and those of a child; the whole burgeoning possibility of all that the phrase "motherless child" can mean; the subtle differences in meaning—the power of context—that occur when it is a Negro who feels this and when it is a white; the speculative possibilities of the title as social commentary or psychological analysis; the peculiar force of the ungrammatical "like"—these suggest something of the "life" going on in and around the idea. Definition,

1374

analogy, assumption, implication, context, illustration are some of the familiar terms we use to describe this kind of life.

There is, of course, another and more obvious kind of vitality which an idea has: its applicability to the affairs of men in everyday life. Both the kind and extent of an idea's relevance are measures of this vitality. When an essayist wishes to exploit both the life in an idea and the life it comprehends, he often turns to narration, because there he sees the advantage of lifelike characters and events, and of showing through them the liveliness of ideas in both the senses we have noted. Ideas about life can be illustrated in life. And, besides, people like stories. The writer's care must be to keep the reader's interest focused on the ideas, rather than on the life itself; otherwise, he has ceased being essentially the essayist and has become the short-story writer or novelist.

The parable and the moral fable are ideal forms for his purpose. In both, the idea is the heart of the composition; in both the ideas usually assume the form of a lesson about life, some moral truth of general consequence to men; and in both there are characters and actions. Jesus often depended on parables in his teaching. Simple, economical, pointed, the parables developed a "story," but more importantly, applied a moral truth to experience. Peter asked Jesus how often he must forgive the brother who sins against him, and Jesus answered with the parable of the king and his servants, one of whom asked and got forgiveness of the king for his debts but who would not in turn forgive a fellow servant his debt. The king, on hearing of this harshness, retracted his own benevolence and punished the unfeeling servant. Jesus concluded to Peter, "So likewise shall my heavenly Father do also unto you, if ye from your hearts forgive not every one his brother their trespasses." But before this direct drawing of the parallel, the lesson was clear in the outline of the narrative.

Parables usually have human characters; fables often achieve a special liveliness with animals. In March's "The Fisherman and the Hen," the old hen is clearly just a chicken, clucking, picking at worms, scratching the ground. But when the fisherman has struck her to steal her worm for bait, and the old hen, responding to his compassion for having wronged her, gets another worm in order to be struck and so to be fondled afterwards, the old hen is almost magically transformed into a peculiar psychological truth about human behavior. The story creates its own interest as a story, but by its end the reader realizes that the story exists for the sake of an idea—and that its relevance is a lesson about himself.

The writer will be verging continually on strict prose narrative when he writes the parable or fable, but if he is skillful and tactful, he will preserve the essayist's essential commitment to the definition and development of ideas in relation to experience.]

ANONYMOUS: The Whale[1]

The whale is the largest of all the fishes in the sea. If you saw one floating on the surface, you would think it was an island rising from the sea sands. When he is hungry, this huge fish opens his mouth and sends forth a breath—the sweetest thing on earth—from his gaping jaws. Other fish, enticed by this sweetness, draw near and hover in his mouth, happy in their ignorance of his deception. The whale then snaps shut his jaws, sucking in all these fish. He thus traps the little fish; the great he cannot ensnare.

This fish lives near the bottom of the sea until the time when equinoctial storms stir up all the waters, as winter struggles to supplant summer, and the sea bottom becomes so turbulent that he cannot stay there. Then he leaves his home and rises to the surface, where he lies motionless. In the midst of the storm, ships are tossed about on the sea. The sailors fearing death and hoping to live, look about them and see this fish. They think he is an island, and, overjoyed, they head their ships for him and drop anchor. They step ashore and, striking sparks from stone and steel into their tinder, they make a fire on this marvel, warm themselves, and eat and drink. The fish soon feels the fire and dives to the bottom, drawing the sailors down with him. He kills them all without leaving a wound.

Application: The devil is determined and powerful, with the craftiness of witches. He makes men hunger and thirst after sinful pleasures and draws them to him with the sweetness of his breath. But whoever follows him finds only shame. His followers are the men of little faith; men of great faith he cannot ensnare, for they are steadfast, body and soul, in true belief. Whoever listens to the devil's teachings will at last regret it bitterly; whoever anchors his hope on the devil will be drawn down by him to the gloomy depths of hell.

1. From *A Bestiary*, an anonymous thirteenth-century English work, translated by Alan B. and Lidie M. Howes.

MARTIN BUBER: The Demon in the Dream

"What do you see?" asked the demon in the dream.

"A very long wall," I said.

"That is," he explained, "the boundary wall between the land of things and the land of thoughts. On this wall we demons live. It seems narrow to you, does it not, and not very roomy? But for us it is broad and comfortable enough. And we feel at home on it as well. Yes, I even allow myself to fancy that our feelings are better than yours, for you think yourself at home in both lands and are really at home in neither.

"You man! You act as if this wall were only a boundary which is otherwise not there, so to speak; as if one could neither squat on the wall, as I am squatting on it now, nor dance on it, as you saw me doing a moment ago. You believe such a foolish thing only because you know nothing of us. And if one knows nothing of us, how shall he know anything of the world or of the subtlest of its kingdoms, this wall?

"You know nothing of us. You only 'suspect' something. Oh, your suspicions! They arouse disgust in all beings—things and thoughts and demons. There, out of the darkness, a slimy grasping arm shoots towards you and then past you. Ugh, man, how unappetizing! I should rather be a crude tree-trunk and experience only what is necessary than be a being full of suspicions.

"You have a suspicion of us, then. But we know you to your very ground and deeper, too. We know you better than anything else, and in another way. But you are also more important to us than anything else. Yes, reluctantly I admit it, we are directly dependent on you. For we live off you. We can receive the strength of the world only through you. We can enjoy all things only through you. Your experience is our food, and we have no other.

"The more forcefully you live, the more avidly do we enjoy ourselves. The content of your living does not much matter to us; your joy and anger, sin and holiness, heroism and despair, are all the same to us. But whether you live fully or faintly, that does concern us. Your moderation is a meager crumb, your temperance a tough morsel that sticks in the throat. But where some fellow is horrified at the world and rushes against it and rages over its appeasements and is shattered on the wall of the great indifference; or where some fellow falls madly in love and again and again draws forth new power from out of his extravagance and converts it into amorousness until he revolves around some envisioned axis like a hundred-spoked fire-wheel, flaring up and crackling in a blissful smoke—there we feast, there we thrive.

"What you call contents is for us only gaily-colored variety, a cupboard of agreeable spices, no more. It does not occur to us to prefer one kind to another. Whether your passion pursues sensuality or politics, business or deeds of mercy, that does not affect our enjoyment; it only plays round it. But on the violence of your passion, on that we do depend.

"You have a No for every Yes, and for every value a disvalue. You effect transitions from one to the other, and you call the Yes good and the No bad, or vice versa, and are very concerned about whether your passion is on the side of the Yes or on the side of the No. But we are not especially interested in all this. The juggling amuses us, yet I assure you that we cannot otherwise express our esteem for your virtue and your moderate high-mindedness than by leaving it alone.

"But you must not think that we amuse ourselves on this wall and coolly await what ascends to us from excited human power. We would have a hard life then! For you are accustomed to 'let things happen' and to allow the possibilities in you to remain merely possibilities. It is fatiguing and disagreeable, you think, to give all of yourself; it is not even seemly. If it were not for us you would sleep through all your opportunities. We descend to you, we become things or thoughts in order not to startle you, we mingle with you, and—we tempt you. We taste the food, and when we find it flat we undertake the temptation: thereupon the bite becomes tasty. We rustle your passion out of its hiding-place. We inflame to feeling your capacity to feel. We actualize you. Naturally we do all this for our own sake; but, incidentally, what would become of you if we did not stir you up!

"There are some among you who imagine that one is tempted only to sin. That attitude fits them well, my dear: for they possess no other art than that which inclines them towards what they call sin. But in reality we are not at all specialized: we desire that out of your *potentia* should come *actus*, nothing more. We do not mix in your sophistries.

"We have, indeed—I may not conceal it from you—our sad chapter. We consume ourselves in the act of tempting. To tempt men is no child's play. We spring head over heels into each new undertaking, and it swallows all we are and all we can be. We could, in fact, say that we risk ourselves. Yes, we do enjoy it; but the enjoyment is exclusive and pitiless. When we are finished with this enjoyment, we collapse into ourselves. This collapsing of ours is not like your sleep; it is a dispersion, a scattering, a being wiped away. It lasts until a desire for fresh enjoyment steals over us and collects us. From this you can well imagine how much continuity there is in our lives. Hardly a vague trace remains in memory from one adventure to another! We seem continually to be starting life over again. Indeed it appears each time as if the escapade were really worth while—but that is, after all, a moot point.

"Though we are constantly starting all over again, we cannot remember a real beginning in our lives. Seriously, it seems to me as if we had nothing that might be called a real beginning. At times there descends on me a dull feeling as if I already always existed. But we do have an end, that is certain. Sometimes a final enjoyment will arrive which will swallow me and not deliver me up again. And until then . . .! Well, it is a melancholy bliss, I cannot deny it.

"And once there was even one among us who . . . I shall tell you about it although I can hardly believe you capable of fully understanding; for it is a story with long roots—but you have a nice way of looking at one, as if you . . . no matter!

"There was one demon who was discontented. He longed for continuity. Moments—he loathed moments if he could not advance upright from one to another, but one lay there and was more insignificant than a drunken man! He refused to take part any longer in this foolish rhythm of power and weakness. But you must not fancy that he conducted himself like your famous human rebels and harangued some god. When he realized he was fed up, he stood up and took a step outside of time. Once outside he sat down again.

"There he sat and was no longer affected by the whole game. There was no enjoyment, but there was no more emptiness—for where time no longer beats there is no emptiness, only the shape of the stillness. Thus he who had been discontented waxed in power and in duration. He took on security as a tree takes on rings. His power became ever stronger until he became aware that it could never again flag. Confident that he was wholly his own, it seemed to him as if the world was wholly his possession. You should have seen him when he stepped back into time!

"He began to tempt men again. But because his power had grown so great, each of his temptations drove his victim to his uttermost. Each ability of this man was intensified to the maximum, every longing was strained to its extreme. The uttermost of man, as you may well know, is a wonderful thing. The uttermost of man creates. That is a dangerous activity. It creates modes of being, essence, immortality. It lures men into madness and destruction, but it transforms the uttermost moment into eternity. And it cannot be exhausted through our enjoyment of it; its deep sweetness remains untasted, an eternally inaccessible remainder.

"He who had come back had been able to enjoy himself despite this remainder before he stepped out of time. Now he could do so no longer. Now, under the influence of the stillness, something greater than enjoyment sprang up in him: he sensed the inexhaustible over against him; he suffered, he burned. He was no longer merely discontented as before; he was wretched and alien. And he grew ever more miserable the higher his temptations reached on the ladder of creativeness. His strength, his capacity for enjoyment, was not impaired; it even grew from time to time without slackening. He went upright from one adventure to the next, yet each time the remainder pained him ever more acutely. Ever more silly the enjoyment appeared that could only satiate itself through intensity; ever more furiously he longed for the vision. To grasp the remainder, to fathom the qualities, to take possession of creativity, to see! But a demon can see as little as he can create.

"And while my brother's great game kindled awesome raptures, triumphs, downgoings on earth, driving the human soul upward to perform its greatest deed; while a gigantic burnt offering ascended to the tempter out of tumult and beauty, tyranny and grace, my brother recognized: 'What I enjoy is not the essence, the essence is beyond my reach; the essence is given to this little man with whom I play. While I play with him I evoke in him the essence, I make the essence in him alive.' And in the tempter there awoke this desire: 'I want to become a man: man, plaything—I want immortality—I want a creating soul!' For immortality, he perceived, is nothing but the creating soul."

The demon in my dream had altered. His grin had turned into an awkward smile, like the first smile on an infant's face, and his initially strident voice now sounded like the voice of the winegrowers I once heard sing the ancient melody of the dead to the words of a harvest song. Then sleep loosened, and the intertwined worlds slipped away from each other's embrace.

PLATO: The Allegory of the Cave[1]

And now, I said, let me show in a figure how far our nature is enlightened or unenlightened: Behold! human beings living in an underground den, which has a mouth open towards the light and reaching all along the den; here they have been from their childhood, and have their legs and necks chained so that they cannot move, and can only see before them, being prevented by the chains from turning round their heads. Above and behind them a fire is blazing at a distance, and between the fire and the prisoners there is a raised way; and you will see, if you look, a low wall built along the way, like the screen which marionette players have in front of them, over which they show the puppets.

I see.

And do you see, I said, men passing along the wall carrying all sorts of vessels, and statues and figures of animals made of wood and stone and various materials, which appear over the wall? Some of them are talking, others silent.

You have shown me a strange image, and they are strange prisoners.

Like ourselves, I replied; and they see only their own shadows, or the shadows of one another, which the fire throws on the opposite wall of the cave?

True, he said; how could they see anything but the shadows if they were never allowed to move their heads?

And of the objects which are being carried in like manner they would only see the shadows?

Yes, he said.

1. From Book VII of *The Republic*.

And if they were able to converse with one another, would they not suppose that they were naming what was actually before them?

Very true.

And suppose further that the prison had an echo which came from the other side, would they not be sure to fancy when one of the passers-by spoke that the voice which they heard came from the passing shadow?

No question, he replied.

To them, I said, the truth would be literally nothing but· the shadows of the images.

That is certain.

And now look again, and see what will naturally follow if the prisoners are released and disabused of their error. At first, when any of them is liberated and compelled suddenly to stand up and turn his neck round and walk and look towards the light, he will suffer sharp pains; the glare will distress him and he will be unable to see the realities of which in his former state he had seen the shadows; and then conceive some one saying to him, that what he saw before was an illusion, but that now, when he is approaching nearer to being and his eye is turned towards more real existence, he has a clearer vision—what will be his reply? And you may further imagine that his instructor is pointing to the objects as they pass and requiring him to name them—will he not be perplexed? Will he not fancy that the shadows which he formerly saw are truer than the objects which are now shown to him?

Far truer.

And if he is compelled to look straight at the light, will he not have a pain in his eyes which will make him turn away to take refuge in the objects of vision which he can see, and which he will conceive to be in reality clearer than the things which are now being shown to him?

True, he said.

And suppose once more, that he is reluctantly dragged up a steep and rugged ascent, and held fast until he is forced into the presence of the sun himself, is he not likely to be pained and irritated? When he approaches the light his eyes will be dazzled and he will not be able to see anything at all of what are now called realities.

Not all in a moment, he said.

He will require to grow accustomed to the sight of the upper world. And first he will see the shadows best, next the reflections of men and other objects in the water, and then the objects themselves; then he will gaze upon the light of the moon and the stars and the spangled heaven; and he will see the sky and the stars by night better than the sun or the light of the sun by day?

Certainly.

Last of all he will be able to see the sun, and not mere reflections of him in the water, but he will see him in his own proper place, and not in another; and he will contemplate him as he is.

Certainly.

He will then proceed to argue that this is he who gives the season and the years, and is the guardian of all that is in the visible world, and in a certain way the cause of all things which he and his fellows have been accustomed to behold?

Clearly, he said, he would first see the sun and then reason about him.

And when he remembered his old habitation, and the wisdom of the den and his fellow-prisoners, do you not suppose that he would felicitate himself on the change, and pity them?

Certainly, he would.

And if they were in the habit of conferring honors among themselves on those who were quickest to observe the passing shadows and to remark which of them went before, and which followed after, and which were together; and who were therefore best able to draw conclusions as to the future, do you think that he would care for such honors and glories, or envy the possessors of them? Would he not say with Homer,

> Better to be the poor servant of a poor master,

and to endure anything, rather than think as they do and live after their manner?

Yes, he said, I think that he would rather suffer anything than entertain these false notions and live in this miserable manner.

Imagine once more, I said, such an one coming suddenly out of the sun to be replaced in his old situation; would he not be certain to have his eyes full of darkness?

To be sure, he said.

And if there were a contest, and he had to compete in measuring the shadows with the prisoners who had never moved out of the den, while his sight was still weak, and before his eyes had become steady (and the time which would be needed to acquire this new habit of sight might be very considerable) would he not be ridiculous? Men would say of him that up he went and down he came without his eyes; and that it was better not even to think of ascending; and if any one tried to loose another and lead him up to the light, let them only catch the offender, and they would put him to death.

No question, he said.

This entire allegory, I said, you may now append, dear Glaucon, to the previous argument; the prison-house is the world of sight, the light of the fire is the sun, and you will not misapprehend me if you interpret the journey upwards to be the ascent of the soul into the intellectual world according to my poor belief, which, at your desire, I have expressed—whether rightly or wrongly God knows.

But, whether true or false, my opinion is that in the world of knowledge the idea of good appears last of all, and is seen only with an effort; and, when seen, is also inferred to be the universal author of all things beautiful and right, parent of light and of the lord of light in this visible world, and the immediate source of reason and truth in the intellectual; and that this is the power upon which he who would act rationally either in public or private life must have his eye fixed.

I agree, he said, as far as I am able to understand you.

Moreover, I said, you must not wonder that those who attain to this beatific vision are unwilling to descend to human affairs; for their souls are ever hastening into the upper world where they desire to dwell; which desire of theirs is very natural, if our allegory may be trusted.

Yes, very natural.

And is there anything surprising in one who passes from divine contemplations to the evil state of man, misbehaving himself in a ridiculous manner; if, while his eyes are blinking and before he has become accustomed to the surrounding darkness, he is compelled to fight in courts of law, or in other places, about the images or the shadows of images of justice, and is endeavouring to meet the conceptions of those who have never yet seen absolute justice?

Anything but surprising, he replied.

Any one who has common sense will remember that the bewilderments of the eyes are of two kinds, and arise from two causes, either from coming out of the light or from going into the light, which is true of the mind's eye, quite as much as of the bodily eye; and he who remembers this when he sees any one whose vision is perplexed and weak, will not be too ready to laugh; he will first ask whether that soul of man has come out of the brighter life, and is unable to see because unaccustomed to the dark, or having turned from darkness to the day is dazzled by excess of light. And he will count the one happy in his condition and state of being, and he will pity the other; or, if he have a mind to laugh at the soul which comes from below into the light, there will be more reason in this than in the laugh which greets him who returns from above out of the light into the den.

That, he said, is a very just distinction.

JONATHAN SWIFT: The Spider and the Bee[1]

Things were at this crisis, when a material accident fell out. For, upon the highest corner of a large window, there dwelt a certain spider, swollen up to the first magnitude by the destruction of

---

1. From *The Battle of the Books*.

infinite numbers of flies, whose spoils lay scattered before the gates of his palace, like human bones before the cave of some giant. The avenues of his castle were guarded with turnpikes and palisadoes, all after the modern way of fortification. After you had passed several courts, you came to the center, wherein you might behold the constable himself in his own lodgings, which had windows fronting to each avenue, and ports to sally out upon all occasions of prey or defense. In this mansion he had for some time dwelt in peace and plenty, without danger to his person by swallows from above, or to his palace by brooms from below, when it was the pleasure of fortune to conduct thither a wandering bee, to whose curiosity a broken pane in the glass had discovered itself, and in he went; where expatiating a while, he at last happened to alight upon one of the outward walls of the spider's citadel; which, yielding to the unequal weight, sunk down to the very foundation. Thrice he endeavored to force his passage, and thrice the center shook. The spider within, feeling the terrible convulsion, supposed at first that nature was approaching to her final dissolution; or else that Beelzebub,[2] with all his legions, was come to revenge the death of many thousands of his subjects, whom his enemy had slain and devoured. However, he at length valiantly resolved to issue forth, and meet his fate. Meanwhile the bee had acquitted himself of his toils, and posted securely at some distance, was employed in cleansing his wings, and disengaging them from the ragged remnants of the cobweb. By this time the spider was adventured out, when beholding the chasms, and ruins, and dilapidations of his fortress, he was very near at his wit's end; he stormed and swore like a madman, and swelled till he was ready to burst. At length, casting his eye upon the bee, and wisely gathering causes from events (for they knew each other by sight), "A plague split you," said he, "for a giddy son of a whore. Is it you, with a vengeance, that have made this litter here? Could you not look before you, and be d——nd? Do you think I have nothing else to do (in the devil's name) but to mend and repair after your arse?" "Good words, friend," said the bee (having now pruned himself, and being disposed to droll) "I'll give you my hand and word to come near your kennel no more; I was never in such a confounded pickle since I was born." "Sirrah," replied the spider, "if it were not for breaking an old custom in our family, never to stir abroad against an enemy, I should come and teach you better manners." "I pray have patience," said the bee, "or you will spend your substance, and for aught I see, you may stand in need of it all, towards the repair of your house." "Rogue, rogue," replied the spider, "yet methinks you should have more respect to a person, whom all the world allows to be so much your betters." "By my troth," said the bee, "the comparison will amount

2. The Hebrew god of flies. Pate MS.

to a very good jest, and you will do me a favor to let me know the reasons that all the world is pleased to use in so hopeful a dispute." At this the spider, having swelled himself into the size and posture of a disputant, began his argument in the true spirit of controversy, with a resolution to be heartily scurrilous and angry, to urge on his own reasons, without the least regard to the answers or objections of his opposite, and fully predetermined in his mind against all conviction.

"Not to disparage myself," said he, "by the comparison with such a rascal, what art thou but a vagabond without house or home, without stock or inheritance, born to no possession of your own, but a pair of wings and a drone-pipe? Your livelihood is an universal plunder upon nature; a freebooter over fields and gardens; and for the sake of stealing will rob a nettle as easily as a violet. Whereas I am a domestic animal, furnished with a native stock within myself. This large castle (to show my improvements in the mathematics) is all built with my own hands, and the materials extracted altogether out of my own person."

"I am glad," answered the bee, "to hear you grant at least that I am come honestly by my wings and my voice; for then, it seems, I am obliged to Heaven alone for my flights and my music; and Providence would never have bestowed on me two such gifts, without designing them for the noblest ends. I visit indeed all the flowers and blossoms of the field and the garden; but whatever I collect from thence enriches myself, without the least injury to their beauty, their smell, or their taste. Now, for you and your skill in architecture and other mathematics, I have little to say: in that building of yours there might, for aught I know, have been labor and method enough, but by woful experience for us both, 'tis too plain, the materials are naught, and I hope you will henceforth take warning, and consider duration and matter as well as method and art. You boast, indeed, of being obliged to no other creature, but of drawing and spinning out all from yourself; that is to say, if we may judge of the liquor in the vessel by what issues out, you possess a good plentiful store of dirt and poison in your breast; and, tho' I would by no means lessen or disparage your genuine stock of either, yet I doubt you are somewhat obliged for an increase of both, to a little foreign assistance. Your inherent portion of dirt does not fail of acquisitions, by sweepings exhaled from below; and one insect furnishes you with a share of poison to destroy another. So that in short, the question comes all to this—which is the nobler being of the two, that which by a lazy contemplation of four inches round, by an overweening pride, feeding and engendering on itself, turns all into excrement and venom, produces nothing at last, but flybane and a cobweb; or that which, by an universal range, with long search, much study, true judgment, and distinction of things, brings home honey and wax."

JAMES THURBER: The Glass in the Field

A short time ago some builders, working on a studio in Connecticut, left a huge square of plate glass standing upright in a field one day. A goldfinch flying swiftly across the field struck the glass and was knocked cold. When he came to he hastened to his club, where an attendant bandaged his head and gave him a stiff drink. "What the hell happened?" asked a sea gull. "I was flying across a meadow when all of a sudden the air crystallized on me," said the goldfinch. The sea gull and a hawk and an eagle all laughed heartily. A swallow listened gravely. "For fifteen years, fledgling and bird, I've flown this country," said the eagle, "and I assure you there is no such thing as air crystallizing. Water, yes; air, no." "You were probably struck by a hailstone," the hawk told the goldfinch. "Or he may have had a stroke," said the sea gull. "What do you think, swallow?" "Why, I—I think maybe the air crystallized on him," said the swallow. The large birds laughed so loudly that the goldfinch became annoyed and bet them each a dozen worms that they couldn't follow the course he had flown across the field without encountering the hardened atmosphere. They all took his bet; the swallow went along to watch. The sea gull, the eagle, and the hawk decided to fly together over the route the goldfinch indicated. "You come, too," they said to the swallow. "I—I—well, no," said the swallow. "I don't think I will." So the three large birds took off together and they hit the glass together and they were all knocked cold.

Moral: He who hesitates is sometimes saved.

WILLIAM MARCH: The Fisherman and the Hen

When he reached the brook where he intended to fish, an angler found he had left his bait at home, but after considering matters, he thought he might be able to catch grasshoppers and use them instead. He got down on his hands and knees, but try as he would, he wasn't successful. He had about abandoned the idea of getting bait that way, when he saw an old hen in the grass, seeking her breakfast. As he watched, he realized the old hen, despite her infirmities, was a better grasshopper-catcher than he, for almost at once she pounced on a large, lively one and held it in her bill.

The fisherman crept toward the old hen, hoping to take the grasshopper from her before she could swallow it, but the hen, guessing his intention, flushed her wings and ran through the grass. She might have escaped if the fisherman had not thrown a stick at her. He caught her squarely and she fell in the weeds, her tail feathers twitching from side to side.

He pulled the half-swallowed grasshopper from her throat, put it in his pocket, and turned away; but noticing how pathetic the old hen looked there in the grass, he picked her up and stroked her head. "Poor old thing!" he said. "I'm sorry for what I did just now!" He lifted her higher and rubbed his cheek against her wings. "I was a brute to hit you so hard," he said.

It was the first time the old hen had had any affection in years, and she lay back in the fisherman's arms, making a clucking sound in her throat, until he put her down and went back to his fishing. Shortly thereafter, he dismissed the incident from his mind, being engaged with his own pleasures, so he was somewhat puzzled when he heard a soft, seductive noise behind him. He turned, and there was the old hen with another grasshopper in her beak. When she saw she had his attention, she moved away slowly, glancing back at him over her shoulder, awaiting his blow with resignation, since an old hen will put up with anything if you'll give her a little affection now and then.

WILLIAM MARCH: The Unique Quality of Truth

When the old scholar heard that Truth was in the country, he decided to find her, as he had devoted his life to studying her in all her forms. He set out immediately, and at last he came upon the cottage in the mountains where Truth lived alone. He knocked on the door, and Truth asked what he wanted. The scholar explained who he was, adding that he had always wanted to know her and had wondered a thousand times what she really was like.

Truth came to the door soon afterwards, and the scholar saw that the pictures he had formed of her in his imagination were wrong. He had thought of Truth as a gigantic woman with flowing hair who sat nobly on a white horse, or, at the very least, as a sculptured heroic figure with a wide white brow and untroubled eyes. In reality, Truth was nothing at all like that; instead, she was merely a small shapeless old woman who seemed made of some quivering substance that resembled india rubber.

"All right," said the old lady in a resigned voice. "What do you want to know?"

"I want to know what you are."

The old lady thought, shook her head, and answered, "That I don't know. I couldn't tell you to save my life."

"Then have you any special quality that makes you an individual?" asked the scholar. "Surely you must have some characteristic that is uniquely yours."

"As a matter of fact, I have," said the old lady; then, seeing the question on the scholar's lips, she added, "I'll show you what I mean. It's easier than trying to explain."

The shapeless old woman began to bounce like a rubber ball, up and down on her doorstep, getting a little higher each time she struck the floor. When she was high enough for her purpose, she seized the woodwork above her door and held on; then she said, "Take hold of my legs and walk back the way you came, and when you know what my unique quality is, shout and let me know."

The old scholar did as he was told, racking his brains in an effort to determine what quality it was that distinguished Truth. When he reached the road, he turned around, and there in the distance was Truth still clinging to the woodwork above her door.

"Don't you see by this time?" she shouted. "Don't you understand now what my particular quality is?"

"Yes," said the old scholar. "Yes, I do."

"Then turn my legs loose and go on home," said Truth in a small petulant voice.

THE BOOK OF SAMUEL: Thou Art the Man[1]

And it came to pass, after the year was expired, at the time when kings go forth to battle, that David sent Joab, and his servants with him, and all Israel; and they destroyed the children of Ammon, and beseiged Rabbah. But David tarried still at Jerusalem.

And it came to pass in an eveningtide, that David arose from off his bed, and walked upon the roof of the king's house: and from the roof he saw a woman washing herself; and the woman was very beautiful to look upon. And David sent and enquired after the woman. And one said, Is not this Bathsheba, the daughter of Eliam, the wife of Uriah the Hittite? And David sent messengers, and took her; and she came in unto him, and he lay with her; for she was purified from her uncleanness: and she returned unto her house. And the woman conceived, and sent and told David, and said, I am with child.

And David sent to Joab, saying, Send me Uriah the Hittite. And Joab sent Uriah to David. And when Uriah was come unto him, David demanded of him how Joab did, and how the people did, and how the war prospered. And David said to Uriah, Go down to thy house, and wash thy feet. And Uriah departed out of the king's house, and there followed him a mess of meat from the king. But Uriah slept at the door of the king's house with all the servants of his lord, and went not down to his house. And when they had told David, saying, Uriah went not down unto his house, David

1. II Samuel xi and xii. 1-7.

said unto Uriah, Camest thou not from thy journey? why then didst thou not go down unto thine house? And Uriah said unto David, The ark, and Israel, and Judah, abide in tents; and my lord Joab, and the servants of my lord, are encamped in the open fields; shall I then go into mine house, to eat and to drink, and to lie with my wife? as thou livest, and as thy soul liveth, I will not do this thing. And David said to Uriah, Tarry here to day also, and to morrow I will let thee depart. So Uriah abode in Jerusalem that day, and the morrow. And when David had called him, he did eat and drink before him; and he made him drunk: and at even he went out to lie on his bed with the servants of his lord, but went not down to his house.

And it came to pass in the morning, that David wrote a letter to Joab, and sent it by the hand of Uriah. And he wrote in the letter, saying, Set ye Uriah in the forefront of the hottest battle, and retire ye from him, that he may be smitten, and die. And it came to pass, when Joab observed the city, that he assigned Uriah unto a place where he knew that valiant men were. And the men of the city went out, and fought with Joab: and there fell some of the people of the servants of David; and Uriah the Hittite died also. Then Joab sent and told David all the things concerning the war; and charged the messenger, saying, When thou hast made an end of telling the matters of the war unto the king, and if so be that the king's wrath arise, and he say unto thee, Wherefore approached ye so nigh unto the city when ye did fight? knew ye not that they would shoot from the wall? Who smote Abimelech the son of Jerubbesheth? did not a woman cast a piece of millstone upon him from the wall, that he died in Thebez? why went ye nigh the wall? then say thou, Thy servant Uriah the Hittite is dead also.

So the messenger went, and came and shewed David all that Joab had sent him for. And the messenger said unto David, Surely the men prevailed against us, and came out unto us into the field, and we were upon them even unto the entering of the gate. And the shooters shot from off the wall upon thy servants; and some of the king's servants be dead, and thy servant Uriah the Hittite is dead also. Then David said unto the messenger, Thus shalt thou say unto Joab, Let not this thing displease thee, for the sword devoureth one as well as another: make thy battle more strong against the city, and overthrow it: and encourage thou him.

And when the wife of Uriah heard that Uriah her husband was dead, she mourned for her husband. And when the mourning was past, David sent and fetched her to his house, and she became his wife, and bare him a son. But the thing that David had done displeased the Lord.

And the Lord sent Nathan unto David. And he came unto him, and said unto him, There were two men in one city; the one

rich, and the other poor. The rich man had exceeding many flocks
and herds: but the poor man had nothing, save one little ewe lamb,
which he had bought and nourished up: and it grew up together
with him, and with his children; it did eat of his own meat, and
drank of his own cup, and lay in his bosom, and was unto him as
a daughter. And there came a traveller unto the rich man, and he
spared to take of his own flock and of his own herd, to dress for
the wayfaring man that was come unto him; but took the poor man's
lamb, and dressed it for the man that was come to him. And David's
anger was greatly kindled against the man; and he said to Nathan,
As the Lord liveth, the man that hath done this thing shall surely
die: and he shall restore the lamb fourfold, because he did this
thing, and because he had no pity.

And Nathan said to David, Thou art the man.

MATTHEW: Parables of the Kingdom[1]

The same day went Jesus out of the house, and sat by the sea side.

And great multitudes were gathered together unto him, so that
he went into a ship, and sat; and the whole multitude stood on
the shore.

And he spake many things unto them in parables, saying,
Behold, a sower went forth to sow;

And when he sowed, some seeds fell by the way side, and the
fowls came and devoured them up:

Some fell upon stony places, where they had not much earth:
and forthwith they sprung up, because they had no deepness of
earth:

And when the sun was up, they were scorched; and because they
had no root, they withered away.

And some fell among thorns; and the thorns sprung up, and
choked them:

But other fell into good ground, and brought forth fruit, some
an hundredfold, some sixtyfold, some thirtyfold.

Who hath ears to hear, let him hear.

And the disciples came, and said unto him, Why speakest thou
unto them in parables?

He answered and said unto them, Because it is given unto you
to know the mysteries of the kingdom of heaven, but to them it is
not given.

For whosoever hath, to him shall be given, and he shall have
more abundance: but whosoever hath not, from him shall be taken
away even that he hath.

Therefore speak I to them in parables: because they seeing see

1. Matthew xiii.

not; and hearing they hear not, neither do they understand.

And in them is fulfilled the prophecy of Esaias, which saith, By hearing ye shall hear, and shall not understand; and seeing ye shall see, and shall not perceive:

For this people's heart is waxed gross, and their ears are dull of hearing, and their eyes they have closed; lest at any time they should see with their eyes, and hear with their ears, and should understand with their heart, and should be converted, and I should heal them.

But blessed are your eyes, for they see: and your ears, for they hear.

For verily I say unto you, That many prophets and righteous men have desired to see those things which ye see, and have not seen them; and to hear those things which ye hear, and have not heard them.

Hear ye therefore the parable of the sower.

When any one heareth the word of the kingdom, and understandeth it not, then cometh the wicked one, and catcheth away that which was sown in his heart. This is he which received seed by the way side.

But he that received the seed into stony places, the same is he that heareth the word, and anon with joy receiveth it;

Yet hath he not root in himself, but dureth for a while: for when tribulation or persecution ariseth because of the word, by and by he is offended.

He also that received seed among the thorns is he that heareth the word; and the care of this world, and the deceitfulness of riches, choke the word, and he becometh unfruitful.

But he that received seed into the good ground is he that heareth the word, and understandeth it; which also beareth fruit, and bringeth forth, some an hundredfold, some sixty, some thirty.

Another parable put he forth unto them, saying, The kingdom of heaven is likened unto a man which sowed good seed in his field:

But while men slept, his enemy came and sowed tares among the wheat, and went his way.

But when the blade was sprung up, and brought forth fruit, then appeared the tares also.

So the servants of the householder came and said unto him, Sir, didst not thou sow good seed in thy field? from whence then hath it tares?

He said unto them, An enemy hath done this. The servants said unto him, Wilt thou then that we go and gather them up?

But he said, Nay; lest while ye gather up the tares, ye root up also the wheat with them.

Let both grow together until the harvest: and in the time of harvest I will say to the reapers, Gather ye together first the tares, and bind them in bundles to burn them: but gather the wheat into my barn.

Another parable put he forth unto them, saying, The kingdom of heaven is like to a grain of mustard seed, which a man took, and sowed in his field:

Which indeed is the least of all seeds: but when it is grown, it is the greatest among herbs, and becometh a tree, so that the birds of the air come and lodge in the branches thereof.

Another parable spake he unto them; The kingdom of heaven is like unto leaven, which a woman took, and hid in three measures of meal, till the whole was leavened.

All these things spake Jesus unto the multitude in parables; and without a parable spake he not unto them:

That it might be fulfilled which was spoken by the prophet, saying, I will open my mouth in parables; I will utter things which have been kept secret from the foundation of the world.

Then Jesus sent the multitude away, and went into the house: and his disciples came unto him, saying, Declare unto us the parable of the tares of the field.

He answered and said unto them, He that soweth the good seed is the Son of man;

The field is the world; the good seed are the children of the kingdom; but the tares are the children of the wicked one;

The enemy that sowed them is the devil; the harvest is the end of the world; and the reapers are the angels.

As therefore the tares are gathered and burned in the fire; so shall it be in the end of this world.

The Son of man shall send forth his angels, and they shall gather out of his kingdom all things that offend, and them which do iniquity;

And shall cast them into a furnace of fire: there shall be wailing and gnashing of teeth.

Then shall the righteous shine forth as the sun in the kingdom of their Father. Who hath ears to hear, let him hear.

Again, the kingdom of heaven is like unto treasure hid in a field; the which when a man hath found, he hideth, and for joy thereof goeth and selleth all that he hath, and buyeth that field.

Again, the kingdom of heaven is like unto a merchant man, seeking goodly pearls:

Who, when he had found one pearl of great price, went and sold all that he had, and bought it.

Again, the kingdom of heaven is like unto a net, that was cast into the sea, and gathered of every kind:

Which, when it was full, they drew to shore, and sat down, and gathered the good into vessels, but cast the bad away.

So shall it be at the end of the world: the angels shall come forth, and sever the wicked from among the just,

And shall cast them into the furnace of fire: there shall be wailing and gnashing of teeth.

Jesus saith unto them, Have ye understood all these things? They say unto him, Yea, Lord.

Then said he unto them, Therefore every scribe which is instructed unto the kingdom of heaven is like unto a man that is an householder, which bringeth forth out of his treasure things new and old.

And it came to pass, that when Jesus had finished these parables, he departed thence.

And when he was come into his own country, he taught them in their synagogue, insomuch that they were astonished, and said, Whence hath this man this wisdom, and these mighty works?

Is not this the carpenter's son? is not his mother called Mary? and his brethren, James, and Joses, and Simon, and Judas?

And his sisters, are they not all with us? Whence then hath this man all these things?

And they were offended in him. But Jesus said unto them, A prophet is not without honour, save in his own country, and in his own house.

And he did not many mighty works there because of their unbelief.

FRANZ KAFKA: Parable of the Law[1]

"Before the Law stands a doorkeeper. To this doorkeeper there comes a man from the country who begs for admittance to the Law. But the doorkeeper says that he cannot admit the man at the moment. The man, on reflection, asks if he will be allowed, then, to enter later. 'It is possible,' answers the doorkeeper, 'but not at this moment.' Since the door leading into the Law stands open as usual and the doorkeeper steps to one side, the man bends down to peer through the entrance. When the doorkeeper sees that, he laughs and says: 'If you are so strongly tempted, try to get in without my permission. But note that I am powerful. And I am only the lowest doorkeeper. From hall to hall, keepers stand at every door, one more powerful than the other. And the sight of the third man is already more than even I can stand.' These are difficulties which the man from the country has not expected to meet, the Law, he thinks, should be accessible to every man and at all times, but when he looks more closely at the doorkeeper in his furred robe, with his huge pointed nose and long thin Tartar beard, he decides that he had better wait until he gets permission to enter. The

1. From the chapter, "In the Cathedral," of *The Trial* (1925).

doorkeeper gives him a stool and lets him sit down at the side of the door. There he sits waiting for days and years. He makes many attempts to be allowed in and wearies the doorkeeper with his importunity. The doorkeeper often engages him in brief conversation, asking him about his home and about other matters, but the questions are put quite impersonally, as great men put questions, and always conclude with the statement that the man cannot be allowed to enter yet. The man, who has equipped himself with many things for his journey, parts with all he has, however valuable, in the hope of bribing the doorkeeper. The doorkeeper accepts it all, saying, however, as he takes each gift: 'I take this only to keep you from feeling that you have left something undone.' During all these long years the man watches the doorkeeper almost incessantly. He forgets about the other doorkeepers, and this one seems to him the only barrier between himself and the Law. In the first years he curses his evil fate aloud; later, as he grows old, he only mutters to himself. He grows childish, and since in his prolonged study of the doorkeeper he has learned to know even the fleas in his fur collar, he begs the very fleas to help him and to persuade the doorkeeper to change his mind. Finally his eyes grow dim and he does not know whether the world is really darkening around him or whether his eyes are only deceiving him. But in the darkness he can now perceive a radiance that streams inextinguishably from the door of the Law. Now his life is drawing to a close. Before he dies, all that he has experienced during the whole time of his sojourn condenses in his mind into one question, which he has never yet put to the doorkeeper. He beckons the doorkeeper, since he can no longer raise his stiffening body. The doorkeeper has to bend far down to hear him, for the difference in size between them has increased very much to the man's disadvantage. 'What do you want to know now?' asks the doorkeeper, 'you are insatiable.' 'Everyone strives to attain the Law,' answers the man, 'how does it come about, then, that in all these years no one has come seeking admittance but me?' The doorkeeper perceives that the man is nearing his end and his hearing is failing, so he bellows in his ear: 'No one but you could gain admittance through this door, since this door was intended for you. I am now going to shut it.' "

"So the doorkeeper deceived the man," said K. immediately, strongly attracted by the story. "Don't be too hasty," said the priest, "don't take over someone else's opinion without testing it. I have told you the story in the very words of the scriptures. There's no mention of deception in it." "But it's clear enough," said K., "and your first interpretation of it was quite right. The doorkeeper gave the message of salvation to the man only when it could no longer help him." "He was not asked the question any earlier," said the priest, "and you must consider, too, that he was only a doorkeeper, and as such fulfilled his duty." "What makes you think he fulfilled his duty?" asked K. "He didn't fulfill it. His duty might have been to keep all strangers away, but this man, for whom the door was intended, should have been let in." "You have not enough respect for the written word and you are altering the story," said the priest. "The story contains two important statements made by the doorkeeper about admission to the Law, one at the beginning, the other at the end. The first statement is: that he cannot admit the man at the moment, and the other is: that this door was intended only for the man. If there were a contradiction between the two, you would be right and the doorkeeper would have deceived the man. But there is no contradiction. The first statement, on the contrary, even implies the second. One could almost say that in suggesting to the man the possibility of future admittance the doorkeeper is exceeding his duty. At that time his apparent duty is only to refuse admittance and indeed many commentators are surprised that the suggestion should be made at all, since the doorkeeper appears to be a precisian with a stern regard for duty. He does not once leave his post during these many years, and he does not shut the door until the very last minute; he is conscious of the importance of his office, for he says: 'I am powerful'; he is respectful to his superiors, for he says: 'I am only the lowest doorkeeper'; he is not garrulous, for during all these years he puts only what are called 'impersonal questions'; he is not to be bribed, for he says in accepting a gift: 'I take this only to keep you from feeling that you have left something undone'; where his duty is concerned he is to be moved neither by pity nor rage, for we are told that the man 'wearied the doorkeeper with his importunity'; and finally even his external appearance hints at a pedantic character, the large, pointed nose and the long, thin, black, Tartar beard. Could one imagine a more faithful doorkeeper? Yet the doorkeeper has other elements in his character which are likely to advantage anyone seeking admittance and which make it comprehensible enough that he should somewhat exceed his duty in suggesting the possibility of future admittance. For it cannot be denied that he is a little simple-minded and consequently a little conceited. Take the statements he makes about his power and the power of the other doorkeepers and their dreadful aspect which even he cannot bear to see—I hold that these statements may be true enough, but that the way in which he brings them out shows that his perceptions are confused by simpleness of mind and conceit. The commentators note in this connection: 'The right perception of any matter and a misunderstanding of the same matter do not wholly exclude each other.' One must at any rate assume that such simpleness and conceit, however sparingly manifest, are likely to weaken his defense of the door; they are breaches in the character of the doorkeeper.

To this must be added the fact that the doorkeeper seems to be a friendly creature by nature, he is by no means always on his official dignity. In the very first moments he allows himself the jest of inviting the man to enter in spite of the strictly maintained veto against entry; then he does not, for instance, send the man away, but gives him, as we are told, a stool and lets him sit down beside the door. The patience with which he endures the man's appeals during so many years, the brief conversations, the acceptance of the gifts, the politeness with which he allows the man to curse loudly in his presence the fate for which he himself is responsible—all this lets us deduce certain feelings of pity. Not every doorkeeper would have acted thus. And finally, in answer to a gesture of the man's he bends down to give him the chance of putting a last question. Nothing but mild impatience—the doorkeeper knows that this is the end of it all—is discernible in the words: 'You are insatiable.' Some push this mode of interpretation even further and hold that these words express a kind of friendly admiration, though not without a hint of condescension. At any rate the figure of the doorkeeper can be said to come out very differently from what you fancied." "You have studied the story more exactly and for a longer time than I have," said K. They were both silent for a little while. Then. K. said: "So you think the man was not deceived?" "Don't misunderstand me," said the priest, "I am only showing you the various opinions concerning that point. You must not pay too much attention to them. The scriptures are unalterable and the comments often enough merely express the commentators' despair. In this case there even exists an interpretation which claims that the deluded person is really the doorkeeper." "That's a farfetched interpretation," said K. "On what is it based?" "It is based," answered the priest, "on the simple-mindedness of the doorkeeper. The argument is that he does not know the Law from inside, he knows only the way that leads to it, where he patrols up and down. His ideas of the interior are assumed to be childish, and it is supposed that he himself is afraid of the other guardians whom he holds up as bogies before the man. Indeed, he fears them more than the man does, since the man is determined to enter after hearing about the dreadful guardians of the interior, while the doorkeeper has no desire to enter, at least not so far as we are told. Others again say that he must have been in the interior already, since he is after all engaged in the service of the Law and can only have been appointed from inside. This is countered by arguing that he may have been appointed by a voice calling from the interior, and that anyhow he cannot have been far inside, since the aspect of the third doorkeeper is more than he can endure. Moreover, no indication is given that during all these years he ever made any remarks showing a knowledge of the interior, except for the one remark about the doorkeepers. He may have been forbidden to do so, but there is no mention of that either. On these grounds the conclusion is reached that he knows nothing about the aspect and significance of the interior, so that he is in a state of delusion. But he is deceived also about his relation to the man from the country, for he is inferior to the man and does not know it. He treats the man instead as his own subordinate, as can be recognized from many details that must be still fresh in your mind. But, according to this view of the story, it is just as clearly indicated that he is really subordinated to the man. In the first place, a bondman is always subject to a free man. Now the man from the country is really free, he can go where he likes, it is only the Law that is closed to him, and access to the Law is forbidden him only by one individual, the doorkeeper. When he sits down on the stool by the side of the door and stays there for the rest of his life, he does it of his own free will; in the story there is no mention of any compulsion. But the doorkeeper is bound to his post by his very office, he does not dare go out into the country, nor apparently may he go into the interior of the Law, even should he wish to. Besides, although he is in the service of the Law, his service is confined to this one entrance; that is to say, he serves only this man for whom alone the entrance is intended. On that ground too he is inferior to the man. One must assume that for many years, for as long as it takes a man to grow up to the prime of life, his service was in a sense an empty formality, since he had to wait for a man to come, that is to say someone in the prime of life, and so he had to wait a long time before the purpose of his service could be fulfilled, and, moreover, had to wait on the man's pleasure, for the man came of his own free will. But the termination of his service also depends on the man's term of life, so that to the very end he is subject to the man. And it is emphasized throughout that the doorkeeper apparently realizes nothing of all this. That is not in itself remarkable, since according to this interpretation the doorkeeper is deceived in a much more important issue, affecting his very office. At the end, for example, he says regarding the entrance to the Law: 'I am now going to shut it,' but at the beginning of the story we are told that the door leading into the Law always stands open, and if it always stands open, that is to say at all times, without reference to life or death of the man, then the doorkeeper cannot close it. There is some difference of opinion about the motive behind the doorkeeper's statement, whether he said he was going to close the door merely for the sake of giving an answer, or to emphasize his devotion to duty, or to bring the man into a state of grief and regret in his last moments. But there is no lack of agreement that the doorkeeper will not be able to shut the door. Many indeed profess to find that he is subordinate to the man even in knowledge, toward the end, at least, for the man sees the radiance that issues from the door of the Law while the doorkeeper in his official position must stand with his back to the door, nor does he say anything to show that he has perceived the change." "That is well argued," said K., after repeating to himself in a low voice several passages from the priest's exposition. "It is well argued, and I am inclined to agree that the doorkeeper is deceived. But that has not made me abandon my former opinion, since both conclusions are to some extent compatible. Whether the doorkeeper is clear-sighted or deceived does not dispose of the matter. I said the man is deceived. If the doorkeeper is clear-sighted, one might have doubts about that, but if the doorkeeper himself is deceived, then his deception must of necessity be communicated to the man. That makes the doorkeeper not, indeed, a deceiver, but a creature so simple-minded that he ought to be dismissed at once from his office. You mustn't forget that the doorkeeper's deceptions do himself no harm but do infinite harm to the man." "There are objections to that," said the priest. "Many aver that the story confers no right on anyone to pass judgment on the doorkeeper. Whatever he may seem to us, he is yet a servant of the Law; that is, he belongs to the Law and as such is beyond human judgment. In that case one must not believe that the doorkeeper is subordinate to the man. Bound as he is by his service, even only at the door of the Law, he is incomparably greater than anyone at large in the world. The man is only seeking the Law, the doorkeeper is already attached to it. It is the Law that has placed him at his post; to doubt his dignity is to doubt the Law itself." "I don't agree with that point of view," said K., shaking his head, "for if one accepts it, one must accept as true everything the doorkeeper says. But you yourself have sufficiently proved how impossible it is to do that." "No," said the priest, "it is not necessary to accept everything as true, one must only accept it as necessary." "A melancholy conclusion," said K. "It turns lying into a universal principle."

Zen Parables

Muddy Road

Tanzan and Ekido were once traveling together down a muddy road. A heavy rain was still falling.

Coming around a bend, they met a lovely girl in a silk kimono and sash, unable to cross the intersection.

"Come on, girl," said Tanzan at once. Lifting her in his arms, he carried her over the mud.

Ekido did not speak again until that night when they reached a lodging temple. Then he no longer could restrain himself. "We monks don't go near females," he told Tanzan, "especially not young and lovely ones. It is dangerous. Why did you do that?"

"I left the girl there," said Tanzan. "Are you still carrying her?"

A Parable

Buddha told a parable in a sutra:

A man traveling across a field encountered a tiger. He fled, the tiger after him. Coming to a precipice, he caught hold of the root of a wild vine and swung himself down over the edge. The tiger sniffed at him from above. Trembling, the man looked down to where, far below, another tiger was waiting to eat him. Only the vine sustained him.

Two mice, one white and one black, little by little started to gnaw away the vine. The man saw a luscious strawberry near him. Grasping the vine with one hand, he plucked the strawberry with the other. How sweet it tasted!

Learning to Be Silent

The pupils of the Tendai school used to study meditation before Zen entered Japan. Four of them who were intimate friends promised one another to observe seven days of silence.

On the first day all were silent. Their meditation had begun auspiciously, but when night came and the oil lamps were growing dim one of the pupils could not help exclaiming to a servant: "Fix those lamps."

The second pupil was surprised to hear the first one talk. "We are not supposed to say a word," he remarked.

"You two are stupid. Why did you talk?" asked the third.

"I am the only one who has not talked," concluded the fourth pupil.

OSCAR WILDE: The Doer of Good

It was night-time, and He was alone.

And He saw afar off the walls of a round city, and went towards the city.

And when He came near He heard within the city the tread of the feet of joy, and the laughter of the mouth of gladness, and the loud noise of many lutes. And He knocked at the gate and certain of the gate-keepers opened to Him.

And He beheld a house that was of marble, and had fair pillars of marble before it. The pillars were hung with garlands, and within and without there were torches of cedar. And He entered the house.

And when He had passed through the hall of chalcedony and the hall of jasper, and reached the long hall of feasting, He saw lying on a couch of sea-purple one whose hair was crowned with red roses and whose lips were red with wine.

And He went behind him and touched him on the shoulder, and said to him:

"Why do you live like this?"

And the young man turned round and recognized Him, and made answer, and said: "But I was a leper once, and you healed me. How else should I live?"

And He passed out of the house and went again into the street.

And after a little while He saw one whose face and raiment were painted and whose feet were shod with pearls. And behind her came slowly, as a hunter, a young man who wore a cloak of two colours. Now the face of the woman was as the fair face of an idol, and the eyes of the young man were bright with lust.

And He followed swiftly and touched the hand of the young man, and said to him: "Why do you look at this woman and in such wise?"

And the young man turned round and recognized Him, and said: "But I was blind once, and you gave me sight. At what else should I look?"

And He ran forward and touched the painted raiment of the woman, and said to her: "Is there no other way in which to walk save the way of sin?"

And the woman turned round and recognized Him, and laughed, and said: "But you forgave me my sins, and the way is a pleasant way."

And He passed out of the city.

And when He had passed out of the city, He saw, seated by the roadside, a young man who was weeping.

And he went towards him and touched the long locks of his hair, and said to him: "Why are you weeping?"

And the young man looked up and recognized Him, and made answer: "But I was dead once, and you raised me from the dead. What else should I do but weep?"

On Religion

JAMES THURBER
The Owl Who Was God

Once upon a starless midnight there was an owl who sat on the branch of an oak tree. Two ground moles tried to slip quietly by, unnoticed. "You!" said the owl. "Who?" they quavered, in fear and astonishment, for they could not believe it was possible for anyone to see them in that thick darkness. "You two!" said the owl. The moles hurried away and told the other creatures of the field and forest that the owl was the greatest and wisest of all animals because he could see in the dark and because he could answer any question. "I'll see about that," said a secretary bird, and he called on the owl one night when it was again very dark. "How many claws am I holding up?" said the secretary bird, "Two," said the owl, and that was right. "Can you give me another expression for 'that is to say' or 'namely'?" asked the secretary bird. "To wit," said the owl. "Why does a lover call on his love?" asked the secretary bird. "To woo," said the owl.

The secretary bird hastened back to the other creatures and reported that the owl was indeed the greatest and wisest animal in the world because he could see in the dark and because he could answer any question. "Can he see in the daytime, too?" asked a red fox. "Yes," echoed a dormouse and a French poodle. "Can he see in the daytime, too?" All the other creatures laughed loudly at this silly question, and they set upon the red fox and his friends and drove them out of the region. Then they sent a messenger to the owl and asked him to be their leader.

When the owl appeared among the animals it was high noon and the sun was shining brightly. He walked very slowly, which gave him an appearance of great dignity, and he peered about him with large, staring eyes, which gave him an air of tremendous importance. "He's God!" screamed a Plymouth Rock hen. And the others took up the cry "He's God!" So they followed him wherever he went and when he began to bump into things they began to bump into things, too. Finally he came to a concrete highway and he started up the middle of it and all the other creatures followed him. Presently a hawk, who was acting as outrider, observed a truck coming toward them at fifty miles an hour, and he reported to the secretary bird and the secretary bird reported to the owl. "There's danger ahead," said the secretary bird. "To wit?" said the owl. The secretary bird told him. "Aren't you afraid?" He asked. "Who?" said the owl calmly, for he could not see the truck. "He's God!" cried all the creatures again, and they were still crying "He's God!" when the truck hit them and ran them down. Some of the animals were merely injured, but most of them, including the owl, were killed.

Moral: You can fool too many of the people too much of the time.

HERODOTUS

Croesus and the Oracle[1]

The messengers who had the charge of conveying these treasures to the shrines, received instructions to ask the oracles whether Croesus should go to war with the Persians, and if so, whether he should strengthen himself by the forces of an ally. Accordingly, when they had reached their destinations and presentd the gifts, they proceeded to consult the oracles in the following terms: "Croesus, king of Lydia and other countries, believing that these are the only real oracles in all the world, has sent you such presents as your discoveries deserved, and now inquires of you whether he shall go to war with the Persians, and if so, whether he shall strengthen himself by the forces of a confederate." Both the oracles agreed in the tenor of their reply, which was in each case a prophecy that if Croesus attacked the Persians, he would destroy a mighty empire, and a recommendation to him to look and see who were the most powerful of the Greeks, and to make alliance with them.

At the receipt of these oracular replies Croesus was overjoyed, and feeling sure now that he would destroy the empire of the Persians, he sent once more to Pytho, and presented to the Delphians, the number of whom he had ascertained, two gold staters apiece. In return for this the Delphians granted to Croesus and the Lydians the privilege of precedency in consulting the oracle, exemption from all charges, the most honorable seat at the festivals, and the perpetual right of becoming at pleasure citizens of their town.

1. From "Clio," Book I of the *Histories*.

After sending these presents to the Delphians, Croesus a third time consulted the oracle, for having once proved its truthfulness, he wished to make constant use of it. The question whereto he now desired an answer was—"Whether his kingdom would be of long duration?" The following was the reply of the Pythonesss:

> Wait till the time shall come when a mule is monarch of Media;
> Then, thou delicate Lydian, away to the pebbles of Hermus;
> Haste, oh! haste thee away, nor blush to behave like a coward.

Of all the answers that had reached him, this pleased him far the best, for it seemed incredible that a mule should ever come to be king of the Medes, and so he concluded that the sovereignty would never depart from himself or his seed after him.[2]

* * *

With respect to Croesus himself, this is what befell him at the taking of the town. He had a son, of whom I made mention above, a worthy youth, whose only defect was that he was deaf and dumb. In the days of his prosperity Croesus had done the utmost that he could for him, and among other plans which he had devised, had sent to Delphi to consult the oracle on his behalf. The answer which he had received from the Pythoness ran thus:

> Lydian, wide-ruling monarch, thou wondrous simple Croesus,
> Wish not ever to hear in thy palace the voice thou hast prayed for,
> Utt'ring intelligent sounds. Far better thy son should be silent!
> Ah! woe worth the day when thine ear shall first list to his accents.

When the town was taken, one of the Persians was just going to kill Croesus, not knowing who he was. Croesus saw the man coming, but under the pressure of his affliction, did not care to avoid the blow, not minding whether or no he died beneath the stroke. Then this son of his, who was voiceless, beholding the Persian as he rushed towards Croesus, in the agony of his fear and grief burst into speech, and said, "Man, do not kill Croesus." This was the first time that he had ever spoken a word, but afterwards he retained the power of speech for the remainder of his life.

Thus was Sardis taken by the Persians, and Croesus himself fell into their hands, after having reigned fourteen years, and been besieged in his capital fourteen days; thus too did Croesus fulfill the oracle, which said that he should destroy a mighty empire—by destroying his own.

2. Croesus then took the Spartans as allies and went to war against Cyrus, the Persian king, who turned out to be a "mule," since his parents were of different races and different social classes. Cyrus finally besieged and captured the town to which Croesus had withdrawn with his soldiers.

ROBERT GRAVES
Mythology[1]

Mythology is the study of whatever religious or heroic legends are so foreign to a student's experience that he cannot believe them to be true. Hence the English adjective "mythical," meaning "incredible"; and hence the omission from standard European mythologies of all Biblical narratives even when closely paralleled by myths from Persia, Babylonia, Egypt, and Greece, and of all hagiological legends. * * *

Myth has two main functions. The first is to answer the sort of awkward questions that children ask, such as: "Who made the world? How will it end? Who was the first man? Where do souls go after death?" The answers, necessarily graphic and positive, confer enormous power on the various deities credited with the creation and care of souls—and incidentally on their priesthoods.

The second function of myth is to justify an existing social system and account for traditional rites and customs. The Erechtheid clan of Athens, who used a snake as an amulet, preserved myths of their descent from King Erichthonius, a man-serpent, son of the Smith-god Hephaestus and foster-son of the Goddess Athene. The Ioxids of Caria explained their veneration for rushes and wild asparagus by a story of their ancestress Perigune, whom Theseus the Erechtheid courted in a thicket of these plants; thus incidentally claiming cousinship with the Attic royal house. The real reason may have been that wild asparagus stalks and rushes were woven into sacred baskets, and therefore taboo.

Myths of origin and eventual extinction vary according to the climate. In the cold North, the first human beings were said to have sprung from the licking of frozen stones by a divine cow named Audumla; and the Northern afterworld was a bare, misty, featureless plain where ghosts wandered hungry and shivering. According to a myth from the kinder climate of Greece, a Titan named Prometheus, kneading mud on a flowery riverbank, made human statuettes which Athene—who was once the Libyan Moon-goddess Neith—brought to life, and Greek ghosts went to a sunless, flowerless underground cavern. These afterworlds were destined for serfs or commoners; deserving nobles could count on warm, celestial mead halls in the North, and Elysian Fields in Greece.

Primitive peoples remodel old myths to conform with changes produced by revolutions, or invasions and, as a rule, politely disguise their violence: thus a treacherous usurper will figure as a lost heir

---

1. Introduction to the *Larousse Encyclopedia of Mythology*, 1959.

to the throne who killed a destructive dragon or other monster and, after marrying the king's daughter, duly succeeded him. Even myths of origin get altered or discarded. Prometheus' creation of men from clay superseded the hatching of all nature from a world-egg laid by the ancient Mediterranean Dove-goddess Eurynome—a myth common also in Polynesia, where the Goddess is called Tangaroa.

A typical case-history of how myths develop as culture spreads: Among the Akan of Ghana, the original social system was a number of queendoms, each containing three or more clans and ruled by a Queen-mother with her council of elder women, descent being reckoned in the female line, and each clan having its own animal deity. The Akan believed that the world was born from the all-powerful Moon-goddess Ngame, who gave human beings souls, as soon as born, by shooting lunar rays into them. At some time or other, perhaps in the early Middle Ages, patriarchal nomads from the Sudan forced the Akans to accept a male Creator, a Sky-god named Odomankoma, but failed to destroy Ngame's dispensation. A compromise myth was agreed upon: Odomankoma created the world with hammer and chisel from inert matter, after which Ngame brought it to life. These Sudanese invaders also worshipped the seven planetary powers ruling the week—a system originating in Babylonia. (It had spread to Northern Euope, bypassing Greece and Rome, which is why the names of pagan deities—Tuisto, Woden, Thor, and Frigg—are still attached to Tuesday, Wednesday, Thursday, and Friday.) This extra cult provided the Akan with seven new deities, and the compromise myth made both them and the clan gods bisexual. Towards the end of the fourteenth century A.D., a social revolution deposed Odomankoma in favor of a Universal Sun-god, and altered the myth accordingly. While Odomankoma ruled, a queendom was still a queendom, the king acting merely as a consort and male representative of the sovereign Queen-mother, and being styled "Son of the Moon": a yearly dying, yearly resurrected, fertility godling. But the gradual welding of small queendoms into city-states, and of city-states into a rich and populous nation, encouraged the High King—the king of the dominant city-state—to borrow a foreign custom. He styled himself "Son of the Sun," as well as "Son of the Moon," and claimed limitless authority. The Sun, which, according to the myth, had hitherto been reborn every morning from Ngame, was now worshipped as an eternal god altogether independent of the Moon's life-giving function. New myths appeared when the Akan accepted the patriarchal principle, which Sun-worship brought in; they began tracing succession through the father, and mothers ceased to be the spiritual heads of households.

This case-history throws light on the complex Egyptian corpus of myth. Egypt, it seems, developed from small matriarchal Moon-queendoms to Pharaonic patriarchal Sun-monarchy. Grotesque animal deities of leading clans in the Delta became city-gods, and the cities were federated under the sovereignty of a High King (once a "Son of the Moon"), who claimed to be the Son of Ra the Sun-god. Opposition by independent-minded city-rulers to the Pharaoh's autocratic sway appears in the undated myth of how Ra grew so old and feeble that he could not even control his spittle; the Moon-goddess Isis plotted against him and Ra retaliated by casting his baleful eye on mankind—they perished in their thousands. Ra nevertheless decided to quit the ungrateful land of Egypt, whereupon Hathor, a loyal Cow-goddess, flew him up to the vault of Heaven. The myth doubtless records a compromise that consigned the High King's absolutist pretensions, supported by his wife, to the vague realm of philosophic theory. He kept the throne, but once more became, for all practical purposes, an incarnation of Osiris, consort of the Moon-goddess Isis—a yearly dying, yearly resurrected fertility godling.

Indian myth is highly complex, and swings from gross physical abandon to rigorous asceticism and fantastic visions of the spirit world. Yet it has much in common with European myth, since Aryan invasions in the second millennium B.C. changed the religious system of both continents. The invaders were nomad herdsmen, and the peoples on whom they imposed themselves as a military aristocracy were peasants. Hesiod, an early Greek poet, preserves a myth of pre-Aryan "Silver Age" heroes: "divinely created eaters of bread, utterly subject to their mothers however long they lived, who never sacrificed to the gods, but at least did not make war against one another." Hesiod put the case well: in primitive agricultural communities, recourse to war is rare, and goddess-worship the rule. Herdsmen, on the contrary, tend to make fighting a profession and, perhaps because bulls dominate their herds, as rams do flocks, worship a male Sky-god typified by a bull or a ram. He sends down rain for the pastures, and they take omens from the entrails of the victims sacrificed to him.

When an invading Aryan chieftain, a tribal rainmaker, married the Moon-priestess and Queen of a conquered people, a new myth inevitably celebrated the marriage of the Sky-god and the Moon. But since the Moon-goddess was everywhere worshipped as a triad, in honor of the Moon's three phases—waxing, full, and waning—the god split up into a complementary triad. This accounts for three-bodied Geryon, the first king of Spain; three-headed Cernunnos, the Gallic god; the Irish triad, Brian, Iuchar, and Iucharba, who married the three queenly owners of Ireland; and the invading Greek brothers Zeus, Poseidon, and Hades, who, despite great opposition, married the pre-Greek Moon-goddess in her three aspects, respectively as Queen of Heaven, Queen of the Sea, and Queen of the Underworld.

The Queen-mother's decline in religious power, and the goddesses' continual struggle to preserve their royal prerogatives, appears in the Homeric myth of how Zeus ill-treated and bullied Hera, and how she continually plotted against him. Zeus remained a Thunder-god, because Greek national sentiment forbad his becoming a Sun-god in Oriental style. But his Irish counterpart, a thunder-god named The Dagda, grew senile at last and surrendered the throne to his son Bodb the Red, a war-god—in Ireland, the magic of rainmaking was not so important as in Greece.

One constant rule of mythology is that whatever happens among the gods above reflects events on earth. Thus a father-god named "The Ancient One of the Jade" (Yu-ti) ruled the pre-revolutionary Chinese Heaven: like Prometheus, he had created human beings from clay. His wife was the Queen-mother, and their court an exact replica of the old Imperial Court at Pekin, with precisely the same functionaries: ministers, soldiers, and a numerous family of the gods' sisters, daughters, and nephews. The two annual sacrifices paid by the Emperor to the August One of the Jade—at the winter solstice when the days first lengthen and at the Spring equinox when they become longer than the nights—show him to have once been a solar god. And the theological value to the number 72 suggests that the cult started as a compromise between Moon-goddess worship and Sun-god worship. 72 means three-times-three, the Moon's mystical number, multipled by two-times-two-times-two, the Sun's mystical number, and occurs in solar-lunar divine unions throughout Europe, Asia, and Africa. Chinese conservatism, by the way, kept these gods dressed in ancient court-dress, making no concessions to the new fashions which the invading dynasty from Manchuria had introduced.

In West Africa, whenever the Queen-mother, or King, appointed a new functionary at Court, the same thing happened in Heaven, by royal decree. Presumably this was also the case in China; and if we apply the principle to Greek myth, it seems reasonably certain that the account of Tirynthian Heracles' marriage to Hera's daughter Hebe, and his appointment as Celestial Porter to Zeus, commemorates the appointment of a Tirynthian prince as vizier at the court of the Mycenaean High King, after marriage to a daughter of his Queen, the High Priestess of Argos. Probably the appointment of Ganymede, son of an early Trojan king, as cup-bearer to Zeus, had much the same significance: Zeus, in this context, would be more likely the Hittite king resident at Hattusas.

Myth, then, is a dramatic shorthand record of such matters as invasions, migrations, dynastic changes, admission of foreign cults, and social reforms. When bread was first introduced into

Greece—where only beans, poppyseeds, acorns, and asphodel roots had hitherto been known—the myth of Demeter and Triptolemus sanctified its use; the same event in Wales produced a myth of "The Old White One," a Sow-goddess who went around the country with gifts of grain, bees, and her own young; for agriculture, pig breeding and beekeeping were taught to the aborigines by the same wave of neolithic invaders. Other myths sanctified the invention of wine.

A proper study of myth demands a great store of abstruse geographical, historical, and anthropological knowledge, also familiarity with the properties of plants and trees, and the habits of wild birds and beasts. Thus a Central American stone sculpture, a Toad-god sitting beneath a mushroom, means little to mythologists who have not considered the worldwide association of toads with toxic mushrooms or heard of a Mexican Mushroom-god, patron of an oracular cult; for the toxic agent is a drug, similar to that secreted in the sweat glands of frightened toads, which provides magnificent hallucinations of a heavenly kingdom.

Myths are fascinating and easily misread. Readers may smile at the picture of Queen Maya and her prenatal dream of the Buddha descending upon her disguised as a charming white baby elephant—he looks as though he would crush her to pulp—when "at once all nature rejoiced, trees burst into bloom, and musical instruments played of their own accord." In English-speaking countries, "white elephant" denotes something not only useless and unwanted, but expensive to maintain; and the picture could be misread there as indicating the Queen's grave embarrassment at the prospect of bearing a child. In India, however, the elephant symbolizes royalty—the supreme God Indra rides one—and white elephants (which are not albinos, but animals suffering from a vitiliginous skin disease) are sacred to the Sun, as white horses were for the ancient Greeks, and white oxen for the British druids. The elephant, moreover, symbolizes intelligence, and Indian writers traditionally acknowledge the Elephant-god Ganesa as their patron; he is supposed to have dictated the *Mahabharata*.

Again, in English, a scallop shell is associated either with cookery or with medieval pilgrims returning from a visit to the Holy Sepulcher; but Aphrodite the Greek Love-goddess employed a scallop shell for her voyages across the sea, because its two parts were so tightly hinged together as to provide a symbol of passionate sexual love—the hinge of the scallop being a principal ingredient in ancient love-philters. The lotus-flower sacred to Buddha and Osiris has five petals, which symbolize the four limbs and the head; the five senses; the five digits; and, like the pyramid, the four points of the compass and the zenith. Other esoteric meanings abound, for myths are seldom simple, and never irresponsible.

RONALD A. KNOX

The Nature of Enthusiasm[1]

I have called this book *Enthusiasm*, not meaning thereby to name (for name it has none) the elusive thing that is its subject. I have only used a cant term, pejorative, and commonly misapplied, as a label for a tendency. And, lest I should be accused of setting out to mystify the reader, I must proceed to map out, as best I may, the course of this inquiry. There is, I would say, a recurrent situation in Church history—using the word "church" in the widest sense—where an excess of charity threatens unity. You have a clique, an *élite*, of Christian men and (more importantly) women, who are trying to live a less worldly life than their neighbors; to be more attentive to the guidance (directly felt, they would tell you) of the Holy Spirit. More and more, by a kind of fatality, you see them draw apart from their co-religionists, a hive ready to swarm. There is provocation on both sides; on the one part, cheap jokes at the expense of over-godliness, acts of stupid repression by unsympathetic authorities; on the other, contempt of the half-Christian, ominous references to old wine and new bottles, to the kernel and the husk. Then, while you hold your breath and turn away your eyes in fear, the break comes; condemnation or secession, what difference does it make? A fresh name has been added to the list of Christianities.

The pattern is always repeating itself, not in outline merely but in detail. Almost always the enthusiastic movement is denounced as an innovation, yet claims to be preserving, or to be restoring, the primitive discipline of the Church. Almost always the opposition is twofold; good Christian people who do not relish an eccentric spirituality find themselves in unwelcome alliance with worldlings who do not relish any spirituality at all. Almost always schism begets schism; once the instinct of discipline is lost, the movement breeds rival prophets and rival coteries, at the peril of its internal unity. Always the first fervors evaporate; prophecy dies out, and the charismatic is merged in the institutional. "The high that proved too high, the heroic for earth too hard"—it is a fugal melody that runs through the centuries.

If I could have been certain of the reader's goodwill, I would have called my tendency "ultrasupernaturalism." For that is the real character of the enthusiast; he expects more evident results from the grace of God than we others. He sees what effects religion can have, does sometimes have, in transforming a man's whole life and outlook; these exceptional cases (so we are content to think them) are for him the average standard of religious achievement. He will have no

1. From Chapter I of *Enthusiasm*, 1950.

"almost-Christians," no weaker brethren who plod and stumble, who (if the truth must be told) would like to have a foot in either world, whose ambition is to qualify, not to excel. He has before his eyes a picture of the early Church, visibly penetrated with supernatural influences; and nothing less will serve him for a model. Extenuate, accommodate, interpret, and he will part company with you.

Quoting a hundred texts—we also use them but with more of embarrassment—he insists that the members of his society, saved members of a perishing world, should live a life of angelic purity, of apostolic simplicity; worldly amusements, the artifices of a polite society, are not for them. Poor human nature! Every lapse that follows is marked by pitiless watchers outside the fold, creates a harvest of scandal within. Worse still, if the devout circle has cultivated a legend of its own impeccability; we shall be told, in that case, that actions which bring damnation to the worldling may be inculpable in the children of light. We must be prepared for strange alternations of rigorism and antinomianism as our history unfolds itself.

Meanwhile, it must not be supposed that the new birth which the enthusiast preaches can be limited to a mere reformation of manners. It involves a new approach to religion; hitherto this has been a matter of outward forms and ordinances, now it is an affair of the heart. Sacraments are not necessarily dispensed with; but the emphasis lies on a direct personal access to the Author of our salvation, with little of intellectual background or of liturgical expression. The appeal of art and music, hitherto conceived as a ladder which carried human thought upwards, is frowned upon as a barrier which interferes with the simplicity of true heart-worship. An inward experience of peace and joy is both the assurance which the soul craves for and its characteristic prayer-attitude. The strength of this personal approach is that it dominates the imagination, and presents a future world in all the colours of reality. Its weakness—but we are not concerned here to criticize—is an anthropocentric bias; not God's glory but your own salvation preoccupies the mind, with some risk of scruples, and even of despair.

But the implications of enthusiasm go deeper than this; at the root of it lies a different theology of grace. Our traditional doctrine is that grace perfects nature, elevates it to a higher pitch, so that it can bear its part in the music of eternity, but leaves it nature still. The assumption of the enthusiast is bolder and simpler; for him, grace has destroyed nature, and replaced it. The saved man has come out into a new order of being, with a new set of faculties which are proper to his state; David must not wear the panoply of Saul. Especially, he decries the use of human reason as a guide to any sort of religious truth. A direct indication of the Divine will is communicated to him at every turn, if only he will consent to abandon the "arm of flesh"—Man's miserable intellect, fatally obscured by the Fall. If no oracle from heaven is forthcoming, he will take refuge in sortilege; anything, to make sure that he is leaving the decision in God's hands. That God speaks to us through the intellect is a notion which he may accept on paper, but fears, in practice, to apply.

A new set of faculties, and also a new status; man saved becomes, at last, fully man. It follows that "the seed of grace," God's elect people, although they must perforce live cheek by jowl with the sons of perdition, claim another citizenship and own another allegiance. For the sake of peace and charity, they will submit themselves to every ordinance of man, but always under protest; worldly governments, being of purely human institution, have no real mandate to exercise authority, and sinful folk have no real rights, although, out of courtesy, their fancied rights must be respected. Always the enthusiast hankers after a theocracy, in which the anomalies of the present situation will be done away, and the righteous bear rule openly. Disappointed of this hope, a group of sectaries will sometimes go out into the wilderness, and set up a little theocracy of their own, like Cato's senate at Utica. The American continent has more than once been the scene of such an adventure; in these days, it is the last refuge of the enthusiast.

QUESTIONS

1. What devices does Knox use in constructing his definition of enthusiasm?
2. What explanation does Knox imply for the fact that "enthusiasm" is regarded as a pejorative term?
3. What does Knox mean by "ominous references to old wine and new bottles, to the kernel and the husk"?
4. What illustrations might Knox give for his last sentence?

NICHOLAS OF CUSA
The Icon of God[1]

If I strive in human fashion to transport you to things divine, I must needs use a comparison of some kind. Now among men's works I have found no image better suited to our purposes than that of an image which is omnivoyant—its face, by the painter's cunning art, being made to appear as though looking on all around it. There are many excellent pictures of such faces—for example, that of the archeress in the market-place of Nuremberg; that by the eminent painter, Roger, in his priceless picture in the governor's house at Brussels; the Veronica in my chapel at Coblenz, and, in the castle of

1. Preface to *The Vision of God.*

Brixen, the angel holding the arms of the Church, and many others elsewhere. Yet, lest ye should fail in the exercise, which requireth a figure of this description to be looked upon, I send for your indulgence such a picture as I have been able to procure, setting forth the figure of an omnivoyant, and this I call the icon of God.

This picture, brethren, ye shall set up in some place, let us say, on a north wall, and shall stand round it, a little way off, and look upon it. And each of you shall find that, from whatsoever quarter he regardeth it, it looketh upon him as if it looked on none other. And it shall seem to a brother standing to eastward as if that face looketh toward the east, while one to southward shall think it looketh toward the south, and one to westward, toward the west. First, then, ye will marvel how it can be that the face should look on all and each at the same time. For the imagination of him standing to eastward cannot conceive the gaze of the icon to be turned unto any other quarter, such as west or south. Then let the brother who stood to eastward place himself to westward and he will find its gaze fastened on him in the west just as it was afore in the east. And, as he knoweth the icon to be fixed and unmoved, he will marvel at the motion of its immovable gaze.

If now, while fixing his eye on the icon, he walk from west to east, he will find that its gaze continuously goeth along with him, and if he return from east to west, in like manner it will not leave him. Then will he marvel how, being motionless, it moveth, nor will his imagination be able to conceive that it should also move in like manner with one going in a contrary direction to himself. If he wish to experiment on this, he will cause one of his brethren to cross over from east to west, still looking on the icon, while he himself moveth from west to east; and he will ask the other as they meet if the gaze of the icon turn continuously with him; he will hear that it doth move in a contrary direction, even as with himself, and he will believe him. But, had he not believed him, he could not have conceived this to be possible. So by his brother's showing he will come to know that the picture's face keepeth in sight all as they go on their way, though it be in contrary directions; and thus he will prove that that countenance, though motionless, is turned to east in the same way that it is simultaneously to west, and in the same way to north and to south, and alike to one particular place and to all objects at once, whereby it regardeth a single movement even as it regardeth all together. And while he observeth how that gaze never quitteth any, he seeth that it taketh such diligent care of each one who findeth himself observed as though it cared only for him, and for no other, and this to such a degree that one on whom it resteth cannot even conceive that it should take care of any other. He will also see that it taketh the same most diligent care of the least of creatures as of the greatest, and of the whole universe.

GERARD MANLEY HOPKINS
The Fall of God's First Kingdom

A.M.D.G.[1]

FOR SUNDAY EVENING JAN. 25 1880, SEPTUAGESIMA SUNDAY, AT ST. FRANCIS XAVIER'S, LIVERPOOL—on *the Fall of God's First Kingdom*—"Every kingdom divided against itself shall be made desolate and every city (commonwealth) or house divided against itself shall not stand (Matt. xii 25)."

I am to speak tonight of the fall of God's first kingdom, of the Fall of Man. Those of you who have heard this month's evening sermons will understand how this comes now in due course. God entered in the beginning into a contract with man that they two should make one commonwealth for their common good, which was that God might be glorified in man and man in God; God was the sovereign in this commonwealth and kingdom and man the subject; God by his providence, his laws and appointments and man by his obedience and execution of them undertook to bring this good about; both parties were bound by justice and in justice lived, which in man was called original justice, but lasted / [2] not long. It ended with the Fall, of which I am now to speak.

Before God was king of man he was king of angels and before man fell angels had fallen. Then man was made that he might fill the place of angels. But Satan, who had fallen through pride and selflove, resolved that through pride and selflove man should be brought to fall and that, whereas a breach had been made in God's kingdom in heaven, God's kingdom on earth should be broken utterly to pieces. And as he could not do it by force he would do it by fraud. Now the wise assailant attacks the weakest spot, therefore Satan tempted Eve the woman.

He chose his disguise, he spoke by the serpent's mouth; he watched his time, he found Eve alone. And here some say she should have been warned when she heard a dumb beast speaking reason. But of this we cannot be sure: St. Basil says that all the birds and beasts spoke in Paradise: not of course that they were not dumb and irrational creatures by nature then as now, but if a black spirit could speak by them so could a white and it may be that the angels made use of them as instruments to sing God's praises and to entertain man. Neither would Satan needlessly alarm the woman, rather than that he would invisibly have uttered voices in the air. But when she heard what the serpent said, *then* she should have taken

---

1. Abbreviation for *Ad Maiorem Dei Gloriam*, "for the greater glory of God."
2. This sign is used throughout the sermon as a rhetorical notation for phrasing to be used in its delivery.

alarm. So then to listen to a serpent speaking might be no blame; but how came Eve to be alone? for God had said of Adam /*It is not good for man to be alone: let us make him a helpmate like himself*/; and Eve was without the helpmate not like only but stronger than herself. She was deceived and Adam, as St. Paul tells us, was not nor would have been. Then why was Eve alone?

Now, I know, my brethren, that the Scripture does not tell us this and we cannot with certainty answer the question, but yet it is useful to ask it because it throws a great light on what God's first kingdom was and how it came to fall. Take notice then that, besides those things which we must do whether we like or no, which we cannot help doing, such as breathe, eat, and sleep, there are three sorts of things that we may lawfully do, that are right in us, that we are within our rights in doing. The first are *our bounden duties*, as to hear mass on Sunday: these God commands. The second are *what God sanctions* but does not command nor in any special way approve, as to amuse ourselves. The third are what God does not command but specially approves when done, as to hear mass on a week-day: these are called works *of supererogation*. All these are good, not only the things God commands and the things he specially approves and accepts but also the things he only sanctions, for he sanctions nothing but what is good, that is to say / nothing but what is in itself harmless and which his sanction then makes positively good, and when a man says / *I do this because I like it and God allows me* / he submits himself to God as truly as if it were a duty and he said / *I do this because God wills it and commands me*. But though all are good they are not equally good; far from that. In the things God sanctions and we do for our own pleasure the whole good, the only good, comes from God's sanction and our submission to his sovereign will; for that he may reward us, but not for anything else: for the rest, we are doing our own pleasure and our own pleasure is our work's reward. But when we do what God commands or what God specially approves, then he is ready to reward us not only for our submission of ourselves to his sovereign will but also for the work done, for the pains taken; for we were doing *his* pleasure, not our own. Now you will easily understand, indeed you know, that it is the mark of a truly good will to do the good God approves of but does not bind us to, to do, in other words, works of supererogation: it shews that good is loved of itself and freely. And it is the mark of a cold heart, of poor will, I will not say a bad one, to do nothing that God especially approves, only what he commands or else sanctions: it shews that there is little love of good for good's sake. And though no one can be lost but for sin, yet those who do the least good they lawfully can are very likely indeed to fall into doing *less than that least* and so to sin.

Now if this applies to us now / very strongly does it apply to man unfallen. For Adam and Eve though they were in God's kingdom not sovereign but subject, yet they were king and queen of all this earth, they were like vassal princes to a sovereign prince, God's honor was more in their hands than it is in any one of ours; we are but ourselves, they represented mankind, they represented the commons in God's commonwealth; if I dishonor God today one of you may make up by honoring him, but if they left him unhonored who was to honor him? the beasts and birds and fishes? When Adam obeyed God / mankind was obeying its sovereign; when Adam offered God of his own free will unbidden sacrifice / mankind was all engrossed in a work of supererogation, in giving God fresh glory; when Adam was doing his own pleasure / mankind was in its duty indeed but God's honor was not growing, the commonwealth was idle. Now, brethren, with this thought turn to Eve's temptation and look for what shall appear there.

Eve was alone. It was no sin to be alone, she was in her duty, God had given her freedom and she was wandering free, God had made her independent of her husband and she need not be at his side. Only God had made her for Adam's companion; it was her office, her work, the reason of her being to companion him and she was not doing it. There is no sin, but there is no delicacy of duty, no zeal for the sovereign's honor, no generosity, no supererogation. And Adam, he too was alone. He had been commanded to dress and keep Paradise. What flower, what fruitful tree, what living thing was there in Paradise so lovely as Eve, so fruitful as the mother of all flesh, that needed or could repay his tendance and his keeping as she? There was no sin; yet at the one fatal moment when of all the world care was wanted care was not forthcoming, the thing best worth keeping was unkept. And Eve stood by the forbidden tree, which God had bidden them not to eat of, which *she* said God had bidden them not even touch; she neither sinned nor was tempted to sin by standing near it, yet she would go to the very bounds and utmost border of her duty. To do so was not dangerous of itself, as it would be to us. When some child, one of Eve's poor daughters, stands by a peachtree, eyeing the blush of color on the fruit, fingering the velvet bloom upon it, breathing the rich smell, and in imagination tasting the sweet juice, the nearness, the mere neighborhood is enough to undo her, she looks and is tempted, she touches and is tempted more, she takes and tastes. But in Eve there was nothing of this; she was not mastered by concupiscence, *she* mastered *it*. There she stood, beautiful, innocent, with her original justice *and with nothing else*, nothing to stain it, but nothing to heighten and brighten it: she felt no cravings, for she was mistress of herself and would not let them rise; she felt no generous promptings, no liftings of the heart to give God glory, for she was mistress of herself and gave them no encouragement. Such was Eve before her fall.

Now, brethren, fancy, as you may, that rich tree all laden with its shining fragrant fruit and swaying down from one of its boughs, as the pythons and great snakes of the East do now, waiting for their prey to pass and then to crush it, swaying like a long spray of vine or the bine of a great creeper, not terrible but beauteous, lissome, marked with quaint streaks and eyes or flushed with rainbow colors, the Old Serpent. We must suppose he offered her the fruit, as though it were the homage and the tribute of the brute to man, of the subject to his queen, presented it with his mouth or swept it from the boughs down before her feet; and she declined it. Then came those studied words of double meaning the Scripture tells us of: *What! and has God forbidden you to eat of the fruit of Paradise?* Now mark her answer: you would expect her to reply: No, but of this one fruit only: he has given us free leave for all the trees in Paradise excepting one—but hear her: *Of the fruit of the trees in Paradise we do eat*—no mention of God's bounty here, it is all their freedom, what they do: "we do eat"—*but the fruit of the tree in the midst of Paradise*—as though she would say / of the best fruit of all—*God has commanded us not to eat of, nor so much as touch it, or we shall die*: then she remembers God when it is question of a stern and threatening law. She gave her tempter the clue to his temptation—that God her sovereign was a tyrant, a sullen lawgiver; that God her lord and landlord was envious and grudging, a rackrent; that God her father, the author of her being was a shadow of death. The serpent took the hint and bettered it. Well was he called subtle: he does not put her suggestion into words and make it blacker; she would have been shocked, she would have recoiled; he gives the thing another turn, as much as to say: Why yes, God would be all this if you took his law according to the letter. No no; what does "death" mean? you will not die: you will die to ignorance, if you will, and wake to wisdom: *God knows, on the day you eat of it your eyes will be opened and you will be as gods, knowing good and evil.* And with these words he dealt three blows at once against God's kingdom—at God as a lawgiver and judge, at God as an owner or proprietor, at God as a father; at God as a lawgiver and judge, for the Serpent said / God has made this the tree of the knowledge of good and evil, that is / which shall decide for him whether to call you good or evil, good if you keep from it, evil if you touch it: be your own lawgivers and judges of good and evil; be as God yourselves, be divinely independent, why not? make it *good* to try the tree, *evil* to leave it untasted; at God as a proprietor, for as owner of man and the earth and all therein and sovereign of the commonwealth

God had given the other trees of Paradise to his subjects but reserved this one to the crown: the Serpent advised them to trespass boldly on these rights and seize crown-property; and at God as a father, for God like a fatherly providence found them food and forbad them poison: the Serpent told them the deadly poison was life-giving food. It was enough: Eve would judge for herself. She *saw that the tree was good to eat,* that it was *not* poison, it was the food of life—and here was the pride of life; *that it was beautiful to the eyes,* a becoming object to covet and possess—and here was the desire of the eyes; *and that it was delightful to behold,* that is / sweet and enjoyable in imagination even and forecast, how much more in the eating and the reality!—and here was the desire of the flesh; she freely yielded herself to the three concupiscences; *she took and eat* of this devil's-sacrament; she rebelled, she sinned, she fell.

She fell, but still God's kingdom was not fallen yet, because it turned upon the man's obedience, not the woman's. Then came the meeting between the husband and the wife and she learnt that she was deceived and undone. Then her husband must share her lot for better and worse; this selfish and fallen woman would drag her husband in her fall, as she had had no thought of God's honor in her innocence, so in her sin she had no charity for her husband: she had so little love for him that she said, if he loved her he must share her lot. Most dearly he loved her, and she stood before him now lovely and her beauty heightened by distress, a thing never seen before in Paradise, herself a Tree of Knowledge of Good and Evil and offering him its fruit; herself a Tree of Life, the mother of all flesh to be. For he thought his hope of offspring would go with her. He was wrong: God, who gave back to Abraham for his obedience his all but sacrificed son, would have given back to Adam for his obedience his fallen wife; but he did not pause to make an act of hope. He listened to her voice. He left his heavenly father and clave to his wife and they two were in one fallen flesh; for her he took the stolen goods and harbored the forfeit person of the thief, rebelling against God, the world's great landlord, owner of earth and man, who had bestowed upon him Paradise, who had bestowed upon him the body of his wife; for her he eat the fatal fruit, making a new contract, a new commonwealth with Eve alone, and rebelling against God his lawgiver and judge. With that the contract with God was broken, the commonwealth undone, the kingdom divided and brought to desolation. God was left upon his throne but his subject had deserted to the enemy, God was left with his rights but the tenant had refused him payment, God was left a father but his children were turned to children of wrath. Then followed the disinheriting of the disobedient son; then followed the first and most terrible of evictions, when Cherubim swayed the fiery sword and man was turned from Paradise; then followed the judgment of death and the execution of the sentence which we feel yet. *Wretched men that we are, who shall deliver us from this body of death? The grace of God through Jesus Christ our Lord* (Rom. vii 24, 25.). *For the wages of sin are death, but the grace of God is eternal life in Christ Jesus our Lord* (ib. vi 23.), *a blessing etc.*

L. D. S.[3]

3. Abbreviation for *Laus Deo Semper,* "glory to God for ever."

QUESTIONS

1. Compare Hopkins' account of the fall with the account in Genesis iii. How far does Hopkins' account go beyond the brief recital of the facts in Genesis? What justification does Hopkins have in Genesis for his interpretation? Does he add anything to it?
2. Hopkins speaks of God in the first part of his sermon as a "king" or "sovereign" who "entered . . . into a contract with man" and then later has Eve refer to Him as a "tyrant," a "sullen lawgiver," and a "landlord . . . a rackrent." What are the differences in connotation and denotation of these various metaphors for God? How does Hopkins use them to develop the central idea of his sermon?
3. What is the importance for the discourse of the threefold classification of "things that we may lawfully do"? What other examples might be given for each category?
4. Does Hopkins give Eve's case a fair hearing? Explain.
5. Hopkins said that when he delivered this sermon he was required (presumably by his superiors in the church) to "leave out or reword all passages speaking of God's kingdom as falling." How would these omissions affect the central idea and the forcefulness of the sermon?
6. In the light of his address "But Find the Point Again," what do you think Miller's comments on Hopkins' goals as a preacher and effectiveness as a speaker might be?

JOHN DONNE

Let Me Wither

Let me wither and wear out mine age in a discomfortable, in an unwholesome, in a penurious prison, and so pay my debts with my bones, and recompense the wastefulness of my youth, with the beggary of mine age; Let me wither in a spittle under sharp, and foul, and infamous diseases, and so recompense the wantonness of my youth, with that loathsomeness in mine age; yet if God withdraw not his spiritual blessings, his grace, his patience, If I can call my suffering his doing, my passion his action, All this that is temporal, is but a caterpiller got into one corner of my garden, but a mildew fallen upon one acre of my corn; The body of all, the substance of all is safe, as long as the soul is safe. But when I shall trust to that, which we call a good spirit, and God shall deject, and impoverish, and evacuate that spirit, when I shall rely upon a moral constancy, and God shall shake, and enfeeble, and enervate, destroy and demolish that constancy; when I shall think to refresh my self in the serenity and sweet air of a good conscience, and God shall call up the damps and vapors of hell itself, and spread a cloud of diffidence, and an impenetrable crust of desperation upon my conscience; when health shall fly from me, and I shall lay hold upon riches to succor me, and comfort me in my sickness, and riches shall fly from me, and I shall snatch after favor, and good opinion, to comfort me in my poverty; when even this good opinion shall leave me, and calumnies and misinformations shall prevail against me; when I shall need peace, because there is none but thou, O Lord, that should stand for me, and then shall find, that all the wounds that I have, come from thy hand, all the arrows that stick in me, from thy quiver; when I shall see, that because I have given my self to my corrupt nature, thou hast changed thine; and because I am all evil toward thee, therefore thou hast given over being good toward me; When it comes to this height, that the fever is not in the humors, but in the spirits,[1] that mine enemy is not an imaginary enemy, fortune, nor a transitory enemy, malice in great persons, but a real, and an irresistible, and an inexorable, and an everlasting enemy, The Lord of Hosts himself, The Almighty God himself, the Almighty God himself only knows the weight of this affliction, and except he put in that *pondus gloriae*, that exceeding weight of an eternal glory, with his own hand, into the other scale, we are weighed down, we are swallowed up, irreparably, irrevocably, irrecoverably, irremediably.

1. Not in one of the four chief fluids of the body or "humors" (blood, yellow bile, phlegm, and black bile), but in the more subtle fluids.

QUESTIONS

Both Hopkins and Donne are more famous as poets than as preachers, yet all that any author writes will in one way or another bear the stamp of his thought and personality. Read the following poems, one by Donne, one by Hopkins, and compare the poems to sermons. Does the conception of God suggested by each poem resemble that in the sermon by the same author? Do the poems accomplish any of the same purposes as the sermons? Are the sermons "poetic" in any way? What differences arise from the fact that in the sermons both are speaking to congregations, in the poems both are addressing God?

Thou art indeed just, Lord, if I contend
With thee; but, sir, so what I plead is just.
Why do sinners' ways prosper? and why must
Disappointment all I endeavour end?
   Wert thou my enemy, O thou my friend,
How wouldst thou worse, I wonder, than thou dost
Defeat, thwart me? Oh, the sots and thralls of lust
Do in spare hours more thrive than I that spend,
Sir, life upon thy cause. See, banks and brakes
Now, leavèd how thick! lacèd they are again
With fretty chervil, look, and fresh wind shakes
Them; birds build—but not I build; no, but strain,
Time's eunuch, and not breed one work that wakes.
Mine, O thou lord of life, send my roots rain.

—GERARD MANLEY HOPKINS

Batter my heart, three person'd God; for, you
As yet but knocke, breathe, shine, and seeke to mend.
That I may rise, and stand, o'erthrow mee, and bend
Your force, to breake, blowe, burn and make me new.
I, like an usurpt towne, to another due,
Labour to admit you, but Oh, to no end,
Reason your viceroy in mee, mee should defend,
But is captiv'd, and proves weake or untrue.
Yet dearely I love you, and would be loved faine,
But am bethroth'd unto your enemie;
Divorce mee, untie, or breake that knot againe,
Take mee to you, imprison mee, for I
Except you enthrall mee, never shall be free,
Nor ever chast, except you ravish mee.

—JOHN DONNE

JONATHAN EDWARDS

Sinners in the Hands of an Angry God[1]

Their foot shall slide in due time.[2]
—DEUT. xxxii. 35

In this verse is threatened the vengeance of God on the wicked unbelieving Israelites, who were God's visible people, and who lived under the means of grace; but who, notwithstanding all God's

1. Only the first part of the sermon is printed here; the "application" is omitted.
2. The complete verse reads: "To me belongeth vengeance, and recompence; their foot shall slide in due time: for the day of their calamity is at hand, and the things that shall come upon them make haste." It occurs in the middle of a long denunciatory "song" spoken by Moses to the Israelites.

wonderful works towards them, remained (as ver. 28.)[3] void of counsel, having no understanding in them. Under all the cultivations of heaven, they brought forth bitter and poisonous fruit; as in the two verses next preceding the text. The expression I have chosen for my text, *Their foot shall slide in due time*, seems to imply the following things, relating to the punishment and destruction to which these wicked Israelites were exposed.

1. That they were always exposed to *destruction*; as one that stands or walks in slippery places is always exposed to fall. This is implied in the manner of their destruction coming upon them, being represented by their foot sliding. The same is expressed, Psalm lxxiii. 18. "Surely thou didst set them in slippery places; thou castedst them down into destruction."

2. It implies that they were always exposed to sudden unexpected destruction. As he that walks in slippery places is every moment liable to fall, he cannot foresee one moment whether he shall stand or fall the next; and when he does fall, he falls at once without warning: Which is also expressed in Psalm lxxiii. 18, 19. "Surely thou didst set them in slippery places; thou castedst them down into destruction. How are they brought into desolation as in a moment!"

3. Another thing implied is, that they are liable to fall of *themselves*, without being thrown down by the hand of another; as he that stands or walks on slippery ground needs nothing but his own weight to throw him down.

4. That the reason why they are not fallen already, and do not fall now, is only that God's appointed time is not come. For it is said, that when that due time, or appointed time comes, *their foot shall slide*. Then they shall be left to fall, as they are inclined by their own weight. God will not hold them up in these slippery places any longer, but will let them go; and then, at that very instant, they shall fall into destruction; as he that stands on such slippery declining ground, on the edge of a pit, he cannot stand alone, when he is let go he immediately falls and is lost.

The observation from the words that I would now insist upon is this—"There is nothing that keeps wicked men at any one moment out of hell, but the mere pleasure of God"—By the *mere* pleasure of God, I mean his *sovereign* pleasure, his arbitrary will, restrained by no obligation, hindered by no manner of difficulty, any more than if nothing else but God's mere will had in the least degree, or in any respect whatsoever, any hand in the preservation of wicked men one moment. The truth of this observation may appear by the following considerations.

1. There is no want of *power* in God to cast wicked men into hell at any moment. Men's hands cannot be strong when God rises up.

---

3. Verse 28: "For they are a nation void of counsel, neither is there any understanding in them."

The strongest have no power to resist him, nor can any deliver out of his hands. He is not only able to cast wicked men into hell, but he can most easily do it. Sometimes an earthly prince meets with a great deal of difficulty to subdue a rebel, who has found means to fortify himself, and has made himself strong by the numbers of his followers. But it is not so with God. There is no fortress that is any defense from the power of God. Though hand join in hand, and vast multitudes of God's enemies combine and associate themselves, they are easily broken in pieces. They are as great heaps of light chaff before the whirlwind; or large quantities of dry stubble before devouring flames. We find it easy to tread on and crush a worm that we see crawling on the earth; so it is easy for us to cut or singe a slender thread that any thing hangs by: thus easy is it for God, when he pleases, to cast his enemies down to hell. What are we, that we should think to stand before him, at whose rebuke the earth trembles, and before whom the rocks are thrown down?

2. They *deserve* to be cast into hell; so that divine justice never stands in the way, it makes no objection against God's using his power at any moment to destroy them. Yea, on the contrary, justice calls aloud for an infinite punishment of their sins. Divine justice says of the tree that brings forth such grapes of Sodom, "Cut it down, why cumbereth it the ground?" Luke xiii. 7. The sword of divine justice is every moment brandished over their heads, and it is nothing but the hand of arbitrary mercy, and God's mere will, that holds it back.

3. They are already under a sentence of *condemnation* to hell. They do not only justly deserve to be cast down thither, but the sentence of the law of God, that eternal and immutable rule of righteousness that God has fixed between him and mankind, is gone out against them, and stands against them; so that they are bound over already to hell. John iii. 18. "He that believeth not is condemned already." So that every unconverted man properly belongs to hell; that is his place; from thence he is, John viii. 23. "Ye are from beneath:" And thither he is bound; it is the place that justice, and God's word, and the sentence of his unchangeable law assign to him.

4. They are now the objects of that very same *anger* and wrath of God, that is expressed in the torments of hell. And the reason why they do not go down to hell at each moment, is not because God, in whose power they are, is not then very angry with them; as he is with many miserable creatures now tormented in hell, who there feel and bear the fierceness of his wrath. Yea, God is a great deal more angry with great numbers that are now on earth; yea, doubtless, with many that are now in this congregation, who it may be are at ease, than he is with many of those who are now in the flames of hell.

So that it is not because God is unmindful of their wickedness, and does not resent it, that he does not let loose his hand and cut them off. God is not altogether such an one as themselves, though they may imagine him to be so. The wrath of God burns against them, their damnation does not slumber; the pit is prepared, the fire is made ready, the furnace is now hot, ready to receive them; the flames do now rage and glow. The glittering sword is whet, and held over them, and the pit hath opened its mouth under them.

5. The *devil* stands ready to fall upon them, and seize them as his own, at what moment God shall permit him. They belong to him; he has their souls in his possession, and under his dominion. The scripture represents them as his goods, Luke xi. 12. The devils watch them; they are ever by them at their right hand; they stand waiting for them, like greedy hungry lions that see their prey, and expect to have it, but are for the present kept back. If God should withdraw his hand, by which they are restrained, they would in one moment fly upon their poor souls. The old serpent is gaping for them; hell opens its mouth wide to receive them; and if God should permit it, they would be hastily swallowed up and lost.

6. There are in the souls of wicked men those hellish *principles* reigning, that would presently kindle and flame out into hell fire, if it were not for God's restraints. There is laid in the very nature of carnal men, a foundation for the torments of hell. There are those corrupt principles, in reigning power in them, and in full possession of them, that are seeds of hell fire. These principles are active and powerful, exceeding violent in their nature, and if it were not for the restraining hand of God upon them, they would soon break out, they would flame out after the same manner as the same corruptions, the same enmity does in the hearts of damned souls, and would beget the same torments as they do in them. The souls of the wicked are in scripture compared to the troubled sea, Isa. lvii. 20. For the present, God restrains their wickedness by his mighty power, as he does the raging waves of the troubled sea, saying, "Hitherto shalt thou come, but no further;" but if God should withdraw that restraining power, it would soon carry all before it. Sin is the ruin and misery of the soul; it is destructive in its nature; and if God should leave it without restraint, there would need nothing else to make the soul perfectly miserable. The corruption of the heart of man is immoderate and boundless in its fury; and while wicked men live here, it is like fire pent up by God's restraints, whereas if it were let loose, it would set on fire the course of nature; and as the heart is now a sink of sin, so if sin was not restrained, it would immediately turn the soul into a fiery oven, or a furnace of fire and brimstone.

7. It is no security to wicked men for one moment, that there are no visible means of death at hand. It is no security to a natural

man, that he is now in health, and that he does not see which way he should now immediately go out of the world by any accident, and that there is no visible danger in any respect in his circumstances. The manifold and continual experience of the world in all ages, shows this is no evidence, that a man is not on the very brink of eternity, and that the next step will not be into another world. The unseen, unthought-of ways and means of persons going suddenly out of the world are innumerable and inconceivable. Unconverted men walk over the pit of hell on a rotten covering, and there are innumerable places in this covering so weak that they will not bear their weight, and these places are not seen. The arrows of death fly unseen at noon-day; the sharpest sight cannot discern them. God has so many different unsearchable ways of taking wicked men out of the world and sending them to hell, that there is nothing to make it appear, that God had need to be at the expense of a miracle, or go out of the ordinary course of his providence, to destroy any wicked man, at any moment. All the means that there are of sinners going out of the world, are so in God's hands, and so universally and absolutely subject to his power and determination, that it does not depend at all the less on the mere will of God, whether sinners shall at any moment go to hell, than if means were never made use of, or at all concerned in the case.

8. Natural men's prudence and care to preserve their own lives, or the care of others to preserve them, do not secure them a moment. To this, divine providence and universal experience do also bear testimony. There is this clear evidence that men's own wisdom is no security to them from death; that if it were otherwise we should see some difference between the wise and politic men of the world, and others, with regard to their liableness to early and unexpected death: but how is it in fact? Eccles. ii. 16. "How dieth the wise man? even as the fool."

9. All wicked men's pains and *contrivance* which they use to escape hell, while they continue to reject Christ, and so remain wicked men, do not secure them from hell one moment. Almost every natural man that hears of hell, flatters himself that he shall escape it; he depends upon himself for his own security; he flatters himself in what he has done, in what he is now doing, or what he intends to do. Every one lays out matters in his own mind how he shall avoid damnation, and flatters himself that he contrives well for himself, and that his schemes will not fail. They hear indeed that there are but few saved, and that the greater part of men that have died heretofore are gone to hell; but each one imagines that he lays out matters better for his own escape than others have done. He does not intend to come to that place of torment; he says within himself, that he intends to take effectual care, and to order matters so for himself as not to fail.

But the foolish children of men miserably delude themselves in their own schemes, and in confidence in their own strength and wisdom; they trust to nothing but a shadow. The greater part of those who heretofore have lived under the same means of grace, and are now dead, are undoubtedly gone to hell; and it was not because they were not as wise as those who are now alive: it was not because they did not lay out matters as well for themselves to secure their own escape. If we could speak with them, and inquire of them, one by one, whether they expected, when alive, and when they used to hear about hell, ever to be the subjects of that misery: we doubtless, should hear one and another reply, "No, I never intended to come here: I had laid out matters otherwise in my mind; I thought I should contrive well for myself: I thought my scheme good. I intended to take effectual care; but it came upon me unexpected; I did not look for it at that time, and in that manner; it came as a thief: Death outwitted me: God's wrath was too quick for me. Oh, my cursed foolishness! I was flattering myself, and pleasing myself with vain dreams of what I would do hereafter; and when I was saying, Peace and safety, then suddenly destruction came upon me."

10. God has laid himself under *no* obligation, by any promise to keep any natural man out of hell one moment. God certainly has made no promises either of eternal life, or of any deliverance or preservation from eternal death, but what are contained in the covenant of grace, the promises that are given in Christ, in whom all the promises are yea and amen. But surely they have no interest in the promises of the covenant of grace who are not the children of the covenant, who do not believe in any of the promises, and have no interest in the Mediator of the covenant.

So that, whatever some have imagined and pretended about promises made to natural men's earnest seeking and knocking, it is plain and manifest, that whatever pains a natural man takes in religion, whatever prayers he makes, till he believes in Christ, God is under no manner of obligation to keep him a moment from eternal destruction.

So that, thus it is that natural men are held in the hand of God, over the pit of hell; they have deserved the fiery pit, and are already sentenced to it; and God is dreadfully provoked, his anger is as great towards them as to those that are actually suffering the executions of the fierceness of his wrath in hell, and they have done nothing in the least to appease or abate that anger, neither is God in the least bound by any promise to hold them up one moment; the devil is waiting for them, hell is gaping for them, the flames gather and flash about them, and would fain lay hold on them, and swallow them up; the fire pent up in their own hearts is struggling to break out: and they have no interest in any Mediator, there are no means within reach that can be any security to them. In short, they have no refuge, nothing to take hold of; all that preserves them every moment is in the mere arbitrary will, and uncovenanted, unobliged forbearance of an incensed God.

QUESTIONS

1. Trace the steps by which Edwards gets from his text to his various conclusions about man's state. Are they all logical? What assumptions does he add to those implied by the text in developing his argument? (Before answering these questions you will probably want to check the entire context of the text in Deuteronomy xxxii.)

2. What kinds of evidence does Edwards use in supporting his argument? Are they equally valid?

3. How do the concrete details, the imagery, and the metaphors that Edwards uses contribute to the effectiveness of his argument?

4. One might make the assumption that a society's conception of hell reflects, at least indirectly, some of that society's positive values. What positive values are reflected in Edwards' picture of hell?

5. What can you deduce about the nature of the congregations that Edwards and Hopkins (pp. 1413–1418) are preaching to? About differences between the two men?

6. One of his pupils described Edwards' delivery: "His appearance in the desk was with a good grace, and his delivery easy, natural and very solemn. He had not a strong, loud voice, but appeared with such gravity and solemnity, and spake with such distinctness and precision, his words were so full of ideas, set in such a plain and striking light, that few speakers have been so able to demand the attention of an audience as he. His words often discovered a great degree of inward fervor, without much noise or external emotion, and fell with great weight on the minds of his hearers. He made but little motion of his head or hands in the desk, but spake as to discover the motion of his own heart, which tended in the most natural and effectual manner to move and affect others." Would this manner of delivery be effective for the sermon printed here? Explain.

PAUL TILLICH

The Riddle of Inequality

For to him who has will more be given; and from him who has not, even what he has will be taken away.
—MARK iv. 25

One day a learned colleague called me up and said to me with angry excitement: "There is a saying in the New Testament which I consider to be one of the most immoral and unjust statements ever made!" And then he started quoting our text: "To him who has will more be given," and his anger increased when he continued: "and from him who has not, even what he has will be taken away." We all, I think, feel offended with him. And we cannot easily ignore the offense by suggesting what *he* suggested—that the words may be due to a misunderstanding of the disciples. It appears at least four times in the gospels with great emphasis. And even more, we can clearly see that the writers of the gospels felt exactly as we do. For them it was a stumbling block, which they tried to interpret in different ways. Probably none of these explanations satisfied them fully, for with this saying of Jesus, we are confronted immediately with the greatest and perhaps most painful riddle of life, that of the inequality of all beings. We certainly cannot hope to solve it when neither the Bible nor any other of the great religions and philosophies was able to do so. But we can do two things: We can show the breadth and the depth of the riddle of inequality and we can try to find a way to live with it, even if it is unsolved.

I

If we hear the words, "to him who has will more be given," we ask ourselves: What *do* we have? And then we may find that much is given to us in terms of external goods, of friends, of intellectual gifts and even of a comparatively high moral level of action. So we can expect that more will be given to us, while we must expect that those who are lacking in all that will lose the little they already have. Even further, according to Jesus' parable, the one talent they have will be given to us who have five or ten talents. We shall be richer because they will be poorer. We may cry out against such an injustice. But we cannot deny that life confirms it abundantly. We cannot deny it, but we can ask the question, do we *really* have what we believe we have so that it cannot be taken from us? It is a question full of anxiety, confirmed by a version of our text rendered by Luke. "From him who has not, even what he *thinks* that he has will be taken away." Perhaps our having of those many things is not the kind of having which is increased. Perhaps the having of few things by the poor ones is the kind of having which makes them grow. In the parable of the talents, Jesus confirms this. Those talents which are used, even with a risk of losing them, are those which we really have; those which we try to preserve without using them for growth are those which we do not really have and which are being taken away from us. They slowly disappear, and suddenly we feel that we have lost these talents, perhaps forever.

Let us apply this to our own life, whether it is long or short. In the memory of all of us many things appear which we had without having them and which were taken away from us. Some of them became lost because of the tragic limitations of life; we had to sacrifice them in order to make other things grow. We all were given childish innocence; but innocence cannot be used and increased. The growth of our lives is possible only because we have sacrificed the original gift of innocence. Nevertheless, sometimes there arises in us a melancholy longing for a purity which has been taken from us. We all were given youthful enthusiasm for many things and aims. But this also cannot be used and increased. Most of the objects of our early enthusiasm must be sacrificed for a few, and the few must be approached with soberness. No maturity is possible without this sacrifice. Yet often a melancholy longing for the lost possibilities and enthusiasm takes hold of us. Innocence and youthful enthusiasm: we had them and had them not. Life itself demanded that they were taken from us.

But there are other things which we had and which were taken from us, because we let them go through our own guilt. Some of us had a deep sensitivity for the wonder of life as it is revealed in nature. Slowly under the pressure of work and social life and the lure of cheap pleasures, we lose the wonder of our earlier years when we felt intense joy and the presence of the mystery of life through the freshness of the young day or the glory of the dying day, the majesty of the mountains or the infinity of the sea, a flower breaking through the soil or a young animal in the perfection of its movements. Perhaps we try to produce such feelings again, but we are empty and do not succeed. We had it and had it not, and it has been taken from us.

Others had the same experience with music, poetry, the great novels and plays. One wanted to devour all of them, one lived in them and created for oneself a life above the daily life. We *had* all this and did not have it; we did not let it grow; our love towards it was not strong enough and so it was taken from us.

Many, especially in this group, remember a time in which the desire to learn to solve the riddles of the universe, to find truth has been the driving force in their lives. They came to college and university, not in order to buy their entrance ticket into the upper middle classes or in order to provide for the preconditions of social and economic success, but they came, driven by the desire for knowledge. They had something and more could have been given to them. But in reality they did not have it. They did not make it grow and so it was taken from them and they finished their academic work in terms of expendiency and indifference towards truth. Their love for truth has left them and in some moments they are sick in their hearts because they realize that what they have lost they may never get back.

We all know that any deeper relation to a human being needs watchfulness and growth, otherwise it is taken away from us. And we cannot get it back. This is a form of having and not having which is the root of innumerable human tragedies. We all know about them. And there is another, the most fundamental kind of having and not having—our having and losing God. Perhaps we were rich towards God in our childhood and beyond it. We may remember the moments in which we felt his ultimate presence. We may remember prayers with an overflowing heart, the encounter with the holy in word and music and holy places. We had communication with God; but it was taken from us because we had it and had it not. We did not let it grow, and so it slowly disappeared leaving an empty space. We became unconcerned, cynical, indifferent, not because we doubted about our religious traditions—such doubt belongs to being rich towards God—but because we turned away from that which once concerned us infinitely.

Such thoughts are a first step in approaching the riddle of inequality. Those who have, receive more if they really have it, if they use it and make it grow. And those who have not, lose what they have because they never had it really.

II

But the question of inequality is not yet answered. For one now asks: Why do some receive more than others in the very beginning, before there is even the possibility of using or wasting our talents? Why does the one servant receive five talents and the other two and the third one? Why is the one born in the slums and the other in a well-to-do suburban family? It does not help to answer that of those to whom much is given much is demanded and little of those to whom little is given. For it is just this inequality of original gifts, internal and external, which arouses our question. Why is it given to one human being to gain so much more out of his being human than to another one? Why is so much given to the one that much *can* be asked of him, while to the other one little is given and little *can* be asked? If this question is asked, not only about individual men but also about classes, races and nations, the everlasting question of political inequality arises, and with it the many ways appear in which men have tried to abolish inequality. In every revolution and in every war, the will to solve the riddle of inequality is a driving force. But neither war nor revolution can remove it. Even if we imagine that in an indefinite future most social inequalities are conquered, three things remain: the inequality of talents in body and mind, the inequality created by freedom and destiny, and the fact that all generations before the time of such equality would be excluded from its blessings. This would be the greatest possible inequality! No! In face of one of the deepest and most torturing problems of life, it is unpermittably shallow and foolish to escape into a social dreamland. We have to live now; we have to live this our life, and we must face today the riddle of inequality.

Let us not confuse the riddle of inequality with the fact that each of us is a unique incomparable self. Certainly our being individuals belongs to our dignity as men. It is given to us and must be used and intensified and not drowned in the gray waters of conformity which threaten us today. One should defend every individuality and the uniqueness of every human self. But one should not believe that this is a way of solving the riddle of inequality. Unfortunately, there are social and political reactionaries who use this confusion in order to justify social injustice. They are at least as foolish as the dreamers of a future removal of inequality. Whoever has seen hospitals, prisons, sweatshops, battlefields, houses for the insane, starvation, family tragedies, moral aberrations should be cured from any confusion of the gift of individuality with the riddle of inequality. He should be cured from any feelings of easy consolation.

III

And now we must make the third step in our attempt to penetrate the riddle of inequality and ask: Why do some use and increase what was given to them, while others do not, so that it is taken from them? Why does God say to the prophet in our Old Testament lesson that the ears and eyes of a nation are made insensible for the divine message?

Is it enough to answer: Because some use their freedom responsibly and do what they ought to do while others fail through their own guilt? Is this answer, which seems so obvious, sufficient? Now let me first say that it *is* sufficient if we apply it to ourselves. Each of us must consider the increase or the loss of what is given to him as a matter of his own responsibility. Our conscience tells us that we cannot put the blame for our losses on anybody or anything else than ourselves.

But if we look at others, this answer is not sufficient. On the contrary: If we applied the judgment which we *must* apply to anyone else we would be like the Pharisee in Jesus' parable. You cannot tell somebody who comes to you in distress about himself: Use what has been given to you; for he may come to you just because he is unable to do so! And you cannot tell those who are in despair about what they are: Be something else; for this is just what despair means—the inability of getting rid of oneself. You cannot tell those who did not conquer the destructive influences of their surroundings and were driven into crime and misery that they should have been stronger; for it was just of this strength they had been deprived by heritage or environment. Certainly they all are men, and to all of them freedom is given; but they all are also subject to destiny. It is not up to us to condemn them because they were free, as it is not up to us to excuse them because they were under their destiny. We cannot judge them. And when we judge ourselves, we must be conscious that even this is not the last word, but that we like them are under an ultimate judgment. In it the riddle of inequality is eternally answered. But this answer is not ours. It is our predicament that we must ask. And we ask with an uneasy conscience. Why are they in misery, why not we? Thinking of some who are near to us, we can ask: Are we partly responsible? But even if we are, it does not solve the riddle of inequality. The uneasy conscience asks about the farthest as well as about the nearest: Why they, why not we?

Why has my child, or any of millions and millions of children, died before even having a chance to grow out of infancy? Why is my child, or any child, born feeble-minded or crippled? Why has my friend or relative, or anybody's friend or relative, disintegrated in his mind and lost both his freedom and his destiny? Why has my son or daughter, gifted as I believe with many talents, wasted them and been deprived of them? And why does this happen to any parent at all? Why have this boy's or this girl's creative powers been broken by a tyrannical father or by a possessive mother?

In all these questions it is not the question of our own misery which we ask. It is not the question: Why has this happened to *me*?

It is not the question of Job which God answers by humiliating him and then by elevating him into communion with him. It is not the old and urgent question: Where is the divine justice, where is the divine love towards me? But it is almost the opposite question: Why has this *not* happened to me, why has it happened to the other one, to the innumerable other ones to whom not even the power of Job is given to accept the divine answer? Why—and Jesus has asked the same question—are many called and few elected?

He does not answer; he only states that this is the human predicament. Shall we therefore cease to ask and humbly accept the fact of a divine judgment which condemns most human beings away from the community with him into despair and self-destruction? Can we accept the eternal victory of judgment over love? We cannot; and nobody ever could, even if he preached and threatened in these terms. As long as he could not see himself with complete certainty as eternally rejected, his preaching and threatening would be self-deceiving. And who could see himself eternally rejected?

But if this is not the solution of the riddle of inequality at its deepest level, can we trespass the boundaries of the Christian tradition and listen to those who tell us that this life does not decide about our eternal destiny? There will be occasions in other lives, as our present life is determined by previous ones and what we have achieved or wasted in them. It is a serious doctrine and not completely strange to Christianity. But if we don't know and never will know what each of us has been in the previous or future lives, then it is not really *our* destiny which develops from life to life, but in each life it is the destiny of someone else. This answer also does not solve the riddle of inequality.

There is no answer at all if we ask about the temporal and eternal destiny of the single being separated from the destiny of the whole. Only in the unity of all beings in time and eternity can a humanly possible answer to the riddle of inequality be found. *Humanly* possible does not mean an answer which removes the riddle of inequality, but an answer with which we can live.

There is an ultimate unity of all beings, rooted in the divine life from which they come and to which they go. All beings, non-human as well as human, participate in it. And therefore they all participate in each other. We participate in each other's having and we participate in each other's not-having. If we become aware of this unity of all beings, something happens. The fact that others have-not changes in every moment the character of my having: It undercuts its security, it drives me beyond myself, to understand, to give, to share, to help. The fact that others fall into sin, crime and misery changes the character of the grace which is given to me: It makes me realize my own hidden guilt, it shows to me that those who suffer for their sin and crime, suffer also for me; for I am guilty of their guilt—at least in the desire of my heart—and ought to suffer as they do. The awareness that others who *could* have become fully developed human beings and never *have*, changes my state of full humanity. Their early death, their early or late disintegration, makes my life and my health a continuous risk, a dying which is not yet death, a disintegration which is not yet destruction. In every death which we encounter, something of us dies; in every disease which we encounter, something of us tends to disintegrate.

Can we live with this answer? We can to the degree in which we are liberated from the seclusion within ourselves. But nobody can be liberated from himself unless he is grasped by the power of that which is present in everyone and everything—the eternal from which we come and to which we go, which gives us *to* ourselves and which liberates us *from* ourselves. It is the greatness and the heart of the Christian message that God—as manifest in the Cross of the Christ—participates totally in the dying child, in the condemned criminal, in the disintegrating mind, in the starving one and in him who rejects him. There is no extreme human condition into which the divine presence would not reach. This is what the Cross, the most extreme of all human conditions, tells us. The riddle of inequality cannot be solved on the level of our separation from each other. It is eternally solved in the divine participation in all of us and every being. The certainty of the divine participation gives us the courage to stand the riddle of inequality, though finite minds cannot solve it. Amen.

GEORGE SANTAYANA
Classic Liberty

When ancient peoples defended what they called their liberty, the word stood for a plain and urgent interest of theirs: that their cities should not be destroyed, their territory pillaged, and they themselves sold into slavery. For the Greeks in particular liberty meant even more than this. Perhaps the deepest assumption of classic philosophy is that nature and the gods on the one hand and man on the other, both have a fixed character; that there is consequently a necessary piety, a true philosophy, a standard happiness, a normal art. The Greeks believed, not without reason, that they had grasped these permanent principles better than other peoples. They had largely dispelled superstition, experimented in government, and turned life into a rational art. Therefore when they defended their liberty what they defended was not merely freedom to live. It was freedom to live well, to live as other nations did not, in the public experimental study of the world and of human nature. This liberty to discover and pursue a natural happiness, this liberty to grow wise and to live in friendship with the gods and with one another, was the liberty vindicated at Thermopylae by martyrdom and at Salamis by victory.

As Greek cities stood for liberty in the world, so philosophers stood for liberty in the Greek cities. In both cases it was the same kind of liberty, not freedom to wander at hazard or to let things slip, but on the contrary freedom to legislate more precisely, at least for oneself, and to discover and codify the means to true happiness. Many of these pioneers in wisdom were audacious radicals and recoiled from no paradox. Some condemned what was most Greek: mythology, athletics, even multiplicity and physical motion. In the heart of those thriving, loquacious, festive little ant-hills, they preached impassibility and abstraction, the unanswerable scepticism of silence. Others practised a musical and priestly refinement of life, filled with metaphysical mysteries, and formed secret societies, not without a tendency to political domination. The cynics railed at the conventions, making themselves as comfortable as possible in the role of beggars and mocking parasites. The conservatives themselves were radical, so intelligent were they, and Plato wrote the charter[1] of the most extreme militarism and communism, for the sake of preserving the free state. It was the swan-song of liberty, a prescription to a diseased old man to become young again and try a second life of superhuman virtue. The old man preferred simply to die.

1. The reference is to Plato's *Republic*.

Many laughed then, as we may be tempted to do, at all those absolute physicians of the soul, each with his panacea. Yet beneath their quarrels the wranglers had a common faith. They all believed there was a single solid natural wisdom to be found, that reason could find it, and that mankind, sobered by reason, could put it in practice. Mankind has continued to run wild and like barbarians to place freedom in their very wildness, till we can hardly conceive the classic assumption of Greek philosophers and cities, that true liberty is bound up with an institution, a corporate scientific discipline, necessary to set free the perfect man, or the god, within us.

Upon the dissolution of paganism the Christian church adopted the classic conception of liberty. Of course, the field in which the higher politics had to operate was now conceived differently, and there was a new experience of the sort of happiness appropriate and possible to man; but the assumption remained unchallenged that Providence, as well as the human soul, had a fixed discoverable scope, and that the business of education, law, and religion was to bring them to operate in harmony. The aim of life, salvation, was involved in the nature of the soul itself, and the means of salvation had been ascertained by a positive science which the church was possessed of, partly revealed and partly experimental. Salvation was simply what, on a broad view, we should see to be health, and religion was nothing but a sort of universal hygiene.

The church, therefore, little as it tolerated heretical liberty, the liberty of moral and intellectual dispersion, felt that it had come into the world to set men free, and constantly demanded liberty for itself, that it might fulfil this mission. It was divinely commissioned to teach, guide, and console all nations and all ages by the self-same means, and to promote at all costs what it conceived to be human perfection. There should be saints and as many saints as possible. The church never admitted, any more than did any sect of ancient philosophers, that its teaching might represent only an eccentric view of the world, or that its guidance and consolations might be suitable only at one stage of human development. To waver in the pursuit of the orthodox ideal could only betray frivolity and want of self-knowledge. The truth of things and the happiness of each man could not lie elsewhere than where the church, summing up all human experience and all divine revelation, had placed it once for all and for everybody. The liberty of the church to fulfil its mission was accordingly hostile to any liberty of dispersion, to any radical consecutive independence, in the life of individuals or of nations.

When it came to full fruition this orthodox freedom was far from gay; it was called sanctity. The freedom of pagan philosophers too had turned out to be rather a stiff and severe pose; but in the Christian dispensation this austerity of true happiness was less to be wondered at, since life on earth was reputed to be abnormal from the beginning, and infected with hereditary disease. The full beauty and joy of restored liberty could hardly become evident in this life. Nevertheless a certain beauty and joy did radiate visibly from the saints; and while we may well think their renunciations and penances misguided or excessive, it is certain that, like the Spartans and the philosophers, they got something for their pains. Their bodies and souls were transfigured, as none now found upon earth. If we admire without imitating them we shall perhaps have done their philosophy exact justice. Classic liberty was a sort of forced and artificial liberty, a poor perfection reserved for an ascetic aristocracy in whom heroism and refinement were touched with perversity and slowly starved themselves to death.

Since those days we have discovered how much larger the universe is, and we have lost our way in it. Any day it may come over us again that our modern liberty to drift in the dark is the most terrible negation of freedom. Nothing happens to us as we would. We want peace and make war. We need science and obey the will to believe, we love art and flounder among whimsicalities, we believe in general comfort and equality and we strain every nerve to become millionaires. After all, antiquity must have been right in thinking that reasonable self-direction must rest on having a determinate character and knowing what it is, and that only the truth about God and happiness, if we somehow found it, could make us free. But the truth is not to be found by guessing at it, as religious prophets and men of genius have done, and then damning every one who does not agree. Human nature, for all its substantial fixity, is a living thing with many varieties and variations. All diversity of opinion is therefore not founded on ignorance; it may express a legitimate change of habit or interest. The classic and Christian synthesis from which we have broken loose was certainly premature, even if the only issue of our liberal experiments should be to lead us back to some such equilibrium. Let us hope at least that the new morality, when it comes, may be more broadly based than the old on knowledge of the world, not so absolute, not so meticulous, and not chanted so much in the monotone of an abstracted sage.

SAMUEL H. MILLER
But Find the Point Again[1]

When the climate of a culture changes, people are so preoccupied with their traditional habits and ways of looking at things that they do not see what is happening before their eyes. Revolutions come and go, states and empires fall, miracles rise from the ruins, yet they read their daily papers, eat and drink and sleep, suffer their sorrows, as if everything remained the same. They are supported by the structures of the past, to which they have been accustomed, and the new age coming into being rises unseen all about them. They are anachronisms, belonging to another age yet living in this one.

In religion the conserving tendency of faith exaggerates this indifference to the changing world. Thus the church[2] may long deceive itself by its spectacular success in numbers and prestige without knowing how hollow it has become, or how feeble and unintelligible its message sounds to a world which has moved into new dimensions of knowledge and fear. The pulpit may continue to talk of matters long after their cogency has vanished, except in the sacred vocabulary of the preacher.[3] The ministry may be exhausted by the aggressive zeal of its diversified activities without touching the heart of darkness at the center of our troubled time.

Testy old Carlyle, in all his flamboyance, perceived this fact when he declared:

That a man stand there, and speak of spiritual things to me, it is beautiful; even in its great obscurity and decadence it is among the beautifulest, most touching objects one sees on this earth. This speaking man has indeed,

1. An address delivered at the convocation service of the Harvard Divinity School on September 30, 1959.

2. "Certainly by every test but that of influence the Church had never been stronger than it was at the opening of the twentieth century, and its strength increased steadily. Everyone was a Christian, and almost everyone joined some church, though few for reasons that would have earned them admission to Jonathan Edwards' Northampton congregation. The typical Protestant of the twentieth century inherited his religion as he did his politics, though rather more casually, and was quite unable to explain the differences between denominations. He found himself a church member by accident and persisted in his affiliation by habit; he greeted each recurring Sunday service with a sense of surprise and was persuaded that he conferred a benefit upon his rector and his community by participating in church services. The church was something to be 'supported' like some aged relative whose claim was vague but inescapable. "Never before had the church been materially more powerful or spiritually less effective." Henry Steele Commager, *The American Mind,* (New Haven: Yale University Press, 1950) [Miller's note].

3. "The great Biblical key ideas of sovereign divine creation, election, sin, mercy, judgment, conversion, rebirth, reconciliation, justification, sanctification, Kingdom of God, are utterly alien, and consequently irrelevant to people whose minds are molded and dominated by the conquest of the kingdom of man. They are undecipherable hieroglyphs, with which, strangely enough, Church people still seem to play." Hendrik Kraemer, *The Communication of the Christian Faith* (Philadelphia: Westminster Press, 1956), p. 94 [Miller's note].

in these times, wandered terribly from the point; has, alas, as it were, totally lost sight of the point, yet at bottom whom have we to compare with him? Of all such functionaries boarded and lodged on the industry of modern Europe, is there one worthier of the board he has? ... The speaking function, with all our writing and printing function, has a perennial place, could he but find the point again![4]

Worthy of his bed and board—if he could but find the point again! Age after age he had served well. According to the needs of previous epochs, he had stood in the teeth of the storm and despite unpopularity or even martyrdom, he had not wavered from the point or betrayed the nature of his leadership. Think only of the apostles who had fashioned the profound bases of Christian civilization, sustaining for centuries the life and culture of many peoples; or of the priests who had labored in many fields, in the arts and in philosophy during the Middle Ages, elaborating a world which reached its climax in cathedral and *summa*;[5] or of the reformers who had endured the ordeal of a radical revolution in the ways of faith and modes of action, transforming the institutions of the state and church in terms of new freedoms. Where did Carlyle's speaking man lose the point? Was he meandering, fiddling at inconsequentials? Was he blind, or stupid, or wicked? A world was in the making, as every epoch makes its world, and this man did not keep to his job. He strayed and in his straying the bonds of faith were loosed and the world fell apart.

Now you and I are standing in that man's shoes. We too have been called to minister to the world. Will we have anything to say, not merely to please the world, but to fit its real needs? Will we be able to find the point again, and thus provide a firm base for society, perspectives sufficient for the arts and culture, and an intellectual integrity profound enough to discipline the destructive forces of our present chaos?

Our fundamental embarrassment as we stand face to face with this world is that we may become relevant to its demands all too easily, conforming to that standard which the world sets for us, and losing the very point of being a minister in the world at all. One of the tragedies of our time is that the minister is both overworked and unemployed; overworked in a multitude of tasks that do not have the slightest connection with religion, and unemployed in the serious concerns and exacting labors of maintaining a disciplined spiritual life among mature men and women. It is a scandal of modern Protestantism that young men called to the high venture of the Christian way, disciplined by seminary training in the arduous dimensions of such faith, are graduated into churches where the magnitude of their vocation is as Joseph Sittler has said, *macerated,*

4. Thomas Carlyle, *Past and Present,* Bk. IV, Chap. 1 ("Collected Works," Vol. VII, London: 1870) [Miller's note]. 5. A comprehensive treatise by a church philosopher.

chopped into small pieces, by the pressure of the petty practices of so-called parish progress. One wonders how much of the compulsive frenzy of the parish minister comes from the guilty realization that he has not attended to his prime calling at all, but is merely filling up time with a nervous pandemonium of jerks and jabs in the direction of people in order to make the church popular. Wherever the current ideal of the minister comes from—the big operator, the smart salesman, the successful tycoon—it still remains a puzzle why the minister should fall prey to such false images unless he has completely confused what he is supposed to be doing with what most churches want him to do.

Herman Melville, as flamboyant a rhetorician as Carlyle, yet with profound perceptions of what was involved in the minister's task, described the pulpit in the New Bedford Chapel where the one-time harpooner, Father Mapple, preaches.

> The pulpit is ever this earth's foremost part. All the rest comes in its rear; the pulpit leads the world. From thence it is the storm of God's quick wrath is first described, and the bow must bear the earliest brunt. From thence it is that the God of breezes fair or foul is first invoked for favorable winds. Yes, the world's a ship on its passage out, and not a voyage complete; and the pulpit is its prow.[6]

This might easily have been accepted at face value in the early 19th century but for us it would be easier to believe it was written tongue in cheek, a rather fatuous inflation of words and little more. The truth is that the pulpit, at least now, is certainly not the *prow* of this world, either in generating power or in initiating ideas.[7] It is set back now in quieter waters, out of the haste and the traffic where strife is real and decisions must be made.

The world is still a ship on its passage out. There is no doubt of that, nor that the voyage is incomplete. Indeed, we are more uncertain than Melville as to where we are going. Our charts seem obsolete in the light of new facts and forces, so we prove the unknown with a dread as terrifying as that the first man must have felt when he ventured out of sight of land under strange skies. The minister no less than others has been overwhelmed by the catastrophic changes of history.

If the ministry is to regain its magnitude and integrity, it must be validated at a much more serious level of life than that of success and prestige. To succumb either to sentimental popularity or to institutional professionalism is to betray not only our own calling but the world's need as well. The ministry has a point, a tip of light which breaks the darkness like a sharpened spear, a bright

---

6. Herman Melville, *Moby Dick* (Boston: Houghton Mifflin Co., 1956), p. 50 [Miller's note].

7. Several years ago the *Saturday Review* conducted a survey of sources of ideas in contemporary life. The results were as follows: 49% from radio and TV, 21% from newspapers, 11% from magazines, 11% from movies, and 8% from books [Miller's note].

moment when the diversity and contradictions of life break into a unity, a unity never complete and never permanent, but always redemptive and profoundly satisfying. We prove ourselves at the point where we enter into history, where the world is being made and unmade, where life turns into hell or opens into heaven, where, like Jacob of old, men and women are caught in the middle of the darkness, alone and in agony, wrestling with the unnamed mysteries of existence, striving to exact a blessing from the exigencies of their human lot. We come to life as a profession when we stand forth beyond the superficial safety and the limits of praise and blame, to speak the clumsy, daring word which only faith may speak of things unseen but powerful with portent to be, of realities waiting to be born at the far edge of all things known, of a realm mysterious with blessing for any who can become like little children, able to leap beyond themselves to a greatness dimly surmised.

Yet any man who steps into this kind of pulpit, into this prow where the storms strike first and the dark is thickest, knows right well the terror of his position. The ministry in any age is caught between the offense of God and the offense of the world, between the awful terror of making God plain, of speaking the *verbum dei*, and the terrifying muddle of this world's jumble of circumstances in which human life is crucified. Like a lonely figure, the ministry in our age stands separated from the confident assurance of any infallible or perhaps even divine message easily inherited from the past, and as well from the arrogance of an age which finds all authority in itself. We may stand at the prow, but not with the sustaining authority our forefathers found in their Bibles, their creeds and their churches; and the seething waters that break across our bow are from deeper seas than any man has ever sailed.

This is a world [says J. Robert Oppenheimer] in which each of us, knowing his limitations, knowing the evils of superficiality and the terrors of fatigue, will have to cling to what is close to him, to what he knows, to what he can do, to his friends and his tradition and his love, lest he be dissolved in a universal confusion and know nothing and love nothing. . . .

This balance, this perpetual, precarious, impossible balance between the infinitely open and the intimate, this time—our twentieth century—has been long in coming; but it has come. It is, I think, for us and our children, our only way. . . . This cannot be an easy life. We shall have a rugged time of it to keep our minds open and to keep them deep. . . .[8]

Only the utmost honesty, perhaps the confession of our poverty, will enable us in this extremity to prove ourselves a skilled profession worthy of its bed and board.

Our Fading Heritage

To say the least, our situation is bewildering. T. S. Eliot described

8. J. Robert Oppenheimer, *Man's Right to Knowledge*, 2nd Series (New York: Columbia University Press, 1935), p. 115 [Miller's note].

it by saying that much of our heritage is Christian but it is vastly less so than it used to be. The truth is that the whole imaginative structure of Christian truth, elaborated in myth and symbol, has for the most part crumbled under the impact of the last three centuries of revolutionary thought, scientific methods, and historical studies. The vision of reality articulated in this great Biblical formulary has evaporated and no longer serves as the frame of reference for elucidating the mysteries of being human. We have not deliberately renounced our Christian heritage, but it no longer plays a dynamic role either in the motivation of our actions or in the judgments which evaluate our satisfactions. Men are no longer moved by the words which once thrust men to war or turned them from the world to God. The charts which men have used for centuries now seem quite inadequate in the face of new conditions. The character of reality for human beings has changed, and the ancient vision is no longer sufficient.

It is precisely at this point that we must ask whether we shall labor to create a new Christian culture with materials coming from the new discoveries, disciplines, and attitudes of our time or succumb to an essentially non-religious one, that is, a sub-pagan culture.[9] It has always been the function of faith to supply a structure of myth and symbol, and to enact in appropriate rites a vision of reality capable of sustaining the larger inferences of meaning in the life of a people, thus providing a margin sufficiently suggestive for the exercise of freedom in human possibilities but not reducible to precise, black and white, static literalisms.[1] It is such a symbolic structure of the imagination which both ties together the disparate realities and forces of human existence, and at the same time becomes a vocabulary, verbal, visual, and active, by which a community can be established and under certain conditions can rise to the level of communion. Wherever this symbolic structure evaporates, loses its power of suggestion, becomes dogmatically rigid and then superficially literal, the people lose their means of coherence. The ancient dictum that where there is no vision of commonly recognized reality the people perish as a people, society falls apart, and civilization and culture are thrown into anarchy and self-destruction is still true. Lewis Mumford, in his Bampton Lectures, declared:

Perhaps the fatal course all civilizations have so far followed has been

---

9. "The civilization characteristic of Christendom has not disappeared, yet another civilization has begun to take its place . . . Our whole life and mind is saturated with the slow upward filtration of a new spirit—that of an emancipated atheistic international democracy." George Santayana, *Winds of Doctrine* (New York: Harper & Row,

1957), p. 1 [Miller's note].

1. "The great social ideal for religion is that it should be the common basis for the unity of civilization . . . In that way it justifies its insight beyond the transient clash of brute force." Alfred North Whitehead, *Adventures of Ideas* (New York: The Macmillan Co., 1933), p. 221 [Miller's note].

due, not to natural miscarriages, the disastrous effects of famines and floods and diseases, but to accumulated perversions of the symbolic functions.[2]

Our disorders, I suspect, derive from the fact that the vision of reality conceived in redemptive terms and elaborated by Dante and Aquinas is simply no longer an instrument of suggestiveness for multitudes conditioned by the popular influences of science and industry. The minister, if he is to find the point at all of being useful to the rehabilitation of society and the redemption of the individual, cannot offer the twentieth century the image which the thirteenth century found eminently satisfactory. The new age has a style of its own, a language peculiar to itself, and whatever image of reality is to be conjured up must be of the very substance of our time. On the other hand, the minister can scarcely believe that the twentieth century, unlike all others, has transcended the limitations of time and history so that it is sufficient to itself.[3] A vision of reality limited only to our own epoch is incredibly arrogant and stupidly parochial. The golden-tongued Chrysostom put it well, as he put many things: "A priest must be sober and clear-eyed, with a thousand eyes in every direction."

New Images of Reality

New configurations of experience have arisen in the Renaissance, the Industrial Revolution, and in the rise of science, each with its own system of values and perspectives of discrimination by which life is ordered. We have moved out of the Magical Age, as I. A. Richards has put it, into the Scientific. We have reached a new maturity of freedom from superstition and credulity. With this *Mundigkeit*, or adulthood, as Bonhoeffer describes it, there has occurred an extraordinary activity and excitement in all the creative aspects of man's mind and spirit. New life is erupting in fresh but ambiguous forms needing identification and judgment. To evaluate such a burgeoning mass of new work is not easy, but it is evident that in the midst of it there is much which approximates or reflects the ancient and traditional expressions of religious concerns about the elemental mysteries of human existence.

Into the vacuum left by the slow evaporation of the Biblical image of reality the burgeoning powers of this age have understandably and desperately pushed their way, seeking to formulate a new vision of reality more congenial to the terms of our contemporary sensibilities and knowledge. The arts have gone philosophical. Beckman, Klee, Picasso, Henry Moore deliver their gnomic elucida-

2. Lewis Mumford, *Art. Technics* (New York: Columbia University Press, 1952), p. 51 [Miller's note].

3. "Any modern re-formation of the religion (based upon certain historical occasions scattered irregularly within a period of about 1200 years from the earlier prophets to the stabilization of theology by Augustine) must first concentrate upon the moral and metaphysical intuitions scattered throughout the whole epoch." Whitehead, *op. cit.*, p. 212 [Miller's note].

tions about the nature of reality with religious seriousness. The sciences, too, finding themselves on the brink of this same vacuum, have not always been slow to make a leap of faith concerning ultimate things, or if the scientists themselves modestly desisted, their friends have rushed in with cosmic conclusions. Even business, for all its pragmatic traditions and prejudices, has become quite confidently responsible and evangelical, urging upon men and their families the "business way of life."

Thus the minister must confront these twin terrors of the pulpit —at his back what seems to be an obsolete order of things and before him a confusion from which nothing is exempt. He stands for a whole congeries of notions which have become mere words, the realities seemingly no longer a part of modern existence, and he must deal with a turbulent age doing its best to create a new order of intelligible meaning. Now that the Christian vision no longer reverberates in the life of the contemporary man, how will the minister find the insight or the courage to proclaim "good news"? How will he rehabilitate the heights and depths of sensibility which have atrophied in the recent frenzy of naturalizing the world? How will he demonstrate the reality of life at levels from which man has long since withdrawn to busy himself in other areas? How will he speak to the point when man has nothing in his experience to provide the peg on which to hang such realities as grace and spirit?

Can the minister supply a vision of reality? Can he offer the Bible to a people disabused of its validity? Can he recall heaven and hell to a people who have laughed them out of existence? Can he talk to them of God, when they find God quite unimaginable in such a world, scientifically structured in iron law? Can he explain faith, redemption, grace, while they wonder what such things have to do with the defense mechanisms of the ego or the libidinous expressions of the id? Can he continue to conduct the rites of the church, and speak of "holy" things when life itself has been naturalized and even the church transfers its own significance to statistical categories and popular prestige?

Sharing in this demythologized epoch, he may have no vision of reality to offer. But if there is no vision, there is no preacher, no message, no church. He cannot peddle Dante or Thomas, Luther or Calvin, as if nothing had happened in the world since their time. As Kierkegaard so succinctly put it, one cannot crib the answers to the problems of the age from the back of the book.

The Need for a Learned Ministry

If ever the conditions of the world demanded the highest and most rigorous intellectual preparation for the ministry, they do so now. The founders of this University were profoundly convinced that no well-ordered society could long endure without a "learned ministry." Well into the 18th century this passionate conviction continued to be expressed until the twin forces of pietism and romanticism began to dull the edge of all discipline in American life. Slackness, emotionalism, and a fever of optimism spread through the church and corrupted its ways. There was a general levelling down of all classes in the name of democracy, and a revolt against all theological thoroughness in the name of simplicity and practical concerns. By and large, it was a loose vulgarisation of the Christian faith which by the early 20th century had transformed it into a shadow of the moral enthusiasm and respectability of the secular world. We need again to reassert the fundamental necessity for a learned ministry if the church is to survive as a potent source of that vision by which society unites its life in a meaningful order of truth and goodness. Its present tactics are scarcely more than an effort to keep its body alive by repudiating its soul.

It is only by dint of the severest intellectual discipline that a man may provide a vision of reality for such an age as this. If that vision is in the Christian tradition, he must discover how to unwrap it, reveal its dynamic suggestiveness, make plain its elucidation of the human problem. If it is not in the Christian tradition he must discover where it is and what it is. In all he must be able to make wise and revealing judgments, not confusing truth with novelty, or tradition with truth, but discerning the distinctions between appearance and reality, between the authentic and the popular. To attain the intellectual acumen to be wise about the living past in the present, to be able to confirm the eternal in the temporal, and to discriminate sharply between sophisticated skepticism and skeptical faith is an order of considerable magnitude. It is certainly no job for an ecclesiastical mechanic or a general manager of parish programs. The radical thrust of this work is in the direction of the profoundest perceptiveness, imagination, rational daring, and penetrating insight.

As in other professions, and nowhere more disastrously, American practicality has contrived short cuts in the training of the ministry. Concerned only with shortsighted results, it has reduced theological education to a vulgarized form of a trade school, where facile schemes, glib formulae, and manipulative methods prepare a man for disillusionment and heartsickening bitterness when he discovers all too late that such bright and shining stones are no food for the hunger of honest men and women, touched by this world's tragic pain. If there is to be a vision of reality, if the minister really desires to find the point again and to be worthy of his board, he can do it only by probing the Bible to its deepest ground, exploring the wide reaches of faith in its historical elaboration, and articulating as explicitly as his imagination and reason allow, the theological structure of human relationships and circumstantial mysteries. Certainly no portion of his intellectual ability can be left undeveloped. A great deal of nonsense especially in pietistic circles, supported by a native American anti-intellectualism, has been uttered in this regard. The attainment of the saints has been praised as if it were achieved either without assistance from or in spite of their intelligence. Neither history nor biography corroborate such an illusion. A soft-headed saint is simply no saint. Although the saints may not have been scholars, their intelligence was undeniable. One can scarcely fulfill the love of God in Jesus' prime commandment by avoiding the passionate expression of the "whole mind." Let the minister be sure his mind is sharpened to its utmost, lest he blunder about the world with a rough and stupid carelessness, hoping that he might hit upon the will of God merely because of his good intentions.

The minister has a job cut from monumental dimensions. The specifications for rehabilitating a usable, imaginable, worshipful vision of reality in our time are such as to thrust a man beyond all normal limits of his resources. He must probe the past till he finds the quick of it—and knows beyond the peradventure of a doubt the broad and everlasting realities in it which run like a living stream into our own day. He must probe the present, suffer the full brunt of its tumultuous power and passion, separating with painful threshing the wheat from the chaff in his own mind and heart. He must take the Bible, a very old book fashioned in archaic languages and forms, and unveil the present intimacy of its radical realities. He must handle the mixed and perplexing chaos of mortal circumstance, the old and the new, the great and the inconsequential, the sacred and the profane, and by an alchemy of his own he must make sense of things, or be honest, and humble in knowing he can do no more than to face them wisely and bravely. He must learn to see the primordial truth in small events, the sublime in common unexpected places, the glory of grace in humble persons, the son of God in a "litter of scorn." Everywhere he must have eyes to see what mortal eyes too often miss, and the intelligence both to look for it and to confirm it when it is found.

When André Malraux, the novelist, has one of his characters ask, "How can one make the best of one's life?" the answer is given, "By converting as wide a range of experience into conscious thought as possible." This is in a sense the function of the minister, especially if we keep in mind the tremendous scope of "experience" and the dialectical forces of history producing it. The intelligence of the minister is redemptive, in that he not only turns experience into conscious thought, but he seeks to make sense out of the diversity and incompleteness of experience. It is his task to bring experience to conscious fulfillment, and to articulate that fulfillment in terms of an ultimate whole. The vision of reality is seen in small events and single revelations; it becomes the symbol of the total way of life in which all things work together for good to them that love God. He will sadly know how true it is, as Proust once said, that most lives are like camera film, exposed to passing events but never developed. It is the joy and anguish of the minister to "develop" the experience of men to a vision of reality.

I should like to risk the privilege of using some words of Albert Camus, spoken when he received the Nobel prize, as a thrust of light in this direction. Although he is speaking of art, I should like to substitute our own thoughts of religion.

> To me art is not a solitary delight. It is a means of stirring the greatest number of men with a privileged image of our common joys and sorrows. Hence it forces the artist [minister] not to isolate himself; it subjects him to the humblest and most universal truth.
>
> Not one of us is great enough for such a vocation.... Whatever our personal frailties may be, the nobility of our calling will always be rooted in two commitments difficult to observe: refusal to lie about what we know and resistance to oppression.
>
> Faced with a world threatened by disintegration, in which our grand inquisitors may set up once and for all the kingdoms of death, this generation knows that, in a sort of mad race against time, it ought to reestablish among nations a peace not based on slavery, to reconcile labor and culture again, and to reconstruct with all men an Ark of the Covenant.[4]

"To reconstruct with all men an Ark of the Covenant"! To bind together in one household the humanity of our time, to recover the ground of truth on which we all must stand and the vision of hope in which freedom may be boldly exercised, to lift up our eyes to that higher dream of which Dante spoke in which the exuberance of our epoch may become, not a haunted nightmare or a burden of despair, but a song of joy and peace for all people. This is a calling beyond our strength, and yet nothing less than such a kingdom could demand or deserve our all. It is Dante again who emblazons the text for such a calling in his unforgettable words, "I crown and mitre thee above myself." Not in our strength, not in our wisdom, but in the power of that which waits to be born, in the new Ark of the Covenant, we stake our faith.

The Scope of Theological Training

To train men for such a profession has never been an easy task. In our day an educated man may pass as such by having a wide smattering of slight contacts, innumerable opinions, and a name-dropping vocabulary. Sometimes theological education has contented itself with informing men with more than they can think, and encouraging a kind of lust for knowledge which accumulates a body of inert ideas in lieu of wisdom. Certainly if we can keep in mind that Ark

---

4. Albert Camus, quoted by Charles Rolo, "Albert Camus: A Good Man," *The Atlantic Monthly*, Vol. 201, No. 5 (May 1958) [Miller's note].

of the Covenant for which Camus is striving out of motives far removed from the Christian faith, we too will know that there is something greater than our particular art, or our special skill. The fragmentation of the world is mirrored in our divisive authorities. Our vocabularies tend to become departmental or even private. The paths of communication and of possible unity become clogged with protective devices and defensive barriers for our private satisfaction. The ramifying walls which separate so much of our learning in seemingly water-tight compartments are not in life. We make them ourselves, sometimes for our convenience, often for our prestige; but we must find a way to breach them if we are to train men to love God with their whole mind.[5]

A learned ministry is not necessarily pedantic. Indeed, a minister is in many respects a disciplined amateur. He is amateur because he works forever at the edge of unprecedented possibilities in the freedom by which the spirit fulfills events and needs. He is amateur because he is concerned with everything human across the entire spectrum of sensibility from feeling to idea to action. He is amateur because he is the lover of this world, intent on fulfilling its deepest and most radical reality through its diversified institutions and cultures. As amateur, he will want to draw together insight and perception from every corner of time and space. He will meditate, day and night, on those primordial myths in which the experience of multitudes was strained, concentrated, and objectified in archaic figures and forms. He will read the long and troubled contours of the past, the profound penetrations of prophet and priest, the dreams and corruption and heroism of the church, the anguish of centuries and the hope of eternity. To know, to know accurately and deeply, to respect the fullness of our inheritance, to study it with earnest discipline and to explore it humbly and expectantly for its peculiar gift to the wisdom of the ages and the opening of the deeper levels of present existence requires intelligence of the most disciplined sort, but not pedantry.

Every profession of our time increasingly demands a skill of theoretical knowledge and practical application; and the ministry no less than any other must be a disciplined profession. By and large, we are not so at present. We have bartered our professional birthright of an honored place in the economy of a community by reducing our office to a mad dervish dance of unenlightened public activities. Our duty is still an intellectual one in the highest sense of that term.

I will not say that you cannot be ordained as a minister without

---

5. "The doctor, the teacher, the administrator, the judge, the clergyman, the architect are each in his own way professionally concerned with man as a whole, and the conditions of human life as a whole. Preparation for these professions is unthinking and inhuman if it fails to relate us to the whole." Karl Jaspers, *The Idea of the University* (Boston: Beacon Press, 1959), p. 47 [Miller's note].

some vision of reality by which human experience can be elucidated, its heights and depths articulated, and its risk of waste redeemed for meaning and joy; I will not say you cannot serve the church in many different ways without such a scheme of measurement and discernment; I will not say that you cannot help people in many of their crises when the spirit despairs and life grows dark; but I will say that if you enter the ministry and hope to stand in the pulpit as the prow of the world, in the foremost part where directions are discerned and determined; if you expect to serve the real needs and not the apparent ones of the time in which you live; if you are going to find the point again where the ministry can be validated as a profession competently intent on doing its own job, then you must find a way to pull life together in a frame of reference or in a vision of reality so that men will know the dignity of belonging to this vast venture under God. Only by stretching ourselves to the utmost, by submitting both to the discipline of training and to the conditions of the time under which we work, will we prepare ourselves to make meaning out of the cataclysms of history or the humble events of human experience. Until we find the point again, and stand by it boldly, intelligently, the pulpit will be no more than an easy refuge from the strife and pain of life. But if we find the point again, if the vision is restored and the word is spoken for which every age waits, then no man will claim our place.

QUESTIONS

1. *Miller's piece was delivered as an address at a convocation service of the Harvard Divinity School. How did occasion and audience influence his presentation?*
2. *Miller implies certain goals in the education of students for the ministry. What are these goals and how far are they appropriate for other kinds of students? To what extent would he agree with the goals implied by Robert Frost in "Education by Poetry" (pp. 780–789)?*
3. *On page 1443, Miller mentions distinctions between truth and novelty, tradition and truth, appearance and reality, and the authentic and the popular. How are these distinctions important to his central idea and how are they developed, explicitly and implicitly, elsewhere in his address?*
4. *How does Miller use the metaphor from Melville's Moby Dick? For what purpose does he refer to it again later in his address?*
5. *On page 1443 Miller speaks of "the moral enthusiasm and respectability of the secular world." How does his use of the term "enthusiasm" here differ from Knox's (pp. 1409–1411)?*
6. *On page 1445 Miller distinguishes between "wisdom" and "a kind of lust for knowledge which accumulates a body of inert ideas in lieu of wisdom." Explain how closely this distinction corresponds to Perry's distinction between "bull" and "cow" (p. 333).*

GILBERT HIGHET
The Mystery of Zen

The mind need never stop growing. Indeed, one of the few experiences which never pall is the experience of watching one's own mind, and observing how it produces new interests, responds to new stimuli, and develops new thoughts, apparently without effort and almost independently of one's own conscious control. I have seen this happen to myself a hundred times; and every time it happens again, I am equally fascinated and astonished.

Some years ago a publisher sent me a little book for review. I read it, and decided it was too remote from my main interests and too highly specialized. It was a brief account of how a young German philosopher living in Japan had learned how to shoot with a bow and arrow, and how this training had made it possible for him to understand the esoteric doctrines of the Zen sect of Buddhism. Really, what could be more alien to my own life, and to that of everyone I knew, than Zen Buddhism and Japanese archery? So I thought, and put the book away.

Yet I did not forget it. It was well written, and translated into good English. It was delightfully short, and implied much more than it said. Although its theme was extremely odd, it was at least highly individual; I had never read anything like it before or since. It remained in my mind. Its name was *Zen in the Art of Archery*, its author Eugen Herrigel, its publisher Pantheon of New York. One day I took it off the shelf and read it again; this time it seemed even stranger than before and even more unforgettable. Now it began to cohere with other interests of mine. Something I had read of the Japanese art of flower arrangement seemed to connect with it; and then, when I wrote an essay on the peculiar Japanese poems called *haiku*, other links began to grow. Finally I had to read the book once more with care, and to go through some other works which illuminated the same subject. I am still grappling with the theme; I have not got anywhere near understanding it fully; but I have learned a good deal, and I am grateful to the little book which refused to be forgotten.

The author, a German philosopher, got a job teaching philosophy at the University of Tokyo (apparently between the wars), and he did what Germans in foreign countries do not usually do: he determined to adapt himself and to learn from his hosts. In particular, he had always been interested in mysticism—which, for every earnest philosopher, poses a problem that is all the more inescapable because it is virtually insoluble. Zen Buddhism is not the only mystical doctrine to be found in the East, but it is one of the most highly developed and certainly one of the most difficult to approach. Herrigel knew that there were scarcely any books which did more than skirt the edge of the subject, and that the best of all books on Zen (those by the philosopher D. T. Suzuki) constantly emphasize that Zen can never be learned from books, can never be studied as we can study other disciplines such as logic or mathematics. Therefore he began to look for a Japanese thinker who could teach him directly.

At once he met with embarrassed refusals. His Japanese friends explained that he would gain nothing from trying to discuss Zen as a philosopher, that its theories could not be spread out for analysis by a detached mind, and in fact that the normal relationship of teacher and pupil simply did not exist within the sect, because the Zen masters felt it useless to explain things stage by stage and to argue about the various possible interpretations of their doctrine. Herrigel had read enough to be prepared for this. He replied that he did not want to dissect the teachings of the school, because he knew that would be useless. He wanted to become a Zen mystic himself. (This was highly intelligent of him. No one could really penetrate into Christian mysticism without being a devout Christian; no one could appreciate Hindu mystical doctrine without accepting the Hindu view of the universe.) At this, Herrigel's Japanese friends were more forthcoming. They told him that the best way, indeed the only way, for a European to approach Zen mysticism was to learn one of the arts which exemplified it. He was a fairly good rifle shot, so he determined to learn archery; and his wife co-operated with him by taking lessons in painting and flower arrangement. How any philosopher could investigate a mystical doctrine by learning to shoot with a bow and arrow and watching his wife arrange flowers, Herrigel did not ask. He had good sense.

A Zen master who was a teacher of archery agreed to take him as a pupil. The lessons lasted six years, during which he practiced every single day. There are many difficult courses of instruction in the world: the Jesuits, violin virtuosi, Talmudic scholars, all have long and hard training, which in one sense never comes to an end; but Herrigel's training in archery equaled them all in intensity. If I were trying to learn archery, I should expect to begin by looking at a target and shooting arrows at it. He was not even allowed to aim at a target for the first four years. He had to begin by learning how to hold the bow and arrow, and then how to release the arrow; this took ages. The Japanese bow is not like our sporting bow, and the stance of the archer in Japan is different from ours. We hold the bow at shoulder level, stretch our left arm out ahead, pull the string and the nocked arrow to a point either below the chin or sometimes past the right ear, and then shoot. The Japanese hold the bow above the head, and then pull the hands apart to left and right until the left hand comes down to eye level and the right hand comes to rest above the right shoulder; then there is a pause, during which the bow is held at full stretch, with the tip of the three-foot arrow projecting only a few inches beyond the bow; after that, the arrow is loosed. When Herrigel tried this, even without aiming, he found it was almost impossible. His hands trembled. His legs stiffened and grew cramped. His breathing became labored. And of course he could not possibly aim. Week after week he practiced this, with the Master watching him carefully and correcting his strained attitude; week after week he made no progress whatever. Finally he gave up and told his teacher that he could not learn: it was absolutely impossible for him to draw the bow and loose the arrow.

To his astonishment, the Master agreed. He said, "Certainly you cannot. It is because you are not breathing correctly. You must learn to breathe in a steady rhythm, keeping your lungs full most of the time, and drawing in one rapid inspiration with each stage of the process, as you grasp the bow, fit the arrow, raise the bow, draw, pause, and loose the shot. If you do, you will both grow stronger and be able to relax." To prove this, he himself drew his massive bow and told his pupil to feel the muscles of his arms: they were perfectly relaxed, as though he were doing no work whatever.

Herrigel now started breathing exercises; after some time he combined the new rhythm of breathing with the actions of drawing and shooting; and, much to his astonishment, he found that the whole thing, after this complicated process, had become much easier. Or rather, not easier, but different. At times it became quite unconscious. He says himself that he felt he was not breathing, but being breathed; and in time he felt that the occasional shot was not being dispatched by him, but shooting itself. The bow and arrow were in charge; he had become merely a part of them.

All this time, of course, Herrigel did not even attempt to discuss Zen doctrine with his Master. No doubt he knew that he was approaching it, but he concentrated solely on learning how to shoot. Every stage which he surmounted appeared to lead to another stage even more difficult. It took him months to learn how to loosen the bowstring. The problem was this. If he gripped the string and arrowhead tightly, either he froze, so that his hands were slowly pulled together and the shot was wasted, or else he jerked, so that the arrow flew up into the air or down into the ground; and if he was relaxed, then the bowstring and arrow simply *leaked* out of his grasp before he could reach full stretch, and the arrow went nowhere. He explained this problem to the Master. The Master understood perfectly well. He replied, "You must hold the drawn bowstring like a child holding a grownup's finger. You know how firmly a child grips; and yet when it lets go, there is not the slightest jerk—because the child does not think of itself, it is not self-conscious, it does not say, 'I will now let go and do something else,' it merely acts instinctively. That is what you must learn to do. Practice, practice, and practice, and then the string will loose itself at the right moment. The shot will come as effortlessly as snow slipping from a leaf." Day after day, week after week, month after month, Herrigel practiced this; and then, after one shot, the Master suddenly bowed and broke off the lesson. He said "Just then it shot. Not you, but *it*." And gradually thereafter more and more right shots achieved themselves; the young philosopher forgot himself, forgot that he was learning archery for some other purpose, forgot even that he was practicing archery, and became part of that unconsciously active complex, the bow, the string, the arrow, and the man.

Next came the target. After four years, Herrigel was allowed to shoot at the target. But he was strictly forbidden to aim at it. The Master explained that even he himself did not aim; and indeed, when he shot, he was so absorbed in the act, so selfless and unanxious, that his eyes were almost closed. It was difficult, almost impossible, for Herrigel to believe that such shooting could ever be effective; and he risked insulting the Master by suggesting that he ought to be able to hit the target blindfolded. But the Master accepted the challenge. That night, after a cup of tea and long meditation, he went into the archery hall, put on the lights at one end and left the target perfectly dark, with only a thin taper burning in front of it. Then, with habitual grace and precision, and with that strange, almost sleepwalking, selfless confidence that is the heart of Zen, he shot two arrows into the darkness. Herrigel went out to collect them. He found that the first had gone to the heart of the bull's eye, and that the second had actually hit the first arrow and splintered it. The Master showed no pride. He said, "Perhaps, with unconscious memory of the position of the target, I shot the first arrow; but the second arrow? *It* shot the second arrow, and *it* brought it to the center of the target."

At last Herrigel began to understand. His progress became faster and faster; easier, too. Perfect shots (perfect because perfectly unconscious) occurred at almost every lesson; and finally, after six years of incessant training, in a public display he was awarded the diploma. He needed no further instruction: he had himself become a Master. His wife meanwhile had become expert both in painting and in the arrangement of flowers—two of the finest of Japanese arts. (I wish she could be persuaded to write a companion volume, called *Zen in the Art of Flower Arrangement;* it would have a wider general appeal than her husband's work.) I gather also from a hint or two in his book that she had taken part in the archery lessons. During one of the most difficult periods in Herrigel's training, when his Master had practically refused to continue teaching him—because Herrigel had tried to cheat by *consciously* opening his hand at the moment of loosing the arrow— his wife had advised him against that solution, and sympathized with him when it was rejected. She in her own way had learned more quickly than he, and reached the final point together with him. All their effort had not been in vain: Herrigel and his wife had really acquired a new and valuable kind of wisdom. Only at this point, when he was about to abandon his lessons forever, did his Master treat him almost as an equal and hint at the innermost doctrines of Zen Buddhism. Only hints he gave; and yet, for the young philosopher who had now become a mystic, they were enough. Herrigel understood the doctrine, not with his logical mind, but with his entire being. He at any rate had solved the mystery of Zen.

Without going through a course of training as absorbing and as complete as Herrigel's, we can probably never penetrate the mystery. The doctrine of Zen cannot be analyzed from without: it must be lived.

But although it cannot be analyzed, it can be hinted at. All the hints that the adherents of this creed give us are interesting. Many are fantastic; some are practically incomprehensible, and yet unforgettable. Put together, they take us toward a way of life which is utterly impossible for westerners living in a western world, and nevertheless has a deep fascination and contains some values which we must respect.

The word Zen means "meditation." (It is the Japanese word, corresponding to the Chinese Ch'an and the Hindu Dhyana.) It is the central idea of a special sect of Buddhism which flourished in China during the Sung period (between A.D. 1000 and 1300) and entered Japan in the twelfth century. Without knowing much about it, we might be certain that the Zen sect was a worthy and noble one, because it produced a quantity of highly distinguished art, specifically painting. And if we knew anything about Buddhism itself, we might say that Zen goes closer than other sects to the heart of Buddha's teaching: because Buddha was trying to found, not a religion with temples and rituals, but a way of life based on meditation. However, there is something eccentric about the Zen life which is hard to trace in Buddha's teaching; there is an active energy which he did not admire, there is a rough grasp on reality which he himself eschewed, there is something like a sense of humor, which he rarely displayed. The gravity and serenity of the Indian preacher are transformed, in Zen, to the earthy liveliness of Chinese and Japanese sages. The lotus brooding calmly on the water has turned into a knotted tree covered with spring blossoms.

In this sense, "meditation" does not mean what we usually think of when we say a philosopher meditates: analysis of reality, a long-sustained effort to solve problems of religion and ethics, the logical dissection of the universe. It means something not divisive, but whole; not schematic, but organic; not long-drawn-out, but immediate. It means something more like our words "intuition" and "realization." It means a way of life in which there is no division between thought and action; none of the painful gulf, so well known to all of us, between the unconscious and the conscious mind; and no absolute distinction between the self and the external world, even between the various parts of the external world and the whole.

When the German philosopher took six years of lessons in archery in order to approach the mystical significance of Zen, he was not given direct philosophical instruction. He was merely shown how to breathe, how to hold and loose the bowstring, and finally how to shoot in such a way that the bow and arrow used him as an instrument. There are many such stories about Zen teachers. The strangest I know is one about a fencing master who undertook to train a young man in the art of the sword. The relationship of teacher and pupil is very important, almost sacred, in the Far East; and the pupil hardly ever thinks of leaving a master or objecting to his methods, however extraordinary they may seem. Therefore this young fellow did not at first object when he was made to act as a servant, drawing water, sweeping floors, gathering wood for the fire, and cooking. But after some time he asked for more direct instruction. The master agreed to give it, but produced no swords. The routine went on just as before, except that every now and then the master would strike the young man with a stick. No matter what he was doing, sweeping the floor or weeding in the garden, a blow would descend on him apparently out of nowhere; he had always to be on the alert, and yet he was constantly receiving unexpected cracks on the head or shoulders. After some months of this, he saw his master stooping over a boiling pot full of vegetables; and he thought he would have his revenge. Silently he lifted a stick and brought it down; but without any effort, without even a glance in his direction, his master parried the blow with the lid of the cooking pot. At last, the pupil began to understand the instinctive alertness, the effortless perception and avoidance of danger, in which his master had been training him. As soon as he had achieved it, it was child's play for him to learn the management of the sword: he could parry every cut and turn every slash without anxiety, until his opponent, exhausted, left an opening for his counterattack. (The same principle was used by the elderly samurai for selecting his comrades in the Japanese motion picture *The Magnificent Seven.*)

These stories show that Zen meditation does not mean sitting and thinking. On the contrary, it means acting with as little thought as possible. The fencing master trained his pupil to guard against every attack with the same immediate, instinctive rapidity with which our eyelid closes over our eye when something threatens it. His work was aimed at breaking down the wall between thought and act, at completely fusing body and senses and mind so that they might all work together rapidly and effortlessly. When a Zen artist draws a picture, he does it in a rhythm almost the exact reverse of that which is followed by a Western artist. We begin by blocking out the design and then filling in the details, usually working more and more slowly as we approach the completion of the picture. The Zen artist sits down very calmly; examines his brush carefully; prepares his own ink; smooths out the paper on which he will work; falls into a profound silent ecstasy of contemplation—during which he does not think anxiously of various details, composition, brushwork, shades of tone, but rather attempts to become the vehicle through which the subject can express itself in painting; and then, very quickly and almost unconsciously, with sure effortless strokes, draws a picture containing the fewest and most effective lines. Most of the paper is left blank; only the essential is depicted, and that not completely. One long curving line will be enough to show a mountainside; seven streaks will become a group of bamboos bending in the wind; and yet, though technically incomplete, such pictures are unforgettably clear. They show the heart of reality.

All this we can sympathize with, because we can see the results. The young swordsman learns how to fence. The intuitional painter produces a fine picture. But the hardest thing for us to appreciate is that the Zen masters refuse to teach philosophy or religion directly, and deny logic. In fact, they despise logic as an artificial distortion of reality. Many philosophical teachers are difficult to understand because they analyze profound problems with subtle intricacy: such is Aristotle in his *Metaphysics.* Many mystical writers are difficult to understand because, as they themselves admit, they are attempting to use words to describe experiences which are too abstruse for words, so that they have to fall back on imagery and analogy, which they themselves recognize to be poor media, far coarser than the realities with which they have been in contact.

But the Zen teachers seem to deny the power of language and thought altogether. For example, if you ask a Zen master what is the ultimate reality, he will answer, without the slightest hesitation, "The bamboo grove at the foot of the hill" or "A branch of plum blossom." Apparently he means that these things, which we can see instantly without effort, or imagine in the flash of a second, are real with the ultimate reality; that nothing is more real than these; and that we ought to grasp ultimates as we grasp simple immediates. A Chinese master was once asked the central question, "What is the Buddha?" He said nothing whatever, but held out his index finger. What did he mean? It is hard to explain; but apparently he meant "Here. Now. Look and realize with the effortlessness of seeing. Do not try to use words. Do not think. Make no efforts toward withdrawal from the world. Expect no sublime ecstasies. Live. All *that* is the ultimate reality, and it can be understood from the motion of a finger as well as from the execution of any complex ritual, from any subtle argument, or from the circling of the starry universe."

In making that gesture, the master was copying the Buddha himself, who once delivered a sermon which is famous, but was hardly understood by his pupils at the time. Without saying a word, he held up a flower and showed it to the gathering. One man, one alone, knew what he meant. The gesture became renowned as the Flower Sermon.

In the annals of Zen there are many cryptic answers to the final question, "What is the Buddha?"—which in our terms means "What is the meaning of life? What is truly real?" For example, one master, when asked "What is the Buddha?" replied, "Your name is Yecho." Another said, "Even the finest artist cannot paint him." Another said, "No nonsense here." And another answered, "The mouth is the gate of woe." My favorite story is about the monk who said to a Master, "Has a dog Buddha-nature too?" The Master replied, "Wu"—which is what the dog himself would have said.

Now, some critics might attack Zen by saying that this is the creed of a savage or an animal. The adherents of Zen would deny that—or more probably they would ignore the criticism, or make some cryptic remark which meant that it was pointless. Their position—if they could ever be persuaded to put it into words—would be this. An animal is instinctively in touch with reality, and so far is living rightly, but it has never had a mind and so cannot perceive the Whole, only that part with which it is in touch. The philosopher sees both the Whole and the parts, and enjoys them all. As for the savage, he exists only through the group; he feels himself as part of a war party or a ceremonial dance team or a ploughing-and-sowing group or the Snake clan; he is not truly an individual at all, and therefore is less than fully human. Zen has at its heart an inner solitude; its aim is to teach us to live, as in the last resort we do all have to live, alone.

A more dangerous criticism of Zen would be that it is nihilism, that its purpose is to abolish thought altogether. (This criticism is handled, but not fully met, by the great Zen authority Suzuki in his *Introduction to Zen Buddhism*.) It can hardly be completely confuted, for after all the central doctrine of Buddhism is—Nothingness. And many of the sayings of Zen masters are truly nihilistic. The first patriarch of the sect in China was asked by the emperor what was the ultimate and holiest principle of Buddhism. He replied, "Vast emptiness, and nothing holy in it." Another who was asked the searching question "Where is the abiding-place for the mind?" answered, "Not in this dualism of good and evil, being and nonbeing, thought and matter." In fact, thought is an activity which divides. It analyzes, it makes distinctions, it criticizes, it judges, it breaks reality into groups and classes and individuals. The aim of Zen is to abolish that kind of thinking, and to substitute—not unconsciousness, which would be death, but a consciousness that does not analyze but experiences life directly. Although it has no prescribed prayers, no sacred scriptures, no ceremonial rites, no personal god, and no interest in the soul's future destination, Zen is a religion rather than a philosophy. Jung points out that its aim is to produce a religious conversion, a "transformation": and he adds, "The transformation process is incommensurable with intellect." Thought is always interesting, but often painful; Zen is calm and painless. Thought is incomplete; Zen enlightenment brings a sense of completeness. Thought is a process; Zen illumination is a state. But it is a state which cannot be defined. In the Buddhist scriptures there is a dialogue between a master and a pupil in which the pupil tries to discover the exact meaning of such a state. The master says to him, 'If a fire were blazing in front of you, would you know that it was blazing?'

"Yes, master."

"And would you know the reason for its blazing?"

"Yes, because it had a supply of grass and sticks."

"And would you know if it were to go out?"

"Yes, master."

"And on its going out, would you know where the fire had gone? To the east, to the west, to the north, or to the south?"

"The question does not apply, master. For the fire blazed because it had a supply of grass and sticks. When it had consumed this and had no other fuel, then it went out."

"In the same way," replies the master, "no question will apply to the meaning of Nirvana, and no statement will explain it."

Such, then, neither happy nor unhappy but beyond all divisive description, is the condition which students of Zen strive to attain.

Small wonder that they can scarcely explain it to us, the unillu-
minated.

QUESTIONS

1. What difficulties does Highet face in discussing Zen? How does
   he manage to give a definition in spite of his statement that Zen
   "cannot be analyzed"?
2. Why does Highet describe the training in archery in such detail?
3. On page 1456 Highet says that "Zen is a religion rather than
   a philosophy." How has he led up to this conclusion? What
   definitions of "religion" and "philosophy" does he imply?
4. By what means does Highet define "meditation"? Would other
   means have worked as well? Explain.
5. To what extent is Zen "the creed of a savage or an animal"?
   How does Highet go about refuting this charge?

G. B. SANSOM

Shintō[1]

The outstanding feature of Shintō observances is the attention
paid to ritual purity. Things which are offensive to the gods were
called by the early Japanese *tsumi*, a word which is now rendered
by dictionaries as "guilt" or "sin." Avoidance of these things was
called *imi*, a word meaning taboo. The Imibe were a class of
professional "abstainers," whose duty it was to keep free from pollution so that they might approach the gods without offense. Chief
among the offenses to be avoided was uncleanness. It might arise in
many ways, none of which necessarily involved what in other religions would be moral guilt. Uncleanness of the person, from mere
dirt, was scrupulously avoided, and it was a necessary preparation
for religious observances to wash the body and to put on fresh garments. Sexual intercourse, menstruation, and childbirth were
regarded as causing ceremonial impurity, which must be removed
by lustration, abstention, and prayer. In the earliest myth there is
mention of "parturition huts," isolated sheds to which pregnant
women withdrew so that the dwelling-house should not be defiled
by childbirth, and we are told also of "nuptial huts," in which, for
a like reason, marriages were consummated. Disease, wounds, and
death were also sources of uncleanness. Death—or rather the contamination of death—was abhorrent to the early Japanese. The
Han travelers from China noticed that the time of mourning was
short, that after death friends came to dance and sing, and that
after the funeral the whole family went into the water to wash.
The house in which a death took place became unclean, and it was

1. From Chapter 3 in *Japan: A Short Cultural History*, rev. ed., 1962.

doubtless on this account that until the beginning of the 8th century the capital, or at least the palace, was removed to another site upon the death of a sovereign.[2]

Wounds were a source of pollution, and the word for wound, *kega*, still in use, means defilement. Sickness and all the external signs of disease, such as sores, eruptions, and discharges, or contact with sick persons, were also defilements. Eating flesh was not originally unclean, except perhaps for priests preparing themselves for worship, but it appears to have become taboo under Buddhist influence. Intoxicating liquors are not taboo. In fact they figure prominently among offerings to the gods at all times.

So far, it will be noticed, the list of offenses does not reveal any distinction between ceremonial impurity and moral guilt. The consummation of a marriage is no less defiling than adulterous intercourse, a blow or a wound pollutes both parties to a conflict, and generally we find that the early religion is almost entirely deficient in abstract ideas of morality. Its code is not ethical but customary and ceremonial. It reprobates as sins only such acts or states as are visibly or immediately repulsive. It is worthwhile to examine more closely this question, for out of the early conception of morality grows the whole complex of religious and social organization in later times, shaping and modifying even the powerful influences of Chinese philosophy and Buddhist doctrine.

In the great Purification Ritual, which is of uncertain date but which embodies matter of great antiquity, there is a list of offenses (*Tsumi*) from which the gods are asked to cleanse the people. These are divided into heavenly offenses and earthly offenses. The heavenly offenses are so called because they are those committed by the god Susa-no-wo in heaven, and were given a prominent place in the myth because they were offenses against a community whose principal occupation was agriculture. The earthly offenses are wounding and killing; desecration of corpses; leprosy; tumors; incest (though, it appears, intercourse between children of one father by different mothers was not considered incestuous); bestiality (but not, it appears, sodomy); calamity from creeping things, from the gods on high, from birds and animals, and from witchcraft. The offenses in this second category are, it will be observed, calamities affecting the welfare of individuals, and are not even necessarily the result of their own actions or their own fault.[3] What is abhorrent,

---

2. The traditional accession ceremony, performed as lately as 1928, includes an impressive survival of this practice. The Emperor enters a ritual hall, containing a couch-throne, and goes through an elaborate communion meal with the national deities; then, during the same night, he proceeds to another ritual hall close by, identically furnished, and repeats the communion meal [Sansom's note].

3. It is hardly necessary to add that the ritual offenses just named were not the only offenses recognized by early Japanese society, and that there were virtues prized as well as ceremonial purity. The Han historians record with admiration the chastity and gentleness of Japanese women, state that theft is unknown, and that laws and customs are strict [Sansom's note].

what must be washed away and expiated is not guilt but pollution. The conception of sin, as distinct from uncleanness, is wanting, or rudimentary, and throughout their history the Japanese seem to have retained in some measure this incapacity to discern, or this reluctance to grapple with a problem of Evil. Such a statement, once committed to writing, forthwith challenges contradiction in the writer's own mind, but it represents, if imperfectly, a truth; and much that is baffling in the study of their history, from ancient to modern times, becomes clearer when one remembers that they have never been tortured by the sense of sin.

At the core of all Shintō ceremonial is the idea of purity, and at the core of all Shintō beliefs is the idea of fertility. As "celestial offenses" typify those misdeeds which interfere with the production of food, so the chief celestial blessings demanded are those most desirable to farmers and fishermen, such as, in the words recited at the Harvest Festival in honor of every deity in the pantheon, "crops in ears long and in ears abundant, things growing in the great moor-plain, sweet herbs and bitter herbs, things that dwell in the blue sea-plain, the board of fin and the narrow of fin, seaweed from the offing, seaweed from the shore, clothing, bright stuffs and shining stuffs, coarse stuffs and fine stuffs." The most important ceremonies have, in one way or another, to do with food. The chief festivals of the year are the Tasting of the First Fruits (Nii-namé), the Divine Tasting (Kannamé), celebrated in the imperial palace and at the Ise shrines, the Together-Tasting (Ainamé) in which the emperor joins with the gods in partaking of the new season's rice and *sake* of the new brew, and the most solemn festivals of all, the Great Food Offering (Ōnie, later called Daijōe), an elaborate form of the festival of the First Fruits, celebrated after an emperor's succession to the throne, to give a sacramental authority to his sovereignty. There are, it is true, other elements in the accession ceremonies, but the essential characteristics of the Daijōe and its preparatory rites is that "they have preserved from ancient times a primitive technique for the production and preservation of food," and are "deeply stamped with an interest in safeguarding the growth and fertility of crops." Many other celebrations, national and local, are wholly or in part thanksgivings or prayers for harvest. It is a significant fact that at Yamada in Ise, the center of the cult of the Sun Goddess and the resting place of the sacred mirror, there is a shrine, only next in holiness to that of Ama-terasu, devoted to the worship of the goddess of food, Toyo-uke-himi, the Rich-Food-Princess; and there are some reasons for believing that the Sun Goddess was enshrined in this place by the ruling house because it was already in ancient times of great holiness through its association with a popular cult. Further evidence that it was the principle of growth and fertility which inspired, more than anything else, the beliefs and observances of the early Japanese is to be found in the prevalence of phallic worship and its strong power of survival. Phallic emblems are found in neolithic sites, and a phallic significance was seen in trees and stones of appropriate form, doubtless because they suggested procreation and fruitfulness. Even today, in remote districts, there can be seen sometimes stones of phallic shape, set up at the edge of fields, and bearing rude inscriptions such as "God of the Rice." In the earliest chronicles there are several references to phallic worship, and there are numerous records of festivals and liturgies in honor of "gods of the crossways," who were represented by phallic emblems set up by the roadside.

It is hardly necessary to add that though the early Shintō was in essence a nature worship, it developed in special directions under official auspices. It is important to distinguish from the traditional body of popular belief and observance the institutional religion which was fostered by the ruling classes. The former is a simple ritualism based on an animistic creed and tinctured with magic, the latter an organized and elaborate cult closely bound up with the political system. It is equally important to realize that, although Shintō is often described as a form of ancestor worship, this is a loose and misleading statement. Ancestor worship, as practiced in Japan, is a cult imported from China. The objects of worship of the early Japanese were nature deities, and not their own deified ancestors. It is true that the noble families claimed descent from the gods whom they worshipped, but making your god into an ancestor and making your ancestor into a god are not the same thing. The worship of a clan god (*ujigami*) by all the members of a clan (*uji*) at first sight seems to be a form of ancestor worship. The clan god, however, was not necessarily a family god, and might be even a tutelary local deity. There were even cases where the identity of the clan god was disputed. In no case do we find, before the introduction of the Chinese cult, instances of the worship of deified men by their descendants. The worship of deceased emperors, even supposing it to have been practiced before the importation of Chinese theories of kingship—a supposition for which there is no evidence—is a special case, for the emperors were in their lifetime tinged with divinity.

To complete the foregoing account of early religious beliefs and observances, it is necessary to describe briefly how and in what place the gods were worshipped. In the earliest stages of the animistic creed, trees, rocks, and springs were doubtless worshipped *in situ*, and obeisance made to the sun itself. Subsequently, it seems, ceremonies were conducted in an enclosure marked off by branches of evergreen trees thrust into the ground. Later, with the use of objects such as jewels and mirrors to symbolize the presence of a god, came the need for a dwelling in which to enshrine them. The word for a shrine (*miya: ya* "house," with an honorific prefix, *mi*) is the same as that used for the house of a chieftain, and it is clear that for centuries there was no distinction in type between a dwelling-house and a shrine. The special characteristic of Shintō shrines is the simplicity of their construction and ornament as contrasted with the great buildings of Buddhism. The shrines of Ise, which are pulled down and rebuilt in exact replica every twenty years, are thought to represent the purest and most ancient style of Japanese architecture, and they are essentially nothing more than thatched wooden huts, somewhat idealized. The Idzumo shrines, though larger and a little more elaborate, are still comparatively simple in design. There is no provision made for joint worship by a congregation, so that no more space is needed than will accommodate an altar and the priests or other attendants. The individual worshipper does not enter the shrine, but stands outside and makes his obeisance and his petition. It is not known how many shrines existed before the 8th century, but there were over 3,000 officially recognized shrines in A.D. 737, and of these about one-fourth were maintained at the expense of the government.

Worship consisted of obeisance, offerings and prayer. The offerings were primarily food and drink. Later, cloth was added, and eventually a symbolic offering came into use, by which strips of paper, representing strips of cloth, were attached to a wand and placed on the altar. Then, by a curious development, these symbolic offerings (known as *gohei*) themselves came to be regarded as sanctified, and even as representing the deity, who was sometimes mystically supposed to descend into them. Thus, in course of time the *gohei* became objects of worship themselves, and were presented by priests to the devout, who set them up on their domestic altars; while strips of paper, cut in a prescribed way, and attached to a straw rope, to this day confer a special sanctity on places where they are suspended.

Purification was essential before worship and was achieved by various methods, exorcism (*harai*), cleansing (*misogi*), and abstention (*imi*). Exorcism was performed by a priest, and was intended to remove the pollution caused by an offense. It consists essentially of the presentation of offerings by way of fine, after which the priest brandishes before the person to be purified a wand in the form of a brush and pronounces a formula of purification. The exaction of fines gave to the *harai* a certain penal character. It is not clear how early this developed, but there are records under dates in the early part of the 5th century from which it would appear that at that time submission to the *harai* was a recognized punishment for civil as well as religious offenses. Thus in 405 the head of the corporation of carters appropriated to his own service some peasants attached to the glebe of a shrine. He was commanded to perform expiatory rites, though his offense was as much civil as religious. In 469 a certain young nobleman debauched a court lady, and was made to purge his offense by the payment of eight horses and eight swords. He was unrepentant, and boasted in verse, saying that the adventure was well worth eight horses, whereupon the emperor confiscated all his property. We shall see that, with the growth of an administrative system on Chinese lines, there was later a clear division between secular and religious offenses, the *harai* and its accompanying fines being confined to specified breaches of ecclesiastical law.

The *misogi* was a cleansing rite, intended to remove accidental defilement acquired by contact with unclean things, from simple dirt to the pollution of death and disease. It was effected by ablutions, or the mere sprinkling of water or salt. A number of practices common today are vestiges, or even complete survivals, of this ancient custom. In the courtyard of every temple and shrine is a font at which the worshippers wash their hands and rinse their mouths before worship. Outside the privy in the humblest house stands a basin of water and a ladle, used for rinsing the hands in a manner so perfunctory as to be merely symbolic. The indulgence of the Japanese in hot baths, though it is a habit which has survived because of its value in pleasure and health, doubtless owes something to the primitive belief in lustration. Salt is placed in little piles on the threshold of a house, at the edge of a well, or at the corners of a wrestling ring, and it is scattered about the floor after a funeral, with the object of purification. Offerings at a shrine invariably include a number of small dishes of salt.

The third, and perhaps the most interesting method of purification is *imi*, or abstention. Exorcism and lustration confer purity by removing uncleanness, whereas abstention is a method of acquiring a positive purity by avoidance of the sources of pollution. It was therefore the duty of priests rather than of laymen to practice the needful austerities, which consisted chiefly of the observance of certain prohibitions. They must avoid contact with sickness, death, mourning; they must eat only certain kinds of food and those only if cooked over a "pure" fire; they must wear only specially purified garments; and they must remain indoors, remote from noise, dancing and singing. Scrupulous care must be taken to avoid contamination of the sanctuary, the offerings, and the utensils.

Private devotions seem from early times to have been confined to the deposit of offerings before a shrine accompanied by some reverent gesture, such as bowing, or clapping—not merely folding—the hands. It is curious that, in a country where kneeling and prostration are part of every-day social ceremony, kneeling before a shrine was not usual and prostration apparently not practiced at all as a form of worship. Private, individual prayer seems to have been uncommon, and to have consisted at the most of some simple formula. Many examples of official liturgies are recorded in a book of Institutes compiled in the beginning of the 10th century. Some are inclined to regard them as preserving with a high degree of exactitude the form and content of very ancient addresses to the gods, but the probability is that they do not antedate the 7th century at earliest, and that when they were first committed to writing they underwent considerable change at the hands of scribes anxious to give them a certain literary elegance. In the present writer's view they smell too much of the lamp to be genuine survivals, by oral tradition, from a period much earlier than the spread of writing in Japan. They must contain, however, some ancient elements; and it is therefore worth quoting a few passages to show their style and purport. The following is an extract from Aston's translation of the Litany recited at the Ceremony of National Purification.

Then shall no offenses remain unpurged, from the court of the august child of the gods even to the remotest ends of the realm. As the many-piled clouds of heaven are scattered at the breath of the Wind Gods; as the morning breezes and the evening breezes disperse the morning vapors and the evening vapors; as a huge ship moored in a great harbor, casting off its stern moorings, casting off its bow moorings, drives forth into the vast ocean; as yonder thick brushwood is smitten and cleared away by the sharp sickle forged in the fire—so shall all offenses be swept utterly away. To purge and purify them, let the goddess Seori-tsu-hime, who dwells in the rapids of the swift stream whose cataracts tumble headlong from the high mountains and from the low mountains, bear them out into the great sea plains. There let the goddess Haya-akitsu-hime, who dwells in the myriad meeting places of the tides of the myriad sea paths, swallow them up, and let the god Ibukido Nushi (i.e. the master of the spurting-out place), who dwells in Ibukido, spurt them out away to the nether region. Then let the goddess Hayasa-sura-hime, who dwells in the nether region, dissolve and destroy them.

The language is not without a certain elevation but the translation has a sweep and a finish which flatter the rather poorly articulated original. The chief characteristic of its style is a solemn pleonasm, as in the phrase "in the myriad ways of the tides of the myriad sea paths." Some idea of the rhythm of the native words can be gained from the original: *Ara-shio no shio no yaoji no yashioji no shio no yaoai.*

The literary value of the remaining rituals is not great, but they include picturesque and interesting passages, such as this declaration to the Sun Goddess in the great prayer for Harvest:

. . . I do humbly declare in the mighty presence of the Great Heaven-shining Deity who dwells in Ise. Because the Great Deity has bestowed on him lands of the four quarters over which her glance extends as far as where the wall of Heaven rises, as far as where the bounds of Earth stand up, as far as the blue clouds are diffused, as far as where the white clouds settle down opposite; by the blue sea-plain, as far as the prows of ships can go without letting dry their poles and oars; by land, as far as the hoofs of horses can go, with tightened baggage-cords, treading their way among rock-roots and tree-roots where the long road extends, continuously widening the narrow regions and making the steep regions level, drawing together, as it were, the distant regions by throwing over them (a net of) many ropes,—therefore will the first-fruits for the Sovran Great Deity be piled up in her mighty presence like a range of hills, leaving the remainder for him tranquilly to partake of.

And this, from a blessing of the Imperial Palace, after a recital of the circumstances in which the reigning dynasty received the celestial mandate:

And for the Sovran Grandchild who in Heavenly Sun-succession rules the Under-Heaven, to which he had descended, trees are now cut down with the sacred axes of the Imbe in the great valleys and the small valleys of the secluded mountains, and sacrifice having been made of their tops and bottoms to the God of the mountains, the middle parts are brought forth and set up as sacred pillars with sacred mattocks to form a fair Palace wherein the Sovran Grandchild finds shelter from the sky and shelter from the sun. To thee, therefore... I address these heavenly, wondrous, auspicious words of calm and blessing.

HENRY SLOANE COFFIN
What Crucified Christ?[1]

Some years ago a well-known British journalist, the late W. T. Stead, after witnessing the Passion Play at Oberammergau, came away saying to himself: "This is the story which has transformed the world." And he seemed to hear an echo from the Bavarian hills about him: "Yes, and will transform it."

Each generation stresses particular aspects of the Gospel; and it must be confessed that in our day, and especially in those circles where Christianity is interpreted in terms of contemporary thought, the cross does not hold the central place in preaching. With many men the Incarnation has taken the place formerly occupied by the Atonement, and the character of Jesus is proclaimed as the supreme revelation of God and the ideal for man. In other circles it has been the religious experience of Jesus which is oftenest preached, and men are bidden follow His way of life with God and man. In still other quarters it is His teaching which is dwelt on and men are enlisted as devotees of the Kingdom of God. But the cross, while it is mentioned as a significant unveiling of Jesus' character, or as the most draining ordeal for which He drew on spiritual resources, or as the climax of His devotion to His cause, is seldom preached as a

1. Chapter 1 of *The Meaning of the Cross.*

redemptive act. Indeed few of those who have accepted the current liberal theology devote many sermons to the cross of Christ. They feel themselves incapable of treating the theme.

There are various reasons for this. Our exaggerated individualism renders it difficult for us to think of One bearing the sins of others. Our easy optimism makes us think lightly of sin as an obsession of minds which hold unwholesome views of man and of God. Above all, the luxurious circumstances in which modern American Christians have found themselves have dulled our capacities for appreciating sacrifice. We have surrounded ourselves with conveniences and comforts, and we have tried to banish pain. The tortured form of One spiked on a beam of wood and done to death does not belong in our mental picture. Our ideals and manner of life are incompatible with this tragic and heroic symbol. Preachers have felt an unreality in attempting to explore with their people the meaning of the crucifixion.

This neglect of the cross has had something to do with the lack of transforming power in our message. No one can look complacently upon the present condition of our churches. Hundreds of them are barely holding on: they make no gains from the lives about them. In hundreds more, where there is bustle and stir, the activity is about trifles, and lives are not radically altered nor their communities made over. In very few does one find comrades of the conscience of Christ. In most the majority of communicants show no marks of the Lord Jesus in the purposes to which they devote themselves, in their attitudes towards their neighbors, in the opinions which they hold on public questions. Ministers can count on their fingers the number of their people ready to give themselves for an advance of the Kingdom. The wealth in Christian hands in this country is fabulous, but almost all Church Boards are crippled for want of support. More money is taken in at the gates of a single champion prizefight than a million Church members contribute in a whole year to the spread of the Gospel throughout the world. Above all repentance—a fundamental Christian experience— "repentance unto life" as the Westminster divines termed it—is a saving grace seldom seen. That which has most moved other centuries to repentance unto life has been the preaching of Christ crucified. Commenting upon Dwight L. Moody's insistence upon the efficacy of the sacrifice of Christ to do away with sin, Gamaliel Bradford writes:

To some of us, at any rate, whether we can accept this doctrine or not, it seems that the enormous, unparalleled growth and power and majesty of Christianity in the last nineteen hundred years depend upon it.

One would not harshly criticize brethren in the ministry who have shrunk from the word of the cross. We preachers are pitiable men, doomed to be haunted week after week with a sense of the insufficiency of our treatment of subjects obviously too high for us, and on which we are still constrained to speak. We become most abysmally aware of our incompetence when we attempt to set forth the meaning of the suffering and death of the Son of Man. John Milton, who had marvelously celebrated the birth of Jesus in the "Ode on the Morning of Christ's Nativity," attempted a sequel upon the Passion, but after a few exquisite stanzas he ceased in despair, and the fragment is published with the significant note:

This Subject the Author finding to be above the years he had when he wrote it, and nothing satisfied with what was begun, left it unfinished.

And years do not of themselves mature us to deal with this theme. Happily we discover that sermons which seriously try to interpret that supreme event possess a moving power out of proportion to the wisdom of their content.

How are we to preach Christ crucified? We want an interpretation of the cross for our generation which shall move to repentance and faith. In order to remain in close touch with reality, suppose we begin with two questions of history: First, How came it that the Life which subsequent centuries have looked up to as the best ever lived on our earth seemed so intolerable to the dominant groups of His day that they executed Him? Second, Why did Jesus force the issue that made His execution inevitable?

Let us attempt to answer the first question in this initial chapter remembering that we are not attempting a doctrine of the cross for classroom discussion, but for general presentation. How came it that He whom succeeding generations have revered as the best of men was put to death as a criminal? Who were the crucifiers of Christ?

First and foremost the religious leaders whom Church folk respected. It is a tribute to the force conferred by religious conviction that believing men are so often the prime movers in momentous occurrences, both in the blackest crimes and in the brightest triumphs of mankind. Faith, like fire, empowers its possessors whether for woe or for weal. We must not forget that there was ardent faith in God and conscientious loyalty to Him in the Pharisees who contrived the cruel death of our earth's divinest figure. Like one of their own school, they verily thought themselves under compulsion to act as they did.

That is why Church folk should study them carefully. Who were they? The successors of a brave and patriotic company of stalwart believers who had saved the Jewish faith when foreign conquerors attempted to compromise and wreck it by introducing their own customs and worship. They were known for that essential element in vital religion—detachment: they were called Separatists, Pharisees. They were the heirs of a noble army of martyrs. They knew and honored the Bible as the Law of God. They reverenced the scholars who had spent their lives in explaining it and applying it to life. They were the backbone of the synagogues throughout the land. They prayed; they believed in God's present government of His world and in His immediate control of events. They thought His angelic messengers spoke in the consciences of devout folk and watched for good over their steps. They looked forward to the resurrection of the righteous and their life in the Messiah's everlasting kingdom. They were intense lovers of home and country: in their households there was family religion, and boys, like Saul of Tarsus, were brought up to become devotees and leaders of the Church. They supplied the candidates for the ministry—the scribes who studied and interpreted the Torah. They furnished the missionaries who had enthusiasm to compass sea and land for a single proselyte, and had built up around the synagogues of the whole Mediterranean world companies of the God-fearing who had espoused the faith of Israel.

Men who sincerely try to order their lives by God's will usually work out a system of obligations, to which they hold themselves and seek to hold others. Now some matters can readily be embodied in rules—keeping the Sabbath, observing sacred festivals and fasts, adopting methodical times and habits of prayer, setting aside a tenth of one's gains for religious purposes. And some matters cannot be thus codified—having clean thoughts and generous sympathies, being conciliatory, honoring every human being, however unadmirable, as kin to God, serving him as his heavenly Father understandingly cares for him. And matters which can be incorporated in rules tend to be stressed above those which cannot be precisely defined. And when men have their beliefs and duties clearly stated, and are earnestly living by them, they are not apt to distinguish between more and less important items in their religious code: all of it is precious to them. They do not wish any of it changed. Sincere religion is inherently conservative. It deals with tested values.

Jesus scandalized them by disregarding practices which they considered God's Law. He broke the Sabbath shockingly. When asked to speak in the synagogues, His addresses upset many in the congregation. He associated with disreputable people—with loose women and with unpatriotic profiteering farmers of revenue. He touched the academic pride of their scholars: how should a carpenter correct their explanation of Scriptures which they had spent their lives in studying and for which they had the authority of recognized experts? Many of them had never heard Him for themselves, and at second or tenth hand, when the intervening hands are unfriendly, His sayings and doings appeared even more insufferable. From the outset He was surrounded in their minds with an atmosphere of suspicion. They sent spies to watch Him, and spies have a way of hearing what they fancy they are sent to hear. The Pharisees felt themselves guardians of the faith of Israel. Their fathers had fought and bled for it; their own lives were wrapped up in it; they were holding it in the dark days of Roman dominion for their children and children's children. Could they allow this Innovator, this Charlatan who made preposterous claims for Himself, to go on deceiving simple folk and perhaps wreck the Church? Quite apart from the embittering encounters Jesus had with some of them— encounters which may have been colored in our gospels by the subsequent strife between the Synagogue and the growing Christian Church, there was enough difference between His faith and life and theirs to rouse determined antagonism. In loyalty to God they must put an end to His mischievous career.

A second group were the inheritors of a lucrative commercial privilege—the aristocratic Sadducean priests who controlled the Temple area. They also were churchmen, but in comparison with the Pharisees, their religion was a subordinate and moderate interest. It was an inheritance which they cherished with an antiquarian's regard for its more primitive form. Their thought of Deity was of a remote and unaggressive Being, who left men to work out their own affairs, who certainly did not interfere or help by sending angelic spirits. God wished from Israel a seemly recognition in the maintenance of the time-honored ceremonies. For the rest they were broadminded. Their predecessors had welcomed the culture and customs of the Greeks, and they probably had a much more tolerant attitude in religion than the Pharisees. One might have picked up a Greek poem or drama in their homes; they were interested in the on-goings of the larger world; and after the manner of cultivated liberals they smiled in superior fashion on the narrow preoccupations of scribes with the details of the religious code. They were much more concerned with politics and finance than with religion. So long as Jesus remained in Galilee, they may never have heard of Him; or if some rumor of Him came to their ears, they would pay little attention to it. The alarm of the Pharisees over His teaching would have seemed to them a petty squabble which was no concern of theirs.

But when Jesus invaded the Temple precincts and created a commotion by overturning the tables of the money-changers, these gentlemen were roused. Here was a dangerous social Radical. Doubtless their leasing of space for booths in the outer court of the Temple had been criticized before, and there was popular talk over the prices of doves and lambs, and grumbling at the rate of exchange for the half-shekel. But this was the usual proletarian murmuring. Did they not provide a public convenience in these business arrangements? Were they not assisting worshippers in their religious duties? Did not the ancient Law clearly enjoin that the Temple tax should be paid in a particular coin? And must not someone supply facilities for exchanging the various currencies which pilgrims brought with them from all over the Empire for the proper silver piece? Was not four per cent a moderate broker's fee for such an exchange? The idea of this upcountry Agitator appearing and, without a word to anybody in authority, making this disturbance in the Temple court, and infecting the populace with the absurd notion that there should be no charge for perfectly legitimate ecclesiastical business! Where did He think animals for sacrifice would be procured? What did He consider a reasonable charge for exchange, if He called four per cent robbery? Who was He, anyhow, to take upon Himself to reform the financial methods of men whose forebears had derived their incomes unquestioned from these leases? His attack was a reflection not only upon them, but upon their honored fathers. Annas and Caiaphas had never seen the court of the Temple without booths and stalls; it was to them part of the natural order of things that cattle and doves should be sold there and money exchanged. Further they had been born to the tradition that the sacred area of the Temple belonged to the hereditary priesthood, and that they were to derive their support from its ceremonies. How could they understand the indignant feelings of Jesus? The charge, which the false witnesses brought, that He had threatened to destroy the Temple, may have had some slight basis in fact. Such statements are seldom made out of whole cloth. Jesus may have expressed the feeling that, if this Temple made with hands were destroyed, real religion might not lose much. That would disturb these gentlemen in their family sentiment, in their inherited faith, in their economic interests.

And they were politicians with a keen eye for the political situation. At the moment they were on fair terms with the Roman Empire and were allowed some freedom in the management of local affairs. A demagogue of this sort, as Caiaphas remarked, might stir up a political mess, and embroil them with the Roman authorities. Could they risk allowing Him to go on?[2]

A third figure among the crucifiers is the representative of imperialistic government. He seems to have been impressed by Jesus— more impressed than the scribes or the priests. We pity him as part of a system which our age feels to be inherently faulty. In theory at least we do not believe in one people governing another. It is bad

---

2. Doctor L. P. Jacks has said of our contemporary churches: "The gravamen of the charge against the Church is not so much that there are definite abuses in its corporate life as that there is a general atmosphere of acquiescence in all that is worldly and conventional. No one knows exactly what ideal of life the Church stands for, unless that it is that of a kindly and good-natured toleration of things as they are, with a mild desire that they may grow better in time, so far as that is compatible with the maintenance of existing vested interests." That is the position of the Sadducee; and Jesus touched it at its most sensitive point when He assailed vested interests [Coffin's note].

for both peoples. It creates such attitudes as one sees in this scene—the priests fawning upon the governor and Pilate overbearing toward them and insulting the nation by the derisive title he orders nailed above the Victim on the cross. But among imperialistic peoples few have understood their business as well as the Romans. They probably kept Judaea in better order than any native leader could have kept it. They governed brutally, but there are still many who think that inferiors must be made to know their place. Jesus had been struck with their haughty attitude: "Ye know that the rulers of the Gentiles lord it." It may have been partially a patriot's unwillingness to speak against His own countrymen before an overlord which sealed His lips in the judgment hall.

All our narratives agree that the governor was most reluctant to execute this Prisoner. He suggested expedient after expedient to obviate it. He tried everything except the direct course of following his conscience and seeking to deal justly towards the Man before him. The system of which he was a part entangled him. Rome asked her procurators to keep the tribute flowing steadily from their provinces and to maintain quiet. No governor wished complaints lodged against him with his superiors. Pilate had to live with these priests, and in the end it seemed easier to let them have their way with this Peasant from Galilee. He was poor and insignificant, and to this day justice is never the same for the unfriended sons of poverty as for the wealthy and influential. Paul, claiming his rights as a Roman citizen, was to have days in court his Master could not command.

To the last Pilate was uncomfortable about the case. He did his best to shift responsibility—on Herod, on the crowd, on the priests. But the priests knew their man and played skillfully upon his loyalties and his fears. The fourth evangelist makes them say: "If thou release this man, thou art not Cæsar's friend." Fidelity to Cæsar was both a Roman's patriotism and his religion. They were appealing to Pilate's principles, and they won their point. Pilate washed his hands, but throughout the centuries his name has been coupled with this event as responsible for it on the lips of thousands who repeat "crucified under Pontius Pilate."

A fourth figure among crucifiers, although he is hardly a decisive factor, is a man of the gay world—Herod Antipas. A scion of an able family, born to wealth and position, brought up in Rome at the imperial court, admitted to the fashionable society of the capital in the golden age of Augustus, a member of the smart set, he knew all about the latest delicacies of the table, had a keen eye for a beautiful dancer, and surrounded by boon companions lived for pleasure. Like many in similar circumstances in contemporary America he had a shabby marital record, having become infatuated with his half-brother's wife, for whom he divorced his own wife and whom he stole from her husband. But divorces even of this sordid variety were not bad form then, any more than they are among ourselves today, and bad form was the only taboo Herod revered. He had a reputation for political shrewdness, and he had burnt his fingers in handling one prophet, John, and was wary of repeating the blunder. Jesus dreaded what He called "the leaven of Herod"—loose morals, lavish outlay, and sharp politics. He had spoken of this tetrarch as "that fox." Now these two were face to face.

Herod displayed a man-of-the-world's versatility in asking Him "many questions"—one wonders what they were. He was clever and was pleased to display his knowledge of religious fine points before his companions and before the priests. It was a chance to impress them. But Herod could make nothing of Jesus. And Jesus could make nothing of Herod. He had borne witness to His Messiahship before Caiaphas and the Sanhedrin; He had admitted His kingship to Pontius Pilate; but He had not a syllable to utter to Antipas. The tetrarch had heard of him as a wonder-worker and craved the chance to see Him do something startling. But Jesus' mighty works are not tricks to entertain and astonish. Herod had a conscience; could not Jesus appeal to that with some piercing story such as Nathan told adulterous David?[3] Did the Saviour ever confront a needier sinner? But He had not a word for him.

Herod was apparently "past feeling," and Jesus gave him up. This clownish roysterer and his cronies could think of nothing to do with their disappointing Prisoner but tog Him out in mock finery and make game of Him. Fancy the mind of Jesus while this went on! It cost Pilate some struggle to condemn Him; but when He was sent away from the tetrarch's palace, Herod had been laughing at Him as a buffoon, and was now smiling at his own shrewdness in outwitting the governor, and handing his awkward case back to him.

A fifth figure among the crucifiers is a disillusioned idealist. We have no reason to think that the man of Kerioth did not enlist in the cause of Jesus from the same high motives as the other disciples. If anything it was harder for him, the only Judaean in the group, than for Galileans. He heard all that they heard and he shared all that they shared, and, like them, he was disappointed. He had looked for a different issue. Jesus outdistanced his ideals; he fancied that Jesus did not measure up to his ideals and he grew critical. With many the attempt "to go beyond themselves and wind themselves too high" is followed by a reaction. What he had hoped for, and hoped for immediately, did not happen, and Judas became bitter. He felt himself duped. The confident attitude of Jesus as He set His face to what seemed to Judas folly and defeat, irritated him.

3. See "Thou Art the Man" (pp. 1388–1390).

He was no longer the reasonable man he had been. It was that perhaps which led the disciples in retrospect to recall that the devil entered into him. They felt that he was at war with himself. And in such plight men not infrequently turn on those to whom they have been most warmly attached. Their disgust with themselves they are apt to vent on those who make them uncomfortable. Iago says of Cassio: "He hath a daily beauty in his life that makes me ugly." Jesus became hateful to Judas Iscariot. There may be a shred of truth in the theories which make his betrayal of the Master an attempt to force His hand, and compel Him to assume his power.

For what was it that Judas betrayed to the priests? Obviously not merely the spot where their police could arrest Jesus. That was not worth paying for. The police could follow him and find out His haunts. Probably Judas betrayed, as many modern interpreters think, the secret of Jesus' Messiahship, which was talked of in the inner circle but not published abroad. That was not clear to the priests or to the public even after the entry amid hosannas, for the shouts of a crowd are not evidence. Now they had a basis for trial, so Judas was in a sense forcing Jesus to declare Himself. But our narratives imply that Judas did it vindictively, not affectionately.

Disillusioned idealists become sour and cynical. And in cynicism conscience's unravel: Judas may easily have grown careless in handling the money in his custody. Avarice cannot have been the main motive in the betrayal, but greed has a place in most ignoble stories. Very trifling sums induce people still to hideous crimes. When a man is embittered, he is capable of anything, and it was a cynic who drove the shabby bargain with the chief priests and went out with thirty pieces of silver jingling in his purse and a betrayed Master on his conscience.

A sixth factor among the crucifiers is a crowd. The individuals who composed it were decent men, kind to their families and neighbors, and personally they would not have been cruel to this Prophet from Galilee. They had a prejudice against Him, and that prejudice was worked up until they were fused into a howling mob. In such a mass a man is lifted out of himself, loses control of his feelings, and his passions surge unchecked and augmented by the passions of the throng around him. He becomes a thousand times himself emotionally. Shakespeare's Bassanio speaks of

> The buzzing pleased multitude
> Whose every something being blent together
> Turns to a wild of nothing save of joy.

And the reverse is true when the crowd is prejudiced and their every something being blended together turns to a wild of nothing save of cruelty.

A crowd, being emotionally intense, is very suggestible. A catchword will set it off. Our propagandists and advertisers have taught us how we can be worked on in masses by names, phrases, pictures. And crowds are much more readily suggestible to the more primitive and coarser sentiments than to the finer. Man is a thinly varnished savage at best, lump him together in throngs and the varnish melts at the touch. When Pilate appeared unwilling to grant the priests' request, the crowd was swayed by nationalism; the priests were their own, and the governor the representative of the hated oppressor. They had a traditional right to claim clemency for a prisoner at the Passover. They will use it, and natural self-assertion impels them not to ask for One whom Pilate would gladly let them have. A suggestion is given them—Barabbas, a popular revolutionary of the crude type—a slogan for the emotions of a crowd.

Jesus can hardly have been popular. How much better "copy" for our own press Barabbas would be than the Teacher of Nazareth! Besides Barabbas is the nationalistic type Pilate would least like to release. Mobs feel and scarcely think. Could these men as individuals have calmly weighed Jesus and Barabbas, the result might have been different; but they were atingle with their cruder instincts. And a crowd which takes to shouting works itself to a violent pitch, and when thwarted can become fiendishly brutal. The spectators who packed the tiers of the Coliseum, turned down their thumbs at some fallen gladiator and yelled themselves hoarse demanding his death, would not have done anything of the sort by themselves. Each man in the crowd has lost his sense of personal responsibility. It is what men do in a social set, a political party, an economic group, a nation, a religious assembly, that is likely to be least moral and most diabolically savage. Pilate did his weak best not to execute Jesus; Herod found loutish amusement in Him, but showed no desire for His blood; Judas wished Him out of his way, but jail would have satisfied him; the crowd, with their tribal feelings roused—the instincts of the hunting pack—shouted "Crucify Him, crucify Him!"

A seventh factor among the crucifiers was a guard of soldiers. Jesus never spoke harshly of the military profession. One of His rare compliments was paid to an officer who had expressed his faith in terms of soldierly obedience. And probably it was in extenuation of the legionaries charged with the grim details of His execution that He prayed: "Father, forgive them, for they know not what they do." But it was by men prepared for their task by military discipline that He was done to death at Golgotha.

That system is deliberately planned to depersonalize those whom it trains. They are educated not to decide for themselves, but to give machine-like response to a command. Such a system, while it has noble associations with courage, loyalty, honor, and self-effacement, counteracts that which Christianity tries hardest to create—a reasoning conscience. The soldiers who scourged Jesus and spiked His hands and feet to the beams of the cross never thought what they were doing—they were victims of a discipline which had crucified their moral judgments.

Their occupation was held in high honor as the typical and most essential patriotic service. Rome ruled by physical might. She believed in awing inferior peoples and encouraged her soldiers to strike terror into them. The scourging which Pilate ordered—"the terrible preface," as it was called, to capital punishment—was forbidden for Roman citizens, but it was customary for provincials. A small guard was ordered to inflict on Jesus this appalling indignity in public—stripping Him, binding Him to a stake in a stooping position with hands behind Him, and beating Him with thongs at the ends of which were leaden balls or sharp-pointed bones.

And when that prostrating ordeal was over they took Him for further maltreatment to the privacy of the guardroom. Brutal mockery of the condemned was allowed the soldiers in order to maintain their *morale*. All the finer feelings must be overcome in those whose trade is iron and blood. And privacy seems to be an inevitable temptation to men with fellow-beings in their power. Schoolboys, jailors, keepers of the weak in mind or body, generation after generation, have to be watched against outbreaks of savagery to their victims. It was expected of the soldiers—a crude comic interlude of their rough day. But in fairness to these systematically hardened men let us recall that when the Prisoner was uplifted on the cross, slowly bleeding to death in agony, educated and revered religious leaders, professors of divinity, vented their detestation of Him with gibes. Theological animosity renders men as callous as professional hangmen.

Perhaps more so, for these soldiers had to restrain themselves from feeling by gambling at the foot of the cross. They had to sit by while the crucified writhed, and groaned, and cried, in their prolonged misery. It is not surprising that they resorted to the excitement of playing dice as a mental relief. They are typical representatives of callings into which men cannot put themselves—their minds and consciences and hearts. Such callings rob those who engage in them of moral vitality and make them fit agents of tragic occurrences like Calvary.

But there is still an eighth factor without which the crucifixion would not have taken place—the public. Behind the chief actors in the drama at Golgotha we see thousands of obscure figures—the populace of the city. One fancies them getting up in the morning and hearing rumors of a case on before the governor. The city, crowded with Passover pilgrims, would be more excitable and talkative than usual, and news of events at the palace, involving the Sanhedrin, would spread rapidly. Then, as people were in the midst of their morning's work, they would catch sight of that sinister procession tramping through the streets on the way to the place of execution outside the city wall. We can overhear such remarks as "Hello! another hanging today? Who's to be hung? Those two bandits? Who's the third prisoner? That Prophet from Galilee? Oh, they got Him very quickly, didn't they?" And as prisoners and guards filed past, the day's work was resumed.

Behind all earth's tragedies there is a public whose state of mind has much to do with the central event. Even under the least democratic government the authorities dare not go more than a certain distance without the popular will. The thousands of uncaring nobodies, to whom what was done with Jesus was a matter of indifference, gave scribes and priests and governor their chance. These obscure folk felt themselves without responsibility. What had they to do with this Prophet from the north country who had ridden into the city, hailed by a crowd of provincial pilgrims? Possibly it was of them that Jesus was thinking—the public of the capital city—when He said: "O Jerusalem, Jerusalem, that killeth the prophets."

The public is never of one mind; it represents various shades of opinion and feeling—sympathetic, hostile, indifferent; and all shades were there in Jerusalem. But if enough of its inhabitants had really cared about Jesus, He would never have been crucified. The chief handicap of the public is ignorance. The mass of the dwellers in Jerusalem knew next to nothing about the Prophet from Galilee. But Jesus did not weep over them merely because of their lack of information. Religious capitals, like cathedral towns, are proverbially hard to move. Religion was an old story to those who lived in the neighborhood of the venerable Temple and were familiar with the figures of the great doctors of the Law. They were complacent in sacred traditions of the past and not open to fresh incomings of the Most High. Jesus wept over their apathy. To Him it seemed that even unfeeling stones must respond to One who so manifestly represented God. They did not know the things which belonged to peace because they did not wish to know them. Jerusalem slew the Son of God not only because He had won the sharp ill-will of the powerful few, but also because the many did not want to be bothered with Him. And the public of Jerusalem, who thought the fate of this Stranger none of their business, had to bear the doom with their as-yet-unborn children; for judgment brings home social obligations and convinces us that by a myriad unsuspected cords men are tied up in one bundle of life in cities, in nations, in races, and in a world of men. These thousands of citizens of Jerusalem never went through the form of washing their hands, like Pilate. They were unaware of any accountability for this execution. But history with its destruction of the city rendered its verdict upon them.

Such a survey of the factors which crucified Jesus—and a course
rather than a single sermon is obviously necessary to treat them
with sufficient explicitness—forces men to think. This was the
world which executed the Life subsequent generations until this
hour revere as the best earth has seen. And plainly it is the world in
which we still live. All these forces are present and active in our
society—religious intolerance, commercial privilege, political expediency, pleasure-loving irresponsibility, unfaithfulness, the mob
spirit, militarism, public apathy. These are perennial evils. They are
deep-seated in the very structure of human society. The forms of
political and economic and ecclesiastical organization may alter,
but these remain under all forms. We should find them in a socialist republic or a communist state, as surely as in an imperial despotism or a capitalist regime. Moreover, they act and react upon each
other. The priests help Judas to his treachery and incite the mob;
Pilate stimulates the priests to play politics; the political methods
of both governor and religious leaders keep the public morally
indifferent; their sinister motives interweave into a corporate force
for evil. Together they make up what Jesus called "the power of
darkness," the satanic kingdom.

It is significant that the national and ecclesiastical capital is the
slayer of the prophets. Evil organizes itself with this inherent solidarity and possesses a group—a church, a nation, a race. These
forces were present in the villages and towns of Galilee, but they
came to a focus where the organization of the Jewish Church and
the Jewish nation had its seat, and where the representative of
imperial government exercised his power. Wickedness is a racial
force. It propagates itself generation after generation. Jesus recognized the unity of the factors with which He was struggling with
similar factors, which had always been present in the life of His
people, when He spoke of this generation which was crucifying
Him having upon it "all the righteous blood shed on earth," from
the blood of Abel on the first pages of the Jewish Bible to the
blood of Zachariah recorded on its last pages. Evil spreads itself
laterally, building up a corporate force of wickedness, and passes
itself on from age to age, linking the generations in a solidarity of
sin.

When we examine the factors which slew Jesus, we recognize
them at once as contemporaries. We can attach modern names to
them. There is nothing abnormal or unusual about these men who
rear the cross: they are acting true to type—a type which recurs
century after century throughout history. They are average folk.
We must not blacken their characters. John Stuart Mill, whose ethical judgments are singularly dispassionate, says of them:

They were not worse than men commonly are, but rather the contrary, men who possessed in a full, or somewhat more than a full measure the religious, moral, and patriotic feelings of their people; the very kind of men who in all times, our own included, have every chance of passing through life blameless and unspotted.

We can think of no more high-minded young man than the student of Gamaliel, Saul of Tarsus, and we know how cordially he approved the course taken by the leaders of Israel in putting Jesus out of the way.

We can easily multiply from history and literature men far more villainous—a Caesar Borgia or an Iago, for instance. Indeed we can find more depraved figures in almost any community, if we look for them. But the purpose of Jesus and the purposes of even good people clash. The inevitableness of the crucifixion is brought home to us. The issue between the motives of Jesus and those of the mass of mankind is thrown into light. They are irreconcilable. Life is a desperately real struggle between mutually destroying forces. If the motives of Jesus prevail, the factors that slew Him will cease to be. If the motives of Caiaphas and Pilate, of the mob, the soldiers, and the public prevail—there is an execution: "Away with such a fellow from the earth."

There are three crosses on Calvary: on two of them society is trying to rid itself of predatory bandits, on the third it placed One whom it considered also its enemy, perhaps a worse enemy since He was placed on the central cross. We level up with our standards of right, and we also level down. He who is above the conscience of the community is as likely to be slain as he who is below. This is our world; this is the society in which we move; these are the types of people with whom we associate; this is the public to which we belong. The slayers of Jesus are our relatives, kinsmen in thought and feeling. A sense of complicity in what they did comes upon us. We are bound up with them in this bundle of human life. The corporate evil which dominated first-century Palestine and moved these men to kill their Best dominates our world and is compassing similar fell results. Trails of blood lead to our doors. Wretched men that we are, who shall deliver us out of this social body of death?

And these factors are not only about us, they are also within us. As we scan these men who sent Jesus to His death—devout Pharisee and conservative Sadducee, Roman politician and false friend, emotional mob and unthinking soldiers, the host of indifferent or approving faces of the public behind them—their motives and feelings have been and are our own. You may recall in Hawthorne's *Mosses from an Old Manse* the scene where, going through the virtuoso's collection, he nearly falls over a huge bundle, like a peddler's pack, done up in sackcloth and very securely strapped and corded. " 'It is Christian's burden of sin,' said the virtuoso. 'O pray, let me see it,' cried I. 'For many a year I have longed to know its contents.' 'Look into your own conscience and memory,' replied the virtuoso. 'You will there find a list of whatever it contained.' " It is so with the motives of those who planned and carried out the death of Jesus. We do not need to ask: "Lord, is it I?" We are aware of belonging in this same realm of darkness, and of having dealt with His brethren very much as He was dealt with. As we think of ourselves, we shudder—"God, be merciful to me, a sinner."

Men speak of the absence of the sense of sin in our time. It has never been vigorous in any age, save as some judgment of history or the disturbing presence of the ideal has created it. We have witnessed a judgment on a colossal scale in the World War—a judgment upon our entire civilization. Some of us said to ourselves, feeling mankind in the grip of overmastering social forces of passion and greed and brutality: "Now is your hour and the power of darkness." And we know ourselves a long way yet from redemption from the motives which brought it on. Underneath the ease and comfort of our day there is restless discontent. Some of it is crassly materialistic—the common envy of the have-nots for the haves, the craving of the have-littles to have more. But souls are never satisfied with things. Life is in relationships, human and divine, in purposes. And men are dissatisfied with the quality of life. To take them to Calvary and show them the factors which nailed Jesus on the cross is to uncover for them a far more terrible world than they dreamed they were in, and to uncover for them themselves.

This gives us an inkling of Jesus' reason for putting Himself into men's hands and letting them do with Him as they would. His broken and bleeding body on the cross is the exposure of a murderous world. The Crucified becomes one with the unrecognized and misused and cruelly treated in every age. The nail-pierced Figure on Calvary haunts our race as a symbol of what is forever taking place generation after generation, and of what each of us has his part in.

Readers of Ibsen's drama *Emperor and Galilean* will recall how Julian is made to ask—

Where is He now? Has He been at work elsewhere since that happened at Golgotha?

I dreamed of Him lately. I dreamed that I had subdued the whole world. I ordained that the memory of the Galilean should be rooted out on earth; and it was rooted out. Then the spirits came and ministered to me, and bound wings on my shoulders, and I soared aloft into infinite space, till my feet rested on another world.

It was another world than mine. Its curve was vaster, its light more golden, and many moons circled around it. Then I looked down at my own earth—the Emperor's earth that I had made Galileanless—and I thought that all that I had done was very good.

But behold there came a procession by me on the strange earth where I stood. There were soldiers and judges and executioners at the head of it and weeping women followed. And lo, in the midst of the slow-moving array, was the Galilean, alive and bearing a cross on His back. Then I called to Him and said, "Whither away, Galilean?" And He turned His face to me and smiled, nodded slowly and said, "To the place of the skull."

Where is He now? What if that at Golgotha, near Jerusalem, was but a wayside matter, a thing done as it were in passing! What if He goes on and on, and suffers and dies, and conquers, again and again, from world to world!

It is a vivid way of picturing the solidarity of the worlds of every generation, each offering its Golgotha. It is there that men come to themselves and realize their plight and the plight of society. Walter Pater said that "the way to perfection is through a series of disgusts." To let men see the factors which enact the tragedy outside the wall of Jerusalem is to disgust them with their world and with themselves. If some protest that this is not a wholesome state of mind, one may answer in the words of that robust thinker, Walter Bagehot: "So long as men are very imperfect, a sense of great imperfection should cleave to them." It is a necessary part of the process towards genuine healthy-mindedness. When they realize what caused the torture and execution of Jesus, they cry, "O not that! Such a world is intolerable!" And made conscious that they are builders of such worlds, and that their hands are stained, they hunger and thirst after righteousness.

QUESTIONS

1. Indicate each of the principal groups and figures who, by Coffin's account, contributed to the crucifixion of Christ. What leading motive does Coffin ascribe to each? How does Coffin show these motives to be perennial ones, operative now as then? Why does he do so?

2. Examine each of the transitions Coffin makes. How does he proceed from one part to another in his essay? How does he relate part to part? What order of progression is discernible in the essay?

3. Coffin accords the Pharisees considerable praise. Why? What does he imply to be the essential fault of the Pharisees? In what respects does he compare and contrast the Pharisees and Sadducees?

4. Coffin refers (p. 1477) to the "motives of Jesus," but he does not delineate these or discuss them in full. To what extent has he indirectly indicated them in his account of the principal groups and figures contributing to the crucifixion?

5. Consider Coffin's title. Why has he asked precisely that question? Might he just as well have given as title "Who Crucified Christ?" Explain.

C. S. LEWIS
On "Special Providences"[1]

In this book the reader has heard of two classes of events and two only—miracles and natural events. The former are not interlocked with the history of Nature in the backward direction—i.e., in the time before their occurrence. The latter are. Many pious people, however, speak of certain events as being "providential" or "special providences" without meaning that they are miraculous. This generally implies a belief that, quite apart from miracles, some events are providential in a sense in which some others are not. Thus some people thought that the weather which enabled us to bring off so much of our army at Dunkirk was "providential" in some way in which weather as a whole is not providential. The Christian doctrine that some events, though not miracles, are yet answers to prayer, would seem at first to imply this.

I find it very difficult to conceive an intermediate class of events which are neither miraculous nor merely "ordinary." Either the weather at Dunkirk was or was not that which the previous physical history of the universe, by its own character, would inevitably produce. If it was, then how is it "specially" providential? If it was not, then it was a miracle.

It seems to me, therefore, that we must abandon the idea that there is any special class of events (apart from miracles) which can be distinguished as "specially providential." Unless we are to abandon the conception of Providence altogether, and with it the belief in efficacious prayer, it follows that all events are equally providential. If God directs the course of events at all then he directs the movement of every atom at every moment; "not one sparrow falls to the ground"[2] without that direction. The "naturalness" of natural events does not consist in being somehow outside God's providence. It consists in their being interlocked with one another inside a common space-time in accordance with the fixed pattern of the "laws."

In order to get any picture at all of a thing, it is sometimes necessary to begin with a false picture and then correct it. The false picture of Providence (false because it represents God and Nature as being both contained in a common Time) would be as follows. Every event in Nature results from some previous event, not from the laws of Nature. In the long run the first natural event, whatever it was, has dictated every other event. That is, when

---

1. An appendix to *Miracles*, 1947.
2. The allusion is to Matthew x. 29-31: "Are not two sparrows sold for a farthing? and one of them shall not fall on the ground without your Father. / But the very hairs of your head are all numbered. / Fear ye not therefore, ye are of more value than many sparrows."

God at the moment of creation fed the first event into the framework of the "laws"—first set the ball rolling—He determined the whole history of Nature. Foreseeing every part of that history, He intended every part of it. If He had wished for different weather at Dunkirk He would have made the first event slightly different.

The weather we actually had is therefore in the strictest sense providential; it was decreed, and decreed for a purpose, when the world was made—but no more so (though more interestingly to us) than the precise position at this moment of every atom in the ring of Saturn.

It follows (still retaining our false picture) that every physical event was determined so as to serve a great number of purposes.

Thus God must be supposed in pre-determining the weather at Dunkirk to have taken fully into account the effect it would have not only on the destiny of two nations but (what is incomparably more important) on all the individuals involved on both sides, on all animals, vegetables and minerals within range, and finally on every atom in the universe. This may sound excessive, but in reality we are attributing to the Omniscient only an infinitely superior degree of the same kind of skill which a mere human novelist exercises daily in constructing his plot.

Suppose I am writing a novel. I have the following problems on my hands: (1) Old Mr. A. has got to be dead before Chapter 15. (2) And he'd better die suddenly because I have to prevent him from altering his will. (3) His daughter (my heroine) has got to be kept out of London for three chapters at least. (4). My hero has somehow got to recover the heroine's good opinion which he lost in Chapter 7. (5) That young prig B., who has to improve before the end of the book, needs a bad moral shock to take the conceit out of him. (6) We haven't decided on B's job yet; but the whole development of his character will involve giving him a job and showing him actually at work. How on earth am I to get in all these six things? . . . I have it. What about a railway accident? Old A. can be killed in it, and that settles him. In fact the accident can occur while he is actually going up to London to see his solicitor with the very purpose of getting his will altered. What more natural than that his daughter should run up with him? We'll have her slightly injured in the accident: that'll prevent her reaching London for as many chapters as we need. And the hero can be on the same train. He can behave with great coolness and heroism during the accident—probably he'll rescue the heroine from a burning carriage. That settles my fourth point. And the young prig B.? We'll make him the signalman whose negligence caused the accident. That gives him his moral shock and also links him up with the main plot. In fact, once we have thought of the railway accident, that single event will solve six apparently separate problems.

No doubt this is in some ways an intolerably misleading image:

firstly because (except as regards the prig B.) I have been thinking not of the ultimate good of my characters but of the entertainment of my readers: secondly because we are simply ignoring the effect of the railway accident on all the other passengers in that train: and finally because it is I who make B. give the wrong signal. That is, though I pretend that he has free will, he really hasn't. In spite of these objections, however, the example may perhaps suggest how Divine ingenuity could so contrive the physical "plot" of the universe as to provide a "providential" answer to the needs of innumerable creatures.

But some of these creatures have free will. It is at this point that we must begin to correct the admittedly false picture of Providence which we have hitherto been using. That picture, you will remember, was false because it represented God and Nature as inhabiting a common Time. But it is probable that Nature is not really in Time and almost certain that God is not. Time is probably (like perspective) the mode of our perception. There is therefore in reality no question of God's at one point in time (the moment of creation) adapting the material history of the universe in advance to free acts which you or I are to perform at a later point in Time. To Him all the physical events and all the human acts are present in an eternal Now. The liberation of finite wills and the creation of the whole material history of the universe (related to the acts of those wills in all the necessary complexity) is to Him a single operation. In this sense God did not create the universe long ago but creates it at this minute—at every minute.

Suppose I find a piece of paper on which a black wavy line is already drawn. I can now sit down and draw other lines (say in red) so shaped as to combine with the black line into a pattern. Let us now suppose that the original black line is conscious. But it is not conscious along its whole length at once—only of each point on that length in turn.

Its consciousness in fact is travelling along that line from left to right retaining point A only as a memory when it reaches B and unable until it has left B to become conscious of C. Let us also give this black line free will. It chooses the direction it goes in. The particular wavy shape of it is the shape it wills to have. But whereas it is aware of its own chosen shape only moment by moment and does not know at point D which way it will decide to turn at point F, I can see its shape as a whole and all at once. At every moment it will find my red lines waiting for it and adapted to it. Of course: because I, in composing the total red-and-black design have the whole course of the black line in view and take it into account. It is a matter not of impossibility but merely of designer's skill for me to devise red lines which at every point have a right relation not only to the black line but to one another so as to fill the whole paper with a satisfactory design.

In this model the black line represents a creature with free will, the red lines represent material events, and I represent God. The model would of course be more accurate if I were making the paper as well as the pattern and if there were hundreds of millions of black lines instead of one—but for the sake of simplicity we must keep it as it is.[3]

It will be seen that if the black line addressed prayers to me I might (if I chose) grant them. It prays that when it reaches point N it may find the red lines arranged around it in a certain shape. That shape may by the laws of design require to be balanced by other arrangements of red lines on quite different parts of the paper —some at the top or bottom so far away from the black line that it knows nothing about them: some so far to the left that they come before the beginning of the black line, some so far to the right that they come after its end. (The black line would call these parts of the paper, "The time before I was born," and, "The time after I'm dead.") But these other parts of the pattern demanded by that red shape which Black Line wants at N, do not prevent my granting its prayer. For his whole course has been visible to me from the moment I looked at the paper and his requirements at point N are among the things I took into account in deciding the total pattern.

Most of our prayers if fully analyzed, ask either for a miracle or for events whose foundation will have to have been laid before I was born, indeed, laid when the universe began. But then to God (though not to me) I and the prayer I make in 1945 were just as much present at the creation of the world as they are now and will be a million years hence. God's creative act is timeless and timelessly adapted to the "free" elements within it: but this timeless adaptation meets our consciousness as a sequence of prayer and answer.

Two corollaries follow:

1. People often ask whether a given event (not a miracle) was really an answer to prayer or not. I think that if they analyze their thought they will find they are asking, "Did God bring it about for a special purpose or would it have happened anyway as part of the natural course of events?" But this (like the old question, "Have you left off beating your wife?") makes either answer impossible. In the play, *Hamlet*, Ophelia climbs out on a branch overhanging a river: the branch breaks, she falls in and drowns. What would you reply if anyone asked, "Did Ophelia die because Shakespeare for poetic reasons wanted her to die at that moment—or because the branch broke?" I think one would have to say, "For both reasons." Every event in the play happens as a result of other events in the

3. Admittedly all I have done is to turn the tables by making human volitions the constant and physical destiny the variable. This is as false as the opposite view; the point is that it is no falser. A subtler image of creation and freedom (or rather, creation of the free and the unfree in a single timeless act) would be the *almost* simultaneous mutual adaptation in the movements of two expert dancing partners [Lewis' note].

play, but also every event happens because the poet wants it to happen. All events in the play are Shakespearian events; similarly all events in the real world are providential events. All events in the play, however, come about (or ought to come about) by the dramatic logic of events. Similarly all events in the real world (except miracles) come about by natural causes. "Providence" and Natural causation are not alternatives; both determine every event because both are one.

2. When we are praying about the result, say, of a battle or a medical consultation the thought will often cross our minds that (if only we knew it) the event is already decided one way or the other. I believe this to be no good reason for ceasing our prayers. The event certainly has been decided—in a sense it was decided "before all worlds." But one of the things taken into account in deciding it, and therefore one of the things that really cause it to happen, may be this very prayer that we are now offering. Thus, shocking as it may sound, I conclude that we can at noon become part causes of an event occurring at ten o'clock. (Some scientists would find this easier than popular thought does.) The imagination will, no doubt, try to play all sorts of tricks on us at this point. It will ask, "Then if I stop praying can God go back and alter what has already happened?" No. The event has already happened and one of its causes has been the fact that you are asking such questions instead of praying. It will ask, "Then if I begin to pray can God go back and alter what has already happened?" No. The event has already happened and one of its causes is your present prayer. Thus something does really depend on my choice. My free act contributes to the cosmic shape. That contribution is made in eternity or "before all worlds"; but my consciousness of contributing reaches me at a particular point in the time-series.

The following question may be asked: If we can reasonably pray for an event which must in fact have happened or failed to happen several hours ago, why can we not pray for an event which we know *not* to have happened? *e.g.*, pray for the safety of someone who, as we know, was killed yesterday. What makes the difference is precisely our knowledge. The known event states God's will. It is psychologically impossible to pray for what we know to be unobtainable; and if it were possible the prayer would sin against the duty of submission to God's known will.

One more consequence remains to be drawn. It is never possible to prove empirically that a given, non-miraculous event was or was not an answer to prayer. Since it was non-miraculous the sceptic can always point to its natural causes and say, "Because of these it would have happened anyway," and the believer can always reply, "But because these were only links in a chain of events, hanging on other links, and the whole chain hanging upon God's will, they may have occurred because someone prayed." The efficacy of prayer, therefore, cannot be either asserted or denied without an exercise of the will—the will choosing or rejecting faith in the light of a whole philosophy. Experimental evidence there can be none on either side. In the sequence M.N.O. event N, unless it is a miracle, is always caused by M and causes O; but the real question is whether the total series (say A–Z) does or does not originate in a will that can take human prayers into account.

This impossibility of empirical proof is a spiritual necessity. A man who knew empirically that an event had been caused by his prayer would feel like a magician. His head would turn and his heart would be corrupted. The Christian is not to ask whether this or that event happened because of a prayer. He is rather to believe that all events without exception are *answers* to prayer in the sense that whether they are grantings or refusals the prayers of all concerned and their needs have all been taken into account. All prayers are heard, though not all prayers are granted. We must not picture destiny as a film unrolling for the most part on its own, but in which our prayers are sometimes allowed to insert additional items. On the contrary; what the film displays to us as it unrolls already contains the results of our prayers and of all our other acts. There is no question *whether* an event has happened because of your prayer. When the event you prayed for occurs your prayer has always contributed to it. When the opposite event occurs your prayer has never been ignored; it has been considered and refused, for your ultimate good and the good of the whole universe. (For example, because it is better for you and for everyone else in the long run that other people, including wicked ones, should exercise free will than that you should be protected from cruelty or treachery by turning the human race into automata.) But this is, and must remain, a matter of faith. You will, I think, only deceive yourself by trying to find special evidence for it in some cases more than in others.

QUESTIONS

1. Why does Lewis find it "necessary to begin with a false picture and then correct it"? Trace the steps by which he makes the "correction."

2. What point does Lewis illustrate with his sketch of the plot of an imaginary novel? Explain whether the illustration is appropriate or not.

3. Compare Lewis' extended analogy of the black wavy line with one of the briefer analogies among the parables in Matthew xiii (pp. 1390–1393). What do they have in common? How do they differ?

4. Why does Lewis add his two corollaries? Explain whether his essay would have been incomplete without them.

5. How might Lewis' piece differ if it had been prepared as a sermon to be preached from a pulpit?

Notes on Composition

Saying Something That Matters

There is no point in the hard labor of writing unless you expect to *do* something to somebody—perhaps add to his store of information, perhaps cause him to change his mind on some issue that you care about. Determining just what that something is is half the battle; hence the importance of knowing your main point, your central purpose in writing, your **thesis**. It may seem that this step—perhaps in the form of a "thesis sentence" or exact statement of the main point—is inevitably prior to everything else in writing, but in actual practice the case is more complicated. Few good writers attain a final grasp of their thesis until they have tried setting down their first halting ideas at some length; to put it another way, you discover more precisely what it is you have to say in the act of trying to say it. Formulating and refining upon a thesis sentence as you work your way through a piece of writing helps you see what needs to be done at each stage; the finished piece, though, instead of announcing its thesis in any one sentence, may simply imply it by the fact of its unity, the determinate way the parts hang together. There is probably no single sentence in Hannah Arendt's "Denmark and the Jews" (p. 1164) that will serve satisfactorily to represent the entire essay in miniature, yet clearly such a sentence could be formulated: Open resistance frankly based on ethical principle achieved a success in Denmark out of all proportion to the Danes' capacity to attain their ends by force. But whether you state the main point or leave it to be inferred, you need to decide what your piece is about, what you want to say about it, why, and to whom.

Sometimes a thesis will rest on a good many **assumptions**, related ideas that the writer may not mention but depends upon his reader to understand and agree to (if he is an honest writer) or to overlook and hence fail to reject (if his real purpose is to mislead). Stanley Milgram (p. 413) appears to assume that practicing deception on another person and even causing him considerable suffering are justifiable in the name of scientific inquiry.

We may feel that the question is highly ambiguous, or we may disagree sharply. But even if we decide, finally, that we can live with Milgram's assumption, we shall have acquired a fuller understanding of what he is saying, and of our own relationship to it, for having scrutinized what is being taken for granted. The habit of scrutiny guards us against the careless or cunning writer whose unstated assumptions may be highly questionable. The same habit, turned on our own minds when we become writers, can save us from the unthinking use of assumptions that we would be hard pressed to defend.

Some theses lend themselves to verification by laboratory methods or the like; they deal with **questions of fact.** The exact order of composition of Shakespeare's plays could conceivably be settled finally if new evidence turned up. Whether or not the plays are great literature, on the other hand, is a **question of opinion**; agreement (though not hard to reach in this instance) depends on the weighing of arguments rather than on tests or measurements. Not that all theses can be neatly classified as assertions either of fact or of opinion (consider "Shakespeare's influence has been greater than Newton's"); still the attempt to classify his own effort can help a writer understand what he is doing.

Sometimes a writer addresses himself more specifically to his readers' **understanding,** sometimes he addresses himself chiefly to their **emotions.** Although the processes of thinking and of feeling are almost always mixed, still it is obvious that a description of a chemical process and a description of a candidate you hope to see elected to office will differ considerably in tone and emphasis. Accordingly you need to give some thought to the kind of result you hope to produce: perhaps simply an addition of information, perhaps a change of attitude, perhaps a commitment of the will to action.

The Means of Saying It

No worthwhile thesis comes without work, and the work of arriving at a thesis is much like the work of writing itself—developing, elaborating, refining upon an idea that is perhaps at first hazy. For convenience the process may be divided into setting bounds, or defining; marshaling evidence; and drawing conclusions.

DEFINING in a broad sense may be thought of as what you do to answer the question "What do you mean?" It sets bounds by doing two things to an idea: grouping it with others like it and showing how it differs from those others. "An island is a tract of land" (like a lot or prairie or peninsula) "completely surrounded by water and too small to be called a continent" (and therefore different from a lot, etc.). This process of classifying and distinguishing may take many forms, depending on the kind of thing you are dealing with and your reason for doing so. (Artifacts, for example, can hardly be defined without reference to purpose; a lock is a device *for securing* a door; a theodolite is an instrument used *to measure* horizontal or vertical angles.) Some of the standard methods are these: by giving **examples,** pointing to an instance as a short way of indicating class and individual characteristics ("*That* is a firebreak"; "A liberal is a man like Jefferson"); by **negating,** explaining what your subject is *not*—i.e., process of elimination ("Love vaunteth not itself, is not puffed up"); by **comparing and contrasting,** noting the resemblances and differences between your subject and something else ("A magazine is sometimes as big as a book but differs in binding and layout"); by **analyzing,** breaking down a whole into its constituent parts ("A play may be seen as exposition, rising action, and denouement"); by seeking a **cause** of the thing in question or an **effect** that it has produced ("Scurvy is the result of a dietary deficiency and often leads to anemia"); or by attributing to a thing an **end** or **means**, seeing it as a way of fulfilling purpose or as the fulfillment of a purpose ("Representation is the end of the electoral system and the means to good government").

When we turn to specimens of writing, we see immediately that the various methods of defining may serve not only for one-sentence "dictionary" definitions but also as methods of organizing paragraphs or even whole essays, where unfolding the subject is in a sense "defining" it, showing where its boundaries lie. John Rader Platt begins by saying in effect, "To understand what is meant by 'style' in science, let us compare two characteristic attitudes toward scientific investigation" (p. 1250). D. H. Lawrence (p. 1032), arguing that liberty as it is known in America is flawed, traces the flaw to what he takes to be its cause in historical circumstances. Walter Lippmann (p. 1006) opens our eyes to realities that are not immediately apparent by showing us that political opposition is indispensable if the party in power is to provide effective leadership. The choice of method in the above examples, it will be noted, is not random; each author selects according to his purpose in writing, and what suits one purpose exactly might be exactly wrong for another.

MARSHALING EVIDENCE. Once you have said what you mean, the next question is likely to be "How do you know?" Marshaling evidence may be thought of as what you do to answer that question. Where the matter at hand involves questions of fact, **factual evidence** will be most directly appropriate. (A diary, a letter—perhaps a cryptogram hidden in the text— might prove even to die-hard Baconians that Shakespeare himself did in fact write the plays which have been credited to him). Writers on scientific subjects inevitably draw chiefly on facts, often intricately arrayed, to support their conclusions. But it should not be assumed that factual evidence turns up mainly in scientific writing. W. H. Lewis' account of the cruel life endured by slaves on seventeenth-century French galleys is obviously based largely on facts in the form of historical documents, and even the preacher John Donne, arguing that the arrow of temptation often overtakes us simply because we cannot bring ourselves to walk resolutely away from it (p. 817), plainly appeals to facts with which most of us are only too familiar.

Factual evidence is generally thought to carry more weight than any other kind, though the force of a fact is greatly diminished if it is not easily verifiable or attested to by reliable witnesses. Where factual evidence is hard to come by (consider the problems of proving that Bacon did not write Shakespeare's plays), the opinion of **authorities** is often invoked, on the assumption that the men most knowledgeable in a field are most likely to judge truly in a particular case. The testimony of authorities is relevant, of course, not only in questions of fact but also in questions of opinion. William G. Perry, Jr. (p. 328), arguing for the student who "bulled" his way through an examination, implicitly invokes college professors *en masse* as authority for the idea that "bull" is closer than might be supposed to the goal of a liberal education. In general, however, the appeal to authority in matters of opinion has lost the rhetorical effectiveness it once had. Edmund Wilson's treatment of Emily Post (p. 472) is representative of a modern tendency—not necessarily unhealthy—to be highly skeptical of "authoritative" opinions.

As changes in the nature of the question draw in a larger and larger number of "authorities," evidence from authority shades into what might be called "the **common consent** of mankind," those generalizations about human experience that large numbers of readers can be counted upon to accept and that often find expression in proverbs or apothegms: "Risk no more than you can afford to lose" and "The first step toward Hell is halfway there." Such generalizations, whether proverbial or not, are a common ground on which writer and reader meet in agreement. The writer's task is to find and present the ones applicable to his particular thesis and then demonstrate that applicability.

DRAWING CONCLUSIONS. One of the ways of determining the consequences of thought—that is, drawing conclusions—is the process of applying generalizations (**deduction**): "If we should risk no more than we can afford to lose, then we had better not jeopardize the independence of our universities by seeking federal aid." Another way of arriving at conclusions is the process of **induction**, which consists in forming generalizations from a sufficient number of observed instances: "Since universities *A*, *B*, and *C* have been accepting federal aid through research grants for years without loss of independence, it is probably safe for any university to do so." Typically deduction and induction work reciprocally, each helping to supply for the other the materials upon which inference operates. We induce from experience that green apples are sour; we deduce from this generalization that a particular green apple is sour. A third kind of inference, sometimes regarded as only a special kind of deduction or induction, is **analogy**, the process of concluding that two things which resemble each other in one way will resemble each other in another way also: "Federal aid has benefited mental hospitals enormously, and will probably benefit universities just as much." An analogy proves nothing, although it may help the reader see the reasonableness of an idea and is often extremely valuable for purposes of illustration, since it makes an unknown clearer by relating it to a known.

Turning to our essays, we can see something of the variety of ways in which these three kinds of inference manifest themselves in serious writing: Thomas Jefferson deducing from certain self-evident truths the inescapable conclusion that the colonies should declare their independence of Great Britain (p. 992); a New Testament parable adumbrating the kingdom of heaven by drawing an analogy between it and a mustard seed (p. 1390); C. S. Lewis explicating a knotty point in the Christian idea of God by likening God to a novelist (p. 1480).

Such a list of examples suggests that in good writing the conclusions the writer draws, the consequences of his thought, are "consequential" in more than one sense: not only do they follow logically from the evidence he has considered, they are also *significant;* they relate directly or indirectly to aspects of our lives that we care about. To the questions suggested earlier as demands for definition and evidence, then, we must add a third. "What do you mean?" calls for precision yet admits answers vast in scope. "How do you know?" trims the vastness down to what can be substantiated but may settle for triviality as the price of certainty. The appropriate question to raise finally, then, is simply "So what?" and the conclusions we as writers draw need to be significant enough to yield answers to that question. We have come full circle back to the idea of saying something that matters.

And the Style

One theory of style in writing sees form and content as distinct: style is the way a thing is said, the thing itself an unchanging substance that can be decked out in various ways. Mr. Smith not only *died,* he *ceased to be,* he *passed away,* he *croaked,* he *was promoted to glory*—all mean "the same thing." According to a second theory, however, they are ways of saying different things: variations in **diction** imply variations in reference. To say that Smith *ceased to be* records a privative and secular event; to say that he *was promoted to glory* (a Salvation Army expression) rejoices in an event of a different order altogether. Content and form in this view are inseparable; a change in one is a change in the other.

In **metaphor** we can see that the two theories, instead of contradicting each other, are more like the two sides of a coin: when one idea is expressed in terms of another, it is the same and yet not the same. To view the passage from life to death as if it were a promotion from one military rank to a higher one is to see a common center of reference and widening circles of association at the same time. This seeing *as if* opens up a whole range of expression, since many meanings reside in the relationship between the two parts of a comparison rather than in either part by itself. John Selden's country bumpkin (p. 380), "who said, if he were King, he would live like a lord, and have * * * a whip that cried Slash," expressed metaphorically a personal realization of power that would have been diminished or altered by any other means of expression.

But style is by no means dependent on diction and metaphor alone. Grammatical relationships yield a host of stylistic devices, most of which can be described in terms of **repetition and variation**. Repetition may exist at every level; as commonly understood, its chief application is to the word (including the pronoun as a word-substitute), but the same principle governs the use of parallelism (repetition of a grammatical structure) within and between sentences, even between paragraphs. Failure to observe that principle—that similarity in idea calls for similarity in form—can be detected wherever a change in form implies that a distinction is being made when actually none is relevant to the context: "Their conversation was interrupted by dinner, but they resumed their discussion afterwards"; "She rolled out the dough, placed it over the pie, and pricked holes in it. She also trimmed off the edge." The corollary of the principle of appropriate repetition is the principle of appropriate variation—that difference in idea calls for difference in form: For every failure to repeat when repetition is called for there is a corresponding failure to vary when variation is called for: "Their discussion was interrupted when class discussion of the day's assignment began"; "It had been raining for many days near the river. It had been rising steadily toward the top of the levee." Failures of this sort, which suggest a similarity in idea or parallelism in thought where none exists, often strike the ear as a lack of euphony or appropriate rhythm: "A boxer must learn to react absolutely instantly"; "The slingshot was made of strips of inner tubes of tires of cars." The principle of appropriate variation applies, too, to sentences as wholes: if a separate sentence is used for each detail, or if every sentence includes many details, the reader may be given a false impression of parallelism or equality of emphasis. Here again variation may be a way to avoid misleading grammatical indications of meaning. In a writer like Samuel Johnson (p. 813), who works deliberately for a high degree of parallelism, correspondence between repetition and sameness of meaning, or variation and difference of meaning, is perhaps most conveniently illustrated.

All stylistic techniques come together to supply an answer to the question "Who is behind these words?" Every writer establishes an impression of himself—his **identity**—through what he says and the way he says it, and the quality of that impression obviously has much to do with his reader's willingness to be convinced. Honesty and straightforwardness come first— though the honesty of an ignoramus and the straightforwardness of a fool are unlikely to win assent. The writer must therefore choose a suitable role for himself and develop some sense of what that role implies: is he an expert or a humble seeker after truth, a wry humorist or a gadfly deliberately exacerbating hidden guilt? Even within the same general circumstances (in this case the academic world), William G. Perry, Jr. (p. 328) is one sort of a person, John Livingston Lowes (p. 1295) clearly another. A self will be revealed in every phrase the writer sets down—even in details of spelling, grammar, and punctuation, which, if ineptly handled, may suggest to his readers a carelessness that destroys their confidence.

Authors

[An * indicates the source of a selection in this anthology.
Only a few of each author's works are cited.]

Mortimer J. Adler (1902-   )

American author and educator, Director of the Institute for Philosophical Research; author of *What Man Has Made of Man, How to Think About War and Peace, The Revolution in Education.*

James Agee (1909-1955)

American journalist, novelist, film critic, screenwriter; author of *A Death in the Family* (novel), *Let Us Now Praise Famous Men* (social commentary).

Richard D. Altick (1915-   )

American literary critic (Ohio State University); author of *Preface to Critical Reading, The Scholar Adventurers, *The Art of Literary Research.*

Robert Ardrey (1908-   )

American zoologist, playwright and novelist; author of *Thunder Rock, *The Territorial Imperative, African Genesis.*

Hannah Arendt (1906-   )

German-born American political analyst; author of *The Origins of Totalitarianism, The Human Condition, *Eichmann in Jerusalem.*

Matthew Arnold (1822-1888)

English man of letters, poet, and literary critic; author of *Poems, Essays in Criticism, *Culture and Anarchy, Literature and Dogma.*

Roger Ascham (1515-1568)

English scholar, tutor of Queen Elizabeth I; author of *Toxophilus* and *The Scholemaster.*

W. H. Auden (1907-   )

English-born American poet, playwright, critic; author of *In Time of War, The Sea and the Mirror, Poems, *The Dyer's Hand;* with Christopher Isherwood, of *Ascent of F-6, The Dog Beneath the Skin* (plays); with Louis MacNeice, of *Letters from Iceland.*

Sir Francis Bacon (1561-1626)

English politician, stateman and philosopher; author of *Essays, Advancement of Learning, *New Organon, New Atlantis.*

Russell W. Baker (1925-   )

American newspaper columnist (*The New York Times*); author of *An American in Washington, No Cause for Panic, All Things Considered.*

James Baldwin (1924-   )

American essayist and novelist; Harlem-bred, onetime expatriot in Paris, political activist for civil-rights causes; author of *Go Tell It on the Mountain, Another Country, Tell Me How Long the Train's Been Gone* (novels), *Notes of a Native Son, Nobody Knows My Name, The Fire Next Time,* and *Going to Meet the Man* (commentaries).

Margaret Culkin Banning (1891-   )

American novelist; author of *Too Young to Marry, Out in Society, *Letters to Susan, The Case for Chastity.*

Arthur Owen Barfield (1898-   )

British literary critic; author of *History in English Words, Poetic Diction, Saving the Appearances.*

Jacques Barzun (1907-   )

French-born American educator; dean (Columbia University); author of *Teacher in America, *The Modern Researcher* (with Henry E. Graff), *Science: The Glorious Entertainment.*

Walter Jackson Bate (1918-   )

American literary critic (Harvard University); author of *From Classic To Romantic, *The Achievement of Samuel Johnson, John Keats* (Pulitzer Prize 1964).

George Wells Beadle (1903-   )

American geneticist, chancellor of the University of Chicago; author, with Alfred H. Sturtevant, of *An Introduction to Genetics;* with Muriel Beadle, of *The Language of Life.*

Carl Becker (1873-1945)

American historian (Cornell); author of *Progress and Power, The Declaration of Independence, *Modern Democracy.*

Sir Max Beerbohm (1872-1956)

English essayist and caricaturist; author of *Zuleika Dobson* (novel); *A Christmas Garland, *And Even Now.*

Henri Bergson (1859-1941)

French philosopher; author of *The Two*

Sources of Morality and Religion, Time and Free Will, *On Laughter.

George Berkeley (1685-1753)

Irish cleric, philosopher; author of *Principles of Human Knowledge, Dialogue between Hylas and Philonous, Theory of Vision.

Bruno Bettelheim (1903-   )

Austrian-born American psychologist (University of Chicago) and psychoanalyst; author of Love Is Not Enough, *The Informed Heart, The Empty Fortress.

Ambrose Bierce (1842-1914?)

American short-story writer and journalist; author of Tales of Soldiers and Civilians, The Cynic's Word Book (retitled *The Devil's Dictionary).

William Blake (1757-1827)

English poet, artist, and engraver; author of Songs of Innocence, Songs of Experience, *The Marriage of Heaven and Hell, The Book of Thel.

Wayne C. Booth (1921-   )

American literary critic, dean (University of Chicago); author of The Rhetoric of Fiction.

C(harlie) D(unbar) Broad (1887-   )

British philosopher (Cambridge University); author of Mind and Its Place in Nature, Ethics and the History of Philosophy, Lectures on Psychical Research.

Jacob Bronowski (1908-   )

British critic and statesman, senior fellow and trustee of Salk Institute for Biological Studies; author of The Poet's Defence, The Common Sense of Science, Science and Human Values, The Identity of Man.

Sir Thomas Browne (1650-1682)

English physician; author of Religio Medici, Vulgar Errors, *Urn Burial.

Jerome S. Bruner (1915-   )

American psychologist (Harvard University); author of The Process of Education, *Toward A Theory of Instruction, Processes of Cognitive Growth.

Martin Buber (1878-1965)

Austrian-born Jewish theologian and biblical scholar who lived in Israel; author of I and Thou, Between Man and Man, Dialogues of Realization, The Kingship of God.

J. B. Bury (1861-1927)

English historian and classical scholar (Cambridge); author of Idea of Progress, History of the Freedom of Thought, History of the Later Roman Empire.

Truman Capote (1924-   )

American novelist, essayist and critic; author of Breakfast at Tiffany's, *The Muses Are Heard, In Cold Blood.

Thomas Carlyle (1795-1881)

Scots essayist, historian; author of *Sartor Resartus; The French Revolution; On Heroes, Hero-Worship, and the Heroic in History; History of Frederick the Great.

Edward Hallett Carr (1892-   )

English historian (Cambridge), journalist, and statesman; author of The Romantic Exiles; The Bolshevik Revolution, 1917–1923; *What Is History?

W. J. Cash (1901-1941)

American journalist; author of *The Mind of the South.

Lord Chesterfield (1694-1773)

Philip Dormer Stanhope, fourth earl; English statesman and diplomat, well-known letter-writer (*Letters to His Son).

Francis Christensen (1902-   )

American professor of English (University of Southern California); author of Notes Toward a New Rhetoric.

Sir Kenneth Clark (1903-   )

English art historian and critic; author of Landscape into Art, The Nude, Leonardo Da Vinci, Looking at Pictures.

Samuel Langhorne Clemens (1835-1910)

"Mark Twain"; American humorist, novelist, essayist, journalist; author of Life on the Mississippi, The Innocents Abroad, *Roughing It, The Adventures of Tom Sawyer, The Adventures of Huckleberry Finn.

Henry Sloane Coffin (1877-1954)

American clergyman and educator; President, Union Theological Seminary; author of *The Meaning of the Cross, Religion Yesterday and Today.

Anthony Ashley Cooper, First Earl of Shaftesbury (1621-1683)

British Tory politician, adversary of James II; satirized in Dryden's "Absalom and Achitophel."

Benedetto Croce (1866-1952)

Italian philosopher and critic; author of *Aesthetic, History as the Story of Liberty, Autobiography.

Sir Geoffrey Crowther (1907-   )

English economist and journalist, former editor of The Economist, Chairman, Central Advisory Council for Education (England), 1956-60.

Clarence Darrow (1857-1938)

American attorney and politician; identified with many prominent cases, including defenses of labor leaders and the Scopes trial; author of An Eye for an Eye; Crime Its Causes and Treatments; The Story of My Life.

Edward S. Deevey, Jr. (1914-   )

American biologist (Yale).

Benjamin DeMott (1924-   )

American journalist, essayist, and novelist (Amherst); author of The Body's Cage, Hells and Benefits.

Thomas De Quincey (1785-1859)

English essayist and literary journalist; author of *Confessions of an English Opium Eater,* *Autobiographic Sketches.*

Isaac Deutscher (1907-   )

Polish-born British political analyst; G. M. Trevelyan Lecturer, Cambridge, 1966-67; author of *Stalin: A Political Biography, The Prophet Outcast,* *The Unfinished Revolution.*

Emily Dickinson (1830-1886)

American poet; a New England recluse whose poetry was published almost entirely posthumously.

John Donne (1573-1631)

English poet and clergyman, Dean of St. Paul's Cathedral, founder and chief exemplar of the Metaphysical School in English poetry; author of *Songs and Sonnets, Devotions upon Emergent Occasions.*

John Dos Passos (1896-   )

American novelist; author of *Three Soldiers, Manhattan Transfer, U. S. A.* (a trilogy containing *The 42nd Parallel, 1919,* and *The Big Money*), *World in a Glass, The Shackles of Power, The Best Times.*

William O. Douglas (1898-   )

American jurist, law professor (Columbia and Yale), since 1939 an Associate Justice of the U. S. Supreme Court, and traveler and mountain climber; author of *Of Men and Mountains,* *Strange Lands and Friendly People, We the Judges, A Living Bill of Rights.*

John Earle (1601?-1665)

English churchman, Bishop of Salisbury; author of *Microcosmographie,* a series of character sketches.

Jonathan Edwards (1703-1758)

American Puritan preacher and theologian in Massachusetts Bay Colony.

Cecil S. Emden (1889-   )

British literary critic and legal authority (Oxford University); author of *Oriel Papers,* *The People and the Constitution, Poets in Their Letters.*

Ralph Waldo Emerson (1803-1882)

American essayist, poet, expositor of the intellectual movement known as Transcendentalism; author of *Nature, Representative Men, English Traits.*

Desiderius Erasmus (1465-1536)

Dutch humanist-scholar, satirist; author of *The Praise of Folly, Colloquies,* *The Education of a Christian Prince.*

Erik H. Erikson (1902-   )

German-born American psychoanalyst (Harvard University); author of *Young Man Luther, Identity and the Life Cycle,* *Insight and Responsibility.*

Henry Fielding (1707-1754)

English magistrate, novelist, essayist, and dramatist; author of *Joseph Andrews,* *Tom Jones, Amelia.*

Donald Fleming (1923-   )

American historian of science (Har-

vard); author of *John William Draper, William Henry Welch and the Rise of Modern Medicine.*

E. M. Forster (1879-   )

English novelist and essayist; author of *The Longest Journey, Howard's End, A Passage to India* (novels); *Aspects of the Novel,* *Two Cheers for Democracy* (criticism).

W. Nelson Francis (1910-   )

American linguist (Brown University); author of *The English Language, The Structure of American English, A Standard Sample of Present-Day English.*

Felix Frankfurter (1882-1965)

American jurist, former professor of law (Harvard) and Associate Justice of the U. S. Supreme Court (1939-1962); author of *The Public and Its Government, Of Law and Men, Law and Politics.*

Benjamin Franklin (1706-1790)

American statesman, delegate to the Continental Congress and Constitutional Convention, ambassador to France during the American Revolution, inventor, newspaper publisher, and practical philosopher; author of *Poor Richard's Almanack,* *Autobiography.*

Douglas Southall Freeman (1886-1953)

American editor (Richmond *News Leader*), professor of journalism (Columbia), historian; biographer of Robert E. Lee (*R. E. Lee, Lee's Lieutenants*).

Paul A. Freund (1908-   )

American lawyer (Harvard Law School); author of *On Understanding the Supreme Court, The Supreme Court in the United States, History of the Supreme Court* (editor-in-chief).

Robert Frost (1874-1963)

American poet, lecturer, teacher.

James Anthony Froude (1818-1894)

English historian, editor, educator; author of *History of England from the Fall of Wolsey to the Defeat of the Spanish Armada, The English in Ireland in the Eighteenth Century,* biographies of Carlyle.

Northrup Frye (1912-   )

Canadian literary critic (University of Toronto); author of *Anatomy of Criticism, Design for Learning,* *The Educated Imagination.*

Thomas Fuller (1608-1661)

English clergyman, historian, gazetteer, biographer; author of *The Holy State and the Profane State, Church History of Britain, The Worthies of England.*

George Gamow (1904-1968)

American theoretical physicist and popularizer of science; author of *Mr. Tompkins in Wonderland,* *One, Two, Three . . . Infinity, The Creation of the Universe, Gravity.*

Garet Garrett (1878-1954)
American journalist and social critic; author of *A Bubble That Broke the World*, *The American Story*, *The Wild Wheel*.

Edward Gibbon (1737-1794)
English historian; author of *History of the Decline and Fall of the Roman Empire*.

Walker Gibson (1919-   )
American professor of English (New York University); author of *The Reckless Spenders*, *Seeing and Writing*, *The Limits of Language*, *Tough, Sweet and Stuffy*.

Bil Gilbert (1927-   )
American sportsman and journalist (*Sports Illustrated*, *Saturday Evening Post*); author of *Bears in the Ladies' Room and Other Beastly Pursuits* and *How Animals Communicate*.

Étienne Gilson (1884-   )
French Catholic philosopher; author of *The Philosophy of St. Thomas Aquinas*, *The Mystical Philosophy of St. Bernard*, *Painting and Reality*.

Herbert Gold (1924-   )
American novelist, short-story writer, critic; author of *Birth of a Hero*, *First Person Singular*, *The Man Who Was Not With It*, *The Optimist*, *Fathers*.

Henry F. Graff (1921-   )
American historian (Columbia University); author of *The Modern Researcher* (with Jacques Barzun), *The Free and the Brave*, *Thomas Jefferson*.

Robert Graves (1895-   )
British man of letters; author of *The White Goddess*, *The Greek Myths*, *Collected Poems*, *Love Respelt*.

James Bradstreet Greenough (1833-1901)
American philologist (Harvard); author of *Analysis of the Latin Subjunctive*, *Latin Grammar* (with J. H. Allen), *Words and Their Ways in English Speech* (with G. L. Kittredge).

Donald Hall (1928-   )
American poet and professor of English (University of Michigan); author of *The Dark Houses*, *Exiles and Marriages*, *String Too Short to Be Saved*, *Henry Moore*.

Edith Hamilton (1867-1963)
American classical and biblical scholar, teacher (Bryn Mawr School); author of *The Greek Way*, *The Roman Way*, *Echo of Greece*, *Witness to the Truth*.

Learned Hand (1872-1961)
American jurist, U. S. District Court of and Circuit Court of Appeals Judge; author of *The Spirit of Liberty*.

Richard M. Hare (1919-   )
British philosopher (Oxford University); author of *The Language of Morals*, *Freedom and Reason*.

Nathaniel Hawthorne (1804-1864)
American novelist, short-story writer, essayist; author of *Twice-told Tales*, *Mosses from an Old Manse*, *The Scarlet Letter*, *The House of the Seven Gables*.

William Hazlitt (1778-1830)
English essayist, critic; author of *Characters of Shakespeare's Plays*; *English Comic Writers*; *Table Talk*, *or Original Essays on Men and Manners*; *Characteristics*.

Ernest Hemingway (1898-1961)
American novelist and story-writer. Pulitzer and Nobel Prizes; author of *The Sun Also Rises*, *A Farewell to Arms*, *Death in the Afternoon*, *For Whom the Bell Tolls*, *The Old Man and the Sea*.

Herodotus (c. 484-424? B.C.)
Greek historian, "father of history"; author of *Histories*, the nine books of which are named after the nine Muses (*Clio*, *Euterpe*, etc.).

Gilbert Highet (1906-   )
Scots-born American classicist and teacher (Columbia); author of *The Classical Tradition*, *The Art of Teaching*, *The Anatomy of Satire*, *Talents and Geniuses*.

Eric Hoffer (1902-   )
American longshoreman and social critic; author of *The True Believer*, *The Passionate State of Mind*, *The Ordeal of Change*.

John Caldwell Holt (1923-   )
American educator; author of *How Children Fail* and *How Children Learn*.

Richard Hooker (1554-1600)
British divine; author of *Laws of Ecclesiastical Polity*.

Gerard Manly Hopkins (1844-1889)
English Jesuit, poet, essayist.

David Hume (1711-1776)
Scots philosopher, historian; author of *Essays Moral and Political*, *Enquiry Concerning Human Understanding*, *History of Great Britain*.

Thomas Henry Huxley (1825-1895)
English biologist, popularizer of science; author of *Evolution and Ethics*, *Scientific Memoirs*, *Darwiniana*.

Jane Jacobs (1916-   )
American editor and sociologist; author of *The Death and Life of Great American Cities*.

Henry James (1843-1916)
American novelist and essayist, brother of William, longtime resident of London; author of *Portrait of a Lady*, *The Ambassadors*, *The Wings of the Dove*, *The American*.

William James (1842-1910)
American philosopher and pioneer psychologist (Harvard), pragmatist, brother of Henry; author of *Principles of Psychology*, *The Varieties of Religious Experience*, *Pragmatism*.

Thomas Jefferson (1743-1826)
Third President of the United States,

first Secretary of State, founder of the University of Virginia, drafter of the *Declaration of Independence and the statute of Virginia for religious freedom, founder of the Democratic party; also renowned for his talents as an architect and inventor.

Samuel Johnson (1709-1784)
English lexicographer, critic, moralist; journalist (*The Idler*, *The Rambler*); author of *A Dictionary of the English Language, Lives of the Poets;* subject of Boswell's *Life.*

Franz Kafka (1883-1924)
Czech novelist and short-story writer; author of *The Trial, The Castle, Amerika.*

X. J. Kennedy (1929-   )
Pseudonym of Joseph C. Kennedy; poet, critic, professor of English (Tufts); author of *Nude Descending a Staircase* and *Introduction to Poetry.*

Sören Kierkegaard (1813-1855)
Danish theologian and philosopher; author of *Fear and Trembling, Either/ Or, Philosophical Fragments.*

Martin Luther King, Jr. (1929-1968)
American Negro clergyman and civil rights leader; President, Southern Christian Leadership Conference; Nobel Peace Prize, 1964; author of *Stride Toward Freedom* and *Why We Can't Wait.*

George Lyman Kittredge (1860-1941)
American philologist and professor of English (Harvard); author of *Words and Their Ways in English Speech* (with J. B. Greenough), *Chaucer and His Poetry, Shakespeare, Sir Thomas Malory,* and editor of *The Complete Works of Shakespeare.*

Ronald Knox (1888-1957)
English Roman Catholic prelate; author of *The Belief of Catholics; The Body in the Silo; Let Dons Delight; *Enthusiasm, a Chapter in the History of Religion.*

Theodora Kroeber (1897-   )
Wife of anthropologist A. L. Kroeber; author of *The Inland Whale* and *Ishi in Two Worlds.*

Joseph Wood Krutch (1893-   )
American literary and social critic; author of *The Modern Temper, The Measure of Man, Human Nature and the Human Condition.*

Charles Lamb (1775-1834)
English essayist, critic; author of *Essays of Elia* and, with his sister, *Tales from Shakespeare.*

François, duc de la Rochefoucauld (1613-1680)
French moralist; author of *Memoirs, *Reflections or Sentences and Moral Maxims.*

D(avid) H(erbert) Lawrence (1885-1930)
British novelist, poet, and critic; author of *Sons and Lovers, The Rainbow,*

*Lady Chatterley's Lover, *Studies in Classic American Literature.*

Stephen Leacock (1869-1944)
Canadian humorist, economist (McGill), and historian; author of *The Unsolved Riddle of Social Justice* and, among his lighter works, *Nonsense Novels* and *Moonbeams from the Larger Lunacy.*

C. S. Lewis (1898-1963)
English literary scholar and critic, novelist, theologian; author of *A Preface to Paradise Lost, The Screwtape Letters, Mere Christianity, *Miracles.*

W. H. Lewis (1895-   )
British historian (Oxford University); author of *The Splendid Century, Assault on Olympus, Louis XIV.*

A. J. Liebling (1904-1963)
American journalist (*The New Yorker*), who counted wine and boxing among many other interests; author of *Back Where I Came From, The Honest Rainmaker, The Earl of Louisiana.*

Abraham Lincoln (1809-1865)
Sixteenth President of the United States; lawyer, Congressman, celebrated for his debates with Stephen Douglas on the question of slavery's extension. His voluminous state papers include the Emancipation Proclamation, the Gettysburg Address, the Second Inaugural.

Walter Lippmann (1889-   )
American political philosopher and journalist-statesman; author of *Public Opinion, A Preface to Morals, The New Imperative, The Public Philosophy, The Communist World and Ours.*

Lester D. Longman (1905-   )
American art historian (University of Iowa); author of *Outline of Art History, History and Appreciation of Art.*

Konrad Lorenz (1903-   )
Austrian-born German scientist; Director of Max Planck Institute for Physiology of Behavior; author of *King Solomon's Ring and So Kam der Mensch auf den Hund (Thus Came the Man to the Dog).*

John Livingston Lowes (1867-1945)
American literary critic, scholar, and teacher (Harvard); author of *Geoffrey Chaucer, The Road to Xanadu.*

Robert Lynd (1879-1949)
Irish essayist, journalist; author of *The Pleasures of Ignorance, Solomon in All His Glory, Dr. Johnson and Company, *It's a Fine World.*

Thomas Babington Macaulay (1800-1859)
English historian, member of Parliament, and first Baron Macaulay; author of *History of England, Lays of Ancient Rome.*

Niccolò Machiavelli (1469-1527)
Florentine statesman and political phi-

losopher during the reign of the Medici; author of *The Art of War, History of Florence, Discourses on Livy, *The Prince.*

Archibald MacLeish (1892-   )

American poet, former Librarian of Congress, professor of English (Harvard); author of the verse play *J.B., Poetry and Experience, The Eleanor Roosevelt Story, Herakles.*

James Madison (1751-1836)

Fourth President of the United States and Secretary of State under Jefferson; drafter of the Virginia plan, the basis of the U. S. Constitution, and keeper of notes of the proceedings of the Constitutional Convention; like Jefferson, a Virginian, proponent of religious freedom, and opponent of slavery; author, with Hamilton and Jay, of *The Federalist,* papers arguing for the ratification of the Constitution.

Norman Mailer (1923-   )

American novelist and social critic; author of *The Naked and the Dead, The Deer Park, The Armies of the Night.*

Katherine Mansfield (1888-1923)

Pseudonym of Katherine Middleton Murry; New Zealand-born English short-story writer; author of *Bliss, The Garden Party, The Dove's Nest.*

William March (1893-1954)

Pseudonym of William Edward March Campbell; American businessman, novelist, short-story writer, fabulist; author of *Company K, The Little Wife and Other Stories, Some Like Them Short, *99 Fables.*

Jacques Maritain (1882-   )

French-born American theologian (Princeton University); author of *Art and Scholasticism and the Frontiers of Poetry, Existence and the Existent, The Responsibility of the Artist.*

Matthew

One of the twelve Apostles of Christ, author of *The Gospel according to St. Matthew.

W. Somerset Maugham (1874-1965)

English novelist, dramatist, short-story writer; author of *Of Human Bondage* (novel), *The Moon and Sixpence* (stories), *The Circle* (play), *The Summing Up* (autobiography).

(Herbert) Marshall McLuhan (1911-   )

American communications specialist and critic (University of Toronto). Author of *Understanding Media, The Mechanical Bride, The Gutenberg Galaxy.*

Margaret Mead (1901-   )

American anthropologist (American Museum of Natural History and Columbia); author of *Coming of Age in Samoa, *Male and Female, New Lives for Old, Continuities in Cultural Evolution,* and *Keep Your Powder Dry.*

Sir Peter B(rian) Medawar (1915-   )

Brazilian-born British biologist; Director of the National Institute of Medical Research, 1962-   ; Nobel Prize, 1960.

Stanley Milgram (1933-   )

American social psychologist (Yale).

John Stuart Mill (1806-1873)

English political and social philosopher, economist, and social reformer, civil servant in India, a proponent of utilitarianism and political freedom; author of *A System of Logic, On Liberty, Utilitarianism, Autobiography.*

Samuel Miller (1900-   )

American clergyman, dean of the Harvard Divinity School; author of *The Life of the Soul, The Life of the Church, Great Realities, Prayers for Daily Use.*

Daniel P. Moynihan (1927-   )

American diplomat and sociologist; director of Joint Center for Urban Studies, M.I.T. and Harvard; co-author of *Beyond the Melting Pot.*

Lewis Mumford (1895-   )

American critic of architecture and city planning; author of *Sticks and Stones, The Brown Decades, *Technics and Civilization, The Culture of Cities, The Human Prospect, The Myth of the Machine.*

John Henry Newman (1801-1890)

English Catholic prelate and cardinal; author of *Tracts for the Times, *The Idea of a University, Apologia pro Vita sua.*

Nicholas of Cusa (c. 1400-1464)

German Catholic prelate (bishop and cardinal) and philosopher, argued in favor of church councils over the pope and for the principle of consent as the basis of government; author of *De concordantia catholica, De docta ignorantia, *De visione Dei (The Vision of God).*

J. Robert Oppenheimer (1904-1967)

American nuclear physicist, one of the key men in harnessing atomic energy, director of the Institute for Advanced Study at Princeton; author of *Science and the Common Understanding, *The Open Mind.*

George Orwell (1903-1950)

Pseudonym of Eric Blair; English novelist, essayist, and social commentator, satirist of totalitarianism; author of *Down and Out in London and Paris, Homage to Catalonia, *Nineteen Eighty-Four, Animal Farm.*

James Packard (1928-   )

American editor and academic administrator (University of Michigan).

Francis Parkman (1823-1893)

American historian of colonial America, including *History of the Conspiracy of Pontiac, *LaSalle and the Discovery of the Great West, Montcalm and Wolfe.*

Blaise Pascal (1623-1662)
French mathematician, moralist, and essayist; author of *Pensées.*

Walter Pater (1839-1894)
English man of letters, interpreter of Renaissance humanism; author of *Studies in the History of the Renaissance, Marius the Epicurean, Appreciations.*

Donald R. Pearce (1917-   )
Canadian professor of English (Santa Barbara); author of *Journal of a War: Northwest Europe, 1944-1945* and *In the President's and My Opinion.*

Jean Paul de Gondi, Cardinal de Retz (1614-1679)
French prelate and politician; author of *Mémoires.*

Charles Sanders Peirce (1839-1914)
American philosopher, scientist, and logician; author of *Chance, Love, and Logic; Essays in the Philosophy of Science, Values in a Universe of Chance.*

William G. Perry, Jr. (1913-   )
American educator, director of the Bureau of Study Counsel at Harvard.

Plato (427?-347 B.C.)
Greek philosopher, pupil and friend of Socrates, teacher of Aristotle, founder of the Academy, proponent of an oligarchy of intellectuals based on the assumption that virtue is knowledge; author of *The Republic.*

John Rader Platt (1918-   )
American physicist (University of Chicago).

Stephen Potter (1900-   )
English writer-producer (BBC), critic, and humorist; author of *D. H. Lawrence, A First Study; The Muse in Chains; A Study in Education,* and, among his lighter things, *Gamesmanship, Lifemanship, One-Upmanship.*

Berton Roueché (1911-   )
American journalist (*The New Yorker*), chronicler of medical history; author of *Eleven Blue Men, The Incurable Wound, The Neutral Spirit.*

(Lord) Bertrand Russell (1872-   )
British philosopher, mathematician and political analyst; Nobel Prize, 1950; author of *The Analysis of Mind, A History of Western Philosophy, Marriage and Morals, *Philosophical Essays.*

Franklin Russell (1922-   )
American naturalist; author of *Argen the Gull, *The Secret Islands, Watchers at the Pond.*

Samuel
The subject of two books of the Old Testament; leader of Israel, anointer of Saul and of David.

Sir George B. Sansom (1883-   )
British orientalist; author of *A History of Japan, *Japan: A Short Cultural History, Japan in World History.*

George Santayana (1863-1952)
American philosopher (Harvard), author of *The Life of Reason, The Realm of Essence, The Realm of Truth,* and *Soliloquies in England.*

Allan Seager (1906-1968)
American novelist and short-story writer, professor of English (University of Michigan); author of *Amos Berry, Hilda Manning, *A Frieze of Girls, The Glass House* (a biography of Theodore Roethke).

John Selden (1584-1654)
English politician, jurist, oriental scholar, and member of Parliament; author of many political tracts and works on law and *Table Talk.*

George Bernard Shaw (1856-1950)
Irish playwright and essayist; author of the plays *Saint Joan, *Man and Superman, *Major Barbara, Caesar and Cleopatra.*

Edward B. Shils (1915-   )
American sociologist (University of Chicago); author of *Automation and Industrial Relations* and *Medicine USA.*

Logan Pearsall Smith (1865-1946)
American social critic and humorist; author of *All Trivia, More Trivia, Stories and Essays.*

Talbot Smith (1899-   )
American jurist, U. S. District Court Judge (in Michigan), former professor of law (University of California) and associate justice of the Supreme Court of Michigan.

Wallace Stegner (1909-   )
American essayist, novelist, professor of English (Stanford); author of *Remembering Laughter, The Women on the Wall, Beyond the Hundredth Meridian, A Shocking Star, *Wolf Willow, All the Little Live Things,* and *Gathering of Zion: The Story of the Mormon Trail.*

John Steinbeck (1902-   )
American novelist, columnist, Nobel prize-winner; author of *In Dubious Battle, Of Mice and Men, The Grapes of Wrath, East of Eden.*

Laurence Sterne (1713-1768)
English cleric, novelist, and humorist; author of *Tristram Shandy, Sentimental Journey, Sermons.*

Charles L. Stevenson (1908-   )
American philosopher (University of Michigan); author of *Ethics and Language* and *Facts and Values.*

John D. Stewart (1930-   )
English essayist, fiction writer, dramatist, civil servant, contributor to English and American magazines.

Jonathan Swift (1667-1745)
Irish satirist, poet, and churchman; author of *Gulliver's Travels, A Tale of a Tub, *"The Battle of the Books."

Theophrastus (c. 371-287 B.C.)
Greek philosopher, naturalist, and suc-

cessor to Aristotle; author of *Characters, Metaphysics, On Plants*.

Dylan Thomas (1914-1953)

Welsh poet, story writer, radio-script writer and broadcaster; author of *Collected Poems (1934-1952)*, *Under Milk Wood* (poems), *Adventures in the Skin Trade and Other Stories*, *Portrait of the Artist as a Young Dog* (novel).

Henry David Thoreau (1817-1862)

American philosopher, essayist, naturalist, poet, disciple of Emerson, foremost exponent of self-reliance; author of *Descent into Hell*, *War in ence*," *Journals*.

Thucydides (c. 460-c. 400 B.C.)

Greek historian; author of *The Peloponnesian War*.

James Thurber (1894-1963)

American humorist, cartoonist, social commentator (*The New Yorker*), playwright; author of *My Life and Hard Times*; *Fables for Our Time*; *Men, Women, and Dogs*; *The Beast in Me and Other Animals*.

Paul Tillich (1886-)

German-born American theologian (Union Theological Seminary and Harvard); author of *The Interpretation of History*, *The Shaking of the Foundations*, *Systematic Theology*, *The Dynamics of Faith*, *Christianity and the Encounter of the World Religions*.

Diana (Mrs. Lionel) Trilling (1905-)

American literary critic and journalist; editor of *The Portable D. H. Lawrence*, *Selected Letters of D. H. Lawrence*, *Mark Twain: Huckleberry Finn*.

Barbara Tuchman (1912-)

American writer and historian; author of *The Zimmerman Telegram*, *The Guns of August* (Pulitzer Prize, 1963), *The Proud Tower*.

Ernest van den Haag (1914-)

Dutch-born American sociologist (New School for Social Research); author or co-author of *The Fabric of Society*, *Education as an Industry*, *Passion and Social Constraint*.

Evelyn Waugh (1903-1966)

British novelist and humorist; author of *Decline and Fall*, *Handful of Dust*, *Vile Bodies*, *The Loved One*, *Men At Arms*, *Officers and Gentlemen*, *The End of Battle*.

E. B. White (1899-)

American essayist, journalist, editor (*The New Yorker*); author of *One Man's Meat*, *The Wild Flag*, *The Second Tree from the Corner*.

Alfred North Whitehead (1861-1947)

English mathematician and philosopher. Author of *Principia Mathematica*

(with Bertrand Russell), *The Aims of Education*, *Adventures of Ideas*, *Dialogues*, and other books.

Benjamin Lee Whorf (1897-1941)

American linguist; author of *Language, Thought and Reality* and *Loanwords in Ancient Mexico*.

Oscar Wilde (1856-1900)

Irish wit, dramatist, poet, story writer, critic; author of *The Picture of Dorian Gray* (novel), *The Importance of Being Earnest* (play).

William B. Willcox (1907-)

American historian (University of Michigan); author of *Gloucestershire: A Study in Local Government*; *Star of Empire: A Study of Britain as a World Power*; *Portrait of a General: Sir Henry Clinton in the War of Independence*.

Roger Williams (c. 1603-1683)

English clergyman, exiled from Massachusetts Bay Colony for advocating separation of church and state, founder of Rhode Island.

Alexander Wilson (1766-1813)

American ornithologist and poet; author of *American Ornithology* and *Poems and Literary Prose*.

Edmund Wilson (1895-)

American man of letters, critic, and novelist; author of *To the Finland Station* (history), *Classics and Commercials*, *Axel's Castle*, and *The Bit Between My Teeth: A Literary Chronicle of 1950-1965* (criticism), *Memoirs of Hecate County* (novel).

William Edward Wilson (1906-)

American professor of English (Indiana University); author of *Big Knife: The Story of George Rogers Clark*.

W. K. Wimsatt (1907-)

American literary critic (Yale University); author of *The Prose Style of Samuel Johnson*, *The Verbal Icon* (with Cleanth Brooks), *Literary Criticism: A Short History*.

John Winthrop (1588-1649)

First governor of Massachusetts Bay Colony, keeper of a journal published posthumously as *The History of New England*.

Roberta Wohlstetter (1912-)

American social scientist (Rand Corporation); author of *Pearl Harbor: Warning and Decision*.

Virginia Woolf (1882-1941)

English novelist, essayist, and critic; author of *Mrs. Dalloway*, *The Common Reader*, *To the Lighthouse*, *Granite and Rainbow*, *The Second Common Reader*.

Harold Zyskind (1917-)

American professor of philosophy (State University of New York).

Alphabetical Index